lonely pl

D0388313

Coastal
California

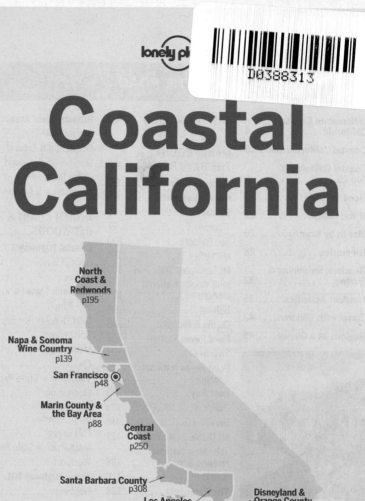

**North
Coast &
Redwoods**
p195

**Napa & Sonoma
Wine Country**
p139

San Francisco ◉
p48

**Marin County &
the Bay Area**
p88

**Central
Coast**
p250

Santa Barbara County
p308

Los Angeles
p347

**Disneyland &
Orange County**
p383

San Diego & Around
p425

THIS EDITION WRITTEN AND RESEARCHED BY

Sara Benson,
Andrew Bender, Alison Bing, Celeste Brash,
Beth Kohn, Adam Skolnick, John A Vlahides

PLAN YOUR TRIP

BIG SUR P275

SANTA BARBARA WINE
COUNTRY P326

PJGAM / GETTY IMAGES ©

ED FREEMAN / GETTY IMAGES ©

ON THE ROAD

Contents

UNDERSTAND

SURVIVAL GUIDE

SPECIAL FEATURES

Welcome to Coastal California

From towering coast redwoods in the foggy north, to the perfect sun-kissed surf beaches of the south, this slice of Pacific Coast is a knockout beauty.

Beaches & Outdoor Fun

In all of your California dreaming, palm trees, golden sands and Pacific sunsets beckon, right? In coastal California, those cinematic fantasies really do come true. You can learn to surf, play a game of pickup volleyball or light an oceanfront bonfire on cool nights. Sunny beach towns from Santa Cruz south to San Diego, each with its own idiosyncratic personality, give you perfect excuses to head outdoors. Heading north of San Francisco, dramatically windswept sands have inspired generations of poets and painters, offering miles of oceanfront for beachcombing and tramping in solitude.

Big Cities, Small Towns

No less astoundingly diverse than the landscapes are the people who have staked their fortunes here. Start out exploring San Francisco's one-of-a-kind neighborhoods, from beatnik North Beach to historic Chinatown, before going celebrity-spotting and people-watching in LA. In between, hang with radical tree-sitting lefties in the Humboldt Nation, live the very good life in California's wine countries, get groovy with new-age gurus in San Diego's North County, or talk fishing with salty dogs in port towns like Eureka, Bodega Bay and Monterey.

Food & Drink

Maybe your coastal sojourn will be an epicurean quest. Finding the most-killer fish tacos in San Diego alone could take days or even weeks. San Francisco and Los Angeles are both culinary capitals, where citizens passionately argue about the best sushi bar or fusion food truck. LA is also a melting pot of multicultural cooking, from Thai Town to the tamale shops of East LA. Outside the cities, follow your nose and let it lead you serendipitously up and down California's coastal highways, stopping at seafood shacks, rollicking brewpubs, farmers markets and vineyards.

Creative Culture

From the mid-19th-century Gold Rush to the dot-com bubble, California has survived extreme booms and busts, often getting by on its wits. Today Hollywood still makes most of the world's movies and TV shows, fed by a vibrant performing arts scene on stages across the state. Trends are usually kick-started in California not by moguls in offices, but by motley crowds of surfers, artists and dreamers concocting the out-there ideas behind everything from skateboarding to biotechnology. If you linger long enough, you might actually see the future coming.

Why I Love Coastal California

By Sara Benson, Coordinating Author

Like almost half of the people who live here, California wasn't where I was born, but it's where I've chosen to make my home. I never tire of road-tripping along the Golden State's coastal highways, seeking out hidden beaches, new peaks to climb and places to paddle a kayak. The rural vineyards and craft breweries of the Central Coast are practically in my backyard, tempting me to play truant on any given weekday. For weekend escapes, I head north to cool, fog-kissed San Francisco Bay or south to sunny, cosmopolitan Los Angeles.

For more about our authors, see page 528.

Above: Big Sur coast (p275)

Coastal California

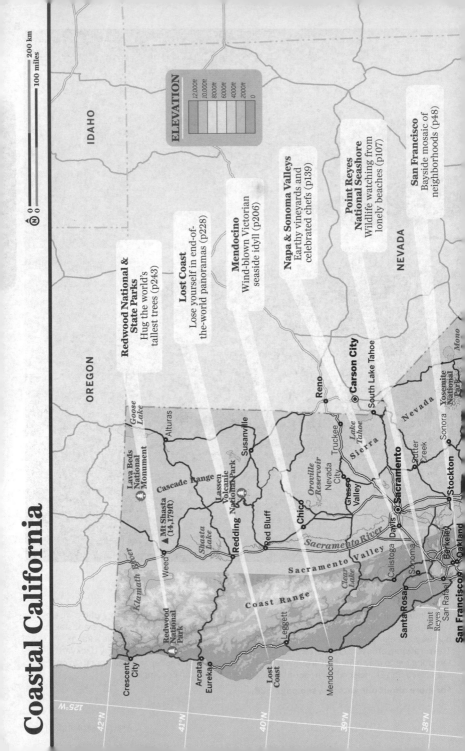

Redwood National & State Parks
Hug the world's tallest trees (p243)

Lost Coast
Lose yourself in end-of-the-world panoramas (p228)

Mendocino
Wind-blown Victorian seaside idyll (p206)

Napa & Sonoma Valleys
Earthy vineyards and celebrated chefs (p139)

Point Reyes National Seashore
Wildlife watching from lonely beaches (p107)

San Francisco
Bayside mosaic of neighborhoods (p48)

ELEVATION

12,000ft
10,000ft
8000ft
6000ft
4000ft
2000ft
0

OREGON

IDAHO

NEVADA

Disneyland Resort
SoCal's biggest
theme park (p386)

San Diego
Wet 'n' wild
surf city (p427)

Monterey
Myriad marine
wonders await (p262)

Big Sur
Get lost with bohemian
beatniks (p275)

San Luis Obispo
Laid-back beaches and
farmers markets (p297)

Santa Barbara
Posh 'American
Riviera' lifestyle (p310)

Channel Islands
SoCal's biodiverse offshore
archipelago (p343)

Los Angeles
See stars on the
boulevards (p347)

Orange County Beaches
Surf style with
arty flair (p397)

ARIZONA

MEXICO

PACIFIC
OCEAN

Coastal California's
Top 25

San Francisco's Neighborhoods

1 As anyone who has clung to the side of a cable car can tell you, this city (p48) gives you a heck of a ride, from the Marina's chic waterfront to the edgy Mission district. And just when you think you have a grasp on the 'Paris of the West,' you turn another corner to find a brightly painted alleyway mural, a filigreed Victorian roofline or a hidden stairway with bay-view panoramas that will entirely change your outlook. Alamo Square (p67)

Big Sur

2 Nestled up against mossy, mysterious-looking redwood forests, the rocky Big Sur (p275) coast is a secretive place. Get to know it like the locals do, especially if you want to find hidden hot springs and beaches where the sand is tinged purple or where giant jade has washed ashore. Time your visit for May, when waterfalls peak, or after summer vacation crowds have left but sunny skies still rule. Crane your neck skyward to catch sight of endangered California condors taking wing above the cliffs.

LIMEWAVE / INSPIRATION TO EXPLORATION / GETTY IMAGES ©

PAUL M O'CONNELL / GETTY IMAGES ©

Los Angeles

3 LA (p347) runs deeper than her beaches and reality-TV entourages might lead you to believe. True, she has spawned tons of pop culture, while popularizing silicone implants and spandex. But the City of Angels has also nurtured artists, architects, writers, performers and film directors alongside yogis and alternative-health gurus. Ultimately, it's LA's ethnic diversity and vibrant global-immigrant culture that make the biggest impression. Open your mind and you'll soon love La La Land as much as we do. Griffith Observatory (p353)

Disneyland Resort

4 Where orange groves and walnut trees once grew, Walt Disney built his dream. Today, Disneyland (p386) and neighboring Disney California Adventure are SoCal's most-visited tourist attraction. Inside Anaheim's mega-popular theme parks, beloved cartoon characters waltz down Main Street, USA, and fireworks explode over Sleeping Beauty Castle. If you're a kid, or just hopelessly young at heart, perhaps this really can be 'The Happiest Place on Earth,' at least for a day. Paradise Pier, Disney California Adventure (p389)

DAVID LIU / GETTY IMAGES ©

YINYANG / GETTY IMAGES ©

Redwood National & State Parks

5 Ditch the cellphone and hug a tree, dude. And why not start with the world's tallest, the redwood? California's towering giants grow along much of the coast, from Big Sur north to the Oregon border. It's possible to cruise past these trees – or even drive right through them at old-fashioned tourist traps – but nothing compares to the awe you'll feel while walking among the ancient ones protected by Redwood National and State Parks (p243).

San Diego

6 San Diego's breezy confidence and sunny countenance are irresistible. The only problem with 'America's Finest City' (p427) is that with 70 miles of coastline and a near-perfect climate, it's tough to decide where to start. When in doubt, do as locals do: grab a fish taco and a surfboard, then hit the beach. Beautiful Balboa Park is where San Diegans come to play when they're not at the beach. You could spend the whole day at the famous zoo or immersed in any of a dozen art, cultural and science museums.

Napa & Sonoma Wine Country

7 As winemaking in the Napa Valley grows ever more dizzyingly upscale, neighboring Sonoma Valley's vineyards are still surrounded by pastoral ranchlands. Yet they share a common passion for the uniqueness of *terroir*. Here in California's best-known wine country (p139), you can take a tour of biodynamic vineyards, shake hands with famous winemakers or sample new vintages from the barrel in naturally cooled underground cellars, then crack open a bottle in the fields outside. Who cares if it's not noon? This is California: conventions need not apply.

WITOLD SKRYPCZAK / GETTY IMAGES ©

Santa Barbara

8 Locals call it the 'American Riviera,' and honestly that's not much of a stretch: Santa Barbara (p310) is so idyllic, you just have to sigh. Waving palm trees, sugar-sand beaches, boats bobbing by the harbor – it'd be a travel cliché if it wasn't the plain truth. California's 'Queen of the Missions' is a beauty, as are downtown's red-roofed, whitewashed adobe buildings, all rebuilt in harmonious Spanish colonial revival style after a devastating earthquake in 1925. Come aspire to the breezy, rich-and-famous lifestyle over a long, lazy weekend. State Street

Hearst Castle

9 A monument to William Randolph Hearst's maniacal obsession with Old World treasures collected from Europe, Hearst Castle (p284) is the biggest showboat attraction on the Central Coast, just south of Big Sur. Take a spin around Hearst's hilltop retreat with its sparkling outdoor Neptune Pool, interiors lavishly decorated in antiquities and jewels, and jaw-dropping coastal sunsets viewed from the balcony. Evening living-history tours will bring you back to the castle's 1930s heyday, when Hollywood celebrities hobnobbed with heads of state. Neptune Pool, Hearst Castle

Malibu

10 What, you didn't see any stars in Hollywood? We're so not surprised. Big-wig producers and A-list stars hide out in beachy Malibu (p357), a quick drive up the Pacific Coast Hwy from LA. Whoever said Malibu is a state of mind more than a place was right though: there's no real center here (apart from shopping malls), just miles of white-sand beaches and rolling Pacific waves backed by million-dollar oceanfront mansions. Luckily, those beautiful beaches are public-access up to the high tide line – any paparazzi photographer can tell you that.

Lost Coast

11 Hellloooo? Anyone out there? This is the coast that time has just about forgotten. Buoyed by the wilderness peaks of the Kings Range and speckled by wild beaches of volcanic origin, the Lost Coast (p228) makes you earn the right to see its natural wonders. Time your multiday backpacking trek to match the flow of the tides and camp out by the crashing surf on a deserted beach along the Lost Coast Trail, or drive yourself to the last outpost of civilization, tiny Shelter Cove.

Mendocino

12 Originally a 19th-century port built by New Englanders, Mendocino (p206) today belongs to bohemians. In summer, fragrant bursts of lavender and jasmine drift on fog-laden winds over the town's unique redwood water towers, while at any time of year nothing restores the soul like a ramble out onto the craggy headland cliffs here. Churning surf is never out of earshot, and driftwood-littered beaches are potent reminders of the sea's power.

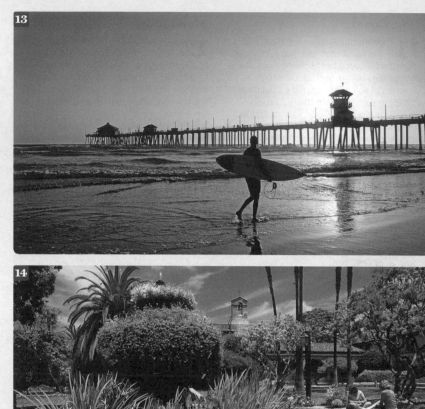

Orange County Beaches

13 In Orange County (p397), there are beaches for all. Huntington draws the surfer crowd, while biker rebels, bodacious babes and anti-establishment types hit Sunset Beach. Families with kids gravitate toward old-fashioned Seal Beach and its pier, but glamorous teens and trophy wives cavort in the fantasyland of Newport Beach. Laguna Beach beckons with its sophisticated blend of money and culture. Oh, and natural beauty too: startlingly beautiful seascapes inspired an artists colony to bloom there. Huntington Beach (p401)

Mission San Juan Capistrano

14 When you visit SoCal, you can't help but follow in the footsteps of early Spanish conquistadors and Catholic priests. Mission San Juan Capistrano (p422) – the 'Jewel of the Missions' – was founded by peripatetic priest Junípero Serra in 1776. Today the mission deserves its nickname, with gardens, stone arcades and fountains, and a chapel adorned with spiritual frescoes. In mid-March the town celebrates the swallows' return from South America to nest in the mission's walls.

Point Reyes National Seashore

15 If just one park could encapsulate Northern California, Point Reyes (p107) would get our vote. Step across the San Andreas Fault, then stand out by the lighthouse at what truly feels like land's end. Peer through binoculars at migratory whales, or witness the raucous birthing and mating antics of endangered elephant seals at Chimney Rock. Then hike among herds of tule elk and drive out to more windswept beaches, where the horizon stretches toward infinity. Tomales Bay

Santa Cruz

16 Nowhere else can you get in touch with Northern California's countercultural roots faster than in Santa Cruz (p252). White sandy beaches for wetsuit-wearing, board-riding dudes and chicks? Check. A carnivalesque downtown flush with crunchy cafes, one-of-a-kind shops and eccentric personalities? Yup. Tree-hugger hippie camps and outsider artists' cabins in the redwood forests? Uh-huh. Left-of-liberal politics, Rastafarian dreadlocks and new-age crystal readings? Of course, man. Hula hooping, Santa Cruz

Channel Islands

17 Tossed like so many lost pearls off the coast, the Channel Islands (p343) are SoCal's answer to the Galapagos. Centuries ago, seafaring Chumash tribespeople established villages on remote rocks. Today the islands support an abundance of marine life, from coral-reef creatures to giant colonies of pinnipeds. Get back to nature in Channel Islands National Park, a wildlife haven with hiking trails and rustic campgrounds, or make a more civilized excursion to Avalon on Catalina Island. Anacapa Island (p344)

Santa Barbara Wine Country

18 Southern California's answer to Napa and Sonoma is the Santa Ynez and Santa Maria Valleys (p326), aka *Sideways* wine country. Less than an hour's drive from Santa Barbara, you can wander through fields of grapes, tipple soft Pinot Noir and sample the sun-drenched good life. Start in dandified Los Olivos, where the streets are packed with wine-tasting rooms and bistros. Then wind north along the Foxen Wine Trail, a two-lane country road, where famous-name wineries and boutique winemakers are neighbors.

San Luis Obispo

19 Almost exactly between San Francisco and Los Angeles, San Luis Obispo (p297) is often dismissed by urban culture vultures, but this collection of organic farms, vineyards and ranchlands is refreshingly down to earth. Detour here for laid-back beach towns, spectacular hiking and camping at state parks and beaches, and, most of all, the locavarian bounty sold at more than a dozen farmers markets. You won't even need a car – arrive in retro style on Amtrak's *Pacific Surfliner* or *Coast Starlight* trains, which trundle past unforgettable coastal scenery. Barbecuing. San Luis Obispo

Monterey

20 Often foggy and wind-tossed, the peninsular fishing village of Monterey (p262) calls to mind John Steinbeck and his gritty novels of American realism. Hop aboard a whale-watching cruise out into the bay's national marine sanctuary, some of whose aquatic denizens also swim in Cannery Row's aquarium. Soak up more maritime atmosphere at the West Coast's oldest lighthouse in Pacific Grove, then wander downtown Monterey's hidden gardens and historic adobe-walled buildings from California's Spanish, Mexican and early American days. Monterey Bay Aquarium (p262)

RICHARD CUMMINS / GETTY IMAGES ©

La Jolla

21 On the most beautiful stretch of San Diego's coastline, La Jolla (p450) is definitely not just another SoCal beach town. Sitting pretty atop rocky bluffs just a whisper's breath from the sea, La Jolla's richly adorned downtown is crowded with fashion-forward boutiques, chic cafes and posh hotels. But what's right on the shoreline is even more of a treasure, especially the all-natural fish bowl of La Jolla Cove, and windswept Torrey Pines State Reserve, further north along the ribbon of coastal highway, where hang-gliders fly.

Venice Beach

22 New-agey bohemians, muscled bodybuilders, goth punks, hippie tribal drummers and genuine freaks all gravitate toward Venice Beach's Ocean Front Walk (p358). It's the place where the crazy side of SoCal really lets it all hang out. Imagine an experimental human zoo, or an outdoor carnival in which audience participation is practically required. Strap on those in-line skates, hop on a pastel-pink beach cruiser or just strut in your bikini and shake what yo' mama gave you.

Whale-Watching

23 Thar she blows! All up and down the coast, and no matter what the season, you can spot migratory whales offshore from California. During summer and fall, blue, humpback and sperm whales cruise by. But the biggest parades happen every winter and spring when gray whales make their annual migrations between the arctic waters of Alaska and balmy breeding and birthing lagoons in the Gulf of Mexico. Jump aboard a whale-watching boat tour to observe these majestic marine mammals up close and personal.

Bolinas

24 Locals keep taking down the highway signs to prevent you from discovering this paradisiacal hamlet (p105) by the sea in Marin County, but once you finally find it, the rewards justify the effort. Take time out to go beachcombing along Agate Beach, drift around the placid waters of Bass Lake on an inner tube, or gin up your courage enough to talk politics with the grizzled old fishers and baby boomers at a saloon while slurping down oyster shooters and an icy beer.

Murals, Bolinas

Sausalito

25 It's not just seabirds and seals – travelers also flock to this little fishing and houseboat community (p95) on San Francisco Bay, just north of the iconic Golden Gate Bridge. Stroll around Sausalito's little downtown on a bike or walk out onto the floating quays in the marina that bob up and down with the gentle waves as kayakers paddle past. Feast on fresh sushi or grilled seafood before hopping on a ferry back across the bay, letting the salty maritime breezes lick your lips.

Need to Know

For more information, see Survival Guide (p497)

Currency
US dollars ($)

Language
English

Visas
Generally not required for stays of 90 days or less for citizens of Visa Waiver Program (VWP) countries with ESTA approval (apply online at least 72 hours in advance).

Money
ATMs widely available. Credit cards usually required for reservations; debit cards sometimes accepted. Traveler's checks (US dollars) rarely used. Tipping is customary, not optional.

Cell Phones
The only foreign phones that will work are GSM multiband models. Buy prepaid SIM cards locally. Coverage can be spotty in remote areas.

Time
Pacific Standard Time (GMT/UTC minus eight hours).

When to Go

Eureka
GO Apr–Oct

San Francisco
GO Apr–Oct

Monterey
GO Apr–Oct

Santa Barbara
GO Apr–Oct

Los Angeles
GO Apr–Oct

San Diego
GO Apr–Nov

- Desert, dry climate
- Dry climate
- Warm to hot summers, mild winters
- Warm to hot summers, cold winters

High Season
(Jun–Aug)

➡ Accommodation prices up 50–100%.

➡ Major holidays are even busier and more expensive.

➡ Thick clouds may blanket the coast during 'June gloom,' which can last into July.

Shoulder Season (Apr–May & Sep–Oct)

➡ Crowds and prices drop off almost everywhere along the coast.

➡ Mild temperatures, with many sunny, cloudless days.

➡ Weather typically wetter in spring, drier in autumn.

Low Season
(Nov–Mar)

➡ Fewest crowds and lowest lodging rates, except around holidays and sometimes in major cities.

➡ Chilly temperatures bring more frequent rainstorms throughout winter.

Websites

California Travel & Tourism Commission (www.visitcalifornia.com) Multilingual trip-planning guides.

Lonely Planet (www.lonelyplanet.com/usa/california) Destination info, hotel bookings, travelers' forums and more.

LA Times (www.latimes.com/travel/california) Travel news, deals and blogs.

Sunset (www.sunset.com/travel/california) Savvy local and insider travel tips.

Important Numbers

All phone numbers have a three-digit area code followed by a seven-digit local number. For long distance and toll-free calls, dial 1 plus all 10 digits.

Country code	☑1
International dialing code	☑011
Operator	☑0
Emergency (ambulance, fire & police)	☑911
Directory assistance (local)	☑411

Exchange Rates

Australia	A$1	$0.89
Canada	C$1	$0.90
Euro zone	€1	$1.27
China	Y10	$1.63
Japan	¥100	$0.92
Mexico	MXN10	$0.74
New Zealand	NZ$1	$0.79
UK	£1	$1.61

For current exchange rates see www.xe.com.

Daily Costs

Budget:
Less than $75

➡ Hostel dorm bed: $25–55

➡ Take-out meal: $6–12

➡ Beach parking: Free–$15

Midrange:
$75–200

➡ Two-star inland motel or hotel double room: $75–200

➡ Sit-down meal in casual restaurant: $20–50

➡ Rental car per day, excluding insurance and gas: $30–75

Top end:
More than $200

➡ Three-star coastal hotel or beach resort room: $150–300

➡ Three-course meal excluding drinks in top restaurant: $75–100

Opening Hours

Businesses, restaurants and shops may close earlier and on additional days during the winter off-season (November to March). Otherwise, standard opening hours are as follows:

Banks 9am–5pm Monday–Thursday, to 6pm Friday, some 9am–1:30pm Saturday

Bars 5pm–2am daily

Business hours (general) 9am–5pm Monday–Friday

Nightclubs 10pm–4am Thursday–Saturday

Post offices 8:30am–4:30pm Monday–Friday, some 9am–noon Saturday

Restaurants 7:30am–10:30am, 11:30am–2:30pm and 5pm–9pm or 10pm daily, some open later Friday and Saturday

Shops 10am–6pm Monday–Saturday, noon–5pm Sunday (malls open later)

Arriving in Coastal California

Los Angeles International Airport (p379) Taxis to most destinations ($30 to $50) take 30 minutes to one hour. Door-to-door shuttles ($16 to $27) operate 24 hours. FlyAway bus ($8) runs to downtown LA. Free shuttles connect with LAX City Bus Center & Metro Rail station.

San Francisco International Airport (p507) Taxis into the city ($35 to $55) take 25 to 50 minutes. Door-to-door shuttles ($16 to $20) operate 24 hours. BART trains ($8.65, 30 minutes) serve the airport, running from 5:30am to 11:45pm daily.

Getting Around

Most people drive themselves around California. You can also fly (it's expensive) or take cheaper long-distance buses or scenic trains. In cities, when distances are too far to walk, hop aboard buses, trains, streetcars, cable cars or trolleys, or grab a taxi.

Car Metro-area traffic can be nightmarish, especially during weekday commuter rush hours (roughly 7am to 10am and 3pm to 7pm). City parking is often an expensive hassle.

Train The fastest way to get around the San Francisco Bay Area and LA, but lines don't go everywhere. Pricier regional and long-distance Amtrak trains connect some destinations.

Bus Usually the cheapest and slowest option, but with extensive metro-area networks. Inter-city, regional and long-distance Greyhound routes are limited and more expensive.

For much more on **getting around**, see p506

If You Like...

Fabulous Food

Infused by immigrant cultures for more than 200 years, California cuisine is all about creatively mixing it up, from kimchi tacos to vegan soul food.

Chez Panisse Berkeley chef Alice Waters revolutionized California cuisine with seasonal, locavorian cooking. (p123)

French Laundry This high-flying kitchen mastered by Thomas Keller is a gastronomic highlight of Napa's wine country. (p153)

Ferry Building Drop by the farmers market, or duck inside for Bay Area artisanal food vendors. (p79)

LA's food trucks They're everywhere now, but LA sparked the mobile foodie revolution, with 200 chefs-on-wheels. (p368)

San Diego's fish tacos Find the perfect snack down south near the Mexico border. (p440)

Marin County Shuck fresh oysters by the sea, taste gourmet cheeses and stop at roadside farms. (p90)

Wine

Napa and Sonoma are ultra-famous, but California's other wine countries more than hold their own. Crack open a bottle from these sun-kissed rural valleys and you'll be a believer.

Napa Valley Pay your respects to California's legendary big-name producers in this premier wine-growing region. (p142)

Sonoma Valley Shake hands with boutique winemakers in sun-dappled biodynamic vineyards. (p164)

Russian River Area Tipple at woodsy wineries after a day of canoeing on the river. (p175)

Santa Barbara County Pastoral country roads wind past famous vintners and smaller family-owned estate wineries. (p326)

Paso Robles Dozens of down-to-earth vineyards produce rich, earthy Zinfandels, with olive-oil farms nearby. (p295)

Anderson Valley Mendocino County's rural valley, where apple orchards abound, hides petite wineries. (p219)

National & State Parks

All along the coast, a chain of public parks protect an astonishing diversity of life zones, extending offshore to marine sanctuaries and wind-tossed islands. Just inland, misty redwood forests beckon.

Redwood National & State Parks Get lost ambling among ancient groves of the world's tallest trees on the foggy North Coast. (p243)

Channel Islands National Park Escape civilization on SoCal's far-flung islands, nicknamed 'California's Galapagos.' (p343)

Point Reyes National Seashore Step on the San Andreas Fault, hike to end-of-the-world beaches and spy wildlife. (p107)

Monterey Bay National Marine Sanctuary Cruise above an undersea canyon on a whale-watching boat, then kayak Elkhorn Slough. (p262)

Big Sur's State Parks Find redwood forest waterfalls and walk along sea cliffs, above which California condors fly. (p275)

Crystal Cove State Park Go scuba diving along gorgeously undeveloped beaches in Orange County. (p417)

Hiking

Californians have been hiking ever since Native Americans made the first footpaths in the wilderness. Oceanside rambles, panorama-view mountain summits and verdant forest idylls await.

North Coast Hardy backpackers challenge the remote Lost Coast Trail, while families ramble among redwood trees. (p195)

Marin County Tawny headlands and wild, windblown Point Reyes tempt hikers across the Golden Gate Bridge. (p90)

Central Coast Seek out Big Sur's secret waterfalls and climb volcanic peaks around San Luis Obispo. (p250)

Los Angeles Run around LA's Griffith Park, or head up into the untamed Santa Monica Mountains. (p347)

Santa Barbara County Venture into the scenic Santa Ynez Mountains or the vast Los Padres National Forest. (p308)

Hot Springs & Spas

Get nekkid and soak in natural hot-springs pools or your own private redwood hot tub under the stars, or be pampered at a wine-country spa.

Calistoga Mud baths are just what the doctor ordered before a day of wine tasting. (p160)

Big Sur Take an sea-cliff dip at Esalen and trek to wilderness Sykes Hot Springs. (p280)

North Coast Take holistic health cures, soak in naturally carbonated springs or go bohemian hot-tubbing. (p222)

Ojai Hike through the forest to hidden hot springs pools to bathe *au naturale*. (p339)

Avila Beach At a mineral-springs spa, book a hillside hot tub for just the two of you. (p302)

Film & TV Locations

All California's a sound stage, it sometimes seems. To witness the magic in action, join a live studio audience or tour a movie studio in LA.

PLAN YOUR TRIP IF YOU LIKE...

Top: Redwood forest, Northern California
Bottom: Tacos, Mijita (p79), San Francisco

Los Angeles Hollywood was born here. You can't throw a director's megaphone without hitting a celluloid sight, from Mulholland Drive to Malibu. (p347)

San Francisco Bay Area Relive film-noir classics like *The Maltese Falcon* and Hitchcock's thrillers *Vertigo* and *The Birds*.

Orange County Where soap operas, 'dramedies' and reality TV series have glamorized pop culture. (p397)

Mendocino For over a century, this tiny North Coast town has starred in dozens of movies, from *East of Eden* to *The Majestic*. (p206)

Santa Barbara Idyllic 'American Riviera' setting for zany rom-coms such as *Sideways* and *It's Complicated*. (p308)

Coronado Where Marilyn Monroe cavorted in *Some Like It Hot*. (p433)

Offbeat & Kitsch

A capital of kookiness, California lets you encounter eccentric characters, oddball places and bizarre experiences, from tiny coastal towns to the maze-like streets of SF and LA.

Venice Boardwalk Gawk at the human zoo of body builders, chainsaw-jugglers and Speedo-clad snake charmers. (p358)

Kinetic Grand Championship Outrageously whimsical, artistic and human-powered sculptures race along the North Coast. (p238)

Madonna Inn Fantastically campy Central Coast hotel advertising 110 bizarrely themed rooms, including 'Caveman.' (p300)

Solvang Danish-flavored village in Santa Barbara's wine country

spirited out of a Hans Christian Andersen fairy tale. (p333)

Bay to Breakers San Francisco's wacky, costumed annual pilgrimage from the Embarcadero to Ocean Beach. (p70)

Mystery Spot Santa Cruz's shamelessly kitschy 1940s tourist trap will turn your whole world upside down. (p256)

Small Towns

When you tire of California's never-ending freeway traffic, make your escape to these in-between spots, whether by the beach or just down the road from vineyards.

Ferndale The North Coast's most charming Victorian farm town, filled with 'butterfat mansions.' (p232)

Bolinas This hamlet in Marin County isn't exactly a secret anymore. (p105)

Seal Beach Orange County surf spot with an old-fashioned main street and wooden pier. (p400)

Ojai Catch a 'pink moment' at sunset over this sleepy, arty little Shangri-La outside LA. (p339)

Mendocino North Coast seaside village perched on ocean bluffs, where landscape painters set up their easels. (p206)

Scenic Drives

Drop the convertible top and step on it! California's coastal routes deliver surreally beautiful ocean vistas and serpentine cliff-side stretches.

Pacific Coast Highway SoCal's stretch of Hwy 1 famously hop-scotches between beach towns in Orange County. (p409)

Avenue of the Giants Roll through groves of redwood trees in NorCal's Humboldt Redwoods State Park. (p230)

17-Mile Drive Postcard Pacific vistas beckon all along this private toll road around the Monterey Peninsula. (p272)

Big Sur Twist and turn atop dizzying sea cliffs along Hwy 1 on the Central Coast. (p275)

San Diego's North County Cruise lazily alongside the Pacific past funky beach towns and famous surf spots. (p450)

Aquariums & Zoos

California is chockablock with futuristic theme parks and other family-friendly attractions to keep kids entertained for days, but for many, it's the local wildlife that are the real stars.

Monterey Bay Aquarium Watch otters play at feeding time, touch tide-pool critters and get chills as sharks swim by. (p262)

San Diego Zoo In leafy Balboa Park, California's best zoo exhibits over 800 different species from around the world. (p429)

San Diego Zoo Safari Park Take a safari-style tram tour through an 'open-range' zoo where giraffes and lions roam. (p43)

Aquarium of the Pacific Meet coastal California's denizens of the deep at Long Beach, just south of LA. (p359)

Los Angeles Zoo Originally a refuge for retired circus animals, this conservation-minded zoo inhabits Griffith Park. (p353)

Marine Mammal Center Marin County's wildlife hospital and oceanic education center has unbeatable eco-credentials. (p91)

Interior of Madonna Inn (p300), San Luis Obispo

History

Native American tribes, Spanish colonial *presidios* (forts), Catholic missions and Mexican *pueblos* (towns) have all left traces here for you to find.

Mission San Juan Capistrano A painstakingly restored jewel along 'El Camino Real,' California's mission trail. (p422)

San Diego's Old Town Time travel back to the late 19th century at California's first civilian Spanish *pueblo*. (p431)

El Pueblo de Los Angeles Get swept up by the atmosphere of LA's earliest days along lively Olvera St. (p349)

Monterey State Historic Park Beautifully preserved brick and adobe buildings from California's Spanish, Mexican and American periods. (p263)

San Francisco Prowl Chinatown's alleys, channel the Beats in North Beach or tour the psychedelic Haight. (p48)

Hearst Castle A fantastical hilltop mansion filled with priceless art and antiquities on the Central Coast. (p284)

Museums

Who says coastal California only has pop culture? You could spend most of your trip viewing multimillion-dollar art galleries, high-tech science exhibits, out-of-this-world planetariums and more.

Balboa Park Spend all day hopping between San Diego's top-notch art, history and science museums. (p429)

Getty Center & Getty Villa LA art museums that are as beautiful as their elevated settings and ocean views. (p355)

California Academy of Sciences Natural history museum in SF's Golden Gate Park breathes 'green' with a living roof. (p75)

Los Angeles County Museum of Art More than 150,000 works of art span the ages and cross all borders. (p354)

Griffith Observatory There's no better place to see stars in Hollywood than at this hilltop planetarium. (p353)

Exploratorium Even adults love the interactive science fun at this indoor/outdoor landmark on San Francisco Bay. (p53)

Month by Month

TOP EVENTS

Tournament of Roses,
January

**Miramar Air Show &
Fleet Week**, October

**Festival of Arts &
Pageant of the Masters**, July & August

Kinetic Grand Championship, May

Tall Ships Festival,
September

January

Typically the wettest
and coldest month in
California, January is
a slow time for coastal
travel, except over the
Martin Luther King Jr Day
holiday weekend.

☆ Tournament of Roses

Held before the Rose Bowl
college football game, this
famous New Year's parade
of flower-festooned floats,
marching bands and prancing equestrians draws over
700,000 spectators to Pasadena, a suburb of LA.

February

Usually another rainy
month for coastal
California, but wildflowers
start blooming. Valentine's
Day is booked solid at
restaurants and hotels.

✹ Chinese New Year

Firecrackers, parades, lion
dances and street food
accompany the lunar new
year, falling in late January
or early February. Some of
California's most colorful
festivities happen in San
Francisco and LA.

March

Winter rains start to end in
California. Coastal travel
picks up again, especially
over spring break (exact
dates vary, depending on
school schedules and the
Easter holiday).

✹ Mendocino Coast Whale Festivals

As the northbound winter
migration of gray whales
peaks, Mendocino, Fort
Bragg and nearby towns
celebrate with food and
wine tastings, art shows
and naturalist-guided
walks and talks over three
weekends in March.

✹ Festival of the Swallows

After wintering in South
America, the famous swallows return to Orange
County's Mission San Juan
Capistrano around March
19. The historic mission
town honors its Spanish
and Mexican heritage with
events all month long.
(p423)

May

California's weather starts
to heat up, although some
coastal areas are blanketed
by fog ('May gray'). Travel
peaks over the Memorial
Day holiday weekend.

🏃 Kinetic Grand Championship

Over Memorial Day weekend, this 'triathlon of
the art world' involves a
three-day race from Arcata
to Ferndale on the North
Coast. Competitors outdo
each other in inventing
human-powered, self-
propelled and sculptural
contraptions. (p238)

June

Once school lets out
for the summer, nearly
everywhere in California
gets busy, even though fog
('June gloom') lingers in
some coastal areas.

☆ Pride Month
Out and proud since 1970, many of California's gay pride events take place throughout June, with costumed parades, coming-out parties, live music, DJs and more, especially in San Francisco and LA. San Diego celebrates in mid-July.

July
Beach season gets into full swing, especially in Southern California, where theme parks are mobbed by families. The July 4th holiday is summer's busiest travel weekend.

☆ Reggae on the River
Come party with the 'Humboldt Nation' of hippies, Rastafarians, tree huggers and other fun NorCal freaks for two days of live reggae bands, arts and crafts, barbecue, juggling, unicycling, camping and swimming in late July and early August. (p227)

✤ Festival of Arts & Pageant of the Masters
Exhibits by hundreds of artists and a pageant of masterpiece paintings 're-created' by actors keep Orange County's Laguna Beach extremely busy during July and August.

August
Sunny weather and warm water temperatures keep beaches packed. Students go back to school, but everywhere along the coast stays busy through

the Labor Day holiday weekend.

☆ Old Spanish Days Fiesta
Santa Barbara revives its early Spanish, Mexican and American *rancho* culture with flashy parades, cowboy rodeo events, arts-and-crafts shows, live music and dancing in early August. (p318)

September
Summer's last hurrah is the Labor Day holiday weekend, when everywhere is extremely crowded. Afterward, the beaches and cities start seeing fewer visitors.

◉ Miramar Air Show & Fleet Week
San Diego's military pride is on display during this week (more like a month) of parades, concerts, shipboard tours and the USA's largest air show in late September or early October. (p437)

🏃 Tall Ships Festival
In early September, the West Coast's biggest gathering of historical tall ships happens at Dana Point in Orange County, with knot-tying and scrimshaw carving demonstrations. (p424)

October
Despite beautifully sunny and balmy weather, coastal travel slows down. Shoulder-season deals abound at beaches and

in cities as temperatures begin to cool off.

♟ Vineyard Festivals
All month long under sunny skies, California's wine countries bring in the harvest with gourmet food-and-wine shindigs, grape-stomping 'crush' parties and barrel tastings.

November
Temperatures drop everywhere in California, as scattered winter rainstorms begin. Coastal areas are less busy, except around the Thanksgiving holiday

✤ Día de los Muertos
Mexican communities honor deceased ancestors on November 2 with costumed parades, sugar skulls, graveyard picnics, candlelight processions and fabulous altars, including in San Francisco, LA and San Diego.

December
Winter rains start to drench coastal California. Christmas and New Year's Eve are extremely busy times, with a short-lived lull in travel between them.

◉ Parade of Lights
Spicing up the Christmas holiday season with nautical cheer, brightly bedecked and illuminated boats float through many coastal California harbors, most famously at Newport Beach and San Diego. (p406 & p438)

Itineraries

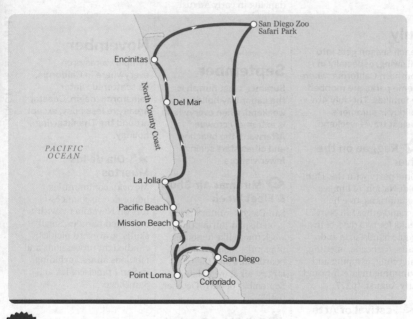

San Diego Zoo
Safari Park

Encinitas

North County Coast

Del Mar

PACIFIC
OCEAN

La Jolla

Pacific Beach

Mission Beach

San Diego

Point Loma   Coronado

3 DAYS San Diego & North County

The best part about San Diego? It's almost always around 68°F (20°C) and sunny. Add insanely good Mexican food, beaches of all stripes, historic sites and one of the best zoos in the world (plus an open-range safari park). Are you sold yet?

Spend a couple of days at San Diego's Pearl-like beaches, stretching all the way up the North County Coast. But before you head northward, drive out to **Point Loma** for sweeping views, or take a ferry over to old-fashioned **Coronado**, with its famous 'Hotel Del.' Ride the Giant Dipper roller coaster at family-friendly **Mission Beach**, join the funky surfers at **Pacific Beach**, dive or snorkel in gorgeous **La Jolla**, bet on horse races or soar in a hot-air balloon at **Del Mar**, and get new-agey in **Encinitas**.

On day three, if you have kids, make a beeline to the suburban **San Diego Zoo Safari Park**, where giraffes, lions and zebras roam. Otherwise, head back to **San Diego** to explore the zoo at museum-loaded Balboa Park and the atmospheric Spanish-Mexican Old Town. End your trip with a wild night out in the city's Gaslamp Quarter downtown.

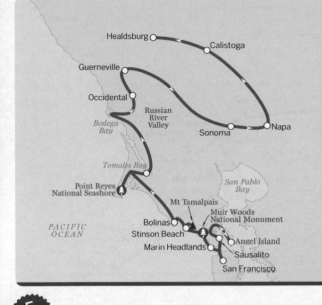

5 DAYS — San Francisco, Marin County & Wine Country

Clamber around the hilly 7-sq-mile peninsula that is dashing, innovative and ever-evolving San Francisco. Then soak up the natural beauty of Marin County before indulging in a wine-splashed weekend in Napa and Sonoma.

Start with a day in **San Francisco** uncovering the alleyways of Chinatown, wandering the Mission District and climbing Coit Tower. Brave the fog on a cruise to Alcatraz from Fisherman's Wharf, or lose yourself on a sunny day in Golden Gate Park, stopping to smell the flowers where hippies danced during 1967's 'Summer of Love.' Wherever you roam, eat everything in sight – especially at the waterfront Ferry Building Marketplace.

Escape the city on day two via the landmark Golden Gate Bridge, which you can trek, cycle or drive across. On the far side of the bay, photograph the floating houseboats of picturesque **Sausalito**, or go hiking and mountain-biking across the **Marin Headlands**, where a swinging footbridge leads to historic Point Bonita Lighthouse. To really get away from it all, hop aboard the ferry from Tiburon over to **Angel Island**, within view of San Francisco's skyscrapers.

Meander north along the Marin County coast on day three, passing the tall redwood trees of **Muir Woods National Monument**, crescent-shaped **Stinson Beach** and the turnoff to quirky small-town **Bolinas**. Veer inland to conquer **Mt Tamalpais** or make your way to wildly beautiful **Point Reyes National Seashore**, where end-of-the-world beaches lead to long rambles, and you can spy whales in winter from the historic lighthouse. Save time for sea kayaking at nearby **Tomales Bay**.

Finish with two days in wine country. From Bodega Bay, country roads wind inland to charming **Occidental** and the vineyards of **Russian River Valley**. Paddle a canoe downriver to **Guerneville**, with its redwood cottages and swimming by the beach in summer. Truck east across Hwy 101, then head south into Northern California's wine country, orbiting stylish **Napa** and its countrified but still-chic cousin **Sonoma**. Soak your road-weary bones in a volcanic mud bath at a hot-springs spa in **Calistoga** before winding down in posh **Healdsburg**.

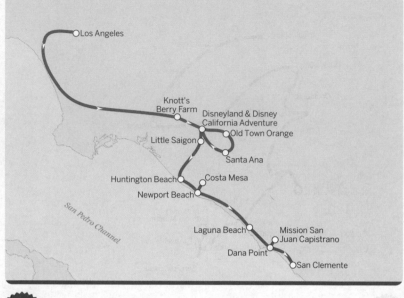

1 WEEK Los Angeles & Orange County

Kick things off in Los Angeles, where top-notch attractions, miles of beaches and tasty food form an irresistible trifecta, before tripping through OC's theme parks and beaches.

On your first two days in **Los Angeles**, traipse along the star-studded sidewalks of clubby Hollywood, dive into the arts and cultural scenes Downtown, and browse the Mid-City's many museums and West LA's hilltop Getty Center. Out at the Pacific's edge, sophisticated Santa Monica beckons with a carnival seaside pier and creative restaurants, while alternative Venice lives and breathes beachy boho-chic style.

Heading inland on day three, make a date with Mickey at perfectly 'imagineered' **Disneyland** and next-door **Disney California Adventure**, celebrating the Golden State. Both parks are in Anaheim, not far from **Knott's Berry Farm**, America's oldest theme park, which pairs Old Western cowboy themes with high-tech roller coasters. If it's too darn hot, cool off at Knott's Soak City Orange County water park.

Drop by the family-friendly, interactive Discovery Science Center or peruse the art galleries of the Bowers Museum in **Santa Ana**. Catch your breath in time-warped **Old Town Orange**, clustered with antiques stores, or **Little Saigon**, where you can trade theme-park hot dogs for a steaming bowl of pho.

On day four, motor west toward the ocean. In **Huntington Beach**, aka 'Surf City,' USA,' rent a board, play beach volleyball, build a bonfire after sunset. Hit **Newport Beach** for soap opera–worthy people-watching by the piers. Make a quick stop for power shopping in **Costa Mesa**, then roll south to **Laguna Beach**, a former artists' colony with more than two dozen public beaches to spoil you, plus fashionable downtown boutiques.

Slingshot back toward the I-5 on your last day, stopping off at **Mission San Juan Capistrano** for a glimpse of Spanish colonial and Mexican history. Or keep up the beach-bum attitude by slacking south to **Dana Point**, with its yacht-filled harbor and beach, and retro **San Clemente**, near Trestles, a year-round surf break.

Top: Hollywood Walk of Fame (p349), Los Angeles. *Hollywood Walk of Fame™ & Design © 2014 HCC. All Rights Reserved*

Bottom: Dana Point harbor (p423)

Plan Your Trip

Beaches, Swimming & Surfing

Beach life and surf culture are part of California's free-wheeling lifestyle, so play hooky on any day of the week and go hit the waves like locals do. Southern California is where you'll find the sunniest swimming beaches, while Northern California's rockier, often foggy strands beckon to beachcombers.

Best Beaches

San Diego
Coronado, Mission Beach, Pacific Beach, La Jolla

Orange County
Newport Beach, Laguna Beach, Crystal Cove State Park, Doheny State Beach

Los Angeles
Santa Monica, Venice, South Bay, Malibu

Santa Barbara
East Beach, El Capitán State Beach, Refugio State Beach, Carpinteria State Beach

Central Coast
Main Beach (Santa Cruz), Moonstone Beach, Cayucos, Pismo State Beach

San Francisco Bay Area
Stinson Beach, Point Reyes National Seashore, Pacifica State Beach

North Coast
Sonoma Coast State Beach, Lost Coast, Trinidad State Beach

Swimming

If lazing on the beach and taking a dip in the Pacific is what your California dreams are made of, look no further than Southern California (SoCal). With miles and miles of wide, sandy beaches, you will find it easy to get wet and wild almost anywhere between Santa Barbara and San Diego. Ocean temperatures in SoCal become tolerable by May or June, peaking in July and August.

Northern California (NorCal) beaches are generally rocky, with dangerously high swell in some places and windy conditions that make swimming less than inviting. NorCal beaches remain chilly year-round – bring or rent a wetsuit!

Building bonfires on the beach at sunset is a California tradition, but they're no longer permitted at most beaches for environmental reasons. Legally, you can build bonfires only in designated fire-pits – show up early in the day to snag one and bring your own firewood. Unless otherwise posted, drinking alcohol is usually prohibited on beaches, except at campgrounds.

During the hottest dog days of summer, another way to keep cool is by swimming at Legoland (p457), in San Diego's North County, or **Soak City Orange County** (☎714-220-5200; www.knotts.com; adult/child 3-11yr & senior $27/22; ☉mid-May–Sep; 🚹) in Anaheim, near Disneyland.

Safety Tips

➡ Most beaches, especially in Southern California, have flags to distinguish between surfer-only sections and sections for swimmers. Flags also alert beachgoers to dangerous water conditions.

➡ Popular beaches (again, mostly in Southern California) have lifeguards, but can still be dangerous places to swim. Obey all posted warning signs and ask about local conditions before venturing out.

➡ Stay out of the ocean for at least three days after a major rainstorm because of dangerously high levels of pollutants flushed out through storm drains.

➡ Water quality varies from beach to beach, and day to day. For current water-safety conditions and beach closures, check the **Beach Report Card** (http://brc.healthebay.org) issued by the nonprofit organization **Heal the Bay** (www.healthebay.org).

Best Family-Friendly Beaches

➡ **Silver Strand State Beach** (p433) Coronado

➡ **Santa Monica State Beach** (p357) Los Angeles

➡ **Leo Carrillo State Beach** (p357) Malibu

➡ **Balboa Peninsula** (p404) Newport Beach

➡ **Carpinteria State Beach** (p316) Santa Barbara County

WARNING! RIPTIDES
If you find yourself being carried offshore by a dangerous ocean current called a riptide, the important thing is to just keep afloat. Don't panic or try to swim against the current, as this will quickly exhaust you and you could drown. Instead, swim parallel to the shoreline and once the current stops pulling you out, swim back to shore.

➡ **Arroyo Burro Beach County Park** (p316) Santa Barbara

➡ **Avila Beach** (p302) San Luis Obispo County

➡ **Natural Bridges State Beach** (p255) Santa Cruz

➡ **Stinson Beach** (p104) Marin County

➡ **Trinidad State Beach** (p241) North Coast

Best Beaches for Bonfires

➡ **Huntington City Beach** (p401) Orange County

➡ **Main Beach** (Corona del Mar State Beach; p417) Orange County

➡ **Mission Beach** (p398) San Diego

➡ **Carmel Beach City Park** (p274) Central Coast

➡ **Ocean Beach** (p74) San Francisco

Best Places for Beach Volleyball

➡ **Manhattan Beach** (p355) LA's South Bay

➡ **Hermosa Beach** (p355) LA's South Bay

➡ **Huntington City Beach** (p401) Orange County

➡ **Mission Bay** (p433) San Diego

➡ **East Beach** (p522) Santa Barbara

Books & Maps

The outstanding *California Coastal Access Guide* (University of California Press, 2014) has comprehensive maps of every public beach, reef, harbor, cover, overlook and coastal campground, with valuable information about parking, hiking trails, facilities and wheelchair access. It's especially helpful for finding secret pockets of uncrowded sand.

Surfing

Surf's up! Are you down? Even if you have never set foot on a board, there's no denying the influence of surfing on every aspect of California beach life, from street clothing to slang. Surfing is an obsession up and down the SoCal coast, particularly in San Diego and Orange Counties.

The most powerful ocean swells arrive along California's coast during late fall and winter. May and June are generally the flattest months, although they do bring warmer water. Speaking of temperature, don't believe all those images of hot blonds surfing in skimpy bikinis; without a wetsuit, you'll likely freeze your butt off except at the height of summer, especially in NorCal.

Crowds can be a problem at many surf spots, as can overly territorial surfers. Befriend a local surfer for an introduction before hitting Cali's most famous waves, such as notoriously agro Windansea Beach and Malibu's Surfrider Beach.

Sharks do inhabit California waters but attacks are rare. Most take place in the so-called 'Red Triangle' between Monterey on the Central Coast, Tomales Bay north of San Francisco and the offshore Farallon Islands.

Rentals & Lessons

You'll find board rentals on just about every patch of sand where surfing is possible. Expect to pay about $20 per half day for a board, with wetsuit rental costing another $10 or so.

Two-hour group lessons for beginners start around $100 per person, while private, two-hour instruction easily costs over $125. If you're ready to jump in the deep end, many surf schools offer more expensive weekend surf clinics and weeklong 'surfari' camps.

Stand-up paddleboarding (SUP) is easier than learning to surf, and it's skyrocketing in popularity. You'll find similarly priced board-and-paddle rentals and lessons popping up all along the coast, from San Diego to north of San Francisco Bay.

Top Surf Spots for Pros

California comes fully loaded with easily accessible world-class surf spots, the lion's share of which are in SoCal. If you're already a wave-sliding expert, check out:

➜ **Huntington Beach** (p401) This beach in Orange County may have the West Coast's most consistent waves, with miles of breaks.

➜ **Trestles** (p423) The OC's premier summer spot, with big but forgiving waves, a fast ride and both right and left breaks.

➜ **Windansea Beach** (p452) This San Diego spot has a powerful reef break, while nearby **Big Rock** (p452) churns out gnarly tubes.

➜ **Surfrider Beach** (p357) A clean right break in Malibu that just gets better with bigger waves.

➜ **Rincon Point** (p315) In Carpinteria, this is another legendary point-break that peels forever.

➜ **Steamer Lane** (p254) Glassy point-breaks and rocky reef-breaks below an old lighthouse that houses a small surfing museum in Santa Cruz.

➜ **Mavericks** (p135) Big-wave surfing at Half Moon Bay. Waves top 50ft when the most powerful winter swells arrive (see www.mavericksinvitational.com to learn about the annual surf competition).

Best Surf Breaks for Beginners

The best spots to learn to surf are at the beach breaks of long, shallow bays where waves are small and rolling. Along California's coast, popular places for beginners, and where many surf schools also offer lessons, include the following:

➜ **San Diego** Mission Beach (p433), Pacific Beach (p433), La Jolla (p450), Oceanside (p459)

➜ **Orange County Beaches** (p397) Huntington Beach, Newport Beach, Laguna Beach

➜ **Los Angeles** Santa Monica (p357), Malibu (p357)

➜ **Santa Barbara County** Leadbetter Beach (p315), Carpinteria (p316)

➜ **Central Coast** Santa Cruz (p253), Cayucos (p287)

Online Resources

➜ Browse the atlas, webcams and reports at **Surfline** (www.surfline.com) for the lowdown from San Diego to Humboldt County.

➜ Orange County–based **Surfer** (www.surfermag.com) magazine's website has travel reports, gear reviews, blogs, forums and videos.

➜ Check out **Surfrider Foundation** (www.surfrider.org), a nonprofit organization that works to protect the coastal environment.

➜ Bone up on your surf-speak at the **Riptionary** (www.riptionary.com).

Books & Maps

➜ Water-resistant *Surfer Magazine's Guide to Southern California Surf Spots* (Chronicle Books, 2006) and *Surfer Magazine's Guide to Northern and Central California Surf Spots* (Chronicle Books, 2006) are jam-packed with expert reviews, information, maps and photos.

Plan Your Trip
Outdoor Activities

California is an all-seasons outdoor playground. Here you can go hiking among wildflowers in spring, swimming in the Pacific warmed by summer sunshine, mountain-biking among fall foliage and whale-watching in winter. For bigger thrills, launch a glider off ocean bluffs or don a wet suit to dive into underwater sanctuaries.

Kayaking

Whether you're looking for an adventure exploring sea caves or just a serene float past coastal bluffs or along inland rivers, kayaking opportunities abound in coastal California. Few water-based sports are as accessible and fun for the whole family, and most people manage to get paddling along quickly with minimal instruction.

Best Places to Kayak

➡ Sea kayaking is fabulous in **Channel Islands National Park**, offshore from Ventura, and **Catalina Island**, closer to Los Angeles and Orange County. Both are ideal overnight getaways for experienced paddlers.

➡ Further south, beginners can paddle around the calm waters of San Diego's **Mission Bay** or at **Huntington Harbor** and **Dana Point** in OC.

➡ You can explore sea caves while floating above kelp forests and reefs of **San Diego–La Jolla Underwater Park Ecological Reserve**.

➡ You'll find more coastal kayaking in **Malibu**, among the coves of Orange County's **Laguna Beach** and around **Gaviota** near Santa Barbara.

➡ Beginners can take a spin around **Morro Bay**, whose waters are protected by a 4-mile sand spit, or float inland for wildlife-watching at **Elkhorn Slough** between Monterey and Santa Cruz.

Best Times to Go

Backpacking & hiking Apr–Oct

Cycling & mountain biking Apr–Oct

Kayaking Jul–Oct

Snorkeling & scuba diving Jul–Oct

Whale-watching Jan–Mar

Windsurfing Apr–Oct

Top Outdoor Experiences

Backpacking Northern California's Lost Coast Trail

Cycling Coastal Hwy 1 through Big Sur

Hiking Redwood National & State Parks

Mountain biking Marin County, especially Mt Tamalpais

Kayaking Channel Islands National Park

Snorkeling & scuba diving La Jolla in San Diego County

Whale-watching Monterey Bay National Marine Sanctuary

Windsurfing San Diego's Mission Bay

Camping in Coastal California

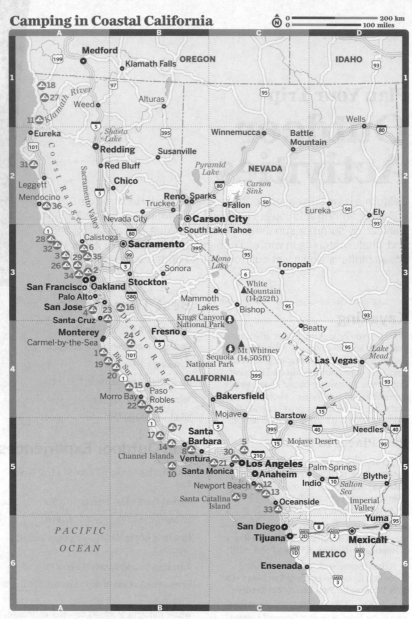

→ In Northern California, brave the choppy waters of **San Francisco Bay**, or head for more sheltered **Richardson Bay** in Sausalito, **Tomales Bay** near Point Reyes, **Bodega Bay** further north, or **Half Moon Bay** south along Hwy 1.

→ In Sonoma's wine country, the **Russian River** is a pretty place to paddle a kayak or canoe, with put-ins at Guerneville, Jenner and Healdsburg.

→ Just outside Mendocino, the **Big River** tidal estuary is a peaceful kayak or canoe trip for families.

Camping in Coastal California

➡ All along the **North Coast**, you'll find challenging points for experienced sea kayakers, as well as gentler lagoons, coves and bays.

Rentals, Lessons & Tours

Most outfitters offer a choice between sit-upon (open) kayaks and sit-in (closed-hull) ones; the latter are slightly more difficult to keep balanced and upright. Kayak rentals average $30 to $50 for a half-day; you'll usually have a choice between single or tandem. A reputable outfitter will make sure you're aware of the tide schedule and wind conditions for your proposed route.

Many kayaking outfitters give lessons and lead guided tours (from $50), including sunrise, sunset and full-moon paddles. There's nothing quite like seeing the reflection of the moon and stars glittering on the water and hearing the gentle splash of water on your kayak's hull. Small-group tours led by guides with natural-history knowledge are best.

Whether you're taking a tour or renting kayaks, try to make reservations at least the day beforehand.

Resources

California Kayak Friends (www.ckf.org) Offers lots of information about everything from safety and popular paddling destinations to recent trip reports and upcoming events.

Kayak Online (www.kayakonline.com/california.html) For dozens of links to local kayaking outfitters, schools and organizations, plus helpful advice.

Scuba Diving & Snorkeling

All along the California coast, rock reefs, shipwrecks and kelp beds teem with sea creatures ready for their close-up. Underwater playgrounds are suited to all skill and experience levels. Ocean waters are warmest in Southern California and between July and September, but wet suits are recommended for divers year-round.

Best Scuba Diving & Snorkeling Spots

➡ **San Diego–La Jolla Underwater Park Ecological Reserve** is a great place for beginning divers, while **La Jolla Cove** attracts snorkelers.

➡ More experienced divers steer towards Orange County's **Crystal Cove State Park**, just south of Newport Beach; **Divers Cove** in Laguna Beach; and **Wreck Alley** near San Diego's Mission Bay.

➡ Some popular dive spots are also good for snorkeling, for example, offshore **Channel Islands National Park** and **Catalina Island**. Boats depart from Los Angeles, Orange County and Ventura County, south of Santa Barbara.

➡ With its national marine sanctuary, **Monterey Bay** offers world-renowned diving and snorkeling; you'll need a thick wet suit.

➡ Just south of Monterey, **Point Lobos State Natural Reserve** is another gem for divers and snorkelers (permit reservations are required here).

Rentals, Lessons & Tours

Local dive shops are your best resource for equipment, guides, instructors and boat trips. If you already have your PADI certification, you can book a one-tank boat dive for $65 to $150; reserve at least a day in advance. To dabble in diving, ask about beginner scuba courses that include basic instruction, followed by a shallow beach or boat dive, for around $150. A multiday open-water certificate course costs anywhere from $250 to $600.

Snorkel kits (including mask, snorkel, fins and maybe a wet suit) can be rented from beach concessionaires and many dive shops for around $20 to $45 per day. If you're going to be taking the plunge more than once or twice, it's probably worth buying your own mask and fins. Remember not to touch anything while you're out snorkeling, don't snorkel alone and always wear a T-shirt or sunblock on your back.

Resources

LA Diver (www.ladiver.com) Although it's not up-dated regularly, this site has encyclopedic listings of dive sites and shops, certification programs, safety resources and weather conditions for the LA area, with links to sister sites for Southern, Central and Northern California.

Scuba Diving (www.scubadiving.com) and **Sport Diver** (www.sportdiver.com) Published by PADI, these magazines have comprehensive websites dedicated to underwater adventures.

Windsurfing & Kiteboarding

Experienced windsurfers tear up the waves along the coast, while newbies or those who want a mellower ride skim along calm bays and protected beaches. There's almost always a breeze, but the best winds blow from September through November. Wet suits are a good idea year-round, especially in Northern California.

Best Places to Windsurf & Kiteboard

Usually any place that has good windsurfing also has good kiteboarding. Look for the people doing aerial acrobatics as their parachute-like kites yank them from the water. In wide-open spaces devoid of obstacles like piers and power lines, you won't have to worry about unexpected flights that could slam you into concrete.

➡ In San Diego, novices should check out **Santa Clara Point** in Mission Bay.

➡ Santa Barbara's **Leadbetter Beach** is another good spot for beginners to learn.

➡ In LA County, you'll see lots of action off **Belmont Shores** near Long Beach and **Point Fermin** near San Pedro.

➡ Offshore from San Francisco's **Crissy Field** is a favorite spot for experienced boarders. The wind literally howls as it squeezes into the bay.

Rentals & Lessons

The learning curve in windsurfing is steeper than other board sports – imagine balancing on a fast-moving plank through choppy waters while trying to read the wind and angle the sail just so. At most windsurfing hot spots, a half-day introductory lesson costs $100 to $150.

Although it's harder to get started kiteboarding, experts say it's easier to advance quickly once the basics are down. Beginner kiteboarding lessons start at over $200, and usually take place over a few days. The first lesson is spent learning kite control on the beach and the second lesson gets you into the water.

Windsurfing gear rentals cost about $50 to $75 per day for a beginner's board and harness. Most windsurfing shops usually won't rent kite gear to people who aren't also taking kiteboarding lessons.

Resources

iWindsurf (www.iwindsurf.com) Wind reports, weather forecasts, live wind-cams and active discussion forums.

iKitesurf (www.ikitesurf.com) Primo locations, wind reports and more for aspiring and experienced kiteboarders.

Whale-Watching

During their annual migration, gray whales can be spotted off the California coast from December to April, while blue, humpback and sperm whales pass by in summer and fall. Just about every port town worth its sea salt along the coast offers whale-watching boat excursions, especially during winter. You can try your luck whale-watching while staying shore-bound (eg from lighthouses) – it's free, but you're less likely to see any whales and you'll be removed from all the action.

Half-day whale-watching boat trips (from $25 to $90 per adult, up to 50% off per child) last from 2½ to four hours, and sometimes include snacks and drinks. Make reservations at minimum a day or two in advance. Better boats limit the number of people and have a trained naturalist on board. Some companies will let you go out again for free if you don't spot any whales on your first cruise.

Bring binoculars and dress in warm, waterproof layers. Choppy seas can be nauseating. To avoid seasickness, sit outside on the boat's second level – but not too close to the diesel fumes in back.

Hiking & Backpacking

No matter where you find yourself in coastal California, you're never far from a trail, even in busy metropolitan areas. The best trails are often amid the jaw-dropping scenery of national and state parks, forests, recreation areas and other public lands. Take your pick of a staggering variety of routes, from easy strolls negotiable by wheelchairs and baby strollers to multiday backpacking treks through the wilderness. Don't miss a ramble among the world's tallest trees, coast redwoods, or California's spring wildflowers that bloom with all the colors of a painter's palette.

Best Places to Hike

➡ **North Coast** Redwood National & State Parks and Humboldt Redwoods State Park offer misty walks through groves of old-growth coast redwoods, or you can discover remote beaches along the challenging Lost Coast Trail.

➡ **San Francisco Bay Area** The Marin Headlands, Muir Woods, Mt Tamalpais and Point Reyes National Seashore, all within a 90-minute drive of San Francisco, are crisscrossed by dozens of superb trails.

➡ **Central Coast & Santa Barbara** Santa Cruz and Big Sur's state parks abound with redwood-forest trails, while Point Lobos State Natural Reserve and Channel Islands National Park offer ocean-view trails with wildlife-watching. The Santa Ynez Mountains and Los Padres National Forest beckon in Santa Barbara County.

➡ **Los Angeles** Ditch your car in urban Griffith Park and wild Santa Monica Mountains National Recreation Area, or head out to the cooler climes of Big Bear Lake. Offshore, day hikers and backpackers trek Catalina Island.

Fees & Wilderness Permits

➡ Many of coastal California's national parks, including Redwood National Park, Point Reyes National Seashore and Channel Islands National Park, are free for entry.

➡ Most California state parks charge a daily parking fee of $4 to $15. There's often no charge for pedestrians or cyclists. Don't park your car just outside the gate and then walk in – California's state parks are chronically underfunded and need your support.

➡ For unlimited admission to national parks, national forests and other federal recreation lands, buy an 'America the Beautiful' annual pass (p500) from national park visitor centers and entry stations or at most USFS ranger stations.

➡ Otherwise, you'll need a **National Forest Adventure Pass** (☏909-382-2623, 909-382-2622; www.fs.fed.us/r5/sanbernardino/ap/; per day $5, annual pass $30) to park in some recreational areas of the San Bernardino, Cleveland, Angeles and Los Padres National Forests. Buy these passes on the spot from USFS ranger stations and authorized local vendors (eg sporting-goods stores), or order them online in advance.

BEWARE: POISON OAK
....

Watch out for western poison oak throughout coastal California, especially in forests and foothills below 5000ft in elevation. This poisonous shrub is most easily identified by its shiny reddish-green tripartite leaves (remember the rhyme 'Leaves of three, let it be!'), which turn crimson in the fall, and its white berries. In winter, when the plant has no leaves, it looks brown and twiggy, but can still cause a serious allergic reaction if even one billionth of a gram of urushiol oil touches your skin. If you brush against poison oak, scrub the affected area immediately with soap and water or an over-the-counter remedy such as Tecnu, a soap specially formulated to remove the plant's itchy urushiol oils.

➡ Often required for overnight backpacking trips, wilderness permits (up to $20 or more, sometimes free) are issued at ranger stations and park visitor centers. Daily quotas may be in effect during peak periods, usually from late spring through early fall. Some permits can be reserved ahead of time and the most popular trails may sell out months in advance.

Resources

At major trailheads, bulletin boards display trail maps and safety information; some also have brochure dispensers.

Free trail maps For short, well-established hikes, the free trail maps handed out at park visitor centers and ranger stations are usually sufficient.

Topographical maps A detailed topographical map may be necessary for longer hikes. Topo maps are sold at park bookstores, visitor centers, stations and outdoor shops such as REI (www.rei.com).

US Geological Survey (USGS; www.store.usgs. gov) Offers its topographic maps as free downloadable PDFs, or order print copies online.

California Coastal Trail Association (www.coastwalk.org) Helping build a 1200-mile trail along California's shoreline – it's already half finished.

Leave No Trace Center for Outdoor Ethics (www.lnt.org) Learn how to minimize your impact on the environment while traipsing through the wilderness.

Cycling & Mountain Biking

The cycling season runs year-round in Southern California, although summers can be blazing hot and coastal fog may rob you of views in winter and also during 'May gray' and 'June gloom.' Late spring through early fall is prime time to pedal around Northern California, where winters are generally cold, rainy and not ideal for cycling.

Road Rules

➡ In national and state parks, bicycles are usually limited to paved and dirt roads and not allowed on trails or in designated wilderness.

➡ Most national forests and Bureau of Land Management (BLM) areas are open to mountain bikers. Stay on already established tracks and always yield to hikers and horseback riders.

Best Places to Cycle

➡ Even the heavily trafficked urban areas of Southern California may sport some good cycling turf. Take, for example, the beachside South Bay Trail in **Los Angeles** or oceanfront recreational paths along **Newport Beach** and **Huntington Beach** in Orange County and in **Santa Barbara** and **Ventura**.

➡ In Northern California's bike-friendly **San Francisco**, you can cruise through Golden Gate Park and over the Golden Gate Bridge, then hop on a ferry from **Sausalito**. **Angel Island** is another great bike-and-ferry combo.

➡ On the Central Coast, the waterfront **Monterey Peninsula Recreational Trail** is an easy pedal, while the scenic **17-Mile Drive** entices more skilled riders. For long-distance cyclists, nothing surpasses coastal **Highway 1**, especially the dizzying stretch through **Big Sur**.

➡ Many of California's many wine countries, including **Napa Valley** and **Sonoma Valley**, offer beautiful guided or DIY bike tours past vineyards, farms and small towns.

Best Places for Mountain Biking

➡ North of San Francisco, **Marin Headlands** offers a bonanza of trails for fat-tire fans, while **Mt Tamalpais State Park** lays claim to being the sport's birthplace. Even **Point Reyes National Seashore** has some single-track.

OTHER COASTAL CALIFORNIA ACTIVITIES

ACTIVITY	LOCATION	REGION
Bird-watching	Channel Islands National Park	Santa Barbara County
	Elkhorn Slough	Central Coast
	Audubon Canyon Ranch	Marin County
	Point Reyes National Seashore	Marin County
	Point Lobos State Natural Reserve	Central Coast
	Humboldt Bay National Wildlife Refuge	North Coast
	Lake Earl Wildlife Area	North Coast
	Clear Lake	North Coast
Caving	Pinnacles National Park	Central Coast
Fishing*	Point Loma & Mission Bay	San Diego
	Bodega Bay	North Coast
	Monterey Bay	Central Coast
	Dana Point	Orange County
Golf	Pebble Beach	Central Coast
	Torrey Pines	San Diego County
	Pacific Grove	Central Coast
Hang-gliding & paragliding	Torrey Pines	San Diego County
	Santa Barbara	Santa Barbara County
Horseback riding	Point Reyes National Seashore	Marin County
	Santa Monica Mountains	Los Angeles
	Bodega Bay	North Coast
	Big Sur	Central Coast
Hot-air ballooning	Del Mar	San Diego County
	Napa Valley	Wine Country
	Temecula	San Diego & Around
Rock climbing	Pinnacles National Park	Central Coast
Skiing	Big Bear Lake	Los Angeles

* For fishing licenses, regulations and location information, consult the **California Department of Fish & Game** (www.wildlife.ca.gov).

➡ You'll find miles of backcountry roads and trails in the **Santa Monica Mountains** north of LA. **Big Bear Lake** is another fat-tire playground, with national forest trails and a ski-resort chairlift that serves mountain bikers in summer.

➡ Coastal state parks especially popular with mountain bikers include Orange County's **Crystal Cove State Park**, NorCal's **Prairie Creek Redwoods State Park**, and **Montaña de Oro State Park** on the Central Coast.

➡ Inland from Monterey, **Fort Ord National Monument** has over 80 miles of dirt single-track and fire roads open to mountain bikers.

Resources

Bike shops and some visitor centers can supply more route ideas, maps and advice.

Adventure Cycling Association (www.adventurecycling.org) Sells long-distance cycling route guides and touring maps.

California Bicycle Coalition (www.calbike.org) Links to free online cycling maps, bike-sharing programs and community bike shops.

League of American Bicyclists (www.bikeleague.org) Find bicycle specialty shops, local cycling clubs, group rides and other special events.

Plan Your Trip
Travel with Children

Coastal California is a tailor-made destination for traveling with kids. The kids will already be begging to go to Southern California's theme parks. Get those over with (you might enjoy them too) and then introduce them to the great outdoors, from sunny southern beaches to magical northern redwood forests.

Best Regions for Kids

Los Angeles

See stars in Hollywood and movie magic at Universal Studios, then hit the beaches and Griffith Park for fun in the sun. What, it's raining? Dive into LA's kid-friendly museums instead.

Orange County & San Diego

Think beaches and theme parks galore: Disneyland, Knott's Berry Farm, the San Diego Zoo & Safari Park, Legoland and more.

San Francisco

Explore hands-on science museums, hear the barking sea lions at Pier 39, traipse through Golden Gate Park and ride the famous cable cars.

Central Coast & Santa Barbara

Santa Cruz's beach boardwalk, Monterey's whale-watching boats and giant aquarium, Big Sur's forests and riverside campgrounds, and laid-back beach towns all attract families.

North Coast & Redwoods

Go tide-pooling at NorCal's rocky beaches and coves, then let your kids stand next to the world's tallest trees, protected by state and national parks.

Coastal California for Kids

There's not too much to worry about when traveling in coastal California with your kids, as long as you keep them covered in sunblock.

Children's discounts are available for everything from museum admission and movie tickets to bus fares and motel stays. The definition of a 'child' varies from 'under 18' to age six and under. At amusement parks, some rides may have minimum-height requirements – let younger kids know about this in advance to avoid disappointment and tears.

It's fine to bring kids along to most restaurants, except top-end places. Casual restaurants usually have high chairs and children's menus and break out paper place mats and crayons for drawing. Generally, dining earlier (say, before 6pm) is better for families with young ones. At theme parks, pack a cooler in the car and have a picnic in the parking lot to save money. On the road, many supermarkets have wholesome, ready-to-eat takeout dishes.

Baby food, infant formula, disposable diapers (nappies) and other necessities are widely sold at supermarkets and pharmacies. Most women are discreet about breastfeeding in public. Many public toilets have a baby-changing table, while private gender-neutral 'family' bathrooms may be available at airports, museums etc.

Children's Highlights

Many outdoor outfitters and tour operators offer family-friendly activities, although minimum-age requirements vary. At national and state parks, ask at visitor centers about family-friendly, ranger-led activities and self-guided 'Junior Ranger' programs, in which kids earn themselves a badge after completing an activity booklet.

Theme Parks

➡ **Disneyland & Disney California** (p386) Adventure Kids of all ages, even teens, and the young-at-heart will adore the 'Magic Kingdom.'

➡ **Knott's Berry Farm** (p395) Near Disney, SoCal's original theme park offers thrills-a-minute, especially on spooky haunted Halloween nights.

➡ **Universal Studios Hollywood** (p359) Movie-themed rides, special-effects shows and a working studio backlot tram tour entertain tweens and teens.

➡ **Legoland** (p457) In San Diego's North County, this fantasyland of building blocks is made for tots and youngsters.

Aquariums & Zoos

➡ **San Diego Zoo** (p429) & **Safari Park** (p458) Journey around the world with exotic wildlife at California's best and biggest zoo, then go on safari in suburban Escondido.

➡ **Monterey Bay Aquarium** (p262) Get acquainted with coastal California's aquatic citizens next door to the Central Coast's biggest marine sanctuary.

➡ **Aquarium of the Pacific** (p359) Long Beach's aquarium houses critters from balmy Baja California to the chilly north Pacific.

➡ **Seymour Marine Discovery Center** (p253) Santa Cruz's university-run aquarium makes interactive science fun, with tide pools for exploring nearby at the beach.

➡ **Birch Aquarium** (p450) La Jolla's kids zone is as entertaining as it is educational, thanks to the super Scripps Institute of Oceanography.

Beaches

➡ **Los Angeles** Have carnival fun on Santa Monica Pier, drop by Manhattan Beach's beach volleyball courts, or drive up Hwy 1 to Malibu's perfect beaches.

➡ **Orange County** Take your pick of Newport Beach's kiddie-sized rides at Balboa Pier, Laguna Beach's miles of million-dollar sands, surf at Huntington Beach (aka 'Surf City, USA'), or old-fashioned Seal Beach.

➡ **San Diego** Head over to Coronado's idyllic Silver Strand, play in Mission Bay by SeaWorld, lap up La Jolla or unwind in a half dozen surf-style beach towns.

➡ **Santa Barbara & Central Coast** Laze on Santa Barbara's golden sands, then roll north past San Luis Obispo's off-the-beaten-track beach towns all the way north to Santa Cruz's famous boardwalk and pier.

➡ **San Francisco Bay Area** Travel north up to Marin County's crescent-shaped Stinson Beach and wilder Point Reyes National Seashore, or south along Hwy 1 to Half Moon Bay.

Parks

➡ **Redwood National & State Parks** (p243) On the fog-laden North Coast, a string of nature preserves protects magnificent wildlife, beaches and the tallest trees on earth.

➡ **Griffith Park** (p353) Bigger than NYC's Central Park, this LA green space has tons of fun for younger kids, from miniature train rides and a merry-go-round to planetarium shows.

➡ **Balboa Park** (p427) Spend all day at the San Diego Zoo and museums, taking time out for the puppet theater. Plazas, fountains and gardens offer plenty of space for younger kids to let off steam.

➡ **Golden Gate Park** (p75) With kids in tow, wander through the indoor rainforest at the California Academy of Sciences, tour the Japanese tea garden and spy on the bison herd.

➡ **Channel Islands National Park** (p343) Sail across to California's version of the Galapagos for wildlife-watching, sea kayaking, hiking and camping adventures, best for teens.

Museums

➡ **San Francisco Bay Area** San Francisco is a mind-bending classroom for kids, with the interactive Exploratorium, multimedia Children's Creative Museum, ecofriendly California

Academy of Sciences and whimsical Musée Mechanique. Then head over to the East Bay's star-powered Chabot Space & Science Center.

➡ **Los Angeles** See stars (the real ones) at the Griffith Observatory and dinosaur bones at the Natural History Museum of Los Angeles County and the Page Museum at the La Brea Tar Pits, then get hands-on at the energetic California Science Center.

➡ **San Diego** Balboa Park is jam-packed with museums such as the Reuben H Fleet Science Center and San Diego Air & Space Museum. Downtown, take younger kids to the engaging New Children's Museum and let tweens and teens clamber aboard the USS Midway Museum.

➡ **Orange County** Bring budding lab geeks to the Discovery Science Center and get a pint-sized dose of arts and culture at the Kidseum at the Bowers Museum, all near Disneyland.

Planning

A word of advice: don't pack your schedule too tightly. Traveling with kids can take longer than expected, especially in metro areas like LA, San Diego and San Francisco, where you'll want to allow extra time for traffic jams and parking.

Accommodations

Rule one: if you're traveling with kids, always mention it when making reservations. At a few places, such as B&Bs, children may not be allowed. Also be sure to request the specific room type you want, although this is often not guaranteed.

Motels and hotels typically have rooms with two beds or an extra sofabed. They also may have roll-away beds or cots, usually available for a surcharge (request these when making reservations). Some offer

'kids stay free' promotions, which may apply only if no extra bedding is required.

Resorts may offer daytime activity programs for kids and child-care services. At other hotels, front desk staff or a concierge might be able to help you make babysitting arrangements. Ask whether babysitters are licensed and bonded, what they charge per hour per child, whether there's a minimum fee, and if they charge extra for transportation and meals.

Transportation

Airlines usually allow infants (up to age two) to fly for free – bring proof of age – while older children require a seat of their own and don't usually qualify for reduced fares. Children receive substantial discounts on most trains and buses.

In cars, any child under age six or weighing less than 60lb must be buckled up in the back seat in a child or infant safety seat. Most car-rental agencies rent these for about $10 per day, but you must specifically book them in advance.

On the road, rest stops are few and far between, and gas stations and fast-food bathrooms tend to be icky. However, you're usually never far from a shopping mall, which generally have well-kept restrooms.

What to Pack

Sunscreen. And bringing sunscreen should remind you to bring hats, swimsuits, flip-flops and goggles. If you like beach umbrellas and sand chairs, pails and shovels, you'll probably want to bring your own or buy them at local supermarkets and pharmacies. At many beaches, you can rent bicycles and water-sports gear.

If you forget some critical piece of equipment, **Traveling Baby Company** (www.travelingbaby.com) and **Baby's Away** (www.babysaway.com) rent cribs, strollers, car seats, backpacks, beach gear and more.

Regions at a Glance

Coastal California's cities have more flavors than a jar of jelly beans. Start in San Francisco, equal parts earth mother and geek chic, or Los Angeles, where dozens of independent cities are rolled into one multicultural mosaic. Later, kick back in surf-style San Diego.

Calling you away from California's metro areas are misty redwood forests on the North Coast, country lanes winding past vineyards in Napa and Sonoma wine country, wildlife spotting on the Central Coast, and the cinematic beaches of Orange County and Santa Barbara.

On sunny days, when the coastal fog lifts, more than 800 miles of Pacific beaches await.

San Francisco

Food
Culture
Museums

California's 'Left Coast' reputation rests on SF, where DIY self-expression, sustainability and spontaneity are the highest virtues. Free thinkers, foodies, innovative techies, groundbreaking arts scenes and top-tier museums are all in the creative mix.

p48

Marin County & the Bay Area

Outdoor Sports
Ecotourism
Food

Outdoors nuts adore Marin County and Hwy 1 south of San Francisco for the beaches, kayaking, and hiking and mountain-biking trails. Taste and tour organic farms that inspire chefs all around the Bay.

p88

Napa & Sonoma Wine Country

Wineries
Food
Cycling & Canoeing

Amid fruit orchards and ranch lands, sunny valleys kissed by cool coastal fog have made the Napa, Sonoma and Russian River Valleys into California's premier wine-growing region and a showcase for bountiful farm-to-table cuisine.

p139

North Coast & Redwoods

Wildlife
Hiking
Scenic Drives

Primeval redwood forests are the prize along NorCal's foggy and wild coastline. Let loose your inner hippy or Rastafarian in Humboldt County, or explore bootstrap fishing villages and wind-tossed beaches from Bodega Bay to Eureka.

p195

Central Coast

Wildlife
Beaches
Scenic Drives

Surf south from hippy-dippy Santa Cruz to collegiate San Luis Obispo, stopping to hop aboard a whale-watching boat at Monterey Bay and to camp and hike in Big Sur's cool redwood forests, where waterfalls spring to life.

p250

Santa Barbara County

Beaches
Wineries
Water Sports

Spanish colonial Santa Barbara prettily presides over white-sand beaches, with fruitful vineyards less than an hour's drive away. Then go snorkeling, diving and sea kayaking in treasured Channel Islands National Park, just offshore.

p308

Los Angeles

Beaches
Food
Nightlife

There's more to life in La La Land than just sunny beaches and air-kissing celebs. Get a dose of art and culture Downtown, then dive into diverse neighborhoods, from historic Little Tokyo to red-carpeted Hollywood.

p347

Disneyland & Orange County

Theme Parks
Beaches
Surfing

The OC's beaches are packed bronze-shoulder-to-shoulder with blond surfers, beach-volleyball nuts and soap opera-esque beauties. Inland, take the kids – heck, load up the whole minivan – to Disney's Magic Kingdom.

p383

San Diego & Around

Beaches
Mexican Food
Museums

With a near perfect climate, lucky residents of California's southernmost city always seem to be slacking off. Take a permanent vacation in laid-back beach towns while devouring fish tacos, or wander Balboa Park's museums and zoo.

p425

On the Road

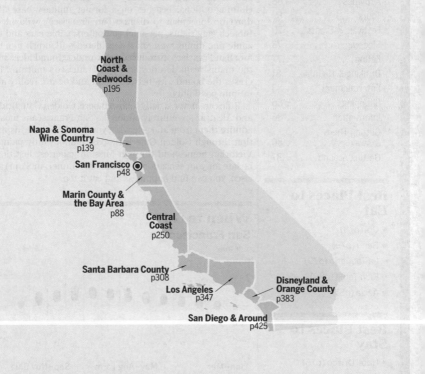

North Coast & Redwoods p195

Napa & Sonoma Wine Country p139

San Francisco p48

Marin County & the Bay Area p88

Central Coast p250

Santa Barbara County p308

Los Angeles p347

Disneyland & Orange County p383

San Diego & Around p425

San Francisco

Best Places to Eat

➜ Coi (p78)
➜ Benu (p79)
➜ La Taqueria (p79)
➜ Rich Table (p80)
➜ Aziza (p81)

Best Places to Stay

➜ Hotel Drisco (p76)
➜ Hotel Vitale (p76)
➜ Hotel Bohème (p74)
➜ Inn San Francisco (p76)
➜ Argonaut Hotel (p74)

Why Go?

Get to know the world capital of weird from the inside out, from mural-lined alleyways named after poets to clothing-optional beaches on a former military base. But don't be too quick to dismiss San Francisco's wild ideas. Biotech, gay rights, personal computers, cable cars and organic fine dining were once considered outlandish too, before San Francisco introduced these underground ideas into the mainstream decades ago. San Francisco's morning fog erases the boundaries between land and ocean, reality and infinite possibility.

Rules are never strictly followed here. Golden Gate Bridge and Alcatraz are entirely optional – San Franciscans mostly admire them from afar – leaving you free to pursue inspiration through Golden Gate Park, past flamboyantly painted Victorian homes and through Mission galleries. Just don't be late for your sensational, sustainable dinner: in San Francisco, you can find happiness and eat it too.

When to Go
San Francisco

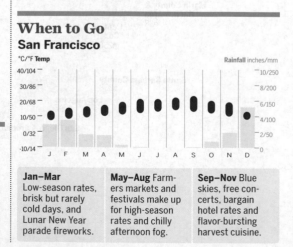

Jan–Mar Low-season rates, brisk but rarely cold days, and Lunar New Year parade fireworks.

May–Aug Farmers markets and festivals make up for high-season rates and chilly afternoon fog.

Sep–Nov Blue skies, free concerts, bargain hotel rates and flavor-bursting harvest cuisine.

Bay Bridge

San Francisco's other landmark bridge was inspired by a madman. Joshua Norton lost his shirt and his mind in the Gold Rush before proclaiming himself 'Emperor of these United States and Protector of Mexico,' and ordering construction of a trans-bay bridge in 1872. Taxpayers took some convincing: the Bay Bridge was completed in 1936. But the eastern span collapsed in the 1989 Loma Prieta earthquake, taking 12 years and $6.4 billion to repair.

Emperor Norton's idea seemed not quite so bright anymore – until artist Leo Villareal installed 25,000 LED lights along the western span, mesmerizing commuters with a 1.8-mile-long light show that shimmers and pulses in never-repeating patterns. The show runs from dusk until 2am nightly until March 2015 – but a crowdfunding campaign may keep the lights twinkling through 2026. For more, see thebaylights.org.

DON'T MISS...

➡ **Saloons** The Barbary Coast is roaring back to life with historically researched whiskey cocktails and staggering gin concoctions in San Francisco's great Western saloon revival (p81).

➡ **Rooftop-garden cuisine** SF chefs are raising the roof on hyperlocal fare with ingredients raised right upstairs: city-bee honey at Jardinière (p80), edible pansies at Coi (p78), herbs at farm:table (p77) and salad greens to feed the homeless at Glide Memorial (p52).

➡ **Green everything** Recent reports rank San Francisco as the greenest city in North America, with its pioneering parklets, citywide composting laws and America's biggest stretch of urban greenery: Golden Gate Park (p75).

SF's Best Free...

➡ **Music** Golden Gate Park hosts free concerts summer through fall, from opera and reggae to Hardly Strictly Bluegrass.

➡ **Speech** City Lights Bookstore (p52) won a landmark free-speech case in 1957 over the publication of Allen Ginsberg's magnificent, incendiary *Howl*; take a seat in the designated Poet's Chair and celebrate your right to read freely.

➡ **Love** Pride fills San Francisco streets with free candy, free condoms and over a million people freely smooching total strangers under rainbow flags.

➡ **Spirits** Anywhere within city limits – and you're free to join in anytime.

DID YOU KNOW?

Despite slacker reputations cultivated at 30 medical marijuana clubs, San Franciscans hold more patents and earn more degrees per capita than residents of any other US city.

SAN FRANCISCO

Fast Facts

➡ **Population** 839,336

➡ **Area** 47 sq miles

➡ **Telephone area code**
☑ 415

Planning Your Trip

➡ **Three weeks before** Book Alcatraz trips and dinner at Coi or Benu.

➡ **Two weeks before** Build stamina for downtown hills, Golden Gate Park adventures and Mission bars.

➡ **One week before** Score tickets to San Francisco Symphony or Opera, and assemble your costume – SF throws parades whenever.

Resources

➡ **SF Bay Guardian** (www. sfbg.com) Hot tips on local entertainment, arts, politics.

➡ **SFGate** (www.sfgate. com) News and event listings.

History

Oysters and acorn bread were prime dinner options in the Mexico-run Ohlone settlement of San Francisco circa 1848 – but a year and some gold nuggets later, Champagne and chow mein were served by the bucket. Gold found in nearby Sierra Nevada foothills turned a sleepy 800-person village into a port city of 100,000 prospectors, con artists, prostitutes and honest folk – good luck telling them apart in the city's 200 saloons.

Panic struck when Australia glutted the market with gold in 1854. Rioters burned waterfront 'Sydney-Town' before turning on SF's Chinese community, who from 1877 to 1945 were restricted to living and working in Chinatown by anti-Chinese exclusion laws. Chinese laborers were left with few employment options besides dangerous work building railroads for San Francisco's robber barons, who dynamited, mined and clearcut their way across the Golden West, and built Nob Hill mansions above Chinatown.

But the city's grand ambitions came crashing down in 1906, when earthquake and fire reduced the city to rubble. Theater troupes and opera divas performed for free amid smoldering ruins, and reconstruction hummed along at an astounding rate of 15 buildings per day.

During WWII, soldiers accused of insubordination and homosexuality were dismissed in San Francisco, as though that would teach them a lesson. Instead San Francisco's counterculture thrived, with North Beach jazz and Beat poetry. When the Central Intelligence Agency (CIA) tested LSD on the willing volunteer and *One Flew Over the Cuckoo's Nest* author Ken Kesey, he slipped some into Kool-Aid and kicked off the psychedelic '60s.

The Summer of Love brought free food, love and music to the Haight, and pioneering gay activists in the Castro helped elect Harvey Milk as San Francisco supervisor – America's first out gay official. When San Francisco witnessed devastating losses from HIV/AIDS in the 1980s, the city rallied to become a global model for epidemic treatment and prevention.

San Francisco's unconventional thinking spawned the web in the 1990s, until the dotcom bubble burst in 2000. But risk-taking SF continues to float outlandish new ideas –

NEIGHBORHOODS IN A NUTSHELL

North Beach & the Hills Poetry and parrots, top-of-the-world views, Italian gossip and opera on the jukebox.

Embarcadero & the Piers Weird science, sea-lion antics, gourmet treats, and getaways to and from Alcatraz.

Downtown & the Financial District The notorious Barbary Coast has gone legit with banks and boutiques, but shows its wild side in redwood parks and provocative art.

Chinatown Pagoda roofs, mahjong games, revolutionary plots, and fortunes made and lost in historic alleyways.

Hayes Valley, Civic Center & the Tenderloin Grand buildings and great performances, dive bars and cable cars, foodie finds and local designs.

SoMa South of Market; where high technology meets higher art, and everyone gets down and dirty on the dance floor.

Mission A book in one hand, a burrito in the other, and murals all around.

Castro Out and proud with samba whistles, rainbow sidewalks and history-making policy platforms.

Haight Flashbacks and fashion-forwardness, free thinking, free music and pricey skateboards.

Japantown, the Fillmore & Pacific Heights Sushi in the fountains, John Coltrane over the altar, and rock at the Fillmore.

Marina & the Presidio Boutiques, organic dining, peace and public nudity at a former army base.

Golden Gate Park & the Avenues SF's great green streak, surrounded by gourmet hangouts for hungry surfers.

San Francisco Highlights

1 Follow your bliss through SF's mile-wide wild streak: **Golden Gate Park** (p53).

2 See how real life is cooler than science fiction at the **Exploratorium** (p53).

3 Watch fog dance atop the deco towers of the **Golden Gate Bridge** (p52).

4 Explore SF's colorful history, captured in renegade **Mission murals** (p69).

5 Plot your escape from **Alcatraz** (p75). SF's notorious island prison.

6 Wander through 150 years of California history in pagoda-topped **Chinatown** (p52).

7 Come out and celebrate GLBT history in **the Castro** (p65), the center of the gay universe.

8 Get breathless from the climb, freshly restored murals and panoramic views at **Coit Tower** (p59).

9 Graze at the **Ferry Building** (p79), SF's local, sustainable food destination.

social media, mobile apps, biotech. Congratulations: you're just in time for San Francisco's next wild ride.

◉ Sights

◉ Union Square, Civic Center & the Tenderloin

★ Asian Art Museum   MUSEUM
(Map p56; ☑ 415-581-3500; www.asianart.org; 200 Larkin St; adult/student/child $12/8/free, 1st Sun of month free; ⊗ 10am-5pm Tue-Sun, to 9pm Thu; ♿; Ⓜ Civic Center, Ⓑ Civic Center) Imaginations race from ancient Persian miniatures to cutting-edge Japanese architecture through three floors spanning 6000 years of Asian arts. Besides the largest Asian art collection outside Asia – 18,000 works – the Asian offers excellent programs for all ages, from shadow-puppet shows and yoga for kids to weeknight Artist's Drawing Club mixers with crosscultural DJ mashups.

City Hall   HISTORIC BUILDING
(Map p56; ☑ art exhibit line 415-554-6080, tour info 415-554-6139; http://sfgsa.org/index.aspx?page=1085; 400 Van Ness Ave; ⊗ 8am-8pm Mon-Fri, tours 10am, noon & 2pm; ♿; Ⓜ Civic Center, Ⓑ Civic Center) FREE That mighty beaux-arts dome has covered San Francisco's greatest civic ambitions and setbacks, from marriage equality to McCarthy hearings. Designed in 1915 to outstyle Paris and outsize the capitol in Washington, DC, the dome was unsteady until its retrofit after the 1989 earthquake, when ingenious technology enabled it to swing on its base.

Glide Memorial United Methodist Church   CHURCH
(Map p56; ☑ 415-674-6090; www.glide.org; 330 Ellis St; ⊗ celebrations 9am & 11am Sun; Ⓜ Powell, Ⓑ Powell) The rainbow-robed, 100-strong Glide gospel choir kicks off Sunday celebrations with a warm welcome for whomever comes through the door. Between celebrations, volunteers help Glide provide a million free meals a year and housing for formerly homeless families. Thursdays from 10am to 2pm, volunteers head upstairs to Glide's sunny Graze the Roof garden, harvesting organic vegetables for its free meals.

Luggage Store Gallery   ART GALLERY
(Map p56; ☑ 415-255-5971; www.luggagestoregallery.org; 1007 Market St; ⊗ noon-5pm Wed-Sat; Ⓜ Civic Center, Ⓑ Civic Center) Bringing signs of life to one of SF's toughest blocks for two decades, this nonprofit gallery has launched renowned SF graffiti-art stars including Barry McGee and Clare Rojas. Don't miss the door camouflaged by spray paint, or the new rooftop mural by Brazilian street-art-duo Os Gemeos.

Union Square   SQUARE
(Map p56; intersection of Geary, Powell, Post & Stockton Sts; 🚋 Powell-Mason, Powell-Hyde, Ⓜ Powell, Ⓑ Powell) Free spirits and socialites converge on Union Square, named after pro-Union Civil War rallies, ringed by department stores and presided over by bare-breasted bronze socialite (and Legion of Honor founder) Alma Spreckels as the Goddess of Victory. Public outcry obliged Apple to revise its Union Square flagship plans in order to preserve SF sculptor Ruth Asawa's beloved Stockton St fountain, featuring SF icons by 250 contributors.

◉ Chinatown & North Beach

★ City Lights Bookstore   BUILDING
(Map p62; ☑ 415-362-8193; www.citylights.com; 261 Columbus Ave; ⊗ 10am-midnight) When founder and Beat poet Lawrence Ferlinghetti and manager Shigeyoshi Murao defended their right to 'willfully and lewdly print' Allen Ginsberg's magnificent *Howl and Other Poems* in 1957, City Lights became a free-

---

DON'T MISS

GOLDEN GATE BRIDGE

Hard to believe the Navy almost nixed SF's signature art-deco landmark (Map p51; www.goldengatebridge.org/visitors; off Lincoln Blvd; northbound free, southbound toll $6, billed electronically to vehicle's license plate; 🚌 28, all Golden Gate Transit buses) by architects Gertrude and Irving Murrow and engineer Joseph B Strauss. Photographers, take your cue from Hitchcock: seen from Fort Point (Map p114; ☑ 415-556-1693; www.nps.gov/fopo; Marine Dr; admission free; ⊗ 10am-5pm Fri-Sun; 🅿; 🚌 28) FREE, the 1937 bridge induces a thrilling case of vertigo. Fog aficionados prefer Marin's Vista Point, watching gusts billow through bridge cables like dry ice at a Kiss concert. For the full effect, hike or bike the 2-mile span.

THREE CHINATOWN ALLEYS THAT MADE HISTORY

➡ **Waverly Place** (Map p62; 🚇 30, 🚋 California St, Powell-Mason) After the 1906 earthquake and fire devastated Chinatown, developers schemed to relocate Chinatown residents left homeless to less-desirable real estate outside the city. But representatives from the Chinese consulate and several gun-toting merchants marched back to Waverly Place, holding temple services amid the rubble at still-smoldering altars. The alley is the namesake of the main character in Amy Tan's bestselling *The Joy Luck Club*.

➡ **Spofford Alley** (Map p62; 🚇 1, 15, 30, 45) Sun Yat-sen plotted the overthrow of China's last emperor at No 36, and the 1920s brought bootleggers' gun battles to this alley – but Spofford has mellowed with age. In the evenings you'll hear shuffling mahjong tiles and *erhu* (two-stringed Chinese fiddle) players warming up at local senior centers.

➡ **Ross Alley** (Map p62; 🚇 1, 30, 45) Alternately known as Manila, Spanish and Mexico St after the working girls who once worked this block, mural-lined Ross Alley is occasionally pimped out for Hollywood productions, including *Karate Kid II* and *Indiana Jones and the Temple of Doom*. Duck into the alley's **Golden Gate Fortune Cookie Factory** (56 Ross Alley; admission free; ⊙ 8am-7pm) for custom cookies hot off the press (50¢ each), and write your own fortune.

speech landmark. Celebrate your freedom to read freely in the designated Poet's Chair upstairs overlooking Jack Kerouac Alley, load up on 'zines on the mezzanine and entertain radical ideas downstairs in the Muckraking and Stolen Continents sections.

Beat Museum MUSEUM
(Map p62; ☎ 1-800-537-6822; www.kerouac.com; 540 Broadway; adult/student $8/5; ⊙ 10am-7pm; 🚇 10, 12, 30, 41, 45, 🚋 Powell-Hyde, Powell-Mason) Grab a ramshackle theater seat redolent with the accumulated odors of literary giants, pets and pot to watch fascinating films about the SF Beat literary scene c 1950–69. Upstairs are shrines to Beat achievements, including *On the Road* and other books that expanded America's outlook to include the margins. Two-hour guided tours at 1pm Wednesday, Saturday and Sunday cover the museum and Beat hangouts (adult/student $30/25).

Chinese Historical Society of America MUSEUM
(CHSA; Map p62; ☎ 415-391-1188; www.chsa.org; 965 Clay St; ⊙ noon-5pm Tue-Fri, 11am-4pm Sat; 🚇 1, 30, 45, 🚋 California St) FREE Picture what it was like to be Chinese in America during the gold rush, transcontinental railroad construction or the Beat heyday in this 1932 landmark, built as Chinatown's YWCA by Julia Morgan (also chief architect of Hearst Castle). The nation's largest Chinese American historical institute is a treasury of artifacts and personal stories, tracing journeys from China that made American history.

👁 Fisherman's Wharf

⭐ **Exploratorium** MUSEUM
(Map p64; ☎ 415-528-4444; www.exploratorium.edu; Pier 15; adult/child $25/19, Thu evening $15; ⊙ 10am-5pm Tue-Sun, over-18yr only Thu 6-10pm; P ♿; M F) 🍴 Is there a science to skateboarding? Do toilets flush conterclockwise in Australia? Find out first-hand with 600-plus fascinating, freaky exhibits. In under an hour you can star in psychedelic fractal music videos, make art from bacteria, and grope your way in total darkness through the Tactile Dome. Founded in 1969 by atom-bomb physicist Frank Oppenheimer, the newly relocated, expanded Exploratorium shows how life is cooler than science fiction.

⭐ **Musée Mécanique** AMUSEMENT PARK
(Map p64; ☎ 415-346-2000; www.musee-mechanique.org; Pier 45, Shed A; ⊙ 10am-7pm Mon-Fri, to 8pm Sat & Sun; ♿; 🚇 47, 🚋 Powell-Mason, Powell-Hyde, M F) Where else can you guillotine a man for a quarter? Creepy, 19th-century arcade games like the macabre French Execution compete for your spare change with the diabolical Ms Pac-Man.

USS Pampanito HISTORIC SITE
(Map p64; ☎ 415-775-1943; www.maritime.org/pamphome.htm; Pier 45; adult/child $12/6; ⊙ 9am-8pm Thu-Tue, to 6pm Wed; ♿; 🚇 19, 30, 47, 🚋 Powell-Hyde, M F) Explore a restored WWII submarine that survived six tours of duty, while you listen to submariner sailors' tales of stealth mode and sudden attacks in a riveting

Alcatraz

Book a ferry from Pier 33 and ride 1.5 miles across the bay to explore America's most notorious former prison. The trip itself is worth the money, providing stunning views of the city skyline. Once you've landed at the **Ferry Dock & Pier 1**, you begin the 580-yard walk to the top of the island and prison; if you're out of shape, there's a twice-hourly tram.

As you climb toward the **Guardhouse 2**, notice the island's steep slope; before it was a prison, Alcatraz was a fort. In the 1850s, the military quarried the rocky shores into near-vertical cliffs. Ships could then only dock at a single port, separated from the main buildings by a sally port (a drawbridge and moat in what became the guardhouse). Inside, peer through floor grates to see Alcatraz' original prison.

Volunteers tend the brilliant **Officer's Row Gardens 3** – an orderly counterpoint to the overgrown rose bushes surrounding the burned-out shell of the **Warden's House 4**. At the top of the hill, by the front door of the **Main Cellhouse 5**, beauty shots unfurl all around, including a **view of the Golden Gate Bridge 6**. Above the main door of the administration building, notice the **historic signs & graffiti 7**, before you step inside the dank, cold prison to find the **Frank Morris cell 8**, former home to Alcatraz' most notorious jail-breaker.

Historic Signs & Graffiti
During their 1969–71 occupation, Native Americans graffitied the water tower: 'Home of the Free Indian Land.' Above the cellhouse door, examine the eagle-and-flag crest to see how the red-and-white stripes were changed to spell 'Free.'

Warden's House
Fires destroyed the warden's house and other structures during the Indian Occupation. The government blamed the Native Americans; the Native Americans blamed agents provocateurs acting on behalf of the Nixon Administration to undermine public sympathy.

Parade Grounds

TOP TIPS

➡ Book at least two weeks prior for self-guided daytime visits, longer for ranger-led night tours. For info on garden tours, see www.alcatraz gardens.org.

➡ Be prepared to hike; a steep path ascends from the ferry landing to the cell block. Most people spend two to three hours on the island. You need only reserve for the outbound ferry; take any ferry back.

➡ There's no food (just water) but you can bring your own; picnicking is allowed at the ferry dock only. Dress in layers as weather changes fast and it's usually windy.

Ferry Dock & Pier
A giant wall map helps you get your bearings. Inside nearby Bldg 64, short films and exhibits provide historical perspective on the prison and details about the Indian Occupation.

View of Golden Gate Bridge

The Golden Gate Bridge stretches wide on the horizon. Best views are from atop the island at Eagle Plaza, near the cellhouse entrance, and at water level along the Agave Trail (September to January only).

Main Cellhouse

During the mid-20th century, the maximum-security prison housed the day's most notorious troublemakers, including Al Capone and Robert Stroud, the 'Birdman of Alcatraz' (who actually conducted his ornithology studies at Leavenworth).

6

Recreation Yard

Water Tower

Power House

5

8

Officers' Club

Frank Morris Cell

Peer into cell 138 on B-Block to see a re-creation of the dummy's head that Frank Morris left in his bed as a decoy to aid his notorious – and successful – 1962 escape from Alcatraz.

7
Lighthouse

3

4

2

Guard Tower

1

Guardhouse

Alcatraz' oldest building dates to 1857 and retains remnants of the original drawbridge and moat. During the Civil War the basement was transformed into a military dungeon – the genesis of Alcatraz as prison.

Officer's Row Gardens

In the 19th century soldiers imported topsoil to beautify the island with gardens. Well-trusted prisoners later gardened – Elliott Michener said it kept him sane. Historians, ornithologists and archaeologists choose today's plants.

Downtown San Francisco & SoMa

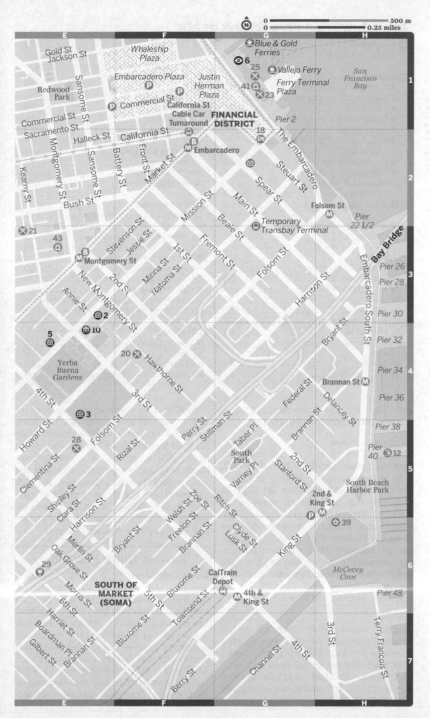

N
0 — 500 m
0 — 0.25 miles

Gold St
Jackson St
Whaleship Plaza
Blue & Gold Ferries
6
San Francisco Bay
Redwood Park
Sansome St
Embarcadero Plaza
P
Justin Herman Plaza
Vallejo Ferry
25
Ferry Terminal Plaza
41
23
Commercial St
P
Commercial St
P
California St
Pier 2
Sacramento St
California St Cable Car Turnaround
FINANCIAL DISTRICT
Halleck St
California St
18
Montgomery St
Sansome St
Battery St
Front St
Market St
B
Embarcadero
The Embarcadero
Kearny St
Bush St
Steuart St
Spear St
Mission St
Main St
Beale St
Folsom St
M
Pier 22 1/2
21
Stevenson St
Jessie St
Minna St
1st St
Fremont St
Temporary Transbay Terminal
Folsom St
43
B
Montgomery St
New Montgomery St
2nd St
Natoma St
Harrison St
Embarcadero South St
Bay Bridge
Pier 26
Pier 28
Annie St
Pier 30
2
Bryant St
Pier 32
5
10
20
Hawthorne St
Yerba Buena Gardens
4th St
3rd St
Federal St
Brannan St M
Pier 34
Pier 36
3
Howard St
Folsom St
Perry St
Stillman St
Delancey St
Pier 38
28
Rizal St
Taber Pl
South Park
2nd St
Brannan St
Pier 40
12
Clementina St
Shipley St
Clara St
Harrison St
Welsh St
Zoe St
Varney St
Stanford St
South Beach Harbor Park
2nd & King St
M
Merlin St
Bryant St
Freelon St
Brannan St
Clyde St
Lusk St
P
39
Oak Grove St
King St
29
Morris St
SOUTH OF MARKET (SOMA)
5th St
Bluxome St
CalTrain Depot
4th & King St
M
McCovey Cove
Pier 48
6th St
Harriet St
Boardman Pl
Brannan St
Bluxome St
Townsend St
3rd St
Terry Francois St
Gilbert St
Berry St
Channel St
4th St
7

Downtown San Francisco & SoMa

audio tour ($3) that makes surfacing afterwards a relief (caution claustrophobes).

**Maritime National
Historical Park** HISTORIC SITE
(Map p64; www.nps.gov/safr; 499 Jefferson St, Hyde St Pier; adult/child $5/free; ⊙9:30am-5pm Oct-May, to 5:30pm Jun-Sep; ⓖ; 🚋19, 30, 47, 🚋Powell-Hyde, Ⓜ F) Historic ships at the Maritime National Historical Park are the Wharf's most authentic attraction. Moored along the Hyde St Pier, standouts include the 1891 schooner *Alma* and the 1895 lumber schooner *CA Thayer*. Also check out the paddle-wheel tugboat *Eppleton Hall* and the iron-hulled *Balclutha*, which hauled coal from Australia and Wales.

Pier 39 PIER
(Map p64; www.pier39.com; Beach St & the Embarcadero; Ⓟ ⓖ; 🚋47, 🚋Powell-Mason, Ⓜ F) Sea lions have lived the California dream since 1989, when they first bellyflopped on Pier 39 yacht docks. You'll find up to 1300 of them January to July, sunbathing, canoodling, and setting SF standards for beach-bumming.

Across the pier, sharks circle overhead inside **Aquarium of the Bay** (Map p64; www.aquariumofthebay.com; Pier 39; adult/child/family $21.95/12.95/64; ⊙10am-7pm Mon-Thu, to 8pm Fri-Sun, daily in summer; ⓖ; 🚋49, 🚋Powell-Mason, Ⓜ F), and your chariot awaits at the vintage **San Francisco Carousel** (Map p64; www.pier39.com; Pier 39; admission $3; ⊙11am-7pm; ⓖ; 🚋47, 🚋Powell-Mason, Ⓜ F). The visitors' center rents strollers, stores luggage, and has free phone-charging stations.

◉ Russian Hill & Nob Hill

Grace Cathedral CHURCH
(Map p56; ☎415-749-6300; www.gracecathedral.org; 1100 California St; suggested donation adult/child $3/2, Sun services free; ⊙8am-6pm Mon-Sat, to 7pm Sun, services 8:30am & 11am Sun; 🚋1, 🚋California St) Rebuilt three times and completed over 40 years, Grace celebrates community and human endeavor with an AIDS memorial chapel altarpiece by Keith Haring, murals honoring the founding of the UN in San Francisco, and Gothic stained-

glass windows featuring Albert Einstein uplifted in swirling atomic particles. Check the website for choral performances with Grace's splendid acoustics.

San Francisco Art Institute ART GALLERY
(Map p64; www.sfai.edu; 800 Chestnut St; admission free; ⊙Walter & McBean Galleries 11am-7pm Tue, to 6pm Wed-Sat, Diego Rivera Gallery 9am-5pm; 🚋Powell-Mason) FREE Founded in the 1870s, SFAI was the vanguard for 1960s Bay Area Abstraction, 1970s conceptual art, and 1990s new-media art – glimpse what's next in contemporary art here at the **Walter & McBean Gallery**. Diego Rivera's 1931 *The Making of a Fresco Showing a Building of a City* sprawls across **Diego Rivera Gallery**, showing the artist pausing to admire the constant work-in-progress that is San Francisco.

Lombard Street STREET
(Map p64; 900 block of Lombard St; 🚋Powell-Hyde) You've seen Lombard's eight downhill switchbacks on postcards, movies *(Vertigo)*, TV *(The Real World)*, even video games (Tony Hawk's *Pro Skater*). Billed incorrectly as 'the world's crookedest street' – SF's Vermont St deserves the honor – scenic Lombard St earns street cred with zigzagging flowerbeds. The street often closes to traffic on busy summer weekends, accommodating pedestrians who brave 250 steps for **Sterling Park** sunsets with Golden Gate Bridge views.

⊙ Japantown

Japan Center BUILDING
(www.sfjapantown.org; 1737 Post St; ⊙10am-midnight; 🚌2, 3, 22, 38, 38L) Welcome to *kawaii* (cuteness) – this 1968 mall is a vintage gem, with rock gardens, wooden bridges and *maneki-neko* (waving cat) figurines atop sushi-bar counters. Lose track of time in photo-sticker booths, karaoke lounges, *ukiyo-e* (woodblock print) galleries and Japanese video-game arcades – then take a breather under the cherry trees by the Peace Plaza pagoda.

Cottage Row STREET
(off Bush St btwn Webster & Fillmore Sts; 🚌2, 3, 22, 38) Detour to the 1860s and '70s via this National Historic Landmark promenade formerly known as 'Japan Street,' where Japanese Americans lived in clapboard cottages, farmed tiny backyard plots and socialized under plum trees until their forced internment in WWII. Forty-five years later, San Francisco's Japanese American Citizens League won a presidential apology for internees – and today, Cottage Row's public mini-park remains a point of community pride.

⊙ The Marina & Presidio

★Crissy Field PARK
(Map p64; www.crissyfield.org; 1199 East Beach; 🚌30, PresidioGo Shuttle) The Presidio's army airstrip has been stripped of asphalt and

---

COIT TOWER

Adding an exclamation mark to San Francisco's landscape, **Coit Tower** (Map p62; ☏415-362-0808; http://sfrecpark.org/destination/telegraph-hill-pioneer-park/coit-tower; Telegraph Hill Blvd; elevator entry (nonresident) adult/child $7/5; ⊙10am-5:30pm Mar-Sep, 9am-4:30pm Oct-Feb; 🚌39) offers views worth shouting about – especially after you climb the giddy, steep Filbert St or Greenwich St steps to the top of Telegraph Hill. This 210ft, peculiar projectile is a monument to San Francisco firefighters financed by eccentric heiress Lillie Hitchcock Coit. Lillie could drink, smoke and play cards as well as any off-duty firefighter, rarely missed a fire or a firefighter's funeral, and even had the firehouse emblem embroidered on her bedsheets.

Even before it opened in 1934, Lillie's tower became a lightning-rod for controversy. Federally funded lobby murals show San Franciscans during the Great Depression at speakeasies, soup kitchens, and dock-workers' unions. Authorities denounced Coit Tower's 25 muralists as communists, but San Franciscans rallied to protect their artwork as a national landmark.

Newly restored in 2014, the bright, bold murals broaden world views just as surely as the 360-degree views from the tower-top viewing platform. To glimpse murals inside Coit Tower's spiral stairwell, join free guided tours at 11am on Saturdays.

POWELL
AND
MARKET

HYDE AND BEACH
FISHERMANS
WHARF

5
6
Powell-Hyde
Cable Car
Turnaround
4
Beach St
North Point St
Powell-Mason
Cable Car Turnaround
7
Chestnut St
NORTH
BEACH
Bay St
The Embarcadero (Herb Caen Way)
San
Francisco
Bay
3
Filbert St
8
Grant Ave
Columbus Ave
Battery St
Sansome St
Lombard St
Jones St
Powell-Mason Cable Car Line
Broadway
Van Ness Ave
Powell-Hyde St Cable Car Line
Stockton St
California St
Cable Car
Turnaround
10 END
Broadway
9 CHINATOWN
California St Cable Car Line
M B Embarcadero
Jackson St
Washington St
NOB HILL
2
Bush St
Market St
Folsom St M
California St
Pine St
Bush St
California St
Cable Car
Turnaround
Powell-Mason &
Powell-Hyde St
Cable Car Lines
M B Montgomery St
Powell St
Mason St
Geary St
Hyde St
Geary Blvd
START 1 M B Powell St
Brannan St M

0   1 km
N   0   0.5 miles

San Francisco by Cable Car

Carnival rides can't compare to cable cars, San Francisco's vintage public transit. Novices slide into strangers' laps but regular commuters just grip leather hand-straps, lean back and ride downhill slides like pro surfers. On this trip, you'll master the San Francisco stance and conquer SF hills without breaking a sweat.

At the ❶ **Powell St Cable Car Turnaround** operators turn the car atop a revolving wooden platform and a vintage kiosk; buy an all-day Muni Passport for $14 instead of paying $6 per ride. Board the Powell-Hyde cable car and begin your journey up Nob Hill.

As your cable car lurches uphill, you can imagine 19th-century horses struggling up this slippery crag. Inventor Andrew Hallidie's cable cars survived the 1906 earthquake and fire that destroyed 'Snob Hill' mansions, returning the faithful to rebuild ❷ **Grace Cathedral** (p58).

Back on the Powell-Hyde car, careen past crooked, flower-lined ❸ **Lombard Street** (p59) toward ❹ **Fisherman's Wharf**. The waterfront terminus is named for Friedel Klussman, who saved cable cars from mayoral modernization plans in 1947. She did the math: cable cars brought in more tourism dollars than they cost in upkeep. The mayor demanded a vote – and lost to 'the Cable Car Lady' by a landslide.

At the wharf you can see SF as sailors did as they emerged from the submarine ❺ **USS Pampanito** (p53). Witness Western saloon brawls in vintage arcade games at the ❻ **Musée Mécanique** (p53) before hitching the Powell-Mason cable car to North Beach.

Hop off to see Diego Rivera's 1934 cityscape at the ❼ **San Francisco Art Institute** (p59) or follow your rumbling stomach directly to ❽ **Liguria Bakery** (p77). Stroll through North Beach and Chinatown alleyways or take the Powell-Mason line to time-travel through the ❾ **Chinese Historical Society of America** (p53). Nearby, catch a ride on the city's oldest line: the California St cable car. The terminus is near the ❿ **Ferry Building** (p79), where champagne-and-oyster happy hour awaits.

Top: Cable Car Turnaround; Bottom: Cable car on Hyde St, heading toward Fisherman's Wharf

Chinatown & North Beach

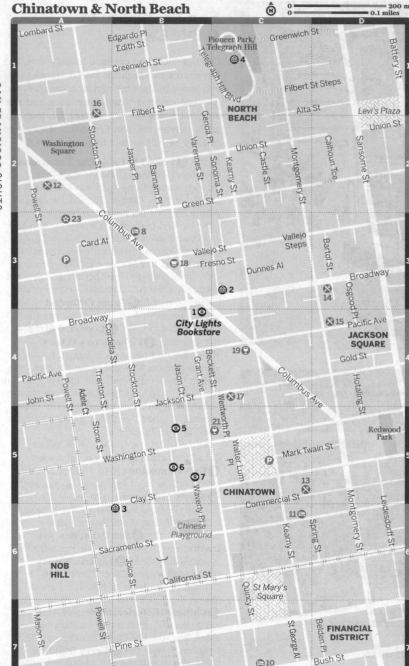

Chinatown & North Beach

reinvented as a haven for coastal birds, kite-fliers and windsurfers enjoying sweeping views of Golden Gate Bridge.

★ **Baker Beach** BEACH
(☉ sunrise-sunset; ☐ 29, PresidiGo Shuttle) Unswimmable waters (except when the tide's coming in) but unbeatable views of the Golden Gate make this former Army beachhead SF's tanning location of choice, especially the clothing-optional north end – at least until the afternoon fog rolls in.

Presidio Visitors Center TOURIST INFORMATION
(www.presidio.gov; Montgomery St & Lincoln Blvd, Bldg 105; ☉ 10am-4pm Thu-Sun; ☐ PresidiGo Shuttle) San Francisco's official motto is 'Oro in Paz, Fierro in Guerra' (Gold in Peace, Iron in War), but it hasn't seen much military action since 1776, when its Spanish *presidio* (military post) was built by conscripted Ohlone. Today the revamped **Officers Club** features archaeological displays and California cuisine from celebrity chef Traci des Jardins. Cultural institutions including the **Walt Disney Family Museum** (Map p64; ☑ 415-345-6800; www.waltdisney.org; 104 Montgomery St, Presidio; adult/student/child $20/15/12; ☉ 10am-6pm Wed-Mon, last entry 5pm; ℗ ⓘ; ☐ 43, PresidiGo Shuttle) line the former **parade grounds**, and a Yoda statue fronts **George Lucas' Letterman Digital Arts Center**.

◉ SoMa

Contemporary Jewish Museum MUSEUM
(Map p56; ☑ 415-344-8800; www.thecjm.org; 736 Mission St; adult/child $12/free, after 5pm Thu $5, 1st Tue of month free; ☉ 11am-5pm Mon-Tue & Fri-Sun, to 8pm Thu; Ⓜ Montgomery, Ⓑ Montgomery) A blue-steel box balancing on one corner brings signs of life to San Francisco's commercial downtown – literally. Architect Daniel Libeskind based his landmark design for the Contemporary Jewish Museum on the shape of the Hebrew word *l'chaim* – 'to life.' Galleries inside a converted power substation illuminate Jewish life and ideals through artists as diverse as Andy Warhol, Maurice Sendak, Marc Chagall and the Bay Area's own Gertrude Stein.

Cartoon Art Museum MUSEUM
(Map p56; ☑ 415-227-8666; www.cartoonart.org; 655 Mission St; adult/student $8/6, 1st Tue of month free; ☉ 11am-5pm Tue-Sun; ⓘ; ☐ 14, 15, 30, 45, Ⓜ Montgomery, Ⓑ Montgomery) Introducing this place to comics fans would be an insult. Of course you know it was funded by *Peanuts*' Charles M Schultz. Naturally you recognize Mike Zeck's *Captain America* covers, own R Crumb's underground classic *Mr Natural,* and can recite Edward Gorey's alphabet ('A is for Amy who fell down the stairs/B is for Basil assaulted by bears...') But even diehard fans learn something new here, from lectures by Pixar animators to celebrations of women cartoonists with SF comics legend Trina Robbins.

Museum of the African Diaspora MUSEUM
(MoAD; Map p56; ☑ 415-358-7200; www.moadsf.org; 685 Mission St; adult/student/child $10/5/free; ☉ 11am-6pm Wed-Sat, noon-5pm Sun; ℗ ⓘ; ☐ 14, 15, 30, 45, Ⓜ Montgomery, Ⓑ Montgomery) MoAD tells the epic story of diaspora across three floors with an international cast of artists, writers and historians. Quarterly exhibits

Fisherman's Wharf, The Marina & Russian Hill

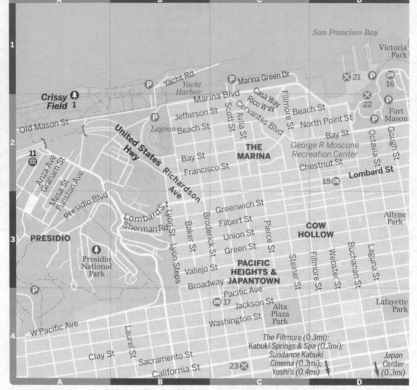

Fisherman's Wharf, The Marina & Russian Hill

have showcased glittering royals by Nigerian British sensation Chris Ofili, Romare Bearden's Harlem jazz portraits, and Siddi family quilts by South Indians descended from African slaves. Don't miss the moving video narrated by Maya Angelou.

The Mission & the Castro

★ 826 Valencia
CULTURAL SITE

(Map p66; ☎415-642-5905; www.826valencia.org; 826 Valencia St; ⊙noon-6pm; ⚫; ➁14, 33, 49, Ⓑ16th St Mission, Ⓜ J) Avast, ye scurvy scalawags! If ye be shipwrecked without yer eye patch or McSweeney's literary anthology, lay down yer dubloons and claim yer booty at this here nonprofit Pirate Store. Below decks, kids be writing tall tales for dark nights asea, and ye can study making video games and magazines and suchlike, if that be yer dastardly inclination...arrrr!

Mission Dolores
CHURCH

(Misión San Francisco de Asís; Map p66; ☎415-621-8203; www.missiondolores.org; 3321 16th St; adult/child $5/3; ⊙9am-4pm Nov-Apr, to 4:30pm May-Oct; ➁22, 33, Ⓑ16th St Mission, Ⓜ J) The city's oldest building was founded in 1776 and rebuilt in 1782 with conscripted Ohlone and Miwok labor – a graveyard memorial hut commemorates 5000 Native laborers who died of hardship and measles epidemics. Today the original adobe is overshadowed by the ornate 1913 Churrigueresque basilica, featuring stained-glass windows of California's 21 missions.

GLBT History Museum
MUSEUM

(Map p66; ☎415-621-1107; www.glbthistory.org/museum; 4127 18th St; admission $5, 1st Wed of month free; ⊙11am-7pm Mon & Wed-Sat, noon-5pm Sun; Ⓜ Castro) America's first gay-history museum captures proud moments and historic challenges: Harvey Milk's campaign literature, interviews with trailblazing bisexual author Gore Vidal, matchbooks from long-gone bathhouses and 1950s penal codes banning homosexuality.

Harvey Milk & Jane Warner Plazas
SQUARE

(Market & Castro Sts; Ⓜ Castro) A huge rainbow flag welcomes arrivals to Harvey Milk

The Mission & The Castro

Plaza (Map p66; 24, 33, F, Castro St), where a display honors the Castro camera-store owner who was assassinated not long after becoming America's first out gay official – but who remains an icon of civil rights and civic pride. By the F-train terminus is **Jane Warner Plaza** (Map p66), named for the Castro's trailblazing lesbian police officer. The community converges here for sun and local color – including thong-clad protestors of SF's 2013 nudity ban.

Human Rights Campaign
Action Center   HISTORIC SITE
(Map p66; ☑415-431-2200; http://shop.hrc.org/san-francisco-hrc-store; 575 Castro St; ⏰10am-8pm Mon-Sat, to 7pm Sun) You may recognize Harvey Milk's former camera storefront, featured in the Oscar-winning movie *Milk*. Now it's home to the civil rights advocacy group, where supporters converge to sign petitions, shop for 'Equality' wedding rings, and admire the mural featuring Milk's famous words: 'If a bullet should enter my brain, let that bullet shatter every closet door.'

◉ The Haight

Haight & Ashbury   LANDMARK
(Map p70; 6, 33, 37, 43, 71) This legendary intersection was the epicenter of the psychedelic '60s and remains a counterculture magnet. On average Saturdays here you can sign Green Party petitions, commission a poem, hear Hare Krishna on keyboards and Bob Dylan on banjo. The clock overhead always reads 4:20 – better known in herbal circles as International Bong-Hit Time. A local clockmaker recently fixed it; within a week it was stuck at 4:20.

Alamo Square Park   PARK
(Map p66; Hayes & Scott Sts; ☎; 5, 21, 22, 24) **FREE** The pastel Painted Ladies of famed Postcard Row on Alamo Square's east side pale in comparison to colorful characters along the park's north side. Here you'll spot Barbary Coast baroque, with facades bedecked with fish-scale shingles and gingerbread trim dripping from peaked roofs. On the northwest corner, the 1889 Westerfield mansion miraculously survived tenancies by czarist Russian bootleggers, Fillmore jazz musicians, and hippie communes – plus watchtower rituals by Church of Satan founder Anton LaVey.

The Mission & The Castro

◎ Top Sights
1 826 Valencia	D5
2 Balmy Alley	F7

◎ Sights
3 Alamo Square Park	A1
4 Clarion Alley	D4
5 GLBT History Museum	A5
6 Harvey Milk Plaza	A4
7 Human Rights Campaign Action Center	A5
8 Jane Warner Plaza	A4
9 Mission Dolores	C4
10 Women's Building	D5

⊕ Activities, Courses & Tours
11 Precita Eyes Mission Mural Tours	F7

⊜ Sleeping
12 Inn on Castro	A4
13 Inn San Francisco	E5
14 Metro Hotel	A2
15 Parker Guest House	B4
16 Parsonage	C1

⊗ Eating
17 Bi-Rite Creamery	C4
18 Craftsman & Wolves	D5
19 Frances	B4
20 La Taqueria	E7
21 Mission Pie	E7
22 Namu Gaji	C4
23 Rich Table	D1
24 Rosamunde Sausage Grill	B2

⊙ Drinking & Nightlife
25 Bar Agricole	F2
26 Lexington Club	D5
27 Ritual Coffee Roasters	D6
28 Stud	F1
29 Toronado	B2

⊗ Entertainment
30 Castro Theatre	A4
31 DNA Lounge	F2
32 Independent	A1
33 ODC Theater	E4
34 Roxie Cinema	D4
35 SFJAZZ Center	D1
36 Slim's	F2
37 The Chapel	D5

⊙ Shopping
38 Betabrand	D5
39 Gravel & Gold	D6

◎ The Richmond

Coastal Trail TRAIL
(Map p72; www.californiacoastaltrail.info; Fort Funston to Lincoln Park; ⊙sunrise-sunset; ☐1, 18, 38) Hit your stride on the 9-mile stretch of Coastal Trail starting near former nuclear bunkers at Fort Funston, crossing 4 miles of sandy Ocean Beach, wrapping around the Presidio and ending at the Golden Gate Bridge. Casual strollers can pick up the trail near the ruins of Sutro Baths, head around cliffside Land's End for end-of-the-world views, then duck into the Legion of Honor at Lincoln Park.

California Palace of the Legion of Honor MUSEUM
(Map p72; ☑415-750-3600; http://legionofhonor. famsf.org; 100 34th Ave; adult/child $10/free, $2 discount with Muni ticket, 1st Tue of month free; ⊙9:30am-5:15pm Tue-Sun; ℗♿; ☐18) Larger-than-life sculptor's model 'Big Alma' Spreckels gifted this museum to lift San Francisco's spirits and pay tribute to Californians killed in WWI. Featured artworks range from Monet waterlilies to John Cage soundscapes, Iraqi ivories to R Crumb comics – part of the Legion's stellar Achenbach Collection of 90,000 graphic artworks.

⋆ Activities

Cycling & Skating

Blazing Saddles CYCLING
(Map p64; ☑415-202-8888; www.blazingsaddles. com/san-francisco; 2715 Hyde St; cycle hire per hr $8-15, per day $32-88, electric bikes per day $48-88; ⊙8am-7:30pm; ♿; ☐Powell-Hyde) Cover the waterfront with bikes from the main shop on Hyde St or seven rental stands around Fisherman's Wharf. They also rent electric bikes, offer 24-hour return service and provide extras (bungee cords, packs etc).

Golden Gate Park Bike & Skate BICYCLING
(Map p72; ☑415-668-1117; www.goldengatepark-bikeandskate.com; 3038 Fulton St; skates per hr $5-6, per day $20-24, bikes per hr $3-5, per day $15-25, tandem bikes per hr/day $15/75, discs $6/25; ⊙10am-6pm; ♿; ☐5, 31, 44) Besides bikes and skates (both quad-wheeled and inline), this little rental shop just outside the park rents disc putters and drivers for the nearby free Frisbee golf course.

Kayaking & Whale-Watching

City Kayak KAYAKING
(Map p56; ☑415-294-1050; www.citykayak.com; Pier 40, South Beach Harbor; kayak rentals per hr $35-65, 3hr lesson & rental $59, tours $58-98;

Ⓜ Brannan) Newbies to kayaking can take lessons and venture calm waters near the Bay Bridge, and experienced paddlers can brave choppy currents beneath the Golden Gate (conditions permitting) – but romantics prefer calm-water moonlight tours.

Oceanic Society   WHALE-WATCHING
(🖉 reservations 415-256-9941; www.oceanic-society.org; tours per person $125; ⊘ reservations 8:30am-5pm Mon-Fri, trips Sat & Sun) Whale sightings aren't a fluke on naturalist-led, ocean-going, weekend boat trips during mid-October through December migrations. In the off-season, trips run to the Farallon Islands, 27 miles west of San Francisco.

Spas
⭐ **Kabuki Springs & Spa**   SPA
(🖉 415-922-6000; www.kabukisprings.com; 1750 Geary Blvd; admission $25; ⊘ 10am-9:45pm, co-ed Tue, women-only Wed, Fri & Sun, men-only Mon, Thu & Sat; 🚇 22, 38) Unwind in these Japanese baths. Scrub down with salt in the steam room, soak in the hot pool, take the cold plunge and reheat in the sauna. Most days are clothing-optional, but bathing suits are required on co-ed Tuesdays. Silence is mandatory – if you hear the gong, it means *Shhhh!*

☞ Tours
Day visits to Alcatraz (www.nps.gov/alca) include captivating audio tours with prisoners and guards recalling cellhouse life, while creepy twilight tours are led by park rangers; book tickets at least two weeks ahead. See also p76.

Alcatraz Cruises   BOAT TOUR
(Map p64; 🖉 415-981-7625; www.alcatrazcruises.com; day tours adult/child/family $30/18/92, night adult/child $37/22) Ferries depart Pier 33 half-hourly 9am to 3:55pm, night tours leave at 6:10pm and 6:45pm.

⭐ Precita Eyes Mission Mural Tours TOUR
(Map p66; 🖉 415-285-2287; www.precitaeyes.org; adult $15-20, child $3; ⊘ see website calendar for tour dates; 🚹) Muralists lead two-hour tours on foot or bike covering 60 to 70 murals in a six- to 10-block radius of mural-bedecked Balmy Alley; proceeds fund mural upkeep at this community arts nonprofit.

Chinatown Alleyway Tours   TOUR
(🖉 415-984-1478; www.chinatownalleywaytours.org; adult/student $18/12; ⊘ 11am Sat; 🚹; 🚌 8X, 8AX, 8BX) Neighborhood teens lead two-hour community nonprofit tours for up-close-and-personal peeks into Chinatown's past (weather permitting). Book five days ahead or pay double for Saturday walk-ins; cash only.

Public Library City Guides   TOUR
(🖉 415-557-4266; www.sfcityguides.org; donations/tips welcome) **FREE** Volunteer historians lead nonprofit tours organized by neighborhood

---

MISSION MURALS

Inspired by Diego Rivera's San Francisco Works Progress Administration (WPA) murals and outraged by US foreign policy in Central America, Mission *muralistas* set out in the 1970s to transform the political landscape, one alley at a time. Today, 400-plus murals line Mission streets, including:

➡ ⭐ **Balmy Alley** (Map p66; 🖉 415-285-2287; www.precitaeyes.org; btwn 24th & 25th Sts; 🚇 10, 12, 27, 33, 48, 🚇 24th St Mission) Between Treat Ave and Harrison St, murals spanning 35 years transform garage doors into artistic and political statements, from an early memorial for El Salvador activist Archbishop Òscar Romero to a homage to the golden age of Mexican cinema.

➡ **Clarion Alley** (Map p66; btwn 17th & 18th Sts, off Valencia St; 🚇 14, 22, 33, 🚇 16th St Mission, Ⓜ J) Only the strongest street art survives in Clarion, where lesser works are peed on or painted over. Very few pieces survive for years, such as Megan Wilson's daisy-covered *Capitalism Is Over (If You Want It)* or Jet Martinez' view of Clarion Alley within a man standing in a forest.

➡ **Women's Building** (Map p66; 3543 18th St; 🚹; Ⓜ 18th St, 🚇 16th St Mission) San Francisco's biggest mural is the 1994 *MaestraPeace*, a show of female strength painted by 90 *muralistas* that hugs the Women's Building. Featured icons range from ancient Mayan and Chinese goddesses to modern trailblazers, including Nobel Prize–winner Rigoberta Menchu, poet Audre Lorde and artist Georgia O'Keeffe.

The Haight

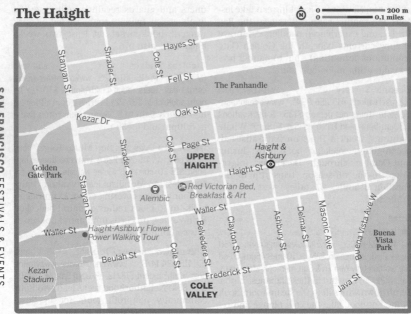

and theme: Art Deco Marina, Gold Rush Downtown, Secrets of Fisherman's Wharf, Telegraph Hill Stairway Hike and more.

Sea Foraging Adventures   TOUR
(www.seaforager.com; tours from $42 per person; ☉calendar & reservations online) California sealife expert Kirk Lombard leads guided adventures to secret foraging spots around San Francisco's waterfront, finding urban edibles ranging from bullwhip seaweed to eels under the Golden Gate Bridge.

Emperor Norton's Fantastic Time Machine   TOUR
(http://emperornortontour.com/; tours depart from Union Square; tours $20; ☉tours 11am & 2:30pm Tue & Sun; ☐2,38, ⓑPowell) Gold Rush through Wild West legends in a 2¾-hour walking tour led by SF's self-proclaimed Emperor Norton, the eccentric schemer and Bay Bridge dreamer reincarnated by SF historian Joseph Amster.

Haight-Ashbury Flower Power Walking Tour   WALKING
(Map p70; ☑ 415-863-1621; www.haightashburytour.com; adult/child under 9yr $20/free; ☉10:30am Tue & Sat, 2pm Thu, 11am Fri; ☐6, 71, ⓜN) Take a long, strange trip through 12 blocks of hippie history in two hours, following the steps of

Jimi, Jerry and Janis – if you have to ask for last names, you totally need this tour. Tours meet at the corner of Stanyan and Waller Sts; reservations required.

✹ Festivals & Events

February

Lunar New Year   CULTURAL
(www.chineseparade.com) Firecrackers, legions of tiny-tot martial artists and a 200ft dancing dragon make this parade the highlight of San Francisco winters.

April & May

SF International Film Festival   FILM
(www.sffs.org) Stars align and directors launch premieres each April at the nation's oldest film festival.

Bay to Breakers   SPORT
(www.baytobreakers.com; race registration $58-89.50) Run costumed from Embarcadero to Ocean Beach (7.5 miles) on the third Sunday in May, while joggers dressed as salmon run upstream.

June

SF Pride Celebration   CULTURAL
A day isn't enough to do SF proud: June begins with **International LGBT Film Festival** (www.frameline.org; ☉mid-Jun) and goes out in

🏃 City Walk
San Francisco Hilltops

START DRAGON GATE
FINISH GRACE CATEHDRAL
LENGTH 2.3 MILES; 2½ HOURS

Conquer San Francisco's three most famous hills – Telegraph, Russian and Nob – for views that are pure poetry.

Enter Chinatown's ❶ **Dragon Gate** and walk up dragon-lantern-lined Grant Ave to Sacramento St. Turn left half a block up, then right onto ❷ **Waverly Place** (p53), where prayer flags grace painted temple balconies. At Clay St, jog left and right again onto ❸ **Spofford Alley** (p53), where Sun Yat-sen plotted revolution. At the end of the block on Washington, take a right and an immediate left onto mural-lined ❹ **Ross Alley** (p53), once San Francisco's bordello byway.

Turn right down Jackson to Grant, then turn right onto ❺ **Jack Kerouac Alley**, where the pavement echoes Kerouac's ode to San Francisco: 'The air was soft, the stars so fine, and the promise of every cobbled alley so great...' Ahead is literary landmark

❻ **City Lights** (p52), where you'll pause to read a poem upstairs in the designated Poet's Chair.

Head left up Columbus and veer right up Vallejo to fuel up with an espresso at ❼ **Caffe Trieste** (p81), where Francis Ford Coppola drafted his script for *The Godfather*. Continue up Vallejo and scale the steps to Montgomery St. Go left three blocks, and turn left onto cottage-lined ❽ **Greenwich Street Steps** to summit Telegraph Hill. Inside ❾ **Coit Tower** (p59), enjoy 1934 city views in newly restored murals downstairs and panoramic Bay views up top.

Head downhill, past wild parrots and tai-chi masters at ❿ **Washington Square**. Turn left on Columbus, right on Vallejo, and up three blocks to take another picturesque stairway path to flower-lined ⓫ **Ina Coolbrith Park**. Any breath you have left will be taken away by sweeping views to Alcatraz. Summit your last hill of the day the easy way: catch the ⓬ **Powell-Mason cable car** up Nob Hill to walk the meditation labyrinth at ⓭ **Grace Cathedral** (p58).

The Richmond, The Sunset & Golden Gate Park

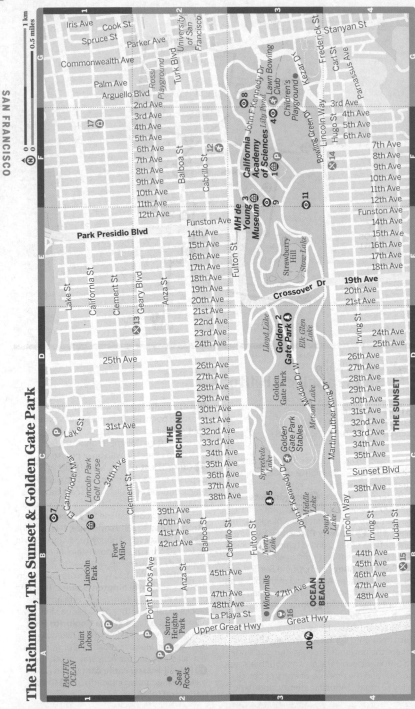

The Richmond, The Sunset & Golden Gate Park

style the last weekend with Pink Saturday's **Dyke March** (www.dykemarch.org) and **Pride Parade** (www.sfpride.org).

August & September

Outside Lands   MUSIC
(www.sfoutsidelands.com/; 1-/3-day $115/375) Three days of major acts – such as Kanye West, Macklemore, The Killers, The Flaming Lips – and outlandish debauchery at Wine Land, Beer Lands and Taste of the Bay.

Folsom Street Fair   STREET FAIR
(www.folsomstreetfair.com) Work that leather look and enjoy public spankings for local charities the last weekend of September.

October & November

Litquake   LITERATURE
(www.litquake.org) Score signed books and grab drinks with authors in October.

Hardly Strictly Bluegrass   MUSIC
(www.strictlybluegrass.com) Three days of free Golden Gate Park concerts and headliners ranging from Elvis Costello to Gillian Welch; early October.

Día de los Muertos   FESTIVAL
(Day of the Dead; www.dayofthedeadsf.org) Party to wake the dead with a spooky costume parade, sugar skulls and fabulous altars in the Mission on November 2.

🛏 Sleeping

🛏 Union Square & the Tenderloin

Hotel des Arts   HOTEL $
(Map p62; ☑415-956-3232, 800-956-4322; www. sfhoteldesarts.com; 447 Bush St; r with bath $129- 199, without bath $99; 🛜; Ⓜ Montgomery, Ⓑ Montgomery) A budget hotel for art freaks, with jaw-dropping murals by underground artists – it's like sleeping inside a painting. Rooms with private bath require seven-night stays. Bring earplugs.

Pacific Tradewinds Hostel   HOSTEL $
(Map p62; ☑415-433-7970, 888-734-6783; www. sanfranciscohostel.org; 680 Sacramento St; dm $35; ◉🛜; 🚏1, ⬛ California St, Ⓑ Montgomery) San Francisco's smartest-looking all-dorm hostel has a blue-and-white nautical theme, fully equipped kitchen, spotless glass-brick showers, no lockout time and great staff. No elevator means hauling bags up three flights.

Hotel Carlton   DESIGN HOTEL $$
(Map p56; ☑415-673-0242, 800-922-7586; www. hotelcarltonsf.com; 1075 Sutter St; r $175-245; ◉🛜🛝; 🚏2, 3, 19, 38, 47, 49) 🍃 World travelers fit right into this freshly renovated hotel off the beaten track – a 10-minute walk to Union Square. Spotless rooms have an upbeat, worldly vibe, with colorful bedspreads and tapestry pillows. Rooftop solar panels help keep the hotel carbon neutral; downstairs is a top-notch Middle Eastern restaurant.

Phoenix Hotel   MOTEL $$
(Map p56; ☑415-776-1380, 800-248-9466; www. thephoenixhotel.com; 601 Eddy St; r $209-244; Ⓟ🛜🏊; 🚏19, 31, 47, 49) The ultimate rocker crash pad earns street cred with courtyard pool parties (bring earplugs), rooms packed with pop art, and a long list of California rebels (Red Hot Chili Peppers, Joan Jett, Keanu Reeves) who frequent this cool converted midcentury motel in the gritty Tenderloin. Free parking and admission to Kabuki Springs & Spa (p69).

OCEAN BEACH

Bundle up for strolls along the blustery 4-mile stretch of **Ocean Beach** (Map p72; ☑ 415-561-4323; www.parksconserv-ancy.org; Great Hwy; ⊘ sunrise-sunset; ☐ 5, 18, 31, Ⓜ N), where Golden Gate Park greenery ends and the great blue Pacific Ocean begins. Dedicated sand-castle architects dot the water's edge year-round, but only hardcore surfers brave these riptides (casual swimmers be-ware). Beachcombers may spot sand dollars and 19th-century shipwrecks along the south end – but stick to paths in fragile dunes, where skittish snowy plover shorebirds shelter in winter. Bon-fires are permitted in artist-designed fire pits only; no alcohol allowed. For drinks, stop by oceanfront **Beach Chalet** (Map p72; ☑ 415-386-8439; www.beachchalet. com; 1000 Great Hwy; ⊘ 9am-10pm Mon-Thu, to 11pm Fri, 8am-11pm Sat, 8am-10pm Sun; ⊞; ☐ 5, 18, 31) for house-brewed beer on the heated patio and 1930s lobby murals.

Golden Gate Hotel HOTEL **$$**
(Map p56; ☑ 415-392-3702, 800-835-1118; www. goldengatehotel.com; 775 Bush St; r with/with-out bath $190/135; @ 奈; ☐ 2, 3, 龱 Powell-Hyde, Powell-Mason) Like an old-fashioned *pen-sione*, this 1913 Edwardian inn has kindly owners and homey mismatched furniture. Rooms are simple and cozy, most with pri-vate baths – request an antique claw-foot tub. Homemade cookies and a resident cat provide comfort after sightseeing.

★**Orchard Garden Hotel** BOUTIQUE HOTEL **$$$**
(Map p62; ☑ 415-399-9807, 888-717-2881; www. theorchardgardenhotel.com; 466 Bush St; r $295-370; ❋@奈; ☐ 2, 3, 30, 45, Ⓑ Montgomery) ⌀ San Francisco's first all-green-practices ho-tel features sustainable wood furnishings, chemical-free cleaning products, and a sun-ny rooftop terrace. Luxe touches include fluffy down pillows and Egyptian-cotton sheets in soothingly quiet rooms.

Hotel Rex BOUTIQUE HOTEL **$$$**
(Map p56; ☑ 415-433-4434, 800-433-4434; www.thehotelrex.com; 562 Sutter St; r $287-309; ❋@奈❋; 龱 Powell-Hyde, Powell-Mason, Ⓜ Powell, Ⓑ Powell) ⌀ French gramophone music evokes New York's Algonquin in the 1920s, and handsome guestrooms feature hand-painted lampshades, local art and plush beds piled with crisp linens and down pillows. Street-facing rooms are bright but noisy; request air-con.

North Beach

San Remo Hotel HOTEL **$$**
(Map p64; ☑ 415-776-8688, 800-352-7366; www. sanremohotel.com; 2237 Mason St; r with shared bath $99-139; @奈❋; ☐ 30, 47, 龱 Powell-Mason) One of the city's best-value stays, this 1906 inn is an old-fashioned charmer with antique furnishings. Bargain rooms have windows facing the corridor; family suites accommodate up to five. No elevator.

★**Hotel Bohème** BOUTIQUE HOTEL **$$$**
(Map p62; ☑ 415-433-9111; www.hotelboheme. com; 444 Columbus Ave; r $214-275; @奈; ☐ 10, 12, 30, 41, 45) A love letter to the Beat era, with vintage photos, parasol lights and moody 1950s color schemes. Rooms are smallish and some face noisy Columbus Ave – but the vibrant North Beach neighborhood scene could inspire your next novel.

Fisherman's Wharf

★**HI San Francisco Fisherman's Wharf** HOSTEL **$**
(Map p64; ☑ 415-771-7277; www.sfhostels.com; Bldg 240, Fort Mason; dm incl breakfast $30-42, r $75-109; Ⓟ@奈; ☐ 28, 30, 47, 49) A former army hospital building offers bargain-priced private rooms and dorms (some co-ed) with four to 22 beds and a huge kitchen. No curfew, but no heat during the day – bring warm clothes. Limited free parking.

★**Argonaut Hotel** BOUTIQUE HOTEL **$$$**
(Map p64; ☑ 415-563-0800, 800-790-1415; www. argonauthotel.com; 495 Jefferson St; r $389-449, with view $489-529; ❋奈❋; ☐ 19, 47, 49, 龱 Powell-Hyde) ⌀ Built as a cannery in 1908, Fisherman's Wharf's best inn has century-old wooden beams, exposed brick walls and an over-the-top nautical theme that includes porthole-shaped mirrors. Ultra-comfy beds and iPod docks are standard, though some rooms are small and dark – pay extra for mesmerising bay views.

The Marina & Pacific Heights

Coventry Motor Inn MOTEL **$$**
(Map p64; ☑ 415-567-1200; www.coventrymo-torinn.com; 1901 Lombard St; r $155-165; Ⓟ❋奈;

GOLDEN GATE PARK

When San Franciscans refer to 'the park,' there's only one that gets the definite article. Everything they hold dear is in **Golden Gate Park** (Map p72; http://sfrecpark.org; 🚹🚻; 🚌5, 18, 21, 28, 29, 33, 44, 71, Ⓜ N) 🍴, including free spirits, free music, Frisbee and bison.

At the east end you can join year-round drum circles at **Hippie Hill**, sweater-clad athletes at the historic **Lawn Bowling Club**, toddlers clinging for dear life onto the 100-year-old **carousel** and meditators in the contemplative **AIDS Memorial Grove** (Map p72). To the west, turtles paddle past model yachts at **Spreckels Lake**, offerings are made at pagan altars behind the **baseball diamond** and free concerts are held in the **Polo Fields**, site of 1967's hippie Human Be-In.

This scenery seems far-fetched now, but impossible when proposed in 1866. When New York's Central Park architect Frederick Law Olmsted balked at transforming 1017 acres of dunes into the world's largest developed park, San Francisco's green scheme fell to tenacious young civil engineer William Hammond Hall. He insisted that instead of casinos, resorts, race tracks and an igloo village, park features should include **botanical gardens** (Strybing Arboretum; Map p72; ☎415-661-1316; www.strybing.org; 1199 9th Ave; adult/child $7/5, 2nd Tue of month free; ⏰9am-6pm Apr-Oct, to 5pm Nov-Mar, bookstore 10am-4pm; 🚹; 🚌6, 43, 44, 71, Ⓜ N) 🍴, a dedicated **bison paddock** (Map p72) and waterfalls at **Stow Lake**.

Today the park offers 7.5 miles of bicycle trails, 12 miles of equestrian trails, an archery range, fly-casting pools, four soccer fields and 21 tennis courts. Sundays, when JFK Dr closes to traffic around 9th Ave, don't miss **roller disco** and **lindy-hopping** in the park. Other times, catch these park highlights:

MH de Young Museum (Map p72; ☎415-750-3600; http://deyoung.famsf.org/; 50 Hagiwara Tea Garden Dr; adult/child $10/6, discount with Muni ticket $2, 1st Tue of month free, online booking fee $1 per ticket; ⏰9:30am-5:15pm Tue-Sun, to 8:45pm Fri Apr-Nov; 🚌5, 44, 71, Ⓜ N) Follow sculptor Andy Goldsworthy's artificial earthquake fault in the sidewalk into Herzog + de Meuron's faultlessly sleek, copper-clad building that's oxidizing green to blend into the park. Don't be fooled by the de Young's camouflaged exterior: shows here boldly broaden artistic horizons, from Oceanic ceremonial masks and Bulgari jewels to California photographer Anthony Friedkin's 1970s portraits of gay liberation.

California Academy of Sciences (Map p72; ☎415-379-8000; www.calacademy.org; 55 Music Concourse Dr; adult/child $34.95/24.95, discount with Muni ticket $3; ⏰9:30am-5pm Mon-Sat, 11am-5pm Sun; 🅿🚹; 🚌5, 6, 31, 33, 44, 71, Ⓜ N) Architect Renzo Piano's landmark, LEED-certified green building houses 38,000 weird and wonderful animals, with a four-story rainforest and split-level aquarium under a 'living roof' of California wildflowers. After the penguins nod off to sleep, the wild rumpus starts at kids'-only Academy Sleepovers and over-21 NightLife Thursdays, when rainforest-themed cocktails encourage strange mating rituals among shy first dates.

Japanese Tea Garden (Map p72; ☎tea ceremony reservations 415-752-1171; www.japanese-teagardensf.com; 75 Hagiwara Tea Garden Dr; adult/child $7/2, before 10am Mon, Wed & Fri free; ⏰9am-6pm Mar-Oct, to 4:45pm Nov-Feb; 🅿🚹; 🚌5, 44, 71, Ⓜ N) Since 1894, this 5-acre garden has blushed with cherry blossoms in spring, turned flaming red with maple leaves in fall, and lost all track of time in the meditative **Zen Garden**. The 100-year-old **bonsai grove** is the legacy of founder Makoto Hagiwara, who tended them until his family's forced deportation to WWII Japanese American internment camps, and spent decades afterwards restoring these priceless miniature evergreens. Don't miss green tea and fortune cookies (invented for the garden's opening) at the **tea pavilion**.

Conservatory of Flowers (Map p72; ☎info 415-831-2090; www.conservatoryofflowers.org; 100 John F Kennedy Dr; adult/child $7/2, 1st Tue of month free; ⏰10am-4:30pm Tue-Sun; 🚌5, Ⓜ N) Flower power thrives inside this restored 1878 Victorian greenhouse, where orchids dangle from the ceiling like trapeze artists, lilies float contemplatively and creepy carnivorous plants make lunch of passing insects.

ⓘ DEALS & HIDDEN COSTS

San Francisco is the birthplace of the boutique hotel, offering stylish rooms for a price: $150-plus for most midrange rooms, plus 16% hotel tax (hostels exempt) and $35 to $50 for overnight parking. For last-minute vacancies and deals, check **Lonely Planet** (http://hotels.lonelyplanet.com) and San Francisco–based accommodations specialists **HotelTonight** (www.hotel tonight.com), **Airbnb** (www.airbnb. com), **Bed & Breakfast SF** (www. bbsf.com), **Hipmunk** (www.hipmunk. com) and **Hotwire** (www.hotwire.com).

🚍22, 28, 30, 43) Of the many motels lining Lombard St (Hwy 101), the generic Coventry has the highest quality-to-value ratio with spacious, plain, well-maintained rooms and extras like air-con and covered parking.

⭐**Hotel Drisco**   BOUTIQUE HOTEL **$$$**
(Map p64; ☑415-346-2880, 800-634-7277; www.hoteldrisco.com; 2901 Pacific Ave; r incl breakfast $375-425; @📶; 🚍3, 24) A stately apartment-hotel tucked between Pacific Heights mansions, with elegant architecture, attentive service and understated-chic room decor. At this lofty ridgeline location, spring for city-view rooms and taxis.

🛏 SoMa

Hotel Vitale   BOUTIQUE HOTEL **$$$**
(Map p56; ☑415-278-3700, 888-890-8688; www.hotelvitale.com; 8 Mission St; r $419-509; ✳@📶🛁; Ⓜ Embarcadero, Ⓑ Embarcadero) Behind that tinted glass is a laid-back luxury waterfront hotel. The clever Vitale has thought of everything: 450-thread-count sheets, on-site spa with two rooftop hot tubs and a sleek downstairs lounge. Get bayfront rooms for spectacular Bay Bridge views.

Good Hotel   MOTEL **$$$**
(Map p56; ☑415-621-7001, 800-444-5819; www. thegoodhotel.com; 112 7th St; r $199-279; @📶🖼; Ⓜ Civic Center, Ⓑ Civic Center) 🖈 SF's hip green motel, with reclaimed-wood headboards, upcycled-bottle chandeliers, and fleece bedspreads made from recycled soda bottles. Drawbacks are the sketchy neighborhood and street noise; book rooms in back.

🛏 The Mission & the Castro

Inn San Francisco   B&B **$$**
(Map p66; ☑800-359-0913, 415-641-0188; www. innsf.com; 943 S Van Ness Ave; r incl breakfast $185-310, with shared bath $135-200; Ⓟ@📶; 🚍14, 49) 🖈 An impeccably maintained 1872 Italianate-Victorian mansion, this inn has period antiques, fresh-cut flowers, and fluffy featherbeds; some have Jacuzzi tubs. There's also a freestanding garden cottage that sleeps up to six. Outside there's an English garden and redwood hot tub. Limited parking: reserve ahead.

Inn on Castro   GLBT, B&B **$$**
(Map p66; ☑415-861-0321; www.innoncastro.com; 321 Castro St; r incl breakfast $165-185, without bath $125-145, self-catering apt $165-210; 📶; Ⓜ Castro) Flashback to the Castro's disco heyday inside this Edwardian townhouse with '70s-mod furnishings. Rooms are retro-cool and breakfasts exceptional – the owner is a chef. Ask about nearby apartments also available for rent.

Parker Guest House   B&B **$$$**
(Map p66; ☑415-621-3222, 888-520-7275; www. parkerguesthouse.com; 520 Church St; r incl breakfast $209-259; @📶; 🚍33, Ⓜ J) Welcome to the Castro's stateliest gay digs, inside twin Edwardian mansions sharing a garden and steam room. Elegant rooms have cushy beds with down duvets; bath fixtures gleam.

🛏 The Haight & Hayes Valley

Metro Hotel   HOTEL **$**
(Map p66; ☑415-861-5364; www.metrohotelsf. com; 319 Divisadero St; r $88-100; @📶; 🚍6, 24, 71) A central Haight hotel providing cheap, clean rooms with private bath, 24-hour reception, a garden patio and excellent pizza downstairs. No elevator.

Chateau Tivoli   B&B **$$**
(☑415-776-5462, 800-228-1647; www.chateau-tivoli.com; 1057 Steiner St; r incl breakfast $175-215, with shared bath $115-135; 📶; 🚍5, 22) This glorious chateau off Alamo Sq once hosted Isadora Duncan and Mark Twain, and shows plenty of character with turrets, carved woodwork and (rumor has it) the ghost of a Victorian opera diva. No elevator, no TV.

Red Victorian Bed, Breakfast & Art   B&B **$$**
(Map p70; ☑415-864-1978; www.redvic.net; 1665 Haight St; r incl breakfast $179-189, without bath $119-149; 📶; 🚍33, 43, 71) 🖈 The trippy '60s

live on inside this 1904 Victorian, with theme rooms like Sunshine, Flower Children and Summer of Love. Only four of 18 rooms have baths, but all include breakfast in the organic Peace Café downstairs. Reduced rates for longer stays; no elevator.

Hayes Valley Inn HOTEL **$$**
(Map p56; ✆415-431-9131, 800-930-7999; www.hayesvalleyinn.com; 417 Gough St; d incl breakfast $93-115, queen $103-126; @🖥🐾; 🚇21, Ⓜ Van Ness) Amid tempting boutiques and bistros, this amazingly reasonable find has simple, small rooms with shared baths, kindly staff and a good-natured resident dog. Bring ear plugs and expect a walk to the nearest bathroom; no elevator.

Parsonage B&B **$$$**
(Map p66; ✆415-863-3699; www.theparsonage.com; 198 Haight St; r $220-270; @🖥; 🚇6, 71, streetcar F) The charming owners are justly proud of their 23-room Italianate-Victorian's gorgeous original details, including brass chandeliers and Carrara-marble fireplaces. Airy rooms are bedecked with oriental rugs and period antiques. Take breakfast in the formal dining room, and nightcaps of brandy and chocolate by the fire.

✗ Eating

✗ Union Square

farm:table AMERICAN **$**
(Map p56; ✆415-292-7089; www.farmtablesf.com; 754 Post St; dishes $6-9; ⏱7:30am-2pm Tue-Fri, 8am-3pm Sat & Sun; 🚇2, 3, 27, 38) 🍃 A tiny storefront with one wooden communal table inside, two tables and a stand-up outdoor counter, farm:table uses local organics and rooftop-grown herbs in daily menus posted on Twitter (@farmtable). Cash only.

Sweet Woodruff CAFE, CALIFORNIAN **$**
(Map p56; ✆415-292-9090; www.sweetwoodruffsf.com; 798 Sutter St; dishes $8-14; ⏱8am-9:30pm Mon-Fri, 9:30am-9:30pm Sat & Sun; 🚇2, 3, 27) 🍃 Little sister to neighboring Michelin-starred Sons & Daughters, this storefront features top-end, seasonal-regional ingredients in small plates like roasted padron peppers with fromage blanc and sea-urchin baked potatoes with bacon. No waiters, no frills, just tasty.

Cafe Claude FRENCH **$$**
(Map p56; ✆415-392-3505; www.cafeclaude.com; 7 Claude Lane; mains $15-23; ⏱11:30am-10:30pm Mon-Sat, 5:30pm-10:30pm Sun; Ⓜ Montgomery, Ⓑ Montgomery) Hidden in an alleyway, Cafe Claude is a sweet downtown retreat with outdoor tables and effortlessly charming staff. Lunch is served until 5pm, jazz combos play weekends, and coq au vin and a stellar wine list make dream dates.

✗ Chinatown & North Beach

★Liguria Bakery BAKERY **$**
(Map p62; ✆415-421-3786; 1700 Stockton St; focaccia $4-5; ⏱8am-1pm Tue-Fri, from 7am Sat; ✗🚻; 🚇8X, 30, 39, 41, 45, 🚋 Powell-Mason) Bleary-eyed art students and Italian grandmothers line up by 8am for cinnamon-raisin focaccia hot from the 100-year-old oven, leaving 9am dawdlers a choice of tomato or classic rosemary. Take yours in wax paper or boxed for picnics; cash only.

City View CHINESE **$**
(Map p62; ✆415-398-2838; 662 Commercial St; dishes $3-8; ⏱11am-2:30pm Mon-Fri, from 10am Sat & Sun; 🚇8X, 10, 12, 30, 45, 🚋 California St) Order off the menu or hail carts loaded with shrimp dumplings, garlicky Chinese broccoli, tangy spare ribs and other tantalizing dim sum. Arrive before noon for first picks from fragrant bamboo steamers.

★Cotogna ITALIAN **$$**
(Map p62; ✆415-775-8508; www.cotognasf.com; 490 Pacific Ave; mains $17-29; ⏱11:30am-11pm Mon-Thu, 11:30am-midnight Fri & Sat, 5-9:30pm Sun; ✗; 🚇10, 12) Rustic Italian pastas, wood-fired pizzas and rotisserie meats spiked with rooftop-grown herbs show chef Michael Tusk's finesse with well-chosen, balanced ingredients. Book ahead or plan a late lunch.

Z & Y CHINESE **$$**
(Map p62; ✆415-981-8988; www.zandyrestaurant.com; 655 Jackson St; mains $9-20; ⏱11am-9:30pm Mon-Thu, to 10:30pm Fri-Sun; 🚇8X, 🚋 Powell-Mason, Powell-Hyde) Graduate from so-so sweet-and-sour and middling *mu-shu* pork to sensational Szechuan dishes that go down in a blaze of glory: spicy pork dumplings, heat-blistered string beans, housemade noodles, and fish poached in flaming chili oil. Go early; expect a wait.

Cinecittà PIZZA **$$**
(Map p62; ✆415-291-8830; www.cinecittarestaurant.com; 663 Union St; pizza $12-15; ⏱noon-10pm Sun-Thu, to 11pm Fri & Sat; ✗🚻; 🚇8X, 30, 39, 41, 45, 🚋 Powell-Mason) Squeeze in at the counter for thin-crust pizza served with local brews on tap and sass by Roman owner Romina.

❶ SF MEALS & DEALS

Hope you're hungry: there are more restaurants per capita in San Francisco than in any other US city. Scan for deals at www.blackboardeats.com and www.opentable.com – and since SF's top restaurants are quite small, reserve now. Some restaurants brazenly tack on a 4% surcharge to cover city-mandated healthcare for SF food workers. Factor in 9.5% tax on top of your meal price, plus 15% to 25% for the tip.

North Beach loyalties are divided between the Roman Travestere (mozzarella, arugula and prosciutto) and Neapolitan O Sole Mio (capers, olives, mozzarella and anchovies).

★ Coi   CALIFORNIAN $$$
(Map p62; ☏415-393-9000; www.coirestaurant.com; 373 Broadway; set menu $195; ⏱5:30-10pm Tue-Sat; ☐8X, 30, 41, 45, ☐Powell-Mason) ✔ Chef Daniel Patterson's restlessly imaginative eight-course tasting menu is like licking California's coastline: rooftop-raised pansies grace Sonoma duck's tongue, and wild-caught abalone surfaces in pea-shoot tidepools. Settle in among the shaggy cushions and spot-lit stoneware to enjoy only-in-California wine pairings ($115; generous enough for two).

✕ Fisherman's Wharf & Russian Hill

Fisherman's Wharf Crab Stands   SEAFOOD $
(Map p64; foot of Taylor St; mains $5-15; ☑F) Brawny-armed men stir steaming cauldrons of Dungeness crab at takeaway crab stands at the foot of Taylor St. Crab season runs winter through spring, but you'll find shrimp and seafood year-round. Take your haul to Pier 43 Promenade benches, or duck through glass doors marked 'Passageway to the Boats' at 8/9 Fisherman's Wharf for dockside lunches.

★ Gary Danko   CALIFORNIAN $$$
(Map p64; ☏415-749-2060; www.garydanko.com; 800 North Point St; 3-/5-course menu $76/111; ⏱5:30-10pm; ☐19, 30, 47, ☐Powell-Hyde) The true test of SF romance is whether you're willing to share Gary Danko's crèmes brûlée trio. Smoked-glass windows prevent passersby from tripping over their tongues at roast lobster with trumpet mushrooms,

duck breast with rhubarb compote, and the lavish cheese cart. Reservations required.

✕ The Marina, Japantown & Pacific Heights

Off the Grid   FOOD TRUCK $
(Map p64; www.offthegridsf.com; 2 Marina Blvd; dishes $5-10; ⏱5-11pm Fri; ❙; ☐22, 28) Some 30 food trucks converge Fridays for SF's largest mobile-gourmet hootenanny (other nights/ locations attract fewer trucks; see website). Arrive before 6:30pm or expect 20-minute waits for Chairman Bao's roast duck buns, Roli Roti's free-range herbed roast chicken, and Crème Brûlée Man desserts. Cash only; enjoy takeout dockside with Golden Gate Bridge sunsets.

★ Greens   VEGETARIAN, CALIFORNIAN $$
(Map p64; ☑415-771-6222; www.greensrestaurant.com; Bldg A, Fort Mason Center, cnr Marina Blvd & Laguna St; lunch $15-18, dinner $18-25; ⏱11:45am-2:30pm & 5:30-9pm Tue-Fri, from 11am Sat, 10:30am-2pm & 5:30-9pm Sun, 5:30-9pm Mon; ☑❙; ☐28) ✔ Career carnivores won't realize there's zero meat in hearty roasted-eggplant panini and black-bean chili with crème fraîche and pickled jalapeños – they're packed with flavor-bursting ingredients grown on a Zen farm in Marin. Make reservations on weekends, or get take-out to enjoy on a wharf-side bench.

State Bird Provisions   CALIFORNIAN $$
(☑415-795-1272; statebirdsf.com; 1529 Fillmore St; ⏱5:30-10pm Sun-Thu, to 11pm Fri & Sat; ☐22, 38) James Beard dubbed State Bird America's best new restaurant in 2013 for its wildly inventive take on dim sum, with esoteric local ingredients like fennel pollen and garum (fish extract). Book ahead, or arrive by 5pm for a coveted walk-in bar spot. Prices are deceptive; all those small plates add up.

Tataki   JAPANESE $$
(Map p64; ☏415-931-1182; www.tatakisushibar.com; 2815 California St; dishes $12-20; ⏱11:30am-2pm & 5:30-10pm Mon-Thu, 11:30am-2pm & 5:30-10:30pm Fri, 5-10:30pm Sat, 5-9:30pm Sun; ☐1, 24) ✔ Pioneering sustainable sushi chefs Kin Lui, Raymond Ho and Kenny Zhu rescue dinner and the oceans with silky farmed Arctic char with yuzu-citrus and the Golden State Roll – a California dream of spicy, line-caught scallop, Pacific tuna, organic avocado and apple slivers.

✗ SoMa

Zero Zero   PIZZA $$

(Map p56; ☑ 415-348-8800; www.zerozerosf.com; 826 Folsom St; pizzas $12-19; ⊙ 11:30am-2:30pm & 4-10pm Mon-Thu, to 11pm Fri, 11:30am-11pm Sat, 11:30am-10pm Sun; M Powell, B Powell) The name is a throw-down of Neapolitan pizza credentials – '00' flour is used for Naples' famous puffy-edged crust – and these pies deliver on that promise, with inspired SF-themed toppings. The Geary is a crossover hit with Manila clams, bacon and chilies, but the real crowd-pleaser is the Castro, turbo-loaded with housemade sausage.

★ Benu   CALIFORNIAN, FUSION $$$

(Map p56; ☑ 415-685-4860; www.benusf.com; 22 Hawthorne St; tasting menu $195; ⊙ 5:30-8:30pm Tue-Sat; ☐ 10, 12, 14, 30, 45) SF has refined fusion cuisine over 150 years, but no one rocks it quite like chef/owner Corey Lee (formerly of Napa's French Laundry), who remixes local, sustainable, fine-dining staples and Pacific Rim flavors with a SoMa DJ's finesse. Dungeness crab and truffle bring such outsize flavor to his faux-shark's-fin soup, you'll swear there's Jaws in there.

✗ The Mission & the Castro

★ La Taqueria   MEXICAN $

(Map p66; ☑ 415-285-7117; 2889 Mission St; burritos $6-8; ⊙ 11am-9pm Mon-Sat, to 8pm Sun; ⚹; ☐ 12, 14, 48, 49, B 24th St Mission) SF's definitive burrito has no debatable saffron rice, spinach tortilla or mango salsa – just perfectly grilled meats, slow-cooked beans and classic tomatillo or mesquite salsa wrapped in flour tortillas.

★ Ichi Sushi   SUSHI $$

(☑ 415-525-4750; www.ichisushi.com; 3282 Mission St; sushi $4-8; ⊙ 5:30-10pm Mon-Thu, to 11pm Fri & Sat; ☐ 14, 49, B 24th St Mission, M J) Ichi Sushi is a sharp cut above other fish joints. Silky, sustainably sourced fish is sliced with a jeweler's precision, balanced atop well-packed rice, and topped with powerfully tangy dabs of gelled yuzu and microscopically diced chili daikon that make soy sauce unthinkable.

★ Namu Gaji   KOREAN, CALIFORNIAN $$

(Map p66; ☑ 415-431-6268; www.namusf.com; 499 Dolores St; small plates $10-21; ⊙ 11:30am 4pm Wed-Fri, from 10:30am Sat & Sun, 5-10pm Tue-Thu & Sun, 5-11pm Fri & Sat; ☐ 22, 33, M J, B 16th St Mission) ✔ SF's culinary advantages are

THE FERRY BUILDING

San Francisco's monument to food, the **Ferry Building** (Map p56; ☑ 415-983-8000; www.ferrybuildingmarketplace.com; Market St & the Embarcadero; ⊙ 10am-6pm Mon-Fri, 9am-6pm Sat, 11am-5pm Sun; P ⚹; M Embarcadero, B Embarcadero) still doubles as a trans-bay transit hub – but with dining options like these, you may never leave.

Ferry Plaza Farmers Market (Map p56; ☑ 415-291-3276; www.cuesa.org; Market St & the Embarcadero; ⊙ 10am-2pm Tue & Thu, 8am-2pm Sat; M Embarcadero, B Embarcadero) Star chefs troll farmers-market stalls for rare heirloom varietals, foodie babies blissfully teethe on organic apricots, and organic tamale trucks have rock-star fan bases. Pass time in line exchanging recipe tips, then haul your picnic to Pier 2.

Slanted Door (Map p56; ☑ 415-861-8032; www.slanteddoor.com; 1 Ferry Bldg; lunch $16-36, dinner $18-45; ⊙ 11am-4:30pm & 5:30-10pm Mon-Sat, 11:30am-4:30pm & 5:30-10pm Sun; M Embarcadero, B Embarcadero) Charles Phan earns his 2014 James Beard Outstanding Chef title with California-fresh, Vietnamese-inspired fare that rivals the sparkling Bay views – especially five-spice duck with figs. Reserve ahead or hit the takeout window.

Hog Island Oyster Company (Map p56; ☑ 415-391-7117; www.hogislandoysters.com; 1 Ferry Bldg; 4 oysters $13; ⊙ 11:30am-9pm Mon-Thu, to 10pm Fri, 11am-10pm Sat, 11am-9pm Sun; M Embarcadero, B Embarcadero) ✔ Slurp sustainably farmed Tomales Bay oysters as you please: drizzled with tangy caper buerre blanc, spiked with bacon and paprika, or au naturel with Sonoma bubbly.

Mijita (Map p56; ☑ 415-399-0814; www.mijitasf.com; 1 Ferry Bldg; dishes $4-10; ⊙ 10am-7pm Mon-Thu, to 8pm Fri, 9am-8pm Sat, 8:30am-3pm Sun; ✎ ⚹; M Embarcadero, B Embarcadero) Sustainable fish tacos reign supreme and *agua fresca* (fruit punch) is made with fresh juice at chef-owner Traci des Jardin's bayfront Cal-Mex joint.

showcased in Namu's Korean-inspired soul food. Menu standouts include ultra-savory shiitake mushroom dumplings, meltingly tender marinated beef tongue, and a sizzling stone pot of rice with organic vegetables, grass-fed steak and a Sonoma farm egg.

★ **Frances** CALIFORNIAN $$$
(Map p66; ☑ 415-621-3870; www.frances-sf. com; 3870 17th St; mains $20-27; ☺ 5-10pm Sun-Thu, to 10:30pm Fri & Sat; Ⓜ Castro) Chef/ owner Melissa Perello ditched downtown fine dining to start this bistro showcasing bright, seasonal flavors and luxurious textures: cloudlike sheep's-milk ricotta gnocchi with crunchy broccolini, grilled calamari with preserved Meyer lemon, and artisan wine served by the ounce, directly from Wine Country.

🍴 The Haight & Hayes Valley

Second Act FOOD ARTISANS $
(http://secondactsf.com/; 1727 Haight St; dishes $5-12; ☺ 8am-6pm, to 8pm Fri) When collectively run Red Vic movie house ended its 30-year run, neighbors demanded an encore – now Second Act Marketplace houses local

food makers and a neighborhood events space. Stop by for dumplings at Anda Piroshki, High Cotton Kitchen soul food, and the cherry-lavender ice cream at Eatwell Farm – and stay for Friday happy hours and indie-movie premieres (see website).

★ **Rich Table** CALIFORNIAN $$$
(Map p66; ☑ 415-355-9085; http://richtablesf. com; 199 Gough St; meals $17-30; ☺ 5:30-10pm Sun-Thu, to 10:30pm Fri & Sat; ☐ 5, 6, 21, 47, 49, 71, Ⓜ Van Ness) 🍴 Licking plates is the obvious move after finishing chilled apricot soup with pancetta or rabbit cannelloni with nasturtium cream. Married co-chefs/co-owners Sarah and Evan Rich invent playful, exquisite Californian food like the Dirty Hippie: silky goat-buttermilk pannacotta topped with nutty sunflower seeds and hemp. Book two to four weeks ahead (call the restaurant directly) or arrive early for bar seating.

★ **Jardinière** CALIFORNIAN $$$
(Map p56; ☑ 415-861-5555; www.jardiniere.com; 300 Grove St; mains $18-32; ☺ 5-10:30pm Tue-Sat, to 10pm Sun & Mon; ☐ 5, 21, 47, 49, Ⓜ Van Ness) 🍴 *Iron Chef, Top Chef* Master and James Beard Award–winner Traci Des Jardins

TOP SAN FRANCISCO TREATS

Life is sweet in San Francisco, where chocolate bars were invented in the Gold Rush and velvet ropes keep ice-cream lines from getting ugly. Before you dismiss dessert, consider these temptations.

➡ ★ **Craftsman & Wolves** (Map p66; ☑ 415-913-7713; http://craftsman-wolves.com; 746 Valencia St; pastries $3-7; ☺ 7am-7pm Mon-Thu, to 8pm Fri, 8am-8pm Sat, 8am-7pm Sun; ☐ 14, 22, 33, 49, Ⓑ 16th St Mission, Ⓜ J) A sleek counter fit to showcase diamonds offers something far better: exquisite salted-caramel eclairs and black-sesame checkered cake.

➡ **Bi-Rite Creamery** (Map p66; ☑ 415-626-5600; www.biritecreamery.com; 3692 18th St; ice cream $3-7; ☺ 11am-10pm Sun-Thu, to 11pm Fri & Sat; 🍴; ☐ 33, Ⓑ 16th St Mission, Ⓜ J) 🍴 Organic ice cream worth the line even in foggy weather – especially salted caramel and balsamic strawberry.

➡ **Tout Sweet** (Map p56; ☑ 415-385-1679; www.toutsweetsf.com; Geary & Stockton Sts, Macy's, 3rd fl; baked goods $2-8; ☺ 10am-8pm Mon-Wed, until 9pm Thu-Sat, 11am-7pm Sun; ☐ 2, 38, 🚋 Powell-Mason, Powell-Hyde, Ⓑ Powell St) Bypass sales and head directly to Macy's 3rd floor, where *Top Chef* winner Yigit Pura reinvents French macarons in irreverent SF flavors like sour cherry/bourbon and peanut butter and jelly.

➡ **Benkyodo** (☑ 415-922-1244; www.benkyodocompany.com; 1747 Buchanan St; mochi $1.25-2; ☺ 8am-5pm Mon-Sat; ☐ 2, 3, 22, 38) Legendary *mochi* (rice cakes) made in-house daily – come early for perennially popular green tea, peanut butter, and chocolate-filled strawberry flavors.

➡ **Mission Pie** (Map p66; ☑ 415-282-1500; www.missionpie.com; 2901 Mission St; pie slices $3.50-4; ☺ 7am-10pm Mon-Fri, from 8am Sat, from 9am Sun; 📶 🍴; ☐ 12, 14, 48, 49, Ⓑ 24th St Mission) 🍴 Warm, flaky, heirloom apple pie served with free organic whipped cream in a sunny, certified-green Victorian storefront with toys for kids.

champions sustainable, salacious California cuisine. She lavishes housemade tagliatelle with bone marrow and tops velvety scallops with satiny sea urchin. Go Mondays, when $55 scores three decadent courses with wine pairings.

The Richmond & the Sunset

★ Outerlands
CALIFORNIAN $$

(Map p72; ☑ 415-661-6140; www.outerlandssf. com; 4001 Judah St; sandwiches & small plates $7-14, mains $18-22; ☺ 10am-3pm Tue-Fri, from 9am Sat & Sun, 5:30-10pm Tue-Sun; ⊞; ☐ 18, Ⓜ N) 🍴 When windy Ocean Beach leaves you feeling shipwrecked, drift into this beach-shack bistro for organic, seed-to-table California comfort food. Brunch demands Dutch pancakes in iron skillets with housemade ricotta, and lunch brings grilled artisan-cheese combos with farm-inspired soup. Reserve ahead or enjoy wine while you wait.

Nopalito
MEXICAN $$

(Map p72; ☑ 415-233-9966; www.nopalitosf.com; 1224 9th Ave; ☺ 11:30am-10pm; ⊞; ☐ 6, 43, 44, 71, Ⓜ N) 🍴 Head south of Golden Gate Park's border for upscale, sustainably sourced Cal-Mex, including tasty *tortas* (flatbread sandwiches), tender *carnitas* (braised pork) tacos and cinnamon-laced Mexican hot chocolate. No reservations; call one to two hours ahead to join the wait list.

★ Aziza
MOROCCAN, CALIFORNIAN $$$

(Map p72; ☑ 415-752-2222; www.aziza-sf.com; 5800 Geary Blvd; mains $19-29; ☺ 5:30-10:30pm Wed-Mon; ☐ 1, 29, 31, 38) *Iron Chef* champ Mourad Lahlou's inspiration is Moroccan and his ingredients organic Californian, but the flavors are out of this world: Sonoma duck confit and caramelized onion fill flaky pastry *basteeya*, and slow-cooked Marin lamb tops saffron-infused barley. Pastry chef Melissa Chou's apricot bavarian is a goodnight kiss.

🍸 Drinking & Nightlife

🍷 Union Square

★ Rickhouse
BAR

(Map p62; ☑ 415-398-2827; www.rickhousebar. com; 246 Kearny St; ☺ 5pm-2am Mon, 3pm-2am Tue-Fri, 6pm-2am Sat; Ⓜ Montgomery, Ⓑ Montgomery) Like a shotgun shack plunked downtown, Rickhouse is lined with bourbon casks and shelving from an Ozark Mountains nunnery that once secretly brewed

hooch. The emphasis is on rare bourbon, but groups guzzle authentic Pisco Punch by the garage-sale punchbowl.

Irish Bank
PUB

(Map p62; ☑ 415-788-7152; www.theirishbank.com; 10 Mark Lane; ☺ 11:30am-2am; Ⓜ Montgomery, Ⓑ Montgomery) Perfectly pulled pints, thick-cut fries with malt vinegar, and sausages with lashings of mustard are staples at this genuinely friendly Irish pub. Cozy snugs are great for conversation, but tables under alley awnings appeal to smokers.

🍷 Chinatown & North Beach

★ Caffe Trieste
CAFE

(Map p62; ☑ 415-392-6739; www.caffetrieste.com; 601 Vallejo St; ☺ 6:30am-11pm Sun-Thu, to midnight Fri & Sat; 🛜; ☐ 8X, 10, 12, 30, 41, 45) Poetry on bathroom walls, opera on the jukebox, live accordion jams weekly and sightings of Beat poet laureate Lawrence Ferlinghetti: Trieste has been a North Beach landmark since the 1950s. Sip espresso under the Sicilian mural, where Francis Ford Coppola drafted *The Godfather*. Cash only.

★ Comstock Saloon
BAR

(Map p62; ☑ 415-617-0071; www.comstocksaloon. com; 155 Columbus Ave; ☺ noon to 2am Mon-Fri, from 4pm Sat, 4pm-midnight Sun; ☐ 8X, 10, 12, 30, 45, ☐ Powell-Mason) Cocktails at this Victorian saloon remain period-perfect: Pisco Punch is made with pineapple gum and martini-precursor Martinez features gin, vermouth, bitters and maraschino liqueur. Call ahead for booths or tufted-velvet parlor seating and to get dates when ragtime-jazz bands play.

Specs'
BAR

(☑ 415-421-4112; 12 William Saroyan Pl; ☺ 4:30pm-2am Mon-Fri, from 5pm Sat & Sun) Order pitchers of Anchor Steam, admire walls plastered with merchant-marine memorabilia and join salty old-timers plotting mutinies against last call.

Li Po
BAR

(Map p62; ☑ 415-982-0072; www.lipolounge. com; 916 Grant Ave; ☺ 2pm-2am; ☐ 8X, 30, 45, ☐ Powell-Mason, Powell-Hyde) Beat a hasty retreat to red vinyl booths where Allen Ginsberg and Jack Kerouac debated the meaning of life alongside a bemused golden Buddha. Enter the 1937 faux-grotto doorway and dodge red lanterns to order beer or a sweet, sneaky-strong Chinese mai tai made with *baiju* (rice liquor). Bathrooms and random DJ appearances are in the basement.

Downtown & SoMa

★ Bar Agricole BAR

(Map p66; ☎415-355-9400; www.baragricole.com; 355 11th St; ☉6-10pm Tue-Thu & Sun, 5:30-11pm Fri & Sat; ☐9, 12, 27, 47) Drink your way to a history degree with these cocktails: Bellamy Scotch Sour with egg whites passes the test, but Tequila Fix with lime, pineapple gum and hellfire bitters earns honors. Don't miss the sea-urchin deviled eggs.

Blue Bottle Coffee Company CAFE

(www.bluebottlecoffee.net; 66 Mint St; ☉7am-7pm Mon-Fri, 8am-6pm Sat & Sun) The mad-scientist $20,000 coffee siphon yields superior fairtrade, organic drip coffee, rivaled only by bittersweet mochas and an off-menu invention called the Gibraltar.

Local Edition LOUNGE

(☎415-795-1375; www.localeditionsf.com; 691 Market st; ☉5pm-2am Mon-Fri, from 7pm Sat) Get the scoop on SF's cocktail scene at this new speakeasy in the historic Hearst newspaper building's basement. Lights are so dim you might bump into typewriters, but all is forgiven when you get the Pulitzer – a scotch-sherry cocktail that goes straight to your head.

DNA Lounge CLUB

(Map p66; www.dnalounge.com; 375 11th St; admission $3-25; ☉9pm-3am Fri & Sat, other nights vary; ☐12, 27, 47) One of SF's last megaclubs hosts live bands, mash-up dance party Bootie, epic drag at Trannyshack, and Monday's 18-plus Goth Death Guild.

The Mission

Ritual Coffee Roasters CAFE

(Map p66; ☎415-641-1011; www.ritualroasters.com; 1026 Valencia St; ☉6am-8pm Mon-Thu, to 10pm Fri, 7am-10pm Sat, 7am-8pm Sun; ☎; ☐14, 49, ⒷBoston 24th St Mission) Cults wish they inspired the same devotion as Ritual, where devotees queue for house-roasted espresso drinks and specialty drip coffees with genuinely bizarre flavor profiles – believe descriptions of beans with cashew and grapefruit-peel notes.

GAY/LESBIAN/BI/TRANS SAN FRANCISCO

Singling out the best places to be queer in San Francisco is almost redundant. Though the Castro is a gay hub and the Mission is a magnet for lesbians, dancing queens and party bois head to SoMa for thump-thump clubs. Top GLBT venues include:

➡ **The Stud** (Map p66; www.studsf.com; 399 9th St; admission $5-8; ☉noon-2am Tue, from 5pm Wed & Sat, 5pm-3am Thu & Fri, 5pm to midnight Sun; ☐12, 19, 27, 47) Rocking the gay scene since 1966, and branching out beyond leather daddies with rocker-grrrl Mondays, Tuesday drag variety shows, raunchy comedy/karaoke Wednesdays, Friday art-drag dance parties, and performance-art cabaret whenever hostess/DJ Anna Conda gets it together.

➡ **Lexington Club** (Map p66; ☎415-863-2052; www.lexingtonclub.com; 3464 19th St; ☉5pm-2am Mon-Thu, from 3pm Fri-Sun; ☐14, 33, 49, Ⓑ16th St Mission) Odds are eerily high you'll develop a crush on your ex-girlfriend's hot new girlfriend over strong drinks, pinball and tattoo comparisons; live dangerously at SF's most famous/notorious full-time lesbian bar.

➡ **Aunt Charlie's** (Map p56; ☎415-441-2922; www.auntcharlieslounge.com; 133 Turk St; admission $2-5; ☉noon-2am Mon-Fri, from 10am Sat, 10am-midnight Sun; ⓂPowell, ⒷPowell) Total dive, with the city's best classic drag show Fridays and Saturdays at 10pm. Thursday nights, art-school boys freak for bathhouse disco at Tubesteak ($5).

➡ **Endup** (Map p56; ☎415-646-0999; www.theendup.com; 401 6th St; admission $5-20; ☉10pm Thu-4am Fri, 11pm Fri-11am Sat, 10pm Sat-4am Mon, 10pm Mon-4am Tue; ☐12, 27, 47) Home of Sunday 'tea dances' since 1973, though technically the party starts Saturday, EndUp watching the sunrise Monday over the freeway on-ramp.

➡ **Rickshaw Stop** (Map p56; ☎415-861-2011; www.rickshawstop.com; 155 Fell St; admission $5-35; ☉variable, check online; ⓂVan Ness) Freak beats keep sweaty 18-plus crowds up past their bedtimes at this all-ages, all-orientations, all-fabulous shoebox club; lesbian go-go and bhangra nights rule.

➡ **Sisters of Perpetual Indulgence** (Map p56; www.thesisters.org) For guerrilla antics and wild fundraisers, check the website of the self-described 'leading-edge order of queer nuns,' a charitable organization and San Francisco institution.

El Rio
CLUB

(✆415-282-3325; www.elriosf.com; 3158 Mission St; admission $3-8; ⊗1pm-2am; ☐12,14,27,49, Ⓑ24th St Mission) The DJ mix takes its cue from El Rio regulars: eclectic, funky and internationally sexy, no matter your orientation. Margaritas get crowds bopping to disco-punk mashups and flirting shamelessly in the back garden. Come for shuffleboard and free oysters Fridays at 5:30pm. Cash only.

🍷 The Haight & Hayes Valley

★ Smuggler's Cove
BAR

(Map p56; ✆415-869-1900; www.smugglerscovesf. com; 650 Gough St; ⊗5pm-1:15am; ☐5, 21, 49, ⓂVan Ness) Yo-ho-ho and a bottle of rum…or perhaps a Dead Reckoning with bitters, Nicaraguan rum, tawny port and vanilla liqueur. Pirates are bedeviled by choice at this shipwreck tiki speakeasy – with 400 rums and 70 cocktails, you won't be dry-docked long.

★ Toronado
PUB

(Map p66; ✆415-863-2276; www.toronado.com; 547 Haight St; ⊗11:30am-2am; ☐6, 22, 71, ⓂN) Glory hallelujah, beer lovers: your prayers are answered with 50-plus brews on tap and hundreds more bottled. Bring cash and pair seasonal ales with sausages from **Rosamunde** (Map p66; ✆415-437-6851; http://rosamundesausagegrill.com; 545 Haight St; sausages $6.50-7; ⊗11:30am-10pm Sun-Wed, to 11pm Thu-Sat; ☐6,22, 71, ⓂN) next door – it may get too loud to hear your date, but you'll hear angels sing.

Alembic
BAR

(Map p70; ✆415-666-0822; www.alembicbar.com; 1725 Haight St; ⊗4pm-2am Mon-Fri, from noon Sat & Sun; ☐6,33,37,43,71, ⓂN) The floors are well-stomped and the tin ceilings hammered – and you will be too, if you gulp Alembic's potent concoctions made with 250 specialty spirits. Honor the Haight with a Lava Lamp (rosé bubbly with walnut bitters) or be rendered speechless by Charlie Chaplin (sloe gin, lime and apricot liqueur).

☆ Entertainment

Live Music

★ SFJAZZ Center
JAZZ

(Map p66; ✆866-920-5299; www.sfjazz.org; 201 Franklin St; ⊗showtimes vary; ☐5, 7, 21, ⓂVan Ness) America's newest, largest jazz center draws legendary artists-in-residence like Wynton Marsalis, Regina Carter and Tony Bennett (who left his heart here, after all) – but the real thrills are experimental performances, like pianist Jason Moran's jam session with SF skateboarders pounding a ramp inside the auditorium. Upper-tier cheap seats are more like stools, but offer clear stage views and ledges for drinks.

★ The Chapel
LIVE MUSIC

(Map p66; ✆415-551-5157; www.thechapelsf. com; 777 Valencia St; tickets $15-22; ☐14, 33, ⓂJ, Ⓑ16th St Mission) Musical prayers are answered in a 1914 California Craftsman landmark where heavenly acoustics. The 40ft roof is raised by shows like Preservation Hall Jazz Band jams with Nick Lowe, Polyphonic Spree's full-choir ruckus and Radiohead's *OK Computer* lipsynched by an all-star drag revue. Many shows are all-ages, except when comedians like W Kamau Bell test edgy material.

The Fillmore
CONCERT VENUE

(✆415-346-3000; www.thefillmore.com; 1805 Geary Blvd; tickets from $20; ⊗shows nightly) Hendrix, Zeppelin, Janis – they all played the Fillmore. The legendary venue that launched the psychedelic era has the posters to prove it upstairs, and hosts arena acts in a 1250-seat venue where you can squeeze in next to the stage.

Slim's
LIVE MUSIC

(Map p66; ✆415-255-0333; www.slimspresents. com; 333 11th St; tickets $12-30; ⊗box office 10:30am-6pm Mon-Fri & show nights; ☐9, 12, 27, 47) Guaranteed good times by Gogol Bordello, the Expendables and the Mekons fit the bill at this midsized club, where Prince and Elvis Costello have played sets unannounced. Shows are all-ages, though shorties may have a hard time seeing once the floor starts bouncing. Reserve dinner ($25) to score balcony seats.

Great American Music Hall
LIVE MUSIC

(Map p56; ✆415-885-0750; www.gamh.com; 859 O'Farrell St; admission $12-35; ⊗box office 10:30am-6pm Mon-Fri & show nights; ☐19, 38, 47, 49) Once a bordello, the Great American Music Hall is full of surprises: Black Rebel Motorcycle Club playing acoustic, hardcore bluegrass jams, and burly bouncers swaying to Vetiver. Arrive early to claim balcony seats, or find standing room near the stage.

Independent
LIVE MUSIC

(Map p66; ✆415-771-1421; www.theindependentsf. com; 628 Divisadero St; tickets $12-45; ⊗box office 11am-6pm Mon-Fri, to 9:30pm show nights; ☐5, 6, 21, 71) Shows earn street cred here, featuring indie dreamers (Magnetic Fields, Rogue Wave), rock legends (Courtney Love, Marky Ramone), alterna-pop (Imagine Dragons, Vampire Weekend) and wacky events like the US Air Guitar Championships.

Yoshi's   JAZZ, LIVE MUSIC
(☑ 415-655-5600; www.yoshis.com; 1330 Fillmore St; ⊙ shows 8pm &/or 10pm Tue-Sun, dinner 5:30-9pm Tue & Wed, 5:30-10pm Thu, 5:30-10:30pm Fri & Sat, 5-9pm Sun; ▣ 22, 31) The Fillmore Jazz District was once called 'the Harlem of the West,' and Yoshi's still draws top global talent like guitarist Leon Redbone, singer Nancy Wilson and Sufi electronica artist Niyaz – and it throws Black Panther reunions and serves mean sushi besides.

Mezzanine   LIVE MUSIC
(Map p56; ☑ 415-625-8880; www.mezzaninesf.com; 444 Jessie St; admission $10-40; Ⓜ Powell, Ⓑ Powell) Beats boom off brick walls at shows by Wyclef Jean, Quest Love, Method Man, Nas and Snoop Lion (aka Dogg), plus throwback alt-classics like the Dandy Warhols and Psychedelic Furs.

Theater

★ American Conservatory Theater THEATER
(ACT; Map p56; ☑ 415-749-2228; www.act-sf.org; 415 Geary St; ⊙ box office noon-6pm Mon, to curtain Tue-Sun; ▣ 38, ▣ Powell-Mason, Powell-Hyde) Breakthrough shows destined for Broadway premiere at ACT's Geary Theater, including Tony Kushner's *Angels in America* and Robert Wilson's *Black Rider*, with a libretto by William S Burroughs and music by the Bay Area's Tom Waits.

Beach Blanket Babylon   CABARET
(BBB; Map p62; ☑ 415-421-4222; www.beachblanketbabylon.com; 678 Green St; admission $25-100; ⊙ shows 8pm Wed, Thu & Fri, 6:30pm & 9:30pm Sat, 2pm & 5pm Sun; ▣ 8X, ▣ Powell-Mason) Snow White searches for Prince Charming in San Francisco: what could possibly go wrong? SF's signature musical-comedy cabaret since 1974 stays fresh with topical comedy and

---

ⓘ HOT TICKETS

At **TIX Bay Area** (www.tixbayarea.org), half-price tickets are sold on show day for cash only. For advance tickets to concerts and Broadway shows, check **Ticketmaster** (www.ticketmaster.com) and **SHN** (www.shnsf.com).

---

wigs big as parade floats. Pop icons and heads of state are spoofed mercilessly – even when President Obama, Queen Elizabeth and the SF Giants attended.

Cobb's Comedy Club   COMEDY
(Map p64; ☑ 415-928-4320; www.cobbscomedyclub.com; 915 Columbus Ave; admission $12.50-45, plus 2-drink minimum; ⊙ showtimes vary; ▣ 8X, 30, 39, 41, 45, ▣ Powell-Mason) Bumper-to-bumper shared tables make an intimate audience for breakthrough talent and big-name acts from Dave Chappelle to Louis CK. Check the website for shows and comically twisted events – Father's Day Burlesque Brunch, anyone?

AsiaSF   DRAG CABARET
(Map p56; ☑ 415-255-2742; www.asiasf.com; 201 9th St; per person from $39; ⊙ 7:15-11pm Wed, Thu & Sun, 7:15pm-2am Fri, 5pm-2am Sat; Ⓜ Civic Center, Ⓑ Civic Center) Cocktails and Asian-inspired dishes are served with surplus sass and one little secret: your servers are drag stars. Hostesses rock the bar/runway hourly, but once drinks kick in, everyone mingles on the downstairs dance floor. Bring cash for tips.

Classical Music, Opera & Dance

★ Davies Symphony Hall   CLASSICAL MUSIC
(Map p56; ☑ rush tickets 415-503-5577, 415-864-6000; www.sfsymphony.org; 201 Van Ness Ave; Ⓜ Van Ness, Ⓑ Civic Center) SF Symphony has racked up nine Grammys, and you can see why: conductor Michael Tilson Thomas keeps the audience rapt through Beethoven, Mahler, even Metallica. The season runs September to July; call the rush-ticket hotline for $20 next-day tickets, and don't miss free pre-show talks.

★ San Francisco Opera   OPERA
(Map p56; ☑ 415-864-3330; www.sfopera.com; War Memorial Opera House, 301 Van Ness Ave; tickets $10-350; Ⓑ Civic Center, Ⓜ Van Ness) SF Opera rivals New York's Met with original operas like Stephen King's *Dolores Claiborne* and Verdi and Puccini revivals by acclaimed Tuscan director Nicola Luisotti. Book ahead, or score $10 same-day, standing-room tickets at 10am and two hours before curtain.

★ ODC Theater   DANCE
(Map p66; ☑ 415-863-9834; www.odctheater.org; 3153 17th St; ⊙ box office noon-3pm Mon-Fri) For 40 years, ODC has redefined dance with risky, raw performances September through December – plus year-round guest performers and 200 dance classes a week.

San Francisco Ballet DANCE
(Map p56; ☑ 415-861-5600, tickets 415-865-2000; www.sfballet.org; War Memorial Opera House, 301 Van Ness Ave; tickets $10-120; Ⓜ Van Ness, Ⓑ Civic Center) SF Ballet performs 100 gloriously staged shows annually at the War Memorial Opera House January to May; check website for dates and ticket deals.

Cinemas

★ **Castro Theatre** CINEMA
(Map p66; ☑ 415-621-6120; www.castrotheatre.com; 429 Castro St; adult/child $11/8.50; ☺ showtimes vary; Ⓜ Castro) The crowd sings along to pre-show Mighty Wurlitzer organ tunes, especially the theme song to the 1936 classic *San Francisco*. Don't miss silver-screen revivals, and cult classics preceded by live re-enactments – in drag. Cash only.

★ **Roxie Cinema** CINEMA
(Map p66; ☑ 415-863-1087; www.roxie.com; 3117 16th St; regular screening/matinee $10/7; ☐ 14, 22, 33, 49, Ⓑ 16th St Mission) A little neighborhood nonprofit cinema with major international clout for indie premieres, controversial films and documentaries banned elsewhere. No ads, plus personal introductions to every film.

Sundance Kabuki Cinema CINEMA
(☑ 415-346-3243; www.sundancecinemas.com; 1881 Post St; adult $9.75-15, child $9.50-12; ☐ 2, 3, 22, 38) ⫸ Robert Redford's Sundance Institute runs this innovative green multiplex with first-run flicks, festival premieres and no ads – get comfortable in reserved recycled-fiber seating and booze in 21-plus screenings.

Sports

San Francisco Giants BASEBALL
(Map p56; ☑ 415-972-2000; www.sfgiants.com; AT&T Park, 24 Willie Mays Plaza; tickets $5-135) Watch and learn how the World Series is won.

🔒 Shopping

San Francisco has big department stores and name-brand boutiques around Union Sq, including **Macy's** (Map p56; www.macys.com; 170 O'Farrell St; ☺ 10am-9pm Mon-Sat, 11am-7pm Sun; ☐ Powell-Mason, Powell-Hyde, Ⓜ Powell, Ⓑ Powell) and **Westfield San Francisco Centre** (Map p56; www.westfield.com/sanfrancisco; 865 Market St; ☺ 10am-8:30pm Mon-Sat, to 7pm Sun; ♿; ☐ Powell-Mason, Powell-Hyde, Ⓜ Powell, Ⓑ Powell) – but only-in-SF scores are found in the Haight, Castro, Mission and Hayes Valley.

SAN FRANCISCO FOR CHILDREN

Imaginations come alive in this storybook city, with wild parrots squawking around Coit Tower (p59) and sunning sea lions gleefully nudging one another off the docks at Pier 39 (p58). For thrills, try rickety, seatbelt-free cable cars. Kids will find playmates at Golden Gate Park (p75) and Crissy Field (p59). The **Children's Creativity Museum** (Map p56; ☑ 415-820-3320; www.zeum.org; 221 4th St; admission $11; ☺ 10am-4pm Wed-Sun Sep-May, Tue-Sun Jun-Aug; ♿; Ⓜ Powell, Ⓑ Powell) features technology that's too cool for school: robots, live-action video games, and 3D animation workshops.

See also: Exploratorium (p53), California Academy of Sciences (p75), Cartoon Art Museum (p63), Musée Mécanique (p53), Japan Center (p59), and 826 Valencia (p65).

★ **Under One Roof** GIFTS
(Map p56; ☑ 415-503-2300; www.underoneroof.org; Crocker Galleria, 50 Post St; ☺ 10am-6pm Mon-Fri) AIDS service organizations receive 100% of the proceeds from goods donated by local designers and retailers, so show volunteer salespeople some love.

★ **Gravel & Gold** HOUSEWARES, GIFTS
(Map p66; ☑ 415-552-0112; www.gravelandgold.com; 3266 21st St; ☺ noon-7pm Mon-Sat, to 5pm Sun; Ⓜ 24th St Mission, Ⓑ 24th St Mission) Get back to the land and in touch with California roots with Gravel & Gold's trippy silkscreened totes, hippie homesteader smock-dresses, 1960s Osborne/Woods ecology posters, and rare books on '70s beach-shack architecture.

★ **Park Life** ART, GIFTS
(Map p72; ☑ 415-386-7275; www.parklifestore.com; 220 Clement St; ☺ noon-8pm Mon-Thu, from 11am Fri & Sat, 11am-7pm Sun; ☐ 1, 2, 33, 38, 44) Design store, indie publisher and art gallery in one. Park Life presents are too good to wait for birthdays, including Golden State pendants, Sean O'Dell utopia catalogs, and Ian Johnson's portrait of John Coltrane radiating rainbow vibes.

★ **Heath Ceramics** HOUSEWARES
(Map p56; ☑ 415-399-9284; www.heathceramics.com; 1 Ferry Bldg; ☺ 10am-7pm Mon-Fri, 8am-6pm Sat, 11am-5pm Sun; Ⓜ Embarcadero,

B Embarcadero) No SF tablescape is complete without handmade modern Heath stoneware, thrown by potters in Heath's Sausalito studio since 1948. Pieces are priced for fine dining except studio seconds, sold on weekends.

★ **Betabrand** CLOTHING
(Map p66; ☑ 800-694-9491; www.betabrand.com; 780 Valencia St; ⊙ 11am-7pm Mon-Fri, to 8pm Sat, noon-6pm Sun; ☐ 14, 22, 33, 49, B 16th St Mission) Experimental designs are put to online votes and winners produced in limited editions. Recent designs include lunch-meat-patterned socks, reversible smoking jackets, and bike-to-work pants with reflective-strip cuffs.

ⓘ Information

DANGERS & ANNOYANCES
Keep your city smarts and wits sharp, especially at night in SoMa, the Mission and the Haight. Unless you know where you're going, avoid the seedy, depressing Tenderloin (bordered east–west by Powell and Polk Sts and north–south by O'Farrell and Market Sts), Skid Row (6th St between Market and Folsom Sts) and Bayview–Hunters Point. Panhandlers and homeless people are part of San Francisco's community. People will probably ask you for spare change, but donations to local nonprofits stretch further. Don't engage with panhandlers at night or around ATMs. A simple 'I'm sorry,' is a polite response.

EMERGENCY & MEDICAL SERVICES
Haight Ashbury Free Clinic (☑ 415-762-3700; www.healthright360.org; 558 Clayton St; ⊙ by appointment; ☐ 6, 33, 37, 43, 71, Ⓜ N) Provides substance abuse and mental health services by appointment.

San Francisco General Hospital (☑ emergency 415-206-8111, main hospital 415-206-8000; www.sfdph.org; 1001 Potrero Ave; ⊙ 24hr; ☐ 9, 10, 33, 48) Provides care to uninsured patients; no documentation required.

Walgreens (☑ 415-861-3136; www.walgreens. com; 498 Castro St, cnr 18th St; ⊙ 24hr; ☐ 24, 33, 35, Ⓜ F, K, L, M) Pharmacy and over-the-counter meds; locations citywide (see website).

INTERNET ACCESS
SF has free wi-fi hot spots citywide – locate one nearby with www.openwifispots.com.

Apple Store (☑ 415-392-0202; www.apple. com/retail/sanfrancisco; 1 Stockton St; ⊙ 9am-9pm Mon-Sat, 10am-8pm Sun; 🛜; Ⓜ Powell St) Free wi-fi and internet terminal usage.

San Francisco Main Library (☑ 415-871-4294; www.sfpl.org; 100 Larkin St; ⊙ 10am-6pm Mon & Sat, 9am-8pm Tue-Thu, noon-6pm Fri, noon-5pm Sun; 🛜; Ⓜ Civic Center) Free 15-minute internet terminal usage; spotty wi-fi access.

MONEY
Bank of America (www.bankamerica.com; 1 Market Plaza; ⊙ 9am-5pm Mon-Thu, to 6pm Fri)

POST
Rincon Center Post Office (Map p56; www. usps.gov; 180 Steuart St; ⊙ 7:30am-5pm Mon-Fri, 9am-2pm Sat; Ⓜ Embarcadero, B Embarcadero)

US Post Office (Map p56; www.usps.gov; Macy's, 170 O'Farrell St; ⊙ 10am-9pm Mon-Sat; ☐ Powell-Mason & Powell-Hyde, Ⓜ Powell St, B Powell St) At Macy's department store.

TOURIST INFORMATION
California Welcome Center (Map p64; ☑ 415-981-1280; www.visitcwc.com; Pier 39, Bldg P, Suite 241b; ⊙ 9am-7pm)

San Francisco Visitor Information Center (Map p56; ☑ 415-391-2000, events hotline 415-391-2001; www.onlyinsanfrancisco.com; lower level, Hallidie Plaza, Market & Powell Sts; ⊙ 9am-5pm Mon-Fri, to 3pm Sat & Sun; ☐ Powell-Mason, Powell-Hyde, Ⓜ Powell St, B Powell St) Provides practical information and runs a 24-hour events hotline.

USEFUL WEBSITES
Craig's List (http://sfbay.craigslist.org) Events, activities, partners, freebies and dates.

Eater (http://sf.eater.com) Food and bars.

Flavorpill (www.flavorpill.com) Live music, lectures, art openings and movie premieres.

The Bold Italic (www.thebolditalic.com) SF trends, openings and opinions.

Urban Daddy (www.urbandaddy.com) Bars, shops, restaurants and events.

ⓘ Getting There & Away

AIR
San Francisco is served by three major airports:
➧ **San Francisco International Airport** Most international flights arrive/depart SFO, 14 miles south of downtown SF off Hwy 101.

➧ **Oakland International Airport** Travelers from other US cities may find flights that arrive across the Bay on discount airlines such as JetBlue and Southwest.

➧ **Norman Y Mineta San Jose International Airport** Just 50 miles south of San Francisco along Hwy 101, and accessible via Caltrain.

BUS
Until the new terminal is completed in 2017, SF's intercity hub remains the **Temporary Transbay Terminal** (Map p56; Howard & Main Sts), where you can catch buses on **AC Transit** (www. actransit.org) to the East Bay, **Golden Gate Transit** (http://goldengatetransit.org) north to Marin and Sonoma, and **SamTrans** (www.

samtrans.com) south to Palo Alto and the Pacific coast. **Greyhound** (☎800-231-2222; www.greyhound.com) buses leave daily for Los Angeles ($59, eight to 12 hours), Truckee near Lake Tahoe ($31, 5½ hours), and other destinations.

CAR & MOTORCYCLE

Major car-rental operators have offices at airports and downtown.

FERRY

Blue & Gold Ferries (Map p56; ☎415-705-8200; www.blueandgoldfleet.com; one-way $6.25) Runs the Alameda–Oakland ferry from Pier 41 and the Ferry Building.

Golden Gate Ferry (☎415-455-2000; www.goldengateferry.org; adult/child $9.75/4.75; ⊙6am-9:30pm Mon-Fri, 10am-6pm Sat & Sun) Ferry service from the Ferry Building to Sausalito and Larkspur.

Vallejo Ferry (Map p56; ☎877-643-3779; www.baylinkferry.com; adult/child $13/6.50) Get to Napa car-free via Vallejo Ferry with departures from Ferry Building docks 6:30am to 7pm weekdays and 11am to 7:30pm weekends; bikes permitted. From Vallejo Ferry Terminal, take Napa Valley Vine bus 10.

TRAIN

Amtrak (☎800-872-7245; www.amtrakcalifornia.com) Serves San Francisco via Oakland stations, with free shuttle buses to San Francisco. Scenic routes with sleeping cars include the 35-hour Los Angeles–Seattle run via Oakland on the *Coast Starlight*, and the 51-hour Chicago–Oakland journey on the *California Zephyr*.

CalTrain (www.caltrain.com; cnr 4th & King Sts) Links San Francisco to the South Bay, ending in San Jose.

ⓘ Getting Around

For Bay Area transit options, departures and arrivals, check ☑511 or www.511.org.

TO/FROM THE AIRPORT

➡ **BART** Direct 30-minute ride to/from downtown.

➡ **SuperShuttle** (☎800-258-3826; www.supershuttle.com) Door-to-door vans depart baggage-claim areas, taking 45 minutes to most SF locations; $17.

➡ **Taxis** To/from downtown costs $35 to $50.

BART

Bay Area Rapid Transit (Bay Area Rapid Transit; www.bart.gov; one way $8.25) links SFO, the Mission, downtown and the East Bay. Within SF, one-way fares start at $1.75.

BICYCLE

Bicycling is safest in Golden Gate Park and along the waterfront; rentals are readily available.

CAR

Avoid driving in San Francisco: street parking is rare and meter readers ruthless. Convenient downtown parking lots are at 5th and Mission Sts, Union Sq, and Sutter and Stockton Sts. Daily rates run $25 to $50.

If your car is towed for parking violations, retrieve it from **Autoreturn** (☎415-865-8200; www.autoreturn.com; 450 7th St, SoMa; ⊙24hr; Ⓜ27, 42). Fines run $73, plus towing and storage ($453.75 for the first four hours).

Members of **American Automobile Association** (AAA; ☎800-222-4357, 415-773-1900; www.aaa.com; 160 Sutter St; ⊙8:30am-5:30pm Mon-Fri) can call anytime for emergency service.

MUNI

MUNI (Municipal Transit Agency; www.sfmuni.com) operates bus, streetcar and cable-car lines. The standard fare for buses or streetcars is $2, and tickets are good for transfers for 90 minutes; hang onto your ticket to avoid a $100 fine. The cable-car fare is $6 per ride.

MUNI Passport (1-/3-/7-days $14/22/28) allows unlimited travel on all MUNI transport, including cable cars; it's sold at San Francisco Visitor Information Center and many hotels.

Key routes include:

➡ **California cable car** California St between Market St and Van Ness Ave

➡ **F** Fisherman's Wharf to Castro

➡ **J** Downtown to Mission

➡ **K, L, M** Downtown to Castro

➡ **N** Caltrain to Haight and Ocean Beach

➡ **Powell-Mason** and **Powell-Hyde cable cars** Powell and Market Sts to Fisherman's Wharf

➡ **T** Embarcadero to Caltrain

RIDESHARE & TAXI

SF-based rideshare companies including **Uber** (www.uber.com) and **Lyft** (www.lyft.com) offer rides from mostly non-professional drivers at set rates, starting around $15 for in-city rides. Expect fast dispatch and fares charged to your account; signup and/or app download required.

San Francisco taxi fares run $2.75 per mile, plus 10% tip ($1 minimum); meters start at $3.50. SF taxis have their own app to hail and pay cabs, downloadable at www.flywheel.com. Major cab companies include:

DeSoto Cab (☎415-970-1300; www.desotogo.com)

Green Cab (☎415-626-4733) Fuel-efficient hybrids; worker-owned collective.

Luxor (☎415-282-4141; www.luxorcab.com)

Yellow Cab (☎415-333-3333; www.yellow-cabsf.com)

Marin County & the Bay Area

Why Go?

The region surrounding San Francisco encompasses a bonanza of natural vistas and wildlife. Cross the Golden Gate Bridge to Marin and visit wizened ancient redwoods body-blocking the sun and herds of elegant tule elk prancing along the bluffs of Tomales Bay. Gray whales show some fluke off the cape of wind-scoured Point Reyes, and hawks surf the skies in the pristine hills of the Marin Headlands.

On the cutting edge of intellectual thought, Stanford University and the University of California at Berkeley draw academics and students from around the world. The city of Berkeley sparked the locavore food movement and continues to be on the forefront of environmental and left-leaning political causes. South of San Francisco, Hwy 1 traces miles of undeveloped coastline and sandy pocket beaches.

Best Places to Eat

➜ Chez Panisse (p123)
➜ Sushi Ran (p97)
➜ Lake Chalet (p113)
➜ Duarte's Tavern (p137)
➜ Ippuku (p123)

Best Places to Stay

➜ HI Pigeon Point Lighthouse Hostel (p137)
➜ Cavallo Point (p95)
➜ Mountain Home Inn (p101)
➜ Hotel Shattuck Plaza (p123)

When to Go
Berkeley

Dec–Mar Elephant seal pupping season and the peak of gray whale migrations.

Mar–Apr Wildflowers hit their peak on trails throughout the region.

Jun–Sep Farmers markets overflow with sweet seasonal fruit.

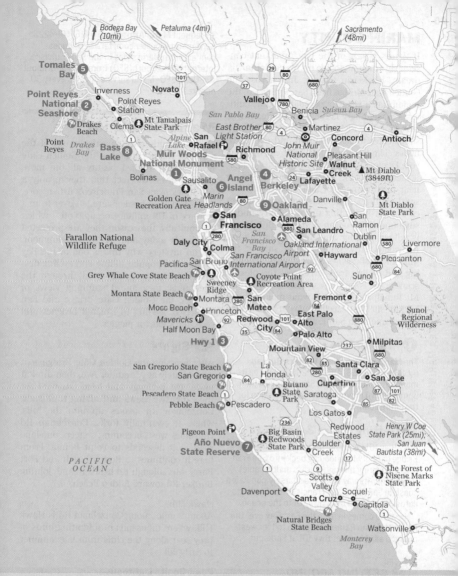

Marin County & the Bay Area Highlights

① Gazing up at the majestic redwood canopy at **Muir Woods National Monument** (p103).

② Cavorting with elk and gray whales at the **Point Reyes National Seashore** (p107).

③ Touring the beach-cove coastline along **Hwy 1** from Pacifica to Santa Cruz.

④ Feasting your way through the delectable **Gourmet Ghetto** (p120) in Berkeley.

⑤ Kayaking **Tomales Bay** (p107) amid harbor seals and splendid shorelines.

⑥ Hiking or cycling the perimeter of panoramic **Angel Island** (p98).

⑦ Spying on the elephant seals at **Año Nuevo State Reserve** (p137).

⑧ Cooling off with a cannonball splash at blissful **Bass Lake** (p105).

⑨ Heading to Oakland's **Chabot Space & Science Center** (p112) to marvel at the stars.

MARIN COUNTY

If there's a part of the Bay Area that consciously attempts to live up to the California dream, it's Marin County. Just across the Golden Gate Bridge from San Francisco, the region has a wealthy population that cultivates a seemingly laid-back lifestyle. Towns may look like idyllic rural hamlets, but the shops cater to cosmopolitan and expensive tastes. The 'common' folk here eat organic, vote Democrat and drive hybrids.

Geographically, Marin County is a near mirror image of San Francisco. It's a south-pointing peninsula that nearly touches the north-pointing tip of the city, and is surrounded by ocean and bay. But Marin is wilder, greener and more mountainous. Redwoods grow on the coast side of the hills, the surf crashes against cliffs, and hiking and cycling trails crisscross the blessed scenery of Point Reyes, Muir Woods and Mt Tamalpais. Nature is what makes Marin County such an excellent day trip or weekend escape from San Francisco.

❶ Information

The **Marin Convention & Visitors Bureau** (☑ 866-925-2060, 415-925-2060; www.visit-marin.org; 1 Mitchell Blvd, San Rafael; ⊙ 9am-5pm Mon-Fri) provides tourist information for the entire county.

❶ Getting There & Around

Busy Hwy 101 heads north from the Golden Gate Bridge ($7 toll when heading back into San Francisco), spearing through Marin's middle; quiet Hwy 1 winds its way along the sparsely populated coast. In San Rafael, Sir Francis Drake Blvd cuts across west Marin from Hwy 101 to the ocean.

Hwy 580 comes in from the East Bay over the Richmond–San Rafael bridge ($5 toll for westbound traffic) to meet Hwy 101 at Larkspur.

> ### ❶ GETTING AROUND
> ....
> Visitors taking multiple forms of public transportation throughout the Bay Area should note that the regional **Clipper card** (www.clippercard.com) can be used on the Caltrain, BART, SamTrans, VTA, Golden Gate Transit and the Golden Gate Ferry systems. It can be a handy way to avoid buying multiple tickets, and offers some small discounts, plus almost 50% off on the Golden Gate Ferry system.

Frequent **Marin Airporter** (☑ 415-461-4222; www.marinairporter.com; fare $20) buses connect from Marin stops to the San Francisco International Airport (SFO) from 4am until about 10:30pm; SFO–Marin service departs every 30 minutes.

Marin Headlands

The headlands rise majestically out of the water at the north end of the Golden Gate Bridge, their rugged beauty all the more striking given the fact that they're only a few miles from San Francisco's urban core. A few forts and bunkers are left over from a century of US military occupation – which is, ironically, the reason they are protected parklands today and free of development. It's no mystery why this is one of the Bay Area's most popular hiking and cycling destinations. As the trails wind through the headlands, they afford stunning views of the sea, the Golden Gate Bridge and San Francisco, leading to isolated beaches and secluded spots for picnics.

◉ Sights

After crossing the Golden Gate Bridge, exit immediately at Alexander Ave, then dip left under the highway and head out west for the expansive views and hiking trailheads. Conzelman Rd snakes up into the hills, where it eventually forks. Conzelman Rd continues west, becoming a steep, one-lane road as it descends to Point Bonita. From here it continues to Rodeo Beach and Fort Barry. McCullough Rd heads inland, joining Bunker Rd toward Rodeo Beach.

Hawk Hill   HILL
About 2 miles along Conzelman Rd is Hawk Hill, where thousands of migrating birds of prey soar along the cliffs from late summer to early fall.

Point Bonita Lighthouse   LIGHTHOUSE
(www.nps.gov/goga/pobo.htm; off Field Rd; ⊙ 12:30-3:30pm Sat-Mon) **FREE** At the end of Conzelman Rd, this lighthouse is a breathtaking half-mile walk from a small parking area. From the tip of Point Bonita, you can see the distant Golden Gate Bridge and beyond it the San Francisco skyline. It's an uncommon vantage point of the bay-centric city, and harbor seals haul out nearby in season. To reserve a spot on one of the free monthly full-moon tours of the promontory, call ☑ 415-331-1540.

WHY IS IT SO FOGGY?

When the summer sun's rays warm the air over the chilly Pacific, fog forms and hovers offshore; to grasp how it moves inland requires an understanding of California's geography. The vast agricultural region in the state's interior, the Central Valley, is ringed by mountains like a giant bathtub. The only substantial sea-level break in these mountains occurs at the Golden Gate, to the west, which happens to be the direction from which prevailing winds blow. As the inland valley heats up and the warm air rises, it creates a deficit of air at surface level, generating wind that gets sucked through the only opening it can find: the Golden Gate. It happens fast and it's unpredictable. Gusty wind is the only indication that the fog is about to roll in. But even this is inconsistent: there can be fog at the beaches south of the Golden Gate and sun a mile to the north. Hills block fog – especially at times of high atmospheric pressure, as often happens in summer. Because of this, weather forecasters speak of the Bay Area's 'microclimates.' In July it's not uncommon for inland areas to reach 100°F (38°C), while the mercury at the coast barely reaches 70°F (21°C).

Nike Missile Site SF-88 HISTORIC SITE
(☑ 415-331-1453; www.nps.gov/goga/nike-missile-site.htm; off Field Rd; ⊙12:30pm-3:30pm Thu-Sat) FREE File past guard shacks with uniformed mannequins to witness the area's not-too-distant military history at this fascinating Cold War museum staffed by veterans. Watch them place a now-warhead-free missile into position, then ride a missile elevator to the cavernous underground silo to see the multikeyed launch controls that were thankfully never set in motion.

Marine Mammal Center ANIMAL RESCUE CENTER
(☑ 415-289-7325; www.marinemammalcenter.org; ⊙10am-5pm; ♿) FREE Set on the hill above Rodeo Lagoon, the Marine Mammal Center rehabilitates injured, sick and orphaned sea mammals before returning them to the wild, and has educational exhibits about these animals and the dangers they face. During the spring pupping season the center can have up to several dozen orphaned seal pups on site and you can often see them before they're set free.

Headlands Center for the Arts GALLERY
(☑ 415-331-2787; www.headlands.org; 944 Simmonds Rd; ⊙noon-5pm Sun-Thu) FREE In Fort Barry, refurbished barracks converted into artist work spaces host open studios with its artists-in-residence, as well as talks, performances and other events.

🏃 Activities

Hiking

At the end of Bunker Rd sits Rodeo Beach, protected from wind by high cliffs. From here the **Coastal Trail** meanders 3.5 miles inland, past abandoned military bunkers, to the Tennessee Valley Trail. It then continues 6 miles along the blustery headlands all the way to Muir Beach.

All along the coastline you'll find cool old battery sites – abandoned concrete bunkers dug into the ground with fabulous views. Evocative **Battery Townsley**, a half-mile walk or bike ride up from the Fort Cronkite parking lot, opens for free subterranean tours from noon to 4pm on the first Sunday of the month.

Tennessee Valley Trail HIKING
This trail offers beautiful views of the rugged coastline and is one of the most popular hikes in Marin (expect crowds on weekends), especially for families. It has easy, level access to the cove beach and ocean, and is a short 3.8-mile round trip. From Hwy 101, take the Mill Valley–Stinson Beach–Hwy 1 exit and turn left onto Tennessee Valley Rd from the Shoreline Hwy; follow it to the parking lot and trailhead.

ℹ️ GOLDEN GATE BRIDGE TOLL

The bridge toll ($7) crossing from Marin to San Francisco is now all electronic; drivers can no longer stop to pay. Rental-car drivers may use their car company's toll program or pay in advance online, and motorists in private vehicles are billed by mail if they haven't prepaid online. See www.goldengate.org/tolls/tolltipsforvisitors.php for payment information.

Marin County

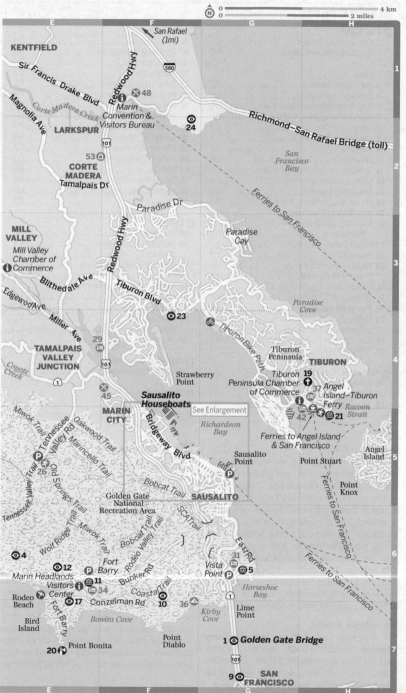

0 4 km
0 2 miles

San Rafael
(1mi)

KENTFIELD

Sir Francis Drake Blvd

Magnolia Ave

Redwood Hwy

Corte Madera Creek

Marin
Convention &
Visitors Bureau

LARKSPUR

Richmond–San Rafael Bridge (toll)

San
Francisco
Bay

CORTE
MADERA
Tamalpais Dr

Paradise Dr

MILL
VALLEY

Mill Valley
Chamber of
Commerce

Blithedale Ave

Edgewood Ave

Miller Ave

Redwood Hwy

Tiburon Blvd

Paradise
Cay

Paradise
Cove

Ferries to San Francisco

TAMALPAIS
VALLEY
JUNCTION

Coyote
Creek

Tiburon Bike Path

Tiburon
Peninsula

TIBURON

Strawberry
Point

Tiburon
Peninsula Chamber
of Commerce

Tiburon 19
Angel
Island–Tiburon
Ferry

Racoon
Strait

Miwok Trail

Tennessee Valley Trail

Tennessee Valley Rd

Oakwood Trail

Marincello Trail

Old Springs Trail

Sausalito
Houseboats

MARIN
CITY

Bridgeway Blvd

See Enlargement

Richardson
Bay

Ferries to Angel Island
& San Francisco

Point Stuart

Angel
Island

Sausalito
Point

Sausalito
Point

Point
Knox

Bobcat Trail

Golden Gate
National
Recreation Area

SAUSALITO

SCA Trail

Ferries to San Francisco

Wolf Ridge Trail

Miwok Trail

Bobcat Trail

Rodeo Valley Trail

Fort
Barry

Bunker Rd

East Rd

Vista
Point

Marin Headlands
Visitors Center

Fort Barry

Conzelman Rd

Coastal Trail

Rodeo
Beach

Bird
Island

Bonita Cove

Point
Diablo

Point Bonita

Horseshoe
Bay

Kirby
Cove

Lime
Point

Golden Gate Bridge

SAN
FRANCISCO

Marin County

Mountain Biking

The Marin Headlands have some excellent mountain-biking routes, and it's an exhilarating ride across the Golden Gate Bridge.

For a good 12-mile dirt loop, choose the **Coastal Trail** west from the fork of Conzelman and McCullough Rds, winding down to Bunker Rd where it meets **Bobcat Trail**, which joins **Marincello Trail** and descends into the Tennessee Valley parking area. The **Old Springs Trail** and the **Miwok Trail** take you back to Bunker Rd a bit more gently than the Bobcat Trail, though any attempt to avoid at least a couple of hefty climbs is futile.

Horseback Riding

For a ramble on all fours, **Miwok Livery Stables** (☎415-383-8048; www.miwokstables. com; 701 Tennessee Valley Rd; trail ride $75) offers hillside trail rides with stunning views of Mt Tam and the ocean. Reservations required.

🛏 Sleeping

There are four small campgrounds in the headlands, and two involve hiking (or cycling) in at least 1 mile from the nearest parking lot. **Hawk**, **Bicentennial** and **Haypress** campgrounds are inland, with free camping, but sites must be reserved through the Marin Headlands Visitors Center. None have water available.

Kirby Cove Campground   CAMPGROUND **$**
(☎877-444-6777; www.recreation.gov; tent sites $25; ⊙Apr-Oct) In a spectacular shady nook near the entrance to the bay, there's a small beach with the Golden Gate Bridge arching over the rocks nearby. At night you can watch the phantom shadows of cargo ships passing by (and sometimes be lulled to sleep by the dirge of a fog horn). Reserve far ahead.

HI Marin Headlands Hostel HOSTEL **$**
(☑415-331-2777; www.norcalhostels.org/marin;
Fort Barry, Bldg 941; dm $26-30, r $72-92, all with
shared bath; @) ✈ Wake up to grazing deer
and dew on the ground at this spartan 1907
military compound snuggled in the woods. It
has comfortable beds and two well-stocked
kitchens, and guests can gather round a fireplace in the common room, shoot pool or
play ping-pong. Hiking trails beckon outside.

Cavallo Point HOTEL **$$$**
(☑888-651-2003, 415-339-4700; www.caval-
lopoint.com; 601 Murray Circle; r from $359;
❄@☎❄❄) ✈ Spread out over 45 acres of
the Bay Area's most scenic parkland, Cavallo
Point is a buzz-worthy lodge that flaunts a
green focus, a full-service spa and easy ac-
cess to outdoor activities. Choose from rich-
ly renovated rooms in the landmark Fort
Baker officers' quarters or more contempo-
rary solar-powered accommodations with
exquisite bay views (including a turret of the
Golden Gate Bridge).

ℹ Information

Information is available from the **Golden Gate
National Recreation Area** (GGNRA; ☑415-
561-4700; www.nps.gov/goga) and the **Marin
Headlands Visitors Center** (☑415-331-1540;
www.nps.gov/goga/marin-headlands.htm; Fort
Barry; ◷9:30am-4:30pm), in an old chapel off
Bunker Rd near Fort Barry.

ℹ Getting There & Away

By car, take the Alexander Ave exit just after
the Golden Gate Bridge and dip left under the
freeway. Conzelman Rd, to the right, takes you
up along the bluffs; you can also take Bunker Rd,
which leads to the headlands through a one-way
tunnel. It's also a snap to reach these roads from
the bridge via bicycle.

On weekdays, **Golden Gate Transit** (☑415-
455-2000, 511; www.goldengatetransit.org)
buses 2, 4 and 92 service Sausalito ($4.75) and
the eastern Headlands. On Saturday, Sunday
and holidays, **MUNI** (☑511, 415-701-2311; www.
sfmta.com) bus 76X runs hourly from San Fran-
cisco's Financial District to the Marin Headlands
Visitors Center and Rodeo Beach. Both lines are
equipped with bicycle racks.

Sausalito

Perfectly arranged on a secure little harbor
on the bay, Sausalito is undeniably lovely.
Named for the tiny willows that once pop-
ulated the banks of its creeks, it's a small
settlement of pretty houses that tumble
neatly down a green hillside into a well-
heeled downtown. Much of the town affords
the visitor uninterrupted views of San Fran-
cisco and Angel Island, and due to the ridge-
line at its back, fog generally skips past it.

Sausalito began as a 19,000-acre land
grant to an army captain in 1838. When it
became the terminus of the train line down
the Pacific Coast, it entered a new stage as a
busy lumber port with a racy waterfront. Dra-
matic changes came in WWII when Sausalito
became the site of Marinship, a huge ship-
building yard. After the war a new bohemian
period began, with a resident artists' colony
living in 'arks' (houseboats moored along

HIKING & CYCLING THE GOLDEN GATE BRIDGE

Walking or cycling across the Golden Gate Bridge to Sausalito is a fun way to avoid traf-
fic, get some great ocean views and bask in that refreshing Marin County air. It's a fairly
easy journey, mostly flat or downhill when heading north from San Francisco (cycling
back to the city involves one big climb out of Sausalito). You can also simply hop on a
ferry back to SF.

The trip is about 4 miles from the south end of the bridge and takes less than an
hour. Pedestrians have access to the bridge's east walkway between 5am and 9pm daily
(until 6pm in winter). Cyclists generally use the west side, except on weekdays between
5am and 3:30pm, when they must share the east side with pedestrians (who have the
right-of-way). After 9pm (6pm in winter), cyclists can still cross the bridge on the east
side through a security gate. Check the bridge **website** (www.goldengatebridge.org/bikes-
bridge/bikes.php) for changes.

For more ambitious cyclists, the Cal Park Hill Tunnel is a safe subterranean passage
from Larkspur (another ferry terminus) to San Rafael.

More information and resources are available at the websites of the **San Francisco
Bicycle Coalition** (www.sfbike.org) and the **Marin County Bicycle Coalition** (www.
marinbike.org).

the bay). Hundreds of these floating abodes remain.

Sausalito today is a major tourist haven, jam-packed with souvenir shops and costly boutiques. It's the first town you encounter after crossing the Golden Gate Bridge, so daytime crowds turn up in droves and make parking difficult. Ferrying from San Francisco makes a more relaxing excursion.

◉ Sights

Sausalito is actually on Richardson Bay, a smaller bay within San Francisco Bay. The commercial district is mainly one street, Bridgeway Blvd, on the waterfront.

★ Sausalito Houseboats   ARCHITECTURE
Bohemia still thrives along the shoreline of Richardson Bay, where free spirits inhabit hundreds of quirky homes that bobble in the waves amongst the seabirds and seals. Structures range from psychedelic mural-splashed castles to dilapidated salt-sprayed shacks and immaculate three-story floating mansions. It's a tight-knit community, where residents tend sprawling dockside gardens and stop to chat on the creaky wooden boardwalks as they wheel their groceries home.

You can poke around the houseboat docks located off Bridgeway between Gate 5 and Gate 6½ Rds.

Bay Model Visitors Center   MUSEUM
(☑ 415-332-3871; www.spn.usace.army.mil/Missions/Recreation/BayModelVisitorCenter.aspx; 2100 Bridgeway Blvd; ☺ 9am-4pm Tue-Sat, plus 10am-5pm Sat & Sun in summer; ⊞) One of the coolest things in town, fascinating to both kids and adults, is the Army Corps of Engineers' solar-powered visitor center. Housed in one of the old (and cold!) Marinship warehouses, it's a 1.5-acre hydraulic model of San Francisco Bay and the delta region. Self-guided tours take you over and around it as the water flows.

Bay Area Discovery Museum   MUSEUM
(☑ 415-339-3900; www.baykidsmuseum.org; 557 McReynolds Rd; admission $11, free 1st Wed each month; ☺ 9am-5pm Tue-Sun; ⊞) Just under the north tower of the Golden Gate Bridge, at East Fort Baker, this excellent hands-on activity museum is specifically designed for children. Permanent (multilingual) exhibits include a wave workshop, a small underwater tunnel and a large outdoor play area

with a shipwreck to romp around. A small cafe has healthy nibbles.

Plaza Viña Del Mar   PARK
Near the ferry terminal, the plaza has a fountain flanked by 14ft-tall elephant statues from the 1915 Panama–Pacific Exposition in San Francisco.

🏃 Activities

Sausalito is great for bicycling, whether for a leisurely ride around town, a trip across the Golden Gate Bridge or a longer-haul journey. From the ferry terminal, an easy option is to head south on Bridgeway Blvd, veering left onto East Rd toward the Bay Area Discovery Museum. Another nice route heads north along Bridgeway Blvd, then crosses under Hwy 101 to Mill Valley. At Blithedale Ave, you can veer east to Tiburon; a bike path parallels parts of Tiburon Blvd.

Sea Trek Kayak & SUP   KAYAKING
(☑ 415-332-8494; www.seatrek.com; Schoonmaker Point Marina; single/double kayaks per hr $20/35) On a nice day, Richardson Bay is irresistible. Kayaks and stand-up paddleboards can be rented here, near the Bay Model Visitor Center. No experience is necessary, and lessons and group outings are also available.

Also on offer are guided kayaking excursions around Angel Island from $75 per person, including overnight camping ($125). Tours include equipment and instructions. May through October is the best time to paddle.

Sausalito Bike Rentals   BICYCLE RENTAL
(☑ 415-331-2453; www.sausalitobikerentals.com; 34a Princess St; bicycle per hour $10; ☺ 10am-6pm) Rent road, mountain, tandems ($25 per hour) and electric ($20 per hour) bicycles to explore the area.

🛏 Sleeping

All of the lodgings below charge an additional $15 to $20 per night for parking.

Hotel Sausalito   HISTORIC HOTEL $$
(☑ 415-332-0700; www.hotelsausalito.com; 16 El Portal; r $180-225, ste $305-320; ⊞⊞) Steps away from the ferry in the middle of downtown, this grand 1915 hotel has loads of period charm, paired with modern touches like MP3-player docking stations. Each guest room is decorated in Mediterranean hues, with sumptuous bathrooms and park or partial bay views.

Inn Above Tide   INN $$$

(📞415-332-9535,   800-893-8433; www.in-
nabovetide.com; 30 El Portal; r incl breakfast $345-
625, ste $735-1100; 🌐 @ 🛜) Next to the ferry
terminal, ensconce yourself in one of the 31
modern and spacious rooms – most with
private decks and wood-burning fireplaces –
that practically levitate over the water. With
envy-inducing bay views from your window,
scan the horizon with the in-room binoculars. Free loaner bicycles available.

Gables Inn   INN $$$

(📞415-289-1100; www.gablesinnsausalito.com; 62
Princess St; r incl breakfast $199-545; @ 🛜) Tran-
quil and inviting, this inn has nine guest
rooms in a historic 1869 home, and six in a
newer building. The more expensive rooms
have spa baths, fireplaces and balconies
with spectacular views, but even the smaller, cheaper rooms are stylish and tranquil.
Evening wine and cheese is included.

✖ Eating

Bridgeway Blvd is packed with moderately
priced cafes, a few budget ethnic food options and some more expensive bay-view
restaurants.

Avatar's   INDIAN $$

(www.enjoyavatars.com; 2656 Bridgeway Blvd;
mains $10-17; ⏲11am-3pm & 5-9:30pm Mon-Sat;
�🍴) Boasting a cuisine of 'ethnic confusion,'
the Indian fusion dishes here incorporate
Mexican, Italian and Caribbean ingredients
and will bowl you over with their flavor and
creativity. Think Punjabi enchilada with cur-
ried sweet potato or spinach and mushroom
ravioli with mango and rose petal alfredo
sauce. All diets (vegan, gluten-free, etc) are
graciously accommodated.

Fish   SEAFOOD $$

(📞415-331-3474; www.fish311.com; 350 Harbor Dr;
mains $14-28; ⏲11:30am-8:30pm; 🍴) 🌿 Chow
down on seafood sandwiches, oysters and
Dungeness crab roll with organic local butter at redwood picnic tables facing Richardson Bay. A local leader in promoting fresh
and sustainably caught fish, this place has
wonderful wild salmon in season, and refus-
es to serve the farmed stuff. Cash only.

Sushi Ran   JAPANESE $$$

(📞415-332-3620; www.sushiran.com; 107 Caledo-
nia St; sushi $4-33; ⏲11:45am-2:30pm Mon-Fri,
5-10pm Sun-Thu, to 11pm Fri & Sat; 🚗) Many Bay
Area residents claim this place is the best sushi spot around. If you didn't reserve ahead,
the wine and sake bar next door eases the
pain of the long wait for a table.

Murray Circle   MODERN AMERICAN $$$

(📞415-339-4750; www.cavallopoint.com/dine.
html; 601 Murray Circle, Fort Baker; dinner mains
$23-34; ⏲7-11am & 11:30am-2pm Mon-Fri, to
2:30pm Sat & Sun, 5:30-10pm Sun-Thu, to 11pm
Fri & Sat) At the Cavallo Point lodge, dine on
locally sourced meats, seafood and produce,
like grass-fed organic beef burgers or Dungeness crab BLT, in a clubby dining room
topped by a pressed-tin ceiling. Reservations
recommended for dinner.

ℹ Information

The **Sausalito Visitors Center** (📞415-332-
0505; www.sausalito.org; 780 Bridgeway Blvd;
⏲11:30am-4pm Tue-Sun) has local information.
There's also an information kiosk at the ferry
terminal.

ℹ Getting There & Away

Driving to Sausalito from San Francisco, take the
Alexander Ave exit (the first exit after the Golden
Gate Bridge) and follow the signs into Sausalito.
There are five municipal parking lots in town,
and street parking is difficult to find.

Golden Gate Transit (📞415-455-2000; www.
goldengatetransit.org) bus 10 runs daily to Sausalito from downtown San Francisco ($4.75). On
weekends and holidays from late May through
early September, the **West Marin Stagecoach**
(📞415-526-3239; www.marintransit.org/stage.
html) bus 61 extends to Sausalito and Fort
Baker, with six daily departures for Mt Tamalpais
State Park, Stinson Beach and Bolinas.

The ferry is a fun and easy way to travel to Sausalito. **Golden Gate Ferry** (📞415-455-2000;
www.goldengateferry.org; one-way $10.25)
operates to and from the San Francisco Ferry
Building six to nine times daily and takes 30 minutes. The **Blue & Gold Fleet** (📞415-705-8200;
www.blueandgoldfleet.com; Pier 41, Fisherman's
Wharf; one-way $11) sails to Sausalito four to
five times daily from the Fisherman's Wharf
area in San Francisco. Both ferries operate year-
round and transport bicycles for free.

Tiburon

At the end of a small peninsula pointing out
into the center of the bay, Tiburon is blessed with gorgeous views. The name comes
from the Spanish *Punta de Tiburon* (Shark
Point). Take the ferry from San Francisco,
browse the shops on Main St, grab a bite
to eat and you've seen Tiburon. The town

WORTH A TRIP

ANGEL ISLAND

Angel Island (📞 415-435-5390; www.parks.ca.gov/?page_id=468), in San Francisco Bay, has a mild climate with fresh bay breezes, which makes it pleasant for hiking and cycling. For a unique treat, picnic in a protected cove overlooking the close but distant urban surroundings. The island's varied history – it was a hunting and fishing ground for the Miwok people, served as a military base, an immigration station, a WWII Japanese internment camp and a Nike missile site – has left it with some evocative old forts and bunkers to poke around in. There are 12 miles of roads and trails around the island, including a hike to the summit of 781ft **Mt Livermore** (no bicycles) and a 5-mile perimeter trail.

The **Immigration Station** (📞 415-435-5537; www.aiisf.org/visit; ☉ 11am-3pm Mon-Fri, 11am-4pm Sat & Sun), which operated from 1910 to 1940, was the Ellis Island of the West Coast. But this facility was primarily a screening and detention center for Chinese immigrants, who were at that time restricted from entering the US under the Chinese Exclusion Act. Many detainees were held here for long periods before ultimately being returned home, and one of the most unusual sights on the island is the sad and longing Chinese poetry etched into the barrack walls. The site is now a museum with excellent interpretive exhibits; more extensive **tours** (adult/child $7/5) include admission fees and can be reserved ahead or purchased first-come first-served on-site.

Sea Trek (www.seatrek.com) runs **kayaking** excursions around the island. You can rent **bicycles** at Ayala Cove (per hour/day $12.50/40), and there are **tram tours** ($15) around the island. Two-hour tours on Segway scooters ($68) and electric scooters ($50) are another option, and should be booked in advance. Tour schedules vary seasonally; go to www.angelisland.com for more information.

You can camp on the island, and when the last ferry sails off for the night, the place is your own – except for the very persistent raccoons. The dozen hike-, bicycle- or kayak-in **campsites** (📞 800-444-7275; www.reserveamerica.com; tent sites $30) are usually reserved months in advance. Near the ferry dock, there's a **cafe** serving sandwiches and snacks.

Getting There & Away

From San Francisco, take a **Blue & Gold Fleet ferry** (Map p86; 📞 415-773-1188; www.blueandgoldfleet.com; round-trip adult/child $17/9.50) from Pier 41. From May to September there are three ferries a day on weekends and two on weekdays; during the rest of the year the schedule is reduced.

From Tiburon, take the **Angel Island–Tiburon** (📞 415-435-2131; www.angelislandferry.com; round-trip adult/child/bike $13.50/11.50/1) ferry.

From Oakland, **San Francisco Bay Ferry** (📞 415-705-8291; www.sanfranciscobayferry.com; round-trip adult/child $14.50/8.50) has one round-trip on summer weekends.

is also a jumping-off point for nearby Angel Island.

⊙ Sights & Activities

The central part of town is comprised of Tiburon Blvd, with Juanita Lane and charming Main St arcing off. Main St, which is also known as Ark Row, is where the old houseboats have taken root on dry land and metamorphosed into classy shops and boutiques.

Railroad & Ferry Depot Museum   MUSEUM
(www.landmarkssociety.com; 1920 Paradise Dr; suggested donation $5; ☉ 1-4pm Wed-Sun Apr-Oct) Formerly the terminus for a 3000-person ferry to San Francisco and a railroad that once reached north to Ukiah, this late-19th-

century building showcases a scale model of Tiburon's commercial hub, circa 1909. The restored stationmaster's quarters can be visited upstairs.

Old St Hilary's Church   CHURCH
(201 Esperanza; ☉ 1-4pm Sun Apr-Oct) There are great views from the lovely hillside surrounding this fine 19th-century example of Carpenter Gothic.

Richardson Bay Audubon Center   NATURE RESERVE
(📞 415-388-2524; http://richardsonbay.audubon.org/; 376 Greenwood Beach Rd; ☉ 9am-5pm Mon-Sat; 🅿) Off Tiburon Blvd, this center is home to a huge variety of water birds.

Angel Island–Tiburon Ferry BOAT TOUR
(☑415-435-2131; www.angelislandferry.com; round-trip adult/child/bike $13.50/11.50/1, sunset cruise adult/child 6-12/child 3-5 $20/10/5) Also runs sunset cruises on Friday and Saturday evenings from May through October. Reservations recommended.

🛏 Sleeping

Lodge at Tiburon HOTEL $$
(☑415-435-3133; www.lodgeattiburon.com; 1651 Tiburon Blvd; r from $179; ❄@🛜🐕) 🐾 Now a stylish and comfortable contemporary hotel with a grill restaurant, the concrete hallways and staircases testify to the more basic motel it once was. The best value in town, it's a short stroll to anywhere – including the ferry – and there's a pool, DVD library, rental bikes, free parking and a rooftop deck with fireplace and heady Mt Tamalpais views.

Water's Edge Hotel HOTEL $$$
(☑415-789-5999; www.watersedgehotel.com; 25 Main St; r incl breakfast $249-539; ❄@🛜) 🐾 This hotel, with its deck extending over the bay, is exemplary for its tasteful modernity. Rooms have an elegant minimalism that combines comfort and style, and all afford an immediate view of the bay. The rooms with rustic, high wood ceilings are quite romantic. Perks include complimentary bicycles and evening wine and cheese.

🍴 Eating

Sam's Anchor Cafe SEAFOOD $$
(☑415-435-4527; www.samscafe.com; 27 Main St; mains $14-32; ☺11am-9:30pm Mon-Fri, 9:30am-10pm Sat & Sun; 🍴) Sam's has been slinging seafood and burgers since 1920, and though the entrance looks like a shambling little shack, the area out back has unbeatable views. On a warm afternoon, you can't beat a cocktail or a tasty plate of sautéed prawns on the deck.

Caprice AMERICAN $$$
(☑415-435-3400; www.thecaprice.com; 2000 Paradise Dr; mains $17-58; ☺5-10pm Tue-Sun, plus 11am-3pm Sun) Splurge-worthy and romantic, book a table here at sunset for riveting views of Angel Island, the Golden Gate Bridge and San Francisco. Caprice mostly features seafood, though other standouts include the artichoke bisque and the filet mignon. Take a peek at the fireplace downstairs – it's constructed into the coast bedrock. A three-course midweek dinner ($30) is easier on the wallet.

❶ Information

The **Tiburon Peninsula Chamber of Commerce** (☑415-435-5633; www.tiburonchamber.org; 96b Main St) can provide information about the area.

❶ Getting There & Away

Golden Gate Transit (☑415-455-2000; www.goldengatetransit.org) commute bus 8 runs directly between San Francisco and Tiburon ($4.75) during the week.

On Hwy 101, look for the off-ramp for Tiburon Blvd, E Blithedale Ave and Hwy 131; driving east, it leads into town and intersects with Juanita Lane and Main St.

Blue & Gold Fleet (☑415-705-8200; one-way $11) sails daily from Pier 41 or the Ferry Building (weekdays commute times only) in San Francisco to Tiburon. You can transport bicycles for free. From Tiburon, ferries also connect regularly to Angel Island.

Sir Francis Drake Blvd & Around

The towns along and nearby the Sir Francis Drake Blvd corridor – including Larkspur, Corte Madera, Ross, San Anselmo and Fairfax – evoke charmed small-town life, even though things get busy around Hwy 101.

Starting from the eastern section in **Larkspur**, window-shop along Magnolia Ave or explore the redwoods in nearby **Baltimore Canyon**. On the east side of the freeway is the hulking mass of **San Quentin State Penitentiary**, California's oldest and most notorious prison, founded in 1852. Johnny Cash recorded an album here in 1969 after scoring a big hit with his live *At Folsom Prison* album a few years earlier.

Take the bicycle and pedestrian bridge from the ferry terminal across the road to the **Marin Country Mart**, a shopping center with a dozen excellent eateries and comfortable outdoor seating. One favorite is the **Marin Brewing Company** (www.marinbrewing.com; 1809 Larkspur Landing Cir, Marin Country Mart, Bldg 2, Larkspur; mains $12-19; ☺11:30am-midnight Sun-Thu, to 1am Fri & Sat; 🛜) brewpub, where you can see the glassed-in kettles behind the bar. The head brewer, Arne Johnson, has won many awards, and the Mt Tam Pale Ale complements the menu of pizza, burgers and hearty sandwiches.

Just south, **Corte Madera** is home to one of the Bay Area's best bookstores, **Book Passage** (☑415-927-0960; www.bookpassage.com;

51 Tamal Vista Blvd; ⊙9am-9pm), in the Marketplace shopping center. It has a strong travel section, plus frequent author appearances.

Continuing west along Sir Francis Drake, **San Anselmo** has a cute, small downtown area along San Anselmo Ave, including several antique shops. The attractive center of neighboring **Fairfax** has ample dining and shopping options, and cyclists congregate at **Gestalt Haus Fairfax** (28 Bolinas Rd, Fairfax; ⊙11:30am-11pm Sun & Mon, 11:30am-midnight Tue & Wed, 11:30am-2am Thu-Sat) for the indoor bicycle parking, board games, European draft beers and sausages of the meaty or vegan persuasion.

Arti (www.articafe.com; 7282 Sir Francis Drake Blvd, Lagunitas; mains $10-14; ⊙noon-9pm; 🍴), 🍴, between Hwys 1 and 101 in the tiny hamlet of **Lagunitas**, is a tempting stop for organic Indian fare. There's a cozy, casual dining room and an outdoor patio for warm days, and folks from miles around adore its sizzling chicken tikka platter.

Six miles east of Olema on Sir Francis Drake Blvd, **Samuel P Taylor State Park** (☎415-488-9897; www.parks.ca.gov/?page_id= 469; parking $8, tent & RV sites $35, cabin $100) has beautiful, secluded campsites in redwood groves and a coveted handful of new five-person cabins with electricity and wood stoves. The park's also located on the paved **Cross Marin Trail**, with miles of creekside landscape to explore along a former railroad grade.

❶ Getting There & Around

Golden Gate Ferry (☎415-455-2000; www. goldengateferry.org) runs a daily ferry service ($9.50, 50 minutes) from the Ferry Building in San Francisco to Sir Francis Drake Blvd in Larkspur, directly east of Hwy 101. You can take bicycles on the ferry.

San Rafael

The oldest and largest town in Marin, San Rafael is slightly less upscale than most of its neighbors but doesn't lack atmosphere. It's a common stop for travelers on their way to Point Reyes. Just north of San Rafael, Lucas Valley Rd heads west to Point Reyes Station, passing George Lucas' Skywalker Ranch. Fourth St, San Rafael's main drag, is lined with cafes and shops. If you follow it west out of downtown San Rafael, it meets Sir Francis Drake Blvd and continues west to the coast.

◉ Sights

China Camp State Park   PARK
(☎415-456-0766; www.parks.ca.gov/?page_id= 466; per car $5) About 4 miles east of San Rafael, this is a pleasant place to stop for a picnic or short hike. From Hwy 101, take the N San Pedro Rd exit and continue 3 miles east. A Chinese fishing village once stood here, and a small museum exhibits interesting artifacts from the settlement.

Mission San Rafael Arcángel   MISSION
(www.saintraphael.com; 1104 5th Ave) The town began with this mission, founded in 1817, which served as a sanatorium for Native Americans suffering from European diseases. The present building is a replica from 1949.

🛏 Sleeping & Eating

China Camp State Park   CAMPGROUND $
(☎800-444-7275; www.reserveamerica.com; tent sites $35) The park has 30 walk-in campsites with showers and pleasant shade.

Panama Hotel   B&B $$
(☎415-457-3993; www.panamahotel.com; 4 Bayview St; s/d with shared bath $75/90, r $120-195; ❄️ 🐾 🛜 🐕) The 10 artsy rooms at this B&B, in a building dating from 1910, each have their own unique style and charming decor – such as crazy quilts and vibrant accent walls. The hotel restaurant has an inviting courtyard patio.

**★Sol Food Puerto Rican
Cuisine**   PUERTO RICAN $$
(☎415-451-4765; www.solfoodrestaurant.com; cnr Lincoln Ave & 3rd St; mains $7.50-16; ⊙7am-midnight Mon-Thu, to 2am Fri, 8am-2am Sat, to midnight Sun) 🍴 Lazy ceiling fans, a profusion of tropical plants and the pulse of Latin rhythms create a soothing atmosphere for delicious dishes such as a *jíbaro* sandwich and other meals concocted with plantains, organic veggies and free-range meats.

☆ Entertainment

Rafael Film Center   CINEMA
(☎415-454-1222; www.cafilm.org/rfc; 1118 4th St) A restored downtown cinema offering innovative art-house programming on three screens in state-of-the-art surroundings.

❶ Getting There & Away

Numerous **Golden Gate Transit** (☎415-455-2000, 511; www.goldengatetransit.org) buses operate between San Francisco and the San Rafael Transit Center at 3rd and Hetherton Sts ($5.75, one hour).

Mill Valley

Nestled under the redwoods at the base of Mt Tamalpais, tiny Mill Valley is one of the Bay Area's most picturesque hamlets. Mill Valley was originally a logging town, its name stemming from an 1830s sawmill – the first in the Bay Area to provide lumber. Though the 1892 Mill Valley Lumber Company still greets motorists on Miller Ave, the town's a vastly different place today, packed with wildly expensive homes, fancy cars and pricey boutiques.

Mill Valley also served as the starting point for the scenic railway that carried visitors up Mt Tamalpais. The tracks were removed in 1940, and today the Depot Bookstore & Cafe occupies the space of the former station.

◉ Sights & Activities

Old Mill Park   PARK
Several blocks west of downtown along Throckmorton Ave is Old Mill Park, perfect for a picnic. Here you'll also find a replica of the town's namesake sawmill. Just past the bridge at Old Mill Creek, the **Dipsea Steps** mark the start of the Dipsea Trail.

★ Dipsea Trail   HIKING
A beloved though demanding hike is the 7-mile Dipsea Trail, which climbs over the coastal range and down to Stinson Beach, cutting through a corner of Muir Woods. This classic trail starts at Old Mill Park with a climb up 676 steps in three separate flights, and includes a few more ups and downs before reaching the ocean. **West Marin Stagecoach** (www.marintransit.org/stage.html) route 61 runs from Stinson Beach to Mill Valley, making it a doable one-way day hike.

The few slaloms between staircases aren't well-signed, but locals can point the way.

🎪 Festivals & Events

Mill Valley Film Festival   FILM
(www.mvff.com; ⊙ Oct) Each October the Mill Valley Film Festival presents an innovative, internationally regarded program of independent films.

🛏 Sleeping

Acqua Hotel   BOUTIQUE HOTEL $$
(☑ 415-380-0400, 888-662-9555; www.marinhotels.com; 555 Redwood Hwy; r incl breakfast from $159; ❋ @ 🖕) 🏊 With views of the bay and Mt Tamalpais, and a lobby with a soothing

fireplace and fountain, the Acqua doesn't lack for pleasant eye candy. Contemporary rooms are sleekly designed with beautiful fabrics.

Mountain Home Inn   INN $$$
(☑ 415-381-9000; www.mtnhomeinn.com; 810 Panoramic Hwy; r incl breakfast $195-345; 🖕) Set amid redwood, spruce and pine trees on a ridge of Mt Tamalpais, this retreat is both modern and rustic. The larger (more expensive) rooms are rugged beauties, with unfinished timbers forming columns from floor to ceiling, as though the forest is shooting up through the floor. Smaller rooms are cozy dens for two. The positioning of a good local trail map on the dresser makes it clear that it's a place to breathe and unwind.

✗ Eating & Drinking

Depot Bookstore & Cafe   CAFE $
(www.depotbookstore.com; 87 Throckmorton Ave; mains under $10; ⊙ 7am-7pm; 🖕) Smack in the town center, Depot serves cappuccinos, sandwiches and light meals. The bookstore sells lots of local publications, including trail guides.

Buckeye Roadhouse   AMERICAN $$
(☑ 415-331-2600; www.buckeyeroadhouse.com; 15 Shoreline Hwy; mains $18-37; ⊙ 11:30am-10:30pm Mon-Sat, 10:30am-10pm Sun) Originally opened as a roadside stop in 1932, the Buckeye is a Marin County gem, and its upscale American cuisine is in no danger of being compared to truck-stop fare. Stop off for chili-lime 'brick' chicken, baby back ribs or oysters Bingo and a devilish wedge of s'more pie before getting back on Hwy 101.

Mill Valley Beerworks   PUB
(www.millvalleybeerworks.com; 173 Throckmorton Ave; mains $18-32; ⊙ 5:30-10:30pm Mon-Fri, 11:30am-10:30pm Sat & Sun, kitchen closed 3-5:30pm) 🍴 With 60 bottled varieties of brew and a few of its own (from the Fort Point Brewing Company in San Francisco) amongst the dozen or so on tap, beer lovers can pair their favorites with the kitchen's delicious farm-to-table cuisine. The unsigned setting is stark and stylish, with unfinished wood tables and a pressed-tin wall.

❶ Information

Visitor information is available from the **Mill Valley Chamber of Commerce** (☑ 415-388-9700; www.millvalley.org; 85 Throckmorton Ave; ⊙ 10am-4pm Tue-Fri).

ⓘ Getting There & Away

From San Francisco or Sausalito, take Hwy 101 north to the Mill Valley–Stinson Beach–Hwy 1 exit. Follow Hwy 1 (also called the Shoreline Hwy) to Almonte Blvd (which becomes Miller Ave), then follow Miller Ave into downtown Mill Valley.

From the north, take the E Blithedale Ave exit from Hwy 101, then head west into Mill Valley.

Golden Gate Transit (☑ 415-455-2000; www.goldengatetranist.org) bus 4 runs directly from San Francisco to Mill Valley ($4.75) on weekdays; route 17 ($2) runs between there from the Sausalito ferry terminal daily.

Mt Tamalpais State Park

Standing guard over Marin County, majestic Mt Tamalpais (Mt Tam) has breathtaking 360-degree views of ocean, bay and hills rolling into the distance. The rich, natural beauty of the 2571ft mountain and its surrounding area is inspiring – especially considering it lies within an hour's drive from one of the state's largest metropolitan areas.

Mt Tamalpais State Park (☑ 415-388-2070; www.parks.ca.gov/mttamalpais; parking $8) was formed in 1930, partly from land donated by congressman and naturalist William Kent (who also donated the land that became Muir Woods National Monument in 1907). Its 6300 acres are home to deer, foxes, bobcats and many miles of hiking and cycling trails.

Mt Tam was a sacred place to the coastal Miwok people for thousands of years before the arrival of European and American settlers. By the late 19th century, San Franciscans were escaping the bustle of the city with all-day outings on the mountain, and in 1896 the 'world's crookedest railroad' (281 turns) was completed from Mill Valley to the summit. Though the railroad was closed in 1930, Old Railroad Grade is today one of Mt Tam's most popular and scenic hiking and cycling paths.

⊙ Sights

Panoramic Hwy climbs from Mill Valley through the park to Stinson Beach. From Pantoll Station, it's 4.2 miles by car to **East Peak Summit**; take Pantoll Rd and then panoramic Ridgecrest Blvd to the top. A 10-minute hike leads to a fire lookout at the very top and awesome sea-to-bay views.

Mountain Theater   THEATER
(☑ 415-383-1100; www.mountainplay.org; adult/child $40/20) The park's natural-stone, 4000-seat theater hosts the annual 'Mountain Play' series on a half dozen weekend afternoons between mid-May and late June. Free shuttles are provided from Mill Valley. Free monthly **astronomy programs** (www.friendsofmttam.org/astronomy.html; ⊙ Apr-Oct) also take place here on Saturday nights around the new moon.

🏃 Activities

Hiking

The park map is a smart investment, as there are a dozen worthwhile hiking trails in the area. From Pantoll Station, the **Steep Ravine Trail** follows a wooded creek on to the coast (about 2.1 miles each way). For a longer hike, veer right (northwest) after 1.5 miles onto the **Dipsea Trail**, which meanders through trees for 1 mile before ending at Stinson Beach. Grab some lunch, then walk north through town and follow signs for the **Matt Davis Trail**, which leads 2.7 miles back to Pantoll Station, making a good loop. The Matt Davis Trail continues on beyond Pantoll Station, wrapping gently around the mountain with superb views.

Another worthy option is **Cataract Trail**, which runs along Cataract Creek from the end of Pantoll Rd; it's approximately 3 miles to Alpine Lake. The last mile is a spectacular rooty staircase as the trail descends alongside **Cataract Falls**.

Mountain Biking

Cyclists must stay on the fire roads (and off the single-track trails) and keep to speeds under 15mph. Rangers are prickly about these rules, and a ticket can result in a steep fine.

The most popular ride is the **Old Railroad Grade**. For a sweaty, 6-mile, 2280ft climb, start in Mill Valley at the end of W Blithedale Ave and cycle up to East Peak. It takes about an hour to reach the West Point Inn from Mill Valley. For an easier start, begin part way up at the Mountain Home Inn and follow the **Gravity Car Grade** to the Old Railroad Grade and the West Point Inn. From the inn, it's an easy half-hour ride to the summit.

From just west of Pantoll Station, cyclists can either take the **Deer Park fire road**, which runs close to the Dipsea Trail, through giant redwoods to the main entrance of Muir Woods, or the southeastern extension of the **Coastal Trail**, which has breathtaking views of the coast before joining Hwy 1 about 2 miles north of Muir

Beach. Either option requires a return to Mill Valley via Frank Valley/Muir Woods Rd, which climbs steadily (800ft) to Panoramic Hwy and then becomes Sequoia Valley Rd as it drops toward Mill Valley. A left turn on Wildomar and two right turns at Mill Creek Park lead to the center of Mill Valley.

For further information on bicycle routes and rules, contact the Marin County Bicycle Coalition (p95), whose Marin Bicycle Map is the gold standard for local cycling.

🛏 Sleeping & Eating

★Steep Ravine   CAMPGROUND, CABIN $
(Map p48; ☎ 800-444-7275; www.reserveamerica. com; Nov-Sep; tent site $25, cabin $100) Just off Hwy 1, about 1 mile south of Stinson Beach, this jewel has seven beachfront campsites and nine rustic five-person cabins with wood stoves overlooking the ocean. Both options are booked out months in advance and reservations can be made up to seven months ahead.

Bootjack Campground   CAMPGROUND $
(Panoramic Hwy; tent sites $25) Recently re-opened after decades of closure, its 15 first-come, first-served walk-in sites are right on two of the park's best hiking trails and adjacent to Redwood Creek, with open vistas to the south. It's a half-mile northeast of Pantoll Station.

Pantoll Campground   CAMPGROUND $
(Panoramic Hwy; tent sites $25) From the parking lot it's a 100yd walk or bicycle ride to the campground, with 16 first-come, first-served tent sites but no showers.

West Point Inn   LODGE, CABIN $
(☎ info 415-388-9955, reservations 415-646-0702; www.westpointinn.com; 100 Old Railroad Grade Fire Rd, Mill Valley; r per adult/child $50/25) Load up your sleeping bag and hike in to this rustic 1904 hilltop hideaway built as a stopover for the Mill Valley and Mt Tamalpais Scenic Railway. It also hosts monthly pancake breakfasts ($10) on Sundays during the summer.

ℹ Information

Pantoll Station (☎ 415-388-2070; www.parks. ca.gov/?page_id=471; 801 Panoramic Hwy; ⊙ variable hours; 🛜) is the park headquarters. Detailed park maps are sold here. The **Mt Tamalpais Interpretive Association** (www.mttam. net; ⊙ 11am-4pm Sat & Sun) staffs a small visitor center at East Peak.

ℹ Getting There & Away

To reach Pantoll Station by car, take Hwy 1 to the Panoramic Hwy and look for the Pantoll signs. **West Marin Stagecoach** (☎ 415-526-3239; www.marintransit.org/stage.html) route 61 runs daily minibuses ($2) from Marin City (via Mill Valley; plus weekend and holiday service from the Sausalito ferry) to both the Pantoll Station and Mountain Home Inn.

Muir Woods National Monument

Walking through an awesome stand of the world's tallest trees is an experience to be had only in Northern California and a small part of southern Oregon. The old-growth redwoods at **Muir Woods** (☎ 415-388-2595; www.nps.gov/muwo; Muir Woods Rd, Mill Valley; adult/child $7/free; ⊙ 8am-sunset), just 12 miles north of the Golden Gate Bridge, is the closest redwood stand to San Francisco. The trees were initially eyed by loggers, and Redwood Creek, as the area was known, seemed ideal for a dam. Those plans were halted when congressman and naturalist William Kent bought a section of Redwood Creek and, in 1907, donated 295 acres to the federal government. President Theodore Roosevelt made the site a national monument in 1908, the name honoring John Muir, naturalist and founder of environmental organization the Sierra Club.

Muir Woods can become quite crowded, especially on weekends. Try to come midweek, early in the morning or late in the afternoon, when tour buses are less of a problem. Even at busy times, a short hike will get you out of the densest crowds and onto trails with huge trees and stunning vistas. A lovely cafe serves local and organic goodies and hot drinks that hit the spot on foggy days.

🏃 Activities

The 1-mile **Main Trail Loop** is a gentle walk alongside Redwood Creek to the 1000-year-old trees at **Cathedral Grove**; it returns via **Bohemian Grove**, where the tallest tree in the park stands 254ft high. The **Dipsea Trail** is a good 2-mile hike up to the top of aptly named **Cardiac Hill**.

You can also walk down into Muir Woods by taking trails from the Panoramic Hwy, such as the **Bootjack Trail** from the Bootjack picnic area, or from Mt Tamalpais' Pantoll Station campground, along the **Ben Johnson Trail**.

❶ Getting There & Away

The parking lot is insanely full during busy periods, so consider taking the seasonal **Muir Woods Shuttle** (Route 66F; www.marintransit. org; round trip adult/child $5/free; ☺ weekends & holidays late-Mar–Oct). The 40-minute shuttle connects with Sausalito ferries arriving from San Francisco before 3pm.

To get there by car, drive north on Hwy 101, exit at Hwy 1 and continue north along Hwy 1/ Shoreline Hwy to the Panoramic Hwy (a right-hand fork). Follow that for about 1 mile to Four Corners, where you turn left onto Muir Woods Rd (there are plenty of signs).

Muir Beach

The turnoff to Muir Beach from Hwy 1 is marked by the longest row of mailboxes on the north coast. Muir Beach is a quiet little town with a nice beach, but it has no direct bus service. Just north of Muir Beach there are superb views up and down the coast from the **Muir Beach Overlook**; during WWII, watch was kept from the surrounding concrete lookouts for invading Japanese ships.

🛏 Sleeping & Eating

Green Gulch Farm & Zen Center   LODGE $$
(☑415-383-3134; www.sfzc.org; 1601 Shoreline Hwy; s $90-155, d $160-225, d cottage $350-400, all with 3 meals; @🐾) 🍴 Green Gulch Farm & Zen Center is a Buddhist retreat in the hills above Muir Beach. The center's accommodations are elegant, restful and modern, and delicious buffet-style vegetarian meals are included. A hilltop retreat cottage is 25 minutes away by foot.

Pelican Inn   PUB $$$
(☑415-383-6000; www.pelicaninn.com; 10 Pacific Way; mains $14-34; 🍴) The oh-so-English Tudor-style Pelican Inn is Muir Beach's only commercial establishment. Hikers, cyclists and families come for pub lunches inside its timbered restaurant and cozy bar, perfect for a pint, a game of darts and warming up beside the open fire. The British fare is respectable, but it's the setting that's magical. Upstairs are seven luxe rooms (from $206) with cushy half-canopy beds.

Stinson Beach

Just 5 miles north of Muir Beach, Stinson Beach is positively buzzing on warm weekends. The town flanks Hwy 1 for about three blocks and is densely packed with galleries, shops, eateries and B&Bs. The beach itself is often blanketed with fog, and when the sun's shining it's blanketed with surfers, families and gawkers. There are views of Point Reyes and San Francisco on clear days, and the beach is long enough for a vigorous stroll.

◉ Sights

Stinson Beach   BEACH
Three-mile-long Stinson Beach is a popular surf spot, but swimming is advised from late May to mid-September only; for updated weather and surf conditions call ☑415-868-1922. The beach is one block west of Hwy 1.

Red Rock Beach   BEACH
Around 1 mile south of Stinson Beach is Red Rock Beach. It's a clothing-optional beach that attracts smaller crowds, probably because it can only be accessed by a steep trail from Hwy 1.

★**Audubon Canyon Ranch**   WILDLIFE RESERVE
(☑415-868-9244; www.egret.org; donations requested; ☺ usually 10am-4pm Sat, Sun & holidays mid-Mar–mid-Jul) Audubon Canyon Ranch is about 3.5 miles north of Stinson Beach on Hwy 1, in the hills above the Bolinas Lagoon. A major nesting ground for great blue herons and great egrets, viewing scopes are set up on hillside blinds where you can watch these magnificent birds congregate to nest and hatch their chicks in tall redwoods. At low tide, harbor seals often doze on sand bars in the lagoon. Confirm hours, as a recent nesting failure may alter future public access.

🛏 Sleeping & Eating

Sandpiper   MOTEL, CABINS $$
(☑415-868-1632; www.sandpiperstinsonbeach. com; 1 Marine Way; r $145-225; 🐾) Just off Hwy 1 and a quick stroll to the beach, the ten comfortable rooms and cabins of the Sandpiper have gas fireplaces and kitchenettes, and are ensconced in a lush garden and picnic area. Prices dip from November through March; two-night minimum stay on weekends.

Parkside Cafe   AMERICAN $$
(☑415-868-1272; www.parksidecafe.com; 43 Arenal Ave; mains $9-25; ☺ 7:30am-9pm, coffee from 6am) 🍴 Parkside Cafe is famous for its hearty breakfasts and lunches, and noted far and wide for its excellent coastal cuisine. Reservations are recommended for dinner.

ℹ️ Getting There & Away

West Marin Stagecoach (☏ 415-526-3239; www.marintransit.org/stage.html) route 61 runs daily minibuses ($2) from Marin City, and weekend and holiday services to the Sausalito ferry. By car from San Francisco, it's nearly an hour's drive, though on weekends plan for toe-tapping traffic delays.

Bolinas

For a town that is so famously unexcited about tourism, Bolinas offers some fairly tempting attractions for the visitor. Known as Jugville during the Gold Rush days, the sleepy beachside community is home to writers, musicians and fisherfolk, and deliberately hard to find. The highway department used to put signs up at the turnoff from Hwy 1; locals kept taking them down, so the highway department finally gave up.

👁 Sights & Activities

★ Point Blue

Conservation Science   BIRD OBSERVATORY
(☏ 415-868-0655; www.pointblue.org) Off Mesa Rd west of downtown and formerly known as the Point Reyes Bird Observatory, its Palomarin Field Station has bird-banding and netting demonstrations, a visitors center and nature trail. Banding demonstrations are held in the morning every Tuesday to Sunday from May to late November, and on Wednesday, Saturday and Sunday the rest of the year.

Bolinas Museum   MUSEUM
(☏ 415-868-0330; www.bolinasmuseum.org; 48 Wharf Rd; ⊙ 1-5pm Fri, noon-5pm Sat & Sun) FREE
This courtyard complex of five galleries exhibits local artists and showcases the region's history. Look for the weathered Bolinas highway sign affixed to the wall, since you certainly didn't see one on your way into town.

Agate Beach   BEACH
There are tide pools along some 2 miles of coastline at Agate Beach, around the end of Duxbury Point.

2 Mile Surf Shop   SURFING
(☏ 415-868-0264; www.2milesurf.com; 22 Brighton Ave; ⊙ 9am-6pm May-Oct, 10am-5pm Nov-Apr) Surfing's popular in these parts, and this shop behind the post office rents boards and wetsuits and also gives lessons. Call ☏ 415-868-2412 for the surf report.

Hiking
Beyond the observatory is the Palomarin parking lot and access to various **walking trails** in the southern part of the Point Reyes National Seashore, including the easy (and popular) 3-mile trail to lovely **Bass Lake**. A sweet inland spot buffered by tall trees, this small lake is perfect for a pastoral swim on a toasty day. You can dive in wearing your birthday suit (or not), bring an inner tube to float about, or do a long lap all the way across.

If you continue 1.5 miles northwest, you'll reach the unmaintained trail to **Alamere Falls**, a fantastic flume plunging 50ft off a cliff and down to the beach. But sketchy beach access makes it more enjoyable to walk another 1.5 miles to **Wildcat Beach** and then backtrack a mile on sand.

🛏 Sleeping & Eating

Smiley's Schooner Saloon & Hotel MOTEL $$
(☏ 415-868-1311; www.smileyssaloon.com; 41 Wharf Rd; r $104-124; 🛜🐾) A crusty old place dating back to 1851, Smiley's has simple but decent rooms, and last-minute weekday rates can be a bargain. The bar, which serves some food, has live bands Thursday through Saturday and is frequented by plenty of salty dogs and grizzled deadheads.

Bolinas People's Store   CAFE, MARKET $
(14 Wharf Rd; ⊙ 8:30am-6:30pm; ✎) ⏹ An awesome little co-op grocery store hidden behind the community center, the People's Store serves Fair Trade coffee and sells organic produce, fresh soup and excellent tamales. Eat at the tables in the shady courtyard, and have a rummage through the Free Box, a shed full of clothes and other waiting-to-be-reused items.

Coast Café   AMERICAN $$
(www.bolinascoastcafe.com; 46 Wharf Rd; mains $10-22; ⊙ 11:30am-3pm & 5-8pm Tue-Thu, to 9pm Fri, 8am-3pm & 5-9pm Sat, to 8pm Sun; ✎🐾) ⏹ The only 'real' restaurant in town, everyone jockeys for outdoor seats among the flowerboxes for fish and chips, barbecued oysters, or buttermilk pancakes with damn good coffee. Live music Thursday and Sunday nights.

ℹ️ Getting There & Away

Route 61 of the **West Marin Stagecoach** (☏ 415-526-3239; www.marintransit.org/stage.html) goes daily ($2) from the Marin City transit hub (weekend and holiday service from the Sausalito ferry) to downtown Bolinas. By car, follow Hwy

1 north from Stinson Beach and turn west for Bolinas at the first road north of the lagoon. At the first stop sign, take another left onto Olema–Bolinas Rd and follow it 2 miles to town.

Olema & Nicasio

About 10 miles north of Stinson Beach near the junction of Hwy 1 and Sir Francis Drake Blvd, Olema was the main settlement in west Marin in the 1860s. Back then, there was a stagecoach service to San Rafael and there were *six* saloons. In 1875, when the railroad was built through Point Reyes Station instead of Olema, the town's importance began to fade. In 1906 it gained distinction once again as the epicenter of the Great Quake.

The **Bolinas Ridge Trail**, a 12-mile series of ups and downs for hikers or bikers, starts about 1 mile west of Olema, on Sir Francis Drake Blvd. It has great views.

In the former Olema Inn, a creaky 1876 building, hyper-local **Sir & Star** (⌨415-663-1034; www.sirandstar.com; cnr Sir Francis Drake Blvd & Hwy 1; mains $20, prix fixe Sat/other nights $75/48; ☺5-9pm Wed-Sun, plus earlier hours in summer; ☎) ✿ restaurant delights with Marin-sourced seasonal bounty such as Tomales Bay oysters, Dungeness crab and duck 'faux' gras. Reservations recommended.

About a 15-minute drive inland from Olema, at the geographic center of Marin County, is Nicasio, a tiny town with a low-key rural flavor. In the town center, its music venue, **Rancho Nicasio** (⌨415-662-2219; www.ranchonicasio.com; 1 Old Rancheria Rd; ☺11:30am-3pm & 5-9pm Mon-Thu, to 10pm Fri, 11am-3pm & 5-10pm Sat, to 9pm Sun), is a rustic saloon that regularly attracts local and national blues, rock and country performers.

❶ Getting There & Away

Route 68 of the **West Marin Stagecoach** (⌨415-526-3239; www.marintransit.org/stage.html) runs daily to Olema and Samuel P Taylor State Park from the San Rafael Transit Center ($2).

Nicasio is located at the west end of Lucas Valley Rd, 10 miles from Hwy 101.

Point Reyes Station

Though the railroad stopped coming through in 1933 and the town is small, Point Reyes Station is nevertheless the hub of west Marin. Dominated by dairies and ranches, the region was invaded by artists in the 1960s. Today it's an interesting blend of art galleries and tourist shops. The town has a rowdy saloon and the occasional smell of cattle on the afternoon breeze.

🛏 Sleeping & Eating

Cute little cottages, cabins and B&Bs are plentiful in and around Point Reyes. The **West Marin Chamber of Commerce** (⌨415-663-9232; www.pointreyes.org) has numerous listings, as does the **Point Reyes Lodging Association** (⌨415-663-1872, 800-539-1872; www.ptreyes.com).

Windsong Cottage Guest Yurt YURT $$
(⌨415-663-9695; www.windsongcottage.com; 25 McDonald Lane; d yurt $185-210; ☎) A wood-burning stove, private outdoor hot tub, comfy king bed and kitchen stocked with breakfast supplies make this round sky-lighted abode a cozy slice of heaven.

Bovine Bakery BAKERY $
(www.thebovinebakery.com; 11315 Hwy 1; pastry $3; ☺6:30am-5pm Mon-Fri, 7am-5pm Sat & Sun) ✿ Don't leave town without sampling something buttery from possibly the best bakery in Marin. A sweet bear-claw pastry and an organic coffee are a good way to kick off your morning.

Tomales Bay Foods & Cowgirl Creamery DELI, MARKET $
(www.cowgirlcreamery.com; 80 4th St; sandwiches $6-12; ☺10am-6pm Wed-Sun; ☛) ✿ A market in an old barn selling picnic items, including gourmet cheeses and organic produce. Reserve a spot in advance for the small-scale artisanal cheesemaker's demonstration and tasting ($5); watch the curd-making and cutting, then sample a half dozen of the fresh and aged cheeses. All of the milk is local and organic, with vegetarian rennet in the soft cheeses.

Osteria Stellina ITALIAN $$
(⌨415-663-9988; www.osteriastellina.com; 11285 Hwy 1; mains $15-24; ☺11:30am-2:30pm & 5-9pm; ☛) ✿ This place specializes in rustic Italian cuisine made from locally sourced produce, including pizza and pasta dishes and Niman Ranch meats. For dessert, the water-buffalo-milk gelato is the way to go.

Pine Cone Diner DINER $$
(www.pineconediner.com; 60 4th St; mains $9-13; ☺8am-2:30pm; ☛) ✿ The Pine Cone serves big breakfasts and lunches inside a cute

retro dining room and at shaded al fresco picnic tables. Try the buttermilk biscuits, the chorizo or tofu scramble, or the fried oyster sandwich.

☆ Entertainment

Old Western Saloon LIVE MUSIC, BAR
(☑415-663-1661; cnr Shoreline Hwy & 2nd St; ☺10am-midnight or 2am) A rustic 1906 saloon with live bands and cool tables emblazoned with horseshoes. Prince Charles stopped in here for an impromptu pint during a local visit in 2006.

❶ Getting There & Away

Hwy 1 becomes Main St in town, running right through the center. Route 68 of the **West Marin Stagecoach** (☑415-526-3239; www.marintransit.org/stage.html) runs here daily from the San Rafael Transit Center ($2).

Inverness

This tiny town, the last outpost on your journey westward, is spread along the west side of Tomales Bay. It's got good places to eat and, among the surrounding hills and picturesque shoreline, multiple rental cottages and quaint B&Bs. Several great beaches are only a short drive north.

🏃 Activities

Blue Waters Kayaking KAYAKING
(☑415-669-2600; www.bluewaterskayaking.com; rentals/tours from $50/68; 🚻) At the Tomales Bay Resort and across the bay in Marshall (on Hwy 1, eight miles north of Point Reyes Station), this outfit offers various Tomales Bay tours, or you can rent a kayak and paddle around secluded beaches and rocky crevices on your own; no experience necessary.

🛏 Sleeping

Cottages at Point Reyes Seashore BUNGALOW $$
(☑800-416-0405, 415-669-7250; www.invernessvalleyinn.com; 13275 Sir Francis Drake Blvd; r $139-219; 🐾⊠) ❂ Cottages at Point Reyes Seashore is a family-friendly place hidden away in the woods, just a mile from town. It offers clean, modern kitchenette rooms in A-frame structures, and has a tennis court, hot tub, horseshoe pitches, barbecue pits and in-room DVD players. There's also a large garden and private nature trail. It's

past the town, on the way down the Point Reyes peninsula.

Tomales Bay Resort MOTEL $$
(☑415-669-1389; www.tomalesbayresort.com; 12938 Sir Francis Drake Blvd; r $125-275; 🐾⊠) The bayside Tomales Bay Resort has 36 motel rooms and a pool (unheated). When rates drop – Sunday through Thursday and in the winter – it's one of the best bargains around.

Dancing Coyote Beach Cottages BUNGALOW $$$
(☑415-669-7200; www.dancingcoyotebeach.com; 12794 Sir Francis Drake Blvd; cottages $200-260; 🐾⊠) Serene and comfortable, these four modern cottages back right onto Tomales Bay, with skylights and decks extending the views in all directions. Full kitchens contain tasty breakfast foods and fireplaces are stocked with firewood for foggy nights.

❶ Getting There & Away

From Hwy 1, Sir Francis Drake Blvd leads straight into Inverness. Route 68 of the **West Marin Stagecoach** (☑415-526-3239; www.marintransit.org/stage.html) makes daily stops here from San Rafael ($2).

Point Reyes National Seashore

The windswept peninsula **Point Reyes** (Map p48; www.nps.gov/pore) FREE is a rough-hewn beauty that has always lured marine mammals and migratory birds as well as scores of shipwrecks. It was here in 1579 that Sir Francis Drake landed to repair his ship, the *Golden Hind*. During his five-week stay he mounted a brass plaque near the shore claiming this land for England. Historians believe this occurred at Drakes Beach and there is a marker there today. In 1595 the first of scores of ships lost in these waters, the *San Augustine*, went down. She was a Spanish treasure ship out of Manila laden with luxury goods, and to this day bits of her cargo wash up on shore. Despite modern navigation, the dangerous waters here continue to claim the odd boat.

Point Reyes National Seashore has 110 sq miles of pristine ocean beaches, and the peninsula offers excellent hiking and camping opportunities. Be sure to bring warm clothing, as even the sunniest days can quickly turn cold and foggy.

ℹ️ POINT REYES SHUTTLE

On good-weather weekends and holidays from late December through mid-April, the road to Chimney Rock and the lighthouse is closed to private vehicles. Instead you must take a shuttle ($5, children under 17 free) from Drakes Beach.

◉ Sights & Activities

For an awe-inspiring view, follow the **Earthquake Trail** from the park headquarters at Bear Valley. The trail reaches a 16ft gap between the two halves of a once-connected fence line, a lasting testimonial to the power of the 1906 earthquake that was centered in this area. Another trail leads from the visitors center a short way to **Kule Loklo**, a reproduction of a Miwok village.

Limantour Rd, off Bear Valley Rd about 1 mile north of Bear Valley Visitor Center, leads to the Point Reyes Hostel and **Limantour Beach**, where a trail runs along Limantour Spit with Estero de Limantour on one side and Drakes Bay on the other. The **Inverness Ridge Trail** heads from Limantour Rd up to Mt Vision (1282ft), from where there are spectacular views of the entire national seashore. You can drive almost to the top of Mt Vision from the other side.

About 2 miles past Inverness, Pierce Point Rd splits off to the right from Sir Francis Drake Blvd. From here you can get to two nice swimming beaches on the bay: Marshall Beach requires a mile-long hike from the parking area, while Hearts Desire, in **Tomales Bay State Park**, is accessible by car.

Pierce Point Rd continues to the huge windswept sand dunes at **Abbotts Lagoon**, full of peeping killdeer and other shorebirds. At the end of the road is Pierce Point Ranch, the trailhead for the 3.5-mile **Tomales Point Trail** through the **Tule Elk Reserve**. The plentiful elk are an amazing sight, standing with their big horns against the backdrop of Tomales Point, with Bodega Bay to the north, Tomales Bay to the east and the Pacific Ocean to the west.

★**Point Reyes Lighthouse**　　LIGHTHOUSE
(☺ lighthouse 10am-4:30pm Fri-Mon, lens room 2:30-4pm Fri-Mon) **FREE** At the very end of Sir Francis Drake Blvd, with wild terrain and ferocious winds, this spot feels like the end of the earth and offers the best **whale-**watching along the coast. The lighthouse sits below the headlands; to reach it requires descending more than 300 stairs. Nearby **Chimney Rock** is a fine short hike, especially in spring when the wildflowers are blossoming. A nearby viewing area allows you to spy on the park's **elephant seal colony**.

Keep back from the water's edge at the exposed North Beach and South Beach, as people have been dragged in and drowned by frequent rogue waves.

Five Brooks Stables　　HORSEBACK RIDING
(☎ 415-663-1570; www.fivebrooks.com; trail rides from $40; 🖶) Explore the landscape on horseback with a trail ride. Take a slow amble through a pasture or ascend more than 1000ft to Inverness Ridge for views of the Olema Valley. If you can stay in the saddle for six hours, ride along the coastline to Alamere Falls via Wildcat Beach.

🛏️ Sleeping

Wake up to deer nibbling under a blanket of fog at one of Point Reyes' four very popular hike-in **campgrounds** (☎ 877-444-6777; www.recreation.gov; tent sites $20), each with pit toilets, water and tables. Reservations are accepted up to six months in advance, and weekends go fast. Reaching the campgrounds requires a 2- to 6-mile hike or bicycle ride, or you can try for a permit to camp on the beach in Tomales Bay. Check with the Bear Valley Visitor Center for same-day permits.

★**HI Point Reyes Hostel**　　HOSTEL **$**
(☎ 415-663-8811; www.norcalhostels.org/reyes; 1390 Limantour Spit Rd; dm $25, r $82-120, all with shared bath; @) 🖉 Just off Limantour Rd, this rustic HI property has bunkhouses with warm and cozy front rooms, big-view windows and outdoor areas with hill vistas, and a newer LEED-certified building with four private rooms (two-night minimum stay on weekends) and a stunning modern kitchen. It's in a secluded valley 2 miles from the ocean and surrounded by lovely hiking trails.

ℹ️ Information

The park headquarters, **Bear Valley Visitor Center** (☎ 415-464-5100; www.nps.gov/pore; ☺ 10am-5pm Mon-Fri, from 9am Sat & Sun), is near Olema and has information and maps. You can also get information at the Point Reyes Lighthouse and the **Kenneth Patrick Center** (☎ 415-669-1250; ☺ 9:30am-4:30pm Sat, Sun & holidays) at Drakes Beach. All visitor centers have slightly longer hours in summer.

HIKING & CYCLING THE BAY BRIDGE

Why should the Golden Gate get all the outdoor action? Inaugurated in 2013, the **Bay Bridge Trail** (www.baybridgeinfo.org/path) is a separated pedestrian and bicycle path along the new Bay Bridge span between Oakland and Yerba Buena Island. The path has two access points: from outside the Ikea store on Shellmound St in Emeryville (1.5 miles from the MacArthur BART station), and from the corner of Maritime St and Burma Rd in West Oakland. One-way distances are about 5 miles from Emeryville and 3.5 miles from West Oakland, and a number of benches line the trail so you can drink in the open vistas.

Steps from the ferry in Jack London Square, **Bay Area Bikes** (☑510-836-2311; www. bayareabikerentals.net; 427 Water St; rentals per day from $25 ; ⏱10am-5pm Mon-Fri, 9am-6pm Sat & Sun) rents bikes with helmets and locks.

❶ Getting There & Away

By car you can get to Point Reyes a few different ways. The curviest is along Hwy 1, through Stinson Beach and Olema. More direct is to exit Hwy 101 in San Rafael and follow Sir Francis Drake Blvd all the way to the tip of Point Reyes. For the latter route, take the central San Rafael exit and head west on 4th St, which turns into Sir Francis Drake Blvd. By either route, it's about 1½ hours to Olema from San Francisco.

Just north of Olema, where Hwy 1 and Sir Francis Drake Blvd come together, is Bear Valley Rd; turn left to reach the Bear Valley Visitor Center. If you're heading to the further reaches of Point Reyes, follow Sir Francis Drake Blvd through Point Reyes Station and out onto the peninsula (about an hour's drive).

West Marin Stagecoach (www.marintransit. org/stage.html) route 68 makes daily stops at the Bear Valley Visitor Center from San Rafael ($2).

EAST BAY

Berkeley and Oakland are what most San Franciscans think of as the East Bay, though the area includes numerous other suburbs that swoop up from the bayside flats into exclusive enclaves in the hills. While many residents of the 'West Bay' would like to think they needn't ever cross the Bay Bridge or take a BART train under water, a wealth of museums, universities, excellent restaurants, woodsy parklands and better weather are just some of attractions that lure travelers from San Francisco.

Oakland

Named for the grand oak trees that once lined its streets, Oakland is to San Francisco what Brooklyn is to Manhattan. To some degree a less expensive alternative to the nearby city of hills, it's often where people have fled to escape pricey San Francisco housing costs. An ethnically diverse city, Oakland has a strong African American community and a long labor union history. Urban farmers raise chickens in their backyard or occupy abandoned lots to start community gardens, families find more room to stretch out, and self-satisfied residents thumb their noses at San Francisco's fog while basking in a sunnier Mediterranean climate.

◉ Sights & Activities

Broadway is the backbone of downtown Oakland, running from Jack London Sq at the waterfront all the way north to Piedmont and Rockridge. Telegraph Ave branches off Broadway at 15th St and heads north straight to Berkeley via the Temescal neighborhood (located between 40th St and 51st St). San Pablo Ave also heads north from downtown into Berkeley. Running east from Broadway is Grand Ave, leading to the Lake Merritt commercial district.

Downtown BART stations are on Broadway at both 12th and 19th Sts; other stations are near Lake Merritt, Rockridge and Temescal (MacArthur station).

◉ Downtown

Oakland's downtown is full of historic buildings and a growing number of colorful local businesses. With such easy access from San Francisco via BART and the ferry, it's worth spending part of a day exploring here – and nearby Chinatown and Jack London Sq – on foot or by bicycle.

The pedestrianized **City Center**, between Broadway and Clay St, 12th and 14th Sts, forms the heart of downtown Oakland. The twin towers of the **Ronald Dellums Federal Building** are on Clay St, just behind it.

Oakland

0 / 500 m
0 / 0.25 miles

Emeryville (0.25mi)

Bakesale Betty (0.3mi);
Rockridge (1mi)

Lusk St
39th St
Apgar St
41st St
40th St
Manila Ave
Terrace St
22

37th St
W MacArthur Blvd
West St
Market St
MacArthur BART Station
38th St
Shafter Ave
Mountain View Cemetery (0.5mi)
W MacArthur Blvd
Howe St
15

32nd St
San Pablo Ave
33rd St
Brockhurst St
31st St
State Hwy 24
580
36th St
Mosswood Park
Broadway
Piedmont Ave
Yosemite Ave

Chestnut St
28th St
West St
29th St
Martin Luther King Jr Way
Hawthorne Ave
Webster St
30th St
Frisbie St
Oakland Ave

Filbert St
Myrtle St
27th St
26th St
980
28th St
29th St
Vernon St

Mead Ave
Athens Ave
25th St
Sycamore Al
25th St
28
27th St
Valdez St
Harrison St
Grand Lake Theatre (0.5mi);
Boot & Shoe Service (0.5mi);
Arizmendi (0.6mi)

22nd St
West St
23rd St
24th St
27
Grand Ave
22nd St
21st St
Bay Pl Bellevue Ave
Grand Ave

18th St
Greyhound
19th St
20th St
10
William St
19th St
18
24
23
29
30
19th St/Oakland BART Station
17th St
19th St
Lakeside Dr
2
Lakeside Park

17th St
16th St
14th St
Brush St
Castro St
Jefferson St
Clay St
19
3
15th St
6
City Center
Oakland City Center/12th St BART Station
17th St
Harrison St
Alice St
Jackson St
Madison St
19th St
Lake Merritt
Lakeside Park
11

Market St
Brush St
Megabus (1.2km)
Martin Luther King Jr Way
11th St
10th St
9th St
12
17
25
26
12th St
14th St
Oak St
16

6th St
5th St
Jefferson St
Washington St
Franklin St
Webster St
Oakland Museum of California
1
Lake Merritt BART Station
14th St
12th St
Lakeside Dr
1st Ave
2nd Ave

7
31
4
9
14
13 8
Visit Oakland Visitor Center
San Francisco Bay
Jack London Square
20
Clay St
2nd St
3rd St
4th St
5th St
6th St
Water St
2nd St
21
Alice St
Jackson St
8th St
7th St
Channel Park
E 12th St
E 11th St
E 10th St
4th Ave

5
Harrison St
Alameda
Amtrak Station
Oak St
4th St
Fallon St
880
E 8th St
6th Ave
7th Ave

Oakland

MARIN COUNTY & THE BAY AREA OAKLAND

City Hall, at 14th & Clay Sts, is a beautifully refurbished 1914 beaux arts hall.

Old Oakland, along Washington St between 8th and 10th Sts, is lined with historic buildings dating from the 1860s to the 1880s. The buildings have been restored and the area has a lively restaurant and after-work scene. The area also hosts a lively **farmers market** every Friday morning.

East of Broadway and bustling with commerce, **Chinatown** centers on Franklin and Webster Sts, as it has since the 1870s. It's much smaller than the San Francisco version.

◉ Uptown

Continuing north of Oakland's City Center, the Uptown district contains many of the city's art-deco beauties and a proliferating arts and restaurant scene. The area stretches roughly between Telegraph and Broadway, bounded by Grand Ave to the north.

Great Western Power Company CLIMBING, GYM
(☏510-452-2022; www.touchstoneclimbing.com; 520 20th St; day pass $15-20; ⊙6am-10pm Mon-Thu, to 11pm Tue & Thu, 10am-6pm Sat & Sun) Work up a sweat in the belly of this former power plant – you can't miss the smokestack – where climbers can scale a 48-foot-high wall (full gear rental $5), conquer their problems in the 1500-square-foot bouldering area, take yoga classes or use the gym.

◉ Jack London Square

The area where writer and adventurer Jack London once raised hell now bears his name, and recent spasms of redevelopment have added a new cinema complex, condo development, excellent restaurants and some eclectic watering holes. The pretty waterfront location is worth a stroll, especially when the Sunday **farmers market** (⊙10am-2pm) takes over, or get off your feet and kayak around the harbor. Catch a ferry from San Francisco – a worthwhile excursion in and of itself – and you'll land just paces away.

Jack London's Yukon Cabin   LANDMARK
A replica of Jack London's Yukon cabin stands at the eastern end of the square. It's partially built from the timbers of a cabin London lived in during the Yukon Gold Rush. Oddly, people throw coins inside as if it's a fountain. Another interesting stop, adjacent to the tiny cabin, is Heinold's First & Last Chance Saloon.

USS Potomac   HISTORIC SITE
(☏510-627-1215; www.usspotomac.org; admission $10; ⊙11am-3pm Wed, Fri & Sun) Franklin D Roosevelt's 'floating White House,' the 165ft USS *Potomac*, is moored at Clay and Water Sts by the ferry dock, and is open for dockside tours. Two-hour history cruises (adult/child $55/35) are also held several times a month from May through October.

◉ Lake Merritt

An urban respite, Lake Merritt is a popular place to stroll or go running (a 3.5-mile track circles the lake). The two main commercial streets skirting Lake Merritt are Lakeshore Ave on the eastern edge of the lake and Grand Ave, running along the north shore.

★**Oakland Museum of California**   MUSEUM
(OMCA; ☑ 888-625-6873, 510-318-8400; www.museumca.org; 1000 Oak St; adult/child 9-17yr $15/6, 1st Sun each month free; ⊘ 11am-5pm Wed-Sun, to 9pm Fri; ▣) Near the southern end of the lake and one block from the Lake Merritt BART station, this museum has rotating exhibitions on artistic and scientific themes, and excellent permanent galleries dedicated to the state's diverse ecology and history, as well as California art. Admission is half-off on Friday nights, when DJs, food trucks and free kids' art workshops made it a fun hangout spot.

Children's Fairyland   AMUSEMENT PARK
(☑ 510-452-2259; www.fairyland.org; 699 Bellevue Ave; admission $8; ⊘ 10am-4pm Mon-Fri, to 5pm Sat & Sun Jun-Aug, off-season hours vary; ▣) Lakeside Park, at the northern end of the saltwater lake, includes this 10-acre attraction, which dates from 1950 and has charming fairy-tale-themed train, carousel and mini Ferris-wheel rides.

Lake Merritt Boating Center   WATER SPORTS
(☑ 510-238-2196; www2.oaklandnet.com; 568 Bellevue Ave; boat rentals per hour $12-24; ⊘ daily Mar-Oct, Sat & Sun only Nov-Feb) Rents canoes, rowboats, kayaks, pedal boats and sailboats.

◉ Piedmont Ave & Rockridge

North of downtown Oakland, Broadway becomes a lengthy strip of car dealerships called Broadway Auto Row. Just past that is **Piedmont Ave**, wall-to-wall with antique stores, coffeehouses, fine restaurants and an art cinema.

One of Oakland's most popular shopping areas is **Rockridge**, a lively, upscale neighborhood. It is centered on College Ave, which runs from Broadway all the way to the UC Berkeley Campus. College Ave is lined with clothing boutiques, good bookstores, several pubs and cafes, and quite a few upscale restaurants – maybe the largest concentration in the Bay Area. BART at the Rockridge station puts you in the thick of things.

Mountain View Cemetery   CEMETERY
(www.mountainviewcemetery.org; 5000 Piedmont Ave; ⊘ 6:30am-7pm) At the end of Piedmont Ave, this is perhaps the most serene and lovely artificial landscape in all the East Bay. Designed by Frederick Law Olmstead, the architect of New York City's Central Park, it's great for walking and the views are stupendous.

◉ Oakland Hills

The large parks of the Oakland Hills are ideal for day hiking and challenging cycling, and the **East Bay Regional Parks District** (www.ebparks.org) manages more than 1200 miles of trails in 65 regional parks, preserves and recreation areas in the Alameda and Contra Costa counties.

Off Hwy 24, **Robert Sibley Volcanic Regional Preserve** is the northernmost of the Oakland Hills parks. It has great views of the Bay Area from its Round Top Peak (1761ft). From Sibley, Skyline Blvd runs south past **Redwood Regional Park** and adjacent **Joaquin Miller Park** to **Anthony Chabot Regional Park**. A hike or mountain-bike ride through the groves and along the hilltops of any of these sizable parks will make you forget you're in an urban area. At the southern end of Chabot Park is the enormous **Lake Chabot**, with an easy trail along its shore and canoes, kayaks and other boats for rent from the **Lake Chabot marina** (☑ 510-247-2526; www.norcalfishing.com/chabot).

Chabot Space & Science Center   SCIENCE CENTER
(☑ 510-336-7300; www.chabotspace.org; 10000 Skyline Blvd; adult/child $16/12; ⊘ 10am-5pm Wed & Thu, to 10pm Fri & Sat, 10am-5pm Sun, plus 10am-5pm Tue summer; ▣) Stargazers will go gaga over this science and technology center in the Oakland Hills with loads of exhibits on subjects such as space travel and eclipses, as well as cool planetarium shows. When the weather's good, check out the free Friday and Saturday evening viewings (7:30pm to 10:30pm) using a 20in refractor telescope.

⌂ Sleeping

If you like B&Bs, the **Berkeley and Oakland Bed & Breakfast Network** (www.bbonline.com/ca/berkeley-oakland) lists private homes that rent rooms, suites and cottages; prices start from $100 per night and many have a two-night-minimum stay. Reservations recommended.

Anthony Chabot Regional Park
CAMPGROUND **$**

(☑ 510-639-4751, reservations 888-327-2757; www.ebparks.org/parks/anthony_chabot; tent sites $25, RV sites with hookups $25-35; ▩) This 5000-acre park has 75 campsites open year-round and hot showers. Reservations ($8 service charge) at www.reserveamerica.com.

Waterfront Hotel
BOUTIQUE HOTEL **$$**

(☑ 510-836-3800; www.waterfronthoteloakland.com; 10 Washington St; r $149-279; ❉ @ ☎ ▩ ▩) Paddle-printed wallpaper and lamps fashioned from faux lanterns round out the playful nautical theme of this bright, cheerful harborside hotel. A huge brass-topped fireplace warms the foyer, and comfy rooms include MP3-players and coffeemakers, plus microwaves and fridges. Unless you're an avid trainspotter, water-view rooms are preferred, as trains rattle by on the city side.

Washington Inn
HISTORIC HOTEL **$$**

(☑ 510-452-1776; www.thewashingtoninn.com; 495 10th St, r incl breakfast $99-140; ❉ @ ▩) Small and modern with a boutique feel, this historic downtown lodging offers guest rooms with character and efficient sophistication. The dramatic high-ceilinged lobby is a wasted opportunity, outfitted with random chairs instead of velvet divans. Still, the carved lobby bar is perfect for a predinner cocktail, and you're spoiled for choice with several fine restaurants within a few blocks' radius.

Claremont Resort & Spa
RESORT **$$$**

(☑ 800-551-7266, 510-843-3000; www.claremonttresort.com; 41 Tunnel Rd; r $215-309, plus $26 nightly resort fee; ❉ @ ☎ ▩ ▩) Oakland's classy crème de la crème, the Claremont is a glamorous white 1915 building with elegant restaurants, a fitness center, swimming pools, tennis courts and a full-service spa (room/spa packages are available). The bay view rooms are superb. It's located at the foot of the Oakland Hills, off Hwy 13 (Tunnel Rd) near Claremont Ave on the Berkeley border.

✕ Eating

Oakland's fun and sophisticated eateries rival those of its neighbor San Francisco.

✕ Uptown, Downtown & Jack London Square

Ratto's
DELI **$**

(www.rattos.com; 821 Washington St; sandwiches from $6; ☺ 8:30am-4:30pm Mon-Fri, 9:30am-3:30pm Sat; ☑) If you want to eat outside on a sunny day, grab a sandwich from Ratto's, a vintage Oakland grocery (since 1897) with a deli counter (and a few sidewalk tables) that attracts a devoted lunch crowd.

Rudy's Can't Fail Cafe
AMERICAN **$$**

(www.iamrudy.com; 1805 Telegraph Ave; mains $9-13; ☺ 7am-1am; ☑ ⬥) A modern diner with tables crafted from board games and strange toys under glass, it has a goofy punk rock feel, possibly because an owner is the bassist from Green Day. Show up for huevos or tofu rancheros all day, or just chow down on a big burger under the gaze of an army of Barbie dolls. Right next to the Fox Theater.

Bocanova
LATIN AMERICAN **$$**

(☑ 510-444-1233; www.bocanova.com; 55 Webster St; mains $12-28; ☺ 11:30am-9:30pm Mon-Thu, 11am-10:30pm Fri & Sat, to 9:30pm Sun) Facing the water at sun-drenched Jack London Sq, you can people-watch from the outdoor patio or eat inside the chic industrial dining room lit by hanging glass lamps. The focus here is Pan-American cuisine, and standouts include the Dungeness crab deviled eggs and scallops in Brazilian curry sauce. Reservations recommended on Wednesday – when wine bottles are half-price – and weekends.

✕ Lake Merritt

Arizmendi
BAKERY **$**

(http://lakeshore.arizmendi.coop; 3265 Lakeshore Ave; pizza slices $2.50; ☺ 7am-7pm Tue-Sat, to 6pm Sun, to 3pm Mon; ☑) Great for breakfast or lunch but beware – this bakery co-op is not for the weak-willed. The gourmet vegetarian pizza, yummy fresh breads and amazing scones are mouthwateringly addictive.

Boot & Shoe Service
PIZZERIA **$$**

(☑ 510-763-2668; www.bootandshoeservice.com; 3308 Grand Ave; pizza from $10; ☺ 5:30-10pm Tue-Thu, 5-10:30pm Fri & Sat, to 10pm Sun) ◖ The name plays off its former identity as a cobbler shop, but the current patrons pack this brick-walled place for its wood-fired pizzas, original cocktails and creative antipasti made from sustainably sourced fresh ingredients.

Lake Chalet
SEAFOOD **$$$**

(☑ 510-208-5253; www.thelakechalet.com; 1520 Lakeside Dr; mains $17-36; ☺ 11am-10pm Mon-Thu, to 11pm Fri, 10am-11pm Sat, 10am-10pm Sun) Whether you stop by the long pump house

BAY AREA BACKPACKING

For an overnight experience in the wilds just outside the city, grab your gear and set off to one of these local jewels. **Sports Basement** (http://community.sportsbasement.com/rentals/camping) and **REI** (www.rei.com) rent all gear.

➡ **Point Reyes National Seashore** (☑ 877-444-6777; www.recreation.gov; tent sites $20) Established hike- and bike-in campgrounds near the ocean; toilets and potable water.

➡ **Henry W Coe State Park** (p132) Where local backpackers set out when snow engulfs the Sierra, this enormous park has miles of hilly backcountry with seasonal ponds and creeks.

➡ **Hawk Camp** (www.nps.gov/goga/planyourvisit/outdooractivities.htm) Remote Marin Headlands' campsite with the requisite bird's-eye views; toilets but no water.

➡ **Angel Island** (p98) So close to the city and yet so far, you can watch the cargo ships thread under the Golden Gate Bridge.

➡ **Ohlone Wilderness Trail** (www.ebparks.org/parks/ohlone) A 28-mile adventure through mountains and canyons in the East Bay.

view bar for a martini and oysters during the buzzing happy hour (3pm to 6pm and 9pm to close), feast on a whole roasted crab by a window seat in the formal dining room, or cruise Lake Merritt on a Venetian-style **gondola** (www.gondolaservizio.com; per couple from $60), this 100-year-old former park office and boathouse is an enjoyable destination restaurant. Weekend reservations recommended.

✖ Piedmont Ave & Rockridge

À Côté   MEDITERRANEAN **$$**
(☑ 510-655-6469; www.acoterestaurant.com; 5478 College Ave; dishes $8-20; ☻5:30-10pm Sun-Tue, to 11pm Wed & Thu, to midnight Fri & Sat) This small-plates eatery with individual and friendly communal tables is one of the best restaurants along College Ave. What the menu calls 'flatbread' is actually pizza for the gods. Mussels with Pernod is a signature dish.

Commis   CALIFORNIAN **$$$**
(☑ 510-653-3902; www.commisrestaurant.com; 3859 Piedmont Ave; 8-course dinner $95; ☻from 5:30pm Wed-Sat, from 5pm Sun; ☑) The only Michelin-starred restaurant in the East Bay, the signless and discreet dining room counts a minimalist decor and some coveted counter real estate (reservable by phone only) where patrons can watch chef James Syhabout and his team piece together creative and innovative dishes. Reservations highly recommended.

✖ Temescal & Emeryville

Emeryville is a separate bite-sized city, wedged between Oakland and south Berkeley on I-80.

Bakesale Betty   SANDWICHES, BAKERY **$**
(www.bakesalebetty.com; 5098 Telegraph Ave; sandwiches $8; ☻11am-2pm Tue-Sat; ☑) An Aussie expat and Chez Panisse alum, Betty Barakat (in signature blue wig) has patrons licking their lips and lining up out the door for her heavenly strawberry shortcake and scrumptious fried-chicken sandwiches. Rolling pins dangle from the ceiling, and blissed-out locals sit down at ironing-board sidewalk tables.

Emeryville Public Market   INTERNATIONAL **$**
(www.publicmarketemeryville.com; 5959 Shellmound St, Emeryville; mains under $10; ☻7am-9pm Mon-Sat, 7am-8pm Sun; ☎) To satisfy a group of finicky eaters, cross the Amtrak tracks to the indoor area and choose from dozens of ethnic food stalls dishing out a huge range of international cuisines.

Homeroom   AMERICAN **$$**
(☑ 510-597-0400; www.homeroom510.com; 400 40th St; mains $9-16; ☻11am-10pm Tue-Sun; ☑☑) ◗ Mac-n-cheese, the ultimate in American comfort food, gets a long-overdue ovation at this quirky restaurant modeled after a school. A menu of regionally focused options – including the Ivy Leaguer Truffle, Dungeness crab, vegan and the spicy Exchange Student Sriracha – are more gour-

met than anything Mom packed for your lunchbox. Six rotating beers on tap.

🍷 Drinking & Nightlife

★ Café Van Kleef   BAR
(📞510-763-7711; www.cafevankleef.com; 1621 Telegraph Ave; ⊙noon-2am Tue-Fri, 4pm-2am Sat-Mon) Order a greyhound (with fresh-squeezed grapefruit juice) and take a gander at the profusion of antique musical instruments, fake taxidermy heads, sprawling formal chandeliers and bizarro ephemera clinging to every surface possible here. Quirky, kitschy and evocative even *before* you get lit, it features live blues, jazz and the occasional rock band on weekends plus DJs and a drag show other nights.

Awaken Cafe   CAFE
(www.awakencafe.com; 1429 Broadway; ⊙7:30am-10pm Mon-Thu, to midnight Fri, 8:30am-midnight Sat, to 7pm Sun; 🛜) The laptop brigade camps out at this central downtown cafe by day, munching wood-fired bagels and drinking fairly traded Four Barrel coffee. But they get sidelined at 5pm, with live Afro-Cuban, folk, R&B and other events (cover free to $15) taking center stage after 7pm.

Beer Revolution   BEER HALL
(www.beer-revolution.com; 464 3rd St; ⊙noon-11pm Mon-Sat, to 9pm Sun) Go ahead and drool. With almost 50 beers on tap, and more than 500 in the bottle, there's a lifetime of discovery ahead, so kick back on the sunny deck or park yourself at that barrel table embedded with bottle caps. Bonuses include no distracting TVs and a punk soundtrack played at conversation-friendly levels. Check Facebook for meet-the-brewer sessions and Sunday barbecues.

Blue Bottle Coffee Company   CAFE
(www.bluebottlecoffee.net; 300 Webster St; ⊙7am-5:30pm Mon-Fri, from 8am Sat & Sun) 🍴 The java gourmands queue up here for single-origin espressos and what some consider the best coffee in the country, and the very origin-specific beans are roasted on site. Its newer cafe (4270 Broadway; ⊙7am-6pm Mon-Fri, 8am-6pm Sat & Sun) in the historic WC Morse Building (a 1920s truck showroom) has two communal tables, lofty ceilings and a minimalist white decor for drinking an espresso or an Oji cold-drip coffee.

Trappist   PUB
(www.thetrappist.com; 460 8th St; ⊙noon-12:30am Sun-Thu, noon-1:30am Fri & Sat) So popular that it busted out of its original brick-and-wood-paneled shoebox and expanded into a second storefront and back terrace, the specialty here is Belgian ales. More than two dozen drafts rotate through the taps, and tasty stews and sandwiches, and seasonal beer-friendly cuisine ($8.50 to $12) make it easy to linger.

Make Westing   COCKTAIL BAR
(www.makewesting.com; 1741 Telegraph Ave; ⊙4pm-2am) Named for a Jack London story, the free indoor bocce ball courts and eclectic cocktails pack this Uptown hotspot on weekends. Toss back a garden gimlet and satiate the munchies with some cilantro and habañero-infused popcorn.

Heinold's First & Last Chance   BAR
(www.heinolds.com; 48 Webster St; ⊙3-11pm Mon, noon-11pm Tue-Sun, to midnight Fri & Sat) An 1883 bar constructed from wood scavenged from an old whaling ship, you really have to hold on to your beer here. Keeled to a severe slant during the 1906 earthquake, the building's 20% grade might make you feel self-conscious about stumbling before you even order. Its big claim to fame is that author Jack London was a regular patron.

Tribune Tavern   BAR
(www.tribunetavern.com; 401 13th St; ⊙11:30am-10pm Mon-Fri, 10:30am-11pm Sat & Sun) For sophisticated downtown drinks under a pressed-tin ceiling and Edison lights, head to the 1923 Tribune Tower, an Oakland icon with a red-neon clock and former home of the *Oakland Tribune* newspaper.

PINBALL WIZARDS, UNITE!

Put down that video game console, cast aside your latest phone app, and return to the bygone days of pinball play. Lose yourself in bells and flashing lights at **Pacific Pinball Museum** (📞510-769-1349; www.pacificpinball.org; 1510 Webster St, Alameda; adult/child under 16 $15/7.50; ⊙2-9pm Tue-Thu, to midnight Fri, 11am-midnight Sat, to 9pm Sun; 🚼), a pinball parlor with almost 100 games dating from the 1930s to the present, and vintage jukeboxes playing hits from the past. Take AC Transit bus 51A from downtown Oakland.

☆ Entertainment

A monthly street festival, **Oakland First Fridays** (www.oaklandfirstfridays.org) takes place between 5pm and 9pm on the first Friday of the month. Telegraph Ave between 27th St and W Grand Ave closes to car traffic, with thousands turning out for food vendors, live music and performances. There's a concurrent gallery-hop called **Oakland Art Murmur** (www.oaklandartmurmur.com; ⊘6-9pm), which also coordinates a more low-key Saturday Stroll in the afternoons every week.

Music

Uptown   LIVE MUSIC
(☑510-451-8100; www.uptownnightclub.com; 1928 Telegraph Ave; admission free-$20; ⊘Tue-Sun) For an eclectic calendar of indie, punk and experimental sounds, burlesque shows and fun DJ dance parties, this club hits the spot. Come for a good mix of national acts and local talent, and the easy two-block walk to BART.

Yoshi's   JAZZ
(☑510-238-9200; www.yoshis.com/oakland; 510 Embarcadero West; admission $15-49) Yoshi's has a solid jazz calendar, with talent from around the world passing through on a near-nightly basis. Often, touring artists will stop in for a stand of two or three nights. It's also a Japanese restaurant, so you might enjoy a sushi plate before the show. Some events have half-price tickets for students and seniors.

Luka's Taproom & Lounge   DJ
(www.lukasoakland.com; 2221 Broadway; ⊘DJs Wed-Sun) Go Uptown to get down. DJs spin nightly at this popular restaurant and lounge, with a soulful mix of hip-hop, reggae, funk and house. There's generally a $10 cover on Fridays and Saturdays after 11pm.

Theaters & Cinemas

The Fox Theater is the nucleus of evening activity in the Uptown district, with hip restaurants and bars clustered nearby.

Fox Theater   THEATER
(www.thefoxoakland.com; 1807 Telegraph Ave) A phoenix arisen from the urban ashes, this restored 1928 art-deco stunner adds dazzle to downtown and is a cornerstone of the happening Uptown theater district. It's a popular concert venue for national and international acts.

Paramount Theatre   THEATER
(☑510-465-6400; www.paramounttheatre.com; 2025 Broadway) This massive 1931 art-deco masterpiece shows classic films a few times each month and is also home to the **Oakland East Bay Symphony** (www.oebs.org) and **Oakland Ballet** (www.oaklandballet.org). It periodically books big-name concerts. Tours ($5) are given at 10am on the first and third Saturdays of the month.

Grand Lake Theatre   CINEMA
(☑510-452-3556; www.renaissancerialto.com; 3200 Grand Ave) In Lake Merritt, this 1926 beauty lures you in with its huge corner marquee (which sometimes displays left-leaning political messages) and keeps you coming back with a fun balcony and a Wurlitzer organ playing the pipes on weekends.

New Parkway Theater   CINEMA
(☑510-658-7900; www.thenewparkway.com; 474 24th St) This great, laid-back moviehouse shows quality second-run films in a comfy couch setting, and serves reasonably priced beer, wine, sandwiches and pizza, with delivery to your seat.

Sports

Sports teams play at the (insert most recent and ever-changing corporate branding) **Coliseum** or the **Oracle Arena** off I-880 (Coliseum/Oakland Airport BART station). Cheer on the Golden State Warriors, the Bay Area's NBA basketball team, the Oakland A's, the Bay Area's American League baseball team, and the Raiders, Oakland's NFL team; see www.coliseum.com for listings of upcoming events.

ℹ Information

Oakland's daily newspaper is the *Oakland Tribune* (www.insidebayarea.com/oakland-tribune). The free weekly *East Bay Express* (www.eastbay-express.com) has good Oakland and Berkeley listings.

Visit Oakland Visitor Center (☑510-839-9000; www.visitoakland.org; 481 Water St; ⊘9:30am-4pm Tue-Sun) At Jack London Sq.

ℹ Getting There & Away

AIR

Oakland International Airport (p50700) is directly across the bay from San Francisco International Airport, and it's usually less crowded and less expensive to fly here. Southwest Airlines has a large presence.

BART

Within the Bay Area, the most convenient way to get to Oakland and back is by **BART** (☎ 510-465-2278, 511; www.bart.gov). Trains run on a set schedule from 4am to midnight on weekdays, 6am to midnight on Saturday and 8am to midnight on Sunday, and operate at 15- or 20-minute intervals on average.

To get to downtown Oakland, catch a Richmond or Pittsburg/Bay Point train. Fares to the 12th or 19th St stations from downtown San Francisco are $3.30. From San Francisco to Lake Merritt or the Oakland Coliseum/Airport station, catch a BART train that is heading for Fremont or Dublin/Pleasanton. Rockridge is on the Pittsburg/Bay Point line. Between Oakland and downtown Berkeley you can catch a Fremont-Richmond train.

For AC Transit bus connections, take a transfer from the white AC Transit machines in the BART station to save 25¢ off the bus fare.

BUS

Regional company **AC Transit** (☎ 511, 510-817-1717; www.actransit.org; day pass $5) runs convenient buses from San Francisco's Transbay Temporary Terminal at Howard and Main Streets to downtown Oakland and Berkeley, and between the two East Bay cities. Scores of buses go to Oakland from San Francisco during commute hours ($4.20), but only the 'O' line runs both ways all day and on weekends; you can catch the 'O' line at the corner of 5th and Washington Sts in downtown Oakland.

After BART trains stop, late-night transportation between San Francisco and Oakland is with the 800 line, which runs hourly from downtown Market St and the Transbay Temporary Terminal in San Francisco to the corner of 14th St and Broadway.

Between Berkeley and downtown Oakland ($2.10) on weekdays, take the fast and frequent 1R bus along Telegraph Ave between the two city centers. Alternatively, take bus 18 that runs via Martin Luther King Jr Way daily.

Greyhound (☎ 510-832-4730; www.greyhound.com; 2103 San Pablo Ave) operates direct buses from Oakland to Vallejo, San Jose, Santa Rosa and Sacramento. The station is pretty seedy. Discount carrier **Megabus** (across from the south entrance to W Oakland BART station) has daily service to Los Angeles (seven hours), departing from opposite the south entrance to W Oakland BART station.

CAR & MOTORCYCLE

From San Francisco by car, cross the Bay Bridge and enter Oakland via one of two ways: I-580, which leads to I-980 and drops you near the City Center; or I-880, which curves through West Oakland and lets you off near the south end of Broadway. I-880 then continues to the Coliseum, the Oakland International Airport and, eventually, San Jose.

Driving to San Francisco, the bridge toll is $4 to $6, depending on the time and day of the week.

FERRY

With splendid bay views, ferries are the most enjoyable way of traveling between San Francisco and Oakland, though also the slowest and most expensive. From San Francisco's Ferry Building, the **Alameda–Oakland ferry** (☎ 510-522-3300; www.sanfranciscobayferry.com) sails to Jack London Sq (one-way $6.25, 30 minutes, about a dozen times a day, and also departing from Pier 41 on weekends). Ferry tickets include a free transfer, which you can use on AC Transit buses from Jack London Sq.

TRAIN

Oakland is a regular stop for Amtrak trains operating up and down the coast. From Oakland's **Amtrak station** (☎ 800-872-7245; www.amtrak.com; 245 2nd St) in Jack London Sq, you can catch AC Transit bus 72 to downtown Oakland (and the free Broadway Shuttle on weekdays and Saturday night), or take a ferry across the bay to San Francisco.

Amtrak passengers with reservations on to San Francisco need to disembark at the Emeryville Amtrak station, one stop away from Oakland. From there, an Amtrak bus shuttles you to San Francisco's Ferry Building stop. The free **Emery Go Round** (www.emerygoround.com) shuttle runs a circuit that includes the **Emeryville Amtrak station** (☎ 800-872-7245; www.amtrak.com; 5885 Horton St) and MacArthur BART. Emeryville is also the terminus for the California Zephyr (9:10am, one daily departure) to Chicago via Reno, Salt Lake City and Denver.

ⓘ Getting Around

TO/FROM THE AIRPORT

BART is the cheapest and easiest transportation option. From the Coliseum/Oakland Airport BART, the new Oakland Airport Connector train ($6, 15 minutes) runs directly to the airport every five minutes during BART hours.

SuperShuttle (☎ 800-258-3826; www.supershuttle.com) is one of many door-to-door shuttle services operating out of Oakland International Airport. One-way service to San Francisco destinations costs about $27 for the first person and $15 for the second. East Bay service destinations are also served. Reserve ahead.

A taxi from Oakland International Airport to downtown Oakland costs about $30; to downtown San Francisco about $60.

BUS

AC Transit (p117) has a comprehensive bus network within Oakland. Fares are $2.10 and exact change is required.

The free **Broadway Shuttle** (www.meetdowntownoak.com/shuttle.php; ☉7am-7pm Mon-Fri, to 1am Fri, 6pm-1am Sat) runs down Broadway between Jack London Sq and Lake Merritt, stopping at Old Oakland/Chinatown, the downtown BART stations and the Uptown district. The lime-green buses arrive every 10 to 15 minutes.

Berkeley

As the birthplace of the free speech and disability rights movements, and the home of the hallowed halls of the University of California, Berkeley is no bashful wallflower. A national hotspot of (mostly left-of-center) intellectual discourse and one of the most vocal activist populations in the country, this infamous college town has an interesting mix of graying progressives and idealistic undergrads. It's easy to stereotype 'Beserkeley' for some of its recycle-or-else PC crankiness, but the city is often on the forefront of environmental and political issues that eventually go mainstream.

Berkeley is also home to a large South Asian community, as evidenced by an abundance of sari shops on University Ave and a large number of excellent Indian restaurants.

◉ Sights & Activities

Approximately 13 miles east of San Francisco, Berkeley is bordered by the bay to the west, the hills to the east and Oakland to the south. I-80 runs along the town's western edge, next to the marina; from here University Ave heads east to downtown and the campus.

Shattuck Ave crosses University Ave one block west of campus, forming the main crossroads of the downtown area. Immediately to the south is the downtown shopping strip and the downtown Berkeley BART station.

◉ University of California, Berkeley

The Berkeley campus of the University of California (UCB, called 'Cal' by both students and locals) is the oldest university in the state. The decision to found the college was made in 1866, and the first students arrived in 1873. Today UCB has more than 35,000 students, more than 1500 professors and more Nobel laureates than you could point a particle accelerator at.

From Telegraph Ave, enter the campus via Sproul Plaza and Sather Gate, a center for people-watching, soapbox oration and pseudotribal drumming. Or you can enter from Center St and Oxford Lane, near the downtown BART station.

★ UC Berkeley Art Museum   MUSEUM

(☑510-642-0808; www.bampfa.berkeley.edu; 2626 Bancroft Way; adult/child $10/7; ☉11am-5pm Wed-Sun) The museum has 11 galleries showcasing a huge range of works, from ancient Chinese to cutting-edge contemporary. The complex also houses a bookstore, cafe and sculpture garden. The museum and the much-loved Pacific Film Archive are scheduled to move to a new home on Oxford St between Addison and Center Streets in 2016.

★ Campanile   LANDMARK

(Sather Tower; adult/child $3/2; ☉10am-3:45pm Mon-Fri, to 4:45pm Sat, 10am-1:30pm & 3-4:45pm Sun; ☒) Officially called Sather Tower, the Campanile was modeled on St Mark's Basilica in Venice. The 328ft spire offers fine views of the Bay Area, and at the top you can stare up into the carillon of 61 bells, ranging from the size of a cereal bowl to that of a Volkswagen. Recitals take place daily at 7:50am, noon and 6pm, with a longer piece performed at 2pm on Sunday.

Museum of Paleontology   MUSEUM

(☑510-642-1821; www.ucmp.berkeley.edu; ☉8am-10pm Mon-Thu, to 5pm Fri, 10am-5pm Sat, 1-10pm Sun) FREE Housed in the ornate Valley Life Sciences Building (and primarily a research facility that's closed to the public), you can see a number of fossil exhibits in the atrium, including a *Tyrannosaurus rex* skeleton.

Bancroft Library   LIBRARY

(☑510-642-3781; www.bancroft.berkeley.edu; ☉10am-5pm Mon-Fri) The Bancroft houses, among other gems, the papers of Mark Twain, a copy of Shakespeare's First Folio and the records of the Donner Party. Its small public exhibits of historical Californiana include the surprisingly small gold nugget that sparked the 1849 Gold Rush. To register to use the library, you must be 18 years or older (or a high school graduate) and present two forms of identification (one with a photo). The registration desk is on your way in.

Phoebe A Hearst Museum of Anthropology
MUSEUM

(📞510-643-7648; http://hearstmuseum.berkeley. edu; Kroeber Hall) South of the Campanile in Kroeber Hall, this museum includes exhibits from indigenous cultures around the world, including ancient Peruvian, Egyptian and African items. There's also a large collection highlighting native Californian cultures. Closed for renovations until 2015.

👁 South of Campus

Telegraph Ave
STREET

Telegraph Ave has traditionally been the throbbing heart of studentville in Berkeley, the sidewalks crowded with undergrads, postdocs and youthful shoppers squeezing their way past throngs of vendors, buskers and homeless people. Numerous cafes and budget food options cater to students, and most of them are very good.

The frenetic energy buzzing from the university's Sather Gate on any given day is a mixture of youthful posthippies reminiscing about days before their time and young hipsters and punk rockers who sneer at tie-dyed nostalgia. Panhandlers press you for change, and street stalls hawk everything from crystals to bumper stickers to self-published tracts.

People's Park
PARK

This park, just east of Telegraph, between Haste St and Dwight Way, is a marker in local history as a political battleground between residents and the city and state government in the late 1960s. The park has since served mostly as a gathering spot for Berkeley's homeless. A publicly funded restoration spruced it up a bit, and occasional festivals do still happen here, but it's rather run-down.

Elmwood District
NEIGHBORHOOD

South along College Ave is the Elmwood District, a charming nook of shops and restaurants that offers a calming alternative to the frenetic buzz around Telegraph Ave. Continue further south and you'll be in Rockridge.

First Church of Christ Scientist
CHURCH

(www.friendsoffirstchurch.org; 2619 Dwight Way; ☺services Sun) Bernard Maybeck's impressive 1910 church uses concrete and wood in its blend of Arts and Crafts, Asian and Gothic influences. Maybeck was a professor of architecture at UC Berkeley and designed San Francisco's Palace of Fine Arts, plus many landmark homes in the Berkeley Hills. Free tours happen the first Sunday of every month at 12:15pm.

Julia Morgan Theatre
THEATER

(📞510-845-8542; 2640 College Ave) To the southeast of People's Park is this beautifully understated, redwood-infused 1910 theater, a performance space (formerly a church) created by Bay Area architect Julia Morgan. She designed numerous Bay Area buildings and, most famously, the Hearst Castle.

⊙ Downtown

Berkeley's downtown, centered on Shattuck Ave between University Ave and Dwight Way, has far fewer traces of the city's tie-

MARIN COUNTY & THE BAY AREA BERKELEY

WATER SPORTS ON THE BAY

The San Francisco Bay makes a lovely postcard or snapshot, and there are myriad outfits to help you play in it.

California Canoe & Kayak (📞510-893-7833; www.calkayak.com; 409 Water St, Oakland; rental per hour single/double kayak $20/30, canoe $30, stand-up paddleboard $20; ☺10am-6pm) Rents kayaks, canoes and stand-up paddleboards at Oakland's Jack London Sq.

Cal Adventures (📞510-642-4000; www.recsports.berkeley.edu; 124 University Ave, Berkeley; 👤) Run by the UC Berkeley Aquatic Center and located at the Berkeley Marina, Cal offers sailing, windsurfing and sea-kayaking classes and rentals for adults and youth.

Cal Sailing Club (www.cal-sailing.org; Berkeley Marina) An affordable membership-based and volunteer-run nonprofit with sailing and windsurfing programs, based at the Berkeley Marina.

Boardsports School & Shop (www.boardsportsschool.com) Offers lessons and rentals for kiteboarding, windsurfing and stand-up paddleboarding from its three locations in San Francisco, Alameda (East Bay) and Coyote Point.

Sea Trek Kayak & SUP (p96) Located in Sausalito, it has kayaking and stand-up paddleboards, and a fabulous full moon paddle tour.

Central Berkeley

dyed reputation. The area has emerged as an exciting arts district with numerous shops and restaurants and restored public buildings. At the center are the acclaimed thespian stomping grounds of the Berkeley Repertory Theatre and the Aurora Theatre Company and live music at the Freight & Salvage Coffeehouse; a few good movie houses are also nearby.

North Berkeley

Not too far north of campus is a neighborhood filled with lovely garden-front homes, parks and some of the best restaurants in California. The popular **Gourmet Ghetto** stretches along Shattuck Ave north of University Ave for several blocks, anchored by Chez Panisse. Northwest of here, **Solano Ave**, which crosses from Berkeley into Albany, is lined with lots of funky shops and more good restaurants.

On Euclid Ave just south of Eunice St is the **Berkeley Rose Garden** and its eight terraces of colorful explosions. Here you'll find quiet benches and a plethora of almost perpetually blooming roses arranged by hue. Across the street is a picturesque park with a

Central Berkeley

children's playground (including a very fun concrete slide, about 100ft long).

◉ The Berkeley Hills

Tilden Regional Park   PARK
(www.ebparks.org/parks/tilden) This 2079-acre park, in the hills east of town, is Berkeley's crown jewel. It has more than 30 miles of trails of varying difficulty, from paved paths to hilly scrambles, including part of the magnificent Bay Area Ridge Trail. There's also a miniature steam train ($3), a children's farm, a wonderfully wild-looking botanical garden, an 18-hole **golf course** (☑510-848-7373) and environmental education center. **Lake Anza** is good for picnics, and from spring through late fall you can swim ($3.50).

AC Transit bus 67 runs to the park on weekends and holidays from the downtown BART station, but only stops at the entrances on weekdays.

UC Botanical Garden at Berkeley   GARDENS
(☑510-643-2755; www.botanicalgarden.berkeley.edu; 200 Centennial Dr; adult/child $10/2; ⊙9am-5pm, closed 1st Tue each month) With 34 acres and more than 12,000 species of plants in the Strawberry Canyon hills, the garden is one of the most varied collections in the USA.

A fire trail is a woodsy walking loop around Strawberry Canyon that has great views of town and the off-limits Lawrence Berkeley National Laboratory. Enter at the trailhead at the parking lot on Centennial Dr just southwest of the Botanical Garden; you'll emerge near the Lawrence Hall of Science.

The garden can be reached via the Bear Transit shuttle H line.

Lawrence Hall of Science   SCIENCE CENTER
(☑510-642-5132; www.lawrencehallofscience.org; Centennial Dr; adult/senior & child 7-8/child 3-6 $12/9/6; ⊙10am-5pm daily; ⓐ) Near Grizzly Peak Blvd, the science hall is named after Ernest Lawrence, who won the Nobel Prize for his invention of the cyclotron particle accelerator. He was a key member of the WWII Manhattan Project, and he's also the name behind the Lawrence Berkeley and Lawrence Livermore laboratories. The Hall of Science has interactive exhibits for kids and adults (many closed on weekdays) on subjects ranging from earthquakes to nanotechnology, and outside there's a 60ft model of a DNA molecule.

AC Transit bus 65 runs to the hall from the downtown BART station. You can also catch the university's Bear Transit shuttle (H line) from the Hearst Mining Circle.

⊙ West Berkeley

Berkeley Marina   MARINA
At the west end of University Ave is the marina, frequented by squawking seagulls, silent types fishing from the pier, unleashed dogs and, especially on windy weekends, lots of colorful kites. First construction began in 1936, though the pier has much older origins. It was originally built in the 1870s, then replaced by a 3-mile-long ferry pier in 1920 (its length dictated by the bay's extreme shallowness). Part of the original pier is now rebuilt, affording visitors sweeping bay views.

Adventure Playground   PLAYGROUND
(☑510-981-6720; www.cityofberkeley.info/adventureplayground; ☺11am-5pm Sat & Sun & daily mid-Jun–mid-Aug, closed last week of year; ⛵) At the Berkeley Marina, this is one of the coolest play spaces in the country – a free outdoor park encouraging creativity and cooperation where supervised kids of any age can help build and paint their own structures. There's an awesome zip line too. Dress the tykes in play clothes, because they *will* get dirty.

San Pablo Ave   STREET
Formerly US Rte 40, this was the main thoroughfare from the east before I-80 came along. The area north of University Ave is still lined with a few older motels, diners and atmospheric dive bars with neon signs. South of University Ave are pockets of trendiness, such as the short stretch of gift shops and cafes around Dwight Way.

4th St Shopping District   NEIGHBORHOOD
Hidden within an industrial area near I-80 lies a three-block area offering shaded sidewalks for upscale shopping or just strolling, and a few good restaurants.

Takara Sake   MUSEUM
(www.takarasake.com; 708 Addison St; ☺noon-6pm) FREE Stop in to see the traditional wooden tools used for making sake and a short video of the brewing process. Tours of the factory aren't offered, but you can view elements of modern production and bottling through a window. Flights ($5) are available in a spacious tasting room constructed with reclaimed wood and floor tiles fashioned from recycled glass.

🛏 Sleeping

Lodging rates spike during special university events such as graduation (mid-May) and home football games. A number of older motels along University Ave can be handy during peak demand. For B&B options, look up the **Berkeley & Oakland Bed & Breakfast Network** (www.bbonline.com).

YMCA   HOSTEL $
(☑510-848-6800; www.ymca-cba.org/locations/downtown-berkeley-hotel; 2001 Allston Way; s/d with shared bath from $49/81; @🛜🏊) The 100-year-old downtown Y building is still the best budget option in town. Rates for the austere private rooms (all with shared bathroom) include use of the sauna, pool and fitness center, and kitchen facilities, and wheelchair-accessible rooms are available as well. Corner rooms 310 and 410 boast enviable bay views. Entrance on Milvia St.

Berkeley City Club   HISTORIC HOTEL $$
(☑510-848-7800; www.berkeleycityclub.com; 2315 Durant Ave; r/ste incl breakfast from $165; @🛜🏊) Designed by Julia Morgan, the architect of Hearst Castle, the 35 rooms and dazzling common areas of this refurbished 1929 historic landmark building (which is also a private club) feel like a glorious time warp into a more refined era. The hotel contains lush and serene Italianate courtyards, gardens and terraces, and a stunning indoor pool.

Elegant Old World rooms contain no TVs, and those with numbers ending in 4 and 8 have to-die-for views of the bay and the Golden Gate Bridge.

Bancroft Hotel   HISTORIC HOTEL $$
(☑800-549-1002, 510-549-1000; www.bancrofthotel.com; 2680 Bancroft Way; r incl breakfast $135-179; @🛜) 🌿 A gorgeous 1928 Arts and Crafts building that was originally a women's club, the Bancroft is just across the street from campus and two blocks from Telegraph Ave. It has 22 comfortable, beautifully furnished rooms (number 302 boasts a lovely balcony) and a spectacular bay-view rooftop, though no elevator.

Rose Garden Inn   INN $$
(☑800-922-9005, 510-549-2145; www.rosegardeninn.com; 2740 Telegraph Ave; r incl breakfast from $138; @🛜) The decor flirting with flowery, this cute place is a few blocks south from the Telegraph Ave action and very

peaceful, with two old houses surrounded by pretty gardens.

Downtown Berkeley Inn
MOTEL $$

(☎510-843-4043; www.downtownberkeleyinn. com; 2001 Bancroft Way; r $79-129; ❄🛜) A 27-room budget boutique-style motel with good-sized rooms and correspondingly ample flat-screen TVs.

★Hotel Shattuck Plaza
HOTEL $$$

(☎510-845-7300; www.hotelshattuckplaza.com; 2086 Allston Way; r from $195; ❄@🛜) Peace is quite posh following a $15-million renovation and greening of this 100-year-old downtown jewel. A foyer of red Italian glass lighting, flocked Victorian-style wallpaper – and yes, a peace sign tiled into the floor – leads to comfortable rooms with down comforters, and an airy, columned restaurant serving all meals. Accommodations off Shattuck are quietest; cityscape rooms boast bay views.

Hotel Durant
BOUTIQUE HOTEL $$$

(☎510-845-8981; www.hoteldurant.com; 2600 Durant Ave; r from $209; @🛜) 🍽 Located a block from campus, this classic 1928 hotel has been cheekily renovated to highlight the connection to the university. The lobby is adorned with embarrassing yearbook photos and a ceiling mobile of exam books, and smallish rooms have dictionary-covered shower curtains and bongs repurposed into bedside lamps.

🍴 Eating

Telegraph Ave is packed with cafes, pizza counters and cheap restaurants, and Berkeley's Little India runs along the University Ave corridor. Many more restaurants can be found downtown along Shattuck Ave near the BART station. The section of Shattuck Ave north of University Ave is the 'Gourmet Ghetto,' with lots of excellent eating.

🍴 Downtown & Around Campus

Berkeley Farmers Market
MARKET $

(cnr Center St & MLK Way; ⊙10am-3pm Sat) Pick up some organic produce or tasty prepared food at the downtown farmers market, operating year-round, and sit down to munch at MLK Park across from city hall.

Au Coquelet Café
CAFE $

(www.aucoquelet.com; 2000 University Ave; mains $7-13; ⊙6am-1:30am Sun-Thu, to 2am Fri & Sat; 🛜) Open till late, Au Coquelet is a popu-

lar stop for postmovie meals or late-night studying. The front section serves coffee and pastries while the skylit and spacious back room does a big range of omelets, pastas, sandwiches, burgers and salads.

★Ippuku
JAPANESE $$

(☎510-665-1969; www.ippukuberkeley.com; 2130 Center St; small plates $5-18; ⊙Sun-Thu 5-10pm, to 11pm Fri & Sat) Specializing in *shochu* (flights $12), a distilled alcohol made from rice, barley or sweet potato, Japanese expats gush that Ippuku reminds them of *izakayas* (pub-style restaurants) back in Tokyo. Choose from a menu of skewered meats and settle in at one of the traditional wood platform tables (no shoes, please) or cozy booth perches. Reservations essential.

Gather
CALIFORNIAN $$

(☎510-809-0400; www.gatherrestaurant.com; 2200 Oxford St; mains lunch $11-19, dinner $15-25; ⊙11:30am-2pm Mon-Fri, from 10am Sat & Sun, & 5-10pm daily; 🍽) 🍃 When vegan foodies and passionate farm-to-table types dine out together, they often end up here. Inside a salvaged wood interior punctuated by green vines streaking down over an open kitchen, patrons swoon over dishes created from locally sourced ingredients and sustainably raised meats. Reserve for dinner.

La Note
FRENCH $$

(☎510-843-1535; www.lanoterestaurant.com; 2377 Shattuck Ave; breakast mains $10-14, dinner $15-20; ⊙8am-2:30pm Mon-Fri, to 3pm Sat & Sun, & 6-10pm Thu-Sat) A rustic country-French bistro downtown, La Note serves excellent breakfasts. Wake up to a big bowl of café au lait, paired with oatmeal raspberry pancakes or lemon gingerbread pancakes with poached pears. Anticipate a wait on weekends.

🍴 North Berkeley

Cheese Board Pizza
PIZZERIA $

(www.cheeseboardcollective.coop; 1512 Shattuck Ave; slice/half-pizza $2.50/10; ⊙7am-8pm Tue-Sat; 🍽) Stop in to take stock of the more than 300 cheeses available at this worker-owned business, and scoop up some fresh bread to make a picnic lunch. Or sit down for a slice of the fabulously crispy one-option-per-day veggie pizza just next door, where live music's often featured.

★Chez Panisse
CALIFORNIAN $$$

(☎cafe 510-548-5049, restaurant 510-548-5525; www.chezpanisse.com; 1517 Shattuck Ave; cafe dinner mains $22-30, restaurant prix-fixe dinner $65-100; ⊘ cafe 11:30am-2:45pm & 5-10:30pm Mon-Thu, to 3pm & to 11:30pm Fri & Sat; restaurant seatings 5:30-6pm & 8-8:45pm Mon-Thu & half hour later Fri & Sat) 🍴 Foodies come to worship here at the church of Alice Waters, the inventor of California cuisine. It's in a lovely Arts and Crafts house in the Gourmet Ghetto, and you can choose to pull all the stops with a prix-fixe meal downstairs, or go less expensive and a tad less formal in the cafe upstairs. Reservations accepted one month ahead.

The restaurant is as good and popular as it ever was, and despite its fame, the place has retained a welcoming atmosphere.

🍴 West Berkeley

Vik's Chaat Corner   INDIAN $
(☎ 644 4432; www.vikschaatcorner.com; 2390 4th St, at Channing Way; dishes $5-8; ⊘ 11am-6pm Mon-Thu, to 8pm Fri-Sun; 🚗) 🍴 This longtime and very popular *chaat* house has moved to a larger space but still gets mobbed at lunchtime by regulars that include an equal number of hungry office workers and Indian families. Try a *cholle* (spicy garbanzo curry) or one of the many filling *dosas* (savory crepes) on the weekend menu. It's one block east of the waterfront.

Bette's Oceanview Diner   DINER $$
(www.bettesdiner.com; 1807 4th St; mains $6-13; ⊘ 6:30am-2:30pm Mon-Fri, to 4pm Sat & Sun) A buzzing breakfast spot, especially on the weekends, serving yummy baked soufflé pancakes and German-style potato pancakes with applesauce, plus eggs and sandwiches. Superfresh food and a nifty diner interior make it worth the wait. It's about a block north of University Ave.

🍷 Drinking & Nightlife

Caffe Strada   CAFE
(2300 College Ave; ⊘ 6am-midnight; 🛜) A popular, student-saturated hangout with an inviting shaded patio and strong espressos. Try the signature white-chocolate mocha.

Torpedo Room   BEER HALL
(www.sierranevada.com/brewery/california/torpedoroom; 2031 4th St; ⊘ 11am-8pm Tue-Sat, noon-5pm Sun) Sample a flight of 4 oz pours ($2 each) from the sixteen rotating drafts on tap at Sierra Nevada brewery's new tasting room. No pints are served, but growlers are available to go, and a small selection of bar snacks helps keep you fortified. It's one block south of University Ave.

Jupiter   PUB
(www.jupiterbeer.com; 2181 Shattuck Ave; ⊘ 11:30am-1am Mon-Thu, 11:30am-1:30am Fri, noon-1:30am Sat, noon-midnight Sun) This downtown pub has loads of regional microbrews, a beer garden, good pizza and live bands most nights. Sit upstairs for a bird's-eye view of bustling Shattuck Ave.

Albatross   PUB
(www.albatrosspub.com; 1822 San Pablo Ave; ⊘ 6pm-2am Sun-Tue, 4:30pm-2am Wed-Sat) A block north of University Ave, Berkeley's oldest pub is one of the most inviting and friendly in the entire Bay Area. Some serious darts are played here, and boardgames will be going on around many of the worn-out tables. Sunday is Pub Quiz night.

Triple Rock Brewery & Ale House   BREWERY
(www.triplerock.com; 1920 Shattuck Ave; ⊘ 11:30am-1am Mon-Wed, to 2am Thu-Sat, to midnight Sun) Opened in 1986, Triple Rock was one of the country's first brewpubs. The house beers and pub grub are quite good, and the antique wooden bar and rooftop sun deck are delightful.

Guerilla Café   CAFE
(☎ 510-845-2233; www.guerillacafe.com; 1620 Shattuck Ave; ⊘ 7am-2pm Mon, 7am-4:30pm Tue-Fri, 8am-4:30pm Sat & Sun) 🍴 Exuding a 1970s flavor, this small and sparkling cafe has a creative political vibe, with polka-dot tiles on the counter handmade by one of the artist-owners, and order numbers spotlighting guerillas and liberation revolutionaries. Organic and Fair Trade ingredients feature in the breakfasts and panini sandwiches, and locally roasted Blue Bottle coffee is served.

☆ Entertainment

The arts corridor on Addison St between Milvia and Shattuck Sts anchors a lively downtown entertainment scene.

Live Music
Berkeley has plenty of intimate live-music venues. Cover charges range from $5 to $20, and a number of venues are all-ages or 18-and-over.

Freight & Salvage Coffeehouse   FOLK, WORLD
(☎ 510-644-2020; www.thefreight.org; 2020 Addison St; ♿) This legendary club has almost 50 years of history and is conveniently located

in the downtown arts district. It features great traditional folk and world music and welcomes all ages, with half-price tickets for patrons under 21.

La Peña Cultural Center
WORLD

(☑510-849-2568; www.lapena.org; 3105 Shattuck Ave) A few blocks east of the Ashby BART station, this cultural center and Chilean cafe presents dynamic musical and visual arts programming with a peace and justice bent. Look for the vibrant mural on its facade.

Ashkenaz
FOLK, WORLD

(☑510-525-5054; www.ashkenaz.com; 1317 San Pablo Ave; 🖐) Ashkenaz is a 'music and dance community center' attracting activists, hippies and fans of folk, swing and world music who love to dance (lessons offered).

924 Gilman
PUNK ROCK

(www.924gilman.org; 924 Gilman St; ⊘Fri-Sun) This volunteer-run and booze-free all-ages space is a West Coast punk rock institution. From Berkeley BART, take AC Transit bus 25 to Gilman and 8th Sts.

Cinemas

Pacific Film Archive
CINEMA

(PFA; ☑510-642-5249; www.bampfa.berkeley.edu; 2575 Bancroft Way; adult/child $9.50/6.50) A renowned film center with an ever-changing schedule of international and classic films, cineasts should seek this place out. The spacious theater has seats that are comfy enough for hours-long movie marathons.

Theater & Dance

Zellerbach Hall
PERFORMING ARTS

(☑510-642-9988; http://tickets.berkeley.edu) On the south end of campus near Bancroft Way and Dana St, Zellerbach Hall features dance events, concerts and performances of all types by national and international artists. The on-site **Cal Performances Ticket Office** sells tickets without a handling fee.

Berkeley Repertory Theatre
THEATER

(☑510-647-2949; www.berkeleyrep.org; 2025 Addison St; tickets $35-100) This highly respected company has produced bold versions of classical and modern plays since 1968. Most shows have half-price tickets for patrons under 30.

California Shakespeare Theater
THEATER

(☑510-548-9666; www.calshakes.org; box office 701 Heinz Ave) Headquartered in Berkeley, with a fantastic outdoor amphitheater further east in Orinda, 'Cal Shakes' is a warm-weather tradition of al fresco Shakespeare (and other classic) productions, with a season that lasts from about June through September.

Aurora Theatre Company
THEATER

(☑510-843-4822; www.auroratheatre.org; 2081 Addison St) An intimate downtown theater, it performs contemporary and thought-provoking plays staged with a subtle chamber-theater aesthetic.

Marsh
PERFORMING ARTS

(☑510-704-8291; www.themarsh.org; 2120 Allston Way) The 'breeding ground for new performance' in Berkeley has eclectic solo and comedy acts.

Shotgun Players
THEATER

(☑510-841-6500; www.shotgunplayers.org; 1901 Ashby Avenue) ✐ The country's first all-solar-powered theater company stages exciting

WHERE THE EARTH MOVED

Curious to find a few places where the earth shook? Visit these notorious spots in and around the Bay Area:

➡ **Earthquake Trail**, at Point Reyes National Seashore, shows the effects of the big one in 1906.

➡ **Cypress Freeway Memorial Park**, at 14th St and Mandela Parkway, commemorates the forty-two people that died and those who helped rescue survivors when the Cypress Freeway collapsed in West Oakland, one of the most horrifying and enduring images of the 1989 Loma Prieta quake.

➡ In the **Forest of Nisene Marks State Park** (☑831-763-7062; www.parks.ca.gov/?page_id=666; parking $8), near Aptos in Santa Cruz County, a sign on the Aptos Creek Trail marks the actual epicenter of the Loma Prieta quake, and on the Big Slide Trail a number of fissures can be spotted.

➡ At UC Berkeley, the Hayward Fault runs just beneath **Memorial Stadium**.

and provocative work in an intimate space. Across from the Ashby BART station.

Sports

Memorial Stadium, which dates from 1923, is the university's 63,000-seat sporting venue, and the Hayward Fault runs just beneath it. On alternate years, it's the site of the famous football frenzy between the UC Berkeley and Stanford teams.

The **Cal Athletic Ticket Office** (☑800-462-3277; www.calbears.com; 2223 Fulton St) on campus has ticket information on all UC Berkeley sports events. Keep in mind that some sell out weeks in advance.

🛍 Shopping

Branching off the UC campus, Telegraph Ave caters mostly to students, hawking a steady dose of urban hippie gear, handmade jewelry and head-shop paraphernalia. Audiophiles will swoon over the music stores. Other shopping corridors include College Ave in the Elmwood District, 4th St (north of University Ave) and Solano Ave.

Amoeba Music   MUSIC
(☑510-549-1125; 2455 Telegraph Ave; ⊙10:30am-8pm Mon-Thu, to 10pm Fri & Sat, 11am-8pm Sun) If you're a music junkie, you might plan on spending a few hours at the original Berkeley branch of Amoeba Music, packed with massive quantities of new and used CDs, DVDs, tapes and records (yes, lots of vinyl).

Moe's   BOOKS
(☑510-849-2087; 2476 Telegraph Ave; ⊙10am-10pm) A longstanding local favorite, Moe's offers four floors of new, used and remaindered books for hours of browsing.

University Press Books   BOOKS
(☑510-548-0585; 2430 Bancroft Way; ⊙10am-8pm Mon-Fri, to 6pm Sat, noon-5pm Sun) Across

the street from campus, this academic and scholarly bookstore stocks works by UC Berkeley professors and other academic and museum publishers.

Down Home Music   MUSIC
(☑510-525-2129; www.downhomemusic.com; 10341 San Pablo Ave, El Cerrito; ⊙11am-7pm Thu-Sun) North of Berkeley in El Cerrito, this world-class store for roots, blues, folk, Latin and world music is affiliated with the Arhoolie record label, which has been issuing landmark recordings since the early 1960s.

Rasputin   MUSIC
(☑800-350-8700; www.rasputinmusic.com; 2401 Telegraph Ave; ⊙11am-7pm Mon-Thu, to 8pm Sat, noon-7pm Sun) A large music store full of new and used releases.

North Face Outlet   OUTDOOR EQUIPMENT
(☑510-526-3530; cnr 5th & Gilman Sts; ⊙10am-7pm Mon-Sat, 11am-5pm Sun) Discount store for the well-respected Bay Area-based brand of outdoor gear. It's a few blocks west of San Pablo Ave.

REI   OUTDOOR EQUIPMENT
(☑510-527-4140; 1338 San Pablo Ave; ⊙10am-9pm Mon-Fri, to 8pm Sat, to 7pm Sun) This large and busy co-op lures in active folks for camping and mountaineering rentals, sports clothing and all kinds of nifty outdoor gear.

ℹ Information

Alta Bates Summit Medical Center (☑510-204-4444; www.altabatessummit.org; 2450 Ashby Ave) 24-hour emergency services.
Visit Berkeley (☑800-847-4823, 510-549-7040; www.visitberkeley.com; 2030 Addison St; ⊙9am-1pm & 2-5pm Mon-Fri, 10am-1pm & 2-4pm Sat) The helpful Berkeley Convention & Visitors Bureau has a free visitors guide.
UC Berkeley Visitor Services Center (☑510-642-5215; http://visitors.berkeley.edu; 101

WORTH A TRIP

EAST BROTHER LIGHT STATION

East Brother Light Station (☑510-233-2385; www.ebls.org; d incl breakfast & dinner $295-415; ⊙Thu-Sun) Most Bay Area residents have never heard of this speck of an island off the East Bay city of Richmond, and even fewer know that the East Brother Light Station is an extraordinary five-room Victorian B&B. Spend the night in the romantic lighthouse or fog signal building (the foghorn is used from October through March), where every window has stupendous bay views and harbor seals frolic in the frigid currents.

Resident innkeepers serve afternoon hors d'oeuvres and champagne, and between gourmet meals you can stroll around the breezy one-acre islet and rummage through historical photos and artifacts.

Sproul Hall; ⊘ tours usually 10am Mon-Sat & 1pm Sun) Campus maps and information available. Free 90-minute campus tours are given at 10am Monday to Saturday and 1pm Sunday; reservations required.

❶ Getting There & Away

BART

The easiest way to travel between San Francisco, Berkeley, Oakland and other East Bay points is on **BART** (☑ 511, 510-465-2278; www.bart.gov). Trains run approximately every 10 minutes from 4am to midnight on weekdays, with limited service from 6am on Saturday and from 8am on Sunday.

To get to Berkeley, catch a Richmond-bound train to one of three BART stations: Ashby (Adeline St and Ashby Ave), Downtown Berkeley (Shattuck Ave and Center St) or North Berkeley (Sacramento and Delaware Sts). The fare ranges from $3.75 to $4 between Berkeley and San Francisco; $1.85 between Berkeley and downtown Oakland. After 8pm on weekdays, 7pm on Saturday and all day Sunday, there is no direct service operating from San Francisco to Berkeley; instead, catch a Pittsburg/Bay Point train and transfer at 19th St station in Oakland.

A **BART-to-Bus** transfer ticket, available from white AC Transit machines near the BART turnstiles, reduces the connecting bus fare by 25¢.

BUS

The regional company **AC Transit** (☑ 511, 510-817-1717; www.actransit.org) operates a number of buses from San Francisco's Transbay Temporary Terminal to the East Bay. The F line leaves from the Transbay Temporary Terminal to the corner of University and Shattuck Aves approximately every half-hour ($4.20, 30 minutes).

Between Berkeley and downtown Oakland ($2.10) on weekdays, take the fast and frequent 1R bus along Telegraph Ave between the two city centers, or bus 18 that runs daily via Martin Luther King Jr Way. Bus 51B travels along University Ave from Berkeley BART to the Berkeley Marina.

CAR & MOTORCYCLE

With your own wheels you can approach Berkeley from San Francisco by taking the Bay Bridge and then following either I-80 (for University Ave, downtown Berkeley and the UCB campus) or Hwy 24 (for College Ave and the Berkeley Hills).

Driving to San Francisco, the bridge toll is $4 to $6, depending on the time and day of the week.

TRAIN

Amtrak does stop in Berkeley, but the shelter is not staffed and direct connections are few. More convenient is the nearby **Emeryville Amtrak**

station (☑ 800-872-7245; www.amtrak.com; 5885 Horton St), a few miles south.

To reach the Emeryville station from downtown Berkeley, take a Transbay F bus or ride BART to the MacArthur station and then take the free Emery Go Round bus (Hollis route) to Amtrak.

❶ Getting Around

Public transportation, cycling and walking are the best options for getting around central Berkeley.

BICYCLE

Cycling is a popular means of transportation, and safe and well-marked 'bicycle boulevards' with signed distance information to landmarks make crosstown journeys very easy. Just north of Berkeley, **Wheels of Justice** (☑ 510-524-1094; www.wheelsofjustice.com; 1554 Solano Ave, Albany; ⊘ 11am-7pm Thu, 10am-6pm Fri-Wed, to 5pm Sun) has 24-hour mountain-bike rentals for $35.

BUS

AC Transit operates public buses in and around Berkeley, and UC Berkeley's **Bear Transit** (http://pt.berkeley.edu/around/beartransit) runs a shuttle from the downtown BART station to various points on campus ($1). From its stop at the Hearst Mining Circle, the H Line runs along Centennial Dr to the higher parts of the campus.

CAR & MOTORCYCLE

Drivers should note that numerous barriers have been set up to prevent car traffic from traversing residential streets at high speeds, so zigzagging is necessary in some neighborhoods.

Mt Diablo State Park

◉ Sights

Mt Diablo State Park   PARK
(☑ 925-837-2525; www.mdia.org; per vehicle $6-10; ⊘ 8am-sunset) Collecting a light dusting of snowflakes on the coldest days of winter, at 3849ft Mt Diablo is more than 1000ft higher than Mt Tamalpais in Marin County. On a clear day (early on a winter morning is a good bet) the views from Diablo's summit are vast and sweeping. To the west you can see over the bay and out to the Farallon Islands; to the east you can see over the Central Valley to the Sierra Nevada.

The park has more than 50 miles of hiking trails, and can be reached from Walnut Creek, Danville or Clayton. You can also drive to the top, where there's a visitors center.

🛏 Sleeping

Mt Diablo Campgrounds   CAMPGROUND $
(☑800-444-7275; www.reserveamerica.com; tent & RV sites $30) Of the three campgrounds, Juniper and Live Oak have showers, though the campgrounds can be closed during high fire danger and water may be turned off throughout the park if water restrictions are in effect.

ℹ Information

Mt Diablo State Park Visitors Center
(☺10am-4pm) The park office is at the junction of the two entry roads.

John Muir National Historic Site

John Muir Residence   HISTORIC SITE
(☑925-228-8860; www.nps.gov/jomu; 4202 Alhambra Ave, Martinez; ☺10am-5pm Wed-Sun) **FREE** Just 15 miles north of Walnut Creek, the John Muir residence sits in a pastoral patch of farmland in bustling, modern Martinez. Though Muir wrote of sauntering the High Sierra with a sack of tea and bread, it may be a shock for those familiar with the iconic Sierra Club founder's ascetic weather-beaten appearance that the house (built by his father-in-law) is a model of Victorian Italianate refinement, with a tower cupola, a daintily upholstered parlor and splashes of white lace.

Muir's 'scribble den' has been left as it was during his life, with crumpled papers overflowing from wire wastebaskets and dried bread balls – his preferred snack – resting on the mantelpiece.

Acres of his fruit orchard still stand, and visitors can enjoy seasonal samples. The grounds include the 1849 **Martinez Adobe**, part of the rancho on which the house was built, and the oak-speckled hiking trails on nearby **Mt Wanda**.

ℹ Getting There & Away

The park is just north of Hwy 4, and accessible by **County Connection** (www.cccta.org) buses from Amtrak and BART.

Vallejo

For one week in 1852 Vallejo was officially the California state capital – but the fickle legislature changed its mind. It tried Vallejo a second time in 1853, but after a month moved on again (to Benicia). That same year, Vallejo became the site of the first US naval installation on the West Coast (Mare Island Naval Shipyard, now closed).

⊙ Sights

Six Flags Discovery Kingdom AMUSEMENT PARK
(☑707-643-6722; www.sixflags.com/discovery-kingdom; adult/child under 4ft $63/43; ☺approx 10:30am-6pm Fri-Sun spring & fall, to 8pm or 9pm daily summer, variable weekend & holiday hours Dec) The town's biggest tourist draw, this modern wildlife and theme park offers mighty coasters and other rides alongside animal shows featuring sharks and a killer whale. Significant discounts are available on the park's website. Exit I-80 at Hwy 37 westbound, 5 miles north of downtown Vallejo. Parking is $20.

Vallejo Naval & Historical Museum MUSEUM
(☑707-643-0077; www.vallejomuseum.org; 734 Marin St; admission $5; ☺noon-4pm Tue-Sat) This museum tells the story of Vallejo's shortlived history as California's state capital and West Coast naval site.

ℹ Getting There & Away

San Francisco Bay Ferry (☑415-705-8291; www.sanfranciscobayferry.com; one way adult/child $13/6.50) runs ferries from San Francisco's Pier 41 at Fisherman's Wharf and the Ferry Building to Vallejo; the journey takes one hour. Discount admission and transportation packages for Six Flags are available from San Francisco. The ferry is also a gateway to the Wine Country, with connections via the **Napa Valley Vine** (www.ridethevine.com) buses and the **Napa Valley Wine Train** (www.winetrain.com/ferry).

THE PENINSULA

South of San Francisco, squeezed tightly between the bay and the coastal foothills, a vast swath of suburbia continues to San Jose and beyond. Dotted within this area are Palo Alto, Stanford University and Silicon Valley, the center of the Bay Area's immense tech industry. West of the foothills, Hwy 1 runs down the Pacific Coast via Half Moon Bay and a string of beaches to Santa Cruz. Hwy 101 and I-280 both run to San Jose, where they connect with Hwy 17, the quickest route to Santa Cruz. Any of these routes can be combined into an interesting loop or extended to the Monterey Peninsula.

And don't bother looking for Silicon Valley on the map – you won't find it. Because silicon chips form the basis of modern microcomputers, and the Santa Clara Valley – stretching from Palo Alto down through Mountain View, Sunnyvale, Cupertino and Santa Clara to San Jose – is thought of as the birthplace of the microcomputer, it's been dubbed 'Silicon Valley.' The Santa Clara Valley is wide and flat, and its towns are essentially a string of shopping centers and industrial parks linked by a maze of freeways. It's hard to imagine that even after WWII this area was still a wide expanse of orchards and farms.

San Francisco to San Jose

South of the San Francisco peninsula, I-280 is the dividing line between the densely populated South Bay area and the rugged and lightly populated Pacific Coast. With sweeping views of hills and reservoirs, I-280 is a more scenic choice than crowded Hwy 101, which runs through miles of boring business parks. Unfortunately, these parallel north–south arteries are both clogged with traffic during commute times and often on weekends.

A historic site where European explorers first set eyes on San Francisco Bay, **Sweeney Ridge** (www.nps.gov/goga/planyourvisit/upload/sb-sweeney-2008.pdf) straddles a prime spot between Pacifica and San Bruno, and offers hikers unparalleled ocean and bay views. From I-280, exit at Sneath Lane and follow it 2 miles west until it dead ends at the trailhead.

Right on the bay at the northern edge of San Mateo, 4 miles south of San Francisco International Airport, is **Coyote Point Recreation Area** (parking $6; 🚻), a popular park (its playground sports a huge castle) and windsurfing destination. The main attraction – formerly known as the Coyote Point Museum – is **CuriOdyssey** (☑ 650-342-7755; www.curiodyssey.org; adult/child $9/7; ⊙ 10am-5pm Tue-Sat, noon-5pm Sun; 🚻), with innovative exhibits for kids and adults highlighting science and wildlife. Exit Hwy 101 at Coyote Point Dr.

Stanford University

Sprawled over 8200 leafy acres in Palo Alto, **Stanford University** (www.stanford.edu) was founded by Leland Stanford, one of the Central Pacific Railroad's 'Big Four' founders and a former governor of California. When the Stanfords' only child died of typhoid during a European tour in 1884, they decided to build a university in his memory. Stanford University was opened in 1891, just two years before Leland Stanford's death, but the university grew to become a prestigious and

NERDS' NIRVANA

Touted as the largest computer history exhibition in the world, the **Computer History Museum** (☑ 650-810-1010; www.computerhistory.org; 1401 N Shoreline Blvd, Mountain View; adult/student & senior $15/12; ⊙ 10am-5pm Wed-Sun) has rotating exhibits drawn from its 100,000-item collection. Artifacts range from the abacus to the iPod, including Cray-1 supercomputers, a Babbage Difference Engine (a Victorian-era automatic computing engine) and the first Google server.

Don't come looking to ogle the latest iPhone or get a Genius Bar consultation. At **Apple Headquarters** (www.apple.com/companystore; 1 Infinite Loop, Cupertino; ⊙ 10am-5:30pm Mon-Fri), hardcore fans can load up on Apple-branded clothing and ephemera from its company store and commiserate that, yes, Steve Jobs has left the building.

Though there are no official tours of the **Googleplex** (www.google.com/about/company/facts/locations; 1600 Amphitheatre Pkwy, Mountain View), visitors can stroll the campus and gawk at the public art on the leafy grounds, where scads of Googlers zoom about on primary-colored bicycles. Don't miss the 'dessert yard' outside Building 44, with lawn sculptures of Android operating systems (a cupcake! a donut! a robot!), and across the street, a toothy T-Rex festooned in pink flamingos next to the volleyball court.

At the company's headquarters, the **Intel Museum** (☑ 408-765-5050; www.intel.com/museum; 2200 Mission College Blvd, Santa Clara; ⊙ 9am-6pm Mon-Fri, 10am-5pm Sat) FREE has displays on the birth and growth of the computer industry with special emphasis, not surprisingly, on microchips and Intel's involvement. Reserve ahead if you want to schedule a guided tour.

wealthy institution. The campus was built on the site of the Stanfords' horse-breeding farm and, as a result, Stanford is still known as 'The Farm.'

☉ Sights

Main Quad
PLAZA

Auguste Rodin's *Burghers of Calais* bronze sculpture marks the entrance to the university's Main Quad, an open plaza where the original 12 campus buildings, a mix of Romanesque and Mission revival styles, were joined by the **Memorial Church** (also called MemChu) in 1903. The church is noted for its beautiful mosaic-tiled frontage, stained-glass windows and four organs with more than 8000 pipes.

Hoover Tower
TOWER

(adult/child $2/1; ☉10am-4pm, closed during final exams, breaks btwn sessions & some holidays) A campus landmark at the east of the Main Quad, the 285ft-high Hoover Tower offers superb views. The tower houses the university library, offices and part of the right-wing Hoover Institution on War, Revolution & Peace (where Donald Rumsfeld caused a university-wide stir by accepting a position after he resigned as Secretary of Defense).

Cantor Center for Visual Arts
MUSEUM

(http://museum.stanford.edu; 328 Lomita Dr; ☉11am-5pm Wed & Fri-Sun, to 8pm Thu) **FREE** The Cantor Center for Visual Arts is a large museum originally dating from 1894. Its collection spans works from ancient civilizations to contemporary art, sculpture and photography, and rotating exhibits are eclectic in scope.

Rodin Sculpture Garden
SCULPTURE GARDEN

Immediately south of the Cantor Center is the open-air Rodin Sculpture Garden, which boasts the largest collection of bronze sculptures by Auguste Rodin outside of Paris, including reproductions of his towering *Gates of Hell*. More sculpture can be found around campus, including pieces by Andy Goldsworthy and Maya Lin.

ⓘ Information

Stanford Visitor Center (www.stanford.edu/dept/visitorinfo; 295 Galvez St) The Stanford Visitor Center offers free one-hour walking tours of the campus daily at 11am and 3:15pm, except during the winter break (mid-December through early January) and some holidays. Specialized tours are also available.

ⓘ Getting There & Away

Stanford University's free public shuttle, **Marguerite** (http://transportation.stanford.edu/marguerite), provides service from Caltrain's Palo Alto and California Ave stations to the campus, and has bicycle racks. Parking on campus is expensive and trying.

San Jose

Though culturally diverse and historic, San Jose has always been in San Francisco's shadow, awash in Silicon Valley's suburbia. Founded in 1777 as El Pueblo de San José de Guadalupe, San Jose is California's oldest Spanish civilian settlement. Its downtown is small and scarcely used for a city of its size, though it does bustle with 20-something clubgoers on the weekends. Industrial parks, high-tech computer firms and look-alike

---

WINCHESTER MYSTERY HOUSE

Winchester Mystery House (☎408-247-2101; www.winchestermysteryhouse.com; 525 S Winchester Blvd; adult/senior/child 6-12 $33/30/25; ☉9am-5pm Oct-Mar, 9am-7pm Apr-Sep) An odd structure purposefully commissioned to be so by the heir to the Winchester rifle fortune, the Winchester Mystery House is a ridiculous Victorian mansion with 160 rooms of various sizes and little utility, with dead-end hallways and a staircase that runs up to a ceiling all jammed together like a toddler playing architect. Apparently, Sarah Winchester spent 38 years constructing this mammoth white elephant because the spirits of the people killed by Winchester rifles told her to.

No expense was spared in the construction and the extreme results sprawl over 4 acres. Tours start every 30 minutes, and the standard hour-long guided mansion tour includes a self-guided romp through the gardens as well as entry to an exhibition of guns and rifles.

It's west of central San Jose and just north of I-280, across the street from Santana Row.

housing developments have sprawled across the city's landscape, taking over where farms, ranches and open spaces once spread between the bay and the surrounding hills.

◉ Sights

Downtown San Jose is at the junction of Hwy 87 and I-280. Hwy 101 and I-880 complete the box. Running roughly north–south along the length of the city, from the old port town of Alviso on the San Francisco Bay all the way downtown, is 1st St; south of I-280, its name changes to Monterey Hwy.

San Jose State University is immediately east of downtown, and the SoFA district, with numerous nightclubs, restaurants and galleries, is on a stretch of S 1st St south of San Carlos St.

★ **History Park**   PARK
(🖉 408-287-2290; www.historysanjose.org; cnr Senter Rd & Phelan Ave; ⊙11am-5pm Tue-Sun, closed 1st Mon of month) Historic buildings from all over San Jose have been brought together in this open-air history museum, southeast of the city center in Kelley Park. The centerpiece is a dramatic half-scale replica of the 237ft-high 1881 **Electric Light Tower**. The original tower was a pioneering attempt at street lighting, intended to illuminate the entire town center. It was a complete failure but was left standing as a central landmark until it toppled over in 1915 because of rust and wind. Other buildings include an 1888 **Chinese temple** and the **Pacific Hotel**, which has rotating exhibits inside. The **Trolley Restoration Barn** restores historic trolley cars to operate on San Jose's light-rail line, and on weekends you can ride a trolley along the park's own short line.

Tech Museum of Innovation   MUSEUM
(The Tech; 🖉 408-294-8324; www.thetech.org; 201 S Market St; adult/child 3-17 $15/10; ⊙10am-5pm; ♿) This excellent technology museum, opposite Plaza de Cesar Chavez, examines subjects from robotics to space exploration to genetics. The museum also includes an IMAX dome theater (additional $5 admission), which screens different films throughout the day.

San Jose Museum of Art   MUSEUM
(🖉 408-271-6840; www.sjmusart.org; 110 S Market St; adult/student & senior $8/5; ⊙11am-5pm Tue-Sun) With a strong permanent collection of 20th-century works and a variety of imag-

inative changing exhibits, the city's central art museum is one of the Bay Area's finest. The main building started life as the post office in 1892, was damaged by the 1906 earthquake and became an art gallery in 1933. A modern wing was added in 1991.

Rosicrucian Egyptian Museum   MUSEUM
(🖉 408-947-3635; www.egyptianmuseum.org; 1342 Naglee Ave; adult/child/student $9/5/7; ⊙9am-5pm Wed-Fri, 10am-6pm Sat & Sun) West of downtown, this unusual and educational Egyptian Museum is one of San Jose's more interesting attractions, with an extensive collection that includes statues, household items and mummies. There's even a two-room, walk-through reproduction of an ancient subterranean tomb. The museum is the centerpiece of **Rosicrucian Park** (cnr Naglee & Park Aves), west of downtown San Jose.

MACLA   GALLERY
(Movimiento de Arte y Cultura Latino Americana; 🖉 408-998-2783; www.maclaarte.org; 510 S 1st St; ⊙noon-7pm Wed & Thu, noon-5pm Fri & Sat) **FREE** A cutting-edge gallery highlighting themes by both established and emerging Latino artists, MACLA is one of the best community arts spaces in the Bay Area, with open-mic performances, hip-hop and other live-music shows, experimental theater and well-curated and thought-provoking visual arts exhibits. It's also a hub for the popular **South First Fridays** (www.southfirstfridays. com) art walk and street fair.

Plaza de Cesar Chavez   PLAZA
This leafy square in the center of downtown, which was part of the original plaza of El Pueblo de San José de Guadalupe, is the oldest public space in the city. It's named after Cesar Chavez – founder of the United Farm Workers, who lived part of his life in San Jose – and is surrounded by museums, theaters and hotels.

Cathedral Basilica of St Joseph   CHURCH
(80 S Market St) At the top of the Plaza de Cesar Chavez, the pueblo's first church. Originally constructed of adobe brick in 1803, it was replaced three times due to earthquakes and fire; the present building dates from 1877.

Santana Row   MALL
(www.santanarow.com; Stevens Creek & Winchester Blvds) An upscale Main St-style mall, Santana Row is a mixed-use space west of downtown with shopping, dining and entertainment

SAN JOSE FOR CHILDREN

Children's Discovery Museum (☎408-298-5437; www.cdm.org; 180 Woz Way; admission $12; ⊙10am-5pm Tue-Sat, from noon Sun; ▮) Downtown, this science and creativity museum has hands-on displays incorporating art, technology and the environment, with plenty of toys, and very cool play-and-learn areas. The museum is on Woz Way, which is named after Steve Wozniak, the cofounder of Apple.

Great America (☎408-986-5886; www.cagreatamerica.com; 4701 Great America Pkwy, Santa Clara; adult/child under 4ft $60/40; ⊙Apr-Oct; ▮) If you can handle the shameful product placements, kids love the roller coasters and other thrill rides. Note that online tickets cost much less than walk-up prices; parking costs $15 but it's also accessible by public transportation.

Raging Waters (☎408-238-9900; www.rwsplash.com; 2333 South White Rd; adult/child under 4ft $39/29, parking $6; ⊙May-Sep; ▮) A water park inside Lake Cunningham Regional Park, Raging Waters has fast water slides, a tidal pool and a nifty water fort. Online discounts.

along with a boutique hotel, lofts and apartments. Restaurants spill out onto sidewalk terraces, and public spaces have been designed to invite loitering and promenading. On warm evenings, the Mediterranean-style area swarms with an energetic crowd.

🛏 Sleeping

Conventions and trade shows keep the downtown hotels busy year-round, and midweek rates are usually higher than weekends.

Henry W Coe State Park CAMPGROUND $
(☎408-779-2728, reservations 800-444-7275; www.reserveamerica.com; sites $20; ▮) Southeast of San Jose near Morgan Hill, this huge state park has 20 drive-in campsites at the top of an open ridge overlooking the hills and canyons of the park's backcountry. There are no showers. You can't make reservations less than two days in advance, though it rarely fills up except on spring and summer holidays and weekends.

Hikers (permit $5) can overnight in the park's vast wilderness.

Westin San Jose HISTORIC HOTEL $$
(☎866-870-0726, 408-295-2000; www.thesainte-claire.com; 302 S Market St; r weekend/midweek from $129/179; ❀@☎▩) Formerly the Sainte Claire, this atmospheric 1926 landmark hotel overlooking Plaza de Cesar Chavez has a drop-dead beautiful lobby with stretched leather ceilings. Guest rooms are smallish, and were being completely remodeled at research time.

Hotel De Anza HOTEL $$
(☎800-843-3700, 408-286-1000; www.hoteldeanza.com; 233 W Santa Clara St; r Sun-Thu/Fri & Sat $149/239; ❀@☎▩) This downtown hotel is a restored art-deco beauty, although contemporary stylings overwhelm the place's history. Guest rooms offer plush comforts (the ones facing south are a tad larger) and full concierge service is available.

Hotel Valencia BOUTIQUE HOTEL $$$
(☎866-842-0100, 408-551-0010; www.hotelvalencia-santanarow.com; 355 Santana Row; r incl breakfast $199-309; ❀@☎▩) A burbly lobby fountain and deep-red corridor carpeting set the tone for this tranquil 212-room contemporary hotel in the Santana Row shopping complex. In-room minibars and bathrobes and a pool and hot tub create an oasis of luxury with European and Asian design accents.

🍴 Eating

Tofoo Com Chay VEGETARIAN, VIETNAMESE $
(☎408-286-6335; 388 E Santa Clara St; mains $6.50; ⊙9am-9pm Mon-Fri, 10am-6pm Sat; ▯) Conveniently located on the border of the San Jose State University campus, students and vegetarians queue up for the Vietnamese dishes such as the fake-meat *pho* and the heaped combo plates.

Original Joe's ITALIAN $$
(www.originaljoes.com; 301 S 1st St; mains $15-37; ⊙11am-11pm Sun-Thu, 11am-midnight Fri & Sat) Waiters flit about this busy 1950s San Jose landmark, serving standard Italian dishes to locals and conventioneers. The dining room is a curious but tasteful hodgepodge of '50s

brick, contemporary wood paneling and 5ft-tall Asian vases. Expect a wait.

Arcadia
STEAK $$$

(☑ 408-278-4555; www.michaelmina.net/restaurants; 100 W San Carlos St; mains lunch $12-19, dinner $28-50; ☺ 6:30am-2pm daily, 5:30-10pm Mon-Sat) This fine New American steakhouse restaurant in the Marriott Hotel is run by Chef Michael Mina, one of San Francisco's biggest celebrity chefs. It's not the daring, cutting-edge style Mina is known for, but it's slick, expensive and, of course, very good.

🍷 Drinking & Nightlife

The biggest conglomeration of clubs is on S 1st St, aka SoFA, and around S 2nd at San Fernando. Raucous young clubgoers pack the streets on Friday and Saturday nights.

★Singlebarrel
COCKTAIL BAR

(www.singlebarrelsj.com; 43 W San Salvador St; ☺ 5pm-midnight Sun & Tue, 5pm-1:30am Wed-Sat) A speakeasy-style lounge, where bartenders sheathed in tweed vests artfully mix custom cocktails ($12) tailored to customer's preferences, with some recipes dating back to before Prohibition. There's often a line out the door, but you'll be whisked downstairs as soon as they're ready to craft you a drink.

Caffe Frascati
CAFE

(www.caffefrascati.com; 315 S 1st St; ☺ 7am-10pm Mon-Thu, to midnight Fri, 8am-midnight Sat, to 9pm Sun; 🛜) Photos of local theater folks line the walls at this high-ceilinged hangout a few doors down from the California Theatre. Linger over a cappuccino with a pastry or panini, and stop by for live music on Friday and Saturday nights. Opera performances rattle the cups the first Friday of each month.

Trials Pub
PUB

(www.trialspub.com; 265 N 1st St; ☺ from 5pm) If you seek a well-poured pint in a supremely comfortable atmosphere, Trials Pub, north of San Pedro Sq, has many excellent ales on tap (try a Fat Lip), all served in a warm and friendly room with no TVs. There's good pub food and a fireplace in the back room.

Hedley Club
LOUNGE

(www.hoteldeanza.com/hedley_club.asp; 233 W Santa Clara St) Inside the elegant 1931 Hotel De Anza, the Hedley Club is a good place for a quiet drink in swanky art-deco surroundings. Jazz combos play Thursday through Saturday night.

South First Billiards
BAR, POOL HALL

(www.facebook.com/420southfirst; 420 S 1st St; ☺ 4pm-midnight Mon-Thu, 4pm-2am Fri & Sat) It's a great place to shoot some stick, and a welcoming club to boot. Check its Facebook page for live music and DJ nights.

☆ Entertainment

Live Music

Blank Club
LIVE MUSIC

(www.theblankclub.com; 44 S Almaden; ☺ Tue-Sat) A small club near the Greyhound station and off the main party streets. Live bands jam on a stage cascading with silver tinsel, and a glittering disco ball presides over fun retro dance parties.

Theaters

California Theatre
THEATER

(☑ 408-792-4111; www.sanjosetheaters.org/theaters/california-theatre; 345 S 1st St) The absolutely stunning Spanish interior of this landmark entertainment venue is cathedral-worthy. The theater is home to Opera San José, Symphony Silicon Valley, and is a venue for the city's annual film festival, Cinequest (www.cinequest.org), held in late February or early March.

Sports

SAP Center
STADIUM

(☑ 408-287-9200; www.sapcenteratsanjose.com; cnr Santa Clara & N Autumn Sts) Formerly the HP Pavilion, the fanatically popular San Jose Sharks, the city's NHL (National Hockey League) team, plays at this massive glass-

---

PSYCHO DONUTS? QU'EST QUE C'EST?

Who knew that a sugary confection with a hole could induce such devious giggles and fiendish delight? Saunter on over to **Psycho Donuts** (www.psycho-donuts.com; 288 S 2nd St; ☺ 7am-10pm Mon-Thu, to midnight Fri, 8am-midnight Sat, to 10pm Sun; 🅿), where counter staff dressed in saucy medical garb hand out bubble wrap to pop as patrons choose from twisted flavors such as Cereal Killer (topped with marshmallows and Cap'n Crunch breakfast cereal), Headbanger (death-metal visage oozing red jelly) and the tantalizing square S'mores (campfire not included).

and-metal stadium. The NHL season runs from September to April.

San Jose Earthquakes SOCCER (www.sjearthquakes.com) San Jose's Major League Soccer team plays from February through October. Until 2015, when the Quakes' new stadium opens nearby just west of San Jose airport, catch the action at Santa Clara University's **Buck Shaw Stadium** (500 El Camino Real, Santa Clara).

ⓘ Information

To find out what's happening and where, check out the free weekly *Metro* (www.metroactive. com) newspaper or the Friday 'eye' section of the daily *San Jose Mercury News* (www.mercu-rynews.com).

San Jose Convention & Visitors Bureau (☑ 800-726-5673, 408-295-9600; www. sanjose.org)

Santa Clara Valley Medical Center (☑ 408-885-5000; 751 S Bascom Ave; ☺ 24hr)

ⓘ Getting There & Away

AIR

Two miles north of downtown, between Hwy 101 and I-880, Mineta San José International Airport (p50700) has free wi-fi and numerous domestic flights from two terminals.

BART

To access the BART system in the East Bay, **VTA** (☑ 408-321-2300; www.vta.org) bus 181 runs daily between the Fremont BART station and downtown ($4).

BUS

Greyhound buses to Los Angeles ($22 to $59, seven to 10 hours) leave from the **Greyhound station** (☑ 408-295-4151; www.greyhound.com; 70 Almaden Ave). The super-cheap new carrier **Megabus** (us.megabus.com) boasts electrical outlets and free wi-fi, with fares to Los Angeles averaging $10 to $40; departures from Diridon Station.

The VTA Hwy 17 Express bus (route 970) plies a handy daily route between Diridon Station and Santa Cruz ($5, one hour).

CAR & MOTORCYCLE

San Jose is right at the bottom end of the San Francisco Bay, about 40 miles from Oakland (via I-880) or San Francisco (via Hwy 101 or I-280). Expect lots of traffic at all times of the day on Hwy 101. Although I-280 is slightly longer, it's much prettier and usually less congested. Heading south, Hwy 17 leads over the hill to Santa Cruz.

Many downtown retailers offer two-hour parking validation, and on weekends until 6pm parking is free in city-owned lots and garages downtown. Check www.sjdowntownparking.com for details.

TRAIN

A double-decker commuter rail service that operates up and down the Peninsula between San Jose and San Francisco, **Caltrain** (☑ 800-660-4287; www.caltrain.com) makes more than three dozen trips daily (fewer on weekends); the 60-minute (on the Baby Bullet commuter trains) to 90-minute journey costs $9 each way and bicycles can be brought on designated cars. It's definitely your best bet, as traffic can be crazy any day of the week. San Jose's terminal, **Diridon Station** (off 65 Cahill St), is just south of the Alameda.

Diridon Station also serves as the terminal for **Amtrak** (☑ 408-287-7462; www.amtrak.com), serving Seattle, Los Angeles and Sacramento, and **Altamont Commuter Express** (www. acerail.com), which runs to Great America, Livermore and Stockton.

VTA runs a free weekday shuttle (known as the Downtown Area Shuttle or DASH) from the station to downtown.

ⓘ Getting Around

VTA buses run all over Silicon Valley. From the airport, free VTA Airport Flyer shuttles (route 10) run every 10 to 15 minutes to the Metro/Airport Light Rail station, where you can catch the San Jose light rail to downtown San Jose. The route also goes to the Santa Clara Caltrain station. Fares for buses (except express lines) and light-rail trains are $2 for a single ride and $6 for a day pass.

The main San Jose light-rail line runs 20 miles north–south from the city center. Heading south gets you as far as Almaden and Santa Teresa. The northern route runs to the Civic Center, the airport and Tasman, where it connects with another line that heads west past Great America to downtown Mountain View.

San Francisco to Half Moon Bay

One of the real surprises of the Bay Area is how fast the urban landscape disappears along the rugged and largely undeveloped coast. The 70-mile stretch of coastal Hwy 1 from San Francisco to Santa Cruz is one of the most beautiful motorways anywhere. For the most part a winding two-lane blacktop, it passes small farmstands and beach after beach, many of them little sandy coves hidden from the highway. Most beaches along Hwy 1 are buffeted by wild and unpredictable surf, making them more suitable for sunbathing (weather permitting) than swimming. The state beaches along the coast don't charge an access fee, but parking can cost a few dollars.

A cluster of isolated and supremely scenic HI hostels, at Point Montara (22 miles south of San Francisco) and Pigeon Point (36 miles), make this an interesting route for cyclists, though narrow Hwy 1 itself can be stressful, if not downright dangerous, for the inexperienced.

Pacifica & Devil's Slide

Pacifica and Point San Pedro, 15 miles from downtown San Francisco, signal the end of the urban sprawl. South of Pacifica is Devil's Slide, a gorgeous coastal cliff area now bypassed by a car tunnel, though hikers and cyclists can sightsee on the adjacent **Devil's Slide Coastal Trail**, a paved 1.3-mile section of old Hwy 1.

In Pacifica, the main attractions are **Rockaway Beach** and the more popular **Pacifica State Beach** (also known as Linda Mar Beach; per car $3), where the nearby **Nor-Cal Surf Shop** (☑650-738-9283; 5440 Coast Hwy; ◷9am-6pm Sun-Fri, 8am-6pm Sat) rents surfboards ($19 per day) and wetsuits ($16.50).

Gray Whale Cove to Half Moon Bay

One of the coast's popular 'clothing-optional' beaches is **Gray Whale Cove State Beach**, just south of Point San Pedro. Park across the road and cross Hwy 1 to the beach *very* carefully. **Montara State Beach** is just a half-mile south. From the town of Montara, 22 miles from San Francisco, trails climb up from the Martini Creek parking lot into **McNee Ranch**, which has hiking and cycling trails aplenty, including a strenuous ascent to the panoramic viewpoint of Montara Mountain, and access to the new 4000-acre park of **Ranch Corral de Tierra** (www.nps.gov/goga/rcdt.htm).

Starting life as a fog station in 1875, the **Point Montara Lighthouse Hostel** (☑650-728-7177; www.norcalhostels.org/montara; cnr Hwy 1 & 16th St; dm $27, r $75; @🛜) 🖉 is adjacent to the current lighthouse, which dates from 1928. This very popular hostel has a living room, kitchen facilities and an international clientele. There are a few private rooms for couples or families. Reservations are a good

idea, especially on weekends during summer. SamTrans bus 17 stops outside.

The **Fitzgerald Marine Reserve** (☑650-728-3584; www.fitzgeraldreserve.org; 🐾), south of the lighthouse at Moss Beach, is an extensive area of natural tidal pools and a habitat for harbor seals. Walk out among the pools at low tide – wearing shoes that you can get wet – and explore the myriad crabs, sea stars, mollusks and rainbow-colored sea anemone. Note that it's illegal to remove any creatures, shells or even rocks from the marine reserve. From Hwy 1 in Moss Beach, turn west onto California Ave and drive to the end. SamTrans bus 17 stops along Hwy 1.

Overlooking the ocean, the **Moss Beach Distillery** (☑650-728-5595; www.mossbeach-distillery.com; cnr Beach Way & Ocean Blvd; mains $15-36; ◷noon-9pm Mon-Sat, from 11am Sun; 🐾) is a 1927 landmark. In fair weather the restaurant's deck is the best place for miles around to have a leisurely cocktail or glass of vino. Reservations recommended.

South of here is a hamlet named **Princeton**, with a stretch of coast called Pillar Point. Fishing boats bring in their catch at the Pillar Point Harbor, some of which gets cooked up in a bevy of seafront restaurants. In the harbor, **Half Moon Bay Kayak** (☑650-773 6101; www.hmbkayak.com; ◷10am-4pm Wed-Mon) rents kayaks and offers guided trips of Pillar Point and the Fitzgerald Marine Reserve. **Half Moon Bay Brewing Company** (www.hmbbrewingco.com; 390 Capistrano Rd; mains $15-23; ◷11:30am-9pm Mon-Thu, to 10pm Fri, 9:30am-10pm Sat & Sun; 🐾) 🖉 serves seafood, burgers and a tantalizing menu of local brews from a sheltered and heated outdoor patio looking out over the bay, complemented by live music on the weekends.

At the western end of Pillar Point is **Mavericks**, a serious surf break that attracts the world's top big-wave riders to battle its huge, steep and very dangerous waves. The annual Mavericks surf contest, called on a few days' notice when the swells get huge, is usually held between December and March.

Half Moon Bay

Developed as a beach resort back in the Victorian era, Half Moon Bay is the main coastal town between San Francisco (28 miles north) and Santa Cruz (40 miles south). Its long stretches of beach still attract rambling weekenders and hearty surfers. Half Moon Bay spreads out along Hwy 1 (called Cabrillo Hwy in town), but despite the development, it's

SCENIC DRIVE: HIGHWAY 84

Inland, large stretches of the hills are protected in a patchwork of parks that, just like the coast, remain remarkably untouched despite the huge urban populations only a short drive to the north and east. Heading east toward Palo Alto, Hwy 84 winds its way through thick stands of redwood trees and several local parks with mountain biking and hiking opportunities.

A mile in from **San Gregorio State Beach** (per car $8) on Hwy 1, kick off your shoes and stomp your feet to live bluegrass, Celtic and folk music on the weekends at the landmark **San Gregorio General Store** (www.sangregoriostore.com), and check out the wooden bar singed by area branding irons.

Eight miles east is the tiny township of **La Honda**, former home to *One Flew Over the Cuckoo's Nest* author Ken Kesey, and the launching spot for his 1964 psychedelic bus trip immortalized in Tom Wolfe's *The Electric Kool-Aid Acid Test*. Housed in an old blacksmith's shop, **Apple Jack's** (650-747-0331) is a rustic, down-home bar with lots of local color.

To stretch your legs in the redwoods, **Sam McDonald Park** (650-879-0238; http://parks.smcgov.org/sam-mcdonald-park; parking $6), two miles south of La Honda on Pescadero Rd, has a number of worthy trails and a secluded **hike-to cabin** (http://lp.sierraclub.org/hikers_hut/hikers_hut.asp; adult $25-30, child 2-10 $10) available for rent.

still relatively small. The main drag is a five-block stretch called Main St lined with shops, cafes, restaurants and a few upscale B&Bs. Visitor information is available from the **Half Moon Bay Coastside Visitors Bureau** (650-726-8380; www.halfmoonbaychamber.org).

Pumpkins are a major deal around Half Moon Bay, and the pre-Halloween harvest is celebrated in the annual **Art & Pumpkin Festival** (www.pumpkinfest.miramarevents.com). The mid-October event kicks off with the World Championship Pumpkin Weigh-Off, where the bulbous beasts can bust the scales at more than 1000lb.

Around 1 mile north of the Hwy 92 junction, **Sea Horse Ranch** (650-726-9903; www.seahorseranch.org) offers daily horseback rides along the beach. A two-hour ride is $75; an early-bird special leaves at 8am and costs just $50.

SamTrans (800-660-4287; www.samtrans.com) bus 294 operates from the Hillsdale Caltrain station in San Mateo to Half Moon Bay; bus 17 connects up the coast to Moss Beach and Pacifica and has very limited weekday service to Pescadero.

Half Moon Bay to Santa Cruz

With its long coastline, mild weather and abundant fresh water, this area has always been prime real estate. When Spanish missionaries set up shop along the California coast in the late 1700s, it had been Ohlone Native American territory for thousands of years. Pescadero was formally established in 1856, when it was mostly a farming and dairy settlement, although its location along the stagecoach route – now called Stage Rd – transformed it into a popular vacation destination. The Pigeon Point promontory was an active whaling station until 1900, when Prohibition-era bootleggers favored the isolated regional beaches for smuggling booze.

Pescadero

A foggy speck of coastside crossroads between the cities of San Francisco and Santa Cruz, 150-year-old Pescadero is a close-knit rural town of sugar-lending neighbors and community pancake breakfasts. But on weekends the tiny downtown strains its seams with long-distance cyclists panting for carbohydrates and day trippers dive-bombing in from the ocean-front highway. They're all drawn to the winter vistas of emerald-green hills parched to burlap brown in summer, the wild Pacific beaches populated by seals and pelicans, and the food at a revered destination restaurant. With its cornucopia of tide-pool coves and parks of sky-blotting redwood canopy, city dwellers come here to slow down and smell the sea breeze wafting over fields of bushy artichokes.

◉ Sights & Activities

A number of pretty sand beaches speckle the coast, though one of the most interesting places to stop is **Pebble Beach**, a tide-pool jewel a mile and a half south of Pescadero Creek Rd (and part of Bean Hollow State Beach). As the name implies, the shore is awash in bite-sized eye candy of agate, jade and carnelians, and sandstone troughs are pockmarked by groovy honeycombed formations called tafoni. Bird-watchers enjoy **Pescadero Marsh Reserve**, across the highway from Pescadero State Beach, where numerous species feed year-round.

★**Pigeon Point Light Station**   LIGHTHOUSE
(☑ 650-879-2120;   www.parks.ca.gov/?page_id=533) Five miles south along the coast, the 115ft Light Station is one of the tallest lighthouses on the West Coast. The 1872 landmark had to close access to the upper tower when chunks of its cornice began to rain from the sky (restoration is in progress), but the beam still flashes brightly and the bluff is a prime though blustery spot to scan for breaching gray whales. The hostel here is one of the best in the state.

Butano State Park   PARK
(☑ 650-879-2040; per car $10, camping $35 Apr-Nov) About 5 miles south of Pescadero, bobcats and full-throated coyotes reside discreetly in 2800 acres of dense redwood canyon. From Hwy 1, take Gazos Creek Rd.

🛏 Sleeping & Eating

★**HI Pigeon Point Lighthouse Hostel**   HOSTEL $
(☑ 650-879-0633;   www.norcalhostels.org/pigeon; 210 Pigeon Point Rd; dm $26-27, r/t/6-bed $75/101/162, all with shared bath; @ 🖥) 🖉 Not your workaday HI outpost, this highly coveted coastside hostel is all about location. Check in early to snag a spot in the outdoor hot tub, and contemplate roaring waves as the lighthouse beacon races through a starburst sky.

Costanoa   CABIN, CAMPGROUND $$
(☑ 877-262-7848,   650-879-1100;   www.costanoa. com; 2001 Rossi Rd; tent/cabin with shared bath from $89/179, lodge r $203-291; 🖥) Even though the resort includes a **campground** (☑ 800-562-9867;   www.koa.com/campgrounds/santa-cruz-north; tent site $30-34, RV site from $69; 🖥 🐾), no one can pull a straight face to declare they're actually roughing it here. Down bedding swaddles guests in cushy canvas

tent cabins, and chill-averse tent campers can use communal 'comfort stations' with 24-hour dry saunas, fireside patio seating, heated floors and hot showers.

Lodge rooms with private fireplaces and hot tub access fulfill the whims of those without such spartan delusions. There's a **restaurant** (dinner mains $17 to $36) and spa on site; bicycle rentals and horseback riding are available as well.

Pescadero Creek Inn B&B   INN $$
(☑ 888-307-1898;   www.pescaderocreekinn.com; 393 Stage Rd; r $155-225; 🖥) 🖉 Unwind in the private two-room cottage or one of the spotless Victorian rooms in a restored 100-year-old farmhouse with a tranquil creekside garden.

★**Duarte's Tavern**   AMERICAN $$
(☑ 650-879-0464;   www.duartestavern.com; 202 Stage Rd; mains $11-45; ⊙ /am-9pm) You'll rub shoulders with fancy-pants foodies, spandex-swathed cyclists and dusty cowboys at this casual, surprisingly unpretentious fourth-generation family restaurant. Duarte's is the culinary magnet of Pescadero – for many the town and eatery are synonymous. Feast on crab cioppino and a half-and-half split of the cream of artichoke and green chili soups, and bring it home with a wedge of olallieberry pie.

Except for the unfortunate lull of Prohibition, the wood-paneled bar has been hosting the locals and their honored guests since 1894. Reservations recommended.

❶ Getting There & Away

By car, the town is 3 miles east from Hwy 1 on Pescadero Creek Rd, south of San Gregorio State Beach. On weekdays, **SamTrans** (www. samtrans.com) bus 17 runs once a day to/from Half Moon Bay.

Año Nuevo State Reserve

More raucous than a full-moon beach rave, thousands of boisterous elephant seals party down year-round on the dunes of Año Nuevo point, their squeals and barks reaching fever pitch during the winter pupping season. The beach is 5 miles south of Pigeon Point and 27 miles north of Santa Cruz.

Elephant seals were just as fearless two centuries ago as they are today, but unfortunately, club-toting seal trappers were not in the same seal-friendly category as camera-toting tourists. Between 1800 and

THE CULINARY COAST

Pescadero is renowned for Duarte's Tavern, but loads of other tidbits are very close by.

Arcangeli Grocery/Norm's Market (Norm's Market; www.normsmarket.com; 287 Stage Rd, Pescadero; sandwiches $6.50-8.75; ⊙10am-6pm Mon-Thu, 9am-6pm Sat & Sun) Create a picnic with made-to-order deli sandwiches, homemade artichoke salsa and a chilled bottle of California wine. And don't go breezing out the door without nabbing a crusty loaf of the famous artichoke garlic herb bread, fresh-baked almost hourly.

Harley Farms Cheese Shop (☑650-879-0480; www.harleyfarms.com; 250 North St, Pescadero; ⊙10am-5pm Wed-Sun; 🖪) Follow the cool wooden cut-outs of the goat and the Wellington-shod girl with the faraway eyes. Another local food treasure with creamy artisanal goat cheeses festooned with fruit, nuts and a rainbow of edible flowers. Weekend farm tours by reservation, and a new shop selling goat-milk body products and non-toxic paint. Splurge for a seat at one of the monthly five-course farm dinners in the restored barn's airy hayloft.

Pie Ranch (www.pieranch.org; 2080 Cabrillo Hwy, Pescadero; ⊙noon-6pm Thu & Fri, 10am-6pm Sat & Sun; 🖪) 🍴 Hit the brakes for this roadside farmstand in a wooden barn, and pick up fresh produce, eggs and coffee, plus amazing pies made with the fruit grown here. The historic pie-slice-shaped farm is a nonprofit dedicated to leadership development and food education for urban youth. Check the website for details on its monthly farm tours and barn dances. Located 11 miles south of Pescadero Creek Rd.

Swanton Berry Farm (☑650-469-8804; www.swantonberryfarm.com; Coastways Ranch, 640 Cabrillo Hwy, Pescadero; ⊙10am-4pm Fri-Sun) To get a better appreciation of the rigors and rewards of farm life, smoosh up your shirtsleeves and harvest some fruit at this organic pick-your-own farm near Año Nuevo. It's a union outfit (operated by Cesar Chavez's United Farm Workers), with buckets of seasonal kiwis and olallieberries ripe for the plucking. Its **farm stand and strawberry u-pick** (⊙8am-5pm) is 8.5 miles further south near Davenport.

Bonnie Doon Vineyard (☑831-471-8031; www.bonnydoonvineyard.com; 450 Hwy 1, Davenport; ⊙11am-5pm Thu-Mon) Round out your palate with a flight ($10 to $20) at the new roadside tasting room of Randall Grahm's acclaimed winery, where Edison lights and rough-hewn wooden tables entice you to sample a Cigare Volant (yes, that's a flying cigar) and other bottles made with lesser-known varietals.

1850, the elephant seal was driven to the edge of extinction. Only a handful survived around the Guadalupe Islands off the Mexican state of Baja California. With the availability of substitutes for seal oil and the conservationist attitudes of more recent times, the elephant seal has made a comeback, reappearing on the Southern California coast from around 1920. In 1955 they returned to Año Nuevo Beach.

In the midwinter peak season, during the mating and birthing time from December 15 to the end of March, you must plan well ahead if you want to visit the reserve, because visitors are only permitted access through heavily booked guided tours. For the busiest period, mid-January to mid-February, it's recommended you book eight weeks ahead. If you haven't booked, bad weather can sometimes lead to last-minute cancellations.

The rest of the year, advance reservations aren't necessary, but visitor permits from the entrance station are required; arrive before 3pm from September through November and by 3:30pm from April through August.

Although the **park office** (☑650-879-2025, recorded information 650-879-0227; www.parks.ca.gov/?page_id=523) can answer general questions, high-season tour bookings must be made at ☑800-444-4445 or http://anonuevo.reserveamerica.com. When required, these tours cost $7, and entry is $10 per car year-round. From the ranger station it's a 3- to 5-mile round-trip hike on sand, and a visit takes two to three hours. No dogs are allowed on-site, and visitors aren't permitted for the first two weeks of December.

There's another, more convenient viewing site further south in Piedras Blancas.

Napa & Sonoma Wine Country

Best Places to Eat

➡ The Shed (p192)

➡ Oxbow Public Market (p149)

➡ Fremont Diner (p171)

➡ Madrona Manor (p193)

Best Places to Stay

➡ Beltane Ranch (p174)

➡ Cottages of Napa Valley (p148)

➡ Mountain Home Ranch (p161)

➡ El Bonita (p155)

Why Go?

America's premier viticulture region has earned its reputation among the world's best. Despite hype about Wine Country style, it's from the land that all Wine Country lore springs. Rolling hills, dotted with century-old oaks, turn the color of lion's fur under the summer sun and swaths of vineyards carpet hillsides as far as the eye can see. Where they end, lush redwood forests follow serpentine rivers to the sea.

There are over 600 wineries in Napa and Sonoma Counties, but it's quality, not quantity, that sets the region apart – especially in Napa, which competes with France and doubles as an outpost of San Francisco's top-end culinary scene. Sonoma prides itself on agricultural diversity, with goat-cheese farms, you-pick-'em orchards and roadside fruit stands. Plan to get lost on back roads, and, as you picnic atop sun-dappled hillsides, grab a hunk of earth and know firsthand the thing of greatest meaning in Wine Country.

When to Go
Napa

Jan Bright-yellow flowers carpet the valleys during the off-season; room rates plummet.

Apr–May Before summer holidays is perfect for touring, with long days and warm sun.

Sep–Oct 'Crush' time is peak season, when wine-making operations are in full force.

ⓘ Getting There & Away

Napa and Sonoma counties each have an eponymous city and valley. So, the town of Sonoma is in Sonoma County, at the southern end of Sonoma Valley. The same goes for the city, county and valley of Napa.

From San Francisco, public transportation gets you to the valleys, but it's insufficient for vineyard-hopping. For public-transit informa-tion, ⌨ dial 511 from Bay Area telephones, or look online at www.transit.511.org.

Both valleys are 90 minutes' drive from San Francisco. Napa, the further inland, has over 400 wineries and attracts the most visitors (expect heavy traffic on summer weekends). Sonoma County has 260 wineries, 40 in Sonoma Valley, which is less commercial and less congested than Napa. If you have time to visit only one, for ease choose Sonoma.

Napa & Sonoma Wine Country Highlights

❶ Sample California's greatest red wines in **Napa Valley** (p142).

❷ Picnic in sun-dappled shade on the state's largest town square, **Sonoma Plaza** (p168).

❸ Bite into the artisanal food scene at Napa's **Oxbow Public Market** (p149).

❹ Get lost on West County Sonoma back roads, like **Coleman Valley Road** (p182).

❺ Submerge yourself in a volcanic-ash mud bath in **Calistoga** (p159).

❻ Meet kooky locals at the **Occidental Farmers Market** (p182).

❼ Pedal between wineries along pastoral **West Dry Creek Road** (p178), in the Dry Creek Valley.

❽ Float in a canoe or kayak down the **Russian River** (p175).

BUS

Evans Transportation (☎707-255-1559; www.evanstransportation.com) Shuttles ($29) to Napa from San Francisco and Oakland Airports.

Golden Gate Transit (☎415-923-2000; www.goldengate.org) Bus 70/80 from San Francisco to Petaluma ($10.25) and Santa Rosa ($11.25); board at 1st and Mission Sts. Connects with Sonoma County Transit buses.

Greyhound Buses (☎800-231-2222; www.greyhound.com) San Francisco to Santa Rosa ($22 to $30); transfer to local buses.

Napa Valley Vine (☎707-251-2800, 800-696-6443; www.nctpa.net) Operates local bus 10 daily from downtown Napa to Calistoga ($1.50); express bus 29 Monday to Friday from the Vallejo Ferry Terminal ($3.25) and El Cerrito del Norte BART station ($5.50), via Napa, to Calistoga; and local bus 11 daily from the Vallejo Ferry Terminal to downtown Napa ($1.50).

Sonoma County Airport Express (☎800-327-2024, 707-837-8700; www.airportexpressinc.com) Shuttles ($34) between Sonoma County Airport (Santa Rosa) and San Francisco and Oakland Airports.

CAR

From San Francisco, take Hwy 101 north over the Golden Gate Bridge, then Hwy 37 east to Hwy 121 north; continue to the junction of Hwy 12/121. For Sonoma Valley, take Hwy 12 north; for Napa Valley, take Hwy 12/121 east. Plan 70 minutes in light traffic, two hours during the weekday commute.

Hwy 12/121 splits south of Napa: Hwy 121 turns north and joins with Hwy 29 (aka St Helena Hwy); Hwy 12 merges with southbound Hwy 29 toward Vallejo. Hwy 29 backs up weekdays 3pm to 7pm, slowing returns to San Francisco.

From the East Bay (or downtown San Francisco), take I-80 east to Hwy 37 west (north of Vallejo), then northbound Hwy 29.

From Santa Rosa, take Hwy 12 east to access the northern end of Sonoma Valley. From Petaluma and Hwy 101, take Hwy 116 east.

FERRY

Baylink Ferry (☎877-643-3779; sanfranciscobayferry.com) Downtown San Francisco to Vallejo (adult/child $13/6.50, 60 minutes); connect with Napa Valley Vine bus 29 (weekdays) or bus 11 (daily).

TRAIN

Amtrak (☎800-872-7245; www.amtrak.com) Trains travel to Martinez (south of Vallejo), with connecting buses to Napa (45 minutes), Santa Rosa (1¼ hours) and Healdsburg (1¾ hours).

BART trains (☎415 989-2278; www.bart.gov) Run from San Francisco to El Cerrito del Norte ($4.40, 30 minutes). Napa Valley Vine bus 29 runs weekdays from BART to Calistoga, via Napa; on Saturdays take **SolTrans** (☎707-648-4666; www.soltransride.com) from BART to Vallejo ($5, 30 minutes), then connect with Napa Valley Vine bus 11 to Napa and Calistoga; on Sundays there's no connecting bus service from BART.

❶ Getting Around

You'll need a car or bike to winery-hop. Alternatively visit tasting rooms in downtown Napa or downtown Sonoma.

BICYCLE

Touring Wine Country by bicycle is unforgettable. Stick to back roads. We most love pastoral West Dry Creek Rd, northwest of Healdsburg, in Sonoma County. Through Sonoma Valley, take Arnold Dr instead of Hwy 12; through Napa Valley, take the Silverado Trail instead of Hwy 29.

Cycling between wineries isn't demanding – the valleys are mostly flat – but crossing between the Napa and Sonoma Valleys is intense, particularly via steep Oakville Grade and Trinity Rd (between Oakville and Glen Ellen).

Bicycles, in boxes, can be checked on Greyhound buses for $30 to $40; bike boxes cost $10 (call ahead). You can transport bicycles on Golden Gate Transit buses, which usually have free racks available (first-come, first-served).

CAR

Napa Valley is 30 miles long and 5 miles across at its widest point (city of Napa), 1 mile at its narrowest (Calistoga). Two roads run north–south: Hwy 29 (St Helena Hwy) and the more scenic Silverado Trail, a mile east. Drive up one, down the other.

The American Automobile Association ranks Napa Valley among America's most congested rural vacation destinations. Summer and fall weekend traffic is unbearable, especially on Hwy 29 between Napa and St Helena. Plan accordingly.

Cross-valley roads linking Silverado Trail with Hwy 29 – including Yountville, Oakville and Rutherford crossroads – are bucolic and get less traffic. For scenery, the Oakville Grade and rural Trinity Rd (which leads southwest to Hwy 12 in Sonoma Valley) are narrow, curvy and beautiful – but treacherous in rainstorms. Mt Veeder Rd leads through pristine countryside west of Yountville.

Note: Police watch like hawks for traffic violators. *Don't drink and drive.*

There are a number of shortcuts between the Napa and Sonoma Valleys: from Oakville, take Oakville Grade to Trinity Rd; from St Helena, take Spring Mountain Rd into Calistoga Rd; from Calistoga, take Petrified Forest Rd to Calistoga Rd.

PUBLIC TRANSPORTATION

Napa Valley Vine (☑707-251-2800, 800-696-6443; www.nctpa.net) Bus 10 runs daily from downtown Napa to Calistoga ($1.50, 1¼ hours).

Sonoma County Transit (☑800-345-7433, 707-576-7433; www.sctransit.com) Buses from Santa Rosa to Petaluma ($2.45, 70 minutes), Sonoma ($3.05, 1¼ hours) and western Sonoma County, including Russian River Valley towns ($3.05, 30 minutes).

NAPA VALLEY

The birthplace of modern-day Wine Country is famous for regal Cabernet Sauvignons, château-like wineries and fabulous food, attracting more than four million visitors a year, many planning to wine and dine themselves into a stupor, maybe get a massage, and sleep somewhere swell with fine linens and a pool.

A few decades ago, this 5-by-35-mile strip of former stagecoach stops seemed forgotten by time, a quiet agricultural valley dense with orchards. Grapes had grown here since the Gold Rush, but grape-sucking phylloxera bugs, Prohibition and the Great Depression reduced 140 wineries in the 1890s, to around 25 by the 1960s.

In 1968, Napa was declared the 'Napa Valley Agricultural Preserve,' effectively blocking future valley development for non-ag purposes. The law stipulated no subdivision of valley-floor land under 40 acres. This succeeded in preserving the valley's natural beauty, but when Napa wines earned top honors at a 1976 blind tasting in Paris, the wine-drinking world noticed and land values skyrocketed. Only the very rich could afford to build. Hence, so many architecturally jaw-dropping wineries. Independent, family-owned wineries still exist – we highlight a number of them – but much of Napa Valley is now owned by global conglomerates.

The city of Napa anchors the valley, but the real work happens up-valley. Napa isn't as pretty as other towns, but has some noteworthy sights, among them Oxbow Public Market. Scenic towns include St Helena, Yountville and Calistoga – the latter more famous for water than wine.

Napa Valley Wineries

Cab is king in Napa. No varietal captures imaginations like the fruit of the Cabernet Sauvignon vine – Bordeaux is the French equivalent – and no wine fetches a higher price. Napa farmers can't afford *not* to grow Cabernet. Other heat-loving varietals, such as Sangiovese and Merlot, also thrive here.

Napa's wines merit their reputation among the world's finest – complex, with luxurious finishes. Napa wineries sell many 'buy-and-hold' wines, versus Sonoma's 'drink-now' wines.

Artesa Vineyards & Winery   WINERY
(☑707-254-2126; www.artesawinery.com; 1345 Henry Rd, Napa; glass $12, tasting $15-20, incl tour $30; ☺10am-4:30pm) Begin or end the day with a glass of bubbly or Pinot at Artesa, southwest of Napa. Built into a mountainside, the ultra-modern Barcelona-style architecture is stunning, and you can't beat the top-of-the-world vistas over San Pablo Bay. Tours run at 11am and 2pm. Bottles cost $20 to $60.

Vintners' Collective   TASTING ROOM
(Map p147; ☑707-255-7150; www.vintnerscollective.com; 1245 Main St, Napa; tasting $10-30; ☺11am-6pm) Ditch the car and chill in downtown Napa at this tasting bar, inside a former 19th-century brothel, representing 20 high-end boutique wineries too small to have their own tasting rooms.

Twenty Rows   WINERY
(☑707-265-7750; www.twentyrows.com; 880 Vallejo St, Napa; tasting $10; ☺11am-5pm Tue-Sat, by appointment Sun & Mon) Downtown Napa's only working winery crafts light-on-the-palate Cabernet Sauvignon for just $20 a bottle. Taste in a chilly garage, on plastic furniture, with fun dudes who know their wines. Good Sauvignon Blanc, too.

★**Hess Collection**   WINERY, GALLERY
(☑707-255-1144; www.hesscollection.com; 4411 Redwood Rd, Napa; tasting $15, gallery free; ☺10am-5:30pm) ✐ Art lovers: don't miss **Hess Collection**, whose galleries display mixed-media and large-canvas works, including pieces by Francis Bacon and Louis Soutter. In the cave-like tasting room, find well-known Cabernet and Chardonnay, but also try the Viognier. Hess overlooks the valley: be prepared to drive a winding road. Reservations recommended. Bottles: $20 to $60. (NB: Don't confuse Hess Collection with Hess Select, the grocery-store brand.)

Darioush   WINERY
(☑707-257-2345; www.darioush.com; 4240 Silverado Trail, Napa; tasting $18-40; ☺10:30am-5pm)

TOURING NAPA & SONOMA WINE COUNTRY

You have the most flexibility by driving your own vehicle, but to drink and not drive, here are some tour options. Note that some wineries do not allow limousines (because the people in them are often obnoxious and don't buy anything); and limousine companies have set itineraries with little flexibility (ie, you'll have few choices about which wineries you visit).

Bicycle Tours & Rentals

Guided tours start around $90 per day including bikes, tastings and lunch. Daily rentals cost $25 to $85; make reservations.

Backroads (☎800-462-2848; www.backroads.com) All-inclusive guided biking and walking.

Calistoga Bike Shop (☎707-942-9687; www.calistogabikeshop.com; 1318 Lincoln Ave, Calistoga; ☺10am-6pm) Wine-tour rental package ($90) includes wine pickup.

Getaway Adventures (☎800-499-2453, 707-568-3040; http://getawayadventures.com; tours $149) Great guided tours, some combined with kayaking, of Napa, Sonoma, Calistoga, Healdsburg and Russian River. Single- and multiday trips.

Good Time Touring (☎888-525-0453, 707-938-0453; www.goodtimetouring.com) Tours of Sonoma Valley, Dry Creek and West County Sonoma.

Napa River Velo (Map p147; ☎707-258-8729; www.naparivervelo.com; 680 Main St, Napa; ☺10am-7pm Mon-Fri, 9am-6pm Sat, 10am-5pm Sun) Daily rentals and weekend tours with wine pickup.

Napa Valley Adventure Tours (☎707-224-9080, 707-259-1833; www.napavalleyadventuretours.com; 1147 1st St, Napa) Guides tours between wineries, off-road trips, hiking and kayaking. Daily rentals.

Napa Valley Bike Tours (☎707-944-2953; www.napavalleybiketours.com; 6500 Washington St, Yountville; ☺8:30am-5pm) Daily rentals; easy and moderately difficult tours.

Spoke Folk Cyclery (☎707-433-7171; www.spokefolk.com; 201 Center St, Healdsburg; ☺10am-6pm Mon-Fri, to 5pm Sat & Sun) Rents touring, racing and tandem bicycles.

Wine Country Bikes (☎707-473-0610, toll free 866-922-4537; www.winecountrybikes.com; 61 Front St, Healdsburg; rentals per day from $39, multiday guided tours from $595; ☺9am-5pm) Rents bikes in downtown Healdsburg and guides multiday Sonoma County tours.

Other Tours

Wine Country Jeep Tours (☎800-539-5337, 707-546-1822; www.jeeptours.com; 3hr tour $75) Tour Wine Country's back roads and boutique wineries by Jeep, year-round at 10am and 1pm. Also operates tours of Sonoma Coast.

Antique Tours Limousine (☎707-761-3949; www.antiquetours.net) Drive in style in a 1947 Packard convertible; tours cost $120 to $170 per hour.

Beau Wine Tours (☎800-387-2328, 707-938-8001; www.beauwinetours.com) Winery tours in sedans and stretch limos; charges $60 to $95 per hour (four- to six-hour minimum).

Beyond the Label (☎707-363-4023; www.btlnv.com; per couple $995) Personalized tours, including lunch at home with a vintner, guided by a Napa native.

Flying Horse Carriage Company (☎707-849-8989; www.flyinghorse.org; 4hr tour per person $150; ☺Fri-Mon) Trot through Alexander Valley by horse-drawn carriage. Includes picnic.

Magnum Tours (☎707-753-0088; www.magnumwinetours.com) Sedans and specialty limousines from $65 to $125 per hour (four-hour minimum, five hours Saturdays). Exceptional service.

Like a modern-day Persian palace, Darioush ranks high on the fabulosity scale, with towering columns, Le Corbusier furniture, Persian rugs and travertine walls. Though known for Cabernet, Darioush also bottles Chardonnay, Merlot and Shiraz, all made with 100% of their respective varietals. Call about wine-and-cheese pairings. Bottles cost $40 to $95.

Regusci
WINERY

(☑707-254-0403; www.regusciwinery.com; 5584 Silverado Trail, Napa; tasting $25-30, incl tour $30-60; ☺10am-5pm) One of Napa's oldest, unfussy Regusci dates to the late 1800s, with 173 acres of vineyards unfurling around a century-old stone winery that makes Bordeaux-style blends on the valley's quieter eastern side – good when traffic up-valley is bad. No appointment necessary; lovely oak-shaded picnic area. Bottles cost $36 to $140.

★ Robert Sinskey
WINERY

(☑707-944-9090; www.robertsinskey.com; 6320 Silverado Trail, Napa; tasting $25, incl tour $50-75; ☺10am-4:30pm) ✏ Chef-owned Robert Sinskey's dramatic hilltop tasting room, constructed of stone, redwood and teak, resembles a small cathedral – fitting, given the sacred status bestowed upon food and wine here. Sinskey specializes in bright-acid organic Pinot, Merlot and Cabernet, and exceptional Alsatian varietals, Vin Gris, Cabernet Franc and dry Rosé, specifically designed to pair well with food. Tasting fee waived with two-bottle purchase – a rarity. Small bites accompany tastings. Call about culinary tours. Bottles cost $28 to $100.

Robert Mondavi
WINERY

(☑888-766-6328; www.robertmondaviwinery. com; 7801 Hwy 29, Oakville; tasting & tour $20-55; ☺10am-5pm; ﹏) Tour buses flock to this corporate-owned winery, but if you know nothing about wine and can cope with crowds, the worthwhile tours provide excellent insight into winemaking. Otherwise, skip it unless you're considering one of its glorious outdoor summer **concerts**; call for schedules. Bottles cost $25 to $150.

Elizabeth Spencer
TASTING ROOM

(☑707-963-6067; www.elizabethspencerwines. com; 1165 Rutherford Rd, Rutherford; tasting $20; ☺10am-5:30pm) Taste inside an 1872 railroad depot or the outdoor garden at this inviting small winery, featuring monster-sized Pinot Noir, grapefruity Sauvignon Blanc, structured light-body Grenache, and signature Cabernet. Bottles cost $30 to $95.

Mumm Napa
WINERY, GALLERY

(☑800-686-6272; www.mummnapa.com; 8445 Silverado Trail, Rutherford; glass $8; tasting $18-40, tour $25; ☺10am-4:45pm) Valley views are spectacular at Mumm, which makes respectable sparkling wines you can sample while seated on a vineyard-view terrace – ideal when you want to impress conservative parents-in-law. Dodge crowds by coming early, or paying $40 for the reserve-tasting Oak Terrace (reservations advised).

★ Frog's Leap
WINERY

(☑707-963-4704; www.frogsleap.com; 8815 Conn Creek Rd, Rutherford; tasting $15, incl tour $20; ☺by appointment; ﹏☙) ✏ Meandering paths wind through magical gardens and

---

NAPA OR SONOMA?

Napa and Sonoma Valleys run parallel, separated by the narrow, imposing Mayacamas Mountains. The two couldn't be more different. It's easy to mock aggressively sophisticated Napa, its monuments to ego, trophy homes and trophy wives, $1000-a-night inns, $50-plus tastings and wine-snob visitors, but Napa makes some of the world's best wines. Constrained by its geography, it stretches along a single valley, making it easy to visit. Drawbacks are high prices and heavy traffic, but there are 400 nearly side-by-side wineries. And the valley is gorgeous.

There are three Sonomas: the town of Sonoma, which is in Sonoma Valley, which is in Sonoma County. Think of them as Russian dolls. Sonoma County is much more down-to-earth and politically left-leaning. Though it's becoming gentrified, Sonoma lacks Napa's chic factor (Healdsburg notwithstanding), and locals like it that way. The wines are more approachable, but the county's 260 wineries are spread out. If you're here on a weekend, head to Sonoma (County or Valley), which gets less traffic, but on a weekday, see Napa, too. Ideally schedule two to four days: one for each valley, and one or two additional for western Sonoma County.

Spring and fall are the best times to visit. Summers are hot, dusty and crowded. Fall brings fine weather, harvest time and the 'crush,' the pressing of the grapes, but lodging prices skyrocket.

fruit-bearing orchards – pick peaches in July – surrounding an 1884 barn and farmstead with cats and chickens. The vibe is casual and down-to-earth, with a major emphasis on *fun*. Sauvignon Blanc is its best-known wine, but the Merlot merits attention. There's also a dry, restrained Cabernet, atypical of Napa.

All are organic. Appointments required. Bottles cost $22 to $42.

★ Tres Sabores
WINERY

(☎707-967-8027; www.tressabores.com; 1620 South Whitehall Lane, St Helena; tour & tasting $20; ☺by appointment; 🍴) 🚗 At the valley's westernmost edge, where sloping vineyards meet wooded hillsides, Tres Sabores is a portal to old Napa – no fancy tasting room, no snobbery, just great wine in a spectacular setting. Bucking the Cabernet custom, Tres Sabores crafts elegantly structured, Burgundian-style Zinfandel, and spritely Sauvignon Blanc, which the *New York Times* dubbed a top 10 of its kind in California. Reservations essential.

Guinea fowl and sheep control pests on the 35-acre estate, while golden labs chase butterflies through gnarled old vines. After your tour, linger at olive-shaded picnic tables and drink in gorgeous valley views. Bottles cost $22 to $80.

Hall
WINERY

(Map p156; ☎707-967-2626; www.hallwines.com; 401 St Helena Hwy, St Helena; tasting $30, tour $50; ☺10am-5:30pm; 🍴) Owned by Bill Clinton's former ambassador to Austria, Hall specializes in Sauvignon Blanc, Merlot and Cabernet Sauvignon, crafted in big-fruit California style. Its dramatic tasting room has a stand-up bar with 180-degree views of vineyards and mountains through floor-to-ceiling glass, and the glorious art collection includes a giant chrome rabbit leaping over the vines. Bottles cost $22 to $80.

Long Meadow Ranch
TASTING ROOM

(Map p156; ☎707-963-4555; www.longmeadow-ranch.com; 738 Main St, St Helena; tasting $15-25; ☺11am-6pm) 🚗 Long Meadow stands out for olive-oil tastings (free), plus good estate-grown Cabernet, Sauvignon Blanc, Chardonnay and Pinot noir (bottles $20 to $47), served inside an 1874 farmhouse surrounded by lovely gardens.

Pride Mountain
WINERY

(Map p156; ☎707-963-4949; www.pridewines. com; 3000 Summit Trail, St Helena; tasting incl tour

$20-25; ☺by appointment) High atop Spring Mountain, cult-favorite Pride straddles the Napa–Sonoma border and bottles vintages under both appellations. The well-structured Cabernet and heavy-hitting Merlot are the best-known but there's also an elegant Viognier (perfect with oysters) and standout Cab Franc, available only here. Picnicking here is spectacular: choose Viewpoint for drop-dead vistas or Ghost Winery for shade and the historic ruins of a 19th-century winery, but you must first reserve a tasting. Bottles cost $38 to $70.

Titus
WINERY

(Map p156; ☎707-963-3235; www.titusvineyards. com; 2971 Silverado Trail North, St Helena; tasting $20; ☺by appointment; 🚗🍴) Unfussy Titus occupies a tiny oak-shaded 1910 farmhouse, surrounded by white-picket fence and roses. Call ahead to sample good-value, fruit-forward Cabernet Sauvignon and old-vine Zinfandel, which you taste in an old-fashioned kitchen overlooking the vineyards. Afterward, take your glass outside and wander the vineyards. The tasting fee is waived with a purchase and bottles are $20 to $70.

Casa Nuestra
WINERY

(Map p156; ☎866-844-9463; www.casanuestra. com; 3451 Silverado Trail North, St Helena; tasting $10; ☺by appointment) 🚗 A peace flag and portrait of Elvis greet you at this old-school, mom-and-pop winery, which produces unusual blends and interesting varietals (including good Chenin Blanc) and 100% Cabernet Franc. Vineyards are all-organic; the sun provides power. Picnic free (call ahead and buy a bottle) beneath weeping willows shading happy goats. Bottles are $20 to $60.

Cade
WINERY

(Map p156; ☎707-965-2746; www.cadewinery.com; 360 Howell Mountain Rd S, Angwin; tasting $40-70; ☺by appointment) 🚗 Ascend Mt Veeder for drop-dead vistas, 1800ft above the valley, at Napa's oh-so-swank, first-ever organically farmed, LEED-gold-certified winery, partly owned by former San Francisco mayor Gavin Newsom. Hawks ride thermals at eye level as you sample bright Sauvignon Blanc and luscious Cabernet Sauvignon that's more Bordelaise in style than Californian. Reservations required. Bottles cost $44 to $80.

Ladera
WINERY

(Map p156; ☑707-965-2445, 866-523-3728; www. laderavineyards.com; 150 White Cottage Rd S, Angwin; tasting $25; ☺by appointment) ✔ High atop Howell Mountain, Ladera makes wonderful, little-known, estate-grown Cabernet Sauvignon and Sauvignon Blanc in a well-off-the-beaten-path, 1886, stone-walled winery, one of Napa's oldest – ideal when you want to escape the crowds. Bottle are $28 to $85.

Schramsberg
WINERY

(Map p156; ☑707-942-2414; www.schramsberg. com; 1400 Schramsberg Rd, off Peterson Dr; tour & tasting $50; ☺by appointment 10am, 11:30am, 12:30pm, 1:30pm & 2:30pm) Napa's second-oldest winery, Schramsberg makes some of California's best brut sparkling wines, and in 1972 was the first domestic wine served at the White House. Blanc de Blancs is the signature. The appointment-only tasting and tour (book well ahead) is expensive, but you'll sample all the *tête de cuvées*, not just the low-end wines. Tours include a walk through the caves; bring a sweater. Bottles cost $22 to $100.

Castello di Amorosa
WINERY, CASTLE

(Map p156; ☑707-967-6272; www.castellodiamorosa.com; 4045 Hwy 29, Calistoga; admission & tasting $19-29, incl guided tour $34-75; ☺9:30am-6pm, to 5pm Nov-Feb) It took 14 years to build this perfectly replicated, 12th-century Italian castle, complete with moat, hand-cut stone walls, ceiling frescoes by Italian artisans, Roman-style cross-vault brick catacombs, and a torture chamber with period equipment. You can taste without an appointment, but this is one tour worth taking. Oh, the wine? Some respectable Italian varietals, including a velvety Tuscan blend, and a Merlot blend that goes great with pizza. Bottles are $20 to $125.

Lava Vine
WINERY

(Map p156; ☑707-942-9500; www.lavavine.com; 965 Silverado Trail; tasting $10; ☺10am-5pm; ⊕⊛) ✔ Breaking ranks with Napa snobbery, the party kids at Lava Vine take a light-hearted approach to their seriously good wines – don't be surprised if they bust out musical instruments and start jamming. Children and dogs play outside, while you tap your toe to uptempo tunes in the tiny tasting room. Picnicking allowed. Reservations recommended. Bottles cost $25 to $55.

Vincent Arroyo
WINERY

(Map p156; ☑707-942-6995; www.vincentarroyo. com; 2361 Greenwood Ave, Calistoga; ☺by appointment) FREE The tasting room is a garage, where you may even meet Mr Arroyo, known for his all-estate-grown petite Syrah and Cabernet Sauvignon. They're distributed nowhere else and are so consistently good that 75% of production is sold before it's bottled. Tastings are free, but appointments are required. Bottles are $22 to $45.

Napa

The valley's workaday hub was once a nothing-special city of storefronts, Victorian cottages and riverfront warehouses, but booming real-estate values caused an influx of new money that's transforming downtown into a hub of arts and food.

⊙ Sights

Napa lies between Silverado Trail and St Helena Hwy/Hwy 29. For downtown, exit Hwy 29 at 1st St and drive east. Napa's main drag, 1st St, is lined with shops and restaurants.

★Oxbow Public Market
MARKET

(Map p147; ☑707-226-6529; www.oxbowpublicmarket.com; 610 1st St; ☺9am-7pm Mon, Wed & Thu, to 8pm Tue, Fri & Sat, 10am-6pm Sun; ⊕) ✔ Produce stalls, kitchen shops, and everywhere something to taste – Oxbow is foodie central, with emphasis on seasonal eating and sustainability. Come hungry.

★di Rosa Art + Nature Preserve
GALLERY, GARDENS

(☑707-226-5991; www.dirosaart.org; 5200 Hwy 121; admission $5, tours $12-15; ☺10am-4pm Wed-Sun) West of downtown, scrap-metal sheep graze Carneros vineyards at 217-acre di Rosa Preserve, a stunning collection of Northern California art, displayed indoors in galleries and outdoors in sculpture gardens. Reservations recommended for tours.

⊂ Tours

Napa Valley Wine Train
TRAIN TOUR

(☑800-427-4124, 707-253-2111; www.winetrain. com; adult/child from $109/74) A cushy, if tour-

Napa

Napa

◉ Top Sights
1 Oxbow Public Market D1

◉ Sights
2 Vintners' Collective C1

◐ Activities, Courses & Tours
3 Napa River Velo D3

⊜ Sleeping
4 Blackbird Inn A3
5 Napa River Inn D3

✕ Eating
6 Alexis Baking Co B3
7 Angèle D3
8 Bounty Hunter Wine Bar &
  Smokin' BBQ C2

9 Norman Rose Tavern B3
10 Oenotri B3
11 Pizza Azzurro C1

⊙ Drinking & Nightlife
12 Billco's Billiards & Darts C3
13 Downtown Joe's C2

✪ Entertainment
14 City Winery at Napa Valley
   Opera House C2
   Silo's Jazz Club .... (see 5)
15 Uptown Theatre C3

⌂ Shopping
16 Betty's Girl C2
   Napa General Store .... (see 5)

isty, way to see Wine Country, the Wine Train offers three-hour daily trips in vintage Pullman dining cars, from Napa to St Helena and back, with an optional winery tour. Trains depart from McKinstry St, near 1st St.

🛏 Sleeping

Summer demand exceeds supply. Weekend rates skyrocket. Also consider staying in Calistoga.

Chablis Inn MOTEL $$
(☏ 707-257-1944; www.chablisinn.com; 3360 Solano Ave; r Mon-Fri $89-109, Sat & Sun $169-189; ✽ @ 🛜 ☒) Good-value, well-kept motel near Napa's only stretch of freeway. Hot tub.

★ Carneros Inn RESORT $$$
(☏ 707-299-4900; www.thecarnerosinn.com; 4048 Sonoma Hwy; r Mon-Fri $485-570, Sat & Sun $650-900; ✽ @ 🛜 ☒ 🐾) Carneros Inn's contemporary aesthetic and retro, small-town

agricultural theme shatter the predictable Wine Country mold. The semi-detached, corrugated-metal cottages look like itinerant housing, but inside they're snappy and chic, with cherry-wood floors, ultrasuede headboards, wood-burning fireplaces, heated-tile bathroom floors, giant tubs and indoor-outdoor showers. Linger by day at the hilltop pool, by night at the outdoor fireplaces. Two excellent on-site restaurants.

Milliken Creek Inn INN $$$

(☎888-622-5775, 707-255-1197; www.millikencreek-inn.com; 1815 Silverado Trail; r incl breakfast $295-750; ❋@❅) Understatedly elegant Milliken Creek combines small-inn charm, fine-hotel service and B&B intimacy. Rooms are impeccably styled in English-Colonial style, and have top-flight amenities, fireplaces and ultra-high-thread-count linens. Breakfast is delivered. Book a river-view room.

Cottages of Napa Valley BUNGALOW $$$

(☎707-252-7810; www.napacottages.com; 1012 Darns Lane; d $395-500, q $475-575; ❋❅) Eight pristine cottages of quality construction – made for romantic hideaways, with extra-long soaking tubs, indoor gas fireplaces and outdoor campfire pits – surround a big garden shaded by towering pines. Cottages 4 and 8 have private porches and swinging chairs. The only drawback is white noise from traffic, but interiors are silent.

Andaz Hotel HOTEL $$$

(☎707-224-3900; napa.andaz.hyatt.com; 1450 1st St; r $289-389; ❋@❅) Smack downtown, the

---

Andaz was constructed in 2009, and feels like a big-city hotel, with business-class-fancy rooms, styled in sexy retro-70s style. Walkable to restaurants and bars.

Napa River Inn HOTEL $$$

(Map p147; ☎877-251-8500, 707-251-8500; www.napariverinn.com; 500 Main St; r incl breakfast $249-549; ❋@❅❅) Beside the river, in the 1884 Hatt Building, the inn has upper-mid-range rooms, Victoriana to modern, in three satellite buildings. Walkable to restaurants and bars. Dogs get special treatment.

River Terrace Inn HOTEL $$$

(☎707-320-9000, 866-627-2386; www.riverterraceinn.com; 1600 Soscol Ave; r $189-360; ❋❅❅) Upmarket, business-class, chain-style hotel with shopping-mall-bland architecture fronting on the Napa River. Heated outdoor pool.

Casita Bonita BUNGALOW $$$

(☎707-321-4853, 707-259-1980; www.lacasitabonita.com; q $395; ❋❅) Well decorated two-bedroom cottage with full kitchen and veggie garden – kids love the chickens. Perfect for two couples or a family. Two-night minimum. Check the website for location details.

Best Western Ivy Hotel HOTEL $$$

(☎800-253-6272, 707-253-9300; www.ivyhotelnapa.com; 4195 Solano Ave; r $180-295; ❋@❅❅) Redone in 2011, this colorful, smart-looking, two-story hotel, on the suburban strip north of Napa, has extras like fridge, microwave and on-site laundry. Good value when under $250.

Napa Winery Inn HOTEL $$$

(☎800-522-8999, 707-257-7220; www.napawineryinn.com; 1998 Trower Ave; r incl breakfast Mon-Fri $179-279, Sat & Sun $229-339; ❋@❅❅❅) Request a remodeled room at this good-value hotel, north of downtown, decorated with generic. Hot tub, good service.

Blackbird Inn B&B $$$

(Map p147; ☎888-567-9811, 707-226-2450; www.blackbirdinnnapa.com; 1775 1st St; r incl breakfast $185-300; ❋❅) Gorgeous, eight-room Arts and Crafts–style B&B, but anticipate street noise.

Best Western Elm House INN $$$

(☎707-255-1831; www.bestwesternelmhouseinn.com; 800 California Blvd; r incl breakfast $199-299; ❋@❅) Impeccably kept rooms with generic furnishings in soft pastels. Ideal for conservative travelers. Fifteen-minute walk to downtown; easy highway access. Hot tub.

ⓘ CUTTING COSTS IN NAPA

To avoid overspending on tasting fees, it's perfectly acceptable to pay for one tasting to share between two people. Ask in advance if fees are applicable to purchase (they usually aren't). Tour fees cannot be split. Ask at your hotel, or at visitors centers, for free- or discounted-tasting coupons, or download from napatouristguide.com. If you can't afford the hotels, try western Sonoma County, but if you want to be nearer Napa, try the suburban towns of Vallejo and American Canyon, about 20 minutes from downtown Napa. Both have motels for $75 to $125 in high season. Also find chains 30 minutes away in Fairfield, off I-80 exits 41 (Pittman Rd) and 45 (Travis Blvd).

✕ Eating

Make reservations whenever possible. July to mid-August, look for the peach stand at Deer Park Rd and Silverado Trail (across Deer Park Rd from Stewart's farmstand) for juicy-delicious heirloom varieties.

★ **Oxbow Public Market** MARKET $
(☎707-226-6529; www.oxbowpublicmarket.com; 644 1st St; dishes from $3; ◎9am-7pm Mon, Wed & Thu-Sat, to 8pm Tue, 10am-5pm Sun) ◢ Graze this gourmet market and plug into the Northern California food scene. Standouts: **Hog Island** oysters (six for $16); comfort cooking at celeb-chef Todd Humphries' **Kitchen Door** (mains $14 to $24); Venezuelan cornbread sandwiches ($9) at **Pica Pica**; great Cal-Mexican at **C Casa** (tacos $5 to $9); pastries at **Ca'Momi** ($2); and **Three Twins** certified-organic ice cream ($3.75 for a single cone).

Tuesday is locals' night (5pm to 8pm), with many discounts. Tuesday and Saturday mornings, there's a farmers market. Some stalls remain open till 9pm, even on Sundays, but many close earlier.

Alexis Baking Co CAFE $
(Map p147; ☎707-258-1827; www.alexisbakingcompany.com; 1517 3rd St; dishes $7-13; ◎7am-3pm Mon-Fri, 7:30am-3pm Sat, 8am-2pm Sun; ◢⊞) Our fave spot for quality scrambles, granola, focaccia, big cups of joe and boxed lunches to go.

Taqueria Maria MEXICAN $
(☎707-257-6925; www.taqueriamaria.com; 640 3rd St; mains $8-13; ◎9am-8:30pm Sun-Thu, to 9pm Fri & Sat; ◢⊞) Reliably good Mexican cooking that won't break the bank. Also serves breakfast.

Buttercream Bakery DINER $
(☎707-255-6700; www.buttercreambakery.com; 2297 Jefferson St; breakfast $5; ◎5:30am-3pm) For a retro-flashback: this pink-striped diner, favored by Napa's little old ladies, has all-day breakfasts and white-bread lunches, served by matrons in heavy eye shadow.

Soda Canyon Store DELI $
(☎707-252-0285; www.sodacanyonstore.com; 4006 Silverado Trail; ◎6am-5:30pm Mon-Sat, 7:30am-5pm Sun) This roadside deli, with shaded picnic area, makes an easy stop while winery-hopping north of town.

Oenotri ITALIAN $$
(Map p147; ☎707-252-1022; www.oenotri.com; 1425 1st St; dinner mains $17-29, lunch $13-15;

◎11:30am-2:30pm & 5:30-9pm Sun-Thu, to 10pm Fri & Sat) ◢ Housemade salumi and pastas, and wood-fired Naples-style pizzas are the stars at always-busy Oenotri, which draws crowds for daily-changing, locally sourced, rustic-Italian cooking, served in a cavernous brick-walled space.

Carpe Diem Wine Bar CALIFORNIAN $$
(☎707-224-0800; www.carpediemwinebar.com; 1001 2nd St; mains $17-19; ◎4-9pm Mon-Thu, to 10pm Fri & Sat) This busy storefront wine bar and restaurant makes inventive, flavorful small plates, from simple skewers and flatbreads, to elaborate ostrich burgers, salumi platters and – wait for it – duck confit 'quack and cheese.'

Pearl Restaurant NEW AMERICAN $$
(☎707-224-9161; www.therestaurantpearl.com; 1339 Pearl St; mains $15-23; ◎11:30am-2pm & 5:30-9pm Tue-Sat; ⊛) Meet locals at this dog-friendly bistro with pinewood tables and open-rafter ceilings, whose winning down-to-earth cooking includes double-cut pork chops, chicken-verde polenta, steak tacos, and oysters – the specialty.

Pizza Azzuro PIZZA $$
(Map p147; ☎707-255-5552; www.azzurropizzeria.com; 1260 Main St; mains $13-16; ◎11:30am-9pm Sun-Thu, to 9:30pm Fri & Sat; ◢⊞) This Napa classic gets deafeningly loud, but it's worth bearing for tender-crusted pizzas, salad-topped 'manciata' bread, good Caeser salads and pastas.

Norman Rose Tavern PUB FOOD $$
(Map p147; ☎707-258-1516; www.normanrosenapa.com; 1401 1st St; mains $10-24; ◎11:30am-9pm Sun-Thu, to 10pm Fri & Sat; ⊞) This happening gastropub, styled with reclaimed wood and tufted-leather banquettes, is good for a burger and beer. Great fries. Beer and wine only.

HIGH SEASON VS LOW SEASON

Many Wine Country restaurants and hotels diminish operations in wintertime. Make reservations, especially in summertime, or you may not eat. Hotel rates jump during September and October's grape-crushing season – the most popular time.

NAPA & SONOMA WINE COUNTRY NAPA

Bounty Hunter Wine Bar & Smokin' BBQ
BARBECUE $$

(Map p147; 707-226-3976; www.bountyhunter-winebar.com; 975 1st St; mains $13-24; 11am-10pm Sun-Thu, to midnight Fri & Sat;) Inside an 1888 grocery store, Bounty Hunter has an Old West vibe and superb barbecue, made with house-smoked meats. The standout whole chicken is roasted over a can of Tecate. Ten local beers and 40 wines by the glass.

Torc
CALIFORNIAN $$$

(707-252-3292; www.torcnapa.com; 1140 Main St; mains $26-29; 5-9:30pm daily, 10:30am-2:30pm Sat & Sun) Wildly popular Torc plays off the seasons with dynamic combinations of farm-fresh ingredients, such as springtime white asparagus with black-truffle toasts, and squab with artichoke and licorice. Well-arranged for people-watching, the big stone dining room has an open-truss ceiling, and exposed pinewood tables that downplay formality. Reservations essential.

Bistro Don Giovanni
ITALIAN $$$

(707-224-3300; www.bistrodongiovanni.com; 4110 Howard Lane; mains $16-28; 11:30am-10pm Sun-Thu, to 11pm Fri & Sat) This long-running favorite roadhouse serves modern-Italian pastas, crispy pizzas and wood-roasted meats. Reservations essential. Weekends get packed – and loud. Request a vineyard-view table (good luck).

Angèle
FRENCH $$$

(Map p147; 707-252-8115; www.angelerestaurant.com; 540 Main St; lunch mains $14-27, dinner $26-34; 11:30am-10pm) Stalwart Angèle serves reliable provincial-French cooking –

A LOVELY SPOT FOR A PICNIC

Unlike Sonoma, there aren't many places to picnic legally in Napa. Here's a short list, in south-to-north order, but call ahead and remember to buy a bottle (or glass, if available) of your host's wine. If you don't finish it, California law forbids driving with an uncorked bottle in the car (keep it in the trunk).

➡ Regusci (p144)

➡ Napa Valley Museum (p151)

➡ Pride Mountain (p145)

➡ Casa Nuestra (p145)

➡ Lava Vine (p146)

Niçoise salads and *croques messieurs* at lunch, duck confit and beef Bourguignon at dinner – on a river-view deck or cozy dining room, both perfect for lingering with a good bottle of wine.

🍷 Drinking & Nightlife

Empire
LOUNGE

(707-254-8888; www.empirenapa.com; 1400 1st St; 5:30pm-midnight Tue-Thu, to 2am Fri & Sat) Moody and dark, with candlelight and a jellyfish tank, Empire mimics big-city lounges, with good cocktails and uptempo music. Alas, no dance floor.

Billco's Billiards & Darts
SPORTS BAR

(Map p147; www.billcos.com; 1234 3rd St; noon-midnight) Dudes in khakis swill craft beers and throw darts inside this polite pool hall.

Downtown Joe's
SPORTS BAR, BREWERY

(Map p147; www.downtownjoes.com; 902 Main St at 2nd St;) Live music Thursday to Sunday, TV-sports nightly. Often packed, usually messy.

☆ Entertainment

Silo's Jazz Club
LIVE MUSIC

(Map p147; 707-251-5833; www.silosjazzclub.com; 530 Main St; cover varies; 6-10pm Wed-Thu, 7pm-midnight Fri & Sat, varied hrs Sun) A cabaret-style wine-and-beer bar, Silo's hosts jazz and rock acts Friday and Saturday nights; Wednesday and Thursday it's good for drinks. Reservations recommended weekends.

City Winery at Napa Valley Opera House
THEATER

(Map p147; 707-260-1600; www.citywinery.com/napa; 1030 Main St) Napa's vintage-1880s opera theater houses a happening wine bar and restaurant downstairs, and 300-seat cabaret upstairs, hosting acts like Ginger Baker and Graham Nash. Opening hours vary, though it's usually open Thursday to Sunday evenings.

Uptown Theatre
THEATER

(Map p147; 707-259-0333; www.uptowntheatrenapa.com; 1350 3rd St) Big-name acts play this restored 1937 theater.

🛍 Shopping

Betty's Girl
WOMEN'S CLOTHING, VINTAGE

(Map p147; 707-254-7560; www.bettysgirlnapa.com; 968 Pearl St; 11am-6pm Thu & Fri, 10am-2pm Sat) Expert couturier Kim Northrup fits women with fabulous vintage cocktail dresses and custom-made designs, altering and shipping for no additional charge. Open extra hours by appointment.

Napa Valley Olive Oil Mfg Co FOOD
(nvoliveoil.com; 1331 1st St; ☉10am-5:30pm) Sample 30 varieties of fine olive oil and vinegar at this downtown specialty-food boutique, which also carries fancy salts and local jam.

Napa General Store GIFTS
(Map p147; ☑707-259-0762; www.napageneral-store.com; 540 Main St; ☉8am-6pm) Finally, cutesy Wine Country souvenirs reasonably priced. The on-site wine bar is convenient for non-shopping spouses.

ℹ Information

Napa Library (☑707-253-4241; www.county-ofnapa.org/Library; 580 Coombs St; ☉10am-9pm Mon-Thu, to 6pm Fri & Sat; 🛜) Free internet access.

Napa Valley Welcome Center (Map p147; ☑707-251-5895, lodging assistance 707-251-9188, toll free 855-847-6272; www.visitnapaval-ley.com; 600 Main St; ☉9am-5pm; ♿) Lodging assistance, wine-tasting passes, spa deals and comprehensive winery maps.

Queen of the Valley Medical Center (☑707-252-4411; www.thequeen.org; 1000 Trancas St; ☉24hr) Emergency medical.

ℹ Getting Around

Pedi cabs park outside downtown restaurants – especially at the foot of Main St, near the Napa Valley Welcome Center – in summertime. The car-sharing service **Uber** (www.uber.com) also operates in Napa.

Yountville

This onetime stagecoach stop, 9 miles north of Napa, is now a fine-food destination playing to the haute bourgeoisie, with more Michelin stars per capita than any other American town. There are some good inns here, but it's deathly boring by night. You stay in Yountville to drink at dinner without having to drive afterward. Napa, St Helena and Calistoga are more interesting bases. Most businesses are on Washington St.

◉ Sights

Ma(i)sonry GALLERY, TASTING ROOM
(☑707-944-0889; www.maisonry.com; 6711 Washington St; ☉10am-6pm Sun-Thu, to 7pm Fri & Sat) Ma(i)sonry occupies a free-to-browse 1904

stone house and garden, transformed into a fussy winery-collective and gallery of over-priced rustic-modern *meubles* and art, some quite cool. Wine-tasting (by reservation) ranges from $25 to $45.

Napa Valley Museum MUSEUM
(☑707-944-0500; www.napavalleymuseum.org; 55 Presidents Circle, off California Drive; adult/child $5/2.50; ☉10am-5pm Wed-Mon) Yountville's modernist 40,000-sq-ft museum chronicles cultural history and showcases local paintings. From town, it's across Hwy 29.

🛏 Sleeping

Napa Valley Railway Inn INN $$
(☑707-944-2000; www.napavalleyrailwayinn.com; 6523 Washington St; r $125-260; ❇@🛜♨) Sleep in a converted railroad car, part of two short trains parked at a central platform. They've little privacy, but come moderately priced. Bring earplugs.

Maison Fleurie B&B $$$
(☑800-788-0369, 707-944-2056; www.maison-fleurienapa.com; 6529 Yount St; r incl breakfast $160-295; ❇@🛜♨) Rooms at this ivy-covered country inn are in a century-old home and carriage house, decorated in French-provincial style. Big breakfasts, afternoon wine and *hors d'oeuvres,* hot tub.

Bardessono LUXURY HOTEL $$$
(☑877-932-5333, 707-204-6000; www.bardes-sono.com; 6524 Yount St; r $600-800, ste from $800; ❇@🛜♨) 𝄜 The outdoors flows indoors at California's first-ever (for what it's worth) LEED-platinum-certified green hotel, made of recycled everything, styled in Japanese-led austerity, with neutral tones and hard angles that are exceptionally

urban for farm country. Glam pool deck and on-site spa. Tops for a splurge.

Poetry Inn
INN $$$

(☑707-944-0646; www.poetryinn.com; 6380 Silverado Trail; r incl breakfast $650-1400; ✳🅿🛜🏊) There's no better valley view than from this contemporary three-room inn, high on the hills east of Yountville. Decorated with posh restraint, rooms have private balconies, wood-burning fireplaces, 1000-thread-count linens and enormous baths with indoor-outdoor showers. Bring a ring.

Napa Valley Lodge
HOTEL $$$

(☑707-944-2468, 888-944-3545; www.napavalleylodge.com; 2230 Madison St; r $300-475; ✳🛜🏊) It looks like a condo complex, but rooms are spacious and modern; some have fireplaces. Hot tub, sauna and exercise room.

Petit Logis
INN $$$

(☑707-944-2332, 877-944-2332; www.petitlogis.com; 6527 Yount St; r Mon-Fri $195-285, Sat & Sun $265-295; ✳🛜) Simple, cozy and comfortable, this cedar-sided inn has five correct rooms, each with jetted tub and gas fireplace.

✗ Eating

Make reservations or you may not eat. **Yountville Park** (cnr Washington & Madison Sts) has picnic tables and barbecue grills. Find groceries across from the post office. There's a great **taco truck** (6764 Washington St) parked in town.

Bouchon Bakery
BAKERY $

(☑707-944-2253; http://bouchonbakery.com; 6528 Washington St; items from $3; ⏰7am-7pm) Bouchon makes as-good-as-in-Paris French pastries and strong coffee. There's always a line and rarely a seat: get it to go.

Napa Style Paninoteca
CAFE $

(☑707-945-1229; www.napastyle.com; 6525 Washington St; dishes $8-10; ⏰11am-3pm) TV-chef Michael Chiarello's cafe (inside his store, Napa Style) makes camera-ready salads and paninos – try the slow-roasted pork – that pair nicely with his organic wines.

Redd Wood
ITALIAN $$

(☑707-299-5030; www.redd-wood.com; 6755 Washington St; pizzas $12-16, mains $24-28; ⏰11:30am-3pm & 5-10pm, to 11pm Fri & Sat) Celeb-chef Richard Reddington's casual Italian trattoria serves outstanding homemade

Napa Valley South

Napa Valley South

pastas, salumi, and tender-to-the-tooth pizzas from a wood-fired oven.

★ **French Laundry** CALIFORNIAN $$$
(☑ 707-944-2380; www.frenchlaundry.com; 6640 Washington St; prix-fixe dinner $295; ⊙ seatings 11am-1pm Fri-Sun, 5:30pm-9:15pm daily) The pinnacle of California dining, Thomas Keller's French Laundry is epic, a high-wattage culinary experience on par with the world's best. Book two months ahead at 10am sharp, or log onto OpenTable.com precisely at midnight. Avoid tables before 7pm; first-service seating moves a touch quickly.

Ad Hoc CALIFORNIAN $$$
(☑ 707-944-2487; www.adhocrestaurant.com; 6476 Washington St; prix-fixe dinner from $52; ⊙ 5-10pm Mon & Thu-Sat, 10am-1pm & 5-10pm Sun) A winning formula by Yountville's culinary patriarch, Thomas Keller, Ad Hoc serves the master's favorite American home cooking in four-course family-style menus, with no variations (dietary restrictions notwithstanding). Monday is fried-chicken night, which you can also sample weekend lunchtime, takeout only, behind the restaurant at Keller's latest venture, **Addendum** (⊙ 11am-

2pm Thu-Sat), which serves to-go boxed-lunch barbecue (order ahead).

Bouchon FRENCH $$$
(☑ 707-944-8037; www.bouchonbistro.com; 6354 Washington St; mains $19-45; ⊙ 11am-midnight Mon-Fri, from 10am Sat & Sun) Details at celeb-chef Thomas Keller's French brasserie are so impeccable you'd swear you were in Paris. Only the Bermuda-shorts-clad Americans look out of place. On the menu: oysters, onion soup, roasted chicken, leg of lamb, trout with almonds, runny cheeses and perfect profiteroles.

Bistro Jeanty FRENCH $$$
(☑ 707-944-0103; www.bistrojeanty.com; 6510 Washington St; mains $19-30; ⊙ 11:30am-10:30pm) French bistros by classical definition serve comfort food to weary travelers, and that's what French-born chef-owner Philippe Jeanty does, with succulent cassoulet, coq au vin, *steak-frites*, braised pork with lentils, and scrumptious tomato soup.

Mustards Grill CALIFORNIAN $$$
(☑ 707-944-2424; www.mustardsgrill.com; 7399 St Helena Hwy; mains $25-30; ⊙ 11:30am-9pm

Mon-Thu & Sun, to 10pm Fri & Sat; 🎵) The valley's original and always-packed roadhouse makes platters of crowd-pleasing, wood-fired, California comfort food – roasted meats, lamb shanks, pork chops, hearty salads and sandwiches.

Étoile CALIFORNIAN $$$
(☑ 707-944-8844; www.chandon.com; 1 California Dr, Chandon Winery; lunch mains $28-36, dinner mains $29-39; ⊘ 11:30am-2:30pm & 6-9pm Thu-Mon) At Chandon winery, Étoile is perfect for a top-shelf lunch, an ideal one-stop destination when you want to visit a winery, eat a good meal and minimize driving.

🍷 Drinking & Entertainment

Pancha's DIVE BAR
(6764 Washington St; ⊘ noon-2am) Swill tequila with vineyard-workers early, waiters later.

Lincoln Theater THEATER
(☑ box office 707-949-9900; www.lincolntheater.org; 100 California Dr) Various artists, including Napa Valley Symphony, play this theater.

🛍 Shopping

Napa Style FOOD
(☑ 707-945-1229; www.napastyle.com; 6525 Washington St; ⊘ 10am-6pm) The only worthwhile store at Yountville's V Martketplace is this

---

FLYING & BALLOONING

Wine Country is stunning from the air – a multihued tapestry of undulating hills, deep valleys and rambling vineyards. Make reservations.

The **Vintage Aircraft Company** (Map p166; ☑ 707-938-2444; www.vintageaircraft.com; 23982 Arnold Dr, Sonoma) flies over Sonoma in a vintage biplane with an awesome pilot who'll do loop-de-loops on request (add $50). Twenty-minute tours cost $175/260 for one/two adults.

Napa Valley's signature hot-air balloon flights leave early, around 6am or 7am, when the air is coolest; they usually include a champagne breakfast on landing. Adults pay about $200 to $250, and kids $150 to $175. Call **Balloons above the Valley** (☑ 800-464-6824, 707-253-2222; www.balloonrides.com) or **Napa Valley Balloons** (☑ 800-253-2224, 707-944-0228; www.napavalleyballoons.com), both in Yountville.

---

fancy cookware shop by celeb-chef Michael Chiarello.

Oakville & Rutherford

But for its famous grocery, you'd drive through Oakville (pop 71) and never know you'd missed it. Vineyards sprawl everywhere. Rutherford (pop 164) is more conspicuous.

🛏 Sleeping & Eating

There's no budget lodging.

⭐**Auberge du Soleil** LUXURY HOTEL $$$
(☑ 800-348-5406, 707-963-1211; www.aubergedusoleil.com; 180 Rutherford Hill Rd, Rutherford; r $850-1200, ste $1500-4000; ❅ 🐾 🛜 🏊) The top splurge for a no-holds-barred romantic weekend. A meal in its **dining room** (breakfast mains $16 to $19, lunch $31 to $42, three-/four-/six-course prix-fixe dinner $105/125/150) is an iconic Napa experience: come for a fancy breakfast, lazy lunch or will-you-wear-my-ring dinner; valley views are mesmerizing – *don't* sit inside. Make reservations; arrive before sunset.

Rancho Caymus HOTEL $$$
(☑ 800-845-1777, 707-963-1777; www.ranchocaymus.com; 1140 Rutherford Rd, Rutherford; r $179-299; ❅ @ 🛜 🏊) Styled after California's missions, this hacienda-like inn scores high marks for its fountain courtyard, kiva fireplaces, oak-beamed ceilings, and comparitively great rates.

La Luna Market & Taqueria MARKET $
(☑ 707-963-3211; 1153 Rutherford Rd, Rutherford; dishes $4-6; ⊘ 9am-5pm May-Nov) Vineyard workers flock here for burrito lunches and homemade hot sauce.

Oakville Grocery DELI, MARKET $$
(☑ 707-944-8802; www.oakvillegrocery.com; 7856 Hwy 29, Oakville; sandwiches $9-15; ⊘ 6:30am-5pm) The definitive Wine Country deli: excellent cheeses, charcuterie, bread, olives and wine – however pricy. Find tables outside or ask where to picnic nearby.

Rutherford Grill AMERICAN $$
(☑ 707-963-1792; www.rutherfordgrill.com; 1180 Rutherford Rd, Rutherford; mains $15-30) Yes, it's a chain, but its bar provides a chance to rub shoulders with winemakers at lunchtime. The food is consistent – ribs, rotisserie chicken, grilled artichokes – and there's no corkage, so bring that bottle you just bought.

WINE TASTING

The best way to discover the real Wine Country is to avoid factory wineries and visit family-owned boutique houses (producing fewer than 20,000 annual cases) and mid-sized houses (20,000 to 60,000 annual cases). Why does it matter? Think of it. If you were to attend two dinner parties, one for 10 people, one for 1000, which would have the better food? Small wineries maintain tighter control. Also, you won't easily find these wines elsewhere.

Tastings are called 'flights' and include four to six different wines. Napa wineries charge $10 to $50. In Sonoma Valley, tastings cost $5 to $20, often refundable with purchase. In Sonoma County, tastings are free or $5 to $10. You must be 21 to taste.

Do not drink and drive. The curvy roads are dangerous, and police monitor traffic, especially on Napa's Hwy 29.

To avoid burnout, visit no more than three wineries per day. Most open daily 10am or 11am to 4pm or 5pm, but call ahead if your heart's set, or you absolutely want a tour, especially in Napa, where law requires that some wineries accept visitors only by appointment. If you're buying, ask if there's a wine club, which is free to join and provides discounts, but you'll have to agree to buy a certain amount annually.

St Helena

You'll know you're here when traffic halts. St Helena (ha-*lee*-na) is the Rodeo Dr of Napa. Fancy boutiques line the historic downtown's Main St (Hwy 29) and provide excellent window-shopping. Parking, however, is next-to-impossible summer weekends (tip: look behind the visitors center).

◉ Sights

Silverado Museum MUSEUM
(Map p156; ☑707-963-3757; www.silveradomuseum.org; 1490 Library Lane; ☺noon-4pm Tue-Sat) FREE Contains a fascinating collection of Robert Louis Stevenson memorabilia. In 1880, the author – then sick, penniless and unknown – stayed in an abandoned bunkhouse at the old Silverado Mine on Mt St Helena with his wife, Fanny Osbourne; his novel *The Silverado Squatters* is based on his time there. Turn east off Hwy 29 at the Adams St traffic light and cross the railroad tracks.

Farmers Market MARKET
(Map p156; www.sthelenafarmersmkt.org; ☺7:30am-noon Fri May-Oct) Meets at Crane Park, half a mile south of downtown.

☙ Courses

Culinary Institute of America at Greystone COOKING COURSE
(Map p156; ☑707-967-2320; www.ciachef.edu/california; 2555 Main St; mains $25-29, cooking demonstration $20; ☺restaurant 11:30am-9pm, cooking demonstrations 1:30pm Sat & Sun) Inside an 1889 stone chateau, now a cooking school, there's a gadget- and cookbook-filled culinary shop; fine restaurant, weekend cooking demonstrations; and wine-tasting classes by luminaries including Karen MacNeil, author of *The Wine Bible*.

🛏 Sleeping

El Bonita MOTEL $$
(Map p156; ☑707 963 3216; www.elbonita.com; 195 Main St; r $169-239; ❄@🛜🏊🐕) Book in advance to secure this sought-after motel, with up-to-date rooms (quietest are in back), attractive grounds, hot tub and sauna.

Wydown Hotel BOUTIQUE HOTEL $$$
(Map p156; ☑707-963-5100; www.wydownhotel.com; 1424 Main St; r Mon-Fri $269-380, Sat & Sun $379-475; ❄🛜) Opened 2012, this fashion-forward boutique hotel, with good service, sits smack downtown, its 12 oversized rooms smartly decorated with tufted-velvet, distressed leather, subway-tile baths, and California-king beds with white-on-white high-thread-count linens.

Harvest Inn INN $$$
(Map p156; ☑707-963-9463, 800-950-8466; www.harvestinn.com; 1 Main St; r incl breakfast $369-569; ❄@🛜🏊🐕) 🌿 A former estate, this 74-room resort has rooms in satellite buildings on sprawling manicured grounds. The newest building's generic; choose the vineyard-view rooms, which have private hot tubs.

Meadowood RESORT $$$
(Map p156; ☑800-458-8080, 707-963-3646; www.meadowood.com; 900 Meadowood Lane; r from

Napa Valley North

Napa Valley North

$600; ✽@🛜🏊) Hidden in a wooded dell with towering pines and miles of hiking, Napa's grandest resort has cottages and rooms in satellite buildings surrounding a croquet lawn. We most like the hillside fireplace cottages; lawn-view rooms lack privacy but are good for families. The vibe is Republican country club: wear linen and play *Great Gatsby*. Kids love the mammoth pool.

✖ Eating

Make reservations where possible.

Napa Valley Olive Oil Mfg Co　　MARKET $
(Map p156; ☎707-963-4173; www.oliveoilsainthe-lena.com; 835 Charter Oak Ave; ◷8am-5:30pm)
Before the advent of fancy-food stores, this ramshackle market introduced Napa to Italian delicacies – real prosciutto and salami, meaty olives, fresh bread, nutty cheeses and, of course, olive oil. Ask nicely and the owner

will lend you a knife and a board to picnic at the rickety tables in the grass outside. Cash only.

Sunshine Foods
MARKET, DELI $

(Map p156; www.sunshinefoodsmarket.com; 1115 Main St; ⊙ 7:30am-8:30pm) Town's best grocery store; excellent deli.

Model Bakery
CAFE $

(Map p156; ☑ 707-963-8192; www.themodelbakery.com; 1357 Main St; dishes $5-10; ⊙ 6:30am-6pm Mon-Sat, 7am-5pm Sun) Good bakery with scones, muffins, salads, pizzas, sandwiches and exceptional coffee.

Gillwood's Cafe
AMERICAN $

(Map p156; www.gillwoodscafe.com; 1313 Main St; dishes $8-13; ⊙ 7am-3pm; 🖤) Convenient for breakfast and lunch, Gillwood's serves good diner fare – scrambles, pancakes, sandwiches, burgers and salads. Beer and wine, too.

Gott's Roadside
AMERICAN $$

(Map p156; ☑ 707-963-3486; http://gotts.com; 933 Main St; mains $10-15; ⊙ 7am-9pm, to 10pm May-Sep; 🖤) 🍴 Wiggle your toes in the grass and feast on quality burgers – of beef or ahi tuna – plus Cobb salads and fish tacos at this classic roadside drive-in, whose original name, 'Taylor's Auto Refresher,' remains on the sign. Avoid weekend waits by phoning ahead or ordering online. There's another at Oxbow Public Market (p149).

Cindy's Backstreet Kitchen
NEW AMERICAN $$

(Map p156; ☑ 707-963-1200; www.cindysbackstreetkitchen.com; 1327 Railroad Ave; mains $16-28; ⊙ 11:30am-9:30pm) 🍴 The inviting retro-homey decor complements the Cal-American comfort food, such as avocado-and-papaya salad, wood-fired duck, steak with French fries and burgers. The bar makes mean mojitos.

Cook
CAL-ITALIAN $$

(Map p156; ☑ 707-963-7088; www.cooksthelena.com; 1310 Main St; lunch $14-23, dinner $16-28; ⊙ 11:30am-10pm Mon-Sat, 10am-9pm Sun) Locals crowd this tiny storefront bistro, beloved for its earthy Cal-Italian cooking – homemade pasta and risotto, melt-off-the-bone ribs and simple-delicious burgers. Expect a wait, even with reservations.

Armadillo's
MEXICAN $$

(Map p156; www.armadillosnv.com; 1304 Main St; mains $8-12; ⊙ 11am-9pm Sun-Thu, to 10pm Fri & Sat) Respectable, reasonably priced Mexican cooking.

Restaurant at Meadowood
CALIFORNIAN $$$

(Map p156; ☑ 707-967-1205; www.meadowood.com; 900 Meadowood Lane; 9-course menu $225; ⊙ 5:30-10pm Mon-Sat) If you couldn't score reservations at French Laundry (p153), fear not: Meadowood – the valley's only other Michelin-three-star restaurant – has a slightly more sensibly priced menu, elegantly unfussy dining room, and lavish haute cuisine that's not too esoteric. Auberge (p154) has better views, but Meadowood's food and service far surpass it.

Terra
CALIFORNIAN $$$

(Map p156; ☑ 707-963-8931; www.terrarestaurant.com; 1345 Railroad Ave; 4-/5-/6-course menus $78/93/105; ⊙ 6-9pm Wed-Sun) Seamlessly blending Japanese, French and Italian culinary styles, Terra is one of Wine Country's top tables – the signature is broiled sake-marinated black cod with shrimp dumplings in shiso broth. The adjoining bar serves small bites without reservations, but the dining room's the thing.

Goose & Gander
NEW AMERICAN $$$

(Map p156; ☑ 707-967-8779; www.goosegander.com; 1245 Spring St; mains $23-32; ⊙ 5-10pm Sun-Thu, noon-midnight Fri & Sat) Inside a converted Craftsman house, with cathedral ceiling and gorgeous woodwork, Goose & Gander has a clubby vibe conducive to drinking, excellent craft cocktails, and an imaginative (sometimes heavy) menu with some standouts, like the summertime-only shrimp-and-watermelon salad. Consider the garden. Boozy locals favor the basement pub.

Farmstead
NEW AMERICAN $$$

(Map p156; ☑ 707-963-9181; www.farmsteadnapa.com; 738 Main St; mains $16-27; ⊙ 11:30am-9pm) 🍴 An enormous open-truss barn with big leather booths and rocking-chair porch, Farmstead draws a youthful crowd and grows many of its own ingredients – including grass-fed beef – for an earthy menu highlighting wood-fired cooking.

Market
NEW AMERICAN $$$

(Map p156; ☑ 707-963-3799; www.marketsthelena.com; 1347 Main St; mains $18-27; ⊙ 11:30am-9pm) 🍴 We love Market's big portions of simple, fresh American cooking, including hearty salads of local produce, and soul-satisfying mains like buttermilk fried chicken. The stone-walled dining room dates to the 19th century, as does the ornate backbar, where cocktails get muddled to order. Free corkage.

🛍 Shopping

Main St is lined with high-end boutiques (think $100 socks), but some mom-and-pop shops remain.

Woodhouse Chocolates   FOOD
(Map p156; www.woodhousechocolate.com; 1367 Main St; ☻10:30am-5:30pm) Woodhouse looks more like Tiffany than a candy shop, with housemade chocolates similarly priced, but their quality is beyond reproach.

Napa Soap Company   BEAUTY
(Map p156; www.napasoap.com; 651 Main St; ☻10am-5:30pm) 🍃 Eco-friendly bath products, locally produced.

Baksheesh   HOMEWARES
(Map p156; www.baksheeshfairtrade.com; 1327 Main St; ☻10am-6pm) 🍃 Handcrafted fair-trade home decor from 38 countries.

Lolo's Consignment   VINTAGE
(Map p156; www.lolosconsignment.com; 1120 Main St; ☻10:30am-4pm Mon to 5:30pm Tue-Sat, 11am 4pm Sun) Groovy cheap dresses and cast-off cashmere.

Vintage Trunk   VINTAGE
(Map p156; http://vintagetrunkonline.com; 1210 Main St; ☻10:30am-5:30pm) High-end women's designer consignment; prices from $90.

Main Street Books   BOOKS
(Map p156; 1315 Main St; ☻10am-5:30pm Mon-Sat, 11am-3pm Sun) Good used books.

ℹ Information

St Helena Welcome Center (Map p156; ☎707-963-4456; www.sthelena.com; 657 Main St; ☻9am-5pm Mon-Fri, plus 10am-4pm Sat-Sun May-Nov) The visitor center has information and lodging assistance.

Calistoga & Around

The least gentrified town in Napa Valley feels refreshingly simple, with an old-fashioned main street lined with shops, not boutiques, and diverse characters wandering the sidewalks. Bad hair? No problem. Fancy-pants St Helena couldn't feel further away. Many don't go this far north. You should.

Famed 19th-century author Robert Louis Stevenson said of Calistoga: 'the whole neighborhood of Mt St Helena is full of sulfur and boiling springs...Calistoga itself seems to repose on a mere film above a boiling, subterranean lake.'

Indeed, it does. Calistoga is synonymous with mineral water bearing its name, bottled here since 1924. Its springs and geysers have earned it the nickname the 'hot springs of the West.' Plan to visit a spa to indulge in the local specialty: hot-mud baths, made with volcanic ash from nearby Mt St Helena.

The town's odd name comes from Sam Brannan, who founded Calistoga in 1859, believing it would develop like the New York spa town of Saratoga. Apparently Sam liked his drink and at the founding ceremony tripped on his tongue, proclaiming it the 'Cali-stoga' of 'Sara-fornia.' The name stuck.

⊙ Sights

Hwys 128 and 29 run together from Rutherford through St Helena; in Calistoga, they split. Hwy 29 turns east and becomes Lincoln Ave, continuing across Silverado Trail, toward Clear Lake. Hwy 128 continues north as Foothill Blvd (not St Helena Hwy). Calistoga's shops and restaurants line Lincoln Ave.

Sharpsteen Museum   MUSEUM
(Map p156; ☎707-942-5911; www.sharpsteen-museum.org; 1311 Washington St; suggested donation $3; ☻11am-4pm; 🖫) **FREE** Across from the picturesque 1902 City Hall (originally an opera house), the Sharpsteen Museum was created by an ex-Disney animator (whose Oscar is on display) and houses a fantastic diorama of town in the 1860s, big Victorian dollhouse, full-size horse-drawn carriage, cool taxidermy and a restored cottage from Brannan's original resort. (The only Brannan cottage still at its original site is at 106 Wappo Ave).

Bale Grist Mill & Bothe-Napa Valley State Parks   HISTORIC PARK
(☎707-942-4575; parks.ca.gov; 🖫) Both these parks have picnic areas and admission to one includes the other. **Bale Grist Mill State Historic Park** (Map p156; ☎707-963-2236; adult/child $5/2; 🖫) features a 36ft-high **water-powered mill wheel** dating to 1846 – the largest still operating in North America; Saturdays and Sundays (and sometimes Fridays and Mondays) from 10am to 4pm, it grinds flour. A mile-long trail leads to adjacent **Bothe-Napa Valley State Park** (Map p156; ☎707-942-4575; parking $8; ☻8am-sunset; 🖫), where there's a **swimming pool** ($5), and camping (p161), plus hiking through redwood groves.

If you're two or more adults, go first to Bothe and pay $8, instead of the per-head charge at Bale Grist. The mill and both parks are on Hwy 29/128, midway between St Helena and Calistoga. In early October, look for living-history festival **Old Mill Days.**

Old Faithful Geyser
GEYSER

(Map p156; ☑707-942-6463; www.oldfaithfulgeyser.com; 1299 Tubbs Lane; adult/child/under 5yr $14/8/free; ⊙9am-6pm, to 5pm Nov-Mar; 🖈) Calistoga's mini-version of Yellowstone's Old Faithful shoots boiling water 60ft in 100ft into the air, every 30 minutes. The vibe is pure roadside Americana, with folksy hand-painted interpretive exhibits, picnicking and a little petting zoo, where you can come nose-to-nose with llamas. It's 2 miles north of town, off Silverado Trail. Find discount coupons online.

Petrified Forest
FOREST

(☑707-942-6667; www.petrifiedforest.org; 4100 Petrified Forest Rd; adult/child $10/5; ⊙9am-7pm summer, to 5pm winter) Three million years ago at this now roadside-Americana attraction, a volcanic eruption at Mt St Helena blew down a stand of redwoods. The trees fell in the same direction, away from the blast, and over the millennia the mighty giants' trunks turned to stone. Discover them on a short interpretive trail through the woods. The first stumps were discovered in 1870. A monument marks Robert Louis Stevenson's 1880 visit, which he described in *The Silverado Squatters.*

It's 5 miles northwest of town, off Hwy 128.

Safari West
WILDLIFE RESERVE

(☑707-579-2551; www.safariwest.com; 3115 Porter Creek Rd; adult $70-80, child 3-12yr $32; 🖈) Giraffes in Wine Country? Whadya know. Safari West sprawls over 400 acres and protects zebras, cheetahs and other exotic animals, which mostly roam free. See them on a guided two-and-a-half-hour safari in open-sided jeeps; reservations required, no kids under three. If you're feeling adventurous, stay overnight in nifty canvas-sided **tent cabins** (cabin including breakfast $225 to $305) inside the preserve.

Robert Louis Stevenson State Park
PARK

(☑707-942-4575; www.parks.ca.gov; Hwy 29; ⊙sunrise-sunset) FREE At this undeveloped state park 8 miles north of Calistoga, the long-extinct volcanic cone of Mt St Helena marks Napa Valley's end and often gets snow

TOP KID-FRIENDLY WINERIES

➡ Kaz (p167) Play-Doh, playground and grape juice.

➡ Benziger (p167) Open-air tram rides.

➡ Frog's Leap (p144) Cats, chickens and croquet.

➡ Casa Nuestra (p145) Playful goats.

➡ Castello di Amorosa (p146) Bona-fide castle.

➡ Lava Vine (p146) Mellow vibe, grassy play area.

in winter. It's a strenuous 5-mile climb to the peak's 4343ft summit, but what a view – 200 miles on a clear winter's day. Check conditions before setting out. Also consider 2.2-mile one-way **Table Rock Trail** (go south from the summit parking area) for drop-dead valley views.

Temperatures are best in wildflower season, February to May; fall is prettiest, when the vineyards change colors. The park includes the site of the **Silverado Mine** where Stevenson and his wife honeymooned in 1880.

🏃 Activities

Oat Hill Mine Trail
CYCLING, HIKING

(Map p156) One of Northern California's most technically challenging trails, OHM Trail draws hardcore mountain bikers and hikers. Softcore walkers, take heart: a moderately strenuous half-mile up from town, there's a bench with incredible valley views. The trailhead is at the intersection of Hwy 29 and Silverado Trail.

Calistoga Bike Shop
BICYCLE RENTAL

(Map p156; ☑707-942-9687, 866-942-2453; www.calistogabikeshop.com; 1318 Lincoln Ave; ⊙10am-6pm) Rents full-suspension mountain bikes ($75 per day) and hybrids ($12/39 per hour/day), and provides reliable trail information. Wine-touring packages ($90 per day) include wine-rack baskets and free wine pickup.

Spas

Calistoga is famous for hot-spring spas and mud-bath emporiums, where you're buried in hot mud and emerge feeling supple, detoxified and enlivened. (The mud is made with volcanic ash and peat; the higher the ash content, the better the bath.)

Packages take 60 to 90 minutes and cost $70 to $90. You start semi-submerged in hot mud, then soak in hot mineral water. A steam bath and blanket-wrap follow. A massage increases the cost to $130 and up.

Baths can be taken solo or, at some spas, as couples. Variations include thin, painted-on clay-mud wraps (called 'fango' baths, good for those uncomfortable sitting in mud), herbal wraps, seaweed baths and various massage treatments. Discount coupons are sometimes available from the visitors center. Book ahead, especially on summer weekends. Reservations are essential everywhere.

Most spas offer multi-treatment packages. Some offer discounted spa-lodging packages.

★ Indian Springs Spa   SPA

(Map p156; ☑707-942-4913; www.indiansprings-calistoga.com; 1712 Lincoln Ave; ☺by appointment 9am-8pm) California's longest continually operating spa, and original Calistoga resort, has concrete mud tubs and mines its own ash. Treatments include use of the huge, hot-spring-fed pool. Great cucumber body lotion.

Spa Solage   SPA

(Map p156; ☑707-226-0825; www.solagecalistoga.com/spa; 755 Silverado Trail; ☺by appointment 8am-8pm) Chichi, austere, top-end spa, with couples' rooms and a fango-mud bar for DIY paint-on treatments. Also has zero-gravity chairs for blanket wraps, and a clothing-optional pool.

Dr Wilkinson's Hot Springs Resort   SPA

(Map p156; ☑707-942-4102; www.drwilkinson.com; 1507 Lincoln Ave; ☺by appointment 10am-3:30pm) Fifty years running; 'the doc' uses more peat in its mud.

Mount View Spa   SPA

(Map p156; ☑707-942-5789, 800-816-6877; www.mountviewhotel.com; 1457 Lincoln Ave; ☺by appointment 9am-9pm) Traditional full-service, eight-room spa, good for clean-hands people who prefer painted-on mud to submersion.

Lavender Hill Spa   SPA

(Map p156; ☑707-341-6002, 800-528-4772, 707-942-4495; http://lavenderhillspa.com; 1015 Foothill Blvd; ☺by appointment 9am-9pm Thu-Mon, to 7pm Tue & Wed) Small, cute spa that uses much-lighter, less-icky lavender-infused mud; offers couples' treatments.

Golden Haven Hot Springs   SPA

(Map p156; ☑707-942-8000; www.goldenhaven.com; 1713 Lake St; ☺by appointment 8am-8pm) Old-school and unfussy; offers couples' mud baths and couples' massage.

Calistoga Spa Hot Springs   SPA, SWIMMING

(Map p156; ☑866-822-5772, 707-942-6269; www.calistogaspa.com; 1006 Washington St; ☺by appointment 8:30am-4:30pm Tue-Thu, to 9pm Fri-Mon, swimming pools 10am-9pm; ⛲) Traditional mud baths and massage at a motel complex with two huge **swimming pools** where kids can play while you soak (pool passes $25).

🛏 Sleeping

Bothe-Napa Valley State Park
Campground   CAMPGROUND $

(Map p48; ☑800-444-7275; www.reserveamerica.com; 3801 Hwy 128; camping & RV sites $35; ⛺⛲) Three miles south, Bothe has shady camping near redwoods, coin-operated showers, and gorgeous hiking (p159). Sites 28 to 36 are most secluded.

★ Mountain Home Ranch   RESORT $$

(☑707-942-6616; www.mountainhomeranch.com; 3400 Mountain Home Ranch Rd; r $111-121, cabins $71-156; @🛜⛲) 🏊 In continuous operation since 1913, this 340-acre homestead outside town is a flashback to old California. Doubling as a retreat center, the ranch has simple lodge rooms and rustic freestanding cabins, some with kitchens and fireplaces, ideal for families, but you may be here during someone else's family reunion or spiritual quest.

No matter. With miles of oak-woodland trails, a hilltop swimming pool, private lake with canoeing and fishing, and a hike to warm springs in a magical fault-line canyon, you may hardly notice – and you may never make it to a single winery. Breakfast is included, but you'll have to drive 15 minutes to town for dinner. Pack hiking boots, not high heels.

Dr Wilkinson's Motel &
Hideaway Cottages   MOTEL, COTTAGES $$

(Map p156; ☑707-942-4102; www.drwilkinson.com; 1507 Lincoln Ave; r $149-255, cottages $165-270; ⛲@🛜⛲) This good-value vintage-1950s motel has well-kept rooms facing a swimming-pool courtyard with hot tub, three pools (one indoors), and mud baths. Also rents simple, great-value stand-alone cottages with kitchens at the affiliated Hideaway Cottages, also with pool and hot tub.

EuroSpa & Inn
MOTEL $$

(Map p156; ☑707-942-6829; www.eurospa.com; 1202 Pine St; r incl breakfast $145-199; ❄@🕏) Immaculate single-story motel on a quiet side street, with extras like gas-burning fireplaces, afternoon wine and small on-site spa. Excellent service, but tiny pool.

Golden Haven Hot Springs
MOTEL $$

(Map p156; ☑707-942-8000; www.goldenhaven.com; 1713 Lake St; r $165-239; ❄@🕏) This motel-spa has mudbath-lodging packages and good-value well-kept rooms, some with Jacuzzis.

Best Western Stevenson Manor
HOTEL $$

(Map p156; ☑800-528-1238, 707-942-1112; www.stevensonmanor.com; 1830 Lincoln Ave; r weekday $159-189, weekend $249-289; ❄@🕏) This entry-level business-class hotel feels generic, but has good extras, including full hot breakfast. Upstairs rooms are quietest. No elevator.

Calistoga Spa Hot Springs
MOTEL $$

(Map p156; ☑707-942-6269, 866-822-5772; www.calistogaspa.com; 1006 Washington St; r $187-235; ❄@🕏) Great for families, who jam the place weekends, this motel-resort has slightly scuffed generic rooms (request one that's been remodeled) with kitchenettes, and fantastic pools – two full-size, a kiddie-pool with miniwaterfall and a huge adults-only Jacuzzi. Outside are barbecues and snack bar. Wi-fi in lobby.

Calistoga Inn
INN $$

(Map p156; ☑707-942-4101; www.calistogainn.com; 1250 Lincoln Ave; r with shared bath incl breakfast $129-169; 🕏) Upstairs from a busy bar, this inn has 18 clean, basic rooms with shared bath, ideal for no-fuss bargain-hunters. No TVs, no elevator. Bring earplugs.

Solage
RESORT $$$

(Map p156; ☑866-942-7442, 707-226-0800; www.solagecalistoga.com; 755 Silverado Trail; r $530-675; ❄@🕏) 🏊 Calistoga's top spa-hotel ups the style factor, with Cali-chic semidetached cottages and a glam palm-tree-lined deck. Rooms are austere, with vaulted ceilings, zillion-thread-count linens and pebble-floor showers. Cruiser bikes included.

Indian Springs Resort
RESORT $$$

(Map p156; ☑707-942-4913; www.indiansprings-calistoga.com; 1712 Lincoln Ave; lodge r $229-359, cottage $259-429, 2-bedroom cottage $359-499; ❄🕏) The definitive old-school Calistoga resort, Indian Springs has cottages facing a central lawn with palm trees, shuffleboard, bocce, hammocks and Weber grills – not unlike a vintage Florida resort. Some sleep six. There are also top-end, motel-style lodge rooms (adults only). Huge hot-springs-fed swimming pool.

Chateau De Vie
B&B $$$

(Map p156; ☑877-558-2513, 707-942-6446; www.cdvnapavalley.com; 3250 Hwy 128; r incl breakfast $229-429; ❄@🕏) Surrounded by vineyards, with gorgeous views of Mt St Helena, CDV has five modern, elegantly decorated B&B rooms with top-end amenities and zero froufrou. Charming owners serve wine on the sun-dappled patio, then leave you alone. Hot tub, big pool. Gay-friendly.

Meadowlark Country House
B&B $$$

(☑800-942-5651, 707-942-5651; www.meadowlarkinn.com; 601 Petrified Forest Rd; r incl breakfast $210-265, ste $285; ❄@🕏) On 20 acres west of town, Meadowlark has homey rooms decorated in contemporary style, most with decks and Jacuzzis. Outside there's a hot tub, sauna and clothing-optional pool. The truth-telling innkeeper lives elsewhere, offers helpful advice, then vanishes when you want privacy. There's a fabulous cottage for $465. Gay-friendly.

Mount View Hotel & Spa
HISTORIC HOTEL $$$

(Map p156; ☑707-942-6877, 800-816-6877; www.mountviewhotel.com; 1457 Lincoln Ave; r Mon-Fri $209-429, Sat & Sun $279-459; ❄🕏) Smack in the middle of town, this 1917 Mission Revival hotel is decorated in vaguely mod-Italian style at odds with the vintage building, but rooms are clean and fresh-looking nonetheless. Gleaming bathrooms, on-site spa, year-round heated pool. No elevator.

Chanric
B&B $$$

(Map p156; ☑707-942-4535; www.thechanric.com; 1805 Foothill Blvd; r incl breakfast $249-439; ❄🕏) A converted Victorian near the road, this cushy B&B has small, but smartly furnished rooms, plus many free extras including champagne on arrival and lavish three-course breakfasts. Gay-friendly. No elevator.

Hotel d'Amici
HOTEL $$$

(Map p156; ☑707-942-1007; www.hoteldamici.com; 1436 Lincoln Ave; r incl breakfast $200-300; ❄@🕏) All four rooms at this 2nd-floor hotel are remarkably spacious and include continental breakfast, but they're up two flights of stairs (no elevator) and there's no on-site staff.

Cottage Grove Inn
BUNGALOW $$$

(Map p156; ☑707-942-8400, 800-799-2284; www.cottagegrove.com; 1711 Lincoln Ave; cottages $315-450; ❄🖨) Romantic cottages for over-40s, with wood-burning fireplaces, two-person tubs and rocking-chair front porches.

Aurora Park Cottages
COTTAGES $$$

(Map p156; ☑877-942-7700, 707-942-6733; www.aurorapark.com; 1807 Foothill Blvd; cottages incl breakfast $269-299; ❄🖨) Six immaculately kept, sunny-yellow cottages – with polished-wood floors, featherbeds and sundeck – stand in a row beside flowering gardens. Though close to the road, they're quiet by night. The innkeeper couldn't be nicer.

Sunburst Calistoga
MOTEL $$$

(Map p156; ☑707-942-0991; www.thesunburstcalistoga.com; 1880 Lincoln Ave; r $229-289; @🖨❄) This single-story 1950s motor lodge got a makeover in 2013, with mid-century-modern-led aesthetics, but it's basically still a drive-to-the-door motel, only with nicer-than-average furnishings and thin walls.

Chelsea Garden Inn
B&B $$$

(Map p156; ☑707-942-0948; www.chelseagardeninn.com; 1443 2nd St; r incl breakfast $195-350; ❄🖨❄) On a quiet sidestreet, this single-story inn has five floral-print rooms, with private entrances, facing pretty gardens. Never mind the pool's rust spots.

Wine Way Inn
B&B $$$

(Map p156; ☑800-572-0679, 707-942-0680; www.winewayinn.com; 1019 Foothill Blvd; r $189-299; ❄🖨) A small B&B, in a 1910-era house, close to the road; friendly owners.

✖ Eating

Buster's Southern BBQ
BARBECUE $

(Map p156; ☑707-942-5605; www.busterssouthernbbq.com; 1207 Foothill Blvd; dishes $8-12; ⊙10am-7:30pm Mon-Sat, 10:30am-6pm Sun; 🖨) The sheriff dines at this indoor-outdoor barbecue joint, which serves smoky ribs, chicken, tri-tip steak and burgers, but closes early at dinnertime. Beer and wine.

Calistoga Inn & Brewery
AMERICAN $$

(Map p156; ☑707-942-4101; www.calistogainn.com; 1250 Lincoln Ave; lunch mains $11-15, dinner $15-30; ⊙11:30am-3pm & 5:30-9pm) Locals crowd the outdoor beer garden Sundays. Midweek we prefer the country dining room's big oak-wood tables – a homey spot for simple American cooking. Live music summer weekends.

Solbar
CALIFORNIAN $$$

(☑707-226-0850; www.solagecalistoga.com; 755 Silverado Trail; lunch mains $17-20, dinner $24-34; ⊙7am-11am, 11:30am-3pm & 5:30-9pm) ✔ We like the spartan ag-chic look of this Michelin-starred resort restaurant, whose menu maximizes seasonal produce in elegant dishes, playfully composed. And this being a spa (p161), too, the menu is split for calorie-counters into light and hearty dishes. Reservations essential.

JoLé
CALIFORNIAN $$$

(Map p156; ☑707-942-5938; www.jolerestaurant.com; 1457 Lincoln Ave; mains $25-30; ⊙5-9pm) The inventive farm-to-table plates at chef-owned Jolé evolve seasonally, and may include such dishes as local sole with tangy miniature Napa grapes, caramelized brussels sprouts with capers, and organic Baldwin apple strudel with burnt-caramel ice cream. Four courses cost $55. Reservations essential.

Calistoga Kitchen
CALIFORNIAN $$$

(Map p156; ☑707-942-6500; www.calistogakitchen.com; 1107 Cedar St; lunch mains $12-18, dinner $18-29; ⊙5:30-9pm Thu, 11:30am-3pm & 5:30-9pm Fri & Sat, 9:30am-3pm Sun) A sparsely decorated cottage surrounded by a white-picket fence, Calistoga Kitchen is especially good for lunch in the garden. The chef-owner favors simplicity, focusing on quality ingredients in a half-dozen changing dishes, such as a delicious lamb stew. Reservations advised.

All Seasons Bistro
NEW AMERICAN $$$

(Map p156; ☑707-942-9111; www.allseasonsnapavalley.net; 1400 Lincoln Ave; lunch mains $12-18, dinner $18-27; ⊙noon-2pm & 5:30-8:30pm Tue-Sun) ✔ It looks like a white-tablecloth soda fountain, but All Seasons makes very fine meals, from simple *steak-frites* to composed dishes like cornmeal-crusted scallops with summer succotash.

🍷 Drinking & Nightlife

Yo El Rey
CAFE

(Map p156; ☑707-942-1180; www.yoelreyroasting.com; 1217 Washington St; ⊙6:30am-6pm) ✔ Hip kids favor this micro-roastery, which serves stellar small-batch, fair-trade coffee.

Hydro Grill
BAR

(Map p156; ☑707-942-9777; 1403 Lincoln Ave; ⊙8:30am-midnight Sun-Thu, to 2am Fri & Sat)

OUTLET SHOPPING

Max out your credit cards on last season's close-outs.

Napa Premium Outlets (☑707-226-9876; www.premiumoutlets.com; 629 Factory Stores Dr, Napa; ☺10am-9pm Mon-Sat, to 7pm Sun) Fifty stores.

Petaluma Village Premium Outlets (☑707-778-9300; www.premiumoutlets.com; 2200 Petaluma Blvd North, Petaluma; ☺10am-9pm Mon-Sat, to 7pm Sun) Sixty stores, Sonoma County.

Vacaville Premium Outlets (☑707-447-5755; www.premiumoutlets.com/vacaville; 321 Nut Tree Rd, Vacaville; ☺10am-9pm Mon-Sat, to 7pm Sun) 120 stores, northeast of the Wine Country on I-80.

Live music plays weekend evenings at this hoppin' corner bar-restaurant.

Solbar BAR
(Map p156; ☑707-226-0850; www.solagecalistoga.com; 755 Silverado Trail; ☺11am-9pm) Sip craft cocktails beside outdoor fireplaces and a palm-lined pool at this swank resort bar.

Brannan's Grill BAR
(Map p156; ☑707-942-2233; www.brannanscalistoga.com; 1374 Lincoln Ave; ☺11am-11pm) The mahogany bar at Calistoga's handsomest restaurant is great for martinis and microbrews, especially weekends when jazz combos play.

Susie's Bar DIVE BAR
(Map p156; ☑707-942-6710; 1365 Lincoln Ave) Turn your baseball cap sideways, swill beer and shoot pool to a soundtrack of classic rock.

🛍 Shopping

Calistoga Pottery CERAMICS
(Map p156; ☑707-942-0216; www.calistogapottery.com; 1001 Foothill Blvd; ☺9am-5pm) Artisanal pottery, hand-thrown on site.

Coperfield's Bookshop BOOKS
(Map p156; ☑707-942-1616; 1330 Lincoln Ave; ☺10am-7pm Mon-Sat, 10am-6pm Sun) Indie bookshop, with local maps and guides.

ℹ Information

Chamber of Commerce & Visitors Center
(Map p156; ☑707-942-6333, 866-306-5588; www.calistogavisitors.com; 1133 Washington St; ☺9am-5pm)

SONOMA VALLEY

We have a soft spot for Sonoma's folksy ways. Unlike in fancy Napa, nobody cares if you drive a clunker and vote Green. Locals call it 'Slow-noma.' Anchoring the bucolic 17-mile-long Sonoma Valley, the town of Sonoma makes a great jumping-off point for exploring Wine Country – it's an hour from San Francisco – and has a marvelous sense of place, with storied 19th-century historical sights surrounding the state's largest town square. Halfway up-valley, tiny Glen Ellen is straight from a Norman Rockwell painting – in stark contrast to the valley's northernmost town, Santa Rosa, the workaday urban center best known for traffic. If you have more than a day, explore Sonoma's quiet, rustic western side, along the Russian River Valley, and continue to the sea.

Sonoma Hwy/Hwy 12 is lined with wineries, and runs from Sonoma to Santa Rosa, to western Sonoma County; Arnold Dr has less traffic (but few wineries) and runs parallel, up the valley's western side, to Glen Ellen.

Sonoma Valley Wineries

Rolling grass-covered hills rise from 17-mile-long Sonoma Valley. Its 40-some wineries get less attention than Napa's, but many are equally good. If you love Zinfandel and Syrah, you're in for a treat.

Picnicking is allowed at Sonoma wineries. Get maps and discount coupons in the town of Sonoma or, if you're approaching from the south, the Sonoma Valley Visitors Bureau (p170) at Cornerstone Gardens.

Plan at least five hours to visit the valley from bottom to top.

Homewood WINERY
(Map p166; ☑707-996-6353; www.homewoodwinery.com; 23120 Burndale Rd, at Hwy 121/12; tasting $5; ☺10am-4pm; 🐾) Barn cats dart about at this down-home winery, where the tasting room is a garage, and the winemaker crafts standout ports and Rhône-style Grenache, Mourvèdre and Syrah – 'Da redder, da better' – plus some late-harvest dessert wines, including excellent Viognier and Albariño. Bottles are $22 to $42, the tasting fee is waived with a purchase.

Robledo WINERY
(Map p166; ☑707-939-6903; www.robledofamilywinery.com; 21901 Bonness Rd, off Hwy 116; tasting $10-15; ☺by appointment 10am-5pm Mon-Sat,

11am-4pm Sun) Sonoma Valley's feel-good winery, Robledo was founded by a former grape-picker from Mexico who worked his way up to vineyard manager, then land owner, now vintner. His kids run the place. The wines – served at hand-carved furniture in a garage – include a no-oak Sauvignon Blanc, jammy Syrah, spicy Cabernet, and bright-fruit Pinot Noir. Bottles cost $18 to $60.

Gundlach-Bundschu Winery WINERY
(Map p166; ☑707-939-3015; www.gunbun.com; 2000 Denmark St, Sonoma; tasting $10-15, incl tour $20-50; ☺11am-4:30pm, to 5:30pm Jun–mid-Oct; 🏖) 🍷 California's oldest family-run winery looks like a castle, but has a down-to-earth vibe. Founded 1858 by a Bavarian immigrant, its signatures are Gewürztraminer

and Pinot Noir, but 'Gun-Bun' was the first American winery to produce 100% Merlot. Down a winding lane, it's a terrific bike-to winery, with picnicking, hiking and a lake. Tour the 2000-barrel cave ($20) by reservation only. Bottles are $22 to $45.

★ Bartholomew Park Winery WINERY
(☑707-939-3026; www.bartpark.com; 1000 Vineyard Lane, Sonoma; tasting $10, incl tour $20; ☺11am-4:30pm) 🍷 A great bike-to winery, Bartholomew Park occupies a 375-acre preserve, with oak-shaded picnicking and valley-view hiking. The vineyards were originally cultivated in 1857 and now yield certified-organic Sauvignon Blanc, Cabernet Sauvignon softer in style than Napa, and lush Zinfandel. Tours (reservations

A WINE COUNTRY PRIMER

When people talk about Sonoma, they're referring to the *whole* county which, unlike Napa, is huge. It extends all the way from the coast, up the Russian River Valley, into Sonoma Valley and eastward to Napa Valley; in the south it stretches from San Pablo Bay (an extension of San Francisco Bay) to Healdsburg in the north. It's essential to break Sonoma down by district.

West County refers to everything west of Hwy 101 and includes the Russian River Valley and the coast. Sonoma Valley stretches north–south along Hwy 12. In northern Sonoma County, Alexander Valley lies east of Healdsburg, and Dry Creek Valley lies north of Healdsburg. In the south, Carneros straddles the Sonoma–Napa border, north of San Pablo Bay. Each region has its own particular wines; what grows where depends upon the weather.

Inland valleys get hot; coastal regions stay cool. In West County and Carneros, nighttime fog blankets the vineyards. Burgundy-style wines do best, particularly Pinot Noir and Chardonnay. Further inland, Alexander, Sonoma and much of Dry Creek Valleys (as well as Napa Valley) are fog-protected. Here, Bordeaux-style wines thrive, especially Cabernet Sauvignon, Sauvignon Blanc, Merlot and other heat-loving varieties. For California's famous cabernets, head to Napa. Zinfandel and Rhône-style varieties, such as Syrah and Viognier, grow in both regions, warm and cool. In cooler climes, wines are lighter and more elegant; in warmer areas they are heavier and more rustic. As you explore, notice the bases of grapevines: the fatter they are, the older. 'Old vine' grapes yield color and complexity not found in grapes from younger vines.

Some basics: wineries and vineyards aren't the same. Grapes grow in a vineyard, then get fermented at a winery. Wineries that grow their own grapes are called estates, as in 'estate-grown' or 'estate-bottled,' but estates, too, ferment grapes from other vineyards. When vintners speak of 'single-vineyard' or 'vineyard-designate' wines, they mean the grapes all originated from the same vineyard; this allows for tighter quality-control. 'Single varietal' means all the grapes are the same variety (such as 100% merlot), but may come from different vineyards. Reserves are the vintner's limited-production wines; they're usually available only at the winery.

Don't be afraid to ask questions. Vintners love to talk. If you don't know how to taste wine, or what to look for, ask the person behind the counter to help you discover what you like. Just remember to spit out the wine; the slightest buzz will diminish your capacity to taste.

For a handy-dandy reference on the road, pick up a copy of Karen MacNeil's *The Wine Bible* (2001, Workman Publishing) or Jancis Robinson's *The Oxford Companion to Wine* (2006, Oxford University Press) to carry in the car.

required) Friday to Sunday. Bottles are $22 to $45.

Hawkes
TASTING ROOM

(Map p169; ☎707-938-7620; www.hawkeswine. com; 383 1st St W, Sonoma; tasting $10; ⊙11am-6pm) When you're in downtown Sonoma and don't feel like fighting traffic, Hawke's refreshingly unfussy tasting room showcases meaty Merlot and Cabernet Sauvignon, never blended with other varietals. Bottles are $30 to $70, the tasting fee is waived with a purchase over $30.

Little Vineyards
WINERY

(Map p166; ☎707-996-2750; www.littlevineyards. com; 15188 Sonoma Hwy, Glen Ellen; tasting $15; ⊙11am-4:30pm Thu-Mon; 🅿🍷) The name fits at this family-owned small-scale winery surrounded by grapes, with a lazy dog to greet you and a weathered, cigarette-burned tasting bar, at which Jack London formerly drank (before it came here). The big reds include Syrah, petite Syrah, Zin, Cab and several delish blends. Good picnicking on the vineyard-view terrace. Also rents a cottage in the vines. Bottles cost $20 to $45.

BR Cohn
WINERY

(Map p166; ☎800-330-4064, 707-938-4064; www. brcohn.com; 15000 Sonoma Hwy, Glen Ellen; tasting $10; ⊙10am-5pm) Picnic like a rock star at always-busy BR Cohn, whose founder managed '70s-superband the Doobie Brothers before moving on to make outstanding organic olive oils and fine wines – including excellent Cabernet Sauvignon, atypical in Sonoma. The little gourmet shop offers lots to taste, plus limited picnic supplies. In autumn, benefit concerts showcase bands like Skynyrd and the Doobies. Bottles are $16 to $56.

Arrowood
WINERY

(Map p166; ☎707-935-2600; www.arrowoodvineyards.com; 14347 Sonoma Hwy; tasting $20; ⊙10am-4:30pm) 🌱 Arrowood's hilltop tasting room has postcard-perfect valley views and a bourgeois vibe, fussy for Sonoma, but the excellent Chardonnay and Cabernet Sauvignon merit the hype. Tasting fee refunded with two-bottle purchase. Bottles are $25 to $90.

Imagery Estate
WINERY

(Map p166; ☎707-935-4515; www.imagerywinery.com; 14335 Sonoma Hwy; tasting $10-20; ⊙10am-4:30pm; 🅿🍷) 🌱 Imagery produces lesser-known varietals, biodynamically

Sonoma Valley

Sonoma Valley

grown, that you can't buy anywhere else – Cabernet Franc and Sangiovese are standouts. Each bottle sports an artist-designed label, with originals on display in the on-site gallery. Lovely gardens include a grassy picnic area with horseshoes and bocce. Limited picnic supplies available. Bottles are $24 to $45.

Benziger   WINERY
(Map p166; ☑707-935-4527, 888-490-2739; www.benziger.com; 1883 London Ranch Rd, Glen Ellen; tasting $15-20, tram tour adult/under 21yr $25/10; ⊙10am-5pm, tram tours 11:30am-3:30pm; ⊕❀) ✦ If you're new to wine, make Benziger your first stop for Sonoma's best crash course in winemaking. The worthwhile, non-reservable tour includes an open-air tram ride (weather permitting) through biodynamic vineyards, and a five-wine tasting. Great picnicking, plus a playground, make it tops for families. The large-production wine's OK (head for the reserves); the tour's the thing. Bottles are $15 to $80.

Wellington   WINERY
(Map p166; ☑800-816-9463; www.wellingtonvineyards.com; 11600 Dunbar Rd, Glen Ellen; tasting $10; ⊙10:30am-4:30pm) ✦ Known for port (including a white) and meaty reds, Welling-

ton makes great Zinfandel, one from vines planted in 1892 – wow, what color! The noir de noir is a cult favorite. Alas, servers have vineyard views, while you face the warehouse. Bottles are $15 to $30 and the tasting fee is refundable with a purchase.

Loxton   WINERY
(Map p166; ☑707-935-7221; www.loxtonwines.com; 11466 Dunbar Rd, Glen Ellen; ⊙11am-5pm) **FREE** Say g'day to Chris the Aussie winemaker at Loxton, a no-frills winery with million-dollar views and free tastings. The 'tasting room' is actually a small warehouse, where you can taste wonderful Syrah and Zinfandel; non-oaky, fruit-forward Chardonnay; and good port. Bottles cost $16 to $30.

★ Kaz   WINERY
(Map p166; ☑707-833-2536; www.kazwinery.com; 233 Adobe Canyon Rd, Kenwood; tasting $5; ⊙11am-5pm Fri-Mon; ⊕❀) ✦ Sonoma's cult favorite, supercool Kaz is about blends: whatever's in the organic vineyards goes into the wine – and they're blended at crush, not during fermentation. Expect lesser-known varietals like Alicante Bouschet and Lenoir, and a worthwhile Cabernet-Merlot blend. Kids can sample grape juice, then run

around the playground outside. Bottles cost $20 to $48.

Sonoma & Around

Fancy boutiques may be replacing hardware stores lately, but Sonoma still retains an old-fashioned charm, thanks to the plaza and its surrounding frozen-in-time historic buildings. You can legally drink on the plaza – a rarity in California parks – but only between 11:30am and sunset.

Sonoma has rich history. In 1846 it was the site of a second American revolution, this time against Mexico, when General Mariano Guadalupe Vallejo deported all foreigners from California, prompting outraged frontiersmen to occupy the Sonoma Presidio and declare independence. They dubbed California the Bear Flag Republic after the battle flag they'd fashioned.

The republic was short-lived. The Mexican-American War broke out a month later, and California was annexed by the US. The revolt gave California its flag, which remains emblazoned with the words 'California Republic' beneath a muscular brown bear. Vallejo was initially imprisoned, but ultimately returned to Sonoma and played a major role in its development.

Sonoma Hwy (Hwy 12) runs through town. Sonoma Plaza, laid out by Vallejo in 1834, is the heart of downtown, lined with hotels, restaurants, tasting rooms and shops. The visitors bureau has a walking-tour brochure. Immediately north along Hwy 12, expect a brief suburban landscape before the valley's pastoral gorgeousness begins.

◉ Sights

★ Sonoma Plaza   SQUARE
(Map p169; btwn Napa, Spain & 1st Sts) Smack in the center of the plaza, the Mission-revival-style **city hall**, built between 1906 and 1908, has identical facades on four sides, reportedly because plaza businesses all demanded City Hall face their direction. At the plaza's northeast corner, the **Bear Flag Monument** marks Sonoma's moment of revolutionary glory. The weekly **farmers market** (5:30pm to 8pm Tuesday, April to October) showcases Sonoma's incredible produce.

Sonoma State Historic Park   HISTORIC SITE
(☏707-938-9560; www.parks.ca.gov; adult/child $3/2; ☺10am-5pm) The park is comprised of multiple sites, most side-by-side. The 1823

Mission San Francisco Solano de Sonoma anchors the plaza, and was the final California mission. Sonoma Barracks houses exhibits on 19th-century life. The 1886 Toscano Hotel lobby is beautifully preserved – peek inside. The 1852 Vallejo Home lies a half-mile northwest. One ticket allows admission to all, including **Petaluma Adobe** (☏707-762-4871; www.petalumaadobe.com; 3325 Adobe Rd, Petaluma; ☺10am-5pm Sat & Sun), Vallejo's ranch, 15 miles away.

➡ Mission San Francisco Solano de Sonoma
(Map p169; ☏707-938-9560; 114 E Spain St) At the plaza's northeast corner, the mission was built in 1823, partly to forestall Russians at Fort Ross from moving inland. This was the 21st and final California mission – the northernmost point on El Camino Real – and the only one built during the Mexican period (the rest were founded by the Spanish). Five original rooms remain. The not-to-be-missed chapel dates to 1841.

➡ Sonoma Barracks
(Map p169; ☏707-939-9420; parks.ca.gov; 20 E Spain St; adult/child $3/2; ☺10am-5pm) The adobe Sonoma Barracks was built by Vallejo between 1836 and 1840 to house Mexican troops. Today, interpretive displays describe life during the Mexican and American periods. The Barracks became the capital of a rogue nation on June 14, 1846, when American settlers, of varying sobriety, surprised guards and declared an independent 'California Republic' [sic] with a homemade flag featuring a blotchy bear.

The US took over a month later, but abandoned the barracks during the Gold Rush, leaving Vallejo to turn them into (what else?) a winery, in 1860.

➡ Toscano Hotel
(Map p169; ☏707-938-9560; 20 E Spain St) FREE Toscano Hotel opened as a store and library in the 1850s, then became a hotel in 1886. Peek into the lobby from 10am to 5pm; except for the traffic outside, you'd swear you were peering back in time. There are free tours 1pm through 4pm Saturdays and Sundays.

➡ General Vallejo Home
(☏707-938-9559; 363 3rd St W) A half-mile from the plaza, the lovely Vallejo Home, aka Lachryma Montis (Latin for 'Tears of the Mountain'), was built between 1851 and 1852 for General Vallejo and named for the on-site spring; the Vallejo family made good

Sonoma

0   400 m
0   0.2 miles

General Vallejo Home (0.2mi)

Bike Trail

W Spain St

Sonoma Market (0.1mi); El Pueblo Inn (0.2mi); Pearl's Diner (0.3mi); Sonoma Chalet (0.8mi);

W Napa St

Sonoma Plaza

Sonoma Valley Visitors Bureau

E Spain St

E Napa St

Emerald Park

Broadway

McDonell St

Patten St

Andrieux St

Sonoma Valley Cyclery (0.3mi); MacArthur Place (0.5mi)

money piping water to town. The property remained in the family until 1933, when the state of California purchased it, along with its original furnishings. Docents lead tours Saturdays and Sundays at 1pm, 2pm and

3pm. A bike path leads to the house from downtown.

La Haye Art Center ARTS CENTER
(Map p169; ☑707-996-9665; 148 E Napa St; ⊗11am-5pm) FREE At this collective in a converted foundry, you can tour a storefront gallery and meet the artists – sculptor, potter and painters – in their studios.

Sonoma Valley Museum of Art MUSEUM
(Map p169; ☑707-939-7862; www.svma.org; 551 Broadway; adult/family $5/8; ⊗11am-5pm Wed-Sun) Though this museum presents compelling work by local and international artists, such as David Hockney, the annual standout is October's Día de los Muertos exhibition.

Bartholomew Park PARK
(☑707-938-2244; www.bartholomewpark.org; 1000 Vineyard Lane; ⊗10am-6pm) FREE The top near-town outdoors destination is 375-acre Bartholomew Park, off Castle Rd, where you can picnic beneath giant oaks and hike 2 miles of trails, with hilltop vistas to San Francisco. The **Palladian Villa**, at the park's entrance, is a re-creation of Count Haraszthy's original residence, open noon to 3pm Saturdays and Sundays. There's also a good winery, independently operated.

Cornerstone Sonoma GARDENS
(Map p166; ☑707-933-3010; www.cornerstonegardens.com; 23570 Arnold Dr, Hwy 121; ⊗10am-4pm; ✚) FREE There's nothing traditional about Cornerstone Gardens, which showcases 25 walk-through gardens by renowned avant-garde landscape designers who explore the intersection of art and nature. Let the kids run free while you explore top-notch garden shops, taste wine and gather information from the on-site **Sonoma Valley Visitors Bureau** (Map p166; ☑707-935-4747; www.sonomavalley.com; Cornerstone Gardens, 23570 Hwy 121; ⊗10am-4pm); there's also a good, if pricy, on-site cafe. Look for the enormous blue Adirondack chair at road's edge.

We especially love Pamela Burton's 'Earth Walk,' which descends into the ground; and Planet Horticulture's 'Rise,' which exaggerates space.

🏃 Activities

Many local inns provide bicycles.

Traintown AMUSEMENT PARK
(Map p166; ☑707-938-3912; www.traintown.com; 20264 Broadway; ⊗10am-5pm daily late May–mid-Sep, Fri-Sun mid-Sep–late May; ✚) Little

kids adore Traintown, 1 mile south of the plaza. A miniature steam engine makes 20-minute loops ($5.75), and six other vintage amusement-park rides ($2.75 per ride) include a carousel and Ferris wheel.

Sonoma Valley Cyclery BICYCLE RENTAL
(Map p166; ☑707-935-3377; www.sonomacyclery.com; 20091 Broadway/Hwy 12; bikes per day from $30; ⊗10am-6pm Mon-Sat, to 4pm Sun; ✚) Sonoma is ideal for cycling – not too hilly – with multiple wineries near downtown. Book ahead for weekends.

Willow Stream Spa at Sonoma Mission Inn SPA
(Map p166; ☑707-938-9000; www.fairmont.com/sonoma; 100 Boyes Blvd; ⊗7:30am-8pm) Few Wine Country spas compare with glitzy Sonoma Mission Inn, where two treatments on the weekend – or $89 on a weekday (make reservations) – allow use of three outdoor and two indoor mineral pools, gym, sauna, and herbal steam room at the Romanesque bathhouse. No under 18s.

🍽 Courses

Ramekins Sonoma Valley Culinary School COOKING COURSE
(Map p169; ☑707-933-0450; www.ramekins.com; 450 W Spain St; ✚) Offers demonstrations and hands-on classes for home chefs. Also runs weekend 'culinary camps' for adults and kids.

🛏 Sleeping

Off-season rates plummet. Reserve ahead. Ask about parking; some historic inns have no lots. Also consider Glen Ellen and, if counting pennies, Santa Rosa.

Sonoma Chalet B&B $$
(☑800-938-3129, 707-938-3129; www.sonomachalet.com; 18935 5th St W; r $160-180, with shared bath $140, cottages $195-225; 🌐) A historic farmstead surrounded by rolling hills, Sonoma Chalet has rooms in a Swiss chalet–style house adorned with little balconies and country-style bric-a-brac. We love the free-standing cottages; Laura's has a wood-burning fireplace. All rooms come with breakfast, which is served on a deck overlooking a nature preserve. No air-con in rooms with shared bath. No phones, no internet.

Sonoma Hotel HISTORIC HOTEL $$
(Map p169; ☑800-468-6016, 707-996-2996; www.sonomahotel.com; 110 W Spain St; r incl breakfast $170-200, ste $250; ❄🌐) Long on charm, this

good-value, vintage-1880s hotel, decorated with country-style willow-wood furnishings, sits right on the plaza. Double-pane glass blocks the noise, but there's no elevator or parking lot.

Swiss Hotel HISTORIC HOTEL $$
(Map p169; ☑707-938-2884; www.swisshotelsonoma.com; 18 W Spain St; r incl breakfast Mon-Fri $150-170, Sat & Sun $200-240; ❋❡) It opened in 1905, so you'll forgive the wavy floors. The floral prints are likewise dated, but rooms are large, good value and share a plaza-view balcony. Downstairs there's a raucous bar and restaurant. No parking lot or elevator.

Windhaven Cottage COTTAGE $$
(Map p166; ☑707-483-1856, 707-938-2175; www.windhavencottage.com; 21700 Pearson Ave; cottage $155-165; ❋❡) Great-bargain Windhaven has two units: a hideaway cottage with vaulted wooden ceilings and a fireplace, and a handsome 800-sq-ft studio. We prefer the romantic cottage. Both have hot tubs. Tennis facilities, bicycles and barbecues sweeten the deal.

Sonoma Creek Inn MOTEL $$
(Map p166; ☑888-712-1289, 707-939-9463; www.sonomacreekinn.com; 239 Boyes Blvd; r $116-225; ❋❋❡❋) This cute-as-a-button motel has spotless, cheery, retro-Americana rooms, but it's not downtown. Valley wineries are a short drive. When available, last-minute bookings cost just $89.

El Dorado Hotel BOUTIQUE HOTEL $$$
(Map p169; ☑707-996-3220; www.eldoradosonoma.com; 405 1st St W; r Mon-Fri $165-265, Sat & Sun $245-325; P❋❡❋) Stylish touches, such as high-end linens, justify rates and compensate for the rooms' compact size, as do private balconies, which overlook the plaza or rear courtyard (we prefer the plaza view, despite noise). No elevator.

El Pueblo Inn MOTEL $$$
(Map p166; ☑707-996-3651, 800-900-8844; www.elpuebloinn.com; 896 W Napa St; r incl breakfast $189-239; ❋@❡❋) One mile west of downtown, family-owned El Pueblo has surprisingly cushy rooms with great beds. The big lawns and the heated pool are perfect for kids; parents appreciate the 24-hour hot tub.

Sonoma's Best Guest Cottages COTTAGES $$$
(Map p166; ☑800-291-8962, 707-933-0340; www.sonomasbestcottages.com; 1190 E Napa St; cottages $199-349, q $279-395; ❋❡) Each of these four colorful, inviting cottages has a bed-room, living room, kitchen and barbecue, with comfy furniture, stereos, DVDs and bicycles. One mile east of the plaza.

Hidden Oak Inn B&B $$$
(Map p169; ☑707-996-9863; www.hiddenoakinn.com; 214 E Napa St; r incl breakfast $195-245; ❋❡❋) Three-room, 1914 Craftsman B&B with lovely service.

MacArthur Place INN $$$
(☑800-722-1866, 707-938-2929; www.macarthurplace.com; 29 E MacArthur St; r from $350, ste from $499; ❋@❡❋) Sonoma's top full-service inn occupies a former estate with century-old gardens.

✗ Eating

There's creek-side picnicking, with barbecue grills, up-valley at Sugarloaf Ridge State Park (p173). Find late-night taco trucks on Hwy 12, between Boyes Blvd and Aqua Caliente.

Angelo's Wine Country Deli DELI $
(Map p166; ☑707-938-3688; 23400 Arnold Dr; sandwiches $7; ⊙9am 5:30pm) Look for the cow on the roof of this roadside deli, south of town, a fave for fat sandwiches and homemade jerky. In springtime, little lambs graze outside.

Pearl's Diner DINER $
(☑707-996-1783; 561 5th St W; mains $7-10; ⊙7am-2:30pm; ❋) Across from Safeway's west-facing wall, greasy-spoon Pearl's serves giant American breakfasts, including standout bacon and waffles with batter enriched by melted vanilla ice cream.

Sonoma Market DELI, MARKET $
(☑707-996-3411; www.sonoma-glenellenmkt.com; 500 W Napa St; sandwiches from $6; ⊙5:30am-10pm) Sonoma's best groceries and deli sandwiches.

★Fremont Diner AMERICAN $$
(Map p166; ☑707-938-7370; http://thefremontdiner.com; 2698 Fremont Dr; mains $10-16; ⊙8am-3pm Mon-Wed, to 9pm Thu-Sun; ❋) ✐ Lines snake out the door peak times at this farm-to-table roadside diner. We prefer the indoor tables, but will happily accept a picnic table in the big outdoor tent to feast on ricotta pancakes with real maple syrup, chicken and waffles, oyster po' boys, finger-licking barbecue and skillet-baked cornbread. Arrive early, or late, to beat queues.

Sunflower Caffé & Wine Bar
CAFE $$

(Map p169; ☎707-996-6845; www.sonomasunflower.com; 421 1st St W; dishes $8-15; ☺7am-4pm; 🖥) The big back garden at this local hangout is a great spot for breakfast, a no-fuss lunch or afternoon wine.

Red Grape
ITALIAN $$

(Map p169; ☎707-996-4103; http://theredgrape.com; 529 1st St W; mains $10-20; ☺11:30am-10pm; 📵) A reliable spot for an easy meal, Red Grape serves good thin-crust pizzas and big salads in a cavernous, echoey space. Good for takeout, too.

Della Santina's
ITALIAN $$

(Map p169; ☎707-935-0576; www.dellasantinas.com; 135 E Napa St; mains $14-24; ☺11:30am-3pm & 5-9:30pm) The waiters have been here forever, and the 'specials' rarely change, but Della Santina's American-Italian cooking – linguini pesto, veal parmigiana, rotisserie chickens – is consistently good, and the brick courtyard is inviting on warm evenings.

Taste of the Himalayas
INDIAN, NEPALESE $$

(Map p169; ☎707-996-1161; 464 1st St E; mains $10-20; ☺11am-2:30 Tue-Sun, 5-10pm daily) Spicy curries, luscious lentil soup and sizzle-platter meats make a refreshing break from the usual French-Italian Wine Country fare.

★ Cafe La Haye
CALIFORNIAN $$$

(Map p169; ☎707-935-5994; www.cafelahaye.com; 140 E Napa St; mains $20-32; ☺5:30-9pm Tue-Sat) 🖋 One of Sonoma's top tables for earthy New American cooking, La Haye only uses produce sourced from within 60 miles. Its dining room gets packed cheek-by-jowl and service can border on perfunctory, but the clean simplicity and flavor-packed cooking make it many foodies' first choice. Reserve well ahead.

the girl & the fig
FRENCH $$$

(Map p169; ☎707-938-3634; www.thegirlandthefig.com; 11 W Spain St; mains $20-27; ☺11:30am-10pm Mon-Fri, 11am-11pm Sat, 10am-10pm Sun) For a festive evening, book a garden table at this French-provincial bistro, with good small plates ($12 to $14) including steamed mussels with matchstick fries, and duck confit with lentils. Weekday three-course prix-fixe costs $36, add $12 for wine. Stellar cheeses. Reservations essential.

El Dorado Kitchen
CALIFORNIAN $$$

(Map p169; ☎707-996-3030; www.eldorado-sonoma.com; 405 1st St W; lunch mains $12-17, dinner $24-31; ☺8-11am, 11:30am-2:30pm & 5:30-9:30pm) 🖋 The swank plaza-side choice for contemporary California-Mediterranean cooking, El Dorado showcases seasonal-regional ingredients in dishes like duck-confit salad and housemade ravioli, served in a see-and-be-seen dining room with a big community table at its center. The happening lounge serves good small plates ($9 to $15) and craft cocktails. Make reservations.

La Salette
PORTUGUESE $$$

(Map p169; ☎707-938-1927; www.lasalette-restaurant.com; 452 1st St E; lunch mains $12-25, dinner $19-25; ☺11:30am-2pm & 5:30-9pm) 🖋 Contemporary Portuguese cuisine is the focus at this restaurant that serves excellent-value, proper sit-down meals, including a standout seafood stew. Make reservations.

Harvest Moon Cafe
NEW AMERICAN $$$

(Map p169; ☎707-933-8160; www.harvestmoon-cafesonoma.com; 487 1st St W; mains $19-29; ☺5:30-9pm Wed-Mon) 🖋 Inside a cozy 1836 adobe, this casual bistro uses local ingredients in its changing menu, with simple soul-satisfying dishes like duck risotto with Bellwether Farms ricotta. Book the patio in warm weather.

🍷 Drinking & Entertainment

Free **jazz concerts** happen on the plaza every second Tuesday, June to September, 6pm to 8:30pm; arrive early, bring a picnic.

Murphy's Irish Pub
PUB

(Map p169; ☎707-935-0660; www.sonomapub.com; 464 1st St E; ☺noon-11pm) Don't ask for Bud – there're only *real* brews here. Good hand-cut fries and shepherd's pie, too. Live music Thursday through Sunday evenings.

Swiss Hotel
BAR

(Map p169; www.swisshotelsonoma.com; 18 W Spain St; ☺11:30am-midnight) Locals and tourists crowd the 1909 Swiss Hotel for cocktails. There's OK food, but the bar's the thing.

Hopmonk Tavern
BREWERY

(Map p169; ☎707-935-9100; www.hopmonk.com; 691 Broadway; ☺11:30am-10pm) This happening gastro-pub (dishes $10 to $20) and beer garden takes its brews seriously, with 16 on tap, served in type-appropriate glassware. Live music Friday through Sunday.

Enoteca Della Santina
WINE BAR

(Map p169; www.enotecadellasantina.com; 127 E Napa St; ☺4-10pm Mon-Thu, to 11pm Fri, 2-11pm Sat, 2-10pm Sun) Thirty global vintages by the glass let you compare what you're tasting in California with the rest of the world's wines.

Steiner's
BAR

(Map p169; www.steinerstavern.com; 465 1st St W; ⊙6am-2am; 🛜) Sonoma's oldest bar gets crowded Sunday afternoons with cyclists and motorcyclists.

Sebastiani Theatre
CINEMA

(Map p169; ☑707-996-2020; sebastianitheatre. com; 476 1st St E) The plaza's gorgeous 1934 Mission-revival cinema screens art-house and revival films, and sometimes live theater.

🛍 Shopping

Vella Cheese Co
FOOD

(Map p169; ☑707-938-3232; www.vellacheese. com; 315 2nd St E; ⊙9:30am-6pm Mon-Sat) Known for its dry-jack cheeses (made here since the 1930s), Vella also makes good Mezzo Secco with cocoa powder–dusted rind. Staff will vacuum-pack for shipping.

Tiddle E Winks
TOYS

(Map p169; ☑707-939-6933; www.tiddleewinks. com; 115 E Napa St; ⊙10:30am-5:30pm Mon-Sat, 11am-5pm Sun; 🚼) Vintage five-and-dime, with classic, mid-20th-century toys.

Sign of the Bear
HOMEWARES

(Map p169; ☑707-996-3722; 435 1st St W; ⊙10am 6pm) Kitchen-gadget freaks: make a beeline to this indie cookware store.

Chateau Sonoma
HOMEWARES, GIFTS

(Map p169; ☑707-935-8553; www.chateausonoma. com; 153 W Napa St; ⊙10:30am-6pm Mon-Sat, 11am-5pm Sun) France meets Sonoma in one-of-a-kind gifts and arty home decor.

Readers' Books
BOOKS

(Map p169; ☑707-939-1779; readers.indiebound. com; 130 E Napa St; ⊙10am-7pm Mon-Sat, to 6pm Sun) Independent bookseller.

ℹ Information

Sonoma Post Office (Map p169; ☑800-275-8777; www.usps.com; 617 Broadway; ⊙9am-5pm Mon-Fri)

Sonoma Valley Hospital (☑707-935-5000; www.svh.com; 347 Andrieux St) Twenty-four-hour emergency room.

Sonoma Valley Visitors Bureau (Map p169; ☑707-996-1090; www.sonomavalley.com; 453 1st E; ⊙9am-5pm Mon-Sat, 10am-5pm Sun) Arranges accommodations; has a good walking-tour pamphlet and events information. There's another at Cornerstone Gardens (p170).

Glen Ellen & Kenwood

Sleepy Glen Ellen is a snapshot of old Sonoma, with white-picket fences and tiny cottages beside a poplar-lined creek. When downtown Sonoma is jammed, you can wander quiet Glen Ellen and feel far away. It's ideal for a leg-stretching stopover between wineries or a romantic overnight – the nighttime sky blazes with stars. Arnold Dr is the main drag and the valley's back-way route. Kenwood lies just north, along Hwy 12, but has no town center like Glen Ellen's. For services, drive 8 miles south to Sonoma. Glen Ellen's biggest draws are Jack London State Historic Park and Benziger winery (p167).

💿 Sights & Activities

Jack London State Historic Park
PARK

(Map p166; ☑707-938-5216; www.jacklondonpark.com; 2400 London Ranch Rd, Glen Ellen; per car $10, tour adult/child $4/2; ⊙9:30am-5pm) Napa has Robert Louis Stevenson, but Sonoma's got Jack London. This 1400-acre park frames the author's last years; don't miss the excellent on-site museum. Miles of hiking trails (some open to mountain bikes) weave through oak-dotted woodlands, between 600ft and 2300ft elevations; an easy 2-mile loop meanders to a lake, great for picnicking. Watch for poison oak.

Changing occupations from Oakland fisherman to Alaska gold prospector to Pacific yachtsman – and novelist on the side – London (1876–1916) ultimately took up farming. He bought 'Beauty Ranch' in 1905 and moved here in 1910. With his second wife, Charmian, he lived and wrote in a small cottage while his mansion, **Wolf House**, was under construction. On the eve of its completion in 1913, it burned down. The disaster devastated London, and although he toyed with rebuilding, he died before construction got underway. His widow, Charmian, built the **House of Happy Walls**, which has been preserved as a museum. It's a half-mile walk from there to the remains of Wolf House, passing London's grave along the way. Other paths wind around the farm to the cottage where he lived and worked.

Sugarloaf Ridge State Park
HIKING

(Map p166; ☑707-833-5712; www.parks.ca.gov; 2605 Adobe Canyon Rd, Kenwood; per car $8) There's fantastic hiking – when it's not blazingly hot. On clear days, **Bald Mountain** has drop-dead views to the sea; **Bushy Peak**

ℹ WHAT'S CRUSH?

Crush is autumn harvest, the most atmospheric time of year, when the vine's leaves turn brilliant colors and you can smell fermenting fruit on the breeze. Farmers throw big parties for the vineyard workers to celebrate their work. Everyone wants to be here. That's why room rates skyrocket. If you can afford it, come during autumn. To score party invitations, join your favorite winery's wine club.

Trail peers into Napa Valley. Both are moderately strenuous; plan four hours round-trip.

Morton's Warm Springs   SWIMMING
(Map p166; ☑707-833-5511; www.mortonswarmsprings.com; 1651 Warm Springs Rd, Glen Ellen; adult/child $15/5; ☺10am-6pm Sat, Sun & holidays May & Sep, Tue-Sun Jun-Aug; 🖐) This old-fashioned family swim club has two mineral pools, limited hiking, volleyball and BBQ facilities. No credit cards Tuesday to Friday: exact change required. From Sonoma Hwy in Kenwood, turn west on Warm Springs Rd.

Triple Creek Horse Outfit   HORSEBACK RIDING
(☑707-887-8700; www.triplecreekhorseoutfit.com; 60/90min rides $75/95; ☺Wed-Mon) Explore Jack London State Park by horseback for stunning vistas over Sonoma Valley. Reservations required.

🛏 Sleeping

Sugarloaf Ridge State Park   CAMPGROUND $
(Map p166; ☑800-444-7275; www.reserveamerica.com; 2605 Adobe Canyon Rd, Kenwood; tent & RV sites $35; 🐾) Sonoma's nearest camping is north of Kenwood at this lovely hilltop park, with 50 drive-in sites, clean coin-operated showers and great hiking.

Jack London Lodge   MOTEL $$
(Map p166; ☑707-938-8510; www.jacklondonlodge.com; 13740 Arnold Dr, Glen Ellen; r Mon-Fri $124, Sat & Sun $189; ❄🛜🏊) An old-fashioned wood-sided motel, with well-kept rooms decorated with antique repros, this is a weekday bargain – and the manager will sometimes negotiate rates. Outside there's a hot tub; next door, a saloon.

Glen Ellen Cottages   BUNGALOW $$
(Map p166; ☑707-996-1174; www.glenelleninn.com; 13670 Arnold Dr, Glen Ellen; cottage Mon-Fri $139-159, Sat & Sun $209-249; ❄🛜) Hidden behind Glen Ellen Inn, these five creek-side cottages are designed for romance, with oversized jetted tubs, steam showers and gas fireplaces.

★Beltane Ranch   B&B $$$
(Map p166; ☑707-996-6501; www.beltaneranch.com; 11775 Hwy 12, Glen Ellen; d incl breakfast $160-285; 🛜) 🐾 Surrounded by horse pastures and vineyards, Beltane is a throwback to 19th-century Sonoma. The cheerful, lemon-yellow, 1890s ranch house has double porches, lined with swinging chairs and white wicker. Though it's technically a B&B, each country-Americana-style room has a private entrance – nobody will make you pet the cat. Breakfast in bed. No phones or TVs mean zero distraction from pastoral bliss.

Gaige House Inn   B&B $$$
(Map p166; ☑707-935-0237, 800-935-0237; www.gaige.com; 13540 Arnold Dr, Glen Ellen; d incl breakfast from $275, ste from $425; @🛜🏊) Among the valley's most chic inns, Gaige has 23 rooms, five inside an 1890 house decked out in Euro-Asian style. Best are the Japanese-style 'Zen suites,' with requisite high-end bells and whistles, including freestanding tubs made from hollowed-out granite boulders. Fabulous.

Kenwood Inn & Spa   INN $$$
(Map p166; ☑800-353-6966, 707-833-1293; www.kenwoodinn.com; 10400 Sonoma Hwy, Kenwood; r incl breakfast $450-825; ❄@🛜) Lush gardens surround ivy-covered bungalows at this sexy 25-room inn, designed to resemble a Mediterranean château. Two hot tubs (one with a waterfall) and an on-site spa make it ideal for lovers, boring for singles. No kids. Book an upstairs balcony room.

🍴 Eating

Glen Ellen Village Market   DELI, MARKET $
(Map p166; www.sonoma-glenellenmkt.com; 13751 Arnold Dr, Glen Ellen; ☺6am-8pm) Fantastic market with huge deli, ideal for picnickers.

Garden Court Cafe   CAFE $
(Map p166; ☑707-935-1565; www.gardencourtcafe.com; 13647 Arnold Dr, Glen Ellen; mains $9-12; ☺8:30am-2pm Wed-Mon) Basic breakfasts, sandwiches and salads.

fig cafe & winebar   FRENCH, CALIFORNIAN $$
(Map p166; ☑707-938-2130; www.thefigcafe.com; 13690 Arnold Dr, Glen Ellen; mains $18-22; ☺10am-3pm Sat & Sun, 5:30-9pm daily) The fig's earthy California–Provençal comfort food includes flash-fried calamari with spicy-lemon aioli,

duck confit and *moules-frites* (mussels and French fries). Good wine prices and weekend brunch give reason to return.

Yeti
INDIAN $$

(Map p166; ☑707-996-9930; www.yetirestaurant. com; 14301 Arnold Dr, Glen Ellen; mains $12-22; ⊙11:30am-2:30pm & 5-9pm) Surprisingly good Indian and Nepalese cooking, served on a creek-side patio at a converted mill, make Yeti worth seeking out. Great value.

Glen Ellen Inn
AMERICAN $$

(Map p166; ☑707-996-6409; www.glenelleninn. com; 13670 Arnold Dr, Glen Ellen; mains $16-25; ⊙11:30am-9pm Thu-Tue, 5:30-9pm Wed) Oysters, martinis and grilled steaks. Lovely garden, full bar.

Mayo Winery Reserve
WINERY $$

(Map p166; ☑707-833-5504; www.mayofamilywinery.com; 9200 Sonoma Hwy, Kenwood; 7-course menu $35; ⊙by appointment 11am 5pm) Feast on a seven-course small-plates menu, paired with seven wines, for just $35 at this unatmospheric roadside wine-tasting room.

Cafe Citti
ITALIAN $$

(Map p166; ☑707-833-2690; www.cafecitti.com; 9049 Sonoma Hwy, Kenwood; mains $8-15; ⊙11am-3:30pm & 5-9pm; ☻) Locals favor this order-at-the-counter Italian-American deli, with standout roasted chicken, homemade gnocchi and ravioli; lunchtime, there's pizza and house-baked focaccia-bread sandwiches.

Kenwood Restaurant & Bar
CALIFORNIAN $$$

(Map p166; ☑707-833-6326; www.kenwoodrestaurant.com; 9900 Sonoma Hwy, Kenwood; mains $22-30; ⊙11:30am-8:30pm Wed-Sun) ⊘ A stone patio flanks vineyards and flowering gardens at this roadhouse restaurant, lovely for a lingering lunch. The chef showcases quality ingredients by local producers in simple-delicious dishes like pork chops with bacon or roasted chicken. The small-plates menu ($10 to $16) is ideal for a quick bite between wineries. Reservations advised.

Aventine
ITALIAN $$$

(Map p166; ☑707-934-8911; http://glenellen. aventinehospitality.com; 14301 Arnold Dr, Glen Ellen; mains $14-28; ⊙4:30-10pm Tue-Fri, 11am-10pm Sat & Sun) The Sonoma outpost of the popular San Francisco and Hollywood restaurants occupies an atmospheric former grist mill with a sun-dappled outdoor patio, and serves Italian-derived dishes, including mozzarella-stuffed meatball with pesto over polenta. Make reservations.

Olive & Vine
NEW AMERICAN $$$

(Map p166; ☑707-996-9152; oliveandvinerestaurant.com; 14301 Arnold Dr, Glen Ellen; mains $23-36; ⊙5:30-9pm Wed-Sun) ⊘ Inside a repurposed grist mill with mismatched shabby-chic furniture, Olive & Vine showcases seasonal flavors in its cooking. Reservations essential.

🔒 Shopping

Wine Country Chocolates Tasting Bar
FOOD

(Map p166; ☑707-996-1010; www.winecountrychocolates.com; 14301 Arnold Dr, Glen Ellen; ⊙10am-5pm) Sample fine chocolates of varying degrees of cacao.

Figone's Olive Oil
FOOD

(Map p166; ☑707-282-9092; www.figoneoliveoil. com; 9580 Sonoma Hwy, Kenwood; ⊙11am-5pm) Figone's presses its own extra-virgin olive oil, and infuses some with flavors like Meyer-lemon, all free to sample.

RUSSIAN RIVER AREA

Lesser-known western Sonoma County was formerly famous for its apple farms and vacation cottages. Lately vineyards are replacing orchards, and the Russian River has taken its place among California's important wine appellations, especially for pinot noir.

'The River,' as locals call it, has long been a summertime-weekend destination for Northern Californians, who come to canoe, wander country lanes, taste wine, hike redwood forests and live at a lazy pace. In winter the river floods, and nobody's here.

The Russian River begins in the mountains north of Ukiah, in Mendocino County, but the most-known sections lie southwest of Healdsburg, where the river cuts a serpentine course toward the sea. Just north of Santa Rosa, River Rd, the lower valley's main artery, connects Hwy 101 with coastal Hwy 1 at Jenner. Hwy 116 heads northwest from Cotati through Sebastopol, then at Guerneville joins River Rd and cuts west to the sea. Westside Rd connects Guerneville and Healdsburg. West County's winding roads get confusing and there's limited cell service; carry a proper map.

Russian River Area Wineries

Sonoma County's wine-growing regions encompass several diverse areas, each famous

Russian River Area

for different reasons (p165). Pick up the free, useful *Russian River Wine Road* map (www.wineroad.com) in tourist-brochure racks.

Russian River Valley

Nighttime coastal fog drifts up the Russian River Valley, then usually clears by midday. Pinot Noir does beautifully, as does Chardonnay, which also grows in hotter regions, but prefers the longer 'hang time' of cooler climes. The highest concentration of wineries is along Westside Rd, between Guerneville and Healdsburg.

Hartford Family Winery WINERY
(☎707-887-8030; www.hartfordwines.com; 8075 Martinelli Rd, Forestville; tasting $15; ☺10am-4:30pm) 🖉 Surprisingly upscale for West County, Hartford sits in a pastoral valley surrounded by redwood-forested hills, on one of the area's prettiest back roads. It specializes in fine single-vineyard Pinot (12 kinds), Chardonnay and Zinfandel from old-vine fruit. Umbrella-shaded picnic tables dot the garden. Bottles are $38 to $90 and the tasting fee is waived with purchase.

Russian River Area

Korbel
WINERY

(☑707-824-7000, 707-824-7316; www.korbel.com; 13250 River Rd, Guerneville; ⊙10am-5pm; ☯) **FREE** Gorgeous rose gardens (April to October) and an on-site deli make Korbel worth a stop for free tasting; the sparking wine's just OK.

Iron Horse Vineyards
WINERY

(☑707-887-1507; www.ironhorsevineyards.com; 9786 Ross Station Rd, Sebastopol; tasting $20; ⊙10am-4:30pm) Atop a hill with drop-dead views over the county, Iron Horse is known for Pinot Noir and sparkling wines, which the White House often pours. The outdoor tasting room is refreshingly unfussy; when you're done with your wine, pour it in the grass. Sunday noon to 4pm, April to October, they serve oysters ($3). Located off Hwy 116. Bottles cost $27 to $85.

Marimar
WINERY

(☑707-823-4365; www.marimarestate.com; 11400 Graton Rd, Sebastopol; tasting $10-15; ⊙11am-4pm; ☯) *◈* Middle-of-nowhere Marimar specializes in all-organic Pinot – seven different kinds – and Spanish varietals. The hacienda-style hilltop tasting room has a knockout vineyard-view terrace, good for picnics. Also consider tapas-and-wine pairings ($45). Bottles are $29 to $57.

Gary Farrell
WINERY

(☑707-473-2900; www.garyfarrellwines.com; 10701 Westside Rd, Healdsburg; tasting $15-25; ⊙10:30am-4:30pm; ☯) High on a hilltop, overlooking the Russian River, Gary Farrell's tasting room sits perched among second-growth redwoods. The elegant Chardonnay and long-finish Pinot, made by a big-name winemaker, score high marks for consistency. Bottles are $32 to $60.

Porter Creek
WINERY

(☑707-433-6321; www.portercreekvineyards.com; 8735 Westside Rd, Healdsburg; ⊙10:30am-4:30pm; ☯) *◈* **FREE** Inside a vintage-1920s garage, Porter Creek's tasting bar is a former bowling-alley lane, plunked atop barrels. Porter is old-school Northern California, an early pioneer in biodynamic farming. High-acid, food-friendly Pinot Noir and Chardonnay are specialties, but there's silky Zinfandel and other Burgundian- and Rhône-style wines, too. Check out the aviary. Bottles cost $20 to $72 and tastings are free.

Hop Kiln Winery
WINERY

(☑707-433-6491; www.hopkilnwinery.com; 6050 Westside Rd, Healdsburg; tasting $7; ⊙10am-5pm) This photogenic, historic landmark, has a busy tasting room inside a former hop kiln; we especially like the flavored vinegars, which make great $10 gifts.

De La Montanya
WINERY

(☑707-433-3711; www.dlmwine.com; 999 Foreman Lane, Healdsburg; tasting $10; ⊙by appointment Mon-Thu, 11am-4:30pm Fri-Sun; ☯) This tiny winery, tucked amid vineyards, is known for 17 small-batch varieties made with estate-grown fruit. Viognier, Primitivo, Pinot and Cabernet are signatures; the 'summer white' and Gewürztraminer are great back-porch wines. Apple-shaded picnic area, bocce ball and horseshoes add to the fun. Bottles are $20 to $60 and the tasting fee is refundable with a purchase.

J Winery
WINERY

(☑707-431-3646; www.jwine.com; 11447 Old Redwood Hwy, Healdsburg; tasting $20, tour $30; ⊙11am-5pm) *◈* J crafts crisp sparkling wines, among Sonoma's best, but it's pricy. Splurge on seated food-and-wine pairings ($45; Friday to Sunday, May to October, call ahead). Bottles cost $20 to $90.

Dry Creek Valley

Hemmed in by 2000ft-high mountains, Dry Creek Valley is relatively warm, ideal for Sauvignon Blanc and Zinfandel, and in some places Cabernet Sauvignon. It's west of Hwy 101, between Healdsburg and Lake Sonoma. Dry Creek Rd is the fast-moving main thoroughfare. Parallel-running West Dry Creek Rd is an undulating country lane with no center stripe – one of Sonoma's great back roads, ideal for cycling.

Quivira
WINERY

(☑707-431-8333; www.quivirawine.com; 4900 West Dry Creek Rd; tasting $10; ⊙11am-5pm; ☷☯) *◈* Sunflowers, lavender and crowing roosters greet your arrival at this winery and biodynamic farm, with self-guided garden tours and a picnic grove beside the vines. Kids can giggle with pigs and chickens, while you sample Rhône varietals, unusual blends, and lip-smacking Sauvignon Blanc. Bottles are $22 to $45; the tasting fee is refundable with purchase.

Unti Vineyards
WINERY

(☑707-433-5590; www.untivineyards.com; 4202 Dry Creek Rd; tasting $5; ⊙by appointment 10am-4pm; ☯) *◈* Inside a vineyard-view tasting room, Unti pours all estate-grown reds –

Châteauneuf-du-Pape–style grenache, compelling Syrah, and superb Sangiovese – favored by oenophiles for their structured tannins and concentrated fruit. If you love small-batch wines, don't miss Unti. Bottles are $23 to $40 and the tasting fee is refundable with a purchase.

Family Wineries
WINERY

(📞 707-433-0100; familywines.com; 4791 Dry Creek Rd; tasting $10; ⏰ 10:30am-4:30pm) Sample multiple varietals at this cooperative, which showcases six boutique wineries too small to have their own tasting rooms. Tasting fee is refundable with a purchase.

Truett Hurst Vineyards
WINERY

(📞 707-433-9545; www.truetthurst.com; 5610 Dry Creek Rd; tasting $5-10; ⏰ 10am-5pm) 🍴 Pull up an Adirondack chair and picnic creekside at Truett Hurst, Dry Creek's newest biodynamic winery. Sample terrific old-vine zins, standout petite Syrah and Russian River Pinots at the handsome contemporary tasting room, then meander through fragrant butterfly gardens to the creek, where salmon spawn in autumn. Saturdays there are snacks, Sundays **live music** (1pm to 4:30pm). Bottles are $18 to $50.

Bella Vineyards
WINERY

(📞 707-473-9171; www.bellawinery.com; 9711 West Dry Creek Rd; tasting $10; ⏰ 11am-4:30pm) Atop the valley's north end, always-fun Bella has caves built into the hillside. The estate-grown grapes include 110-year-old vines from Alexander Valley. The focus is on big reds – Zin and Syrah – but there's terrific rosé (good for barbecues), and late-harvest Zin (great with brownies). The wonderful vibe and dynamic staff make Bella special. Bottles are $25 to $42.

Preston Vineyards
WINERY

(www.prestonvineyards.com; 9282 West Dry Creek Rd; tasting $5; ⏰ 11am-4:30pm; 🚼) 🍴 An early leader in organics, Lou Preston's 19th-century farm is old Sonoma. Weathered picket fencing frames the 19th-century farmhouse-turned-tasting room, with candy-colored walls and tongue-in-groove ceilings setting a country mood. The signature is citrusy Sauvignon Blanc, but try the Rhône varietals and small-lot wines: Mourvèdre, Viognier, Cinsault and cult-favorite Barbera. Preston also bakes good bread; picnic in the shade of a walnut tree. Monday to Friday, there's bocce ball. Bottles are $24 to

$38, and the tasting fee is refundable with a purchase.

Alexander Valley

Bucolic Alexander Valley flanks the Mayacamas Mountains, with postcard-perfect vistas and wide-open vineyards. Summers are hot, ideal for Cabernet Sauvignon, Merlot and warm-weather Chardonnays, but there's also fine Sauvignon Blanc and Zinfandel. For events info, visit www.alexandervalley.org.

Hanna
WINERY

(📞 800-854-3987, 707-431-4310; http://hannawinery.com; 9280 Hwy 128, Healdsburg; tasting $10-20; ⏰ 10am-4pm; 🚼) Abutting oak-studded hills, Hanna's tasting room has lovely vineyard views and good picnicking. At the bar, find estate-grown Merlot and Cabernet, and big-fruit Zins and Syrah. Sit-down wine-and-cheese tastings are available ($25). Bottles cost $18 to $56.

Hawkes
TASTING ROOM

(📞 707-433-4295; www.hawkeswine.com; 6734 Hwy 128, Healdsburg; tasting $10; ⏰ 10am-5pm; 🚼) Friendly Hawkes' makes an easy stopover while you're exploring the valley. The single-vineyard Cab is damn good, as is the blend; there's also a clean-and-crisp, non-malolactic Chardonnay. Bottles are $30 to $70 and the tasting fee is refundable with a purchase.

Stryker Sonoma
WINERY

(📞 707-433-1944; www.strykersonoma.com; 5110 Hwy 128, Geyserville; tasting $10; ⏰ 10:30am-5pm; 🚼) 🍴 Wow, what a view from the hilltop concrete-and-glass tasting room at Stryker Sonoma. The standouts are fruit-forward Zinfandel and Sangiovese, which you can't buy anywhere else. Good picnicking. Bottles are $20 to $50; tasting fee is refundable with purchase.

Trentadue
WINERY

(📞 888-332-3032, 707-433-3104; www.trentadue.com; 19170 Geyserville Ave, Geyserville; tasting $5-10; ⏰ 10am-5pm; 🚼) Specializes in ports (ruby, not tawny); the chocolate port makes a great gift.

Sebastopol

Grapes have replaced apples as the new cash crop, but Sebastopol's farm-town identity remains rooted in the apple – evidence the much-heralded summertime Gravenstein

Apple Fair. The town center feels suburban because of traffic, but a hippie tinge gives it color. This is the refreshingly unfussy side of Wine Country, and makes a good-value base for exploring the area.

Hwy 116 splits downtown; southbound traffic uses Main St, northbound traffic Petaluma Ave. North of town, it's called Gravenstein Hwy N and continues toward Guerneville; south of downtown, it's Gravenstein Hwy S, which heads toward Hwy 101 and Sonoma.

◉ Sights

Around Sebastopol, look for family-friendly farms, gardens, animal sanctuaries and pick-your-own orchards. For a countywide list, check out the **Sonoma County Farm Trails Guide** (www.farmtrails.org).

★ The Barlow   MARKET
(☑707-824-5600; thebarlow.net; 6770 McKinley St; ◉8:30am-9:30pm; ⓘ) The Barlow occupies a former apple processing plant, covering 12 acres, re-purposed into a village of food producers, artists, winemakers, coffee roasters, spirits distillers and indie restaurateurs, who showcase West County's culinary and artistic diversity. Wander shed to shed, sample everything from house-brewed beer to nitrogen flash-frozen ice cream, and meet artisanal producers in their workshops. Thursdays 4pm to 8pm, mid-June to mid-October, the Barlow hosts a 'street fair,' with live music and local vendors.

Spirit Works Distillery   DISTILLERY
(☑707-634-4793; www.spiritworksdistillery.com; 6790 McKinley St, 100, The Barlow; tasting $5, tour $15; ◉11am-4pm Thu-Sun) ⌀ A bracing alternative to wine-tasting, Spirit Works crafts superb small-batch spirits – vodka, gin, sloe gin and (soon) whiskey – of organic California red-winter wheat. Sample and buy in the warehouse. Tours (by reservation) happen Friday to Sunday at 4pm. Bottles are $27 to $36.

California Carnivores   GARDENS
(☑707-824-0433; www.californiacarnivores.com; 2833 Old Gravenstein Hwy S; ◉10am-4pm Thu-Mon) Even vegans can't help admiring these incredible carnivorous plants – the largest collection in the US – including specimens from around the globe.

Farmers Market   MARKET
(www.sebastopolfarmmarket.org; cnr Petaluma & McKinley Aves; ◉10am-1:30pm Sun) Meets at the downtown plaza.

♨ Festivals & Events

Apple Blossom Festival   CULTURAL
(appleblossomfest.com) Live music, food, drink, wine, a parade and exhibits in April.

Gravenstein Apple Fair   FOOD
(www.gravensteinapplefair.com) Arts, crafts, food, wines and brews, games, live entertainment and farm-life activities in August.

🛏 Sleeping

Staying in Sebastopol is convenient to Russian River Valley, the coast, and Sonoma Valley.

Sebastopol Inn   MOTEL $$
(☑800-653-1082, 707-829-2500; www.sebastopolinn.com; 6751 Sebastopol Ave; r $119-209; ❄ 🐕 ❄) We like this independent, *non*-cookie-cutter motel for its quiet, off-street location, usually reasonable rates and good-looking if basic rooms. Outside are grassy areas for kids and a hot tub.

Fairfield Inn & Suites   HOTEL $$
(☑800-465-4329, 707-829-6677; www.winecountryhi.com; 1101 Gravenstein Hwy S; r $134-249; ❄ @ 🐕 ❄) Generic but modern, this hotel has little extras, such as in-room refrigerators and coffee makers, plus a hot tub.

✕ Eating

Fiesta Market   MARKET $
(Pacific Market; ☑707-823-9735; fiestamkt.com; 550 Gravenstein Hwy N; ◉8am-8pm) Excellent for groceries and picnics; north of downtown.

East-West Cafe   MEDITERRANEAN $
(☑707-829-2822; www.eastwestcafesebastopol.com; 128 N Main St; meals $9-13; ◉8am-9pm Mon-Sat, to 8pm Sun; 🍴ⓘ) ⌀ This unfussy cafe serves everything from grass-fed burgers to macrobiotic wraps, stir-fries to *huevos rancheros* (corn tortilla with fried egg and chili-tomato sauce). Good blue-corn pancakes at breakfast.

Slice of Life   VEGETARIAN $
(☑707-829-6627; www.thesliceoflife.com; 6970 McKinley St; mains under $10; ◉11am-9pm Tue-Fri, 9am-9pm Sat & Sun; 🍴) ⌀ This vegan-vegetarian kitchen doubles as a pizzeria. Breakfast all day. Great smoothies and date shakes.

Screamin' Mimi   ICE CREAM $
(☑707-823-5902; www.screaminmimisicecream.com; 6902 Sebastopol Ave; ◉11am-10pm) Delish homemade ice cream.

Mom's Apple Pie
DESSERTS $

(☑ 707-823-8330; www.momsapplepieusa.com; 4550 Gravenstein Hwy N; whole pies $7-17; ⊙ 10am-6pm; ☑ ⊞) Pie's the thing at this roadside bakery – and yum, that flaky crust. Apple is predictably good, especially in autumn, but the blueberry is our fave, made better with vanilla ice cream.

Forchetta Bastoni
ITALIAN, SOUTHEAST ASIAN $$

(☑ 707-829-9500; www.forchettabastoni.com; 6948 Sebastopol Ave; mains $10-16; ⊙ 11am-9pm Sun-Thu, to 10pm Fri & Sat; ☑) Inside a converted brick-walled warehouse, Forchetta Bastoni has two kitchens that make wildly different food – Southeast Asian and Italian. Pick a cuisine, then be seated on one side or the other for wood-fired pizzas, pastas and roasted meats; or noodles, rice bowls and curries. If you can't decide, sit at the happening bar.

Red's Apple Roadhouse
AMERICAN $$

(☑ 707-861-9338; www.redsappleroadhouse.com; 4550 Gravenstein Hwy N; mains $9-15; ⊙ 8am-9:30pm Tue-Sat, to 5pm Sun) A rustic roadhouse and tavern north of downtown (next door to Mom's Apple Pie), Red's smokes its own bacon and pastrami, bakes its own bread and serves simple, quality American cooking, using locally sourced ingredients in dishes like fried chicken and waffles, pulled-pork sandwiches, biscuits and gravy, and classic mac-n-cheese. Local beer and wine. Live music Wednesday and Friday evenings.

Hopmonk Tavern
PUB FOOD $$

(☑ 707-829-9300; www.hopmonk.com; 230 Petaluma Ave; mains $12-23; ⊙ 11:30am-9pm Sun-Wed, to 9:30pm Thu-Sat, bar to 1:30am; ☜) Inside a converted 1903 railroad station, Hopmonk's serves 76 varieties of beer – served in type-specific glassware – that pair with a good menu of burgers, fried calamari, charcuterie platters and salads.

K&L Bistro
FRENCH $$$

(☑ 707-823-6614; www.klbistro.com; 119 S Main St; lunch $14-20, dinner $19-29; ⊙ 11am-9pm) K&L serves earthy provincial Cal-French bistro cooking in a convivial bar-and-grill space with sidewalk patio. Expect classics like mussels and French fries, and grilled steaks with red-wine reduction. Reservations essential.

Zazu Kitchen & Farm
ITALIAN, NEW AMERICAN $$$

(☑ 707-523-4814; zazukitchen.com; 6770 McKinley St, 150, The Barlow; lunch mains $13-18, dinner $24-29; ⊙ 11:30am-10pm Wed & Thu, to midnight Fri, from 9am Sat & Sun, from 5pm Mon) We love the farm-to-table ethos of Zazu – they raise their own pigs and source everything locally – but some dishes miss, and the industrial-style space gets crazy loud. Still, we love their pizzas, salads, housemade salumi and bacon. Good breakfasts, too.

Drinking & Entertainment

Woodfour Brewing Co.
BREWERY

(☑ 707-823-3144; www.woodfourbrewing.com; 6780 Depot St, The Barlow; ⊙ 11am-9pm Sun-Thu, to 11pm Fri & Sat) Woodfour's solar-powered brewery serves 12 housemade beers, light on alcohol and hops, plus several sours (high-acid beer). It has an exceptionally good menu of small plates, designed to pair with beer, from simple snacks to refined, technique-driven dishes better than any we've had at a California brewery.

Taylor Maid Farms
CAFE

(☑ 707-634-7129; www.taylormaidfarms.com; 6790 Depot St, The Barlow; ⊙ 6am-7pm Sun-Thu, to 9pm Fri & Sat) Choose your brew method (drip, press, etc) at this third-wave coffeehouse that roasts its own organic beans. Exceptional seasonal drinks include lavender lattes.

Hardcore Espresso
CAFE

(☑ 707-823-7588; 1798 Gravenstein Hwy S; ⊙ 6am-7pm; ☜) Meet local hippies and art freaks over coffee and smoothies at this classic Nor-Cal, off-the-grid, indoor-outdoor coffeehouse, south of downtown, that's essentially a corrugated-metal-roofed shack surrounded by umbrella tables.

Jasper O'Farrell's
BAR

(☑ 707-823-1389; 6957 Sebastopol Ave; ⊙ noon-2am) Busy bar with billiards and live music most nights; good drink specials.

Hopmonk Tavern
LIVE MUSIC

(☑ 707-829-7300; www.hopmonk.com; 230 Petaluma Ave; ⊙ 11:30am-11pm Sun-Wed, to midnight Thu-Sat) This always-busy tavern and beer garden has town's most diverse live-music calendar, and sometimes hosts the likes of Jonathan Richman.

Shopping

Antique shops line Gravenstein Hwy S toward Hwy 101.

Aubergine
VINTAGE

(☑ 707-827-3460; 755 Petaluma Ave; ⊙ 10am-6pm) Vast vintage emporium, specializing in cast-off European thrift-shop clothing.

NAPA & SONOMA WINE COUNTRY SEBASTOPOL

Sumbody BEAUTY
(☑707-823-2053; www.sumbody.com; 118 N Main St; ☺10am-7pm Mon-Wed, to 8pm Thu-Sat, to 6pm Sun) Eco-friendly bath products made with all-natural ingredients. Also offers well-priced facials ($49) and massages ($85) at its small on-site spa.

Toyworks TOYS
(☑707-829-2003; www.sonomatoyworks.com; 6940 Sebastopol Ave; ☺10am-6pm Mon-Sat, 11am-5pm Sun; 📶) Indie toy-seller with phenomenal selection of quality games for kids.

Funk & Flash CLOTHING
(☑707-829-1142; www.funkandflash.com; 228 S Main St; ☺11am-7pm) Disco-glam party clothes, inspired by Burning Man.

Antique Society ANTIQUES
(☑707-829-1733; www.antiquesociety.com; 2661 Gravenstein Hwy S; ☺10am-5pm) One-hundred-and-twenty-five antiques vendors under one roof.

Beekind FOOD, HOMEWARES
(☑707-824-2905; www.beekind.com; 921 Gravenstein Hwy S; ☺10am-6pm Mon-Sat, to 4pm Sun) 🖉 Local honey and beeswax candles.

Copperfield's Books BOOKS
(☑707-823-2618; www.copperfields.net; 138 N Main St; ☺10am-7pm Mon-Sat, to 6pm Sun) Indie bookshop with literary events.

Midgley's Country Flea Market MARKET
(☑707-823-7874; mfleamarket.com; 2200 Gravenstein Hwy S; ☺6:30am-4:30pm Sat & Sun) The region's largest flea market.

ℹ Information

Sebastopol Area Chamber of Commerce & Visitors Center (☑877-828-4748, 707-823-3032; www.visitsebastopol.org; 265 S Main St;

☺10am-4pm Mon-Fri) Maps, information and exhibits.

Occidental & Around

Our favorite West County town is a haven of artists, back-to-the-landers and counter-culturalists. Historic 19th-century buildings line a single main street, easy to explore in an hour; continue north by car and you'll hit the Russian River, in Monte Rio. At Christmastime, Bay Area families flock to Occidental to buy trees. The town decorates to the nines, and there's weekend cookie-decorating and caroling at the Union Hotel's Bocce Ballroom.

⊙ Sights & Activities

Occidental Farmers Market MARKET
(www.occidentalfarmersmarket.com; ☺4pm-dusk Fri Jun-Oct) Meet the whole community at Occidental's detour-worthy farmers market, with musicians, craftspeople and – the star attraction – **Gerard's Paella** (www.gerardspaella.com) of TV-cooking-show fame.

Sonoma Canopy Tours OUTDOORS
(☑888-494-7868; www.sonomacanopytours.com; 6250 Bohemian Hwy; adult $99-109, child $69) North of town, fly through the redwood canopy on seven interconnected ziplines, ending with an 80ft-rappel descent; reservations required.

Osmosis SPA
(☑707-823-8231; www.osmosis.com; 209 Bohemian Hwy, Freestone; ☺by appointment) Three miles south in Freestone, tranquility prevails at this Japanese-inspired spa, which indulges patrons with dry-enzyme baths of aromatic cedar fibers (bath-and-blanket wrap $89

WORTH A TRIP

SCENIC DRIVE: COLEMAN VALLEY ROAD

Wine Country's most scenic drive isn't through the grapes, but along these 10 miles of winding West County byway, from Occidental to the sea. It's best late morning, after the fog has cleared. Drive west, not east, with the sun behind you and the ocean ahead. First you'll pass through redwood forests and lush valleys where Douglas firs stand draped in sphagnum moss – an eerie sight in the fog. The real beauty shots lie further ahead, when the road ascends 1000ft hills, dotted with gnarled oaks and craggy rock formations, with the vast blue Pacific unfurling below. The road ends at coastal Hwy 1, where you can explore Sonoma Coast State Beach (p200), then turn left and find your way to the tiny town of Bodega (not Bodega Bay) to see locales where Hitchcock shot his 1963 classic, *The Birds*.

to $99), lovely tea-and-meditation gardens, plus outdoor massages. Make reservations.

🛏 Sleeping

Occidental Hotel
MOTEL $$

(☑877-867-6084, 707-874-3623; www.occidentalhotel.com; 3610 Bohemian Hwy; r $120-160, 2-bedroom q $200-240; ❄ 🤚 🐕 🐾) Rates are sometimes negotiable for these well-kept motel rooms

Valley Ford Hotel
INN $$

(☑707-876-1983; www.vfordhotel.com; r $115-175) Surrounded by pastureland 8 miles south in Valley Ford, this 19th-century, six-room inn has good beds, great rates and a terrific roadhouse restaurant.

Inn at Occidental
INN $$$

(☑707-874-1047, 800-522-6324; www.innatoccidental.com; 3657 Church St; r incl breakfast $249-339; 🐾) One of Sonoma's finest, this beautifully restored 18-room Victorian inn is filled with collectible antiques; rooms have gas fireplaces and cozy feather beds.

🍴 Eating

Howard Station Cafe
AMERICAN $

(☑707-874-2838; www.howardstationcafe.com; 3811 Bohemian Hwy; mains $6-12; ⊙7am-2:30pm Mon-Fri, to 3pm Sat & Sun; 🐾🐕) Big plates of comfort cooking and fresh-squeezed juices. Cash only.

Wild Flour Bread
BAKERY $

(www.wildflourbread.com; 140 Bohemian Hwy, Freestone; items from $3; ⊙8:30am-6:30pm Fri-Mon) Organic brick-oven sourdough breads, giant sticky buns and good coffee.

Bohemian Market
DELI $

(☑707-874-3312; 3633 Main St; ⊙8am-9pm) Occidental's best grocery store has an OK deli.

Rocker Oysterfeller's
NEW AMERICAN $$

(☑707-876-1983; www.rockeroysterfellers.com; 14415 Hwy 1, Valley Ford; mains $13-24; ⊙5pm-8:30pm Thu & Fri, from 3pm Sat, from 10am Sun) We love the flavor-rich cooking at this Valley Ford roadhouse, which features barbecued oysters, local crab cakes, steaks and fried chicken. Great wine bar, too. Sundays there's brunch.

Barley & Hops
PUB FOOD $$

(☑707-874-9037; www.barleynhops.com; 3688 Bohemian Hwy; mains $10-15; ⊙4-9:30pm Mon-Thu, from 11am Fri-Sun) Serves over 100 beers, sandwiches, giant salads and shepherd's pie.

Union Hotel
ITALIAN $$

(☑707-874-3555; www.unionhoteloccidental.com; 3703 Bohemian Hwy; meals $15-25; ⊙11am-9pm; 🐾) Occidental has two old-school American-Italian restaurants that serve family-style meals. The Union is slightly better (neither is great), and has a hard-to-beat lunch special in its 1869 saloon – whole pizza, salad and soda for $12. At dinner, sit in the fabulous Bocce Ballroom.

Bistro des Copains
FRENCH-CALIFORNIAN $$$

(☑707-874-2436; www.bistrodescopains.com; 3728 Bohemian Hwy; mains $24-26, 3-course menu $40-45; ⊙5-9pm Wed-Mon) 🌿 Worth a special trip, this convivial bistro draws boho vivants for Cal-French country cooking, like *steak-frites* and roast duck. Great wines; $10 corkage for Sonoma vintages. Make reservations.

🛍 Shopping

Verdigris
HOMEWARES

(☑707-874-9018; www.1lightartlamps.com; 72 Main St; ⊙11am-6pm Thu-Mon) Crafts gorgeous art lamps.

Hand Goods
CERAMICS

(☑707-874-2161; www.handgoods.net; 3627 Main St; ⊙10am-6pm) Collective of ceramicists and potters.

Guerneville & Around

The Russian River's biggest vacation-resort town, Guerneville gets busy summer weekends with party-hardy gay boys, sun-worshipping lesbians and long-haired, beer-drinking Harley riders, earning it the nickname 'Groin-ville.' Though the town is slowly gentrifying, it hasn't lost its honky-tonk vibe – fun-seeking crowds still come to canoe, hike redwoods and hammer cocktails poolside.

Downriver, some areas are sketchy (due to drugs). The local chamber of commerce has chased most of the tweakers from Main St in Guerneville, but if some off-the-beaten-path areas feel creepy – especially campgrounds – they probably are.

Four miles downriver, tiny Monte Rio has a sign over Hwy 116 declaring it 'Vacation Wonderland' – an overstatement, but the dog-friendly beach is a hit with families. Further west, idyllic Duncans Mills is home to a few dozen souls and has picture-ready historic buildings, now converted into cute shops. Upriver, east of Guerneville, Forestville is where agricultural country resumes.

◉ Sights & Activities

Look for sandy beaches and swimming holes along the river; there's good river access east of town at **Sunset Beach** (www.sonoma-county.org/parks; 11060 River Rd, Forestville; per car $7; ☉7am-sunset). Fishing and watercraft outfitters operate mid-May to early October, after which winter rains dangerously swell the river. A **farmers market** meets downtown on Wednesdays, June through September, from 3pm to 7pm. On summer Saturdays, there's also one at Monte Rio Beach, 11am to 2pm.

Armstrong Redwoods
State Natural Reserve   FOREST
(☑information 707-869-2015, office 707-869-9177, visitor center 707-869-2958; www.parks.ca.gov; 17000 Armstrong Woods Rd; per car $8; ☉8am-sunset; 🚹) A magnificent redwood forest 2 miles north of Guerneville, the 805-acre Armstrong Redwoods State Reserve was saved from the saw by a 19th-century lumber magnate. Short interpretive trails lead into magical forests, with trees 30-stories high. Beyond lie 20 miles of backcountry trails, through oak woodlands, in adjoining **Austin Creek State Recreation Area**, one of Sonoma County's last-remaining wilderness areas. Walk or cycle in for free; pay only to park.

Burke's Canoe Trips   CANOEING
(☑707-887-1222; www.burkescanoetrips.com; 8600 River Rd, Forestville; canoe/kayak rental incl shuttle $65/45; ☉10am-6pm Mon-Fri, 9am-6pm Sat & Sun) You can't beat Burke's for a day on the river. Self-guided canoe and kayak trips include shuttle back to your car. Make reservations; plan four hours. Camping in its riverside redwood grove costs $10 per person.

R3 Hotel Pool   SWIMMING
(Triple R; ☑707-869-8399; www.ther3hotel.com; 16390 4th St, Guerneville; ☉9am-midnight) 𝗙𝗥𝗘𝗘 The gay, adults-only, party-scene swimming pool at the Triple R is free, provided you buy drinks. Bring your own towel. Bathing suits mandatory, but only because state liquor-license laws require them.

Pee Wee Golf & Arcade   GOLF, CYCLING
(☑707-869-9321; 16155 Drake Rd at Hwy 116, Guerneville; 18/36 holes $8/12; ☉11am-10pm Jun-Aug, to 5pm Sat & Sun May & Sep; 🚹) Flashback to 1948 at this impeccably kept, retro-kitsch, 36-hole miniature golf course, just south of the Hwy 116 bridge, with brilliantly painted obstacles, including T Rex and Yogi Bear.

Bring your own cocktails; also rents gas barbecue grills ($20).

King's Sport &
Tackle   FISHING, KAYAKING, CANOEING
(☑707-869-2156; www.kingsrussianriver.com; 16258 Main St, Guerneville; ☉8am-6pm) *The* local source for fishing and river-condition information. Also rents kayaks ($35 to $55), canoes ($55) and fishing gear.

River Rider   BICYCLE RENTAL
(☑707-483-2897; www.riverridersrentals.com; half-/full-day rental $25/45; ☉7am-7pm) Delivers bicycles, along with wine-tasting passes on request; discounts for multiday rentals.

Johnson's Beach   WATER SPORTS
(☑707-869-2022; www.johnsonsbeach.com; 16241 First St, Guerneville; kayak & canoe per hr/day $10/30; ☉10am-6pm May-Sep; 🚹) Canoe, paddleboat and watercraft rental (from $30). Beach admission free, and you can camp here.

Northwood Golf Course   GOLF
(☑707-865-1116; www.northwoodgolf.com; 19400 Hwy 116, Monte Rio; walking $25-27, riding $33-35, 9 holes $25-35, 18 holes $35-53; ☉7:30am-sunset) Vintage-1920s Alistair MacKenzie–designed, par-36, nine-hole course.

✦ Festivals & Events

Monte Rio Variety Show   MUSIC
(www.monterioshow.org) Members of the elite, secretive Bohemian Grove (Google it) perform publicly, sometimes showcasing unannounced celebrities, in July.

Lazy Bear Weekend   CULTURAL
(www.lazybearweekend.com) Read: heavy, furry gay men; August.

Russian River Jazz & Blues Festival   MUSIC
(www.russianriverfestivals.com) A day of jazz, followed by a day of blues in September, with occasional luminaries like BB King.

🛏 Sleeping

Russian River has few budget sleeps; prices drop midweek. For weekends and holidays, book ahead. Many places have no TVs. Because the river sometimes floods, some lodgings have cold linoleum floors: pack slippers.

🏨 Guerneville

Staying downtown means you can walk to restaurants and bars.

Guerneville Lodge CAMPGROUND $
(☑707-869-0102; www.guernevillelodge.com; 15905 River Rd; tent sites $40) The prettiest place to camp in downtown Guerneville is behind this retreat-center lodge, on sprawling grassy lawns fronting on the river. Amenities: hot clean showers, big campsites, refrigerator access, fire pits with grills. When available, lodge rooms cost $189 to $229.

Bullfrog Pond Campground CAMPGROUND $
(☑Mon-Fri reservations & information 707-869-9177, Sat & Sun ranger kiosk 707-869-2015; www.stewardscr.org; sites reserved/non-reserved $35/25; ☒) Reached via a steep road from Armstrong Redwoods State Natural Reserve, 4 miles from the entrance kiosk, Bullfrog Pond has forested campsites, with cold water, and primitive hike-in and equestrian backcountry campsites. Reserve via www.hipcamp.com or by phone.

Schoolhouse Canyon Campground CAMPGROUND $
(☑707-869-2311; www.schoolhousecanyon.com; 12600 River Rd; tent sites $30; ☒) Two miles east of Guerneville, Schoolhouse's well-tended sites lie beneath tall trees, across the main road from the river. Coin-operated hot showers, clean bathrooms, quiet by night.

Johnson's Beach Resort CABIN, CAMPGROUND $
(☑707-869-2022; www.johnsonsbeach.com; 16241 1st St; tent sites $25, RV sites $25-35, cabins $75, per week $400) On the river in Guerneville, Johnson's has rustic, but clean, thin-walled cabins on stilts; all have kitchens. Bring earplugs. There's camping, too, but it's loud. No credit cards.

Fern Grove Cottages CABIN $$
(☑707-869-8105; www.ferngrove.com; 16650 River Rd; cabins incl breakfast $159-219, with kitchen $199-269; @�Bⓡ☒) Downtown Guerneville's cheeriest resort, Fern Grove has vintage-1930s pine-paneled cabins, tucked beneath redwoods and surrounded by lush flowering gardens. Some have Jacuzzis and fireplaces. The pool uses salt, not chlorine; the lovely English innkeeper provides concierge services; and breakfast includes homemade scones.

Highlands Resort CABIN, CAMPGROUND $$
(☑707-869-0333; www.highlandsresort.com; 14000 Woodland Dr; tent sites $20-30, r with bath $90-100, without $70-80, cabins $120-205; ⒮☒☒) Guerneville's mellowest all-gay resort sits on a wooded hillside, walkable to

town, and has simply furnished rooms, little cottages with porches and good camping. The large pool and hot tub are clothing-optional (weekday/weekend day use $10/15).

R3 Hotel RESORT $$
(Triple R; ☑707-869-8399; www.ther3hotel.com; 16390 4th St; r Mon-Fri $80-150, Sat & Sun $105-215; ⒮☒) Ground zero for party-hardy gay lads and lesbians, Triple-R (as it's known) has plain-Jane, motel-style rooms surrounding a bar and pool deck that get so crowded summer weekends, management won't allow guests to bring pets because 'they get hurt' (actual quote). Come for the scene, not for quiet (light sleepers: bring ear plugs). Midweek it's mellow, wintertime dead.

Riverlane Resort CABIN $$
(☑707-869-2323, 800-201-2324; www.riverlaneresort.com; 16320 1st St; cabins $90-140; ⒮☒☒) Right downtown, Riverlane has basic cabins with kitchens, decorated with mismatched furniture, but they're very clean and have decks with barbecues. Best for no-frills travelers or campers wanting an upgrade. Heated pool, private beach and hot tub.

Applewood Inn INN $$$
(☑800-555-8509, 707-869-9093; www.applewoodinn.com; 13555 Hwy 116; r incl breakfast $215-345; ⒮@ⓡ☒) A hideaway estate on a wooded hilltop south of town, cushy Applewood has marvelous 1920s-era detail, with dark wood and heavy furniture that echo the forest. Rooms have Jacuzzis, couples' showers and top-end linens; some have fireplaces. Small on-site spa.

Boon Hotel + Spa BOUTIQUE HOTEL $$$
(☑707-869-2721; www.boonhotels.com; 14711 Armstrong Woods Rd; r $165-275; ⓡ☒☒) ⚑ Rooms surround a swimming-pool courtyard (with Jacuzzi) at this mid-century-modern, 14-room motel-resort, gussied up in minimalist style. The look is austere but fresh, with organic-cotton linens and spacious rooms; most have wood-burning fireplaces. Drive to town, or ride the free bicycles.

Santa Nella House B&B $$$
(☑707-869-9488; www.santanellahouse.com; 12130 Hwy 116; r incl breakfast $199-219; @ⓡ☒) All four spotless rooms at this 1871 Victorian, south of town, have wood-burning fireplaces and frilly Victorian furnishings. Upstairs rooms are biggest. Outside there's a hot tub and sauna. Best for travelers who appreciate the B&B aesthetic.

🛏 Forestville

Raford Inn   B&B $$$
(📞800-887-9503, 707-887-9573; http://rafordinn.
com; 10630 Wohler Rd, Healdsburg; r $185-270;
❄@🤝) 🐾 We love this 1880 Victorian
B&B's secluded hilltop location, surrounded by tall palms and rambling vineyards.
Rooms are big and airy, done with lace and
antiques; some have fireplaces. And wow,
those sunset views.

Farmhouse Inn   INN $$$
(📞800-464-6642, 707-887-3300; www.farm-
houseinn.com; 7871 River Rd; r $445-795;
❄@🤝❄) Think love nest. The area's premier inn has spacious rooms and cottages,
styled with cushy amenities like saunas,
steam-showers and wood-burning fireplaces. Small on-site spa and top-notch restaurant. Check in early to maximize time.

🛏 Monte Rio

Village Inn   INN $$
(📞707-865-2304; www.villageinn-ca.com; 20822
River Blvd; r $145-235; 🤝) 🐾 A retired con-
cierge owns this cute, old-fashioned, 11-room
inn, beneath towering trees, right on the
river. Some rooms have river views; all have
fridge and microwave. No elevator.

Rio Villa Beach Resort   INN $$
(📞877-746-8455, 707-865-1143; www.riovilla.com;
20292 Hwy 116; r with kitchen $149-209, without
$139-189; ❄🤝❄) Landscaping is lush at this
small riverside resort with excellent sun exposure (you see redwoods, but you're not under them). Rooms are well kept but simple
(request a quiet room, not by the road); the
emphasis is on the outdoors, evident by the
large riverside terrace, outdoor fireplace and
barbecues. Some air-con.

Highland Dell   INN $$
(📞707-865-2300; highlanddell.com; 21050 River
Blvd; r $109-179; 🕐Apr-Nov; ❄🤝) 🐾 Built in
1906 in grand lodge style, redone in 2007,
the inn fronts right on the river. Above
the giant dining room are 12 bright, fresh-
looking rooms with comfy beds. No elevator.

🛏 Duncans Mills

Casini Ranch   CAMPGROUND $
(📞800-451-8400, 707-865-2255; www.casin-
iranch.com; 22855 Moscow Rd; tent sites $45-52,
RV sites partial hookups $47-58, full hookups $53-
56; 🤝❄) In quiet Duncans Mills, beautifully

set on riverfront ranchlands, Casini is an
enormous, well-run campground. Amenities
include kayaks and paddleboats (day use $5
to $10); bathrooms are spotless.

🍴 Eating

🍴 Guerneville

There's a good **taco truck**, in the Safeway
parking lot at 16451 Main St.

Big Bottom Market   MARKET, CAFE $
(📞707-604-7295; www.bigbottommarket.com;
16228 Main St; sandwiches $7-10; 🕐8am-5pm
Sun-Thu, to 6pm Fri & Sat) 🐾 Gourmet deli and
wine shop with scrumptious pastries and
grab-and-go picnic supplies.

Coffee Bazaar   CAFE $
(📞707-869-9706; www.mycoffeeb.com; 14045
Armstrong Woods Rd; dishes $5-9; 🕐6am-8pm;
🤝) Happening cafe with salads, sandwiches
and all-day breakfasts; adjoins a good used
bookstore.

Taqueria La Tapatia   MEXICAN $
(📞707-869-1821; 16632 Main St; mains $7-14;
🕐11am-9pm) Reasonable choice for traditional Mexican.

Garden Grill   BARBECUE $
(📞707-869-3922; www.gardengrillbbq.com; 17132
Hwy 116, Guernewood Park; mains $6-12; 🕐8am-
8pm) One mile west of Guerneville, this roadhouse barbecue joint, with redwood-shaded
patio, serves good house-smoked meats, but
the fries could be better. Breakfast till 3pm.

Food for Humans   MARKET $
(📞707-869-3612; 16385 1st St; 🕐9am-8pm; 🥗)
🐾 Organic groceries; better alternative than
neighboring Safeway, but no meat.

Seaside Metal Oyster Bar   SEAFOOD $$
(📞707-604-7250; seasidemetal.com; 16222 Main
St; dishes $11-16; 🕐5-10pm Wed-Sun) Unexpect-
edly urban for Guerneville, this storefront
raw bar is an offshoot of San Francisco's Bar
Crudo – one of the city's best – and showcases oysters, clams, lobster and exquisitely
prepared raw-fish dishes. There's limited hot
food, but it's overwrought: stick to raw.

Dick Blomster's
Korean Diner   KOREAN, AMERICAN $$
(📞707-896-8006; 16236 Main St; mains $15-20;
🕐5-10pm Sun-Thu, to 2am Fri & Sat Jun-Aug, to
11pm Fri & Sat Sep-May) By day a vintage-1940s
coffee shop, by night a Korean-American

diner with full bar, Dick Blomster's serves playfully tongue-in-cheek dishes, including fried PB&J sandwiches and 'the other KFC – Korean fried crack' – fried chicken with sugary-sweet brown sauce, which sure hits the spot after a night's drinking.

Boon Eat + Drink
CALIFORNIAN $$$
(☑707-869-0780; http://eatatboon.com; 16248 Main St; lunch mains $14-18, dinner $15-26; ⊙11am-3pm Mon, Tue, Thu & Fri, 5-9pm Mon-Fri, 10am-3pm & 5-10pm Sat & Sun) Locally sourced ingredients inform the seasonal, Cali-smart cooking at this tiny, always-packed, New American bistro, with cheek-by-jowl tables that fill every night. Make reservations or expect to wait.

Applewood Inn Restaurant
CALIFORNIAN $$$
(☑707-869-9093; www.applewoodinn.com; 13555 Hwy 116; mains $20-28; ⊙5:30-8:30pm Wed-Sun) Cozy up by the fire in the treetop-level dining room and sup on quality Euro-Cal cooking that maximizes seasonal produce, with dishes like rack of lamb with minted *chimichuri* (garlic-parsley vinaigrette) and smoked trout with corn and crayfish. Sunday nights there's a $35 prix-fixe menu. Reservations essential.

🍴 Forestville

Canneti Roadhouse
ITALIAN $$
(☑707-887-2232; http://cannetirestaurant.com; 6675 Front St; lunch mains $12-24, dinner $15-28; ⊙11:30am-3pm Wed-Sat, to 5pm Sun, 5:30-9pm Tue-Sun) 🌱 A Tuscan-born chef makes bona fide *cucina Italiana*, using quality ingredients from local farms, at this austere restaurant in downtown Forestville, worth the 15-minute drive from Guerneville. The menu ranges from simple brick-oven pizzas to an all-Tuscan, five-course tasting menu ($55, dinner only). When it's warm, sit on the patio beneath a giant redwood. Make reservations.

Farmhouse Inn
NEW AMERICAN $$$
(☑707-887-3300; www.farmhouseinn.com; 7871 River Rd; 3-/4-course dinner $69/84; ⊙from 5.30pm Thu-Mon) 🌱 Special-occasion worthy, Michelin-starred Farmhouse changes its seasonal Euro-Cal menu daily using locally raised, organic ingredients like Sonoma lamb, wild salmon and rabbit – the latter is the house specialty. Details are impeccable, from aperitifs in the garden to tableside cheese service, but detractors call it precious. Make reservations.

🍴 Monte Rio

Don's Dogs
FAST FOOD $
(☑707-865-4190; cnr Bohemian Hwy & Hwy 116; sandwiches $4-12; ⊙9am-4pm Thu-Mon Oct-May, to 7pm daily Jun-Sep; 🛜) Gourmet hot dogs, wine, beer, simple breakfasts and coffee, behind the Rio Theater.

Highland Dell
GERMAN $$$
(☑707-865-2300; http://highlanddell.com; 21050 River Blvd; mains $20-22; ⊙4-10pm Fri-Tue Apr-Nov) A dramatic, three-story-high, chalet-style dining room with a river-view deck, Highland Dell makes pretty good German-inspired cooking, including steaks and schnitzel. Full bar.

Village Inn
AMERICAN $$$
(☑707-865-2304; www.villageinn-ca.com; 20822 River Blvd; mains $19-26; ⊙5-8pm Wed-Sun) The straightforward steaks-and-seafood menu is basic American and doesn't distract from the wonderful river views. Great local wine list, full bar.

🍴 Duncans Mills

Cape Fear Cafe
AMERICAN $$
(☑707-865-9246; 25191 Main St; lunch mains $9-15, dinner $15-25; ⊙10am-8pm Mon & Thu, to 3pm Tue & Wed, to 9pm Fri-Sun) A country-Americana diner in a 19th-century grange, Cape Fear is visually charming, but it's erratic – except at weekend brunch, when the kitchen makes excellent Benedicts. Good stopover en route to the coast.

🍸 Drinking & Nightlife

Stumptown Brewery
BREWERY
(www.stumptown.com; 15045 River Rd, Guerneville; ⊙11am-midnight Sun-Thu, to 2am Fri & Sat) Guerneville's best straight bar, 1 mile east of downtown, is gay-friendly and has a foot-stompin' jukebox, billiards, riverside beer garden, and several homemade brews. Pretty-good pub grub includes house-smoked barbecue.

Rainbow Cattle Company
GAY
(www.queersteer.com; 16220 Main St, Guerneville; ⊙noon-midnight Sun-Thu, to 2am Fri & Sat) The stalwart gay watering hole has pinball and shuffleboard.

Sophie's Cellars
WINE BAR
(☑707-865-1122; www.sophiescellars.com; 25179 Main St/Hwy 116, Duncans Mills; glasses $7-15; ⊙11am-5pm Mon, Thu, Sat & Sun, to 7pm Fri) The

perfect stopover between river and coast, Sophie's rural wine bar, in Duncans Mills, pours glasses and tastes of local wine, and carries cheese, salami and a well-curated selection of bottles. Friday's 'locals happy hour' (4pm to 7pm) brings hors d'oeuvres, drink specials and a big crowd.

☆ Entertainment

Rio Theater
CINEMA
(☎707-865-0913; www.riotheater.com; cnr Bohemian Hwy & Hwy 116, Monte Rio; adult/child $8/5; 🐾) Dinner and a movie take on new meaning at this vintage-WWII Quonset hut converted to a cinema in 1950, with a concession stand serving gourmet hot dogs with a drink and chips for just $7. In 2014 they finally added heating, but still supply blankets. Only in Monte Rio. Shows nightly (and sometimes Sunday afternoons), but call ahead, especially off-season.

Main Street Station
CABARET
(☎707-869-0501; www.mainststation.com; 16280 Main St, Guerneville; ⊘7-10pm or 11pm; 🐾) FREE Hosts live acoustic-only jazz, blues and cabaret nightly in summer (weekends in winter), and families are welcome because the cabaret doubles as an American-Italian restaurant (stick to pizza).

Rio Nido Roadhouse
LIVE MUSIC
(☎707-869-0821; www.rionidoroadhouse.com; 14540 Canyon Two, Rio Nido) Raucous roadhouse bar, off River Rd, 4 miles east of Guerneville, with eclectic lineup of live bands. Shows start 6pm Saturday and sometimes Friday and Sunday, too; check website.

🛍 Shopping

Eight miles west of Guerneville, tiny Duncans Mills (pop 85) has good shopping in a handful of side-by-side businesses within weathered 19th-century cottages.

Mr Trombly's Tea & Table
FOOD & DRINK
(www.mrtromblystea.com; 25185 Main St, Duncans Mills; ⊘10am-5pm Sun-Thu, to 6pm Sat & Sun) Different kinds of tea and teapots, plus quality kitchen gadgets and well-priced tableware.

Pig Alley
JEWELRY
(☎707-865-2698; www.pigalleyshop.com; 25193 Main St, Duncans Mills; ⊘10:30am-5:30pm) Vast selection of handcrafted American-made jewelry, notable for gorgeous earrings.

ℹ Information

Russian River Chamber of Commerce & Visitors Center (☎707-869-9000, 877-644-9001; www.russianriver.com; 16209 1st St, Guerneville; ⊘10am-4:45pm Mon-Sat, plus 10am-3pm Sun May-Sep) For information and lodging referrals.

Russian River Visitors Center (☎707-869-4096; ⊘10am-3pm Oct-Apr, to 4pm May-Sep) At Korbel Cellars.

Santa Rosa

Wine Country's biggest city and the Sonoma County seat, Santa Rosa claims two famous native sons – a world-renowned cartoonist and a celebrated horticulturalist – whose legacies include museums and gardens enough to keep you busy for an afternoon. Otherwise, there ain't much to do, unless you need your car fixed or you're here in July during the **Sonoma County Fair** (www.sonomacountyfair.com), at the fairgrounds on Bennett Valley Rd. Santa Rosa is mostly known for traffic and suburban sprawl. It generally lacks charm (except downtown, where redwood trees serve as landscaping and tower over buildings), but has reasonably priced accommodations and easy access to Sonoma County and Valley.

◉ Sights & Activities

The main shopping stretch is 4th St, which abruptly ends at Hwy 101, but re-emerges across the freeway at historic Railroad Sq. Downtown parking garages (75¢ hour, $8 max) are cheaper than street parking. East of town, 4th St becomes Hwy 12 into Sonoma Valley.

Luther Burbank Home & Gardens GARDENS
(☎707-524-5445; www.lutherburbank.org; cnr Santa Rosa & Sonoma Aves; ⊘8am-dusk) FREE Pioneering horticulturist Luther Burbank (1849–1926) developed many hybrid plant species, including the Shasta daisy, here at his 19th-century, Greek-revival home. The extensive gardens are lovely. The house and adjacent **Carriage Museum** (guided tour adult/child $7/free; ⊘10am-3:30pm Tue-Sun Apr-Oct) have displays on Burbank's life and work, you can take a self-guided cell phone tour for free. Across the street from Burbank's home, **Julliard Park** has a playground.

Charles M Schulz Museum
MUSEUM

(☎707-579-4452; www.schulzmuseum.org; 2301 Hardies Lane; adult/child $10/5; ⏰11am-5pm Mon & Wed-Fri, 10am-5pm Sat & Sun; ⓐ) Charles Schulz, Santa Rosa resident and creator of *Peanuts* cartoons, was born in 1922, published his first drawing in 1937, introduced Snoopy and Charlie Brown in 1950, and produced *Peanuts* cartoons until his death in 2000. This modern museum honors his legacy with a Snoopy labyrinth, *Peanuts*-related art, and a re-creation of Schulz's studio. Skip Snoopy's Gallery gift shop; the museum has the good stuff.

Farmers Markets
MARKET

(4th & B Sts; ⏰5-8:30pm Wed mid-May–Aug) Sonoma County's largest farmers market. Another year-round market meets 8:30am to 1pm Saturdays at Santa Rosa Veterans Building, 1351 Maple Ave.

Redwood Empire Ice Arena
SKATING

(☎707-546-7147; www.snoopyshomeice.com; 1667 West Steele Lane; adult incl skates $9-12, child $7-10; ⓐ) This skating rink was formerly owned and deeply loved by Schulz. It's open most afternoons (call for schedules). Bring a sweater.

Children's Museum of Sonoma County
SCIENCE CENTER

(☎707-546-4069; www.cmosc.org; 1835 Steele Lane; admission $7; ⏰9am-4pm Tue-Sat, noon-4pm Sun; ⓐ) Geared to little children 10 and under, this happy learning center inspires discovery, exploration and creativity with hands-on exhibits, most outdoors, focused on nature and science. Picnicking welcome. No adults without kids.

🛏 Sleeping

Find chain hotels near Railroad Sq. Nothing-special motels line Cleveland Ave, fronting Hwy 101's western side, between the Steele Lane and Bicentennial Lane exits; skip Motel 6. Nearby Windsor has two chain hotels (Hampton Inn and Holiday Inn) off Hwy 101 at exit 'Central Windsor.'

Spring Lake Park
CAMPGROUND $

(☎707-539-8092, reservations 707-565-2267; www.sonomacountyparks.org; 5585 Newanga Ave; sites $32; ⓐ) 🅿 Lovely lakeside park, 4 miles from downtown; make reservations ($8.50 fee) online or 10am to 3pm weekdays by phone. The park is open year-round, with lake swimming in summer; the campground operates May to September, weekends Oc-

---

OLIVE-OIL TASTING

When you weary of wine-tasting, pop by one of the following olive-oil makers and dip some crusty bread – it's free. Harvest and pressing happen in November.

➡ BR Cohn (p166)

➡ Napa Valley Olive Oil Mfg Co (p151)

➡ Long Meadow Ranch (p145)

➡ Figone's Olive Oil (p175)

tober to April. Take 4th St eastbound, turn right on Farmer's Lane, pass the first Hoen St and turn left on the second Hoen St, then left on Newanga Ave.

Hillside Inn
MOTEL $

(☎707-546-9353; www.hillside-inn.com; 2901 4th St; s/d Nov-Mar $70/82, Apr-Oct $74/86; 🛜🅿) Santa Rosa's best-value motel, Hillside is close to Sonoma Valley; add $4 for kitchens. Furnishings are dated and service peculiar, but everything is scrupulously maintained. Adjoins an excellent breakfast cafe.

Hotel La Rose
HISTORIC HOTEL $$

(☎707-579-3200; www.hotellarose.com; 308 Wilson St; r Mon-Fri $139-199, Sat & Sun $159-229; 🅿🛜) 🅿 At Railroad Sq, Hotel La Rose has rooms in a well-kept historic 1907 brick hotel, and across the street in a 1980s-built 'carriage house,' which feels like a small condo complex with boxy, spacious rooms. All are decorated in out-of-fashion pastels, but have excellent beds with quality linens and down duvets; some have jetted tubs.

Flamingo Resort Hotel
HOTEL $$

(☎800-848-8300, 707-545-8530; www.flamingoresort.com; 2777 4th St; r $159-269; 🅿🛜🅿) 🅿 Sprawling over 11 acres, this mid-century modern hotel doubles as a conference center. Rooms are business-class-generic, but the pool is gigantic – and kept 82°F year-round. Kids love it. On-site health-club and gym. Prices double summer weekends.

Best Western Garden Inn
MOTEL $$

(☎888-256-8004, 707-546-4031; www.thegardeninn.com; 1500 Santa Rosa Ave; r Mon-Fri $119-139, Sat & Sun $199-229; 🅿🛜🅿) Well-kept motel, south of downtown, with two pools. Rear rooms open to grassy gardens, but you may hear kids in the pool; book up front for quiet. The street gets seedy by night, but the hotel is secure, clean and comfortable.

Vintners Inn INN $$$
(☑800-421-2584, 707-575-7350; www.vintnersinn. com; 4350 Barnes Rd; r $245-495; ❉@✿) 🖋 Surrounded by vineyards north of town (near River Rd), Vintner's Inn caters to the gated-community crowd with business-classy amenities. Jacuzzi, no pool. Check for last-minute specials.

✗ Eating

Jeffrey's Hillside Cafe AMERICAN $
(www.jeffreyshillsidecafe.com; 2901 4th St; dishes $8-12; ⊘7am-2pm; 🖫) 🖋 East of downtown, near Sonoma Valley, chef-owned Jeffrey's is excellent for breakfast or brunch before wine-tasting.

Rosso Pizzeria & Wine Bar PIZZA $$
(☑707-544-3221; www.rossopizzeria.com; 53 Montgomery St, Creekside Shopping Centre; pizzas $13-17; ⊘11am-10pm; 🖫) 🖋 Fantastic wood-fired pizzas, inventive salads and standout wines make Rosso worth seeking out.

Naked Pig CAFE $$
(☑707-978-3231; 435 Santa Rosa Ave; mains $11-14; ⊘8am-3pm Wed-Sun) 🖋 This tiny cafe in a former bus depot makes everything from scratch and serves simple-delicious, farm-to-table breakfasts and lunches at communal tables.

El Coqui CARIBBEAN $$
(☑707-542-8868; http://elcoqui2eat.com; 400 Mendocino Ave; lunch mains $10-14, dinner $14-19; ⊘11am-10pm Mon-Sat, noon-9pm Sun) Unique in Wine Country, El Coqui serves yummy Puerto Rican food, including stuffed plantains. Beer and wine.

Spinster Sisters CALIFORNIAN $$$
(☑707-528-7100; www.thespinstersisters.com; 401 South A St; lunch mains $10-16, dinner $23-26; ⊘8am-3pm Mon, to 10pm Tue-Fri, 9am-10pm Sat & Sun) 🖋 At Santa Rosa's culinary vanguard, this casual market-driven restaurant makes its own bagels, cheese and charcuterie meats. The diverse tapas-like small plates ($7 to $14) pair well with the extensive wine list.

🍺 Drinking & Nightlife

★ Russian River Brewing Co BREWERY
(www.russianriverbrewing.com; 729 4th St; ⊘11am-midnight Sun-Thu, to 1am Fri & Sat) Santa Rosa's justly famous brewery crafts outstanding double IPA, called Pliny the Elder, plus top-grade sour beer aged in wine barrels. Good pizza and pub grub, too.

ℹ Information

California Welcome Center & Santa Rosa Visitors Bureau (☑800-404-7673, 707-577-8674; www.visitsantarosa.com; 9 4th St; ⊘9am-5pm Mon-Sat, 10am-5pm Sun) Same-day lodging assistance. At Railroad Sq, west of Hwy 101; take downtown exit from Hwy 12 or 101.

Santa Rosa Memorial Hospital (☑707-546-3210; 1165 Montgomery St)

Healdsburg & Around

Once a sleepy ag town best known for its Future Farmers of America parade, Healdsburg has emerged as northern Sonoma County's culinary capital. Foodie-scenester restaurants and cafes, wine-tasting rooms and fancy boutiques line Healdsburg Plaza, the town's sun-dappled central square (bordered by Healdsburg Ave and Center, Matheson and Plaza Sts). Traffic grinds to a halt summer weekends, when second-home-owners and tourists jam downtown. Old-timers aren't happy with the Napa-style gentrification, but at least Healdsburg retains its historic look, if not its once-quiet summers. It's best visited weekdays – stroll tree-lined streets, sample locavore cooking and soak up the NorCal flavor.

◉ Sights

Tasting rooms surround the plaza. Free **summer concerts** play Tuesday afternoons.

Healdsburg Museum MUSEUM
(☑707-431-3325; www.healdsburgmuseum.org; 221 Matheson St, Healdsburg; donation requested; ⊘11am-4pm Wed-Sun) Exhibits include compelling installations on northern Sonoma County history, with an emphasis on Healdsburg. Pick up the walking-tour pamphlet.

Healdsburg Public Library LIBRARY
(☑707-433-3772; sonomalibrary.org; cnr Piper & Center Sts; ⊘10am-6pm Tue, Thu & Fri, to 8pm Wed, to 4pm Sat) Wine Country's leading oenology-reference library.

Healdsburg Veterans Memorial Beach BEACH
(☑707-433-1625; www.sonomacountyparks.org; 13839 Healdsburg Ave, Healdsburg; parking $7; ⊘7am-sunset; 🖫) You can swim at this beach – lifeguards are on duty summer weekends –

NAPA & SONOMA WINE COUNTRY HEALDSBURG & AROUND

but if you're squeamish, confirm current water quality online (www.sonoma-county.org/health/services/freshwater.asp).

Locals Tasting Room TASTING ROOM
(☑707-857-4900; www.tastelocalwines.com; Geyserville Ave & Hwy 128, Geyserville; ⊙11am-6pm) **FREE** Eight miles north of Healdsburg, tiny Geyserville is home to this indie tasting room, which represents 12 small-production wineries with free tastings.

Farmers Markets MARKET
(www.healdsburgfarmersmarket.org; Healdsburg) Discover Healdsburg's agricultural abundance at the **Tuesday market** (cnr Vine & North Sts; ⊙3:30pm-6pm Wed Jun-Oct) and **Saturday market** (⊙9am-noon Sat May-Nov), the latter held one block west of the plaza.

🏃 Activities

After you've walked around the plaza, there isn't much to do in town. Go wine-tasting in Dry Creek Valley or Russian River Valley (p175). Bicycling on winding West Dry Creek Rd is brilliant, as is paddling the Russian River, which runs through town. Rent bikes from Spoke Folk Cyclery (p143).

Coppola Winery Swimming Pool SWIMMING, WINERY
(☑707-857-1400, 877-590-3329; www.francisfordcoppolawinery.com; 300 Via Archimedes, Geyserville; adult/child $30/15; ⊙11am-6pm daily Jun-Sep, Fri-Sun Apr, May & Oct; 🚸) The two huge interconnected pools at Francis Ford Coppola Winery are a glam way to spend a hot day with kids. To ensure admission, reserve in advance a cabine ($135), which includes chairs for four and wine-tasting passes; day passes include towel and lawn seating, not chairs; summer weekends sell out immediately – arrive before 10:45am.

Russian River Adventures CANOEING
(☑707-433-5599; russianriveradventures.com; 20 Healdsburg Ave, Healdsburg; adult/child $50/25; 🚸🐾) Paddle a secluded stretch of river in quiet inflatable canoes, stopping for rope swings, swimming holes, beaches and bird-watching. This ecotourism outfit points you in the right direction and shuttles you back at day's end. Or they'll guide your kids downriver while you go wine-tasting (guides $125 per day). Reservations required.

Getaway Adventures CYCLING, KAYAKING
(☑800-499-2453, 707-763-3040; www.getawayadventures.com) Guides spectacular morning vineyard cycling in Dry Creek Valley, followed by lunch and optional kayaking on Russian River ($150 to $175).

River's Edge Kayak & Canoe Trips BOATING
(☑707-433-7247; www.riversedgekayakandcanoe.com; 13840 Healdsburg Ave, Healdsburg) Rents hard-sided canoes ($90/110 per half/full day) and kayaks ($40/55). Self-guided rentals include shuttle.

🎓 Courses

The Shed COURSE
(☑707-431-7433; healdsburgshed.com; 25 North St, Healdsburg) 🍴 Healdsburg's culinary center (p192) leads classes and workshop on topics related to food and sustainability, from seed-saving and bee-keeping, to home-brewing and kombucha-fermenting. Also hosts important lecturers, such as Michael Pollan.

Relish Culinary Adventures COOKING COURSE
(☑707-431-9999, 877-759-1004; www.relishculinary.com; 14 Matheson St, Healdsburg; ⊙by appointment) Plug into the locavore food scene with culinary day trips, demo-kitchen classes or winemaker dinners.

🎉 Festivals & Events

Russian River Wine Road Barrel Tasting WINE
(www.wineroad.com) Sample wine, directly from the cask, before it's bottled or released for sale, in March.

Future Farmers Parade CULTURAL
(www.healdsburgfair.org) The whole town shows up for this classic-Americana farm parade in May.

Wine & Food Affair FOOD
(www.wineroad.com/events) Special food and wine pairings at over 100 wineries in November.

🛏 Sleeping

Healdsburg is expensive: demand exceeds supply. Rates drop winter to spring, but not significantly. Guerneville is much less expensive, and just 20 minutes away. Most Healdsburg inns are within walking distance of the plaza; several B&Bs are in surrounding countryside. Find motels at Hwy 101's Dry Creek exit.

Cloverdale Wine Country KOA CAMPGROUND $
(☑800-368-4558, 707-894-3337; www.winecountrykoa.com; 1166 Asti Ridge Rd, Cloverdale; tent/RV sites from $50/65, 1-/2-bedroom cabins $85/95;

⊕⊠⊛) Six miles from central Cloverdale (exit 520) off Hwy 101; hot showers, pool, hot tub, laundry, paddleboats and bicycles.

L&M Motel
MOTEL $$

(⊘707-433-6528; www.landmmotel.com; 70 Healdsburg Ave, Healdsburg; r $150-180; ⊛⊕⊠⊛) Simple, clean, old-fashioned motel, with big lawns and barbecue grills, great for families. Dry sauna and Jacuzzi. Winter rates plummet.

Geyserville Inn
MOTEL $$

(⊘877-857-4343, 707-857-4343; www.geyservilleinn.com; 21714 Geyserville Ave, Geyserville; r Mon-Fri $129-169, Sat & Sun $269-289; ⊛⊕⊠⊛) Eight miles north of Healdsburg, this immaculately kept upmarket motel is surrounded by vineyards. Rooms have unexpectedly smart furnishings and quality extras, like feather pillows. Request a remodeled room. Hot tub.

Best Western Dry Creek
MOTEL $$

(⊘707-433-0300; www.drycreekinn.com; 198 Dry Creek Rd, Healdsburg; r Mon-Fri $109-149, Sat & Sun $219-319; ⊛@⊕⊠) This generic midrange motel has good service and an outdoor hot tub. New rooms have jetted tubs and gas fireplaces.

Hotel Healdsburg
HOTEL $$$

(⊘707-431-2800, 800-889-7188; www.hotelhealdsburg.com; 25 Matheson St, Healdsburg; r incl breakfast from $450; ⊛@⊕⊠) Smack on the plaza, the fashion-forward HH has a coolly minimalist style of concrete and velvet, with requisite top-end amenities, including sumptuous beds and extra-deep tubs. Full-service spa.

H2 Hotel
HOTEL $$$

(⊘707-431-2202, 707-922-5251; www.h2hotel.com; 219 Healdsburg Ave, Healdsburg; r incl breakfast Mon-Fri $289-389, Sat & Sun $409-509; ⊛@⊕⊠⊛) ⌀ Little sister to Hotel Healdsburg, H2 has the same angular concrete style, but was built LEED-gold-certified from the ground up, with a living roof, reclaimed everything, and fresh-looking rooms with cush organic linens. Tiny pool, free bikes.

Madrona Manor
HISTORIC HOTEL $$$

(⊘800-258-4003, 707-433-4231; www.madronamanor.com; 1001 Westside Rd, Healdsburg; r incl breakfast Mon-Fri $260-305, Sat & Sun $385-515; ⊛⊕⊠) The first choice of lovers of country inns and stately manor homes, the regal 1881 Madrona Manor exudes Victorian elegance. Surrounded by 8 acres of woods and gorgeous century-old gardens, the hilltop mansion is decked out with many original furnishings. A mile west of downtown, it's convenient to Westside Rd wineries.

Belle de Jour Inn
B&B $$$

(⊘707-431-9777; www.belledejourinn.com; 16276 Healdsburg Ave, Healdsburg; r $225-295, ste $355; ⊛⊕) Charming Belle de Jour's sunny, uncluttered rooms have American-country furnishings, with extras like private entrances, sun-dried sheets and jetted tubs. The manicured gardens are ready-made for a moonlight tryst.

Healdsburg Inn on the Plaza
INN $$$

(⊘800-431-8663, 707-433-6991; www.healdsburginn.com; 110 Matheson St, Healdsburg; r $295-375; ⊛⊕⊠) The spiffy, clean-lined rooms, conservatively styled in khaki and beige, feel bourgeois summer-house casual, with fine linens and gas fireplaces; some have jetted double tubs. The plaza-front location explains the price.

Honor Mansion
INN $$$

(⊘707-433-4277, 800-554-4667; www.honormansion.com; 891 Grove St, Healdsburg; r incl breakfast $330-595; ⊛⊕⊠) Elegant 1883 Victorian mansion with spectacular resort-like grounds, cushy rooms and great service.

Camellia Inn
B&B $$$

(⊘707-433-8182, 800-727-8182; www.camelliainn.com; 211 North St, Healdsburg; r $139-395; ⊛⊕⊠) Elegantly furnished 1869 mansion, with (among others) one budget room ($139), plus a two-bed family room ($259).

Haydon Street Inn
B&B $$$

(⊘707-433-5228, 800-528-3703; www.haydon.com; 321 Haydon St, Healdsburg; r $195-325, cottage $425; ⊛⊕) Two-story Queen Anne with big front porch and separate cottage.

Piper Street Inn
INN $$$

(⊘707-433-8721, 877-703-0370; www.piperstreetinn.com; 402 Piper St, Healdsburg; r $295; ⊛⊕⊠) Cozy garden cottage.

✕ Eating

Healdsburg is the gastronomic capital of Sonoma County. Your hardest decision will be choosing where to eat. Reservations essential.

★The Shed
CAFE, MARKET $

(⊘707-431-7433; healdsburgshed.com; 25 North St, Healdsburg; dishes $3-15; ⊙8am-7pm Wed-Mon; ⊞) ⌀ At the vanguard of locavore eating, the Shed integrates food at all stages of production, milling its own locally sourced flours, pressing olive oils, fermenting vinegars and kombucha from local fruit, and growing its own produce. It comprises a cafe with wood-fired dishes, fermentation bar with housemade shrubs, coffee bar with stellar pastries, and a market with prepared to-go foods.

Healdsburg Bar & Grill   PUB FOOD $$
(☎707-433-3333;   www.healdsburgbarandgrill.com; 245 Healdsburg Ave, Healdsburg; mains $9-15; ☺8am-9pm) 'Top Chef Masters' winner Doug Keane's gastropub is perfect when you're famished, but don't want to fuss. Expect simple classics – mac-n-cheese, pulled-pork sandwiches, top-end burgers and truffle-parmesan fries. At breakfast, look for homemade bagels and waffles. Sit in the garden.

Oakville Grocery   DELI $$
(☎707-433-3200; www.oakvillegrocery.com; 124 Matheson St, Healdsburg; sandwiches $10; ☺8am-7pm) Luxurious smoked fish and caviar, fancy sandwiches and grab-and-go gourmet picnics. It's overpriced, but the plaza-view fireside terrace is ever-fun for scouting Botox blonds, while nibbling cheese and sipping vino.

Scopa   ITALIAN $$
(☎707-433-5282;   www.scopahealdsburg.com; 109A Plaza St, Healdsburg; mains $15-24; ☺5:30-10pm Tue-Sun) Space is tight inside this converted barbershop, but it's worth cramming in for perfect thin-crust pizza and rustic Italian home cooking, like Nonna's slow-braised chicken, with sautéed greens, melting into toasty polenta. A lively crowd and good wine prices create a convivial atmosphere.

Diavola   ITALIAN $$
(☎707-814-0111; www.diavolapizzera.com; 21021 Geyserville Ave, Geyserville; pizzas $15-18; ☺11:30am-9pm; ♿) ✐ Ideal for lunch while wine-tasting in Alexander Valley, Diavola makes oustanding salumi and thin-crust pizzas, served in an Old West, brick-walled space, loud enough to drown out the kids.

Ravenous   NEW AMERICAN $$
(☎707-431-1302;   117   North   St,   Healdsburg; lunch mains $12-17, dinner $20-24) Chalkboard-scrawled menu, with California comfort cooking and excellent burgers, served in a tiny eight-table dining room inside a former theater lobby.

Costeaux French Bakery & Cafe   CAFE $$
(☎707-433-1913; www.costeaux.com; 417 Healdsburg Ave, Healdsburg; mains $10-13; ☺7am-3pm Mon-Sat, to 1pm Sun; 🐾) This cavernous bakery-cafe is good for an easy lunch of salads and sandwiches on house-baked bread, plus all-day breakfast dishes including omelets and scrambles.

★Madrona Manor   CALIFORNIAN $$$
(☎800-258-4003, 707-433-4231; www.madronamanor.com; 1001 Westside Rd, Healdsburg; 6-/11-course menu $106/$129; ☺6-9pm Wed-Sun) ✐ You'd be hard-pressed to find a lovelier place to propose than this retro-formal Victorian mansion's garden-view verandah – though there's nothing old-fashioned about the artful haute cuisine: the kitchen churns its own butter, each course comes with a different variety of just-baked bread, lamb and cheese originate down the road, and desserts include ice cream flash-frozen tableside. Reserve a pre-sunset table on the verandah.

Mateo's Cucina Latina   MEXICAN $$$
(☎707-433-1520; www.mateoscocinalatina.com; 214 Healdsburg Ave, Healdsburg; small plates $11-15, mains $21-25; ☺11:30am-9pm Thu-Tue, 4-9pm Wed, closed Tue Nov-Apr) ✐ This is not Mexican food as you may know it. Here the up-market Yucatan-inspired cooking integrates fine technique and all-local ingredients for standout small plates, such as wild-nettle empanadas and slow-roasted suckling pig, whose subtle flavors shine through the spice. The full bar showcases rare tequilas and mescals. Make reservations; request a garden table.

Barndiva   CALIFORNIAN $$$
(☎707-431-0100; www.barndiva.com; 231 Center St, Healdsburg; lunch mains $15-22, dinner $28-38; ☺noon-2:15 & 5:30pm-9pm Wed-Sat, from 11am Sun) ✐ Impeccable seasonal-regional cooking, happening bar, beautiful garden, but service sometimes misses.

Self-Catering
Dry Creek General Store   DELI $
(☎707-433-4171; www.drycreekgeneralstore1881.com; 3495 Dry Creek Rd, Healdsburg; sandwiches $8-10; ☺6:30am-6pm) Stop at this vintage general store, where locals and cyclists gather for coffee on the creaky front porch. Perfect picnic supplies include Toscano-salami-and-manchego   sandwiches   on chewy-dense ciabatta.

Cheese Shop FOOD $
(☑707-433-4998; www.sharpandnutty.com; 423 Center St, Healdsburg; ⊙11am-6pm Mon-Sat) Top-notch imported and local cheeses.

Shelton's Natural Foods MARKET, DELI $
(☑707-431-0530; www.sheltonsmarket.com; 428 Center St, Healdsburg; ⊙8am-8pm) 🍴 Indie alternative for groceries and picnic supplies; reasonably priced.

Moustache Baked Goods BAKERY $
(☑707-395-4111; moustachebakedgoods.com; 381 Healdsburg Ave, Healdsburg; cupcakes $3; ⊙11am-7pm) 🍴 Incredible locavore small-batch sweets (some gluten-free), including scrumptious cupcakes in unusual combos like maple-bacon.

Noble Folk Ice Cream & Pie Bar DESSERTS $
(☑707-395-4426; 116 Matheson St, Healdsburg; slice $5.25, single cone $3.25; ⊙noon-9pm) 🍴 Handcrafted ice cream and classic American pie, made with top-quality, all-local ingredients.

Downtown Bakery & Creamery BAKERY $
(☑707-431-2719; www.downtownbakery.net; 308A Center St, Healdsburg; ⊙7am-5:30pm) Healdsburg's classic bakery makes perfect breakfast pastries and specialty breads.

Jimtown Store DELI, MARKET $$
(☑707-433-1212; www.jimtown.com; 6706 Hwy 128; sandwiches $6-14; ⊙7:30am-3pm Mon, Wed & Thu, to 5pm Fri-Sun) One of our favorite Alexander Valley stopovers, Jimtown is great for picnic supplies and sandwiches made with housemade condiment spreads.

🍸 Drinking & Entertainment

Flying Goat Coffee CAFE
(www.flyinggoatcoffee.com; 324 Center St, Healdsburg; ⊙7am-7pm) 🍴 See ya later, Starbucks. Flying Goat is what coffee should be – fair-trade and house-roasted – and locals line up for it every morning.

Bear Republic Brewing Company BREWERY
(☑707-433-2337; www.bearrepublic.com; 345 Healdsburg Ave, Healdsburg; ⊙11am-9:30pm Sun-Thu, to 11pm Fri & Sat) Bear Republic features handcrafted award-winning ales, non-award-winning pub grub, and live music weekends.

Alexander Valley Bar COCKTAIL BAR
(AVB; ☑707-431-1904; 3487 Alexander Valley Rd, Medlock Ames Winery; ⊙5-9pm Sun-Thu, to 11pm Fri & Sat) Vineyard sunsets are incredible at this speakeasy-style bar in Alexander Valley, which crafts cocktails ($10) using whatever's growing in the garden outside.

Raven Theater & Film Center THEATER
(☑707-433-5448; www.raventheater.com; 115 N Main St, Healdsburg) Hosts concerts, events and first-run art-house films.

🔒 Shopping

The Shed GARDEN, CULINARY
(☑707-431-7433; healdsburgshed.com; 25 North St, Healdsburg; ⊙8am-7pm Wed-Mon) 'Tools and supplies for growing, preparing and sharing food,' including heritage seeds by local farmers, house-milled California flour, and practical cookware.

Jimtown Store GIFTS
(☑707-433-1212; www.jimtown.com; 6706 Hwy 128) Forage antique bric-a-brac, candles and Mexican oilcloths at this roadside deli and store in Alexander Valley.

Gardener GARDENS
(☑707-431-1063; www.thegardener.com; 516 Dry Creek Rd, Healdsburg) 🍴 Garden-shop lovers: don't miss this rural beauty.

One World GIFTS, HOMEWARES
(☑707-473-0880; www.oneworldfairtrade.net; 104 Matheson St, Healdsburg; ⊙10am-6pm Mon-Sat, to 5:30pm Sun) 🍴 Household goods from fair-trade collectives.

Options Gallery CRAFTS, JEWELRY
(☑707-431-8861; www.optionsgallery.com; 126 Matheson St, Healdsburg; ⊙10:30am-5:30pm Mon-Sat, 11am-4pm Sun) Gifts, crafts and jewelry by local artists, including lovely earrings.

Copperfield's Books BOOKS
(☑707-433-9270; copperfieldsbooks.com; 104 Matheson St, Healdsburg; ⊙9am-6pm Sun-Thu, to 7pm Fri & Sat) Good general-interest books.

Levin & Company BOOKS, MUSIC
(☑707-433-1118; 306 Center St, Healdsburg; ⊙9am-9pm Mon-Sat, 10am-6pm Sun) Fiction and CDs; co-op art gallery.

ℹ️ Information

Healdsburg Chamber of Commerce & Visitors Bureau (☑707-433-6935, 800-648-9922; www.healdsburg.com; 217 Healdsburg Ave, Healdsburg; ⊙9am-5pm Mon-Fri, to 3pm Sat, 10am-2pm Sun) A block south of the plaza. Has winery maps and information on ballooning, golf, tennis, spas and nearby farms (get the *Farm Trails* brochure); 24-hour walk-up booth.

North Coast & Redwoods

Why Go?

There's a stretch of the coast with no road access called the 'Lost Coast,' but even the rest of the region, reached by a circuitous two-lane blacktop, feels far from the world's radar. The North Coast is no Beach Boys' song; there are no bikinis and few surfboards. The jagged edge of the continent is wild, scenic and even slightly foreboding, where spectral fog and an outsider spirit have fostered the world's tallest trees, most potent weed and a string of idiosyncratic two-stoplight towns. Explore hidden coves with a blanket and a bottle of local wine, scan the horizon for migrating whales and retreat at night to fire-warmed Victorians. As you travel further north, find valleys of redwood, wide rivers and mossy, overgrown forests. Befitting this dramatic clash of land and water are its unlikely mélange of residents: timber barons and tree huggers, pot farmers and political radicals of every stripe.

Best Places to Eat

➜ Café Beaujolais (p210)

➜ Brick & Fire (p236)

➜ Café Aquatica (p201)

➜ Mario's Lost Coast Cafe (p233)

➜ Table 128 (p220)

Best Places to Stay

➜ Mar Vista Cottages (p204)

➜ Philo Apple Farm (p220)

➜ Benbow Inn (p227)

➜ Alegria (p209)

➜ Gold Bluffs Beach (p245)

When to Go

Eureka

Jun–Jul The driest season in the Redwoods is spectacular for day hikes and big views.

Aug–Oct Warm weather and clear (or clearer) skies are the best for hiking the Lost Coast.

Dec–Apr Whales migrate off the coast. In early spring look for mothers and calves.

North Coast & Redwoods Highlights

1 Explore the gargantuan forests and dramatic coast of **Redwood National & State Parks** (p243).

2 Feel small amongst the standing and fallen giants in **Humboldt Redwoods State Park** (p230).

3 Hike the lush, remote and wild **Lost Coast** (p228).

4 Find a hidden cove on the **Sonoma Coast** (p200).

5 Get pampered at the B&Bs of **Mendocino** (p206).

6 Drink the sampler at McKinleyville's **Six Rivers Brewery** (p240), NorCal's best brewpub.

7 Climb to the top of **Point Arena Lighthouse** (p204) for views over the jagged coast.

8 Tour the laid-back vineyards of the **Anderson Valley** (p219).

9 Indulge in some all-American roadside kitsch along Hwy 101 like **Trees of Mystery** (p247).

10 Feel like you've been transported to the wholesome 1950s in the dairy town of **Ferndale** (p232).

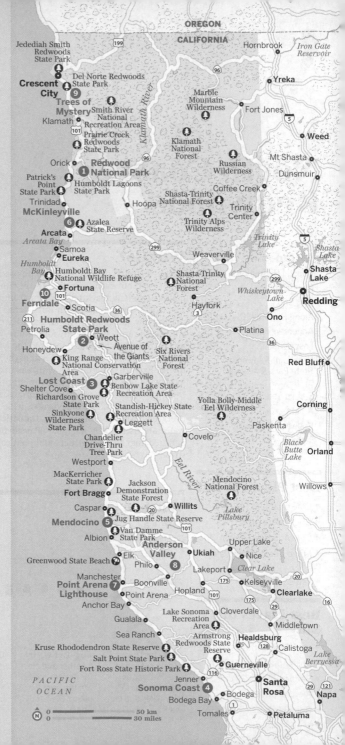

ℹ Getting Around

Although Hwy 1 is popular with cyclists and there are bus connections, you will almost certainly need a car to explore this region. Those headed to the far north and on a schedule should take Hwy 101, the faster, inland route and then cut over to the coast. Windy Hwy 1 hugs the coast, then cuts inland and ends at Leggett, where it joins Hwy 101. Neither Amtrak nor Greyhound serve cities on coastal Hwy 1.

Amtrak (☑ 800-872-7245; www.amtrakcalifornia.com) operates the *Coast Starlight* between Los Angeles and Seattle. From LA, Amtrak buses connect to several North Coast towns including Leggett ($85, 11 hours, two daily) and Garberville ($87, 11½ hours, two daily).

Brave souls willing to piece together bus travel through the region will face a time-consuming headache, but connections are possible to almost every town in the region. **Greyhound** (☑ 800-231-2222; www.greyhound.com) runs buses between San Francisco and Ukiah, ($44, three hours, one daily) Willits ($44, 3½ hours, one daily), Rio Dell (near Fortuna, $57, six hours, one daily), Eureka ($57, 6¾ hours, one daily) and Arcata ($57, seven hours, one daily).

The **Mendocino Transit Authority** (MTA; ☑ 800-696-4682, 707-462-1422; www.4mta. org; fares $3.25-7.75) operates bus 65, which travels between Mendocino, Fort Bragg, Willits, Ukiah and Santa Rosa daily, with an afternoon return. Bus 95 runs between Point Arena and Santa Rosa, via Jenner, Bodega Bay and Sebastopol. Bus 75 heads north every weekday from Gualala to the Navarro River junction at Hwy 128, then runs inland through the Anderson Valley to Ukiah, returning in the afternoon. The North Coast route goes north between Navarro River junction and Albion, Little River, Mendocino and Fort Bragg, Monday to Friday. The best long-distance option is a daily ride between Fort Bragg and Santa Rosa via Willits and Ukiah ($21, three hours).

North of Mendocino County, the **Redwood Transit System** (☑ 707-443-0826; www.hta. org) operates buses ($3) Monday through Saturday between Scotia and Trinidad (2½ hours), stopping en route at Eureka (1¼ hours) and Arcata (1½ hours). **Redwood Coast Transit** (☑ 707-464-9314; www.redwoodcoasttransit. org) runs buses Monday to Saturday between Crescent City, Klamath ($1.50, one hour, five daily) and Arcata ($30, two hours, three daily), with numerous stops along the way.

COASTAL HIGHWAY 1

Down south it's called the 'PCH,' or Pacific Coast Hwy, but North Coast locals simply call it 'Hwy 1.' However you label it, get ready for a fabulous coastal drive, which cuts a winding course on isolated cliffs high above the crashing surf. Compared to the famous Big Sur coast, the serpentine stretch of Hwy 1 up the North Coast is more challenging, more remote and more *real*; passing farms, fishing towns and hidden beaches. Drivers use roadside pull-outs to scan the hazy Pacific horizon for migrating whales and explore a coastline dotted with rock formations that are relentlessly pounded by the surf. The drive between Bodega Bay and Fort Bragg takes four hours of daylight driving without stops. At night in the fog, it takes steely nerves and much, much longer. The most popular destination is the cliffside charmer of Mendocino.

Considering their proximity to the Bay Area, Sonoma and Mendocino counties remain unspoiled, and the austere coastal bluffs are some of the most spectacular in the country. But the trip north gets more rewarding and remote with every mile. By the time Hwy 1 cuts inland to join Hwy 101, the land along the Pacific – called the Lost Coast – the highway disappears and offers the state's best-preserved natural gifts.

Coastal accommodations (including campgrounds) can fill from Memorial Day to Labor Day (late May to early September) and on fall weekends, and often require two-night stays, so reserve ahead. Try to visit during spring or fall, especially in September and October; when the fog lifts, the ocean sparkles and most other visitors have gone home.

Bodega Bay

Bodega Bay is the first pearl in a string of sleepy fishing towns that line the North Coast and was the setting of Hitchcock's terrifying 1963 avian psycho-horror flick *The Birds*. The skies are free from bloodthirsty gulls today (though you best keep an eye on the picnic); it's Bay Area weekenders who descend en masse for extraordinary beaches, tide pools, whale-watching, fishing, surfing and seafood. Mostly a few restaurants, hotels and shops on both sides of Hwy 1, the downtown is not made for strolling, but it is a great base for exploring the endless nearby coves of the Sonoma Coast State Beach (p200).

Originally inhabited by the Pomo people, the bay takes its name from Juan Francisco de la Bodega y Quadra, captain of the Spanish sloop *Sonora*, which entered the bay in 1775. The area was then settled by Russians in the early 19th century, and farms were established to grow wheat for the Russian fur-trapping empire, which stretched from Alaska all the way down the coast to Fort Ross. The Russians pulled out in 1842, abandoning fort and farms, and American settlers moved in.

Hwy 1 runs through town and along the east side of Bodega Bay. On the west side, a peninsula juts out to sea, forming the entrance to Bodega Harbor.

◉ Sights & Activities

Surfing, beach combing and sportfishing are the main activities here – the latter requires advance booking. From December to April, the fishing boats host whale-watching trips, which are also good to book ahead. Just about everyone in town sells kites which are great for flying at Bodega Head. The excellent *Farm Trails* (www.farmtrails.org) guide at the Sonoma Coast Visitor Center (p200) has suggestions for tours of local ranches, orchards, farms and apiaries.

Bodega Head LOOKOUT

At the peninsula's tip, Bodega Head rises 265ft above sea level. To get there (and see the open ocean), head west from Hwy 1 onto Eastshore Rd, then turn right at the stop sign onto Bay Flat Rd. It's great for whale-watching. Landlubbers enjoy hiking above the surf, where several good trails include a 3.75-mile trek to Bodega Dunes Campground and a 2.2-mile walk to Salmon Creek Ranch.

Bodega Marine Laboratory & Reserve SCIENCE CENTER

(☎707-875-2211; www.bml.ucdavis.edu; 2099 Westside Rd; ☺2-4pm Fri) FREE Run by University of California (UC) Davis, this spectacularly diverse teaching and research reserve surrounds the research lab, which has studied Bodega Bay since the 1920s. The 263-acre reserve hosts many marine environments, including rocky intertidal coastal areas, mudflats and sandflats, salt marsh, sand dunes and freshwater wetlands. On most Friday afternoons docents give tours of the lab and surrounds.

Ren Brown Collection Gallery GALLERY

(www.renbrown.com; 1781 Hwy 1; ☺10am-5pm Wed-Sun) The renowned collection of modern Japanese prints and California works at this small gallery is a tranquil escape from the elements. Check out the Japanese garden at the back.

Chanslor Ranch HORSEBACK RIDING

(☎707-785-8849; www.chanslorranch.com; 2660 N Hwy 1; rides from $40) Just north of town, this friendly outfit leads horseback expeditions along the coastline and the rolling inland hills. Ron, the trip leader, is an amiable, sun-weathered cowboy straight from central casting; he recommends taking the Salmon Creek ride or calling ahead for weather-permitting moonlight rides. The 90-minute beach rides are donation based, and support a horse-rescue program.

Overnight trips in simple platform tents, which are excellent for families, can also be arranged. If you book a ride, you can park your RV at the ranch for free.

BLOODTHIRSTY BIRDS OF BODEGA BAY

Bodega Bay has the enduring claim to fame as the setting for Alfred Hitchcock's *The Birds*. Although special effects radically altered the actual layout of the town, you still get a good feel for the supposed site of the farm owned by Mitch Brenner (played by Rod Taylor). The once-cozy Tides Restaurant, where much avian-caused havoc occurs in the movie, is still there but since 1962 it has been transformed into a vast restaurant complex. Venture 5 miles inland to the tiny town of Bodega and you'll find two icons from the film: the schoolhouse and the church. Both stand just as they did in the movie – a crow overhead may make the hair rise on your neck. The **Bodega Country Store** (☺8am-8pm) claims to have more *The Birds* artifacts than anywhere else in the world.

The movie's star Tipi Hedren, now in her 80s, visits Bodega Bay at least once a year to help with local events and fundraisers. She also was in town for the movie's 50th anniversary festival in 2013 and there are hopes that the event will become annual.

Coincidentally, right after production of *The Birds* began, a real-life bird attack occurred in Capitola, the sleepy seaside town south of Santa Cruz. Thousands of seagulls ran amok, destroying property and attacking people.

Bodega Bay
Sportfishing Center   FISHING, WHALE-WATCHING
(☏707-875-3344; www.bodegacharters.com; 1410 Bay Flat Rd) Beside the Sandpiper Cafe, this outfit organizes full-day fishing trips ($135) and whale-watching excursions (three hours adult/child $50/35). It also sells bait, tackle and fishing licenses. Call ahead to ask about recent sightings.

Bodega Bay Surf Shack   SURFING
(☏707-875-3944; http://bodegabaysurf.com; 1400 N Hwy 1; surfboard/wetsuit/kayak rentals from $17/17/45) If you want to get on the water, this easygoing one-stop shop has all kinds of rentals, lessons and good local information.

✨ Festivals & Events
Bodega Seafood, Art & Wine Festival   FOOD, WINE
(www.winecountryfestivals.com; ✎) In late August, this festival of food and drink brings together the best beer- and wine-makers of the area, tons of seafood and activities for kids. It takes place in the town of Bodega.

Bodega Bay Fishermen's Festival   CULTURAL
(www.bbfishfest.org) At the end of April, this festival culminates in a blessing of the fleet, a flamboyant parade of vessels, an arts-and-crafts fair, kite-flying and feasting.

🛏 Sleeping
There's a wide spread of options – RV and tent camping, quaint motels and fancy hotels. All fill up early during peak seasons. Campers should consider heading just north of town to the state-operated sites.

Sonoma County
Regional Parks   CAMPGROUND $
(☏707-565-2267; www.parks.sonomacounty. ca.gov; tent sties $7, RV sites without hookups $32) There are a few walk-in sites at the **Doran Regional Park** (201 Doran Beach Rd), at the quiet Miwok Tent Campground, and **Westside Regional Park** (2400 Westshore Rd), which is best for RVs. It caters primarily to boaters and has windy exposures, beaches, hot showers, fishing and boat ramps. Both are heavily used. Excellent camping is also available at the Sonoma Coast State Beach (p200).

Bodega Harbor Inn   MOTEL $$
(☏707-875-3594; www.bodegaharborinn.com; 1345 Bodega Ave; r $80-155, cottages $135-175; 🛜🐾) Half a block inland from Hwy 1, surrounded by grassy lawns and furnished with both real and faux antiques, this modest yet adorable blue-and-white shingled motel is the town's most economical option. Pets are allowed in some rooms for a fee of $15 plus a security deposit of $50. They also offer a variety of cottages and rentals around town.

Chanslor Guest Ranch   RANCH $$
(☏707-875-2721; www.chanslorranch.com; 2660 Hwy 1; campsites $40, furnished tents from $80, r from $175) A mile north of town, this working horse ranch has rooms and options for upscale camping. Wildlife programs and guided horse tours make this one sweet place, with sweeping vistas across open grasslands to the sea.

Bodega Bay Lodge & Spa   LODGE $$$
(☏888-875-2250, 707-875-3525; www.bodegabay-lodge.com; 103 Hwy 1; r $190-470; @🛜🏊) Bodega's plushest option, this small oceanfront resort has an ocean-view swimming pool, golf course, a Jacuzzi and a state-of-the-art fitness club. In the evenings it hosts wine tastings. The more expensive rooms have commanding views, but all have balconies. The other pluses on-site include Bodega Bay's best spa and the **Duck Club** (☏707-875-3525; mains $16-37; ⏱7:30-11am & 6-9pm), which is the fanciest dining in town.

Bay Hill Mansion   B&B $$$
(☏877-468-1588; www.bayhillmansion.com; 3919 Bay Hill Rd; d $279-299; 🛜🐾) A luxe B&B in a spacious, modern mansion. The decor is tasteful without much imagination but the cleanliness and comfort standards here are some of the best we've ever seen. Get a private yoga class or massage then the helpful hosts can direct you to the area's best spots. Views overlook trees with just a peek at the bay.

🍴 Eating & Drinking
For the old-fashioned thrill of seafood by the docks there are two options: **Tides Wharf & Restaurant** (835 Hwy 1; breakfast $8-22, lunch $13-28, dinner $16-28; ⏱7:30am-9:30pm Mon-Thu, 7:30am-10pm Fri, 7am-10pm Sat, 7am-9:30pm Sun; ✎) and **Lucas Wharf Restaurant & Bar** (595 Hwy 1; mains $9-28; ⏱11:30am-9pm Mon-Fri, 11am-10pm Sat; ✎). Both have views and similar menus of clam chowder, fried fish and coleslaw, and markets for picnic supplies. Tides boasts a great fish market, though Lucas Wharf feels less like a factory. Don't be surprised if a bus pulls up outside either of them.

Spud Point Crab Company
SEAFOOD $

(www.spudpointcrab.com; 1910 Westshore Rd; dishes $4-11; ◎9am-5pm; 🚗) In the classic tradition of dockside crab shacks, Spud Point serves salty-sweet crab cocktails and *real* clam chowder, served at picnic tables overlooking the marina. Take Bay Flat Rd to get here.

The Birds Cafe
MEXICAN, AMERICAN $

(1407 Hwy 1; meals $6-14; ◎11:30am-5pm) The menu consists of just a few things – usually fish tacos, fish 'n' chips, chowder and a few salads. Barbecued oysters are available seasonally. Order at the bar then take it to an outdoor picnic table overlooking the harbor. There's beer and wine available. Bliss.

Terrapin Creek Cafe & Restaurant
CALIFORNIAN $$

(☑707-875-2700; www.terrapincreekcafe.com; 1580 Eastshore Dr; lunch mains $12-19, dinner mains $23-30; ◎11am-2:30pm & 4:30-9pm Thu-Sun; ☑) 🍃 Bodega Bay's most exciting upscale restaurant is run by a husband-wife team who espouse the slow food movement and serve local dishes sourced from the surrounding area. Comfort-food offerings like black cod roasted in lemon grass and coconut broth are artfully executed, while the Dungeness crab salad is fresh, briny and perfect. Jazz and warm light complete the atmosphere.

Gourmet Au Bay
WINE BAR

(913 Hwy 1; ◎11am-6pm Thu-Tue) The back deck of this wine bar offers a salty breeze with wine tasting.

ⓘ Information

Sonoma Coast Visitor Center (☑707-875-3866; www.bodegabay.com; 850 Hwy 1; ◎9am-5pm Mon-Thu & Sat, to 6pm Fri, 10am-5pm Sun) Opposite the Tides Wharf. Stop by for the best help on the coast and for a copy of the *North Coaster*, a small-press indie newspaper of essays and brilliant insights on local culture.

Sonoma Coast State Beach

Stretching 17 miles north from Bodega Head to Vista Trail, the glorious **Sonoma Coast State Beach** (☑707-875-3483) is actually a series of beaches separated by several beautiful rocky headlands. Some beaches are tiny, hidden in little coves, while others stretch far and wide. Most of the beaches are connected by vista-studded coastal **hiking trails** that wind along the bluffs. Exploring this area makes an excellent day-long adventure, so bring a picnic. Be advised however: the surf is often too treacherous to wade, so keep an eye on children. While this system of beaches and parks has some camping, you can't just pitch a tent anywhere; most are for day-use only.

◎ Sights & Activities

Beaches

Salmon Creek Beach
BEACH

Situated around a lagoon, this has 2 miles of hiking and good waves for surfing.

Portuguese Beach & Schoolhouse Beach
BEACHES

Both are very easy to access and have sheltered coves between rocky outcroppings.

Duncan's Landing
BEACH

Small boats unload near this rocky headland in the morning. A good place to spot wildflowers in the spring.

Shell Beach
BEACH

A boardwalk and trail leads out to a stretch perfect for tide-pooling and beachcombing.

Goat Rock
BEACH

Famous for its colony of harbor seals, lazing in the sun at the mouth of the Russian River.

🛏 Sleeping

Bodega Dunes
CAMPGROUND $

(☑800-444-7275; www.reserveamerica.com; 3095 Hwy 1, Bodega Bay; tent & RV sites $35, day use $8) The largest campground in the Sonoma Coast State Beach system of parks, it is also closest to Bodega Bay. It gets a lot of use. Sites are in high dunes and have hot showers but be warned – the fog horn sounds all night.

Wright's Beach Campground
CAMPGROUND $

(☑800-444-7275; www.reserveamerica.com; tent & RV sites $35, day use $8) Of the few parks that allow camping along Sonoma Coast State Beach, this is the best, even though sites lack privacy. Sites can be booked six months in advance, and numbers 1–12 are right on the beach. There are BBQ pits for day use and it's a perfect launch for sea kayakers.

Everyone else, stay out of the water; according to camp hosts the treacherous rip tides claim a life every season.

Jenner

Perched on the hills looking out to the Pacific and above the mouth of the Russian River, tiny Jenner offers access to the coast and the Russian River wine region. A **harbor-seal colony** sits at the river's mouth and pups are born here from March to August. There are restrictions about getting too close to the chubby, adorable pups – handling them can be dangerous and cause the pups to be abandoned by their mothers. Volunteers answer questions along the roped-off area where day trippers can look on at a distance. The best way to see them is by kayak and most of the year you will find **Water Treks Ecotours** (☏707-865-2249; 2hr rental from $25; ⊙10am-3pm) renting kayaks on the highway. Heading north on Hwy 1 you will begin driving on one of the most beautiful, windy stretches of California highway. You'll also probably lose cell-phone service – possibly a blessing.

🛏 Sleeping & Eating

Jenner Inn & Cottages   INN $$
(☏707-865-2377; www.jennerinn.com; 10400 Hwy 1; r incl breakfast creekside $118-278, cottages $228-298; @) It's difficult to sum up this collection of properties dispersed throughout Jenner – some are in fairly deluxe oceanview cottages with kitchen and ready-to-light fireplaces, others are small and upland near a creek. All have the furnishings of a stylish auntie from the early 1990s.

★**Café Aquatica**   CAFE $
(www.cafeaquatica.com; 10439 Hwy 1; sandwiches $10-13; 🛜) This is the kind of North Coast coffee shop you've been dreaming of: fresh pastries, organic coffee and chatty locals. The view of the Russian River from the patio and gypsy sea-hut decor make it hard to leave.

★**River's End**   CALIFORNIAN $$$
(☏707-865-2484; www.rivers-end.com; 11048 Hwy 1; lunch mains $14-26, dinner mains $25-39; ⊙noon-3pm & 5-8:30pm Thu-Mon; 🅿) Unwind in style at this picture-perfect restaurant that overlooks the river's mouth and the grand sweep of the Pacific Ocean. It serves world-class meals at world-class prices, but the real reward is the view. Its ocean-view **cottages** (rooms and cottages $159 to $229) are wood paneled and have no TVs, wi-fi or phones. Children under 12 are not recommended.

Fort Ross State Historic Park

A curious glimpse into Tsarist Russia's exploration of the California coast, the salt-washed buildings of **Fort Ross State Historic Park** (☏707-847-3286; www.fortrossstatepark.org; 19005 Hwy 1; per car $8; ⊙10:30am-4pm Sat & Sun) offer a fascinating insight into the pre-American Wild West. It's a quiet, picturesque place with a riveting past.

In March 1812, a group of 25 Russians and 80 Alaskans (including members of the Kodiak and Aleutian tribes) built a wooden fort here, near a Kashaya Pomo village. The southernmost outpost of the 19th-century Russian fur trade on America's Pacific Coast, Fort Ross was established as a base for sea-otter hunting operations and trade with Alta California, and for growing crops for Russian settlements in Alaska. The Russians dedicated the fort in August 1812 and occupied it until 1842, when it was abandoned because the sea otter population had been decimated and agricultural production had never taken off.

Fort Ross State Historic Park, an accurate reconstruction of the fort, is 11 miles north of Jenner on a beautiful point. The original buildings were sold, dismantled and carried off to Sutter's Fort during the Gold Rush. The **visitor center** (☏707-847-3437) has a great museum with historical displays and an excellent bookshop on Californian and Russian history. Ask about hikes to the Russian cemetery.

On **Fort Ross Heritage Day**, the last Saturday in July, costumed volunteers bring the fort's history to life; check the website www.parks.ca.gov or call the visitor center for other special events.

If you pass by on a weekday when the fort is closed (due to budget cuts), you still may be able to walk down and have a peek inside if a school group is there.

🛏 Sleeping

Stillwater Cove Regional Park CAMPGROUND $
(☏reservations 707-565-2267; www.sonoma-county.org/parks; 22455 N Hwy 1; tent & RV sites $28) Two miles north of Timber Cove, this park has hot showers and hiking under Monterey pines. Sites 1, 2, 4, 6, 9 and 10 have ocean views.

Timber Cove Inn   INN $$
(☏800-987-8319, 707-847-3231; www.timbercoveinn.com; 21780 N Hwy 1; r from $155, ocean view from $183) A dramatic and quirky '60s-modern seaside inn that was once a top-of-the-line luxury lodge. Though the price remains high, it has slipped a bit. The rustic architectural

shell is still stunning, though, and a duet of tinkling piano and crackling fire fills the lobby. The quirky rooms facing the ocean have a treehouse feel, with rustic redwood details, balconies, fireplaces and lofted beds. Even those who don't bunk here should wander agape in the shadow of Benny Bufano's 93ft peace statue, a spectacular totem on the edge of the sea. The expensive restaurant on-site is nothing to write home about and the staff were grumpy when we passed by.

Salt Point State Park

Stunning 6000-acre **Salt Point State Park** (☑707-847-3321; per car $8; ⊙visitor center 10am-3pm Sat & Sun Apr-Oct) has sandstone cliffs that drop dramatically into the kelp-strewn sea and hiking trails that crisscross windswept prairies and wooded hills, connecting pygmy forests and coastal coves rich with tidepools. The 6-mile-wide park is bisected by the San Andreas Fault – the rock on the east side is vastly different from that on the west. Check out the eerily beautiful *tafonis*, honeycombed-sandstone formations, near Gerstle Cove. For a good roadside photo op, there's a pullout at mile-marker 45, with views of decaying redwood shacks, grazing goats and headlands jutting out to the sea.

Though many of the day use areas have been closed off due to budget cuts, trails lead off Hwy 1 pull-outs to views of the pristine coastline. The platform overlooking **Sentinel Rock** is just a short stroll from the Fisk Mill Cove parking lot at the park's north end. Further south, seals laze at **Gerstle Cove Marine Reserve**, one of California's first underwater parks. Tread lightly around tidepools and don't lift the rocks: even a glimpse of sunlight can kill some critters. If you're here between April and June, you *must* see **Kruse Rhododendron State Reserve**. Growing abundantly in the forest's filtered light, magnificent, pink rhododendrons reach heights of over 30ft, making them the tallest species in the world; turn east from Hwy 1 onto Kruse Ranch Rd and follow the signs. Be sure to walk the short **Rododendron Loop Trail**.

🛏 Sleeping

Woodside & Gerstle Cove Campgrounds CAMPGROUND $
(☑800-444-7275; www.reserveamerica.com; tent & RV sites $35; ⊙Woodside Apr-Sep) Two campgrounds, Woodside and Gerstle Cove, both signposted off Hwy 1, have campsites with cold water. Inland Woodside is well protected by Monterey pines. Gerstle Cove's trees burned over a decade ago and have only grown halfway back, giving the gnarled, blackened trunks a ghostly look when the fog twirls between the branches.

Ocean Cove Lodge Bar & Grill MOTEL $
(☑707-847-3158; www.oceancovelodge.com; 23255 Hwy 1; r from $69; ❋ 🛜) Just a few minutes south of Salt Point State Park is Ocean Cove Lodge Bar & Grill, a godsend for those on a budget. It's just a basic motel but the location is fabulous, there's a hot tub and a surprisingly good American-style restaurant on the premises.

Stuart Point Store & Retreat TENT CABINS, GROCERY $$
(32000 Hwy 1; d tents Mon-Fri $155, Sat & Sun $225-250; ⊙8am-5pm) For snacks, coffee and photo ops, don't miss a stop at Stuart Point Store just north of Salt Point State Park. This may be the oldest continuously family-run business west of the Mississippi (it opened in 1868), and while the decor has stayed true to its heritage, the gourmet fare on offer is deliciously modern. The owner's house is in the antique-looking ranch next door and about a quarter of a mile south down Hwy 1 are the eerie remains of the old schoolhouse.

'Glamping' is now available on the wild, 1200-acre property with canvas tents perched 400ft over stunning sea cliffs, all equipped with queen-sized beds and luxury linens. It's a bit pricey considering there's no electricity (tents are lit by battery-powered lanterns) and showers are outdoors, but the setting is unparalleled.

Sea Ranch

Though not without its fans, the exclusive community of Sea Ranch is a sort of weather-beaten Stepford-by-the-Sea. The ritzy subdivision that sprawls 10 miles along the coast is connected with a well-watched network of private roads. Approved for construction prior to the existence of the watchdog Coastal Commission, the community was a precursor to the concept of 'slow growth,' with strict zoning laws requiring that houses be constructed of weathered wood only. According to *The Sea Ranch Design Manual:* 'This is not a place for the grand architectural statement; it's a place to explore the subtle nuances of fitting in...' Indeed. Though there are some lovely and recommended short-term rentals here, don't break any community rules – like throwing wild parties – or security will come knockin'. For supplies and gasoline, go to Gualala.

After years of litigation, public throughways onto private beaches have been legally mandated and are now well marked. Hiking trails lead from roadside parking lots to the sea and along the bluffs, but don't dare trespass on adjacent lands. **Stengel Beach** (Hwy 1, Mile 53.96) has a beach-access staircase, **Walk-On Beach** (Hwy 1, Mile 56.53) provides wheelchair access and **Shell Beach** (Hwy 1, Mile 55.24) also has beach-access stairs; parking at all three areas costs $6. For hiking details, including maps, contact the **Sea Ranch Association** (www.tsra.org).

Sea Ranch Lodge (707-785-2371; www.searanchlodge.com; 60 Sea Walk Dr; r incl breakfast $199-369;) , a marvel of '60s-modern California architecture, has spacious, luxurious, minimalist rooms, many with dramatic views to the ocean; some have hot tubs and fireplaces. The fine contemporary **restaurant** (lunch mains $12-18, dinner mains $22-38; 8am-9pm) has a menu for discerning guests; expect everything from duck breast to local fish tacos. North of the lodge you'll see Sea Ranch's iconic nondenominational **chapel**; it's on the inland side of Hwy 1, mileage marker 55.66. For those short on time or on a budget, this is the best reason to pull over in Sea Ranch.

Depending on the season, it can be surprisingly affordable to rent a house in Sea Ranch; contact **Rams Head Realty** (www.ramshead-realty.com), **Sea Ranch Rentals** (www.searanchrentals.com), or **Sea Ranch Escape** (www.searanchescape.com).

Gualala & Anchor Bay

At just 2½ hours north of San Francisco, Gualala – pronounced by most locals as 'Wah-la-la' – is northern Sonoma coast's hub for a weekend getaway as it sits square in the middle of the 'Banana Belt,' a stretch of coast known for unusually sunny weather. Founded as a lumber town in the 1860s, the downtown stretches along Hwy 1 with a bustling commercial district that has a great grocery store and some cute, slightly upscale shops.

Just north, quiet Anchor Bay has several inns, a tiny shopping center and, heading north, a string of secluded, hard-to-find

beaches. Both are excellent jumping-off points for exploring the area.

Sights & Activities

Seven miles north of Anchor Bay, pull off at mile-marker 11.41 for **Schooner Gulch**. A trail into the forest leads down cliffs to a sandy beach with tidepools. Bear right at the fork in the trail to reach iconic **Bowling Ball Beach**, where low tide reveals rows of big, round rocks resembling bowling balls. Consult tide tables for Arena Cove. The forecast low tide must be lower than +1.5ft on the tide chart for the rocks to be visible.

Gualala Arts Center　　ARTS CENTER
(707-884-1138; www.gualalaarts.org; 9am-4pm Mon-Fri, noon-4pm Sat & Sun) Inland along Old State Rd, at the south end of town and beautifully built entirely by volunteers, this center hosts changing exhibitions, organizes the **Art in the Redwoods Festival** in late August and has loads of info on local art.

Adventure Rents　　KAYAKING
(888-881-4386, 707-884-4386; www.adventurerents.com) In the summer, a sand spit forms at the mouth of the river, cutting it off from the ocean and turning it into a warm-water lake. This outfit rents **canoes** (two hours/half-day/full day $70/80/90) and **kayaks** (two hours/half-day/full day $35/40/45) out of a van and provides instruction.

Sleeping & Eating

Of the two towns, Gualala has more services and is a more practical hub for exploring –

there are a bunch of good motels and a pair of nice grocery stores. Get fresh veggies at the **farmers market** (Gualala Community Center; ☺10am-12:30pm Sat Jun-Oct) and organic supplies and local wine at the **Anchor Bay Village Market** (35513 S Hwy 1).

Gualala Point Regional Park   CAMPGROUND $
(http://parks.sonomacounty.ca.gov; 42401 Highway 1, Gualala; campsites $32) Shaded by a stand of redwoods and fragrant California Bay laurel trees, a short trail connects this creekside campground to the windswept beach. The quality of sites, including several secluded hike-in spots, makes it the best drive-in camping on this part of the coast.

Gualala River Redwood Park   CAMPGROUND $
(☑707-884-3533; www.gualalapark.com; day use $6, tent & RV sites $42-49) Another excellent Sonoma County Park. Inland along Old State Rd, you can camp and do short hikes along the river.

★**St Orres Inn**   INN $$
(☑707-884-3303; www.saintorres.com; 36601 Hwy 1, Gualala; B&B $95-135, cottages $140-445; 🐾🖥) Famous for its striking Russian-inspired architecture: dramatic rough-hewn timbers, stained glass and burnished copper domes, there's no place quite like St Orres. On the property's fairytale-like, wild-mushroom-strewn 90 acres, hand-built cottages range from rustic to luxurious. The inn's fine **restaurant** (☑707-884-3335; dinner mains $40-50) serves worth-the-splurge, inspired Californian cuisine in one of the coast's most romantic rooms.

North Coast Country Inn   B&B $$
(☑800-959-4537, 707-884-4537; www.northcoastcountryinn.com; 34591 S Hwy 1, Gualala; r incl breakfast $185-235; 🐾🖥) Perched on an inland hillside beneath towering trees, surrounded by lovely gardens, the perks of this adorable place begin with the gregarious owner and a hot tub. The six spacious, country-style rooms are decorated with lovely prints and boast exposed beams, fireplaces, board games and private entrances.

★**Mar Vista Cottages**   CABIN $$$
(☑877-855-3522, 707-884-3522; www.marvista-mendocino.com; 35101 S Hwy 1, Gualala; cottages $175-305; 🐾🖥) ✐ The elegantly renovated 1930s fishing cabins offer a simple, stylish seaside escape with a vanguard commitment to sustainability. The harmonious environment is the result of pitch-perfect

details: linens are line-dried over lavender, guests browse the organic vegetable garden to harvest their own dinner and chickens cluck around the grounds laying the next morning's breakfast. It often requires two-night stays.

Laura's Bakery & Taqueria   MEXICAN $
(☑707-884-3175; 38411 Robinson Reef Rd, at Hwy 1, Gualala; mains $7-12; ☺7am-7pm Mon-Sat; ✐) Laura's is a refreshing, low-key break from Hwy 1 upscale dining. The menu's taqueria staples are fantastic (the Baja-style fish tacos are a steal) but the fresh *mole* dishes and distant ocean view are the real surprises.

Bones Roadhouse   BARBECUE $$
(www.bonesroadhouse.com; 39350 S Hwy 1, Gualala; mains $9-20; ☺11:30am-9pm Sun-Thu, to 10pm Fri & Sat) Savory smoked meats and a busy biker bar vibe make this Gualala's most fun lunch stop. On weekends a codgerly blues outfit may be growling out 'Mustang Sally.'

❶ Information

Redwood Coast Visitors Center (www.redwoodcoastchamber.com; 39150 Hwy 1, Gualala; ☺12-5pm Thu-Sat) Has local information.

Point Arena

This laid-back little town combines creature comforts with relaxed, eclectic California living and is the first town up the coast where the majority of residents don't seem to be retired Bay Area refugees. Sit by the docks a mile west of town at **Arena Cove** and watch surfers mingle with fishermen and hippies.

◉ Sights

Point Arena Lighthouse   LIGHTHOUSE
(☑707-882-2777; www.pointarenalighthouse.com; 45500 Lighthouse Rd; adult/child $7.50/1; ☺10am-3:30pm, to 4:30pm late May-early Sep) Two miles north of town, this 1908 lighthouse (the tallest on the US West Coast) stands 10 stories high and is the only lighthouse in California you can ascend. Check in at the museum, then climb the 145 steps to the top and see the Fresnel lens and the jaw-dropping view. You an stay on-site (p205).

Stornetta Public Lands   NATURE RESERVE
For fabulous bird-watching, hiking on terraced rock past sea caves and access to hidden coves, head 1 mile down Lighthouse Rd from Hwy 1 and look for the Bureau of Land Management (BLM) signs on the left

indicating these 1132-acre public lands. The best, most dramatic walking trail leads along the coast and also begins on Lighthouse Rd from a small parking area about a quarter-mile before the Lighthouse parking area.

Sleeping & Eating

Wharf Master's Inn HOTEL $$
(800-932-4031, 707-882-3171; www.wharfmasters.com; 785 Iversen Ave; r $100-195;) This is a cluster of small, modern rooms on a cliff overlooking fishing boats and a stilt pier. Tidy and very clean, rooms have the character of a chain hotel.

Coast Guard House Inn INN $$
(707-882-2442; www.coastguardhouse.com; 695 Arena Cove; r $165-265;) Come here if you want to soak up old-world oceanside charm and are willing to deal with historic plumbing. It's a 1901 Cape Cod–style house and cottage, with water-view rooms.

Coast Guard Homes VACATION RENTAL $$
(877-725-4448; 45500 Lighthouse Rd; houses $135-235) True lighthouse buffs should look into staying at the plain three-bedroom, kitchen-equipped former Coast Guard homes at the Lighthouse. They're quiet, wind-swept retreats.

Franny's Cup & Saucer BAKERY $
(www.frannyscupandsaucer.com; 213 Main St; items from $2; 8am-4pm Wed-Sat) The cutest patisserie on this stretch of coast is run by Franny and her mother, Barbara (a veteran of Chez Panisse). The fresh berry tarts and creative housemade chocolates seem too beautiful to eat, until you take the first bite and immediately want to order another. Several times a year they pull out all the stops for a Sunday garden brunch ($25).

Arena Market ORGANIC, DELI $
(www.arenaorganics.org; 183 Main St; 7:30am-7pm Mon-Sat, 8:30am-6pm Sun;) The deli in front of this fully stocked organic grocer makes excellent to-go veg and gluten-free options, often sourced from local farms. The serve-yourself soup is delish.

Pizzas N Cream PIZZA $$
(www.pizzasandcream.com; 790 Port Rd; pizzas $10-18; 11:30am-9pm;) In Arena Cove, this friendly place whips up exquisite pizzas and fresh salads, and serves beer and ice cream.

Drinking & Entertainment

215 Main BAR
(www.facebook.com/215Main; 215 Main St; 2pm-2am Tue-Sun) Head to this open, renovated historic building to drink local beer and wine. There's jazz on the weekends.

Arena Cinema CINEMA
(www.arenatheater.org; 214 Main St) Shows mainstream, foreign and art films in a beautifully restored movie house. Sue, the ticket seller, has been in that booth for 40 years. Got a question about Point Arena? Ask Sue.

Manchester

Follow Hwy 1 for about 7 miles north of Point Arena, through gorgeous rolling fields dropping down from the hills to the blue ocean, and a turnoff leads to **Manchester State Beach**, a long, wild stretch of sand. The area around here is remote and beautiful (only one grocery store), but it's a quick drive to Point Arena for more elaborate provisions.

Ross Ranch (707-877-1834; www.rossranch.biz) at Irish Beach, another 5 miles to the north, arranges two-hour horseback beach ($60) and mountain ($50) rides; reservations recommended.

Mendocino Coast KOA (707-882-2375; www.manchesterbeachkoa.com; tent/RV sites from $29/49, cabins $64-78;) is an impressive private campground with tightly packed campsites beneath enormous Monterey pines, a cooking pavilion, hot showers, a hot tub and bicycles. The cabins are a great

---

TOP WHALE-WATCHING SPOTS

Watch for spouts, sounding and breaching whales and pods. Anywhere coastal will do, but the following are some of the north coast's best:

→ Bodega Head (p198)

→ Mendocino Headlands State Park (p207)

→ Jug Handle State Reserve (p211)

→ MacKerricher State Park (p215)

→ Shelter Cove & Lost Coast (p228)

→ Trinidad Head Trail (p241)

→ Klamath River Overlook (p246)

option for families who want to get the camping experience without roughing it.

A quarter-mile west, the sunny, exposed campground at **Manchester State Park** (www.parks.gov.ca; tent & RV sites $29-39) has cold water and quiet sites right by the ocean. Sites are nonreservable. Budget cuts have all but eliminated ranger service.

Elk

Thirty minutes north of Point Arena, itty-bitty Elk is famous for its stunning cliff-top views of 'sea stacks,' towering rock formations jutting out of the water. Otherwise, it's one of the cutest yet gentrified-looking villages before Mendocino. There is *nothing* to do after dinner, so bring a book if you're a night owl. And you can forget about the cell phone, too; reception here is nonexistent. Elk's **visitor center** (5980 Hwy 1; ⊙11am-1pm Sat & Sun mid-Mar–Oct) has exhibits on the town's logging past. At the southern end of town, **Greenwood State Beach** sits where Greenwood Creek meets the sea.

Tucked into a tiny house looking across the road to the ocean, the **Elk Studio Gallery & Artist's Collective** (www.artists-collective.net; 6031 S Hwy 1; ⊙10am-5pm) is cluttered with local art – everything from carvings and pottery to photography and jewelry.

🛏 Sleeping & Eating

Griffin House INN $$
(☑707-877-3422; www.griffinn.com; 5910 S Hwy 1; cottages incl breakfast $138-260; 🕾🐾) This is the most affordable choice, with an adorable cluster of simple, powder-blue bluffside cottages with wood-burning stoves.

Elk Cove Inn & Spa INN $$$
(☑800-725-2967; www.elkcoveinn.com; 6300 S Hwy 1; r $100-375, cottages $275-355; 🕾🐾) Several upmarket B&Bs take advantage of the views. You simply can't beat those from Elk Cove Inn & Spa, located on a bluff with steps leading down to the driftwood-strewn beach below. Prices in the wide selection of rooms and cottages include breakfast, wine, champagne and cocktails plus you can relax even further at their deluxe spa.

Harbor House Inn INN $$$
(☑800-720-7474, 707-877-3203; www.theharborhouseinn.com; 5600 S Hwy 1; r & cottages incl breakfast & dinner $360-490; 🕾) Harbor House Inn, located in a 1915 Arts and Crafts–style mansion (closed for renovations when we

passed), has gorgeous cliff-top gardens and a private beach. Rates include a superb four-course dinner for two in the ocean-view room with a lauded wine list.

Queenie's Roadhouse Cafe CAFE $
(☑707-877-3285; 6061 S Hwy 1; dishes $6-10; ⊙8am-3pm Thu-Mon; 🍴) Everyone swears by excellent, retro-chic Queenie's Roadhouse Cafe for a creative range of breakfast (try the wild-rice waffles) and lunch treats.

Bridget Dolan's AMERICAN $$
(☑707-877-1820; 5910 S Hwy 1; mains $10-15; ⊙4:30-8pm) Sweet, little Bridget Dolan's serves straight-forward cookin' like pot pies, and bangers and mash.

Van Damme State Park

Three miles south of Mendocino, this gorgeous 1831-acre **park** (☑707-937-5804; www.parks.ca.gov; per car $8) draws divers, beachcombers and kayakers to its easy-access beach. It's also known for its **pygmy forest**, where the acidic soil and an impenetrable layer of hardpan just below the surface create a bonsai forest with decades-old trees growing only several feet high. A wheelchair-accessible boardwalk provides access to the forest. Turn east off Hwy 1 onto Little River Airport Rd, a half-mile south of Van Damme State Park, and drive for 3 miles. Alternatively, hike or bike up from the campground on the 3.5-mile **Fern Canyon Scenic Trail**, which crosses back and forth over Little River.

The **visitor center** (☑707-937-4016; ⊙10am-3pm Fri-Sun) has nature exhibits, videos and programs; a half-hour **Marsh Loop Trail** starts nearby.

Two pretty **campgrounds** (☑800-444-7275; www.reserveamerica.com; tent & RV sites $35; 🕾) are excellent for family car camping. They both have hot showers: one is just off Hwy 1, the other is in a highland meadow, which has lots of space for kids to run around. Nine **environmental campsites** (tent sites $25) lie just a 1¼-mile hike up Fern Canyon; there's untreated creek water.

For sea-cave kayaking tours ($60), contact **Kayak Mendocino** (☑707-937-0700; www.kayakmendocino.com).

Mendocino

Leading out to a gorgeous headland, Mendocino is the North Coast's salt-washed perfect village, with B&Bs surrounded by rose gardens, white-picket fences and New England–style redwood water towers. Bay Area weekenders walk along the headland among berry bramble and wildflowers, where cypress trees stand over dizzying cliffs. Nature's power is evident everywhere, from driftwood-littered fields and cave tunnels to the raging surf. The town itself is full of cute shops – no chains – and has earned the nickname 'Spendocino,' for its upscale goods. In summer, fragrant bursts of lavender and jasmine permeate the foggy wind, tempered by salt air from the churning surf, which is never out of earshot.

Built by transplanted New Englanders in the 1850s, Mendocino thrived late into the 19th century, with ships transporting redwood timber from here to San Francisco. The mills shut down in the 1930s, and the town fell into disrepair until it was rediscovered in the 1950s by artists and bohemians. Today the culturally savvy, politically aware, well-traveled citizens welcome visitors, but eschew corporate interlopers – don't look for a Big Mac or Starbucks. To avoid crowds, come midweek or in the low season, when the vibe is mellower – and prices more reasonable.

◉ Sights

Mendocino is lined with all kinds of interesting galleries, which hold openings on the second Saturday of each month from 5pm to 8pm.

Mendocino Art Center GALLERY
(☏707-937-5818, 800 653 3328; www.mendocinoartcenter.org; 45200 Little Lake St; ☺10am-5pm Apr-Oct, to 4pm Tue-Sat Nov-Mar) Behind a yard of twisting iron sculpture, the city's art center takes up a whole tree-filled block, hosting exhibitions, the 81-seat **Helen Schonei Theatre** and nationally renowned art classes. This is also where to pick up the *Mendocino Arts Showcase* brochure, a quarterly publication listing all the happenings and festivals in town.

Kelley House Museum MUSEUM
(www.mendocinohistory.org; 45007 Albion St; admission $2; ☺11am-3pm Thu-Tue Jun-Sep, Fri-Mon Oct-May) With a research library and changing exhibits on early California and Mendocino, the 1861 museum hosts seasonal, two-hour **walking tours** for $10; call for times.

Kwan Tai Temple TEMPLE
(www.kwantaitemple.org; 45160 Albion St) Peering in the window of this 1852 temple reveals an old altar dedicated to the Chinese god of war. Tours are available by appointment.

Point Cabrillo Lighthouse LIGHTHOUSE
(www.pointcabrillo.org; Point Cabrillo Dr; ☺11am-4pm Sat & Sun Jan & Feb, daily Mar-Oct, Fri-Mon Nov & Dec) FREE Restored in 1909, this stout lighthouse stands on a 300-acre wildlife preserve north of town, between Russian Gulch and Caspar Beach. **Guided walks** of the preserve leave at 11am on Sundays from May to September. You can also stay in the lighthouse keeper's house and cottages which are now vacation rentals (p209).

🏃 Activities

Wine tours, whale-watching, shopping, hiking, cycling: there's more to do in the area than a thousand long weekends could accomplish. For navigable river and ocean kayaking, launch from tiny Albion, which hugs the north side of the Albion River mouth, 5 miles south of Mendocino.

Catch A Canoe & Bicycles Too! CANOEING, KAYAKING
(☏707-937-0273; www.catchacanoe.com; Stanford Inn by the Sea, 44850 Comptche-Ukiah Rd; kayak & canoe rental adult/child from $28/14; ☺9am-5pm) This friendly outfit at the Stanford Inn south of town rents bikes, kayaks and stable outrigger canoes for trips up the 8-mile Big River tidal estuary, the longest undeveloped estuary in Northern California. No highways or buildings, only beaches, forests, marshes, streams, abundant wildlife and historic logging sites. Bring a picnic and a camera to enjoy the ramshackle remnants of century-old train trestles and majestic blue herons.

Mendocino Headlands State Park OUTDOORS
A spectacular park surrounds the village, with trails crisscrossing the bluffs and rocky coves. Ask at the visitor center about guided weekend walks, including spring wildflower walks and whale-watching.

🎊 Festivals & Events

For a complete list of Mendocino's many festivals, check with the visitor center or www.gomendo.com.

Mendocino Whale Festival WILDLIFE
(www.mendowhale.com) Early March, with wine and chowder tastings, whale-watching and music.

Mendocino

Mendocino

◎ Sights
1	Kelley House Museum	C2
2	Kwan Tai Temple	A3
3	Mendocino Art Center	A2
4	Mendocino Headlands State Park	A1

🛏 Sleeping
5	Alegria	D2
6	Headlands Inn	C2
7	MacCallum House Inn	B2
8	Mendocino Coast Reservations	B2
9	Mendocino Hotel	B3
10	Packard House	B2
11	Raku House	D2
12	Sea Gull Inn	C2

✖ Eating
13	955 Ukiah Street	C2
14	Café Beaujolais	D2

15	Farmers Market	C2
16	Flow	B3
17	GoodLife Cafe & Bakery	C2
	MacCallum House Restaurant	(see 7)
	Mendocino Cafe	(see 12)
18	Mendocino Market	B2
19	Mendosa's	C2
20	Patterson's Pub	C2

◐ Drinking & Nightlife
21	Dick's Place	B3

◉ Shopping
22	Compass Rose Leather	B3
23	Gallery Bookshop	B3
24	Moore Used Books	D2
25	Out Of This World	B3
26	Twist	A3
27	Village Toy Store	C2

Mendocino Music Festival   MUSIC
(www.mendocinomusic.com; 🔊) Mid-July, with orchestral and chamber music concerts on the headlands, children's matinees and open rehearsals.

Mendocino Wine & Mushroom Festival   FOOD, WINE
(www.mendocino.com) Early November, guided mushroom tours and symposia.

🛏 Sleeping

Standards are high and so are prices; two-day minimums often crop up on weekends. Fort Bragg, 10 miles north, has cheaper lodgings. All B&B rates include breakfast; only a few places have TVs. For a range of cottages and B&Bs, contact **Mendocino Coast Reservations** (☎800-262-7801, 707-937-5033; www.mendocinovacations.com; 45084 Little Lake St; ⊙9am-5pm).

Russian Gulch State Park CAMPGROUND $

(📞reservations 800-444-7275; www.reserveameri-ca.com; tent & RV sites $35) In a wooded canyon 2 miles north of town, with secluded drive-in sites, hot showers, a small waterfall and the Devil's Punch Bowl (a collapsed sea arch).

Andiron CABIN $$

(📞800-955-6478, 707-937-1543; http://theand-iron.com; 6051 N Hwy 1, Little River; most cabins $109-299; 🐾🛜) 🏖 Styled with hip vintage decor, this cluster of 1950s roadside cottages is a refreshingly playful option amid the cab-bage-rose and lace aesthetic of Mendocino. Each cabin houses two rooms with comple-menting themes: 'Read' has old books, com-fy vintage chairs and hip retro eyeglasses, while the adjoining 'Write' features a huge chalk board and a ribbon typewriter.

A favorite for travelers? 'Here' and 'There,' themed with old maps, 1960s airline par-aphernalia and collectables from North Coast's yesteryear.

MacCallum House Inn B&B $$

(📞800-609-0492, 707-937-0289; www.maccallum-house.com; 45020 Albion St; r & cottages from $149, water tower from $225; @🛜🐾) 🏖 The finest B&B option in town with gardens in a riot of color. There are cheerful cottages, and a modern luxury home, but the most memora-ble space is within one of Mendocino's iconic historic water towers – living quarters fill the ground floor, a sauna is on the 2nd floor and there's a view of the coast from the top.

All accommodations have cushy extras like robes, DVD players, stereos and plush linens.

Packard House B&B $$

(📞888-453-2677, 707-937-2677; www.packard-house.com; 45170 Little Lake St; r $175-225; 🛜) Decked out in contemporary style, this place is Mendocino's most chic and sleek B&B choice, with beautiful fabrics, colorful min-imalist paintings and limestone bathrooms.

Headlands Inn B&B $$

(📞707-937-4431; www.headlandsinn.com; cnr Albi-on & Howard Sts; r $139-249; 🛜) Homey saltbox with featherbeds, English gardens and fire-places. Quiet rooms have sea views and staff will bring you the gourmet breakfast in bed.

Sea Gull Inn B&B $$

(📞888-937-5204, 707-937-5204; www.seagullbb.com; 44960 Albion St; r $130-198, barn $200; 🛜) With pristine white bedspreads, organic breakfasts and a flowering garden, this cute, converted motel is extremely comfortable, fairly priced, and right in the thick of the action.

Lighthouse Inn at Point Cabrillo HISTORIC B&B $$

(📞866-937-6124, 707-937-6124; www.pointcabril-lo.org; Point Cabrillo Dr; lightkeeper's house from $461, cottages from $132; 🛜) On 300 acres, in the shadow of Point Cabrillo Lighthouse, the stately lightkeeper's house and the staff's two turn-of-the-century cottages have been turned into vacation rentals. All options have verandahs and lush period decor but are not very private.

★ Alegria B&B $$$

(📞800-780-7905, 707-937-5150; www.ocean-frontmagic.com; 44781 Main St; r $239-299; 🛜) A perfect romantic hideaway, beds have views over the coast, decks have ocean views and all rooms have wood-burning fireplac-es. Outside a gorgeous path leads to a big, amber-grey beach. Ever-so-friendly inn-keepers whip up amazing breakfasts served in the sea-view dining area. Less expensive rooms are available across the street at bright and simple **Raku House** (www.raku-house.com; r from $159).

Glendeven B&B $$$

(📞707-937-0083; www.glendeven.com; 8205 N Hwy 1; r $165-320; 🛜) 🏖 This elegant estate 2 miles south of town has organic gardens, grazing llamas (with daily feedings at dusk), forest and oceanside trails, and a wine bar serving only Mendocino wines – and that's just the start. Romantic rooms have neutral-toned, soothing decor, fireplaces and top-notch linens. Farm-to-table dinners are available at the bistro.

Brewery Gulch Inn B&B $$$

(📞800-578-4454, 707-937-4752; www.brewer-ygulchinn.com; 9401 N Hwy 1; d incl breakfast $245-495; 🛜) 🏖 Just south of Mendocino, this bright, woodsy place has 10 modern rooms (all with flat-screen televisions, gas fireplaces and spa bathtubs), and guests enjoy touches like feather beds and leath-er reading chairs. The hosts pour heavily at the complimentary wine hour and leave out sweets for midnight snacking. Made-to-order breakfast is served in a small dining room overlooking the distant water.

Stanford Inn by the Sea INN $$$

(📞800-331-8884, 707-937-5615; www.stanfordinn.com; cnr Hwy 1 & Comptche-Ukiah Rd; r $211-299;

@ 🏫 💺 🍴) 🍳 This masterpiece of a lodge standing on 10 lush acres has wood-burning fireplaces, knotty pine walls, original art, stereos and top-quality mattresses in every room. Figure in a stroll in the organic gardens, where they harvest food for the excellent on-site restaurant Ravens (p210), the solarium-enclosed pool and the hot tub, and it's a sublime getaway.

Mendocino Hotel   HISTORIC HOTEL $$$
(📋 800-548-0513, 707-937-0511; www.mendocinohotel.com; 45080 Main St; r with/without bath from $261/186, ste $475; 🅿 🛜) Built in 1878 as the town's first hotel, this is like a piece of the Old West. The modern garden suites sit behind the main building and don't have a shade of old-school class, but are modern and serviceable. As gorgeous as it is, the prices are inflated, especially for the rooms with shared bathrooms.

🍴 Eating

With quality to rival Napa Valley, the influx of Bay Area weekenders have fostered an excellent dining scene that enthusiastically espouses organic, sustainable principles. Make reservations. Gathering picnic supplies is easy at **Mendosa's** (📋 8am-9pm; www.harvestmarket.com; 10501 Lansing St) 🍳 organic grocery store (with deli) and the **farmers market** (cnr Howard & Main St; ⊙ noon-2pm Fri May-Oct).

GoodLife Cafe & Bakery   CAFE $
(http://goodlifecafemendo.com; 10485 Lansing St; light meals $6-10; ⊙ 8am-4pm) 🍳 Here's where locals and tourists mingle in an unpretentious, noisy and cozy cafe setting. Get bakery goods and fair-trade coffee for breakfast and comfort food like mac and cheese or curry bowls at lunch. Lots of gluten-free options are available.

Mendocino Market   DELI $
(45051 Ukiah St; sandwiches $6-9; ⊙ 11am-5pm Mon-Fri, to 4pm Sat & Sun; 🛜) Pick up huge deli sandwiches and picnics here.

Mendocino Cafe   CALIFORNIAN, FUSION $$
(www.mendocinocafe.com; 10451 Lansing St; lunch mains $12-16, dinner mains $21-33; ⊙ 11:30am-8pm; 🍴) One of Mendocino's few fine dinner spots that also serves lovely alfresco lunches on its ocean-view deck surrounded by roses. Try the fish tacos or the 'Healing Bowl' of soba noodles, miso, shitake mushrooms and choice of meat or seafood. At dinner there's grilled steak and seafood.

Ledford House   MEDITERRANEAN $$
(📋 707-937-0282; www.ledfordhouse.com; 3000 N Hwy 1, Albion; mains $14-30; ⊙ 5-8pm Wed-Sun; 🍴) Watch the water pound the rocks and the sun set out of the Mendocino hubbub (8 miles south) at this friendly Cal-Med bistro. Try the cassoulet or the gnocchi. It's a local hangout and gets hoppin' with live jazz most nights.

Flow   CALIFORNIAN $$
(45040 Main St; mains $10-25; ⊙ 8am-10pm; 🛜🍴) Run by the Mendocino Cafe, this new, very busy place has the best views of the ocean in town from its 2nd-story perch. Brunch is a specialty as are Mexican-inspired small plates, artisanal pizzas and a sublime local dungeness crab chowder. Gluten-free and vegan options are available.

Patterson's Pub   PUB FOOD $$
(www.pattersonspub.com; 10485 Lansing St; mains $13-16; ⊙ food till 11pm) If you pull into town late and hungry, you'll thank your lucky stars for this place; it serves quality pub grub – fish and chips, burgers and dinner salads – with cold beer. The only traditional Irish pub ambience spoiler is the plethora of flat-screen TVs. A busy brunch is served on Saturday and Sunday mornings from 10am to 2pm.

⭐ Café Beaujolais   CALIFORNIAN $$$
(📋 707-937-5614; www.cafebeaujolais.com; 961 Ukiah St; dinner mains $23-35; ⊙ 11:30am-2:30pm Wed-Sun, dinner from 5:30pm daily) 🍳 Mendocino's iconic, beloved country-Cal–French restaurant occupies an 1896 house restyled into a monochromatic urban-chic dining room, perfect for holding hands by candlelight. The refined, inspired cooking draws diners from San Francisco, who make this the centerpiece of their trip. The locally sourced menu changes with the seasons, but the Petaluma duck breast served with crispy skin is a gourmand's delight.

Ravens   CALIFORNIAN $$$
(📋 707-937-5615; www.ravensrestaurant.com; Stanford Inn, Comptche-Ukiah Rd; breakfast $11-15, mains $24-30; ⊙ 8-10:30am Mon-Sat, to noon Sun, dinner 5:30-10pm; 🍴) 🍳 Ravens brings haute-contemporary concepts to a completely vegetarian and vegan menu. Produce comes from the idyllic organic gardens of the Stanford Inn (p209), and the bold menu takes on everything from sea-palm strudel and portabella sliders to decadent (guilt-free) desserts.

MacCallum House Restaurant
CALIFORNIAN **$$$**

(☑707-937-0289; www.maccallumhouse.com; 45020 Albion St; cafe dishes $12-18, mains $25-42; ⊘8:15-10am Mon-Fri, to 11am Sat & Sun, 5:30-9pm daily; ☑) ✔ Sit on the verandah or fireside for a romantic dinner of all-organic game, fish or risotto primavera. Chef Alan Kantor makes *everything* from scratch and his commitment to sustainability and organic ingredients is nearly as visionary as his menu. The cafe menu, served at the **Grey Whale Bar**, is one of Mendocino's few four-star bargains.

955 Ukiah Street
CALIFORNIAN **$$$**

(☑707-937-1955; www.955restaurant.com; 955 Ukiah St; mains $18-37; ⊘from 6pm Thu-Sun) One of those semi-secret institutions, the menu here changes with what's available locally. When we passed that meant wonderful things like yogurt and scallion marinated wild jumbo prawns. The dimly lit, bohemian setting overlooks rambling gardens. Check the website for the excellent-value, three-course meal with wine for $25 and other events.

🍸 Drinking & Nightlife

Have cocktails at the Mendocino Hotel or the Grey Whale Bar at the MacCallum House Restaurant. For boisterousness and beer head straight to Patterson's Pub.

Dick's Place
DIVE BAR

(45080 Main St) A bit out of place among the fancy-pants shops downtown, but an excellent spot to check out the *other* Mendocino and do shots with rowdy locals.

🔒 Shopping

Mendocino's walkable streets are great for shopping, and the ban on chain stores ensures unique, often upscale gifts. There are many small galleries in town where one-of-a-kind artwork is for sale.

Compass Rose Leather
LEATHER GOODS

(45150 Main St) From hand-tooled belts and leather-bound journals to purses and peg-secured storage boxes, the craftsmanship here is unquestionable.

Out Of This World
OUTDOOR EQUIPMENT

(45100 Main St) Birders, astronomy buffs and science geeks head directly to this telescope, binocular and science-toy shop.

Village Toy Store
TOYS

(10450 Lansing St) Get a kite or browse the old-world selection of wooden toys and games that you won't find in the chains – hardly anything requires batteries.

Gallery Bookshop
BOOKS

(www.gallerybookshop.com; 319 Kasten St) Stocks a great selection of books on local topics, titles from California's small presses and specialized outdoor guides.

Twist
CLOTHING

(45140 Main St) ✔ Twist stocks ecofriendly, natural-fiber clothing and lots of locally made clothing and toys.

Moore Used Books
BOOKS

(990 Main St) An excellent bad-weather hideout, the stacks here have over 10,000 used titles. The shop is in an old house at the far east end of Main St.

ℹ Information

Ford House Museum & Visitor Center (☑707-537-5397; http://mendoparks.org; 735 Main St; ⊘11am-4pm) Maps, books, information and exhibits, including a scale model of 1890 Mendocino.

Jug Handle State Reserve

Between Mendocino and Fort Bragg, Jug Handle preserves an **ecological staircase** that you can view on a 5-mile (round-trip) self-guided **nature trail**. Five wave-cut terraces ascend in steps from the seashore, each 100ft and 100,000 years removed from the previous one, and each with its own distinct geology and vegetation. One of the terraces has a **pygmy forest**, similar to the better-known example at Van Damme State Park. Pick up a printed guide detailing the area's geology, flora and fauna from the parking lot. The reserve is also a good spot to stroll the headlands, whale-watch or lounge on the beach. It's easy to miss the entrance; watch for the turnoff, just north of Caspar.

Jug Handle Creek Farm & Nature Center (☑707-964-4630; www.jughandlecreekfarm.com; tent sites $14, r & cabins adult $45, student $38; 🐾) is a nonprofit 39-acre farm with rustic cabins and hostel rooms in a 19th-century farmhouse. Call ahead about work-stay discounts. Drive 5 miles north of Mendocino to Caspar; the farm is on the east side of

Hwy 1. Take the second driveway after Fern Creek Rd.

Fort Bragg

In the past, Fort Bragg was Mendocino's ugly stepsister, home to a lumber mill, a scrappy downtown and blue-collar locals who gave a cold welcome to outsiders. Since the mill closure in 2002, the town has started to reinvent itself, slowly warming to a tourism-based economy. What to do with the seaside mill site is the talk of the town, running the gamut from ideas like a marine research center or university to commercial ones like a condo development. The town itself has little say since, including projected acquisitions, it will hold under 100 acres of the 415-acre site; the rest is owned by Georgia Pacific, which is owned by Koch Industries, which is majority owned by the Koch brothers.

In the meantime, Fort Bragg's downtown continues to develop as a wonderfully unpretentious alternative to Mendocino, even if the southern end of town is hideous. Unlike the *entire* franchise-free 180-mile stretch of Coastal Hwy 1 between here and the Golden Gate, in Fort Bragg you can get a Big Mac, grande latte or any of a number of chain store products whose buildings blight the landscape. Don't fret. In downtown you'll find better hamburgers and coffee, old-school architecture and residents eager to show off their little town.

Twisting Hwy 20 provides the main access to Fort Bragg from the east, and most facilities are near Main St, a 2-mile stretch of Hwy 1. Franklin St runs parallel, one block east.

◉ Sights & Activities

Fort Bragg has the same banner North Coast activities as Mendocino – beach combing, surfing, hiking – but basing yourself here is much cheaper and arguably less quaint and pretentious. The wharf lies at Noyo Harbor – the mouth of the Noyo River – south of downtown where you can find **whale-watching cruises** and **deep-sea fishing trips**.

Mendocino Coast Botanical Gardens   GARDENS
(☑707-964-4352; www.gardenbythesea.org; 18220 N Hwy 1; adult/child/senior $14/5/10; ⊙9am-5pm Mar-Oct, to 4pm Nov-Feb) 🍃 This gem of Northern California displays native flora, rhododendrons and heritage roses. The succulent display alone is amazing and the organic garden is harvested by volunteers to feed area residents in need. The serpentine paths wander along 47 seafront acres south of town. Primary trails are wheelchair-accessible.

Glass Beach   BEACH
Named for (what's left of) the sea-polished glass in the sand, remnants of its days as a city dump, this beach is now part of MacKerricher State Park (p215) where visitors comb the sand for multicolored glass. Take the headlands trail from Elm St, off Main St, but leave the glass; as a part of the park system, visitors are not supposed to pocket souvenirs.

Northcoast Artists Gallery   GALLERY
(www.northcoastartists.org; 362 N Main St; ⊙10am-6pm) An excellent local arts cooperative that has the useful *Fort Bragg Gallery & Exhibition Guide*, which directs you to other galleries around town. Openings are the first Fridays of the month. Antique and book stores line Franklin St, one block east.

Triangle Tattoo & Museum   MUSEUM
(www.triangletattoo.com; 356B N Main St; ⊙noon-7pm) FREE Shows multicultural, international tattoo art.

Guest House Museum   MUSEUM
(☑707-964-4251; www.fortbragghistory.org; 343 N Main St; admission $2; ⊙1-3pm Mon, 11am-2pm Tue-Fri, 10am-4pm Sat & Sun May-Oct, 11am-2pm Thu-Sun) A majestic Victorian structure built in 1892 displays historical photos and relics of Fort Bragg's history. As hours vary, call ahead.

★ Skunk Train   HISTORIC TRAIN
(☑866-866-1690, 707-964-6371; www.skunktrain. com; adult/child $54/34; 🐾) Fort Bragg's pride and joy, the vintage train got its nickname in 1925 for its stinky gas-powered steam engines, but today the historic steam and diesel locomotives are odorless. Passing through redwood-forested mountains, along rivers, over bridges and through deep mountain tunnels, the trains run from both Fort Bragg and Willits (p223) to the midway point of Northspur, where they turn around.

If you want to go to Willits, plan to spend the night. The rain depot is downtown at the foot of Laurel St, one block west of Main St.

All-Aboard Adventures FISHING, WHALE-WATCHING
(📞707-964-1881; www.allaboardadventures.com; 32400 N Harbor Dr) Captain Tim leads crabbing and salmon-fishing trips (five hours, $80) and whale-watching during the whale migration (two hours, $35).

Pudding Creek Trestle BOARDWALK
(🚶) The walk along the Pudding Creek Trestle, north of downtown, is fun for the whole family.

⭐ Festivals & Events

Fort Bragg Whale Festival WILDLIFE
(www.mendowhale.com) Held on the third weekend in March, with microbrew tastings, crafts fairs and whale-watching trips.

Paul Bunyan Days CARNIVAL
(www.paulbunyandays.com) Held on Labor Day weekend in September, celebrate California's logging history with a logging show, square dancing, parade and fair.

🛏 Sleeping

Fort Bragg's lodging is cheaper than Mendocino's, but most of the motels along noisy Hwy 1 don't have air-conditioning, so you'll hear traffic through your windows. Most B&Bs do not have TVs and they all include breakfast. The usual chains abound. The best-value bland motel is **Colombi Motel** (📞707-964-5773; www.colombimotel.com; 647 Oak St; 1-/2-bedroom units with kitchenette from $60/70; 🛜) which is in town, not on the highway.

Country Inn B&B $
(📞707-964-3737; www.beourguests.com; 632 N Main St; r $80-220; 🛜🐾) This cute-as-a-button, gingerbread-trimmed B&B is right in the middle of town and is an excellent way to dodge the chain motels for a good-value stay. The lovely family hosts are welcoming and easygoing, and can offer good local tips. Breakfast can be delivered to your room and at night you can soak in a hot tub out back.

California Department of Forestry CAMPGROUND $
(📞707-964-5674; 802 N Main St; ⏰8am-4:30pm Mon, to noon Tue-Thu) Come here for maps, permits and camping information for the **Jackson State Forest**, east of Fort Bragg, where camping is free – which attracts all sorts so this isn't recommended for families or solo women.

NORTH COAST BEER TOUR
....

The craft breweries of the North Coast don't mess around – bold hop profiles, Belgian-style ales and smooth lagers are regional specialties, and they're produced with flair. Some breweries are better than others, but the following tour makes for an excellent long weekend of beer tasting in the region.

➡ Ukiah Brewing Co (p222), Ukiah

➡ Anderson Valley Brewing Company (p219), Boonville

➡ North Coast Brewing Company (p214), Fort Bragg

➡ Six Rivers Brewery (p240), McKinleyville

➡ Eel River Brewing (p232), Fortuna

Shoreline Cottages MOTEL, COTTAGE $$
(📞707-964-2977; www.shoreline-cottage.com; 18725 Shoreline Hwy, Fort Bragg; d $95-165; 🛜🐾) Low-key, four-person rooms and cottages with kitchens surround a central, tree-filled lawn. The family rooms are a good bargain, and suites feature modern artwork and clean sight lines. All rooms have docks for your iPod, snacks and access to a library of DVDs and there's a communal hot tub.

Grey Whale Inn B&B $$
(📞800-382-7244, 707-964-0640; www.greywhaleinn.com; 615 N Main St; r $110-195; 🛜) Situated in a historic building on the north side of town (walking distance from downtown and Glass Beach), this comfortable, family-run inn has simple, straightforward rooms that are good value – especially for families.

Weller House Inn B&B $$$
(📞877-893-5537, 707-964-4415; www.wellerhouse.com; 524 Stewart St; r $200-310; 🛜) Rooms in this beautifully restored 1886 mansion have down comforters, good mattresses and fine linens. The water tower is the tallest structure in town – and it has a hot tub at the top! Breakfast is in the massive redwood ballroom.

🍴 Eating

Similar to the lodging scene, the food in Fort Bragg is less spendy than Mendocino, but there are a number of truly excellent options. Self-caterers should try the **farmers market** (cnr Laurel & Franklin Sts; ⏰3:30-6pm

Wed May-Oct) downtown or the **Harvest Market** (☎707-964-7000; cnr Hwys 1 & 20; ☺5am-11pm) for the best groceries.

Cowlick's Handmade Ice Cream ICE CREAM $
(250B N Main St; scoops from $1.85; ☺11am-9pm)
Just great ice cream in fun flavors from classics like mocha almond fudge to the very unusual like candy cap mushroom (tastes like maple syrup but better), ginger or blackberry chocolate chunk. The sorbets (try the grapefruit Campari) are also delish.

Los Gallitos MEXICAN $
(130 S Main St; burritos $5.25-6.25; ☺11am-8pm Mon-Sat, from 10am Sun) A packed hole-in-the-wall that serves the best Mexican on the coast. Chips are homemade, the guacamole is chunky and the dishes, from the fresh fish tacos to homemade pork tamales and generous *sopas*, are consistently flavorful and well beyond the standard glob of refried beans. It's located across the parking lot from the CVS.

Living Light Café VEGAN $
(☎707-964-2420; 301 N Main St; mains $5-11; ☺8am-5:30pm Mon-Sat, to 4pm Sun; ✎) ✿ As an extension of the renowned Living Light Culinary Institute, one of the nation's leading raw food schools, this bright cafe serves a tasty to-go menu that can rival cooked food at even some of the better restaurants. Try the Sicilian-style pizza on a sprouted-seed crust, raw desserts (the brownies are amazing), salads and fresh juices.

Headlands Coffeehouse CAFE $
(www.headlandscoffeehouse.com; 120 E Laurel St; dishes $4-8; ☺7am-10pm Mon-Sat, to 7pm Sun; ✿✎) The town's best cafe is in the middle of the historic downtown, with high ceilings and lots of atmosphere. The menu gets raves for the Belgian waffles, homemade soups, veggie-friendly salads, panini and lasagna.

Eggheads BREAKFAST $
(www.eggheadsrestaurant.com; 326 N Main St; mains $8-15; ☺7am-2pm) Enjoy the *Wizard of Oz* theme as you tuck into one of 50 varieties of omelet, crepe or burrito, some with local Dungeness crab.

★**Piaci Pub & Pizzeria** ITALIAN $$
(www.piacipizza.com; 120 W Redwood Ave; mains $8-18; ☺11am-9:30pm Mon-Thu, to 10pm Fri & Sat, 4-9:30pm Sun) Fort Bragg's must-visit pizzeria is known for its sophisticated wood-fired, brick-oven pies as much as for its long list of microbrews. Try the 'Gustoso' – with chèvre, pesto and seasonal pears – all carefully orchestrated on a thin crust. It's tiny, loud and fun, with much more of a bar atmosphere than a restaurant. Expect to wait at peak times.

Mendo Bistro AMERICAN $$
(☎707-964-4974; www.mendobistro.com; 301 N Main St; mains $14-28; ☺5-9pm; ⊞) This dining option gets packed with a young crowd on the weekend, offering a choose-your-own-adventure menu, where you select a meat, a preparation and an accompanying sauce from a litany of options. The loud, bustling 2nd-story room is big enough for kids to run around and nobody will notice.

North Coast Brewing Company BREWERY $$
(www.northcoastbrewing.com; 455 N Main St; mains $8-25; ☺7am-9:30pm Sun-Thu, to 10pm Fri & Sat) Though thick, rare slabs of steak and a list of specials demonstrate that they take the food as seriously as the bevvies, it's burgers and garlic fries that soak up the fantastic selection of handcrafted brews. A great stop for serious beer lovers.

☆ Entertainment

Gloriana Opera Company THEATER
(www.gloriana.org; 721 N Franklin St) Stages musical theater and operettas.

🔒 Shopping

There's plenty of window-shopping in Fort Bragg's compact downtown, including a string of antique shops along Franklin St.

Outdoor Store OUTDOOR EQUIPMENT
(www.mendooutdoors.com; 247 N Main St) If you're planning on camping on the coast or exploring the Lost Coast, this is the best outfitter in the region, stocking detailed maps of the region's wilderness areas, fuel for stoves and high-quality gear.

Mendocino Vintage ANTIQUES
(www.mendocinovintage.com; 344 N Franklin St) Of the antique shops on Franklin, this is the hippest by a long shot, with a case full of vintage estate jewelry, antique glassware and old local oddities.

ⓘ Information

Fort Bragg-Mendocino Coast Chamber of Commerce (www.fortbragg.com; 332 N Main St; per 15min $1; ☺9am-5pm Mon-Fri, to 3pm Sat) Internet access.

Mendocino Coast District Hospital (☑707-961-1234; 700 River Dr; ☻24hr) Emergency room.

❶ Getting There & Around

Fort Bragg Cyclery (☑707-964-3509; www.fortbraggcyclery.com; 221a N Main St; bike rental per day from $32) Rents bicycles.

Mendocino Transit Authority (MTA; ☑800-696-4682, 707-462-1422; www.mendocinotransit.org) Runs local route 5 'BraggAbout' buses between Noyo Harbor and Elm St, north of downtown ($2). Service runs throughout the day.

MacKerricher State Park

Three miles north of Fort Bragg, the **MacKerricher State Park** (☑707-964-9112; www.parks.ca.gov) preserves 9 miles of pristine rocky headlands, sandy beaches, dunes and tidepools.

The **visitor center** (☻10am-4pm Mon-Fri, 9am-6pm Sat & Sun Jun-Aug, 9am-3pm Sep-May) sits next to the whale skeleton at the park entrance. Hike the **Coastal Trail** along dark-sand beaches and see rare and endangered plant species (tread lightly). **Lake Cleone** is a 30-acre freshwater lake stocked with trout and visited by over 90 species of birds. At nearby **Laguna Point** an interpretive disabled-accessible boardwalk overlooks harbor seals and, from December to April, migrating whales. **Ricochet Ridge Ranch** (☑707-964-7669; www.horse-vacation.com; 24201 N Hwy 1) offers horseback-riding trips through redwoods or along the beach ($50 for 90 minutes).

Just north of the park is **Pacific Star Winery** (33000 Hwy 1; tastings $5; ☻11am-5pm), in a dramatic, rub-your-eyes-in-disbelief-beautiful location on a bluff over the sea. The wines don't get pros excited but they are very drinkable, the owners are supremely friendly and you're encouraged to picnic at one of the many coast-side tables, stroll some of the short coastal trails along the cliffs and generally enjoy yourself (which isn't hard).

Popular **campgrounds** (☑800-444-2725; www.reserveamerica.com; tent & RV sites $35), nestled in pine forest, have hot showers and water; the first-choice reservable tent sites are numbers 21 to 59. Ten superb, secluded walk-in tent sites (numbers 1 to 10) are first-come, first-served.

Westport

If sleepy Westport feels like the peaceful edge of nowhere, that's because it is. The last hamlet before the Lost Coast, on a twisting 15-mile drive north of Fort Bragg, it is the last town before Hwy 1 veers inland on the 22-mile ascent to meet Hwy 101 in Leggett.

Head 1.5 miles north of town for the ruggedly beautiful **Westport-Union Landing State Beach** (☑707-937-5804; tent sites $25), which extends for 3 miles on coastal bluffs. A rough **hiking trail** leaves the primitive campground and passes by tidepools and streams, accessible at low tide. Bring your own water.

🛏 Sleeping & Eating

Westport Inn　　　　　　　　　INN $
(☑707-964-5135; www.westportinnca.com; 37040 N Hwy 1; r incl breakfast from $70; 🐾) Simple accommodations in town include the blue-and-red, plastic-flower-festooned Westport Inn.

★ **Westport Hotel & Old Abalone Pub**　　　　　　　　INN $$
(☑877-964-3688; www.westporthotel.us; Hwy 1; r $150-225; 🐾) Westport Hotel & Old Abalone Pub is quiet enough to have a motto which brags 'You've finally found nowhere.' The rooms are bright and beautiful – feather duvets, hardwood furniture, simple patterns – and enjoy excellent views. The classy historic pub downstairs is the only option for dinner, so be thankful it's a delicious sampling of whimsical California fusions (like turduken sausage and buttermilk potatoes, and rock shrimp mac and cheese) and hearty, expertly presented pub food.

Howard Creek Ranch　　　RANCH $$
(☑707-964-6725; www.howardcreekranch.com; 40501 N Hwy 1; r $90-198, cabins $105-198; 🐾🐾) Howard Creek Ranch, sitting on 60 stunning acres of forest and farmland abutting the wilderness, has accommodations in an 1880s farmhouse or a few cabins including a carriage barn, whose way-cool redwood rooms have been expertly handcrafted by the owner. Rates include full breakfast. Bring hiking boots, not high heels.

ALONG HIGHWAY 101

To get into the most remote and wild parts of the North Coast on the quick, eschew winding Hwy 1 for inland Hwy 101, which runs north from San Francisco as a freeway, then as a two- or four-lane highway north of Sonoma County, occasionally pausing under the traffic lights of small towns.

Know that escaping the Bay Area at rush hour (weekdays between 4pm and 7pm) ain't easy. You might sit bumper-to-bumper through Santa Rosa or Willits, where trucks bound for the coast turn onto Hwy 20.

Although Hwy 101 may not look as enticing as the coastal route, it's faster and less winding, leaving you time along the way to detour into Sonoma and Mendocino counties' wine regions (Mendocino claims to be the greenest wine region in the country), explore pastoral Anderson Valley, splash about Clear Lake or soak at hot-springs resorts outside Ukiah – time well spent indeed!

Hopland

Cute Hopland is the gateway to Mendocino County's wine country and flaunts its eco-minded, green-living ways at every turn. Hops were first grown here in 1866, but Prohibition brought the industry temporarily to a halt. Today, booze drives the local economy again with wine tasting as the primary draw.

◎ Sights

For an excellent weekend trip, use Hopland as a base for exploring the regional wineries. More information about the constantly growing roster of wineries is available at www.destinationhopland.com. Find a map to the wine region at www.visitmendocino.com.

Real Goods Solar Living Center
ENVIRONMENT CENTER
(www.solarliving.org; 13771 S Hwy 101; ⏰9am-6pm; 🖶) 🍷 This progressive, futuristic 12-acre campus is largely responsible for the area's bold green initiates. The Real Goods Store, which sold the first solar panel in the US, is an impressive straw-bale house showroom that also has free Frey Wine tastings. The suggested donation for tours of the center (11am and 3pm Friday to Sunday, April through October) is $3 to $5.

Sip! Mendocino
WINERY
(www.sipmendocino.com; 13420 S Hwy 101; tastings $5; ⏰11am-6pm) In central Hopland, this is a friendly place to get your bearings, pick up a map to the region and taste several wines without navigating all the back roads.

Amiable proprietors guide you through a tour of 18 wines with delectable appetizer pairings and a blossom-filled courtyard.

Saracina
WINERY
(www.saracina.com; 11684 S Hwy 101; ⏰10am-5pm) 🍷 The highlight of a tour here is the descent into the cool caves. Sensuous whites are all biodynamcially and sustainably farmed.

Fetzer Vineyards Organic Gardens
WINERY
(www.fetzer.com; 13601 Eastside Rd; ⏰9am-5pm) 🍷 Fetzer's sustainable practices have raised the bar, and their gardens are lovely. The wines are excellent value.

Brutocao Schoolhouse Plaza
TASTING ROOM
(www.brutocaoschoolhouseplaza.com; 13500 S Hwy 101; ⏰10am-5pm) In central Hopland, this place has bocce courts and bold reds – a perfect combo.

Graziano Family of Wines
WINERY
(www.grazianofamilyofwines.com; 13251 S Hwy 101; ⏰10am-5pm) Specializes in 'Cal-Ital' wines – nebbiolo, dolcetto, barbera and Sangiovese – at some great prices.

🛏 Sleeping & Eating

Piazza de Campovida
INN $$$
(☎707-744-1977; www.piazzadecampovida.com; 13441 S Hwy 101; ste $250-285; 🖥) Modern Californian meets Italian at this very comfortable spot where all the spacious suites have Jacuzzi tubs, fireplaces and private balconies. The homey pizzeria in front has big tables for communal dining and fantastic artisanal pizzas – there's no corkage fee either so bring your wine find of the day.

Hopland Tap House
PUB FOOD $
(13351 S Hwy 101; mains $6-9; ⏰11:30am-9pm Wed-Mon) Friendly locals, good sandwiches and selection of local beers all served in a bright brick building (plus shuffleboard). What more could you want?

Bluebird Cafe
AMERICAN $
(☎707-744-1633; 13340 S Hwy 101; breakfast & lunch $5-15, dinner $12-22; ⏰7am-2pm Mon-Thu, to 7pm Fri-Sun; 🖥) For conservative tastes, this classic American diner serves hearty breakfasts, giant burgers and homemade pie (the summer selection of peach-blueberry pie is dreamy). For a more exciting culinary adventure, try the wild game burgers, including boar with apple chutney and elk with a bite of horseradish.

Clear Lake

With over 100 miles of shoreline, Clear Lake is the largest naturally occurring freshwater lake in California (Tahoe is bigger, but crosses the Nevada state line). In summer the warm water thrives with algae, giving it a murky green appearance and creating a fabulous habitat for fish – especially bass – and tens of thousands of birds. Mt Konocti, a 4200ft-tall dormant volcano, lords over the scene. Alas, the human settlements don't always live up to the grandeur and thousands of acres near the lake remain scarred from wildfires in 2008.

◎ Sights & Activities

Locals refer to the northwest portion as 'upper lake' and the southeast portion as 'lower lake.' Likeable and well-serviced **Lakeport** (population 4695) sits on the northwest shore, a 45-minute drive east of Hopland along Hwy 175 (off Hwy 101); tiny, Old West style **Kelseyville** (population 3353) is 7 miles south. **Clearlake**, off the southeastern shore, is the biggest (and ugliest) town.

Hwy 20 links the relatively bland northshore hamlets of **Nice** (the northernmost town) and **Lucerne**, 4 miles southeast. **Middletown**, a cute village, lies 20 miles south of Clearlake at the junction of Hwys 175 and 29, 40 minutes north of Calistoga.

Clear Lake State Park　　　STATE PARK
(☏707-279-4293; 5300 Soda Bay Rd, Kelseyville; per car $8) Six miles from Lakeport, on the lake's west shore, the park is idyllic and gorgeous, with hiking trails, fishing, boating and camping. The **bird-watching** is extraordinary. The **visitor center** has geological and historical exhibits.

Redbud Audubon Society　　　BIRD WATCHING
(www.redbudaudubon.org) In lower lake, this conservation group leads birding walks.

🛏 Sleeping & Eating

Make reservations on weekends and during summer, when people flock to the cool water.

🛏 Lakeport & Kelseyville

There are a number of motels along the main drag in Keleysville and Lakeport, but if you want fresh air, Clear Lake State Park has four **campgrounds** (☏800-444-7275; www.reserveamerica.com; tent & RV sites $35) with showers. The weekly **farmers market** (Hwy 29 & Thomas Rd; ◷8:30am-noon Sat May-Oct) is in Kelseyville.

Mallard House　　　MOTEL $
(☏707-262-1601; www.mallardhouse.com; 970 N Main St, Lakeport; r with kitchen $69-149, without $55-99; ❄🐾🛜) Waterfront motels with boat slips include this good-value, cottage-style place. There's a tiny beach in front half covered with reeds.

★**Lakeport English Inn**　　　B&B $$
(☏707-263-4317; www.lakeportenglishinn.com; 675 N Main St, Lakeport; r $185-210, cottages $210; ❄🛜) The finest B&B at Clear Lake is an 1875 Carpenter Gothic with 10 impeccably furnished rooms, styled with a nod to the English countryside. Weekends take high tea (nonguests welcome by reservation) – with real Devonshire cream.

NORTH COAST & REDWOODS CLEAR LAKE

TOP CLEAR LAKE WINERIES

From north to south, the following four wineries are the best; some offer tours by appointment. Tastings generally cost $5 to $10.

Ceago Vinegarden (www.ceago.com; 5115 E Hwy 20, Nice; ◷noon-5pm) Ceago (cee-ay-go) occupies a spectacular spot on the north shore, and pours biodynamic, fruit-forward wines.

Brassfield Estate (www.brassfieldestate.com; 10915 High Valley Rd, Clearlake Oaks; ◷11am-5pm Mar-Nov, from noon Dec-Apr) A stunning, unique property in the remote High Valley appellation, try the Eruption and Serenity blends.

Wildhurst Vineyards (www.wildhurst.com; 3855 Main St, Kelseyville; ◷10am-5pm) The best wine on the lake, but the place lacks atmosphere. Try the Sauvignon Blanc.

Langtry Estate Vineyards (21000 Butts Canyon Rd, Middletown; ◷11am-5pm) The most beautiful vineyard. Try the port.

Skylark Shores Resort
INN $$

(☑800-675-6151; www.lakeportskylarkshores.com; 1120 N Main St, Lakeport; r $84-145; ✳ ☎ ☀) There's a 1960s holiday-camp feel here with a sprawl of well-maintained older units, many of which overlook the lakeside full of wading ducks and splashing kids and a big lawn dotted with smoking barbecues. Some units also have kitchens and there's a public launch boat dock.

Park Place
AMERICAN $

(50 3rd St, Lakeport; mains $7-11; ☺ 11am-9pm Tue-Sun, to 3pm Mon) 🍴 Simple but right on the waterfront, come to this bright and completely unpretentious eatery for basics like pasta, burgers and pizza made from sustainable, local produce at great prices. A local favorite.

Studebaker's Coffee House
DELI $

(3990 Main St, Kelseyville; sandwiches from $6; ☺ 6am-4pm Mon-Fri, 7am-4pm Sat, 7am-2pm Sun) A friendly, old-style diner/fountain place with plenty of character from black-and-white checker linoleum floors to old photos on the wall. Great sandwiches including vegetarian options and the coffee's good too.

★ Saw Shop Gallery Bistro
CALIFORNIAN $$$

(☑707-278-0129; www.sawshopbistro.com; 3825 Main St, Kelseyville; small plates $10-16, mains $15-26; ☺ from 3pm Tue-Sat) The best restaurant in Lake County serves a Californian-cuisine menu of wild salmon and rack of lamb, as well as a small plates menu of sushi, lobster tacos, Kobe-beef burgers and flatbread pizzas. Laid-back atmosphere, too.

🛏 North Shore

Tallman Hotel
HISTORIC HOTEL $$

(☑888-880-5253, 707-274-0200; www.tallmanhotel.com; 9550 Main St, Nice; cottages $169-274; ✳ ☎ ☀ ☀) 🍴 The centerpiece may be the smartly renovated historic hotel – tile bathrooms, warm lighting, thick linens – but the rest of the property's lodging, including several modern, sustainably built cottages, are equally peaceful. The shaded garden, walled-in swimming pool, brick patios and porches exude timeless elegance. Garden rooms come with Japanese soaking tubs heated by an energy-efficient geothermal-solar system.

Featherbed Railroad Co
HOTEL $$

(☑800-966-6322, 707-274-8378; www.featherbedrailroad.com; 2870 Lakeshore Blvd, Nice; cabooses incl breakfast $175-220; ✳ ☀) A treat for train buffs and kids, Featherbed has 10 comfy, real cabooses on a grassy lawn. Some of the cabooses straddle the border between kitschy and tacky (the 'Easy Rider' has a Harley Davidson headboard and a mirrored ceiling), but they're great fun if you keep a sense of humor. There's a tiny beach across the road.

Sea Breeze Resort
COTTAGES $$

(☑707-998-3327; www.seabreezeresort.net; 9595 Harbor Dr, Glenhaven; cottages $125-180; ☺ Apr-Oct; ✳ ☀) Just south of Lucerne on a small peninsula, gardens surround seven spotless lakeside cottages. All have barbecues.

🛏 Middletown

★ Harbin Hot Springs
SPA $$

(☑800-622-2477, 707-987-2377; www.harbin.org; Harbin Hot Springs Rd; tent & RV sites midweek/weekend $30/40, dm $40/60, s $50-75, d $100-190) Harbin is classic Northern California. Originally a 19th-century health spa and resort, it now has a retreat-center vibe and people come to unwind in silent, clothing-optional hot- and cold-spring pools. This is the birthplace of Watsu (floating massage) and there are wonderful body therapies as well as yoga, holistic-health workshops and 1160 acres of hiking.

Accommodations are in Victorian buildings (which could use sprucing up) and share a common vegetarian-only kitchen. Food is available at the market, cafe and restaurant. Day-trippers are welcome Monday through Thursday only; day rates are $20.

The springs are 3 miles off Hwy 175. From Middletown, take Barnes St, which becomes Big Canyon Rd, and head left at the fork.

🍷 Drinking & Entertainment

Library Park, in Lakeport, has free lakeside Friday-evening **summer concerts**, with blues and rockabilly tunes to appeal to middle-aged roadtrippers. Harbin Hot Springs presents a surprising line-up of world music and dances.

Kelsey Creek Brewing
BREWERY

(3945 Main St, Kelseyville; ☺ 2-8pm Tue-Fri, noon-8pm Sat, noon-5pm Sun) A 'hop'-ping fun local's scene with excellent craft beer, peanut shells on the floor and a bring-your-own-food, bring-your-dog kind of laid-back vibe.

Lakeport Auto Movies
CINEMA

(www.lakeportautomovies.com; 52 Soda Bay Rd, Lakeport; 1/2/3 people per car $10/18/25)

Lakeport is home to one of the few surviving drive-in movie theaters, with showings on Friday and Saturday nights.

ℹ Information

Lake County Visitor Information Center (www.lakecounty.com; 6110 E Hwy 120, Lucerne; ⊙9am-5pm Mon-Sat, noon-4pm Sun) Has complete information and an excellent website, which allows potential visitors to narrow their focus by interests.

ℹ Getting Around

Lake Transit (☑707-994-3334, 707-263-3334; www.laketransit.org) operates weekday routes between Middletown and Calistoga ($3, 35 minutes, three daily); on Thursday it connects through to Santa Rosa. Buses serve Ukiah ($5, two hours, four daily), from Clearlake via Lakeport ($3, 1¼ hours, seven daily). Since piecing together routes and times can be difficult, it's best to phone ahead.

Anderson Valley

Rolling hills surround rural Anderson Valley, famous for apple orchards, vineyards, pastures and quiet. Visitors come primarily to winery-hop, but there's good hiking and bicycling in the hills, and the chance to escape civilization. Traveling through the valley is the most common route to Mendocino from San Francisco.

⊙ Sights & Activities

Boonville (population 1488) and **Philo** (population 349) are the valley's principal towns. From Ukiah, winding Hwy 253 heads 20 miles south to Boonville. Equally scenic Hwy 128 twists and turns 60 miles between Cloverdale on Hwy 101, south of Hopland, and Albion on coastal Hwy 1.

Philo Apple Farm FARM (www.philoapplefarm.com; 18501 Greenwood Rd, Philo; ⊙dawn-dusk) For the best fruit, skip the obvious roadside stands and head to this gorgeous farm for organic preserves, chutneys, heirloom apples and pears. It also hosts **cooking classes** with some of the Wine Country's best chefs. You can make a weekend out of it by staying in one of the orchard cottages (p220).

Anderson Valley Brewing Company BREWERY (☑707-895-2337; www.avbc.com; 17700 Hwy 253; ⊙11am-6pm) ⏺ East of the Hwy 128 crossroads, this solar-powered brewery crafts

BOONTLING

Boonville is famous for its unique language, 'Boontling,' which evolved about the turn of the 20th century when Boonville was very remote. Locals developed the language to *shark* (stump) outsiders and amuse themselves. You may hear *codgie kimmies* (old men) asking for a horn of *zeese* (a cup of coffee) or some *bahl gorms* (good food). If you are really lucky, you'll spot the tow truck called Boont Region De-arkin' Moshe (literally 'Anderson Valley Un-wrecking Machine'). Find a fun dictionary at www.andersonvalleymuseum.org.

award-winning beers in a Bavarian-style brewhouse. You can also toss around a disc on the **Frisbee-golf course** while enjoying the brews, but, be warned, the sun can take its toll. Tours leave at 1:30pm and 3pm daily (only Tuesday and Wednesday in winter); call ahead.

Anderson Valley Historical Society Museum MUSEUM (www.andersonvalleymuseum.org; 12340 Hwy 128; ⊙1-4pm Sat & Sun Feb-Nov) In a recently renovated little red schoolhouse west of Boonville, this museum displays historical artifacts.

✸ Festivals & Events

Pinot Noir Festival WINE (www.avwines.com) One of Anderson Valley's many wine celebrations; held in May.

Sierra Nevada World Music Festival MUSIC (www.snwmf.com) In June, the sounds of reggae and roots fill the air, co-mingling with the scent of Mendocino County's *other* cash crop.

Mendocino County Fair FAIR (www.mendocountyfair.com) A county classic in mid-September.

🛏 Sleeping

Accommodations fill on weekends.

Hendy Woods State Park CAMPGROUND $ (☑707-937-5804, reservations 800-444-7275; www.reserveamerica.com; tent & RV sites $40, cabins $60) Bordered by the Navarro River on Hwy 128, west of Philo, the park has hiking,

TOP ANDERSON VALLEY WINERIES

The valley's cool nights yield high-acid, fruit-forward, food-friendly wines. Pinot Noir, Chardonnay and dry Gewürtztraminer flourish. Most **wineries** (www.avwines.com) sit outside Philo. Many are family-owned and offer free tastings, some give tours. The following are particularly noteworthy:

Navarro (www.navarrowine.com; 5601 Hwy 128; ☉10am-6pm) The best option with award-winning Pinot Noir and a delicious Riesling, picnicking is encouraged.

Esterlina (www.esterlinavineyards.com) For big reds, pack a picnic and head high up the rolling hills; call ahead.

Husch (www.huschvineyards.com; 4400 Hwy 128; ☉10am-5pm) The oldest vineyard in the valley serves exquisite tastings inside a rose-covered cottage.

Bink (9000 Hwy 128; ☉11am-5pm Wed-Mon) Small-batch artisanal wines that get rave reviews are served in the Madrones complex.

picnicking and a forested campground with hot showers.

The Other Place　　　COTTAGES **$$**
(☏707-895-3979; www.sheepdung.com; Boonville; cottages $150-350; 🐾👶) Outside of town, 500 acres of ranch land surrounds private, fully equipped hilltop cottages.

★Philo Apple Farm　　　COTTAGES **$$$**
(☏707-895-2333; www.philoapplefarm.com; 18501 Greenwood Rd, Philo; r Mon-Thu $200, Fri-Sun $275) Set within the orchard (p219), guests of Philo's bucolic apple Farm choose from four exquisite cottages, each built with reclaimed materials. With bright, airy spaces, polished plank floors, simple furnishings and views of the surrounding trees, each one is an absolute dream.

Red Door cottage is a favorite because of the bathroom – you can soak in the slipper tub, or shower on the private deck under the open sky. The cottages often get booked with participants of the farm's cooking classes, so book well in advance. For a swim, the Navarro River is within walking distance.

Boonville Hotel　　BOUTIQUE HOTEL **$$$**
(☏707-895-2210; www.boonvillehotel.com; 14050 Hwy 128, Boonville; r $150-360; 🐾) Decked out in a contemporary American-country style with sea-grass flooring, pastel colors and fine linens that would make Martha Stewart proud, this historic hotel's rooms are safe for urbanites who refuse to abandon style just because they've gone to the country.

The Madrones　　　HOTEL **$$$**
(www.themadrones.com; 9000 Hwy 28, Philo; r $160-325; 🐾) Tucked off the back of the Madrones Mediterranean-inspired complex

that includes a restaurant and the wonderful Bink Wines tasting room (p220), the spacious 'guest quarters' here are as modern-country-luxe, with a tinge of Tuscany, as you'd hope they'd be.

✖ Eating

Boonville restaurants seem to open and close as they please, so expect hours to vary based on season and whimsy. There are several places along Hwy 128 which can supply a picnic with fancy local cheese and fresh bread.

Paysenne　　　ICE CREAM **$**
(14111 Hwy 128, Boonville; cone $2; ☉10am-3pm Thu-Mon) Booneville's fantastic ice-cream shop serves the innovative flavors of Three Twins Ice Cream, whose delightful choices include Lemon Cookie and Strawberry Je Ne Sais Quoi (which has a hint of balsamic vinegar).

Boonville General Store　　　DELI **$**
(17810 Farrer Lane, Boonville; dishes $5-12; ☉7:30am-3pm Mon-Thu, 7:30am-3pm & 5:30-8pm Fri, 8:30am-3pm Sat & Sun) Opposite the Boonville Hotel, this deli is good to stock up for picnics, offering sandwiches on homemade bread, thin-crust pizzas and organic cheeses.

★Table 128　　　CALIFORNIAN **$$**
(14050 Hwy 128, Boonville; lunch mains $10-14, dinner mains $19-31; ☉6:30-8:15pm Fri-Sun) Food-savvy travelers love the constantly changing New American menu here, featuring simple dishes done well, like roasted chicken, grilled local lamb, and cheesecake. The family-style service makes dinner here a freewheeling, elegant social affair, with big

farm tables and soft lighting. It also has great wines, craft beers, fine scotch and cocktails.

Lauren's AMERICAN $$
(www.laurensgoodfood.com; 14211 Hwy 128, Boonville; mains $13-16; ☺5-9pm Tue-Sat; 🖋🖶) Locals pack Lauren's for eclectic homemade cookin' and a good wine list. Musicians sometimes jam on the stage by the front window.

ℹ Information

Anderson Valley Chamber of Commerce
(☑707-895-2379; www.andersonvalleychamber. com; 9800 Hwy 128, Boonville) Has tourist information and a complete schedule of annual events.

Ukiah

As the county seat and Mendocino's largest city, Ukiah is mostly a utilitarian stop for travelers to refuel the car and get a bite. But, if you have to stop here for the night, you could do much worse: the town is a friendly place that's gentrifying. There are a plethora of cookie-cutter hotel chains, some cheaper midcentury motels and a handful of very good dining options. The coolest attractions, thermal springs and a sprawling campus for Buddhist studies, lie outside the city limits. Ukiah has a pleasant, walkable shopping district along School St near the courthouse.

◉ Sights

Germain-Robin DISTILLERY
(☑707-462-0314; unit 35, 3001 S State St; ☺by appointment) Makes some of the world's best brandy, which is handcrafted by a fifth-generation brandy-maker from the Cognac region of France. It's by appointment only, but if you're into cognac, you gotta come.

Grace Hudson Museum & Sun House MUSEUM
(www.gracehudsonmuseum.org; 431 S Main St; admission $4; ☺10am-4:30pm Wed-Sat, from noon Sun) One block east of State St, the collection's mainstays are paintings by Grace Hudson (1865–1937). Her sensitive depictions of Pomo people complement the ethnological work and Native American baskets collected by her husband, John Hudson.

🎊 Festivals & Events

Redwood Empire Fairs FAIR
(www.redwoodempirefair.com) At the end of July through early August.

Ukiah Country PumpkinFest CULTURAL
(www.cityofukiah.com; 🖶) In late October, with an arts-and-crafts fair, children's carnival and fiddle contest.

🛏 Sleeping

Every imaginable chain resort is here, just off the highway – the best of these is the **Hampton Inn** (☑707-462-6555; hamptoninn3. hilton.com; 1160 Airport Blvd; r $143-209; ❄🖥🛜🏊). For something with more personality, hot-spring resorts and campgrounds cluster around Ukiah.

Discovery Inn Motel MOTEL $
(☑707-462-8873; www.discoveryinnukiahca.com; 1340 N State St; r $51-95; ❄🛜🏊) Clean, but dated with a 75ft pool and several Jacuzzis.

🍴 Eating

It'd be a crime to eat the fast-food junk located off the highway; Ukiah has a burgeoning food scene that pairs nicely with the surrounding wine country.

★Schat's Courthouse Bakery & Cafe CAFE $
(www.schats.com; 113 W Perkins St; lunch mains $3-7, dinner mains $8-14; ☺5:30am-6pm Mon-Fri, to 5pm Sat) Founded by Dutch bakers, Schat's makes a dazzling array of chewy, dense breads, sandwiches, wraps, big salads, delish hot mains, full breakfasts and homemade pastries.

Ukiah Farmers Market MARKET $
(cnr School & Clay Sts; ☺9am-noon Sat) The market offers farm-fresh produce, crafts and entertainment.

Kilkenny Kitchen CAFE $
(www.kilkennykitchen.com; 1093 S Dora St; sandwiches $8; ☺10am-3pm Mon-Fri; 🖋🖶) Tucked into a neighborhood south of downtown, county workers love this chipper yellow place for the fresh rotation of daily soups and sandwich specials (a recent visit on a blazing-hot day found a heavenly, cold cucumber dill soup). The salads – like the pear, walnut and blue cheese – are also fantastic, and there's a kid's menu.

★Saucy PIZZA $$
(☑707-462-7007; 108 W Satandley St; pizzas $11-19; ☺11:30am-9pm Mon-Thu, to 10pm Fri, noon-10pm Sat) Yes there are arty pizzas with toppings like Calabrian love sausage (really), fennel pollen and almond basil pesto but there are also amazing soups, salads,

pastas and starters – Nana's meatballs are to die for and the 'kicking' minestrone lives up to its name. The small-town ambience is slightly chic but also boistrous at the same time.

Oco Time   JAPANESE **$$**
(☑707-462-2422; www.ocotime.com; 111 W Church St; lunch mains $7-10, dinner mains $8-19; ☺11:15am-2:30pm Tue-Fri, 5:30-8:30pm Mon-Sat; ☕) Shoulder your way through the locals to get Ukiah's best sushi, noodle bowls and *oco* (a delicious mess of seaweed, grilled cabbage, egg and noodles). The 'Peace Café' has a great vibe, friendly staff and interesting special rolls. Downside? The place gets mobbed, so reservations are a good idea.

Patrona   NEW AMERICAN **$$**
(☑707-462-9181; www.patronarestaurant.com; 130 W Standley St; lunch mains $10-16, dinner mains $15-34; ☺11am-9pm; ☕) ✿ Foodies flock to excellent Patrona for earthy, flavor-packed, seasonal and regional organic cooking. The unfussy menu includes dishes like roasted chicken, brined-and-roasted pork chops, housemade pasta and local wines. Make reservations and ask about the prix fixe.

Himalayan Cafe   HIMALAYAN **$$**
(www.thehimalayancafe.com; 1639 S State St; curries $15; ☕) South of downtown, find delicately spiced Nepalese cooking – tandoori breads and curries. Some Sundays there's a Nepalese buffet at 4pm.

🍸 Drinking & Entertainment

Ask at the chamber of commerce about cultural events, including **Sunday summer concerts** at Todd Grove Park, which have a delightfully festive atmosphere, and local **square dances**.

Dive bars and scruffy cocktail lounges line State St.

Ukiah Brewing Co   BREWERY
(www.ukiahbrewingco.com; 102 S State St; 📶) ✿ A great place to drink, this local brewpub makes organic beer and draws weekend crowds.

Black Oak Coffee Roasters   CAFE
(476 N State St; lavender lattes from $4; ☺6:30am-6pm) A big modern coffeehouse with some interesting and delicious choices like a local lavender latte or a matcha chia milkshake. Light breakfasts and lunches are also on offer.

ℹ️ Information

Running north–south, west of Hwy 101, State St is Ukiah's main drag. School St, near Perkins St, is also good for strolling.

Bureau of Land Management (☑707-468-4000; 2550 N State St) Maps and information on backcountry camping, hiking and biking in wilderness areas.

Greater Ukiah Chamber of Commerce (☑707-462-4705; www.gomendo.com; 200 S School St; ☺9am-5pm Mon-Fri) One block west of State St; information on Ukiah, Hopland and Anderson Valley.

Around Ukiah

Ukiah Wineries

You'll notice the acres of grapes stretching out in every direction on your way into town. Winemakers around Ukiah enjoy much of the same climatic conditions that made Napa so famous. Pick up a wineries map from the Ukiah chamber of commerce. Tasting fees are generally around $5.

Parducci Wine Cellars   WINERY
(www.parducci.com; 501 Parducci Rd, Ukiah; ☺10am-5pm) ✿ Sustainably grown, harvested and produced, 'America's Greenest Winery' produces affordable, bold, earthy reds. The tasting room, lined in brick and soft light, is a perfect little cave-like environment to get out of the summer heat, sip wine and chat about sustainability practices.

Nelson Family Vineyards   WINERY
(www.nelsonfamilyvineyards.com; 550 Nelson Ranch Rd, Ukiah; ☺10am-5pm; 🅿) Just north of Ukiah, this winery, vineyard, pear, olive and Christmas-tree farm with wondrous views over the valley is a great place to picnic (in a redwood grove), make friends and sip not-too-sweet Chardonnay and luscious red blends.

Vichy Hot Springs Resort

Opened in 1854, Vichy is the oldest continuously operating mineral-springs spa in California. The water's composition perfectly matches that of its famous namesake in Vichy, France. A century ago, Mark Twain, Jack London and Robert Louis Stevenson traveled here for the water's restorative properties, which ameliorate everything from arthritis to poison oak.

Today, the beautifully maintained historic **resort** ($\boxed{\mathbb{Z}}$ 707-462-9515; www.vichysprings.com; 2605 Vichy Springs Rd, Ukiah; lodge s/d $145/205, creekside r $205/255, cottages from $295; ✿ 🎧 🌀) has the only warm-water, naturally carbonated mineral baths in North America. Unlike others, Vichy requires swimsuits (rentals $2). Day use costs $30 for two hours, $50 for a full day.

Facilities include a swimming pool, outdoor mineral hot tub, 10 indoor and outdoor tubs with natural 100°F (38°C) waters, and a grotto for sipping the effervescent waters. Massages and facials are available. Entry includes use of the 700-acre grounds, abutting Bureau of Land Management (BLM) lands; hiking trails lead to a 40ft waterfall, an old cinnabar mine and 1100ft peaks – great for sunset views.

The resort's suite and two cottages, built in 1854, are Mendocino County's three oldest structures. The cozy rooms have wooden floors, top-quality beds, breakfast and spa privileges, and no TVs.

From Hwy 101, exit at Vichy Springs Rd and follow the state-landmark signs east for 3 miles. Ukiah is five minutes, but a world, away.

Orr Hot Springs

A clothing-optional resort that's beloved by locals, back-to-the-land hipsters, backpackers and liberal-minded tourists, **springs** ($\boxed{\mathbb{Z}}$ 707-462-6277; tent sites $50-60, d $150-180, cottages $215-250; 🌀) has private tubs, a sauna, spring-fed rock-bottomed swimming pool, steam, massage and magical gardens. Day use costs $30.

Accommodation includes use of the spa and communal kitchen; some of the rustic cottages have kitchens. Reservations are essential.

To get there from Hwy 101, take the N State St exit, go north a quarter of a mile to Orr Springs Rd, then 9 miles west. The steep, winding mountain road takes 30 minutes to drive.

Montgomery Woods State Reserve

Two miles west of Orr, this 1140-acre **reserve** (Orr Springs Rd) protects five old-growth redwood groves, and some of the best groves within a day's drive from San Francisco. A 2-mile loop trail crosses the creek, winding through the serene groves, starting near the picnic tables and toilets. It's out of the way, so visitors are likely to have it mostly to themselves. Day use only; no camping.

Lake Mendocino

Amid rolling hills, 5 miles northeast of Ukiah, this tranquil 1822-acre artificial lake fills a valley, once the ancestral home of the Pomo people. On the lake's north side, **Pomo Visitor Center** ($\boxed{\mathbb{Z}}$ 707-467-4200) is modeled after a Pomo roundhouse, with exhibits on tribal culture and the dam. The center was closed indefinitely for upgrades at the time of update, but was still offering information via phone about camping.

Coyote Dam, 3500ft long and 160ft high, marks the lake's southwest corner; the lake's eastern part is a 689-acre protected wildlife habitat. The **Army Corps of Engineers** (www.spn.usace.army.mil/mendocino; 1160 Lake Mendocino Dr; ⊘ 8am-4pm Mon-Fri) built the dam, manages the lake and provides recreation information. Its office is inconveniently located on the lower lake.

There are 300 **tent and RV sites** ($\boxed{\mathbb{Z}}$ 877-444-6777; www.reserveusa.com; sites $25-30), most with hot showers and primitive boat-in sites ($8).

City of Ten Thousand Buddhas

Three miles east of Ukiah, via Talmage Rd, the **site** ($\boxed{\mathbb{Z}}$ 707-462-0939; www.cttbusa.org; 2001 Talmage Rd; ⊘ 8am-6pm) used to be a state mental hospital. Since 1976 it has been a lush, quiet 488-acre Chinese-Buddhist community. Don't miss the temple hall, which really does have 10,000 Buddhas. As this is a place of worship, please be respectful of those who use the grounds for meditating. Stay for lunch in the vegetarian Chinese **restaurant** (4951 Bodhi Way; mains $8-12; ⊘ noon-3pm; 🌀).

Willits

Twenty miles north of Ukiah, Willits mixes NorCal dropouts with loggers and ranchers (the high school has a bull-riding team). Lamp posts of the main drag are decorated with bucking broncos and cowboys, but the heart of the place is just as boho. Though ranching, timber and manufacturing may be its mainstays, tie-dye is de rigueur. For visitors, Willits' greatest claim to fame is as the eastern terminus of the Skunk Train. Fort

Bragg is 35 miles away on the coast; allow an hour to navigate twisty Hwy 20.

◉ Sights & Activities

Ten miles north of Willits, Hwy 162/Covelo Rd makes for a superb drive following the route of the Northwestern Pacific Railroad along the Eel River and through the **Mendocino National Forest**. The trip is only about 30 miles, but plan on taking at least an hour on the winding road, passing exquisite river canyons and rolling hills. Eventually, you'll reach **Covelo**, known for its unusual round valley.

Mendocino County Museum   MUSEUM
(www.mendocinomuseum.org; 400 E Commercial St; adult/child $4/1; ◷10am-4:30pm Wed-Sun) Among the best community museums in this half of the state, this puts the lives of early settlers in excellent historical context – much drawn from old letters – and there's an entire 1920s soda fountain and barber shop inside. You could spend an hour perusing Pomo and Yuki basketry and artifacts, or reading about local scandals and countercultural movements.

Outside, the **Roots of Motive Power** (www.rootsofmotivepower.com) exhibit occasionally demonstrates steam logging and machinery.

Ridgewood Ranch   HISTORIC SITE
(☑reservations 707-459-7910; www.seabiscuitheritage.com; 16200 N Hwy 101; tours $20) Willits' most famous resident was the horse Seabiscuit, which grew up here. Ninety-minute tours operate on Monday, Wednesday and Friday (June to September) at 9:30am; three-hour tours for eight or more people are available by reservation and there are other events listed on the website. Reserve-in-advance, docent-led nature tours of the surrounding natural area are free.

Skunk Train   HISTORIC TRAIN
(☑866-866-1690, 707-964-6371; www.skunktrain.com; adult/child $54/34) The depot is on E Commercial St, three blocks east of Hwy 101. Trains run between Willits and Fort Bragg (p212).

Jackson Demonstration State Forest   HIKING
Fifteen miles west of Willits on Hwy 20, the forest offers day-use recreational activities, including educational hiking trails and mountain biking. You can also camp here.

✴ Festivals & Events

Willits Frontier Days & Rodeo   RODEO
(www.willitsfrontierdays.com) Dating from 1926, Willits has the oldest continuous rodeo in California, occurring in the first week in July.

🛏 Sleeping

Some of the in-town motels – and there seems to be about a hundred of them – are dumps, so absolutely check out the room before checking in. Ask about Skunk Train packages. There are a couple crowded, loud RV parks on the edges of town for only the most desperate campers.

Old West Inn   MOTEL $
(☑707-459-4201; www.theoldwestinn.com; 1221 S Main St; r $79; ❋ 🐾 🛜) The facade looks like a mock up of an Old West main street and each room has a theme from the 'Stable' to the 'Barber Shop.' The decor is simple and comfy with just enough imagination to make it interesting. Besides that this is the cleanest, friendliest and most highly recommended place in town.

Jackson Demonstration State Forest   CAMPGROUND $
(☑707-964-5674; campsites $15) Campsites have barbecue pits and pit toilets, but no water. Get a permit from the on-site host, or from a self-registration kiosk.

Baechtel Creek Inn & Spa   BOUTIQUE HOTEL $$
(☑800-459-9911, 707-459-9063; www.baechtelcreekinn.com; 101 Gregory Lane; d incl breakfast $119-159; ❋ 🐾 🛜 ⛲ 🐾) As Willits' only upscale option, this place draws an interesting mix: Japanese bus tours, business travelers and wine trippers. The standard rooms are nothing too flashy, but they have top-notch linens, iPod docks and tasteful art. Custom rooms come with local wine and more space. The immaculate pool and lovely egg breakfast on the patio are perks.

🍴 Eating

Loose Caboose Cafe   SANDWICHES $
(10 Woods St; sandwiches $7-11; ◷7:30am-3pm) People tend to get a bit flushed when talking about the sandwiches at the Loose Caboose, which gets jammed at lunch. The Reuben and Sante Fe Chicken sandwiches are two savory delights.

Aztec Grill   MEXICAN $
(781 S Main St; burritos $5-8; ◷5am-9pm) Yes this is in the Chevron Gas Station but the

unanimous vote from locals is that this is, hands down, the best Mexican food in town. Cheap too.

Mariposa Market ✓ GROCERIES $
(600 S Main St) Willits' natural food outlet.

Ardella's Kitchen AMERICAN $
(35 E Commercial St; mains $5-11; ☺6am-noon Tue-Sat) For quick eats, this tiny place is tops for breakfast – and is *the* place for gossip. Prices are great, portions are big and fresh and there's an infectious, cheery vibe.

Adam's Restaurant MEDITERRANEAN $$$
(☑707-456-9226; 50 S Main St; mains $22-27) Willits' swankiest address is known for its crab cakes and special occasion-worthy mains like big New York steaks, lamb osso boco or bouillabaisse, perhaps finished off with a blueberry crème brûlée. The ambiance is simple and service stellar.

☕ Drinking & Entertainment

Shanachie Pub BAR
(50 S Main St; ☺Mon-Sat) This is a friendly little garden-side dive with tons on tap.

Willits Community Theatre THEATER
(www.willitstheatre.org; 37 W Van Lane) Stages award-winning plays, readings and comedy.

🛍 Shopping

JD Redhouse & Co CLOTHING, HOMEWARES
(212 S Main St; ☺10am-6pm) Family-owned and operated, this central mercantile is a good reflection of Willits itself, balancing cowboy essentials – boots and grain, tools and denim – with treats for the weekend tourist. The Cowlick's counter (with excellent Mendocino-made ice cream) is a good place to cool off when the heat on the sidewalk gets intense.

Book Juggler BOOKS
(182 S Main St; ☺10am-7pm Mon-Thu, to 8pm Fri, to 6pm Sat, noon-5pm Sun) Has dense rows of new and used books, music books and local papers (pick up the weird, locally printed *Anderson Valley Advertiser* here).

SOUTHERN REDWOOD COAST

There's some real magic in the loamy soil and misty air 'beyond the redwood curtain'; it yields the tallest trees and most potent herb on the planet. North of Fort Bragg, Bay Area weekenders and antique-stuffed B&Bs give way to lumber wars, pot farmers and an army of carved bears. The 'growing' culture here is palpable and the huge profit it brings to the region has evident cultural side effects – an omnipresent population of transients who work the harvests, a chilling respect for 'No Trespassing' signs and a political culture that is an uneasy balance between gun-toting libertarians, ultra-left progressives and typical college-town chaos. Nevertheless, the reason to visit is to soak in the magnificent landscape, which runs through a number of pristine, ancient redwood forests.

ℹ Information

Redwood Coast Heritage Trails (www.redwoods.info) Gives a nuanced slant on the region with itineraries based around lighthouses, Native American culture, the timber and rail industries, and maritime life.

Leggett

Leggett marks the redwood country's beginning and Hwy 1's end. There ain't much but a creepy and expensive gas station (cash only), pizza joint and two markets (not always open).

Visit 1000-acre **Standish-Hickey State Recreation Area** (☑707-925-6482; www.parks.ca.gov; 69350 Hwy 101; per car $8; ♿), 1.5 miles to the north, for picnicking, swimming and fishing in the Eel River and hiking trails among virgin and second-growth redwoods. Year-round **campgrounds** (☑800-444-7275; www.reserveamerica.com; tent & RV sites $35) with hot showers book up in summer. Avoid highway-side sites.

Chandelier Drive-Thru Tree Park (www.drivethrutree.com; 67402 Drive Thru Tree Road, Leggett; per car $5; ☺8:30am-9pm; ♿) has 200 private acres of virgin redwoods with picnicking and nature walks. And yes, there's a redwood with a hole carved out, which cars can drive through. Only in America.

The 1949 tourist trap of **Confusion Hill** (www.confusionhill.com; 75001 N Hwy 101; adult/child Gravity House $5/4, train rides $8.50/6.50; ☺9am-6pm May-Sep, 10am-5pm Oct-Apr; ♿) is an enduring curiosity and the most elaborate of the old-fashioned stops that line the route north. The Gravity House challenges queasy visitors to keep their balance while standing at a 40-degree angle (a rad photo

Southern Redwood Coast

(📞 707-925-6444; 69501 Hwy 101; ⏱ 8am-9pm) north of Leggett on Hwy 101.

Richardson Grove State Park

Fifteen miles to the north of Leggett, and bisected by the Eel River, serene **Richardson Grove** (📞 707-247-3318; www.parks.ca.gov; per car $8) occupies 1400 acres of virgin forest. Many trees are over 1000 years old and 300ft tall, but there aren't many hiking trails. In winter, there's good fishing for silver and king salmon. For the last few years, CalTrans has been considering widening the road through Richardson Grove, which has sparked an intense protest.

The **visitor center** (⏱ 9am-2pm) sells books inside a 1930s lodge, which often has a fire going during cool weather. The park is primarily a **campground** (📞 reservations 800-444-7275; www.reserveamerica.com; tent & RV sites $35) with three separate areas with hot showers; some remain open year-round. Summer-only Oak Flat on the east side of the river is shady and has a sandy beach.

Benbow Lake

On the Eel River, 2 miles south of Garberville, the 1200-acre **Benbow Lake State Recreation Area** (📞 summer 707-923-3238, winter 707-923-3318; per car $8) exists when a seasonal dam forms the 26-acre Benbow Lake, mid-June to mid-September. In mid-August avoid swimming in the lake or river until two weeks after the **Reggae on the River** festival, when 25,000 people use the river as a bathtub. The water is cleanest in early summer. You can avoid the day use fee by parking near the bridge and walking down to the river. According to a ranger, you can float from here all the way through the redwood groves along the Avenue of the Giants.

🛏 Sleeping

Campground   CAMPGROUND **$**
(📞 reservations 800-444-7275; www.reserveamerica.com; tent & RV sites $35) The year-round riverside campground is subject to wintertime bridge closures due to flooding. This part of the Eel River has wide banks and is also excellent for swimming and sunbathing.

op). Kids and fans of kitsch go nuts for the playhouse quality of the space and the narrow-gauge train rides are exciting for toddlers.

For basic supplies, a burger and some good Americana visit **Price's Peg House**

★ **Benbow Inn** HISTORIC HOTEL **$$$**
(☎ 707-923-2124, 800-355-3301; www.benbowinn.com; 445 Lake Benbow Dr, Garberville; r $99-315, cottage $230-315; ✲ ☎ ✳ ⚋) This inn is a monument to 1920s rustic elegance; the Redwood Empire's first luxury resort is a national historic landmark. Hollywood's elite once frolicked in the Tudor-style resort's lobby, where you can play chess by the crackling fire, and enjoy complimentary afternoon tea and evening hors d'oeuvres.

Rooms have top-quality beds, antique furniture and crystal sherry decanters (including complimentary sherry). The window-lined **dining room** (breakfast and lunch $10 to $15, dinner mains $22 to $32) serves excellent meals and the rib eye earns raves.

Garberville

The main supply center for southern Humboldt County is the primary jumping-off point for both the Lost Coast, to the west, and the Avenue of the Giants, to the north. There's an uneasy relationship between the old-guard loggers and the hippies, many of whom came in the 1970s to grow sinsemilla (potent, seedless marijuana) after the feds chased them out of Santa Cruz. At last count, the hippies were winning the culture wars, but it rages on: a sign on the door of a local bar reads simply: 'Absolutely NO patchouli oil!!!' Two miles west, Garberville's ragtag sister, Redway, has fewer services. Garberville is about four hours north of San Francisco, one hour south of Eureka.

✵ Festivals & Events

The **Mateel Community Center** (www.mateel.org), in Redway, is the nerve center for many of the area's long-running annual festivals, which celebrate everything from hemp to miming.

Reggae on the River MUSIC
(www.reggaeontheriver.com) In mid-July, this fest draws huge crowds for reggae, world music, arts and craft fairs, camping and swimming in the river.

Avenue of the Giants Marathon MARATHON
(www.theave.org) Among the nation's most picturesque marathons, held in May.

Harley-Davidson
Redwood Run MOTORCYCLE RALLY
(www.redwoodrun.com) The redwoods rumble with the sound of hundreds of shiny bikes in June.

🛏 Sleeping

Garberville is lined with motels and many of them, although serviceable, rent out long-term and can house questionable characters. South of town, Benbow Inn blows away the competition. For cheaper lodging try **Humboldt Redwoods Inn** (☎ 707-923-2451; www.humboldtredwoodsinn.com; 987 Redwood Dr; r $65-110; ✲ ☎ ✳), the least dodgy of the low-budget places.

Riverwood Inn INN **$**
(☎ 707-943-1766; www.riverwoodinn.info; 2828 Avenue of the Giants, Phillipsville; r $80-98; ✲) Six miles north of Garberville is this rockin', vintage 1937, all-American roadhouse with a big bar at the front, an OK Mexican restaurant at the back and simple lodge rooms (some with lovely terraces) downstairs. There's live music most weekend nights when you can get rowdy with the locals and traveling motorbikers then sleep it off downstairs.

✗ Eating & Drinking

Woodrose Café BREAKFAST **$$**
(www.woodrosecafe.com; 911 Redwood Dr; meals $9-16; ⊙ 8am-12pm; ☑ ☖) Garberville's beloved cafe serves organic omelets, veggie scrambles and buckwheat pancakes with *real* maple syrup in a cozy room. Lunch brings crunchy salads, sandwiches with all-natural meats and good burritos. Plenty of gluten-free options.

Cecil's New Orleans Bistro CAJUN **$$$**
(www.cecilsgarberville.com; 733 Redwood Dr; dinner mains $18-28; ⊙ 5-9pm Thu-Mon) This 2nd-story eatery overlooks Main St and serves ambitious dishes that may have minted the California-Cajun style. Start with fried green tomatoes before launching into the smoked boar gumbo. Check the website for music events.

Branding Iron Saloon BAR
(744 Redwood Dr) Craft beer, nice locals and a hopping pool table. We'll forgive the stripper pole in the middle of the room.

❶ Information

Find out what's really happening by tuning in to community radio **KMUD FM91** (www.kmud.org).

(www.garberville.org; 784 Redwood Dr; ⊙10am-4pm May-Aug, Mon-Fri Sep-Apr) Inside the Redwood Drive Center.

Lost Coast

The North Coast's superlative backpacking destination is a rugged, mystifying stretch of coast where narrow dirt trails ascend rugged coastal peaks. Here you'll find volcanic beaches of black sand and ethereal mist hovering above the roaring surf as majestic Roosevelt elk graze the forests. The rugged King Range boldly rises 4000ft within 3 miles of the coast between where Hwy 1 cuts inland north of Westport to just south of Ferndale. The coast became 'lost' when the state's highway system deemed the region impassable in the early 20th century.

The best hiking and camping is within the King Range National Conservation Area and the Sinkyone Wilderness State Park, which make up the central and southern stretch of the region. The area north of the King Range is more accessible, if less dramatic.

In autumn, the weather is clear and cool. Wildflowers bloom from April through May and gray whales migrate from December through April. The warmest, driest months are June to August, but days are foggy. Note that the weather can quickly change.

❶ Information

Aside from a few one-horse villages, Shelter Cove, the isolated unincorporated town 25 long miles west of Garberville, is the only option for services. Get supplies in Garberville, Fort Bragg, Eureka or Arcata. The area is a patchwork of government-owned land and private property; visit the Bureau of Land Management office for information, permits and maps. There are few circuitous routes for hikers, and rangers can advise on reliable (if expensive) shuttle services in the area.

A few words of caution: lots of weed is grown around here and it's wise to stay on trail and respect no trespassing signs, lest you find yourself at the business end of someone's right to bear arms. And pot farmers don't pose the only threat: you'll want to check for ticks (Lyme disease is common) and keep food in bear-proof containers, which are required for camping.

Bureau of Land Management (BLM; ☑707-825-2300, 707-986-5400; 768 Shelter Cove Rd; ⊙8am-4:30pm Mon-Sat Sep-May, 8am-4:30pm Mon-Fri Jun-Aug) Nine miles east of Shelter Cove, the Bureau of Land Management has maps and directions for trails and campsites; they're posted outside after hours.

Sinkyone Wilderness State Park

Named for the Sinkyone people who once lived here, this 7367-acre wilderness extends south of Shelter Cove along pristine coastline. The Lost Coast Trail passes through here for 22 miles, from Whale Gulch south to Usal Beach Campground, taking at least three days to walk as it meanders along high ridges, providing bird's-eye views down to deserted beaches and the crashing surf (side trails descend to water level). Near the park's northern end, you can register at the (haunted!) **Needle Rock Ranch** (☑707-986-7711; tent sites $35) for the adjacent campsites. This is the only source of potable water. For information on when the ranch is closed (most of the time), call Richardson Grove State Park (p226).

To get to Sinkyone, drive west from Garberville and Redway on Briceland-Thorn Rd, 21 miles through Whitethorn to Four Corners. Turn left (south) and continue for 3.5 miles down a very rugged road to the ranch house; it takes 1½ hours.

There's access to the **Usal Beach Campground** (tent sites $25) at the south end of the park from Hwy 1 (you can't make reservations). North of Westport, take the unpaved County Rd 431 beginning from Hwy 1's Mile 90.88 and travel 6 miles up the coast to the campground. The road is graded yearly in late spring and is passable in summer via 2WD vehicles. Most sites are past the message board by the beach. Use bear canisters or keep food in your trunk. Look for giant elk feeding on the tall grass – they live behind sites No 1 and 2 – and osprey by the creek's mouth.

North of the campground, Usal Rd (County Rd 431) is much rougher and recommended only if you have a high-clearance 4WD and a chainsaw. Seriously.

King Range National Conservation Area

Stretching over 35 miles of virgin coastline, with ridge after ridge of mountainous terrain plunging to the surf, the 60,000-acre area tops out at namesake King's Peak (4087ft). The wettest spot in California, the range receives over 120in – and sometimes as much as 240in – of annual rainfall, causing frequent landslides; in winter, snow falls

HIKING THE LOST COAST

The best way to see the Lost Coast is to hike, and the best hiking is through the southern regions within the Sinkyone and Kings Range Wilderness areas. Some of the best trails start from Mattole Campground, just south Petrolia, which is on the northern border of the Kings Range. It's at the ocean end of Lighthouse Rd, 4 miles from Mattole Rd (sometimes marked as Hwy 211), southeast of Petrolia.

Both Wailaki and Nadelos have developed **campgrounds** (tent sites $8) with toilets and water. There are another four developed campgrounds around the range, with toilets but no water (except Honeydew, which has purifiable creek water). There are multiple primitive walk-in sites. You'll need a bear canister and backcountry permit, both available from Bureau of Land Management (BLM) offices.

Lost Coast Trail The Lost Coast Trail follows 24.7 miles of coastline from Mattole Campground in the north to Black Sands Beach at Shelter Cove in the south. The prevailing northerly winds make it best to hike from north to south; plan for three or four days. In October and November, and April and May, the weather is iffy and winds can blow south to north, depending on whether there's a low-pressure system overhead. The best times to come are summer weekdays in early June, at the end of August, September and October. The trail is 'discovered' and will often have hikers; busiest times are Memorial Day, Labor Day and summer weekends. The only reliable shuttle with permits to transport backpackers through the area is pricey **Lost Coast Shuttle** (☑ 707-223-1547; www. lostcoastshuttle.com; 2 people $200-450, extra passenger $25). Transport prices depend on the distance you want to travel.

Highlights include an abandoned lighthouse at Punta Gorda, remnants of early shipwrecks, tidepools and abundant wildlife including sea lions, seals and some 300 bird species. The trail is mostly level, passing beaches and crossing over rocky outcrops. Along the Lost Coast Trail, **Big Flat** is the most popular backcountry destination. Carry a tide table, lest you get trapped: from Buck Creek to Miller Creek, you can only hike during an outgoing tide.

Punta Gorda Lighthouse Hike A good day hike starts at the Mattole Campground trailhead and travels 3 miles south along the coast to the Punta Gorda lighthouse (return against the wind).

Ridgeline Trails To ditch the crowds, take any of the (strenuous) upland trails off the beach toward the ridgeline. For a satisfying, hard, 21-mile-long hike originating at the Lost Coast Trail, take Buck Creek Trail to King Crest Trail to Rattlesnake Ridge Trail. The 360-degree views from **King Peak** are stupendous, particularly with a full moon or during a meteor shower. Note that if you hike up, it can be hellishly hot on the ridges, though the coast remains cool and foggy; wear removable layers. Carry a topographical map and a compass: signage is limited.

on the ridges. (By contrast, nearby sea-level Shelter Cove gets only 69in of rain and no snow.) Two-thirds of the area is awaiting wilderness designation.

See the Bureau of Land Management (BLM; p228) for information. For overnight hikes, you'll need a backcountry-use permit. Don't turn left onto Briceland-Thorn Rd to try to find the 'town' of Whitethorn; it doesn't exist. Whitethorn is the BLM's name for the general area. To reach the BLM office from Garberville/Redway, follow signs to Shelter Cove; look for the roadside information panel, a quarter mile past the post office. Information and permits are also available from the BLM in Arcata (p240).

Fire restrictions begin July 1 and last until the first soaking rain, usually in November. During this time, there are no campfires allowed outside developed campgrounds.

North of the King Range

Though it's less of an adventure, you can reach the Lost Coast's northern section year-round via paved, narrow Mattole Rd. Plan on three hours to navigate the sinuous 68 miles from Ferndale in the north to the coast at Cape Mendocino, then inland to Humboldt

Redwoods State Park (p230) and Hwy 101. Don't expect redwoods; the vegetation is grassland and pasture. It's beautiful in spots – lined with sweeping vistas and wildflowers that are prettiest in spring.

You'll pass two tiny settlements, both 19th-century stage-coach stops. **Petrolia** has an all-in-one **store** (⏺707-629-3455; ⏰9am-5pm) which rents bear canisters and sells supplies for the trail, good beer and gasoline. **Honeydew** also has a **general store**. The drive is enjoyable, but the Lost Coast's wild, spectacular scenery lies further south in the more remote regions.

Shelter Cove

The only sizable community on the Lost Coast, Shelter Cove is surrounded by the King Range National Conservation Area and abuts a large south-facing cove. It's a tiny seaside subdivision with an airstrip in the middle – indeed, many visitors are private pilots. Fifty years ago, Southern California swindlers subdivided the land, built the airstrip and flew in potential investors, fast-talking them into buying seaside land for retirement. But they didn't tell buyers that a steep, winding, one-lane dirt road provided the *only* access and that the seaside plots were eroding into the sea.

Today, there's still only one route, but now it's paved. Cell phones don't work here: this is a good place to disappear. The town, though sleepy and bland, offers surfing (beginners to advanced), sea kayaking, fishing, whale-watching from the shore and fantastic tide pooling; a short drive brings you to the stunning **Black Sands Beach** stretching for miles northward. You can rent surf boards, kayaks, wetsuits and more at the **Lost Coast Surf Shack** (surfboards $25 per day, kayaks half/full-day $45/70; ⏰10:30am-4:30pm).

🛏 Sleeping

Shelter Cove RV Park, Campground & Deli   CAMPGROUND $
(⏺707-986-7474; 492 Machi Rd; tent/RV sites $33/43) The services may be basic, but the fresh gusts of ocean air can't be beat – the deli has good fish and chips.

Oceanfront Inn & Lighthouse   INN $$
(⏺707-986-7002; www.sheltercoveoceanfrontinn. com; 10 Seal Court; r $150-250; 🛜) It looks funky on the outside but the big, bright rooms have phenomenal sea views and are

tidy and modern with microwaves, refrigerators and balconies. Plus **Cove Restaurant** downstairs is the best place to eat in town.

Tides Inn   HOTEL $$
(⏺707-986-7900; www.sheltercovetidesinn.com; 59 Surf Pt; r $165, ste with kitchen $190-380; 🛜) Perched above tidepools teeming with starfish and sea urchins, the squeaky-clean rooms here offer excellent views (go for the mini-suites on the 3rd floor). The suite options are good for families, and kids are greeted warmly by the innkeeper with an activity kit.

Inn of the Lost Coast   INN $$
(⏺888-570-9676, 707-986-7521; www.innofthelost-coast.com; 205 Wave Dr; r $160-250; 🛜🐾) This is the most family-friendly hotel in town with clean rooms with basic cooking facilities, breathtaking ocean views and fireplaces. Downstairs there's a serviceable take-out pizza place and **coffeehouse** as well as ping pong and a hot tub.

Spy Glass Inn   INN $$$
(⏺707-986-4030; www.spyglassinnsheltercove. com; 118 Dolphin Dr; ste $295-335; 🛜) Up on a hill a short walk from town, the relatively new, luxurious suites here all have sea-view Jacuzzi tubs, full kitchens and windows lit up by the expansive shoreline beyond.

🍴 Eating

Shelter Cove General Store   GROCERIES $
(⏺707-986-7733; 7272 Shelter Cove Rd) For those who are self-catering, Shelter Cove General Store is 2 miles beyond town. Get groceries and gasoline here.

Cove Restaurant   AMERICAN $$
(⏺707-986-1197; 10 Seal Ct; mains $8-25; ⏰10am-2pm & 5-9pm Thu-Sun) The first-choice place to eat, Cove has everything from veggie stir-fries to New York steaks.

Humboldt Redwoods State Park & Avenue of the Giants

Don't miss this magical drive through California's largest redwood park, **Humboldt Redwoods State Park** (www.humboldtred-woods.org), which covers 53,000 acres – 17,000 of which are old-growth – and contains some of the world's most magnificent trees. It also boasts three-quarters of the world's tallest 100 trees. Tree huggers take note: these groves rival (and some say surpass) those in Redwood National Park (p243), which is a long drive further north, although the landscapes here are less diverse.

Exit Hwy 101 when you see the 'Avenue of the Giants' sign, take this smaller alternative to the interstate; it's an incredible, 32-mile, two-lane stretch. You'll find free driving guides at roadside signboards at both the avenue's southern entrance, 6 miles north of Garberville, near Phillipsville, and at the northern entrance, south of Scotia, at Pepperwood; there are access points off Hwy 101.

Three miles north, the **California Federation of Women's Clubs Grove** is home to an interesting four-sided hearth designed by renowned San Franciscan architect Julia Morgan in 1931 to commemorate 'the untouched nature of the forest.'

Primeval **Rockefeller Forest**, 4.5 miles west of the avenue via Mattole Rd, appears as it did a century ago. It's the world's largest contiguous old-growth redwood forest, and contains about 20% of all such remaining trees. Walk the 2.5-mile **Big Trees Loop** (note that at the time of research a footbridge had been taken out and you'll have to walk across a fallen tree to cross the river where the trail starts). You quickly walk out of sight of cars and feel like you have fallen into the time of dinosaurs.

In **Founders Grove**, north of the visitor center, the **Dyerville Giant** was knocked over in 1991 by another falling tree. A walk along its gargantuan 370ft length, with its wide trunk towering above, helps you appreciate how huge these ancient trees are.

The park has over 100 miles of trails for hiking, mountain biking and horseback riding. Easy walks include short nature trails in Founders Grove and Rockefeller Forest and **Drury-Chaney Loop Trail** (with berry picking in summer). Challenging treks include popular **Grasshopper Peak Trail**, south of the visitor center, which climbs to the 3379ft fire lookout.

Sleeping & Eating

If you want to stay along the avenue, several towns have simple lodgings of varying calibers and levels of hospitality, but camping at Humboldt Redwoods is by far the best option.

Humboldt Redwoods State Park Campgrounds CAMPGROUND $
(800-444-7275; www.reserveamerica.com; campsites from $35) The park runs three campgrounds, with hot showers, two environmental camps, five trail camps, a hike/bike camp and an equestrian camp. Of the developed spots, **Burlington Campground** is open year-round beside the visitor center and near a number of trailheads. **Hidden Springs Campground**, 5 miles south, and **Albee Creek Campground**, on Mattole Rd past Rockefeller Forest, are open mid-May to early fall.

Miranda Gardens Resort RESORT $$
(707-943-3011; www.mirandagardens.com; 6766 Avenue of the Giants, Miranda; cottages with kitchen $165-300, without kitchen $115-200;) The best indoor stay along the avenue. The slightly rustic cottages have redwood paneling, some with fireplaces, and are spotlessly clean. The grounds – replete with outdoor ping pong and a play area for kids and swaying redwoods – have wholesome appeal for families.

Chimney Tree AMERICAN $
(1111 Avenue of the Giants, Phillipsville; burgers $7-11; 10am-7pm May-Sep) If you're just passing through and want something quick, come here. It raises its own grass-fed beef. Alas, the fries are frozen, but those burgers... mmm-mmm!

Riverbend Cellars WINERY $$
(www.riverbendcellars.com; 12990 Avenue of the Giants, Myers Flat; 11am-5pm) For something a bit posh, pull over here. The El Centauro red – named for Pancho Villa – is an excellent estate-grown blend.

DRIVE-THRU TREES

Three carved-out (but living) redwoods await along Hwy 101, a bizarre holdover from a yesteryear road trip.

➡ **Chandelier Drive-Thru Tree** (p225) Fold in your mirrors and inch forward, then cool off in the über-kitschy gift shop; in Leggett and arguably the best one.

➡ **Shrine Drive-Thru Tree** (13078 Avenue of the Giants, Myers Flat; walk/drive through $3/6; sunrise-sunset;) Look up to the sky as you roll through. The least impressive of the three.

➡ **Tour Thru Tree** (430 Highway 169, Klamath; sunrise-sunset;) Take exit 769 in Klamath, squeeze through a tree and check out an emu.

ℹ Information

Visitor Center (📞 707-946-2263; ⊙ 9am-5pm May-Sep, 10am-4pm Oct-Apr) South of Weott, a volunteer-staffed visitor center shows videos and sells maps.

Scotia

For years, Scotia was California's last 'company town,' entirely owned and operated by the Pacific Lumber Company, which built cookie-cut houses and had an open contempt for long-haired outsiders who liked to get between their saws and the big trees. The company went belly up in 2006, sold the mill to another redwood company and, though the town still has a creepy *Twilight Zone* vibe, you no longer have to operate by the company's posted 'Code of Conduct.'

A history of the town awaits at the **Scotia Museum & Visitor Center** (www.townofscotia.com; cnr Main & Bridge Sts; ⊙ 8am-4:30pm Mon-Fri Jun-Sep), at the town's south end. The museum's **fisheries center** (admission free) is remarkably informative – ironic, considering that logging destroys fish habitats – and houses the largest freshwater aquarium on the North Coast.

There are dingy motels and diners in **Rio Dell** (aka 'Real Dull'), across the river but the best place to stay is Scotia itself at the historic but rather plain **Scotia Inn** (📞 707-764-5338; www.thescotiainn.com; 100 Main St; r $75-150; 📶🐾) with rooms that look like Grandma's house, with lace curtains and flowery wallpaper. Back in the day, Rio Dell is where the debauchery happened: because it wasn't a company town, Rio Dell had bars and hookers. In 1969, the freeway bypassed the town and it withered.

As you drive along Hwy 101 and see what appears to be a never-ending redwood forest, understand that this 'forest' sometimes consists of trees only a few rows deep – called a 'beauty strip' – a carefully crafted illusion for tourists. Most old-growth trees have been cut. **Bay Area Coalition for Headwaters Forest** (www.headwaterspreserve.org) helped preserve over 7000 acres of land with public funds through provisions in a long-negotiated agreement between the Pacific Lumber Company and state and federal agencies.

Up Hwy 101 there's a great pit stop at **Eel River Brewing** (www.eelriverbrewing.com; 1777 Alamar Way; ⊙ 11am-11pm Mon-Sun) where a breezy beer garden and excellent burgers accompany all-organic brews.

Ferndale

The North Coast's most charming town is stuffed with impeccable Victorians – known locally as 'butterfat palaces' because of the dairy wealth that built them. There are so many, in fact, that the entire place is a state and federal historical landmark. Dairy farmers built the town in the 19th century and it's still run by the 'milk mafia': you're not a local till you've lived here 40 years. A stroll down Main St offers a taste of super wholesome, small-town America from galleries to old-world emporiums and soda fountains. Although Ferndale relies on tourism, it has avoided becoming a tourist trap – and has no chain stores. Though a lovely place to spend a summer night, it's dead as a doornail in winter.

◉ Sights

Half a mile from downtown via Bluff St, enjoy short tramps through fields of wildflowers, beside ponds, past redwood groves and eucalyptus trees at 110-acre **Russ Park**. The **cemetery**, also on Bluff St, is amazingly cool with graves dating to the 1800s and expansive views to the ocean. Five miles down Centerville Rd, **Centerville Beach** is one of the few off-leash dog beaches in Humboldt County.

Kinetic Sculpture Museum MUSEUM
(580 Main St; ⊙ 10am-5pm Mon-Sat, noon-4pm Sun; 🎫) This warehouse holds the fanciful, astounding, human-powered contraptions used in the town's annual Kinetic Grand Championship (p238). Shaped like giant fish and UFOs, these colorful piles of junk propel racers over roads, water and marsh in the May event.

Fern Cottage HISTORIC BUILDING
(📞 707-786-4835; www.ferncottage.org; Centerville Rd; group tours per person $10; ⊙ by appointment) This 1866 Carpenter Gothic grew to a 32-room mansion. Only one family ever lived here, so the interior is completely preserved.

✴ Festivals & Events

This wee town has a packed social calendar, especially in the summer. If you're planning a visit, check the events page at www.victorianferndale.com.

Tour of the Unknown Coast BICYCLE RACE
(www.tuccycle.org) A challenging event in May, in which participants in the 100-mile race climb nearly 10,000ft.

Humboldt County Fair FAIR
(www.humboldtcountyfair.org) Held mid-August, the longest-running county fair in California.

Sleeping

Francis Creek Inn MOTEL $
(707-786-9611; www.franciscreekinn.com; 577 Main St; r from $85;) White picket balconies stand in front of this downtown motel, which is family owned and operated (check in at the Red Front convenience store, right around the corner). Rooms are basic, clean and furnished simply; the value is outstanding.

Humboldt County Fairgrounds CAMPGROUND $
(707-786-9511; www.humboldtcountyfair.org; 1250 5th St; tent/RV sites $10/20) Turn west onto Van Ness St and go a few blocks for lawn camping with showers.

Hotel Ivanhoe HISTORIC HOTEL $$
(707-786-9000; www.ivanhoe-hotel.com; 315 Main St; r $95-145;) Ferndale's oldest hostelry opened in 1875. It has four antique-laden rooms and an Old West-style, 2nd-floor gallery, perfect for morning coffee. The adjoining saloon, with dark wood and lots of brass, is an atmospheric place for a nightcap.

Shaw House B&B $$
(800-557-7429, 707-786-9958; www.shawhouse. com; 703 Main St; r $110-159, ste $200-250;) Shaw House, an emblematic 'butterfat palace,' was the first permanent structure in Ferndale, completed by founding father Seth Shaw in 1866. Today, it's California's oldest B&B, set back on extensive grounds. Original details remain, including painted wooden ceilings. Most of the rooms have private entrances, and three have private balconies over a large garden.

Victorian Inn HISTORIC HOTEL $$
(888-589-1808, 707-786-4949; www.victorianvillageinn.com; 400 Ocean Ave; r $105-225;) The bright, sunny rooms inside this venerable, two-story former bank building (1890), are comfortably furnished with thick carpeting, good linens and antiques.

★**Gingerbread Mansion** HISTORIC B&B $$$
(707-786-4000; www.gingerbread-mansion. com; 400 Berding St; r $175-495;) This is the cream of dairyland elegance, an 1898 Queen Anne–Eastlake that's unsurprisingly the town's most photographed building. And the inside is no less extravagant with each room having its own unique (and complex) mix of floral wallpaper, patterned carpeting, grand antique furniture and perhaps a fireplace, wall fresco, stained glass window or Greek statue thrown in for kicks.

Eating

There is an abundance of great places to eat in Ferndale (mostly along Main St) – from pie shops and ice cream to a butcher/deli and chocolate shop – so take this list as a starting point only. A **farmers market** (400 Ocean Ave; 10:30am-2pm Sat May-Oct) has locally grown veggies and locally produced dairy – including the freshest cheese you'll find anywhere.

★**Mario's Lost Coast Cafe** VEGETARIAN, VEGAN $
(468 Main St; sandwiches $7.25; 10am-3:30pm;) Step into Mario's homey kitchen and be blown away. This guy mills his own flour, bakes his own bread and is so passionate and well-versed in all things food that it's no wonder the soups, sandwiches, salads and baked goods are easily the best vegetarian choices north of Fort Bragg. Coffee is on the house. Cash only.

No Brand Burger Stand BURGERS $
(989 Milton St; burgers $7; 11am-5pm) Hiding near the entrance to town by an industrial building, this hole-in-the-wall turns out a juicy jalapeño double cheese burger that ranks easily as the North Coast's best burger. The shakes – so thick your cheeks hurt from pulling on the straw – are about the only other thing on the menu.

Poppa Joe's AMERICAN $
(409 Main St; mains $5-7; 11am-8:30pm Mon-Fri, 6am-noon Sat & Sun) You can't beat the atmosphere at this diner, where trophy heads hang from the wall, the floors slant at a precarious angle and old men play poker all day. The American-style breakfasts are good, too – especially the pancakes.

Entertainment

Ferndale Repertory Theatre THEATER
(707-786-5483; www.ferndale-rep.org; 447 Main St) This top-shelf community company produces excellent contemporary theater in the historic Hart Theatre Building.

🛍 Shopping

Main St is a great place to shop. Look for the handful of secondhand stores selling vintage cowboy boots and used designer jeans at reasonable prices.

Blacksmith Shop & Gallery   METAL GOODS
(☑ 707-786-4216;   www.ferndaleblacksmith.com; 455 & 491 Main St) From wrought-iron art to hand-forged furniture, this is the largest collection of contemporary blacksmithing in America.

Abraxas Jewelry & Leather Goods   JEWELRY
(505 Main St) The pieces of locally forged jewelry here are extremely cool and moderately priced. The back room is filled with tons of hats.

Humboldt Bay National Wildlife Refuge

This pristine **wildlife refuge** (www.fws.gov/humboldtbay) protects wetland habitats for more than 200 species of birds migrating annually along the Pacific Flyway. Between the fall and early spring, when Aleutian geese descend en masse to the area, more than 25,000 geese might be seen in a cackling gaggle outside the visitor center.

The peak season for waterbirds and raptors runs September to March; for black brant geese and migratory shorebirds mid-March to late April. Gulls, terns, cormorants, pelicans, egrets and herons come year-round. Look for harbor seals offshore; bring binoculars. If it's open, drive out South Jetty Rd to the mouth of Humboldt Bay for a stunning perspective.

Pick up a map from the **visitor center** (1020 Ranch Rd; ⊙ 8am-5pm). Exit Hwy 101 at Hookton Rd, 11 miles south of Eureka, turn north along the frontage road, on the freeway's west side. In April look for the **Godwit Days** festival, a celebration of the spring bird migration.

Eureka

One hour north of Garberville, on the edge of the giant Humboldt Bay, lies Eureka, the largest bay north of San Francisco. With strip-mall sprawl surrounding a lovely historic downtown, it wears its role as the county seat a bit clumsily. Despite a diverse and interesting community of artists, writers, pagans and other free-thinkers, Eureka's

wild side slips out only occasionally – the **Redwood Coast Dixieland Jazz Festival** (www.redwoodcoastmusicfestivals.org) is a rollicking festival with events all over town, and **summer concerts** rock out the F Street Pier – but mostly, Eureka goes to bed early. Make for Old Town, a small district with colorful Victorians, good shopping and a revitalized waterfront. For night life head to Eureka's trippy sister up the road, Arcata.

◉ Sights

The free *Eureka Visitors Map*, available at tourist offices, details walking tours and scenic drives, focusing on architecture and history. **Old Town**, along 2nd and 3rd Sts from C St to M St, was once down-and-out, but has been refurbished into a buzzing pedestrian district. The F Street Plaza and Boardwalk run along the waterfront at the foot of F St. **Gallery openings** fall on the first Saturday of every month.

**Blue Ox Millworks &
Historic Park**   HISTORIC BUILDING
(www.blueoxmill.com; adult/child 6-12yr $10/5; ⊙ 9am-4pm Mon-Sat; 🖈) One of only seven of its kind in America, antique tools and mills are used to produce authentic gingerbread trim for Victorian buildings; one-hour self-guided tours take you through the mill and historical buildings, including a blacksmith shop and 19th-century skid camp. Kids love the oxen.

**Romano Gabriel Wooden
Sculpture Garden**   GARDENS
(315 2nd St) The coolest thing to gawk at downtown is this collection of whimsical outsider art that's enclosed by aging glass. For 30 years, wooden characters in Gabriel's front yard delighted locals. After he died in 1977, the city moved the collection here.

Clarke Historical Museum   MUSEUM
(www.clarkemuseum.org; 240 E St; suggested donation $3; ⊙ 11am-4pm Wed-Sat) The best community historical museum on this stretch of the coast houses a set of typically musty relics – needlework hankies and paintings of the area's history-making notables (in this case Ulysses Grant, who was once dismissed from his post at Fort Humboldt for drunkenness). Its best collection is that of intricately woven baskets from local tribes.

Carson Mansion   HISTORIC BUILDING
(143 M St) Of Eureka's fine Victorian buildings the most famous is the ornate 1880s

home of lumber baron William Carson. It took 100 men a full year to build. Today it's a private men's club. The **pink house** opposite, at 202 M St, is an 1884 Queen Anne Victorian designed by the same architects and built as a wedding gift for Carson's son.

Sequoia Park   PARK
(www.sequoiaparkzoo.net; 3414 W St; park free, zoo adult/child $5/3; ⊙zoo 10am-5pm May-Sep, Tue-Sun Oct-Apr; ⊕) A 77-acre old-growth redwood grove is a surprising green gem in the middle of a residential neighborhood. It has biking and hiking trails, a children's playground and picnic areas, and a small **zoo**.

Morris Graves Museum of Art   MUSEUM
(www.humboldtarts.org; 636 F St; admission $5; ⊙noon-5pm Thu-Sun) Across Hwy 101, the excellent museum shows rotating Californian artists and hosts performances inside the 1904 **Carnegie library**, the state's first public library.

Discovery Museum   MUSEUM
(www.discovery-museum.org; 517 3rd St; admission $4; ⊙10am-4pm Tue-Sat, from noon Sun; ⊕) A hands-on kids' museum.

🏃 Activities

Harbor Cruise   CRUISE
(www.humboldtbaymaritimemuseum.com; narrated cruise adult/child $18/10) Board the 1910 *Madaket*, America's oldest continuously operating passenger vessel, and learn the history of Humboldt Bay. Located at the foot of C St, it originally ferried mill workers and passengers until the Samoa Bridge was built in 1972. The $10 sunset cocktail cruise serves from the smallest licensed bar in the state; there's also a 75-minute narrated cruise.

Hum-Boats Sail, Canoe &
Kayak Center   BOAT RENTAL
(www.humboats.com; Startare Dr; ⊙9am-5pm Mon-Fri, to 6pm Sat & Sun Apr-Oct, to 2:30pm Nov-Mar) At Woodley Island Marina, this outfit rents kayaks and sailboats, offering lessons, tours, charters, sunset sails and full-moon paddles.

🛏 Sleeping

Every brand of chain hotel is along Hwy 101. Room rates run high midsummer; you can sometimes find cheaper in Arcata, to the north, or Fortuna, to the south. There are also a handful of motels which cost from $55 to $100 and have no air-conditioning; choose places set back from the road. The cheapest are south of downtown on the suburban strip.

Abigail's Elegant Victorian Mansion   INN $$
(☑707-444-3144; www.eureka-california.com; 1406 C St; r $115-145; ☎) Inside this National Historic Landmark that's practically a living-history museum, the sweet-as-could-be innkeepers lavish guests with warm hospitality.

Eureka Inn   HISTORIC HOTEL $$
(☑877-552-3985, 707-497-6903; www.eurekainn. com; cnr 7th & F Sts; r from $109; ☎) This magestic and enormous historic hotel is slowly being renovated. The style is cozy, in an early-20th-century-lodger, vagely Wild West sort of way. The staff are extremely friendly and there's a decent bar and restaurant on the premises.

Bayview Motel   MOTEL $$
(☑866-725-6813, 707-442-1673; www.bayviewmotel.com; 2844 Fairfield St; r $94-175; ☎🐾) Spotless rooms are of the chain-motel standard; some have patios overlooking Humboldt Bay.

Eagle House Inn   HISTORIC INN $$
(☑707-444-3344; www.eaglehouseinn.com; 139 2nd St; r $105-250; ☎) This hulking Victorian hotel in Old Town has 24 rooms above a turn-of-the-century ballroom that's used for everything from theater and movie performances to special events. Rooms and common areas are tastefully done with precious period decor. The coolest rooms are in the corner and have sitting areas in turrets looking over the street.

Daly Inn   B&B $$
(☑800-321-9656, 707-445-3638; www.dalyinn. com; 1125 H St; r with bath $170-185, without bath $130) This impeccably maintained 1905 Colonial Revival mansion has individually decorated rooms with turn-of-the-20th-century European and American antiques. Guest parlors are trimmed with rare woods; outside are century-old flowering trees.

Carter House Inns   B&B $$$
(☑800-404-1390, 707-444-8062; http://carter-house.com; 301 L St, Eureka; r incl breakfast $179-385; ☎🐾) Recently constructed in period style, this hotel is a Victorian lookalike, holding rooms with top-quality linens and modern amenities; suites have in-room Jacuzzis and marble fireplaces. The same owners operate three sumptuously decorated houses: a single-level 1900 house, a honeymoon-

hideaway cottage and a replica of an 1880s San Francisco mansion, which the owner built himself, entirely by hand.

Unlike elsewhere, you won't see the innkeeper unless you want to. Guests have an in-room breakfast or can eat at the understated, elegant restaurant.

Eating

Eureka is blessed with two excellent natural food grocery stores – **Eureka Co-op** (cnr 5th & L Sts) and **Eureka Natural Foods** (1626 Broadway) – and two weekly **farmers markets** (cnr 2nd & F Sts; ⊗10am-1pm Tue Jun-Oct) and the **Henderson Center** (⊗10am-1pm Thu Jun-Oct). The vibrant dining scene is focused in the Old Town district.

Ramone's BAKERY, DELI $
(2223 Harrison St; mains $6-10; ⊗7am-6pm Mon-Sat, 8am-4pm Sun) For grab-and-go sandwiches, fresh soups and wraps.

★**Brick & Fire** CALIFORNIAN $$
(☑707-268-8959; 1630 F St; pizzas from $14, mains $15-25; ⊗11:30am-8:30pm Mon, Wed & Thu, 11:30am-9pm Fri, 5-9pm Sat & Sun) Eureka's best restaurant is in an intimate, warm-hued, bohemian-tinged setting that is almost always busy. Choose from thin-crust pizzas, delicious salads (try the pear and blue cheese) and an ever-changing selection of appetizers and mains that highlight local produce and wild mushrooms. There's a weighty wine list and servers are well-versed in pairings.

Kyoto JAPANESE $$
(☑707-443-7777; 320 F St; sushi $4-6, mains $15-27; ⊗11:30am-3pm & 5:30-9:30pm Wed-Sat) Renowned as the best sushi in Humboldt County, dine in a tiny, packed room, where conversation with the neighboring table is inevitable. A menu of sushi and sashimi is rounded out by grilled scallops and fern-tip salad. North Coast travelers who absolutely need sushi should phone ahead for a reservation.

Waterfront Café Oyster Bar SEAFOOD $$
(102 F St; lunch $8-17, dinner $15-24; ⊗9am-9pm) With a nice bay view and baskets of steamed clams, fish and chips, oysters and chowder, this is a solid bayside lunch for the atmosphere more than anything. A top spot for Sunday brunch, with jazz and Ramos fizzes.

Restaurant 301 CALIFORNIAN $$$
(☑800-404-1390; www.carterhouse.com; 301 L St; dinner mains $23-32; ⊗6-9pm) Eureka's top

table, romantic, sophisticated 301 serves a contemporary Californian menu, using produce from its organic gardens (tours available). Mains are pricey, but the prix-fixe menu is a good way to taste local food in its finest presentation. The eight-course Chef's Grand Menu ($96) is only worthy of *really* special occasions.

Drinking & Nightlife

Lost Coast Brewery BREWERY
(☑707-445-4480; 617 4th St; 10 tasters for $12; ⊗11am-10pm Sun-Thu, to 11pm Fri & Sat; ☏) The roster of the regular brews at Eureka's colorful brewery might not knock the socks off a serious beer snob (and can't hold a candle to some of the others on the coast), but highlights include the Downtown Brown Ale, Great White and Lost Coast Pale Ale. After downing a few pints, the fried pub grub starts to look pretty tasty.

2 Doors Down WINE BAR
(1626 F St; glass/bottle from $5/19; ⊗4:40-9:30pm Wed-Mon) Wonderfully cozy and inviting, this Victorian-feeling wine bar lets you create your own flights and will open any bottle on their list of 80 plus wines if you're getting two or more glasses from it. Plenty of snacks are available or order from Brick & Fire (p236) next door.

Shanty DIVE BAR
(213 2nd St; ⊗noon-2am; ☏) The coolest spot in town is grungy and fun. Play pool, Donkey Kong, Ms Pac Man or ping pong, or kick it on the back patio with local 20- and 30-something hipsters.

Old Town Coffee & Chocolates CAFE
(211 F St; ⊗7am-9pm) You'll smell roasting coffee blocks before you see this place. It's a local hang out with plenty of tables, baked goods and a board where you can give a cup of whatever to your favorite regular.

Entertainment

For gay events, log onto www.queerhumboldt.com.

Morris Graves
Museum of Art PERFORMING ARTS
(www.humboldtarts.org; 636 F St; suggested donation $4; ⊗noon-5pm Thu-Sun) Hosts performing-arts events between September and May, usually on Saturday evenings and Sunday afternoons.

The Alibi   CLUB
(www.thealibi.com; 744 9th St) Live music on
Wednesdays and Saturdays.

🔒 Shopping

Eureka's streets lie on a grid; numbered
streets cross lettered streets. For the best
window shopping, head to the 300, 400 and
500 blocks of 2nd St, between D and G Sts.
The town's low rents and cool old spaces
harbor lots of indie boutiques.

Shipwreck   VINTAGE
(430 3rd St; ⊙10am-6pm Mon-Fri, noon-5pm Sun)
The quality of vintage goods here – *genuinely* distressed jeans and leather jackets,
1940s housedresses and hats – is compli-
mented by handmade local jewelry and paper products.

Going Places   BOOKS
(328 2nd St; ⊙10:30am-5:30pm Mon-Sat, 11am-
5pm Sun) Guidebooks, travel gear and international goods are certain to give a thrill
to any vagabond. It's one of three excellent
bookshops in Old Town.

ⓘ Information

Eureka Chamber of Commerce (☑800-356-
6381, 707-442-3738; www.eurekachamber.
com, 2112 Broadway; ⊙8:30am-5pm Mon-Fri;
🛜) The main visitor information center is on
Hwy 101.

Six Rivers National Forest Headquarters
(☑707-442-1721; 1330 Bayshore Way; ⊙8am-
4:30pm Mon-Fri) Maps and information.

ⓘ Getting There & Around

The Arcata/Eureka Airport (ACV) is a small,
expensive airport which connects regionally. The
Greyhound station is in Arcata.

Eureka Transit Service (☑707-443-0826;
www.eurekatransit.org) operates local buses
($1.70), Monday to Saturday.

Samoa Peninsula

Grassy dunes and windswept beaches extend along the half-mile-wide, 7-mile long
Samoa Peninsula, Humboldt Bay's western
boundary. Stretches of it are spectacular,
particularly the dunes, which are part of a
34-mile-long dune system – the largest in
Northern California – and the wildlife viewing is excellent. The shoreline road (Hwy
255) is a backdoor route between Arcata and
Eureka.

At the peninsula's south end, **Samoa
Dunes Recreation Area** (⊙sunrise-sunset) is
good for picnicking and fishing. For wildlife,
head to **Mad River Slough & Dunes**; from
Arcata, take Samoa Blvd west for 3 miles,
then turn right at Young St, the Manila turnoff. Park at the community center lot, from
where a trail passes mudflats, salt marsh
and tidal channels. There are over 200 species of birds: migrating waterfowl in spring
and fall, songbirds in spring and summer,
shorebirds in fall and winter, and waders
year-round.

These undisturbed dunes reach heights of
over 80ft. Because of the environment's fra-
gility, access is by guided tour only. **Friends
of the Dunes** (www.friendsofthedunes.org)
leads free guided walks; register via email
through the website and check online for
departure locations and information.

The lunch place on the peninsula is the
Samoa Cookhouse (☑707-442-1659; www.sa-
moacookhouse.net; 908 Vance Ave; breakfast $12,
lunch $13, dinner $16; ⊙7am-3pm & 5-8pm; 🛗),
the last surviving lumber camp cookhouse
in the West, where you can shovel down
all-you-can-eat meals at long red-checkered
tables. Kids eat for half-price. The cookhouse is five minutes northwest of Eureka,
across the Samoa Bridge, follow the signs.
From Arcata, take Samoa Blvd (Hwy 255).

Arcata

The North Coast's most progressive town,
Arcata surrounds a tidy central square that
fills with college students, campers, tran-
sients and tourists. Sure, it occasionally
reeks of patchouli and its politics lean far
left, but its earnest embrace of sustainability
has fostered some of the most progressive
civic action in America. Here, garbage trucks
run on biodiesel, recycling gets picked up
by tandem bicycle, wastewater gets filtered
clean in marshlands and almost every street
has a bike lane.

Founded in 1850 as a base for lumber
camps, today Arcata is defined as a magnet for 20-somethings looking to expand
their minds: either at Humboldt State University (HSU), and/or on the highly potent
marijuana which grows around here like,
um, weeds. After a 1996 state proposition
legalized marijuana for medical purposes,
Arcata became what one *New Yorker* article
referred to as the 'heartland of high grade

marijuana.' The economy of the regions has become inexorably tied to the crop since.

Roads run on a grid, with numbered streets traveling east–west and lettered streets going north–south. G and H Sts run north and south (respectively) to HSU and Hwy 101. The plaza is bordered by G and H and 8th and 9th Sts.

◉ Sights

Around **Arcata Plaza** are two National Historic Landmarks: the 1857 **Jacoby's Storehouse** (cnr H & 8th Sts) and the 1915 **Hotel Arcata** (cnr G & 9th Sts). Another great historic building is the 1914 **Minor Theatre** (1013 10th St), which some local historians claim is the oldest theater in the US built specifically for showing films.

Humboldt State University UNIVERSITY
(HSU; www.humboldt.edu; 1 Harpst St) The University on the northeastern side of town holds the Campus Center for Appropriate Technology (CCAT), a world leader in developing sustainable technologies; on Fridays at 2pm you can take a self-guided tour of the **CCAT House**, a converted residence that uses only 4% of the energy of a comparably sized dwelling.

Arcata Marsh & Wildlife Sanctuary WILDLIFE RESERVE
On the shores of Humboldt Bay, this has 5 miles of walking trails and outstanding birding. The **Redwood Region Audubon Society** (🖉826 7031; www.rras.org; donation welcome) offers guided walks Saturdays at 8:30am, rain or shine, from the parking lot at I St's south end. Friends of Arcata Marsh offer guided tours Saturdays at 2pm from the **Arcata Marsh Interpretive Center** (🖉707-826-2359; 569 South G St; tours free; ◉9am-5pm).

🏃 Activities

Finnish Country Sauna & Tubs DAY SPA, MASSAGE
(🖉707-822-2228; http://cafemokkaarcata.com; cnr 5th & J Sts; 30min per adult/child $9.50/2; ◉noon-11pm Sun-Thu, to 1am Fri & Sat) Like some kind of Euro-crunchy bohemian dream, these private, open-air redwood hot tubs (half-hour/hour $9/17) and sauna are situated around a small frog pond. The staff is easygoing, and the facility is relaxing, simple and clean. Reserve ahead, especially on weekends.

HSU Center Activities OUTDOORS
(www.humboldt.edu/centeractivities) An office on the 2nd floor of the University Center, beside the campus clock tower, sponsors myriad workshops, outings and sporting-gear rentals; nonstudents welcome.

Arcata Community Pool SWIMMING
(ww.arcatapool.com; 1150 16th St; adult/child $7/4.50; ◉5:30am-9pm Mon-Fri, 9am-6pm Sat, 1-4pm Sun; 🛋) Has a co-ed hot tub, sauna and exercise room.

Adventure's Edge OUTDOORS
(www.adventuresedge.com; 650 10th St; ◉9am-6pm Mon-Sat, 10am-5pm Sun) Rents, sells and services outdoor equipment.

🎊 Festivals & Events

Kinetic Grand Championship RACE
(www.kineticgrandchampionship.com) Arcata's most famous event is held Memorial Day weekend: people on amazing self-propelled contraptions travel 38 miles from Arcata to Ferndale.

Arcata Bay Oyster Festival FOOD
(www.oysterfestival.net) A magical celebration of oysters and beer happens in June.

North Country Fair FAIR
(www.sameoldpeopl.org) A fun September street fair, where bands with names like the Fickle Hillbillies jam.

🛏 Sleeping

Arcata has affordable but limited lodgings. A cluster of hotels – Comfort Inn, Hampton Inn, etc – is just north of town, off Hwy 101's Giuntoli Lane. There's cheap camping further north at Clam Beach.

Fairwinds Motel MOTEL $
(🖉707-822-4824; www.fairwindsmotelarcata.com; 1674 G St; s $70-75, d $80-90; 🛜) Serviceable rooms in a standard-issue motel, with some noise from Hwy 101. It's more expensive than the chain motels but has the advantage of being in town.

Hotel Arcata HISTORIC HOTEL $$
(🖉707-826-0217; www.hotelarcata.com; 708 9th St; r $89-156; 🛜) Anchoring the plaza, this renovated 1915 brick landmark has friendly staff, high ceilings and comfortable, old-world rooms of mixed quality. The rooms in front are an excellent perch for people-watching on the square, but the quietest face the back.

Lady Anne Inn   B&B $$
(☎707-822-2797; www.ladyanneinn.com; 902 14th
St; r $115-140) Roses line the walkway to this
1888 mansion full of Victorian bric-a-brac.
The frilly rooms are pretty, but there's no
breakfast.

Arcata Stay   VACATION RENTALS $$
(☎877-822-0935, 707-822-0935; www.arcatastay.
com; apt from $169) A network of excellent
apartment and cottage rentals. There is a
two-night minimum and prices go down the
longer you stay.

✗ Eating

Great food abounds in restaurants throughout Arcata, almost all casual.

There are fantastic **farmers markets**, at
the **Arcata Plaza** (⊘9am-2pm Sat Apr-Nov)
and in the parking lot of Wildberries Market. Just a few blocks north of downtown,
there is a cluster of the town's best restaurants on G St.

Wildberries Marketplace   MARKET, DELI $
(www.wildberries.com; 747 13th St, Arcata; sandwiches $4-10; ⊘6am-midnight; 🖉) Wildberries
Marketplace is Arcata's best grocery, with
natural foods, a good deli, bakery and juice
bar.

North Coast Co-op   GROCERIES $
(cnr 8th & I Sts; ⊘6am-9pm) The gigantic North
Coast Co-op carries organic foods and is a
community staple; check the kiosk out front.

Japhy's Soup & Noodles   NOODLES $
(1563 G St; mains $5-9; ⊘11:30am-8pm Mon-Fri)
Big salads, tasty coconut curry, cold noodle
salads and homemade soups – and cheap!

Stars Hamburgers   BURGERS $
(1535 G St; burgers $3-6; ⊘11am-8pm Mon-Thu,
to 9pm Fri, to 7pm Sat, noon-6pm Sun; 🖪) Uses
grass-fed beef to make fantastic burgers.

Los Bagels   BAGELS $
(1061 I St; bagels from $3.75; ⊘6:30am-5pm
Mon-Fri, 7am-5pm Sat, 7am-3pm Sun) Mixing
'traditional Jewish food with the taste of
Mexico.' Get all kinds of creative spreads and
toppings on fresh bagels. Locals swear the
Swedish dill sauce served here (from Trinidad's Larrapin Restaurant) is one of the best
things on earth.

Don's Donuts   FAST FOOD $
(933 H St; donuts 80¢-$1.35, sandwiches from $6;
⊘24hr) Tasty Southeast Asian sandwiches
and doughnuts, even at 3am.

Arcata Scoop   ICE CREAM $
(1068 I St; cones from $3.50; ⊘12-10:30pm)
Creamy and wonderful flavors inspired by
seasonal ingredients. Try the honey vanilla
lavender. These are the same folks who run
the ever-popular Fairfax Scoop in Marin
County, California.

★**3 Foods Cafe**   FUSION $$
(www.cafeattheendoftheuniverse.com; 835 J St;
dishes $4-14; ⊘5:30am-10pm Tue-Thu, to 11pm Fri
& Sat, to 9pm Sun; 🖉) A perfect fit with the
Arcata dining scene: whimsical, creative,
worldly small plates (think Thai-style tacos
or buttermilk fried chicken) at moderate
prices (a prix fixe is sometimes available for
$20). The lavender-infused cocktails start
things off on the right foot. The 'uber' mac
and cheese is the crowd favorite.

Wildflower Cafe & Bakery   CAFE $$
(☎707-822-0360; 1604 G St; breakfast & lunch
$5-8, dinner mains $15-16; ⊘8am-8pm Sun-Wed;
🖉) Tops for vegetarians, this tiny storefront
serves fab frittatas, pancakes and curries,
and big crunchy salads.

Machine Works   CALIFORNIAN $$
(937 10th St; mains $10-20; ⊘5-10pm Mon-Sun,
10am-2pm Sat & Sun) Inside the Robert Good-
man Winery, this place gets raves from lo-
cals for its brunch (think: crab Benedict or

eggs baked in chèvre mousse) and dinner fare from a killer French onion soup to burgers and hoisin-braised short ribs. It's also a fab spot for creative cocktails.

Folie Douce   MODERN AMERICAN **$$$**
(☑ 707-822-1042; www.foliedoucearcata.com; 1551 G St; dinner mains $24-37; ⊙ 5:30-9pm Tue-Thu, to 10pm Fri & Sat; ☑) ✐ Just a slip of a place, but with an enormous reputation. The short but inventive menu features seasonally inspired bistro cooking, from Asian to Mediterranean, with an emphasis on local organics. Wood-fired pizzas ($16 to $22) are renowned. Sunday brunch, too. Reservations essential.

🍸 Drinking & Nightlife

Dive bars and cocktail lounges line the plaza's northern side. Arcata is awash in coffeehouses and brewpubs.

★ Six Rivers Brewery   BREWERY
(www.sixriversbrewery.com; 1300 Central Ave, McKinleyville; ⊙ 11:30am-midnight Tue-Sun, from 4pm Mon) One of the first female-owned breweries in California, the 'brew with a view' kills it in every category: great beer, amazing community vibe, occasional live music and delicious hot wings. The spicy chili-pepper ale is amazing. At first glance the menu might seem like ho-hum pub grub (mains $11 to $18), but portions are fresh and huge. They also make a helluva pizza.

Redwood Curtain Brewery   BREWERY
(550 S G St, suite 6; ⊙ 3-11pm Mon-Fri, 12-11pm Sat & Sun) A newer brewery (started in 2010), this tiny gem has a varied collection of rave-worthy craft ales and live music most Thursdays and Saturdays. Plus they offer free wheat thins and goldfish crackers to munch on.

Humboldt Brews   BAR
(www.humbrews.com; 856 10th St) This popular beer house has been elegantly remodeled and has a huge selection of carefully selected beer taps, fish tacos and buffalo wings (pub grub $5 to $10). Live music nightly.

Cafe Mokka   CAFE
(www.cafemokkaarcata.com; cnr 5th & J Sts) Bohos head to this cafe at Finnish Country Sauna & Tubs (p238) for a mellow, old-world vibe, good coffee drinks and homemade cookies (snacks $4).

☆ Entertainment

Arcata Theatre   CINEMA
(www.arcatatheater.com; 1036 G St) An exquisite remodeling has revived this classic movie house, which shows art films, rock documentaries, silent films and more. Serves beer.

Center Arts   PERFORMING ARTS
(☑ tickets 707-826-3928; www.humboldt.edu/centerarts) Hosts events on campus and you'd be amazed at who shows up: from Diana Krall and Dave Brubeck to Ani DiFranco. The place to buy tickets is at the University Ticket Office in the HSU Bookstore on the 3rd floor of the University Center.

🛍 Shopping

Tin Can Mailman   BOOKS
(www.tincanbooks.com; 1000 H St) Used volumes on two floors; excellent for hard-to-find books.

ℹ Information

Arcata Eye (www.arcataeye.com) Free newspaper listing local events; the 'Police Log' column is hysterical.

Bureau of Land Management (BLM; ☑ 707-825-2300; 1695 Heindon Rd) Has information on the Lost Coast.

California Welcome Center (☑ 707-822-3619; www.arcatachamber.com; ⊙ 9am-5pm) At the junction of Hwys 299 and 101 is a California Welcome Center, with area info.

ℹ Getting There & Around

United (www.united.com) makes regional connections (which are predictably expensive) to the Arcata/Eureka Airport.

Greyhound (www.greyhound.com) serves Arcata; from San Francisco budget $57 and seven hours. **Redwood Transit buses** (www.hta.org) serve Arcata and Eureka on the Trinidad–Scotia routes ($3, 2½ hours), which don't run on Sunday.

Arcata city buses (☑ 707-822-3775; ⊙ Mon-Sat) stop at the **Arcata Transit Center** (☑ 707-825-8934; 925 E St at 9th St). For shared rides, read the bulletin board at the North Coast Co-op (p239).

Revolution Bicycle (www.revolutionbicycle.com; 1360 G St) and **Life Cycle Bike Shop** (www.lifecyclearcata.com; 1593 G St; ⊙ Mon-Sat) rent, service and sell bicycles.

Only in Arcata: borrow a bike from **Library Bike** (www.arcata.com/greenbikes; 865 8th St) for a $20 deposit, which gets refunded when you return the bike – up to six months later! They're beaters, but they ride.

NORTHERN REDWOOD COAST

Congratulations, traveler, you've reached the middle of nowhere, or at least the top of the middle of nowhere. Here, the trees are so large that the tiny towns along the road seem even smaller. The scenery is pure drama: cliffs and rocks, native lore, legendary salmon runs, mammoth trees, redneck towns and RVing retirees. It's certainly the *weirdest* part of the California Coast. Leave time to dawdle and bask in the haunting grandeur of it all and, even though there are scores of mid-century motels, you simply must make an effort to sleep outdoors if possible.

Trinidad

Cheery, tiny Trinidad perches prettily on the side of the ocean, combining upscale homes with a mellow surfer vibe. Somehow it feels a bit off-the-beaten-path even though tourism augments fishing to keep the economy going. Trinidad gained its name when Spanish sea captains arrived on Trinity Sunday in 1775 and named the area La Santisima Trinidad (the Holy Trinity). It didn't boom, though, until the 1850s, when it became an important port for miners.

◉ Sights & Activities

Trinidad is small: approach via Hwy 101 or from the north via Patrick's Point Dr (which becomes Scenic Dr further south). To reach town, take Main St.

The free town map at the information kiosk (p243) shows several fantastic hiking trails, most notably the **Trinidad Head Trail** with superb coastal views; excellent for **whale-watching** (December to April). Stroll along an exceptionally beautiful cove at **Trinidad State Beach**; take Main St and bear right at Stagecoach, then take the second turn left (the first is a picnic area) into the small lot.

Scenic Dr twists south along coastal bluffs, passing tiny coves with views back toward the bay. It peters out before reaching the broad expanses of **Luffenholtz Beach** (accessible via the staircase) and serene white-sand **Moonstone Beach**. Exit Hwy 101 at 6th Ave/Westhaven to get there. Further south Moonstone becomes **Clam Beach County Park**.

Surfing is good year-round, but potentially dangerous: unless you know how to judge conditions and get yourself out of trouble – there are no lifeguards here – surf in better-protected Crescent City.

HSU Telonicher Marine Laboratory AQUARIUM
(☑707-826-3671; www.humboldt.edu/marinelab; 570 Ewing St; self-guided tours $1; ⊙9am-4:30pm Mon-Fri, 10am-5pm Sat & Sun mid-Sep–mid-May; 🅿) Near Edwards St, this marine lab has a touch tank, several aquariums (look for the giant Pacific octopus), an enormous whale jaw and a cool 3D map of the ocean floor. You can also join a naturalist on **tidepooling expeditions** (90 minutes, $3). All tours are by appointment only so call ahead and be sure to ask about conditions.

🛏 Sleeping

Many of the inns line Patrick's Point Dr, north of town. **Trinidad Retreats** (www.trinidadretreats.com) and **Redwood Coast Vacation Rentals** (www.redwoodcoastvacationrentals.com) handle local property rentals.

Clam Beach CAMPGROUND $
(tent sites per car $15) South of town off Hwy 101, this beach has excellent camping, but can get very crowded and it's a favorite with traveling homeless folks. Pitch your tent in the dunes (look for natural windbreaks). Facilities include pit toilets, cold water, picnic tables and fire rings.

View Crest Lodge LODGE $$
(☑707-677-3393; www.viewcrestlodge.com; 3415 Patrick's Point Dr; sites $27, 1-bedroom cottages $95-240; 🐾) On a hill above the ocean on the inland side, some of the well-maintained, modern and terrific-value cottages have views and Jacuzzis; most have kitchens. There's also a good campground.

Trinidad Inn INN $$
(☑707-677-3349; www.trinidadinn.com; 1170 Patrick's Point Dr; r $75-195; 🐾🅿) Sparklingly clean and attractively decorated rooms (many with kitchens) fill this upmarket, gray-shingled motel under tall trees. Most rooms have fully equipped kitchens.

★**Trinidad Bay B&B** B&B $$$
(☑707-677-0840; www.trinidadbaybnb.com; 560 Edwards St; r incl breakfast $200-300; 🐾) Opposite the lighthouse, this gorgeous light-filled Cape Cod–style place overlooks the harbor

Northern Redwood Coast

and Trinidad Head. Breakfast is delivered to your uniquely styled room and in the afternoon the house fills with the scent of freshly baked cookies. The Trinity Alps room has a kitchenette and is well-set up for families.

Lost Whale Inn B&B $$$
(☎707-677-3425; www.lostwhaleinn.com; 3452 Patrick's Point Dr; r incl breakfast $199-325, ste $408-750; ☎) Perched atop a grassy cliff, high above crashing waves and braying sea lions, this spacious, modern, light-filled B&B has jaw-dropping views out to the sea. The lovely gardens have a 24-hour hot tub. Kids under seven are not permitted.

Turtle Rocks Oceanfront Inn B&B $$$
(☎707-677-3707; www.turtlerocksinn.com; 3392 Patrick's Point Dr; r incl breakfast $195-335) Enjoy truly stunning sea vistas from every room at this plush, modern place on three peaceful, windswept acres.

🍴 Eating & Drinking

Lighthouse Café FAST FOOD $
(☎707-677-0390; 355 Main St; mains $6-9; ⏰11am-7pm Tue-Sun; 🅿) 🍴 Across from the Chevron, this fun little arty joint makes good food fast, using mostly organic ingredients – try the creative soups, fish and chips with hand-cut fries, local grass-fed beef burgers and homemade ice creams. Order at the counter and then sit inside or out.

Katy's Smokehouse & Fishmarket SEAFOOD $
(www.katyssmokehouse.com; 740 Edwards St; ⏰9am-6pm) 🍴 Makes its own chemical-free and amazingly delicious smoked and canned fish, using line-caught sushi-grade seafood. There's no restaurant, just grab some for a picnic.

The Seascape SEAFOOD $$
(1 Bay St; mains $12-35; ⏰7am-8:30pm) Go to this old-school, diner-type place for a panoramic view of the sea more than the food. It's a lovely spot to watch the daily catch come in over a slice of pie or a bowl of yummy clam chowder.

Larrupin Cafe CALIFORNIAN $$$
(☎707-677-0230; www.larrupin.com; 1658 Patrick's Point Dr; mains $20-37; ⏰5-9pm) Everybody loves Larrupin, where Moroccan rugs, chocolate-brown walls, gravity-defying floral arrangements and deep-burgundy Oriental carpets create a moody atmosphere perfect for a lovers' tryst. On the menu expect consistently good mesquite-grilled seafood and

meats – the smoked beef brisket is amazing. In the summer book a table on the garden patio for live music Wednesday and Friday nights.

Moonstone Grill SEAFOOD $$$
(Moonstone Beach; mains $20-90; ⊙5:30-8:30pm Wed-Sun) Enjoy drop-dead sunset views over a picture-perfect beach while supping on the likes of oysters on the half-shell, Pacific wild king salmon or spice-rubbed rib eye. If the high price tag is a bit out-of-budget, drop in for a glass of wine.

Beachcomber Café CAFE
(☑707-677-0106; 363 Trinity St; ⊙7am-4pm Mon-Fri, 8am-4pm Sat & Sun) Head here for the best homemade cookies and to meet locals. Bring your own cup if you want a drink to go. Friday rocks live music and beer's on tap.

❶ Information

Information Kiosk (cnr Patrick's Point Dr & Main St) Just west of the freeway. The pamphlet *Discover Trinidad* has an excellent map.

Trinidad Chamber of Commerce (☑707-667-1610; www.trinidadcalif.com) Information on the web, but no visitor center.

Patrick's Point State Park

Coastal bluffs jut out to sea at 640-acre **Patrick's Point** (☑707-677-3570; www.parks.ca.gov; 4150 Patrick's Point Dr; per car $8), where sandy beaches abut rocky headlands. Five miles north of Trinidad, with supereasy access to dramatic coastal bluffs, it's a best-bet for families. Stroll scenic overlooks, climb giant rock formations, watch whales breach, gaze into tidepools, or listen to barking sea lions and singing birds from this manicured park.

Sumêg (⊙daily) **FREE** is an authentic reproduction of a Yurok village, with hand-hewn redwood buildings where Native Americans gather for traditional ceremonies. In the native plant garden you'll find species for making traditional baskets and medicines.

On **Agate Beach** look for stray bits of jade and sea-polished agate. Follow the signs to tidepools, but tread lightly and obey regulations. The 2-mile **Rim Trail**, a old Yurok trail around the bluffs, circles the point with access to huge rocky outcroppings. Don't miss **Wedding Rock**, one of the park's most romantic spots. Other trails lead around unusual formations like **Ceremonial Rock** and **Lookout Rock**.

The park's three well-tended **campgrounds** (☑reservations 800-444-7275; www.reserveamerica.com; tent & RV sites $35) have coin-operated hot showers and very clean bathrooms. Penn Creek and Abalone campgrounds are more sheltered than Agate Beach.

Humboldt Lagoons State Park

Stretching out for miles along the coast, Humboldt Lagoons has long, sandy beaches and a string of coastal lagoons. **Big Lagoon** and the even prettier **Stone Lagoon** are both excellent for kayaking and birdwatching. Sunsets are spectacular, with no artificial structures in sight. Picnic at Stone Lagoon's north end. The Stone Lagoon Visitor Center, on Hwy 101, has closed due to staffing shortages, but there's a toilet and a bulletin board displaying information.

A mile north, **Freshwater Lagoon** is also great for birding. South of Stone Lagoon, tiny **Dry Lagoon** (a freshwater marsh) has a fantastic day hike and good agate hunting. Park at Dry Lagoon's picnic area and hike north on the unmarked trail to Stone Lagoon; the trail skirts the southwestern shore and ends up at the ocean, passing through woods and marshland rich with wildlife. Mostly flat, it's about 2.5 miles one way – and nobody takes it because it's unmarked.

All campsites are first-come, first-served. The park runs two **environmental campgrounds** (tent sites $20; ⊙Apr-Oct); bring water. Stone Lagoon has six boat-in environmental campsites. Check in at Patrick's Point State Park, at least 30 minutes before sunset.

Humboldt County Parks (☑707-445-7651; tent sites $20) operates a lovely cypress-grove picnic area and campground beside Big Lagoon, a mile off Hwy 101, with flush toilets and cold water, but no showers.

Redwood National & State Parks

A patchwork of public lands jointly administered by the state and federal governments, the Redwood National & State Parks include Redwood National Park, Prairie Creek Redwoods State Park, Del Norte Coast Redwoods State Park and Jedediah Smith Redwoods State Park. A smattering

THE ENDANGERED MARBLED MURRELET: KEEPER OF THE FORESTS

Notice how undeveloped the Redwood National & State Parks have remained? Thank the marbled murrelet, a small white and brown-black auk that nests in old-growth conifers. Loss of nesting territory due to logging has severly depleted the bird's numbers but Redwood National Park scientists have discovered that corvid predators (ravens, jays etc) are also to blame. Because corvids are attracted to food scraps left by visitors, the number of snacking, picnicking or camping humans in the park greatly affects predation on the marbled murrelet. Restrictions on development to prevent food scraps and thus protect the birds are so strict that it's nearly impossible to build anything new.

of small towns break up the forested area, making it a bit confusing to get a sense of the parks as a whole. Prairie Creek and Jedediah Smith parks were originally land slated for clear-cutting, but in the '60s activists successfully protected them and today all these parks are an International Biosphere Reserve and World Heritage Site. At one time the national park was to absorb at least two of the state parks, but that did not happen, and so the cooperative structure remains.

Little-visited compared to their southern brethren, the world's tallest living trees have been standing here for time immemorial, predating the Roman Empire by over 500 years. Prepare to be impressed.

The small town of Orick (population 650), at the southern tip of the park, in a lush valley, is barely more than a few storefronts, the only gas station between Trinidad and Klamath, and a vast conglomeration of woodcarving.

Redwood National Park

Just north of the southern visitor center, turn east onto Bald Hills Rd and travel 2 miles to Lady Bird Johnson Grove, one of the park's most spectacular groves, and also one of the busiest, accessible via a gentle 1-mile loop trail. Continue for another 5 miles up Bald Hills Rd to Redwood Creek

Overlook. On the top of the ridgeline, at 2100ft, get views over the forest and the entire watershed – provided it's not foggy. Just past the overlook lies the gated turnoff for Tall Trees Grove, the location of several of the world's tallest trees. Rangers issue 50 vehicle permits. Pick one up, along with the gate-lock combination, from the visitor centers. Allow four hours for the round-trip, which includes a 6-mile drive down a rough dirt road (speed limit 15mph) and a steep 1.3-mile one-way hike, which descends 800ft to the grove.

Several longer trails include the awe-inspiring Redwood Creek Trail, which also reaches Tall Trees Grove. You'll need a free backcountry permit to hike and camp (highly recommended, as the best backcountry camping on the North Coast), but the area is most accessible from Memorial Day to Labor Day, when summer footbridges are up. Otherwise, getting across the creek can be perilous or impossible.

For hikes, kayaking, fishing or a slew of other tours, book with Redwood Adventures (☑ 866-733-9637; www.redwoodadventures.com; 7 Valley Green Camp Rd, Orick) whose guides know the area better than anyone and will get you to places you may not otherwise find on your own. For horseback riding from May to November call the Redwood Creek Bukarettes (☑ 707-499-2943; www.redwoodcreekbukarettes.com; 1000 Drydens Rd, Orick; 1½hr trail rides from $60).

🛏 Sleeping

Elk Meadow Cabins   CABINS $$$
(☑ 866-733-9637; www.redwoodadventures.com; 7 Valley Green Camp Rd, Orick; cabins $179-279; 🛜🐾) These spotless and bright cabins with equipped kitchens and all the mod-cons are in a perfect mid-parks location – they're great if you're traveling in a group and the most comfy choice even if you're not. Expect to see elk on the lawn in the mornings. Cabins sleep six to eight people and there's an additional $45 cleaning fee.

ℹ Information

Unlike most national parks, there are no fees and no highway entrance stations at Redwood National Park, so it's imperative to pick up the free map at the park headquarters in Crescent City (p249) or at the infomation center in Orick. Rangers here issue permits to visit Tall Trees Grove and loan bear-proof containers for backpackers.

For in-depth redwood ecology, buy the excellent official park handbook. The **Redwood Parks Association** (www.redwoodparksassociation.org) provides good information on its website, including detailed descriptions of all the parks hikes.

Redwood Information Center (Kuchel Visitor Center; ☑707-464-6101; www.nps.gov/redw; Hwy 101; ⊙9am-6pm June-Aug, to 5pm Sep-Oct & Mar-May, to 4pm Nov-Feb) On Hwy 101, a mile south of tiny Orick.

Prairie Creek Redwoods State Park

Famous for some of the world's best virgin redwood groves and unspoiled coastline, this 14,000-acre section of Redwood National & State Parks has spectacular scenic drives and 70 miles of hiking trails, many of which are excellent for children. Pick up maps and information and sit by the river-rock fireplace at **Prairie Creek Visitor Center** (☑707-464-6101; ⊙9am-5pm Mar-Oct, 10am-4pm Nov-Feb; ☞). Kids will love the taxidermy dioramas with push-button, light-up displays. Outside, elk roam grassy flats.

 Activities

There are 28 mountain-biking and hiking trails through the park, from simple to strenuous. Only a few of these will appeal to hard-core hikers, who should take on the Del Norte Coast Redwoods State Park. Those tight on time or with mobility impairments should stop at **Big Tree**, an easy 100yd walk from the car park. Several other easy nature trails start near the visitor center, including **Revelation Trail** and **Elk Prairie Trail**. Stroll the recently reforested logging road on the **Ah-Pah Interpretive Trail** at the park's north end. The most challenging hike in this corner of the park is the truly spectacular 11.5-mile **Coastal Trail** which goes through primordial redwoods.

Just past the Gold Bluffs Beach Campground the road dead ends at **Fern Canyon**, the second busiest spot in the parks, where 60ft fern-covered sheer-rock walls can be seen from Steven Spielberg's *Jurassic Park 2: The Lost World*. This is one of the most photographed spots on the North Coast – damp and lush, all emerald green – and *totally* worth getting your toes wet to see.

Newton B Drury Scenic Parkway DRIVING
Just north of Orick is the turn off for the 8-mile parkway, which runs parallel to Hwy 101 through untouched ancient redwood forests. This is a not-to-miss short detour off the freeway where you can view the magnificence of these trees. Numerous trails branch off from roadside pullouts, including family-friendly options and trails that fit ADA (American Disabilities Act) requirements, including Big Tree and Revelation Trail.

Sleeping

Welcome to the great outdoors: without any motels or cabins, the only choice here is to pitch a tent in the campgrounds at the southern end of the park.

★**Gold Bluffs Beach** CAMPGROUND **$**
(tent sites $35) This gorgeous campground sits between 100ft cliffs and wide-open ocean, but there are some windbreaks and solar-heated showers. Look for sites up the cliff under the trees. No reservations.

Elk Prairie Campground CAMPGROUND **$**
(☑reservations 800 444 7275, www.reserveamerica.com; tent & RV sites $35) Elk roam this popular campground, where you can sleep under redwoods or at the prairie's edge. There are hot showers, some hike-in sites and a shallow creek to splash in. Sites 1–7 and 69–76 are on grassy prairies and get full sun; sites 8–68 are wooded. To camp in a mixed redwood forest, book sites 20–27.

Del Norte Coast Redwoods State Park

Marked by steep canyons and dense woods north of Klamath, half the 6400 acres of this park (☑707-464-6101, ext 5120; per car day-use $8) are virgin redwood forest, crisscrossed by 15 miles of hiking trails. Even the most cynical of redwood-watchers can't help but be moved.

Pick up maps and inquire about guided walks at the Redwood National & State Parks Headquarters (p249) in Crescent City or the Redwood Information Center in Orick.

Hwy 1 winds in from the coast at rugged, dramatic **Wilson Beach**, and traverses the dense forest, with groves stretching off as far as you can see.

Picnic on the sand at **False Klamath Cove**. Heading north, tall trees cling precipitously to canyon walls that drop to the rocky, timber-strewn coastline, and it's almost impossible to get to the water, except via the

WORTH A TRIP

SMITH RIVER NATIONAL RECREATION AREA

West of Jedediah Smith Redwoods State Park, the Smith River, the state's last remaining undammed waterway, runs right beside Hwy 199. Originating high in the Siskiyou Mountains, its serpentine course cuts through deep canyons beneath thick forests. Chinook salmon (October to December) and steelhead trout (December to April) annually migrate up its clear waters. Camp (there are four developed campgrounds), hike (75 miles of trails), raft (145 miles of navigable white water) and kayak here, but check regulations if you want to fish. Stop by the **Six Rivers National Forest Headquarters** (☑707-457-3131; www.fs.fed.us/r5/sixrivers; 10600 Hwy 199, Gasquet; ☉8am-4:30pm daily May-Sep, Mon-Fri Oct-Apr) to get your bearings. Pick up pamphlets for the **Darlingtonia Trail** and **Myrtle Creek Botanical Area**, both easy jaunts into the woods, where you can see rare plants and learn about the area's geology.

gorgeous but steep **Damnation Creek Trail** or **Footsteps Rock Trail**.

Between these two, serious hikers will be most greatly rewarded by the Damnation Creek Trail. It's only 4 miles long, but the 1100-ft elevation change and cliff-side redwood makes it the park's best hike. The unmarked trailhead starts from a parking area off Hwy 101 at Mile 16.

Crescent Beach Overlook and picnic area has superb wintertime whale-watching. At the park's north end, watch the surf pound at **Crescent Beach**, just south of Crescent City via Enderts Beach Rd.

Mill Creek Campground (☑800-444-7275; www.reserveamerica.com; tent & RV sites $35) has hot showers and 145 sites in a redwood grove, 2 miles east of Hwy 101 and 7 miles south of Crescent City. Sites 1-74 are woodsier; sites 75-145 sunnier. Hike-in sites are prettiest.

Jedediah Smith Redwoods State Park

The northernmost park in the system of Redwood National & State Parks, the dense stands at **Jedediah Smith** (☑707-464-6101, ext 5112; day use $8) are 10 miles northeast of Crescent City (via Hwy 101 east to Hwy 197). The redwood stands are so thick that few trails penetrate the park, but the outstanding 11-mile **Howland Hill scenic drive** cuts through otherwise inaccessible areas (take Hwy 199 to South Fork Rd; turn right after crossing two bridges). It's a rough road, impassable for RVs, but if you can't hike, it's the best way to see the forest.

Stop for a stroll under enormous trees in **Simpson-Reed Grove**. If it's foggy at the coast it may be sunny here. There's a swimming hole and picnic area near the park entrance. An easy half-mile trail, departing from the far side of the campground, crosses the **Smith River** via a summer-only footbridge, leading to **Stout Grove**, the park's most famous grove. The **visitor center** (☑707-464-6101; ☉10am-4pm daily Jun-Aug, Sat & Sun Sep-Oct & Apr-May) sells hiking maps and nature guides. If you wade in the river, be careful in the spring when currents are swift and the water cold.

🛏 Sleeping

Campground   CAMPGROUND $
(☑reservations 800-444-7275; www.reserveamerica.com; tent & RV sites $35) The popular campground has gorgeous sites tucked through the redwoods beside the Smith River.

Hiouchi Motel   MOTEL $
(☑888-881-0819, 707-458-3041; www.hiouchimotel.com; 2097 Hwy 199; s $50, d $65-71; @ 🛜) If you don't camp, try the renovated Hiouchi Motel offering clean, straightforward motel rooms.

Klamath

Giant metal-cast golden bears stand sentry at the bridge across the Klamath River announcing Klamath, one of the tiny settlements that break up Redwood National & State Parks between Prairie Creek Redwoods State Park and Del Norte Coast Redwoods State Park. With a gas station/market, diner and a casino, Klamath is basically a wide spot in the road with some seriously great roadside kitsch at its edges. The **Yurok Tribal Headquarters** is in the town center and the entire settlement and much of the surrounding area is the tribe's ancestral land. Klamath is roughly an hour north of Eureka.

Sights & Activities

The mouth of the **Klamath River** is a dramatic sight. Marine, riparian, forest and meadow ecological zones all converge and the **birding** is exceptional. For the best views, head north of town to Requa Rd and the **Klamath River Overlook** and picnic on high bluffs above driftwood-strewn beaches. On a clear day, this is one of the most spectacular viewpoints on the North Coast, and one of the best whale-watching spots in California (this is one of the mammal's first feeding stops as they come south from Alaska). For a good hike, head north along the **Coastal Trail**. You'll have the sand to yourself at **Hidden Beach**; access the trail at the northern end of Motel Trees.

Just south of the river, on Hwy 101, the scenic **Coastal Drive**, a narrow, winding country road traces extremely high cliffs over the ocean. Due to erosion a 3.3 mile section of the 9.5 mile loop (between Carruther's Cove trailhead and the intersection of the Coastal Drive with Alder Camp Rd) has been closed to motor traffic since 2011 but it's still walkable and bikeable. Though technically in Redwood National Park, this drive is much closer to Klamath.

Klamath Jet Boat Tours   BOAT TOURS
(www.jetboattours.com; 17635 US 101; 2hr tours adult/child $45/25) Book jet-boat excursions and fishing trips run by the Yukon Tribe.

Sleeping & Eating

Woodsy Klamath is cheaper than Crescent City, but there aren't as many places to eat or buy groceries, and there's nothing to do at night but play cards. There are ample private RV parks in the area.

Flint Ridge Campground   CAMPGROUND
(707-464-6101) **FREE** Four miles from the Klamath River Bridge via Coastal Drive, this tent-only, hike-in campground sits among a wild, overgrown meadow of ferns and moss. It's a 10-minute walk (half a mile) east, uphill from the parking area. There's no water, plenty of bear sightings (bear boxes on site) and you have to pack out trash. But, hey, it's free.

Ravenwood Motel   MOTEL $
(866-520-9875, 707-482-5911; www.ravenwood-motel.com; 131 Klamath Blvd; r/ste with kitchen $75/125;) The spotlessly clean rooms are better than anything in Crescent City and individually decorated with furnishings and flair you'd expect in a city hotel, not a small-town motel.

★**Historic Requa Inn**   HISTORIC HOTEL $$
(707-482-1425; www.requainn.com; 451 Requa Rd, Klamath; r $119-199;) A woodsy country lodge on bluffs overlooking the mouth of the Klamath, the creaky and bright 1914 Requa Inn is a North Coast favorite and – even better – it's a carbon-neutral facility. Many of the charming old-time-America–style rooms have mesmerizing views over the misty river, as does the dining room, which serves new Native American, organic cuisine.

Crescent City

Though Crescent City was founded as a thriving 1853 seaport and supply center for inland gold mines, the town's history was quite literally washed away in 1964, when half the town was swallowed by a tsunami. Of course, it was rebuilt (though mostly with the utilitarian ugliness of ticky-tacky buildings), but its marina was devastated by the 2011 Japan earthquake and tsunami, when the city was evacuated. Crescent City remains California's last big town north of Arcata, though the constant fog (and sounding fog horn) and damp, '60s sprawl makes it about as charming as a wet bag of dirty laundry. The economy depends heavily on shrimp and crab fishing, hotel tax and on Pelican Bay maximum-security prison, just

---

TREES OF MYSTERY

It's hard to miss the giant statues of Paul Bunyan and Babe the Blue Ox towering over the parking lot at **Trees of Mystery** (707-482-2251; www.treesofmystery.net; 15500 Hwy 101; adult/child & senior $14/7; 8am-7pm Jun-Aug, 9am-4pm Sep-May;), a shameless tourist trap with a gondola running through the redwood canopy and a fun 'Tall Tales Forest' where chainsaw sculptures tell the tale of Paul Bunyan. It's perfect for families, anyone unable to take a strenuous hike or lovers of kitsch. The surprisingly wonderful **End of the Trail Museum** located behind the Trees of Mystery gift shop has an outstanding collection of Native American arts and artifacts, and it's free.

north of town, which adds tension to the air and lots of cops to the streets.

Hwy 101 splits into two parallel one-way streets, with the southbound traffic on L St, northbound on M St. To see the major sights, turn west on Front St toward the lighthouse. Downtown is along 3rd St.

◉ Sights & Activities

If you're in town in August, the **Del Norte County Fair** features a rodeo, and lots of characters. Jedediah Smith Redwoods State Park (p246) is 10 miles inland.

North Coast Marine Mammal Center   SCIENCE CENTER
(📞707-465-6265; www.northcoastmmc.org; 424 Howe Dr; admission by donation; ⏲10am-5pm; ♨) ✐ Just east of Battery Point, this is the ecologically minded foil to the garish Ocean World: the clinic treats injured seals, sea lions and dolphins and releases them back into the wild (donation requested).

Battery Point Lighthouse   LIGHTHOUSE
(📞707-467-3089; www.delnortehistory.org; adult/child $3/1; ⏲10am-4pm Wed-Sun Apr-Oct) The 1856 lighthouse, at the south end of A St, still operates on a tiny, rocky island that you can easily reach at low tide. You can also get a tour of the on-site **museum** for $3. Note that the listed hours are subject to change due to tides and weather.

Beachfront Park   PARK
(Howe Dr; ♨) Between B and H Sts, this park has a harborside beach with no large waves, making it perfect for little ones. Further east on Howe Dr, near J St, you'll come to **Kidtown**, with slides and swings and a make-believe castle.

⌂ Sleeping

Most people stop here for one night while traveling; motels are overpriced, but you'll pass a slew of hotels on the main arteries leading into and out of town. The county operates two excellent first-come, first-served campgrounds just outside of town.

★Curly Redwood Lodge   MOTEL $
(📞707-464-2137; www.curlyredwoodlodge.com; 701 Hwy 101 S; r $56-98; ✷ 🛜) The Redwood Lodge is a marvel: it's entirely built and paneled from a single curly redwood tree which measured over 18in thick in diameter. Progressively restored and polished into a gem of mid-century kitsch, the inn is a delight

for retro junkies. Rooms are clean, large and comfortable (request one away from the road). For truly modern accommodations, look elsewhere.

Bay View Inn   HOTEL $
(📞800-742-8439; www.ccbvi.com; 2844 Fairfield; r $55-135; ✷ 🛜) Bright, modern, updated rooms with microwaves and refrigerators fill this centrally located independent hotel. It may seem a bit like a better-than-average highway exit chain, but colorful bedspreads and warm hosts add necessary homespun appeal. The rooms upstairs in the back have views of the lighthouse and the harbor.

Crescent Beach Motel   MOTEL $
(📞707-464-5436; www.crescentbeachmotel.com; 1455 Hwy 101 S; r $84-136; ✷ 🛜) Just south of town, this basic, old-fashioned motel is the only place in town to stay right on the beach, offering views that distract you from the somewhat plain indoor environs. Skip rooms without a view.

Florence Keller Park   CAMPGROUND $
(📞707-464-7230; http://www.co.del-norte.ca.us; 3400 Cunningham Lane; sites $10) County-run Florence Keller Park has 50 sites in a beautiful grove of young redwoods (take Hwy 101 north to Elk Valley Cross Rd and follow the signs).

Ruby Van Deventer Park   CAMPGROUND $
(4705 N Bank Rd; sites $15; ♨) The county's Ruby Van Deventer Park has 18 sites along the Smith River, off Hwy 197.

✕ Eating

Good Harvest Café   AMERICAN $
(575 Hwy 101 S; mains $7-14; ⏲7am-9pm Mon-Sat, from 8am Sun; ✐♨) This popular local cafe is in a spacious location across from the harbor. It's got a bit of everything – all pretty good – from soups and sandwiches to full meals and smoothies. Good beers, a crackling fire and loads of vegetarian options make this the best dining spot in town.

Tomasini's Enoteca   ITALIAN, AMERICAN $
(960 3rd St; mains $4-11; ⏲7:30am-2pm; ✐) Stop in for salads, sandwiches or jazz on weekend nights. Hands down the most happening place downtown.

Chart Room   SEAFOOD $$
(130 Anchor Way; dinner mains $10-28; ⏲6:30am-7pm Sun-Thu, to 8pm Fri & Sat; ♨) At the tip of the South Harbor pier, this joint is

renowned far and wide for its fish and chips: batter-caked golden beauties which deliver on their reputation. It's often a hive of families, retirees, Harley riders and local businessmen, so grab a beer at the small bar and wait for a table.

ℹ️ Information

Crescent City-Del Norte Chamber of Commerce (☑ 800-343-8300, 707-464-3174; www.northerncalifornia.net; 1001 Front St; ⊘ 9am-5pm May-Aug, Mon-Fri Sep-Apr) Local information.

Redwood National & State Parks Headquarters (☑ 707-464-6101; 1111 2nd St; ⊘ 9am-5pm Oct-May, to 6pm Jun-Sep) On the corner of K St; you'll find rangers here and information about all four parks under its jurisdiction.

ℹ️ Getting There & Around

United Express (☑ 800-241-6522) flies into tiny **Crescent City Airport** (CEC), north of town. **Redwood Coast Transit** (www.redwoodcoast-transit.org) serves Crescent City with local buses ($1), and runs buses Monday to Saturday to Klamath ($1.50, one hour, two daily) and Arcata ($30, two hours, two daily) with stops in between.

Tolowa Dunes State Park & Lake Earl Wildlife Area

Two miles north of Crescent City, this **state park and wildlife area** (☑ 707-464-6101, ext 5112; ⊘ sunrise-sunset) encompasses 10,000 acres of wetlands, dunes, meadows and two lakes, **Lake Earl** and **Lake Tolowa**. This major stopover on the Pacific Flyway route brings over 250 species of birds here. Listen for the whistling, warbling chorus. On land, look for coyotes and deer, angle for trout, or hike or ride 20 miles of trails; at sea, spot whales, seals and sea lions.

The park and wildlife area are a patchwork of lands administered by California State Parks and the Department of Fish and Game (DFG). The DFG focuses on single-species management, hunting and fishing; the State Parks' focus is on ecodiversity and recreation. You might be hiking a vast expanse of pristine dunes, then suddenly hear a shotgun or a whining 4WD. Strict regulations limit where and when you can hunt and drive; trails are clearly marked.

Register for two primitive, nonreservable **campgrounds** (tent sites $20) at Jedediah Smith (p246) or Del Norte Coast Redwoods State Park (p245) campgrounds. The mosquitoes are plentiful in the spring and early summer.

Pelican State Beach

Never-crowded **Pelican State Beach** (☑ 707-464-6101, ext 5151) occupies five coastal acres on the Oregon border. There are no facilities, but it's great for kite flying; pick one up at the shop just over the border in Oregon.

🛏️ Sleeping

Clifford Kamph Memorial Park CAMPGROUND **$**
(☑ 707-464-7230; 15100 Hwy 101; tent sites $10) Pitch a tent by the ocean (no windbreaks) at Clifford Kamph Memorial Park; no RVs. It's a steal for the beachside location and, even though sites are exposed in a grassy area and there isn't much privacy, all have BBQs.

Casa Rubio BOUTIQUE HOTEL **$$**
(☑ 707-487-4313; www.casarubio.com; 17285 Crissey Rd; r $98-178; 🅴🅴) The best reason to visit Pelican State Beach is to stay at secluded, charming Casa Rubio, where three of the four ocean-view rooms have kitchens.

Central Coast

Best Places to Eat

➜ Passionfish (p273)

➜ Ember (p307)

➜ Cracked Crab (p307)

➜ San Luis Obispo Farmers Market (p299)

➜ Penny Ice Creamery (p257)

Best Places to Stay

➜ Post Ranch Inn (p281)

➜ Dream Inn (p256)

➜ Cass House Inn (p288)

➜ HI Santa Cruz Hostel (p256)

➜ Pfeiffer Big Sur State Park Campground (p280)

Why Go?

Too often forgotten or dismissed as 'flyover' country between San Francisco and LA, this stretch of California coast is packed with wild beaches, misty redwood forests, and rolling golden hills of fertile vineyards and farm fields.

Coastal Hwy 1 pulls out all the stops, scenery-wise. Flower-power Santa Cruz and the historic port town of Monterey are gateways to the rugged wilderness of the bohemian Big Sur coast. It's an epic journey snaking down to vainglorious Hearst Castle, past lighthouses and edgy cliffs atop which endangered condors soar.

Get acquainted with California's agricultural heartland along inland Hwy 101, called El Camino Real (the King's Highway) by Spanish conquistadors and Franciscan friars. Colonial missions still line the route, which passes through Paso Robles' flourishing wine country. Then soothe your nature-loving soul in collegiate San Luis Obispo, ringed by sunny beach towns and volcanic peaks.

When to Go
Santa Cruz

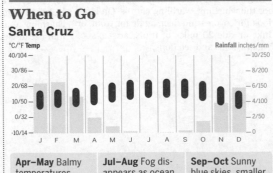

Apr–May Balmy temperatures, but fewer tourists than summer; wildflowers bloom.

Jul–Aug Fog disappears as ocean waters warm up for beach season.

Sep–Oct Sunny blue skies, smaller crowds and wine country harvest festivals.

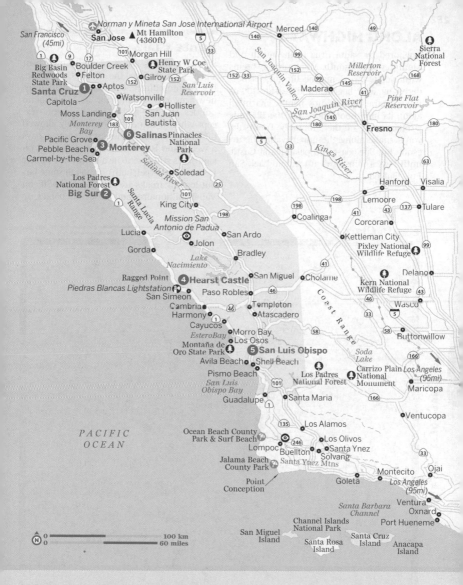

Central Coast Highlights

1 Screaming your head off aboard the Giant Dipper on the beach boardwalk, then learning to surf in **Santa Cruz** (p252).

2 Cruising Hwy 1, where the sky touches the sea, along the rocky coastline of mystical **Big Sur** (p275).

3 Being mesmerized by aquatic denizens of the 'indoor ocean' at the kid-friendly **aquarium** (p262) in Monterey.

4 Marveling in disbelief at the grandiosity of **Hearst Castle** (p284) after meeting the neighbors: ginormous elephant seals.

5 Hanging loose in college-town **San Luis Obispo** (p297), surrounded by beaches, vineyards and mountains.

6 Exploring down-to-earth novelist John Steinbeck's blue-collar world in the agricultural small town of **Salinas** (p292).

ALONG HIGHWAY 1

Anchored by Santa Cruz to the north and Monterey to the south, Monterey Bay teems with richly varied marine life and is bordered by wild beaches and seaside towns full of character and idiosyncratic charm all along its half-moon shore. On the 125-mile stretch south of the Monterey Peninsula, you'll snake along the unbelievably picturesque Big Sur coast and past Hearst Castle until Hwy 1 joins Hwy 101 in laid-back San Luis Obispo.

Santa Cruz

Santa Cruz has marched to its own beat since long before the Beat Generation. It's counterculture central, a touchy-feely, new-agey city famous for its leftie-liberal politics and live-and-let-live ideology – except when it comes to dogs (rarely allowed off-leash), parking (meters run seven days a week) and Republicans (allegedly shot on sight). It's still cool to be a hippie or a stoner here (or better yet, both), although some far-out-looking freaks are just slumming Silicon Valley millionaires and trust-fund babies.

Santa Cruz

CENTRAL COAST SANTA CRUZ

Santa Cruz is a city of madcap fun, with a vibrant but chaotic downtown. On the waterfront is the famous beach boardwalk, and in the hills redwood groves embrace the University of California, Santa Cruz (UCSC) campus. Plan to spend at least half a day here, but to appreciate the aesthetic of jangly skirts, crystal pendants and Rastafarian dreadlocks, stay longer and plunge headlong into the rich local brew of surfers, students, punks and eccentric characters.

⊙ Sights

One of the best things to do in Santa Cruz is simply stroll, shop and watch the sideshow along **Pacific Ave** downtown. A 15-minute walk away is the beach and **Municipal Wharf** (Map p252), where seafood restaurants, gift shops and barking sea lions compete for attention. Ocean-view **West Cliff Dr** follows the waterfront southwest of the wharf, paralleled by a paved recreational path.

★ Santa Cruz Beach Boardwalk
AMUSEMENT PARK

(Map p252; ☑831 423-5590; www.beachboardwalk.com; 400 Beach St; per ride $3-6, all-day pass $32-40; ⊙ daily Apr–early Sep, seasonal hours vary; ⊛) The West Coast's oldest beachfront amusement park, this 1907 boardwalk has a glorious old-school Americana vibe. The smell of cotton candy mixes with the salt air, punctuated by the squeals of kids hanging upside down on carnival rides. Famous thrills include the Giant Dipper, a 1924 wooden roller coaster, and the 1911 Looff carousel, both National Historic Landmarks. During summer, catch free mid-week movies and Friday night concerts by rock veterans you may have thought were already dead.

Closing times and off-season hours vary. All-day parking costs $6 to $15.

★ Seymour Marine Discovery Center
MUSEUM

(Map p260; ☑831-459-3800; http://seymourcenter.ucsc.edu; 100 Shaffer Rd; adult/child 3-16yr $8/6; ⊙10am-5pm Tue-Sun year-round, also 10am-5pm Mon Jul & Aug; ⊛) ◢ By Natural Bridges State Beach, this kids' educational center is part of UCSC's Long Marine Laboratory. Interactive natural-science exhibits include tidal touch pools and aquariums, while outside you can gawk at the world's largest blue-whale skeleton. Guided one-hour tours happen at 1pm, 2pm and 3pm daily, with a special 30-minute tour for families with younger children at 11am; sign up for tours in person an hour in advance (no reservations).

Sanctuary Exploration Center
MUSEUM

(Map p252; ☑831-421-9993; http://montereybay.noaa.gov; 35 Pacific Ave; ⊙10am-5pm Wed-Sun; ⊛) ◢ **FREE** Operated by the Monterey Bay National Marine Sanctuary, this educational museum near the beach boardwalk is an interactive multimedia experience that teaches kids and adults about the bay's marine treasures, watershed conservation and high-tech underwater exploration for scientific research.

Santa Cruz Surfing Museum — MUSEUM

(Map p260; www.santacruzsurfingmuseum.org; 701 W Cliff Dr; admission by donation; ⊙ 10am-5pm Wed-Mon Jul 4-early Sep, noon-4pm Thu-Mon early Sep-Jul 3) A mile southwest of the wharf along the coast, this museum inside an old lighthouse is packed with memorabilia, including vintage redwood surfboards. Fittingly, Lighthouse Point overlooks two popular surf breaks.

University of California, Santa Cruz — UNIVERSITY

(Map p260; UCSC; www.ucsc.edu) Check it: the school mascot is a banana slug! Established in 1965 in the hills above town, UCSC is known for its creative, liberal bent. The rural campus has fine stands of redwoods and architecturally interesting buildings – some made with recycled materials – designed to blend in with rolling pastureland. Amble around the peaceful arboretum (http://arboretum.ucsc.edu; cnr High St & Arboretum Rd; adult/child 6-17yr $5/2, free 1st Tue of each month; ⊙ 9am-5pm) and picturesquely decaying 19th-century structures from Cowell Ranch, upon which the campus was built.

Santa Cruz Museum of Natural History — MUSEUM

(Map p260; ☑ 831-420-6115; www.santacruzmuseum.org; 1305 E Cliff Dr; adult/child under 18yr $4/free, free 1st Fri of each month; ⊙ 10am-5pm Tue-Sun; ⊞) The collections at this pint-sized museum include stuffed animal mounts, Native Californian cultural artifacts and a touch-friendly tide pool that shows off sea critters living by the beach right across the street.

Museum of Art & History — MUSEUM

(Map p252; ☑ 831-429-1964; www.santacruzmah.org; McPherson Center, 705 Front St; adult/child 12-17yr $5/2, free 1st Fri of each month; ⊙ 11am-5pm Tue-Thu, Sat & Sun, to 9pm Fri) Rotating displays by contemporary California artists and exhibits on local history are worth a quick look.

🏃 Activities

DeLaveaga Disc Golf Club — GOLF

(Map p260; www.delaveagadiscgolf.com; Upper Park Rd) FREE Touring pros and families with kids toss discs across this challenging hillside layout that peaks at Hole No 27, nicknamed 'Top of the World.' It's a couple of miles northeast of downtown, off Branciforte Dr.

Surfing

Year-round, water temperatures average under 60°F, meaning that without a wetsuit, body parts quickly turn blue. Surfing is incredibly popular, especially at experts-only Steamer Lane and beginners' Cowell's, both off West Cliff Dr. Other favorite surf spots include Pleasure Point Beach, on East Cliff Dr toward Capitola, and Manresa State Beach off Hwy 1 southbound.

Santa Cruz Surf School — SURFING

(Map p252; ☑ 831-345-8875, 831-426-7072; www.santacruzsurfschool.com; 131 Center St; 2hr group/1hr private lesson $90/120; ⊞) Wanna learn to surf? Near the wharf, friendly male and female instructors will have you standing and surfing on your first day out.

Richard Schmidt Surf School — SURFING

(Map p260; ☑ 831-423-0928; www.richardschmidt.com; 849 Almar Ave; 2hr group/1hr private lesson $90/120) Award-winning surf school can get you out there, all equipment included. Summer surf camps hook adults and kids alike.

O'Neill Surf Shop — SURFING

(Map p260; ☑ 831-475-4151; www.oneill.com; 1115 41st Ave; wetsuit/surfboard rental from $10/20; ⊙ 9am-8pm Mon-Fri, from 8am Sat & Sun) Head east toward Pleasure Point to worship at this internationally renowned surfboard maker's flagship store, with branches on the beach boardwalk and downtown.

Cowell's Beach Surf Shop — SURFING

(Map p252; ☑ 831-427-2355; www.cowellssurfshop.com; 30 Front St; 2hr group lesson $90; ⊙ 8am-6pm, to 5pm Nov-Mar; ⊞) Rent surfboards, boogie boards, wetsuits and other beach gear near the wharf, where veteran staff offer local tips and lessons.

Kayaking

Kayaking lets you discover the craggy coastline and kelp beds where sea otters float.

Venture Quest — KAYAKING

(Map p252; ☑ 831-425-8445, 831-427-2267; www.kayaksantacruz.com; Municipal Wharf; kayak rental/tour from $30/55; ⊙ 10am-7pm Mon-Fri, from 9am Sat & Sun late-May–late-Sep, hours vary late-Sep–mid-May) Convenient rentals on the wharf, plus whale-watching and coastal sea-cave tours, moonlight paddles and kayak-sailing trips. Book ahead for kayak-surfing lessons.

Kayak Connection — WATER SPORTS

(Map p260; ☑ 831-479-1121; www.kayakconnection.com; Santa Cruz Harbor, 413 Lake Ave; kayak

TOP SANTA CRUZ BEACHES

Sun-kissed Santa Cruz has warmer beaches than San Francisco or Monterey. *Baywatch* it isn't, but 29 miles of coastline reveal a few Hawaii-worthy beaches, craggy coves, some primo surf spots and big sandy stretches where your kids will have a blast. Fog may ruin many a summer morning; it often burns off by the afternoon.

West Cliff Dr is lined with scramble-down-to coves and plentiful parking. If you don't want sand in your shoes, park yourself on a bench and watch enormous pelicans dive for fish. You'll find bathrooms and showers at the lighthouse parking lot.

Locals favor less-trampled **East Cliff Dr** beaches, which are bigger and more pro-tected from the wind, meaning calmer waters. Except at a small metered lot at 26th Ave, parking is by permit only on weekends (buy a $8 per day permit at 9th Ave).

Main Beach *The* scene, with a huge sandy stretch, volleyball courts and swarms of people. Park on East Cliff Dr and walk across the Lost Boys trestle to the beach boardwalk.

Its Beach (Map p260; 🐾) The only official off-leash beach for dogs (before 10am and after 4pm) is just west of the lighthouse.

Natural Bridges State Beach (Map p260; www.parks.ca.gov; 2531 W Cliff Dr; per car $10; ⊙8am–sunset; 🖈) Best for sunsets, this family favorite has lots of sand, tide pools and mon-arch butterflies from mid-October through mid-February. It's at the far end of W Cliff Dr.

Twin Lakes State Beach (Map p260; www.parks.ca.gov; E Cliff Dr & 9th Ave; ⊙8am–sunset; 🖈) Big beach with bonfire pits and a lagoon, good for kids and often fairly empty. It's off E Cliff Dr.

Moran Lake County Park (Map p260; www.scparks.com; E Cliff Dr; ⊙8am–sunset) With a good surf break and bathrooms, this pretty all-around sandy spot is further east of 26th Ave off E Cliff Dr.

New Brighton State Beach (Map p260; ☎831-464-6330; www.parks.ca.gov; 500 Park Rd, Capitola; per car $10; ⊙8am–sunset) Heading east of Santa Cruz to Capitola, New Brighton State Beach is a quieter place for a swim, paddleboarding or camping on a forested bluff.

Seacliff State Beach (☎831-685-6442; www.parks.ca.gov; State Park Rd, Aptos; per car $10; ⊙8am–sunset) Seacliff State Beach harbors a 'cement boat,' a quixotic freighter built of concrete that floated OK, but ended up here as a coastal fishing pier.

Manresa State Beach (☎831-761-1975; www.parks.ca.gov; San Andreas Rd, Watsonville; per car $10; ⊙8am–sunset) Near Watsonville, the La Selva Beach exit off Hwy 1 leads here to this sparsely populated beach.

Sunset State Beach (☎831-763-7062; www.parks.ca.gov; San Andreas Rd, Watsonville; per car $10; ⊙8am–sunset) The La Selva Beach exit off Hwy 1, near Watsonville, brings you here, where you can have miles of sand and surf almost all to yourself.

rental/tour from $35/45; 🖈) Rents kayaks and offers lessons and tours, including whale-watching, sunrise, sunset and full-moon trips. Also rents stand-up paddleboarding (SUP) sets (from $25), wetsuits ($10) and boogie boards ($10).

Whale-Watching & Fishing

Winter whale-watching trips run from December through April, though there's plenty of marine life to see on a summer bay cruise. Many fishing trips depart from the wharf, where a few shops rent fishing tackle and poles.

Stagnaro's　　　　　　　　　　BOAT TOUR
(Map p260; ☎info 831-427-0230, reservations 888-237-7084; www.stagnaros.com; 2896 Soquel Ave; adult/child under 14yr cruise from $20/13, whale-watching tour from $47/33) Longstand-ing tour operator offers scenic and sunset cruises around Monterey Bay and whale-watching tours year-round.

☆ Festivals & Events

Woodies on the Wharf　　　　　CULTURE
(www.santacruzwoodies.com) Classic car show features vintage surf-style station wagons on Santa Cruz's Municipal Wharf in late June.

MYSTERY SPOT

A kitschy, old-fashioned tourist trap, Santa Cruz's **Mystery Spot** (📞831-423-8897; www.mysteryspot.com; 465 Mystery Spot Rd; admission $6; ⊘10am-4pm Mon-Fri, to 5pm Sat & Sun Sep-May, 10am-6pm Mon-Fri, 9am-7pm Sat & Sun Jun-Aug) has scarcely changed since it opened in 1940. On a steeply sloping hillside, compasses seem to point crazily, mysterious forces push you around and buildings lean at silly angles. Make reservations, or risk getting stuck waiting for a tour. It's about 4 miles northeast of downtown, up into the hills via Branciforte Dr. Parking costs $5. Don't forget your bumper sticker!

Wharf to Wharf Race　　　　SPORTS
(www.wharftowharf.com) More than 15,000 runners cruise from Santa Cruz to Capitola accompanied by 50 different live-entertainment acts in late July.

Open Studio Art Tour　　　　CULTURE
(www.ccscc.org) Step inside local artists' creative workshops over three weekends in October. The arts council also sponsors 'First Friday' art exhibitions on the first Friday of each month.

🛏 Sleeping

Santa Cruz does not have enough beds to satisfy demand: expect outrageous prices at peak times for nothing-special rooms. Places near the beach boardwalk run the gamut from friendly to frightening. If you're looking for a straightforward motel, cruise Ocean St inland or Mission St (Hwy 1) near the UCSC campus.

★**HI Santa Cruz Hostel**　　　　HOSTEL $
(Map p252; 📞831-423-8304; www.hi-santacruz.org; 321 Main St; dm $26-29, r $60-110, all with shared bath; ⊘check-in 5-10pm; @) Budget overnighters dig this hostel at the century-old Carmelita Cottages surrounded by flowering gardens, just two blocks from the beach. Cons: midnight curfew, daytime lockout (10am to 5pm) and three-night maximum stay. Reservations are essential. Street parking costs $2.

California State Park Campgrounds　　　　CAMPGROUND $
(📞reservations 800-444-7275; www.reserveamerica.com; tent & RV sites $35-65; 🐾) Book well

ahead to camp at state beaches off Hwy 1 south of Santa Cruz or up in the foggy Santa Cruz Mountains off Hwy 9. Family-friendly campgrounds include Henry Cowell Redwoods State Park in Felton and New Brighton State Beach in Capitola.

★**Adobe on Green B&B**　　　　B&B $$
(Map p252; 📞831-469-9866; www.adobeongreen.com; 103 Green St; r incl breakfast $169-219; 🛜) 🐾 Peace and quiet are the mantras at this place, a short walk from Pacific Ave. The hosts are practically invisible, but their thoughtful touches are everywhere, from boutique-hotel amenities in spacious, stylish and solar-powered rooms to breakfast spreads from their organic gardens.

Pelican Point Inn　　　　INN $$
(Map p260; 📞831-475-3381; www.pelicanpointinn-santacruz.com; 21345 E Cliff Dr; ste $139-219; 🛜🐾) Ideal for families, these roomy apartments near a kid-friendly beach come with everything you'll need for a lazy vacation, including kitchenettes. Weekly rates available. Pet fee $20.

Mission Inn　　　　MOTEL $$
(Map p260; 📞800-895-5455, 831-425-5455; www.mission-inn.com; 2250 Mission St; r incl breakfast $130-220; ❄🛜) Perfectly serviceable two-story motel with a garden courtyard, hot tub and complimentary continental breakfast. It's on busy Hwy 1 near the UCSC campus, away from the beach.

Sunny Cove Motel　　　　MOTEL $$
(Map p260; 📞831-475-1741; www.sunnycovemotel.com; 21610 E Cliff Dr; r $90-250; ❄🐾) No-frills retro hideaway east of downtown is a staunch surfers' fave. The long-time Santa Cruzian owner rents well-worn rooms and kitchenette suites.

Dream Inn　　　　HOTEL $$$
(Map p252; 📞866-774-7735, 831-426-4330; www.dreaminnsantacruz.com; 175 W Cliff Dr; r $249-479; ❄@🛜🐾) Overlooking the wharf from a spectacular hillside perch, this chic boutique hotel is as stylish as Santa Cruz gets. Rooms have all mod cons, while the beach is just steps away. Don't miss happy hour at Aquarius restaurant's ocean-view bar. Parking is $25.

Pacific Blue Inn　　　　B&B $$$
(Map p252; 📞831-600-8880; www.pacificblueinn.com; 636 Pacific Ave; r incl breakfast $189-289; 🛜) 🐾 This downtown courtyard B&B is an eco-conscious gem, with water-saving fixtures

and renewable and recycled building materials. Refreshingly elemental rooms have pillowtop beds, electric fireplaces and flat-screen TVs with DVD players. Free loaner bikes.

West Cliff Inn
INN $$$
(Map p252; 800-979-0910, 831-457-2200; www.westcliffinn.com; 174 W Cliff Dr; r incl breakfast $195-325;) In a classy Victorian house west of the wharf, this boutique inn's quaint rooms mix sea-grass wicker, dark wood and jaunty striped curtains. The most romantic suites have gas fireplaces and let you spy on the breaking surf. Rates include a breakfast buffet and afternoon wine, tea and snacks.

Sea & Sand Inn
MOTEL $$$
(Map p252; 831-427-3400; www.santacruzmotels.com; 201 W Cliff Dr; r $199-419;) With a grassy lawn at the cliff's edge, this spiffy, if seriously overpriced motel overlooks Main Beach and the wharf. Fall asleep to braying sea lions! Rooms are smallish, but ocean views can be stellar. Rates include complimentary afternoon refreshments. Their contempo sister property, Carousel Beach Inn, is cheaper and closer to the beach boardwalk.

Babbling Brook Inn
B&B $$$
(Map p260; 831-427-2437, 800-866-1131; www.babblingbrookinn.com; 1025 Laurel St; r incl breakfast $229-309;) Built around a running stream with meandering gardens, the inn has cozy rooms decorated in French-provincial style. Most have gas fireplaces, some have whirlpool tubs and all have featherbeds. There's afternoon wine and hors d'oeuvres, plus a full breakfast.

Hotel Paradox
HOTEL $$$
(Map p260; 855-425-7200, 831-425-7100; www.thehotelparadox.com; 611 Ocean St; r from $189;) Downtown boutique hotel brings the great outdoors inside, with nature prints on the walls, textured wood panels and earth-toned furnishings. Relax in a cabana by the pool or next to an outdoor fire pit. Weekday rates can be reasonable, but summer weekends are high-priced. Parking is $10.

Eating

Downtown is chockablock with casual cafes. If you're looking for seafood, wander the wharf's takeout counter joints. Mission St, near UCSC, and 41st Ave offer cheaper eats.

★ Penny Ice Creamery
ICE CREAM $
(Map p252; www.thepennyicecreamery.com; 913 Cedar St; snacks $2-4; noon-11pm;) With a cult following, this artisan ice-cream shop crafts zany flavors like bourbon candied ginger, lemon verbena blueberry and ricotta apricot all from scratch using local, organic and wild-harvested ingredients. Even vanilla is special: it's made using Thomas Jefferson's original recipe. Also at a downtown kiosk (1520 Pacific Ave; noon-6pm Sun-Thu, to 9pm Fri & Sat;) and near Pleasure Point (820 41st Ave; noon-9pm Sun-Thu, to 11pm Fri & Sat;).

Picnic Basket
DELI $
(Map p252; http://thepicnicbasketsc.com; 125 Beach St; dishes $3-10; 7am-4pm Mon-Thu, to 9pm Fri-Sun;) Across the street from the beach boardwalk, this locavarian kitchen puts together creative sandwiches such as beet with lemony couscous or 'fancy pants' grilled cheese with fruit chutney, plus homemade soups, breakfast burritos and baked goods. Ice-cream treats are sweet.

Walnut Ave Cafe
BREAKFAST $
(Map p252; www.walnutavecafe.com; 106 Walnut Ave; mains $7-11; 7am-3pm Mon-Fri, 8am-4pm Sat & Sun;) Line up at this clean, well lit breakfast spot for fluffy Belgian waffles, blackened ahi tuna eggs benny, Mexican huevos rancheros with pulled pork and all kinds of veggie scrambles. Lunch brings less-exciting sandwiches, salads and soups. Dogs are welcome on the outdoor patio.

Bagelry
DELI $
(Map p252; www.bagelrysantacruz.com; 320a Cedar St; dishes $1-9; 6:30am-5:30pm Mon-Fri, 7am-4:30pm Sat, 7:30am-4pm Sun;) The bagels here are twice-cooked (boiled, then baked), and come with fantastic spreads like crunchy 'Tofu del Fuego' or hummus with sprouts.

Tacos Moreno
MEXICAN $
(Map p260; www.tacosmoreno.com; 1053 Water St; dishes $2-6; 10am-10pm Mon-Fri, 11am-7pm Sat & Sun) Who cares how long the line is at lunchtime? Find taquería heaven with these marinated pork, chicken or beef soft tacos. Also on 41st Ave in Capitola.

New Leaf Community Market
SUPERMARKET $
(Map p252; www.newleaf.com; 1134 Pacific Ave; 8am-9pm;) Organic and local produce, natural-foods groceries and deli take-out meals downtown and also off Hwy 1 near the UCSC campus. The 41st Ave branch has a healthy-minded Beet Cafe.

Santa Cruz Farmers Market
MARKET $
(Map p252; www.santacruzfarmersmarket.org; cnr Lincoln & Center Sts; 1:30-6:30pm Wed;)

🍽 Organic produce, baked goods and arts-and-crafts and food booths all give you an authentic taste of the local vibe. Shorter fall and winter hours.

Pono Hawaiian Grill
FUSION $$

(Map p252; www.ponohawaiiangrill.com; 120 Union St; mains $7-15; ⊙11am-10pm Sun-Wed, to 11pm Thu-Sat) Inside the Reef bar, this kitchen runs on 'island time' as it mixes up your fresh ahi tuna, salmon, shellfish or veggie *poke* (cubed raw salad) in a bowl or ladled on a plate with two-scoop rice and creamy macaroni or tossed green salad. The *loco moco* burrito with spicy gravy is a huge hit.

Engfer Pizza Works
PIZZERIA $$

(Map p260; www.engferpizzaworks.com; 537 Seabright Ave; pizzas $8-23; ⊙usually 4-9:30pm Tue-Sun; ⚐🐾) Detour to find this old factory, where wood-fired oven pizzas are made from scratch – the no-name specialty is like a giant salad on roasted bread. Play ping-pong and down draft microbrews while you wait.

Soif
BISTRO $$$

(Map p252; ☑831-423-2020; www.soifwine.com; 105 Walnut Ave; small plates $5-17, mains $19-25; ⊙5-9pm Sun-Thu, to 10pm Fri & Sat) Bon vivants swoon over a heady selection of three dozen international wines by the glass, paired with a sophisticated, seasonally driven Euro-Cal menu. Expect tastebud-ticklers like roasted beet salad with fava beans and maple vinaigrette or squid-ink linguini with spicy chorizo.

Laili
AFGHANI $$$

(Map p252; ☑831-423-4545; www.lailirestaurant.com; 101b Cooper St; mains $13-28; ⊙11:30am-2:30pm Tue-Sun, 5-9pm Tue-Thu & Sun, to 10pm Fri & Sat) A chic downtown dining oasis, family-owned Laili invites diners in with an elegant high-ceilinged dining room and garden patio. Share apricot-chicken flatbread, tart pomegranate eggplant, roasted cauliflower with saffron, succulent lamb kebabs and more. Service is spotty. Reservations advised.

🍷 Drinking & Nightlife

Downtown overflows with bars, lounges and coffee shops. Heading west on Mission St (Hwy 1), several Santa Cruz Mountains winery tasting rooms hide out along Ingalls St.

★Verve Coffee Roasters
CAFE

(Map p252; www.vervecoffeeroasters.com; 1540 Pacific Ave; ⊙6:30am-9pm; 🕷) To sip finely roasted artisan espresso or a cup of rich pour-over coffee, join the surfers and hipsters at this industrial-zen cafe. Single-origin brews and house blends rule.

Caffe Pergolesi
CAFE

(Map p252; www.theperg.com; 418 Cedar St; ⊙7am-11pm; 🕷) Discuss conspiracy theories over stalwart coffee, tea or beer at this landmark Victorian house with a big ol' tree-shaded verandah. There's live music some evenings.

Vino Prima
WINE BAR

(Map p252; www.vinoprimawines.com; 55 Municipal Wharf; ⊙2-8pm Mon-Tue, 2-10pm Wed-Fri, noon-

LOCAL KNOWLEDGE

TOP SANTA CRUZ COUNTY BREWERIES

We asked Derek Wolfgram, home brewer and local beer columnist, to share with us his favorite places for a pint:

Boulder Creek Brewery (p260) High up in the mountains, these guys brew amber 'Redwood Ale' and 'Dragon's Breath' American IPA.

Sante Adairius Rustic Ales (Map p260; www.rusticales.com; 103 Kennedy Dr; ⊙3-8pm Tue-Fri, from noon Sat & Sun) Off Hwy 1 east of Santa Cruz, Belgian-inspired and barrel-aged beers are a beer geek's dream.

Discretion Brewing (Map p260; www.discretionbrewing.com; 2703 41st Ave, Soquel; ⊙11:30am-9pm) Rye IPA, English ales and traditional Belgian and German brews are always on tap, off Hwy 1.

Santa Cruz Mountain Brewing (Map p260; www.scmbrew.com; 402 Ingalls St; ⊙11:30am-10pm) Bold organic beers make this tiny locals' tasting room crowded. Oddest flavor? Lavender IPA.

Santa Cruz Ale Works (Map p260; www.santacruzaleworks.com; 150 Dubois St; ⊙11am-6pm; 🐾🐕) Hefeweizen and 'Dark Night' oatmeal stout are commendable at this dog-friendly brewpub with a deli.

10pm Sat, noon-8pm Sun) With dreamy ocean views, this spot pours California boutique wines, including hard-to-find bottles from around Santa Cruz and Monterey Counties.

Surf City Billiards & Café   BAR
(Map p252; www.surfcitybilliardscafe.com; 931 Pacific Ave; ⊙5pm-midnight Sun-Thu, to 2am Fri & Sat) An escape from downtown's dives, this upstairs pool hall has Brunswick Gold Crown tables for shooting stick, darts, shuffleboard and big-screen sports TVs.

Hula's Island Grill   BAR
(Map p252; www.hulastiki.com; 221 Cathcart St; ⊙4:30-9:30pm Mon-Thu, 11:30am-11pm Fri & Sat, 11:30am-9:30pm Sun) Pull up a seat at this Hawaii-themed tiki bar for mai tais, *lilikoi* (passion fruit) margaritas, zombie cocktails and happy-hour *pupus* (appetizers).

☆ Entertainment

Free tabloid *Santa Cruz Weekly* (www.santacruzweekly.com) and *Good Times* (www.gtweekly.com) cover music, arts and nightlife scenes.

Catalyst   LIVE MUSIC
(Map p252; ✆831-423-1338; www.catalystclub.com; 1011 Pacific Ave) Over the years, this stage for local bands has seen big-time national acts perform, from Queens of the Stone Age to Snoop Dogg. Expect loads of punk attitude.

Kuumbwa Jazz Center   LIVE MUSIC
(Map p252; ✆831-427-2227; www.kuumbwajazz.org; 320 Cedar St) Hosting jazz luminaries since 1975, this nonprofit theater is for serious jazz cats snapping their fingers for famous-name performers in an intimate room.

Moe's Alley   LIVE MUSIC
(Map p260; ✆831-479-1854; www.moesalley.com; 1535 Commercial Way) In a way-out industrial wasteland, this joint puts on live sounds almost every night: jazz, blues, reggae, roots, salsa and acoustic world-music jams.

🛍 Shopping

Stroll Pacific Ave and downtown side streets to find one-of-a-kind, locally owned boutiques (not just smoke shops, dude). For vintage clothing and surf shops, amble 41st Ave around Portola Dr.

Annieglass   HOMEWARES
(Map p252; www.annieglass.com; 110 Cooper St; ⊙10:30am-6pm Mon-Sat, to 5pm Sun) Handcrafted sculptural glassware by an artist

whose work is displayed at the Smithsonian American Art Museum is made right here in wackadoodle Santa Cruz.

Bookshop Santa Cruz   BOOKS
(Map p252; ✆831-423-0900; www.bookshopsantacruz.com; 1520 Pacific Ave; ⊙9am-10pm Sun-Thu, to 11pm Fri & Sat) Vast selection of new books, a few used ones, and 'Keep Santa Cruz Weird' bumper stickers.

Donnelly Fine Chocolates   FOOD
(Map p260; www.donnellychocolates.com; 1509 Mission St; ⊙10:30am-6pm Mon-Fri, from noon Sat & Sun) The Willy Wonka of Santa Cruz makes stratospherically priced chocolates on par with the big city. Try the cardamom or chipotle truffles.

ℹ️ Information

FedEx Office (www.fedex.com; 712 Front St; per min 30-40¢; ⊙6am-midnight Mon-Fri, 8am-9pm Sat, 9am-9pm Sun; 🖥) Pay-as-you-go internet workstations and photo-printing kiosks.

KPIG 107.5 FM (www.kpig.com) Streams the classic Santa Cruz soundtrack – think Bob Marley, Janis Joplin and Willie Nelson.

Public Library (www.santacruzpl.org; 224 Church St; ⊙10am-7pm Mon-Thu, 10am-5pm Fri & Sat, 1-5pm Sun; 🖥) Free wi-fi and public internet terminals for California public library cardholders (out-of-state visitors $10).

Santa Cruz Visitor Center (✆800-833-3494, 831-429-7281; www.santacruzca.org; 303 Water St; ⊙9am-noon & 1-4pm Mon-Fri, 11am-3pm Sat & Sun) Free public internet terminal, maps and brochures.

ℹ️ Getting There & Around

Santa Cruz is 75 miles south of San Francisco via coastal Hwy 1 or Hwy 17, a nail-bitingly narrow, winding mountain road. Monterey is about an hour's drive further south via Hwy 1.

Santa Cruz Airport Shuttles (✆831-421-9883; www.santacruzshuttles.com) runs shared shuttles to/from the airports at San Jose ($50), San Francisco ($80) and Oakland ($80), with a $5 cash discount; the second passenger pays $10.

Greyhound (✆800-231-2222; www.greyhound.com; Metro Center, 920 Pacific Ave) has a few daily buses to San Francisco ($16.50, three hours), Salinas ($14, one hour), Santa Barbara ($53, six hours) and Los Angeles ($59, nine hours).

Santa Cruz Metro (✆831-425-8600; www.scmtd.com; single-ride/day pass $2/6) operates local and countywide bus routes that converge on downtown's **Metro Center** (920 Pacific

Ave). Hwy 17 express buses link Santa Cruz with San Jose's Amtrak/CalTrain station ($5, 50 minutes, once or twice hourly).

From late May through early September, the **Santa Cruz Trolley** (www.santacruztrolley.com; per ride 25¢) shuttles between downtown and the beach from 11am until 9pm daily.

Around Santa Cruz

Santa Cruz Mountains

Winding between Santa Cruz and Silicon Valley, Hwy 9 is a 40-mile backwoods byway through the Santa Cruz Mountains, passing tiny towns, towering redwood forests and fog-kissed vineyards. Many wineries are only open for 'Passport Days' on the third Saturday of January, April, July and November. The **Santa Cruz Mountains Winegrowers Association** (www.scmwa.com) publishes a free winery map, available at tasting rooms, including those that have opened more convenient tasting rooms in Santa Cruz, mostly west of downtown off Hwy 1.

Heading north from Santa Cruz, it's 7 miles to Felton, passing **Henry Cowell Redwoods State Park** (☑info 831-335-4598, reservations 800-444-7275; www.parks.ca.gov; 101 N Big Trees Park Rd, Felton; entry per car $10, campsites $35; ☉sun-

rise-sunset; ⓘ), which has miles of hiking trails through old-growth redwood groves along the San Lorenzo River and camping. In Felton, **Roaring Camp Railroads** (☑831-335-4484; www.roaringcamp.com; 5401 Graham Hill Rd, Felton; tours adult/child 2-12yr from $26/19, parking $8; ☉call for schedules; ⓘ)operates narrow-gauge steam trains up into the redwoods and a standard-gauge train down to the Santa Cruz Beach Boardwalk. Seven miles further north on Hwy 9, you'll drive through the rustic town of **Boulder Creek**, a decent place to grab a bite or a pint at **Boulder Creek Brewery & Cafe** (☑831-338-7882; www.bouldercreekbrewery.net; 13040 Hwy 9, Boulder Creek; mains $9-18; ☉11:30am-10pm Sun-Thu, to 10:30pm Fri & Sat).

Follow Hwy 236 northwest for nine miles to **Big Basin Redwoods State Park** (☑831-338-8860; www.bigbasin.org; 21600 Big Basin Way, Boulder Creek; entry per car $10, campsites $35; ☉sunrise-sunset), where nature trails loop past giant old-growth redwoods and beside shady campgrounds. A 12.5-mile one-way section of the **Skyline to the Sea Trail** ends at Waddell Beach, almost 20 miles northwest of Santa Cruz on Hwy 1. On weekends between mid-March and mid-December, you can usually ride **Santa Cruz Metro** (☑831-425-8600; www.scmtd.com) bus 35A up to Big Basin in the morning and get picked up by bus 40 at the beach in the afternoon.

Around Santa Cruz

Capitola

Six miles east of Santa Cruz, the diminutive beach town of Capitola nestles quaintly between ocean bluffs. Show up for mid-September's **Capitola Art & Wine Festival**, or the famous **Begonia Festival** (www.begoniafestival.com), held over Labor Day weekend, with a flotilla of floral floats along Soquel Creek.

By the beach, downtown is laid out for strolling, where cutesy shops and touristy restaurants inhabit seaside houses. Drop by family-friendly **Capitola Beach Company** (Map p260; ✆831-462-5222; www.capitolabeachcompany.com; 131 Monterey Ave; ⏰10am-6pm; ☻) or **Capitola Surf & Paddle** (Map p260; ✆831-435-6503; www.capitolasurfandpaddle.com; 208 San Jose Ave; ⏰10am-6pm) to rent water-sports gear or, if you book ahead, take surfing and stand-up paddleboarding lessons.

Catch an organic, fair-trade java buzz at **Mr Toots Coffeehouse** (Map p260; www.tootscoffee.com; 2nd fl, 231 Esplanade; ⏰7am-10pm; ☎), which has an art gallery, live music and ocean-view deck. Head inland to **Gayle's Bakery & Rosticceria** (Map p260; www.gaylesbakery.com; 504 Bay Ave; dishes $4-10; ⏰6:30am-8:30pm; ☻), which has a deli for assembling beach picnics. A few miles farther east in Aptos, **Aptos St BBQ** (www.aptosslbbq.com; 8059

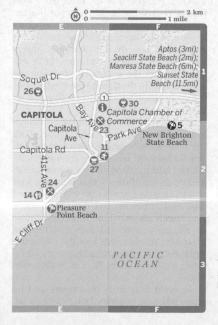

Aptos St, Aptos; mains $5-23; ⏰11:30am-9pm) pairs smoked tri-tip beef and pulled pork with California craft beers and live music.

The **Capitola Chamber of Commerce** (✆800-474-6522; www.capitolachamber.com; 716g Capitola Ave; ⏰10am-4pm) offers travel tips. Driving downtown can be a nightmare in summer and on weekends; use the parking lot behind City Hall, off Capitola Ave by Riverview Dr.

Moss Landing & Elkhorn Slough

Hwy 1 swings back toward the coast at Moss Landing, just south of the Santa Cruz County line, almost 20 miles north of Monterey. From the working fishing harbor, **Sanctuary Cruises** (✆831-917-1042; www.sanctuarycruises.com; 7881 Sandholdt Rd; adult/child 12yr & under $50/40; ☻) ☏ operates whale-watching and dolphin-spotting cruises year-round aboard biodiesel-fueled boats (reservations essential). Devour dock-fresh seafood at warehouse-sized **Phil's Fish Market** (✆831-633-2152; www.philsfishmarket.com; 7600 Sandholdt Rd; mains $11-21; ⏰10am-8pm Sun-Thu, to 9pm Fri & Sat; ☻) or, after browsing the antiques shops, lunch at **Haute Enchilada** (✆831-633-5483; www.hauteenchilada.com; 7902 Moss Landing Rd; mains $13-26; ⏰11am-9pm Mon-Thu, from 9am Fri-Sun) ☏, an inspired Mexican restaurant inside a Frida Kahlo-esque art gallery.

On the east side of Hwy 1, **Elkhorn Slough National Estuarine Research Reserve** (✆831-728-2822; www.elkhornslough.org; 1700 Elkhorn Rd, Watsonville; adult/child 16yr & under $4/free; ⏰9am-5pm Wed-Sun) is popular with bird-watchers and hikers. Docent-led tours typically depart at 10am and 1pm on Saturdays and Sundays, or sign up for an electric-boat cruise with **Whisper Charters** (✆800-979-3370; www.whispercharters.com; 2370 Hwy 1, Moss Landing; 2hr tour adult/child 12yr & under $49/39; ☻) ☏. Kayaking is a fantastic way to see the slough, though not on a windy day or when the tides are against you. Reserve ahead for kayak or SUP rentals, guided tours and paddling instruction with **Kayak Connection** (✆831-724-5692; www.kayakconnection.com; 2370 Hwy 1, Moss Landing; kayak rental $35-65, tours adult/child from $45/35; ⏰9am-5pm Mon-Fri, to 6pm Sat & Sun) or **Monterey Bay Kayaks** (✆800-649-5357, 831-373-5357; www.montereybaykayaks.com; 2390 Hwy 1, Moss Landing; kayak rental/tour from $30/55).

CENTRAL COAST AROUND SANTA CRUZ

Around Santa Cruz

CENTRAL COAST MONTEREY

Monterey

Working-class Monterey is all about the sea. What draws many visitors is a world-class aquarium overlooking **Monterey Bay National Marine Sanctuary**, which protects dense kelp forests and a sublime variety of marine life, including seals and sea lions, dolphins and whales. The city itself possesses the best-preserved historical evidence of California's Spanish and Mexican periods, with many restored adobe buildings. An afternoon's wander through downtown's historic quarter promises to be more edifying than time spent in the tourist ghettos of Fisherman's Wharf and Cannery Row.

⊙ Sights

★**Monterey Bay Aquarium**   AQUARIUM
(⌨info 831-648-4800, tickets 866-963-9645; www.montereybayaquarium.org; 886 Cannery Row; adult/child 3-12yr/youth 13-17yr $40/25/30; ⊙9:30am-6pm daily Jun, 9:30am-6pm Mon-Fri, to 8pm Sat & Sun Jul-Aug, 10am-5pm or 6pm daily Sep-May; ▥) ✎ Monterey's most mesmerizing experience is its enormous aquarium, built on the former site of the city's largest sardine cannery. All kinds of aquatic creatures are featured, from kid-tolerant sea stars and slimy sea slugs to animated sea otters and surprisingly nimble 800lb tuna.

The aquarium is much more than an impressive collection of glass tanks – thoughtful placards underscore the bay's cultural and historical contexts.

Every minute, up to 2000 gallons of seawater is pumped into the three-story **kelp forest**, re-creating as closely as possible the natural conditions you see out the windows to the east. The large fish of prey are at their charismatic best during mealtimes; divers hand-feed at 11:30am and 4pm. More entertaining are the sea otters, which may be seen basking in the **Great Tide Pool** outside the aquarium, where they are readied for reintroduction to the wild.

Even new-agey music and the occasional infinity-mirror illusion don't detract from the astounding beauty of jellyfish in the **Jellies Gallery**. To see marine creatures – including hammerhead sharks, ocean sunfish and green sea turtles – that outweigh kids many times over, ponder the awesome **Open Sea** tank. Upstairs and downstairs you'll find **touch pools**, where you can get close to sea cucumbers, bat rays and tidepool creatures. Younger kids love the interactive **Splash Zone**, with interactive bilingual exhibits and penguin feedings at 10:30am and 3pm.

To avoid long lines in summer and on weekends and holidays, buy tickets in advance. A visit can easily become a full-day affair, so get your hand stamped and break for lunch. Metered on-street parking is limited. Parking lots offering daily rates are plentiful just uphill from Cannery Row.

Cannery Row   HISTORIC SITE
(🏛) John Steinbeck's novel *Cannery Row* immortalized the sardine-canning business that was Monterey's lifeblood for the first half of the 20th century. A bronze **bust** of the Pulitzer Prize–winning writer sits at the bottom of Prescott Ave, just steps from the unabashedly touristy experience that the famous row has devolved into. The historical **Cannery Workers Shacks** at the base of flowery Bruce Ariss Way provide a sobering reminder of the hard lives led by Filipino, Japanese, Spanish and other immigrant laborers.

Back in Steinbeck's day, Cannery Row was a stinky, hardscrabble, working-class melting pot, which the novelist described as 'a poem, a stink, a grating noise, a quality of light, a tone, a habit, a nostalgia, a dream.' Sadly, there's precious little evidence of that era now, as overfishing and climatic changes caused the sardine industry's collapse in the 1950s.

★ Monterey State Historic Park   HISTORIC SITE
(📱 audio tour 831-998-9458, info 831-649-7118; www.parks.ca.gov) 🎧 **FREE** Old Monterey is home to an extraordinary assemblage of 19th-century brick and adobe buildings, administered as Monterey State Historic Park, all found along a 2-mile self-guided walking tour portentously called the 'Path of History.' You can inspect dozens of buildings, many with charming gardens; expect some to be open while others aren't, according to a capricious schedule dictated by unfortunate state-park budget cutbacks.

➡ **Pacific House**
(📱 831-649-7118; www.parks.ca.gov; 20 Custom House Plaza; admission incl Custom House $3, incl walking tour $5; ⊙ 10am-4pm Fri-Sun) Find out what's currently open at Monterey State Historic Park, grab a free map and buy tickets for guided walking tours inside this 1847 adobe building, which has fascinatingly in-depth exhibits covering the state's early Spanish, Mexican and American eras.

Nearby are some of the state park's historical highlights, including an **old whaling station** and **California's first theater**. A 10-minute walk south is the **old Monterey** **jail** featured in John Steinbeck's novel *Tortilla Flat.*

➡ **Custom House**
(Custom House Plaza; admission incl Pacific House Museum $3, incl walking tour $5; ⊙ 10am-4pm Fri-Sun) In 1822, a newly independent Mexico ended the Spanish trade monopoly and stipulated that any traders bringing goods to Alta (Upper) California must first unload their cargoes here for duty to be assessed. In 1846 when the US flag was raised over the Custom House, *voilà!* California was formally annexed from Mexico. Restored to its 1840s appearance, today this adobe building displays an exotic selection of goods that traders once brought to exchange for California cowhides.

➡ **Stevenson House**
(www.parks.ca.gov; 530 Houston St; ⊙ 1-4pm Sat Apr-early Sep) **FREE** Scottish writer Robert Louis Stevenson came to Monterey in 1879 to court his wife-to-be, Fanny Osbourne. This building, then the French Hotel, was where he stayed while reputedly devising his novel *Treasure Island.* The boarding-house rooms were primitive and Stevenson was still a penniless unknown. Today the house displays a superb collection of the writer's memorabilia.

Cooper-Molera Adobe   HISTORIC BUILDING
(📱 tour reservations 831-649-7172; 525 Polk St; ⊙ shop 10am-4pm, gardens from 9am, tours by appointment only) This stately early-19th-century adobe home was built by John Rogers Cooper, a New England sea captain, and three generations of his family resided here. Over time, the original adobe buildings were partitioned and expanded, gardens were added and later everything was willed to the National Trust for Historic Preservation. Worth a browse, the bookshop sells nostalgic toys and household goods.

Museum of Monterey   MUSEUM
(📱 831-372-2608; www.museumofmonterey.org; 5 Custom House Plaza; adult/child under 13yr $8/free, free 1st Wed of each month; ⊙ 10am-7pm Tue-Sat & noon-5pm Sun late-May–early Sep, 10am-5pm Wed-Sat & noon-5pm Sun early Sep–late-May; 🏛) Near the waterfront, this voluminous modern exhibition hall illuminates Monterey's salty past, from early Spanish explorers to the roller-coaster-like rise and fall of the local sardine industry that brought Cannery Row to life in the mid-20th century. Highlights include a ship-in-a-bottle collection and the

Monterey

N 0   500 m
0   0.25 miles

Monterey Bay Aquarium
1

Eardley Ave
32
David Ave
Irving St
5
28
37
4
40
38
26
Prescott Ave
Hoffman Ave
Foam St
Wave St
Cannery Row
18
43
42
29
23
Scholze Park
17
McClellan Ave
Lighthouse Ave
Hawthorne St
Reeside Ave
Dickman Ave
Drake Ave
Laine St

Monterey Peninsula
Recreation Trail
Monterey Bay
San Carlos Beach Park
Coast Guard Wharf

Bolio Rd
Coast Guard Headquarters

Presidio of Monterey
Lower Presidio Park
13
Infantry St
Shoreline Park
Municipal Wharf 2
Artillery St
Fisherman's Wharf
Lighthouse Tunnel
Seeno St
22
Scott St
31
12
7
3
10
2
Monterey State Historic Park
36
33
Monterey State Beach
16
Portola Plaza
21
45
Franklin St
Del Monte Ave
41
39
Jefferson St
34
30
35
Larkin St
Van Buren St
Tyler St
Washington St
Adams St
19
Monterey Visitors Center
Lake El Estero
Anthony St
11
Madison St
Dutra St
Pacific St
Calle Principal
Alvarado St
Polk St
9
Transit Plaza
44
6
15
Houston St
Abrego St
Alma St
Figueroa St
El Estero Park
20
Pearl St
Hartnell St
Church St
24
14
Hartnell Gulch
Fremont St
25
27
Perry Ln
8
El Dorado St
Cass St
Munras Ave
Abrego St
Camino El Estero
Mesa Rd
Fishnet Rd

Monterey

historic Fresnel lens from Point Sur's lighthouse.

Monterey Museum of Art MUSEUM
(MMA; www.montereyart.org; adult/child 18yr & under $10/free; ⊙11am-5pm Thu-Mon) Downtown, **MMA Pacific Street** (☏831-372-5477; 559 Pacific St) is particularly strong in California contemporary art and modern landscape painters and photographers, including Ansel Adams and Edward Weston. Temporary exhibits fill **MMA La Mirada** (☏831-372-3689; 720 Via Mirada), a silent-film star's villa, whose humble adobe origins are exquisitely concealed. You can visit both locations on the same admission ticket.

Royal Presidio Chapel & Heritage Center Museum CHURCH
(☏831-373-2628; www.sancarloscathedral.org; 500 Church St; admission by donation; ⊙10am-noon Wed, to 3pm Fri, to 2pm Sat, 1-3pm Sun, also 10am-12pm 2nd & 4th Mon of each month) Built of sandstone in 1794, this graceful chapel is California's oldest continuously functioning church and first stone building. The original 1770 mission church stood here before being moved to Carmel. As Monterey expanded under Mexican rule in the 1820s, older buildings were gradually destroyed, leaving behind this National Historic Landmark as the strongest reminder of the defeated Spanish colonial presence.

Presidio of Monterey Museum MUSEUM
(www.monterey.org/museums; Bldg 113, Corporal Ewing Rd; ⊙10am-1pm Mon, to 4pm Thu-Sat, 1-4pm Sun) **FREE** On the grounds of the original Spanish fort, this museum of interest only to history buffs looks at Monterey's history from a military perspective through the Native American, Mexican and American periods.

🏃 Activities

Like its larger namesake in San Francisco, Monterey's **Fisherman's Wharf** is a tacky tourist trap, but also a jumping-off point for deep-sea fishing trips and whale-watching cruises. A short walk east at workaday **Municipal Wharf 2**, fishing boats bob and sway in the bay.

Dennis the Menace Park PLAYGROUND
(www.monterey.org; 777 Pearl St; ☉10am-dusk, closed Tue Sep-May; 🚹) **FREE** The brainchild of Hank Ketcham, the creator of the classic *Dennis the Menace* comic strip, this ain't your standard dumbed-down playground suffocated by Big Brother's safety regulations. With lightning-fast slides, a hedge maze, a suspension bridge and towering climbing walls, even some adults can't resist playing here.

Cycling & Mountain Biking
Along an old railway line, the **Monterey Peninsula Recreational Trail** travels for 18 car-free miles along the waterfront, passing Cannery Row en route to Lovers Point in Pacific Grove. Road-cycling enthusiasts can make the round trip to Carmel along the **17-Mile Drive**. Mountain bikers head to **Fort Ord National Monument** to pedal more than 80 miles of single-track and fire roads; the **Sea Otter Classic** (www.seaotterclassic. com) races there in mid-April.

Adventures by the Sea CYCLING, KAYAKING
(☎831-372-1807; www.adventuresbythesea.com; 299 Cannery Row; rental per day kayak or bicycle $30, SUP set $50, tours from $60; 🚹) Beach cruisers, electric bike and water-sports gear rentals and tours available at multiple locations on Cannery Row and **downtown** (☎831-372-1807; www.adventuresbythesea.com; 210 Alvarado St; 🚹).

Bay Bikes CYCLING
(☎831-655-2453; www.baybikes.com; 585 Cannery Row; bicycle rental per hour/day from $8/32) Cruiser, tandem, hybrid and road-bike rentals near the aquarium and also **downtown** (☎831-655-2453; www.baybikes.com; 486 Washington St).

Whale-Watching
You can spot whales off the coast of Monterey Bay year-round. The season for blue and humpback whales runs from April to early December, while gray whales pass by from mid-December through March. Tour boats depart from Fisherman's Wharf and Moss Landing (p261). Reserve trips at least a day in advance; be prepared for a bumpy, cold ride.

Monterey Whale Watching BOAT TOUR
(☎831-205-2370, 888-223-9153; www.montereywhalewatching.com; 96 Fisherman's Wharf; 2½hr tour adult/child 5-11yr $45/35; 🐾) Several daily departures; no children under age five or pregnant women allowed.

Monterey Bay Whale Watch BOAT TOUR
(☎831-375-4658; www.montereybaywhalewatch. com; 84 Fisherman's Wharf; 3hr tour adult/child 4-12yr from $40/27; 🚹) Morning and afternoon departures; young children are welcome on board.

Diving & Snorkeling
Monterey Bay offers world-renowned diving and snorkeling, including off **Lovers Point** in Pacific Grove and at Point Lobos State Natural Reserve (p273) south of Carmel-by-the-Sea. You'll want a wetsuit year-round. In summer upwelling currents carry cold water from the deep canyon below the bay, sending a rich supply of nutrients up toward the surface level to feed the bay's diverse marine life. These frigid currents also account for the bay's chilly water temperatures and the summer fog that blankets the peninsula.

Aquarius Dive Shop DIVING
(☎831-375-1933; www.aquariusdivers.com; 2040 Del Monte Ave; snorkel/scuba-gear rental $35/65, dive tours from $65) Talk to this five-star PADI operation for gear rentals, classes and guided dives into Monterey Bay.

Monterey Bay Dive Charters DIVING
(☎831-383-9276; www.mbdcscuba.com; scuba-gear rental $75, shore/boat dive from $65/85) Arrange shore or boat dives and rent a full scuba kit with wetsuit from this well-reviewed outfitter.

Kayaking & Surfing

Monterey Bay Kayaks KAYAKING
(☎831-373-5357, 800-649-5357; www.montereybaykayaks.com; 693 Del Monte Ave; kayak or SUP set rental per day from $30, tours from $55) Rents kayaks and SUP equipment, offers paddling lessons and leads guided tours of Monterey Bay, including full-moon and sunrise trips.

Sunshine Freestyle Surf & Sport SURFING
(☎831-375-5015; www.sunshinefreestyle.com; 443 Lighthouse Ave; rental surfboard/wetsuit/boogie board from $20/10/7) Monterey's oldest surf shop rents and sells all the surfing gear you'll need. Staff grudgingly dole out local tips.

✨ Festivals & Events

Castroville Artichoke Festival FOOD
(www.artichoke-festival.org) Head north of Monterey for 3D 'agro art' sculptures, cooking

demos, a farmers market and field tours in May or June.

Blues, Brews & BBQ FOOD, MUSIC
(www.bluesbrewsandbarbecue.com) Rockin' bands, California craft beers and barbecue-pit masters at the county fairgrounds in late July.

Strawberry Festival at Monterey Bay FOOD
(www.mbsf.com) Berry-licious pie-eating contests and live bands in Watsonville, north of Monterey, in early August.

Monterey County Fair CARNIVAL, FOOD
(www.montereycountyfair.com) Old-fashioned fun, carnival rides, horse-riding and live-stock competitions, wine tasting and live music in late August and early September.

★ Monterey Jazz Festival MUSIC
(www.montereyjazzfestival.org) One of the world's longest-running jazz festivals (since 1958) showcases big-name headliners over a long weekend in mid-September.

Monterey Bay Birding Festival OUTDOORS
(www.montereybaybirding.org) Enthusiastic birders and naturalists gather for field trips, workshops and lectures in Monterey and surrounding counties in late September.

🛏 Sleeping

Book ahead for special events, on weekends and in summer. To avoid the tourist congestion and jacked-up prices of Cannery Row, look to Pacific Grove. Cheaper motels line Munras Ave, south of downtown, and N Fremont St, east of Hwy 1.

HI Monterey Hostel HOSTEL $
(☏831-649-0375; www.montereyhostel.org; 778 Hawthorne St; dm with shared bath $26-35; ☺check-in 4-10pm; @🛜) Four blocks from Cannery Row and the aquarium, this simple, clean hostel houses single-sex and mixed dorms, as well as private rooms (call for rates). Budget backpackers stuff themselves silly with make-your-own pancake breakfasts. Reservations strongly recommended. Take MST bus 1 from downtown's Transit Plaza.

Veterans Memorial Park Campground CAMPGROUND $
(☏831-646-3865; www.monterey.org; tent & RV sites $27) Tucked into the forest, this municipal campground has 40 grassy, nonreservable sites near a nature preserve's hiking trails. Amenities include coin-op hot showers, flush toilets, drinking water and barbecue fire pits. Three-night maximum stay.

Casa Munras BOUTIQUE HOTEL $$
(☏800-222-2446, 831-375-2411; www.hotelcasamunras.com; 700 Munras Ave; r from $120; @🛜🛟🐾) Built around an adobe hacienda once owned by a 19th-century Spanish colonial don, chic modern rooms come with lofty beds and some gas fireplaces, all inside two-story motel-esque buildings. Splash in a heated outdoor pool, unwind at the tapas bar or take a sea-salt scrub in the tiny spa. Pet fee $50.

Hotel Abrego BOUTIQUE HOTEL $$
(☏800-982-1986, 831-372-7551; www.hotelabrego.com; 755 Abrego St; r from $140; 🛜🛟🐾) At this downtown boutique hotel, most of the spacious, clean-lined contemporary rooms have gas fireplaces and chaise longues. Work out in the fitness studio, take a dip in the outdoor pool or warm up in the hot tub. Pet fee $30.

Monterey Hotel HISTORIC HOTEL $$
(☏800-966-6490, 831-375-3184; www.montereyhotel.com; 406 Alvarado St; r $80-220; 🛜) In the heart of downtown and a short walk from Fisherman's Wharf, this 1904 edifice harbors five-dozen small, somewhat noisy, but freshly renovated rooms with Victorian-styled furniture and plantation shutters. No elevator. Parking $17.

Colton Inn MOTEL $$
(☏800-848-7007, 831-649-6500; www.coltoninn.com; 707 Pacific St; r incl breakfast $119-209; 🛜) Downtown, this dated two-story motel prides itself on cleanliness and friendliness. There's no pool and zero view, but staff loan out DVDs, some rooms have real log-burning fireplaces, hot tubs or kitchenettes, and there's even a dry sauna.

★ InterContinental–Clement HOTEL $$$
(☏866-781-2406, 831-375-4500; www.ictheclementmonterey.com; 750 Cannery Row; r from $200; 🅿@🛜🛟) Like an upscale version of a New England millionaire's seaside mansion, this all-encompassing resort presides over Cannery Row. For the utmost luxury and romance, book an ocean-view suite with a balcony and private fireplace, then breakfast in bayfront C Restaurant downstairs. Parking is $23.

Sanctuary Beach Resort HOTEL $$$
(☏877-944-3863, 831-883-9478; www.thesanctuarybeachresort.com; 3295 Dunes Dr, Marina;

r $179-329; ✴ @ 🛜 🐾 🐟) Be lulled to sleep by the surf at this low-lying retreat hidden in the sand dunes north of Monterey. Reached via golf carts, townhouses harbor petite rooms with gas fireplaces and binoculars for whale-watching. Sunset bonfires bring out s'mores. The beach is an off-limits nature preserve, but there are public beaches and walking trails nearby. Pet fee $40.

Jabberwock   B&B $$$
(📋 888-428-7253, 831-372-4777; www.jabberwock-inn.com; 598 Laine St; r incl breakfast $169-309; @ 🛜) High atop a hill and barely visible through a shroud of foliage, this 1911 arts-and-crafts house hums a playful *Alice in Wonderland* tune through its seven immaculate rooms, a few with fireplaces and whirlpool tubs. Over afternoon tea and cookies or evening wine and hors d'oeuvres, ask the genial hosts about the house's many salvaged architectural elements.

✖ Eating

Uphill from Cannery Row, Lighthouse Ave is chock-a-block with casual, budget-friendly eateries, from Hawaiian barbecue to Middle Eastern kebabs.

Old Monterey Marketplace   MARKET $
(www.oldmonterey.org; Alvarado St, btwn Del Monte Ave & Pearl St; ⊗ 4-7pm Tue Sep-May, to 8pm Jun-Aug; 🖶) 🍴 Rain or shine, head downtown on Tuesdays for farm-fresh fruit and veggies, artisan cheeses, international food stalls and a scrumptious 'baker's alley.'

Crêpes of Brittany   FRENCH $
(www.crepesofbrittany.com; 6 Fisherman's Wharf; crepes $5-10; ⊗ 8am-3pm Mon-Fri, to 4pm Sat & Sun Sep-May, 8am-6:30pm Mon-Fri, to 8pm Sat & Sun Jun-Aug; 🖉 🖶) Authentic savory and sweet crepes are swirled by a French expat – the homemade caramel is a treat. Expect long lines on weekends. Cash only.

First Awakenings   AMERICAN $$
(www.firstawakenings.net; American Tin Cannery, 125 Oceanview Blvd; mains $8-12; ⊗ 7am-2pm Mon-Fri, to 2:30pm Sat & Sun; 🖶) Sweet and savory, all-American breakfasts and lunches and bottomless pitchers of coffee merrily weigh down outdoor tables at this cafe uphill from the aquarium. Try the unusual 'bluegerm' pancakes or a spicy Sonoran frittata.

LouLou's Griddle in the Middle   AMERICAN $$
(www.louolousgriddle.com; Municipal Wharf 2; mains $8-16; ⊗ usually 7:30am-3pm & 5-8:30pm

Wed-Mon; 🖶 🖶) Stroll down the municipal wharf to this zany diner, best for breakfasts of ginormous pancakes and omelets with Mexican pico de gallo salsa or fresh seafood for lunch. Breezy outdoor tables are dog-friendly.

Montrio Bistro   CALIFORNIAN $$$
(📋 831-648-8880; www.montrio.com; 414 Calle Principal; mains $17-29; ⊗ 5-10pm Sun-Thu, to 11pm Fri & Sat; 🖶) Inside a 1910 firehouse, Montrio looks dolled up with leather walls and iron trellises, but the tables have butcher paper and crayons for kids. The eclectic seasonal menu mixes local, organic fare with Californian, Asian and European flair, including tapas-style small bites and mini desserts.

Monterey's Fish House   SEAFOOD $$$
(📋 831-373-4647; 2114 Del Monte Ave; mains $9-28; ⊗ 11:30am-2:30pm Mon-Fri, 5-9:30pm daily; 🖶) Watched over by photos of Sicilian fishermen, dig into oak-grilled or blackened swordfish, barbecued oysters or, for those stout of heart, the Mexican squid steak. Reservations are essential (it's *so* crowded), but the vibe is island-casual: Hawaiian shirts seem to be de rigueur for men.

Sandbar & Grill   SEAFOOD $$$
(📋 831-373-2818; www.sandbarandgrillmonterey.com; Municipal Wharf 2; mains $18-30; ⊗ 11am-9pm; 🖶) Watch otters play outside the bay-view windows at this floating seafood kitchen on the wharf. Stick with the classics such as creamy clam chowder, grilled sand dabs and jumbo crab club sandwiches. Reservations strongly recommended. Ring the bell to let them know you've arrived.

🍷 Drinking & Nightlife

Prowl downtown's Alvarado St, touristy Cannery Row and locals-only Lighthouse Ave for more watering holes.

A Taste of Monterey   WINE BAR
(www.atasteofmonterey.com; 700 Cannery Row; tasting fee $10-20; ⊗ 11am-7pm Sun-Wed, to 8pm Thu-Sat) Sample medal-winning Monterey County wines from as far away as the Santa Lucia Highlands while soaking up dreamy sea views, then peruse thoughtful exhibits on barrel-making and cork production.

East Village Coffee Lounge   CAFE, LOUNGE
(www.eastvillagecoffeelounge.com; 498 Washington St; ⊗ 6am-late Mon-Fri, from 7am Sat & Sun; 🛜) Downtown coffee shop on a busy corner

brews with fair-trade, organic beans. At night, it pulls off a big-city lounge vibe with film, open-mic and live-music nights and an all-important booze license.

Crown & Anchor
PUB

(www.crownandanchor.net; 150 W Franklin St; ⊙11am-1:30am) At this basement British pub, the first thing you'll notice is the red plaid carpeting, then the plentiful draft beers and single-malt scotches, not to mention damn fine fish-and-chips.

Cannery Row Brewing Co
BAR

(www.canneryrowbrewingcompany.com; 95 Prescott Ave; ⊙11am-midnight Sun-Thu, to 2am Fri & Sat) Dozens of craft beers from around the world bring folks into this Cannery Row bar-and-grill, as does an outdoor deck with roaring fire pits.

Sardine Factory Lounge
LOUNGE

(www.sardinefactory.com; 701 Wave St; ⊙5pm-midnight) The legendary restaurant's fireplace lounge pours wines by the glass, delivers filling appetizers to your table and has a live piano player most nights.

☆ Entertainment

For comprehensive entertainment listings, browse the free tabloid *Monterey County Weekly* (www.montereycountyweekly.com).

Sly McFly's Fueling Station
LIVE MUSIC

(☑831-649-8050; www.slymcflys.net; 700 Cannery Row; ⊙11:30am-midnight Sun-Thu, to 2am Fri & Sat) Waterfront dive showcases live local blues, jazz and rock bands nightly after 8:30pm or 9pm. Skip the food, though.

Osio Cinemas
CINEMA

(☑831-644-8171; www.osiocinemas.com; 350 Alvarado St; adult $10, before 6pm $6.50) Downtown cinema screens indie dramas, cutting-edge documentaries and offbeat Hollywood films. Drop by its Cafe Lumiere for locally roasted coffee, loose-leaf tea, decadent cheesecake and wi-fi.

🔒 Shopping

Cannery Row is jammed with claptrap shops, while downtown's side streets hide more one-of-a-kind finds.

Wharf Marketplace
FOOD & DRINK

(www.thewharfmarketplace.com; 290 Figueroa St; ⊙7am-7pm Wed-Mon, to 2pm Tue) 🌊 Inside an old railway station, this gourmet-food emporium carries bountiful farm goodness and artisanal products from Monterey County and beyond.

Monterey Peninsula Art Foundation Gallery
ART

(www.mpaf.org; 425 Cannery Row; ⊙11am-5pm) Taking over a cozy sea-view house, more than 30 local artists sell plein-air paintings and sketches alongside contemporary works in all media.

Cannery Row Antique Mall
ANTIQUES

(www.canneryrowantiquemall.com; 471 Wave St; ⊙10am-5:30pm Mon-Fri, to 6pm Sat, to 5pm Sun) Inside a historic 1920s cannery building, two floors are stacked high with beguiling flotsam and jetsam from decades past.

Old Capitol Books
BOOKS

(559 Tyler St; ⊙10am-6pm Wed-Mon, to 7pm Tue) Tall shelves of new, used and antiquarian books, including rare first editions, California titles and John Steinbeck's works.

ℹ️ Information

Doctors on Duty (☑831-649-0770; www.doctorsonduty.com; 501 Lighthouse Ave; ⊙8am-8pm Mon-Sat, 8am-6pm Sun) Walk-in, nonemergency medical clinic.

FedEx Office (www.fedex.com; 799 Lighthouse Ave; per min 30-40¢; ⊙7am-10pm Mon-Fri, 8am-9pm Sat, 9am-9pm Sun; 🛜) Pay-as-you-go internet computer workstations.

Monterey Public Library (www.monterey.org; 625 Pacific St; ⊙noon-8pm Mon-Wed, 10am-6pm Thu-Sat, 1-5pm Sun; 🛜) Free wi-fi and public internet terminals.

Monterey Visitors Center (☑877-666-8373, 831-657-6400; www.seemonterey.com; 401 Camino El Estero; ⊙9am-6pm Mon-Sat, to 5pm Sun, closing 1hr earlier Nov-Mar) Free tourist brochures; ask for a *Monterey County Literary & Film Map*.

ℹ️ Getting There & Around

A few miles east of downtown off Hwy 68, Monterey Peninsula Airport (p50700) has flights with United (LA, San Francisco and Denver), American (LA), Alaska (San Diego), Allegiant Air (Las Vegas) and US Airways (Phoenix).

Monterey Airbus (☑831-373-7777; www.montereyairbus.com; 🛜) links Monterey with international airports in San Jose ($40, 1½ hours) and San Francisco ($50, 2½ hours) almost a dozen times daily; book online for discounts.

To get here on public transportation, first take a Greyhound bus or Amtrak train to Salinas, then catch a Thruway bus (for Amtrak train passengers only) or MST bus 20 to Monterey ($3.50, one hour, every 30 to 60 minutes).

Monterey Peninsula

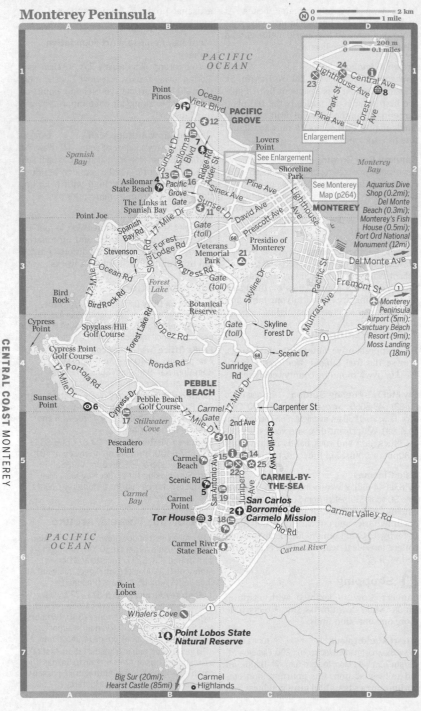

Monterey Peninsula

Monterey-Salinas Transit (MST; ☑ 888-678-2871; www.mst.org; single-ride $1.50-3.50, day pass $10) operates local and regional buses; routes converge on downtown's **Transit Plaza** (cnr Pearl & Alvarado Sts). From late May until early September, MST's free **trolley** loops around downtown, Fisherman's Wharf and Cannery Row between 10am and 7pm or 8pm daily.

Pacific Grove

Founded as a tranquil Methodist summer retreat in 1875, PG maintained its quaint, holier-than-thou attitude well into the 20th century. The selling of liquor was illegal up until 1969, making it California's last 'dry' town. Today, leafy streets are lined by stately Victorian homes and a charming, compact downtown orbits Lighthouse Ave.

◉ Sights & Activities

Aptly named **Ocean View Blvd** affords views from Lovers Point Park west to Point Pinos, where it becomes **Sunset Dr**, offering tempting turnouts where you can stroll by pounding surf, rocky outcrops and teeming tide pools all the way to **Asilomar State Beach**. This seaside route is great for cycling too – some say it rivals the famous 17-Mile Drive for beauty, and even better, it's free.

Point Pinos Lighthouse   LIGHTHOUSE
(☑ 831-648-3176; www.pointpinos.org; 90 Asilomar Ave; suggested donation adult/child 6-17yr $2/1; ☺ 1-4pm Thu-Mon) The West Coast's oldest continuously operating lighthouse has been warning ships off the hazardous tip of the Monterey Peninsula since 1855. Inside are modest exhibits on the lighthouse's history and alas, its failures – local shipwrecks.

Monarch Grove Sanctuary   PARK
(www.ci.pg.ca.us; off Ridge Rd, btwn Lighthouse Ave & Short St; ☺ dawn-dusk; ☀) 🄵🅁🄴🄴 Between October and February, more than 25,000 migratory monarch butterflies cluster in this thicket of tall eucalyptus trees, secreted inland. During peak season, volunteer guides answer all of your questions.

Pacific Grove Museum of Natural History   MUSEUM
(☑ 831-648-5716; www.pgmuseum.org; 165 Forest Ave; admission by donation; ☺ 10am-5pm Tue-Sat; ☀) With a gray-whale sculpture out front, this small kid-oriented museum has old-fashioned exhibits about sea otters, coastal bird life, butterflies, the Big Sur coast and Native Californian tribes.

Pacific Grove Golf Links   GOLF
(☑ 831-648-5775; www.pggolflinks.com; 77 Asilomar Blvd; green fees $25-65) Can't afford to play at famous Pebble Beach? This historic

CENTRAL COAST PACIFIC GROVE

18-hole municipal course, where deer freely range, has impressive sea views, and it's a lot easier (not to mention cheaper) to book a tee time here.

🛏 Sleeping

Antique-filled B&Bs have taken over many stately Victorian homes around downtown and by the beach. Motels cluster at the peninsula's western end, off Lighthouse and Asilomar Aves.

Asilomar Conference Grounds   LODGE $$

(✆888-635-5310, 831-372-8016; www.visitasilomar.com; 800 Asilomar Ave; r incl breakfast from $145; @ 🖥 🏊) This state-park lodge sprawls by sand dunes in pine forest. Skip ho-hum motel rooms and opt for historic houses designed by early-20th-century architect Julia Morgan (of Hearst Castle fame) – the thin-walled, hardwood-floored rooms may be small, but share a fireplace lounge. Head to the lodge lobby for ping-pong and pool tables and wi-fi. Bike rentals available.

Sunset Inn   MOTEL $$

(✆831-375-3529; www.gosunsetinn.com; 133 Asilomar Blvd; r $90-235; 🖥) At this small motor lodge near the golf course and the beach, attentive staff hand out keys to crisply redesigned rooms that have hardwood floors, king-sized beds with cheery floral-print comforters and sometimes a hot tub and a fireplace.

Deer Haven Inn   MOTEL $$

(✆831-373-7784; www.deerhaveninn.com; 750 Crocker Ave; r incl breakfast $109-209; 🖥) Stylish renovations have brought this two-story motel into the modern age. Every room has a gas fireplace, and it's a quick walk to the beach.

🍴 Eating

Downtown PG teems with European-style bakeries, coffee shops and neighborhood cafes.

Red House Cafe   CAFE $$

(✆831-643-1060; www.redhousecafe.com; 662 Lighthouse Ave; mains breakfast & lunch $8-

---

SCENIC DRIVE: 17-MILE DRIVE

What to See

Pacific Grove and Carmel are linked by the spectacularly scenic, if overhyped, 17-Mile Drive, which meanders through Pebble Beach, a wealthy private resort. It's no chore staying within the 25mph limit – every curve in the road reveals another postcard vista, especially when wildflowers are in bloom. Cycling the drive is enormously popular: try to do it during the week, when traffic isn't as heavy, and ride with the flow of traffic from north to south.

Using the self-guided touring map you'll receive at the toll gate, you can easily pick out landmarks such as **Spanish Bay**, where explorer Gaspar de Portolá dropped anchor in 1769; treacherously rocky **Point Joe**, which was often mistaken for the entrance to Monterey Bay and thus became the site of shipwrecks; and **Bird Rock**, also a haven for harbor seals and sea lions. The ostensible pièce de résistance is the trademarked **Lone Cypress**, which has perched on a seaward rock for possibly more than 250 years.

Besides the coastal scenery, star attractions at Pebble Beach include world-famous **golf courses**, where a celebrity and pro tournament happens every February. The luxurious **Lodge at Pebble Beach** (✆800-654-9300, 831-624-3811; www.pebblebeach.com; 1700 17-Mile Drive; r from $765; ❄ @ 🖥 🏊) embraces a spa and designer shops where the most demanding of tastes are catered to. Even if you're not a trust-fund baby, you can still soak up the rich atmosphere in the resort's art-filled public spaces and bay views from the cocktail lounge.

The Route

Operated as a toll road by the Pebble Beach Company, the **17-Mile Drive** (www.pebblebeach.com; per car/bicycle $10/free) is open from sunrise to sunset. The toll can be refunded later as a discount on a $30 minimum food purchase at Pebble Beach restaurants.

Time & Mileage

There are five separate gates for the 17-Mile Drive; how far you drive and how long you take is up to you. To take advantage of the most scenery, enter off Sunset Dr in Pacific Grove and exit onto San Antonio Ave in Carmel-by-the-Sea.

14, dinner $12-23; ⊙8am-2:30pm daily, 5-9pm Tue-Sun; 🌐) Crowded with locals, this shingled late-19th-century house dishes up comfort food with haute touches, including cinnamon-brioche French toast, grilled eggplant-fontina sandwiches or spinach-cheese ravioli in lemon beurre blanc sauce. Oatmeal-apricot-pecan cookies are what's for dessert. Reservations helpful.

★**Passionfish**   SEAFOOD **$$$**
(📞831-655-3311; www.passionfish.net; 701 Lighthouse Ave; mains $16-32; ⊙5-9pm Sun-Thu, to 10pm Fri & Sat) 🍃 Fresh, sustainable seafood is artfully presented in any number of inventive ways, and a seasonally inspired menu also carries slow-cooked meats and vegetarian dishes spotlighting local farms. The earth-tone decor is spare, with tables squeezed conversationally close together. An ambitious world-ranging wine list is priced near retail, and there are twice as many Chinese teas as wines by the glass.

Reservations strongly recommended.

❶ Information

Pacific Grove Chamber of Commerce
(📞800-656-6650, 831-373-3304; www.pacificgrove.org; 584 Central Ave; ⊙9:30am-5pm Mon-Fri, 10am-3pm Sat) Free maps and brochures.

❶ Getting There & Around

MST (📞888-678-2871; www.mst.org) bus 1 connects downtown Monterey and Cannery Row with Pacific Grove, continuing to Asilomar ($2.50, every 30 to 60 minutes).

Carmel-by-the-Sea

With borderline fanatical devotion to its canine citizens, quaint Carmel has the well-manicured feel of a country club. Watch the parade of behatted ladies toting fancy-label shopping bags to lunch and dapper gents driving top-down convertibles along Ocean Ave, the village's slow-mo main drag.

Founded as a seaside resort in the 1880s – fairly odd, given that its beach is often blanketed in fog – Carmel quickly attracted famous artists and writers, such as Sinclair Lewis and Jack London, and their hangers-on. Artistic flavor survives in more than 100 galleries that line downtown's immaculate streets, but sky-high property values have long obliterated any salt-of-the-earth bohemia.

Dating from the 1920s, Comstock cottages, with their characteristic stone chimneys and pitched gable roofs, still dot the town, making it look vaguely reminiscent of the English countryside. Even payphones, garbage cans and newspaper vending boxes are quaintly shingled.

◉ Sights & Activities

Escape downtown's harried shopping streets and stroll tree-lined neighborhoods on the lookout for domiciles charming and peculiar. The Hansel and Gretel houses on Torres St, between 5th and 6th Avenues, are just how you'd imagine them. Another eye-catching house in the shape of a ship, made from local river rocks and salvaged ship parts, is on Guadalupe St near 6th Ave.

★**Point Lobos State Natural Reserve** PARK
(📞831-624-4909; www.pointlobos.org; Hwy 1; per car $10; ⊙8am-7pm, closing 30min after sunset early Nov–mid-Mar; 🌐) They bark, they bathe and they're fun to watch – sea lions are the stars here at Punta de los Lobos Marinos (Point of the Sea Wolves), almost 4 miles south of Carmel, where a dramatically rocky coastline offers excellent tide-pooling. The full perimeter hike is 6 miles, but shorter walks take in wild scenery too, including Bird Island, shady cypress groves, the historical Whaler's Cabin and Devil's Cauldron, a whirlpool that gets splashy at high tide.

The kelp forest at **Whalers Cove** is popular with snorkelers and scuba divers; without donning a wetsuit, you can still get an idea of the underwater terrain with a 3D model located by the parking lot. Reserve snorkeling, scuba-diving, kayaking and SUP permits (per person $5 to $10) up to 60 days in advance online.

Arrive early on weekends; parking is limited. Don't skip paying the entry fee by parking outside the park gates on the highway shoulder – California's state parks are chronically underfunded and need your help.

★**San Carlos Borroméo de Carmelo Mission** CHURCH
(www.carmelmission.org; 3080 Rio Rd; adult/child 7-17yr $6.50/2; ⊙9:30am-7pm) Monterey's original mission was established by Franciscan friar Junípero Serra in 1770, but poor soil and the corrupting influence of Spanish soldiers forced the move to Carmel two years later. Today this is one of California's most strikingly beautiful missions, an oasis of solemnity bathed in flowering gardens. The

WORTH A TRIP

CARMEL VALLEY

Where sun-kissed vineyards rustle beside farm fields, Carmel Valley is a peaceful side trip, just a 20-minute drive east of Hwy 1 along eastbound Carmel Valley Rd. At organic **Earth-bound Farm Stand** (☎805-625-6219; www.ebfarm.com; 7250 Carmel Valley Rd; ☉8am-6:30pm Mon-Sat, 9am-6pm Sun; ☻) ✐, sample homemade soups and salads or harvest your own herbs from the garden. Several wineries further east offer tastings – don't miss the Pinot Noir bottled by **Boekenoogen** (www. boekenoogenwines.com; 24 W Carmel Valley Rd; tasting fee $8-10; ☉11am-5pm). Afterwards, stretch your legs in the village of Carmel Valley, chock-a-block with genteel shops and bistros.

mission's adobe chapel was later replaced with an arched basilica made of stone quarried in the Santa Lucia Mountains. Museum exhibits are scattered throughout the meditative complex.

The spartan cell attributed to Serra looks like something out of *The Good, the Bad and the Ugly,* while a separate chapel houses his memorial tomb. Don't overlook the gravestone of 'Old Gabriel,' a Native American convert whom Serra baptized, and whose dates put him at 151 years old when he died. People say he smoked like a chimney and outlived seven wives. There's a lesson in there somewhere.

★ **Tor House**   HISTORIC BUILDING
(☎831-624-1813; www.torhouse.org; 26304 Ocean View Ave; adult/child 12-17yr $10/5; ☉tours hourly 10am-3pm Fri & Sat) Even if you've never heard of 20th-century poet Robinson Jeffers, a pilgrimage to this house built with his own hands offers fascinating insights into both the man and the bohemian ethos of Old Carmel. A porthole in the Celtic-inspired **Hawk Tower** reputedly came from the wrecked ship that carried Napoleon from Elba. The only way to visit the property is to reserve a tour (children under 12 years old not allowed), although the tower can be glimpsed from the street.

Carmel Beach City Park   BEACH
(off Scenic Rd; ☻) FREE Not always sunny, Carmel Beach is a gorgeous blanket of white sand, where pampered pups excitedly run off-leash. South of 10th Ave, bonfires crackle after sunset.

✮✭ Festivals & Events

Carmel Art Festival   CULTURE
(www.carmelartfestival.org) Meet plein-air painters and sculptors in Devendorf Park over a long weekend in mid-May.

Carmel Bach Festival   MUSIC
(www.bachfestival.org) Classical and chamber-music performances are staged around town in July.

Pebble Beach Concours d'Elegance PARADE
(www.pebblebeachconcours.net) Rare vintage and classic cars roll onto the fairways at Pebble Beach in mid-August.

Carmel Art & Film Festival   CULTURE, FILM
(www.carmelartandfilm.com) Contemporary fine art, live music and more than 100 independent film screenings in mid-October.

🛏 Sleeping

Shockingly overpriced boutique hotels, inns and B&Bs fill up quickly, especially in summer. Ask the chamber of commerce about last-minute deals. For better-value lodgings, head north to Monterey.

Carmel Village Inn   MOTEL $$
(☎800-346-3864, 831-624-3864; www.carmel-villageinn.com; cnr Ocean & Junípero Aves; d incl breakfast buffet from $129; ☜) With cheerful flowers decorating its exterior, this well-located motel across from Devendorf Park has cheapish rooms, some with gas fireplaces, and nightly quiet hours.

Cypress Inn   BOUTIQUE HOTEL $$$
(☎831-624-3871, 800-443-7443; www.cypress-inn. com; Lincoln St, at 7th Ave; r incl breakfast from $245; ☜☻) Done up in Spanish Colonial style, this 1929 inn is co-owned by movie star Doris Day. Airy terra-cotta hallways with colorful tiles give it a Mediterranean feel, while sunny rooms face the courtyard. Pet fee $30.

Sea View Inn   B&B $$$
(☎831-624-8778; www.seaviewinncarmel.com; El Camino Real, btwn 11th & 12th Aves; r incl breakfast $145-295; ☜) Retreat from downtown's hustle to fireside nooks tailor-made for reading. The cheapest rooms with slanted ceilings are short on cat-swinging space. Rates in-

clude afternoon wine and noshes on the front porch.

Mission Ranch　　　　　　INN $$$
(☎800-538-8221, 831-624-6436; www.mission-ranchcarmel.com; 26270 Dolores St; r incl breakfast $135-300; ☎) If woolly sheep grazing on green fields by the beach doesn't convince you to stay here, maybe knowing Hollywood icon Clint Eastwood restored this historic ranch will. Accommodations are shabby-chic, even a tad rustic.

✖ Eating

Carmel's staid dining scene is more about old-world atmosphere than value.

Bruno's Market & Deli　　DELI, MARKET $
(www.brunosmarket.com; cnr 6th & Junípero Aves; sandwiches $6-9; ☎7am-8pm) Small supermarket deli counter makes a saucy sandwich of oakwood-grilled tri-tip beef and stocks all the accoutrements for a beach picnic, including Sparkys root beer from Pacific Grove.

Mundaka　　　　　　SPANISH, TAPAS $$
(☎831-624-7400; www.mundakacarmel.com; San Carlos St, btwn Ocean & 7th Aves; small plates $6-25; ☎5:30-10pm Sun-Wed, to 11pm Thu-Sat) This stone courtyard hideaway is a svelte escape from Carmel's stuffy 'newly wed and nearly dead' crowd. Taste Spanish tapas and housemade sangria while world beats spin.

Katy's Place　　　　　BREAKFAST $$
(www.katysplacecarmel.com; Mission St, btwn 5th & 6th Aves; mains $8-16; ☎7am-2pm) It's pricey, but what isn't in Carmel? Start your day with an apple-cinnamon Belgian waffle, Swedish pancakes or one of 16 Californicized variations on eggs benedict.

♟ Drinking & Entertainment

Scheid Vineyards　　　　　WINE BAR
(www.scheidvineyards.com; San Carlos St, at 7th Ave; tasting fee $10-20; ☎noon-6pm Sun-Thu, to 7pm Fri & Sat) Wine-tasting rooms abound downtown. Pop into Scheid Vineyards to sip a prodigious variety of grape varietals, all grown in Monterey County.

Forest Theater　　　　　　THEATER
(☎831-626-1681; www.foresttheatercarmel.org; cnr Mountain View Ave & Santa Rita St) At this 1910 venue, community-theater musicals, dramas and comedies and film screenings take place under the stars by flickering fire pits.

ℹ Information

Downtown buildings have no street numbers, so addresses specify the street and nearest intersection only.

Carmel Chamber of Commerce (☎800-550-4333, 831-624-2522; www.carmelcalifornia.org; San Carlos St, btwn 5th & 6th Aves; ☎10am-5pm) Free maps and brochures, including local art gallery guides.

Carmel Pine Cone (www.pineconearchive.com) Free weekly newspaper packed with local personality and color – the police log is a comedy of manners.

ℹ Getting There & Around

Carmel is about 5 miles south of Monterey via Hwy 1. There's free parking (no time limit) in a **municipal lot** (cnr 3rd & Junípero Aves) behind the Vista Lobos building.

MST (☎888-678-2871; www.mst.org) 'Grapevine Express' bus 24 ($2.50, hourly) connects Monterey's Transit Plaza with downtown Carmel, the mission and Carmel Valley. Bus 22 ($3.50) stops in downtown Carmel and at the mission en route to/from Point Lobos and Big Sur three times daily between late May and early September, and twice daily on Saturday and Sunday only the rest of the year.

Big Sur

Big Sur is more a state of mind than a place you can pinpoint on a map. There are no traffic lights, banks or strip malls, and when the sun goes down, the moon and the stars are the only streetlights – if summer's dense fog hasn't extinguished them, that is. Much ink has been spilled extolling the raw beauty and energy of this precious piece of land shoehorned between the Santa Lucia Range and the Pacific Ocean, but nothing quite prepares you for your first glimpse of the craggy, unspoiled coastline.

In the 1950s and '60s, Big Sur – so named by Spanish settlers living on the Monterey Peninsula, who referred to the wilderness as *el país grande del sur* ('the big country to the south') – became a retreat for artists and writers, including Henry Miller and Beat Generation visionaries such as Lawrence Ferlinghetti. Today Big Sur attracts self-proclaimed artists, new-age mystics, latter-day hippies and city slickers seeking to unplug and reflect more deeply on this emerald-green edge of the continent.

Big Sur

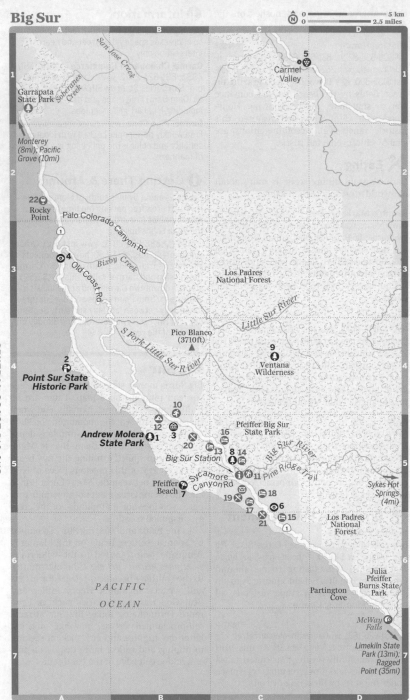

0 ____ 5 km
0 ____ 2.5 miles

A   B   C   D

San Jose Creek

Carmel Valley **5**

Garrapata State Park

Soberanes Creek

Monterey (8mi); Pacific Grove (10mi)

22 Rocky Point

Palo Colorado Canyon Rd

(1)

4

Bixby Creek

Old Coast Rd

Los Padres National Forest

Little Sur River

S Fork Little Sur River

Pico Blanco (3710ft)

9 Ventana Wilderness

2

Point Sur State Historic Park

10

12 **3**

Andrew Molera State Park **1**

Pfeiffer Big Sur State Park

16

20

13 **8** **14**

Big Sur Station

Big Sur River

Pine Ridge Trail

Sykes Hot Springs (4mi)

11

Pfeiffer Beach

Sycamore Canyon Rd

7

19   **18**

17

6

21   **15**

(1)

Los Padres National Forest

PACIFIC OCEAN

Partington Cove

Julia Pfeiffer Burns State Park

McWay Falls

Limekiln State Park (13mi); Ragged Point (35mi)

Big Sur

◉ Sights

At Big Sur's state parks, your parking fee ($10) receipt is valid for same-day entry to all except Limekiln. Please don't skip paying the entry fee by parking illegally outside the parks along Hwy 1 – California's state parks have suffered severe budget cutbacks, and every dollar helps.

Garrapata State Park PARK
(☎831-624-4909; www.parks.ca.gov; off Hwy 1; ☻) **FREE** Over 4 miles south of Point Lobos on Hwy 1, pull over to hike coastal headlands, where you might spot whales cruising by offshore during winter, or into canyons of wildflowers and redwood trees. *Garrapata* is Spanish for tick, of which there are many in the canyon and woods, so wearing long sleeves and pants is smart. Leashed dogs are allowed on the beach only.

Bixby Bridge LANDMARK
Less than 15 miles south of Carmel, this landmark spanning Rainbow Canyon is one of the world's highest single-span bridges. Completed in 1932, it was built by prisoners eager to lop time off their sentences. There's a perfect photo-op pull-off on the bridge's north side. Before Bixby Bridge was constructed, travelers had to trek inland on what's now called the **Old Coast Rd**, a rough dirt route that reconnects after 11 miles with Hwy 1 near Andrew Molera State Park.

When the weather is dry enough, the old road is usually navigable by 4WD or a mountain bike.

★**Point Sur State Historic Park** LIGHTHOUSE
(☎831-625-4419; www.pointsur.org; off Hwy 1; adult/child 6-17yr from $12/5; ☺tours usually at 1pm Wed, 10am Sat & Sun Nov-Mar, 10am & 2pm Wed & Sat, 10am Sun Apr-Oct, also 10am Thu Jul & Aug) A little more than 6 miles south of Bixby Bridge, Point Sur rises like a velvety green fortress out of the sea. It looks like an island, but is actually connected to land by a sandbar. Atop the volcanic rock sits an 1889 stone lightstation, which was staffed until 1974. During three-hour guided tours, ocean views and tales of the lighthouse keepers' family lives are engrossing. Meet your tour guide at the locked farm gate ¼-mile north of Point Sur Naval Facility.

Special monthly moonlight tours are given between April and October. Call ahead to confirm all tour schedules. Show up early because space is limited (no reservations, some credit cards accepted).

★**Andrew Molera State Park** PARK
(☎831-667-2315; www.parks.ca.gov; Hwy 1; per car $10; ☺30min before sunrise-30min after

sunset; 🚶) Named after the farmer who first planted artichokes in California, this oft-overlooked park is a trail-laced pastiche of grassy meadows, ocean bluffs and rugged sandy beaches offering excellent wildlife watching. Look for the entrance just a little more than 8 miles south of Bixby Bridge.

South of the parking lot, you can learn all about endangered California condors inside the **Big Sur Discovery Center** (☑ 831-624-1202; www.ventanaws.org/discovery_center/; ☉ 10am-4pm Sat & Sun late-May–early Sep; 🚶) 🅵 **FREE**. At the bird-banding lab inside a small shed, naturalists carry out long-term species monitoring programs.

From the main parking lot, a short walk along the beach-bound trail passes through a first-come, first-served campground, from where a gentle spur trail leads to the 1861 redwood **Cooper Cabin**, Big Sur's oldest building. Keep hiking on the main trail out toward a wild beach where the Big Sur River runs into the ocean; condors may be spotted circling overhead and migrating whales sometimes cruise by offshore.

Pfeiffer Big Sur State Park   PARK

(☑ 831-667-2315; www.parks.ca.gov; 47225 Hwy 1; per car $10; ☉ 30min before sunrise-30min after sunset; 🚶) Named after Big Sur's first European settlers who arrived in 1869, this is Big Sur's largest state park, where hiking trails loop through stately redwood groves. The most popular hike – to 60ft-high **Pfeiffer Falls**, a delicate cascade hidden in the forest, which usually runs from December to May – is a 2-mile round-trip. Built in the 1930s by the Civilian Conservation Corps (CCC), rustic Big Sur Lodge stands near the park entrance, about 13 miles south of Bixby Bridge.

Pfeiffer Beach   BEACH

(www.fs.usda.gov/lpnf; end of Sycamore Canyon Rd; per car $10; ☉ 9am-8pm; 🐾) This phenomenal, crescent-shaped and dog-friendly beach is known for its huge double rock formation, through which waves crash with life-affirming power. It's often windy, and the surf is too dangerous for swimming. But dig down into the wet sand – it's purple! That's because manganese garnet washes down from the craggy hillsides above. To get here from Hwy 1, make a sharp right onto Sycamore Canyon Rd, marked by a small yellow sign that says 'narrow road' at the top.

From the turnoff, which is a half-mile south of Big Sur Station on the ocean side of Hwy 1, it's two narrow, twisting miles down to the beach (RVs and trailers prohibited).

Henry Miller Memorial Library   ARTS CENTER

(☑ 831-667-2574; www.henrymiller.org; 48603 Hwy 1; ☉ 11am-6pm) 'It was here in Big Sur I first learned to say Amen!' wrote novelist Henry Miller, a Big Sur denizen from 1944 to 1962. More of a beatnik memorial, alt-cultural venue and bookshop, this community gathering spot was never Miller's home. The house belonged to Miller's friend, painter Emil White, until his death and is now run by a nonprofit group. Stop by to browse and hang out on the front deck. It's about 0.4 miles south of Nepenthe restaurant.

Inside are copies of all of Miller's written works, many of his paintings and a collection of Big Sur and Beat Generation material, including copies of the top 100 books Miller said most influenced him. Check the online calendar for upcoming events.

Partington Cove   BEACH

(off Hwy 1) 🅵 **FREE** It's a raw, breathtaking spot where crashing surf salts your skin. On the steep, half-mile dirt hike down to the cove, you'll cross a cool bridge and go through an even cooler tunnel. The cove's water is unbelievably aqua and within it grow tangled kelp forests. Look for the unmarked trailhead turnoff inside a hairpin turn on the ocean side of Hwy 1, about 6 miles south of Nepenthe restaurant and 2 miles north of Julia Pfeiffer Burns State Park.

The trail starts just beyond the locked vehicle gate. There's no real beach access and ocean swimming isn't safe, but some people scamper on the rocks and look for tide pools as waves splash ominously. Originally used for loading freight, Partington Cove allegedly became a landing spot for Prohibition-era bootleggers.

★ Julia Pfeiffer Burns State Park   PARK

(☑ 831-667-2315; www.parks.ca.gov; Hwy 1; per car $10; ☉ 30min before sunrise-30min after sunset; 🚶) If you're chasing waterfalls, swing into this state park named for a Big Sur pioneer. From the parking lot, the 1.3-mile round-trip Overlook Trail rushes downhill toward the ocean, passing through a tunnel underneath Hwy 1. Everyone comes to photograph 80ft-high **McWay Falls**, which tumbles year-round over granite cliffs and freefalls into the sea – or the beach, depending on the tide. The park entrance is on the east side of Hwy 1, about 8 miles south of Nepenthe restaurant.

McWay Falls is the classic Big Sur postcard shot, with tree-topped rocks jutting above a golden beach next to swirling blue pools and crashing white surf. From trailside benches, you might spot migrating whales during winter.

Limekiln State Park
PARK

(☑ 831-434-1996; www.parks.ca.gov; 63025 Hwy 1; per car $8; ⊘ 8am-sunset) Two miles south of Lucia, this park gets its name from the four remaining wood-fired kilns originally built here in the 1880s to smelt quarried limestone into powder, a key ingredient in cement building construction from Monterey to San Francisco. Tragically, pioneers chopped down most of the steep canyon's old-growth redwoods to fuel the kilns' fires. A one-mile round-trip trail leads through a redwood grove to the historic site, passing a creekside spur trail to a delightful 100ft-high waterfall.

Los Padres National Forest
FOREST

(☑ 831-667-2315; www.fs.usda.gov/lpnf; ☻) The tortuously winding 40-mile stretch of Hwy 1 south of Lucia to Hearst Castle is even more sparsely populated, rugged and remote, mostly running through national forest lands. Around 5 miles south of Kirk Creek Campground and Nacimiento-Fergusson Rd, almost opposite Plaskett Creek Campground, is **Sand Dollar Beach** (http://campone.com; Hwy 1; per car $10, free with paid local USFS campground fee; ⊘ 9am-8pm; ☻). From the picnic area, it's a five-minute walk to

southern Big Sur's longest sandy beach, a crescent-shaped strip of sand protected from winds by high bluffs.

In 1971, in the waters of nearby **Jade Cove** (http://campone.com; Hwy 1; ⊘ sunrise-sunset; ☻) FREE, local divers recovered a 9000lb jade boulder that measured 8ft long and was valued at $180,000. People still comb the beach today. The best time to find jade, which is black or blue-green and looks dull until you dip it in water, is during low tide or after a big storm. Keep an eye out for hang gliders flying in for a movie-worthy landing on the beach. Trails down to the water start from several mostly unmarked roadside pulloffs immediately south of Plaskett Creek Campground.

If you have any sunlight left, keep trucking down the highway to **Salmon Creek Falls** (www.fs.usda.gov/lpnf/; Hwy 1; ☂ ☻) FREE, which usually flows from December through May. Tucked up in a forested canyon, this double-drop waterfall can be glimpsed from the hairpin turn on Hwy 1, about 8 miles south of Gorda. Roadside parking gets very crowded, as everyone takes the 0.3-mile walk up to the falls to splash around in the pools, where kids shriek and dogs happily bark.

Before leaving Lucia, make sure you've got at least enough fuel in the tank to reach the expensive gas stations at Gorda, about 11 miles south of Limekiln State Park, or Ragged Point, another 12 miles further south.

Ragged Point
LANDMARK

(19019 Hwy 1) Your last – or first – taste of Big Sur's rocky grandeur comes at this craggy

---

CALIFORNIA'S COMEBACK CONDORS

When it comes to endangered species, one of the state's biggest success stories is the California condor. These gigantic, prehistoric birds weigh over 20lb with a wingspan of up to 10ft, letting them fly great distances in search of carrion. They're easily recognized by their naked pink head and large white patches on the underside of each wing.

This big bird became so rare that in 1987 there were only 27 left in the world, and all were removed from the wild to special captive-breeding facilities. Read the whole gripping story in journalist John Moir's book *Return of the Condor: The Race to Save Our Largest Bird from Extinction*.

There are more than 400 California condors alive today, with increasing numbers of captive birds being released back into the wild, where it's hoped they will begin breeding naturally, although it's an uphill battle. Wild condors are still dying of lead poisoning caused by hunter's bullets in the game carcasses that the birds feed on.

The Big Sur coast and Pinnacles National Park (p294) offer excellent opportunities to view this majestic bird. In Big Sur, the **Ventana Wildlife Society** (www.ventanaws.org) occasionally leads two-hour guided condor-watching tours ($50) using radio telemetry to track the birds; for sign-up details, check the website or ask inside the Big Sur Discovery Center.

WORTH A TRIP

VENTANA WILDERNESS

The 240,000-acre **Ventana Wilderness** is Big Sur's wild backcountry. It lies within the northern Los Padres National Forest, which straddles the Santa Lucia Range running parallel to the coast. Most of this wilderness is covered with oak and chaparral, though canyons cut by the Big Sur and Little Sur Rivers support virgin stands of coast redwoods and the rare endemic Santa Lucia fir, which grows on steep, rocky slopes too.

Partly reopened after devastating wildfires in 2008, Ventana Wilderness remains popular with adventurous backpackers. A much-trammeled overnight destination is **Sykes Hot Springs**, natural 100°F (35°C) mineral pools framed by redwoods. It's a moderately strenuous 10-mile one-way hike along the **Pine Ridge Trail**, starting from **Big Sur Station** (☑831-667-2315; www.parks.ca.gov; Hwy 1; ☺8am-4pm, closed Mon & Tue Nov-Mar), where you can get free campfire permits and pay for overnight trailhead parking ($5). Don't expect solitude on weekends during peak season (April through September) and always follow **Leave No Trace** (www.lnt.org) principles.

cliff outcropping with fabulous views of the coastline in both directions, about 15 miles north of Hearst Castle. Once part of the Hearst empire, it's now taken over by a sprawling, ho-hum lodge with a pricey gas station. Heading south, the land grows increasingly wind-swept as Hwy 1 rolls gently down to the water's edge.

🏇 Activities

Molera Horseback Tours HORSEBACK RIDING
(☑831-625-5486; www.molerahorsebacktours.com; Hwy 1; per person $48-74; 🖘) Across Hwy 1 from Andrew Molera State Park, Molera offers guided trail rides on the beach and through redwood forest. Walk-ins and novices are welcome; children must be at least six years old, with most rides recommended for ages 12 and up.

Esalen Institute RETREAT CENTER
(☑888-837-2536; www.esalen.org; 55000 Hwy 1) Marked only by a lit sign reading 'Esalen Institute – By Reservation Only,' this spot is like a new-age hippie camp for adults. Esoteric workshops treat anything 'relating to our greater human capacity,' from shapeshifting to Thai massage. Esalen's famous **baths** (☑831-667-3047; per person $25, credit cards only; ☺public entry 1am-3am nightly, reservations accepted 8am-8pm Mon-Thu & Sat, 8am-noon Fri & Sun), fed by a natural hot spring, sit on a ledge above the ocean. The entrance is on the ocean side of Hwy 1, a little more than 11 miles south of Nepenthe restaurant and 10 miles north of Lucia.

Dollars to donuts you'll never take another dip that compares panorama-wise with the one here, especially on stormy winter nights. Only two small outdoor pools perch directly over the waves, so once you've stripped down (bathing is clothing-optional) and taken a quick shower, head outside immediately to score the best views. Otherwise, you'll be stuck with a tepid, no-view pool or even worse, a rickety bathtub.

Things have sure changed a lot since Hunter S Thompson was the gun-toting caretaker here in the 1960s.

🛌 Sleeping

With few exceptions, Big Sur's lodgings do not have TVs and rarely have telephones. This is where you come to escape the world. There aren't a lot of rooms overall, so demand often exceeds supply and prices can be steep. Bigger price tags don't necessarily buy you more amenities either. In summer and on weekends, reservations are essential everywhere from campgrounds to deluxe resorts.

⭐**Pfeiffer Big Sur State Park Campground** CAMPGROUND $
(☑reservations 800-444-7275; www.reserveamerica.com; 47225 Hwy 1; tent & RV sites $35-50; 🖘) Best for novice campers and families with young kids, here more than 200 campsites nestle in a redwood-shaded valley. Facilities include drinking water, fire pits and coin-op hot showers and laundry.

Andrew Molera State Park Campground CAMPGROUND $
(www.parks.ca.gov; Hwy 1; tent sites $25) Two-dozen primitive tent sites (no reservations) in a grassy meadow come with fire pits and drinking water, but no ocean views. The campground is a 0.3-mile walk from the parking lot.

Limekiln State Park
Campground
CAMPGROUND $

(www.parks.ca.gov; 63025 Hwy 1; tent & RV sites $35; 🐕) In southern Big Sur, this quiet state park has two-dozen campsites huddled under a bridge next to the ocean. Drinking water, fire pits and coin-op hot showers are available.

Julia Pfeiffer Burns State
Park Campground
CAMPGROUND $

(www.parks.ca.gov; Hwy 1; tent sites $30) Two small walk-in campsites sit up on a semi-shaded ocean bluff, with fire pits and vault toilets but no water. All campers must check in first at Pfeiffer Big Sur State Park, 11 miles north.

USFS Plaskett Creek
Campground
CAMPGROUND $

(🖉 reservations 877-477-6777; www.recreation.gov; Hwy 1; tent & RV sites $25) Nearly 40 spacious, shady campsites with drinking water and vault toilets circle a forested meadow near Sand Dollar Beach in southern Big Sur.

USFS Kirk Creek Campground
CAMPGROUND $

(🖉 reservations 877-444-6777; www.recreation.gov; Hwy 1; tent & RV sites $25) More than 30 exposed ocean-view blufftop campsites with drinking water and fire pits cluster close together, nearly 2 miles south of Limekiln State Park.

Big Sur Campground & Cabins
CABIN,
CAMPGROUND $$

(🖉 831-667-2322; www.bigsurcamp.com; 47000 Hwy 1; tent/RV sites from $50/60, cabins $120-345; 🐕) On the Big Sur River and shaded by redwoods, cozy housekeeping cabins sport full kitchens and fireplaces, while canvas-sided tent cabins are dog-friendly (pet fee $20). The riverside campground, where neighboring sites have little privacy, is popular with RVs. There are hot showers, a coin-op laundry, playground and general store.

Ripplewood Resort
CABIN $$

(🖉 831-667-2242; www.ripplewoodresort.com; 47047 Hwy 1; cabins $105-225; 🛜) North of Pfeiffer Big Sur State Park, Ripplewood has struck a blow for fiscal equality by charging the same rates year-round. Throwback Americana cabins mostly have kitchens and sometimes even wood-burning fireplaces. Quiet riverside cabins are surrounded by redwoods, but roadside cabins can be noisy. Wi-fi in restaurant only.

Deetjen's Big Sur Inn
LODGE $$

(🖉 831-667-2377; www.deetjens.com; 48865 Hwy 1; d $90-260) Nestled among redwoods and wisteria, this creekside conglomeration of rustic, thin-walled rooms and cottages was built by Norwegian immigrant Helmuth Deetjen in the 1930s. Some antiques-furnished rooms are warmed by wood-burning fireplaces, while cheaper ones share bathrooms. This timeless escape isn't for everyone.

Ragged Point Inn
MOTEL $$

(🖉 805-927-4502; www.raggedpointinn.net; 19019 Hwy 1; r $169-319; 🛜🐕) At Big Sur's southern edge, split-level motel rooms are nothing special, except for those with ocean horizon views. Pet fee $50.

★ Post Ranch Inn
RESORT $$$

(🖉 831-667-2200; www.postranchinn.com; 47900 Hwy 1; d incl breakfast from $675; 🛜🐕) The last word in luxurious coastal getaways, the exclusive Post Ranch pampers demanding guests with slate spa tubs, wood-burning fireplaces, private decks and walking sticks for coastal hikes. Ocean-view rooms celebrate the sea, while treehouses lack views and have a bit of sway. Paddle around the clifftop infinity pool after a shamanic healing session or yoga class in the spa. No children allowed.

Panoramic sea-view Sierra Mar restaurant has mostly disappointing food, except for the gourmet breakfast buffet served to guests only.

Ventana Inn & Spa
RESORT $$$

(🖉 800-628-6500, 831-667-2331; www.ventanainn.com; 48123 Hwy 1; d incl breakfast from $510; 🛜🐕) 🍃 Almost at odds with Big Sur's hippie-alternative vibe, Ventana injects a little soul into its deluxe digs. Honeymooning couples and paparazzi-fleeing celebs pad from tai chi class to the Japanese baths and outdoor pools (one is famously clothing-optional), or hole up all day next to the wood-burning fireplace in their own private villa, hot-tub suite or ocean-view cottage.

Treebones Resort
LODGE $$$

(🖉 877-424-4787, 805-927-2390; www.treebonesresort.com; 71895 Hwy 1; d with shared bath incl breakfast from $215; 🛜🐕) Don't let the word 'resort' throw you. Yes, they've got an ocean-view hot tub, heated pool and massage treatments. But a unique woven 'human nest' and canvas-sided yurts with polished pine floors, quilt-covered beds, sink vanities and redwood decks are more like glamping, with little privacy. Communal bathrooms and showers are a short stroll away. Wi-fi in main lodge only.

Children must be at least six years old. Look for the signposted turnoff a mile north of Gorda, at the southern end of Big Sur.

Glen Oaks Motel MOTEL, CABIN **$$$**
(☑831-667-2105; www.glenoaksbigsur.com; 47080 Hwy 1; d $225-390; ☜) ✐ At this 1950s redwood-and-adobe motor lodge, rustic rooms and cabins seem effortlessly chic. Dramatically transformed by eco-conscious design, snug romantic hideaway rooms all have gas fireplaces. Woodsy cabins in a red-wood grove have kitchenettes and share outdoor fire pits, or retreat to the one-bedroom house with a full kitchen.

Big Sur Lodge LODGE **$$$**
(☑800-424-4787, 831-667-3100; www.bigsurlodge.com; 47225 Hwy 1; d $205-365; ☒) What you're really paying for is a peaceful location, right inside Pfeiffer Big Sur State Park. Fairly rustic duplexes each have a deck or balcony looking out into the redwood forest, while family-sized rooms may have a kitchenette or wood-burning fireplace. The outdoor swimming pool is closed in winter.

Lucia Lodge MOTEL **$$$**
(☑831-667-2718, 866-424-4787; www.lucialodge.com; 62400 Hwy 1; d $195-275) Vertiginous clifftop views from an ocean-view deck, but tired 1930s cabin rooms.

✖ Eating

Like Big Sur's lodgings, restaurants and cafes alongside Hwy 1 are often overpriced, overcrowded and underwhelming.

Big Sur Deli & General Store DELI, MARKET **$**
(www.bigsurdeli.com; 47520 Hwy 1; dishes $2-7; ☉7am-8pm) With the most reasonable prices in Big Sur, this family-owned deli slices custom-made deli sandwiches and piles up tortillas with carne asada, pork *carnitas*, veggies or beans and cheese. The small market carries camping food, snacks and beer and wine.

**Big Sur Burrito Bar &
General Store** DELI, MARKET **$**
(www.bigsurriverinn.com; 46840 Hwy 1; mains $8-10; ☉11am-7pm; ⊕) Order a San Francisco-sized burrito or wrap sandwich with a fresh-fruit smoothie from the back of the Big Sur River Inn's well-stocked general store, which carries snacks, drinks and camping supplies.

**Big Sur Lodge Restaurant
& General Store** CALIFORNIAN **$$**
(☑831-667-3100; www.bigsurlodge.com/dining; 47225 Hwy 1; mains $10-30; ☉8am-9:30pm; ⊕) Inside Pfeiffer Big Sur State Park, pull up a wooden table in the cabin-esque dining room or on an outdoor riverside deck to fill up on wild salmon, roasted veggie pasta and generous salads, all made with hungry hikers in mind. The lodge's small general store stocks camping groceries, snacks, drinks and ice-cream treats.

★Restaurant at Ventana CALIFORNIAN **$$$**
(☑831-667-4242; www.ventanainn.com; Ventana Inn & Spa, 48123 Hwy 1; lunch $16-26, 4-course dinner menu $75; ☉7-10:30am, 11:30am-4:30pm & 6-9pm; ☜) The old truism about the better the views, the worse the food just doesn't seem to apply here. The resort's clifftop terrace restaurant and cocktail bar are Big Sur's gathering spot for foodies and bon vivants. Feast on grilled swordfish with lemony couscous, a house-smoked pork sandwich or salads flavored with herbs grown in the garden right outside. Reservations essential.

Nepenthe CALIFORNIAN **$$$**
(☑831-667-2345; www.nepenthebigsur.com; 48510 Hwy 1; mains $15-42; ☉11:30am-4:30pm & 5-10pm) Nepenthe comes from a Greek word meaning 'isle of no sorrow,' and indeed, it's hard to feel blue while sitting by the fire pit on this aerial terrace. Just-okay California cuisine (try the renowned Ambrosia burger) takes a backseat to the views and Nepenthe's history – Orson Welles and Rita Hayworth briefly owned a cabin here in the 1940s. Reservations essential.

Downstairs, cheaper but still expensive Café Kevah delivers coffee, baked goods, light brunches and head-spinning ocean views on its outdoor deck (closed during winter and bad weather).

Big Sur Roadhouse CALIFORNIAN, CAJUN **$$$**
(☑831-667-2370; www.bigsurroadhouse.com; 47080 Hwy 1; breakfast & lunch $6-12, dinner $19-30; ☉7:30am-9pm) This Southern-spiced roadhouse glows with color-splashed artwork and an outdoor fire pit. At riverside tables, fork into a New Orleans–born chef's hearty fried chicken, white grits with serrano peppers, po' boy sandwiches and blackened locally caught fish with a dollop of fresh herb aioli. Reservations advised for dinner, or just stop by for drinks and small bites such as buttermilk biscuits.

Big Sur Bakery & Restaurant CALIFORNIAN $$$
(☑831-667-0520; www.bigsurbakery.com; 47540 Hwy 1; bakery items $3-14, mains $14-36; ☺bakery from 8am daily, restaurant 9:30am-3:30pm Mon-Fri, 10:30am-2:30pm Sat & Sun, 5:30pm-close Tue-Sat) Behind the Shell station, this warmly lit, funky house has seasonally changing menus, on which wood-fired pizzas share space with more refined dishes such as butter-braised halibut. Fronted by a pretty patio, the bakery makes addictive fruit-and-ginger scones and super-stuffed sandwiches. Expect long waits and standoffish service. Dinner reservations essential.

Deetjen's Restaurant AMERICAN $$$
(☑831-667-2378; www.deetjens.com; Deetjen's Big Sur Inn, 48865 Hwy 1; mains $26-38; ☺breakfast 8am-noon Mon-Fri, to 12:30pm Sat & Sun, dinner 6-9pm daily) 🍃 At a quaint yesteryear lodge, the cozy, candle-lit dining room has a daily changing menu of steaks, cassoulets and other hearty country fare, primarily sourced from organic local produce, hormone-free meat and sustainable seafood. Breakfast is a much better bet than dinner.

Big Sur River Inn AMERICAN $$$
(☑831-667-2700; www.bigsurriverinn.com; 46840 Hwy 1; breakfast & lunch $9-18, dinner $15-32; ☺8-11am, 11:30am-4:30pm & 5-9pm; 🔊👪) Woodsy supper club with a deck overlooks a creek teeming with throaty frogs. The wedding-reception-quality food is mostly classic American seafood, grilled meats and pastas, but diner-style breakfasts and lunches – like berry pancakes and BLT sandwiches – satisfy.

🍺 Drinking & Entertainment

Big Sur Taphouse BAR
(www.bigsurtaphouse.com; 47520 Hwy 1; ☺noon-10pm Mon-Thu, to midnight Fri & Sat, 10am-10pm Sun; 🔊) Down California craft beers and regional wines on the back deck or by the fireplace inside this high-ceilinged wooden bar with board games, sports TVs and pub grub from the next-door deli.

Maiden Publick House PUB
(☑831-667-2355; Village Center Shops, Hwy 1; ☺noon-2am) Just south of the Big Sur River Inn, this dive has an encyclopedic beer bible and motley local musicians jamming, mostly on weekends.

Rocky Point BAR
(www.rocky-point.com; 36700 Hwy 1; ☺11:30am-8pm) Come for the hillside ocean-view terrace, where cocktails are served all day long. It's about 2.5 miles north of Bixby Bridge.

Henry Miller Memorial Library PERFORMING ARTS
(☑831-667-2574; www.henrymiller.org; 48603 Hwy 1; 🔊) Just south of Nepenthe, this nonprofit alternative space hosts a bohemian carnival of live-music concerts, author readings, open-mic nights and indie film screenings outdoors, especially during summer.

❶ Information

Visitors often wander into businesses along Hwy 1 and ask, 'How much further to Big Sur?' In fact, there is no town of Big Sur as such, though you may see the name on maps. Commercial activity is concentrated along the stretch north of Pfeiffer Big Sur State Park. Sometimes called 'the Village,' this is where you'll find most of the lodging, restaurants and shops, some of which offer free wi-fi. Cellphone reception is spotty to non-existent.

Big Sur Chamber of Commerce (☑831-667-2100; www.bigsurcalifornia.org; ☺9am-1pm Mon, Wed & Fri) Pick up the free *Big Sur Guide* newspaper at local businesses; it's also available online as a free PDF download.

Big Sur Station (☑831-667-2315; www.fs.usda.gov/lpnf; 47555 Hwy 1; ☺8am-4pm, closed Mon & Tue Nov-Mar) About 1.5 miles south of Pfeiffer Big Sur State Park, this multiagency ranger station has information and maps for state parks, the Los Padres National Forest and Ventana Wilderness.

Henry Miller Memorial Library (www.henrymiller.org; 48603 Hwy 1; ☺11am-6pm; 🔊) Free wi-fi and public internet terminals (donation requested).

Post Office (☑800-275-8777; www.usps.com; 47500 Hwy 1; ☺8:30-11am & 1-4pm Mon-Fri) Just north of Big Sur Bakery.

---

❶ DRIVING HWY 1 IN BIG SUR

Driving this narrow two-lane highway through Big Sur and beyond is very slow going. Allow about three hours to cover the distance between the Monterey Peninsula and San Luis Obispo, much more if you want to explore the coast. Traveling after dark can be risky and more to the point, it's futile, because you'll miss out on the seascapes. Watch out for cyclists and make use of signposted roadside pullouts to let faster-moving traffic pass.

❶ Getting There & Around

Big Sur is best explored by car, since you'll be itching to stop frequently and take in the rugged beauty and vistas that reveal themselves after every hairpin turn. Even if your driving skills are up to these narrow switchbacks, others' aren't: expect to average 35mph or less along the route. Parts of Hwy 1 are battle-scarred, evidence of a continual struggle to keep them open after landslides and washouts. Check current highway conditions with **CalTrans** (www.dot.ca.gov) and fill up your gas tank beforehand.

MST (☑ 888-678-2871; www.mst.org) bus 22 ($3.50, 1¼ hours) travels from Monterey via Carmel and Point Lobos as far south as Nepenthe restaurant, stopping en route at Andrew Molera State Park and the Big Sur River Inn. Buses run three times daily between late May and early September, and twice daily on Saturdays and Sundays only the rest of the year.

Point Piedras Blancas

Many lighthouses still stand along California's coast, but few offer such a historically evocative seascape. Federally designated an outstanding natural area, the jutting, windblown grounds of this 1875 **light station** (☑ 805-927-7361; www.piedrasblancas.gov; tours adult/child 6-17yr $10/5; ⊙ tours usually 9:45am Mon-Sat mid-Jun–Aug, 9:45am Tue, Thu & Sat Sep–mid-Jun) have been laboriously replanted with native flora. Picturesquely, everything looks much the way it did when the first lighthouse keepers helped ships find safe harbor at the whaling station at San Simeon Bay. Guided tours meet at the old Piedras Blancas Motel, 1.5 miles north of the lighthouse gate on Hwy 1. No reservations are taken; call ahead to check tour schedules.

At a signposted vista point, around 4.5 miles north of Hearst Castle, you can observe a colony of northern elephant seals bigger than the one at Año Nuevo State Reserve near Santa Cruz. During peak winter season, about 18,000 seals seek shelter in the coves and beaches along this stretch of coast. On sunny days the seals usually 'lie around like banana slugs,' in the words of one volunteer. Interpretive panels along a beach boardwalk and blue-jacketed **Friends of the Elephant Seal** (www.elephantseal.org) guides demystify the behavior of these giant beasts.

Hearst Castle

The most important thing to know about William Randolph Hearst (1863–1951) is that he did not live like *Citizen Kane*. Not that Hearst wasn't bombastic, conniving and larger than life, but the moody recluse of Orson Welles' movie? Definitely not. Hearst also didn't call his 165-room estate a castle, preferring its official name, *La Cuesta Encantada* ('The Enchanted Hill'), or more often calling it simply 'the ranch.' From the 1920s into the '40s, Hearst and Marion Davies, his longtime mistress (Hearst's wife refused to grant him a divorce), entertained a steady stream of the era's biggest movers and shakers. Invitations were highly coveted, but Hearst had his quirks – he despised drunkenness, and guests were forbidden to speak of death.

Hearst Castle is a wondrous, historic (Winston Churchill penned anti-Nazi essays here in the 1930s), over-the-top homage to material excess, perched high on a hill. California's first licensed woman architect Julia Morgan based the main building, Casa Grande, on the design of a Spanish cathedral, and over the decades she catered to Hearst's every design whim, deftly integrating the spoils of his fabled European shopping sprees including artifacts from antiquity and pieces of medieval monasteries. The estate sprawls across acres of lushly landscaped gardens, accentuated by shimmering pools and fountains, statues from ancient Greece and Moorish Spain and the ruins of what was in Hearst's day the world's largest private zoo (drivers on Hwy 1 can sometimes spot the remnant zebra herd grazing on the hillsides of adjacent Hearst Ranch).

Much like Hearst's construction budget, the castle will devour as much of your time and money as you let it. To see anything of this **state historic monument** (☑ info 805-927-2020, reservations 800-444-4445; www. hearstcastle.org; 750 Hearst Castle Rd, San Simeon; tours adult/child 5-12yr from $25/12; ⊙ from 9am daily except Thanksgiving, Christmas & New Year's Day, closing time varies), you must take a tour. In peak summer months, show up early enough and you might be able to get a same-day ticket. For holiday and evening tours, book at least two weeks in advance. Dress in plenty of layers: gloomy fog at the sea-level visitors center can turn into sunny skies at the castle's hilltop location, and vice versa.

Tours usually depart starting at 9am daily, with the last tour leaving the visitor center for the 10-minute ride to the hilltop by 4pm (later in summer). There are four main tours: the guided portion of each lasts about

EYEING ELEPHANT SEALS

The elephant seals that visit coastal California each year follow a precise calendar. In November and December, bulls (adult males) return to their colony's favorite California beaches and start the ritual struggles to assert superiority. Only the largest, strongest and most aggressive 'alpha' males gather a harem of nubile females. In January and February, adult females, already pregnant from last year's beach antics, give birth to pups and soon mate with the dominant males, who promptly depart on their next feeding migration. The bulls' motto is 'love 'em and leave 'em.'

At birth an elephant seal pup weighs about 75lb; while being fed by its mother, it puts on about 10lb a day. Female seals leave the beach in March, abandoning their offspring. For up to two months the young seals, now known as 'weaners,' lounge around in groups, gradually learning to swim, first in tidal pools, then in the ocean. The weaners depart by May, having lost 20% to 30% of their weight during a prolonged fast.

Between June and October, elephant seals of all ages and both sexes return in smaller numbers to the beaches to molt. Always observe elephant seals from a safe distance (minimum 25ft) and do not approach or otherwise harass these unpredictable wild animals, who surprisingly can move faster on the sand than you can!

45 minutes, after which you're free to wander the gardens and terraces, photograph the iconic Neptune Pool and soak up views. Best of all are Christmas holiday and springtime evening tours, featuring living-history reenactors who escort you back in time to the castle's 1930s heyday.

At the visitor center, a five-story-high **theater** shows a 40-minute historical film (free admission included with most tour tickets) about the castle and the Hearst family. Other visitor-center facilities are geared for industrial-sized mobs; it's better to grab lunch at Sebastian's General Store (p286) across Hwy 1. Before you leave, take a moment to visit the often-overlooked museum area at the back of the visitor center.

RTA (☑805-541-2228; www.slorta.org) bus 15 makes a few daily round-trips to Hearst Castle via Cambria and Cayucos from Morro Bay ($2, 55 minutes), where you can transfer to bus 12 to San Luis Obispo.

San Simeon

Little San Simeon Bay sprang to life as a whaling station in 1852, by which time California sea otters had been hunted almost to extinction by Russian fur traders. Shoreline whaling was practiced to catch gray whales migrating between Alaskan feeding grounds and birthing waters in Baja California. In 1865 Senator George Hearst purchased 45,000 acres of ranch land and established a small settlement beside the sea. Designed by architect Julia Morgan, the historic

19th-century houses today are rented to employees of the Hearst Corporation's 82,000-acre free range cattle ranch.

⊙ Sights & Activities

William Randolph Hearst Memorial State Beach BEACH
(www.parks.ca.gov; Hwy 1; ⊙dawn-dusk) FREE
Across from Hearst Castle, this bayfront beach is a pleasantly sandy stretch punctuated by rock outcroppings, kelp forests, a wooden pier (fishing permitted) and picnic areas with barbecue grills.

Coastal Discovery Center MUSEUM
(☑805-927-6575; www.montereybay.noaa.gov; Hwy 1; ⊙11am-5pm Fri-Sun mid-Mar–Oct, 10am-4pm Fri-Sun Nov–mid-Mar; ⊕) FREE Educational displays include a talking artificial tide pool that kids can touch and videos of deep-sea diving and a WWII-era shipwreck just offshore.

Kayak Outfitters KAYAKING
(☑800-717-5225, 805-927-1787; www.kayakcambria.com; Hwy 1; single/double kayak rentals from $10/20, tours $50-110; ⊙10am-4pm or later mid-Jun–early Sep, call for off-season hours) Right on the beach, you can rent sea kayaks, wetsuits, stand-up paddleboarding (SUP) sets, bodyboards and surfboards, or take a kayak-fishing trip or a guided paddle around San Simeon Cove.

🛏 Sleeping & Eating

A few miles south of Hearst Castle, the modern town of San Simeon is nothing more than a strip of unexciting motels and lackluster restaurants. There are better-value places to stay and eat in Cambria and beach towns further south, such as Cayucos and Morro Bay.

San Simeon State Park Campground
CAMPGROUND $

(🖳 reservations 800-444-7275; www.reserveamerica.com; Hwy 1; tent & RV sites $20-25) About 5 miles south of Hearst Castle are two state-park campgrounds: **San Simeon Creek**, with coin-op hot showers and flush toilets; and undeveloped **Washburn**, located along a dirt road. Drinking water is available at both.

Morgan
MOTEL $$

(🖳 800-451-9900, 805-927-3828; www.hotel-morgan.com; 9135 Hearst Dr; r incl breakfast $139-235; 🛜🐾🖳) Although rates are high for these revamped motel-style accommodations, the oceanfront setting makes up for a lot, as do gas fireplaces in deluxe rooms. Complimentary continental breakfast and board games to borrow. Pet fee $25.

Sebastian's General Store
DELI, GROCERIES $

(442 SLO-San Simeon Rd; mains $7-12; ⊙11am-5pm, kitchen closes at 4pm) Down a side road across Hwy 1 from Hearst Castle, this tiny historic market sells cold drinks, Hearst Ranch beef burgers, giant deli sandwiches and salads for beach picnics at San Simeon Cove. Hearst Ranch Winery tastings are available at the copper-top bar.

Cambria

With a whopping dose of natural beauty, the coastal idyll of Cambria is a lone pearl cast along the coast. Built on lands that once belonged to Mission San Miguel, one of the village's first nicknames was Slabtown, after the rough pieces of wood that pioneer buildings were constructed from. Today, just like at neighboring Hearst Castle, money is no object in this wealthy community, whose motto 'Pines by the Sea' is affixed to the back of BMWs that toodle around town.

◉ Sights & Activities

Although its milky-white moonstones are long gone, **Moonstone Beach** still attracts romantics to its oceanfront boardwalk and truly picturesque rocky shoreline. For more solitude, take the Windsor Blvd exit off Hwy 1 and drive down to where the road

dead-ends, then follow a 2-mile round-trip blufftop hiking trail across **East West Ranch**, where **Outback Trail Rides** (🖳805-286-8772; www.outbacktrailrides.com; tours $65-95; ⊙Wed-Mon May-Sep, by reservation only) offers horseback rides (reserve in advance).

A 10-minute drive south of Cambria, past the Hwy 46 turnoff to Paso Robles' wine country, tiny **Harmony** is a slice of rural Americana. An 1865 creamery now houses artists' workshops and a charming **cafe** (2177 Old Creamery Rd, Harmony; dishes $3-10; ⊙usually 10am-4pm) run by an Italian chef, or visit the hillside winery, **Harmony Cellars** (www.harmonycellars.com; 3255 Harmony Valley Rd, Harmony; tasting fee $5; ⊙10am-5pm, to 5:30pm Jul & Aug). A few miles further south inside peaceful **Harmony Headlands State Park** (www.parks.ca.gov; Hwy 1; ⊙6am-sunset) FREE, a 4.5-mile round-trip hiking trail winds out to coastal bluffs with inspiring sea views.

🛏 Sleeping

Cambria's choicest motels and hotels line Moonstone Beach Dr, while quaint B&Bs cluster around the village.

HI Cambria Bridge Street Inn
HOSTEL $

(🖳805-927-7653; www.bridgestreetinncambria.com; 4314 Bridge St; dm from $28, r $49-84, all with shared bath; ⊙check-in 5-9pm; 🛜) Inside a 19th-century parsonage, this tiny hostel seems more like a grandmotherly B&B. It has floral charm and a communal kitchen, but the shabby-chic rooms are thin-walled. Book ahead.

Bluebird Inn
MOTEL $$

(🖳805-927-5215, 800-552-5434; www.bluebirdmotel.com; 1880 Main St; r $80-180; 🛜) Surrounded by peaceful gardens, this friendly East Village motel offers basic, tidy rooms, some with fireplaces and private creekside patios or balconies. Wi-fi can be erratic.

Cambria Palms Motel
MOTEL $$

(🖳805-927-4485; www.cambriapalmsmotel.com; 2662 Main St; r $109-149; ⊙check-in 3-9pm; 🛜) A 1950s motor lodge at the east edge of town, here simple wooden-floored rooms are spruced up by colorful wall art and above-average beds. The outdoor fire pit crackles after dark.

Blue Dolphin Inn
MOTEL $$$

(🖳800-222-9157, 805-927-3300; www.cambriainns.com; 6470 Moonstone Beach Dr; r incl breakfast from $199; 🛜🐾) This sand-colored two-story, slat-sided building may not look as upscale as other oceanfront motels, but rooms have romantic fireplaces, pillowtop mattresses and to-go breakfast picnics to take to the beach. If it's full, try its sister property, the Sand Pebbles Inn. Pet fee $25.

Fogcatcher Inn
HOTEL $$$

(☎ 800-425-4121, 805-927-1400; www.fogcatcherinn.com; 6400 Moonstone Beach Dr; r incl breakfast from $220; 🖳❄🐾) Moonstone Beach Dr hotels are nearly identical, but this one stands out with its pool and hot tub. Faux English Tudor–style cottages harboring quietly luxurious modern rooms, some with fireplaces and ocean views. Pet fee $75.

Cambria Shores Inn
MOTEL $$$

(☎ 800-433-9179, 805-927-8644; www.cambriashores.com; 6276 Moonstone Beach Dr; r incl breakfast from $219; 🖳🐾) A stone's throw from Moonstone Beach, this ocean-view motel offers pampering amenities for pooches, including a welcome doggie basket. Rates include a breakfast basket delivered to your door. Pet fee $15.

✖ Eating & Drinking

It's a short walk between cutesy cafes in the East Village.

Linn's Easy as Pie Cafe
AMERICAN $

(www.linnsfruitbin.com; 4251 Bridge St; dishes $4-9; ⊙10am-6pm Oct-Apr, to 7pm May-Sep; 🛋) If you don't have time to visit Linn's original farm stand out on Santa Rosa Creek Rd (a 20-minute drive east via Main St), you can fork into their famous olallieberry pie at this take-out counter that delivers soups, salads, sandwiches and comfort fare such as chicken pot pie to a sunny deck.

Boni's Tacos
MEXICAN $

(www.bonistacos.com; 2253 Main St; dishes $2-9; ⊙10am-4pm Sat & Sun) Honest Mexican food is slung from this family-owned taco trailer parked in the East Village. Fiery tacos, taquitos, quesadillas and burritos all fly out of the busy window.

★ Indigo Moon
CALIFORNIAN $$$

(☎ 805-927-2911; www.indigomooncafe.com; 1980 Main St; lunch $9-14, dinner $14-33; ⊙10am-9pm) Inside this artisan cheese-and-wine shop, breezy bistro tables complement superb salads and toasty sandwiches served with sweet-potato fries. Locals gossip over lunch on the back patio, where dinner dates order wild-mushroom risotto or crab-stuffed trout.

Cambria Pub & Steakhouse
AMERICAN $$$

(☎ 805-927-0782; www.thecambriapub.com; 4090 Burton Dr; pub mains $9-12, steakhouse mains $20-35; ⊙11am-9pm Thu & Sun-Tue, to 10pm Fri & Sat; 🐾) Over in the East Village, pull up a barstool and order a burger while you watch big-screen sports TVs, or reserve a table in the contemporary-casual steakhouse to dig into Angus beef steaks (regrettably not from Hearst Ranch). The outdoor patio is dog-friendly.

ℹ Information

Cambria has three distinct parts. In the tourist-choked East Village, antiques shops, art galleries and cafes hug Main St. The newer West Village, along Main St closer to Hwy 1, is where you'll find the **chamber of commerce** (☎ 805-927-3624; www.cambriachamber.org; 767 Main St; ⊙9am-5pm Mon-Fri, noon-4pm Sat & Sun). Hotel-lined Moonstone Beach Dr is west of Hwy 1.

ℹ Getting There & Around

From San Luis Obispo, **RTA** (☎ 805-541-2228; www.slorta.org) bus 15 makes a few daily trips from Morro Bay via Cayucos to Cambria ($2, 35 minutes), stopping along Main St and Moonstone Beach Dr. Most buses continue north to Hearst Castle.

Cayucos

With its historic storefronts housing antiques shops and eateries, the main drag of amiable, slow-paced Cayucos recalls an Old West frontier town. Just one block west of Ocean Ave, surf's up by the pier.

◉ Sights & Activities

Fronting a broad white-sand beach, Cayucos' long wooden pier is popular with fishers. It's also a sheltered spot for beginner surfers.

Estero Bluffs State Park
PARK

(www.parks.ca.gov; Hwy 1; ⊙sunrise-sunset) FREE Ramble along coastal grasslands and pocket beaches at this small state park, accessed from unmarked roadside pulloffs north of Cayucos. Look among the scenic sea stacks to spot harbor seals hauled out on tide-splashed rocks.

Good Clean Fun
WATER SPORTS

(☎ 805-995-1993; www.goodcleanfuncalifornia. com; 136 Ocean Front Ln; group surfing lesson or kayak tour from $75) By the beach, this friendly surf shop has all kinds of rental gear –

wetsuits, boogie boards, surfboards, SUP sets and kayaks. Book in advance for surfing lessons and kayak (or kayak-fishing) tours.

Cayucos Surf Company   SURFING
(☑805-995-1000; www.cayucossurfcompany. com; 95 Cayucos Dr; 1hr private/2hr group lesson $90/100; ⊙10am-5pm Sun-Thu, to 6pm Fri & Sat) Near the pier, this landmark local surf shop rents surfboards, boogie boards and wetsuits. Call ahead for learn-to-surf lessons.

🛏 Sleeping

Cayucos doesn't lack for motels or beach-front inns. If there's no vacancy or prices look too high, head 6 miles south to Morro Bay.

Shoreline Inn on the Beach   HOTEL $$
(☑800-549-2244, 805-995-3681; www.cayucosshorelineinn.com; 1 N Ocean Ave; r $139-199; 🐕) There are few beachside lodgings on Hwy 1 where you can listen to the surf from your balcony for such a reasonable price tag. Standard-issue rooms are spacious, perked up by sea-foam painted walls, and also dog-friendly (pet fee $35).

Seaside Motel   MOTEL $$
(☑800-549-0900, 805-995-3809; www.seasidemotel.com; 42 S Ocean Ave; d $80-160; 🛜) Expect a warm welcome from the hands-on owners of this vintage motel with a pretty garden. Country-kitsch rooms may be on the small side, though some have kitchenettes. Cross your fingers for quiet neighbors.

Cypress Tree Motel   MOTEL $$
(☑805-995-3917; www.cypresstreemotel.com; 125 S Ocean Ave; d $80-120; 🛜🐕) Retro motor court has lovingly cared-for, but kinda hokey theme rooms, such as 'Nautical Nellie' with a net of seashells suspended behind the bed, plus a shared barbecue grill on the lawn. Pet fee $10.

Cayucos Beach Inn   MOTEL $$
(☑800-482-0555, 805-995-2828; www.cayucosbeachinn.com; 333 S Ocean Ave; d incl breakfast $99-215; 🐕🛜🐕) At this remarkably dog-friendly motel, even the doors have special peepholes for canine companions. Big rooms look bland, but grassy picnic areas and barbecue grills await out front. Rates include continental breakfast. Pet fee $10.

Cass House Inn   INN $$$
(☑805-995-3669; www.casshouseinn.com; 222 N Ocean Ave; d incl breakfast $195-365; 🛜) Inside a charmingly renovated 1867 Victorian inn,

five boutique rooms beckon, some with ocean views, deep-soaking tubs and antique fireplaces to ward off chilly coastal fog. All rooms have plush beds, flat-screen TVs with DVD players and tasteful, romantic accents, while the beachy cottage comes with a full kitchen. Reservations essential.

🍴 Eating & Drinking

Ruddell's Smokehouse   SEAFOOD $
(www.smokerjim.com; 101 D St; dishes $4-13; ⊙11am-6pm; 🐕🌿) 'Smoker Jim' transforms fresh-off-the-boat seafood into succulently smoked slabs, sandwiches topped with spicy mustard and fish tacos slathered in a unique apple-celery relish. Squeeze yourself in the door to order. Dogs allowed at sidewalk tables.

Brown Butter Cookie Co   BAKERY $
(www.brownbuttercookies.com; 98 N Ocean Ave; snacks from $2; ⊙9am-6pm; 🐕) Seriously addictive, dearly priced cookies baked in all sorts of flavors – almond, citrus, cocoa, coconut-lime and original butter. Also in Paso Robles.

★ Cass House
Restaurant   CALIFORNIAN, FRENCH $$$
(☑805-995-3669; www.casshouseinn.com; Cass House Inn, 222 N Ocean Ave; tasting menu without/ with wine pairings $85/125; ⊙5:30-7:30pm Thu-Mon) 🌿 The inn's chef-driven restaurant defies expectations. Linger over a locally sourced, seasonally inspired menu that ambitiously ranges from stone-fruit salad with whipped homemade ricotta and crispy abalone fritters to milk-and-honey almond cake, all paired with top-notch regional wines. Some diners lament portions are so modestly sized. Reservations essential.

Schooners Wharf   BAR
(www.schoonerswharf.com; 171 N Ocean Ave; ⊙11am-midnight) Come for drinks on the ocean-view deck, rather than the fried seafood.

ℹ Getting There & Away

RTA (☑805-541-2228; www.slorta.org) bus 15 travels three to five times daily from Morro Bay ($2, 15 minutes) to Cayucos, continuing north to Cambria ($2, 20 minutes) and Hearst Castle ($2, 35 minutes).

Morro Bay

Home to a commercial fishing fleet, Morro Bay's biggest claim to fame is Morro Rock, a volcanic peak jutting dramatically from the ocean floor. It's one of the Nine Sisters, a 21-million-year-old chain of rocks stretching all the way south to San Luis Obispo. The town's less boast-worthy landmark comes courtesy of the power plant, whose three cigarette-shaped smokestacks mar the bay views. Along this humble, working-class stretch of coast you'll find fantastic opportunities for kayaking, hiking and camping.

◉ Sights & Activities

This town harbors natural riches that are easily worth a half day's exploration. The bay itself is a deep inlet separated from the ocean by a 5-mile-long sand spit. South of Morro Rock is the **Embarcadero**, a small waterfront boulevard jam-packed with souvenir shops and eateries.

Morro Rock   LANDMARK
Chumash tribespeople are the only people legally allowed to climb this volcanic rock, now the protected nesting ground of peregrine falcons. You can laze at the small beach on the rock's north side, but you can't drive all the way around it. Instead, rent a kayak to paddle the giant estuary, inhabited by two-dozen threatened and endangered species, including brown pelicans, snowy plovers and sea otters.

Morro Bay State Park   PARK
(☏805-772-2694; www.parks.ca.gov; park entry free, museum admission adult/child under 17yr $3/free; ☺museum 10am-5pm) This woodsy waterfront park is strewn with hillside hiking trails. A small **natural history museum** has interactive exhibits geared toward kids that demonstrate how the forces of nature affect us all. North of the museum, a eucalyptus grove harbors one of California's last remaining great blue heron rookeries.

Kayak Horizons   WATER SPORTS
(☏805-772-6444; www.kayakhorizons.com; 551 Embarcadero; kayak or SUP rental from $12, 3hr kayak tour $59; ☺9am-5pm) One of several places on the Embarcadero offering kayak rentals and tours for novices, as well as SUP set and canoes rentals. When paddling out on your own, be aware of the tide schedules: ideally, you'll want to ride the tide out and then back in. Winds are generally calmest in the mornings.

Kayak Shack   WATER SPORTS
(☏805-772-8796; www.morrobaykayakshack.com; 10 State Park Rd; kayak or SUP rental from $12;

☺usually 9am-4pm late-May–Jun, to 5pm Jul-early Sep, 9am-4pm Fri-Sun early-Sep–late-May) No one gets you out on the water faster than this laid-back kayak, canoe and SUP rental spot by the marina in Morro Bay State Park. A no-frills DIY operation, this is a calmer place to start paddling than the Embarcadero.

Cerro Alto   HIKING
(www.fs.usda.gov/lpnf; Cerro Alto Rd, Atascadero; per car $5; ☻) A 7-mile drive inland from Morro Bay on Hwy 41, a USFS campground is the start of a challengingly steep 4-mile round-trip trail up Cerro Alto (2624ft). From the summit, 360° views sweep from mountains to the sea. With more gradual switchbacks, an alternative route (5.5 miles round trip) also begins near campsite No 18. Leashed dogs allowed.

Morro Bay Golf Course   GOLF
(☏805-782-8060; www.slocountyparks.com; 201 State Park Rd; green fees $13-49) South of the Embarcadero, adjacent to the state park, this 18-hole golf course boasts tree-lined fairways and ocean views. A driving range and rental clubs and carts are available.

☞ Tours

Sub-Sea Tours   BOAT TOUR
(☏805-772-9463; www.subseatours.com; 699 Embarcadero; 45min tour adult/child 3-12yr $14/7; ☺hourly departures usually 11am-5pm; ☻) For pint-sized views of kelp forests and schools of fish, take the kids on a spin around the bay in a yellow semi-submersible with underwater viewing windows.

Virg's Landing   FISHING
(☏800-762-5263, 805-772-1222; www.morrobaysportfishing.com; 1169 Market Ave; tours from $59) Salty dogs ready for a little sportfishing can book half-day or all-day trips between May and December with this long-running local outfit.

Central Coast Outdoors   GUIDED TOUR
(☏888-873-5610, 805-528-1080; www.centralcoastoutdoors.com; tours $65-150) Leads kayaking tours (including sunset and full-moon paddles), guided hikes and cycling trips along the coast and to Paso Robles and Edna Valley vineyards.

⭒⭒ Festivals & Events

Morro Bay Winter Bird Festival   OUTDOORS
(www.morrobaybirdfestival.org) Every January, bird-watchers flock here for guided hikes, kayaking tours and naturalist-led field trips,

during which more than 200 species can be spotted along the Pacific Flyway.

🛌 Sleeping

Dozens of motels cluster along Hwy 1 and around Harbor and Main Sts, between downtown and the Embarcadero.

California State Park Campgrounds
CAMPGROUND $

(🖳 reservations 800-444-7275; www.reserveamerica.com; tent & RV sites $35-50; 🐾) In Morro Bay State Park, more than 240 campsites are fringed by eucalyptus and cypress trees; amenities include coin-op hot showers and an RV dump station. At the north end of town off Hwy 1, Morro Strand State Beach has 75 simpler oceanfront campsites.

Pleasant Inn Motel
MOTEL $$

(📞 805-772-8521; www.pleasantinnmotel.com; 235 Harbor St; r $75-209; 🐾🐾) Two blocks uphill from the Embarcadero, this spiffy motel has nautical-esque rooms (some with full kitchens) sporting sailboat photos on the walls, open-beam wooden ceilings and blue-and-white rugs underfoot. Pet fee $20.

Beach Bungalow Inn & Suites
MOTEL $$

(📞 805-772-9700; www.morrobaybeachbungalow.com; 1050 Morro Ave; d $149-250; 🐾🐾) This motor court's chic, contemporary rooms are dressed up with hardwood floors, with rugs, pillowtop mattresses and down comforters for foggy nights. Pet fee $20.

Anderson Inn
INN $$$

(📞 866-950-3434, 805-772-3434; www.andersoninnmorrobay.com; 897 Embarcadero; d $239-299; 🐾) Like a small boutique hotel, this waterfront inn has just a handful of spacious, soothingly earth-toned rooms. If you're lucky, you'll get a gas fireplace, spa tub and harbor views.

Inn at Morro Bay
MOTEL $$$

(📞 800-321-9566, 805-772-5651; www.innatmorrobay.com; 60 State Park Rd; d $119-289; 🐾🐾) Dated two-story waterfront lodge with a kidney-shaped pool has an enviable waterfront setting inside the state park. Bicycle rentals available for guests.

🍴 Eating & Drinking

Predictably touristy seafood shacks line the Embarcadero.

Taco Temple
CALIFORNIAN, SEAFOOD $$

(2680 Main St; mains $8-20; ⏰11am-9pm Wed-Mon; 🐾) Overlook the Hwy 1 frontage-road location for huge helpings of Cal-Mex fusion flavor. At the next table, there might be fishers talking about the good ol' days or starving surfers. Try one of the specials – they deserve the name. Cash only.

Giovanni's Fish Market & Galley
SEAFOOD $$

(www.giovannisfishmarket.com; 1001 Front St; mains $6-15; ⏰9am-6pm; 🐾) At this family-run joint on the Embarcadero, folks line up for batter-fried fish and chips and killer garlic fries. You'll have to dodge beggar birds on the outdoor deck. Inside there's a market with all the fixin's for a beach campground fish-fry.

Stax Wine Bar
WINE BAR

(www.staxwine.com; 1099 Embarcadero; ⏰noon-8pm Sun-Thu, to 10pm Fri & Sat) Perch on barstools in front of the harbor-view windows for a hand-selected tasting flight of California wines. Toasted panini, salads and artisan cheese and cured-meat plates keep sippers fueled.

Libertine Pub
PUB

(www.thelibertinepub.com; 801 Embarcadero; ⏰noon-11pm Mon-Wed, to midnight Thu-Sun) Stroll down to the Embarcadero for barrel-aged house beer and sour cider or to try one of the almost 50 American craft beers on tap.

ℹ️ Information

Morro Bay Visitor Center (📞 805-225-1633, 800-231-0592; www.morrobay.org; 255 Morro Bay Blvd; ⏰9am-5pm) A few blocks uphill from the Embarcadero, in the less touristy downtown area.

ℹ️ Getting There & Around

From San Luis Obispo, **RTA** (📞 805-541-2228; www.slorta.org) bus 12 travels hourly on weekdays and a few times daily on weekends along Hwy 1 to Morro Bay ($2.50, 25 minutes). Three to five times daily, bus 15 heads north to Cayucos ($2, 15 minutes), Cambria ($2, 35 minutes) and Hearst Castle ($2, 55 minutes).

From late May through early October, a **trolley** (single-ride $1, day pass $3) loops around the waterfront, downtown and north Morro Bay, operating varying hours (no service Tuesday to Thursday).

Montaña de Oro State Park

In spring the hillsides are blanketed by bright California native poppies, wild mustard and other wildflowers, giving this **park** (🕿805-772-7434; www.parks.ca.gov; 3550 Pecho Valley Rd, Los Osos; ⏰6am-10pm) **FREE** its Spanish name, meaning 'mountain of gold.' Wind-tossed coastal bluffs with wild, wide-open sea views make it a favorite spot with hikers, mountain bikers and horseback riders. The northern half of the park features sand dunes and an ancient marine terrace visible due to seismic uplifting.

Once used by smugglers, **Spooner's Cove** is now a postcard-perfect sandy beach and picnic area. If you go tidepooling, only touch the marine creatures such as sea stars, limpets and crabs with the back of one hand to avoid disturbing them, and never remove them from their aquatic homes. You can hike along the grassy ocean bluffs, or drive uphill past the **visitor center** inside a historic ranch house to the start of the exhilarating 7-mile loop trail tackling **Valencia Peak** (1346ft) and **Oats Peak** (1347ft).

🛏 Sleeping

Montaña de Oro State Park Campground　　　　CAMPGROUND $
(🕿reservations 800-444-7275; www.reserveamerica.com; tent & RV sites $20-25) Tucked into a small canyon, this minimally developed campground has pleasantly cool drive-up and environmental walk-in sites. Limited amenities include vault toilets, drinking water and fire pits.

❶ Getting There & Away

From the north, exit Hwy 1 in Morro Bay at South Bay Blvd; after 4 miles, turn right onto Los Osos Valley Rd (which runs into Pecho Valley Rd) for 6 miles. From the south, exit Hwy 101 in San Luis Obispo at Los Osos Valley Rd, then drive northwest around 16 miles.

ALONG HIGHWAY 101

Driving inland along Hwy 101 is a quicker way to travel between the Bay Area and Southern California. Although it lacks the striking scenery of coastal Hwy 1, the historic El Camino Real (King's Highway), established by Spanish conquistadors and missionaries, has a beauty of its own, from the fertile fields of Salinas, immortalized by novelist John Steinbeck, to the oak-dappled golden hills of San Luis Obispo and beaches beyond. Along the way are ghostly missions,

jaw-dropping Pinnacles National Park and wineries worth stopping for.

Gilroy

About 30 miles south of San Jose, the self-proclaimed 'garlic capital of the world' hosts the jam-packed **Gilroy Garlic Festival** (www.gilroygarlicfestival.com) over the last full weekend in July. Show up for the chow – garlicky fries, garlic-flavored ice cream and more – and cooking contests under the blazing-hot sun.

Unusual **Gilroy Gardens** (🕿408-840-7100; www.gilroygardens.org; 3050 Hecker Pass Hwy; adult/child 3-10yr $50/40; ⏰11am-5pm Mon-Fri early Jun–mid-Aug, plus 10am-6pm Sat & Sun late Mar-Nov; 🅿) is a nonprofit family-oriented theme park focused on food and plants rather than Disney-esque cartoon characters. You've got to really love flowers, fruit and veggies to get your money's worth, though Most rides such as the 'Mushroom Swing' are tame. Buy tickets online to save. From Hwy 101, follow Hwy 152 west; parking is $12.

Heading east on Hwy 152 toward I-5, **Casa de Fruta** (🕿408-842-7282; www.casadefruta.com; 10021 Pacheco Pass Hwy, Hollister; per ride $2.50-4; ⏰seasonal hours vary; 🅿) **FREE** is a commercialized farm stand with an old-fashioned carousel and choo-choo train rides for youngsters.

San Juan Bautista

In atmospheric old San Juan Bautista, where you can practically hear the whispers of the past, California's 15th mission is fronted by the state's only original Spanish plaza remaining. In 1876 the railroad bypassed the town, which has been a sleepy backwater ever since. Along 3rd St, evocative historic buildings mostly shelter antiques shops and petite garden restaurants. Hark! That cock you hear crowing is one of the town's roosters, which are allowed by tradition to stroll the streets at will.

◉ Sights

Mission San Juan Bautista　　　　CHURCH
(🕿831-623-4528; www.oldmissionsjb.org; 406 2nd St; adult/child 5-17yr $4/2; ⏰9:30am-4:30pm) Founded in 1797, this mission claims the largest church among California's original 21 missions. Unknowingly built directly atop the San Andreas Fault, the mission has been rocked by earthquakes. Bells hanging

in the tower today include chimes that were salvaged after the 1906 San Francisco earthquake toppled the original mission. Scenes from Alfred Hitchcock's thriller *Vertigo* were shot here, although the bell tower in the movie's climactic scene was just a special effect.

Below the mission cemetery, you can spy a section of El Camino Real, the Spanish colonial road built to link California's first missions.

San Juan Bautista State Historic Park

PARK

(☎831-623-4881; www.parks.ca.gov; 2nd St, btwn Mariposa & Washington Sts; museum entry adult/child $3/free; ⊙10am-4:30pm Tue-Sun) Buildings around the old Spanish plaza opposite the mission anchor this small historical park. Cavernous **stables** hint at San Juan Bautista in its 1860s heyday as a stagecoach stop. The 1859 **Plaza Hotel**, which started life as a single-story adobe building, now houses a little historical museum. Next door to the hotel, the **Castro-Breen Adobe** once belonged to Mexican general and governor José Castro. In 1848 it was bought by the Breen family, survivors of the Donner Party disaster.

Fremont Peak State Park

PARK

(☎observatory 831-623-2465; www.parks.ca.gov; San Juan Canyon Rd; per car $6; ♿) Equipped with a 30in telescope, Fremont Peak's **astronomical observatory** (www.fpoa.net) is usually open to the public on many Saturday nights between April and October, starting at 8pm or 8:30pm. Afternoon solar viewing happens monthly between March and October. It's about 11 miles south of town.

🛏 Sleeping

Fremont Peak State Park Campground

CAMPGROUND $

(☎reservations 800-444-7275; www.reserveamerica.com; San Juan Canyon Rd; tent & RV sites $25) A pretty, but primitive 25-site campground with vault toilets (no water) is shaded by oak trees on a hilltop with distant views of Monterey Bay.

🍴 Eating

On 3rd St, you'll find a long line-up of Mexican American restaurants; none are especially memorable.

San Juan Bakery

BAKERY $

(319 3rd St; snacks $2-4; ⊙usually 7am-5pm Wed-Mon) Get there early for fresh loaves of cinnamon bread, hot-cross buns and guava or apricot turnovers, as they often sell out.

Vertigo Coffee

CAFE $

(www.vertigocoffee.com; 81 4th St; dishes $3-10; ⊙7am-7pm Tue-Fri, from 8am Sat & Sun) Rich espresso and pour-over brews, wood-fired pizzas and garden salads make this coffee roaster's shop a find.

❶ Getting There & Away

San Juan Bautista is on Hwy 156, a few miles east of Hwy 101, about a 20-minute drive south of Gilroy. Further south, Hwy 101 enters the sun-dappled eucalyptus grove that James Stewart and Kim Novak drove through in *Vertigo*.

Salinas

Best known as the birthplace of John Steinbeck and nicknamed the 'Salad Bowl of the World,' Salinas is a working-class agricultural center with down-and-out streets. It makes a thought-provoking contrast with the affluence of the Monterey Peninsula, a fact of life that helped shape Steinbeck's novel *East of Eden*. Historic downtown stretches along Main St, with the National Steinbeck Center capping off its northern end.

◉ Sights

National Steinbeck Center

MUSEUM

(☎831-775-4721; www.steinbeck.org; 1 Main St; adult/child 6-12yr/youth 13-17yr $15/6/8; ⊙10am-5pm; ♿) This museum will interest almost anyone, even if you don't know a lick about Salinas' Nobel Prize–winning native son, John Steinbeck (1902–68), a Stanford University dropout. Tough, funny and brash, he portrayed the troubled spirit of rural, working-class Americans in novels such as *The Grapes of Wrath*. Interactive, kid-accessible exhibits and short video clips chronicle the writer's life and works in an engaging way. Gems include Rocinante, the camper in which Steinbeck traveled around the USA while researching *Travels with Charley*.

Take a moment and listen to Steinbeck's Nobel acceptance speech – it's grace and power combined. Temporary exhibitions cover anything from agricultural history and political activism to California landscape photography.

Steinbeck House

HISTORIC BUILDING

(☎831-424-2735; www.steinbeckhouse.com; 132 Central Ave; tour $10; ⊙restaurant 11:30am-2pm

Tue-Sat, gift shop 11am-3pm Tue-Sat) Steinbeck was born and spent much of his boyhood in this house, four blocks west of the museum. It's now a twee lunch cafe, which we're not sure he'd approve of. Guided tours are given on select summer Sundays; check online for details.

Garden of Memories Memorial Park
CEMETERY

(850 Abbott St) Steinbeck is buried in the family plot at this cemetery, less than 2 miles southeast of downtown.

Tours

Farm
GUIDED TOUR

(☑ 831-455-2575; www.thefarm-salinasvalley.com; 7 Foster Rd; call for tour prices; ☺ usually 10am-5pm or 6pm May-Dec, tours by reservation only) This family-owned organic fruit-and-veggie stand offers educational walking tours of its fields. On the drive in, watch for the giant sculptures of farm workers by local artist John Cerney, which also stand along Hwy 101. The farm is off Hwy 68 at Spreckels Blvd, about 3 miles southwest of downtown.

Ag Venture Tours
GUIDED TOUR

(☑ 831-761-8463; www.agventuretours.com; tours adult/child 5-16yr from $70/60) Take an in-depth look at commercial and organic farm fields around the Salinas Valley.

⚜️ Festivals & Events

California Rodeo Salinas
RODEO

(www.carodeo.com) Bull riding, calf roping, cowboy poetry and carnival rides in late July.

Steinbeck Festival
CULTURE

(www.steinbeck.org) Three-day festival in early May features films, lectures, live music and guided bus and walking tours.

California International Airshow
OUTDOORS

(www.salinasairshow.com) Professional stunt flying and vintage and military aircraft take wing in late September.

🛏️ Sleeping

Salinas has plenty of motels off Hwy 101, including at the Market St exit.

Super 8 Salinas
MOTEL $

(☑ 800-454-3213, 831-758-4693; www.super8.com; 131 Kern St; r incl breakfast from $79; ❄️@🛜🏊) Revamped rooms have surprisingly stylish accents, from geometric patterned bed-

spreads to vanity mirrors. Complimentary breakfast buffet.

Laurel Inn
MOTEL $

(☑ 831-449-2474; www.laurelinnmotel.com; 801 W Laurel Dr; r from $80; ❄️🛜🏊) If chain motels don't do it for you, this sprawling, family-owned cheapie has predictably worn rooms that are nevertheless spacious.

🍴 Eating & Drinking

Bakery Station
BAKERY, DELI $

(www.thebakerystation.com; 202 Monterey St; dishes $3-9; ☺ 6am-4pm Mon-Fri, 7am-2pm Sat; 🍴) Inside a converted gas station one block east of Main St, the breads, pastries and cookies are baked fresh daily. Tasty sandwiches are stuffed full of farm-fresh goodness.

Pica Fresh Mex
MEXICAN $$

(157 Main St; mains $6-12; ☺ 11am-9pm Mon-Thu, to 10pm Fri & Sat, 2-9pm Sun; 🛜) Just south of the National Steinbeck Center, this storefront Mexican kitchen gets a stamp of approval for handmade tortillas, smoky chipotle salsa, carne asada tacos, burritos and *brochetas* (meat kebabs).

First Awakenings
AMERICAN $$

(www.firstawakenings.net; 171 Main St; mains $8-12; ☺ 7am-2pm; 🍴) Fork into diner-style breakfasts of fruity pancakes, crepes and egg skillets, or turn up later in the day for hand-crafted sandwiches and market-fresh salads.

XL Public House
BAR

(www.facebook.com/XLPublichouse; 127 Main St; tasting fee $5; ☺ noon-10pm) Stumble into this brick-walled bottle shop for craft beers on tap, board games and retro video arcade consoles.

Monterey Coast Brewing Co
BREWERY

(165 Main St; ☺ 11am-11pm Tue-Sun, to 4pm Mon) At this lively downtown microbrewery, an eight-beer tasting sampler costs just 10 bucks. The pub grub is bland.

ℹ️ Information

Salinas 411 (☑ 831-435-4636; www.oldtown-salinas.com; 222 Main St; ☺ 9am-7pm) Free information, maps and self-guided walking-tour brochures.

ℹ️ Getting There & Away

Amtrak (☑ 800-872-7245; www.amtrak.com; 11 Station Pl) runs daily *Coast Starlight* trains north to Oakland ($16, three hours) and south to Paso

Robles ($19, two hours), San Luis Obispo ($27, 3¼ hours), Santa Barbara ($39, 6¼ hours) and LA ($56, 9¼ hours).

Greyhound (☑ 800-231-2222; www.greyhound.com; 19 W Gabilan St) has a few daily buses north to Santa Cruz ($15, 65 minutes) and San Francisco ($27, 3½ to five hours) and south to San Luis Obispo ($32, 2½ hours) and Santa Barbara ($53, 4¾ hours). From the nearby **Salinas Transit Center** (110 Salinas St), **MST** (☑ 888-678-2871; www.mst.org) bus 20 goes to Monterey ($3.50, one hour, every 30 to 60 minutes).

Pinnacles National Park

Named for the towering spires that rise abruptly out of the chaparral-covered hills east of Salinas Valley, this off-the-beaten-path **park** (☑ 831-389-4486; www.nps.gov/pinn; per car $5) protects the remains of an ancient volcano. A study in geological drama, its craggy monoliths, sheer-walled canyons and twisting caves are the result of millions of years of erosion.

Sights & Activities

Besides **rock climbing** (for route information, click to www.pinnacles.org), the park's biggest attractions are its two talus caves, formed by piles of boulders. **Balconies Cave** is almost always open for exploration. Scrambling through it is not an exercise recommended for claustrophobes, as it's pitch-black inside, making a flashlight essential. Be prepared to get lost a bit too. The cave is found along a 2.5-mile hiking loop from the west entrance. Nearer the east entrance, **Bear Gulch Cave** is closed seasonally, so as not to disturb a resident colony of Townsend's big-eared bats.

To really appreciate Pinnacles' stark beauty, you need to hike. Moderate loops of varying lengths and difficulty ascend into the **High Peaks** and include thrillingly narrow clifftop sections. In the early morning or late afternoon, you may spot endangered California condors soaring overhead. Get an early start to tackle the 9-mile round-trip trail to the top of **Chalone Peak**, granting panoramic views.

Rangers lead guided full-moon hikes and star-gazing programs on some weekend nights, usually in spring or fall. Reservations are required: call ☑ 831-389-4485 in advance or check for last-minute vacancies at the visitor center.

Sleeping

Pinnacles National Park Campground   CAMPGROUND $
(☑ 877-444-6777; www.recreation.gov; tent/RV sites $23/36; ▨▨) On the park's east side, this popular family-oriented campground has more than 130 sites (some with shade), drinking water, coin-op hot showers, fire pits and an outdoor pool (usually closed from October to March).

Information

The best time to visit Pinnacles National Park is during spring or fall; summer heat is extreme. Information, maps and books are available on the park's east side from the small **NPS visitor center** (☑ 831-389-4485; ☉ 9:30am-5pm daily, to 8pm Fri late Mar-early Sep) inside the **campground store** (☑ 831-389-4538; ☉ 3-4pm Mon-Thu, noon-6pm Fri, 9am-6pm Sat & Sun), which sells bottled water, snacks and sundries.

Getting There & Away

There is no road connecting the two sides of the park. To reach the less-developed **west entrance** (☉ 7:30am-8pm), exit Hwy 101 at Soledad and follow Hwy 146 northeast for 14 miles. The **east entrance** (☉ 24hr), where you'll find the visitor center and campground, is accessed via lonely Hwy 25 in San Benito County, southeast of Hollister and northeast of King City.

Mission San Antonio De Padua

Remote, tranquil and evocative, this historical **mission** (☑ 831-385-4478; www.missionsanantonio.net; end of Mission Rd, Jolon; adult/child 12yr & under $5/3; ☉ usually 10am-4pm) sits in the Valley of the Oaks, once part of Hearst Ranch's sprawling land holdings. Today it's inside the boundaries of the US Army's Fort Hunter Liggett.

The mission was founded in 1771 by Franciscan priest Junípero Serra. Built with Native American labor, the church has been restored to its early-19th-century appearance, with a wooden pulpit, canopied altar and decorative flourishes on whitewashed walls. A creaky door leads to a cloistered garden anchored by a fountain. The museum has a small collection of such utilitarian items as an olive press and a weaving loom once used in the mission's workshops. Around the grounds, you can inspect the remains of a mill and irrigation system with aqueducts.

It's seldom crowded here, and you may have the vast site all to yourself, except during **Mission Days** in early April and **La Fiesta** on the second Sunday of June. Pick up a visitor's pass from a military checkpoint on the way in; bring photo ID and proof of your vehicle's registration. From the north, take the Jolon Rd exit off Hwy 101 before King City and follow Jolon Rd (County Rte G14) about 18 miles south to Mission Rd. From the south, take the Jolon Rd (County Rte G18) exit off Hwy 101 and drive 22 miles northwest to Mission Rd.

San Miguel

San Miguel is a small farming town off Hwy 101, where life seems to have remained almost unchanged for decades. Founded in 1797, **Mission San Miguel Arcángel** (☎805-467-3256; www.missionsanmiguel.org; 775 Mission St; adult/child 5-17yr $3/2; ☉10am-4:30pm) suffered heart-breaking damage during a 2003 earthquake. Although repairs are still underway, the church, cemetery, museum and gardens are open. An enormous cactus out front was planted during the early days of the mission.

Hungry? Inside a converted retro gas station downtown, **San Miguel Coffee Station** (www.sanmiguelcoffeestation.com; 1199 Mission St; dishes $3-8; ☉6:30am-5pm Mon-Wed, to 8pm Thu-Sat) vends live-wire cups o' coffee, sweet baked goods, pulled-pork sandwiches and stuffed Cal-Mex burritos.

Paso Robles

In northern San Luis Obispo County, Paso Robles is the heart of a historic agricultural region where grapes are now the biggest money-making crop. Scores of wineries along Hwy 46 produce a brave new world of more-than-respectable bottles. The Mediterranean climate is yielding another bounty too: olive oil. Paso's historic downtown centers on Park and 12th Sts, where boutique shops and wine-tasting rooms await.

◉ Sights & Activities

You could spend days wandering country back roads off Hwy 46, running east and west of Hwy 101. Most wineries have tasting rooms and a few offer vineyard tours. For dozens more wineries and olive-oil farms to visit, browse www.pasowine.com.

Eastside

J Lohr Vineyards & Wines   WINERY
(www.jlohr.com; 6169 Airport Rd; tasting fee free-$10; ☉10am-5pm) A Central Coast wine pioneer, J Lohr owns vineyards in Napa Valley, Monterey's Santa Lucia Highlands and Paso's pastoral countryside. Knowledgeable staff guide you through a far-reaching wine list.

Tobin James Cellars   WINERY
(www.tobinjames.com; 8950 Union Rd; ☉10am-6pm) Anti-serious Old West saloon pours bold reds, including an outlaw 'Ballistic' Zinfandel and 'Liquid Love' dessert wine. No tasting fee.

Eberle Winery   WINERY
(www.eberlewinery.com; 3810 E Hwy 46; tasting fee free-$10; ☉10am-5pm Oct-Mar, 10am-6pm Apr-Sep) Offers lofty vineyard views and hourly tours of its wine caves. Sociable tastings run the gamut of white and red varietals and Rhône blends.

Cass Winery   WINERY
(www.casswines.com; 7350 Linne Rd; tasting fee $10; ☉11am-5pm) All that rich Rhône varietal wine-tasting, from Roussanne to Syrah, going straight to your head? An epicurean market cafe here serves lunch until 5pm daily.

Westside

Tablas Creek Vineyard   WINERY
(www.tablascreek.com; 9339 Adelaida Rd; tasting fee from $10; ☉10am-5pm) 🌿 Breathe easy at this organic estate vineyard reached via a pretty winding drive up into the hills. Known for Rhône varietals, the signature blends also rate highly. Free tours at 10:30am and 2pm daily (reservations advised).

Castoro Cellars   WINERY
(www.castorocellars.com; 1315 N Bethel Rd; tasting fee $5; ☉10am-5:30pm) Husband-and-wife team produces 'dam fine wine' (the mascot is a beaver, get it?), including from custom-crushed and organic grapes. Outdoor vineyard concerts happen during summer.

Chronic Cellars   WINERY
(www.chroniccellars.com; 2020 Nacimiento Lake Dr; tasting fee $10; ☉11:30am-5:30pm) Everyone's favorite irreverent winery, where Día de Los Muertos designs cover bottles of bold blends. Play billiards in the tasting room or a game of horseshoes outside on the grass.

Re:Find Distillery & Villicana Winery   WINERY
(www.villicanawinery.com; 2725 Adelaida Rd; tasting fee $10; ☉11am-5pm) Paso Robles' first

micro-distillery makes clean-tasting botanical brandy (read: gin), which you can taste along with dry rosé in the adjoining wine-tasting room.

Thacher Winery
WINERY

(www.thacherwinery.com; 8355 Vineyard Rd; tasting fee $10; ⏱11am-5pm Thu-Mon) Breathe deeply as you drive up the dirt road to this historic ranch that makes memorable Rhône blends – 'Controlled Chaos' is a perennial fave.

✦ Festivals & Events

Wine Festival
WINE, FOOD

(www.pasowine.com) Oenophiles come for Paso's premier Wine Festival in mid-May, but the Vintage Paso weekend, focusing on Zinfandel wines, in mid-March and the Harvest Wine Weekend in mid-October are just as fun.

California Mid-State Fair
CARNIVAL, MUSIC

(www.midstatefair.com) In mid-July, 12 days of live rock and country-and-western concerts, farm exhibits, carnival rides and a rodeo draw huge crowds.

⌂ Sleeping

Chain motels and hotels line Hwy 101. B&Bs and vacation rentals are scattered among the vineyards outside town.

Melody Ranch Motel
MOTEL $

(☎ 800-909-3911, 805-238-3911; 939 Spring St; r $70-100; ✱ ☏ ☒) At this small, family-owned, 1950s motor court downtown, ultra-basic rooms mean prices that are almost as small as the outdoor pool.

Adelaide Inn
MOTEL $$

(☎800-549-7276, 805-238-2770; www.adelaideinn.com; 1215 Ysabel Ave; r incl breakfast $115-165; ✱ @ ☏ ☒) Fresh-baked cookies, muffins for breakfast, mini golf and a fitness room keep families happy at this motel just off Hwy 101.

Summerwood Inn
B&B $$$

(www.summerwoodwine.com; 2175 Arbor Rd; d incl breakfast from $275) ⊘ Along Hwy 46 within an easy drive of dozens of wineries, this gorgeously renovated inn mixes vintage and modern elements. Each room has a gas fireplace and balcony overlooking the vineyards. Indulge with the chef's gourmet breakfast, afternoon hors d'oeuvres and evening desserts.

Inn Paradiso
B&B $$$

(☎805-239-2800; www.innparadiso.com; 975 Mojave Ln; ste incl breakfast $350; ☏ ☒) An inti-

mate B&B pulls off no-fuss luxury with three suites decorated with art and antiques, and perhaps a fireplace, a deep soaking tub, a canopy king-sized bed or French balcony doors. Pet fee $50.

Zenaida Cellars
B&B $$$

(☎866-936-5638; www.zenaidacellars.com; 1550 W Hwy 46; ste $250-375; ☏) Steal yourself away among the pastoral vineyards of Paso Robles' westside. The winemaker's loft above the tasting room sleeps four adults and has a full kitchen.

✕ Eating & Drinking

Restaurants and wine-tasting rooms surround downtown's grassy central square, off Spring St between 11th and 12th Sts.

La Reyna Market
MEXICAN $

(www.lareynamarket.com; 532 24th St; dishes $2-8; ⏱8am-9pm Mon-Thu, to 9:30pm Fri-Sun) Off Hwy 101, this authentic Mexican grocery store and butcher's deli makes savory *tortas* (sandwiches), wet burritos and street-food tacos (the *al pastor* edges out the carne asada) on hot, homemade tortillas.

★ Artisan
CALIFORNIAN $$$

(☎805-237-8084; www.artisanpasorobles.com; 843 12th St; shared plates $11-19, mains $30-38; ⏱11:30am-9pm Mon-Thu, to 10pm Fri & Sat, 10am-9pm Sun) ⊘ Chef Chris Kobayashi often ducks out of the kitchen just to make sure you're loving his impeccable contemporary renditions of modern American cuisine, featuring sustainably farmed meats, wild-caught seafood and artisan California cheeses. Impressive wine, beer and cocktail menus. Reservations essential.

Fish Gaucho
MEXICAN, SEAFOOD $$$

(www.fishgaucho.com; 1244 Spring St; mains $17-26; ⏱kitchen 3-9:30pm, from 11:30am Fri-Sun, bar till midnight daily) Hand-made furnishings, antiques and decor imported from Mexico fill this Baja-style seafood joint and tequila bar. Smoky, spicy and fruity cocktails wash down stuffed poblano chiles, braised short-rib tacos and oyster shooters with chorizo and cotija crumbles. Reservations recommended.

Firestone Walker Brewing Company
BREWERY

(☎805-225-5911; www.firestonebeer.com; 1400 Ramada Dr; ⏱noon-7pm) Bring your buddies to the taproom to sample the famous Double Barrel Ale or seasonal Velvet Merlin oatmeal stout, plus barrel-aged vintages and experimental brews. Book ahead for free brewery tours.

BarrelHouse Brewing Co BREWERY
(www.barrelhousebrewing.com; 3055 Limestone Way; ⊘ 2-8pm Wed-Thu, 11am-9pm Fri & Sat, 11am-8pm Sun) Detour south of downtown, where locals chill outside at picnic tables with pints of ales, stout and fruity Belgian-style beers, while live bands frequently play.

🛍 Shopping

Around the downtown square, side streets are full of wine-country boutiques.

Paso Robles General Store FOOD, GIFTS
(www.generalstorepr.com; 841 12th St; ⊘ 10am-7pm) Stock up on picnic provisions including California-made pistachio butter, fresh local baguettes, fruit jams and more, plus home goods such as lavender soap.

We Olive FOOD
(www.weolive.com/paso-robles; 1311 Park St; ⊘ 10am-6pm Mon-Sat, 11am-4pm Sun) Step right up to the tasting bar to sample local growers' olive oils and fruit-infused balsamic vinegars. Also in downtown San Luis Obispo.

ℹ Information

Paso Robles Chamber of Commerce (☑ 805-238-0506; www.pasorobleschamber.com; 1225 Park St; ⊘ 8:30am-4:30pm, closed Sun Sep-May) Information and free winery maps.

ℹ Getting There & Away

From an unstaffed **Amtrak** (☑ 800-872-7245; www.amtrak.com; 800 Pine St) station, daily *Coast Starlight* trains head north to Salinas ($19, two hours) and Oakland ($30, 4¾ hours) and south to Santa Barbara ($28, 4¼ hours) and LA ($41, 7½ hours). Several daily Thruway buses link to more-frequent regional trains, including the *Pacific Surfliner*.

From the train station, **Greyhound** (☑ 800-231-2222; www.greyhound.com; 800 Pine St) runs a few daily buses along Hwy 101 south to Santa Barbara ($57, 2¾ hours) and LA ($81, six hours) and north to San Francisco ($74, six hours) via Santa Cruz ($57, 3¼ hours).

RTA (☑ 805-541-2228; www.slorta.org) bus 9 travels between San Luis Obispo and Paso Robles ($2.50, 70 minutes) hourly Monday to Friday, and a few times daily on weekends.

San Luis Obispo

Almost midway between LA and San Francisco, at the junction of Hwys 101 and 1, San Luis Obispo is a popular overnight stop for road trippers. With no must-see attractions, SLO might not seem to warrant much of your time. Even so, this low-key town has an enviably high quality of life – in fact, it has been named America's happiest city. CalPoly university students inject a healthy dose of hubbub into the city's streets, bars and cafes throughout the school year. Nestled at the base of the Santa Lucia foothills, SLO is just a grape's throw from Edna Valley wineries too.

⊙ Sights

San Luis Obispo Creek, once used to irrigate mission orchards, flows through downtown. Uphill from Higuera St, **Mission Plaza** is a shady oasis with restored adobe buildings and fountains overlooking the creek. Look for the **Moon Tree**, a coast redwood grown from a seed that journeyed on board Apollo 14's lunar mission.

Mission San Luis Obispo de Tolosa CHURCH
(☑ 805-543-6850; www.missionsanluisobispo.org; 751 Palm St; donation $2; ⊘ 9am-5pm late Mar-Oct, to 4pm Nov–mid-Mar) Those satisfyingly reverberatory bells heard around downtown emanate from this active parish dating from 1772. The fifth California mission founded by Junipero Serra, it was named for a 13th-century French saint. The modest church has an unusual L-shape and whitewashed walls decorated with Stations of the Cross. An adjacent building contains an old-fashioned museum about daily life during the Chumash tribal and Spanish colonial periods.

San Luis Obispo Museum of Art MUSEUM
(www.sloma.org; 1010 Broad St; ⊘ 11am-5pm, closed Tue early Sep-early Jul) **FREE** By the creek, this small gallery showcases the work of local painters, sculptors, printmakers and fine-art photographers, as well as traveling California art exhibitions.

Bubblegum Alley STREET
(off 700 block of Higuera St) SLO's weirdest sight is colorfully plastered with thousands of wads of ABC ('already been chewed') gum. Watch where you step!

🏃 Activities

For more hiking with ocean views, head to Montaña de Oro State Park (p291), not far away.

Bishop Peak HIKING
SLO's most popular hike summits Bishop Peak (1546ft), the tallest of the Nine Sisters,

San Luis Obispo

a chain of volcanic peaks that stretches north to Morro Bay. The 2.2-mile one-way trail starts in a grove of live oaks (watch out for poison oak) and heads uphill along rocky, mostly exposed switchbacks. Carefully scramble up boulders at the tippy-top for panoramic views.

To get to the trailhead, drive northwest from downtown on Santa Rosa St (Hwy 1), turn left onto Foothill Dr, then right onto Patricia Dr; after 0.8 miles, look for three black posts and a trailhead sign on your left.

Margarita Adventures   ZIP LINING, KAYAKING
(☑ 805-438-3120; www.margarita-adventures.com; 22719 El Camino Real, Santa Margarita; adult/child zip-line tour $99/79, kayak tour $79/59; ☺ closed Tue & Wed; ⛄) Whoosh down five zip lines across the vineyards or paddle around a lake beneath the Santa Lucia Mountains at this historic ranch, about a 10-mile drive northeast of SLO via Hwy 101. Reservations required.

✶✶ Festivals & Events

Concerts in the Plaza   MUSIC, FOOD
(www.downtownslo.com) Every Friday night from early June through early September, downtown's Mission Plaza rocks out with local bands and food vendors.

Savor the Central Coast   FOOD, WINE
(www.savorcentralcoast.com) Behind-the-scenes farm, aquaculture and ranch tours, wine-tasting competitions and celebrity chefs' dinners in late September or early October.

⛏ Sleeping

Motels cluster off Hwy 101, especially off Monterey St northeast of downtown and around Santa Rosa St (Hwy 1).

HI Hostel Obispo   HOSTEL $
(☑ 805-544-4678; www.hostelobispo.com; 1617 Santa Rosa St; dm $27-31, r from $60, all with shared bath; ☺ check-in 4:30-10pm; @ 🛜) ⛅ On a tree-lined street near the train station, this

San Luis Obispo

solar-empowered, avocado-colored hostel inhabits a converted Victorian, which gives it a bit of a B&B feel. Amenities include a kitchen, bike rentals (from $10 per day) and complimentary sourdough pancakes and coffee for breakfast. BYOT (bring your own towel).

Peach Tree Inn MOTEL $$
(📞800-227-6396, 805-543-3170; www.peachtree-inn.com; 2001 Monterey St; r incl breakfast $89-140; ⊙office 7am-11pm; @🛜) The folksy, nothing-fancy motel rooms here are inviting, especially those right by the creek or with rocking chairs on wooden porches overlooking grassy lawns, eucalyptus trees and rose gardens. Continental breakfast features homemade breads.

San Luis Creek Lodge HOTEL $$$
(📞800-593-0333, 805-541-1122; www.sanluis-creeklodge.com; 1941 Monterey St; r incl breakfast $149-269; ✳@🛜) Rubbing shoulders with

neighboring motels, this boutique inn has fresh, spacious rooms with divine beds (and some have gas fireplaces and jetted tubs) inside three whimsically mismatched buildings built in Tudor, California arts-and-crafts and Southern plantation styles. DVDs, chess sets and board games are free to borrow.

Petit Soleil INN $$$
(📞800-676-1588, 805-549-0321; www.petitsoleils-lo.com; 1473 Monterey St; d incl breakfast $169-299; ⊙office 7am-10pm; 🛜🐾) This French-themed, gay-friendly 'bed et breakfast' is a mostly charming retrofit of a courtyard motel. Each room is tastefully decorated with Provençal flair, and breakfast is a gourmet feast. The front rooms catch some street noise. Pet fee $25.

🍴 Eating

★ **San Luis Obispo Farmers Market** MARKET
(www.downtownslo.com; ⊙6-9pm Thu) The county's biggest and best weekly farmers market turns downtown SLO's Higuera St into a giant street party, with smokin' barbecues, overflowing fruit and veggie stands, live music and free sidewalk entertainment, from salvation peddlers to wackadoodle political activists. Rain cancels it.

Firestone Grill BARBECUE $
(www.firestonegrill.com; 1001 Higuera St; dishes $4-10; ⊙11am-10pm Sun-Wed, to 11pm Thu-Sat; 🚸) If you can stomach huge lines, long waits for a table, and sports-bar-style service, you'll get to sink your teeth into an authentic Santa Maria–style tri-tip steak sandwich on a toasted garlic roll and a basket of super-crispy fries.

SLO Donut Company SNACKS $
(www.slodoco.com; 793 E Foothill Blvd; snacks from $2; ⊙24hr; 🛜) Home of unusually good flavor combos like bacon-maple and mint-chip donuts, served with cups of organic, fair-trade, locally roasted coffee. It's northwest of downtown off Santa Rosa St (Hwy 1).

Whole Foods GROCERY, FAST FOOD $
(www.wholefoodsmarket.com; 1531 Froom Ranch Way; ⊙8am-9pm) 🌿 For organic groceries, deli picnic meals and a hot-and-cold salad bar. It's 4 miles southwest of downtown via Hwy 101 (exit Los Osos Valley Rd).

Meze Wine Bar & Bistro MEDITERRANEAN $$
(www.mezewinebar.com; 1880 Santa Barbara Ave; mains $10-20; ⊙11am-9pm Mon-Wed, to 10pm

CENTRAL COAST SAN LUIS OBISPO

MADONNA INN

'Oh, my!' is one of the more printable exclamations overheard from visitors at the **Madonna Inn** (☑805-543-3000, 800-543-9666; www.madonnainn.com; 100 Madonna Rd; r $189-309; ❄@🅰♨), a garish confection visible from Hwy 101. You'd expect outrageous kitsch like this in Las Vegas, not SLO, but here it is, in all its campy extravagance. Japanese tourists, vacationing Midwesterners and hipster, irony-loving urbanites all adore the 110 themed rooms – including Yosemite Rock, Caveman and hot-pink Floral Fantasy. Check out photos of the different rooms online, or wander the halls and spy into the ones being cleaned. The urinal in the men's room is a bizarre waterfall. But the most irresistible reason to stop here? Old-fashioned cookies from the storybook-esque bakery.

Thu-Sat) Hidden downhill from the Amtrak station, this tiny wine shop, gourmet market and tapas-style bar is an eclectic gem. Gather with friends around the cheese and charcuterie board, or stop in for a hand-crafted sandwich with a quinoa salad.

Big Sky Café CALIFORNIAN $$
(www.bigskycafe.com; 1121 Broad St; dinner mains $11-22; ⊙7am-9pm Mon-Thu, to 10pm Fri, 8am-10pm Sat, to 9pm Sun; 🖉) 🍴 Big Sky is a big room, and still the wait can be long – its tagline is 'analog food for a digital world.' Vegetarians have almost as many options as carnivores, and many of the ingredients are sourced locally. Big-plate dinners can be a bit bland, but breakfast (served until 1pm daily) gets top marks.

★ Luna Red FUSION $$$
(☑805-540-5243; www.lunaredslo.com; 1023 Chorro St; shared plates $6-20, mains $20-39; ⊙11am-9pm Mon-Wed, to 11:30pm Thu-Fri, 9:30am-11:30pm Sat, to 9pm Sun; 🖉) 🍴 Local bounty from the land and sea, artisan cheeses and farmers-market produce pervade the chef's Californian, Asian and Mediterranean small-plates menu. Cocktails and glowing lanterns enhance a sophisticated ambience indoors, or linger over brunch on the mission-view garden patio. Reservations recommended.

Novo FUSION $$$
(☑805-543-3986; www.novorestaurant.com; 726 Higuera St; mains $15-34; ⊙11am-9pm Mon-Thu, to 1am Fri & Sat, 10am-9pm Sun) Novo spins out hit-and-miss European, Latin and Asian-inspired tapas, but with an artistic eye towards presentation. Pick from dozens of international beers, wines or sakes, then savor the view from tables on the creekside deck.

Sidecar CALIFORNIAN $$$
(☑805-540-5340; www.sidecarslo.com; 1127 Broad St; mains $14-28; ⊙11am-10pm Mon-Fri, from 10am Sat & Sun) 🍴 A long saloon-style bar where locals mingle with serious cocktails, and a casual Californian menu – try the fried brussels sprouts or the signature house burger with smoked mozzarella – make this downtown eatery a social spot.

🍷 Drinking & Nightlife

Downtown, Higuera St is littered with college-student-jammed bars.

Downtown Brewing Co BREWERY
(☑805-543-1843; www.slobrew.com; 1119 Garden St) Nicknamed SLO Brew, this study in rafters and exposed brick has plenty of craft beers to go, along with filling pub grub. Downstairs, you'll find DJs or live bands (including some surprisingly famous acts) on many nights.

Tap It Brewing BREWERY
(☑805-545-7702; www.tapitbrewing.com; 675 Clarion St; ⊙noon-6pm Sun-Wed, to 8pm Thu-Sat) Head toward the airport to this brewery's tap room, where cacti grow inside an old Jeep and live bands sometimes rock on the patio.

Mother's Tavern PUB
(www.motherstavern.com; 725 Higuera St; ⊙11am-1:30am; 🎵) Cavernous two-story 'MoTav' draws in writhing CalPoly student masses with a no-cover dance floor, DJ and karaoke nights, and big-screen sports TVs.

Kreuzberg CAFE
(www.kreuzbergcalifornia.com; 685 Higuera St; ⊙7:30am-10pm; 🎵) Shabby-chic coffeehouse and roaster has earned a fervent following with its comfy couches, sprawling bookshelves, local art and occasional live music.

Granada Bistro COCKTAIL BAR
(www.granadahotelandbistro.com; 1126 Morro St; ⊙5-10pm Sun-Thu, to 11pm Fri & Sat) A swank indoor/outdoor hotel cocktail lounge, adorned with wrought-iron candelabras and outdoor fire pits, classes up SLO's downtown scene.

Luis Wine Bar WINE BAR
(www.luiswinebar.com; 1021 Higuera St; ⊙ 3-11pm Mon-Thu, to midnight Fri, noon-midnight Sat, noon-11pm Sun) Evincing urbane style and unpretentious sophistication, this downtown wine bar has wide-open seating, a strong craft beer list and small noshes.

Creekside Brewing Co BREWERY
(www.creeksidebrewingcom.ipage.com; 1040 Broad St; ⊙ 4pm-close Mon-Thu, from noon Fri-Sun) On the tiny patio overhanging a bubbling creek, you can sample respectable homemade and imported craft beers and ciders.

☆ Entertainment

Palm Theatre CINEMA
(☑ 805-541-5161; www.thepalmtheatre.com; 817 Palm St; tickets $5-8) ⚐ This small-scale movie house showing foreign and indie flicks just happens to be the USA's first solar-powered cinema. Look for the **SLO International Film Festival** (www.slofilmfest.org) in March.

Performing Arts Center PERFORMING ARTS
(PAC; ☑ 805-756-4849, 888-233-2787; www.pacslo.org; 1 Grand Ave) On the CalPoly campus, SLO's biggest cultural venue presents an internationally spiced variety of concerts, theater, dance recitals, stand-up comedy and other shows, including by big-name performers.

Sunset Drive-In CINEMA
(☑ 805-544-4475; www.facebook.com/sunset-drivein; 255 Elks Ln; ⊞) Recline your seat, put your feet up on the dash and munch on bottomless bags of popcorn at this classic Americana drive-in. Sticking around for the second feature (usually a B-list Hollywood blockbuster) doesn't cost extra. It's 2 miles southwest of downtown off Higuera St.

🔒 Shopping

Downtown Higuera and Marsh Sts, along with all of the arcades and cross streets in between, are full of unique boutiques. Just take a wander.

DON'T MISS

EDNA VALLEY WINERIES

A gorgeous bicycle ride into the rolling hills southeast of downtown SLO, Edna Valley wineries are best known for producing crisp Chardonnay and subtle Pinot Noir, as well as spicy and smoky Syrah. Annual events worth showing up for include 'Roll Out the Barrels' in mid-June and harvest celebrations in mid-November. For a winery map and more information, visit www.slowine.com.

Tolosa Winery (www.tolosawinery.com; 4910 Edna Rd; tasting fee $12-25; ⊙ 11am-4:45pm) No-oak Chardonnay, barrel-selected Pinot Noir and bold estate Syrah, with artisanal cheese, charcuterie and chocolate pairings on weekends.

Edna Valley Vineyard (www.ednavalleyvineyard.com; 2585 Biddle Ranch Rd; tasting fee $10-15; ⊙ 10am-5pm) Sip Paragon Vineyard estate Chardonnay by panoramic windows overlooking fields of grapes.

Baileyana (Niven Family Wine Estates; www.baileyana.com; 5828 Orcutt Rd; tasting fee $8-12; ⊙ 10am-5pm) Samples from six different labels inside an early-20th-century wooden schoolhouse, with a bocce ball court outside.

Talley Vineyards (www.talleyvineyards.com; 3031 Lopez Dr, Arroyo Grande; tasting fee $8-15; ⊙ 10:30am-4:30pm) Unpretentious, value-priced wines set among rolling hillsides, with vineyard tours ($10, including wine-tasting flight $15) by appointment.

Kynsi Winery (www.kynsi.com; 2212 Corbett Canyon Rd, Arroyo Grande; tasting fee $10; ⊙ 11am-5pm, closed Tue & Wed Nov-Jan) Small, family-run vineyard pours cult-worthy Pinot Noir inside a cozy brick tasting room.

Chamisal Vineyards (www.chamisalvineyards.com; 7525 Orcutt Rd; tasting fee $15; ⊙ 11am-5pm) In a rust-colored barn tasting room, tipple hand-crafted, small-lot wines grown mostly organically.

Sextant Wines (www.sextantwines.com; 1653 Old Price Canyon Rd; tasting fee $10; ⊙ 10am-4pm Mon-Fri, to 5pm Sat & Sun) Boisterous tasting room pours different varietals from Edna Valley and Paso Robles, with a tiny gourmet deli.

Hands Gallery
ARTS & CRAFTS

(www.handsgallery.com; 777 Higuera St; ⊙10am-6pm Mon-Wed, to 9pm Thu, to 8pm Fri & Sat, 11am-5pm Sun) Brightly lit downtown shop sells vibrant contemporary pieces by California artisans, including jewelry, fiber arts, sculptures, ceramics and blown glass.

Mountain Air Sports
OUTDOOR EQUIPMENT

(www.mountainairsports.com; 667 Marsh St; ⊙10am-6pm Mon-Sat, to 8pm Thu, 11am-4pm Sun) At this local outdoor outfitter, pick up anything from campstove fuel and tents to brand-name clothing and hiking boots.

Finders Keepers
CLOTHING

(www.finderskeepersconsignment.com; 1124 Garden St; ⊙10am-5pm Mon-Sat) Seriously stylish secondhand women's fashions that match SLO's breezy, laid-back coastal lifestyle, plus hand-picked handbags, coats and jewelry.

ⓘ Information

SLO's compact downtown is bisected by the parallel one-way arteries Higuera St and Marsh St. Banks with 24-hour ATMs are off Marsh St, near the post office. Most downtown coffee shops offer free wi-fi.

FedEx Office (www.fedex.com; 1127 Chorro St; per min 30-40¢; ⊙7am-11pm Mon-Fri, 8am-9pm Sat, 9am-9pm Sun; ☎) Pay-as-you-go internet workstations.

French Hospital (☎805-543-5353; www.frenchmedicalcenter.org; 1911 Johnson Ave; ⊙24hr) Emergency-room services.

San Luis Obispo Library (☎805-781-5991; www.slolibrary.org; 995 Palm St; ⊙10am-5pm Wed-Sat, to 8pm Tue; ☎) Free wi-fi and public internet terminals.

San Luis Obispo Visitor Center (☎805-781-2777; www.visitslo.com; 895 Monterey St; ⊙10am-5pm Sun-Wed, to 7pm Thu-Sat) Free maps and tourist brochures.

ⓘ Getting There & Around

Off Broad St, a little more than 3 miles southeast of downtown, San Luis Obispo County Regional Airport (p50700) has scheduled flights with United (San Francisco and LA) and US Airways (Phoenix).

Amtrak (☎800-872-7245; www.amtrak.com; 1011 Railroad Ave) runs daily Seattle–LA *Coast Starlight* and twice-daily SLO–San Diego *Pacific Surfliner* trains. Both routes head south to Santa Barbara ($27, 2¾ hours) and Los Angeles ($41, 5½ hours). The *Coast Starlight* connects north via Paso Robles to Salinas ($27, three hours) and Oakland ($39, six hours). Several daily Thruway buses link to more regional trains.

Inconveniently stopping off Hwy 101, nearly 4 miles southwest of downtown, **Greyhound** (☎800-231-2222; www.greyhound.com; 1460 Calle Joaquin) operates a few daily buses south to Los Angeles ($30, five hours) via Santa Barbara ($28, 2¼ hours) and north to San Francisco ($53, seven hours) via Santa Cruz ($42, four hours).

San Luis Obispo Regional Transit Authority (RTA; ☎805-541-2228; www.slorta.org; single-ride fares $1.50-3, day pass $5) operates daily county-wide buses with limited weekend services. All buses are equipped with bicycle racks. Lines converge on downtown's **transit center** (cnr Palm & Osos Sts).

SLO Transit (☎805-541-2877; www.slocity.org) runs local city buses ($1.25) and a trolley (50¢) that loops around downtown every 20 minutes between 5pm and 9pm on Thursdays year-round, on Fridays from June to early September and on Saturdays from April through October.

Avila Beach

Quaint, sunny Avila Beach lures crowds with its strand of golden sand and a shiny seafront commercial district of restaurants, cafes and shops. Two miles west of downtown, Port San Luis is a working fishing harbor with a rickety old pier.

◉ Sights & Activities

For a lazy summer day at the beach, you can rent beach chairs and umbrellas, surfboards, boogie boards and wetsuits underneath Avila Pier, off downtown's waterfront promenade. Over by the port, the beach has bonfire pits and the barking of sea lions accompanies your stroll atop Harford Pier, one of the Central Coast's most authentic fishing piers.

Point San Luis Lighthouse
LIGHTHOUSE

(☑guided hike reservations 805-541-8735, trolley tour reservations 855-533-7843; www.sanluislighthouse.org; lighthouse admission adult/child under 12yr $5/free, trolley tour incl admission per adult/child 3-12yr $20/15; ⊙guided hikes usually 8:45am-1pm Wed & Sat, trolley tours usually noon & 2pm Wed & Sat, also 1pm Sat) Just getting to this scenic 1890 lighthouse, overshadowed by Diablo Canyon nuclear power plant, is an adventure. The cheapest way to reach the lighthouse is via a rocky, crumbling, 3.75-mile round-trip hiking trail, for which guided hike reservations are required. If you'd rather take it easy and ride out to the lighthouse, join an afternoon trolley tour, for which reservations are also required. Inside the lighthouse you can inspect an original Fresnel lens and authentic Victorian period furnishings.

The Pecho Coast Trail to the lighthouse is open only for guided hikes led by Pacific Gas & Electric (PG&E) docents, weather permitting. These guided hikes are free; children under nine years old are not allowed. Call for reservations at least two weeks in advance and bring plenty of water.

Avila Valley Barn   FARM
(www.avilavalleybarn.com; 560 Avila Beach Dr; ⊙ usually 9am-6pm mid-Mar–late Dec; 🚻) At this rural farmstand and pick-your-own berry farm, park alongside the sheep and goat pens, lick an ice-cream cone, then grab a basket and walk out into the fields to harvest jammy olallieberries in late spring and early summer, mid-summer peaches and nectarines, or autumn apples and pumpkins.

Sycamore Mineral Springs   SPA
(📞 805-595-7302; www.sycamoresprings.com; 1215 Avila Beach Dr; 1hr per person $13.50-17.50; ⊙ 8am-midnight, last reservation 10:45pm) Make time for a therapeutic soak in one of these private redwood hot tubs discreetly laddered up a woodsy hillside. Call in advance for reservations, especially during summer and after dark on weekends.

Central Coast Kayaks   KAYAKING
(📞 805-773-3500; www.centralcoastkayaks.com; 1879 Shell Beach Rd, Shell Beach; kayak or SUP set rental $20-60, classes $50-105, tours $60-120) Paddle out among sea otters and seals and through mesmerizing sea caves, rock grottos, arches and kelp forests. Wetsuits, paddle jackets and booties available (small surcharge applies) with kayak rentals.

Patriot Sportfishing   BOAT TOUR
(📞 805-595-7200; www.patriotsportfishing.com; Harford Pier, off Avila Beach Dr; 2hr whale-watching tour adult/child under 13yr $35/25) Long-running local biz organizes deep-sea fishing trips and tournaments, as well as whale-spotting cruises between December and April.

Avila Hot Springs   HOT SPRINGS
(📞 805-595-2359; www.avilahotsprings.com; 250 Avila Beach Dr; adult/child under 16yr $10/8; ⊙ usually 8am-9pm Sun-Tue & Thu, to 10pm Wed, Fri & Sat) Slightly sulfuric, lukewarm public swimming pool has kiddie waterslides that are usually open from noon to 5pm on Saturday and Sunday.

🛏 Sleeping

Port San Luis Campground   CAMPGROUND $
(📞 805-903-3395; www.portsanluis.com; RV sites without/with hookups from $40/65) First-come, first-served roadside parking spaces by the harbor have ocean views, but are for RVs only (no tents allowed).

Avila Lighthouse Suites   HOTEL $$$
(📞 800-372-8452, 805-627-1900; www.avilalighthousesuites.com; 550 Front St; ste incl breakfast from $289; ❇ @ 🛜 ❇) Any closer to the ocean, and your bed would actually be sitting on the sand. With families in mind, this apartment-style hotel offers suites and villas with kitchenettes. But it's the giant heated outdoor pool, ping-pong tables, putting green and life-sized checkers board that keeps kids amused. Ask about steep off-season discounts.

Avila La Fonda   INN $$$
(📞 805-595-1700; www.avilalafonda.com; 101 San Miguel St; d from $329; @ 🛜) Downtown, this small boutique hotel is a harmonious mix of Mexican and Spanish colonial styles, with hand-painted tiles, stained-glass windows, wrought iron and rich wood. Gather around the fireplace for nightly wine and hors d'oeuvres. Complimentary beach gear to borrow for guests.

🍴 Eating

At Port San Luis, Harford Pier is home to shops that sell fresh catch right off the boats.

Avila Beach Farmers Market   MARKET $
(www.avilabeachpier.com; ⊙ 4-8pm Fri early Apr-late Sep) 🍴 With local farmers, food booths and rockin' live music, this outdoor street party takes over downtown's oceanfront promenade weekly from spring to fall.

Olde Port Inn   SEAFOOD $$$
(📞 805-595-2515; www.oldeportinn.com; Harford Pier, off Avila Beach Dr; mains $14-46; ⊙ 11:30am-9pm Sun-Thu, to 10pm Fri & Sat; 🚻) Clam chowder and cioppino are standouts at this seriously old-school seafood restaurant at the tip of Harford Pier. A few tables have see-through glass tops and floors, so lucky diners can peer down into the ocean. Reservations recommended.

ⓘ Getting There & Around

Between 10am and 4pm on Saturdays and Sundays from late March until mid-October, a free **trolley** (SCT; 📞 805-781-4472; www.slorta.org) loops from Pismo Beach around downtown Avila

San Luis Obispo Bay

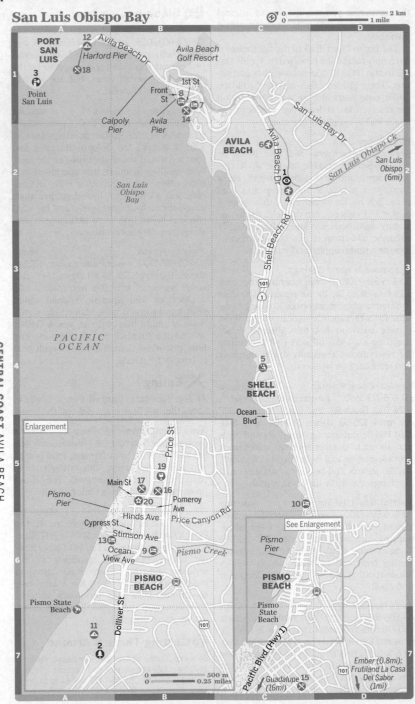

Beach to Port San Luis; from early June to early September, extended hours are 10am to 6pm Thursday through Sunday.

Pismo Beach

Backed by a wooden pier that stretches toward the setting sun, Pismo Beach is where James Dean once trysted with Pier Angeli. Fronted by an invitingly wide, sandy beach, this 1950s-retro town feels like somewhere straight out of *Rebel Without a Cause* or *American Graffiti*. If you're looking for a sand-and-surf respite from coastal road tripping, break your journey here.

◉ Sights & Activities

Pismo likes to call itself the 'Clam Capital of the World,' but these days the beach is pretty much clammed out. You'll have better luck catching something fishy off the pier, where you can rent rods. To rent a wetsuit, boogie board or surfboard, cruise nearby surf shops.

**Pismo Beach Monarch
Butterfly Grove**   PARK
(www.monarchbutterfly.org;   ☉ sunrise-sunset; ♿) FREE From late October until February, more than 25,000 black-and-orange monarchs make their winter home here. Forming dense clusters in the tops of eucalyptus trees, they might easily be mistaken for leaves. Between 10am and 4pm during the roosting season, volunteers can tell you all about the insects' incredible journey, which outlasts any single generation of butterflies. Look for a gravel parking pull-out on the ocean side

of Pacific Blvd (Hwy 1), just south of Pismo State Beach's North Beach Campground.

✦ Festivals & Events

Wine, Waves & Beyond   CULTURE, FOOD
(www.winewavesandbeyond.com) Surfing competitions, surf-themed movies, wine tasting and a big bash on the beach with live music and food in late April or early May.

Classic at Pismo Beach   CULTURE
(www.theclassicatpismobeach.com) Show up in mid-June when hot rods and muscle cars roar off Hwy 1.

Clam Festival   FOOD
(www.pismochamber.com) In mid-October, celebrate the formerly abundant and still tasty mollusk with a clam dig, chowder cookoff, food vendors and live music.

⊟ Sleeping

Pismo Beach has dozens of motels, but rooms fill up quickly and prices skyrocket in summer, especially on weekends. Resorts and hotels roost on cliffs north of town via Price St and Shell Beach Rd, while motels cluster near the beach and along Hwy 101.

**Pismo State Beach –
North Beach Campground**   CAMPGROUND $
(✆ reservations 800-444-7275; www.reserveamerica.com; 399 S Dolliver St; tent & RV sites $35; ♿) About a mile south of downtown, off Hwy 1, the state park's North Beach Campground is shaded by eucalyptus trees and has more than 170 well-spaced, grassy sites with fire pits. The campground offers easy beach access, flush toilets and coin-op hot showers.

SCENIC DRIVE: HWY 1 SOUTH OF PISMO BEACH

What to See

Hwy 1 ends its fling with Hwy 101 at Pismo Beach, veering off toward the coast. Some truly wild, hidden beaches beckon along this back-door route to Santa Barbara.

Guadalupe Dunes

You almost expect to have to dodge tumbleweeds as you drive into the agricultural town of Guadalupe. Five miles further west at **Rancho Guadalupe Dunes Preserve** (www. countyofsb.org/parks; off Hwy 166; ☉7am-sunset) **FREE**, enormous Egyptian-esque film sets from Cecil B DeMille's 1923 Hollywood epic *The Ten Commandments* still lie buried in the sand. Learn more about the 'Lost City of DeMille,' the ecology of North America's largest coastal dunes, and the mystical Dunites who lived here during the 1930s back at downtown's small **Dunes Center** (www.dunescenter.org; 1055 Guadalupe St; donation requested; ☉10am-4pm Wed-Sun) museum.

Surf & Ocean Beaches

These wind-whipped beaches, one with a lonely Amtrak train whistlestop platform station, sidle up to Vandenberg Air Force Base. On the 10-mile drive west of Lompoc and Hwy 1 (take Hwy 246/W Ocean Ave), you'll pass odd-looking structures supporting spy and commerical satellite launches. Between March and September, **Ocean Beach County Park** (www.countyofsb.org/parks; Ocean Park Rd, off Hwy 246; ☉8am-sunset, closed Mar-Sep) **FREE** is closed to the public and **Surf Beach** (www.vandenberg.af.mil/ploverup-date.asp; off Hwy 246; ☉8am-6pm, subject to closure Mar-Oct) is also often closed to protect endangered snowy plovers during their nesting season.

Jalama Beach

Leaving Hwy 1 about 5 miles east of Lompoc, Jalama Rd follows 14 miles of twisting tarmac across ranch and farm lands before arriving at utterly isolated **Jalama Beach County Park** (☎recorded info 805-736-3616; www.countyofsb.org/parks; 9999 Jalama Rd, Lompoc; per car $10). As you soak up the views, munch on a grilled seafood or beef burger from the **Jalama Beach Store** (www.jalamabeachstore.net; dishes $4-12; ☉usually 8am-7pm in summer). To stay overnight, reserve a cabin in advance or arrive by 8am to get on the waiting list for a campsite in the crazily popular **campground** (www.sbparks.org/res-ervations; tent/RV sites from $23/38, cabins $110-210) – look for the 'campground full' sign back near Hwy 1 to avoid a wasted trip.

The Route

Heading south of Pismo Beach, Hwy 1 slowly winds along, passing through Guadalupe and Lompoc, where you can detour to La Purísima Mission State Historic Park (p332). Past Lompoc, Hwy 1 curves east to rejoin Hwy 101 south of Santa Barbara's wine country, near Gaviota.

Time & Mileage

With all of the detours described above, it's a 165-mile drive from Pismo Beach to Santa Barbara. The drive takes at least 3½ hours without any stops or traffic delays.

Beachwalker Inn & Suites MOTEL $$
(☎805-773-2725; www.pismobeachwalkerinn.com; 490 Dolliver St; r from $120; ☜☒) Two blocks uphill from the beach, this renovated motel with a small outdoor heated pool lets you sleep peacefully atop deluxe mattresses. Suites have kitchenettes. Rates include morning coffee and pastries.

Pismo Lighthouse Suites HOTEL $$$
(☎800-245-2411, 805-773-2411; www.pismolight-housesuites.com; 2411 Price St; ste incl breakfast from $275; @☜☒☒) With everything a vacationing family needs – from kitchenettes to a life-sized outdoor chessboard, a putting green, table tennis and badminton courts – this contemporary all-suites hotel right on the beach is hard to tear yourself away from. Ask about off-season discounts. Pet fee $30.

Sandcastle Inn
HOTEL $$$

(☎800-822-6606, 805-773-2422; www.sand-castleinn.com; 100 Stimson Ave; r incl breakfast $169-435; ☎❄) Many of these Eastern Sea-board–styled rooms are mere steps from the sand. The top-floor ocean-view patio is perfect for cracking open a bottle of wine at sunset or after dark by the fireplace. One-time pet fee $75.

✕ Eating

Doc Burnstein's Ice Cream Lab
ICE CREAM $

(www.docburnsteins.com; 114 W Branch St, Arroyo Grande; snacks $3-8; ⏰11am-9:30pm Sun-Thu, to 10:30pm Fri & Sat; 🖤) In neighboring Arroyo Grande, Doc's scoops up fantastical flavors such as Merlot raspberry truffle and the 'Elvis Special' (peanut butter with banana swirls). Live ice-cream lab shows start at 7pm sharp on Wednesday. From Hwy 101 southbound, exit at Grand Ave.

Old West Cinnamon Rolls
BAKERY $

(www.oldwestcinnamon.com; 861 Dolliver St; snacks $2-5; ⏰6:30am-5:30pm) The name says it all at this gobsmacking bakery by the beach.

Bunn Thai Bistro
THAI $$

(☎805-473-2824; www.bunnthaibistro.com; 968 W Grand Ave, Grover Beach; mains $10-18; ⏰11am-3pm & 4-9pm Thu-Tue; 🖤) In the next-door town of Grover Beach, this nouveau Thai restaurant is splashed into tropical colors. Making side trips into Asian fusion, it caters to omnivores, vegans, vegetarians and gluten-free folks. Lunch specials are a steal. Follow Hwy 1 south from Pismo Beach, turning left onto Grand Ave.

Frutiland La Casa Del Sabor
MEXICAN $$

(803 E Grand Ave, Arroyo Grande; mains $7-13; ⏰9:30am-7pm Mon & Wed, to 3:30pm Thu, to 8pm Fri & Sat, 10am-6pm Sun; 🖤) Oversized, overstuffed Mexican *tortas* (sandwiches) will feed two, and there are two dozen varieties to choose from. Or order a platter of blue-corn-tortilla fish tacos with a mango or papaya *agua fresca* (fruit drink). To find this taco shack in Arroyo Grande, exit Hwy 101 southbound at Halcyon Rd.

★ Ember
CALIFORNIAN $$$

(☎805-474-7700; 1200 E Grand Ave, Arroyo Grande; shared dishes $8-20, mains $16-30; ⏰4-9pm Wed-Thu & Sun, to 10pm Fri & Sat; 🖤) 🍷 Chef Brian Collins, who once cooked at Alice Waters' revered Chez Panisse, has returned to his roots in SLO County. Out of this heart-warming restaurant's wood-burning oven come sa-vory flatbreads, artfully charred squid and hearty red-wine-smoked short ribs. No reservations, so show up at 4pm or after 7:30pm, or be prepared for a very long wait for a table.

Sociable seating in the bar, where you can order off the full menu, is first-come, first-served. The restaurant is west of Hwy 101 (southbound exit Halcyon Rd) in Arroyo Grande.

★ Cracked Crab
SEAFOOD $$$

(☎805-773-2722; www.crackedcrab.com; 751 Price St; mains $12-45; ⏰11am-9pm Sun-Thu, to 10pm Fri & Sat; 🖤) Fresh seafood and regional wines are the staples at this super-casual, family-owned grill. When the famous bucket o'seafood, full of flying bits of fish, Cajun sausage, red potatoes and cob corn, gets dumped on your butcher-paper-covered table, make sure you're wearing one of those silly-looking plastic bibs. No reservations, but the wait is worth it.

🍷 Drinking & Entertainment

Taste of the Valleys
WINE BAR

(www.pismowineshop.com; 911 Price St; ⏰noon-9pm Mon-Thu, to 10pm Fri & Sat, to 8pm Sun) Inside a wine shop stacked floor to ceiling with hand-picked vintages from around California and beyond, ask for a taste of anything they've got open, or sample from an astounding list of 500 wines poured by the glass.

Pismo Bowl
BOWLING ALLEY

(www.pismobeachbowl.com; 277 Pomeroy Ave; game per person $4, shoe rental $3; ⏰noon-10pm Sun-Thu, to midnight Fri & Sat; 🖤) Epitomizing Pismo Beach's retro vibe, this old-fashioned bowling alley is just a short walk uphill from the pier. Blacklight 'cosmic' and karaoke bowling rule Friday and Saturday nights.

ℹ Information

Pismo Beach Visitors Information Center (☎800-443-7778, 805-773-4382; www.classiccalifornia.com; 581 Dolliver St; ⏰9am-5pm Mon-Fri, 11am-4pm Sat) Free maps and brochures. Smaller kiosk on the pier is open from 11am to 4pm on Sunday.

ℹ Getting There & Around

Hourly from Monday to Friday, and a few times daily on weekends, **RTA** (☎805-541-2228; www.slorta.org) bus 10 links San Luis Obispo with Pismo's Premium Outlets mall ($2, 30 minutes), a mile from the beach, before continuing to downtown Arroyo Grande ($1.50, 15 minutes).

Santa Barbara County

Best Places to Eat

➡ Lark (p322)

➡ Lure Fish House (p342)

➡ Santa Barbara Shellfish Company (p321)

➡ Succulent Café (p335)

➡ Lucky Penny (p320)

Best Places to Stay

➡ El Encanto (p319)

➡ Inn of the Spanish Garden (p319)

➡ Santa Barbara Auto Camp (p318)

➡ Blue Iguana Inn (p340)

➡ Hamlet Inn (p335)

Why Go?

Frankly put, this area is damn pleasant to putter around. Low-slung between lofty mountains and the shimmering Pacific, chic Santa Barbara's red-tiled roofs, white stucco buildings and Mediterranean vibe give credence to its claim of being the 'American Riviera.' It's a surprisingly bewitching place to loll on the beach, eat and drink extraordinarily well, shop a bit and push all your cares off to another day. The city's car-free campaign has brought electric shuttle buses, urban bike trails and earth-friendly wine tours. Mother Nature returns the love with hiking, biking, surfing, kayaking, scuba diving and camping opportunities galore, from offshore Channel Islands National Park to arty Ojai, surrounded by hot springs. Meanwhile, winemaking is booming in the bucolic Santa Ynez Mountains, where over a hundred wineries vie for your attention. But if all you want to do is relax, no worries – plenty of sunny beaches await.

When to Go
Santa Barbara

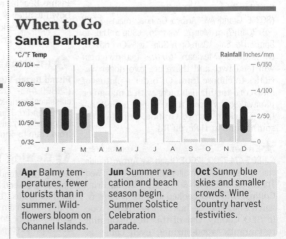

Apr Balmy temperatures, fewer tourists than in summer. Wildflowers bloom on Channel Islands.

Jun Summer vacation and beach season begin. Summer Solstice Celebration parade.

Oct Sunny blue skies and smaller crowds. Wine Country harvest festivities.

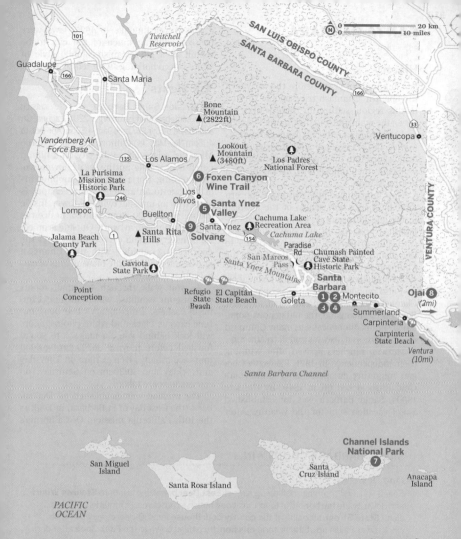

Santa Barbara County Highlights

① Strolling **Stearns Wharf** (p311), then lazing on Santa Barbara's cinematic **beaches**.

② Ambling between wine-tasting rooms, hip bars, art galleries and shops in Santa Barbara's **Funk Zone** (p322).

③ Exploring Spanish-colonial historic sites, such as **Mission Santa Barbara** (p310).

④ Eyeing panoramic views atop the *Vertigo*-esque clock tower of the **Santa Barbara County Courthouse** (p311).

⑤ Pedaling past vineyards and organic farms through the **Santa Ynez Valley** (p331).

⑥ Following the **Foxen Canyon Wine Trail** (p329) to taste top-rated pinot noir.

⑦ Kayaking sea caves and watching whales in **Channel Islands National Park** (p343).

⑧ Rejuvenating your body and soul in new-agey **Ojai** (p339).

⑨ Eating *ableskivers* (panacke popovers) by a kitschy windmill in the Danish village of **Solvang** (p333).

SANTA BARBARA

POP 89,640

History

For hundreds of years before the arrival of the Spanish, Chumash tribespeople thrived in this region, setting up trade routes between the mainland and the Channel Islands and constructing redwood canoes known as *tomol*s. In 1542 explorer Juan Rodríguez Cabrillo sailed into the channel and claimed it for Spain, then quickly met his doom on a nearby island.

The Chumash had little reason for concern until the permanent return of the Spanish in the late 18th century. Catholic priests established missions up and down the coast, ostensibly to convert Native Americans to Christianity. Spanish soldiers often forced the Chumash to construct the missions and presidios (military forts) and provide farm labor; they also rounded up the tribespeople on the Channel Islands and forced them to leave. Back on the mainland, the indigenous population shrank dramatically, as many Chumash died of European diseases and ill treatment.

Mexican ranchers arrived after winning their independence in 1821. Easterners began migrating en masse after California's Gold Rush kicked off in 1849. By the late 1890s, Santa Barbara was an established SoCal vacation spot for the wealthy. After a massive earthquake in 1925, laws were passed requiring much of the city to be rebuilt in a faux-Spanish-colonial style of white-stucco buildings with red-tiled roofs.

◉ Sights

★ **Mission Santa Barbara** CHURCH
(www.santabarbaramission.org; 2201 Laguna St; adult/child 5-15yr $6/1; ⊙9am-4:30pm Apr-Oct, to 4:15pm Nov-Mar; P) California's 'Queen of the Missions' reigns above the city on a hilltop perch over a mile northwest of downtown. Its imposing Doric facade, an architectural homage to an ancient Roman chapel, is topped by an unusual twin bell tower. Inside the mission's 1820 stone church, notice the striking Chumash artwork. Outside is an eerie cemetery – skull carvings hang over the door leading outside – with 4000 Chumash graves and the elaborate mausoleums of early California settlers.

As you walk through 10 small rooms of museum exhibits, which include Chumash baskets, a missionary's bedroom and time-capsule black-and-white photos, doors will lock behind you, so make sure you're finished before moving on. Docent-guided tours are usually given at 11am on Thursday and Friday and 10:30am on Saturday; no reservations are taken.

The mission was established on December 4 (the feast day of St Barbara) in 1786, as the 10th California mission. Of California's

---

SANTA BARBARA COUNTY IN...

One Day

Spend your first morning soaking up rays at **East Beach**, walking out onto **Stearns Wharf** and down by the **harbor**. After lunch, visit downtown's museums, landmarks and shops along **State Street**, stopping at the **county courthouse** for 360-degree views from its clock tower. Finish up at the historic **mission**, then head down to the **Funk Zone** after dark.

Two Days

Cycle along the coast, go surfing or sea kayaking, or hike in the Santa Ynez foothills. In the afternoon, detour east to posh **Montecito** for shopping and people-watching or hang loose in **Carpinteria**, a retro beach town.

Three Days

Head up to Santa Barbara's Wine Country. Enjoy a do-it-yourself vineyards tour via car, motorcycle or bicycle along a scenic wine trail – **Foxen Canyon** and the **Santa Rita Hills** are exceptionally beautiful. Pack a picnic lunch or grab a bite in charming **Los Olivos** or Danish-esque **Solvang**.

Four Days

On your way back to LA, make time for a detour to arty **Ojai** up in the mountains for its hot springs and spas or book a day trip from **Ventura** by boat to **Anacapa Island** in rugged **Channel Islands National Park**.

original 21 Spanish-colonial missions, it's the only one that escaped secularization under Mexican rule. Continuously occupied by Catholic priests since its founding, the mission is still an active parish church.

From downtown, take MTD bus 22.

Santa Barbara County Courthouse
HISTORIC SITE

(☑ 805-962-6464; www.courthouselegacyfoundation.org; 1100 Anacapa St; ⊙ 8:30am-4:45pm Mon-Fri, 10am-4:15pm Sat & Sun) **FREE** Built in Spanish-Moorish Revival style in 1929, the courthouse features hand-painted ceilings, wrought-iron chandeliers, and tiles from Tunisia and Spain. Step inside the hushed mural room depicting Spanish-colonial history on the 2nd floor, then climb El Mirador, the 85ft clock tower, for arch-framed panoramas of the city, ocean and mountains. You're free to explore on your own, but you'll get a lot more out of a free docent-guided tour, usually at 2pm daily and 10:30am on weekdays (except Thursday).

Stearns Wharf
HISTORIC SITE

(www.stearnswharf.org; **P**) **FREE** The southern end of State St gives way onto Stearns Wharf, a rough wooden pier lined with souvenir shops, snack stands and seafood shacks. Built in 1872, it's the oldest continuously operating wharf on the West Coast, although the actual structure has been rebuilt more than once. During the 1940s it was co-owned by tough-guy actor Jimmy Cagney and his brothers. If you've got kids, tow them inside the Ty Warner Sea Center (p314).

Parking on the wharf costs $2.50 per hour; the first 90 minutes are free with merchant validation. But trust us, you'd rather walk than drive over the wharf's bumpy wooden slats. The wharf entrance is a stop on MTD's downtown and waterfront shuttles.

Santa Barbara Museum of Art
MUSEUM

(☑ 805-963-4364; www.sbma.net; 1130 State St; adult/child 6-17yr $10/6, all free 5-8pm Thu; ⊙ 11am-5pm Tue-Wed & Fri-Sun, to 8pm Thu) This thoughtfully curated, bite-sized art museum displays European and American masters – think Matisse and Diego Rivera – along with contemporary photography, classical antiquities and though-provoking temporary exhibits. Traipse up to the 2nd floor, where impressive Asian art collections include an intricate, colorful Tibetan sand mandala and the iron-and-leather armor of a Japanese warrior. Guided tours usually

MEETING MONARCHS

If you're here in late fall or winter, ask at the Outdoors Santa Barbara Visitors Center (p324) about the best places to see migratory monarch butterflies roosting in the trees – an extraordinary sight. See p467 for more information on roosting.

start at 1pm daily. There's also an interactive children's space, a museum shop and a cafe.

Santa Barbara Maritime Museum
MUSEUM

(☑ 805-962-8404; www.sbmm.org; 113 Harbor Way; adult/child 6-17yr $7/4, all free 3rd Thu of each month; ⊙ 10am-5pm, to 6pm late May–early Sep; **P** **♿**) On the harborfront, this jam-packed, two-story exhibition hall celebrates the town's briny history with nautical artifacts, memorabilia and hands-on exhibits, including a big-game fishing chair from which you can 'reel in' a trophy marlin. Take a virtual trip through the Santa Barbara Channel, stand on a surfboard or watch deep-sea diving documentaries in the theater. There's 90 minutes of free parking in the public lot or take the Lil' Toot water taxi from Stearns Wharf.

Santa Barbara Historical Museum
MUSEUM

(☑ 805-966-1601; www.santabarbaramuseum.com; 136 E De La Guerra St; ⊙ 10am-5pm Tue-Sat, from noon Sun) **FREE** Embracing a romantic cloistered adobe courtyard, this peaceful little museum has an endlessly fascinating collection of local memorabilia, ranging from the simply beautiful, such as Chumash woven baskets and Spanish-colonial-era textiles, to the intriguing, such as an intricately carved coffer that once belonged to Junípero Serra. Learn about the city's involvement in toppling the last Chinese monarchy, among other interesting footnotes in local history. Guided tours are usually offered at 2pm on Saturday and Sunday.

Santa Barbara Botanic Garden
GARDEN

(☑ 805-682-4726; www.sbbg.org; 1212 Mission Canyon Rd; adult/child 2-12yr/youth 13-17yr $10/6/8; ⊙ 9am-6pm Mar-Oct, to 5pm Nov-Feb; **P** **♿**) Take a soul-satisfying jaunt around this 40-acre botanic garden, devoted to California's native flora. More than 5 miles of partly wheelchair-accessible trails meander past cacti, redwoods and wildflowers and by the old mission dam, originally built by Chumash tribespeople to irrigate the

Downtown Santa Barbara

0   480 m
0   0.25 miles

Santa Barbara Auto Camp (0.8mi);
Agave Inn (1.4mi)

Mission St

Mission Santa Barbara (0.25mi);
Santa Barbara Museum of
Natural History (0.5mi);
Santa Barbara Botanic
Garden (1.8mi)

El Encanto
(0.12mi)

Alameda Padre Serra

W Pedregosa St

W Islay St

W Valerio St

29

W Arrellaga St   E Arrellaga St

Laguna St

W Michelforena St

Alameda
Park

De La Vina St

State St

Anacapa St

W Sola St   57

30   41   50

E Victoria St

Santa Barbara
Bowl (0.12mi)

53   32   51

W Anapamu St   4   8   E Anapamu St

59   5

MTD Transit
Center

W Figueroa St

El Buen
Gusto (0.1mi)

W Carrillo St   22   Greyhound

52   3   27

W Cañon Perdido St

Paseo
Nuevo

58   44

Garden St

Laguna St

Olive St

Salsipuedes St

Castillo St

Chapala St

W De La Guerra St   43   60   37   6   E De La Guerra St

W Ortega St   49   E Ortega St

Ortega
Park

Quarantina St

56

San Pascual St

W Cota St   E Cota St

39   40

62

101   W Haley St   E Haley St

25   15
54

31   61   E Gutierrez St   47   16

35

Montecito St

Cliff Dr   21   46

Helena Ave

Gray Ave

34   45   38

FUNK
ZONE

Garden St

E Yanonali St

Rancheria St

Castillo St

Lazy Acres (1.6mi);
Arroyo Burro Beach
County Park (2.5mi)

23
24

Natoma Ave

26   36   55

28   W Mason St

Pershing
Park

20
19   48

63

14   W Cabrillo Blvd   18

Anacapa St

Leadbetter Beach (0.3mi);
One Thousands Steps
Beach (1.35mi)

11

12

West
Beach

East
Beach

2   1

E Cabrillo Blvd

Four Seasons
Biltmore (3mi)

Lil' Toot
Water Taxi   7   17

33

Santa
Barbara Harbor

Sand
Bar

Stearns
Wharf   42

13   10

9

Chase Palm
Park

Blue Sands Motel (0.3mi);
Motel 6 Santa
Barbara–Beach (1.35mi)

Downtown Santa Barbara

mission's fields. Leashed, well-behaved dogs are welcome. Guided tours typically depart at 11am and 2pm on Saturday and Sunday, and 2pm on Monday. On weekends, MTD bus 22 from the mission stops at the gardens upon request. If you're driving, head north from the mission to Foothill Blvd (Hwy 192), turn right and then left to continue on Mission Canyon Rd.

El Presidio de Santa Barbara State Historic Park HISTORIC SITE
(☏805-965-0093; www.sbthp.org; 123 E Cañon Perdido St; adult/child under 17yr $5/free; ◎10:30am-4:30pm) Founded in 1782 to defend the mission, this adobe-walled fort built by Chumash laborers was Spain's last military stronghold in Alta California. But its purpose wasn't solely to protect – the

presidio also served as a social and political hub, and as a stopping point for traveling Spanish military. Today this small urban park harbors some of the city's oldest structures. On a self-guided walking tour, be sure to stop at the chapel, its interior radiant with rich hues.

Admission also includes entry to nearby **Casa de La Guerra**, a 19th-century colonial adobe home displaying Spanish, Mexican and California heritage exhibits.

Karpeles Manuscript Library Museum

MUSEUM

(☑805-962-5322; www.rain.org/~karpeles; 21 W Anapamu St; ☺noon-4pm Wed-Sun) FREE Stuffed with a hodgepodge of historical written artifacts, this detour is for history nerds and book and music lovers. One of a dozen Karpeles manuscript museums nationwide, the rotating exhibits at this museum often spotlight literary masterworks, from Shakespeare to Sherlock Holmes.

🏃 Activities

Cycling

A paved **recreational path** stretches 3 miles along the waterfront in both directions from Stearns Wharf, west to Leadbetter Beach beyond the harbor and east just past East Beach. For more pedaling routes, **Bike Santa Barbara County** (www.bike-santabarbara.

org) offers free downloadable DIY cycling tours of the city, mountains and Wine Country, along with links to bicycle rentals and specialty shops.

Wheel Fun Rentals CYCLING (☑805-966-2282; www.wheelfunrentals.com) **Cabrillo Blvd** (www.wheelfunrentals.com; 23 E Cabrillo Blvd; ☺8am-8pm Mar-Oct, to 6pm Nov-Feb; 🚻); **State St** (www.wheelfunrentals.com; 22 State St; ☺8am-8pm Mar-Oct, to 6pm Nov-Feb; 🚻) Hourly rentals of beach cruisers ($10), mountain bikes ($11) and two-/four-person surreys ($29/39), with discounted half-day and full-day rates.

Santa Barbara Bikes To-Go CYCLING (☑805-628-2444; www.sbbikestogo.com; 812 E Gutierrez St) Delivers top-quality road and hybrid mountain bikes to your hotel. Rentals (per day $45 to $105) include helmets and emergency-kit saddle bags. Discounts for multiday, weekly and monthly rentals; reservations essential. Over-18s only.

Kayaking

Paddle the calm waters of Santa Barbara's harbor or the coves of the Gaviota coast, or hitch a ride to the Channel Islands for awesome sea caves.

Paddle Sports Center KAYAKING (☑805-617-3425; www.channelislandso.com; 117b Harbor Way; single/double kayak rental per

---

SANTA BARBARA FOR CHILDREN

Santa Barbara abounds with family-friendly fun for kids of all ages, from tots to tweens.

Ty Warner Sea Center (☑805-962-2526; www.sbnature.org; 211 Stearns Wharf; adult/child 2-12yr/youth 13-17yr $10/7/8; ☺10am-5pm; 🅿🚻) From touch tanks full of tide-pool critters and crawl-through aquariums to whale sing-alongs, it's interactive and educational. Hourly parking on the wharf costs $2.50.

Santa Barbara Museum of Natural History (☑805-682-4711; www.sbnature.org; 2559 Puesta del Sol; adult/child 2-12yr/youth 13-17yr $11/7/8, incl planetarium show $15/11/12; ☺10am-5pm; 🅿🚻) Giant skeletons, an insect wall and a pitch-dark planetarium captivate kids' imaginations. It's a half-mile drive uphill from the mission.

Santa Barbara Maritime Museum (p311) Peer through a periscope, reel in a virtual fish, watch underwater films or check out the model ships.

Santa Barbara Sailing Center Short, one-hour sails around the harbor ($15) let young 'uns spot sea lions up close.

Lil' Toot water taxi (p326) Take a joyride along the waterfront on this tiny yellow boat.

Chase Palm Park (323 E Cabrillo Blvd; 🚻) Antique carousel rides ($2, cash only) plus a shipwreck-themed playground decked out with seashells and a miniature lighthouse.

Arroyo Burro Beach County Park (Hendry's; www.countyofsb.org/parks/; Cliff Dr at Las Positas Rd; ☺8am-sunset; 🅿🚻) A wide, sandy beach, away from the tourists but not too far from downtown.

hr $25/40, per day $50/65; ⊙usually 8am-6pm) Long-established Channel Islands outfitter also guides harbor and coastal kayaking tours ($75 to $95) for beginner to advanced paddlers. Kayak rentals are available year-round at the harbor and Goleta Beach, and from late May through early September on West Beach. Book ahead online or by phone.

Santa Barbara Adventure Company
KAYAKING
(☎877-885-9283, 805-884-9283; www.sbadventureco.com; 32 E Haley St; kayak tours $49-209; ⊕) Leads all kinds of guided kayaking trips, from family-friendly harbor excursions and sunset floats to Gaviota coastal paddles and day and overnight trips to the Channel Islands. Some trips require a two- or four-person minimum.

Santa Barbara Sailing Center
KAYAKING
(☎805-962-2826; www.sbsail.com; off Harbor Way; single/double kayak rental per hr $10/15, 2hr kayak tour $50; ⊕) Just about the cheapest kayak rental and guided tours around, with paddling instruction available by prior arrangement. Call for seasonal hours.

Boating & Whale-Watching
Some tour companies offer year-round whale-watching boat trips, mostly to see grays in winter and spring, and humpbacks and blues in summer.

Condor Express
CRUISE
(☎888-779-4253, 805-882-0088; www.condorcruises.com; 301 W Cabrillo Blvd; adult/child 5-12yr 2½hr cruise $50/30, 4½hr cruise from $89/50; ⊕) Take a whale-watching excursion aboard the high-speed catamaran *Condor Express*. Whale sightings are guaranteed, so if you miss out the first time, you'll get a free voucher for another cruise.

Santa Barbara Sailing Center
CRUISE, SAILING
(☎805-962-2826; www.sbsail.com; off Harbor Way; cruises $15-65, sailing courses from $615; ⊕) Climb aboard the *Double Dolphin,* a 50ft sailing catamaran, for a two-hour coastal or sunset cruise. Seasonal whale-watching trips and quick one-hour spins around the harbor to view sea lions are also kid-friendly. If you want to learn to pilot your own sailboat, sign up for a 20-hour instructional course.

Sunset Kidd's Sailing Cruises
CRUISE
(☎805-962-8222; www.sunsetkidd.com; 125 Harbor Way; 2hr cruise $40-50) Float in an 18-passenger sailboat on a two-hour

whale-watching trip or a morning, afternoon, sunset cocktail or full-moon cruise. Reservations recommended.

Swimming
Los Baños del Mar
SWIMMING
(☎805-966-6110; www.friendsoflosbanos.org; 401 Shoreline Dr; admission $6; ⊕call for public swim schedules; ⊕) Beyond the beaches in and around Santa Barbara, you can also swim at this municipal outdoor pool near West Beach that's good for recreational and lap swimming. For kids under eight years old, there's a wading pool with a lifeguard that's open daily in summer, weather permitting.

Surfing
Unless you're a novice, conditions are too mellow in summer – come back in winter when ocean swells kick back up. Santa Barbara's **Leadbetter Point** is best for beginners. Experts-only **Rincon Point** awaits just outside Carpinteria.

Paddle Sports Center
SURFING
(☎805-617-3425; www.channelislandso.com; off Harbor Way; rental per 2hr/day wetsuit $5/15, boogie board or surfboard $10/30, SUP set $40/100; ⊕usually 8am-6pm) Rent a boogie board, surfboard or stand-up paddleboarding (SUP) set, along with a wetsuit, conveniently right at the harbor.

Santa Barbara Adventure Company
SURFING
(☎877-885-9283, 805-884-9283; www.sbadventureco.com; 32 E Haley St; 2hr surfing or SUP lesson $89, half-/two-day surfing lessons $109/199; ⊕) Learn the art of surfing or stand-up paddleboarding (SUP) from this family-friendly outfitter. Two-person minimum; children must be at least 7 years old.

TOP 10 BEACHES AROUND SANTA BARBARA

Although Santa Barbara's beaches are beauty-pageant prize winners, don't expect sunsets over the ocean because most of this coast faces south.

East Beach (E Cabrillo Blvd) Santa Barbara's largest and most popular beach is a long, sandy stretch sprawling east of Stearns Wharf, with volleyball nets for pick-up games, a children's play area and a snack bar. On Sunday afternoons, artists set up booths along the sidewalk, near the bike path.

Butterfly Beach (Channel Dr east of Butterfly Ln) Armani swimsuits and Gucci sunglasses abound at this narrow but chic swimming beach in front of the historic Biltmore hotel. Don't be surprised if you spot a celeb. The beach faces west, so you can catch a sunset here.

West Beach (W Cabrillo Blvd) Between Stearns Wharf and the harbor you'll find calm waters for kayaking, sailing and stand-up paddleboarding (SUP). It's most popular for sunbathing with tourists staying nearby. For lap swimming, head indoors to Los Baños del Mar (p315).

Leadbetter Beach (Shoreline Dr at Loma Alta Dr) Further west of the harbor, this is a fantastic spot for swimming or learning to surf or windsurf. A grassy picnic area atop the cliffs makes it just that much more family friendly.

One Thousand Steps Beach (foot of Santa Cruz Blvd at Shoreline Dr; ⏱ sunrise-10pm) Descend the cliffs on a historic staircase (don't worry, there aren't actually 1000 steps) for some windy beachcombing and tide-pooling (best at low tide), but no swimming. Neighboring **Shoreline Park** has a grassy area with picnic tables and a children's playground.

Arroyo Burro Beach County Park (p314) Near the junction of Cliff Dr and Las Positas Rd, this gem has a picnic area and the family-style Boathouse restaurant. The beach is flat, wide, away from tourists and great for kids, who can go tide-pooling. It's also a popular local surf spot. Look for an off-leash dog area at Douglas Family Preserve, on the cliffs above the beach.

Goleta Beach County Park (www.countyofsb.org/parks; Sandspit Rd, Goleta; ⏱ 8am-sunset) In the western suburbs near the University of California Santa Barbara (UCSB) campus, this beach is a locals' scene. There's a 1500ft-long fishing pier, a bike path and wide, sandy stretches for sunbathing after taking a dip or surfing easy waves. From Hwy 101, take Hwy 217 westbound.

Carpinteria State Beach (p338) About 12 miles east of Santa Barbara off Hwy 101, this mile-long beach has beautifully calm waters that are great for swimming, wading and tide-pooling, especially for younger kids.

El Capitán State Beach (www.parks.ca.gov; El Capitan State Beach Rd, Goleta; per car $10; ⏱ 8am-sunset; P ⏱) & **Refugio State Beach** (www.parks.ca.gov; 10 Refugio Beach Rd, Goleta; per car $10; ⏱) These twin beauties are worth the trip over 20 miles west of Santa Barbara via Hwy 101. Popular swimming and camping spots, they're connected by a bike path.

Surf-n-Wear's Beach House　　SURFING
(✆ 805-963-1281; www.surfnwear.com; 10 State St; rental per hr/day wetsuit from $8/12, boogie board $10/16, surfboard $10/35, SUP set per day $50; ⏱ 9am-6pm Sun-Thu, to 7pm Fri & Sat) Not far from Stearns Wharf, rent soft (foam) boards, boogie boards, wetsuits and SUP sets from this 1960s surf shop that also sells collectible vintage boards.

Hiking

Gorgeous day hikes await in the foothills of the Santa Ynez Mountains and elsewhere in the Los Padres National Forest. Most trails cut through rugged chaparral and steep canyons – sweat it out and savor jaw-dropping coastal views. Spring and fall are the best seasons for hiking, when temperatures are moderate. Always carry plenty of extra water and watch out for poison oak.

To find even more local trails to explore, browse **Santa Barbara Hikes** (www.santabarbarahikes.com) online or visit the **Los Padres National Forest Headquarters** (☑805-968-6640; www.fs.usda.gov/lpnf; 6755 Hollister Ave, Goleta; ⊙8:30am-noon & 1-4:30pm Mon-Fri), west of the airport (from Hwy 101, exit Glen Annie Rd southbound onto Storke Rd).

Gliding

For condor's-eye ocean views, **Eagle Paragliding** (☑805-968-0980; www.eagleparagliding.com) and **Fly Above All** (☑805-965-3733; www.flyaboveall.com) offer paragliding lessons (from $200) and tandem flights ($100 to $200). For hang-gliding lessons and tandem flights, talk to Eagle Paragliding or **Fly Away** (☑805-403-8487; www.flyawayhanggliding.com).

👉 Tours

⭐Architectural Foundation of Santa Barbara   WALKING TOUR

(☑805-965-6307; www.afcb.org; adult/child under 12yr $10/free; ⊙usually 10am Sat & Sun) 🐾 Take time out of your weekend morning for a fascinating 90-minute guided walking tour of downtown's art, history and architecture. No reservations required; call or check the website for meet-up times and places.

Land & Sea Tours   GUIDED TOUR

(☑805-683-7600; www.out2seesb.com; adult/child 2-9yr $25/10; ⊙usually noon & 2pm daily year-round, also 4pm daily May-Oct; 👶) If you dig James Bond-style vehicles, take a narrated tour of the city on the *Land Shark,* an amphibious vehicle that drives right into the water. Trips depart from Stearns Wharf; buy tickets before boarding (no reservations).

Santa Barbara Trolley   BUS TOUR

(☑805-965-0353; www.sbtrolley.com; adult/child 3-12yr $18/9; 👶) 🐾 Biodiesel-fueled trolleys make a narrated 90-minute one-way loop around major tourist attractions, starting from Stearns Wharf (hourly departures 10am to 4pm). Hop-on, hop-off tickets are valid all day; pay the driver directly, or buy discounted tickets online in advance. One child under age 12 rides free with each paid adult ticket.

Santa Barbara Adventure Company   GUIDED TOUR

(☑805-884-9283, 877-885-9283; www.sbadventureco.com; 32 E Haley St) Maximize your outdoors time with a horseback ride on the beach or a Wine Country cycling tour, either costing around $150 per person (two person minimum).

🎉 Festivals & Events

To find out what's happening now, check the events calendars at www.santabarbaraca.com and www.independent.com online.

Santa Barbara International Film Festival   FILM

(http://sbiff.org) Film buffs and Hollywood A-list stars show up for screenings of more than 200 independent US and foreign films in late January and early February.

TOP DAY HIKES AROUND SANTA BARBARA

TRAIL NAME	ROUND-TRIP DISTANCE (MI)	DESCRIPTION	TRAILHEAD	DIRECTIONS
Inspiration Point	3.5	Popular with locals walking their dogs and for daily workouts	Tunnel Rd	Turn left off Mission Canyon Dr before reaching the Santa Barbara Botanic Garden
Rattlesnake Canyon	3.5	Offering shade and waterfalls as you ascend into the canyon; leashed dogs OK	Las Canoas Rd	Turn right off Mission Canyon Dr before reaching the Santa Barbara Botanic Garden
Cold Spring & Montecito Park	up to 9	Steady uphill hike past small cascades with a spur trail to a summit	Mountain Dr	From Montecito, follow Olive Mill Rd north of Hwy 101, continuing past Hwy 192 on Hot Springs Rd, then turn left

ⓘ SANTA BARBARA ART WALKS

Prime time for downtown gallery hopping is **First Thursday** (www.santabarbaradowntown.com), from 5pm to 8pm on the first Thursday of every month, when art galleries on and off State St throw open their doors for new exhibitions, artists' receptions, wine tastings and live music, all free. Closer to the beach, the **Funk Zone Art Walk** (http://funkzone.net) happens from 1pm to 5pm on the second Saturday of each month, featuring free events and entertainment at offbeat art galleries, bars and restaurants.

I Madonnari Italian Street Painting Festival

ART, FOOD

(www.imadonnarifestival.com; ⊕) Colorful chalk drawings adorn Mission Santa Barbara's sidewalks over Memorial Day weekend, with Italian food vendors and arts-and-crafts booths too.

★ Summer Solstice Celebration

FESTIVAL

(www.solsticeparade.com) Kicking off summer in late June, this wildly popular and wacky float parade down State St feels like something out of Burning Man. Live music, kids' activities, food stands, a wine-and-beer garden and an arts-and-craft show happen all weekend long.

French Festival

CULTURE, ART

(www.frenchfestival.com) In mid-July, California's biggest Francophile celebration has lots of food and wine, world music and dancing, a mock Eiffel Tower and Moulin Rouge, and even a poodle parade.

Santa Barbara County Fair

FAIR

(www.santamariafairpark.com; ⊕) In mid-July, this old-fashioned county fair combines agriculture exhibits, carnival rides, and lots of food and wine. The fairgrounds are in Santa Maria, over an hour's drive northwest of Santa Barbara via Hwy 101.

★ Old Spanish Days Fiesta

CULTURE, ART

(www.oldspanishdays-fiesta.org) The entire city fills up during late July and early August for this long-running – if slightly overblown – festival celebrating Santa Barbara's Spanish and Mexican colonial heritage. Festivities include outdoor bazaars and food markets, live music, flamenco dancing, horseback and rodeo events, and a big ol' parade.

🛏 Sleeping

Prepare for sticker shock: basic motel rooms by the beach command over $200 in summer. Don't show up at the last minute without reservations and expect to find any reasonably priced rooms, especially not on weekends. Cheaper motels cluster along upper State St and Hwy 101 northbound to Goleta and southbound to Carpinteria, Ventura and Camarillo.

★ Santa Barbara Auto Camp

CAMPGROUND $$

(☎888-405-7553; http://autocamp.com/sb; 2717 De La Vina St; d $175-215; P❄🐾🛜🐕) 🐾 Bed down with vintage style in one of five shiny metal Airstream trailers parked near upper State St, north of downtown. All five architect-designed trailers have unique perks, such as a clawfoot tub or extra twin-size beds for kiddos, as well as a full kitchen and complimentary cruiser bikes to borrow. Book ahead; two-night minimum may apply. Pet fee $25.

Hotel Indigo

BOUTIQUE HOTEL $$

(☎805-966-6586, 877-270-1392; www.indigo-santabarbara.com; 121 State St; r from $170; P❄@🛜🐕) 🐾 Poised between downtown and the beach, this petite Euro-chic boutique hotel has all the right touches: curated contemporary-art displays, rooftop patios and ecofriendly green-design elements like a living-plant wall. Peruse local-interest and art history books in the library nook, or retreat to your room and wrap yourself up in a plush bathrobe. Parking $14.

Agave Inn

MOTEL $$

(☎805-687-6009; http://agaveinnsb.com; 3222 State St; r incl breakfast from $119; P❄🛜) While it's still just a motel at heart, this boutique-on-a-budget property's 'Mexican pop meets modern' motif livens things up with a color palette from a Frieda Kahlo painting. Flat-screen TVs, microwaves, minifridges and air-con make it a standout option. Family-sized rooms have kitchenettes and pull-out sofa beds. Continental breakfast included.

Harbor House Inn

MOTEL $$

(☎888-474-6789, 805-962-9745; www.harborhouseinn.com; 104 Bath St; r from $180; P🛜🐕)

Down by the harbor, this converted motel offers brightly lit studios with hardwood floors and a beachy design scheme. A few have full kitchens and fireplaces, but there's no air-con. Rates include a welcome basket of breakfast goodies (with a two-night minimum stay) and beach towels, chairs and umbrellas and three-speed bicycles to borrow. Pet fee $20.

Marina Beach Motel   MOTEL $$
(☑805-963-9311, 877-627-4621; www.marinabeachmotel.com; 21 Bath St; r incl breakfast from $155; P✳☎☜⛟) Family-owned since 1942, this flower-festooned, one-story motor lodge that wraps around a grassy courtyard is worth a stay just for the location. Right by the beach, tidy remodeled rooms are comfy enough, and some have kitchenettes. Complimentary continental breakfast and beach-cruiser bikes to borrow. Small pets OK (fee $15).

Blue Sands Motel   MOTEL $$
(☑805-965-1624; www.thebluesands.com; 421 S Milpas St, r from $120; P☎☜⛟) With affable owners, this tiny two-story motel may be a bit kitschy, but who cares when you're just steps from East Beach? Book a remodeled room, or for a bigger splurge, one with a fireplace or a full kitchen and ocean views. No air-con. Two-night minimum stay on weekends. Pet fee $10.

Franciscan Inn   MOTEL $$
(☑805-963-8845; www.franciscaninn.com; 109 Bath St; r incl breakfast $155-215; P☎☜) Settle into the relaxing charms of this Spanish-colonial two-story motel just over a block from the beach. Rooms differ in shape and decor, but many have kitchenettes and all evince French-country charm. Embrace the friendly vibe, afternoon cookies and outdoor pool and hot tub. Free continental breakfast. No air-con.

Holiday Inn Express Santa Barbara   HOTEL $$
(☑877-834-3613, 805-963-9757; www.hotelvirginia.com; 17 W Haley St; r incl breakfast $185-250; P✳@☎) ⚐ Formerly the Hotel Virginia, this early-20th-century hotel has heaps of character, starting from the tile-filled lobby with a fountain. Upgraded rooms are serviceable, but its location just off downtown's State St merits a stay. Parking $12.

Motel 6 Santa Barbara–Beach   MOTEL $$
(☑805-564-1392, 800-466-8356; www.motel6.com; 443 Corona del Mar; r $100-210; P✳☎⛟) The very first Motel 6 to 'leave the light on for you' has been remodeled with IKEA-esque contemporary design, flat-screen TVs and multimedia stations. It fills nightly; book ahead. Wi-fi costs $3 extra every 24 hours. Pet fee $10.

★El Encanto   LUXURY HOTEL $$$
(☑805-845-5800, 800-393-5315; www.elencanto.com; 800 Alvarado Pl; d from $475; P☎@☜⛟) Triumphantly reborn, this 1920s icon of Santa Barbara style is a hilltop hideaway for travelers who demand the very best of everything. An infinity pool gazes out at the Pacific, while flower-filled gardens, fireplace lounges, a full-service spa and private bungalows with sun-drenched patios concoct the glamorous atmosphere perfectly fitted to SoCal socialites. Grab sunset drinks on the ocean-view terrace. Parking $35.

★Inn of the Spanish Garden   BOUTIQUE HOTEL $$$
(☑866-564-4700, 805-564-4700; www.spanishgardeninn.com; 915 Garden St; d incl breakfast from $309; P✳@☎☜) At this Spanish-colonial-style inn, casual elegance, top-notch service and an impossibly romantic central courtyard will have you lording about like the don of your own private villa. Beds have

---

CAMPING & CABINS AROUND SANTA BARBARA

You won't find a campground anywhere near downtown Santa Barbara, but less than a half-hour drive west via Hwy 101, right on the ocean, are **El Capitán & Refugio State Beaches** (☑reservations 800-444-7275; www.reserveamerica.com; off Hwy 101; tent & RV drive-up sites $35-55, hike-and-bike tent sites $10; P⛟). Amenities include flush toilets, hot showers, picnic tables and convenience stores; parking costs an additional $10. You'll find family-friendly campgrounds with varying amenities in the mountainous Los Padres National Forest (p327) and at **Cachuma Lake Recreation Area** (☑info 805-686-5054, reservations 805-686-5055; http://reservations.sbparks.org; 2225 Hwy 154; campsites $28-48, yurts $65-85, cabins $110-210; P⛟☜) off Hwy 154, closer to Santa Barbara's Wine Country.

luxurious linens, bathrooms have oversized bathtubs and concierge service is top-notch. Palms surround a small outdoor pool, or unwind with a massage in your room.

El Capitan Canyon
CABIN, CAMPGROUND $$$

(📞805-685-3887, 866-352-2729; www.elcapitancanyon.com; 11560 Calle Real; safari tent $155, yurt $205, cabins $225-795; 🅿🛜♨🐾) 🏄 Inland from El Capitán State Beach, this 'glamping' resort is for those who hate to wake up with dirt under their nails. No cars are allowed up-canyon during peak season, making this woodsy resort more peaceful. Safari tents are rustic and share bathrooms, while creekside cabins are more deluxe, some with kitchenettes; all have their own outdoor firepit.

Borrow a bicycle to head over to the beach, or schedule a massage. The property is about 20 miles west of Santa Barbara, off Hwy 101.

Simpson House Inn
B&B $$$

(📞805-963-7067, 800-676-1280; www.simpsonhouseinn.com; 121 E Arrellaga St; d incl breakfast $255-610; 🅿❄♨) Whether you book an elegant suite with a clawfoot bathtub or a sweet cottage with a wood-burning fireplace, you'll be pampered at this Victorian-era estate ensconced in English gardens. From gourmet vegetarian breakfasts through evening wine, hors d'oeuvres and sweets, you'll be well fed. In-room mod cons include streaming internet radio and movies. Complimentary bicycles and beach gear to borrow.

Four Seasons Biltmore
RESORT $$$

(📞info 805-969-2261, reservations 805-565-8299; www.fourseasons.com/santabarbara; 1260 Channel Dr; r from $425; 🅿❄@🛜♨🐾) Wear white linen and live like Jay Gatsby at the oh-so-cushy 1927 Biltmore hotel on Butterfly Beach. Every detail is perfect, from bathrooms with Spanish tiles, French-milled soaps, deep soaking tubs and waterfall showers to bedrooms decked out with ultra-high-thread-count sheets. Indulge yourself at the spa or any of the oceanfront bars and restaurants.

Canary Hotel
BOUTIQUE HOTEL $$$

(📞805-884-0300, 877-468-3515; www.canary-santabarbara.com; 31 W Carrillo St; r $325-575; 🅿❄@🛜♨) 🏄 On a busy block downtown, this haute multistory hotel has a rooftop pool and sunset-watching perch for cocktails. Stylish accommodations show off four-poster Spanish-framed beds and all mod cons. In-room spa services, yoga mats and bathroom goodies will soothe away stress, but ambient street noise may leave you sleepless. Complimentary fitness center access and cruiser bicycles. Parking $25.

Hungry? Taste local farm goodness at the hotel's downstairs restaurant, **Finch & Fork**.

White Jasmine Inn
B&B $$$

(📞805-966-0589; www.whitejasmineinnsantabarbara.com; 1327 Bath St; d $160-330; 🅿🛜) Tucked behind a rose-entwined wooden fence, this cheery inn stitches together a California bungalow and two quaint cottages. Sound-insulated rooms all have private bathrooms and fireplaces, and some are air-conditioned and come with Jacuzzi tubs. Full breakfast basket delivered daily to your door. No children under 12 years old allowed.

Brisas del Mar
HOTEL $$$

(📞800-468-1988, 805-966-2219; www.sbhotels.com; 223 Castillo St; r incl breakfast from $230; 🅿❄@🛜♨🐾) Kudos for all the freebies (DVDs, continental breakfast, afternoon wine and cheese, evening milk and cookies) and the newer Mediterranean-style front section, although some rooms are noisy. It's three blocks north of the beach. The hotel's sister properties, especially those further inland, may charge slightly less.

🍴 Eating

Restaurants abound along downtown's State St and by the waterfront, where you'll find a few gems among the touristy claptrap. More creative kitchens are found down in the Funk Zone. East of downtown, Milpas St is lined with Mexicali taco shops.

★ Lucky Penny
PIZZERIA $

(www.luckypennysb.com; 127 Anacapa St; mains $7-10, pizzas $10-15; ⏱7am-9pm Mon-Sat, from 9am Sun; 🍴) With shiny exterior walls covered in copper pennies, this pizzeria next to Lark restaurant is always jam-packed. It's worth the wait for a crispy pizza topped with smoked mozzarella and pork-and-fennel sausage or a wood oven-fired lamb meatball sandwich. Turn up before 11am for crazily inventive breakfast pizzas and farm-fresh egg skillets.

Lilly's Taquería
MEXICAN $

(http://lillystacos.com; 310 Chapala St; items from $1.60; ⏱10:30am-9pm Sun-Mon & Wed-Thu, to 10pm Fri & Sat) There's almost always a line roping around this downtown taco shack at lunchtime. But it goes fast, so you'd best be snappy with your order – the *adobada* (marinated pork) and *lengua* (beef tongue) are stand-out choices. Second location in Goleta west of the airport, off Hwy 101.

Backyard Bowls
HEALTH FOOD $

(www.backyardbowls.com; 331 Motor Way; items $5-11; ⊗7am-5pm Mon-Fri, from 8am Sat & Sun) 🍐 This eco-minded little shop serves up real-fruit smoothies and heaping acaí bowls with all kinds of health-conscious add-ons like fresh berries, granola, coconut milk, honey, bee pollen, almonds and loads of other locally sourced, sustainably harvested ingredients.

Metropulos
DELI $

(www.metrofinefoods.com; 216 E Yanonali St; dishes $2-10; ⊗8:30am-5:30pm or 6pm Mon-Fri, 10am-4pm Sat) Before a day at the beach, pick up custom-made sandwiches and fresh salads at this gourmet deli in the Funk Zone. Artisan breads, imported cheeses, cured meats, and California olives and wines will be bursting out of your picnic basket.

El Buen Gusto
MEXICAN $

(836 N Milpas St; dishes $2-8; ⊗8am-9pm; P) At this red-brick strip-mall joint, order authentic south-of-the-border tacos, tortas, quesadillas and burritos with an *agua fresca* (fruit drink) or cold Pacifico beer. Mexican music videos and soccer games blare from the TVs. *Menudo* (tripe soup) and *birria* (spicy meat stew) are weekend specials.

Silvergreens
CALIFORNIAN $

(www.silvergreens.com; 791 Chapala St; items $3-11; ⊗7:30am-10pm; 🖳) 🍐 Who says fast food can't be fresh and tasty? With the tag line 'Eat smart, live well,' this sun-drenched corner cafe makes nutritionally sound salads, soups, sandwiches, burgers, breakfast burritos and more.

★ Santa Barbara Shellfish Company
SEAFOOD $$

(www.sbfishhouse.com; 230 Stearns Wharf; dishes $4-19; ⊗11am-9pm; P 🖳) 'From sea to skillet to plate' sums up this end-of-the-wharf seafood shack that's more of a buzzing counter joint than a sit-down restaurant. Chase away the seagulls as you chow down on garlic-baked clams, crab cakes and coconut-fried shrimp at wooden picnic tables outside. Awesome lobster bisque, ocean views and the same location for over 25 years.

Olio Pizzeria
ITALIAN $$

(☑ 805-899-2699; www.oliopizzeria.com; 11 W Victoria St; shared plates $7-24, lunch mains $9-17; ⊗usually 11:30am-10pm) Just around the corner from State St, this high-ceilinged pizzeria with a happening wine bar proffers crispy, wood oven-baked pizzas, platters of imported cheeses and meats, garden-fresh *insalate* (salads), savory traditional Italian antipasti and sweet *dolci* (desserts). The entrance is off the parking lot alleyway.

Brophy Brothers
SEAFOOD $$

(☑ 805-966-4418; www.brophybros.com; 119 Harbor Way; mains $11-25; ⊗11am-10pm; P) 🍐 A longtime favorite for its fresh-off-the-dock fish and seafood, rowdy atmosphere and salty harborside setting. Slightly less claustrophobic tables on the upstairs deck are worth the long wait – they're quieter and have the best ocean views. Or skip the long lines and start knocking back oyster shooters and Bloody Marys with convivial locals at the bar.

DIY DINING IN SANTA BARBARA

Stock up on fresh fruits and veggies, nuts and honey at the midweek **Santa Barbara Farmers Market** (www.sbfarmersmarket.org; 500 & 600 blocks of State St; ⊗4-7:30pm mid-Mar–early Nov, 3-6:30pm mid-Nov–mid-Mar; 🖳) 🍐, which also happens on Saturday morning from 8:30am until 1pm at the corner of Santa Barbara and Cota Sts. Fill up a Wine Country picnic basket inside the **Santa Barbara Public Market** (http://sbpublicmarket.com; 38 W Victoria St; ⊗7am-10:30pm Mon-Thu, to 11pm Fri & Sat, 11am-8pm Sun) 🍐, where gourmet food purveyors and quick-fix food stalls are open every day of the week. The best place for healthy, organic groceries is **Lazy Acres** (www.lazyacres.com; 302 Meigs Rd; ⊗7am-11pm Mon-Sat, to 10pm Sun; P🗐) 🍐, south of Hwy 101 via W Carrillo St. Downtown, **McConnell's Fine Ice Creams** (www.mcconnells.com; 728 State St; ⊗noon-9:30pm Sun-Wed, to 10:30pm Thu-Sat; 🖳) scoops up premium frozen treats. For more sweet endings, pop sea-salt or passion-fruit truffles from **Chocolate Maya** (www.chocolatemaya.com; 15 W Gutierrez St; ⊗10am-6pm Mon-Fri, to 5pm Sat, to 4pm Sun).

Sojourner Café HEALTH FOOD $$
(www.sojournercafe.com; 134 E Cañon Perdido St; mains $8-13; ⊙ usually 11am-10pm; 🍴) 🍃 Vegetarians rejoice – the menu is extensive at this cozy, wholesome 1970s-era cafe. While supporting local farms, cooks get fairly creative with vegetables, tofu, tempeh, fish, seeds and other healthy ingredients. Daily desserts including vegan, dairy-free and wheat-free treats. Fair-trade coffee and local beers and wines are poured.

★**Lark** CALIFORNIAN $$$
(✆ 805-284-0370; www.thelarksb.com; 131 Anacapa St; shared plates $5-32, mains $24-38; ⊙ 5-10pm Tue-Sun, bar till midnight) 🍃 There's no better place in Santa Barbara County to taste the bountiful farm and fishing goodness of this stretch of SoCal coast. Named after an antique Pullman railway car, this chef-run restaurant in the Funk Zone morphs its menu with the seasons, presenting unique flavor combinations like fried olives with chorizo aioli and chile-spiced mussels in lemongrass-lime broth. Make reservations.

Bouchon CALIFORNIAN $$$
(✆ 805-730-1160; www.bouchonsantabarbara.com; 9 W Victoria Street; mains $25-36; ⊙ 5-9pm Sun-Thu, to 10pm Fri & Sat) 🍃 The perfect, unhurried follow-up to a day in the Wine Country is to feast on the bright, flavorful California cooking at pretty Bouchon (meaning

'wine cork'). A seasonally changing menu spotlights locally grown farm produce and ranched meats that marry beautifully with three dozen regional wines available by the glass. Lovebirds, book a table on the candle-lit patio.

Palace Grill CAJUN, CREOLE $$$
(✆ 805-963-5000; http://palacegrill.com; 8 E Cota St; mains lunch $10-22, dinner $17-32; ⊙ 11:30am-3pm daily, 5:30-10pm Sun-Thu, to 11pm Fri & Sat; 🎵) With all the exuberance of Mardi Gras, this N'awlins-style grill makes totally addictive baskets of housemade muffins and breads, and ginormous (if so-so) plates of jambalaya, gumbo ya-ya, blackened catfish and pecan chicken. Stiff cocktails and indulgent desserts make the grade. Act unsurprised when the staff lead the crowd in a rousing sing-along.

🍷 Drinking & Nightlife

On lower State St, most of the meat-market watering holes have happy hours, tiny dance floors and rowdy college nights. Just south of Hwy 101, the arty Funk Zone's eclectic mix of bars and wine-tasting rooms is a trendy scene.

★**Figueroa Mountain Brewing Co** BAR
(www.figmtnbrew.com; 137 Anacapa St; ⊙ 11am-11pm) Father and son brewers have brought their gold medal-winning hoppy IPA, Dan-

---

DON'T MISS

URBAN WINE TRAIL

No wheels to head up to Santa Barbara's Wine Country? No problem. Ramble between over a dozen wine-tasting rooms (and microbreweries, too) downtown and in the Funk Zone near the beach. Pick up the **Urban Wine Trail** (www.urbanwinetrailsb.com) anywhere along its route. Most tasting rooms are open every afternoon or sometimes into the early evening. On weekends, join the beautiful people rubbing shoulders as they sip outstanding glasses of regional wines and listen to free live music.

For a sociable scene, start at **Municipal Winemakers** (www.municipalwinemakers.com; 22 Anacapa St; tastings $12; ⊙ 11am-6pm; 🎵) or **Corks n' Crowns** (corksandcrowns.com; 32 Anacapa St; tastings $7-12; ⊙ 11am-7pm, last call for tastings 6pm) bottle shop. Then head up to Yanonali St, turning left for **Riverbench Winery Tasting Room** (✆ 805-324-4100; www.riverbench.com; 137 Anacapa St; tastings $10; ⊙ 11am-6pm); **Cutler's Artisan Spirits** (http://cutlersartisan.com; 137 Anacapa St; ⊙ 1-6pm Thu-Sun) distillery, a storefront where you can sample bourbon whiskey, vodka and apple liqueur; and Figueroa Mountain Brewing Co Walk further west to find more wine-tippling spots, one inside an old tire shop.

Or turn right on Yanonali St and stop at AVA Santa Barbara for a liquid education about Santa Barbara's five distinct wine-growing regions. It's less than a mile's detour to the refined **Carr Winery** (http://carrwinery.com; 414 N Salsipuedes St; tastings $10-12; ⊙ 11am-6pm Sun-Wed, to 7pm Thu-Sat) barrel room, next door to **Telegraph Brewing Company** (www.telegraphbrewing.com; 416 N Salsipuedes St; ⊙ 3-9pm Tue-Thu, 2-10pm Fri & Sat, 1-7pm Sun), which makes robust ales and a 'rhinoceros' rye wine.

ish red lager, and double IPA from Santa Barbara's Wine Country to the Funk Zone. Clink pint glasses on the taproom's open-air patio while acoustic acts play. Enter on Yanonali St.

AVA Santa Barbara
BAR

(www.avasantabarbara.com; 116 E Yanonali St; ⊗noon-7pm) From the sidewalk, passersby stop just to peek through the floor-to-ceiling glass windows at a wall-sized map of Santa Barbara's Wine Country, all hand-drawn in chalk. Inside, wine lovers lean on the tasting bar while sipping flights of cool-weather Chardonnay or pinot noir and sun-loving sauvignon blanc, grenache, Syrah and cabernet, all grown locally.

Handlebar Coffee Roasters
CAFE

(www.handlebarcoffee.com; 128 E Cañon Perdido St; ⊗7am-5pm Mon-Sat, from 8am Sun; ⊠) Bicycle-themed coffee shop brews rich coffee and espresso drinks from small-batch roasted beans. Sit and sip yours on the sunny patio.

Brewhouse
BREWERY

(sbbrewhouse.com; 229 W Montecito St; ⊗11am-11pm Sun-Thu, to midnight Fri & Sat; ⊠⊠) Down by the railroad tracks, the boisterous Brewhouse crafts its own unique small-batch beer (Saint Barb's Belgian-style ales rule), serves wines by the glass and has cool art and rock-in' live music Wednesday to Saturday nights.

Press Room
PUB

(http://pressroomsb.com; 15 E Ortega St; ⊗11am-2am) This tiny pub can barely contain the college students and European travelers who cram the place to its seams. Pop in to catch soccer games, stuff the jukebox with quarters and enjoy jovial banter with the British bartender.

Marquee
COCKTAIL BAR

(http://marqueesb.com; 1212 State St; ⊗4pm-2am) At downtown's Granada Theatre, flickering candles and glowing lights fill this bar mixing unusual cocktails, pouring wines by the glass and dishing up Mediterranean tapas. Look for jazz, open-mic and comedy nights.

Hollister Brewing Company
BREWERY

(www.hollisterbrewco.com; Camino Real Marketplace, 6980 Marketplace Dr, Goleta; ⊗11am-10pm) With over a dozen microbrews on tap, this place draws serious beer geeks out to Goleta, near the UCSB campus, off Hwy 101. IPAs are the permanent attractions, along with nitrogenated stout. Skip the food, though.

☆ Entertainment

Santa Barbara's appreciation of the arts is evidenced not only by the variety of performances available on any given night, but also its gorgeous, often historic venues. For a current calender of live music and special events, check www.independent.com online or pick up Friday's *Scene* guide in the *Santa Barbara News-Press*.

Santa Barbara Bowl
MUSIC

(☑805-962-7411; http://sbbowl.com; 1122 N Milpas St; most tickets $35-125) Built by Works Progress Administration (WPA) artisans during the Depression in the 1930s, this naturally beautiful outdoor stone amphitheater has ocean views from the highest cheap seats. Kick back in the sunshine or under the stars for live rock, jazz and folk concerts in summer. Big-name acts like Jack Johnson, Sarah McLachlan and The National have all taken the stage here.

Granada Theatre
THEATER, MUSIC

(☑805-899-2222; www.granadasb.org; 1216 State St) This beautifully restored 1930s Spanish Moorish-style theater is home to the city's symphony, ballet and opera, as well as touring Broadway shows and big-name musicians.

Lobero Theatre
THEATER, MUSIC

(☑888-456-2376, 805-963-0761; www.lobero.com; 33 E Cañon Perdido St) One of California's oldest theaters presents modern dance, chamber music, jazz and world-music touring acts and stand-up comedy nights.

Arlington Theatre
CINEMA

(☑805-963-4408; www.thearlingtontheatre.com; 1317 State St) Harking back to 1931, this Mission Revival–style movie palace has a Spanish courtyard and a star-spangled ceiling. It's a drop-dead gorgeous place to attend a film festival screening.

Soho
MUSIC

(☑805-962-7776; www.sohosb.com; ste 205, 1221 State St; most tickets $8-25) One unpretentious brick room plus live music almost nightly equals Soho, upstairs inside a downtown office complex behind McDonald's. Lineups range from indie rock, jazz, folk and funk to world beats. Some all-ages shows.

Velvet Jones
MUSIC, COMEDY

(☑805-965-8676; http://velvet-jones.com; 423 State St; most tickets $10-15) Long-running downtown punk and indie dive for rock, hip-hop, comedy and 18-plus DJ nights for the city's college crowd. Many bands stop here between gigs in LA and San Francisco.

Zodo's Bowling & Beyond   BOWLING
(☑ 805-967-0128; www.zodos.com; 5925 Calle Real, Goleta; bowling per game $4-8, shoe rental $4; ◉ 8:30am-2am Tue-Sat, to midnight Sun & Mon; ▣) With over 40 beers on tap, pool tables and a video arcade (Skee-Ball!), this bowling alley near UCSB is good ol' family fun. Call ahead to get on the wait list and for schedules of open-play lanes and 'Glow Bowling' blacklight nights with DJs. From Hwy 101 west of downtown, exit Fairview Ave north.

🛍 Shopping

Downtown's **State St** is packed with shops of all kinds, and even chain stores conform to the red-roofed architectural style. Cheapskates stick to lower State St, while trust-fund babies should head uptown. For more local art galleries and indie shops, dive into the **Funk Zone**, south of Hwy 101, spreading east of State St.

Paseo Nuevo   MALL
(www.paseonuevoshopping.com; 651 Paseo Nuevo; ◉ 10am-9pm Mon-Fri, to 8pm Sat, 11am-6pm Sun) This busy open-air mall is anchored by Macy's and Nordstrom department stores and clothing chains. Browse Kitson for cutting-edge styles from LA, Bettie Page Clothing's retro pin-up fashions and the eco-green goddesses' bath, body and beauty shop Lush. First 75 minutes of parking free in the underground garage.

Surf-n-Wear's Beach House   CLOTHING
(www.surfnwear.com; 10 State St; ◉ 9am-6pm Sun-Thu, to 7pm Fri & Sat) Modern and vintage surfboards dangle from the ceiling at this beach-minded emporium where unique T-shirts and hoodies, colorful bikinis, shades, beachbags and flip-flops jostle for your attention. This shop has been around since before 1967's Summer of Love.

REI   OUTDOOR EQUIPMENT
(www.rei.com; 321 Anacapa St; ◉ 10am-9pm Mon-Fri, to 7pm Sat, to 6pm Sun) If you forgot your tent or rock-climbing carabiners at home, the West Coast's most popular independent co-op outdoor retailer is the place to pick up outdoor recreation gear, active clothing, sport shoes and topographic maps.

Channel Islands Surfboards   OUTDOOR EQUIPMENT
(www.cisurfboards.com; 36 Anacapa St; ◉ 10am-7pm Mon-Sat, 11am-5pm Sun) Are you ready to take home a handcrafted, Southern California-born surfboard? Down in the Funk Zone, this surf shack is the place for innovative pro-worthy board designs, as well as surfer threads and beanie hats.

CRSVR Sneaker Boutique   SHOES, CLOTHING
(www.crsvr.com; 632 State St; ◉ 10am-8pm) Check out this sneaker boutique run by DJs, not just for limited-editions Nikes and other athletic-shoe brands, but also T-shirts, jackets, hats and more urban styles for men.

La Arcada   MALL
(www.laarcadasantabarbara.com; 1114 State St; ◉ individual shop hr vary) Filled with specialty boutiques, restaurants and whimsical art galleries, this historic red-tile-roofed passageway was designed by Myron Hunt (builder of Pasadena's Rose Bowl) in the 1920s. Savor handmade French candies from Chocolats du Calibressan as you wander around.

Diani   CLOTHING, SHOES
(www.dianiboutique.com; 1324 State St, Arlington Plaza; ◉ 10am-6pm Mon, 10am-7pm Tue-Sat, noon-6pm Sun) Carries high-fashion, Euro-inspired designs, with a touch of funky California soul thrown in for good measure. Think Humanoid dresses, Rag & Bone skinny jeans, Stella McCartney sunglasses and Chloé shoes.

El Paseo   MALL
(800 block of State St; ◉ individual shop hr vary) A smattering of locally owned boutiques surround a tiny, flower-festooned courtyard, constructed in Spanish-colonial style in the 1920s. It cameoed in the romantic comedy *It's Complicated*.

ℹ Information

FedEx Office (www.fedex.com; 1030 State St; per min 30-40¢; ◉ 7am-11pm Mon-Fri, 8am-9pm Sat, 9am-9pm Sun) Self-service online computer workstations.

Outdoors Santa Barbara Visitors Center (☑ 805-884-1475; 4th fl, 113 Harbor Way; ◉ 11am-4pm) Inside the same building as the maritime museum, this volunteer-staffed visitor center offers info on Channel Islands National Park and a harbor-view deck.

Santa Barbara Central Library (☑ 805-962-7653; www.sbplibrary.org; 40 E Anapamu St; ◉ 10am-7pm Mon-Thu, to 5:30pm Fri & Sat, 1-5pm Sun; ☎) Free walk-in internet terminals (photo ID required).

Santa Barbara Cottage Hospital (☎805-682-7111; www.cottagehealthsystem.org; 400 W Pueblo St; ⊙24hr) Emergency room (ER) open 24 hours.

Santa Barbara Independent (www.independent.com) Free alternative weekly tabloid with eating and entertainment listings and reviews, plus an events calendar.

Santa Barbara News-Press (www.newspress.com) Daily newspaper offers an events calendar and Friday's arts-and-entertainment supplement *Scene*.

Santa Barbara Visitors Center (☎805-568-1811, 805-965-3021; www.santabarbaraca.com; 1 Garden St; ⊙9am-5pm Mon-Sat & 10am-5pm Sun Feb-Oct; 9am-4pm Mon-Sat Nov-Jan) Pick up maps and brochures while consulting with the helpful but busy staff. The website offers free downloadable DIY touring maps and itineraries, from famous movie locations to wine trails, art galleries and outdoors fun. Self-pay metered parking lot nearby.

❶ Getting There & Away

The small Santa Barbara Airport (p50700), less than 10 miles west of downtown via Hwy 101, has scheduled flights to/from LA, Las Vegas, San Francisco and other western US cities. A taxi to downtown or the waterfront costs about $30

to $35 plus tip. Car-rental agencies with airport lots include Alamo, Avis, Budget, Enterprise, Hertz and National; reserve in advance.

Santa Barbara Airbus (☎800-423-1618, 805-964-7759; www.sbairbus.com) shuttles between Los Angeles International Airport (LAX) and Santa Barbara ($46/88 one way/round-trip, 2½ hours, eight departures daily). The more people in your party, the cheaper the fare. For more discounts, prepay online.

Amtrak (☎800-872-7245; www.amtrak.com; 209 State St) trains run south to LA ($31, three hours) via Carpinteria, Ventura and Burbank's airport, and north to San Luis Obispo ($27, 2¾ hours) and Oakland ($82, 8¾ hours), with stops in Paso Robles, Salinas and San Jose.

Greyhound (☎800-231-2222, 805-965-7551; www.greyhound.com) operates a few buses daily to LA ($15, three hours), San Luis Obispo ($28, 2¼ hours), Santa Cruz ($53, six hours) and San Francisco ($57, nine hours).

Vista (☎800-438-1112; www.goventura.org) runs frequent daily 'Coastal Express' buses to Carpinteria ($3, 20 to 30 minutes) and Ventura ($3, 40 to 70 minutes); check online or call for schedules.

If you're driving on Hwy 101, take the Garden St or Carrillo St exits for downtown.

GO GREEN IN SANTA BARBARA

Santa Barbara's biggest eco-travel initiative is **Santa Barbara Car Free** (www.santabarbaracarfree.org). Browse the website for tips on seeing the city without your car, plus valuable discounts on accommodations, vacation packages, rail travel and more. Still don't believe it's possible to tour Santa Barbara without a car? Let us show you how to do it.

From LA, hop aboard the *Pacific Surfliner* for a memorably scenic three-hour coastal ride to Santa Barbara's Amtrak station, a few blocks from the beach and downtown. Then hoof it or catch one of the electric shuttles that zips north-south along State St and east-west along the waterfront. Take MTD bus line 22 to reach the famous mission and the botanic gardens. For a DIY cycling tour, Wheel Fun Rentals (p314) is a short walk from the train station.

Even Santa Barbara's Wine Country is getting into the sustainable swing of things. More and more vineyards are implementing biodynamic farming techniques and following organic guidelines. Many vintners and oenophiles are starting to think that the more natural the growing process, the better the wine, too. Sustainable Vine Wine Tours (p332) whisks you around family-owned sustainable vineyards. Minimize your carbon footprint even further by following Santa Barbara's Urban Wine Trail (p322) on foot. If you love both wine and food, **Edible Santa Barbara** (http://ediblecommunities.com/santabarbara/) magazine publishes insightful articles about vineyards and restaurants that are going green. It's available free at many local markets, restaurants and wineries.

Santa Barbara County abounds with ecofriendly outdoor activities, too. Take your pick of hiking trails, cycling routes, ocean kayaking, swimming, surfing or stand-up paddleboarding (SUP). If you're going whale-watching, ask around to see if there are any alternative-fueled tour boats with trained onboard naturalists.

ⓘ Getting Around

Local buses operated by the **Metropolitan Transit District** (MTD; ☎ 805-963-3366; www.sbmtd.gov) cost $1.75 per ride (exact change, cash only). Equipped with front-loading bike racks, these buses travel all over town and to adjacent communities; ask for a free transfer upon boarding. **MTD Transit Center** (1020 Chapala St) has details about routes and schedules.

BUS	DESTINATION	FREQUENCY
5	Arroyo Burro Beach	hourly
11	State St, UCSB campus	every 30 minutes
20	Montecito, Summerland, Carpinteria	hourly
22	Mission, Museum of Natural History and (weekends only) Botanic Garden	seven or eight buses daily

MTD's electric **Downtown Shuttle** buses run along State St down to Stearns Wharf every 10 to 30 minutes from 9am to 6pm daily. A second **Waterfront Shuttle** travels from Stearns Wharf west to the harbor and east to the zoo every 15 to 30 minutes from 9am or 10am to 6pm daily. Between late May and early September, both routes also run every 15 minutes from 6pm to 9pm on Fridays and Saturdays. The fare is 50¢ per ride; transfers between routes are free.

Lil' Toot water taxi (☎ 888-316-9363; www.sbwatertaxi.com; 113 Harbor Way; one-way fare adult/child 2-12yr $4/1; ☺ usually noon-6pm Apr-Oct, hr vary Nov-Mar; ▣) provides an eco-friendly, biodiesel-fueled ride between Stearns Wharf and the harbor, docking in front of the maritime museum. Look for ticket booths on the waterfront. Trips run every half-hour, weather permitting.

For bicycle rentals, Wheel Fun Rentals (p314) has two locations by Stearns Wharf. Downtown, **Pedego** (☎ 805-963-8885; http://pedegosb.com; 436 State St; ☺ 9:30am-6:30am Tue-Sun) rents electric bicycles (per hour/day from $16/70) and pedal-it-yourself models (from $10/40).

Taxis are metered around $3 at flagfall, with an additional $3 to $4 for each mile. Call **Yellow Cab** (☎ 805-965-5111, 800-549-8294; www.santabarbarayellowcab.com).

Downtown street parking or in any of a dozen municipal lots is free for the first 75 minutes; each additional hour costs $1.50.

SANTA BARBARA WINE COUNTRY

Oak-dotted hillsides, winding country lanes, rows of sweetly heavy grapevines stretching as far as the eye can see – it's hard not to gush about the Santa Ynez and Santa Maria Valleys and the Santa Rita Hills wine regions. From fancy convertibles and Harleys to ecofriendly touring vans and road bikes, you'll find an eclectic, friendly mix of travelers sharing these bucolic back roads.

You may be inspired to visit by the Oscar-winning film *Sideways,* which is like real life in at least one respect: this Wine Country is ideal for do-it-yourself-exploring with friends. Locals here are friendly, from longtime landowners and farmers displaying small-town graciousness to vineyard owners who've fled big cities to follow their passion. Ever more winemakers are showing their passion for the vine in earth-conscious ways, implementing organic practices and biodynamic farming techniques. Many happily share their knowledge and intriguing personal histories, as well as their love of the land, in intimate vineyard tasting rooms.

With more than 100 wineries spread out across the landscape, it can seem daunting at first. But the Santa Ynez Valley's five small towns – Los Olivos, Solvang, Buellton, Santa Ynez and Ballard – are all clustered within 10 miles of one another, so it's easy to stop, shop and eat whenever and wherever you feel like it. Don't worry about sticking to a regimented plan or following prescriptive wine guides. Instead, let yourself be captivated by the scenery and pull over wherever signs looks welcoming.

Wineries

The big-name appellations for Santa Barbara's Wine Country are the Santa Ynez Valley, Santa Maria Valley and Santa Rita Hills, plus smaller Happy Canyon and upstart Ballard Canyon. Wine-tasting rooms abound in Los Olivos and Solvang, handy for anyone with limited time.

The Santa Ynez Valley, where you'll find most of the wineries, lies south of the Santa Maria Valley. Hwy 246 runs east–west, via Solvang, across the bottom of the Santa Ynez Valley, connecting Hwy 101 with Hwy 154.

SCENIC DRIVE: HIGHWAY 154 (SAN MARCOS PASS RD)

What to See

As Hwy 154 climbs from the coast, you'll leave oh-so civilized Santa Barbara behind and enter the rugged Santa Ynez Mountains. You'll notice places where the hillsides have been scarred by wildfires, but don't be alarmed: wildfires are part of the natural process of forest birth and regrowth.

Chumash Painted Cave State Historic Park

This tiny, off-the-beaten path **historic site** (www.parks.ca.gov; ⊘dawn-dusk) **FREE** shelters pictographs painted by Chumash tribespeople over 400 years ago. The sandstone cave is now protected from graffiti and vandalism by a metal screen, so bring a flashlight to get a good look. The turnoff to Painted Cave Rd is off Hwy 154 below San Marcos Summit, about 6 miles from Hwy 101. The two-mile twisting side road to the site is extremely narrow, rough and steep (no RVs). Look for a small signposted pull-off on your left.

Cold Spring Tavern

Cold Spring Tavern (☑805-967-0066; www.coldspringtavern.com; 5995 Stagecoach Rd; mains breakfast & lunch $9-14, dinner $22-31; ⊘11am-8:30pm Mon-Fri, from 8am Sat & Sun) is an 1860s stagecoach stop that's still a popular watering hole. A rough-hewn plank floor connects a warren of dimly lit rooms decorated with an odd assortment of Western memorabilia. Call ahead to check if the barbecue grill is open, then order the Santa Maria-style tri-tip barbecue sandwich. The tavern's signposted turnoff from Hwy 154 is about a mile downhill beyond the mountain summit, then follow the signs for another 1.5 miles around the loop road.

Los Padres National Forest

The **Los Padres National Forest** (☑805-967-3481; www.fs.usda.gov/lpnf) stretches over 200 miles from the Carmel Valley to the western edge of LA County. It's a giant playground for hiking, camping, horseback riding and mountain biking.

Several scenic hiking trails lead off Paradise Rd, which crosses Hwy 154 north of San Marcos Pass, over 10 miles from Hwy 101. On the 1-mile round-trip **Red Rock Pools Trail**, the Santa Ynez River deeply pools among rocks and waterfalls, creating a swimming and sunbathing spot; the trailhead is at the end of Paradise Rd.

Stop at the **ranger station** (☑805-967-3481; 3505 Paradise Rd; ⊘8am-4:30pm Mon-Fri, also 8am-4:30pm Sat late May-early Sep) for posted trail maps and information and a National Forest Adventure Pass (per day $5), which is required for parking (unless you have an 'America the Beautiful' Annual Pass (p472)). Family-friendly **campgrounds** (☑877-444-6777; www.recreation.gov; campsites $19-35) with drinking water, flush toilets and both first-come, first-served and reservable sites are along Paradise Rd.

Cachuma Lake Recreation Area

This county-run **park** (☑cruise reservations 805-686-5050/5055; www.countyofsb.org/parks; admission per vehicle $10, 2hr cruise adult/4-12yr $15/7; ⊘open daily, seasonal hr vary; ▣) is a haven for anglers and boaters, with wildlife-watching cruises offered year-round. There's also a child-friendly **nature center** (☑805-693-0691; www.clnaturecenter.org; ⊘10am-4pm Tue-Sat, to 2pm Sun; ▣) and a large campground (p319) with hot showers. First-come, first-served sites fill quickly; book ahead on weekends or for ecofriendly yurts.

The Route

From Hwy 101 west of downtown Santa Barbara, Hwy 154 (San Marcos Pass Rd) heads northwest, winding up through the Los Padres National Forest and passing Cachuma Lake. Beyond the Hwy 246 turnoff west to Solvang, Hwy 154 bisects the Santa Ynez Valley before rejoining Hwy 101 past Los Olivos.

Time & Mileage

It's 35 miles from downtown Santa Barbara to Los Olivos, taking 40 minutes without stops or traffic jams. Returning to Santa Barbara, it's under an hour's trip via Hwy 101.

Santa Barbara Wine Country

North–south secondary roads bordered by vineyards include Alamo Pintado Rd from Hwy 246 to Los Olivos, and Refugio Rd between Santa Ynez and Ballard.

A half-day trip will allow you to see one winery or tasting room, have lunch and return to Santa Barbara. Otherwise make it a full day and plan to have lunch and possibly dinner before returning to the city.

Santa Barbara Wine Country

Foxen Canyon Wine Trail

The scenic **Foxen Canyon Wine Trail** (www.foxencanyonwinetrail.com) runs north from Hwy 154, just west of Los Olivos, deep into the heart of the rural Santa Maria Valley. It's a must-see for oenophiles or anyone wanting to get off the beaten path. For the most part, it follows Foxen Canyon Rd.

★**Foxen** WINERY
(☑ 805-937-4251; www.foxenvineyard.com; 7200 & 7600 Foxen Canyon Rd, Santa Maria; tastings $10; ⊙ 11am-4pm) On what was once a working cattle ranch, Foxen crafts warm Syrah, steel-cut Chardonnay, full-fruited pinot noir and rich Rhône-style wines, all sourced from standout vineyards. The newer tasting room is solar-powered, while the old 'shack' – a dressed-down space with a corrugated-metal roof, funky-cool decor and leafy patio – pours Bordeaux-style and Cal-Ital varietals under the 'Foxen 7200' label.

Demetria Estate WINERY
(☑ 805-686-2345; www.demetriaestate.com; 6701 Foxen Canyon Rd, Los Olivos; tastings $20; ⊙ by appt only) ⊘ This hilltop retreat has the curving arches and thick wooden doors of your hospitable Greek uncle's country house, with epic views of vineyards and rolling hillsides. Tastings are by appointment only, but worth it just to sample the biodynamically farmed Chardonnay, Syrah and viognier, plus rave-worthy Rhône-style red blends.

Zaca Mesa Winery WINERY
(www.zacamesa.com; 6905 Foxen Canyon Rd, Los Olivos; tastings $10; ⊙ 10am-4pm daily year-round, to 5pm Fri & Sat late May–early Sep) Stop by this barn-style tasting room for a rustic, sipping-on-the-farm ambience. Santa Barbara's highest-elevation winery, Zaca Mesa is known not only for its estate-grown Rhône varietals and signature Z Cuvée red blend and Z Blanc white blend, but also a life-sized outdoor chessboard, a tree-shaded picnic

❶ WINE COUNTRY CELEBRATIONS

Santa Barbara Vintners (☎805-668-0881; www.sbcountywines.com) publishes a free touring map brochure of the county's vineyards and wine trails, which you can pick up at just about any winery or visitors center, or download their free mobile app. Special events worth planning your trip around include the **Spring Weekend** (www.sbvintnersweekend.com) in mid-April and mid-October's **Celebration of Harvest** (www.celebrationofharvest.com).

area that's dog-friendly and a short, scenic trail overlooking the vineyards.

Firestone Vineyards WINERY

(☎805-688-3940; www.firestonewine.com; 5017 Zaca Station Rd, Los Olivos; tastings $15, incl tour $20; ☺10am-5pm) Founded in the 1970s, Firestone is Santa Barbara's oldest estate winery. Sweeping views of the vineyard from the sleek, wood-paneled tasting room are nearly as satisfying as the value-priced Chardonnay, sauvignon blanc, merlot and Bordeaux-style blends. Arrive in time for a winery tour, usually offered at 11:15am, 1:15pm and 3:15pm daily (no reservations).

Curtis Winery WINERY

(www.curtiswinery.com; 5249 Foxen Canyon Rd, Los Olivos; tastings $10; ☺10:30am-5:30pm) Just up the road from Firestone Vineyards, artisan winemaker Andrew Murray specializes in Rhône-style wines, including estate-grown Syrah, Mourvèdre, viognier, grenache blanc and Roussanne. The same wines are poured at Andrew Murray Vineyards' tasting room in downtown Los Olivos.

Kenneth Volk Vineyards WINERY

(☎805-938-7896; www.volkwines.com; 5230 Tepusquet Rd, Santa Maria; tastings $10; ☺10:30am-4:30pm) Only an established cult winemaker could convince oenophiles to drive so far out of their way to taste rare heritage varietals like floral-scented Malvasia and inky Negrette, as well as standard-bearing pinot noir, Chardonnay, cabernet sauvignon and merlot.

Riverbench Vineyard & Winery WINERY

(www.riverbench.com; 6020 Foxen Canyon Rd, Santa Maria; tastings $10; ☺10am-4pm) Riverbench has been growing prized pinot noir and

Chardonnay grapes since the early 1970s. The rural tasting room is inside a butter-yellow Arts and Crafts farmhouse with panoramic views across the Santa Maria Valley. Out back is a picnic ground and bocce ball court. You can also sample their wines on Santa Barbara's Urban Wine Trail.

Fess Parker Winery & Vineyard WINERY

(www.fessparkerwines.com; 6200 Foxen Canyon Rd; tastings $12; ☺10am-5pm) Besides its on-screen appearance as Frass Canyon in the movie *Sideways,* the winery's other claim to fame is its late founder Fess Parker, best known for playing Davy Crockett on TV. Even though Fess has now passed on, his winery still gives away coonskin-cap-etched souvenir glasses. Savor the pricey, award-winning Chardonnay and pinot noir.

Rancho Sisquoc Winery WINERY

(www.ranchosisquoc.com; 6600 Foxen Canyon Rd, Santa Maria; tastings $10; ☺10am-4pm Mon-Thu, to 5pm Fri-Sun) This tranquil gem is worth the extra mileage, not necessarily for its hit-and-miss wines, but for the charmingly rustic tasting room surrounded by pastoral views. Turn off Foxen Canyon Rd when you spot **San Ramon Chapel** (www.sanramonchapel.org), a little white church built in 1875. Incidentally, *sisquoc* is the Chumash term for 'gathering place.'

Santa Rita Hills Wine Trail

When it comes to country-road scenery, eco-conscious farming practices and top-notch pinot noir, the less-traveled **Santa Rita Hills** (www.staritahills.com) region holds its own. Almost a dozen tasting rooms line an easy driving loop west of Hwy 101 via Santa Rosa Rd and Hwy 246. Be prepared to share the roads with cyclists and an occasional John Deere tractor. More artisan winemarkers hide out in the industrial warehouses of Buellton near Hwy 101 and farther afield in Lompoc's 'Wine Ghetto' (www.lompoctrail.com).

Alma Rosa Winery & Vineyards WINERY

(☎805-688-9090; www.almarosawinery.com; tastings $5-15; ☺11am-4:30pm) ✎ Richard Sanford left the powerhouse winery bearing his name to start this new winery with his wife, Thekla, using sustainable, organic farming techniques. Cacti and cobblestones welcome you to the ranch, reached via a long, winding gravel driveway. Vineyard-designated pinot noir and fine pinot blanc and pinot gris are what's poured. Call ahead for directions to the new tasting room.

Sanford Winery

WINERY

(www.sanfordwinery.com; 5010 Santa Rosa Rd, Lompoc; tastings $15-20, incl tour $25; ☺11am-4pm Sun-Thu, to 5pm Fri & Sat Mar-Oct, 11am-4pm daily Nov-Feb) Be enchanted by this romantic tasting room built of stone and handmade adobe bricks, all embraced by estate vineyards on the historic Rancho La Rinconda property. Watch the sun sink over the vineyards from the back patio with a glass of silky pinot noir or citrusy Chardonnay in hand. Winery tours are typically given at 11:30am daily (no reservations).

Babcock

WINERY

(www.babcockwinery.com; 5175 E Hwy 146, Lompoc; tastings $12-15; ☺10:30am-5pm) Family-owned vineyards overflow with different grape varietals – Chardonnay, Sauvignon Blanc, Pinot Gris, pinot noir, Syrah, Cabernet Sauvignon, merlot and more – that let innovative small-lot winemaker Bryan Babcock be the star. 'Slice of Heaven' pinot noir alone is worthy of a pilgrimage to this eclectically furnished tasting room with elevated views.

Ampelos Cellars

TASTING ROOM

(☏805-736-9957; www.ampeloscellars.com; 312 N 9th Ave, Lompoc; tastings $10; ☺11am-5pm Thu-Sat, to 4pm Mon) ◢ Danish grower Peter Work and wife Rebecca display their passion for the vine through biodynamic farming techniques and encyclopedic knowledge of their lots. Their pinot noir, Syrah and grenache shine. Sample them in Lompoc's Wine Ghetto, an industrial area far from the vineyards, where most of the family-run tasting rooms (Flying Goat Cellars is a fave) are open only on weekends.

Mosby Winery

WINERY

(☏805-688-2415; www.mosbywines.com; 9496 Santa Rosa Rd, Buellton; tastings $10; ☺10am-4pm Mon-Thu, to 4:30pm Fri-Sun) Just west of Hwy 101, by a hillside olive orchard, this casual red carriage house pours unusual Cal-Italian varietals, including a lip-puckering, fruit-forward Dolcetto and a crisp, citrusy estate-grown Cortese. Be forewarned: the 80-proof grappa distilled from estate-grown Traminer grapes is a knock-out punch.

Santa Ynez Valley

Popular wineries cluster between Los Olivos and Solvang along Alamo Pintado Rd and Refugio Rd, south of Roblar Ave and west of Hwy 154. Noisy tour groups, harried staff and stingy pours often disappoint, but thankfully that's not the case at better wine-tasting rooms.

Beckmen Vineyards

WINERY

(www.beckmenvineyards.com; 2670 Ontiveros Rd, Solvang; tastings $10-15; ☺11am-5pm) ◢ Bring a picnic to the pondside gazebo at this tranquil winery, where estate-grown Rhône varieties flourish on the unique terroir of Purisima Mountain. Using biodynamic farming principles, natural (not chemical), means are used to prevent pests. To sample superb Syrah and a rare cuvée blend with grenache, Mourvèdre and Counoise, follow Roblar Ave west of Hwy 154 to Ontiveros Rd.

Lincourt Vineyard

WINERY

(www.lincourtwines.com; 1711 Alamo Pintado Rd, Solvang; tastings from $10; ☺10am-5pm) Respected winemaker Bill Foley, who runs Firestone Vineyard on the Foxen Canyon Wine Trail, founded this vineyard first in the late 1990s on a former dairy farm. Today you can still see the original 1926 farmhouse built from a Sears catalog kit. Inside

---

SANTA BARBARA WINE COUNTRY 101

Although large-scale winemaking has only been happening here since the 1980s, the climate of Santa Barbara's Wine Country has always been perfect for growing grapes. Two parallel, transverse mountain ranges – Santa Ynez and San Rafael – cradle the region and funnel coastal fog eastward off the Pacific into the valleys between. The farther inland you go, the warmer it gets.

To the west, fog and low clouds may hover all day, keeping the weather crisp even in summer, while only a few miles inland, temperatures approach 100°F in July. These delicately balanced microclimates support two major types of grapes. Nearer the coast in the cooler Santa Maria Valley, pinot noir – a particularly fragile grape – and other Burgundian varieties such as Chardonnay thrive. Inland in the hotter Santa Ynez Valley, Rhône-style grapes do best, including Syrah and viognier.

the yellow cottage's tasting room, sip finely crafted Syrah, pinot noir and a dry French-style rosé, all made from grapes grown in the Santa Maria Valley and Santa Rita Hills.

Kalyra Winery WINERY
(www.kalyrawinery.com; 343 N Refugio Rd, Santa Ynez; tastings $10-12; ⊙11am-5pm Mon-Fri, from 10am Sat & Sun) Australian Mike Brown has traveled halfway around the world to combine his two loves: surfing and winemaking. Try one of his full-bodied red blends, unusual white varietals or sweet dessert wines (the orange muscat is a crowd-pleaser), all in bottles with Aboriginal art-inspired labels. Kalyra also pours at a smaller tasting room on Santa Barbara's Urban Wine Trail.

Sunstone Vineyards & Winery WINERY
(www.sunstonewinery.com; 125 N Refugio Rd, Santa Ynez; tastings $10-15; ⊙11am-5pm) 🐾 Wander inside what looks like an 18th-century stone farmhouse from Provence and into a cool hillside cave housing wine barrels. Sunstone crafts Bordeaux-style wines made from 100% organically grown grapes. Bring a picnic to eat in the courtyard beneath gnarled oaks.

Buttonwood Farm Winery & Vineyard WINERY
(www.buttonwoodwinery.com; 1500 Alamo Pintado Rd, Solvang; tastings $10-15; ⊙11am-5pm; 🎞) 🐾 Bordeaux and Rhône varieties do well in the sun-dappled limestone soil at this friendly winery, best for wine-tasting neophytes and dog owners. The trellised back patio, bordering a fruit-tree orchard, is a pleasant spot to relax with a bottle of zingy sauvignon blanc.

🧭 Tours

Full-day wine-tasting tours average $105 to $160 per person; most leave from Santa Barbara, and some require a minimum number of participants.

Santa Barbara Wine Country Cycling Tours CYCLING
(☎888-557-8687, 805-686-9490; www.wine-countrycycling.com; 3630 Sagunto St, Santa Ynez; ⊙8:30am-4:30pm Mon-Sat, by appt Sun) Guided and DIY cycling tours start from the Santa Ynez storefront, which also rents road and hybrid mountain bikes (from $35/45 per half/full day).

Wine Edventures GUIDED TOUR
(☎805-965-9463; www.welovewines.com) Serves up a fun-lovin' side dish of local history and wine education on its shuttle-driven wine-tasting tours, one of which visits a microbrewery, too.

Sustainable Vine Wine Tours GUIDED TOUR
(☎805-698-3911; www.sustainablevine.com) 🐾 Biodiesel-van tours of wineries implementing organic and sustainable agricultural practices include a local picnic lunch in the vineyards.

Los Olivos

POP 1130

The posh ranching town of Los Olivos is many visitors' first stop when exploring Santa Barbara's Wine Country. Its four-block-long main street is lined with rustic wine-tasting rooms, bistros and boutiques seemingly airlifted straight out of Napa.

◉ Sights

Clairmont Farms FARM
(☎805-688-7505; www.clairmontfarms.com; 2480 Roblar Ave; ⊙usually 10am-6pm Mon-Sat, to 5pm Sun) 🐾 Natural beauty awaits just outside town at this organic family-owned farm, where purple lavender fields bloom like a Monet masterpiece, usually peaking from mid-June to late July. Peruse lavender honey and sea salt and aromatherapy, bath and body products in the small shop.

WORTH A TRIP

MISSION LA PURÍSIMA

One of the most evocative of Southern California's missions, **La Purísima Mission State Historic Park** (☎805-733-3713; www.lapurisimamission.org; 2295 Purísima Rd, Lompoc; per car $6; ⊙9am-5pm; 🚼) 🐾 was completely restored in the 1930s by the Civilian Conservation Corps (CCC). Today its buildings are furnished just as they were during Spanish-colonial times. The mission's fields still support livestock, while outdoor gardens are planted with medicinal plants and trees once used by Chumash tribespeople. Surrounding the mission are miles of peaceful hiking trails. One-hour guided tours begin at 1pm daily. The mission is about 16 miles west of Hwy 101, via Hwy 146 from Buellton.

📖 Sleeping & Eating

Ballard Inn & Restaurant B&B $$$
(☑805-688-7770, 800-638-2466; www.ballardinn.com; 2436 Baseline Ave, Ballard; r incl breakfast $265-345; 🐾) For romantics, this quaint inn awaits in the 19th-century stagecoach town of Ballard, south of Los Olivos heading toward Solvang. Wood-burning fireplaces make en-suite rooms feel even more cozy, though some are dearly in need of updating. Rates include a full hot breakfast and weekend wine tastings. Reservations are essential for rooms and also dinner at the inn's chef-driven Eurasian restaurant.

Los Olivos Grocery MARKET, DELI $
(http://losolivosgrocery.com; 2621 W Hwy 154, Santa Ynez; ⊘7am-9pm) This tiny local market heaps barbecue tri-tip sandwiches, artisan breads, specialty cheeses and everything you'll need for a vineyard picnic, or grab a table on the front porch.

Panino SANDWICHES $$
(http://paninorestaurants.com; 2900 Grand Ave; sandwiches $10-12; ⊘10am-4pm; ☑) Take your pick of gourmet deli sandwiches and salads: curry chicken is a perennial fave, but there are robust vegetarian options too. Order at the counter, then eat outside at an umbrella-covered table.

**Los Olivos Café & Wine
Merchant** CALIFORNIAN, MEDITERRANEAN $$$
(☑805-688-7265; www.losolivoscafe.com; 2879 Grand Ave; mains breakfast $9-12, lunch & dinner $12-29; ⊘11:30am-8:30pm daily, also 8-10:30am Sat & Sun) With white canopies and a wisteria-covered trellis, this wine-country landmark (as seen in *Sideways*) swirls up a casual-chic SoCal ambience. It stays open between lunch and dinner for antipasto platters, hearty salads and crispy pizzas and wine flights at the bar.

Sides Hardware & Shoes AMERICAN $$$
(☑805-688-4820; http://brothersrestaurant.com; 2375 Alamo Pintado Ave; mains lunch $14-18, dinner $26-34; ⊘11am-2:30pm daily, 5-8:30pm Sun-Thu, to 9pm Fri & Sat) Inside a historic storefront, this bistro delivers haute country cooking like 'hammered pig' sandwiches topped by apple slaw, fried chicken with garlicky kale and Colorado lamb sirloin alongside goat-cheese gnocchi. Book ahead for dinner.

Petros GREEK $$$
(☑805-686-5455; www.petrosrestaurant.com; Fess Parker Wine Country Inn & Spa, 2860 Grand Ave; mains lunch $13-20, dinner $16-32; ⊘7am-10pm Sun-Thu, to 11pm Fri & Sat) In a sunny dining room, sophisticated Greek cuisine makes a refreshing change from Italianate wine-country kitsch. Housemade *meze* (appetizers) will satisfy even picky foodies.

🍷 Drinking

Grand Ave and Alamo Pintado Rd are lined with wine and beer tasting rooms, which you can amble between all afternoon long.

Los Olivos Tasting Room WINE BAR
(☑805-688-7406; http://site.thelosolivostastingroom.com; 2905 Grand Ave; tastings $10; ⊘11am-5pm) Inside a rickety 19th-century general store, this tasting room stocks rare vintages you won't find anywhere else. Well-oiled servers are by turns loquacious and gruff, but refreshingly blunt in their opinions about local wines, and pours are generous.

Sarloos + Sons WINE BAR
(☑805-688-1200; http://saarloosandsons.com; 2971 Grand Ave; tastings $10; ⊘11am-5pm Wed-Fri & Sun, to 6pm Sat, last pour 30min before closing) Wine snobs are given the boot at this shabby-chic tasting room pouring estate-grown, small-lot Syrah, grenache noir, pinot noir and sauvignon blanc. Pair your wine flight with a 'cupcake flight' ($10, available Thursday through Sunday).

Carhartt Vineyard Tasting Room WINE BAR
(☑805-693-5100; www.carharttvineyard.com; 2990A Grand Ave; tastings $10; ⊘11am-6pm) An unpretentious tasting room inside a red-trimmed wooden shack leads onto a shady garden patio out back, where a fun-loving younger crowd sips unfussy Syrah, sauvignon blanc and 'Chase the Blues Away' rosé.

🔒 Shopping

Jedlicka's Western Wear CLOTHING, SHOES
(www.jedlickas.com; 2883 Grand Ave; ⊘9am-5:30pm Mon-Sat, 10am-4:30pm Sun) Wranglers and prairie babes should mosey over to Jedlicka's for name-brand boots – Lucchese, Justin and Tony Lama – as well as genuine cowboy hats, jeans and jackets.

Solvang
POP 5345

My God, cap'n, we've hit a windmill! Which can only mean one thing in Wine Country: Solvang, a Danish village founded in 1911 on what was once a 19th-century

LOCAL KNOWLEDGE

CHRIS BURROUGHS: TASTING ROOM MANAGER

Alma Rosa Winery's tasting-room manager is already familiar to moviegoers for his appearance in the 2004 indie hit *Sideways* as – what else? – a cowboy-hat-wearing tasting-room manager. He shared a few smart wine-tasting tips with us.

Novices Never Fear

Don't let a lack of wine savvy keep you away. Winemakers enjoy sharing their passion and knowledge, and beginners are often their favorite guests.

Travel Light

Most tasting rooms aren't equipped for large crowds. Traveling in small groups means you'll have more time to chat with the staff.

Less is More

Don't keep a scorecard on the number of wineries visited. Spend time at only a handful of tasting rooms on any given day. Wine drinking is a social vehicle (not a mobile party crawl).

Be Open-Minded

At most tasting rooms you'll sample six wines: three whites and three reds. Don't tell the staff you never drink Chardonnay – who knows, the wine you try that day may change your mind.

Nice Guys Finish First

Smoking and heavy perfume? Not so considerate of others, and smoking dulls your wine-tasting senses besides. Be friendly, too. I'd rather drink a mediocre bottle of wine with a cool person than special wine with a jerk.

Spanish-colonial mission and later a Mexican *rancho* land grant. This Santa Ynez Valley town holds tight to its Danish heritage, or at least stereotypical images thereof. With its knickknack stores and cutesy motels, the town is almost as sticky-sweet as the Scandinavian pastries foisted upon the wandering crowds of day trippers. Solvang's kitschy charms make it worth visiting if only to gawk.

◉ Sights

Old Mission Santa Ínes　　　CHURCH
(☑ 805-688-4815; www.missionsantaines.org; 1760 Mission Dr; adult/child under 12yr $5/free; ☺ 9am-4:30pm) Off Hwy 246 just east of downtown's Alisal Rd, this historic Catholic mission set the stage for a Chumash revolt against Spanish-colonial cruelty in 1824. Ask for a free (albeit historically biased) audioguide tour of the gardens, small museum and restored church, still an active parish today.

Elverhøj Museum　　　MUSEUM
(www.elverhoj.org; 1624 Elverhoy Way; suggested donation adult/child under 12yr $5/free; ☺ 11am-4pm Wed-Sun) South of downtown, tucked away on residential side streets, the delightful little museum has modest but thoughtful exhibits on Solvang's Danish heritage, as well as Danish culture, art and history.

Wildling Museum　　　MUSEUM
(☑ 805-688-1802; www.wildlingmuseum.org; 1511 Mission Dr; adult/child 6-17yr $5/3; ☺ 11am-5pm Mon & Wed-Fri, from 10am Sat & Sun) Need a break from boozing? This petite art museum exhibits wilderness-themed paintings and photography that may inspire you to go hiking in the mountains outside town.

Hans Christian Andersen Museum　MUSEUM
(2nd fl, 1680 Mission Dr; ☺ 10am-5pm) **FREE** If you remember childhood fairy tales with fondness, stop by this tiny two-room museum where original letters and first-edition copies of the Danish storyteller's illustrated books are on display.

🏃 Activities

Solvang is best known by cyclists for the **Solvang Century** (www.bikescor.com) races in March. For self-guided cycling tours, visit www.solvangusa.com and www.bike-santabarbara.org online and drop by Wheel Fun Rentals (p314), which has a second location in town at 1465 Copenhagen Dr.

🛏 Sleeping

Sleeping in Solvang isn't cheap, not even at older motels with faux-Danish exteriors. On weekends, rates skyrocket and rooms fill fast, so book ahead or make it a day trip.

★ Hamlet Inn
MOTEL **$$**

(☑ 805-688-4413; http://thehamletinn.com; 1532 Mission Dr; r $90-230; ❄ 🐾 🛜) This remodeled motel is to wine-country lodging what IKEA is to interior design: a budget-friendly, trendy alternative. Crisp, modern rooms have bright Danish flag bedspreads and iPod docking stations. Free loaner bicycles and a bocce ball court for guests.

Hadsten House
BOUTIQUE HOTEL **$$**

(☑ 800-457-5373, 805-688-3210; www.hadstenhouse.com; 1450 Mission Dr; r incl breakfast $165-215; ❄ 🛜 🏊) This revamped motel has luxuriously updated just about everything, except for its routine exterior. Inside, rooms are surprisingly plush, with flat-screen TVs, comfy duvets and high-end bath products. Spa suites come with jetted tubs. Rates include a breakfast buffet.

Hotel Corque
HOTEL **$$$**

(☑ 805-688-8000, 800-624-5572; www.hotelcorque.com; 400 Alisal Rd; r $169-350; ❄ @ 🛜 🏊) Downtown, this clean-lined hotel is a relief from all things Danish. Overpriced rooms may look anonymous, but they're quite spacious. Amenities include an outdoor swimming pool and hot tub, plus access to the next-door fitness center, where you can work off all those Danish butter rings.

🍴 Eating

El Rancho Market
SUPERMARKET **$**

(http://elranchomarket.com; 2886 Mission Dr; ⏰ 6am-11pm) East of downtown, this upscale supermarket – with a full deli, smokin' barbecued meats and an espresso bar – is the best place to fill your picnic basket before heading out to the wineries.

Solvang Restaurant
BAKERY **$**

(www.solvangrestaurant.com; 1672 Copenhagen Dr; items from $4; ⏰ 6am-3pm or 4pm Mon-Fri, to 5pm Sat & Sun; 🍴) Duck around the Danish-inscribed beams with decorative borders to order *ableskivers* – round pancake popovers covered in powdered sugar and raspberry jam. They're so popular, there's even a special take-out window.

Solvang Bakery
BAKERY **$**

(www.solvangbakery.com; 438 Alisal Rd; items from $2; ⏰ 7am-6pm Sun-Thu, to 7pm Fri & Sat; 🍴) Tubs of Danish butter cookies and rich almond kringles are popular takeaway treats.

Mortensen's Danish Bakery
BAKERY **$**

(www.mortensensbakery.com; 1588 Mission Dr; ⏰ 7:30am-5:30pm, to 8pm Jun-Aug) Gobble a custardy Danish butter ring, fruit-filled Danish pastry or apple strudel for breakfast.

New Frontiers Natural Marketplace
SUPERMARKET **$**

(https://newfrontiersmarket.com; 1984 Old Mission Dr; ⏰ 8am-8pm Mon-Sat, to 7pm Sun; 🍴) 🌿 To keep things healthy, organic and local, pick up a tasty variety of deli sandwiches, salads and take-out dishes for picnicking.

★ Succulent Café
CALIFORNIAN **$$**

(☑ 805-691-9235; www.succulentcafe.com; 1555 Mission Dr; mains breakfast & lunch $9-13, dinner $19-29; ⏰ breakfast 8:30am-noon Sat & Sun; lunch 11am-3pm Mon & Wed-Fri, to 4pm Sat & Sun; dinner 5:30-9pm Mon & Wed-Sun) 🌿 An inspired menu allows farm-fresh ingredients to speak for themselves at this family-owned gourmet cafe and market. Fuel up on breakfast biscuits stuffed with cinnamon-cumin pork tenderloin and pineapple chutney with bacon gravy, buttermilk-fried chicken salad and artisan grilled-cheese sandwiches for lunch, or pumpkin seed-crusted lamb for dinner. On sunny days, eat outside on the patio.

Root 246
AMERICAN **$$$**

(☑ 805-686-8681; www.root-246.com; 420 Alisal Rd; dinner mains $19-35, brunch buffet per adult/child 6-12yr $27/11; ⏰ 5-9pm Tue-Thu, 5-10pm

---

ⓘ BEST SANTA BARBARA WINERIES FOR PICNICS

You won't have any problem finding picnic fare in Santa Barbara's Wine Country. The region is chock-full of local markets, delis and bakeries serving up portable sandwiches and salads. When picnicking at a winery, remember it's polite to buy a bottle of wine before spreading out your feast.

➜ Beckmen Vineyards (p331)

➜ Sunstone Vineyards & Winery (p332)

➜ Zaca Mesa Winery (p329)

➜ Lincourt Vineyard (p331)

➜ Rancho Sisquoc (p330)

Fri & Sat, 10am-2pm & 5-9pm Sun) 🖋 Next to the Hotel Corque, chef Bradley Ogden's creative farm-to-table cuisine shows an artful touch. It's hard to beat the pastrami short ribs or Sunday brunch buffet. Make reservations or seat yourself in the sleek fireplace lounge to sip California wines by the glass after 4pm.

🍺 Drinking & Entertainment

Sorry, but after dinner this town is deader than an ancient Viking.

Chumash Casino Resort CASINO, LIVE MUSIC
(☑ 800-248-6274; www.chumashcasino.com; 3400 E Hwy 246; ⊙ 24hr) Drive east on Hwy 246 to cutesy Solvang's vice-minded doppelganger, where the slots are plentiful, the cocktails watered-down and the cigarette smoke so thick you could cut it with a Danish butter knife. Get last-minute tickets for concerts by yesterday's pop and rock superstars.

Maverick Saloon BAR
(☑ 805-686-4785; www.mavericksaloon.org; 3687 Sagunto St, Santa Ynez; ⊙ noon-2am Mon-Fri, from 10am Sat & Sun) Off Hwy 246 east of Solvang, the one-horse town of Santa Ynez is home to this Harley-friendly honky-tonk dive bar with live country-and-western and rock bands, dancing and DJs.

🛍 Shopping

Downtown Solvang's notoriously kitschy shops cover a half dozen blocks south of Mission Dr (Hwy 246) between Atterdag Rd and Alisal Rd. For Danish cookbooks, handcrafted quilts and other homespun items, visit the Elverhøj Museum (p334).

Gaveasken GIFTS
(433 Alisal Rd; ⊙ 9:30am-5pm Mon-Sat, from 10am Sun) If decorative Danish plates, elegant silver trays and heart-warming, handmade Christmas ornaments top your shopping list, you'll be crossing off items like mad at 'The Gift Box,' which stocks a primo mix of authentic Scandinavian wares.

Solvang Antique Center ANTIQUES
(http://solvangantiques.com; 1693 Copenhagen Dr; ⊙ 10am-6pm) For truly fine furnishings, antique clocks and music boxes, decorative art and jewelry from around Europe and America, step inside this museum-like emporium.

Book Loft BOOKS
(www.bookloftsolvang.com; 1680 Mission Dr; ⊙ 9am-8pm Tue-Thu, to 9pm Fri & Sat, to 6pm Sun & Mon) Downstairs from the Hans Christian Anderson Museum, this independent bookshop carries antiquarian and Scandinavian titles and children's storybooks.

ℹ Information

Solvang is the busiest hub for wine-country visitors.

Solvang Coffee Company (1680 Mission Dr, Solvang; ⊙ 6am-6pm Sun-Tue, to 7pm Wed-Sat; 🛜) Enjoy wi-fi with your espresso next to the Book Loft and Hans Christian Anderson Museum.

Solvang Conference & Visitors Bureau (☑ 805-688-6144, 800-468-6765; www.solvangusa.com; 1639 Copenhagen Dr, Solvang; ⊙ 9am-5pm) Pick up free tourist brochures and winery maps at this kiosk in the town center, by the municipal parking lot and public restrooms.

Buellton
POP 4905

A mostly humdrum gateway to Santa Barbara's Wine Country, tiny Buellton is best known for the cartoonish landmark towering over the intersection of Hwys 101 and 246: Anderson's Pea Soup Restaurant, where you can get heaping bowls of the green stuff (though we would advise against it).

🛏 Sleeping & Eating

Buellton has slightly less expensive, but more well-worn chain motels and hotels than Solvang, 3 miles further east along Hwy 246.

Ellen's Danish Pancake House BREAKFAST $$
(☑ 805-688-5312; www.ellensdanishpancakehouse.com; 272 Ave of Flags; mains $7-12; ⊙ 6am-8pm Mon-Sat, to 2pm Sun) West of Hwy 101, this old-fashioned, always-busy diner is where locals congregate for the Wine Country's best Danish pancakes, Danish sausages and not-so-Danish Belgian waffles. Breakfast served all day.

Hitching Post II STEAKHOUSE $$$
(☑ 805-688-0676; www.hitchingpost2.com; 406 E Hwy 246; mains $23-50; ⊙ 5-9:30pm; 🅟) As seen in the movie *Sideways*, this dark-paneled chophouse offers oak-grilled steaks, pork ribs, smoked duck breast and rack of lamb. Every old-school meal comes with a veggie tray, garlic bread, shrimp cocktail or soup, salad and potatoes. The Hitching Post makes its own pinot noir, and it's damn good (wine tastings at the bar start at 4pm).

🍸 Drinking & Nightlife

Avant Tapas & Wine WINE BAR
(☑805-686-4742; www.avantwines.com; 35 Industrial Way; ⊙11am-9pm) Hidden upstairs in an industrial-chic space, Avant's Enomatic dispensing system pours tastes of over 30 boutique wines barreled in the warehouse – just walk out onto the catwalk and take a look. Happy hour runs 3pm to 5pm on weekdays.

Figueroa Mountain Brewing Co BREWPUB
(☑805-694-2252; www.figmtnbrew.com; 45 Industrial Way; ⊙4-9pm Mon-Thu, from 11am Fri-Sun) Fig Mountain's original brewpub hosts live-music, comedy and quiz nights. Across the valley in Los Olivos, their cottage taproom also pours tasting samplers of their award-winning brews such as Danish Red Lager and Hoppy Poppy IPA.

ℹ️ Getting There & Around

From Santa Barbara, you can drive to Wine Country in under an hour. Via Hwy 101, it's 45 miles from Santa Barbara to Buellton. Hwy 246 runs east–west from Buellton to Solvang, then across the bottom of the Santa Ynez Valley to Hwy 154. From Santa Barbara, Hwy 154 is a more scenic route; it's fewer miles than taking Hwy 101, but takes longer because the road is often only two lanes wide, with slow-moving traffic. North of Hwy 246, Hwy 154 leads to Los Olivos.

Central Coast Shuttle (☑805-928-1977, 800-470-8818; www.cclax.com) will bus you from LAX to Buellton for $75/138 one way/round-trip, slightly less if you prepay 24 hours in advance. **Amtrak** (☑800-872-7245; www.amtrak.com) provides a couple of daily connecting Thruway buses to and from Solvang, but only if you're catching a train (or arriving on one) in Santa Barbara.

Santa Ynez Valley Transit (☑805-688-5452; www.syvt.com) runs local buses equipped with bike racks on a loop around Buellton, Solvang, Santa Ynez, Ballard and Los Olivos. Buses operate roughly between 7am and 7pm Monday through Saturday; one-way rides cost $1.50 (exact change only).

AROUND SANTA BARBARA

Can't quit your day job to follow your bliss? Don't despair: a long weekend in the mountains, valleys and beaches between Santa Barbara and LA will keep you inspired until you can. In this land of daydreams, perfect waves beckon off Ventura's coast, shady trails wind skyward in the Los Padres National Forest and spiritual Zen awaits you in Ojai Valley. Surf, stroll, seek – if outdoor rejuvenation is your goal, this is the place.

And then there's Channel Islands National Park, a biodiverse chain of islands shimmering just off the coast where you can kayak majestic sea caves, scuba dive in wavy kelp forests, wander fields of wildflower blooms or simply disappear from civilization at a remote wilderness campsite.

Montecito

POP 8965

The well-heeled community of Montecito, just east of Santa Barbara, is like a hitherto-unknown cousin who just inherited the family fortune. This leafy village in the Santa Ynez foothills is not just home to the rich and famous but to the obscenely rich and the uber-famous: it's the type of guarded enclave that would have incited revolutions in eras past.

Though many homes hide behind manicured hedges, a taste of the Montecito lifestyle of yesteryear can be experienced by taking a tour of **Casa del Herrero** (☑805-565-5653; http://casadelherrero.com; 1387 E Valley

---

WORTH A TRIP

LOTUSLAND

In 1941 the eccentric opera singer and socialite Madame Ganna Walska bought the 37 acres that make up **Lotusland** (☑info 805-969-3767, reservations 805-969-9990; www.lotusland.org; 695 Ashley Rd; adult/child 3-18yr $45/20; ⊙tours by appt 10am & 1:30pm Wed-Sat mid-Feb–mid-Nov; ℗) with money from the fortunes she inherited after marrying – and then divorcing – a string of wealthy men. She spent the next four decades tending and expanding this incredible collection of rare and exotic plants from around the world; there are over 120 varieties of aloe alone. Come in summer when the lotuses bloom, typically during July and August. Reservations are required for tours, but the phone is only attended from 9am to 5pm weekdays, 9am to 1pm Saturday.

Rd; 90min tour $20; ⊙10am & 2pm Wed & Sat; Ⓟ), a gorgeously well-preserved 1920s estate built in Spanish-colonial style and bordered by strolling gardens.

Montecito's cafe and boutique-filled main drag is Coast Village Rd (exit Hwy 101 at Olive Mill Rd). **Dressed & Ready** (☑805-565-1253; www.dressedonline.com; 1253 Coast Village Rd; ⊙10am-5pm Mon-Sat, 11am-4pm Sun) are twin couture shops that cater to a star-quality crowd with flirty women's fashions by hand-picked designers. For breakfast or weekend brunch, nab a table on the patio at **Jeannine's** (http://jeannines.com; 1253 Coast Village Rd; mains $9-14; ⊙7am-3pm; ⊕) bakery and cafe, where from-scratch kitchen goodness includes challah French toast with caramelized bananas in Kahlua sauce.

From Santa Barbara, MTD buses 14 and 20 run to and from Montecito ($1.75, 20 minutes, hourly); bus 20 also connects Montecito with Summerland and Carpinteria.

Summerland

POP 1450

This drowsy seaside community was founded in the 1880s by HL Williams, a real-estate speculator. Williams was also a spiritualist, whose followers believed in the power of mediums to connect the living with the dead. Spiritualists were rumored to keep hidden rooms in their homes for séances with the dearly departed – a practice that earned the town the indelicate nickname of 'Spookville.'

Today, those wanting to connect to the past wander the town's antique shops, where you won't find any bargains, but you can ooh and ahh over beautiful furniture, jewelry and art from decades or even centuries gone by. From Hwy 101 southbound, take exit 91 and turn north, then right onto Lillie Ave. To find the beach, turn south off exit 91 instead and cross the railroad tracks to cliffside **Lookout Park** (www.countyofsb. org/parks; Lookout Park Rd; ⊙8am-sunset; ⓢ) FREE, with a kids' playground, picnic tables, barbecue grills and access to a wide, relatively quiet stretch of sand (leashed dogs OK).

Grab breakfast or brunch at the Victorian seaside-style **Summerland Beach Café** (☑805-969-1019; www.summerlandbeachcafe. com; 2294 Lillie Ave; mains $7-14; ⊙7am-3pm Mon-Fri, to 4pm Sat & Sun; ⊕ⓢ), known for its fluffy omelets, and enjoy the ocean breezes on the patio. Or walk over to **Tinker's** (2275 Ortega Hill Rd; items $5-10; ⊙11am-8pm; ⊕), an eat-out-of-a-basket burger shack that delivers seasoned curly fries and old-fashioned milkshakes.

From Santa Barbara, MTD bus 20 runs to Summerland ($1.75, 25 minutes, hourly) via Montecito, continuing to Carpinteria.

Carpinteria

POP 13,230

Lying 11 miles east of Santa Barbara, the time-warped beach of Carpinteria – so named because Chumash tribespeople once built seafaring canoes here – is a laid-back place. You could easily spend an hour or two wandering in and out of antiques shops and beachy boutiques along Linden Ave, downtown's main street. To gawk at the world's largest vat of guacamole, show up for the **California Avocado Festival** (www.avofest. com) in early October.

⊙ Sights & Activities

If you're an expert surfer, **Rincon Point** has long, glassy, right point-break waves. It's about 3 miles southeast of downtown, off Hwy 101 (exit Bates Rd)

Carpinteria State Beach   BEACH
(☑805-968-1033; www.parks.ca.gov; end of Linden Ave; per car $10; ⊙7am-sunset; ⊕) It's an idyllic, mile-long strand where kids splash around in calm waters and go tide-pooling along the shoreline. In winter, you may spot harbor seals and sea lions hauled out on the sand, especially if you hike over a mile south along the coast to a blufftop overlook.

Surf Happens   SURFING
(☑805-966-3613; http://surfhappens.com; 2hr group/private lesson from $110/160; ⊕) Welcoming families, beginners and 'Aloha Surf Sisters,' these highly reviewed classes and weekend camps led by expert staff incorporate the Zen of surfing. In summer, you'll begin your spiritual wave-riding journey off Hwy 101 (exit Santa Claus Ln). Make reservations in advance.

🛏 Sleeping

Carpinteria's cookie-cutter chain motels and hotels are unexciting, but usually less expensive than those just up the road in Santa Barbara.

**Carpinteria State Beach
Campground** CAMPGROUND **$**
(📞 800-444-7275; www.reserveamerica.com; tent
& RV drive-up sites $35-80, hike-and-bike tent sites
$10; 🚐) Often crowded, this oceanfront
campground offers lots of family-friendly
amenities including flush toilets, hot
showers, picnic tables and barbecue grills.
Book ahead.

🍴 Eating & Drinking

Padaro Beach Grill AMERICAN **$**
(3766 Santa Claus Ln; items $3-11; ⊙ usually
10:30am-8pm Mon-Sat, from 11am Sun; 🚐) Off
Hwy 101 west of downtown, this oceanfront
grill makes darn good burgers, grilled fish
tacos, sweet-potato fries and thick, hand-
mixed milkshakes.

Tacos Don Roge MEXICAN **$**
(751 Linden Ave; items from $1.50; ⊙ 10am-9pm)
This Mexican taquería stakes its reputation
on a rainbow-colored salsa bar with up to a
dozen different sauces to drizzle on piquant
meat-stuffed, double-rolled corn tortillas –
try the jalapeño or pineapple versions.

Corktree Cellars CALIFORNIAN **$$**
(📞 805-684-1400; www.corktreecellars.com; 910
Linden Ave; small plates $5-15; ⊙ usually 11:30am-
9pm Tue-Thu, to 10pm Fri & Sat, 10am-9pm Sun)
Downtown's contemporary wine bar and
bistro offers tasty California-style tapas,
charcuterie and cheese plates, and a dizzy-
ing number of wine flights. Neglectful ser-
vice can try diners' patience.

Island Brewing Co BREWERY
(www.islandbrewingcompany.com; 5049 6th St,
off Linden Ave; ⊙ 2-9pm Mon-Fri, from 11am Sat &
Sun; 🐾) Wanna hang loose with beach bums
and drink bourbon barrel-aged brews? Find
this locals-only, industrial space with an
outdoor, dog-friendly patio by the railroad
tracks.

ℹ️ Getting There & Away

Carpinteria is 11 miles east of Santa Barbara
via Hwy 101 (southbound exit Linden Ave,
northbound Casitas Pass Rd). From Santa
Barbara, take MTD bus 20 ($1.75, 45 min-
utes, hourly) via Montecito and Summerland.
Amtrak (📞 800-872-7245; www.amtrak.com;
475 Linden Ave) has an unstaffed platform
downtown; buy tickets online or by phone be-
fore catching one of five daily *Pacific Surfliner*
trains south to Ventura ($11, 25 minutes) or LA
($29, 2¾ hours).

Ojai
POP 7560 / ELEV 745FT
Hollywood director Frank Capra chose the
Ojai Valley to represent a mythical Shangri-
la in his 1937 movie *Lost Horizon*. Today Ojai
('oh-hi', from the Chumash word for 'moon')
attracts artists, organic farmers, spiritual
seekers and anyone ready to indulge in day-
spa pampering. Bring shorts and flip-flops:
Shangri-la sure gets hot in summer.

⊙ Sights & Activities

Inside downtown's historic firehouse, **Ojai
Vineyard** (📞 805-798-3947; www.ojaivineyard.
com; 109 S Montgomery St; tastings $15; ⊙ noon-
5pm) pours tastes of its delicate, small-batch
wines. It's best known for standard-bearing
Chardonnay, pinot noir and Syrah, but the
crisp sauvignon blanc, dry Riesling and zip-
py rosé are also worth sampling. Outside
town, take a free guided tour of the olive or-
chards and sample fruity and herb-infused
oils at family-owned **Ojai Olive Oil Compa-
ny** (📞 805-646-5964; www.ojaioliveoil.com; 1811
Ladera Rd; ⊙ usually hourly tours 1-4pm Wed &
10am-3pm Sat) **FREE**.

For the ultimate in relaxation, book a day
at top-tier **Spa Ojai** (📞 877-597-3731; www.
ojairesort.com/spa-ojai/; Ojai Valley Inn & Spa, 905
Country Club Rd), where non-resort guests
pay an extra $20 to access two swimming
pools, a workout gym and mind/body fitness
classes. Or unwind with an aromatherapy or
hot-rock massage in a hobbitlike cottage at
Day Spa of Ojai (📞 805-640-1100; www.theday-
spa.com; 1434 E Ojai Ave), about a mile east of
downtown.

Running beside the highway, the 9-mile
Ojai Valley Trail, converted from defunct
railway tracks, is popular with walkers,
runners, cyclists and equestrians. Pick it
up downtown two blocks south of Ojai Ave,
then pedal west through the valley. Rent
bikes downtown at the **Mob Shop** (📞 805-
272-8102; www.themobshop.com; 110 W Ojai Ave;
bicycle rental per day $25-50; ⊙ 1-6pm Mon, 10am-
5pm Tue-Fri, 9am-5pm Sat, 9am-4pm Sun).

Gather camping tips and trail maps
for hiking to hot springs, waterfalls and
mountaintop viewpoints in the **Los Pa-
dres National Forest** at the **Ojai Ranger
Station** (📞 805-646-4348; http://www.fs.usda.
gov/lpnf; 1190 E Ojai Ave; ⊙ 8am-4:30pm Mon-Fri)
or on weekends at **Wheeler Gorge Visi-
tors Center** (http://lpforest.org/wheeler; 17017

OJAI'S PINK MOMENT

Ojai is famous for the rosy glow that emanates from its mountains at sunset, the so-called 'Pink Moment.' The ideal vantage point for catching the show is the peaceful lookout atop **Meditation Mount** (https://meditationmount.org; 10340 Reeves Rd; ⊙10am-sunset Wed-Sun) FREE. Head east of downtown on Ojai Ave (Hwy 150) for about 2 miles, turn left at Boccali's farm-stand restaurant and drive another 2.5 miles on Reeves Rd until it dead-ends.

Maricopa Hwy; ⊙9am-3pm Sat & Sun), 8 miles north of Hwy 150 via Hwy 33.

🛏 Sleeping

★ Blue Iguana Inn   INN $$

(☑805-646-5277; www.blueiguanainn.com; 11794 N Ventura Ave; r $129-199, ste from $159, all incl breakfast; 🛋🐾🐾) Artsy iguanas lurk everywhere at this funky architect-designed inn – on adobe walls around Mediterranean-tiled fountains and anywhere else that reptilian style could bring out a smile. Roomy bungalow and cottage suites are unique, and the pool is a social scene for LA denizens. Rates include continental breakfast; two-night minimum stay on weekends. Some pets allowed with prior approval only.

For a more romantic atmosphere, try the sister Emerald Iguana Inn, just north of downtown.

Ojai Retreat   B&B $$

(☑805-646-2536; www.ojairetreat.com; 160 Besant Rd; d incl breakfast $99-299; 🐾@🛋) On a hilltop on the outskirts of town, this peaceful nonprofit inn has a back-to-nature collection of remodeled, country Arts and Crafts–style guest rooms and cottage suites, all perfect for unplugging. Find a quiet nook for reading or writing, ramble through the woods or practice your downward dog in a yoga class. Rates include a healthy breakfast buffet.

Ojai Rancho Inn   MOTEL $$

(☑805-646-1434; http://ojairanchoinn.com; 615 W Ojai Ave; r $120-200; 🐾🛋🐾🐾) At this low-slung motel next to the highway, pine-paneled rooms each have a king bed. Cottage rooms come with fireplaces, and some have Jacuzzi tubs and kitchenettes. Besides competitive rates, the biggest bonuses of staying here are a small pool and sauna, shuffleboard, fire pit and bicycles to borrow for the half-mile ride to downtown. Pet fee $20.

Ojai Valley Inn & Spa   RESORT $$$

(☑855-697-8780, 805-646-1111; www.ojairesort.com; 905 Country Club Rd; r from $329; 🐾@ 🛋🐾🐾) At the west end of town, this pampering resort has landscaped gardens, tennis courts, swimming pools, a championship golf course and a fabulous spa. Luxurious rooms are outfitted with all mod cons, and some sport a fireplace and balcony. Recreational activities run the gamut from kids' camps and bike rentals to full-moon yoga and astrological readings. Nightly 'service' surcharge $25.

🍴 Eating

Ojai Certified Farmers Market   MARKET $

(www.ojaicertifiedfarmersmarket.com; 300 E Matilija St; ⊙9am-1pm Sun; 🚗🐾) 🌿 Mingle with Ojai's bohemians at this rain-or-shine farmers market, where you'll find eggs, oils, jams, homemade bread and locally grown, organic-certified fruit, nuts and vegetables.

Farmer & the Cook   MEXICAN, VEGETARIAN $$

(http://farmerandcook.com; 339 W Roblar Ave; mains $7-14; ⊙8am-8:30pm; 🚗🐾) 🌿 The flavorful goodness of organic, homemade Mexican cooking bursts out of this tiny roadside market, which has its own farm nearby. Come for the squash and goat cheese tacos with fresh corn tortillas, saucy huevos rancheros or at dinner on weekends, creative pizzas and a salad bar.

Boccali's   ITALIAN $$

(☑805-646-6116; http://boccalis.com; 3277 Ojai-Santa Paula Rd; mains $10-18; ⊙4-9pm Mon & Tue, from noon Wed-Sun; 🐾) This roadside farm stand with red-and-white-checkered tablecloths does simple Italian cooking. Much of the produce is grown behind the restaurant, and the fresh tomato salad is often still warm from the garden. The real draw is wood oven-baked pizzas, which take time to make. No credit cards. It's over 2 miles east of downtown via Ojai Ave.

Hip Vegan VEGETARIAN **$$**
(www.hipvegancafe.com; 928 E Ojai Ave; mains $9-13; ⊙11am-5pm; 🖉🚼) 🖉 Tucked back from the street in a tiny garden, this locals' kitchen stays true to Ojai's granola-crunchy hippie roots with sprout-filled wraps, raw salads, fake-meat Reuben sandwiches and classic SoCal date shakes.

Knead BAKERY, CAFE **$$**
(http://kneadbakingcompany.com; 469 E Ojai Ave; items $3-16; ⊙8am-4pm Wed-Sun) Family-run artisan bakery mixes batters with the best of Ojai's fresh fruit, herbs, honey and nuts. Get a slice of a sweet tart or savory quiche, or a made-to-order breakfast sandwich. No credit cards.

🛍 Shopping

Arcade Plaza, a maze of Mission Revival-style buildings on Ojai Ave (downtown's main drag), is stuffed with gifty boutiques.

Bart's Books BOOKS
(www.bartsbooksojai.com; 302 W Matilija St; ⊙9:30am-sunset) One block north of Ojai Ave, this unique indoor-outdoor space sells new and well-loved tomes. It demands at least a half-hour's browse – just don't step on the lurking but surprisingly nimble cat.

Ojai Clothing CLOTHING
(http://ojaiclothing.com; 325 E Ojai Ave; ⊙noon-5pm Mon & Wed-Thu, noon-5:30pm Fri, 10am-5:30pm Sat, 11am-5pm Sun) Equally comfy for doing an interpretive dance or just hanging out, these earth-toned and vibrantly patterned casual pieces for women and men are made from soft cotton knits and woven fabrics.

Human Arts Gallery ARTS & CRAFTS
(www.humanartsgallery.com; 246 E Ojai Ave; ⊙11am-5pm Mon-Fri, to 6pm Sat, noon-5pm Sun) Browse the colorful handmade jewelry, sculpture, woodcarvings, glassworks, folk-art furnishings and more.

Soul Centered GIFTS, BOOKS
(www.soulcentered.com; 311 N Montgomery St; ⊙10:30am-6pm) A 'metaphysical shoppe' echoes Ojai's hippie-dippie vibe with healing crystals, dream therapy and magic books.

ℹ Information

Ojai Valley Chamber of Commerce (📞805-646-8126; www.ojaichamber.org; 206 N Signal St; ⊙9am-4pm Mon-Fri) Pick up free tourist maps and brochures here.

Ojai Library (111 E Ojai Ave; ⊙10am-8pm Mon-Thu, noon-5pm Fri-Sun) Free online computer terminals for public use.

ℹ Getting There & Away

Ojai is 33 miles east of Santa Barbara via scenic Hwy 150, or 15 miles inland (north) from Ventura via Hwy 33. On Main St at Ventura Ave in downtown Ventura, catch **Gold Coast Transit** (📞805-487-4222; www.goldcoasttransit.org) bus 16 to downtown Ojai ($1.50, 40 minutes, hourly).

Ventura

POP 107,735

The primary pushing-off point for Channel Island boat trips, the beach town of San Buenaventura may not look to be the most enchanting coastal city, but it has seaside charms, especially on the historic pier and

---

OFF THE BEATEN TRACK

SANTA PAULA

Now calling itself 'the citrus capital of the world,' the small town of Santa Paula once found its treasure in black gold. If you've seen the movie *There Will Be Blood*, loosely based on the Upton Sinclair novel *Oil!*, then you already know that SoCal's early oil boom was a bloodthirsty business. Today the **California Oil Museum** (📞805-933-0076; www.oilmuseum.net; 1001 E Main St; adult/child 6-17yr $4/1; ⊙10am-4pm Wed-Sun) tells the story of Santa Paula's 'black bonanza' with modest historical exhibits that include an authentic 1890s drilling rig and a collection of vintage gas pumps. Afterward take a walk around downtown Santa Paula's historic district, painted with interesting outdoor murals. Pick up a free self-guided walking tour map inside the museum or one block north at the **chamber of commerce** (📞805-525-5561; www.discoversantapaula.com; 200 N 10th St, Santa Paula; ⊙10am-2pm Mon-Fri, gift shop 10am-noon & 1-4pm Mon-Fri, noon-4pm Sat & Sun). Santa Paula is a 16-mile drive east of Ventura or Ojai, at the intersection of Hwys 126 and 150.

downtown along Main St, north of Hwy 101 via California St.

◎ Sights & Activities

South of Hwy 101 via Harbor Blvd, **Ventura Harbor** is the main departure point for boats to Channel Islands National Park.

San Buenaventura State Beach BEACH
(☑805-968-1033; www.parks.ca.gov; enter off San Pedro St; per car $10; ☉dawn-dusk; ⊕) Along the waterfront off Hwy 101, this long white-sand beach is ideal for swimming, surfing or just lazing on the sand. A recreational cycling path connects to nearby **Emma Wood State Beach**, another popular spot for swimming, surfing and fishing.

Mission San Buenaventura CHURCH
(☑805-643-4318; www.sanbuenaventuramission.org; 211 E Main St; adult/child under 18yr $4/1; ☉10am-5pm Mon-Fri, 9am-5pm Sat, 10am-4pm Sun) Ventura's Spanish-colonial roots go back to this last mission founded by Junípero Serra in California. A stroll around the mellow parish church leads you through a garden courtyard and a small museum, past statues of saints, centuries-old religious paintings and unusual wooden bells.

Limoneira FARM
(☑805-525-5541; www.limoneira.com; 1131 Cummings Rd, Santa Paula; tours $20-40; ☉call for hrs) ☞ A 20-minute drive from downtown, this working farm lets you get up close to sniff the fruit Ventura is most famous for growing: lemons. Drop by the historical ranch store and play bocce outside, or book ahead for a guided tour of the modern packing house and sea-view orchards.

Museum of Ventura County MUSEUM
(☑805-653-0323; http://venturamuseum.org; 100 E Main St; adult/child 6-17yr $5/1; ☉11am-5pm Tue-Sun) This tiny downtown museum has a mishmash of displays including Chumash baskets, vintage wooden surfboards and a massive stuffed California condor with wings outspread. Temporary exhibits usually spotlight local history and art.

⌂ Sleeping & Eating

Midrange motels and high-rise beachfront hotels cluster off Hwy 101 in Ventura. For better deals, keep driving on Hwy 101 southbound about 15 miles to Camarillo, where chain lodgings abound.

In downtown Ventura, Main St is chockablock with Mexicali taco shops, casual cafes and globally flavored kitchens.

Ventura Certified Farmers Market MARKET $
(http://vccfarmersmarkets.com; cnr Santa Clara & Palm Sts; ☉8:30am-noon Sat; ☞⊕) ☞ Over 45 farmers and food vendors show up each week, offering fresh fruits and vegetables, homebaked bread and ready-made meals – Mediterranean, Mexican and more. Another farmers market sets up at midtown's Pacific View Mall from 9am to 1pm on Wednesdays.

Jolly Oyster SEAFOOD $$
(911 San Pedro St; items $5-16; ☉noon-7pm Fri, from 11am Sat & Sun; ⊕) ☞ At San Buenaventura State Beach, this happy-go-lucky seafood shack vends its own farm-raised Kumamoto and Pacific oysters and Manila clams. Seat yourself at picnic tables to shuck 'em raw or cook 'em yourself on barbecue grills. A short menu of tacos, tostadas, ceviche and salads changes weekly. One-hour parking free.

★Lure Fish House SEAFOOD $$$
(☑805-567-4400; www.lurefishhouse.com; 60 S California St; mains lunch $10-22, dinner $15-33; ☉11:30am-9pm Sun-Tue, to 10pm Wed-Thu, to 11pm Fri & Sat; ⊕) ☞ For seafood any fresher, you'd have to catch it yourself off Ventura pier. Go nuts ordering off a stalwart menu of sustainably caught seafood, organic regional farm produce and California wines. Make reservations or turn up at the bar during happy hour (4pm to 6pm Monday to Friday, 11:30am to 6pm Sunday) for strong cocktails, fried calamari and charbroiled oysters.

♟ Drinking & Nightlife

You'll find plenty of rowdy dives down by the harbor.

Surf Brewery BREWERY
(☑805-644-2739; http://surfbrewery.com; suite A, 4561 Market St; ☉4-9pm Tue-Thu, from 1pm Fri, noon-9pm Sat, noon-7pm Sun) Ventura's newest microbrewery makes big waves with its hoppy and black IPAs and rye American pale ale. Beer geeks and food trucks gather at the sociable taproom in an industrial area, about 5 miles from downtown (take Hwy 101 southbound, exit Donlon St).

Wine Rack WINE BAR
(☑805-653-9463; http://thewineracklounge.com; 14 S California St; ☉2-10pm Tue-Thu, to midnight Fri, noon-midnight Sat, noon-6pm Sun) At this upbeat wine shop, novices can sidle up to

the bar for a wine flight, loiter over a cheese plate, flatbread pizza or fondue and listen to live music Thursday to Saturday nights.

🔒 Shopping

B on Main   GIFTS
(www.bonmain.com; 337 E Main St; ⊙10:30am-6pm Mon-Fri, 10am-8pm Sat, 11am-5pm Sun) For coastal living, B sells nifty reproductions of vintage surf posters, shabby-chic furnishings, SoCal landscape art, locally made jewelry and beachy clothing for women.

Ormachea   JEWELRY
(www.ormacheajewelry.com; 451 E Main St) Run by a third-generation Peruvian jewelry craftsman, Ormachea skillfullly hammers out one-of-a-kind, handmade rings, pendants and bangles in a downtown studio.

ARC Foundation Thrift Store   VINTAGE
(www.arcvc.org; 265 E Main St; ⊙9am-6pm Mon-Sat, 10am-5pm Sun) Loads of thrift stores, antiques malls and secondhand and vintage shops cluster downtown. Most are on Main St, west of California St, where ARC is always jam-packed with bargain hunters.

Rocket Fizz   FOOD & DRINK
(www.rocketfizz.com; 105 S Oak St; ⊙10:30am-7pm Sun-Thu, to 9pm Fri & Sat) Retro-style soda pop and old-fashioned candy store is genius for stocking your cooler before a day at the beach.

Camarillo Premium Outlets   MALL
(www.premiumoutlets.com/camarillo; 740 E Ventura Blvd, Camarillo; ⊙10am-9pm Mon-Sat, to 8pm Sun) For steeply discounted designer duds, from LA's Kitson to Nike, Neiman Marcus and North Face, drive about 20 minutes from Ventura on Hwy 101 southbound.

ℹ Information

Ventura Visitors & Convention Bureau
(☑805-648-2075, 800-483-6214; www.ventura-usa.com; 101 S California St; ⊙9-5pm Mon-Sat, 10am-4pm Sun Mar-Oct, till 4pm daily Nov-Feb) Downtown visitor center hands out free maps and tourist brochures.

ℹ Getting There & Away

Ventura is about 30 miles southeast of Santa Barbara via Hwy 101. **Amtrak** (☑800-872-7245; www.amtrak.com; Harbor Blvd at Figueroa St) operates five daily trains north to Santa Barbara ($15, 45 minutes) via Carpinteria and south to LA ($24, 2¼ hours). Amtrak's platform station is unstaffed; buy tickets in advance online or by phone. **Vista** (☑800-438-1112; www.goventura. org) runs several daily 'Coastal Express' buses between downtown Ventura and Santa Barbara ($3, 40 to 70 minutes) via Carpinteria; check online or call for schedules.

Channel Islands National Park

Don't let this off-the-beaten-path **national park** (www.nps.gov/chis) FREE loiter for too long on your lifetime to-do list. It's easier to access than you might think, and the payoff is immense. Imagine hiking, kayaking, scuba diving, camping and whale-watching, and doing it all amid a raw, end-of-the-world landscape. Rich in unique species of flora and fauna, tide pools and kelp forests, the islands are home to 145 plant and animal species found nowhere else in the world, earning them the nickname 'California's Galapagos.'

Geographically, the Channel Islands are an eight-island chain off the Southern California coast, stretching from Santa Barbara

---

CALIFORNIA'S CHANNEL ISLANDS: PARADISE LOST & FOUND

Human beings have left a heavy footprint on the Channel Islands. Livestock overgrazed, causing erosion, and rabbits fed on native plants. The US military even used San Miguel as a practice bombing range. In 1969 an offshore oil spill engulfed the northern islands in an 800-sq-mile slick, killing off uncountable seabirds and mammals. Meanwhile, deep-sea fishing has caused the destruction of three-quarters of the islands' kelp forests, which are key to the marine ecosystem.

Despite past abuses, the future isn't all bleak. Brown pelicans – decimated by the effects of DDT and reduced to one surviving chick on Anacapa Island in 1970 – have rebounded. On San Miguel Island, native vegetation has returned a half century after overgrazing sheep were removed. On Santa Cruz Island, the National Park Service and the Nature Conservancy have implemented multiyear plans to eliminate invasive plants and feral pigs, and hopefully their recovery efforts will meet with success.

ISLAND OF THE BLUE DOLPHINS

For bedtime reading aloud around the campfire, pick up Scott O'Dell's Newberry Medal–winning *Island of the Blue Dolphins*. This children's novel was inspired by the true life story of a Native American girl left behind on San Nicolas Island during the early 19th century, when indigenous people were forced off the Channel Islands. Incredibly the girl survived mostly alone on the island for 18 years, living in a whale-bone hut and sourcing water from a spring, before being rescued in 1853. However, fate was still not on her side: she died just seven weeks after being brought to the mainland. Today her body lies buried in the graveyard at Mission Santa Barbara, where a commemorative plaque is inscribed with her Christian baptismal name, Juana María.

to San Diego. Five of them – San Miguel, Santa Rosa, Santa Cruz, Anacapa and tiny Santa Barbara – comprise Channel Islands National Park. Originally the islands were inhabited by Chumash tribespeople, who were forced to move to mainland Catholic missions by Spanish military forces in the early 1800s. The islands were subsequently taken over by Mexican and American ranchers during the 19th century and the US military in the 20th, until conservation efforts began in the 1970s and '80s.

Sights & Activities

Anacapa and Santa Cruz, the park's most popular islands, are within an hour's boat ride of Ventura. Anacapa is a doable day trip, while Santa Cruz is better suited for overnight camping. Bring plenty of water, because none is available on either island except at Scorpion Ranch Campground on Santa Cruz.

Most visitors arrive during summer, when island conditions are hot, dusty and bone-dry. Better times to visit are during the spring wildflower bloom or in early fall, when the fog clears. Winter can be stormy, but it's also great for wildlife-watching, especially whales.

Before you shove off from the mainland, stop by Ventura Harbor's NPS Visitor Center (p346) for educational natural history exhibits, a free 25-minute nature film and on weekends and holidays, family-friendly activities and ranger talks.

Anacapa Island

Actually three separate islets totaling just over 1 sq mi, Anacapa gives a memorable introduction to the islands' ecology. It's the best option if you're short on time. Boats dock year-round on the East Island and after a short climb, you'll find 2 miles of trails offering fantastic views of island flora, a historic lighthouse, and rocky Middle and West Islands. Kayaking, diving, tide-pooling and watching seals and sea lions are popular activities here. Inside the small museum at the island's visitors center, scuba divers with video cameras occasionally broadcast images to a TV monitor you can watch during spring and summer.

Santa Cruz Island

Santa Cruz, the largest island at 96 sq miles, claims two mountain ranges and the park's tallest peak, Mt Diablo (2450ft). The western three-quarters of Santa Cruz is mostly wilderness owned and managed by the **Nature Conservancy** (www.nature. org) and it can only be accessed with a permit (apply online at www.nature.org/cruzpermit). However, the remaining eastern quarter, managed by the National Park Service (NPS), packs a wallop – ideal for those wanting an action-packed day trip or a more laid-back overnight trip. You can swim, snorkel, scuba dive and kayak. Rangers meet incoming boats at Scorpion Anchorage, a short walk from historic **Scorpion Ranch**.

There are rugged hikes too, which are best not attempted at midday as there's little shade. It's a 1-mile climb to captivating **Cavern Point**. Views don't get much better than from this windy spot. For a longer jaunt, continue 1.5 miles west mostly along scenic bluffs to **Potato Harbor**. From Scorpion Anchorage, the 4.5-mile **Scorpion Canyon Loop** heads uphill to an old oil well for fantastic views, then drops through Scorpion Canyon to the campground. Alternatively, follow Smugglers Rd all the way to the cobblestone beach at **Smugglers Cove**, a strenuous 7.5-mile round-trip from Scorpion Anchorage.

Other Islands

The Chumash called **Santa Rosa** 'Wima' (driftwood) because of the redwood logs that often came ashore here, with which they built plank canoes called *tomols*. This 84-sq-mile island has rare Torrey pines, sandy beaches and hundreds of plant and bird species. Beach, canyon and grasslands hiking trails abound, but high winds can make swimming, diving and kayaking tough for anyone but experts.

While 14-sq-mile **San Miguel** can guarantee solitude and a remote wilderness experience, it's often windy and shrouded in fog. Some sections are off-limits to prevent disruption of the island's fragile ecosystem, which includes a caliche forest (containing hardened calcium-carbonate castings of trees and vegetation) and seasonal colonies of seals and sea lions.

Santa Barbara, only 1 sq mile in size and the smallest of the islands, is a jewel-box for nature lovers. Big, blooming coreopsis, cream cups and chicory are just a few of the island's memorable plant species. You'll also find the humongous northern elephant seal here as well as Scripps's murrelets, a bird that nests in cliff crevices. Get more information from the island's small visitor center.

Tours

Most trips require a minimum number of participants, and may be canceled due to high surf or weather conditions.

Island Packers　　　　　　CRUISE
(☎805-642-1393; www.islandpackers.com; 1691 Spinnaker Dr, Ventura; 3hr cruise adult/child 3-12yr from $36/26) Offers wildlife cruises year-round, including seasonal whale-watching excursions from late December to mid-April (gray whales) and mid-May through mid-September (blue and humpback whales).

Santa Barbara Adventure Company　　　　　KAYAKING
(☎805-884-9283, 877-885-9283; www.sbadventureco.com; 32 E Haley St, Santa Barbara; ▣) This family-friendly outfitter runs a variety of guided paddling tours, from the sea caves of Santa Cruz to the sea arches of Anacapa. Choose from day trips ($180 to $210) or overnight camping expeditions (from $329).

Channel Islands Outfitters　　　KAYAKING, SNORKELING
(☎805-899-4925; www.channelislandso.com; 117b Harbor Way, Santa Barbara) Expertly guided kayaking and snorkeling trips visit Anacapa, Santa Cruz or Santa Barbara ($99 to $225, plus ferry tickets); wetsuits are included.

Truth Aquatics　　　　　DIVING, KAYAKING
(☎805-962-1127; www.truthaquatics.com; 301 W Cabrillo Blvd, Santa Barbara) Based in Santa Barbara, this long-running outfitter organizes diving, kayaking and hiking day trips and multiday excursions aboard specially designed dive boats. See website for prices.

Raptor Dive Charters　　　　　DIVING
(☎805-650-7700; www.raptordive.com; 1559 Spinnaker Dr, Ventura) For certified and experienced divers, boat trips to Anacapa and Santa Cruz, including night dives, cost $110 to $125; equipment rentals available for a surcharge.

Aquasports　　　　　　　　KAYAKING
(☎800-773-2309, 805-968-7231; www.islandkayaking.com) Led by naturalist guides, day and overnight kayaking trips to Santa Cruz, Anacapa and Santa Barbara ($125 to $245, plus ferry tickets) leave from Ventura Harbor.

Channel Islands Kayak Center　　KAYAKING
(☎805-984-5995; www.cikayak.com; 1691 Spinnaker Dr, Ventura; ☺by appt only) Book ahead to rent kayaks (single/double per day $35/55)

CHANNEL ISLANDS NATIONAL PARK CAMPGROUNDS

CAMPGROUND	NUMBER OF SITES	ACCESS FROM BOAT LANDING	DESCRIPTION
Anacapa	7	0.5-mile walk with over 150 stairs	High, rocky, sun-exposed and isolated
Santa Cruz (Scorpion Ranch)	31	Flat 0.5-mile walk	Popular with groups; often crowded and partly shady
Santa Barbara	10	Steep 0.25-mile walk uphill	Large, grassy and surrounded by trails
San Miguel	9	Steep 1-mile walk uphill	Windy, often foggy with volatile weather
Santa Rosa	15	Flat 1.5-mile walk	Eucalyptus grove in a windy canyon

ℹ CHANNEL CROSSINGS

The open seas on the boat ride out to the Channel Islands may feel choppy to landlubbers. To avoid seasickness, sit outside on the upper deck, away from the diesel fumes in back. The outbound trip is typically against the wind and a bit bumpier than the return. Over-the-counter motion-sickness pills (eg Dramamine) can make you drowsy. Staring at the horizon may help. Boats usually brake when dolphins or whales are spotted – always a welcome distraction from any nausea.

or arrange a private guided kayaking tour of Santa Cruz or Anacapa (from $200 per person, two-person minimum).

🛏 Sleeping

Each island has a primitive year-round **campground** (🖉 reservations 877-444-6777; www.recreation.gov; tent sites $15) with pit toilets and picnic tables. Water is only available on Santa Rosa and Santa Cruz Islands. You must pack everything in and out, including trash. Due to fire danger, campfires aren't allowed, but enclosed gas campstoves are OK. Advance reservations are required for all island campsites.

ℹ Information

NPS Visitor Center (🖉 805-658-5730; www.nps.gov/chis; 1901 Spinnaker Dr, Ventura; ⊙8:30am-5pm; 🖪) Trip-planning information, books and maps are available on the mainland at the far end of Ventura Harbor.

ℹ Getting There & Away

You can access the national park by taking a boat from Ventura or Oxnard or a plane from Camarillo. Trips may be canceled anytime due to high surf or weather conditions. Reservations are essential for weekends, holidays and summer trips.

Island Packers (🖉 805-642-1393; www.islandpackers.com; 1691 Spinnaker Dr, Ventura; round-trip fare adult/child 3-12yr from $59/41) From Ventura Harbor and Oxnard, Island Packers offers regularly scheduled boat service to all islands. Day trips to Anacapa and Santa Rosa are less expensive than visiting other islands; campers pay an additional surcharge. Be forewarned: if you camp overnight and seas are rough the following day, you could get stuck for an extra night or more.

Channel Islands Aviation (🖉 805-987-1301; www.flightstothechannelislands.com; 305 Durley Ave, Camarillo) If you're prone to seasickness, you can take a 25-minute scenic flight to Santa Rosa Island from Camarillo. Half-day packages (per person $160 to $220) include hiking or a guided 4WD tour, while overnight camping excursions (per person $300) are more DIY. Ask about surf-fishing charter trips.

Los Angeles

Best Places to Eat

➜ Bestia (p368)

➜ Sushi Gen (p368)

➜ Fishing with Dynamite (p355)

➜ Bar Ama' (p369)

➜ Elf Cafe (p370)

Best Places to Stay

➜ Palihouse (p367)

➜ Chateau Marmont (p364)

➜ Terranea (p355)

➜ Ace Hotel (p363)

➜ Vibe Hotel (p363)

Why Go?

LA runs deeper than her blonde beaches, bosomy hills and ubiquitous beemers would have you believe. She's a myth. A beacon for countless small-town dreamers, rockers and risk-takers, an open-minded angel who encourages her people to live and let live without judgment or shame. She has given us Quentin Tarantino, Jim Morrison and Serena and Venus Williams, spawned skateboarding and gangsta rap, popularized implants, electrolysis and Spandex, and has nurtured not just great writers, performers and directors, but also the ground-breaking yogis who first brought Eastern wisdom to the Western world.

LA is best defined by those simple life-affirming moments. A cracked-ice, jazz-age cocktail on Beverly Blvd, a hike high into the Hollywood Hills sagebrush, a swirling pod of dolphins off Point Dume, a pink-washed sunset over a thundering Venice Beach drum circle, the perfect taco. And her night music. There is always night music.

When to Go
Los Angeles

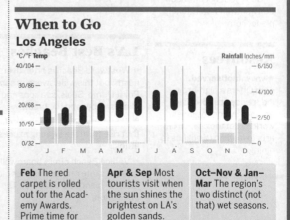

Feb The red carpet is rolled out for the Academy Awards. Prime time for celeb-spotting.

Apr & Sep Most tourists visit when the sun shines the brightest on LA's golden sands.

Oct–Nov & Jan–Mar The region's two distinct (not that) wet seasons.

DON'T MISS

On a balmy summer evening, there are few better places to find yourself than at art deco Dodger Stadium (p376), where the sunsets are stunning, the beer cold, the crowd passionate and the ball club a consistent winner.

Fast Facts: LA County

➤ **Population** 9,963,000

➤ **Area** 4,060 sq miles

➤ **Major movie studios** six

➤ **Unsold screenplays** countless

Planning Your Trip

Think about what you want to see and where you want to hang out, and book accommodation accordingly. We suggest moving around the city, staying for a few nights each in different neighborhoods.

Book your accommodation at http://hotels.lonelyplanet.com.

Resources

➤ **www.laobserved. com** Offers a high-brow, independent and incisive perspective on the inner workings of the city – from arts to fashion to politics to dining.

LA Now

Now is an exciting time to visit LA. Downtown is booming, tech money has turned Santa Monica and Venice into Silicon Beach, and Echo Park and Highland Park bring the Eastside cool. The economy is thriving, and an open and experimental climate energizes the art, architecture, music and fashion scenes, while LA's eclectic palate is challenged and sated by progressive chefs who source from local growers, who flaunt their earthy goods at hundreds of weekly outdoor farmers markets throughout the city.

DON'T MISS

The sheer abundance of world-class musicians within LA's orbit, paired with spectacular and historic venues, make it a minor tragedy to leave town without a concert in the memory files. The Hollywood Bowl, which aside from being the summer home of the LA Philharmonic, has hosted countless legends from Ella to Radiohead. Sitting beneath and among the stars, in a natural bowl tucked into the Hollywood Hills, while music washes over you will make you feel all kinds of glamorous. A second, and only slightly less tasty, summertime venue is the Greek Theatre (p374) – another nature-cupped outdoor amphitheater, which hosts rock and pop acts from MGMT to Gary Clark Jr to Wilco.

The music doesn't stop when the weather turns. The Walt Disney Concert Hall, the winter base for the LA Phil, is an architectural masterwork and also hosts jazz giants.

Acoustic troubadours hold pre-tour residencies at the **Bootleg Theater** (www.bootlegtheater.org; 2220 Beverly Blvd) in Silver Lake, and the recently renovated United Artists Theatre (p374) (adjacent to uber-cool Ace Hotel (p363) downtown), launched with a stirring show by Spiritualized.

LA's Best Beaches

➤ Westward Beach is often overshadowed by Zuma to the north, but this wide sweep of sand rambles all the way to Point Dume. Seals, sea lions and dolphins are frequently glimpsed beyond the break.

➤ El Matador State Beach is defined by sandstone rock spires that rise from the swirling azure sea, and its top-optional ethos.

➤ Venice Beach offers boardwalk, body builders, street ballers, skate rats and hippies old and new peddling goods bizarre, bland and beautiful. The Sunday drum circle is an institution.

⊙ Sights & Activities

⊙ Downtown Los Angeles

Downtown Los Angeles is historical, multi-layered and fascinating. It's a city within a city, blessed with landmark architecture and superb kitchens for all budgets. It's a power nexus with City Hall, the courts and the hall of records, and an ethnic mosaic. Yet just 15 years ago it was still a relative ghost town at night when it was abandoned to the skid-row tramps and addicts, and the ravers who braved the scene for a warehouse or loft party in rickety relics. But today its streets are alive with young professionals, designers and artists who have snapped up stylish lofts in rehabbed art-deco buildings, and the growing gallery district along Main and Spring Sts draws thousands to its monthly art walks. And speaking of art, street art is everywhere. It's as if an entire city has something to say in just a few blocks. Start at **Olvera Street** (Map p352; www.calleolvera.com; 🚇), where the original Mexican city was founded, then stroll from **Little Tokyo** to **Chinatown** (www.chinatownla.com) to the **Fashion District** (Map p352; www.fashiondistrict.org). Don't miss the molten blend of steel music and psychedelic architecture that is Frank Gehry's **Walt Disney Concert Hall** (Map p352; ☑ info 213-972-7211, tickets 323-850-2000; www.laphil.org; 111 S Grand Ave; ⊙ guided tours usually noon & 1pm Tue-Sat; **P**) FREE. **Union Station** (Map p352; ⊙ 6am-6:30pm Mon-Fri) is an architectural classic from a bygone era. **Museum of Contemporary Art** (MOCA; Map p352; ☑ 213-626-6222; www.moca.org; 250 S Grand Ave; adult/child $12/free, 5-8pm Thu free; ⊙ 11am-5pm Mon & Fri, to 8pm Thu, to 6pm Sat & Sun) is downtown's best museum, followed closely by the **Grammy Museum** (Map p352; www.grammymuseum.org; 800 W Olympic Blvd; adult/child $13/11, after 6pm $8; ⊙ 11:30am-7:30pm Mon-Fri, from 10am Sat & Sun; 🚇) in the **LA Live** (Map p352; www.lalive.com; 800 W Olympic Blvd) complex.

⊙ Hollywood

Dear sweet Hollywood, the vortex of a global entertainment industry, has some backstory. First, there was the Golden Age, the dawn of motion pictures, when industry strongmen ruled and owned it all. Then the '70s happened, which brought edgy productions even while studios fled in search of more space in Burbank and Studio City. Soon the only 'stars' left were embedded in the sidewalk. Worse, you had to hopscotch around runaways and addicts to see them. In the late '90s the momentum began to shift, and over the next 10 years, big, intelligent dollars, along with a touch of smart design flooded the area and transformed it into what it is today. A gleaming, bustling, gritty, dazzling mosh pit of fun, food and questionable behavior.

★**Hollywood Bowl**   LANDMARK
(www.hollywoodbowl.com; 2301 Highland Ave; rehearsals free, performance costs vary; ⊙ Apr-Sep; **P**) Summers in LA wouldn't be the same without this chill spot for symphonies under the stars, and big-name acts from Baaba Maal and Sigur Rós to Radiohead and Paul McCartney. A huge natural amphitheater, the Hollywood Bowl has been around since 1922 and has great sound.

Hollywood Walk of Fame   LANDMARK
(Map p356; www.walkoffame.com; Hollywood Blvd) Big Bird, Bob Hope, Marilyn Monroe and Aretha Franklin are among the stars being sought out, worshipped, photographed and stepped on along the Hollywood Walk of Fame. Since 1960 more than 2400 performers – from legends to bit-part players – have been honored with a pink-marble sidewalk star.

Grauman's Chinese Theatre   LANDMARK
(Map p356; ☑ 323-463-9576; www.tclchinesetheatres.com; 6925 Hollywood Blvd; tours & movie tickets adult/child/senior $13.50/6.50/11.50) Ever wondered what it's like to be in George Clooney's shoes? Just find his footprints in the forecourt of this world-famous movie palace. The exotic pagoda theater – complete with temple bells and stone heaven dogs from China – has shown movies since 1927 when Cecil B DeMille's *The King of Kings* first flickered across the screen.

Hollywood Sign   LANDMARK
(Map p358) LA's most famous landmark first appeared in the hills in 1923 as an advertising gimmick for a real-estate development called 'Hollywoodland'. Each letter is 50ft tall and made of sheet metal. Once aglow with 4000 light bulbs, the sign even had its own caretaker who lived behind the 'L' until 1939.

Hollywood Museum   MUSEUM
(Map p356; ☑ 323-464-7776; www.thehollywoodmuseum.com; 1660 N Highland Ave; adult/child $15/5; ⊙ 10am-5pm Wed-Sun) We quite like this musty temple to the stars, crammed with

Los Angeles Highlights

1 Watching surfers carve waves at **Surfrider Beach** (p357) in Malibu.

2 Shopping like a star at **Malibu Country Mart** (p378).

3 Swerving along breathtaking Palos Verdes Drive, then hunting for starfish and anemones in the tide pools of **Abalone Cove Shoreline Park** (p355).

4 Getting your freak on while milling with snake charmers, tarot readers and athletes on the **Venice Boardwalk** (p358).

5 Feeling your spirits soar surrounded by the fantastic art, architecture, views and gardens of the **Getty Center** (p355).

6 Getting gourmet at one of several outstanding **downtown restaurants** (p368).

7 Joining the buff, the famous and their canine companions on a hike through **Runyon Canyon** (p355).

8 Hitting the bars and clubs of **Hollywood** (p373) for a night of tabloid-worthy decadence and debauchery.

kitsch posters, costumes and rotating props. The museum is housed inside the handsome 1914 art-deco Max Factor Building, where the make-up pioneer once worked his magic on Marilyn Monroe and Judy Garland.

Technically, it's illegal to hike up to the sign, but viewing spots are plentiful, including Hollywood & Highland, the top of Beachwood Dr and the Griffith Observatory.

Dolby Theatre THEATER
(Map p356; www.dolbytheatre.com; 6801 Hollywood Blvd; tours adult/child, senior & student $17/12; ☉10:30am-4pm) The Academy Awards are handed out at the Dolby Theatre, which has also hosted the *American Idol* finale, the ESPY awards, the Miss USA pageant and a recent Neil Young residency. On the tour you get to sniff around the auditorium, admire a VIP room and see Oscar up close.

☉ Los Feliz & Griffith Park

Twenty years ago, when Swingers mania tore through LA like a proto-hipster storm, Los Feliz, (mis-) pronounced Fee-lez by the hordes, emerged as LA's next great neighborhood, not least because of the wonderful Griffith Park. A gift to the city in 1896 by mining mogul Griffith J Griffith, and five

Downtown Los Angeles

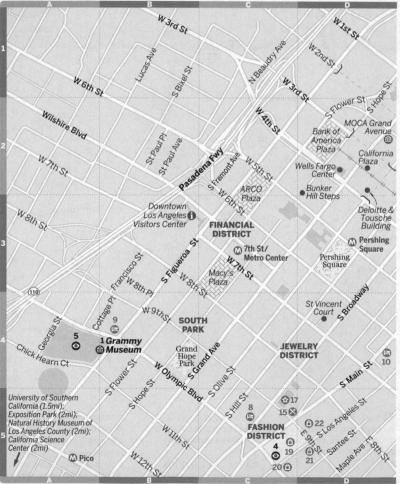

times the size of New York's Central Park, **Griffith Park** (Map p358; ☎ 323-913-4688; www.laparks.org/dos/parks/griffithpk; 4730 Crystal Springs Dr; ⏰ 5am-10:30pm, trails sunrise-sunset; **P** ♿) **FREE** is one of the country's largest urban green spaces. There you'll find a major outdoor theater, the city zoo, two museums, golf courses, playgrounds, 53 miles of **hiking trails**, Batman's caves and the Hollywood sign. It's crowned by the iconic 1935 **Observatory** (Map p358; ☎ 213-473-0800; www. griffithobservatory.org; 2800 E Observatory Rd; admission free, planetarium shows adult/child $7/3; ⏰ noon-10pm Tue-Fri, from 10am Sat & Sun; **P** ♿)

FREE, a first-class planetarium and wonderful Instagram photo-op. Don't miss it.

◉ Silver Lake & Echo Park

Behold the Silver Lake ideal – revitalized modernist homes, groovy bistros, coffeehouses and boutiques patronized by a real community of upwardly mobile, progressive creatives. Which is to say, Silver Lake, a once-gritty Eastside hub has long since gentrified. Rents have soared, working-class Latino families were pushed out and yuppie babies came along with gaggles of Eastside soccer moms pushing jogger strollers

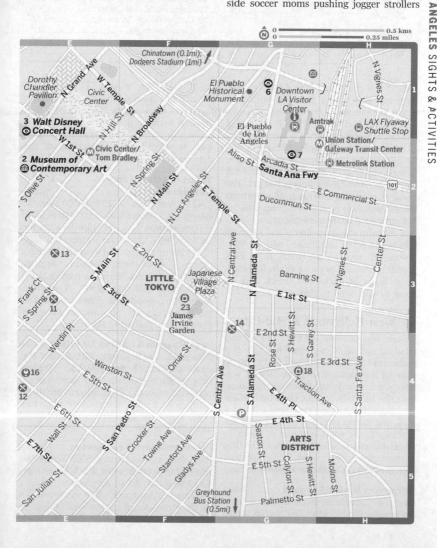

around the reservoir. Silver Lake's terrific shopping and dining are still worthy of praise, yet gone is the grit and the funk.

But you'll find both in Echo Park. One of LA's oldest neighborhoods, it is punctuated by a lake featured in Polanski's *Chinatown,* and for decades has been home to working-class Latinos. The artists and hipsters have arrived, but not in Silver Lake numbers just yet. The *panaderias* and *cevicherias* and lively streets are still here. Let's hope they stick around.

Surrounded by shingled craftsmen homes that rise with the steep streets and looming hills to the north, and blessed with keyhole downtown views to the south, Echo Park Lake is patronized by cool rockers, laid-back vatos, flocks of ducks and crows, and it's home to wild, wind-rustled palms.

⊚ West Hollywood & Mid-City

Upscale and low-rent (but not that low), gay fabulous and Russian-ghetto chic, this is a bastion of LA's fashionista best and home to some of the trashiest shops you'll ever see. Here you can find raw kitchens, bright market cafes and dark-edged tequila bars. Rainbow flags fly proudly over Santa Monica Blvd, and the set piece Sunset Strip still has gravitas. To the south and east of WeHo is an amorphous area we have called Mid-City. It encompasses the groovy Fairfax District with the Farmers Market, and Museum Row.

★ Farmers Market & Around   MARKET
(Map p362; www.farmersmarketla.com; 6333 W 3rd St, Fairfax District; ⊙ 9am-9pm Mon-Fri, to 8pm

Sat, 10am-7pm Sun; P ⟨⟩) **FREE** Long before the city was flooded with farmers markets, there was the Farmers Market. From fresh produce to roasted nuts, to doughnuts to cheeses to blinis – you'll find them, along with wonderful people-watching, at this 1934 landmark. Perfect for families.

★ Los Angeles County
Museum of Art   MUSEUM
(LACMA; Map p362; ☎ 323-857-6000; www.lacma.org; 5905 Wilshire Blvd; adult/child $15/free; ⊙ 11am-5pm Mon, Tue & Thu, to 9pm Fri, 10am-7pm Sat & Sun; P) LA's premier art museum, LACMA's galleries are stuffed with all the major players – Rembrandt, Cézanne, Magritte, Mary Cassat, Ansel Adams, to name a few – plus several millennia worth of ceramics from China, woodblock prints from Japan, pre-Columbian art, and ancient sculpture from Greece, Rome and Egypt.

Page Museum & La Brea Tar Pits   MUSEUM
(Map p362; www.tarpits.org; 5801 Wilshire Blvd; adult/child/student & senior $7/2/4.50; ⊙ 9:30am-5pm; P ⟨⟩) Mammoths and saber-toothed cats used to roam LA's savanna in prehistoric times. We know this because of an archaeological trove of skulls and bones unearthed at La Brea Tar Pits.

Petersen Automotive Museum   MUSEUM
(Map p362; www.petersen.org; 6060 Wilshire Blvd; adult/child/student & senior $15/5/10; ⊙ 10am-6pm Tue-Sun; P) A four-story ode to the auto, the Petersen Automotive Museum reveals LA as the birthplace of gas stations, billboards, drive-in restaurants and drive-in movie

theaters. Glimpse hot rods, movie cars and celebrity-owned rarities.

Ace Gallery   GALLERY
(Map p362; www.acegallery.net; 5514 Wilshire Blvd; ⊙10am-6pm Tue-Sat) An amazing gallery sprawls the entire 2nd floor of the Desmond building (c 1927). The art is all modern-edged works from the likes of Bernar Venet, Gary Lang, Gisele Colon and Peter Alexander.

Sunset Strip   STREET
(Map p362; Sunset Blvd) A visual cacophony of billboards, giant ad banners and neon signs, the sinuous stretch of Sunset Blvd running between Laurel Canyon and Doheny Dr has been nightlife central since the 1920s.

These days, it seems to be coasting on its legacy. The young, hip and fickle have moved west to Abbot Kinney and east to Downtown, leaving the Strip to the cashed-up suburbanites, though midweek and during awards season the celebs still appear.

Runyon Canyon   HIKING
(www.lamountains.com; 2000 N Fuller Ave; ⊙dawn-dusk) A chaparral-draped cut in the Hollywood Hills, this 130-acre public park is as famous for its beautiful, bronzed and buff runners, as it is for the panoramic views from the upper ridge. Follow the wide, partially paved fire road up, then take the smaller track down the canyon where you'll pass the remains of the Runyon estate.

◉ Beverly Hills & the Westside

With its reputation for old-Hollywood glamour, top-end couture and posh dining still circulating in the collective consciousness, Beverly Hills remains impressive to those who stroll Beverly Blvd and Rodeo Drive for the first time.

West and south of Beverly Hills are a string of well-to-do 'hoods that make up LA's Westside, including Westwood, Bel Air, Brentwood and Culver City.

The chief sight in the area is Richard Meier's wonderfully designed **Getty Center** (☑310-440-7300; www.getty.edu; 1200 Getty Center Dr, off I-405 Fwy; ⊙10am-5:30pm Tue-Fri & Sun, to 9pm Sat; ℗) **FREE**, whose five buildings hold collections of manuscripts, drawings,

DON'T MISS

SOUTH BAY BEACHES

This string of beach towns will soothe the big city mess from your psyche in one sunset. It all starts just 15 minutes from the airport with **Manhattan Beach**, a tony town with high-end shopping and dining, and homes stacked high on steep streets because of the sublime stretch of sand and sea out front. USC frat boys and sorority girls, financially challenged surfers and the beautiful boys and girls who love them call **Hermosa Beach** home. The rents are lower here, and the scene trashier, but that's part of the charm. As the coast winds to the south end of Santa Monica Bay you can follow it to diverse **Redondo Beach**, with its signature **pier**, and onto the stunning **Palos Verdes Peninsula**, where you'll find Lloyd Wright's spectacular, glass-walled **Wayfarers Chapel** (☑310-377-1650; www.wayfarerschapel.org; 5755 Palos Verdes Dr S; ⊙10am-5pm; ℗) and the swanky seaside resort, **Terranea** (☑310-265-2800; www.terranea.com; 100 Terranea Way, Palos Verdes; r $350-500, ste $655-2150; ℗@🛜🏊). Also on the peninsula is **Abalone Cove Shoreline Park** (www.palosverdes.com; Palos Verdes Dr; entry per vehicle $5; ⊙9am-4pm; ℗🚹). The best place to hunt for starfish, anemones and other tidepool critters is in and around this rock-strewn eco-preserve. The walk down to the beach gets pretty steep in some sections, so watch your footing.

South Bay gastropubs are a staple. We enjoy **Simmzy's** (www.simmzys.com; 229 Manhattan Beach Blvd; mains $10-14; ⊙11am-1am) in Manhattan Beach and **Abigaile** (☑310-798-8227; www.abigailerestaurant.com; 1301 Manhattan Ave; mains $10-30; ⊙5pm-late Mon-Fri, from 11am Sat & Sun) in Hermosa, but our favorite place to eat is Manhattan Beach's wonderful raw bar, **Fishing with Dynamite** (☑310-893-6299; www.eatfwd.com; 1148 Manhattan Ave; oysters from $2.25, dishes $9-19; ⊙11:30am-10pm Sun-Wed, to 10:30pm Thu-Sat), and the most inventive is **Standing Room** (☑310-374-7575; www.facebook.com/thestandingroomRB; 144 N Catalina Ave, Redondo Beach; burgers & sandwiches $7-14, plates $13-20; ⊙11am-9:30pm Mon-Sat, noon-8pm Sun), a fusion greasy spoon tucked into the back of a Redondo Beach liquor store. Find it.

Hollywood

Hollywood

photographs, furniture, decorative arts and a strong assortment of pre-20th-century European paintings. Must-sees include Van Gogh's *Irises*, Monet's *Wheatstacks*, Rembrandt's *The Abduction of Europa* and Titian's *Venus and Adonis*. Don't miss the lovely Cactus Garden on the remote South Promontory for amazing city views.

Art lovers should also find **Blum & Poe** (www.blumandpoe.com; 2727 S La Cienega Blvd; ☯10am-6pm Tue-Sat) gallery in Culver City and the **Hammer Museum** (Map p366; http://hammer.ucla.edu; 10899 Wilshire Blvd; ☯11am-8pm Tue-Fri, to 5pm Sat & Sun) FREE has one of the great gift shops and is set in Westwood near the **University of California, Los Angeles** (UCLA; Map p366; www.ucla.edu; Ⓟ) campus.

◎ Malibu

Malibu enjoys near-mythical status thanks to its large celebrity population and the incredible beauty of its coastal mountains, pristine coves, wide sweeps of golden sand and epic waves. Stretched out for 27 miles, there are several small commercial strips, but the heart of town is at the foot of Pepper-

dine, where you'll find the Malibu Country Mart and the Malibu Civic Center.

The beach is king, of course, and whether you find a sliver of sand among the sandstone rock towers and topless sunbathers at **El Matador** (32215 Pacific Coast Hwy; parking $8; Ⓟ) or enjoy the wide loamy blonde beaches of **Zuma & Westward**, you'll have a special afternoon. **Topanga Canyon State Park** (www.parks.ca.gov; Entrada Rd; per vehicle $10; ☯8am-dusk) offers 36 miles of hiking trails and the **Getty Villa** (☎310-430-7300; www.getty.edu; 17985 Pacific Coast Hwy; ☯10am-5pm Wed-Mon; Ⓟ) FREE, a replica of a 1st-century Roman villa, is stocked with Greek and Roman antiquities.

Surfrider Beach   BEACH
(26000 Pacific Coast Hwy; Ⓟ) Surf punks descend on this cove that shapes some of the best waves in Southern California. There are several breaks here: the first is well formed for beginners and long boarders, the second and third breaks demand short boards and advanced-level skills. Whichever way you ride, know your etiquette before paddling out.

★**Mishe Mokwa Trail
& Sandstone Peak**   HIKING
(www.nps.gov/samo; 12896 Yerba Buena Rd) On warm spring mornings when the snowy blue *ceonothus* perfumes the air with honeysuckle, there's no better place to be than this 6-mile loop trail that winds through a red-rock canyon, through the oak oasis at **Split Rock** and up to the tallest mountain in the Santa Monica Mountains, Mount Allen, aka Sandstone Peak.

Malibu Surf Shack   SURFING
(www.malibusurfshack.com; 22935 Pacific Coast Hwy; kayaks per day $30, surf boards per day $20-35, SUP per hour/day $45/75, wetsuits per day $10-15, surf/stand-up paddleboard lessons per person $125/100; ☯10am-6pm) This barefoot surf shop rents (and sells) kayaks, SUP (stand-up paddleboard) kits and surfboards. Surf and SUP lessons take place on Surfrider beach, last 90 minutes and include a full day's rental of the board and wetsuit. The paddling between here and Point Dume is excellent, with frequent dolphin and sea-lion sightings.

◎ Santa Monica

Here's a place where real-life Lebowskis sip white Russians next to martini-swilling Hollywood producers, and celebrity chefs and soccer mom's shop shoulder to shoulder at

Griffith Park & Around

abundant farmers markets. It's a small city with forward-thinking social and environmental ideals (and fascist parking codes) alive with surf rats, skate punks, string bikinis, yoga freaks, psychics, street performers and a prodigious homeless population. Most, if not all, of which can be found along a stretch of sublime coastline that cradles the city to the west, and laps at the heels of an undulating mountain range that defines the entire LA area to the north. This is Santa Monica – LA's hippie-chic little sister, its karmic counterbalance and, to many, its salvation.

Once the very end of the mythical Route 66, and still a tourist love affair, the **Santa Monica Pier** (Map p368; ☑ 310-458-8900; www. santamonicapier.org; 🚻) dates back to 1908, is stocked with rides and arcade games and blessed with spectacular views, and is the city's most compelling landmark. After a stroll on the pier, hit the **beach** (Map p368; ☑ 310-458-8411; http://www.smgov.net/portals/ beach/; 🚍 BBB 1). We like the stretch just north of Ocean Park Blvd. Or rent a bike or some skates from **Perry's Cafe** (Map p368; ☑ 310-939-0000; www.perryscafe.com; Ocean Front Walk; mountain bikes & Rollerblades per hr/day $10/30, bodyboards per hr/day $7/17; ☉ 9:30am-5:30pm) and explore the 22-mile **South Bay Bicycle Trail**.

👁 Venice

If you were born too late, and have always been jealous of the hippie heyday, come down to the Boardwalk and inhale an incense-scented whiff of Venice, a boho beach town and longtime haven for artists, New Agers, road-weary tramps, freaks and free spirits. This is where Jim Morrison and the Doors lit their fire, where Arnold Schwarzenegger pumped himself to stardom and where the late Dennis Hopper once lived.

The **Venice Boardwalk** (Ocean Front Walk; Map p368; Venice Pier to Rose Ave; ☉24hr), officially known as Ocean Front Walk, is a wacky carnival alive with altered-states hoola-hoop acrobats, old-timey jazz combos, solo distorted garage rockers and artists – good and bad, but as far as LA experiences go, it's a must. Rent a **bike** (Map p368; ☑ 310-396-2453; 517 Ocean Front Walk; per hr/2hr/day bikes $7/12/20, surfboards $10/20/30, skates $7/12/20) and join the parade, glimpse **Muscle Beach** (Map p368; www.musclebeach.net; 1800 Ocean Front Walk; per day $10; ☉8am-7pm May-Sep, to 6pm Oct-Apr) or hit the **Skate Park** (Map p368; 1800 Ocean Front Walk; ☉dawn-dusk). The Sunday afternoon **drum circle** is always wild.

Just a couple of blocks away from the Boardwalk madness is an idyllic neighbor-

LOS ANGELES SIGHTS & ACTIVITIES

hood of eclectic homes laced with 3 miles of the original **canals** (Map p368), built as an homage to the late Abbot Kinney's beloved Venezia. Hence the name.

◉ Long Beach & San Pedro

Over the past two decades, LA's southernmost seaside enclave has reinvented its gritty downtown making it an attractive place to live and party. On any Saturday night the restaurants, clubs and bars along lower Pine Ave and the Promenade, a new upscale loft district, are abuzz with everyone from buttoned-down conventioneers to hipsters to the testosterone-fuelled frat pack. Additional eateries line Shoreline Village, the departure point for boat cruises.

'San Pedro is real quiet,' Bukowski once observed. That's still true today, except for the distant clanging of containers being hoisted on and off gigantic cargo vessels. LA's own 'Golden Gate', the 1500ft-long suspended Vincent Thomas Bridge, links San Pedro with Terminal Island.

Long Beach's most mesmerizing experience, the **Aquarium of the Pacific** (☑ tickets 562-590-3100; www.aquariumofpacific. org; 100 Aquarium Way, Long Beach; adult/child/senior$29/15/26; ☉9am-6pm; ☕) is a vast, high-tech indoor ocean where sharks dart, jellyfish dance and sea lions frolic. The **Queen Mary** (www.queenmary.com; 1126 Queens Hwy, Long Beach; tours adult/child from $26/15; ☉10am-6:30pm; ℗), a supposedly haunted British luxury liner from yesteryear, is another flagship attraction. The special **Museum of Latin American Art** (www.molaa.org; 628 Alamitos Ave, Long Beach; adult/child /student & senior $9/free/6, Sun free; ☉11am-5pm Wed, Thu, Sat & Sun, to 9pm Fri; ℗) is worth seeking out.

◉ San Fernando Valley

Home to most of LA's major movie studios – including Warner Bros, Disney and Universal – 'the Valley' is an exercise in sprawl. Attractions are few and scattered about; Burbank has Disney and **Warner Bros** (Map p358; ☑ 818-972-8687, 877-492-8687; www.wbstudiotour.com; 3400 W Riverside Dr, Burbank; tours from $54; ☉8:15am-4pm Mon-Sat, hours vary Sun), and North Hollywood, west of here, is home to a growing arts scene. Studio City has some superb sushi on Ventura Blvd. At last count there were 21 sushi bars within a six-block radius, which is why some call it LA's Sushi Row. But the chief attraction is the **Universal Studios Hollywood** (Map p358; www.universalstudioshollywood.com; 100 Universal City Plaza, Universal City; admission from $87, under 3yr free; ☉ open daily, hours vary; ℗ ☕) theme park. Here are stage shows, thrill rides, back lot tours and major family fun.

◉ Pasadena

One could argue that there is more blueblood, meat-eating, robust Americana in

Los Feliz & Silver Lake

Los Feliz & Silver Lake

Pasadena than in all other LA neighborhoods combined. Here is a community with a preppy old soul, a historical perspective, an appreciation for art and jazz and a slightly progressive undercurrent.

The Rose Parade and **Rose Bowl** (☎ 626-577-3100; www.rosebowlstadium.com; 1001 Rose Bowl Dr, Pasadena) football game may have given Pasadena its long-lasting fame, but it's the spirit of this genteel city and its location beneath the lofty San Gabriel Mountains

that make it a charming and attractive place year-round. Don't miss the **Huntington Library** (☎ 626-405-2100; www.huntington.org; 1151 Oxford Rd, San Marino; adult weekday/weekend & holidays $20/23, child $8, 1st Thu each month free; ◷ 10:30am-4:30pm Wed-Mon Jun-Aug, noon-4:30pm Mon & Wed-Fri, from 10:30am Sat, Sun & holidays Sep-May; P), with it's tranquil Zen gardens, **Norton Simon Museum** (www.nortonsimon.org; 411 W Colorado Blvd, Pasadena; adult/child $10/free; ◷ noon-6pm Wed-Mon, to 9pm Fri; P), home to many a masterpiece, and when the **Descanso Gardens** (www.descansogardens.org; 1418 Descanso Dr, La Cañada Flintridge; adult/5-12yr/ student & senior $9/4/6; ◷ 9am-5pm; P) bloom in January and February, they're magic.

The two-lane **Angeles Crest Scenic Byway** (www.byways.org/explore/byways/10245/ travel.html; Hwy 2) treats you to fabulous views of big-shouldered mountains, the Mojave Desert and deep valleys on its 55-mile meander from La Cañada to the resort town of

Wrightwood. The road skirts LA County's tallest mountain, officially called Mt San Antonio (10,064ft), but better known as Old Baldy for its treeless top.

◉ South Central & Exposition Park

South Central LA burst into global consciousness with the rat-a-tat-tat rhythm and rhyme of some of hip-hop's greatest pioneers in the 1980s, and was suddenly defined by its gangs, drugs, poverty, crime and drive-by shootings, which never told the whole story.

After WWII more than five million African Americans left what at the time was a violently racist South and moved to northern cities in the Second Great Migration. Some of those families moved west, from Mississippi, Louisiana and Texas to Los Angeles. They found manufacturing jobs, bought property and built working-class communities south of downtown. Life wasn't perfect, but it was a step up. Fast-forward 30 years and suddenly the high-wage manufacturing jobs dried up, drug addiction soared, families fell apart, guns became accessible, gang violence bloomed, and South Central began to earn its reputation. But recent investment and expanded rail service has helped turn the tide somewhat.

Most folks come for the excellent **Natural History Museum** (☑ 213-763-3466; www.nhm. org; 900 Exposition Blvd; adult/child /student & senior $12/5/9; ☺ 9:30am-5pm; ⊛) and **California Science Center** (☑ film schedule 213-744-2109, info 323-724-3623; www.californiasciencecenter. org; 700 Exposition Park Dr; IMAX movie adult/child $8.25/5; ☺ 10am-5pm; ⊛) **FREE**, home to the recently decommissioned **Space Shuttle Endeavor**. Both are located at **Exposition Park** (www.expositionpark.org; 700 Exposition Park Dr) next door to the **University of Southern California** (USC; ☑ 213-740-6605; www.usc.edu; Exposition Blvd & Figueroa St) **FREE**, where the Trojans play football, George Lucas studied film, and Will Ferrell became, well, Will Ferrell.

For a blast of African American culture find **Leimert Park** (Degnan Blvd & 43rd St). A fun time to visit South Central is during the annual **Pan African Film Festival** (www. paff.org; ☺ February) when filmmakers from across the African diaspora congregate for two weeks each February, and show their films at the **Rave Theaters** (www.baldwin-hillscrenshawplaza.com; 3650 W Martin Luther King Jr Blvd; adult/child $14/7). A wonderful arts and handicrafts bazaar takes over both floors of the attached shopping center as well.

And don't miss the wonderful **Watts Towers** (www.wattstowers.us; 1761-1765 E 107th St; adult/under 12yr/teen & senior $7/free/$3; ☺ 11am-3pm Fri, 10:30am-3pm Sat, 12:30-3pm Sun; ℗), one of the world's great folk-art monuments.

⌖ Tours

★ Esotouric   BUS TOUR
(☑ 323-223-2767; www.esotouric.com; tours $58) Discover LA's lurid and fascinating underbelly on these offbeat, insightful and entertaining walking and bus tours themed around famous crime sites (Black Dahlia anyone?), literary lions (Chandler to Bukowski) and more.

Melting Pot Tours   WALKING TOUR
(☑ 424-247-9666; www.meltingpottours.com; adult/child from $59/45) Duck into aromatic alleyways, stroll through fashionable shopping districts, and explore LA landmarks while tasting some of the city's best ethnic eats in Pasadena, Mid-City and East LA.

Dearly Departed   BUS TOUR
(☑ 1-855-600-3323; www.dearlydepartedtours.com; tours $48-75) This long running, occasionally creepy, frequently hilarious tour will clue you in on where celebs kicked the bucket, George Michael dropped his trousers, Hugh Grant received certain services and the Charles Manson gang murdered Sharon Tate. Not for kids.

TMZ Tours   HOLLYWOOD TOUR
(Map p356; ☑ 855-4TMZ-TOUR; www.tmz.com/tour; 6925 Hollywood Blvd; adult/child $55/45; ☺ approx 10 tours daily) Cut the shame, do you really want to spot celebrities, glimpse their homes, and gawk and laugh at their dirt? Join this branded tour devised by paparazzi who have themselves become famous.

⛏ Festivals & Events

From the Rose Parade to the Hollywood Christmas Parade, from the Oscars to the *LA Times* Festival of Books, from the progressive, hard-rocking Sunset Junction street fair to the candy-colored mayhem of Halloween in WeHo, LA has its share of annual festivities.

Rose Parade   PARADE
(www.tournamentofroses.com) A cavalcade of flower-festooned floats snakes through Pasadena on New Year's Day. Get close-ups during post-parade viewing at Victory Park. Avoid traffic and take the Metro Rail Gold Line to Memorial Park.

West Hollywood & Mid-City

Toyota Grand Prix of Long Beach SPORTS (www.gplb.com) World-class drivers tear up city streets at this week-long racing spectacle by the sea.

Fiesta Broadway CARNIVAL (http://fiestabroadway.la) One of the world's largest Cinco de Mayo parties brings half a million folks to Downtown LA; in 2014 it was held in late April. See website for details.

🛏 Sleeping

🛏 Downtown Los Angeles

Stay
HOTEL, HOSTEL **$**

(Map p352; ☏213-213-7829; www.stayhotels.com; 640 S Main St; dm $39, r $89; 🅿@📶❄) Formerly the Hotel Cecil, Stay has marble floors and shared baths, retro furnishings and bedspreads, iPod docks and accent walls. Gleaming shared baths serve just two dorm rooms each and include showers hewn from marble. Rooms all have private baths.

Figueroa Hotel
HISTORIC HOTEL **$$**

(Map p352; ☏800-421-9092, 213-627-8971; www.figueroahotel.com; 939 S Figueroa St; r $148-184, ste $225-265; 🅿❄@📶❄) It's hard not to be charmed by this rambling owner-operated oasis. Global-chic rooms blend Moroccan mirrors, Iraqi quilts and Kurdish grain-sack floor cushions, with paper lanterns from Chinatown.

Ace Hotel
HOTEL **$$$**

(Map p352; ☏213-623-3233; www.acehotel.com/losangeles; 929 S Broadway Ave; r from $250, stes from $400) Either lovably cool, a bit too hip or a touch self-conscious depending upon your purview, there is no denying that the minds behind Downtown's newest sleep care deeply about their product. Some rooms are cubby-box small, but the 'medium' rooms are doable.

🛏 Hollywood

Vibe Hotel
HOSTEL **$**

(Map p356; ☏323-469-8600; www.vibehotel.com; 5920 Hollywood Blvd; dm $22-25, r $85-95; 🅿@📶) A funky motel-turned-hostel with both co-ed and female-only dorms – each with a flat screen and kitchenette – and several recently re-done private rooms that sleep three. You'll share space with a happening international crowd.

USA Hostels Hollywood
HOSTEL **$**

(Map p356; ☏800-524-6783, 323-462-3777; www.usahostels.com; 1624 Schrader Blvd; dm $30-40, r with shared bath $81-104; ❄@📶) This sociable hostel puts you within steps of the Hollywood party circuit. Private rooms are a bit cramped, but making new friends is easy during staff-organized barbecues, comedy nights and $25 all-you-can-drink limo tours. Freebies include a cook-your-own-pancake breakfast. They have cushy lounge seating on the front porch and free beach shuttles.

**West Hollywood
Halloween Carnaval**
CARNIVAL

(www.visitwesthollywood.com) This street fair brings 350,000 revelers – many in over-the-top and/or X-rated costumes – out for a day of dancing, dishing and dating on Halloween.

West Hollywood & Mid-City

★**Magic Castle Hotel**   HOTEL **$$**
(Map p356; ☑323-851-0800; http://magiccastle-hotel.com; 7025 Franklin Ave; r incl breakfast from $174; P❋@🛜🏊) Walls at this perennial pleaser are a bit thin, but otherwise it's a charming base of operation with large, modern rooms, exceptional staff and a petite courtyard pool where days start with fresh pastries and gourmet coffee. Enquire about access to the Magic Castle, a fabled members-only magic club in an adjacent Victorian mansion. Parking costs $10.

🛏 West Hollywood & Mid-City

Orbit   HOSTEL **$**
(Banana Bungalow; Map p362; ☑323-655-1510; www.orbithotels.com; 603 N Fairfax Ave; dm $22-25, r $69-79) This popular, well-run hostel occupies a converted art-deco-styled nursing home. The local bubbies are gone and the young nomads have moved in to private rooms that have their own baths, TV and mini-fridge or into one of the six 12-bed dorms.

★**Pali Hotel**   BOUTIQUE HOTEL **$$**
(Map p362; ☑323-272-4588; www.pali-hotel.com; 7950 Melrose Ave; r from $179; P@🛜) We love the rustic wood-paneled exterior, the polished concrete floor in the lobby, the Thai massage spa (just $35 for 30 minutes), and the 32 contemporary rooms with two-tone paint jobs, wall-mounted flat screen and

enough room for a sofa too. Some have terraces. A terrific all-around value.

★**Chateau Marmont**   HOTEL **$$$**
(Map p362; ☑323-656-1010; www.chateaumarmont.com; 8221 W Sunset Blvd; r $435, ste from $550; P🛜🏊) Its French-flavored indulgence may look dated, but this faux castle has long lured A-listers with its five-star mystique and legendary discretion. Howard Hughes used to spy on bikini beauties from the same balcony suite that became Bono's favorite.

Standard Hollywood   HOTEL **$$$**
(Map p362; ☑323-650-9090; www.standardhotel.com; 8300 Sunset Blvd; r from $235, ste from $335; ❋@🛜🏊) Kind of yesterday's news but still a good standby, this Sunset Strip haunt has you shacking up in sizable shagadelic rooms with beanbag chairs, orange-tiled bathrooms and Warhol poppy-print curtains. South-facing rooms have the views.

🛏 Beverly Hills & the Westside

★**Mr C**   HOTEL **$$$**
(☑877-334-5623; www.mrchotels.com; 1224 Beverwil Dr; r from $320) A long-standing tower hotel has been re-imagined by the Cipprioni brothers, who have been so involved in their passion project that they've designed everything right down to the furniture. North-facing rooms have spectacular views.

City Walk
Downtown Revealed

START UNITED ARTISTS THEATRE
END WOODSPOON
LENGTH 2.5 MILES; THREE HOURS

Start at the **1** **United Artists Theatre** (p374), grab a coffee at the **2** **Ace Hotel** (p363) next door, then head north on Broadway through the old theater district. This heady mixture of beaux-arts architecture, discount jewelers and new bars, restaurants and shops sums up the Downtown renaissance in just a few short blocks. Take note of the **3** **State Theatre** and **4** **St Vincent Court**, **5** **Los Angeles Theatre** and the **6** **Palace Theatre**.

Turn right at 6th St, continue along for two blocks, then turn left onto Main, where you'll see a flowering of new restaurants and bars at nearly every turn. Turn left on 5th St and continue for several blocks, passing **7** **Pershing Square** and glimpsing the **8** **Biltmore Hotel**. At Grand Ave turn right

and walk past the **9** **Deloitte & Tousche** building, then bisect **10** **MOCA** (p349) on one side and the **11** **Broad** on the other, continuing until you reach the stunning **12** **Walt Disney Concert Hall** (p349) and the **13** **Music Center**. You'll see the **14** **Cathedral of Our Lady of Angels** beckoning. Duck inside, then follow the traffic down the steps of **15** **Grand Park** until you reach Broadway once more.

Make a right on Broadway, and grab lunch at the **16** **Grand Central Market**. Afterward, walk another block south, turn left on 4th St, and then right on lively Spring St, which is dotted with still more cafes and bars. Enjoy the street life and the people-watching until Spring dead ends at Main St, just above 9th St. Say hello to the Cheri Rae at **17** **Peace Yoga** (you kind of have to meet her), and hang a right on 9th to Broadway. If you're hungry for dinner by now, grab a table at **18** **Woodspoon** (p368).

Bel Air & Westside

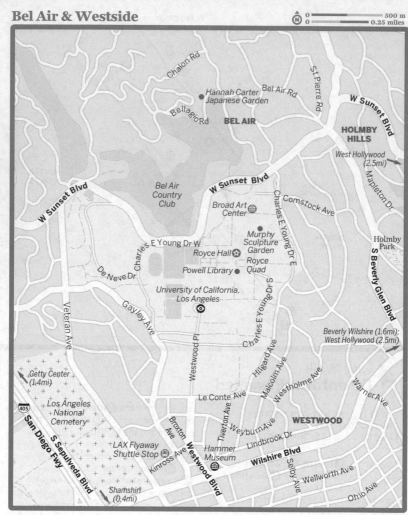

Avalon Hotel

HOTEL **$$$**

(☎800-670-6183, 310-277-5221; www.viceroyhotelgroup.com/avalon; 9400 W Olympic Blvd; r from $200; ✷ @ ☎ ☎ ☎) Mid-century modern gets a 21st-century spin at this fashion-crowd fave, which was Marilyn Monroe's old pad in its days as an apartment building. Funky retro rooms are all unique.

Crescent

HOTEL **$$$**

(☎310-247-0505; www.crescentbh.com; 403 N Crescent Dr; r from $217; ℗ @ ☎) Single rooms are a tight squeeze, but Queen rooms are spacious and good value. There's jazz in the lounge every Thursday night.

🛏 Malibu

Leo Carrillo State Park Campground

CAMPGROUND **$**

(☎800-444-7275; www.reserveamerica.com; 35000 W Pacific Coast Hwy; tent sites $45, per vehicle $12; ☎) This kid-friendly campground sits on a famous 1.5-mile stretch of beach. Offshore kelp beds, caves, tide pools, plus the wilderness of the Santa Monica Mountains create a natural playground. There are 140 flat, tree-shaded sites, flush toilets and coin-operated hot showers. Bookings for summer weekends should be made months in advance.

★ **Malibu Country Inn** INN **$$**
(☎310-457-9622; www.malibucountryinn.com;
6506 Westward Beach Rd; r $160-275; P🐾)
Overlooking Westward Beach is this humble shingled inn with an array of fairly large rooms drenched in corny florals. They all have sun patios and some have sea views.

🛏 **Santa Monica**

HI Los Angeles-Santa Monica HOSTEL **$**
(Map p368; ☎310-393-9913; www.hilosangeles.org;
1436 2nd St; dm $38-49, r $99-159; ❋@🐾) Near the beach and promenade, this hostel has an enviable location on the cheap. Its 200 beds in single-sex dorms and bed-in-a-box doubles with shared bathrooms are clean and safe, and there are plenty of public spaces to lounge and surf, but those looking to party are better off in Venice or Hollywood.

★ **Palihouse** BOUTIQUE HOTEL **$$$**
(Map p368; ☎310-394-1279; www.palihousesantamonica.com; 1001 3rd St; r $279-319, studios $319-379; P❋@🐾) LA's grooviest new hotel brand (not named Ace) has taken over the 36 rooms, studios and one-bedroom apartments of the historic Embassy Hotel (c 1927). Expect a lobby with terra-cotta floors, beamed ceilings and coffee bar, plus booths and leather sofas on which you can canoodle and surf.

Shore Hotel HOTEL **$$$**
(Map p368; ☎310-458-1515; www.shorehotel.com; 1515 Ocean Ave; r from $309) Massive, clean-lined and modern, featuring wood and glass rooms each with private terraces, this is one of the newest hotels on Ocean Ave, and the only gold LEED-certified hotel in Santa Monica, which means it has a reasonably light footprint. Case in point: the lovely back garden is seeded with drought-tolerant plants.

🛏 **Venice**

Venice Beach Inn & Suites BOUTIQUE HOTEL **$$**
(Map p368; ☎310-396-4559; www.venicebeachsuites.com; 1305 Ocean Front Walk; r from $159; P🐾) This place right on the Boardwalk scores big for its bend-over-backwards staff, and its bevy of beach toys for rent. There are exposed-brick walls, kitchenettes, wood floors and built-in closets. It's ideal for long stays. Kitchen suites are big enough for dinner parties.

Hotel Erwin BOUTIQUE HOTEL **$$$**
(Map p368; ☎800-786-7789; www.hotelerwin.com; 1697 Pacific Ave; r from $263; P❋@🐾)

An old motor inn has been dressed up and otherwise funkified in retro style. Think: eye-popping oranges, yellows and greens, framed photos of graffiti art, flat screens, and ergo sofas in the spacious rooms. Book online for the best deals. That rooftop lounge is a wonderful place for a sundowner.

🛏 **Long Beach & San Pedro**

Queen Mary Hotel SHIP **$$**
(☎562-435-3511; www.queenmary.com; 1126 Queens Hwy, Long Beach; r from $99; ❋@🐾) There's an irresistible romance to ocean liners such as the *Queen Mary,* a nostalgic retreat that time-warps you back to a long-gone, slower-paced era. Yes, the rooms are small, but the 1st-class staterooms are nicely refurbished with original art-deco details. Avoid the cheapest cabins on the inside – claustrophobic!

Hotel Maya BOUTIQUE HOTEL **$$**
(☎562-435-7676; www.hotelmayalongbeach.com; 700 Queens Way, Long Beach; r from $179; P@🐾🏊) This once boutique property hits you with hip immediately upon entering the rusted-steel and glass lobby, and continues in the rooms (think: coral tile, river-rock headboards), which are set in four 1970s-era hexagons with views of downtown Long Beach. The poolside cabanas aren't bad either.

🛏 **Pasadena**

★ **Bissell House B&B** B&B **$$**
(☎626-441-3535626-441-3535; www.bissellhouse.com; 201 S Orange Grove Blvd, Pasadena; r $159-259; P🐾) Antiques, hardwood floors and a crackling fireplace make this secluded Victorian B&B on 'Millionaire's Row' a bastion of warmth and romance. The hedge-framed garden feels like a sanctuary, and there's a pool for cooling off on hot summer days. The Prince Albert room has gorgeous wallpaper and a claw-foot tub. All seven rooms have private baths.

Langham RESORT **$$$**
(☎626-568-3900; www.pasadena.langhamhotels.com; 1401 S Oak Knoll Ave, Pasadena; r from $230; P@🐾🏊) Opened as the Huntington Hotel in 1906, this place spent the last several decades as the Ritz Carlton before recently donning the robes of Langham. But some things don't change: this incredible 23-acre, palm-dappled, beaux-arts country estate – complete with rambling gardens, giant swimming pool and covered picture bridge – has still got it. Rates are reasonable.

Eating

Downtown Los Angeles

Cole's SANDWICHES $
(Map p352; www.213nightlife.com/colesfrench-dip; 118 E 6th St; sandwiches $6-9; ☺11am-10pm Sun-Wed, to 11pm Thu, to 1am Fri & Sat) A funky old basement tavern known for originating the French Dip sandwich way back in 1908, when those things cost a nickel. You know the drill – french bread piled with sliced lamb, beef, turkey, pork or pastrami, dipped once or twice in *au jus*.

★ Sushi Gen JAPANESE $$
(Map p352; ☑213-617-0552; www.sushigen.org; 422 E 2nd St; sushi $11-21; ☺11:15am-2pm & 5:30-9:45pm) Seven chefs stand behind the blond-wood bar, carving thick slabs of melt-in-your-mouth salmon, buttery toro, and a wonderful Japanese snapper, among other staples. The sashimi special at lunch ($18) is a steal. Sushi Gen doesn't do jazzy rolls, and you best come early to grab a seat.

Woodspoon BRAZILIAN $$
(Map p352; ☑213-629-1765; www.woodspoonla.com; 107 W 9th St; mains $11-20; ☺11am-2:45pm & 5-10pm Tue-Fri, noon-3pm & 6-11pm Sat, closed Sun) We love it all: the hand-picked china, the vintage Pyrex pots of black beans and rice, and the Brazilian owner-operator who still chefs it up in the back. Her pork ribs fall off the bone, in a bath of grits and gravy. Her take on steak frites substitutes wedges of fried yucca for fries, and her pot pie put this place on the map.

Maccheroni Republic ITALIAN $$
(Map p352; ☑213-346-9725213-346-9725; 332 S Broadway Ave; mains $10-14; ☺11:30am-3pm & 5:30-10pm Mon-Fri, 5:30-10pm Sat, 4:30-9pm Sun) Tucked away on a still ungentrified corner is this gem with a lovely heated patio and tremendous Italian slow food. Don't miss the *polpettine di gamberi*, flattened ground shrimp cakes fried in olive oil. It serves a range of delicious housemade pastas, but doesn't have beer or wine. Bring your own.

★ Bestia ITALIAN $$$
(☑213-514-5724; www.bestia.com; 2121 7th Pl; dishes $10-29; ☺6-11pm Sun-Thu, to midnight Fri & Sat) The most sought-after reservation in town can be found at this new and splashy Italian kitchen in the Arts District. The antipasti ranges from crispy lamb pancetta to sea urchin crudo to veal tartare crostino. Did

Santa Monica & Venice Beach

LOS ANGELES EATING

Santa Monica & Venice Beach

LOS ANGELES EATING

we mention the lamb's heart? Yeah, you may have to leave the vegan at home.

There are tasty pizzas and pastas, squid-ink risotto stuffed with chunks of lobster, mussels, clams and calamari, and roast chops and whole fish. A worthy splurge indeed.

★ Bar Ama' MEXICAN, FUSION $$$
(Map p352; ☑ 213-687-8002; www.bar-ama.com; 118 W 4th St; dishes $8-25, dinners $32-36; ⊙ 11:30am-2:30pm & 5:30-11pm Mon-Thu, 11:30am-3pm & 5:30pm-midnight Fri, 11:30am-midnight Sat, to 10pm Sun) One of three exquisite downtown restaurants with profound Mexican influences offered by Josef Centeno. This one fries pig ears, braises short rib and smothers enchiladas with mole sauce. Brussels sprouts are garnished with pickled red onions, and the roasted cauliflower and cilantro pesto, served with cashew and pine nuts, is a tremendous veggie choice.

✕ Hollywood

Jitlada THAI $$
(☑ 323-667-9809; jitladala.com; 5233 W Sunset Blvd; appetizers $5-10, mains $11-30; ⊙ lunch & dinner; 🅿) A transporting taste of southern Thailand. Its crab curry and fried *som tum* (papaya salad) are fantastic, as is its Thai-style burger. The vivacious owner operator counts Ryan Gosling and Natalie Portman among her loyal, mostly *farang* (European American) customers. Look for the wall of fame near the bathrooms.

Pikoy PUB $$
(Map p362; ☑ 323-850-5400; www.thepikeyla.com; 7617 W Sunset Blvd; dishes $12-28; ⊙ noon-2am Mon-Fri, from 11am Sat & Sun) A tasteful kitchen that began life as Coach & Horses, one of Hollywood's favorite dives before it was reimagined into a place where you can get broccoli roasted with bacon, Arctic char crudo with grapefruit and jalapenos, seared squid with curried chickpeas, and a slow-roasted duck leg. The cocktails rock.

★ Pizzeria & Osteria Mozza ITALIAN $$$
(☑ 323-297-0100; www.mozza-la.com; 6602 Melrose Ave; pizzas $11-19, dinner mains $27-38; ⊙ pizzeria noon-midnight daily, osteria 5:30-11pm Mon-Fri, 5-11pm Sat, 5-10pm Sun) Osteria Mozza is all about fine dining crafted from market fresh, seasonal ingredients, but being a Mario Batali joint you can expect adventure (think: squid-ink chitarra freddi with Dungeness crab, sea urchin and jalapeno) and consistent excellence. Reservations are recommended.

Little Fork SOUTHERN $$$
(Map p356; ☑ 323-465-3675; www.littleforkla.com; 1600 Wilcox Ave; dishes $9-28; ⊙ 11am-3pm Sat & Sun, 5-10pm Sun-Thu, to midnight Fri & Sat; 🅿) The stucco exterior of this converted studio is a horror show, but inside all is dark and moody. More importantly, the kitchen churns out plates of house-smoked trout, brick-roasted chicken, potato gnocchi cooked in bacon lard, tarragon and cream, and a 1lb lobster roll!

✕ Los Feliz & Griffith Park

Yuca's
MEXICAN $

(Map p360; ☑ 323-662-1214; www.yucasla.com; 2056 Hillhurst Ave; items $4-10; ⏱ 11am-6pm Mon-Sat) The tacos, *tortas,* burritos and other Mexi faves at this snack shack earned the Herrera family the coveted James Beard Award in 2005.

★ Mess Hall
PUB $$

(☑ 323-660-6377; www.messhallkitchen.com; 4500 Los Feliz Blvd; mains $15-31; ⏱ 11:30am-3pm & 4-11pm Mon-Thu, to midnight Fri, 10am-3pm & 5pm-midnight Sat, 10am-3pm & 4-11pm Sun) On Tuesdays there are $1 oysters and $5 beers. It's been written up for having one of the best burgers in LA, and it does a nice pulled-pork sandwich and a kale caesar.

Alcove
CAFE $$

(Map p360; ☑ 323-644-0100; www.thealcovecafe. com; 1929 Hillhurst Ave; mains $10-17; ⏱ 6am-midnight; P �456) Hillhurst's choice breakfast hangout, this sunny cafe spills onto a multi-level, streetside brick patio. It's housed in a restored 1897 Spanish-style duplex, and the food is quite good.

✕ Silver Lake & Echo Park

★ Elf Cafe
VEGETARIAN $$

(☑ 213-484-6829; www.elfcafe.com; 2135 Sunset Blvd; mains $12-20; ☑) Simply one of the best vegetarian (not vegan) restaurants in LA, if not the very best. Start with feta wrapped in grape leaves and some spiced olives and almonds, move onto a kale salad dressed with citrus, wild-mushroom risotto and a kebab of seared oyster mushrooms that is fantastic.

Sage
VEGAN $$

(☑ 310-456-1492; www.sageveganbistro.com; 1700 W Sunset Blvd; mains $10-14; ⏱ 11am-10pm Mon-Wed, to 11pm Thu & Fri, 9am-4pm & 5-11pm Sat, to 10pm Sun; ☑ 456) An organic vegan kitchen with sandwiches and veggie burgers, and tacos stuffed with jackfruit or butternut squash. All served in heaping portions. And the menu is the second-best thing here. The best? That would be Kind Kreme's good-for-you, raw ice cream. Taste to believe.

★ L&E Oyster Bar
SEAFOOD $$$

(Map p360; ☑ 323-660-2255; www.leoysterbar. com; 1637 Silver Lake Blvd; mains $17-28; ⏱ 5-10pm Mon-Thu, to 11pm Fri & Sat) Silver Lake's seafood house opened to rave reviews in 2012, and is still a neighborhood darling

where locals and celebs claim tables in the intimate dining room and heated porch to feast on raw and grilled oysters, smoked mussels and whole roasted fish dressed in miso, pickled ginger, chili and garlic.

✕ West Hollywood & Mid-City

Pingtung
ASIAN $

(Map p362; ☑ 323-866-1866; www.pingtungla. com; 7455 Melrose Ave; dishes $6-12; ⏱ 11:30am-10:30pm; ☎) Our new favorite place to eat on Melrose is this Pan-Asian market cafe where the dim sum seaweed and green papaya salads, and rice bowls piled with curried chicken and BBQ beef are all worthy of praise. It has an inviting back patio with ample seating, wi-fi and good beer on tap.

Mercado
MEXICAN $$

(Map p362; ☑ 323-944-0947; www.mercadorestaurant.com; 7910 W 3rd St; dishes $9-26; ⏱ 5-10pm Mon-Wed, to 11pm Thu & Fri, 4-11pm Sat, 10am-3pm & 4-10pm Sun) Terrific *nuevo* Mexican food served in a dining room that is beneath dangling bird-cage chandeliers and anchored by a terrific marble tequila bar. The slow-cooked *carnitas* (pork cubes) melt in your mouth. Mercado also does spit-roast beef and grilled sweet corn, and folds tasty tacos and enchiladas. The Hora Feliz (happy hour) is among the best in the city.

Joan's on Third
CAFE $$

(Map p362; ☑ 323-655-2285; www.joansonthird. com; 8350 W 3rd St; mains $10-16; ⏱ 8am-8pm Mon-Sat, to 7pm Sun; ☑ 456) One of the first market cafes in the LA area is still one of the best. The coffee and pastries are absurdly good and the deli churns out tasty gourmet sandwiches and salads. Hence all the happy people eating alfresco on buzzy 3rd St.

★ Ray's
MODERN AMERICAN $$$

(Map p362; ☑ 323-857-6180; www.raysandstarkbar. com; 5905 Wilshire Blvd; dishes $11-27; ⏱ 11:30am-3pm & 5-10pm Mon-Fri, from 10am Sat & Sun; ☐ MTA 20) Ray's changes the menu twice daily, but if it's offered order the shrimp and grits: it's rich and buttery, afloat with chunks of andouille sausage, okra and two king prawns. The *burrata* (fresh Italian cheese made from mozzarella and cream) melts with tang, the yellow tail collar is crisp and moist, and the bacon-wrapped rabbit sausage will wow you.

★ Connie & Ted's
SEAFOOD $$$

(Map p362; ☑ 323-848-2722; www.connieandteds.com; 8171 Santa Monica Blvd; mains $12-26;

5-11pm Mon & Tue, noon-11pm Wed-Sun) The design is instant classic, there are always up to a dozen oyster varieties on the stocked raw bar. Fresh fish is pan fried or grilled to order. The lobster roll can be served cold with mayo and hot with drawn butter, and the shellfish marinara is a sacred thing.

Beverly Hills & the Westside

Still hungry? **Little Osaka**, West LA's Asian bloom, which runs along Sawtelle for about two blocks north from Olympic Blvd to La Grange Ave, is not exclusively Japanese. Among the karaoke bars, grocers, cafes and boutiques are restaurants devoted to ramen and Korean-style tofu, shabu-shabu, macaroons, dim sum, *pho* and *yakitori*.

Shamshiri   PERSIAN $$
(www.shamshiri.com; 1712 Westwood Blvd, Westwood; appetizers $4-16, mains $13-22; 11:30am-10pm Mon-Thu, to 11pm Fri & Sat, noon-10pm Sun; P) One of a string of Persian kitchens, this place bakes its own pita, which is then used to wrap chicken, beef and lamb shwarma, kebabs and falafel served with a green, *shirazi* or tabouli salad. It also does broiled lamb and seafood platters, and vegan stews. Come for one of its great-value lunch specials ($8 to $10).

Nate 'n Al   DELI $$
(310-274-0101; www.natenal.com; 414 N Beverly Dr; dishes $6.50-13; 7am-9pm;) Dapper seniors, chatty girlfriends, busy execs and even Larry King have kept this New York–style nosh spot busy since 1945. The huge menu brims with corned beef, lox and other old-school favorites, but we're partial to the pastrami, made fresh on-site.

Picca   SOUTH AMERICAN $$$
(310-277-0133; www.piccaperu.com; 9575 W Pico Blvd; dishes $8-28; 6-11pm) Start with a crispy chicken tail, move onto a skirt steak topped with a fried egg and served with fried bananas and chickpeas and finish with a vanilla-bean pisco flan. Or better yet, dive deep and wide into the spectacular raw bar – filled with a variety of ceviche, sashimi and other succulent seafood concoctions.

Bouchon   FRENCH $$$
(310-279-9910; www.bouchonbistro.com; 235 N Cañon Dr; mains $17-59; 11:30am-9pm Mon, to 10:30pm Tue-Fri, 11am-10:30pm Sat, to 9pm Sun; P) Quiche and salad, oysters on the half-shell or mussels steamed opened in white-wine sauce, steak frittes or roast leg of lamb with artichoke, Thomas Keller's Bouchon empire brings you classic French bistro cuisine in classy environs. Taste the goods at a discount at **Bar Bouchon** downstairs.

Ivy   CALIFORNIAN $$$
(Map p362; 310-274-8303; www.theivyrestaurants.com; 113 N Robertson Blvd; mains $22-97; 8am-11pm) With a long history of celebrity power-lunches, this is where Southern comfort food (like fried chicken and crab cakes) have been elevated to haute cuisine. Service is refined and impeccable, and paparazzi etiquette (among one another and their prey) is a fluid, dynamic beast.

Malibu

Café Habana   MEXICAN, CUBAN $$
(310-317-0300; www.habana-malibu.com; 3939 Cross Creek Rd; mains $14-22; 11am-11pm Sun-Wed, to 1am Thu-Sat; P) A Mexican joint disguised as a Cuban joint with terrific margaritas, sumptuous booths on the heated patio, salsa on the sound system and two dishes that prevail above all else: the shrimp and carne asada tacos. Both come piled with either chili- and lime-sautéed rock shrimp, or cubes of ancho-rubbed and grilled steak.

Duck Dive   PUB $$
(310-589-2200; www.duckdivegastropub.com; 29169 Heathercliff Rd; small plates $5-13, mains $9-32; 11:30am-10pm Sun-Thu, to late Fri & Sat) A fantastic little concrete-floor pub with stainless-steel bar and patio seating. It pours craftsman draught brews, and serves hand-cut fries sizzled in duck fat. The smoked mac 'n' cheese can be ramped up with jalapeños and pork belly. It also offers a housemade veggie burger and hearty meat ones too.

Nobu Malibu   JAPANESE $$$
(310-317-9140; www.noburestaurants.com; 22706 Pacific Coast Hwy; dishes $8-46; 11am-3pm & 5:30pm-late; P) South of the pier and born again in landmark quality digs, here's a cavernous, modern-wood chalet with a long sushi bar on the back wall and a dining room that spills onto a patio that overlooks the swirling sea. Remember, it's the cooked food that built the brand.

Santa Monica

⭐**Santa Monica Farmers Markets**   MARKET $
(Map p368; www.smgov.net/portals/farmersmarket; Arizona Ave, btwn 2nd & 3rd Sts; 8:30am-1:30pm

Wed, to 1pm Sat; 🎫) 🎐 You haven't really experienced Santa Monica until you've explored one of its weekly outdoor farmers markets stocked with organic fruits, vegetables, flowers, baked goods and fresh-shucked oysters.

Bay Cities   DELI, ITALIAN $

(Map p368; www.baycitiesitaliandeli.com; 1517 Lincoln Blvd; sandwiches $5-9; ⊘9am-7pm Tue-Sat, to 6pm Sun) Not just the best Italian deli in LA, this is arguably the best deli, period. With sloppy, spicy godmothers (piled with salami, mortadella, coppacola, ham, prosciutto, provolone, and pepper salad), house-roasted tri-tip, tangy salads, imported meats, cheeses, breads, oils and extras. Get your sandwich with the works. And, yes, it's worth the wait.

★ Milo and Olive   ITALIAN $$

(☑310-453-6776; www.miloandolive.com; 2723 Wilshire Blvd; dishes $7-20; ⊘7am-11pm) We love it for its small-batch wines, incredible pizzas and terrific breakfasts (creamy polenta and poached eggs anyone?), breads and pastries, all of which you may enjoy at the marble bar or shoulder to shoulder with new friends at one of two common tables. It's a cozy, neighborhoody kind of joint; no reservations.

★ Bar Pintxo   SPANISH $$

(Map p368; ☑310-458-2012; www.barpintxo.com; 109 Santa Monica Blvd; tapas $4-16, paella $30; ⊘4-10pm Mon-Wed, to 11pm Thu, to midnight Fri, noon-midnight Sat, to 10pm Sun) A Barcelona-inspired tapas bar. It's small, it's cramped, it's a bit loud and a lot of fun. Tapas include pork belly braised in duck fat, filet mignon skewers, lamb meatballs and a tremendous seared calamari.

🍴 Venice

Wurstkuche   GERMAN $

(www.wurstkuche.com; 625 Lincoln Blvd; dishes $4-8; ⊘11am-midnight, bar to 2am) Set in a brick-house loft, but sealed off from the on-rushing madness of Lincoln Blvd, this German sausage and beer *haus* specializes in three things: gourmet and classic grilled sausages; fine Belgian, German and North American beers; and Belgian fries with ample dipping sauces.

★ Gjelina   ITALIAN $$$

(Map p368; ☑310-450-1429; www.gjelina.com; 1429 Abbot Kinney Blvd; dishes $8-26; ⊘11:30am-midnight Mon-Fri, from 9am Sat & Sun; 🎫) Carve out a slip on the communal table between the hipsters and yuppies, or get your own slab of wood on the elegant, tented stone ter-

race, and dine on imaginative small plates (think raw yellowtail spiced with chili and mint and drenched in olive oil and blood orange), and sensational thin crust, wood-fired pizza. It serves until midnight.

Tasting Kitchen   ITALIAN $$$

(Map p368; ☑310-392-6644; www.thetasting-kitchen.com; 1633 Abbot Kinney Blvd; mains $16-40; ⊘10:30am-2pm Sat & Sun, 6pm-late daily) From the salt-roasted branzino to the procini-crusted hangar steak to the burger and the quail, it's all very good here. Especially the pastas (that bucatini is a gift from the gods), and the cocktails, of course. Which is why it's almost always packed. Book ahead.

Scopa   ITALIAN $$$

(☑310-821-1100; www.scopaitalianroots.com; 2905 Washington Blvd; dishes $6-49; ⊘5pm-2am) Spacious and open with polished concrete floors and an expansive marble L-shaped bar. The crudo bar serves scallops and steak tartare, four varieties of oysters, uni and mussels, while mains include a whole roasted branzino and a 24oz T-bone.

🍴 Long Beach & San Pedro

Pier 76   SEAFOOD $$

(☑562-983-1776; www.pier76fishgrill.com; 95 Pine Ave, Long Beach; mains $8-19; ⊘11am-9pm) A terrific, affordable seafood house in downtown Long Beach. Step to the counter and order yellowtail, salmon, trout, mahi mahi or halibut glazed and grilled, and served with two sides. The fries and kale salad are both good. It does fish tacos and sandwiches, poke and ceviche too, and a $19 lobster.

James Republic   MODERN AMERICAN $$

(☑562-901-0235; www.jamesrepublic.com; 500 E 1st St, Long Beach; mains $11-26; ⊘7-10:30am & 11:30am-2:30pm Mon-Fri, 10:30am-3pm Sat & Sun, 6-10pm Mon-Sat, 6-9pm Sun) The best new restaurant in Long Beach offers farm-to-table Modern American eating, though some dishes have a South Asian twist. It grills cauliflower and hangar steaks, spoons a rabbit bucatini, and makes grass-fed burgers, a pastrami sandwich with gruyere and beer mustard, and a wonderful roast chicken.

San Pedro Fish Market &
Restaurant   SEAFOOD $$

(www.sanpedrofishmarket.com; 1190 Nagoya Way, San Pedro; meals $13-18; ⊘8am-8pm; 🅿🎫) Seafood feasts don't get more decadent than at this family-run, harbor-view institution.

Pick from the day's catch, have it spiced and cooked to order with potatoes, tomatoes and peppers, lug your tray to a picnic table, fold up your sleeves and devour meaty crabs, plump shrimp, melty yellowtail and tender halibut.

San Fernando Valley

★**Daichan** JAPANESE $$
(Map p358; 11288 Ventura Blvd, Studio City; mains $8.50-19; ⊙11:30am-3pm & 5:30-9pm Mon-Sat; 🅿) Stuffed with knickknacks, pasted with posters, and staffed by the sunny and sweet owner-operator, this offbeat Japanese diner offers the best (and one of the tastiest) deals on sushi row. The fried seaweed tofu *gyoza* are divine and so are the bowls – especially the *negitoro* bowl, where fatty tuna is served over rice, lettuce and seaweed.

Kazu Sushi JAPANESE $$$
(Map p358; ☑818-763-4836; 11440 Ventura Blvd, Studio City; dishes $10-19; ⊙noon-2pm & 6-10pm Mon-Sat; 🅿) Stuck in a cramped and otherwise nondescript, split level minimall that's easy to miss is one of the best-kept secrets among LA's sushi aficionados. It's Michelin-rated, very high end, has a terrific sake selection, and is worth the splurge.

Pasadena

★**Little Flower** CAFE $
(☑626-304-4800; www.littleflowercandyco.com; 1424 W Colorado Blvd, Pasadena; mains $8-15; ⊙7am-7pm Mon-Sat, 9am-4pm Sun) Locally loved cafe set just a mile over the Colorado Bridge from Old Town. It does exquisite pastries, *bánh mì* sandwiches with chicken, roast beef or tempeh, and bowls stuffed with such things as dahl, raita, curried eggplant and steamed spinach, or salmon, shredded carrots and daikon, micro greens and ponzu.

🍷 Drinking & Nightlife

🍸 Downtown Los Angeles

Las Perlas BAR
(Map p352; 107 E 6th St; ⊙7pm-2am Mon-Sat, 8pm-2am Sun) With Old Mexico whimsy, a chalkboard menu of more than 80 tequilas and mescals, and friendly barkeeps who mix things such as egg whites, blackberries and port syrup into new-school takes on the margarita, there's a reason we love downtown's best tequila bar. But if you truly want to dig tequila, select a highland variety and sip it neat.

Varnish BAR
(Map p352; ☑213-622-9999; www.213nightlife.com/thevarnish; 118 E 6th St; ⊙7pm-2am) Tucked into the back of Cole's, is this cubbyhole-sized speakeasy, where good live jazz burns Sunday to Tuesday.

🍸 Hollywood

La Descarga LOUNGE
(☑323-466-1324; www.ladescargala.com; 1159 N Western Ave; ⊙8pm-2am Wed-Sat) This tastefully frayed, sublimely sweaty rum and cigar lounge is a revelation. Behind the marble bar are more than 100 types of rum from Haiti and Guyana, Guatemala and Venezuela.

★**No Vacancy** BAR
(Map p356; ☑323-465-1902; www.novacancyla.com; 1727 N Hudson Ave; ⊙8pm-2am) An old, shingled Victorian has been converted into LA's hottest night out at research time. Even the entrance is theatrical. You'll follow a rickety staircase into a narrow hall and enter the room of a would-be Madame (dressed in fishnet), who will press a button to reveal another staircase down into the living room and out into a courtyard of mayhem.

Dirty Laundry BAR
(Map p356; ☑323-462-6531; dirtylaundrybarla.com; 1725 N Hudson Ave; ⊙10pm-2am) Under a cotton-candy-pink apartment block of no particular import is a funky den of musty odor and great times, low ceilings, exposed pipes, good whiskey, groovy funk on the turntables and plenty of uninhibited pretty people. There are velvet-rope politics at work here, so reserve a table to make sure you slip through.

Sayers Club CLUB
(Map p356; ☑323-871-8416; www.sbe.com/nightlife/locations/thesayersclub-hollywood; 1645 Wilcox Ave; cover varies; ⊙8pm-2am Tue, Thu & Fri) When rock royalty such as Prince, established stars like the Black Keys and even movie stars like Joseph Gordon Levitt decide to play secret shows in intimate environs, they find the back room at this brick-house Hollywood nightspot, where the booths are leather, the lighting moody and the music – whether live, or spun by DJs – satisfies.

🍸 Silver Lake & Echo Park

Short Stop CLUB
(☑213-482-4942; 1455 W Sunset Blvd; ⊙5pm-2am Mon-Fri, from 2pm Sat & Sun) Echo Park's beloved and deceptively sprawling dive has a

dance floor in one room, a bar strobing ball-games on flat screens in another, and a pool table and pinball machines in still another section. Echo Park locals and hipsters bump shoulders, especially on Motown Mondays, when vintage jams fill the room with joy.

West Hollywood & Mid-City

El Carmen   BAR
(Map p362; 8138 W 3rd St; ⊗5pm-2am Mon-Fri, from 7pm Sat & Sun) A pair of mounted bull heads and *lucha libre* (Mexican wrestling) masks create a 'Tijuana North' look and pull in an industry-heavy crowd at LA's ultimate tequila and mescal tavern.

Bar Marmont   BAR
(Map p362; ☑323-650-0575; www.chateaumarmont.com/barmarmont.php; 8171 Sunset Blvd; ⊗6pm-2am) Elegant, but not stuck up. Been around, yet still cherished. With high ceilings, molded walls and terrific martinis, the famous, and the wish-they-weres, still flock here. If you time it right, you might see Thom Yorke, or perhaps Lindsey Lohan? Come midweek. Weekends are for amateurs.

Formosa Cafe   BAR
(Map p362; ☑323-850-9050; 7156 Santa Monica Blvd; ⊗4pm-2am Mon-Fri, 6pm-2am Sat & Sun) Humphrey Bogart and Clark Gable used to knock 'em back at this dark railcar of a watering hole so authentically noir that scenes from *LA Confidential* were filmed here.

Malibu

Sunset   BAR
(www.thesunsetrestaurant.com; 6800 Westward Rd; ⊗noon-10pm; 🖼) A perfectly strange oasis after a day at the beach. Mostly because the Happy Hour crowd gets weird. Like rich, celebrity, plastic surgery, comb-over weird.

Santa Monica

★Basement Tavern   BAR
(Map p368; www.basementtavern.com; 2640 Main St; ⊗5pm-2am) This creative speakeasy is our favorite well in Santa Monica. We love it for its cocktails, cozy booths and nightly live-music calendar that features blues, jazz, bluegrass and rock. It gets too busy on weekends, but weeknights can be special.

Misfit   LOUNGE
(Map p368; ☑310-656-9800; www.themisfitbar.com; 225 Santa Monica Blvd; ⊗noon-late Mon-Fri,

from 11am Sat & Sun) This darkly lit emporium of food, drink and fun is notable for the decent – not great – menu, and phenomenal cocktails made from craftsman spirits. Set in a historic building decked out with a retro interior, it's busy from brunch to last call.

Venice

Townhouse & Delmonte Speakeasy   BAR
(Map p368; www.townhousevenice.com; 52 Windward Ave; ⊗5pm-2am Mon-Thu, noon-2am Fri-Sun) Upstairs is a cool, dark and perfectly dingy bar with pool tables, booths and good booze. Downstairs is the speakeasy, where DJs spin pop, funk and electronic music, comics take the mic and jazz players set up and jam. It's a reliably good time almost any night.

☆ Entertainment

Live Music

Orpheum Theatre   LIVE MUSIC
(Map p352; ☑877-677-4386; www.laorpheum.com; 842 S Broadway) In the early 20th century, cacophonous Broadway was a glamorous shopping and theater strip, where megastars such as Charlie Chaplin leapt from limos to attend premieres at lavish movie palaces like this one. The Orpheum was the first to be fully restored. Jam band Gods, Widespread Panic, and younger phenoms, MGMT, played here recently.

United Artists Theatre   LIVE MUSIC, DANCE
(Map p352; ☑213-623-3233; www.acehotel.com/losangeles/theatre; 929 S Broadway) A historic gem of a theater, restored by Ace Hotel, which curates the calendar as well. It's homebase for LA's best modern-dance company and stages indie and up-and-coming bands.

★Greek Theatre   LIVE MUSIC
(Map p358; ☑323-665-5857; www.greektheatrela.com; 2700 N Vermont Ave; ⊗May-Oct) A more intimate version of the Hollywood Bowl, this 5800-seat outdoor amphitheater tucked into a woodsy hillside of Griffith Park is much beloved for its vibe and variety – Los Lobos to MGMT to Willie Nelson. Parking is stacked, so plan on a post-show wait.

Royce Hall   LIVE MUSIC
(Map p366; www.uclalive.org; UCLA; tickets from $22) An exceptional theater housed in UCLA's historic heart. The brick building reeks of academia, but **UCLA Live** has been known

GAY & LESBIAN LOS ANGELES

LA is one of the country's gayest cities (the city has made a number of contributions to gay culture), and the rainbow flag flies especially proudly in Boystown, along Santa Monica Blvd in West Hollywood (WeHo). Thursday through Sunday nights are prime time.

If nightlife isn't your scene, there are plenty of other ways to meet, greet and engage. Outdoor activities include the **Frontrunners** (www.lafrontrunners.com) running club and the **Great Outdoors** (www.greatoutdoorsla.org) hiking club. There's gay theater all over town, but the **Celebration Theatre** (Map p362; www.celebrationtheatre.com; 7051 Santa Monica Blvd, West Hollywood) ranks among the nation's leading stages for LGBT plays.

The **LA Gay & Lesbian Center** (Map p356; ☎ 323-993-7400; www.laglc.org; 1625 Schrader Blvd, Hollywood; ⊙ 9am-8pm Mon-Fri, to 1pm Sat) is a one-stop service, and its affiliated **Village at Ed Gould Plaza** (www.laglc.org; 1125 N McCadden Pl, Hollywood; ⊙ 6-10pm Mon-Fri, 9am-5pm Sat) offers art exhibits and theater programs around a leafy courtyard.

The festival season kicks off in mid- to late May with the **Long Beach Pride Celebration** (www.longbeachpride.com) and continues with the three-day **LA Pride** (www.lapride.org) in early June with a parade down Santa Monica Blvd. On **Halloween** (October 31), the same street brings out 350,000 outrageously costumed revelers of all persuasions.

WeHo

Abbey (Map p362; www.abbeyfoodandbar.com; 692 N Robertson Blvd; mains $9-13; ⊙ 11am-2am Mon-Thu, from 10am Fri, from 9am Sat & Sun) Once a humble coffeehouse, the Abbey has developed into WeHo's bar/club/restaurant of record. Always cool and fun, it has so many different-flavored martinis and mojitos that you'd think they were invented here. It also has a full menu. Match your mood to the many different spaces, from outdoor patio to goth lounge to chill room. On weekends they're all busy.

Micky's (Map p362; www.mickys.com; 8857 Santa Monica Blvd; ⊙ 5pm-2am Sun-Thu, to 4am Fri & Sat) A two-story, quintessential WeHo dance club, with go-go boys, expensive drinks, attitude and plenty of eye candy. There is a marble circle bar, exposed steel girders and doors that open all the way to the street. Check online for special events.

Trunks (Map p362; www.trunksbar.com; 8809 Santa Monica Blvd; ⊙ 1pm-2am) With pool tables and sports on the flat screens, this brick house, low-lit dive is a long-running boulevard staple that is less fabulous and more down-to-earth than most in WeHo.

Hamburger Habit (Map p362; ☎ 310-659-8774; 8954 Santa Monica Blvd; mains $5-8; ⊙ 10am-midnight) The greasy burgers are middling, but the evening scene, which may include sing-alongs and topless men dancing on tables, is as unique as it is wonderful.

Beyond WeHo

Akbar (Map p360; www.akbarsilverlake.com; 4356 W Sunset Blvd; ⊙ 4pm-2am) Best jukebox in town, Casbah-style atmosphere, and a great mix of people that's been known to change from hour to hour – gay, straight, on the fence or just hip, but not too hip for you.

Casita del Campo (Map p360; www.casitadelcampo.net; 1920 Hyperion Ave; mains lunch $8, dinner $14-17; ⊙ 11am-11pm Sun-Wed, to midnight Thu, to 2am Fri & Sat; ℗) What's not to love about this Mexican cantina? It's cozy, it's fun, and you might even catch a drag show in the tiny Cavern Club Theater.

Faultline (Map p360; www.faultlinebar.com; 4216 Melrose Ave; ⊙ 5pm-2am Wed-Fri, 2pm-2am Sat & Sun) Indoor-outdoor venue that's party central for manly men, with nary a twink in sight. Take off your shirt and join the Sunday-afternoon beer bust (it's an institution), but get there early or expect a long wait.

to bring in authors such as David Sedaris and Anthony Bourdain for lively readings, and spectacular musicians like piano man Chick Corea, and the Philip Glass ensemble.

El Rey   LIVE MUSIC
(Map p362; www.theelrey.com; 5515 Wilshire Blvd; cover varies) An old art-deco dance hall decked out in red velvet and chandeliers and flaunting an awesome sound

system with excellent sightlines. Although it can hold 800 people, it feels quite small. Performance-wise, it's popular with indie acts and the rockers who love them.

★ Echo
LIVE MUSIC

(www.attheecho.com; 1822 W Sunset Blvd; cover varies) Eastsiders hungry for an eclectic alchemy of sounds pack this funky-town dive that's basically a sweaty bar with a stage and a smoking patio. It books indie bands, and also has regular club nights. The Funky Sole party every Saturday is always a blast.

Comedy & Theater

★ Upright Citizens Brigade Theatre
COMEDY

(Map p356; ☑ 323-908-8702; www.losangeles. ucbtheatre.com; 5919 Franklin Ave; tickets $5-10) Founded in New York by *SNL* alums Amy Poehler and Ian Roberts along with Matt Besser and Matt Walsh, this sketch-comedy group cloned itself in Hollywood in 2005 and is arguably the best improv theater in town. Most shows are $5 or $8, but Sunday's 'Asssscat' is freeeee.

Groundlings
COMEDY

(Map p362; ☑ 323-934-4747; www.groundlings. com; 7307 Melrose Ave; tickets $10-20) This improv school and company has launched Lisa Kudrow, Will Ferrell, Maya Rudolph and other top talent. Their sketch comedy and improv can bring on belly-laughs, especially on Thursdays when the main company, alumni and surprise guests get to riff together in 'Cookin' with Gas.'

Anateus Company
THEATER, COMEDY

(☑ 818-506-5436; www.antaeus.org; 5112 Lankershim Blvd, North Hollywood; tickets $30-34) A theater, among the better reviewed in LA, offering plays and stand-up comedy.

Noho Arts Center Ensemble
THEATER

(www.thenohoartscenter.com; 11136 Magnolia Blvd, North Hollywood; tickets $25; ⊘ shows 8pm Fri & Sat, 3pm Sun) The crown jewel of North Hollywood's budding theater scene offers reimagined classic and new cutting-edge theater.

Sports

Dodger Stadium
BASEBALL

(☑ 866-363-4377; www.dodgers.com; 1000 Elysian Park Ave; ⊘ Apr-Sep) Few clubs can match the Dodgers organization when it comes to history (Jackie Robinson, Sandy Koufax, Kirk Gibson, and Vin Scully), winning and fan loyalty. The club's current owners bought the

organization for roughly two billion dollars, an American team sports record at the time.

🔒 Shopping

🔒 Downtown Los Angeles

★ Raggedy Threads
VINTAGE

(Map p352; ☑ 213-620-1188; www.raggedythreads. com; 330 E 2nd St; ⊘ noon-8pm Mon-Sat, to 6pm Sun) A vintage Americana store just off the main Little Tokyo strip. You'll find plenty of beautifully raggedy denim and overalls, soft T-shirts, a few Victorian dresses, and a wonderful turquoise collection at great prices. Sensational glasses frames and watches too.

Apolis
FASHION

(Map p352; ☑ 213-613-9626; www.apolisglobal.com; 806 E 3rd St) A tremendous, not cheap, men's wear brand that does tailored chinos, jeans and T-shirts, and blazers too. Owned by two Santa Barbarian brothers, the line fits comfortably between J Crew and James Perse. It's all about fair trade, and proves it with development projects in American inner cities and Peruvian, Bangladeshi and Ugandan villages.

🔒 Hollywood

Amoeba Music
MUSIC

(Map p356; ☑ 323-245-6400; www.amoeba. com; 6400 W Sunset Blvd; ⊘ 10:30am-11pm Mon-Sat, 11am-9pm Sun) When a record store not only survives but thrives in this techno age, you know it's doing something right. Flip through half-a-million new and used LPs, CDs, DVDs, videos and vinyl at this granddaddy of music stores. Handy listening stations and its outstanding *Music We Like* booklet keep you from buying lemons.

🔒 West Hollywood & Mid-City

This is by far the best and most diverse shopping territory in a city that often feels like it's built by, and for, shopoholics.

★ Reformation
FASHION

(Map p362; www.thereformation.com; 8253 Melrose Ave; ⊘ 11am-7pm) Here's classic, retro-inspired, fashionable outer wear that's eco-conscious without the granola. The tagline is 'change the world without changing your style.' Products use only pre-existing materials, which means no additional dying of fabrics and half the water use of other fashion brands. Everything is made downtown.

LA'S FASHION DISTRICT DEMYSTIFIED

Bargain hunters love this frantic, 90-block warren of fashion in southwestern downtown. Deals can be amazing, but first-timers are often bewildered by the district's size and immense selection. For orientation, check out www.fashiondistrict.org, where you can download a free app and a map to the area.

Basically, the area is subdivided into several distinct retail areas:

➡ Women – Los Angeles St between Olympic and Pico Blvds; 11th St between Los Angeles and San Julian Sts

➡ Children – Wall St between 12th St and Pico Blvd

➡ Men and bridal – Los Angeles St between 7th and 9th Sts

➡ Textiles – 9th St between Santee and Wall Sts

➡ Jewelry and accessories – Santee St between Olympic Blvd and 13th St

➡ Designer knockoffs – Santee Alley and New Alley (enter on 11th St between Maple and Santee Aves)

Shops are generally open from 10am to 5pm daily, with Saturday being the busiest because that's when many wholesalers open up to the public. Cash is king and haggling may get you 10% or 20% off, especially when buying multiple items. Refunds or exchanges are a no-no, so choose carefully and make sure items are in good condition. Most stores don't have dressing rooms.

Sample Sales

Every last Friday of the month, clued-in fashionistas descend upon the corner of 9th St and Los Angeles St armed with cash and attitude to catfight it out for designer clothes priced below wholesale. Their destination: the hip showrooms at the **Gerry Building** (Map p352; www.gerrybuilding.com; 910 S Los Angeles St), **Cooper Design Space** (Map p352; ☏ 213-627-3754; www.cooperdesignspace.com; 860 S Los Angeles St) and the **New Mart** (Map p352; ☏ 213-627 0671; www.newmart.net; 127 E 9th St). They each specialize in contemporary and young fashions – though the Cooper and the Gerry are considered the hippest of the bunch. The **California Market Center** (Map p352; ☏ 213-630-3600; www.californiamarketcenter.com; 110 E 9th St) has a great fashion bookstore on the ground floor, among make-up and fragrance retailers, and houses both clothing and home-furnishing wholesalers. Open from 9am to 3pm, this is the only time the general public is allowed in these trade-only buildings. Come early and leave your modesty at home, as you'll either be trying things on in front of others or not at all. During Christmas season there are often several sales each week. Check the websites for dates and participating showrooms.

Fahey/Klein Gallery GALLERY
(Map p362; www.faheykleingallery.com; 148 S La Brea Ave; ⊙10am-6pm Tue-Sat) The best in vintage and contemporary fine-art photography by icons such as Annie Leibovitz, Bruce Weber and the late, great rock-and-roll shutterbug, Jim Marshall. It even has his lesser-known civil rights catalog in its vast archives.

Espionage VINTAGE
(Map p362; ☏ 323-272-4942; www.espionagela. com; 7456 Beverly Blvd; ⊙11am-6pm Mon, to 7pm Tue-Fri, 10:30am-7pm Sat, to 6pm Sun) A fabulous boutique blessed with a tasteful mélange of new and vintage goods. Their jewelry is fantastic, so are the chunky vin-

tage perfume bottles and ash trays. Those leather chairs work perfectly with their brass and glass end tables and they offer a collection of vintage couture clothing sold on consignment.

Supreme FASHION
(Map p362; ☏ 323-655-6205; supremenewyork. com; 439 N Fairfax Ave) When we rolled by, this beloved skate punk hip-hop mashup of a label had just re-opened its doors, and the heads lined up for half a block to get a taste of the new line. So, yes, it's a *thing*. Also, it has a half pipe in the store, and that's maybe the best of things.

Melrose Trading Post
MARKET

(Map p362; http://melrosetradingpost.org; Fairfax High School, 7850 Melrose Ave; admission $2; ⊙9am-5pm Sun) Threads, jewelry, housewares and other offbeat items proffered by more than 100 purveyors. Held in the Fairfax High parking lot; proceeds help fund school programs.

Fred Segal
FASHION

(Map p362; ☑323-651-4129; www.fredsegal.com; 8100 Melrose Ave; ⊙10am-7pm Mon-Sat, noon-6pm Sun) Celebs and beautiful people circle for the very latest from Babakul, Aviator Nation and Robbi & Nikki at this warren of high-end boutiques under one impossibly chic but slightly snooty roof. The only time you'll see bargains (sort of) is during the two-week blowout sale in September.

Beverly Hills & the Westside

While Beverly Hills and **Rodeo Drive** (btwn Wilshire & Santa Monica Blvds) get most of the hype, the best boutiques are on Robertson, between Beverly Blvd and Burton Way.

Barneys New York
DEPARTMENT STORE

(☑310-276-4400; www.barneys.com; 9570 Wilshire Blvd; ⊙10am-7pm Mon-Wed, Fri & Sat, to 8pm Thu, noon-6pm Sun) Four floors of straight-up chic. Prices are steep, so keep any eye out for one of its twice-annual warehouse sales. There's a special deli on the top floor worth trying too.

Scoop
FASHION

(☑310-362-6100; www.scoopnyc.com; 265 N Beverly Dr; ⊙10am-7pm Mon-Sat, 11am-6pm Sun) A grab bag of designer denim and limited-edition sneakers, funky belts and designer camo jackets. The women's line is more chic than sporty, sprinkled with dresses, handbags, and heels. It's set in the ground floor of the fabulous blue-glass MGM building.

Malibu

Malibu Country Mart
MALL

(www.malibucountrymart.com; 3835 Cross Creek Rd) Across from Surfrider Beach, this mall spans both sides of Cross Creek Rd. Which is why it's affectionately known as Cross Creek by the sun-kissed local beach girls and boys who gather at this high-end outdoor shopping mall to flirt, grub and shop.

Santa Monica

For big chains such as Anthropologie, the flagship Apple, Guess and Converse make your way to the **Third Street Promenade** (Map p368). **Santa Monica Place** (Map p368; www.santamonicaplace.com; 395 Santa Monica Pl; ⊙10am-9pm Mon-Thu, to 10pm Fri & Sat, 11am-8pm Sun) offers more upscale corporate consumption. For indie-minded boutiques, such as **Planet Blue** (Map p368; www.shopplanetblue.com; 2940 Main St; ⊙10am-6pm), head to **Montana Ave** and **Main St.**

Venice

Boho-chic **Abbot Kinney Blvd** (www.abbotkinneyonline.com) has become one of LA's top shopping destinations. Come see it on the monthly **First Friday** (www.abbotkinney-1stfridays.com) gathering, when galleries stay open late.

Alexis Bittar
JEWELRY

(Map p368; ☑310-452-6901; www.alexisbittar.com; 1612 Abbot Kinney Blvd; ⊙11am-7pm Mon-Sat, noon-6pm Sun) High-end jewelry known for Bittar's use of lucite, which is hand carved and painted in his Brooklyn studio. Some of it looks like stone. He started by selling it on the streets in Manhattan where he was picked up by the MOMA store. Now, he's kind of a big deal.

Will
LEATHER GOODS

(Map p368; www.willleathergoods.com; 1360 Abbot Kinney Blvd; ⊙10am-8pm) A terrific leather-goods store out of Portland, and one of just three nationwide. It does fine leather bags, briefcases, backpacks, belts, wallets and sandals for men and women. Our favorite was the bike messenger bag inlaid with colorful remnant Oaxacan wool.

ⓘ Information

EMERGENCY

Police, Fire, Ambulance (☑911)

Police (☑877-275-5273; www.lapdonline.org) For nonemergencies within the city of LA.

Rape & Battering Hotline (☑310-392-8381, 213-626-3393; ⊙24hr)

INTERNET ACCESS

Internet cafes in LA seem to have the lifespan of a fruit fly, but dozens of cafes and restaurants around town offer free wi-fi.

MEDIA

KCRW 89.9 FM (www.kcrw.com) LA's cultural pulse and the best station in the city. Beams National Public Radio (NPR), eclectic and indie music, intelligent talk, and hosts shows and events throughout Southern California.

La Opinión (www.laopinion.com) Spanish-language daily.

LA Weekly (www.laweekly.com) Free alternative news, live music and entertainment listings.

Los Angeles Downtown News (www.downtownnews.com) The finger on the cultural, political and economic pulse of the booming downtown district.

Los Angeles Times (www.latimes.com) Major daily newspaper.

MEDICAL SERVICES

Cedars-Sinai Medical Center (☑310-423-3277; http://cedars-sinai.edu; 8700 Beverly Blvd, West Hollywood; ⊙24hr) Emergency room.

Rite Aid Pharmacies (☑800-748-3243; www.riteaid.com)

MONEY

Travelex Santa Monica (☑310-260-9219; www.travelex.com; 201 Santa Monica Blvd, Suite 101, Santa Monica; ⊙9am-5pm Mon-Thu, to 6pm Fri); West Hollywood (☑310-659-6093, www.travelex.com; US Bank, 8901 Santa Monica Blvd, West Hollywood; ⊙9:30am-5pm Mon-Thu, 9am-6pm Fri, 9am-1pm Sat).

POST

Call ☑800-275-8777 for the nearest post office branch.

TOURIST INFORMATION

Downtown LA Visitor Center (Map p352; www.discoverlosangeles.com; 800 N Alameda St, Downtown; ⊙8:30am-5pm Mon-Fri)

Hollywood Visitor Information Center (Map p356; ☑323-467-6412; http://discoverlosangeles.com; Hollywood & Highland complex, 6801 Hollywood Blvd, Hollywood; ⊙10am-10pm Mon-Sat, to 7pm Sun) In the Dolby Theatre walkway.

Long Beach Area Convention & Tourism Bureau (☑562-628-8850; www.visitlongbeach.com; 3rd fl, One World Trade Center, 301 E Ocean Blvd, Long Beach; ⊙11am-7pm Sun-Thu, 11:30am-7:30pm Fri & Sat Jun-Sep, 10am-4pm Fri-Sun Oct-May)

Santa Monica (Map p368; ☑800-544-5319; www.santamonica.com; 2427 Main St, Santa Monica) Roving information officers patrol on and around the promenade (on Segways!).

❶ Getting There & Away

AIR

The main LA gateway is **Los Angeles International Airport** (LAX; ☑310-646-5252; www.lawa.org/lax; 1 World Way; 🛜), a U-shaped, bilevel complex with nine terminals linked by the free **Shuttle A** leaving from the lower (arrival) level.

Cabs and hotel and car-rental shuttles stop here as well. A free minibus for travelers with a disability can be ordered by calling ☑310-646-6402. Ticketing and check-in are on the upper (departure) level. The hub for most international airlines is the Tom Bradley International Terminal.

Domestic flights operated by Alaska, American, Southwest, United and other major US airlines also arrive at Bob Hope/Burbank Airport (p50600), which is handy if you're headed for Hollywood, downtown or Pasadena.

To the south, on the border with Orange County, the small Long Beach Airport (p50700) is convenient for Disneyland and is served by Alaska, US Airways and Jet Blue.

BUS

The main bus terminal for **Greyhound** (☑213-629-8401; www.greyhound.com; 1716 E 7th St) is in a grimy part of downtown, so avoid arriving after dark. Take bus 18 to the 7th St subway station or bus 66 to Pershing Square Station, then hop on the Metro Rail Red Line to Hollywood or Union Station with onward service around town. Some Greyhound buses go directly to the terminal in **Hollywood** (1715 N Cahuenga Blvd).

CAR & MOTORCYCLE

All the major car-rental agencies have branches at area airports. **Eagle Rider** (☑888-600-6020; www.eaglerider.com; 11860 S La Cienega Blvd, Hawthorne; per day from $99; ⊙9am-5pm) and Route 66 (p51100) rent Harleys.

TRAIN

Amtrak trains roll into downtown's historic **Union Station** (☑800-872-7245; www.amtrak.com; 800 N Alameda St). The *Pacific Surfliner* travels daily between San Diego, Santa Barbara and San Luis Obispo via LA.

❶ Getting Around

TO/FROM THE AIRPORT

All services mentioned below leave from the lower terminal level of LAX. Door-to-door shuttles, such as those operated by **Prime Time** (☑800-733-8267; www.primetimeshuttle.com) and Super Shuttle (www.supershuttle.com) charge $21, $27 and $16 for trips to Santa Monica, Hollywood or downtown, respectively.

Curbside dispatchers will be on hand to summon a taxi. The flat rate to downtown LA is $47, while going to Santa Monica costs $30 to $35, to West Hollywood around $40, to Hollywood $50 and to Disneyland $90.

LAX FlyAway (☑866-435-9529; www.lawa.org; one-way $8) buses travel nonstop to downtown's Union Station ($8, 45 minutes), Van Nuys ($8, 45 minutes), Westwood Village near UCLA ($10, 30 minutes), and to the Expo Line Light Rail station at La Brea and Exposition Blvd ($7,

1¼ hours) for connections to South Central, Hollywood and Union Station.

For Santa Monica or Venice, catch the free Shuttle C bus to the **LAX Transit Center** (96th St & Sepulveda Blvd), then change to the Santa Monica Rapid 3 ($1, one hour). The center is the hub for buses serving all of LA. If you're headed for Culver City, catch Culver City bus 6 ($1, 20 minutes). For Manhattan or Hermosa Beach, hop aboard Beach Cities Transit 109 ($1), which also stops at Lot G. For Redondo Beach head to Lot C and hop aboard the Metro Local 232 ($1.50).

BICYCLE

Most buses have bike racks, and bikes ride for free, although you must load and unload them yourself. Bicycles are allowed on Metro Rail trains except during rush hour (6:30am to 8:30am and 4:30pm to 6:30pm Monday to Friday).

CAR & MOTORCYCLE

Unless time is no factor – or money is extremely tight – you're going to want to spend some time behind the wheel, although this means contending with some of the worst traffic in the country. Avoid crossing town at rush hour (7am to 9am and 3:30pm to 7pm).

Parking at motels and cheaper hotels is usually free, while fancier ones charge anywhere from $8 to $40 for the privilege. Valet parking at nicer restaurants and hotels is commonplace with rates ranging from $5 to $10.

PUBLIC TRANSPORTATION

Most public transportation is handled by **Metro** (☎ 323-466-3876; www.metro.net), which offers trip-planning help through its website.

The regular base fare is $1.75 per boarding or $7 for a day pass with unlimited rides. Weekly passes are $25 and valid from Sunday to Saturday. Monthly passes are $100 and valid for 30 days.

Single tickets and day passes are available from bus drivers and vending machines at each train station. Weekly and monthly passes must be bought at one of 650 locations around town.

Metro operates about 200 bus lines, most of them local routes stopping every few blocks. Metro Rapid buses stop less frequently.

Metro Rail is a network of six light-rail lines and two subway lines, with five of them converging in downtown. The Expo Line linking Exposition Park and downtown LA with Culver City is expected to reach Santa Monica by 2015.

Red Line The most useful for visitors, it links downtown's Union Station to North Hollywood (San Fernando Valley) via central Hollywood and Universal City.

Blue Line Downtown to Long Beach; connects with the Red Line at 7th St/Metro Center station and the Green Line at the Imperial/Wilmington stop.

Gold Line East LA to Little Tokyo, Chinatown and Pasadena via Union Station, Mt Washington and Highland Park; connects with the Red Line at Union Station.

Green Line Norwalk to Redondo Beach; connects with the Blue Line at Imperial/Wilmington.

Purple Line Subway between downtown LA and Koreatown; shares six stations with the Red Line.

Orange Line Links downtown and Hollywood with the west San Fernando Valley; connects with the Red Line in North Hollywood.

Expo Line Links USC and Exposition Park with Culver City to the west and downtown LA to the northeast, where it connects with the Red Line at Union Station. The Santa Monica extension is scheduled to open in 2015.

Santa Monica–based **Big Blue Bus** (☎ 310-451-5444; www.bigbluebus.com; fares from $1) burns clean fuel and serves Santa Monica, Venice, Westwood and LAX ($1). Its express bus 10 runs from Santa Monica to downtown ($2, one hour).

The **Culver CityBus** (www.culvercity.org) provides service throughout Culver City and the Westside, including LAX ($1). **Long Beach Transit** (www.lbtransit.com) serves Long Beach and surrounding communities.

DASH Buses, operated by the **LA Department of Transportation** (LADOT; www.ladottransit.com), offer 33 routes serving local communities (50¢ per boarding) until 7pm.

TAXI

Getting around by cab will cost you. Cabs are best organized over the phone, though some prowl the streets late at night. In the city of LA, taxi rates are $2.85 at flagfall plus about $2.70 per mile. Cabs leaving from LAX charge a $4 airport fee. For details, check www.taxicabsla.org. In Santa Monica, call **Taxi Taxi** (☎ 310-444-4444; www.santamonicataxi.com).

Uber and UberX (www.uber.com) are extremely popular for cheap and more luxurious rides in LA.

AROUND LOS ANGELES

Ditch the congestion, crowds and smog, and use LA as a hub to all the natural glory of California. Get an early start to beat the traffic (or catch a ferry, Greyhound bus or ride the Amtrak rails), point the compass across the ocean or up into the mountains.

Catalina Island

Mediterranean-flavored Catalina Island is a popular getaway for harried Angelenos, but sinks under the weight of day-trippers in summer. Stay overnight, though, and feel the ambience go from frantic to romantic.

It's a nice stroll along the Avalon waterfront to the art-deco **Casino** (1 Casino Way), which has murals, a movie theater and a fabulous upstairs ballroom; the last can only be seen on guided one-hour tours ($23). There's good snorkeling at **Lovers' Cove** and at **Casino Point Marine Park**, a marine reserve that's also the best shore dive. **Descanso Beach Ocean Sports** (www.kayakcatalinaisland.com; kayak rentals per hr/day from $22/52, SUP rentals per hr/day $24/60) rents snorkeling gear, stand up paddleboard kits and kayaks.

About 1.5 miles inland from Avalon harbor is the peaceful **Wrigley Memorial & Botanical Gardens** (📞 310-510-2595; 1400 Avalon Canyon Rd; adult/child /senior $7/free/5; ⊙ 8am-5pm), where you'll enjoy sweeping garden views from a monument awash in colorful local tile.

To get into the protected backcountry, hop on the **Safari Bus** (📞 310-510-2800; tickets $10-32; ⊙ mid-Jun–early Sep), which goes all the way to Two Harbors. You must book in advance and get a permit (and maps) from the **Catalina Conservancy** (📞 310-510-2595; www.catalinaconservancy.org; 125 Claressa Ave, Avalon; biking/hiking $35/free) if you're going to be hiking or mountain biking.

Certified scuba divers should find **Catalina Dive Shop** (www.catalinadiveshop.com; Lovers Cove; per trip $99-129) to glimpse local shipwrecks and kelp forests. It rents snorkel gear here too. **Two Harbors Dive and Recreation Center** (www.visitcatalinaisland.com; guided dive trips $100-140) accesses pristine dive sites off the island's less-developed coast.

In Avalon nest at the laid-back **Pavilion Hotel** (📞 877-778-8322; www.visitcatalinaisland.com/hotels-packages/avalon/pavilion-hotel; 513 Crescent Ave; r from $185) or splashier **Hotel Metropole** (📞 800-300-8528; www.hotel-metropole.com; 205 Crescent Ave; r from $175). In Two Harbors, it's all about the **Banning House Lodge** (📞 877-778-8322; www.visitcatalinaisland.com/hotels-packages/two-harbors/banning-house-lodge; 1 Banning House Rd; r from $129), a 1910 California Craftsman classic. For camping information, see www.visitcatalinaisland.com/avalon/camping.php.

Bluewater Grill (📞 310-510-3474; www.bluewatergrill.com; 306 Crescent Ave; mains $19-39; ⊙ 11am-10pm) offers sumptuous seafood dinners and **CC Gallagher** (www.ccgallagher.com; 523 Crescent Ave; ⊙ 7am-midnight Sun-Thu, to 1am Fri & Sat), part wine shop, part cafe, part sushi bar, does it all quite well.

❶ Getting There & Away

Reservations are recommended in the summer for ferries to Avalon and Two Harbors.

Catalina Express (www.catalinaexpress.com; round-trip adult/child $75/60) Ferries to Avalon from San Pedro, Long Beach and Dana Point (Orange County), and to Two Harbors from San Pedro. It takes one to 1½ hours, with up to three ferries daily. Ride free on your birthday!

Catalina Flyer (📞 800-830-7744; www.catalinaferries.com; round-trip adult/under 12yr/senior $70/53/65) Catamaran to Avalon and Two Harbors from Balboa Harbor in Newport Beach (one to 1½ hours).

Big Bear Lake

Big Bear Lake is a low-key and family-friendly mountain resort (elevation 6750ft) about 110 miles northeast of LA. Snowy winters lure scores of skiers and boarders to its two mountains; summers bring hikers, mountain bikers and water-sports enthusiasts wishing to escape the stifling heat down in the basin. Blessed with postcard canyon views, the **Rim of the World Scenic Byway** (Hwy 18) is one of America's great drives. We suggest diverging from the trodden path early, and visiting the sculpted sandstone of **Mormon Rocks**. From there take Hwy 138 past **Silverwood Lake** and **Lake Gregory**, then climb Hwy 18 into quaint **Blue Jay** and **Lake Arrowhead**. This is where the vistas get serious and the hairpins exciting. Lake Arrowhead's fashionable mall and ski resort makes a nice respite from the road. Once back on the highway, the most jaw-dropping stretch of road takes you into Big Bear Lake.

🏃 Activities

Big Bear's two ski mountains are jointly managed by **Big Bear Mountain Resorts** (www.bigbearmountainresorts.com; adult/child lift ticket $56/46). The higher of the two, **Bear Mountain** (8805ft) is nirvana for freestyle freaks with more than 150 jumps, 80 jibs, and two pipes including a 580ft in-ground superpipe. **Snow Summit** (8200ft) is more about traditional downhill and has trails for everyone. Altogether the mountains are served by 26 lifts and crisscrossed by more than 55 runs. Ski and boot rentals are about $30.

In summer Snow Summit issues its siren call to mountain bikers. Several pro and amateur races take place here each year. The 9-mile **Grandview Loop** is great for getting your feet in gear. The **Scenic Sky**

Around Los Angeles

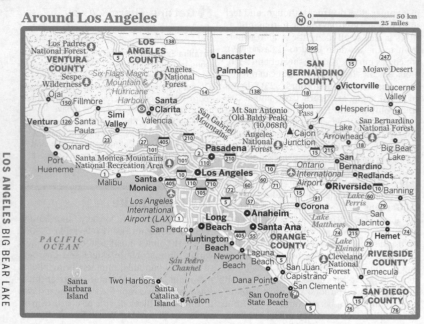

Chair (one-way/day $12/25; ☺May–start of ski season) provides easy access to the top. Maps, tickets and bike rentals are available from **Bear Valley Bikes** (www.bvbikes.com; 40298 Big Bear Blvd; bikes per hr incl helmet $10-20, per day $40-70). It charges higher rates for full suspension, and has fat bikes too.

To get off the beaten track, take your car for an off-road spin along the **Gold Fever Trail**, a 20-mile self-guided romp on a graded dirt road around an old gold-mining area.

🛏 Sleeping & Eating

For cheap sleeps tuck into the clean and friendly **Big Bear Hostel** (☏909-866-8900; www.adventurehostel.com; 527 Knickerbocker Rd; r $20-40; P@⊜). **Switzerland Haus** (☏800-335-3729, 909-866-3729; www.switzerlandhaus.com; 41829 Switzerland Dr; r incl breakfast $125-249; @⊜) offers comfy rooms with mountain-view patios and a Nordic sauna. **Himalayan** (www.himalayanbigbear.com; 672 Pine Knot Ave; mains $8-17; ☺11am-9pm Sun-Tue, to 10pm Fri & Sat; 🍴🚭) is a popular Nepali and Indian kitchen with speedy service. **North Shore Cafe** (☏909-866-5879; www.dininginbigbear.com; 39226 North Shore Dr/Hwy 38, Fawnskin; breakfast & lunch mains $6-12; ☺8am-4pm Wed-Thu, 8am-9pm Fri, 7am-9pm Sat, 7am-6pm Sun Oct-Apr, also 8am-4pm Mon May-Sep; ⊜🚭) is a dear

sweet diner set in a cabin with tasty breakfasts. Hit **Peppercorn Grille** (☏909-866-5405; www.peppercorngrille.com; 553 Pine Knot Ave; mains $8.95-15.95; ☺11am-9pm Sun-Thu, to 10pm Fri & Sat) for candlelight and tablecloths.

ℹ Information

Big Bear Blvd (Hwy 18), the main road, runs south of the lake, skirting the pedestrian-friendly village with cutesy shops, galleries, restaurants and the **visitors center** (www.bigbear.com; 630 Bartlett Rd; ☺8am-5pm Mon-Fri, 9am-5pm Sat & Sun). The ski resorts are east of the village. Quiet N Shore Dr (Hwy 38) provides access to campgrounds and trails.

If you're driving, pick up a National Forest Adventure Pass, available at the **Big Bear Discovery Center** (☏909-382-2790; www.bigbeardiscoverycenter.com; 40971 N Shore Dr, Fawnskin; ☺8am-4:30pm, closed Wed & Thu mid-Sep–mid-May) on the North Shore.

ℹ Getting There & Away

Big Bear is on Hwy 18, an offshoot of Hwy 30 in San Bernardino. A quicker approach is via Hwy 330, which starts in Highland and intersects with Hwy 18 in Running Springs. **Mountain Area Regional Transit Authority** (Marta; ☏909-878-5200; www.marta.cc) buses connect Big Bear with the Greyhound and Metrolink stations in San Bernardino ($2.50, 1¼ hours).

Disneyland & Orange County

Best Places to Eat

➡ Walt's Wharf (p400)

➡ Napa Rose (p393)

➡ 242 Cafe Fusion Sushi (p421)

➡ Bear Flag Fish Company (p407)

➡ Ramos House Café (p423)

Best Places to Stay

➡ Shorebreak Hotel (p402)

➡ Disney's Grand Californian Hotel & Spa (p391)

➡ The Tides Inn (p420)

➡ Crystal Cove Beach Cottages (p417)

➡ Resort at Pelican Hill (p406)

Why Go?

Chances are that Orange County, that stretch between Los Angeles and San Diego, has seeped into your consciousness even if you've never been here.

No doubt Mickey Mouse and friends have been a part of that (Disneyland is California's biggest attraction). So too have TV series from *Real Housewives* to MTV's *Laguna Beach,* from *The OC* to *Arrested Development*, which have all been set here, taking the county's image from humdrum to hip, a place of mythically (gl)amorous teens, gorgeous beaches and socialite catfights.

While there's a whiff of truth to those stereotypes of life behind the 'Orange Curtain' – big, boxy mansions, fortress-like shopping malls, the overly entitled tossing Happy Meals out of their Humvees – this diverse county's 789 sq miles, 34 cities and three million people create deep pockets of individuality, beauty and different ways of thinking, keepin' the OC 'real,' no matter one's reality.

When to Go

Anaheim

May Visitation dips after spring break until Memorial Day. Mostly sunny days, balmy temperatures.

Jul & Aug Summer vacation and beach season peak. Surfing and art festivals by the coast.

Sep Blue skies, cooler temperatures inland, fewer crowds. Tall Ships Festival at Dana Point.

SURFING WALK OF FAME

The OC's answer to Hollywood Boulevard immortalizes surf legends steps from the Huntington Beach Pier.

Top Shows & Parades at Disney Resort

➡ **World of Color** (DCA)

➡ **Fantasmic!** (Disneyland)

➡ **Mickey's Soundsational Parade** (Disneyland)

➡ **Pixar Play Parade** (DCA)

California Culture

Culture vultures: don't miss some of California's best-known cultural institutions: Segerstrom Center for the Arts (p408), South Coast Repertory (p408), Bowers Museum (p396) and Laguna Beach's Festival of Arts (p419) and Pageant of the Masters (p420).

For Local News

➡ **Coastline Pilot** (www.coastlinepilot.com) Laguna Beach.

➡ **Daily Pilot** (www. dailypilot.com) Newport Beach and Costa Mesa.

➡ **OC Weekly** (www. ocweekly.com) Alternative paper for arts and politics.

➡ **Orange County Register** (www.ocregister.com) National and regional news, culture and sports.

Theme-Park Passes

Visiting a lot of SoCal theme parks? The **Southern California CityPass** (www.citypass.com/southern-california; adult/child 3-9yr from $328/284) covers three-day 'Park Hopper' admission to Disneyland Resort, plus one-day admission to SeaWorld San Diego (p633) and Universal Studios Hollywood (p567). The CityPass price is at least $100 less than the combined regular ticket prices. Otherwise, look online for specials (eg five-day Park Hopper passes for the three-day price) or seasonal discounts on annual passports for Southern California residents and their guests.

FEELING THE HEAT AT DISNEYLAND

When Walt Disney opened Disneyland on July 17, 1955, he declared it the 'Happiest Place on Earth.' However, its opening day was a disaster. Temperatures over 100°F (38°C) melted asphalt underfoot, leaving women's high heels stuck in the tar. There were plumbing problems: all of the drinking fountains quit working. Hollywood stars didn't show up on time, and more than twice the number of expected guests – some 28,000 by day's end – crowded through the gates, some holding counterfeit tickets. None of this kept eager Disney fans away for long; more than 50 million tourists visited in its first decade alone. Nowadays, more than 14 million kids, grandparents, honeymooners and international tourists come to Walt's playground every year.

Disneyland To-Do List

➡ Make hotel reservations or book a Disneyland package.

➡ Sign up online for Disney Fans Insider e-newsletters and resort updates.

➡ Check the parks' opening hours and live show and entertainment schedules online.

➡ Make dining reservations for sit-down restaurants or special meals with Disney characters.

➡ Buy print-at-home tickets and passes online.

➡ Recheck the park opening hours and Anaheim Resort Transportation (ART) or hotel-shuttle schedules.

➡ Pack a small day pack with sunscreen, hat, sunglasses, swimwear, change of clothes, jacket or hoodie, lightweight plastic rain poncho, and extra batteries and memory cards for digital and video cameras.

➡ Fully charge your electronic devices, including cameras and phones.

➡ Download a Disneyland app to your smartphone.

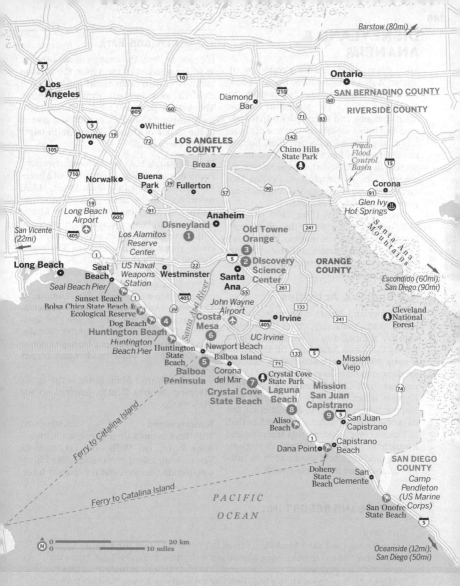

Disneyland & Orange County Highlights

1 Screaming your head off on Space Mountain at **Disneyland** (p386).

2 Experiencing the eye of a hurricane at the **Discovery Science Center** (p396).

3 Shopping for vintage treasures and slurping milkshakes in **Old Towne Orange** (p396).

4 Building a beach bonfire after a day of surfing at **Huntington Beach** (p401).

5 Cycling the as-seen-on-TV sands of Newport Beach's **Balboa Peninsula** (p404).

6 Discovering Orange County's alternative side at the Lab and the Camp 'anti-malls' in **Costa Mesa** (p408).

7 Falling asleep to the sound of the surf at **Crystal Cove State Beach** (p417).

8 Watching the sun dip below the horizon at **Laguna Beach** (p418).

9 Being awed by the Spanish colonial history and the beauty of **Mission San Juan Capistrano** (p422).

DISNEYLAND & ANAHEIM

Mickey is one lucky mouse. Created by animator Walt Disney in 1928, this irrepressible mouse caught a ride on a multimedia juggernaut (film, TV, publishing, music, merchandising and theme parks) that rocketed him into a global stratosphere of recognition, money and influence. Plus, he lives in the 'Happiest Place on Earth,' an 'imagineered' hyper-reality where the streets are always clean, the employees – called 'cast members' – are always upbeat and there are parades every day of the year.

Since opening his Disneyland home in 1955, he has been a pretty thoughtful host. For the more than 14 million kids, grandparents, honeymooners and international tourists who visit every year, Disneyland remains a magical experience.

◉ Sights & Activities

The Disneyland Resort is open 365 days a year, though hours vary; check the website. One-day admission to *either* Disneyland or Disney California Adventure (DCA) currently costs $96 for adults and $90 for children aged three to nine. To visit *both* parks in one day costs $135/129 per adult/child on a 'Park Hopper' ticket. A variety of multiday Park Hopper tickets cost up to $305/289 for five days of admission within a two-week period.

Tickets cover all attractions and rides and a variety of parades and shows throughout the day and fireworks most nights in summer and selected times year-round.

◉ Disneyland Park

It's hard to deny the change in atmosphere as you're whisked by tram from the parking lot into the heart of the resort and wide-eyed children lean forward with anticipation. This is their park, but adults who can willingly suspend disbelief may well also give in to the 'magic of Disney'; Uncle Walt's taken care of every detail.

Main Street, U.S.A.   RIDES, ATTRACTIONS
Fashioned after Walt's hometown of Marceline, Missouri, bustling Main Street, U.S.A. resembles the classic turn-of-the-20th-century all-American town. It's an idyllic, relentlessly upbeat representation, complete with barbershop quartet, penny arcades, ice-cream shops and a steam train. The music playing in the background is from American musicals, and there's a flag-retreat ceremony every afternoon.

Great Moments with Mr. Lincoln, a 15-minute Audio-Animatronics presentation on Honest Abe, sits inside the fascinating Disneyland Story exhibit. Nearby, kids love seeing old-school Disney cartoons like *Steamboat Willie* inside Main Street Cinema.

Lording it over Main Street is the iconic Sleeping Beauty Castle, featured on the Disney logo.

Tomorrowland   RIDES, ATTRACTIONS
This 'land' honors three timeless futurists – Jules Verne, HG Wells, and Leonardo da Vinci – while major corporations like Microsoft, Honda, Siemens and HP sponsor futur-

---

DISNEYLAND RESORT IN...

One Day
Get to Disneyland early. Stroll Main Street, U.S.A. toward Sleeping Beauty Castle. Enter Tomorrowland to ride Space Mountain. In Fantasyland (p387) don't miss the classic "it's a small world" ride. Race down the Matterhorn Bobsleds or take tots to Mickey's Toontown. Grab a FASTPASS for the Indiana Jones™ Adventure or Pirates of the Caribbean (p388) before lunching in New Orleans Square (p388). Plummet down Splash Mountain (p388), then visit the Haunted Mansion (p388) before the fireworks and Fantasmic! shows begin.

Two Days
At Disney California Adventure (p392), take a virtual hang-gliding ride on Soarin' Over California (p390) and let kids tackle the Redwood Creek Challenge Trail (p390) before having fun at Paradise Pier (p390), with its roller coaster, Ferris wheel and carnival games. Watch the Pixar Play Parade, then explore Cars Land (p390) or cool off on the Grizzly River Run (p390). After dark, drop by The Twilight Zone Tower of Terror (p389) and World of Color show.

ⓘ FASTPASS

Disneyland and DCA's FASTPASS system can significantly cut your wait times on many of the most popular rides and attractions.

➡ At FASTPASS ticket machines – located near entrances to select rides – insert your park entrance ticket. You'll receive an additional ticket showing a return time.

➡ Show up within the window of time on the ticket and join the ride's FASTPASS line. There'll still be a wait, but it's shorter (typically 15 minutes or less). Hang on to your FASTPASS ticket until you board the ride.

➡ If you miss the time window printed on your FASTPASS ticket, you can still try joining the FASTPASS line.

---

istic robot shows and interactive exhibits in the **Innoventions** pavilion.

The retro high-tech **monorail** glides to a stop in Tomorrowland, its rubber tires traveling a 13-minute, 2.5-mile round-trip route to Downtown Disney. Kiddies will want to shoot laser beams on **Buzz Lightyear's Astro Blaster** and drive their own miniature cars in the classic **Autopia** ride (don't worry, they're on tracks).

Then jump aboard the **Finding Nemo Submarine Voyage** to look for the world's most famous clownfish from within a refurbished submarine and rumble through an underwater volcanic eruption.

Star Tours – The Adventure Continues clamps you into a Starspeeder shuttle for a wild and bumpy 3D ride through the desert canyons of Tatooine on a space mission, so you can ride it again and again. **Space Mountain**, Tomorrowland's signature attraction and one of the USA's best roller coasters, hurtles you into complete darkness at frightening speed. Another classic is Captain EO, a special-effects tribute film starring Michael Jackson.

Fantasyland RIDES, ATTRACTIONS
Fantasyland is home to **"it's a small world,"** a boat ride past hundreds of creepy Audio-Animatronics children from different cultures all singing the annoying theme song in an astounding variety of languages, joined by Disney characters. Another classic, the **Matterhorn Bobsleds**, mimics a ride down a mountain. The old-school, *Wind in the Willows*–inspired **Mr. Toad's Wild Ride** is a loopy jaunt in an open-air jalopy through London.

Younger kids love whirling around the **Mad Tea Party** teacup ride and **King Arthur Carrousel**, then cavorting with characters in **Mickey's Toontown**, a topsy-turvy mini-metropolis where kiddos can traipse

through Mickey and Minnie's houses and dozens of storefronts.

Frontierland RIDES, ATTRACTIONS
Frontierland's Tom Sawyer Island – the only attraction in the park personally designed by Uncle Walt – has been reimagined as **Pirate's Lair on Tom Sawyer Island**, and now honors Tom in name only. After a raft ride to the island, wander among roving Jack Sparrow–inspired pirates, cannibal cages, ghostly apparitions and buried treasure.

Cruise around the island on the **Mark Twain Riverboat**, a Mississippi-style paddle-wheel boat, or the 18th-century replica sailing ship **Columbia**. The rest of Frontierland gives a nod to the rip-roarin' Old West with a shooting gallery and **Big Thunder Mountain Railroad**, a mining-themed roller coaster.

Adventureland RIDES, ATTRACTIONS
The hands-down highlight of jungle-themed Adventureland is the safari-style **Indiana Jones™ Adventure**. Enormous Humvee-type vehicles lurch and jerk their way through the wild for spine-tingling re-creations of stunts from the famous film trilogy. Nearby, little ones love climbing the stairways of **Tarzan's Treehouse™**.

Cool down with a **Jungle Cruise** featuring exotic Audio-Animatronics animals from the Amazon, Ganges, Nile and Irrawaddy Rivers. Drop by the **Enchanted Tiki Room** to look at the carvings of Hawaiian gods and goddesses, and animatronic birds singing a

ⓘ SINGLE-RIDER LINES

If you're here alone, look for a separate, shorter single-rider line. Availability may depend on the size of the crowd – and also on how that particular cast member is feeling that day, so be nice!

Disneyland Resort

corny song so good natured it's hard not to love.

New Orleans Square RIDES, ATTRACTIONS
New Orleans was Walt's and his wife Lillian's favorite city, and this stunning square has all the charm of the French Quarter minus the marauding drunks. **Pirates of the Caribbean** is the longest ride in Disneyland (17 minutes) and inspired the popular movies. Tawdry pirates and dead buccaneers perch atop their mounds of booty and Jack Sparrow pops up occasionally.

At the **Haunted Mansion**, 999 happy spirits, goblins and ghosts appear while

you ride in a cocoonlike 'Doom Buggy' through web-covered graveyards of dancing skeletons.

Critter Country RIDES, ATTRACTIONS
Critter Country's main attraction is **Splash Mountain**, a flume ride that transports you through the story of Brer Rabbit and Brer Bear, based on the controversial 1946 film *Song of the South*. Your picture is taken at the top, and occasionally guests will lift their shirts, leading to the ride's sometime nickname 'Flash Mountain' (naughty photos are deleted!). Just past Splash Mountain, hop in a mobile beehive on **The Many Ad-**

Disneyland Resort

DISNEYLAND & ORANGE COUNTY DISNEYLAND & ANAHEIM

ventures of **Winnie the Pooh**. Nearby on the Rivers of America, you can paddle **Davy Crockett's Explorer Canoes** on summer weekends.

⊙ **Disney California Adventure**

Across the plaza from Disneyland, Disney California Adventure (DCA) is a G-rated ode to California. Opened in 2001, it covers more acres than Disneyland and feels less crowded, and it has more modern rides and attractions.

Hollywood Land   RIDES, ATTRACTIONS

California's biggest factory of dreams is presented here in miniature, with soundstages, movable props and – of course – a studio store. **The Twilight Zone Tower of Terror** is a 13-story drop down an elevator chute situated in a haunted hotel eerily resembling the historic **Hollywood Roosevelt Hotel** (www.hollywoodroosevelt.com; 7000 Hollywood Blvd; ⊗24hr; 🅿) FREE. From the upper floors of the tower, you'll have views of the Santa Ana mountains, if only for a few heart-pounding seconds.

DISNEYLAND & ORANGE COUNTY DISNEYLAND & ANAHEIM

TOP 10 RIDES FOR TEENS

For the adventure seekers in your brood, try the following;

➡ Indiana Jones™ Adventure (p387); Adventureland

➡ Space Mountain (p387); Tomorrowland

➡ Twilight Zone Tower of Terror (p389); Hollywood Land, DCA

➡ Splash Mountain (p388); Critter Country

➡ California Screamin'; Paradise Pier, DCA

➡ Soarin' Over California; Golden State, DCA

➡ Big Thunder Mountain Railroad (p387); Frontierland

➡ Grizzly River Run; Golden State, DCA

➡ Matterhorn Bobsleds (p387); Fantasyland

➡ Radiator Springs Racers; Cars Land, DCA

Less brave children can navigate a taxicab through 'Monstropolis' on the **Monsters, Inc: Mike & Sulley to the Rescue!** ride heading back toward the street's beginning.

The air-conditioned **Muppet Vision 3D** theater shows a special-effects film. Learn how to draw like Disney in the Animation Academy, discover how cartoon artwork becomes 3D at the Character Close-Up or simply be amazed by the interactive Sorcerer's Workshop, all housed inside the **Animation Building**.

Golden State   RIDES, ATTRACTIONS
Golden State highlights California's natural and human achievements. **Soarin' Over California** is a virtual hang-gliding ride using Omnimax technology that 'flies' you over the Golden Gate Bridge, Yosemite Falls, Lake Tahoe, Malibu and, of course, Disneyland. Keep your senses open for breezes and aromas of the sea, orange groves and pine forests.

Grizzly River Run takes you 'rafting' down a faux Sierra Nevada river – you will get wet, so come when it's warm. Kids can tackle the **Redwood Creek Challenge Trail**, with its 'Big Sir' redwoods, wooden towers and lookouts, and rock slide and climbing traverses. Get a behind-the-scenes looks at what's in the works next for Disneyland's theme parks inside **Walt Disney Imagineering Blue Sky Cellar**.

Paradise Pier   RIDES, ATTRACTIONS
Paradise Pier, which looks like a combination of all the beachside amusement piers in California, presents carnival rides like **California Screamin'**; this state-of-the-art roller coaster resembles an old wooden coaster, but it's got a smooth-as-silk steel track.

At **Toy Story Midway Mania!**, a 4D ride, earn points by shooting at targets while your carnival car swivels and careens through an oversize, old-fashioned game arcade. **Mickey's Fun Wheel** is a 15-story Ferris wheel where gondolas pitch and yaw in little loops as well as the big one. **Silly Symphony Swings** is a hybrid carousel with tornado-like chair swings, the pre-school set can ride a more sedate version on the **Golden Zephyr** and bounce along on the **Jumpin' Jellyfish**. **Goofy's Sky School** is a cute and relatively tame cartoon-themed coaster ride.

Cars Land   RIDES, ATTRACTIONS
Based on Disney·Pixar's popular *Cars* movies, this place gives top billing to the wacky **Radiator Springs Racers**, a race-car ride that bumps and jumps around a track painstakingly decked out like the Great American West. Tractor-towed trailers swing their way around the 'dance floor' at **Mater's Junkyard Jamboree**. Steer your bumper car (well, bumper tire, to be exact) through **Luigi's Flying Tires** (enter via the Casa Della Tires shop) or ride along with Route 66–themed gift shops and diners like the tepee-style Cozy Cone Motel.

🛏 Sleeping

🛏 Disneyland Resort

Each of the resort's **hotels** (☎ 800-225-2024, reservations 714-956-6425; www.disneyland.com) has a swimming pool with waterslide, kids' activity programs, fitness center, restaurants and bars, business center, and valet or complimentary self-parking for registered guests. Every standard room can accommodate up to five guests and has a mini-refrigerator and a coffeemaker. Look for discounted lodging-and-admission packages and early park entry times for resort guests.

★ **Disney's Grand Californian Hotel & Spa**   LUXURY HOTEL **$$$**
(✎info 714-635-2300, reservations 714-956-6425; disneyland.disney.go.com/grand-californian-hotel; 1600 S Disneyland Dr; d from $360; P❋@🛜🛌) Soaring timber beams rise above the cathedral-like lobby of this six-story homage to the Arts and Crafts architectural movement. Cushy rooms have triple-sheeted beds, down pillows, bathrobes and all-custom furnishings. Outside there's a faux-redwood waterslide into the pool. At night, kids wind down with bedtime stories by the lobby's giant stone hearth. For a little adult pampering, your coconut rub and milk ritual wrap awaits at the Mandara Spa.

Paradise Pier Hotel   HOTEL **$$$**
(✎info 714-999-0990, reservations 714-956-6425; http://disneyland.disney.go.com/paradise-pier-hotel; 1717 S Disneyland Dr; d from $240; P❋🛜🛌) Sunbursts, surfboards and a giant superslide are all on deck at the Paradise Pier Hotel, the smallest (472 rooms), cheapest and maybe the most fun of the Disney hotel trio. Kids will love the beachy decor and game arcade, not to mention the roof-deck pool and the tiny-tot video room filled with mini Adirondack chairs.

Disneyland Hotel   HOTEL **$$$**
(✎714-778-6600; www.disneyland.com; 1150 Magic Way; r $210-395; P@🛜🛌) Built in 1955, the park's original hotel has expanded to three towers with themed lobbies (adventure, fantasy and frontier), and good-sized rooms boasting Mickey-hand wall sconces and headboards lit like the fireworks over Sleeping Beauty Castle. This 972-room hotel also has the best swimming pool of the three Disney hotels, plus cartoon character–themed Signature Suites.

🛏 **Anaheim**

Apart from Disneyland, Anaheim is a year-round convention destination. Room rates spike accordingly. Look for packages including tickets to Disneyland or other local attractions, or free Disneyland shuttles, or modestly priced shuttles operated by Anaheim Resort Transportation (p395).

Hotel Indigo Anaheim Main Gate   BOUTIQUE HOTEL **$$**
(✎714-772-7755; F; 435 W Katella Ave; $159-279; P@🛜🛌🏊) New in 2013, this 104-room hotel has a clean, mid-century-modernist look and a dancing fountain out front. It also

has a fitness center, pool and guest laundry. Mosaic murals are modeled after the walnut trees that once bloomed here. It's about 20 minutes' walk or a quick drive from Disneyland's main gate. Free parking.

★ **Anabella**   HOTEL **$$**
(✎800-863-4888, 714-905-1050; www.anabella-hotel.com; 1030 W Katella Ave; r $89-199, ste $109-199; P@🛜🛌) This 7-acre complex has the feel of a laid-back country club, complete with golf carts that ferry guests from the lobby to their buildings. Large rooms have wooden floors and a whisper of Spanish Colonial style, with extras like minifridges and TV entertainment systems. Bunk-bedded kids' suites have Disney-inspired decor.

Best Western Plus Stovall's Inn   MOTEL **$$**
(✎800-854-8175, ext 3, 714-778-1880; www.bestwestern.com; 1110 W Katella Ave; r incl breakfast $90-170; P❋@🛜🛌) The 290 remodeled, sleek and sophisticated motel rooms sparkle; all have a microwave and minifridge, and there's a hot breakfast included. Walk to Disneyland in 15 minutes. Parking $10.

Camelot Inn & Suites   MOTEL **$$**
(✎714-635-7275, 800-828-4898; www.camelotanaheim.com; 1520 S Harbor Blvd; r $99-179, ste $190-269; P@🛜🛌) This five-story, 200-room motel with accents of English Tudor style has minifridges and microwaves in every room, plus on-site laundry, a pool and hot tub. You can walk to Disneyland in 10 minutes. The pool deck and some top-floor rooms have fireworks views. Parking is $9.

Park Vue Inn   MOTEL **$$**
(✎714-772-3691, 800-334-7021; www.parkvueinn.com; 1570 S Harbor Blvd; r $105-163; P❋@🛌) This two-story, 86-room motel gets rotating hordes of families, but well-scrubbed, contemporary-style rooms come with microwaves and minifridges, and downstairs it has an outdoor pool and hot tub. It's almost opposite Disneyland's main gate.

TOP FIVE THEME-PARK AREAS FOR YOUNG KIDS
• •
➡ Fantasyland (p387), Disneyland
➡ Mickey's Toontown, Disneyland
➡ Critter Country (p388), Disneyland
➡ Paradise Pier, DCA
➡ Cars Land, DCA

✗ Eating

From Mickey-shaped pretzels ($4) and jumbo turkey legs ($10) to deluxe, gourmet dinners (sky's the limit), there's no shortage of eating options inside the Disney parks, though they're mostly pretty expensive and mainstream. Phone Disney Dining (☏ 714-781-3463) to make reservations up to 60 days in advance.

Driving just a couple miles into Anaheim will expand the offerings and price points considerably.

✗ Disneyland Park

Jolly Holiday
Bakery & Cafe   RESTAURANT, BAKERY $

(Main Street, U.S.A.; mains $7-10; ⊘ breakfast, lunch & dinner) At this *Mary Poppins*–themed restaurant, the Jolly Holiday combo (grilled cheese sandwich and tomato basil soup for $9) is a decent deal. The cafe does other sandwiches on the sophisticated side, like the mozzarella *caprese* or turkey on ciabatta. Great people-watching from outdoor seating.

Café Orleans   CAJUN, CREOLE $$

(New Orleans Square; mains $16-20; ⊘ seasonal hours vary; ⊕) The next best thing to Blue Bayou is this Southern-flavored restaurant, famous for its Monte Cristo sandwiches at lunch.

Plaza Inn   AMERICAN $$

(Main Street, U.S.A.; mains $12-17, breakfast buffet adult/child 3-9yr $27/13; ⊘ breakfast, lunch & din-

ner) Finger-lickin'-good fried chicken platter and pot roast come with mashed potatoes, buttermilk biscuits and veggies at this 1950s original. There's a fun breakfast buffet with Disney characters. The rest of the day, if you can snag an outdoor table, you'll also get great people-watching here.

Blue Bayou   SOUTHERN $$$

(☏ 714-781-3463; New Orleans Sq; lunch $26-40, dinner $30-46; ⊘ lunch & dinner) Surrounded by the 'bayou' inside the Pirates of the Caribbean attraction, this is the top choice for sit-down dining in Disneyland, serving Creole and Cajun specialties at dinner.

✗ Disney California Adventure

★ Carthay Circle   AMERICAN $$

(Buena Vista St; lunch $20-30, dinner $25-44; ⊘ lunch & dinner) Decked out like a Hollywood country club, new Carthay Circle is the best dining in either park, with steaks, seafood, pasta, smart service and a good wine list. Your table needs at least one order of fried biscuits, stuffed with white cheddar, bacon, and jalapeño and served with apricot honey butter. Inquire about special packages including dinner and the *World of Color* show.

Wine Country Terrace   CALIFORNIAN $$

(Golden State; mains $13-17; ⊘ lunch & dinner) This sunny Cal-Italian terrace restaurant is a fine spot. Fork into Italian pastas, salads or veggie paninis. Decent wine list.

> **WORTH A TRIP**
>
> ### ANAHEIM PACKING DISTRICT & CENTER STREET
>
> To paraphrase *Aladdin*, there's a whole new Anaheim outside Disneyland's gates. Case in point: the **Anaheim Packing District** (anaheimpackingdistrict.com; S Anaheim Bl), around a long-shuttered 1925 car dealership and 1919 orange-packing house a couple miles away, near the city's actual downtown. It relaunched in 2013-14 with chic new restaurants like Umami Burger, the **Anaheim Brewery** (www.anaheimbrew.com; 336 S Anaheim Blvd; ⊘ 5-9pm Tue-Thu, 4-9pm Fri, 11am-9pm Sat, 11am-6pm Sun), an evolving collection of shops and a park for events.
>
> About a quarter-mile from here is **Center Street** (www.centerstreetanaheim.com; W Center St), a quietly splashy redeveloped neighborhood with an ice rink designed by starchitect Frank Gehry, and a couple of blocks of hipster-friendly shops like the **Good** (161 W Center St Promenade) for men's clothing, the **Look** (201 Center St Promenade) for women's, **Barbeer** (165 Center St Promenade) for a shave, haircut and brewski, and the writerly **Ink & Bean** (www.inkandbeancoffee.com; 115 W Center St Promenade) coffee saloon. Dining offerings include **118 Degrees** (185 W Center St; ☑), dedicated to the raw diet, and **Good Food**, a mini food court where you might indulge in healthy junk at **Healthy Junk** (www.healthyjunk.com; 201 Center St Promenade).

Pacific Wharf Cafe AMERICAN **$$**
(Golden State; mains $9-12; ☺breakfast, lunch
& dinner) Hearty soups in sourdough bread
bowls, farmers-market salads and deli sand-
wiches are pretty filling.

Downtown Disney & Hotels

Downtown Disney is often packed, but the
restaurant selection is better than inside the
parks.

Earl of Sandwich SANDWICHES **$**
(☑714-817-7476; Downtown Disney; mains $4-7;
☺8am-11pm Sun-Thu, 8am-midnight Fri & Sat)
This counter-service spot near the Disney-
land Hotel serves grilled sandwiches that
are both kid- and adult-friendly. The 'orig-
inal 1762' is roast beef, cheddar and horse-
radish, or look for chipotle chicken with
avocado, or holiday turkey. There are also
pizza, salad and breakfast options.

★**Napa Rose** CALIFORNIAN **$$$**
(☑714-300-7170; Grand Californian Hotel & Spa,
mains $39-45, 4-course prix-fixe dinner from $90;
☺5:30-10pm; ⊞) Soaring windows, high-back
Arts and Crafts-style chairs, leaded-glass
windows and towering ceilings befit the Disneyland Resort's top-drawer restaurant. On
the plate, impeccably crafted, seasonal 'California Wine Country' cuisine. Kids' menu
available. Reservations essential.

Steakhouse 55 AMERICAN **$$$**
(☑714-781-3463; 1150 Magic Way, Disneyland
Hotel; breakfast $8-12, dinner $30-40, 3-course
prix-fixe menu $40; ☺breakfast & dinner) Dry-
rubbed bone-in rib eye, Australian lobster
tail, heirloom potatoes and green beans with
applewood-smoked bacon uphold a respect-
able chophouse menu. Kids' menu available.
Good wine list.

Anaheim

Most restaurants immediately surrounding
Disneyland are chains, although **Anaheim
Garden Walk** (☑714-635-7400; www.ana-
heimgardenwalk.com; 321 W Katella Ave) has some
upscale ones (California Pizza Kitchen, Mc-
Cormick & Schmick's, Johnny Rocket's, etc).

Umami Burger HAMURGERS **$$**
(☑714-991-8626; www.umamiburger.com; 338 S
Anaheim Blvd; mains $11-15; ☺11am-11pm Sun-Thu,
to midnight Fri & Sat) In the Anaheim Packing
District. Burgers span classic to truffled and
the Hatch burger with roasted green chilies.

Get 'em with deep-fried 'smushed' potatoes
with housemade ketchup, and top it off
with a salted-chocolate-ice-cream sandwich.
Good beer selection too.

★**Olive Tree** MIDDLE EASTERN **$$**
(☑714-535-2878; 512 S Brookhurst St; mains $8-
16; ☺9am-9pm) In Anaheim's Little Arabia,
this simple restaurant in a nondescript strip
mall flying flags of Arab nations has earned
accolades from local papers and from
Saveur magazine. You *could* get standards
like falafel and kebabs, but daily specials are
where it's at; Saturday's *kabseh* is righteous,
fall-off-the-bone lamb shank over spiced rice
with currants and onions.

🍷 Drinking & Entertainment

🍸 Disneyland Resort

It's tiki to the max and good, clean fun at
Trader Sam's Enchanted Tiki Lounge
(1150 Magic Way, Disneyland Hotel). Score a per-
sonal leather recliner and watch the game
on 175-plus screens at **ESPN Zone** (www.esp-
nzone.com; Downtown Disney), or hear big-name
acts at **House of Blues** (☑714-778-2583; www.
houseofblues.com; Downtown Disney) or jazz at
**Ralph Brennan's New Orleans Jazz Kitch-
en** (http://rbjazzkitchen.com; Downtown Disney).
There's also a 12-screen cinema in Down-
town Disney.

🍷 Anaheim

As one of California's largest cities, Anaheim
has a variety of entertainment options, from
the tasting room of Anaheim Brewery in the
Anaheim Packing District to professional
sports at the **Honda Center** (☑800-745-
3000; www.hondacenter.com; 2695 E Katella Ave)
for hockey and **Angel Stadium** (☑714-940-
2000, 888-796-4256; www.angelsbaseball.com;
2000 Gene Autry Way) for baseball, and rock
concerts at the **City National Grove of
Anaheim** (☑714-712-2700; www.thegroveofa-
naheim.com; 2200 E Katella Ave). At the **Block
at Orange** (☑714-769-4001; www.simon.com;
20 City Blvd W, Orange; 🖥) are a video game
arcade, a skate park and a bowling and bil-
liards establishment.

🛍 Shopping

Each 'land' has its own shopping, appropri-
ate to its particular theme, a mind-boggling
variety of souvenirs, clothing and Disneyana,
from T-shirts to mouse ears.

Downtown Disney, too, is a triumph of marketing – once inside the dozens of shops here (not just Disney stuff either), it may be hard to extract yourself. **Disney Vault 28** (Downtown Disney) traffics in a hipster inventory of distressed Cinderella-print T-shirts, familiar brands like Betsey Johnson and Disney-only boutique lines like Disney Couture. **D Street** (Downtown Disney) gives the same treatment to wannabe gangstas, skate rats and surfers. Shop hours are timed to the theme park hours.

ℹ Information

Before you arrive, visit **Disneyland Resort** (✆ live assistance 714-781-7290, recorded info 714-781-4565 ; www.disneyland.com) website for up-to-date information.

INTERNET RESOURCES & MOBILE APPS

Disneyland Explorer Official Disney-released app for iPhone and iPad.
Lonely Planet (www.lonelyplanet.com/usa/california/disneyland-and-anaheim) For planning advice, author recommendations, traveler reviews and insider tips.
MousePlanet (www.mouseplanet.com) One-stop fansite for all things Disney, with news updates, podcasts, trip reports, reviews and discussion boards.
MouseWait (www.mousewait.com) Free iPhone app offers up-to-the-minute updates on ride wait times and what's happening in the parks.

LOCKERS

Self-service lockers with in-and-out privileges cost $7 to $15 per day. You'll find them near entry gates to Disneyland and DCA and at the picnic area just outside.

MEDICAL SERVICES

You'll find first-aid facilities at Disneyland (Main Street, U.S.A.), DCA (Pacific Wharf) and Downtown Disney (next to Ralph Brennan's Jazz Kitchen).
Western Medical Center (WMC; ✆ 714-533-6220; 1025 S Anaheim Blvd, Anaheim; ⊘24hr) Hospital emergency room.

MONEY

Disneyland's City Hall offers foreign-currency exchange. In DCA, head to the guest relations lobby. Multiple ATMs are found in both theme parks and at Downtown Disney.
Travelex (✆ 714-502-0811; Downtown Disney; ⊘10am-4pm Mon-Fri) Foreign exchange.

POST

Holiday Station (www.usps.com; 1180 W Ball Rd, Anaheim; ⊘9am-5pm Mon-Fri) Full-service post office.

TOURIST INFORMATION

Inside the parks, visit Disneyland's City Hall or DCA's guest relations lobby, or just ask any cast member.
Anaheim/Orange County Visitor & Convention Bureau (✆ 855-405-5020; www.anaheimoc.org; Anaheim Convention Center) Offers information on countywide lodging, dining and transportation. Convention Center parking is $15.

ℹ Getting There & Away

AIR

Most international travelers arrive at Los Angeles International Airport (LAX), but for easy-in, easy-out domestic travel, the manageable John Wayne Airport (p50700) in Santa Ana is served by all major US airlines and Canada's WestJet. It's near the junction of Hwy 55 and I-405 (San Diego Fwy).

From LAX, Super Shuttle (www.supershuttle.com) offers one-way fares of $16 per person to Disneyland-area hotels.

BUS

Southern California Gray Line/Coach America (✆ 714-978-8855, 800-828-6699; www.graylineanaheim.com) runs Disneyland Resort Express buses from LAX and SNA to Disneyland-area hotels every 30 minutes to one hour from 7:30am until 10pm.

Greyhound (✆ 714-999-1256, 800-231-222; www.greyhound.com; 100 W Winston Rd, Anaheim) has several daily buses to/from Downtown LA ($12, 40 minutes) and San Diego ($18, 2¼ hours). The bus station is a half mile east of the Disneyland Resort, accessible via taxi or the ART shuttle.

The **Orange County Transportation Authority** (✆ 714-560-6282; www.octa.net; ride/day pass $2/5) operates buses throughout the county. Fares and passes are sold on board (cash only, exact change).

CAR & MOTORCYCLE

Disneyland Resort is just off I-5 (Santa Ana Fwy), about 30 miles southeast of Downtown LA.

TRAIN

Trains stop at the newly opened **Anaheim Regional Transit Intermodal Center** (ARTIC) next to Angel Stadium, a quick ART shuttle or taxi ride east of Disneyland. **Amtrak** (✆ 714-385-1448; www.amtrak.com; 2150 E Katella Ave) has almost a dozen daily trains to/from LA's Union Station ($15, 40 minutes) and San Diego ($28, two hours). Less frequent **Metrolink** (✆ 800-371-5465; www.metrolinktrains.com; 2150 E Katella Ave) commuter trains connect Anaheim to LA's Union Station ($9, 50 minutes), Orange

($5.25, five minutes) and San Juan Capistrano ($8.75, 40 minutes).

❶ Getting Around

CAR & MOTORCYCLE

All-day parking costs $16 ($20 for oversize vehicles). Enter the 'Mickey & Friends' parking structure from southbound Disneyland Dr, off Ball Rd, and board the free tram to the parks.

Downtown Disney parking, reserved for diners, shoppers and movie-goers, offers the first three hours free.

SHUTTLE

Anaheim Resort Transportation (ART; ☑714-563-5287; www.rideart.org; single ride $3, day pass adult/child $5/2) operates some 20 shuttle routes between Disneyland and area hotels, transit center, convention center and other points of interest, saving traffic and parking headaches. Departures are typically two to three times per hour. Purchase single or multiday ART passes at kiosks near ART shuttle stops or online in advance.

TRAM & MONORAIL

With a ticket to Disneyland, you can ride the monorail between Tomorrowland and the far end of Downtown Disney, near the Disneyland Hotel.

AROUND DISNEYLAND

Within 10 easy miles of the Mouse House you'll find a big scoopful of sights and attractions that are worth a visit in their own right.

Knott's Berry Farm

America's oldest **theme park** (☑714-220-5200; www.knotts.com; 8039 Beach Blvd, Buena Park; adult/child $62/33; ⊘ from 10am, closing time varies 6-11pm; ⊛), Knott's is smaller and less frenetic than Disneyland, but it can be more fun, especially for thrill-seeking teens, roller coaster fanatics and younger kids.

The park opened in 1932, when Walter Knott's boysenberries (a blackberry-raspberry hybrid) and his wife Cordelia's fried-chicken dinners attracted crowds of local farmhands. Mr Knott built an imitation ghost town to keep them entertained, and eventually hired local carnival rides and charged admission.

Today Knott's keeps the Old West theme alive and thriving with shows and demonstrations at **Ghost Town**, but it's the thrill

---

> **DON'T MISS**
>
> ### KNOTT'S SCARY FARM
>
> Every year, Knott's Berry Farm puts on SoCal's scariest Halloween party. On select days from late September through October 31, the park closes and reopens at night as Knott's Scary Farm. Horror-minded thrills include a dozen creepy mazes, monster-themed shows and a thousand employees trying to scare the bejeezus out of you in 'scare zones'. Boo!

rides that draw the big crowds. The **Sierra Sidewinder** roller coaster rips through banks and turns while rotating on its axis. The suspended, inverted **Silver Bullet** screams through a corkscrew, a double spiral and an outside loop. **Xcelerator** is a 1950s-themed roller coaster that blasts you from 0mph to 82mph in under 2½ seconds with a hair-raising twist at the top. **Perilous Plunge** whooshes at 75mph down a 75-degree angled water chute that's almost as tall as Niagara Falls.

Minimum height restrictions apply for many rides and attractions. For the little(st) ones, **Camp Snoopy** is a kiddy wonderland populated by the *Peanuts* characters.

Opening hours vary seasonally, and online savings can be substantial (eg $10 off adult admission for buying print-at-home tickets).

Next door to Knott's Berry Farm is the affiliated water park **Soak City Orange County** (☑714-220-5200; www.soakcityoc.com; 8039 Beach Blvd, Buena Park; adult/child 3-11yr $36/26; ⊘10am-5pm, 6pm or 7pm mid-May–mid-Sep), boasting a 750,000-gallon wave pool and dozens of high-speed slides, tubes and flumes. You must have a bathing suit without rivets or metal pieces to go on some slides. Bring a beach towel and a change of dry clothes.

🍴 Sleeping & Eating

Knott's Berry Farm Resort Hotel (☑714-995-1111, 866-752-2444; www.knottshotel.com; 7675 Crescent Ave, Buena Park; r $79-169; @ 🛜 ☒) is a high-rise with bland rooms, outdoor pool, fitness center and tennis and basketball courts. For young Charlie Brown fans, ask about Camp Snoopy rooms, where kids are treated to *Peanuts*-themed decor (dog house headboards? Awesome!), telephone bedtime stories and a goodnight 'tuck-in' visit from Snoopy himself. Overnight parking costs $7.

The park has plenty of carnival-quality fast food, but the classic meal is the button-busting fried chicken and mashed potato dinner at the nuthin'-fancy **Mrs Knott's Chicken Dinner Restaurant** (☑714-220-5055; 8039 Beach Blvd, Buena Park; mains $7-17, chicken dinner $17; ⊙8am-8:30pm Mon-Thu, 7am-9pm Fri, 7am-9:30pm Sat, 7am-8:30pm Sun). It and other eateries are in the California Marketplace, a shopping center outside the park's main gate.

ⓘ Getting There & Away

Knott's Berry Farm is about 6 miles northwest of Disneyland, off the I-5 Fwy or Hwy 91 (Artesia Fwy). All-day parking costs $12. There's free three-hour parking for California Marketplace visitors only.

Discovery Science Center

Follow the giant 10-story cube – balanced on one of its points – to the doors of the best educational kiddie attraction in town, the **Discovery Science Center** (☑714-542-2823; www.discoverycube.org; 2500 N Main St, Santa Ana; adult/child 3-14yr & senior $16/13, 4D movies $2 extra; ⊙10am-5pm; ⊛), about 5 miles southeast of Disneyland via the I-5. More than 100 interactive displays await in exhibit areas with names such as Discovery Theater (playing 4D movies), Dino Quest and more. Step into the eye of a hurricane – your hair will get mussed – or grab a seat in the Shake Shack to virtually experience a magnitude 6.4 quake.

Bowers Museum & Kidseum

The under-the-radar **Bowers Museum** (☑714-567-3600, 877-250-8999; www.bowers.org; 2002 N Main St, Santa Ana; Tue-Fri adult/child 6-17yr & senior $13/10, Sat & Sun $15/12, special-exhibit surcharge varies; ⊙10am-4pm Tue-Sun) explodes onto the scene every year or two with a remarkable exhibit that reminds LA-centric museum-goers not to get too smug. The museum's permanent exhibits are impressive, too, a rich collection of pre-Columbian, African, Oceanic and Native American art.

General admission tickets to the Bowers Museum include entry to the family-focused **Kidseum** (☑714-480-1520; 1802 N Main St, Santa Ana; admission $3, child under 3yr free; ⊙10am-3pm Tue-Fri, 11am-3pm Sat & Sun; ⊛), two blocks south.

The museums are 6 miles southeast of Disneyland, off I-5 in Santa Ana. Admission is free on the first Sunday of each month. Public parking in nearby lots costs $2.

Old Towne Orange

Settlers began arriving en masse in Orange County after the Civil War, lured by cheap land and fertile fields. Today the city of Orange, 7 miles southeast of Disneyland, retains its charming historical center. Locals, antique hounds, SoCal nostalgia buffs and foodies continue to flock here.

✗ Eating

Browse Old Towne Orange's traffic circle and Glassell St for more than a dozen cafes, restaurants, wine bars and brewpubs.

★**Filling Station** DINER $
(www.fillingstationcafe.com; 201 N Glassell St; mains $7-14; ⊙6:30am-9pm, to 10pm Fri & Sat; ⊛) For breakfast, nothing beats this former vintage gas station now serving haute pancakes, chorizo eggs, Cobb salads and patty melts, instead of unleaded. Check out the vintage SoCal photographs on the walls. Sit on the outdoor patio (which is dog-friendly), or grab a shiny counter stool or booth inside. Breakfast is served all day, lunch from 11am.

Watson Drug DINER $$
(www.watsonsdrugs.com; 116 E Chapman Ave; mains $6-15; ⊙7am-9pm Mon-Sat, 8am-6pm Sun) Old-fashioned soda-fountain treats such as malts, milkshakes and sundaes, as well as burgers and all-day breakfast burritos, set inside an 1899 pharmacy with a vintage lunch counter and a contemporary ice-pop stand next door.

Felix Continental Cafe LATIN AMERICAN $$$
(☑714-633-5842; www.felixcontinentalcafe.com; 36 Plaza Sq; mains $8-17; ⊙11am-10pm Mon-Fri, 8am-10pm Sat & Sun) Longtime downtown favorite serves spiced-just-right Caribbean, Cuban, and Spanish dishes, most accompanied by a hefty serving of plantains, black beans and rice. Paella is the house specialty, and the roast pork is popular too. Scope out a patio table if you can. Lunch served until 5pm.

LITTLE SAIGON

Vietnamese immigrants began arriving in Orange County after the end of the Vietnam War in the early 1970s, carving out their own vibrant commercial district (largely of strip malls) about 7 miles from Disneyland, south of Hwy 22 (Garden Grove Fwy) and east of the I-405 (San Diego Fwy).

Start at **Asian Garden Mall** (9200 Bolsa Ave; 🛜), a behemoth packed with scores of food shops, boutiques, herbalists, silver jewelers and anime-inspired clothing and goods. Newbies can chow at the mall's **Lee's Sandwiches** (www.leessandwiches.com; 9200 Bolsa Ave, Suite 305; sandwiches from $4; ⊘8am-7pm; 🛜) or just west of the mall at **Ba Le** (9152 Bolsa Ave; sandwiches from $3; ⊘6am-6pm Mon-Sat, 7am-6pm Sun), both fast-growing chains serving budget-friendly Vietnamese sandwiches on French baguette rolls. The traditional toppings on these belly-fillers provide a delish, not-too-spicy kick – try the pork. Another classic, inexpensive, casual eatery in the mall is **Pho 79** (9200 Bolsa Ave, Suite 117; mains from $6; ⊘8am-7:30pm), which dishes up a variety of noodle and vegetable dishes. The *pho ga* (chicken noodle soup) has a hearty broth.

🛍 Shopping

Old Towne has the OC's most concentrated collection of antiques, collectibles, and vintage and consignment shops.

Woody's Antiques ANTIQUES
(173 N Glassell St) Woody's Antiques feels like walking on to a *Mad Men* set, with mid-century modern and art-deco furnishings and accent pieces.

Elsewhere Vintage VINTAGE CLOTHING
(www.elsewherevintage.com; 131 W Chapman Ave) A hipsters' love affair, this store hangs sundresses next to hats, leather handbags and fabulous costume jewelry.

Joy Ride VINTAGE CLOTHING
(133 W Chapman Ave) Sells men's clothing such as 1950s bowling shirts and immaculately maintained wool blazers.

ⓘ Getting There & Away

The drive from Anaheim takes under 20 minutes: take I-5 south to Hwy 22 east, then drive north on Grand Ave, which becomes Glassell St. Both **Amtrak** (📞800-872-7245; www.amtrak. com) and **Metrolink** (📞800-371-5465; www. metrolinktrains.com) commuter trains stop at Orange's **train station** (191 N Atchison St), a few blocks west of the plaza.

Richard Nixon Library & Museum

About 10 miles northeast of Anaheim, the **Richard Nixon Presidential Library & Museum** (📞714-993-5075; www.nixonfoundation. org; 18001 Yorba Linda Blvd, Yorba Linda; adult/child 7-11yr/student/senior $12/5/7/8.50; ⊘10am-5pm Mon-Sat, 11am-5pm Sun) offers a fascinating walk though America's modern history and that of this controversial native son of Orange County. Noteworthy exhibits include excerpts from the Nixon and Kennedy debates, a full-size replica of the White House's East Room, audiotapes of conversations with Apollo 11 astronauts while on the moon and access to the ex-presidential helicopter, complete with wet bar and ashtrays.

That said, it's the exhibits about Watergate, the infamous scandal that ultimately brought down Nixon's administration, that rightfully garner the most attention. The museum's original Watergate exhibit called it a 'coup' instigated by Nixon's rivals and provided favorably edited White House tapes. That changed when the library was transferred to federal control in 2007, with oversight by the National Archives. The old exhibit was completely torn out, and now the story unfolds from many perspectives, like a spy thriller. It was a bold move, considering that 'Tricky Dick' and First Lady Pat Nixon lie buried just outside.

To get here, take Hwy 57 north and exit east on Yorba Linda Blvd, then continue straight and follow the signs.

ORANGE COUNTY BEACHES

Orange County's 42 miles of beaches are a land of gorgeous sunsets, prime surfing, just-off-the-boat seafood and serendipitous discoveries. Whether you're learning to surf

DISNEYLAND & ORANGE COUNTY RICHARD NIXON LIBRARY & MUSEUM

Southern California's Best Beaches

Hundreds of miles of Pacific beaches edge SoCal's golden coast – which makes choosing just one to visit almost impossible. Take your pick depending on what you prefer doing: launching your surfboard onto a world-famous break; snapping on a snorkel mask and peeking at colorful marine life; or just lazing on the sand.

1. Santa Monica (p357)
A carnival pier with a solar-powered Ferris wheel and a tiny aquarium for the kiddos sits atop this idyllic, 3-mile long strand, where LA comes to play.

2. Malibu (p357)
Celebrity residents aren't keen to share their paradisaical pocket beaches, but with persistence and some insider tips, you too can share these million-dollar views.

3. Huntington Beach (p401)
Officially 'Surf City, USA,' Huntington Beach is everything you imagined SoCal beach life to be, from surfing by the pier to sunset bonfires on the sand.

4. Mission Beach (p433)
A day trip to San Diego's most fun-crazed beach should begin with a ride on the Giant Dipper wooden roller coaster and end with sunset along Ocean Front Walk.

5. Crystal Cove State Park (p417)
Tired of manicured beaches filled with bikini babes? Escape instead to this wilder, undeveloped Orange County gem for beachcombing and scuba diving.

6. Coronado (p433)
Pedal a beach cruiser along the Silver Strand, or frolic like Marilyn Monroe did on the golden sand fronting San Diego's landmark Hotel Del.

7. East Beach (p316)
Next to historic Stearns Wharf, where Santa Barbara meets the sea, this easy-access beach fills in summer with swimmers, volleyball players and even sea kayakers.

8. Carpinteria State Beach (p338)
Even tots can get their feet wet or poke around the tide pools at this Santa Barbara County classic, where palm trees wave above soft sands.

the waves in Seal Beach, playing Frisbee oceanside with your pooch, piloting a boat around Newport Harbor, wandering around eclectic art displays in Laguna Beach, or spotting whales on a cruise out of yacht-filled Dana Point harbor, you'll discover that each beach town has its own brand of quirky charm.

Seal Beach

The first enclave over the LA County line is one of the last great California beach towns and a refreshing alternative to the more-crowded coast further south. Look for 1.5 miles of pristine beach and Main St, a stoplight-free zone bustling with mom-and-pop restaurants and indie shops that are low on 'tude and high on charisma.

◉ Sights & Activities

Amble Main St and check out the laid-back local scene – barefoot surfers, friendly shopkeepers and silver-haired foxes scoping the way-too-young beach bunnies. Where Main St ends, walk out onto **Seal Beach Pier**, extending 1865ft over the ocean.

M&M Surfing School   SURFING
(☎714-846-7873; www.surfingschool.com; 802 Ocean Ave; 3hr group lesson from $72, wetsuit/surfboard rental $15/25; 👪) Learn to surf.

✗ Eating

Crema Café   BAKERY, CAFE $
(☎562-493-2501; cremacafe.com; 322 Main St; mains $5-13; ⊙6:30am-3pm Mon-Fri, 7am-4pm Sat & Sun) The specialty at this breezy, open-air cafe is crepes, from the 'simple' French crepe covered with cinnamon sugar, whipped cream and caramel sauce to savory and fruit-filled varieties. In a hurry? Made-from-scratch pastries and muffins are fab, as

are garden-fresh salads and toasted panini sandwiches.

★**Walt's Wharf**   SEAFOOD, STEAKHOUSE $$$
(☎562-598-4433; www.waltswharf.com; 201 Main St; lunch $11-23, dinner $20-45; ⊙11am-3:30pm & 4-9pm) Everybody's favorite for fresh fish (some drive in from LA), Walt's packs them in on weekends. You can't make reservations for dinner (though they're accepted for lunch), but it's worth the wait for the oak fire–grilled seafood and steaks in the many-windowed ground floor or upstairs in captain's chairs. Otherwise, eat at the bar.

🍷 Drinking

Bogart's Coffee House   CAFE
(www.bogartscoffee.com; 905 Ocean Ave; ⊙6am-9pm Mon-Thu, to 10pm Fri, 7am-10pm Sat, 7am-9pm Sun; 🛜) Sip espresso on the leopard-print sofa and play Scrabble by the beach view as you watch the surf roll in. Bogart's sometimes hosts live music, psychic readings, book clubs and morning meditations by the sea.

☆ Entertainment

Jazz, folk and bluegrass bands play by the pier at the foot of Main St from 6pm to 8pm every Wednesday during July and August for the annual **Summer Concerts in the Park**.

🔒 Shopping

Walk the full three blocks of Main St and browse the eclectic shops, including for surf gear and clothing at **Harbour Surfboards** (www.harboursurfboards.com; 329 Main St) and **Endless Summer** (124 Main St), toys at **Knock Knock** (www.knockknocktoystore.com; 219½ Main St) and even kites at **Up, Up & Away** (http://upupandawaykites.com; 139½ Main St), plus plenty of cafes and watering holes.

ⓘ Getting There & Around

OCTA (☎714-560-6282; www.octa.net) bus 1 connects Seal Beach with the OC's other beach towns and LA's Long Beach every hour; the one-way fare is $2 (exact change).

There's two-hour free parking along Main St between downtown Seal Beach and the pier – if you can snag a spot. Public parking lots by the pier cost $3 per two hours, $6 all day. Free parking along residential side streets is subject to posted restrictions.

Huntington Beach

With consistently good waves, surf shops, a surf museum, beach bonfires, a canine-friendly beach and a sprinkling of hotels and restaurants with killer views, HB is an awesome place for sun, surf and sand.

Hawaiian-Irish surfing star George Freeth gave demonstrations here in 1914, and the city has been a surf destination ever since, with the trademarked nickname 'Surf City, USA' (Santa Cruz lost that fight, sorry). The sport is big business, with a **Surfing Walk of Fame** (www.hsssurf.com/shof) and test-marketing for surf products and clothing.

◉ Sights

Huntington Pier   HISTORIC SITE
(☉5am-midnight) The 1853ft-long Huntington Pier has been here – in one form or another – since 1904. On the pier, rent a fishing pole from **Let's Go Fishin'** bait and tackle shop.

International Surfing Museum   MUSEUM
(www.surfingmuseum.org; 411 Olive Ave; donations welcome; ☉noon-5pm Mon-Fri, 11am-6pm Sat & Sun) This small museum is an entertaining stop for surf-culture enthusiasts, chock-ablock with photos, vintage surfboards, movie memorabilia, surf music and knowledgeable, all-volunteer staff.

Huntington City Beach   BEACH
(☉5am-midnight) One of SoCal's best beaches. Surrounding the pier at the foot of Main St, it gets packed on summer weekends with surfers, volleyball players, swimmers and families. Check at the visitor center for dog-friendly beaches and parks.

By night, volleyball games give way to beach bonfires. Stake out one of the 1000 cement fire rings early in the day, and you can buy firewood from concessionaires.

🏃 Activities

If you forgot to pack beach gear, you can rent umbrellas, beach chairs, volleyballs, bikes and other essentials from Zack's Pier Plaza. Just south of the pier on the Strand, friendly **Dwight's Beach Concession** (201 Pacific Coast Hwy), around since 1932, rents bikes, boogies boards, umbrellas and chairs.

Surfing

Surfing in HB is competitive. If you're a novice, take lessons, or risk annoying the locals.

Zack's   SURF GEAR
(☏714-536-0215; www.zackshb.com; 405 Pacific Coast Hwy) Offers one-hour lessons ($75 to $100) at the beach that include all-day board and wetsuit rental. For board rentals, you'll pay $12/35 per hour/day, plus $5/15 each for bodyboards and wetsuits.

Huntington Surf & Sport   SURF GEAR
(☏714-841-4000; www.hsssurf.com; 300 Pacific Coast Hwy) Megastore at the corner of Pacific Coast Hwy and Main St rents surfboards for $10/30 per hour/day (wetsuit $8/15).

Cycling & Skating

Explore the coast while zipping along the 8.5-mile **paved recreational path** from Huntington State Beach north to Bolsa Chica State Beach. Rent beach cruisers ($10/30 per hour/day) or tandem bikes ($18/50) at Zack's Pier Plaza.

Frisbee

Throw a disc back and forth for hours on the beach, or test your skills at the **Huntington Beach Disc Golf Course** (Huntington Central Park, 18381 Goldenwest St; admission $1-2). Aim for baskets at this scenic 18-hole course, downhill from the sports complex. The on-site pro shop sells discs.

🎊 Festivals & Events

Every Tuesday brings Surf City Nights, a street fair on the first three blocks of Main St, with live music, farmers market goodies, a petting zoo and bounce house for kids, and crafts and sidewalk sales for grownups.

Car buffs, get up early on Saturday mornings for the **Donut Derelicts Car Show** (www.donutderelicts.com), a weekly gathering of woodies, beach cruisers and pimped-out street rods at the corner of Magnolia St and Adams Ave, 2.5 miles inland from Pacific Coast Hwy.

US Open of Surfing   SURFING
(www.usopenofsurfing.com; ☉late Jul & early Aug) In late July and early August, this six-star competition lasts several days and draws more than 600 world-class surfers. Festivities include beach concerts, motocross shows and skateboard jams.

Huntington Harbor Cruise of Lights   CHRISTMAS
(www.cruiseoflights.org; ☉Dec) If you're here for the Christmas holidays, don't miss the evening boat tour past harborside homes twinkling with holiday lights.

WORTH A TRIP

BOLSA CHICA STATE BEACH

A 3-mile-long strip of sand favored by surfers, volleyball players and fishers, **Bolsa Chica State Beach** (www.parks. ca.gov; Pacific Coast Hwy, btwn Seapoint & Warner Aves; parking $15; ☺6am-10pm; P) stretches alongside the Pacific Coast Hwy north of Huntington Dog Beach. Even though it faces a monstrous offshore oil rig, Bolsa Chica (meaning 'little pocket' in Spanish) gets mobbed on summer weekends. All-day parking costs $15. You'll find picnic tables, fire rings and beach showers, plus a bike path.

Across Pacific Coast Hwy, **Bolsa Chica Ecological Reserve** (http://bolsachica.org; ☺sunrise-sunset) may look desolate, but its restored salt marsh is an environmental success story and teems with more than 200 species of birds on over 1200 acres, which were saved by a band of determined locals.

🛏 Sleeping

Huntington Surf Inn   MOTEL $$
(☎714-536-2444; www.huntingtonsurfinn.com; 720 Pacific Coast Hwy; r $159-209; P🐾) You're paying for location at this two-story motel just south of Main St and across from the beach. Nine of its rooms were recently redesigned by surf company Hurley in conjunction with surfers – cool, brah. There's a small common deck area with a beach view.

★Shorebreak Hotel   BOUTIQUE HOTEL $$$
(☎714-861-4470; www.shorebreakhotel.com; 500 Pacific Coast Hwy, Huntington Beach; r $189-495; P❋@🐾🐾) Stow your surfboard (lockers provided) as you head inside HB's hippest hotel, a stone's throw from the pier. The Shorebreak has a surf concierge, a fitness center and yoga studio, beanbag chairs in the lobby, and rattan and hardwood furniture in geometric-patterned rooms. Have sunset cocktails on the upstairs deck at Zimzala restaurant. Parking is $27.

Hilton Waterfront Beach Resort   RESORT $$$
(☎714-845-8000, 800-445-8667; www.waterfrontbeachresort.hilton.com; 21100 Pacific Coast Hwy; r $279-390; P@🐾🐾) The backdrop: miles and miles of gorgeous deep-blue sea. This 100% nonsmoking hotel has a giant tower from which every room has an angled balcony for ocean view. Rooms are plush but tempered with earth tones. Bicycle rentals available. Parking $30.

🍴 Eating

Sancho's Tacos   MEXICAN $
(☎714-536-8226; www.sanchostacos.com; 602 Pacific Coast Hwy; mains $3-10; ☺8am-9pm Mon-Sat, to 8pm Sun) There's no shortage of taco stands in HB, but locals are fiercely dedicated to Sancho's, across from the beach. This two-room shack with patio grills flounder, shrimp and tri-tip to order. Trippy Mexican-meets-skater art.

Sugar Shack   CAFE $
(www.hbsugarshack.com; 213½ Main St; mains $4-10; ☺6am-4pm Mon-Tue & Thu, to 8pm Wed, to 5pm Fri-Sun; 🚲) Expect a wait at this HB institution, or get here early to see surfer dudes don their wetsuits. Breakfast is served all day on the bustling Main St patio and inside, where you can grab a spot at the counter or a two-top. Photos of surf legends plastering the walls raise this place almost to shrine status.

Duke's   SEAFOOD, HAWAIIAN $$
(☎714-374-6446; www.dukeshuntington.com; 317 Pacific Coast Hwy; lunch $7-16, dinner $19-32; ☺11:30am-2:30pm Tue-Fri, 10am-2pm Sun, 5-9pm Tue-Sun) It may be touristy, but this Hawaiian-themed restaurant – named after surfing legend Duke Kahanamoku – is a kick. With unbeatable views of the beach, a long list of fresh fish and a healthy selection of sassy cocktails, it's a primo spot to relax and show off your tan.

Sandy's   CALIFORNIAN $$
(☎714-374-7273; www.sandyshb.com; 315 Pacific Coast Hwy; lunch $10-17, dinner $11-32; ☺11:30am-8:30pm Mon, to 9:30pm Tue-Fri, 9am-9:30pm Sat, 9am-8:30pm Sun) At beach-volleyball level with a generous beachside deck and an easy breezy dining room. Features dishes ranging from breakfast pizza and short rib breakfast burrito for weekend brunch, to pecan-crusted seabass with shrimp couscous, or the jalapeño-date burger.

🍸 Drinking

It's easy to find a bar in HB. Walk up Main St and you'll spot them all.

Hurricanes Bar & Grill   BAR
(www.hurricanesbargrill.com; 2nd fl, 200 Main St) Two words: meat market. But then again,

any strip of beach bars worth its margarita salt needs at least one. DJs nightly, ocean-view patios, a laser-light dance floor, 22 beer taps and loads of special cocktails.

Huntington Beach Beer Co   BAR
(www.hbbeerco.com; 2nd fl, 201 Main St; ⊙from 11am; ⊛) Two-decade-old, cavernous brew-pub with a big balcony, specializing in ales brewed in a half dozen giant, stainless-steel kettles on site, like the HB Blonde, Brickshot Red and seasonal beers flavored with sage to cherry. Try the sampler. DJs and dancing Thursday to Saturday nights.

🛍 Shopping

Huntington Surf & Sport   SPORTS, CLOTHING
(www.hsssurf.com; 300 Pacific Coast Hwy) This massive store supports the Surf City way of life with rows of surfboards, beachwear, surfing accessories and test-marketing for OC-based Hurley.

ℹ Information

Huntington Beach Hospital (☑714-843-5000; www.hbhospital.com; 17772 Beach Blvd; ⊙24hr) 24-hour emergency room.

Main St Library (www.hbpl.org; 525 Main St; internet per hr $5; ⊙10am-7pm Tue-Fri, 9am-5pm Sat; ⊛) Small but just five blocks from the beach; free wi-fi.

Visitors Bureau (☑800-729-6232; www.surfcityusa.com) Main St (☑714-969-3492; www.surfcityusa.com; 2nd fl, 301 Main St; ⊙9am-5pm); Pier Plaza (www.surfcityusa.com; Pier Plaza; ⊙11am-7pm) Hard-to-spot upstairs office on Main St provides maps and information, but the Pier Plaza booth is more convenient.

ℹ Getting There & Around

Public parking lots by the pier and beach – when you can even get a spot – are $1.50 per hour, $15 daily maximum. On-street parking meters cost $1 per 40 minutes.

OCTA (☑714-560-6282; www.octa.net) bus 1 connects HB with the rest of OC's beach towns every hour; one-way/day pass $2/5, payable on board (exact change). At press time, a free **Surf City Downtown Shuttle** (☑714-536-5542) operates from 10am until 8pm on weekends during summer, making a 3.5-mile loop around downtown to the pier, starting from the free public parking lot at **City Hall** (2000 N Main St).

Newport Beach

There are really three Newport Beaches demographics: wealthy Bentley- and Porsche-driving yachtsmen and their trophy wives; surfers and stoners who populate the beachside dives and live for the perfect wave; and everyone else trying to live day-to-day, chow on seafood and enjoy glorious sunsets. Somehow, these diverse communities all seem to live – mostly – harmoniously.

For visitors, the pleasures are many: just-off-the-boat seafood, boogie-boarding the human-eating waves at the Wedge, and the ballet of yachts in the harbor. Inland is posh Fashion Island, one of the OC's biggest shopping centers.

⊙ Sights

Balboa Fun Zone   AMUSEMENT PARK
(www.thebalboafunzone.com; 600 E Bay Ave; ⊙Ferris wheel 11am-8pm Sun-Thu, to 9pm Fri, to 10pm Sat) On the harbor side of Balboa Peninsula, the Fun Zone has delighted locals

---

DON'T MISS

BALBOA ISLAND

For a quick pleasure trip across Newport Harbor, the **Balboa Island Ferry** (www.balboaislandferry.com; 410 S Bay Front; adult/child $1/50¢, car incl driver $2; ⊙6:30am-midnight Sun-Thu, to 2am Fri & Sat) leaves from the Balboa Fun Zone about every 10 minutes. It's tiny, holding just three cars packed single file between open-air seats for the 800ft, sub-five-minute trip.

The ferry lands a half mile west of Marine Ave, the main drag on **Balboa Island** (www.balboa-island.net). It's lined with beachy boutique shops, cafes and restaurants, and old-fashioned ice-cream shops vending Balboa bars (vanilla ice cream dipped in chocolate, peanuts, sprinkles and crushed Oreo cookies on a stick).

For close-ups of the island's beautiful, well-maintained homes, take a stroll along its shoreline. It's only about 1.5 miles around. Then catch the ferry back.

You can also reach Balboa Island by driving south of Pacific Coast Hwy along Jamboree Rd to Marine Ave. But what fun is that?

Newport Beach

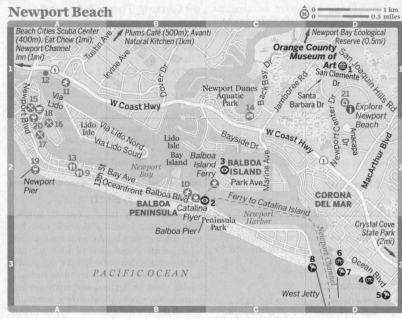

and visitors since 1936. There's a small Ferris wheel ($4 per ride, where Ryan and Marissa shared their first kiss on *The OC*), arcade games, touristy shops and restaurants, and frozen banana stands (just like the one in the TV sit-com *Arrested Development*). The landmark 1905 **Balboa Pavilion** is beautifully illuminated at night.

ExplorOcean   MUSEUM
(☎949-675-8915; www.explorocean.org; 600 E Bay Ave, Balboa Fun Zone; adult/child 4-12yr $5/3; ⏰11am-3:30pm Mon-Thu, to 6pm Fri & Sat, to 5pm Sun) In the Balboa Fun Zone, this newly refurbished museum calls itself an 'ocean literacy center' with critter-filled touch tanks, remotely operated vehicles, the rowboat used by adventurer Roz Savage on her five-year, round-the-world solo voyage, and an innovation lab.

★ **Orange County Museum of Art**   MUSEUM
(☎949-759-1122; www.ocma.net; 850 San Clemente Dr; adult/student/child under 12yr $10/8/free; ⏰11am-5pm Wed-Sun, to 8pm Thu) This engaging museum highlights California art and cutting-edge contemporary artists, with exhibitions rotating through two large spaces. There's also a sculpture garden, eclectic gift shop and theater screening classic, foreign and art-related films.

🏃 Activities

Balboa Peninsula   BEACHES
Four miles long but less than a half mile wide, the Balboa Peninsula has a white-sand beach on its ocean side, great people-watching and countless stylish homes.

Hotels, restaurants and bars cluster around the peninsula's two famous piers: **Newport Pier** near the western end and **Balboa Pier** at the eastern end. Near Newport Pier, several shops rent umbrellas, beach chairs, volleyballs and other necessities. For swimming, families will find a more relaxed atmosphere and calmer waves at **Mothers Beach** (10th St & 18th St).

Surfing
Surfers flock to the breaks at the small jetties surrounding the Newport Pier. At the tip of Balboa Peninsula, by the West Jetty, the **Wedge** is a bodysurfing, bodyboarding and knee-boarding spot famous for its perfectly hollow waves that can swell up to 30ft high. Warning: locals can be territorial, and newcomers should head a few blocks west.

Rent surf, body surfing and stand-up paddleboard equipment and gear at **15th Street Surf Shop** (☎949-673-5810; www.15thstreetsurfshop.com; 103 15th St; boogie

Newport Beach

boards per hr/day $2.50/8, surfboards $6/20) or **Paddle Power** (☏ 949-675-1215; www.paddle-powerh2o.com; 1500 W Balboa Blvd).

Boating

Take a boat tour or rent your own kayak, sailboat or outboard motorboat. Even better, rent a flat-bottomed electric boat that you pilot yourself and cruise with up to 12 friends. Find boats at **Duffy Electric Boat Rentals** (☏ 949-645-6812; www.duffyofnewportbeach.com; 2001 W Pacific Coast Hwy; per hr weekday/weekend $85/100; ⊘10am-8pm) or **Balboa Boat Rentals** (☏ 949-673-7200; http://boats4rent.com; 510 E Edgewater Pl; kayaks

per hr from $15, sailboats $45, powerboats from $70, electric boats from $75).

Cycling & Skating

For fabulous ocean views, ride along the paved **recreational path** that encircles almost the entire Balboa Peninsula. Inland, cyclists like the paved **scenic loop** around Newport Bay Ecological Reserve (p406).

There are many places to rent bikes near Newport and Balboa Piers. **Easyride's Back Alley Bicycles** (☏ 949-566-9850; www.easyridebackalleybikes.com; 204 Washington St; beach cruisers per day $20, tandem bicycles per hr/day $15/30, surreys per hr from $25) even rents surreys (you know, with the fringe on top), but think twice because locals are known to pelt them with water balloons.

Diving

There's terrific diving just south of Newport Beach at the underwater park at Crystal Cove State Park (p417), where divers can check out reefs, anchors and an old military plane crash site. For dive-boat trips, stop by **Beach Cities Scuba Center** (☏ 949-650-5440; www.beachcitiesscuba.com; 4537 W Coast Hwy), where full equipment rental costs $60 per day.

☞ Tours

Fun Zone Boat Co   BOAT TOUR
(☏ 949-673-0240; www.funzoneboats.com; 600 Edgewater Pl; 45min cruise per adult/senior/child 5-11yr from $14/7/11) Sea lion–watching and celebrity home tours depart beneath the Ferris wheel in the Fun Zone.

Davey's Locker   BOAT TOUR
(☏ 949-673-1434; www.daveyslocker.com; 400 Main St; 2½hr whale-watching cruise per adult/child 3-12yr & senior from $32/26, half-day sportfishing $41.50/34) At Balboa Pavilion; offers whale-watching and sportfishing trips.

Gondola Adventures   BOAT TOUR
(☏ 949-646-2067, 888-446-6365; www.gondola.com; 3101 W Coast Hwy; 1hr cruise per couple from $135) Totally cheesy Venetian-esque gondola rides with chocolates and sparkling cider for your sweetie.

★ Festivals & Events

Newport Beach
Wine & Food Festival   FOOD, WINE
(newportwineandfood.com; ⊘mid-Sep) Flashy food-and-wine fest shows off local restaurateurs, top chefs, prestigious winemakers and

brewmasters, with live rock concerts staged near Fashion Island.

Christmas Boat Parade CHRISTMAS
(www.christmasboatparade.com; ⊗ Dec) The week before Christmas brings thousands of spectators to Newport Harbor to watch a tradition dating back over a century. The 2½-hour parade of up to 150 boats, which includes some fancy multimillion-dollar yachts all decked out with Christmas lights and holiday cheer, begins at 6:30pm. You can watch for free from the Fun Zone or Balboa Island, or book ahead for a harbor boat tour.

🛌 Sleeping

A Newport stay ain't cheap, but outside peak season, rates listed here often drop 40% or more.

Newport Channel Inn MOTEL $$
(☑ 800-255-8614, 949-642-3030; www.newportchannelinn.com; 6030 W Coast Hwy; r $129-199; 🅿 ✳ 🛜) The ocean is just across Pacific Coast Hwy from this spotless 30-room, two-story 1960s-era motel. Other perks include large rooms with microwaves and mini-fridges, a big common sundeck, beach equipment for loan and genuinely friendly owners with lots of local knowledge. Enjoy a vacation-lodge vibe under the A-frame roof of Room 219, which sleeps up to seven.

```
WORTH A TRIP
```

NEWPORT BAY ECOLOGICAL RESERVE

Inland from the harbor, where runoff from the San Bernardino Mountains meets the sea, the brackish water of 752-acre **Newport Bay Ecological Reserve** (from $20 per person) 🚶 supports nearly 200 bird species. It's one of SoCal's few preserved estuaries and an important stopover on the migratory Pacific Flyway. It's also under the flyway for planes taking off from John Wayne Airport, but this annoyance doesn't overly detract from the wildlife viewing. Stop by the **Muth Interpretive Center** (☑ 949-923-2290; www.ocparks.com/unbic; 2301 University Dr, off Irvine Ave; ⊗ 10am-4pm Tue-Sun; 🚻), made from sustainable and renewable materials and home to kid-friendly exhibits.

Newport Dunes Waterfront RV Resort & Marina CABINS, CAMPING $$
(☑ 949-729-3863, 800-765-7661; www.newportdunes.com; 1131 Back Bay Dr; campsites from $55, studios/cottages from $150/200; 🅿 @ 🛜 ⊠ 🐾) RVs and tents aren't required for a stay at this upscale campground: two dozen tiny A-frame studios and one-bedroom cottages are available, all within view of Newport Bay. A fitness center and walking trails, kayak rentals, board games, family bingo, ice-cream socials, horseshoe and volleyball tournaments, an outdoor pool and playground, and summertime movies on the beach await.

Resort at Pelican Hill RESORT $$$
(☑ 949-467-6800, 800-315-8214; www.pelican-hill.com; 22701 Pelican Hill Rd S; r from $495; 🅿 @ 🛜 ⊠) At this Tuscan-themed resort, secluded in the Newport Coast hills, mature trees and Palladian columns line the way to over 300 deluxe air-con bungalows and villas. Pleasures include a circular mosaic-inlaid swimming pool (diameter: 136ft), two 18-hole championship golf courses, a soothing spa, top-notch Northern Italian fare at Andrea restaurant and multilingual concierge staff who define solicitous. Rates: sky high. Pampering: priceless.

🍴 Eating

Newport has some of the county's best restaurants.

Eat Chow CALIFORNIAN $$
(☑ 949-423-7080; www.eatchownow.com; 211 62nd St; mains $8-15; ⊗ 8am-9pm Mon-Thu, to 10pm Fri, 7am-10pm Sat, 7am-9pm Sun) Hidden a block off W Coast Hwy, the crowd is equal parts tatted hipsters and ladies who lunch, which makes it very Newport indeed. They all queue happily for dishes like ribeye Thai beef salad, grilled salmon tacos with curry slaw, and bodacious burgers like the Chow BBQ burger with home-made barbecue sauce, smoked gouda, crispy onions and more.

Crab Cooker SEAFOOD $$
(☑ 949-673-0100; www.crabcooker.com; 2200 Newport Blvd; mains $12-23, lobster $40; ⊗ 11am-9pm Sun-Thu, to 10pm Fri & Sat; 🚻) Expect a wait at this always-busy joint, a landmark since 1951. It serves great seafood and fresh crab on paper plates to an appreciative crowd wearing flip-flops and jeans. Don't miss the

delish chowder. If you're in a hurry, there's a to-go counter.

★**Bear Flag Fish Company** SEAFOOD $$
(☑949-673-3434; www.bearflagfishco.com; 407 31st St, Newport Beach; mains $8-15; ☺11am-9pm Tue-Sat, to 8pm Sun & Mon; 🖶) This squat glass box is *the* place for generously sized, grilled and panko-breaded fish tacos, ahi burritos, spankin' fresh ceviche and oysters. Pick out what you want from the ice-cold display cases, then grab a picnic-table seat.

Bluewater Grill SEAFOOD $$
(☑949-675-3474; www.bluewatergrill.com; 630 Lido Park Dr; mains $10-39; ☺11am-10pm Mon-Thu, to 11pm Fri & Sat, 10am-10pm Sun) Sit on the wooden deck and watch the boats at this polished harborside restaurant and oyster bar, which serves incredibly fresh fish. Great for Bloody Marys and a leisurely lunch – maybe swordfish tacos and coleslaw, beer-battered fish and chips or seared ahi with white-bean hummus.

🍸 **Drinking**

Alta Coffee Warehouse COFFEEHOUSE
(www.altacoffeeshop.com; 506 31st St; ☺6am-10:30pm Mon-Thu, 7am-11pm Fri & Sat, 7am-10:30pm Sun) Hidden on a side street, this cozy coffeehouse in a beach bungalow with a covered patio lures locals with live music and poetry readings, art on the brick walls, tasty vittles and honest baristas.

Newport Beach Brewing Company BREWPUB
(www.newportbeachbrewingcompany.com; 2920 Newport Blvd; ☺11:30am-11pm Sun-Thu, to 1am Fri & Sat; 🛜) The town's only microbrewery (try the signature Newport Beach Blonde or Bisbee's ESB), 'Brewco' is a laid-back place to catch the big game or just kick it over burgers, pizzas and fried fare with your buds after a day at the beach.

Mutt Lynch BEACH BAR
(www.muttlynchs.com; 2301 W Oceanfront; ☺7am-midnight) Rowdy dive by the beach offers pool tables, schooners filled with dozens of beers on tap and martinis made with soju (Korean vodka). Food is large portions, especially at breakfast. Best on 'Sunday Fundays.'

🛍 **Shopping**

On Balboa Island, **Marine Ave** is lined with darling shops in an old-fashioned village atmosphere, a good place to pick up something for the kids, unique gifts, beachy souvenirs, jewelry, art or antiques. At the other end of the scale and of town, chic, outdoor mall **Fashion Island** (☑949 721 2000; 550 Newport Center Dr; ☺10am-9pm Mon-Fri, 11am-7pm Sat, 11am-6pm Sun) sits inland with more than 400 specialty stores and department stores Bloomingdale's, Macy's and Neiman Marcus.

ℹ **Information**

Balboa Branch Library (www.city.newport-beach.ca.us/nbpl; 100 E Balboa Blvd; ☺9am-6pm Tue & Thu-Sat, to 9pm Mon & Wed; 🛜) Near the beach; ask for a free internet-terminal guest pass.

Hoag Memorial Hospital Presbyterian (☑949-764-4624; www.hoaghospital.org; 1 Hoag Dr; ☺24hr) With 24-hour emergency room.

Explore Newport Beach (www.visitnewportbeach.com; 401 Newport Center Dr, Fashion Island, Atrium Court, 2nd fl; ☺10am-9pm Mon-Fri, to 7pm Sat, to 6pm Sun) The city's official visitor center.

ℹ **Getting There & Around**

BUS

OCTA (☑714-560-6282; www.octa.net) bus 1 connects Newport Beach with the OC's other beach towns, including Corona del Mar just east, every 30 minutes to one hour. From the intersection of Newport Blvd and Pacific Coast Hwy, bus 71 heads south along the Balboa Peninsula to Main Ave around every hour or so. On all routes, the one-way fare is $2 (make sure you have exact change).

BOAT

The West Coast's largest passenger catamaran, the **Catalina Flyer** (☑800-830-7744; www.catalinainfo.com; 400 Main St; round-trip adult/child 3-12yr/senior $70/53/65, per bicycle $7), makes a daily round-trip to Catalina Island (p590), taking 75 minutes each way. It leaves Balboa Pavilion around 9am and returns before 6pm; check online for discounts.

CAR & MOTORCYCLE

The municipal lot beside Balboa Pier costs 50¢ per 20 minutes, or $15 per day. Street parking meters on the Balboa Peninsula cost 50¢ to $1 per hour. Free parking on residential streets, a block or two from the sand, is time-limited and subject to other restrictions. In summer, expect to circle like a hawk for a space.

Around Newport Beach

Costa Mesa

At first glance the Costa Mesa looks like just another landlocked suburb transected by the I-405, but three top venues attract some 24 million visitors each year. South Coast Plaza is SoCal's largest mall, and steps away are Orange County's prime performing-arts venues: Segerstrom Center for the Arts and South Coast Repertory, one of the nation's most-acclaimed theater companies. A pair of 'anti-malls' (the Lab and the Camp) brings hipster cool to the shopping scene, while strip malls reveal surprisingly tasty cafes and ethnic-food holes-in-the-wall.

✕ Eating

Avanti Natural Kitchen VEGETARIAN $
(www.avantinatural.com; 259 E 17th St; mains $8-11; ⊙11am-10pm Mon-Fri, 10:30am-10pm Sat, 10:30am-8pm Sun; ☕) ✔ A mom-and-pop vegetarian cafe so good, even carnivores will leave feeling sated. It looks like just another strip-mall storefront, but step inside for the creative chef duo's magic with pizzas, roasted stuffed portobello mushrooms and the hot taco brunch. The menu features organic produce from local farms.

Plums Café CALIFORNIAN $$
(☎949-722-7586; www.plumscafe.com; 369 E 17th St; mains $10-25; ⊙8am-3pm, dinner from 5pm) Raise your breakfast game at this gourmet caterer's bistro tucked in the corner of a cookie-cutter strip mall. With its exposed brick walls and sleek designs, Plums will have you feeling oh-so-chic as you nibble Dutch baby pancakes with Oregon pepper bacon, or alderwood smoked salmon hash. Breakfast served until 11:30am weekdays, brunch till 3pm on weekends.

Habana LATIN AMERICAN $$
(☎714-556-0176; the Lab, 2930 Bristol St; lunch $6-13, dinner $15-36; ⊙11:30am-4pm & 5-11pm Sun-Thu, to midnight Fri & Sat) With flickering votive candles, ivy-covered courtyard and spicy Cuban, Mexican and Jamaican specialties, this sultry cantina whispers rendezvous. Paella, *ropa vieja* (shredded flank steak in tomato sauce) and salmon *al parilla* (grilled) come with plantains and black beans on the side. On weekends, the bar gets jumpin' late-night.

Memphis Café Bar SOUTHERN $$
(☎714-432-7685; memphiscafe.com; 2920 Bristol St; mains lunch $7-12, dinner $12-22; ⊙8am-10pm Mon-Wed, to 10:30pm Thu-Sat, 8am-3pm & 5-9:30pm Sun) Inside a vintage mid-century modern building, this fashionable eatery is all about down-home flavor – think pulled-pork sandwiches, popcorn shrimp, gumbo and buttermilk-battered fried chicken. Happy hour at the bar is best.

🍷 Drinking

Milk + Honey CAFE
(the Camp, 2981 Bristol St; ⊙8am-10pm Mon-Thu, to 11pm Fri & Sat, 10am-10pm Sun; ☎) Fair-trade, shade-grown and organic coffee, chai tea and strong espresso drinks, plus fruit smoothies, seasonal frozen-yogurt flavors and Japanese-style shaved ice with flavors like strawberry, red bean and almond.

Wine Lab WINE BAR
(www.winelabcamp.com; the Camp, 2937 Bristol St, Suite A101B; ⊙noon-10pm Tue-Thu, to 11pm Fri & Sat, to 9pm Sun, 4-9pm Mon) This friendly wine shop offers New World wine and craft-beer tasting flights, plus small plates of artisan cheeses and charcuterie.

☆ Entertainment

Segerstrom Center for the Arts THEATER, CONCERT HALL
(☎714-556-2787; www.scfta.org; 600 Town Center Dr) Orchestral and dance performances.

South Coast Repertory THEATER
(☎714-708-5555; www.scr.org; 655 Town Center Dr) One of the nation's most-acclaimed theater companies.

🔒 Shopping

South Coast Plaza MALL
(www.southcoastplaza.com; 3333 Bristol St; ⊙10am-9pm Mon-Fri, to 8pm Sat, 11am-6:30pm Sun) The stats at SoCal's premier luxury shopping destination speak for themselves. About $2 billion in annual sales, nearly 300 luxury brand and chain shops, five department stores, five valet stations and 12,750 parking spaces. Grab a map from a concierge booth. South Coast Plaza offers thrice-daily shuttles (☎888-288-5823) from Anaheim hotels.

Lab MALL
(www.thelab.com; 2930 Bristol St) This outdoor, ivy-covered 'anti-mall' is an in-your-face alternative to South Coast Plaza. Indie-

JAMES RANDKLEV / GETTY IMAGES ©

Pacific Coast Highways

Snaking more than 1000 miles along dizzying sea cliffs and over landmark bridges, passing ancient redwoods, historic lighthouses and quirky beach towns, California's two-lane coastal highways trace the edge of the continent as they connect the dots between perpetually sunny San Diego, star-powered Los Angeles and eclectic San Francisco.

Contents

Above Highway 1, Big Sur (p275)

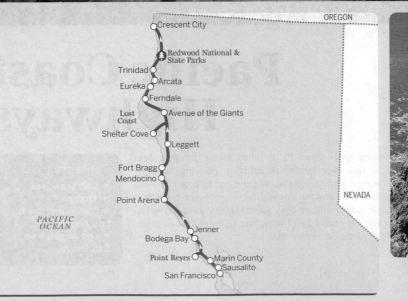

OREGON

Crescent City

Redwood National &
State Parks

Trinidad

Arcata

Eureka

Ferndale

Avenue of the Giants

**Lost
Coast**

Shelter Cove

Leggett

Fort Bragg

Mendocino

Point Arena

NEVADA

*PACIFIC
OCEAN*

Jenner

Bodega Bay

Point Reyes

Marin County

Sausalito

San Francisco

San Francisco to Oregon

4 DAYS

Northern California's redwood forests and fishing villages sprawl along the coast on Hwy 1 north of San Francisco and all the way up to Oregon on Hwy 101. Political radicals, artists, pot farmers and nature-loving hippies all gravitate here.

Get a primer on NorCal's left-leaning beatnik scene starting in **San Francisco**, a multicultural mosaic of neighborhoods. Explore top-notch museums and wide-open spaces in Golden Gate Park, then gather your friends around a sunset bonfire at Ocean Beach.

Jaunting north, outdoorsy **Marin County** has gorgeous beaches and grassy headlands for exploring. Across the Golden Gate Bridge you'll find the houseboat village of **Sausalito**, or go tramping around Muir Woods and Mt Tamalpais.

After more hiking and wildlife spotting at **Point Reyes**, devour fresh oysters at roadside stands alongside Hwy 1. Made infamous by Hitchcock's thriller *The Birds,* **Bodega Bay** is the gateway to the windswept Sonoma Coast. At **Jenner**, where the Russian River meets the sea, it's tempting to make a quick detour inland to wine country.

Keep going north after climbing the **Point Arena** lighthouse to the Victorian village of **Mendocino** sitting atop rocky headlands. Beyond the windy fishing port of **Fort Bragg**, Hwy 1 snakes inland to join Hwy 101 at **Leggett**, where the Redwood Empire begins. Trundle north to the **Avenue of the Giants**.

To really get away from it all, detour west to **Shelter Cove** and the remote **Lost Coast**. When you crave civilization again, head north to the farm town of **Ferndale**; the salty sea-dogs' lair of **Eureka**; the trippy, hippie-dippy university town of **Arcata**; and postcard-perfect bayside **Trinidad**.

Onward to the reason you've driven all this way: California's redwoods, the tallest trees on earth. In **Redwood National and State Parks**, take time out for Tall Trees Grove, Fern Canyon, Gold Bluffs Beach and the winding Newton B Drury Scenic Parkway before rolling into **Crescent City**, with its 19th-century lighthouse.

Top: Hiking the redwood forest (p195)
Bottom: Point Reyes Lighthouse (p108)

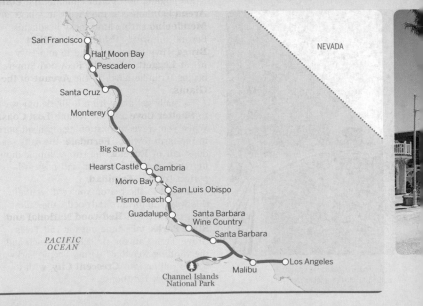

San Francisco

Half Moon Bay

Pescadero

Santa Cruz

Monterey

Big Sur

Hearst Castle

Cambria

Morro Bay

San Luis Obispo

Pismo Beach

Guadalupe

Santa Barbara
Wine Country

Santa Barbara

Malibu

Los Angeles

Channel Islands
National Park

PACIFIC
OCEAN

NEVADA

San Francisco to Los Angeles

4 DAYS

Get away from the boring inland freeways that zip between San Francisco and LA and you'll delightfully discover the Central Coast is a natural wonderland, from Monterey Bay's marine sanctuary and Big Sur's mystical redwood forests to the wildlife-rich Channel Islands just offshore.

Driving along Hwy 1 south of **San Francisco** via **Half Moon Bay** feels like you're dangling off the edge of the world. Pull over in the rural town of **Pescadero** for local farm bounty like organic strawberries and goat cheese.

If you love California's weird, wacky side, stop in **Santa Cruz**. Surfers hit the bodacious beaches, while kids go nuts on the carnival beach boardwalk. On the other side of the bay, **Monterey** has the rough-and-ready seafaring atmosphere of a John Steinbeck novel – don't miss feeding time at the giant aquarium.

Hwy 1 plunges into **Big Sur**, where modern-day hippies, beatniks and bohemians gather. Seek out hot springs and waterfalls, hike through misty redwood forests and keep looking skyward to spot endangered California condors soaring above ocean cliffs.

Hwy 1 tumbles downhill past **Hearst Castle**, a monumental hilltop mansion, before lazing in the seaside village of **Cambria**. Rent a kayak to paddle around **Morro Bay**, with its landmark volcanic rock. Slow down for the college town of **San Luis Obispo**, surrounded by fruitful vineyards and farms.

Soak up the sunshine at **Avila Beach** or go fishing off the pier at **Pismo Beach**. Follow Hwy 1 to detour out to the monumental sand dunes of **Guadalupe**, then head back inland and cross Hwy 101 for bucolic back roads that wind through **Santa Barbara Wine Country**.

Let yourself fall under the spell of the Mediterranean climate, red-tiled roofs and golden beaches of **Santa Barbara**. From Ventura, sail out to **Channel Islands National Park** to get truly wet and wild. Hwy 1 keeps cruising south through star-studded **Malibu**, where celebrity sightings are as predictable as the tides, before hitting **Los Angeles**.

Top: Santa Cruz Beach Boardwalk (p253)
Bottom: Avila Beach (p302)

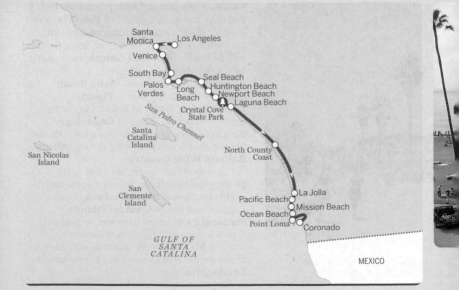

Santa Monica
Los Angeles
Venice
South Bay
Seal Beach
Palos Verdes
Huntington Beach
Long Beach
Newport Beach
Laguna Beach
Crystal Cove State Park

San Pedro Channel

Santa Catalina Island

San Nicolas Island

North County Coast

San Clemente Island

La Jolla
Pacific Beach
Mission Beach
Ocean Beach
Point Loma
Coronado

GULF OF SANTA CATALINA

MEXICO

3 DAYS Los Angeles to San Diego

It's time to drop the convertible top and cue up the California beach-life soundtrack. On this short stretch of Hwy 1, you can dive headfirst into a dreamscape of beautiful beach, epic waves and surf towns. Start in glam LA before cruising through Orange County's coast and laid-back San Diego.

Los Angeles, aka 'La La Land,' is California's biggest, boldest and most diverse metropolis. At the city's western edge, take a spin on the solar-powered Ferris wheel atop the seaside pier at **Santa Monica** and Rollerblade along the beach boardwalk in oddball **Venice**.

Fashionistas, tanned surfers and bikini-clad beach-volleyball stars head to LA's **South Bay**, streaming past chic Manhattan Beach, funky Hermosa Beach and touristy Redondo Beach. Follow Hwy 1 around the **Palos Verdes** peninsula for mesmerizing sea views, then drop by the aquarium in family-friendly **Long Beach**.

Cross the Orange County line for old-fashioned **Seal Beach**, whose quaint main street leads out to a wooden pier. Next up is party-animal **Huntington Beach**, which legally owns the name 'Surf City, USA.' Don strappy sandals and Gucci sunglasses for the white sands of the Balboa Peninsula in **Newport Beach**, where yachties and trophy wives mingle. Pause for a breath of fresh air and beachcombing at wild **Crystal Cove State Park**. Further south, the artists' colony of **Laguna Beach** is another movie-star beautiful hamlet you may never want to leave.

Easy does it along San Diego's **North County Coast**, where a colorful grab-bag of beach towns jostle between Hwy 1 and the ocean. Keep rolling south to fancy-pants **La Jolla**, a coastal village full of ritzy restaurants and boutiques, as well as gorgeous coves and nature reserves.

In San Diego, hang with regular folks at **Pacific Beach**, ride the roller coaster at **Mission Beach** or scarf down fish tacos and get a tattoo in bohemian **Ocean Beach**. Snap a panoramic photo from **Point Loma** before finishing with a cocktail at the swanky 'Hotel Del' in **Coronado**.

Top: Skater, Venice Boardwalk (p358)
Bottom: La Jolla beachfront (p450)

Newport Beach (p403), Orange County

minded shoppers can sift through vintage clothing, unique sneakers, art galleries in trailers, and trendy duds for teens, tweens and 20-somethings.

Camp   MALL
(www.thecampsite.com; 2937 Bristol St) 🏄
Vegans, tree-huggers and rock climbers, lend me your ears. The Camp offers one-stop shopping for all your outdoor and natural-living needs. Active Ride Shop, fair-trade Seed People's Market and the tox-in-free nail salon Lollipop are among the stores clustered along a leafy outdoor walkway. The parking lot is painted with inspirational quotes like 'Show Up for Life.'

ℹ Information

Travelex (South Coast Plaza, 1st fl, 3333 Bristol St; ⊙10am-9pm Mon-Fri, to 8pm Sat, 11am-6:30pm Sun) Foreign-currency exchange inside the mall, between Sears and Bloomingdale's.

ℹ Getting There & Around

Costa Mesa is inland from Newport Beach via Hwy 55.

Several **OCTA** (☑714-560-6282; www.octa. net) routes converge on South Coast Plaza, including bus 57 running along Bristol Ave south to Newport Beach's Fashion Island ($2, 20 minutes, every half hour).

Corona del Mar

Savor some of SoCal's most celebrated ocean views from the bluffs of Corona del Mar, a chichi community stretching along Pacific Coast Hwy and hugging the eastern flank of Newport Channel. In addition to stellar lookouts, several postcard-perfect beach-

es, rocky coves and child-friendly tidepools beckon along this idyllic stretch of coast.

A half mile long, **Main Beach** (Map p404; ☑949-644-3151; ⊙6am-10pm; **P**), aka Corona del Mar State Beach lies at the foot of rocky cliffs. There are restrooms, fire rings (arrive early to snag one) and volleyball courts. All-day parking costs $15, but spaces fill by 9am on weekends. Scenes from the classic TV show *Gilligan's Island* were shot at waveless, family-friendly **Pirates Cove**; take the nearby stairs off the north end of the Main Beach parking lot.

Crystal Cove State Park

With 3.5 miles of open beach and over 2300 acres of undeveloped woodland, this is both a **state beach** (☑949-494-3539; www.parks. ca.gov; 8471 N Coast Hwy; per car $15, campsites $25-75) and an underwater park. Scuba enthusiasts can check out two historic anchors dating from the 1800s as well as the crash site of a Navy plane that went down in the 1940s. Alternatively just go tide pooling, fishing, kayaking and surfing along the undeveloped shoreline.

🛏 Sleeping & Eating

★**Crystal Cove Beach Cottages**   CABIN **$$**
(☑reservations 800-444-7275; www.crystalcovebeachcottages.com; 35 Crystal Cove, Newport Beach; r with shared bath $42-127, cottages $162-249; ⊙check-in 4-9pm) Snag these historic oceanfront cottages in the park's historic district. Book on the first day of the month six months before your intended stay – or pray for last-minute cancellations.

Ruby's Crystal Cove Shake Shack   DINER **$**
(www.rubys.com; 7703 E Coast Hwy; shakes $5; ⊙6:30am-9pm, to 10pm Fri & Sat) A SoCal institution, this been-here-forever wooden shake stand is now part of a chain, but the ocean views are as good as ever. Try the date shake.

Beachcomber Café   AMERICAN **$$**
(☑949-376-6900; www.thebeachcombercafe. com; 15 Crystal Cove; breakfast $9-18, lunch $13-21, dinner $23-36; ⊙7am-9:30pm; **P**) This atmospheric cafe lets you soak up the vintage 1950s beach vibe as you tuck into macadamia-nut pancakes, roasted turkey club sandwiches or more serious surf-and-turf. Sunset is the magic hour for Polynesian tiki drinks. Validated parking with purchase over $15.

Laguna Beach

It's easy to love Laguna: secluded coves, romantic cliffs, azure waves and waterfront parks imbue the city with a Riviera-like feel.

But nature isn't the only draw. Laguna has a strong tradition in the arts, starting with the 'plein air' impressionists who lived and worked here in the early 1900s. Today it's the home of renowned arts festivals, several dozen galleries, a well-known museum and exquisitely preserved Arts and Crafts cottages and bungalows.

◎ Sights

With 30 public beaches sprawling along 7 miles of coastline, there's always another stunning view or hidden cove just around the bend. Just look for 'beach access' signs, and be prepared to pass through people's backyards to reach the sand. Rent beach equipment from **Main Beach Toys** (☑949-494-8808; 150 Laguna Ave; chairs/umbrellas/boards per day $10/10/15; ☺9am-9pm).

★**Laguna Art Museum**   MUSEUM
(☑949-494-8971;   www.lagunaartmuseum.org; 307 Cliff Dr; adult/student & senior/child $7/5/free, 1st Thu of month free; ☺11am-5pm Fri-Tue, to 9pm Thu) This breezy museum has changing exhibitions featuring contemporary Californian artists, and a permanent collection heavy on Californian landscapes, vintage photographs and works by early Laguna bohemians.

Pacific Marine Mammal Center ANIMAL PARK
(☑949-494-3050; www.pacificmmc.org; 20612 Laguna Canyon Rd; admission by donation; ☺10am-4pm) ✐ A nonprofit organization dedicated to rescuing and rehabilitating injured or ill marine mammals, this center northeast of town has a small staff and many volunteers who help nurse rescued pinnipeds – mostly sea lions and seals – before releasing them back into the wild. There are several outside pools and holding pens – but remember, this is a rescue center, not SeaWorld.

⚡ Activities

Central Beaches   BEACHES
Near downtown's village, **Main Beach** has volleyball and basketball courts, a playground and restrooms. It's Laguna's best beach for swimming. Just north at **Picnic Beach**, it's too rocky to surf; tide pooling is best. Pick up a tide table at the visitors bu-

reau. (Tide pool etiquette: tread lightly on dry rocks only and don't pick anything up that you find living in the water or on the rocks.)

Above Picnic Beach, the grassy, bluff-top **Heisler Park** offers vistas of craggy coves and deep-blue sea. Bring your camera – with its palm trees and bougainvillea-dotted bluffs, the scene is definitely one for posterity. A scenic walkway also connects Heisler Park to Main Beach.

North of downtown, Crescent Bay has big hollow waves good for bodysurfing, but parking is difficult; try the bluffs atop the beach; the views here are reminiscent of the Amalfi Coast.

Southern Beaches   BEACHES
About 1 mile south of downtown, secluded **Victoria Beach** has volleyball courts and **La Tour**, a Rapunzel's-tower-like structure from 1926. Skimboarding (at the south end) and scuba diving are popular here. Take the stairs down Victoria Dr; there's limited parking along Pacific Coast Hwy.

Further south, **Aliso Beach County Park** (www.ocparks.com/alisobeach; 31131 S Pacific Coast Hwy; parking per hr $1; ☺6am-10pm) is popular with surfers, boogie boarders and skimboarders. With picnic tables, fire pits and a play area, it's also good for families. Pay-and-display parking costs $1 per hour, or drive south and park on Pacific Coast Hwy for free.

Jealously guarded by locals, **Thousand Steps Beach** is hidden about 1 mile south of Aliso Beach. Just past Mission Hospital, park along Pacific Coast Hwy or residential side streets. At the south end of 9th St, more than 200 steps (OK, so it's not 1000) lead down to the sand. Though rocky, the beach is great for sunbathing, surfing and bodysurfing.

Diving & Snorkeling
With its coves, reefs and rocky outcroppings, Laguna is one of the best SoCal beaches for diving and snorkeling. **Divers Cove** just below Heisler Park is part of the **Glenn E Vedder Ecological Reserve**, an underwater park stretching to the northern border of Main Beach. Check weather and surf conditions (☑949-494-6573) beforehand. **Laguna Sea Sports** (☑949-494-6965; www.beachcitiesscuba.com; 925 N Coast Hwy; ☺10am-6pm Mon-Thu, to 7pm Fri, 7am-7pm Sat, 8am-5pm Sun) rents gear and offers classes.

Laguna Beach

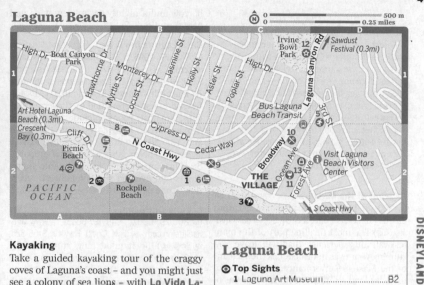

N 0 _____ 500 m
0 _____ 0.25 miles

Kayaking

Take a guided kayaking tour of the craggy coves of Laguna's coast – and you might just see a colony of sea lions – with **La Vida Laguna** (☑ 949-275-7544; www.lavidalaguna.com; 1257 S Coast Hwy; 2hr guided tour $95). Make reservations at least a day in advance.

Hiking

Surrounded by a green belt – a rarity in SoCal – Laguna has great nature trails for hikes. At **Alta Laguna Park**, a locals-only park up-canyon from town, the moderate 1.25-mile **Park Avenue Nature Trail** takes you through fields of spring wildflowers and past panoramic views. Open to hikers and mountain bikers, the 2.5-mile **West Ridge Trail** follows the ridgeline of the hills above Laguna. To reach the trailheads, take Park Ave to Alta Laguna Blvd then turn left.

☞ Tours

Stop by the visitors bureau for brochures about self-guided tours on foot and by public bus, including heritage walks and public art.

⚝ Festivals & Events

Festival of Arts   ART SHOW
(www.foapom.com; 650 Laguna Canyon Rd; admission $7-10; ☺ usually 10am-11:30pm Jul & Aug) A two-month celebration of original artwork in almost all its forms. About 140 exhibitors display works ranging from paintings and handcrafted furniture to scrimshaw, plus kid-friendly art workshops and live music and entertainment daily.

Laguna Beach

◉ Top Sights
1 Laguna Art Museum B2

◉ Sights
2 Heisler Park A2
3 Main Beach C2

✪ Activities, Courses & Tours
4 Divers Cove A2
5 Worldwide Opportunities on
     Organic Farms D1

⊜ Sleeping
6 Inn at Laguna Beach B2
7 Laguna Cliffs Inn A2
8 The Tides Inn B2

✪ Eating
9 242 Cafe Fusion Sushi C2
10 Zinc Cafe & Market C2

◉ Drinking & Nightlife
11 Ocean Brewing Company C2

✪ Entertainment
12 Laguna Playhouse C1

◉ Shopping
13 Hobie Surf Shop C2

Sawdust Festival   ART SHOW
(☑ 949-494-3030; www.sawdustartfestival.org; 935 Laguna Canyon Rd; adult/child 6-12yr/ senior $8.50/4/7; ☺ 10am-10pm late Jun-early Aug, to 6pm Sat & Sun late Nov–mid-Dec) Independent-minded festival that takes place in late autumn.

ℹ FIRE!

Forest fires are an ever-present danger all over Southern California, a truth Laguna Beach knows too well, due to fires large and small over the years. The canyons act like chimneys and small grass fires can quickly become infernos. Use extreme caution when lighting matches and don't just toss your cigarette butts – extinguish them with water or dirt, and once they're completely out, dispose of them properly.

Pageant of the Masters PERFORMANCE ART
(✆800-487-3378; www.foapom.com; 650 Laguna Canyon Rd; tickets from $15; ⊙8:30pm daily mid-Jul–Aug) The most thrilling part of the main festival, an experience that will leave you rubbing your eyes in disbelief, is the Pageant of the Masters performance, where human models blend seamlessly into re-creations of famous paintings. Tickets are hard to get unless you order them more than six months in advance, but you may be able to snag last-minute cancellations.

🛏 Sleeping

Most lodging in Laguna is on busy Pacific Coast Hwy (called Coast Hwy here), so expect traffic noise; bring earplugs or ask for a room away from the road.

★The Tides Inn MOTEL $$
(✆888-777-2107, 949-494-2494; www.tideslaguna.com; 460 N Coast Hwy; r $175-285; P❋🛜⛱🐾) A bargain for Laguna, especially considering its convenient location just three long blocks north of the village. It feels rather upscale, with plush bedding, beachy-keen decor and inspirational quotes painted into each room. Each room is different; some have kitchenettes. Shared facilities include saltwater pool, barbecue grill and a fireplace for toasting marshmallows. Pet fee $25 to $40.

Inn at Laguna Beach HOTEL $$$
(✆949-497-9722, 800-544-4479; www.innatlagunabeach.com; 211 N Coast Hwy; r $210-600; P❋🛜⛱🐾) Pride of place goes to this three-story white concrete hotel, at the north end of Main Beach. Its 70 keen rooms were recently renovated with rattan furniture, blond woods, marble, French blinds and thick featherbeds. Some have balconies overlooking the water. Extras include DVD and CD players, bathrobes, beach gear to borrow and a nightly ocean-view wine and beer reception.

Casa Laguna Inn & Spa B&B $$$
(✆949-494-2996, 800-233-0449; www.casalaguna.com; 2510 S Coast Hwy; r $159-389, ste from $279; P❋@🛜🐾) Laguna's most romantic B&B is built around a historic 1920s Mission Revival house surrounded by flowering gardens. Smallish rooms include those inside former artists' bungalows from the 1930s and '40s. All have fluffy beds and some have Jacuzzis. There's also a full chef-prepared breakfast made with local, organic ingredients and evening wine-and-cheese reception. Some pets OK (fee $25).

Laguna Cliffs Inn HOTEL $$$
(✆800-297-0007, 949-497-6645; www.lagunacliffsinn.com; 475 N Coast Hwy; r $165-325; P❋@⛱) Be it good feng shui, friendly staff or proximity to the beach, something just feels right at this renovated 36-room courtyard inn. From the big earth-tone pillows and hardwood floors to air-con and flat-screen TVs, the decor is contemporary, comfy and clean. Settle into the outdoor heated Jacuzzi with a glass of wine as the sun drops over the ocean.

🍴 Eating

Taco Loco MEXICAN $
(http://tacoloco.net; 640 S Coast Hwy; mains $3-14; ⊙11am-midnight Sun-Thu, to 2am Fri & Sat; 🍴) Throw back Coronas with the surfers while watching the passersby at this Mexican sidewalk cafe. Taco, quesadilla and nacho options seem endless: blackened calamari or tofu, swordfish, veggie (potato, mushroom, tofu) and shrimp to name a few. For dessert: hemp brownies. Order at the counter, dude.

Zinc Cafe & Market CAFE $
(www.zinccafe.com; 350 Ocean Ave, Laguna Beach; mains $6-11; ⊙market 7am-6pm, cafe to 4pm; 🍴) Ground zero for see-and-be-seen vegetarians, this gourmet market has a hedge-enclosed patio where you can munch on tasty vegetarian and vegan meals such as garden-fresh salads and pizzas. Strong espresso too.

Orange Inn DINER $
(✆949-494-6085; www.orangeinnlagunabeach.com; 703 S Coast Hwy; mains $5-10; ⊙6:30am-5pm, to 7pm Sat & Sun) Surfers fuel up, at this little shop from 1931, found in the *Guinness Book of Records* for inventing the smoothie. Also look for date shakes, big

breakfasts, homemade muffins and deli sandwiches on whole-wheat or sourdough bread.

House of Big Fish & Cold Beer   SEAFOOD $$
(☑949-715-4500; www.houseofbigfish.com; 540 S Coast Hwy; mains $7-15; ⊙11:30am-10:30pm) The name says it all (what else do you need?): Hawaii-style *poke* (marinated raw fish), Baja-style fish tacos, coconut shrimp and the fresh catch o' the day. Fish are sustainably raised, and there are dozens of beers with about one-third from California. Make reservations, or wait, like, forever.

★ 242 Cafe Fusion Sushi   JAPANESE $$$
(www.fusionart.us; 242 N Coast Hwy; mains $18-45; ⊙4:30-10pm Sun-Thu, to 10:30pm Fri & Sat) One of the only female sushi chefs in Orange County, Miki Izumisawa slices and rolls organic rice into Laguna's best sushi, artfully presented. The place seats maybe two dozen people at a time, so expect a wait or come early. The 'sexy' handroll – spicy ahi and scallops with mint, cilantro, avocado and crispy potato – is date-enhancing.

Mozambique   AFRICAN FUSION $$$
(☑949-715-7777; www.mozambiqueoc.com; 1740 S Coast Hwy; dinner $14-69; ⊙11am-11pm Sun-Thu, to midnight Fri & Sat) Macaws and toucans welcome guests to this trendy, sophisticated, three-level ode to exotically spiced dishes from southern Africa – peri-peri prawns, chicken pops, grilled pineapple, soaring steaks and seafood, ranging from small plates to pricey surf and turf. Who knows? You might see a *Real Housewife* hiding out in the rooftop bar, where there's live music on weekends.

🍷 Drinking

There are almost as many watering holes in downtown's village as there are art galleries. Most cluster along S Coast Hwy and Ocean Ave, making for an easy pub crawl. If you drink, don't drive; local cops take DUI's very seriously.

Ocean Brewing Company   PUB
(www.oceanbrewing.com; 237 Ocean Ave) Does pub grub and microbrews, excellent after a day of surfing, or look for music and karaoke at night.

Rooftop Lounge   BAR
(www.rooftoplagunabeach.com; 1289 S Coast Hwy) Perched atop **La Casa del Camino** (☑855-634-5736, 949-497-2446; www.lacasadelcamino.

com; 1289 S Coast Hwy; r from $159; P✳@🛜), this bar, has 270-degree coastal views, mango and wild berry mojitos and tasty plates like meatballs in guava BBQ sauce.

Koffee Klatsch   COFFEEHOUSE
(1440 S Coast Hwy; ⊙7am-11pm Sun-Thu, to midnight Fri & Sat) A low-key coffee shop that draws a mixed gay/straight/hipster crowd for coffees, breakfasts, salads and ginormous cakes.

☆ Entertainment

Laguna Playhouse   THEATER
(☑949-497-2787, www.lagunaplayhouse.com; 606 Laguna Canyon Rd) Orange County's oldest continuously operating community theater stages lighter plays in summer, more serious works in winter.

🛍 Shopping

Downtown's village is awash with shops in hidden courtyards and eclectic little bungalows. Forest Ave has the highest concentration of chic boutiques from sleek beachwear to **Hobie Surf Shop** (www.hobie.com; 294 Forest Ave) – Hobie Alter started his internationally known surf line in his parents' Laguna Beach garage in 1950. South of downtown, Pacific Coast Hwy teems with fashionable, eclectic and arty shops where you can shop for goddess clothing, balance your chakras or find vintage rock albums and posters.

For a DIY **art gallery walk**, Laguna has three distinct districts: Gallery Row, along the 300 to 500 blocks of N Coast Hwy; in downtown's village, along Forest Ave and Pacific Coast Hwy; and further south on S Coast Hwy between Oak St and Bluebird Canyon Dr. Pick up an art-walk map at the visitors bureau.

DISNEYLAND & ORANGE COUNTY LAGUNA BEACH

ℹ Information

INTERNET ACCESS

Visit Laguna Beach's Visitor Center for free wi-fi and internet terminal access.

Laguna Beach Library (www.ocpl.org/libloc/lbch; 363 Glenneyre St; ⊘10am-8pm Mon-Wed, to 6pm Thu, to 5pm Fri & Sat; 🛜) Free wi-fi and walk-in online computer access.

MEDICAL SERVICES

Mission Hospital Laguna Beach (📞949-499-1311; www.missionforhealth.com; 31872 Coast Hwy; ⊘24hr) 24-hour emergency room, 4 miles south of downtown along PCH.

TOURIST INFORMATION

Visit Laguna Beach Visitors Center (📞949-497-9229; www.lagunabeachinfo.com; 381 Forest Ave; ⊘10am-5pm; 🛜) Helpful staff, bus schedules, restaurant menus and free brochures on everything from hiking trails to self-guided walking tours.

ℹ Getting There & Away

From I-405, take Hwy 133 (Laguna Canyon Rd) southwest. Hwy 1 goes by several names in Laguna Beach: south of Broadway, downtown's main street, it's called South Coast Hwy; north of Broadway it's North Coast Hwy. Locals also call it Pacific Coast Hwy or just PCH.

OCTA (📞714-560-6282; www.octa.net) bus 1 heading along the coast connects Laguna Beach with Orange County's other beach towns, including Dana Point heading south, every 30 to 60 minutes. The one-way fare is $2 (exact change).

ℹ Getting Around

Laguna Beach Transit (www.lagunabeachcity.net; 375 Broadway) has its central bus depot in downtown's village, served by three routes including to festival sites. Rides cost 75¢ (exact change) or are free during July and August.

Through town, Pacific Coast Hwy moves slowly in summer, especially on weekends.

Parking lots in downtown's village charge between $10 and $20 per entry; they fill up early in the day during summer. Street parking can be hard to find near the beaches during summer, especially in the afternoons and on weekends – arrive early. Coin- and credit-card-operated meters cost from $1 per hour and pay-and-display lots cost $2 per hour. Alternatively, park for free in residential areas, but obey time limits and posted restrictions, otherwise your car will be towed.

Around Laguna Beach

San Juan Capistrano

Famous for the swallows that fly back to town every March, San Juan Capistrano is also home to the 'jewel of the California missions.' It's a little town, about 11 miles south and inland of Laguna Beach, but there's enough history and charm here to make almost a day of it.

⊙ Sights & Activities

★**Mission San Juan Capistrano**   CHURCH
(📞949-234-1300; www.missionsjc.com; 26801 Ortega Hwy, San Juan Capistrano; adult/child $9/6; ⊘9am-5pm) Padre Junipero Serra founded the mission on November 1, 1776, and tended it personally for many years. Particularly moving are the towering remains of the Great Stone Church, almost completely destroyed by a powerful earthquake on December 8, 1812. The **Serra Chapel** – whitewashed outside with restored frescoes inside – is believed to be the oldest existing building in California (1778). Plan on spending at least an hour poking around the sprawling mission's tiled roofs, covered arches, lush gardens, fountains and courtyards – including the padre's quarters, soldiers' barracks and the cemetery.

Admission includes a worthwhile free audio tour with interesting stories narrated by locals.

Los Rios Historic District   HISTORIC BUILDINGS
One block southwest of the Mission, next to the Capistrano train depot, this peaceful assemblage of a few dozen historic cottages and adobes now mostly houses cafes and gift shops. Pick up a free walking-tour guide at the information kiosk off Verdugo St, by the railroad tracks.

✕ Eating & Drinking

★**El Campeon**   MEXICAN $
(31921 Camino Capistrano; mains $2-9; ⊘6:30am-9pm; 🖑) Real-deal Mexican food, in a strip

FIESTA DE LA GOLONDRINAS

Swallows return to nest in the walls of Mission San Juan Capistrano every year around March 19, the feast of St Joseph, after wintering in South America. Their flight covers about 7500 miles each way. The highlight of the town's month-long **Festival of the Swallows** (www. swallowsparade.com) is the big parade and outdoor *mercado* (market), held on a Saturday in mid-March.

mall south of the Mission. There's a simple counter-service restaurant, *panadería* (bakery) and *mercado* (grocery store). Look for tacos, tostadas and burritos in freshly made tortillas, *aguas frescas* (fruit drinks) in flavors like watermelon and grapefruit, and breads and pastries starting at 59¢.

★**Ramos House Café**   CALIFORNIAN $$
(www.ramoshouse.com; 31752 Los Rios St; mains $15-20; ⊗8:30am-3pm Tue-Sun) The best spot for breakfast or lunch near the Mission, this Old West–flavored wood built house from 1881 is famous for organically raised comfort food flavored with herbs grown on-site.

El Adobe de Capistrano   MEXICAN $$
(www.eladobedecapistrano.com; 31891 Camino Capistrano; lunch $11-21, dinner $11-34; ⊗11am-9pm Mon-Thu, to 10pm Fri & Sat, 10am-9pm Sun) In a building that traces its origins to 1797, this sprawling, beamed-ceilinged restaurant and bar does big business, from the standards (enchiladas, fajitas) to blackened fish or lobster tacos and grilled steaks. It was a favorite of President Nixon, who lived in nearby San Clemente, which might be good or bad depending on your outlook.

Coach House   CLUB
(☑949-496-8930; www.thecoachhouse.com; 33157 Camino Capistrano) Long-running live-music venue features a roster of local and national rock, indie, alternative and retro bands; expect a cover charge of $15 to $40. Recent performers include classic rockers like Marshall Tucker and Johnny Winter, tribute bands and comedy shows like the *Funniest Housewives of Orange County*.

❶ Getting There & Away

From Laguna Beach, ride **OCTA** (☑714-560-6282; www.octa.net) bus 1 south to Dana Point.

At the intersection of Pacific Coast Hwy and Del Obispo St, catch bus 91 northbound toward Mission Viejo, which drops you near the Mission. Buses run every 30 to 60 minutes. The trip takes about an hour. You'll have to pay the one-way fare ($2, exact change) twice.

Drivers should take I-5 exit 82 (Ortega Hwy), then head west about 0.25 miles. There's free three-hour parking on streets and in municipal lots.

The **Amtrak** (☑800-872-7245; www.amtrak. com; 26701 Verdugo St) depot is one block south and west of the Mission. You could arrive by train from LA ($21, 75 minutes) or San Diego ($22, 90 minutes). A few daily **Metrolink** (☑800-371-5465; www.metrolinktrains.com) commuter trains link San Juan Capistrano to Orange ($8, 45 minutes), with limited connections to Anaheim.

Dana Point

Dana Point's built-up, parking-lotted harbor detracts from its charm, but it still gets lots of visitors its lovely beaches and port and for whale watching and sport fishing.

TRESTLES

World-renowned **Trestles**, southeast of Dana Point and next to San Diego County, is famous for its natural surf break, which consistently churns out perfect waves, even in summer. It's also endangered; for years surfers and environmentalists have been fighting the extension of a nearby toll road that they contend would negatively affect the waves. Visit http://savetrestles.surfrider. org to learn more.

Trestles lies inside protected **San Onofre State Beach** (www.parks.ca.gov; parking $15 per day), which has rugged bluff-top walking trails, swimming beaches and a developed inland **campground** (☑800-444-7275; www. reserveamerica.com; sites $35-60) with flush toilets, indoor hot showers, picnic tables and fire pits. To get here, exit I-5 at Basilone Rd or Los Christianos Rd (for the campground), then hoof to Trestles along the nature trail.

◉ Sights & Activities

Doheny State Beach   BEACH
(☑949-496-6172; www.dohenystatebeach.org; entry per vehicle $15; ⊗6am-10pm, to 8pm Nov-Feb; P ♨) This mile-long beach is great for swimmers, surfers, surf fishers and tidepoolers. You'll also find picnic tables with grills, volleyball courts and a butterfly exhibit.

Rent bicycles at **Wheel Fun Rentals** (☑949-496-7433; www.wheelfunrentals.com; 25300

Dana Point Harbor Dr; cruiser rental per hr/day $10/28; ☺9am-sunset daily late May-early Sep, Sat & Sun early Sep-late May), just south of the picnic area at Doheny State Beach. Off Dana Point Harbor Dr, **Capo Beach Watercraft Rentals** (☑949-661-1690; www.capobeachwatercraft.com; 34512 Embarcadero Pl) and **Dana Point Jet Ski & Kayak Center** (☑949-661-4947; www.danapointjetski.com; 34671 Puerto Pl) both rent kayaks for harbor paddling. For scuba rentals and dive-boat trips (from $115), try **Beach Cities Scuba** (☑949-443-3858; www.beachcitiesscuba.com; 34283 Pacific Coast Hwy).

Ocean Institute   MUSEUM
(☑949-496-2274; www.ocean-institute.org; 24200 Dana Pt Harbor Dr; adult/child $6.50/4.50; ☺10am-3pm Sat & Sun; ⛟) On Sundays, admission to this child-friendly eco-center includes the guided tours aboard a replica of an early 19th-century tall ship, the brig **Pilgrim**, sailed by Richard Dana during his journey around Cape Horn to California.

Make reservations for the **R/V Sea Explorer** (adult/child 4 to 12 years from $35/22), a 70ft-long floating lab, for a science-focused snorkeling cruise or blue whale safari, or join a 'pyrate' adventure or gray-whale-watching cruise on the **Spirit of Dana Point** (adult/child 4 to 12 years $40/23), a replica of an American Revolution–era ship.

⚲ Tours

In Mariner's Village off Dana Point Harbor Dr, Dana Wharf is the starting point for most boat tours and trips to Catalina Island. Contact **Capt Dave's Dolphin and Whale Safari** (☑949-488-2828; www.dolphinsafari.com; 34451 Ensenada Pl; adult/child 3-12yr from $59/39) or **Dana Wharf Sportfishing** (☑949-496-5794, 888-224-0603; www.danawharf.com; 34675 Golden Lantern St; sportfishing trips adult/child 3-12yr from $46/29, whale-watching tours from $45/25). For more kid-friendly whale-watching tours and coastal cruises, book ahead with the **Ocean Institute**.

✷ Festivals & Events

Festival of Whales   SEA FESTIVAL
(www.dpfestivalofwhales.com; ☺early–mid-Mar) A parade, street fair, nature walks and talks, canoe races, surfing clinics, art exhibitions, live music, and surf 'woody' wagon and hot-rod show make up the merriment.

Doheny Blues Festival   MUSIC FESTIVAL
(www.omegaevents.com/dohenyblues; ☺mid-May) Blues legends such as Buddy Guy and Keb Mo perform alongside up-and-comers over a weekend of funky live-music performances and family fun at Doheny State Beach.

Tall Ships Festival   SEA FESTIVAL
(www.tallshipsfestival.com; ☺early Sep) The Ocean Institute hosts the West Coast's largest gathering of tall ships, with living-history encampments, scrimshaw carving demonstrations and lots more family-friendly marine-themed activities.

🛏 Sleeping & Eating

Mostly chain midrange motels and luxury resorts are what you'll find along Pacific Coast Hwy. The latter include the oceanfront **Ritz-Carlton Laguna Niguel** (☑949-240-2000; www.ritzcarlton.com; 1 Ritz-Carlton Dr; r from $420; @🏱🛜🏊), well-positioned for catching sunsets at Salt Creek Beach. **Doheny State Beach** (☑800-444-7275; www.reserveamerica.com; 25300 Dana Point Harbor Dr; inland/beachfront campsites $35/60) is regularly voted the county's best campground.

Restaurants around Dana Point Harbor serve straight-off-the-boat seafood. At Dana Wharf, **Turk's** (☑949-496-9028; 34683 Golden Lantern St; mains $5-16; ☺8am-2am, shorter hours winter) dive bar is so dark it feels like you're drinking while jailed in the brig of a ship, but never mind. There's plenty of good pub grub (including burgers and fish-and-chips), Bloody Marys and beers, a mellow crowd and a groovy jukebox.

ⓘ Information

Visitors Center (☑949-248-3501; www.danapoint.org; ☺9am-4pm Fri-Sun late May-early Sep) Stop at this tiny booth at the corner of Golden Lantern St and Dana Point Harbor Dr for tourist brochures and maps. Gung-ho volunteers sure love their city.

ⓘ Getting There & Around

From the harbor, **Catalina Express** (☑800-481-3470; www.catalinaexpress.com; 34675 Golden Lantern St; round-trip adult/child 2-11yr/ senior $76.50/70/61) makes daily round-trips to Catalina Island, taking 90 minutes each way.

OCTA (☑714-560-6282; www.octa.net) bus 1 connects Dana Point with the OC's other beach towns every 30 to 60 minutes. The one-way fare is $2 (exact change).

Four-hour public parking at the harbor is free, or pay $5 per day (overnight $10).

San Diego & Around

Why Go?

New York has its cabbie, Chicago its bluesman and Seattle its coffee-drinking boho. San Diego, meanwhile, has the valet guy in a polo shirt, khaki shorts and crisp new sneakers. With his perfectly tousled hair, great tan and gentle enthusiasm, he looks like he's on a perennial spring break, and when he wishes you welcome, he really means it.

This may sound pejorative, but our intention is the opposite. San Diego calls itself 'America's Finest City' and its breezy confidence and sunny countenance filter down even to folks you encounter every day on the street.

What's not to love? San Diego bursts with world-famous attractions for the entire family, including the zoo, Legoland, the museums of Balboa Park and SeaWorld, plus a bubbling downtown and beaches ranging from ritzy to raucous, and America's most perfect weather.

Best Places to Eat

➡ Cucina Urbana (p441)

➡ Puesto at the
Headquarters (p443)

➡ Urban Solace (p442)

➡ Fish 101 (p457)

Best Places to Stay

➡ Hotel del Coronado (p439)

➡ Legoland Hotel (p459)

➡ La Pensione Hotel (p438)

➡ Hotel Solamar (p438)

When to Go

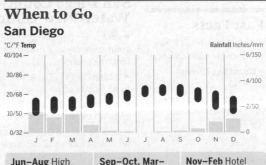

San Diego

Jun–Aug High season. Temperatures and hotel rates are highest.

Sep–Oct, Mar–May Shoulder seasons; moderate rates.

Nov–Feb Hotel rates fall while most of America is hard at work.

MISSION SAN DIEGO DE ALCALÁ

Although the first California mission was on Presidio Hill by present-day Old Town, in 1774 Padre Junípero Serra moved it about 7 miles upriver, closer to water and more arable land. Now the Mission Basilica San Diego de Alcalá (p432) has been lovingly restored into a pretty white church and ancillary buildings (including California's oldest) and welcomes visitors.

Up-and-Coming Neighborhoods

➡ East Village

➡ Little Italy

➡ North Park

Population

With a population of 1,322,553, San Diego is the USA's eighth largest city. San Diego County, at 3,095,313, is fifth largest.

Fast Facts

➡ **Area** 372 sq miles (city); 4526 square miles (county)

➡ **Coastline** 70 miles (county)

➡ **Telephone area codes** ☑ 619, ☑ 858, ☑ 760, ☑ 442

Balboa Park

San Diego's best-known attraction, the zoo, is ensconced in Balboa Park, one of America's great urban spaces. Balboa Park rose to fame with a world's fair about 100 years ago, the Panama-California Exposition of 1915-16. Grand Spanish-colonial revival-style pavilions were constructed, which dominated the California design sense for generations. Here's the thing, though: they were temporary, made largely of stucco, chicken wire, plaster, hemp and horsehair like Hollywood movie sets, but they proved so popular that many were later replaced with the durable concrete structures that you see today. And among the park's many stages and amphitheaters, the jewel is the 600-seat Old Globe, modeled after the London theater where Shakespeare's works were performed. At 1200 acres, Balboa Park is more than 50% bigger than Central Park in New York City (778 acres).

GAY & LESBIAN SAN DIEGO

Historians trace the roots of San Diego's thriving gay community to WWII. Amid the enforced intimacy of military life, gay men from around the US were suddenly able to create strong if clandestine social networks. Postwar, many of these new friends stayed, and by the late 1960s, a newly politicized gay community made its unofficial headquarters in the Hillcrest neighborhood, which still has the highest concentration of LGBT bars, restaurants, cafes and shops, though the center is gradually branching out to other neighborhoods including nearby North Park. Visitors and locals alike find San Diego's gay scene generally more casual and friendly than in San Francisco or LA.

San Diego County's Best Water-View Dining

➡ Anthony's Fish Grotto (p443) Seafood classic next to the great naval ships of the Embarcadero, by Downtown San Diego's seashore.

➡ Bali Hai (p443) Tiki to the max, baby; watch the sailboats go by off Point Loma.

➡ World Famous (p444) This spot in Pacific Beach has never given up the surfer vibe.

➡ George's at the Cove (p453) Consistently rated one of America's top restaurants, with three venues for your dining pleasure. The rooftop lounge has awesome views.

➡ Jake's Del Mar (p456) After a day at the races, stop for a cocktail and an awesome happy hour.

CENTRAL & COASTAL SAN DIEGO

Whoosh – here comes a skateboarder. And there goes a wet-suited surfer toting his board to the break, while a Chanel-clad lady lifts a coffee cup off a porcelain saucer. Downtown San Diego and its nearby coastal communities offer all that and more.

◉ Sights

◉ San Diego Zoo & Balboa Park

San Diego's Zoo is a highlight of any trip to California and should be a high priority for first-time visitors. It's in Balboa Park, which itself is packed with museums and gardens.

To visit the zoo, all 14 museums, half-dozen botanical gardens and more would take days;

San Diego & Around Highlights

❶ Cooing at koalas and pandering to pandas at the **San Diego Zoo** (p429).

❷ Museum-hopping in **Balboa Park** (p429).

❸ Sunning and skating seaside in **Pacific Beach** (p433).

❹ Swilling margaritas in **Old Town** (p431) and pub-crawling downtown's **Gaslamp Quarter** (p444).

❺ Cheering for Shamu at **SeaWorld** (p433).

❻ Marveling at the history and architecture of the **Hotel del Coronado** (p433).

❼ Hang gliding, kayaking or giving your credit card a workout in **La Jolla** (p450).

❽ Sampling fish tacos or the next great taste in **Hillcrest and North Park** (p441).

❾ Mingling with the hoi polloi at **Del Mar Racetrack** (p453).

Metropolitan San Diego

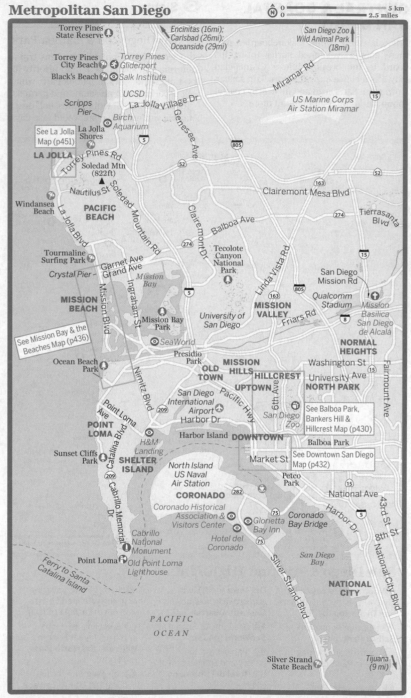

0 — 5 km
0 — 2.5 miles

Torrey Pines
State Reserve

Encinitas (16mi);
Carlsbad (26mi);
Oceanside (29mi)

San Diego Zoo
Wild Animal Park
(18mi)

Torrey Pines
City Beach
Black's Beach

Torrey Pines
Gliderport
Salk Institute

Miramar Rd

UCSD

La Jolla Village Dr

US Marine Corps
Air Station Miramar

Scripps
Pier

Birch
Aquarium

See La Jolla
Map (p451)

La Jolla
Shores

LA JOLLA

Genesee Ave

Torrey Pines Rd

Soledad Mtn
(822ft)

Nautilus St

Clairemont Mesa Blvd

Windansea
Beach

PACIFIC
BEACH

Soledad Mountain Rd

Balboa Ave

Tierrasanta
Blvd

Clairemont Dr

Tourmaline
Surfing Park

Garnet Ave
Grand Ave

Tecolote
Canyon
National
Park

San Diego
Mission Rd

Crystal Pier

Mission
Bay

Qualcomm
Stadium

Mission
Basilica
San Diego
de Alcalá

MISSION
BEACH

Ingraham St

Mission Blvd

Mission Bay
Park

University of
San Diego

MISSION
VALLEY

Friars Rd

See Mission Bay & the
Beaches Map (p436)

SeaWorld

NORMAL
HEIGHTS

Ocean Beach
Park

Nimitz Blvd

Presidio
Park

OLD
TOWN

MISSION
HILLS

Washington St

University Ave

Point Loma
Ave

San Diego
International
Airport

UPTOWN

HILLCREST

NORTH PARK

POINT
LOMA

Catalina Blvd

Harbor Dr

Pacific Hwy

6th Ave

San Diego
Zoo

See Balboa Park,
Bankers Hill &
Hillcrest Map (p430)

Fairmount Ave

Sunset Cliffs
Park

H&M
Landing

Harbor Island

DOWNTOWN

Balboa Park

SHELTER
ISLAND

North Island
US Naval
Air Station

Market St

See Downtown San Diego
Map (p432)

Cabrillo Memorial Dr

CORONADO

Petco
Park

National Ave

Cabrillo
National
Monument

Coronado Historical
Association &
Visitors Center

Glorietta
Bay Inn

Coronado
Bay Bridge

Harbor Dr

43rd St

8th St

National City Blvd

Ferry to Santa
Catalina Island

Point Loma

Old Point Loma
Lighthouse

Hotel del
Coronado

San Diego
Bay

NATIONAL
CITY

Silver Strand Blvd

PACIFIC
OCEAN

Silver Strand
State Beach

Tijuana
(9 mi)

plan your trip at the **Balboa Park Visitors Center** (Map p430; ☑ 619-239-0512; www.balboapark.org; House of Hospitality, 1549 El Prado; ⊙ 9:30am-4:30pm). Pick up a map (suggested donation $1) and the opening schedule.

★ **San Diego Zoo** ZOO
(Map p430; ☑ 619-231-1515; www.sandiegozoo.org; 2920 Zoo Dr; 1-day pass adult/child from $46/36; 2-visit pass to Zoo and/or Safari Park adult/child $82/64; ⊙ 9am-9pm mid-Jun–early Sep, to 5pm or 6pm early Sep–mid-Jun; P ♿) ✦ This justifiably famous zoo is one of SoCal's biggest attractions, showing more than 3000 animals representing over 800 species in a beautifully landscaped setting, typically in enclosures that replicate their natural habitats. Its sister park is San Diego Zoo Safari Park (p458) in northern San Diego County.

Arrive early, as many of the animals are most active in the morning – though many perk up again in the afternoon. Pick up a map at the entrance to the zoo to find your own favorite exhibits.

Balboa Park Museums MUSEUM
(www.balboapark.org; Balboa Park; Passport (s entry to each museum within 1 week) adult/child $53/29, Stay for the Day (5 museums in 1 day) $43; Combo Pass (Passport plus zoo) adult/child $89/52) Among the park's museums, standouts are the **Reuben H Fleet Science Center** (Map p430; ☑ 619-238-1233; www.rhfleet.org; 1875 El Prado; adult/child $13/11, incl Giant Dome Theater $17/14; ⊙ 10am-5pm Mon-Thu, to 6pm Fri-Sun; ♿), with its Giant Dome movie presentations; the **San Diego Natural History Museum** (Map p430; ☑ 619-232-3821; www.sdnhm.org; 1788 El Prado; adult/child $17/11; ⊙ 10am-5pm; ♿); the **San Diego Museum of Art** (SDMA; Map p430; ☑ 619-232-7931; www.sdmart.org; 1450 El Prado; adult/child $12/4.50; ⊙ 10am-5pm Mon-Tue & Thu-Sat, from noon Sun, also 5-9pm Thu Jun-Sep), the city's largest; the **Timken Museum of Art** (Map p430; ☑ 619-239-5548; www.timkenmuseum.org; 1500 El Prado; ⊙ 10am-4:30pm Tue-Sat, from 1:30pm Sun) FREE, with works by masters such as Rembrandt, Rubens, El Greco, Cézanne and Pissarro; and the **Mingei International Museum** (Map p430; ☑ 619-239-0003; www.mingei.org; 1439 El Prado; adult/child $8/5; ⊙ 10am-5pm Tue-Sun; ♿), featuring folk crafts from around the world.

Other, museums include the **San Diego Model Railroad Museum** (Map p430; ☑ 619-696-0199; www.sdmrm.org; Casa de Balboa, 1649 El Prado; adult/child under 6yr $8/free; ⊙ 11am-4pm Tue-Fri, to 5pm Sat & Sun; ♿), the **Museum of Photographic Arts** (Map p430; ☑ 619-238-7559; www.mopa.org; Casa de Balboa, 1649 El Prado; adult/student/child $8/6/free; ⊙ 10am-5pm Tue-Sun, to 9pm Thu late May–Aug), the **Spanish Village Art Center Artist Colony** (Map p430; ⊙ 11am-4pm) FREE and the **Marie Hitchcock Puppet Theater** (Map p430; ☑ 619-685-5990; www.balboaparkpuppets.com; Balboa Park; admission $5.50; ⊙ 11am, 1pm

SAN DIEGO IN...

It's easy to spend most of a week in San Diego, but if your time is limited, here's a whirlwind itinerary. Things will go more smoothly if you've got access to a car.

One Day

Rub elbows with the locals over breakfast in the **Gaslamp Quarter** then ramble around **Old Town State Historic Park** (p431) for a bit of history before a Mexican lunch. Devote the afternoon to the **San Diego Zoo**, which is among the world's best, and if time permits visit some of the museums or gardens in graceful **Balboa Park** (Map p430). For dinner and a night out on the town, head to the hip **East Village** or back to the Gaslamp Quarter, where many restaurants have terrace seating for people-watching, and the partying ranges from posh to raucous.

Two Days

Take the ferry to Coronado for a sea-view breakfast at the Hotel del Coronado (p433), then enjoy the California beach scene at **Mission and Pacific Beaches. La Jolla** beckons this afternoon: explore **Torrey Pines State Reserve** (p450), **Birch Aquarium at Scripps** (p450), kayak the **sea caves**, try a **glider ride** or head to **La Jolla Village** to browse the 1920s Spanish Revival landmarks and boutiques. As the sun begins its descent over the ocean, head to **Del Mar**, where you can cheer from, or snuggle at, one of the restaurants on the roof of **Del Mar Plaza** (1555 Camino Del Mar) while the sky turns brilliant orange and fades to black.

Balboa Park, Bankers Hill & Hillcrest

& 2:30pm Wed-Sun late May–early Sep, shorter hours early Sep–late May; 👣).

👁 Downtown San Diego

Downtown San Diego was a rough place in the 19th century, full of saloons, gambling joints, bordellos and opium dens. By the 1960s it had declined to a skid row of flophouses and bars.

But thanks to strong bones and a local preservation and restoration movement, historic buildings have been restored and collectively renamed the **Gaslamp Quarter**,

now full of restaurants, nightspots and theaters amid 19th-century-style street lamps, trees and brick sidewalks. A few 'adult entertainment' shops, and a fair number of homeless folks serve as reminders of the old days.

See the Gaslamp's early history at the **Gaslamp Museum & William Heath Davis House** (www.gaslampquarter.org; 410 Island Ave; adult/senior & student $5/4, walking tour $10/8; ⏱10am-6pm Tue-Sat, 9am-3pm Sun, walking tour 11am Sat), **San Diego Chinese Historical Museum** (404 3rd Ave; ⏱10:30am-4pm Tue-Sun) **FREE** and **US Grant Hotel** (☑619-232-3121; 326 Broadway).

Balboa Park, Bankers Hill & Hillcrest

Next door, the East Village is a hub of exciting contemporary architecture like the baseball stadium **Petco Park** (☑619-795-5011; www.padres.com; 100 Park Blvd; tours adult/child/senior $12/8/9; ☉tours 10.30am & 12:30pm Sun-Fri, 10:30am, 12:30pm & 3pm off season; ⅏) and the stunning new **Main Library** (www.sandiego.gov/public-library; 330 Park Blvd; ☉noon-8pm Mon, Wed & Fri, 9:30am-5:30pm Tue & Thu, 9:30am-2:30pm Sat, 1-5pm Sun), both open for visitors.

Museum of Contemporary Art   MUSEUM
(MCASD Downtown; ☑858-454-3541; www.mcasd.org; 1001 Kettner Blvd; adult/child under 25yr/senior $10/free/5, 5-7pm 3rd Thu each month free; ☉11am-5pm Thu-Tue, to 7pm 3rd Thu each month) This museum brings an ever-changing variety of innovative artwork to San Diegans, in the downtown location and the La Jolla branch (p450). Across from the main building, a slickly renovated section of San Diego's train station houses permanent works by Jenny Holzer and Richard Serra. Tickets are valid for seven days in all locations.

★ **New Children's Museum**   MUSEUM
(www.thinkplaycreate.org; 200 W Island Ave; admission $10; ☉noon-4pm Sun, 1am-4pm Mon & Wed-Sat; ⅏) This interactive children's museum opened in 2008. Artists have designed installations so that tykes can learn principles of movement and physics while simultaneously being exposed to art and working out the ants in their pants. Exhibits change roughly every 18 months, so there's always something new.

◎ Little Italy

Little Italy was settled in the mid-19th century by Italian immigrants, mostly fishermen and their families, who lived off a booming fish industry and whiskey trade.

Over the last few years, the Italian community has been joined by exciting contemporary architecture, galleries, gourmet restaurants and design and architecture businesses. Fun bars and restaurants have made this one of San Diego's hippest neighborhoods.

◎ Old Town

In 1821, when California was under Mexican rule, the area below the Presidio (fort) became the first official civilian Mexican settlement in California: the **Pueblo de San Diego**.

In 1968 the area was named **Old Town State Historic Park** (☑619-220-5422; www.parks.ca.gov; 4002 Wallace St; ☉visitor center & museums 10am-4pm Oct-Apr, to 5pm May-Sep; ℗⅏) FREE, archaeological work began, and the few surviving original buildings were restored.

There's the **park visitor center** and an excellent **history museum** in the Robinson-Rose House at the southern end of the plaza. The **Whaley House** (☑619-297-7511; www.whaleyhouse.org; 2476 San Diego Ave; adult/child before 5pm $6/4, after 5pm $10/5; ☉10am-10pm late May-early Sep, 10am-5pm Mon-Tue, to 10pm Thu-Sat early Sep-late May) is the city's

Downtown San Diego

oldest brick building and nearby is **El Campo Santo** (San Diego Ave btwn Arista & Conde Sts), an 1849 cemetery for some 20 souls with their biographies on signage. The **Junipero Serra Museum** (☑ 619-297-3258; www.sandiegohistory.org; 2727 Presidio Dr; adult/child $6/3; ◷ 10am-4pm Sat & Sun mid-Sep–mid-May, to 5pm Sat & Sun mid-May–mid-Sep; P ⚿) is named for the Spanish *padre* who established the first Spanish settlement in California, in 1769, and has artifacts of the city's Mission and Rancho Periods. The **Mission Basilica San Diego de Alcalá** (☑ 619-281-8449; www.missionsandiego.com; 10818 San Diego Mission Rd; adult/child $3/1; ◷ 9am-4:30pm; P) eventually moved 7 miles away and is worth a visit.

👁 Embarcadero & the Waterfront

South and west of the Gaslamp Quarter, San Diego's well-manicured waterfront prom-

enades stretch along Harbor Dr, home to excellent museums of naval and sea life, and are perfect for strolling or jogging (or watching well-built members of the US Navy doing same, if that's your thing!).

★ USS Midway Museum   MUSEUM
(☑ 619-544-9600; www.midway.org; 910 N Harbor Dr; adult/child $20/10; ◷ 10am-5pm, last entry 4pm; P ⚿) The permanent home of this giant aircraft carrier (1945–91). On the flight deck, walk right up to some 25 restored aircraft. Admission includes an audio tour to admiral's war room, brig and primary flight control.

★ Maritime Museum   MUSEUM
(☑ 619-234-9153; www.sdmaritime.org; 1492 N Harbor Dr; adult/child $16/8; ◷ 9am-9pm late May-early Sep, to 8pm early Sep-late May; ⚿) Look for the 100ft-high masts of the iron-hulled square-rigger *Star of India*, a tall ship that plied the England–India trade route.

as easily recognized or as much loved as the 'The Del.' The world's largest resort when it was built in 1888, the all-timber, whitewashed main building offers conical towers, cupolas, turrets, balconies and dormer windows, but its biggest fame came as the backdrop to the 1959 Marilyn Monroe classic *Some Like It Hot.* Acres of polished wood give the interior a warm feel that conjures up daydreams of Panama hats and linen suits.

Point Loma

On maps Point Loma looks like an elephant's trunk guarding the entrance to San Diego Bay. Highlights are the Cabrillo National Monument (at the end of the trunk), the shopping and dining of Liberty Station (p447; at its base) and harborside seafood meals.

Cabrillo National Monument   MONUMENT
(☎ 619-557-5450; www.nps.gov/cabr; 1800 Cabrillo Memorial Dr; per car/person walk-in $5/3, good for 7 days; ⊙ 9am-5pm; 🅿) Atop a hill at the tip of the peninsula, this is San Diego's finest locale for history, views and nature walks. It's also the best place in town to see the gray-whale migration (January to March) from land.

The **visitors center** has a comprehensive, old-school presentation on Portuguese explorer Juan Rodríguez Cabrillo's 1542 voyage up the California coast, plus exhibits on native inhabitants and the area's natural history.

Ocean Beach

San Diego's most bohemian seaside community is a place of seriously scruffy haircuts, facial hair and body art. You can get tattooed, shop for antiques and walk into a restaurant barefoot and shirtless without anyone batting an eye. Newport Ave, the main drag, is a compact business district of bars, surf shops, music stores, used-clothing stores and antiques consignment stores.

Mission Bay & Mission & Pacific Beaches

The big ticket attraction around Mission Bay is SeaWorld, while the nearby Mission, Ocean and Pacific Beaches are the SoCal of the movies.

SeaWorld San Diego   THEME PARK
(☎ 800-257-4268;   www.seaworldsandiego.com; 500 SeaWorld Dr; adult/child 3-9yr $84/78; ⊙ daily; 🅿 ♿) SeaWorld opened in San Diego in 1964

Coronado

Across the bay from Downtown San Diego, Coronado is an escape from the jumble of the city. The story of Coronado is in many ways the story of the Hotel del Coronado, opened in 1888 and the centerpiece of one of the West Coast's most fashionable getaways. Coronado's visitors center (p448) doubles as the **Coronado Museum of History and Art** and offers 90-minute historical walking tours. **Coronado Municipal Beach** (parking up to $8; ♿) is consistently ranked in America's top 10. Four-and-a-half miles south of Coronado Village is **Silver Strand State Beach** (☎ 619-435-5184; www.parks.ca.gov; 5000 Hwy 75; per car $10-15; ♿). Both have warm, calm water, perfect for swimming and good for families.

★**Hotel del Coronado**   HOTEL
(☎ 800-582-2595, 619-435-6611; www.hoteldel.com; 1500 Orange Ave; ♿) Few hotels in the world are

Downtown San Diego

and remains one of California's most popular theme parks. Many visitors spend the whole day here, shuttling between shows, rides and exhibits – you can pick up a map to plan your day around scheduled events.

The attraction is best known for live shows featuring trained dolphins, sea lions and killer whales. **One Ocean** is the most visually impressive, a 30-minute show featuring the famous Shamu and other killer whales gliding through the water while interacting with each other, their trainers and the audience.

There are numerous other installations where you can see and learn about aquatic life: in **Penguin Encounter** several penguin species share a habitat that simulates Antarctic living conditions; while **Shark Encounter** offers the chance to see different species of shark as you walk through a 57ft acrylic tunnel. Several amusement-park-style rides are also available. The new **Manta Ray** roller coaster swoops across the park at up to 43mph; **Journey to Atlantis** is a combination flume ride and roller coaster; and **Wild Arctic** is a simulated helicopter flight followed by a walk past beluga whales and polar bears. Expect long waits for rides, shows and exhibits during peak seasons.

Theme parks like SeaWorld have begun to attract controversy in recent years. While the park maintains that it does its share of animal conservation, rescue, rehabilitation, breeding and research, animal welfare groups disagree, questioning the whole idea of places like SeaWorld and criticizing them for keeping the marine life in captivity, arguing that the conditions and treatment of the animals are harmful and stressful, and that all of this is exacerbated further by human interaction. A bill in the California state legislature in 2014 proposed to do away with killer whale shows; it was sent back for further study.

SeaWorld can also be an expensive day out, what with loud advertisements as you wait in line and omnipresent corporate logos and gift shops encouraging additional souvenir spending. That said, good deals are often available for multiday or combination tickets with other parks, including San Diego Zoo and Wild Animal Park, Universal Studios Hollywood and/or Disneyland. Inquire at tourist offices and hotels. To save on food, all-you-can-eat passes to multiple SeaWorld restaurants are available seasonally, or keep a cooler in the car and picnic at tables outside the gates – get a hand-stamp for re-entry.

To get here by car, take SeaWorld Dr off I-5 less than a mile north of where it intersects with I-8. Parking costs $15. Check with Metropolitan Transit System (p449) for public transit. Some hotels offer shuttles.

Mission Bay
OUTDOOR ACTIVITIES

Just east of Mission and Pacific Beaches is this 7-sq-mile playground, with 27 miles of shoreline and 90 acres of parks on islands, coves and peninsulas. Sailing, windsurfing and kayaking dominate northwest Mission Bay, while waterskiers zip around Fiesta Island. Kite flying is popular in Mission Bay Park, beach volleyball on Fiesta Island, and there's delightful cycling and inline skating on bike paths.

Belmont Park
AMUSEMENT PARK

(Map p436; ☎858-458-1549; www.belmontpark. com; 3146 Mission Blvd; per ride $2-6, all-day pass adult/child $27/16; ⊙from 11am daily, closing time varies; P) At the southern end of Mission Beach, this old-style family amusement park (built 1925), has a large indoor pool, known as the Plunge, and the Giant Dipper, a classic wooden roller coaster that'll shake the teeth right outta your mouth, plus bumper cars, a tilt-a-whirl, carousel and other classics.

🏃 Activities

Surfing

A good number of San Diegans moved here for the surfing (p438), and boy is it good. Even beginners will understand why it's so popular.

For the latest beach, weather and surf reports, call San Diego County Lifeguard Services at ☎619-221-8824.

Rental rates vary, but figure on soft boards from $15/45 per hour/day; wetsuits cost $7/28. Equipment and/or lessons are available from outfits including Pacific Beach Surf School (Map p436; ☎858-373-1138; www.pbsurfshop.com; 4150 Mission Blvd; ⊙store 9am-7pm, lessons hourly until 4pm) and Bob's Mission Surf (Map p436; ☎858-483-8837; www.missionsurf.com; 4320 Mission Blvd, Pacific Beach).

Diving & Snorkeling

Off the coast, divers will find kelp beds, shipwrecks (including the *Yukon*, a WWII destroyer sunk off Mission Beach in 2000) and canyons deep enough to host bat rays, octopuses and squid. Check for hazardous conditions before you set out via San Diego County Lifeguard Services at ☎619-221-8824.

Fishing

The most popular public fishing piers are Imperial Beach Pier, Embarcadero Fishing Pier, Shelter Island Fishing Pier, Ocean Beach Pier and Crystal Pier at Pacific Beach. Generally the best pier fishing is from April to October. For offshore fishing, catches can include barracuda, bass and yellowtail and, in summer, albacore. A state fishing license (one day/two day/calendar year $15/23/46) is required for people over 16 for offshore fishing, available from fishing-trip operators in

---

SAN DIEGO FOR KIDS

Tiny hands down, San Diego is one of America's best destinations for family travel. Here are some highlights to jump start your vacation.

Do the Zoo (p429); it's everything they say and more, and while you're there, spend another day enjoying the rest of Balboa Park (p429), one of the nation's best collections of museums. The Reuben H Fleet Science Center (p429), Model Railroad Museum (p429) and Natural History Museum (p429) are all tailor-made for kids, and the plazas, fountains and gardens offer plenty of space for them to let off steam.

Kids elementary-school age and older will appreciate Old Town State Historic Park (p431) and the Mexican restaurants nearby.

Along the coast, SeaWorld (p433) is another landmark (look for specials and combo tickets to keep costs down). Coronado is a calming getaway for the Hotel Del Coronado (p433) and the kid-friendly public library. Views from Cabrillo National Monument (p433) inspire awe, and a museum tells of the Spanish explorers key to local history.

Teens will be in their element among the surfers, bikers and bladers in Mission and Pacific Beaches, while up the coast in La Jolla the Birch Aquarium at Scripps (p450) entertains as it teaches. More active kids can go snorkeling off La Jolla Cove (p450).

In northern San Diego County, Legoland (p457) is the place for the 12-and-under set (and their parents will thrill at the workmanship of the millions of little bricks). Inland, the San Diego Zoo Safari Park (p458) will have the kids roaring.

SAN DIEGO & AROUND ACTIVITIES

addition to tour fees (from $46/36 per adult/child per half-day), including **H&M Landing** (☑ 619-222-1144; www.hmlanding.com; 2803 Emerson St, Point Loma), **Point Loma Sport Fishing** (☑ 619-223-1627; www.pointlomasportfishing.com; 1403 Scott St, Point Loma) and **Seaforth Sportfishing** (☑ 619-224-3383; www.seaforthlanding.com; 1717 Quivira Rd, Mission Bay).

Boating

You can rent powerboats (from $125 per hour), sailboats (from $24 per hour), and kayaks (from $13 per hour) and canoes on Mission Bay, from **Mission Bay Sportcenter** (Map p436; ☑ 858-488-1004; www.missionbaysportcenter.com; 1010 Santa Clara Pl) and **Resort Watersports** (Map p436; ☑ 858-488-2582; www.resortwatersports.com).

Kayaking

Ocean kayaking is a good way to observe sea life, and explore cliffs and caves inaccessible from land. Guided tours and lessons are available from **Family Kayak** (☑ 619-282-3520; www.familykayak.com; adult/child from $44/18; ☑).

Sailing

Experienced sailors may charter boats ranging from catamarans to yachts. Prices start at about $135 for four hours and rise steeply. Charter operators around Harbor Island (on the west side of San Diego Bay near the airport) include **Harbor Sailboat** (☑ 619-291-9568, 800-854-6625; www.harborsailboats.com; Suite 104, 2040 Harbor Island Dr) and **Harbor Yacht Clubs** (☑ 800-553-7245; www.harboryc.com; 1880 Harbor Island Dr).

Whale-Watching

Gray whales pass San Diego from mid-December to late February on their way south to Baja California, and again in mid-March on their way back up to Alaskan waters. Visit Cabrillo National Monument (p433) to spy whales from land, or go on a tour.

☞ Tours

Old Town Trolley Tours & Seal Tours

TROLLEY TOUR

(☑ 888-910-8687; www.trolleytours.com; adult/child $39/19) Hop-on-hop-off open-air buses loop around the main attractions of Downtown and Coronado. The same company operates 90-minute amphibious Seal Tours, which depart from **Seaport Village** (☑ 619-235-4014; www.seaportvillage.com; ☺ 10am-10pm summer).

Mission Bay & the Beaches

Mission Bay & the Beaches

San Diego Scenic Tours   BUS TOUR
(www.sandiegoscenictours.com; adult/child from $38/19) Half and full-day bus tours around San Diego and Tijuana, Mexico, some of which allow time to shop and dine. You can combine some tours with a harbor cruise.

Flagship Cruises   BOAT TOUR
(🖉 619-234-4111; www.flagshipsd.com; 990 N Harbor Dr, tours adult/child from $23/11.50; 🖈) Harbor tours and seasonal whale-watching cruises from the Embarcadero, from one to several hours long.

✯ Festivals & Events

March/April

San Diego Crew Classic   SPORTING EVENT
(www.crewclassic.org; ⊙ late Mar/early Apr) The national college rowing regatta takes places at Mission Bay.

June

Rock 'n' Roll Marathon   SPORTING EVENT
(www.runrocknroll.competitor.com; ⊙ early Jun) Live bands perform at each mile mark of this 26.2-mile race, with a big concert at the finish line.

San Diego County Fair   COUNTY FAIR
(www.sdfair.com; Del Mar Fairgrounds; ⊙ early Jun-early Jul) Well over a million people watch headline acts, enjoy hundreds of carnival rides and shows, and pig out on 'fair fare' (plus some healthier options).

July

Opening Day at Del Mar Racetrack   SPORTING EVENT
(www.dmtc.com, ⊙ mid-late Jul) Outrageous hats, cocktails and general merriment kicks off the horseracing season, 'where the turf meets the surf.' Racing through early September.

San Diego LGBT Pride   COMMUNITY FESTIVAL
(www.sdpride.org; ⊙ late Jul) The city's gay community celebrates in Hillcrest and Balboa Park at the month's end, with parades, parties, performances, art shows and more.

Comic-Con International   CONVENTION
(www.comic-con.org; San Diego Convention Center; ⊙ late Jul) America's largest event for collectors of comic, pop culture and movie memorabilia has gone from geek chic to trendmaker.

September

Fleet Week   MILITARY
(www.fleetweeksandiego.org; ⊙ mid-Sep–early Oct) More like 'Fleet Month.' The US military shows its pride at events such as a sea and air parade, special tours of ships, the Miramar Air Show (the world's largest) and the Coronado Speed Festival featuring vintage cars.

October

Little Italy Festa   FOOD, CULTURE
(www.littleitalysd.com; ⊙ mid-Oct) Come for the tastes and aromas of old Italia, and stay for Gesso Italiano, chalk-art drawn directly onto the streets.

TOP BEACHES IN SAN DIEGO

Choosing San Diego's best beaches is like comparing jewels at Tiffany. Coronado Municipal Beach (p433) has appeared on just about every Top 10 list; others depend on what you're looking for.

Bodysurfing: Pacific Beach and La Jolla Shores. Experienced bodysurfers can head to La Jolla for the big swells of Boomer Beach near La Jolla Cove, or the *whomp* (forceful tubes that break directly onshore) at Windansea or the beach at the end of Sea Lane.

Family friendly: Shell Beach (La Jolla), 15th St Beach (Del Mar), Moonlight Beach (Encinitas).

Nude beach: Black's Beach.

Surf breaks, from south to north: Imperial Beach (best in winter); Point Loma (reef breaks, less accessible but less crowded; best during winter); Sunset Cliffs (Ocean Beach); Pacific Beach. In La Jolla: Big Rock (California's Pipeline), Windansea (hot reef break, best at medium to low tide), La Jolla Shores (beach break, best in winter) and Black's Beach (a fast, powerful wave). Cardiff State Beach; San Elijo State Beach (Cardiff); Swami's (Encinitas); Carlsbad State Beach and Oceanside.

Teen scene: Mission Beach, Pacific Beach.

December

December Nights　HOLIDAY FESTIVAL
(www.balboapark.org/decembernights; ⊘early Dec) This festival in Balboa Park includes crafts, carols and a candlelight parade.

🛏 Sleeping

San Diego Tourism runs a **room-reservation line** (✓800-350-6205; www.sandiego.org).

🏨 Downtown San Diego

500 West Hotel　HOTEL $
(✓619-234-5252, 866-500-7533; www.500westhotelsd.com; 500 W Broadway; s/d with shared bath from $59/79; @✱) Rooms are shoebox-sized and many bathrooms are down the hallway in this 1920s YMCA building, but hipsters on a budget love the bright decor, tiny TVs, communal kitchen (or diner-style restaurant), gym at the Y ($10) and easy access to trolleys and long-distance buses. No air-con.

HI San Diego Downtown Hostel　HOSTEL $
(✓619-525-1531; www.sandiegohostels.org; 521 Market St; 10-/4-bed dm with shared bath incl breakfast from $22/30, d from $75; ✱@✱) Location, location, location. This Gaslamp Quarter HI facility is steps from public transportation, restaurants and big-city fun, and it has a wide range of rooms, including some with private bath. If the local nightlife doesn't suffice, there are movie nights and group dinners to join. Access is 24-hour.

★**USA Hostels San Diego**　HOSTEL $
(✓619-232-3100, 800-438-8622; www.usahostels.com; 726 5th Ave; dm/r with shared bath incl breakfast from $33/79; @✱) Lots of charm and color at this convivial hostel in a former Victorian-era hotel. Look for cheerful rooms, a full kitchen, a communal lounge for chilling and in-house parties and beach barbecues. Rates include linens, lockers and pancakes for breakfast. And it's smack-dab in the middle of Gaslamp nightlife. No air-con.

★**Hotel Solamar**　BOUTIQUE, CONTEMPORARY $$
(✓877-230-0300, 619-531-8740; www.hotelsolamar.com; 435 6th Ave; r $169-299; P✱@✱✱) A great compromise in the Gaslamp: hip style that needn't break the bank. Lounge beats play in the background as you gaze at the Downtown skyscrapers from the pool deck and bar, and rooms have sleek lines and nautical blue and neo-rococo accents for a touch of fun. It has a fitness center, in-room yoga kit, loaner bikes and a nightly complimentary wine hour. Parking costs $41.

★**La Pensione Hotel**　BOUTIQUE HOTEL $$
(Map p430; www.lapensionehotel.com; 606 W Date St; r $110-159; P✱✱; ⑤5, ⑥Pacific Hwy & W Cedar St) Despite the name, Little Italy's La Pensione isn't a pension but an intimate, friendly, recently renovated hotel of 68 rooms – around a frescoed courtyard – with queen-size beds and private bathrooms. It's only steps from the neighborhood's dining, cafes and galleries, and is within walking dis-

tance of most Downtown attractions. There's an attractive cafe downstairs. Parking is $15.

Sofia Hotel BOUTIQUE HOTEL $$
(☏800-826-0009, 619-234-9200; www.thesofiahotel.com; 150 W Broadway; r from $159; P◑@�☀) Across from Westfield Horton Plaza, the historic Sofia has 211 rooms with fashionable dark wood furniture and sprightly printed fabrics. There are also in-room spa services, concierge, complimentary guided walks around the Gaslamp Quarter (Saturday and Sunday) and a fitness and yoga studio. There are three restaurants, including branches of So-Cal chains Coffee Bean and Tender Greens. Parking costs $30.

★**US Grant Hotel** LUXURY $$$
(☏619-232-3121, 800-237-5029; www.starwood.com; 326 Broadway; r from $249; P✷@☀) This 1910 hotel was built as the fancy city counterpart to the Hotel del Coronado and has hosted everyone from Albert Einstein to Harry Truman. Today's quietly flashy lobby combines chocolate-brown and ocean-blue accents, and rooms boast original artwork on the headboards. Parking costs $39.

🛏 Old Town

Cosmopolitan Hotel HISTORIC B&B $$
(☏619-297-1874; www.oldtowncosmopolitan.com; 2660 Calhoun St; r incl breakfast $150-250; ◷front desk 9am-9pm; P☀) Right in Old Town State Park, this creaky, 10-room hotel from 1870 has oodles of charm, antique furnishings, and a restaurant downstairs for lunch and dinner. Don't go expecting modern conveniences like phones and TV, though there's free wi-fi. Breakfast is a simple affair based on coffee and scones. Free parking.

🛏 Coronado

Glorietta Bay Inn HISTORIC B&B $$
(☏619-435-3101, 800-283-9383; www.gloriettabayinn.com; 1630 Glorietta Blvd; r incl breakfast from $219; P✷@☀) Overshadowed by the neighboring Hotel del Coronado, the Glorietta is built in and around a neoclassical 1908 mansion (11 rooms in the mansion, 89 in boxier two-story buildings). Rooms have handsome furnishings and extras such as triple-sheeted beds and high-end bath products. Mansion rooms are more expensive and have even more luxe amenities.

El Cordova Hotel HISTORIC HOTEL $$
(☏619-435-4131, 800-229-2032; www.elcordovahotel.com; 1351 Orange Ave; r from $199; ✷@☀) This exceedingly cozy Spanish-style former mansion from 1902 has rooms and suites around an outdoor courtyard of shops, restaurants, pool, hot tub and barbecue grills. Rooms are charming in an antiquey sort of way, though nothing fancy.

★**Hotel del Coronado** LUXURY HOTEL $$$
(Hotel Del; ☏619-435-6611, 800-468-3533; www.hoteldel.com; 1500 Orange Ave; r from $289; P◑✷@☀) San Diego's iconic hotel provides the essential Coronado experience: over a century of history, a pool, a full-service spa, shops, restaurants, manicured grounds, a white-sand beach and an ice-skating rink in winter. Even the basic rooms have luxurious marbled bathrooms. For a sense of place, book a room in the original hotel, not in the adjacent 1970s building. Parking is $37.

🛏 Point Loma Area

HI San Diego Point Loma Hostel HOSTEL $
(☏619-223-4778; www.sandiegohostels.org; 3790 Udall St; dm/r per person with shared bath incl breakfast from $19/33; @☀) It's a 20-minute walk from central Ocean Beach to this hostel, in a largely residential area close to a market and library. Cheery private rooms are a great deal. There are often cheap dinners, movie nights and free excursions. Bus 923 runs along nearby Voltaire St. No lock-out times. No air-con.

Pearl MOTEL $$
(☏619-226-6100, 877-732-7574; www.thepearlsd.com; 1410 Rosecrans St; r $129-169; P✷☀) The mid-century-modern Pearl feels more Palm Springs than San Diego. The 23 rooms in its 1959 shell have soothing blue hues, trippy surf motifs and betas in fishbowls. There's a lively pool scene (including 'dive-in' movies on Wednesday nights), or you can play Jenga or Parcheesi in the groovy, shag-carpeted lobby. Light sleepers: request a room away from busy street traffic.

🛏 Ocean Beach

Ocean Beach (OB) is under the outbound flight path of San Diego airport. Light sleepers should stay elsewhere or bring earplugs.

Ocean Beach International Hostel HOSTEL $
(Map p436; ☏619-223-7873, 800-339-7263; www.sandiegohostel.us; 4961 Newport Ave; dm $15-40) Central OB's cheapest option is only a couple

of blocks from the ocean; it's a simple but friendly and fun place reserved for international travelers and educators, with barbecues, music nights, bonfires and more. Free transfer from airport, bus or train station on arrival. No air-con.

Inn at Sunset Cliffs BEACHSIDE INN $$$

(☏619-222-7901, 866-786-2453; www.innatsunsetcliffs.com; 1370 Sunset Cliffs Blvd; r/ste from $175/289; P🅿✳@🏠🌊) At the south end of Ocean Beach, wake up to the sound of surf crashing onto the rocky shore. This low-key 1965 charmer wraps around a flower-bedecked courtyard with small heated pool. Its 24 breezy rooms are compact, but most have attractive stone and tile bathrooms, and some suites have full kitchens. Even if the ocean air occasionally takes its toll on exterior surfaces, it's hard not to love. Free parking.

🛏 Pacific Beach & Mission Beach

Banana Bungalow HOSTEL $

(Map p436; ☏858-273-3060; www.bananabungalowsandiego.com; 707 Reed Ave, Pacific Beach; dm/d $35/100; 🏠; 🖥30) Right on Pacific Beach, the Bungalow has a top location, a beach-party atmosphere and is reasonably clean, but it's very basic and gets crowded. Shared rooms are mixed-gender. The communal patio fronts right on the boardwalk; it's a great place for people-watching and beer drinking. No air-con.

Campland on the Bay CAMPING $

(☏858-581-4260, 800-422-9386; www.campland.com; 2211 Pacific Beach Dr, Mission Bay; RV & campsites $45-238, beachfront from $194; P🅿🏠🌊) On more than 40 acres fronting Mission Bay, amenities include a restaurant, two pools, boat rentals, full RV hookups and outdoor activities from skateboarding to singalongs. Price varies depending on proximity to the water; reservations are recommended. Off-season discounts.

Catamaran Resort Hotel RESORT $$

(Map p436; ☏858-488-1081, 800-422-8386; www.catamaranresort.com; 3999 Mission Blvd; r from $159; P🅿@🏠🌊) Tropical landscaping and tiki decor fill this resort backing onto Mission Bay (there's a luau on some summer evenings!). A plethora of activities make it a perfect place for families (sailing, kayaking, tennis, biking, skating, spa-ing, etc) or board the *Bahia Belle* paddleboat from here. Rooms are in low-rise buildings or in a 14-story tower; some have views and full kitchens.

Tower 23 BOUTIQUE HOTEL $$$

(Map p436; ☏858-270-2323, 866-869-3723; www.t23hotel.com; 723 Felspar St, Pacific Beach; r from $249; P🅿✳@🏠🌊) If you like your oceanfront stay to come with contemporary cool, this modernist place has an awesome location, minimalist decor, lots of teals and mint blues, water features and a sense of humor. There's no pool, but dude, you're right on the beach. The hotel's **JRDN** (Jordan; Map p436; ☏858-270-5736; Tower 23 Hotel, 723 Felspar St; mains breakfast & lunch $9-14, dinner $26-46; ☺9am-9pm Sun-Thu, to 9:30pm Sat & Sun) 🍴 restaurant is expensive but worth it. Parking is $20.

Crystal Pier Hotel & Cottages COTTAGE $$$

(Map p436; ☏858-483-6983, 800-748-5894; www.crystalpier.com; 4500 Ocean Blvd; d $185-525; P🅿🏠) Charming, wonderful and unlike anyplace else in San Diego, Crystal Pier has cottages built right on the pier above the water. Almost all 29 cottages have full ocean views and kitchens; most date from 1936. Newer, larger cottages sleep up to six. Book eight to 11 months in advance for summer reservations. Minimum-stay requirements vary by season. No air-con. Rates include parking.

🍴 Eating

Despite its border location, San Diego's food scene doesn't have the ethnic breadth of LA's, but there's a growing locavore and gourmet scene. Reservations are recommended, especially on weekends.

🍴 Balboa Park

★Prado CALIFORNIAN $$$

(Map p430; ☏619-557-9441; www.pradobalboa.com; House of Hospitality, 1549 El Prado; mains lunch $12-21, dinner $22-35; ☺11:30am-3pm Mon-Fri, from 11am Sat & Sun, 5-9pm Sun & Tue-Thu, to 10pm Fri & Sat) In one of San Diego's most beautiful dining rooms, feast on Cal-eclectic cooking by one of San Diego's most renowned chefs: bakery sandwiches, chicken and orecchiette pasta, and pork prime rib. Go for a civilized lunch on the verandah or for afternoon cocktails and appetizers in the bar.

🍴 Gaslamp Quarter

Café 222 BREAKFAST $

(☏619-236-9902; www.cafe222.com; 222 Island Ave; mains $7-11; ☺7am-1:30pm) Downtown's favorite breakfast place serves renowned peanut butter and banana French toast; buttermilk, orange-pecan or granola pancakes; and

TOP FIVE CHEAP EATS
....
➡ Bread & Cie (p442)

➡ Café 222 (p440)

➡ Porkyland (p452)

➡ Saffron (p442)

➡ East Village Asian Diner (p442)

eggs in scrambles or Benedicts. It also sells lunchtime sandwiches and salads, but we always go for breakfast (available until closing).

Gaslamp Strip Club STEAK $$
(☎ 619-231-3140; www.gaslampsteak.com; 340 5th Ave; mains $14-24; ☺ 5-10pm Sun-Thu, to midnight Fri & Sat) Pull your own bottle from the wine vault, then char your own favorite cut of steak, chicken or fish on the open grills in the retro-Vegas dining room at Downtown's best bargain for steak, salad and grill-your-own garlic bread. No bottle costs more than $36, no steak more than $25. Fab, creative martinis and 'pin-up' art by Alberto Vargas. Tons of fun. No one under 21 allowed.

Dick's Last Resort PUB FOOD $$
(☎ 619-231-9100; www.dickslastresort.com; 345 5th Ave; lunch $9-20, dinner $12-24; ☺ 11am-1:30am) At Dick's, a legendary indoor-outdoor bar and grill with a riotously fun atmosphere, you can carry on in full voice while guzzling beer and chowing down on burgers, pork ribs, fried chicken and fish, while the staff makes you a giant dunce cap out of table paper.

Oceanaire SEAFOOD $$$
(☎ 619-858-2277; www.theoceanaire.com; 400 J St; mains $23-52; ☺ 5-10pm Sun-Thu, to 11pm Fri & Sat) The look is art-deco ocean liner, and the service is just as elegant, with an oyster bar and creations like Maryland blue-crab cakes and horseradish-crusted Alaskan halibut. If you don't feel like a total splurge, happy hour features bargain-priced oysters and fish tacos in the bar (times vary).

✖ East Village

Basic PIZZA $
(☎ 619-531-8869; www.barbasic.com; 410 10th Ave; small/large pizzas from $9/14; ☺ 11:30am-2am) Savvy East Villagers feast on fragrant New Haven–style, thin-crust, brick-oven-baked pizzas under Basic's high-ceilinged roof (it's in a former warehouse). Toppings range from the usual to the newfangled, like

mashed potatoes. Wash them down with beers (craft, naturally) or one of several mule cocktails.

Café Chloe FRENCH $$
(☎ 619-232-3242; www.cafechloe.com; 721 9th Ave; breakfast $7-12, lunch $11-17, dinner $20-29; ☺ 7:30am-10pm Mon-Fri, 8:30am-10:30pm Sat, 8:30am-9:30pm Sun) This delightful corner French bistro has a simple style and gets the standards perfect, and everything else as well. Mac 'n' cheese transforms into macaroni, pancetta and French blue gratin, and the *steak frites* is served with herb butter and salad. Wonderful egg dishes for weekend brunch.

✖ Bankers Hill & Old Town

At the giant Mexican eateries all along San Diego Ave, hard-working ladies churn out an estimated 210,000 fresh tortillas per month and most have great bar scenes too.

★Cucina Urbana CALIFORNIAN, ITALIAN $$
(Map p430; ☎ 619-239-2222; 505 Laurel St, Bankers Hill; lunch $10-23, dinner $12-28; ☺ 11:30am-2pm Tue-Fri, 5-9pm Sun & Mon, 5-10pm Tue-Thu, 5pm-midnight Fri & Sat) In this corner place with modern rustic ambience, business gets done, celebrations get celebrated and friends hug and kiss over refined yet affordable Cal Ital cooking. Look for short rib pappardelle, pizzas like foraged mushroom with taleggio cheese and braised leeks, and smart cocktails and local 'brewskies.'

Fred's MEXICAN $$
(☎ 619-858-8226; 2470 San Diego Ave; mains $9-15; ☺ 11am-11pm Sun, Mon, Wed & Thu, to midnight Tue, Fri & Sat) Every night, party people on a budget crowd into raucous Fred's.

Old Town Mexican Café MEXICAN $$
(☎ 619-297-4330; www.oldtownmexcafe.com; 2489 San Diego Ave; mains $4-16; ☺ 7am-2am; ☞) Rowdy and always crowded.

El Agave MEXICAN $$$
(☎ 619-220-0692; www.elagave.com; 2304 San Diego Ave; lunch $12-20, dinner $22-40; ☺ 11am-10pm; ℗) Subdued, sophisticated El Agave has superb mole and a whopping 1500 different tequila varieties.

✖ North Park & Hillcrest

San Diego's restaurant scene is booming in these neighborhoods north of downtown.

Bread & Cie
BAKERY, CAFE $

(Map p430; www.breadandcie.com; 350 University Ave, Hillcrest; mains $6-11; ⊘7am-7pm Mon-Fri, to 6pm Sat, 8am-6pm Sun; P) Aside from crafting some of San Diego's best breads (including anise and fig, kalamata black olive and three-raisin), this wide-open bakery-deli makes fabulous sandwiches with fillings such as curried-chicken salad and Black Forest ham. Boxed lunches cost $11. Great pastries.

★ Urban Solace
CALIFORNIAN $$

(☑619-295-6464; www.urbansolace.net; 3823 30th St, North Park; mains lunch $10-23, dinner $17-27; ⊘11:30am-10pm Mon-Thu, to 11pm Fri, 5-11pm Sat, 5-9pm Sun) North Park's young hip gourmets revel in creative comfort food here: bluegrass burger; 'not your mama's' meatloaf of ground lamb, fig, pine nuts and feta; 'duckaroni' (mac 'n' cheese with duck confit); and chicken and dumplings. The setting is surprisingly chill for such great eats; maybe it's the cocktails like mojitos made with bourbon.

Waypoint Public
GASTROPUB $$

(☑619-255-8778; www.waypointpublic.com; 3794 30th St, North Park; mains $9-21; ⊘4pm-1am Mon-Fri, from 10am Sat & Sun) The comfort-food menu at chef-driven Waypoint is meant to pair craft beers with its dishes, which range from smoked tomato minestrone with grilled cheese to a burger with mozzarella, pulled pork, tomatillo salsa, fried egg and spicy pickled vegetables. Glass garage doors roll up to the outside, all the better for people-watching in busy North Park.

East Village Asian Diner
ASIAN FUSION $$

(Map p430; ☑619-220-4900; www.eateastvillage.com; 406 University Ave, Hillcrest; mains $9-14; ⊘11:30am-2:30pm Mon-Fri, 5-10pm Mon-Wed, to midnight Fri, 11:30am-midnight Sat, 11:30am-10pm Sun) This den of modernist cool fuses mostly Korean cooking with Western and other Asian influences (witness the 'super awesome' beef and kimchi burrito). Try noodle dishes (thai peanut, beef and broccoli, etc), or build your own 'monk's stone pot,' a super-heated rice bowl to which you can add ingredients ranging from pulled pork to salmon. Sauces are made in-house.

Baja Betty's
MEXICAN $$

(Map p430; ☑619-269-8510; bajabettyssd.com; 1421 University Ave, Hillcrest; mains $6-15; ⊘11am-midnight Mon-Fri, 10am-1am Sat, 10am-midnight Sun) Gay-owned and straight-friendly, this restaurant-bar is always a party with a just-back-from-Margaritaville vibe (and dozens of tequilas to take you back there) alongside dishes like Mexi Queen queso dip, You Go Grill swordfish tacos and Fire in the Hole fajitas. Daily specials.

✕ Little Italy

Little Italy is – surprise! – a happy hunting ground for Italian cooking and cafes, and some non-Italian newcomers round out the scene, like Ballast Point Tasting Room (p445).

Bencotto
ITALIAN $$

(Map p430; ☑619-450-4786; www.lovebencotto.com; 750 W Fir St; mains $14-26; ⊘11:30am-9:30pm Sun-Thu, to 10:30pm Fri & Sat; P) Bencotto melds the old with the new of Little Italy – contemporary, angular, architect-designed, arty and green – and the food is great, too, from fresh-sliced prosciutto to pasta *a modo tuo* (your way), with a over 100 potential combos of fresh pasta and sauce.

Filippi's Pizza Grotto
PIZZA, DELI $$

(Map p430; ☑619-232-5094; 1747 India St; dishes $6-20; ⊘9am-10pm Sun & Mon, to 10:30pm Tue-Thu, to 11:30pm Fri & Sat; ⛨) There are often lines out the door for Filippi's old-school Italian cooking (pizza, spaghetti and ravioli) served on red-and-white-checked tablecloths in the dining room festooned with murals of *la bella Italia*. The front of the shop is an excellent Italian deli.

★ Juniper & Ivy
CONTEMPORARY CALIFORNIAN $$$

(Map p430; ☑619-269-9036; www.juniperandivy.com; 2228 Kettner Bl; small plates $9-17, mains $19-36; ⊘4-10pm Sun-Thu, to 11pm Fri & Sat) Chef Richard Blais has opened San Diego's restaurant of the moment. The menu changes daily, but if we mention molecular gastronomic takes on prawn and pork rigatoni; artisan-farmed strip steak with smoked potato, porcini onion rings and kimchi ketchup; and homemade yodel snack cakes for dessert, do you get the idea?

✕ Mission Hills

Mission Hills is the neighborhood north of Little Italy and west of Hillcrest. On India St, where it meets Washington St, there's a block of well-regarded eateries.

Saffron
THAI $

(☑619-574-0177; www.saffronsandiego.com; 3731 India St; mains $7-10; ⊘10:30am-9pm Mon-Sat, 11am-8pm Sun) This multi-award-winning hole-in-the-wall is actually two shops – Saffron Thai Grilled Chicken and Noodles & Saté, but you can get both at either shop and enjoy it in the noodle shop. Chicken is cooked over a charcoal-grill and comes with a choice of sauces, salad, jasmine rice and a menu of finger foods.

El Indio
MEXICAN $

(☑ 619-299-0333; www.el-indio.com; 3695 India St; dishes $3-9; ⊙ 8am-9pm; P ♠) Counter-service shop famous since 1940 for its *taquitos*, *mordiditas* (tiny *taquitos*), tamales and excellent breakfast burritos. Eat in a rudimentary dining room or at picnic tables under metal umbrellas across the street.

Shakespeare Pub & Grille
PUB FOOD $$

(☑ 619-299-0230; www.shakespearepub.com; 3701 India St; dishes $5-15; ⊙ 10:30am-midnight Mon-Thu, to 1am Fri, 8am-1am Sat, 8am-midnight Sun) One of San Diego's most authentic English ale houses, Shakespeare is the place for darts, soccer by satellite, beer on tap and pub grub, including fish and chips, and bangers and mash. On weekends, load up with a British breakfast: bacon, mushrooms, black and white pudding and more. One thing they don't have in Britain: a great sundeck.

✖ Embarcadero & the Waterfront

★ Puesto at the Headquarters
MEXICAN $$

(☑ 610-233-8800; www.eatpuesto.com; 789 W Harbor Dr, The Headquarters; mains $11-19; ⊙ 11am-10pm) This upscale eatery serves Mexican street food that knocked our *zapatos* off: innovative takes on traditional tacos like chicken (with hibiscus, chipotle, pineapple and avocado) and some out-there fillings like potato soy chorizo. Other highlights: crab guacamole, *barbacoa* short ribs (braised in chili sauce) and Mexican street bowl, ie tropical fruits with chili, sea salt and lime.

Anthony's Fish Grotto & Fishette
SEAFOOD $

(www.gofishanthonys.com; 1360 N Harbor Dr; dinner $14-29, lunch specials $10-15; ♠) Fishette (☑ 619-232-2175; Fishette; mains $10-15; ⊙ 10am-9pm Mon-Fri, 8am-9pm Sat & Sun); Grotto (☑ 619-232-5105; Grotto; lunch $8-15, dinner $12-25; ⊙ 11am-9:30pm Sun-Thu, to 10pm Sat & Sun) This pair of restaurants serves seafood and chowders with views of the tall ships on the harbor. The sit-down Grotto has an old-style nautical theme (ahoy, mateys!), while the counter at the Fishette serves a more limited menu

(think fish and chips or sandwiches) that you eat out on the deck.

✖ Coronado

Clayton's Coffee Shop
DINER $

(☑ 619-435-5425; 979 Orange Ave; mains $8-12; ⊙ 6am-9pm Sun-Thu, to 10pm Fri & Sat; ♠) Some diners are old-fashioned. This one is the real deal from the 1940s, with red leatherette swivel stools and booths with mini-jukeboxes. It does famous all-American breakfasts and some Mexican specialties like *machaca* (Mexican-style marinated beef) with eggs and cheese, and it's not above panini and croque monsieur sandwiches. For dessert: mile-high pie from the counter.

★ 1500 Ocean
CALIFORNIAN $$$

(☑ 619-435-6611; www.hoteldel.com/1500-ocean; Hotel del Coronado, 1500 Orange Ave; mains $33-45; ⊙ 5:30-10pm Tue-Sat, plus Sun summer; P) It's hard to beat the romance of supping at the Hotel del Coronado, especially at a table overlooking the sea from the verandah of its 1st-class dining room, where silver service and coastal cuisine with local ingredients set the perfect tone for popping the question or fêting an important anniversary.

Boney's Bayside Market
MARKET $

(155 Orange Ave; sandwiches $5-7; ⊙ 8:30am-9pm) For picnics, stop by this market near the ferry for (mostly) healthy sandwiches and an assortment of salads and organic products.

✖ Point Loma Area

★ Stone Brewing World Bistro & Gardens
BEER HALL $$

(www.stonelibertystation.com; Liberty Station, 2816 Historic Decatur Rd #116; lunch $14-21, dinner $15-29; ⊙ 11:30am-10pm Mon-Sat, 11am-9pm Sun; P) Local brewer Stone has transformed the former mess hall of the naval training center at Liberty Station into a temple to local craft beer. Tuck into standard-setting span-the-globe dishes (yellowfin *poke* tacos, chicken schnitzel, beef *ssambap* – Korean-style lettuce cups – etc) at long tables or comfy booths under the tall beamed ceiling, or beneath twinkling lights in its courtyard.

Bali Hai
POLYNESIAN $$

(☑ 619-222-1181; www.balihairestaurant.com; 2230 Shelter Island Dr; lunch $13-19, dinner $17-31, Sun brunch adult/child $35/17; ⊙ 11:30am-9pm Mon-Thu, to 10pm Fri & Sat, 9:30am-2pm & 4-9pm Sun; P) Near the tiki-themed hotels of Point

Loma, this long-time special occasion restaurant serves Hawaiian-themed meals like tuna *poke, pupus* (small plates), chicken of the gods (with tangy orange and cream sauces) and a massive Sunday champagne brunch buffet. Views are clear across San Diego Bay through its circular wall of windows.

★ **Point Loma Seafoods**   SEAFOOD $$
(www.pointlomaseafoods.com; 2805 Emerson St; mains $7-16; ⊙ 9am-7pm Mon-Sat, 10am-7pm Sun; P ᵻ) For off-the-boat-fresh seafood sandwiches, salads, fried dishes and icy cold beer, order at the counter at this fish-market-cum-deli and grab a seat at a picnic table on the upstairs, harbor-view deck. In the Shelter Island Marina, it's a San Diego institution dating back to Portuguese fishermen days. It also does great sushi and takeout dishes from ceviche to clam chowder.

⋊ Ocean Beach

★ **Hodad's**   BURGERS $
(Map p436; ☑ 619-224-4623; www.hodadies.com; 5010 Newport Ave, Ocean Beach; dishes $4-13; ⊙ 11am-9pm Sun-Thu, to 10pm Fri & Sat) Since the Flower Power days of 1969, OB's legendary burger joint has served great shakes, massive baskets of onion rings and succulent hamburgers. The walls are covered in license plates, grunge/surf-rock plays (loud!) and your bearded, tattooed server might sidle in to take your order.

Ortega's Cocina   CAFE $
(Map p436; ☑ 619-222-4205; 4888 Newport Ave; mains $4-15; ⊙ 8am-10pm Mon-Sat, to 9pm Sun) Tiny, family-run Ortega's is so popular that people often queue for a spot at the counter (there are indoor and sidewalk tables too). Seafood, *moles, tortas* (sandwiches) and handmade tamales are the specialties, but all its dishes are soulful and classic.

Ocean Beach People's Market   VEGETARIAN $
(Map p436; ☑ 619-224-1387; 4765 Voltaire St; dishes $8, per pound from $7.50; ⊙ 8am-9pm; ᵻ) ◢ For strictly vegetarian groceries and fabulous prepared meals and salads north of central Ocean Beach, this organic cooperative does bulk foods, and excellent counter-service soups, sandwiches, salads and wraps.

⋊ Pacific Beach

World Famous   SEAFOOD $$$
(Map p436; ☑ 858-272-3100; www.worldfamouspb.com; 711 Pacific Beach Dr; breakfast & lunch $9-16,

dinner $15-25; ⊙ 7am-midnight) Watch the surf while enjoying 'California coastal cuisine,' an ever-changing all-day menu of inventive dishes from the sea (lobster Benedict for breakfast or lunch; banana rum mahi-mahi), plus steaks, salads and lunchtime sandwiches and burgers, and occasional specials like fish or lobster taco night.

Kono's Surf Club   CAFE, BREAKFAST $
(Map p436; ☑ 858-483-1669; 704 Garnet Ave; mains $3-6; ⊙ 7am-3pm Mon-Fri, to 4pm Sat & Sun; ᵻ) This place makes four kinds of breakfast burritos that you eat out of a basket in view of Crystal Pier as well as pancakes, eggs and Kono potatoes. It's always crowded but well worth the wait. Cash only.

Green Flash   CAFE $$
(Map p436; ☑ 619-270-7715; www.greenflashrestaurant.com; 701 Thomas Ave; breakfast & lunch $5-15, dinner $11-29; ⊙ 8am-10pm) A terrific casual, beach-view breakfast or lunch spot for eggs, meaty burgers, big salads and triple-decker clubs, the Flash also has weekday sunset special meals ($11; 4:30pm to 6pm Sunday to Thursday), with happy hour until 7pm Monday through Friday. Score a table outside on the patio.

☮ Drinking & Nightlife

San Diego may not have the breadth of LA's nightlife, but the Gaslamp Quarter makes up for it in enthusiasm.

Gay and lesbian nightlife tends to concentrate around Hillcrest and North Park. Try **Urban Mo's** (Map p430; ☑ 619-491-0400; www.urbanmos.com; 308 University Ave, Hillcrest; ⊙ 9am-2am) and **Bourbon Street** (☑ 619-291-4043; www.bourbonstreetsd.com; 4612 Park Blvd, North Park; ⊙ 4pm-2am Tue-Sun, from 11am Sun).

◉ Gaslamp Quarter

★ **Bang Bang**   BAR
(www.bangbangsd.com; 526 Market St; ⊙ closed Mon) Beneath lantern-light, the Gaslamp's hottest new spot hosts local and world-known DJs, and serves sushi and Asian small plates to accompany imaginative cocktails (some in giant goblets meant for sharing with your posse). Bathrooms are shrines to Ryan Gosling and Hello Kitty: in a word, awesome.

Fluxx   CLUB
(www.fluxxsd.com; 500 4th Ave; ⊙ Thu-Sat) Think Vegas in the Gaslamp. San Diego's hottest dance club has amazing design with rotating

SURF & SUDS

'The beer that made San Diego famous' may not quite roll off the tongue, but never mind: America's Finest City is home to some of America's finest brew pubs. The **San Diego Brewers Guild** (www.sandiegobrewersguild.org) counts some 40 member establishments. Here are some pubs to get you started. See also **Stone Brewing Company** (☑760-471-4999; www.stonebrew.com; 1999 Citracado Pkwy, Escondido; ☉tours noon-6pm daily), Ballast Point Tasting Room & Kitchen and **Karl Strauss Brewery & Grill** (☑619-234-2739, 858-551-2739; 1157 Columbia St, cnr Wall St & Herschel Ave; ☉hours vary).

Coronado Brewing Co (www.coronadobrewingcompany.com; 170 Orange Ave, Coronado; ☉from 11am) Delicious Coronado Golden house brew goes well with pizzas, pastas, sandwiches and fries; near the ferry terminal.

Pacific Beach Ale House (Map p436; www.pbalehouse.com; 721 Grand Ave, Pacific Beach; mains $9-25; ☉11am-2am) Contempo-cool setting and a huge menu including lobster mac 'n' cheese, steamed clams and bistro meatloaf.

Pizza Port (☑760-720-7007; www.pizzaport.com; 571 Carlsbad Village Dr; mains $8-20; ☉11am-10pm Sun-Thu, to midnight Fri & Sat; ☻) Rockin' and raucous local pizza chain with surf art, rock music and 'anti-wimpy' pizzas to go with the signature 'sharkbite red' brew. Multiple locations.

To leave the driving to someone else, **Brewery Tours of San Diego** (☑619-961-7999; www.brewerytoursofsandiego.com; per person $65-95) offers bus tours to different breweries for a variety of tastes. Tour price varies by timing and whether a meal is served

themes (jellyfish and mermaids, anyone?), DJs spinning electronic dance music and the occasional celeb sighting. Even a crowded dance floor, expensive cocktails and sometimes steep cover charges can't stop this place from being jam-packed.

Dublin Square IRISH PUB
(www.dublinsquareirishpub.com; 544 4th Ave) Guinness? Check. Corned beef? Check. But what sets this pub apart is its selection of nightly music. Try to go when the band Fooks is playing – check website for schedule.

Quality Social DIVE BAR
(www.qualitysocial.com; 789 6th Ave) It sounds like an oxymoron: an upscale dive bar. This concrete box has big windows out to the street, loud music and lots of beers, but you can snack on charcuterie and artisanal cheeses. Look also for $6 shots and cocktails like 'Not Your Grandma's Gin & Tonic.'

Star Bar BAR
(423 E St) When you're looking for a historic dive bar, head to this bar decorated year-round with Christmas lights for the cheapest drinks in the Gaslamp.

East Village

While out-of-towners frolic happily in the Gaslamp Quarter, locals and hipsters instead head east.

East Village Tavern & Bowl DOWLING
(930 Market St, East Village; ☉11:30am-1am, from 10am Sat & Sun) This large sports bar a few blocks from Petco Park has six bowling lanes (thankfully, behind a wall for effective soundproofing). Pub menu (dishes $6 to $11) is served all day.

Noble Experiment BAR
(☑619-888-4713; http://nobleexperimentsd.com; 777 G St; ☉7pm-2am Tue-Sun) This speakeasy is literally a find. Text for a reservation, and they'll tell you if your requested time is available and how to get there. Once inside, it's a treasure trove with miniature gold skulls on the walls, classical paintings on the ceilings and some 400 cocktails on the list.

Little Italy

Ballast Point Tasting Room & Kitchen PUB
(Map p430; ☑619-255-7213; www.ballastpoint. com; 2215 India St; dishes $7-14; ☉11am-11pm Mon-Sat, to 9pm Sun) The brew pub of this San Diego–based brewery does R&D for the rest of the company. Three four-ounce tasters for just $5 is the best craft-beer deal in town. Enjoy them with a full menu, including housemade pretzels, beer-steamed mussels, salads and grilled dishes.

El Camino LOUNGE
(Map p430; 2400 India St) We're not sure what it means that this buzzy watering hole has

a Día de los Muertos (Mexican Day of the Dead holiday) theme in the flight path of San Diego Airport – watch planes land from the outdoor patio – but whatever, dude. The clientele is cool, the design mod, the drinks strong and the Mexican vittles *fabuloso*.

Waterfront   BAR
(Map p430; 2044 Kettner Blvd) San Diego's first liquor license was granted to this place in the 1930s (it was on the waterfront until the harbor was filled and the airport built). A room full of historic bric-a-brac, big windows looking onto the street and the spirits of those who went before make this a wonderful place to spend the afternoon or evening.

Bankers Hill & Old Town

Harney Sushi   BAR
(3964 Harney St) If you're staying in Old Town and are done with tequila, Harney Sushi is a sushi bar where a DJ takes over at night.

Nunu's Cocktail Lounge   COCKTAIL BAR
(Map p430; www.nunuscocktails.com; 3537 5th Ave, Hillcrest) In Bankers Hill, hipster haven Nunu's Cocktail Lounge started pouring when JFK was president and still looks the part.

North Park

Two spots nicely encapsulate North Park's hipster vibe.

Coin-Op Game Room   BAR, GAME ROOM
(☑619-255-8523; www.coinopsd.com; 3926 30th St, North Park; ☺4pm-1am) The walls of this place are lined with dozens of classic arcade games – from pinball and the Claw to Mortal Kombat – to go along with craft beers, creative cocktails and slider burgers.

★ Polite Provisions   COCKTAIL BAR
(www.politeprovisions.com; 4696 30th St, North Park; ☺11:30am-1:30am) A mile north of central North Park, this cocktail bar custom crafts syrups, sodas and infusions and serves many on tap, with a 'sodas and swine' menu.

Coronado to Pacific Beach

Pacific Beach (PB) is party central on the coast, with mostly 20-somethings on a beach bar bender (drivers: watch for tipsy pedestrians). If you've been there/done that, you might prefer one of the quieter coffee houses or restaurant bars, or head to Ocean Beach or Coronado.

Mc P's Irish Pub   PUB
(www.mcpspub.com; 1107 Orange Ave, Coronado) Dyed-in-the-wool Irish pub that's been there for a generation. Pints o' Guinness complement down-home Irish fare – corned beef, stew, meatloaf – as you listen to nightly live music from rock to Irish folk. Indoor and patio seating.

Jungle Java   CAFE
(Map p436; 5047 Newport Ave, Ocean Beach; ☺7am-6pm Mon, Tue & Thu, to 8pm Wed & Fri-Sun) Funky-dunky, canopy-covered cafe and plant shop, also crammed with crafts and art treasures.

Coaster Saloon   DIVE BAR
(Map p436; ☑858-488-4438; 744 Ventura Pl, Mission Beach) Old-fashioned neighborhood dive bar with front-row views of the Belmont Park roller coaster. It draws an unpretentious crowd for events like Wii-bowling. Good margaritas too.

Society Billiard Cafe   BAR
(Map p436; 1051 Garnet Ave, Pacific Beach; ☺noon-2pm) Why settle for a beat-up pool table in the back of a dark bar when you can visit San Diego's plushest pool hall? The billiard room has about a dozen full-sized tables, snacks and a bar.

Café 976   CAFE
(Map p436; 976 Felspar St, Pacific Beach; ☺7am-11pm) Not everyone in PB spends the days surfing or the nights partying; some drink coffee and read books at this delightful side-street cafe in a converted old wooden house ensconced in rose bushes and flowering trees.

☆ Entertainment

Check out the San Diego *City Beat* or *UT San Diego* for the latest movies, theater, galleries and music gigs around town. **Arts Tix** (☑858-381-5595; www.sdartstix.com; Lyceum Theatre, 79 Horton Plaza), in a kiosk near Westfield Horton Plaza, has half-price tickets for many shows.

Live Music

4th & B   LIVE MUSIC
(www.4thandB.com; 345 B St) A mid-sized venue with a mix of unsigned artists to Snoop Dogg and the Last Comic Standing tour.

Casbah   LIVE MUSIC
(Map p430; ☑619-232-4355; www.casbahmusic.com; 2501 Kettner Blvd; tickets $5-45) Bands from Smashing Pumpkins to Death Cab for

Cutie all rocked the Casbah on their way up the charts and it's still a good place to catch tomorrow's headliners.

House of Blues BLUES, R&B
(www.hob.com; 1055 5th Ave) You know what this is.

Shout House LIVE MUSIC
(☑619-231-6700; 655 4th Ave; cover free-$10) Good, clean fun for everyone from college kids to conventioneers around the dueling pianos at Shout House.

Winston's LIVE MUSIC
(Map p436; www.winstonsob.com; 1921 Bacon St, Ocean Beach) A different happening every night: open mic, karaoke, comedy, cover bands, etc.

710 Beach Club LIVE MUSIC
(Map p436; www.710beachclub.com; 710 Garnet Ave, Pacific Beach) PB's main venue for live music books a solid lineup of rock, karaoke and comedy.

Classical Music

San Diego Symphony CLASSICAL
(www.sandiegosymphony.com; 750 B St, Jacobs Music Center) This accomplished orchestra presents classical and family concerts and Summer Pops concerts at Embarcadero Marina Park South.

Theater

Theater is one of the city's greatest cultural assets. The main stage of the **Old Globe Theaters** (Map p430; www.theoldglobe.org; Balboa Park) is modeled after the 17th-century Globe in England, where Shakespeare's works were originally performed. See also La Jolla Playhouse (p453). Pick up San Diego *CityBeat* (www.sdcitybeat.com) for current listings.

Spectator Sports

San Diego's two big-league sports teams, the **Padres** (www.padres.com; Petco Park, 100 Park Blvd; tickets $11-91; ⊙season Apr-early Oct) baseball team and **Chargers** (www.chargers.com; Qualcomm Stadium, 9449 Friars Rd; tickets from $52; ⊙season Aug-Jan) football team, play in the East Village and Mission Valley, respectively.

🔒 Shopping

Souvenir hunters will find stuffed Shamus at SeaWorld, realistic-looking rubber snakes at the zoo and all manner of beachy souvenirs all over.

On Newport Ave in Ocean Beach are a dozen antiques consignment shops such as **Newport Avenue Antique Center** (Map p436; 4864 Newport Ave). **Cow** (Map p436; 5040 Newport Ave) gives the same treatment to music, and **Galactic** (Map p436; 4981 Newport Ave) to comics and video. Thrift shoppers should head to Garnet Ave in Pacific Beach for vintage and recycled clothing at shops including **Pangaea Outpost** (Map p436; 909 Garnet Ave, Pacific Beach) and **Buffalo Exchange** (Map p436; 1007 Garnet Ave, Pacific Beach). Most stores buy, sell and trade.

Westfield Horton Plaza downtown and **Westfield Mission Valley** (www.westfield. com/missionvalley; 1640 Camino del Rio N; ⊙10am-9pm Mon-Sat, 11am-6pm Sun), **Fashion Valley** (www.simon.com; 7007 Friars Rd; ⊙10am-9pm Mon-Sat, 11am-7pm Sun) and **Hazard Center** (www.hazardcenter.com; 7510-7610 Hazard Center Dr) in Mission Valley offer a feast for mall shoppers.

🛍 Central San Diego

Headquarters at Seaport District MALL
(www.theheadquarters.com; 789 W Harbor Dr) San Diego's newest shopping center (opened 2013) is also one of its oldest buildings, the 1939 former police headquarters now turned into some 30 mostly swanky shopping, dining and entertainment options. The old jail cells are still there, for photo ops.

Liberty Station MALL
(www.libertystation.com; 2640 Historic Decatur Rd) Between downtown and Point Loma, onetime offices and barracks of the decommissioned Naval Training Center are gradually being converted to shopping and dining venues. Look for fishing and outdoor gear and top restaurants including **Corvette Diner** (☑619-542-1476; 2965 Historic Decatur Rd; mains $8-11.50; ⊙11:30am-9pm Sun-Thu, to 11pm Fri & Sat; 📶) and Stone Brewing Co (p445).

Westfield Horton Plaza MALL
(www.westfield.com/hortonplaza) At the edge of the Gaslamp, this five-story, seven-block shopping mall features shops big and small, including Nordstrom, Bebe and Coach. Colorful arches and postmodernist balconies make it feel slightly like an MC Escher drawing. Free three-hour parking with validation.

Seaport Village SHOPPING DISTRICT
(www.seaportvillage.com; ⊙10am-10pm; 📶) Neither seaport nor village, this 14-acre collection of novelty shops and restaurants has a

WORTH A TRIP

TRAVELING TO TIJUANA

Just beyond the most-crossed border in the world, Tijuana, Mexico (population around two million), had fallen on hard times in the last decade, but locals have been reclaiming their city.

Avenida Revolución ('La Revo') is the main tourist drag, its charm marred by cheap clothing and souvenir stores, strip joints and pharmacies selling bargain-priced meds. It's much more appealing around Avenida Constitución: **Catedral de Nuestra Señora de Guadalupe** (Cathedral of our Lady of Guadalupe; cnr Av Niños Héroes & Calle 2a) is Tijuana's oldest church, the atmospheric market hall **Mercado El Popo** (cnr Calle 2a & Av Constitución) sells needs from tamarind pods to religious iconography, and the arcade **Pasaje Rodríguez** (btwn Avenida Revolución & Avenida Constitución, Calles 3 & 4) is filled with youthful art galleries, bars and trendsetters.

A short ride away, **Museo de las Californias** (Museum of the Californias; ☑ from US 011-52-664-687-9600; www.cecut.gob.mx; cnr Paseo de los Héroes & Av Independencia; adult/child under 12yr M$20/free; ☉ 10am-6pm Tue-Sun; ☒) offers an excellent history of the border region from prehistory to the present; there's signage in English. Friday nights, check out **lucha libre** (☑ from US 011-52-664-250-9015; Blvd Díaz Ordaz 12421, Auditorio Municipal Fausto Gutierrez Moreno; admission US$8-35), Mexican wrestling by oversized men in gaudy masks.

The Caesar salad was invented at **Hotel Caesar** (☑ from US 011-52-664-685-1606; Av Revolución 827; Caesar salad $6; ☉ 9am-midnight), prepared tableside in the elegant dining room. Contemporary superstar chef Javier Plascencia runs the fun storefront **Erizo** (☑ from US 011-52-686-3895; 3808 Avenida Sonora; tacos M$18-45, ceviche $62-180, ramen $90-120) for innovative takes on tacos, ceviche and even ramen, worth the 10-minute taxi ride from La Revo.

Turista Libre (www.turistalibre.com) runs public and private tours in English.

A passport is required for the border crossing. The **San Diego Trolley** (www.sdmts.com) runs to the border at San Ysidro. By car, take I-5 south and park on the US side (around $8 for up to 24 hours). Cross the border on foot, and follow signs reading 'Centro Downtown,' a 20-minute walk. If traveling by taxi within Mexico, be sure the car has a meter. Driving into Mexico is not recommended.

faux New England theme. It's touristy but good for souvenir shopping and casual eats.

ⓘ Information

INTERNET ACCESS

All public libraries and most coffeehouses and hotel lobbies offer free wi-fi. Libraries also offer computer terminals for access.

MEDIA

KPBS 89.5 FM (www.kpbs.org) National Public Radio station.

San Diego Magazine (www.sandiegomagazine.com) Glossy monthly.

UT San Diego (www.utsandiego.com) The city's major daily.

Free listings magazines Tabloid-sized magazines, **CityBeat** (www.sdcitybeat.com) and **San Diego Reader** (www.sdreader.com), cover the active music, art and theater scenes. Find them in shops and cafes.

MEDICAL SERVICES

Scripps Mercy Hospital (☑ 619-294-8111; www.scripps.org; 4077 5th Ave) Has a 24-hour emergency room.

POST

For post-office locations, call ☑ 800-275-8777 or log on to www.usps.com.

Downtown Post Office (815 E St; ☉ 9am-5pm Mon-Fri)

Coronado Post Office (1320 Ynez Pl; ☉ 8:30am-5pm Mon-Fri, 9am-noon Sat)

TOURIST INFORMATION

International Visitor Information Center (☑ 619-236-1212; www.sandiego.org; 1140 N Harbor Dr; ☉ 9am-5pm Jun-Sep, to 4pm Oct-May) Across from the B St Cruise Ship Terminal, helpful staff offer detailed neighborhood maps, sell discounted tickets to attractions and maintain a hotel reservation hotline.

Coronado Visitors Center (☑ 619-437-8788, 866-599-7242; www.coronadovisitorcenter.

com; 1100 Orange Ave; ◷ 9am-5pm Mon-Fri, 10am-5pm Sat & Sun)

WEBSITES

Lonely Planet (www.lonelyplanet.com/usa/san-diego)

San Diego Tourism (www.sandiego.org) Search hotels, sights, dining, rental cars and more, and make reservations.

❶ Getting There & Away

AIR

San Diego International Airport-Lindbergh Field (p50700) sits just 3 miles west of downtown. All major US airlines serve San Diego, plus Air Canada, British Airways, Japan Airlines, Mexico's Volaris and the Canadian carrier WestJet.

BUS

Greyhound (☏ 619-515-1100, 800-231-2222; www.greyhound.com; 1313 National Ave) serves San Diego from cities across North America from its new location in East Village. Many discounts and special fares are available only online.

Buses depart frequently for LA (one-way/round-trip $18/36, 2½ to four hours) and several daily to Anaheim ($18/36, about 2¼ hours).

CAR & MOTORCYCLE

Allow two hours from LA in non-peak traffic. With traffic, it's anybody's guess.

TRAIN

Amtrak (☏ 800-872-7245; www.amtrak.com) runs the *Pacific Surfliner* several times daily to Anaheim ($28, two hours), Los Angeles ($37, 2¾ hours) and Santa Barbara ($42, 6½ hours) from the historic **Union Station** (Santa Fe Depot; 1055 Kettner Blvd).

❶ Getting Around

While most people get around by car, municipal buses and trolleys run by the **Metropolitan Transit System** (MTS; ☏ 619-557-4555; www.sdmts.com) can get you most places. The Transit Store dispenses route maps and tickets. Transfers are not available, so purchase a day pass if you're going to be taking more than two rides in a day; one-/two-/three-/four-day passes ($5/9/12/15). A refillable **Compass Card** ($2 one-time purchase) will save hassles.

TO/FROM THE AIRPORT

Bus 992 (the Flyer, $2.25) operates at 10- to 15-minute intervals between the airport and downtown. Taxis between downtown and the airport typically cost between $10 and $16. Airport shuttle services, including **Super Shuttle** (☏ 800-258-3826; www.supershuttle.com), run from about $13 per person to downtown, more to other destinations.

BICYCLE

A few outfits like **Bikes & Beyond** (☏ 619-435-7180; www.bikes-and-beyond.com; 1201 1st St, Coronado; per hr/day from $8/30; ◷ 9am-sunset), **Holland's Bicycles** (☏ 619-435-3153; www.hollandsbicycles.com; 977 Orange Ave, Coronado) and **Cheap Rentals** (Map p436; ☏ 858-488-9070, 800-941-7761; 3689 Mission Blvd, Pacific Beach; ◷ 9am-7pm, shorter hours autumn-spring) rent bicycles, from mountain and road bikes to kids' bikes and cruisers. Expect to pay from about $8 per hour, $15 to $22 per half-day (four hours) and $25 to $30 per day.

BOAT

Flagship Cruises (p437) operates the hourly **Coronado Ferry** (☏ 619-234-4111; www.flagshipsd.com; tickets $4.25; ◷ 9am-10pm) shuttling between the **Broadway Pier** (1050 N Harbor Dr) on the Embarcadero and the ferry landing at the foot of B Ave in Coronado, two blocks south of Orange Ave (15 minutes). Bikes are permitted on board at no extra charge.

BUS

MTS (www.sdmts.com) covers most of the metropolitan area. It's most convenient if you're based downtown and not staying out late. Useful routes to/from downtown:

No 3 Balboa Park, Hillcrest, UCSD Medical Center

No 7 Balboa Park, Zoo, Hillcrest, North Park

No 8/9 Old Town to Pacific Beach, SeaWorld

No 30 Old Town, Pacific Beach, La Jolla, University Towne Centre

No 35 Old Town to Ocean Beach

No 901 Coronado

CAR

All the big-name car-rental companies have desks at the airport, and lesser-known ones may be cheaper. Shop around – prices vary widely, even from day to day within the same company.

TAXI & RIDE SHARE

Plan on about $2.40 to start, plus $2.60 for each additional mile. Established companies include **Orange Cab** (☏ 619-223-5555; www.orange-cabsandiego.com) and **Yellow Cab** (☏ 619-444-4444; www.driveu.com). Recently app-based ride-share companies such as Uber and Sidecar have entered the market with lower fares.

TROLLEY

MTS trolleys operate on three main lines. Most useful for visitors, from the transit center across from the Santa Fe Depot, **Blue Line** trolleys go south to San Ysidro (Mexico border) and north to Old Town Transit Center. The **Green Line** runs from Old Town east through Mission Valley.

LA JOLLA & NORTH COUNTY COAST

Immaculately landscaped parks, white-sand coves, upscale boutiques, top restaurants, and cliffs above deep, clear blue waters make it easy to understand why 'La Jolla' translates from Spanish as 'the jewel' – say la-*hoy*-yah, if you please. The name may actually date from Native Americans who inhabited the area from 10,000 years ago to the mid-19th century, who called the place 'mut la hoya, la hoya' – the place of many caves. Whether your interest is jewels or caves, you'll feel at home in this lovely enclave.

Northward from La Jolla, small beach towns extend like pearls on a strand. 'North County,' as locals call it, begins with pretty Del Mar and continues through Encinitas and Carlsbad (home of Legoland), before hitting Oceanside, largely a bedroom community for Camp Pendleton Marine Base.

La Jolla

◉ Sights

◉ La Jolla Village

★ Museum of Contemporary Art San Diego – La Jolla
ART MUSEUM
(MCASD; ☑ 858-454-3541; www.mcasd.org; 700 Prospect St, La Jolla; adult/child $10/free, 5-7pm 3rd Thu each month free; ⊙ 11am-5pm Thu-Tue, to 7pm 3rd Thu each month) La Jolla's branch of this museum gets changing, world-class exhibitions. The original 1916 building was renovated by Philadelphia's postmodern architect Robert Venturi and has an Andy Goldsworthy sculpture out the front. Tickets are good for one week at all three of the museum's locations (p431).

Athenaeum
LIBRARY
(☑ 858-454-5872; www.ljathenaeum.org; 1008 Wall St; ⊙ 10am-5:30pm Tue-Sat, to 8:30pm Wed) Housed in a graceful Spanish renaissance structure, this space is devoted exclusively to art and music. Its reading room is a lovely place to relax and read, and it hosts a series of concerts from chamber music to jazz.

◉ La Jolla Coast

A wonderful walking path skirts the shoreline for half a mile. At the west it begins at Children's Pool, where a jetty protects the beach from big waves. Originally intended to give La Jolla's youth a safe place to frolic, this beach is now given over to sea lions, which you can view up close as they lounge on the shore.

Atop Point La Jolla, at the path's eastern end, **Ellen Browning Scripps Park** is a tidy expanse of green lawns and palm trees, with **La Jolla Cove** to the north. The cove's gem of a beach provides access to some of the best snorkeling around.

White buoys offshore mark the **San Diego-La Jolla Underwater Park Ecological Reserve**, with a variety of marine life, kelp forests, reefs and canyons.

★ Cave Store
CAVES
(☑ 858-459-0746; www.cavestore.com; 1325 Coast Rd; adult/child $4/3; ⊙ 10am-5pm; ⊕) Waves have carved a series of caves into the sandstone cliffs east of La Jolla Cove. The largest is called Sunny Jim Cave, which you can access via this store. Taller visitors, watch your head as you descend the 145 steps.

Birch Aquarium at Scripps
AQUARIUM
(☑ 858-534-3474; www.aquarium.ucsd.edu; 2300 Exhibition Way, La Jolla; adult/child $17/12.50; ⊙ 9am-5pm; Ⓟ ⊕) ✈ Marine scientists were working at the Birch Aquarium at Scripps Institution of Oceanography (SIO) as early as 1910 and, helped by donations from the ever-generous Scripps family, the institute has grown to be one of the world's largest marine research institutions. It is now a part of the University of California San Diego. Off N Torrey Pines Rd, the aquarium has brilliant displays. The **Hall of Fishes** has more than 30 fish tanks, simulating marine environments from the Pacific Northwest to tropical seas.

Salk Institute
ARCHITECTURE
(☑ 858-453-4100, ext 1287; www.salk.edu; 10010 N Torrey Pines Rd; tours $15; ⊙ tours by reservation 11:45am Mon-Fri; Ⓟ) In 1960 Jonas Salk, the polio-prevention pioneer, founded the Salk Institute for biological and biomedical research, and this building by renowned architect Louis Kahn was completed in 1965. It is regarded as a modern masterpiece, with its classically proportioned travertine marble plaza and cubist, mirror-glass laboratory blocks framing a perfect view of the Pacific. The original buildings were expanded with new laboratories designed by Jack McAllister, a follower of Kahn's work.

Torrey Pines State Natural Reserve
PARK
(☑ 858-755-2063; www.torreypine.org; 12600 N Torrey Pines Rd, La Jolla; ⊙ 7:15am-dusk, visitor

La Jolla

La Jolla

◎ Top Sights
1 Cave Store D1
2 Museum of Contemporary Art San
   Diego – La Jolla A3

◎ Sights
3 Athenaeum C2

🛏 Sleeping
4 La Jolla Village Lodge C3
5 La Valencia C2
6 Pantai Inn B2

🍽 Eating
7 Cottage B4
8 El Pescador B5
9 George's at the Cove C2
10 Harry's Coffee Shop C4
11 Porkyland C4
12 Whisknladle C2

🍷 Drinking & Nightlife
13 Pannikin C5

🎭 Entertainment
14 Comedy Store C5

center 10am-4pm Oct-Apr, 9am-6pm May-Sep; P)
🖋 This reserve preserves the last mainland stands of the Torrey pine (*Pinus torreyana*). The views north and out over the ocean (good for whale-watching) are superb. Rangers lead nature walks weekends and holidays. Several walking trails wind through the reserve and down to the beach.

🏃 Activities

La Jolla Beaches
BEACHES
Some of the county's best beaches are north of the Shores in **Torrey Pines City Park**, between the Salk Institute and Torrey Pines State Reserve. Hang-gliders and paragliders launch into the sea breezes rising over the cliffs at Torrey Pines Gliderport, at the end of Torrey Pines Scenic Dr. It's a beautiful sight – tandem flights are available.

Experienced surfers can head to **Windansea Beach** (take La Jolla Blvd south and turn west on Nautilus St). However, some of the locals can be unfriendly toward outsiders. You'll find a more pleasant welcome at **Big Rock**, California's version of Hawaii's Pipeline, immediately south of Windansea Beach, at the foot of Palomar Ave. For the less experienced, lessons are available from the wonderful women of **Surf Diva** (📞858-454-8273; www.surfdiva.com; 2160 Avenida de la Playa; ⊙store 8:30am-6pm, varies seasonally).

San Diego-La Jolla Underwater Park
SNORKELING, DIVING
Some of California's best and most accessible diving is in this reserve, accessible from La Jolla Cove. With an average depth of 20ft, the 6000 acres of look-but-don't-touch underwater real estate is great for snorkeling, too. Ever-present are the spectacular, bright orange Garibaldi fish – California's official state fish and a protected species (there's a $500 fine for poaching one). Further out you'll see forests of giant California kelp (which can increase its length by up to 3ft per day) and the 100ft-deep La Jolla Canyon.

A number of commercial outfits conduct scuba-diving courses, sell or rent equipment, fill tanks, and conduct boat trips to nearby wrecks and islands. The Cave Store (p450) and other outfitters rent snorkel and fin sets (about $20 for two hours).

🛏 Sleeping

La Jolla Village Lodge
MOTEL $$
(📞858-551-2001, 877-551-2001; www.lajollavillagelodge.com; 1141 Silverado St; r incl breakfast $100-200; P🚗🛜🏊) At the edge of downtown La Jolla, this 30-room 1950s-era motel was recently restored in period style with custom-built tables and chairs, teak headboards and new mattresses. Flat-screen TVs are a concession to the 21st century. A roof deck gives long-distance views.

La Valencia
HISTORIC HOTEL $$$
(📞800-451-0772, 858-454-0771; www.lavalencia.com; 1132 Prospect St; r from $385; P❄@🛜🏊🍽) 🖋 Publicity stills of Lon Cheney, Lillian Gish and Greta Garbo line the hallways of this 1926 landmark: pink-walled, Mediterranean-style and designed by William Templeton Johnson. Among its 112 rooms, the ones in the main building are rather compact (befitting the era), but villas are spacious and in any case the property wins for Old Hollywood romance. Even if you don't stay, consider lifting a toast – and a pinkie – to the sunset from its Spanish Revival lounge, la Sala. Parking is $29.

Pantai Inn
BOUTIQUE HOTEL $$$
(📞858-224-7600, 855-287-2682; www.pantaiinn.com; 1003 Coast Blvd; r from $295; P❄@🛜) About as close as you can stay to the beach and Scripps Park, colorful banners mark the perimeter of this new, Balinese-style inn. Rooms vary in size, but all have kitchens and sitting areas, and suites are filled wtih Balinese art and antiques. Continental breakfast is served in the Gathering Room; enjoy it on multiple ocean-view decks.

🍴 Eating

Harry's Coffee Shop
DINER $
(📞858-454-7381; 7545 Girard Ave; dishes $5-13; ⊙6am-3pm; 👶) This classic 1960s coffee shop has a posse of regulars from blue-haired socialites to sports celebs. The food is standard-issue American – pancakes, tuna melts, burgers and breakfast burritos – but it's the aura of the place that makes it special.

Porkyland
MEXICAN $
(📞858-459-1708; 1030 Torrey Pines Rd; dishes $4-9; ⊙9am-7pm) This tiny Mexican joint in a corner shopping center on the edge of La Jolla Village has only simple indoor-outdoor seating, but the burritos and fish tacos have a devoted following. The *verde carnitas* burrito ($6) will make your taste buds roar (in a good way) and still leave you money for beer.

Whisknladle
CALIFORNIAN $$
(📞858-551-7575; www.wnlhosp.com; 1044 Wall St; lunch $14-21, dinner $15.36; ⊙11:30am-9pm Mon-

Thu, to 10pm Fri, 10am-10pm Sat, 10am-9:30pm Sun) Gourmets and gourmands alike love Whisknladle's 'slow food' preparations of local, farm-fresh ingredients, served on a breezy covered patio and meant for sharing. Every minute preparation from curing to pickling and macerating is done in house. The menu changes daily, but it's always clever. So are the cocktails (the London's Burning mixes gin and jalapeño water).

El Pescador   SEAFOOD **$$**
(☑ 858-456-2526; www.elpescadorfishmarket.com; 634 Pearl St; mains $7-20; ☉ 10am-8pm) You could pay three times as much for seafood at fancier restaurants in town while locals will be at this fish market and restaurant, just moved to spanking new digs on the edge of La Jolla Village. Your catch will be prepared into a sandwich, salad or plate.

Cottage   MODERN AMERICAN **$$**
(☑ 858-454-8409; 7702 Fay Ave; breakfast $9-12, lunch $10-19, dinner $11-26; ☉ 7:30am 9pm) Shhh! Don't tell anybody that the stuffed French toast, eggs La Jolla (with bacon, mushrooms, spinach and garlic and balsamic vinegar) and fish tacos make this place a local favorite. It's crowded enough as it is, especially on weekends for brunch. Expect a wait if you arrive much after 8:30am.

★**George's at the Cove**   CALIFORNIAN **$$$**
(☑ 858-454-4244; www.georgesatthecove.com; 1250 Prospect St, La Jolla; mains $13-50; ☉ 11am-10pm Mon-Thu, to 11pm Fri-Sun) The Euro-Cal cooking here is as dramatic as the oceanfront location thanks to the imagination of chef Trey Foshée. George's has graced just about every list of top restaurants in California and the USA. Three venues allow you to enjoy it at different price points: Ocean Terrace, George's Bar and George's California Modern.

🍷 Drinking & Entertainment

Pannikin   CAFE
(pannikincoffeeandtea.com; 7467 Girard Ave; ☉ 6am-6pm Mon-Fri, 6:30am-6pm Sat & Sun; 🛜) A few blocks from the water, this clapboard shack with a generous balcony is popular for its organic coffees, Italian espresso and Mexican chocolate, and occasional live music. Like all the Pannikins, it's a North County institution.

Comedy Store   COMEDY
(☑ 858-454-9176; www.comedystorelajolla.com; 916 Pearl St) One of the area's most established comedy venues, the Comedy Store also serves meals, drinks and barrels of laughs. Expect a cover charge ($15 to $20 on weekends with a two-drink minimum), and some of tomorrow's big names.

La Jolla Symphony & Chorus CLASSICAL MUSIC
(☑ 858-534-4637; www.lajollasymphony.com; UCSD) Quality concerts at UCSD's Mandeville Auditorium running from October to June.

La Jolla Playhouse   THEATER
(☑ 858-550-1010; www.lajollaplayhouse.org; 2910 La Jolla Village Dr, Mandell Weiss Center for the Performing Arts) This nationally recognized theater has sent dozens of productions to Broadway, including *Jersey Boys* and 2010 Tony winner *Memphis*.

🛍 Shopping

La Jolla's skirt-and-sweater crowd pays retail for cashmere sweaters and expensive art and tchotchkes downtown. Mall shoppers make a bee-line for **Westfield UTC** (UTC; 4545 La Jolla Village Dr).

ℹ Getting There & Away

Via I-5 from downtown San Diego, take the La Jolla Pkwy exit and head west toward Torrey Pines Rd, from where it's a right turn onto Prospect St.

Del Mar

The ritziest of North County's seaside suburbs, with a Tudor aesthetic that somehow doesn't feel out of place, Del Mar boasts good (if pricey) restaurants, unique galleries, high-end boutiques and, north of town, the West Coast's most renowned horse-racing track, also the site of the annual county fair.

⊙ Sights & Activities

Del Mar Racetrack & Fairgrounds RACETRACK
(☑ 858-755-1141; www.dmtc.com; admission from $6; ☉ race season mid-Jul–early Sep) Del Mar's biggest draw was founded in 1937 by a prestigious group including Bing Crosby and Jimmy Durante, and is still worth a visit for its lush gardens and Mediterranean architecture. Go on opening day for the spectacle of ladies wearing over-the-top hats.

Seagrove Park   PARK
At the end of 15th St, this park overlooks the ocean. Perfect for a picnic.

California Dreamin'   BALLOONING
(☑ 800-373-3359; www.californiadreamin.com; per person from $288) Brightly colored hot-air balloons are a trademark of the skies above Del Mar.

North County Coast

0 ▲ N

0 — 5 km
0 — 2.5 miles

Camp Pendleton
(US Marine Corps)

Camp Pendleton
Main Gate

**California
Surf Museum**

15

OCEANSIDE

9 26

Oceanside
Transit Center

28

Oceanside
Coaster Station

29

Carlsbad Coaster Station

VISTA

Vista Fwy

El Vista Way

Santa Fe Ave

CARLSBAD

Carlsbad
State Beach

Agua
Hedionda
Lagoon

El Camino Real

Palomar Airport Rd

27 Cannon Rd

7 5

18 3 16

Carlsbad Poinsettia
Station

Lake San
Marcos

Aviara Pkwy

23 22

Batiquitos
Lagoon

25

La Costa Ave

Carlsbad Blvd

Rancho Santa Fe Rd

Downtown Carlsbad

State St
Grand Ave
38
Carlsbad Village Dr
Oak Ave
San Diego Fwy
Carlsbad Blvd
41
Harding St
Roosevelt St
34
Tylor St

0 — 1 km
0 — 0.5 miles

PACIFIC
OCEAN

31

35

LEUCADIA

ENCINITAS

Moonlight Beach

Encinitas Blvd

Encinitas
Coaster Station

Swami's Beach

11 24

**CARDIFF-
BY-THE-SEA**

33

10

2 Solana Beach
Coaster Station

Lomas Santa Fe Dr

Solana Beach

San Elijo
Lagoon

Via de la Valle

San Dieguito River

Encinitas

0 — 500 m
0 — 0.25 miles

5th St
A St
2nd St
B St
C St
30
Encinitas Blvd
17
E D St
Moonlight
Beach
W D St
40
W E St
S Vulcan Ave
S Coast Hwy
De Witt Ave
Cornish Dr
San Dieguito Dr
W F St
H Street
Viewpoint
Park
37
4th St
3rd St
W H St
W I St
Melba Rd

I Street
Viewpoint
Park
36

13

Swami's Beach

32

12

20 42

21 39

19

DEL MAR

Torrey Pines
State Beach

14

Camino Del Mar

6

76

514

511

Vista Fwy

California
Welcome Center

78

S11

S12

S21

S11

S10

S10

59

56

56

North County Coast

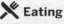

SAN DIEGO & AROUND DEL MAR

🛏 Sleeping

Les Artistes Inn BOUTIQUE HOTEL $$
(☎858-755-4646; www.lesartistesinn.com; 944 Camino Del Mar; r $165-250; P❄@🛜) Behind the eclectic Craftsman-style facade of this inn set back from Camino del Mar, each of the 12 spacious rooms is meticulously furnished in the style of an artist or art movement: Botero through O'Keefe to van Gogh, even Zen.

L'Auberge Del Mar Resort & Spa LUXURY $$$
(☎800-553-1336, 858-259-1515; www.laubergedelmar.com; 1540 Camino Del Mar; r $350-540; P❄@🛜🏊🐕) Rebuilt in the 1990s on the grounds of the historic Hotel del Mar, where 1920s Hollywood celebrities once frolicked, L'Auberge continues a tradition of European-style elegance with luxurious linens, a spa and lovely grounds. It feels so intimate and the service is so individual, you'd never know there are 120 rooms. Parking $25.

Hotel Indigo San Diego Del Mar BOUTIQUE HOTEL $$$
(☎858-755-1501; www.hotelindigosddelmar.com; 710 Camino Del Mar; r from $199; P❄❄@🛜🏊🐕) This collection of white-washed buildings with gray clay-tiled roofs, two pools, a spa and new fitness and business centers received a tip-to-toe renovation for 2014. Rooms boast hardwood floors, mosaic tile accents and horserace- and beach-inspired motifs. Some units have kitchenettes and distant ocean views, and Ocean View Bar & Grill serves breakfast, lunch and dinner.

🍴 Eating

En Fuego MEXICAN $$
(☎858-792-6551; www.enfuegocantina.com; 1342 Camino Del Mar; mains $6-16; ⊙11:30am-midnight Sun-Thu, to 1am Fri & Sat) On the site of Del Mar's first restaurant, this airy, multilevel Nuevo Mexicano spot is both restaurant

and bar. Specialties on the forward-thinking menu include borracho shrimp (sautéed in tequila), filet mignon rancheros and honey habanero chicken (in a sweet spicy glaze), with lots of indoor-outdoor space to enjoy them.

Zel's CALIFORNIAN $$
(☑ 858-755-0076; www.zelsdelmar.com; 1247 Camino Del Mar; mains lunch $9-15, dinner $9-24; ☺ 11am-10pm Mon-Thu, 9am-midnight Sat, 9am-10pm Sun) Zel was a longstanding local merchant, and his grandson continues the family tradition of welcoming locals and visitors, with excellent flatbread pizzas (like chicken with asparagus, truffle oil, arugula and avocado), burgers of bison, quinoa or locally raised beef, and lots of craft beers. Live music Thursday to Sunday.

Americana MODERN AMERICAN $$
(☑ 858-794-6838; 1454 Camino del Mar; mains breakfast & lunch $7-14, dinner $14-21; ☺ 7am-3pm Sun & Mon, to 10pm Tue-Sat) This quietly chichi and much-loved local landmark serves a diverse lineup of regional American cuisine: cheese grits to chicken Reubens, sesame salmon on succotash to seared duck breast with Israeli couscous, plus artisan cocktails, all amid checkerboard linoleum floors, giant windows and homey wainscoting.

Jake's Del Mar SEAFOOD $$$
(☑ 858-755-2002; www.jakesdelmar.com; 1660 Coast Blvd; mains lunch $11-26, dinner $16-36; ☺ 4-9pm Mon, 11:30am-9pm Tue-Fri, 11:30am-9:30pm Sat, 8am-9pm Sun) Head to this beachside classic for ocean-view drinks and half-price appetizers from 4pm to 6pm weekdays and from 2:30pm to 4:30pm on Saturday. The view's great, the atmosphere chic and the food imaginative, like burrata and heirloom tomato salad, ahi tartare tacos and 'surfing steak' with herb-grilled jumbo shrimp, sweet corn cream, sautéed spinach, truffle mash potatoes.

🛍 Shopping

Del Mar Plaza MALL
(www.delmarplaza.com; 555 Camino del Mar) Where 15th St crosses Camino del Mar, the tastefully designed Del Mar Plaza shopping center has restaurants, boutiques and upper-level terraces that look out to sea.

❶ Getting There & Away

N Torrey Pines Rd from La Jolla is the most scenic approach from the south. Heading north, the road (S21) changes its name from Camino del Mar to Coast Hwy 101 to Old Hwy 101.

Cardiff-by-the-Sea

Beachy Cardiff is good for surfing and popular with a laid-back crowd for the miles of restaurants and surf shops along Hwy 101 by **Cardiff** (www.parks.ca.gov; ☺ 7am-sunset; 🅿) and **San Elijo** State Beaches. The other main draw is the 1000-acre **San Elijo Lagoon** (☑ 760-623-3026; www.sanelijo.org; 2710 Manchester Ave; ☺ nature center 9am-5pm) **FREE** ecological preserve, popular with bird-watchers for its herons, coots, terns, ducks, egrets and more than 250 other species.

San Elijo State Beach (☑ 760-753-5091, reservations 800-444-7275; www.parks.ca.gov; 2050 S Coast Hwy 101; summer tent/RV sites from $35/55) has a campground, while **Las Olas** (mains $9-19; ☺ 11am-9pm Mon-Thu, to 9:30pm Fri, 10am-9:30pm Sat, 10am-9pm Sun; 🅿 ♿) serves fish tacos with a sea view; it's so popular that it has its own traffic light. Also across from the beach, **Ki's** (☑ 760-436-5236; 2591 S Coast Hwy 101; breakfast $5-9, lunch $7-14, dinner $13-22; ☺ 8am-8:30pm Sun-Thu, to 10pm Fri, 9pm Sat; 🅿 🖉) is an organic cafe/restaurant and a hub of local activity; there are inspiring beach views from the 2nd-floor bar and dining areas.

Encinitas

Peaceful Encinitas has a decidedly down-to-earth vibe and a laid-back beach-town main street, perfect for a relaxing day trip or weekend escape. North of central Encinitas, yet still part of the city, is **Leucadia**, a leafy stretch of N Hwy 101 with a hippie vibe of used-clothing stores and taco shops.

◉ Sights

Self-Realization Fellowship Retreat RETREAT
(☑ 760-753-1811; www.yogananda-srf.org; 215 K St; ☺ meditation garden 9am-5pm Tue-Sat, 11am-5pm Sun) **FREE** Yogi Paramahansa Yogananda founded his center here in 1937, and the town has been a magnet for holistic healers and natural-lifestyle seekers ever since. The gold lotus domes of the hermitage – conspicuous on South Coast Hwy 101 – mark the southern end of Encinitas and the turn-out for **Swami's Beach**, a powerful reef break surfed by territorial locals. The fellowship's compact but lovely **Meditation Garden** has wonderful ocean vistas, a stream and a koi

pond. If you're interested in more detailed exploration of meditation and the religion's principles, visit the website.

🛏 Sleeping

Best Western Encinitas
Inn & Suites
MOTEL $$

(📞760-942-7455, 866-236-4648; www.bwencinitas.com; 85 Encinitas Blvd; r incl breakfast from $169; 🅿@🛜🏊🐾) Atop a hill between the freeway, shopping center and Coast Hwy is this hexagonal hotel, a few minutes on foot from the sand. Design is nothing fancy, but it's well kept, all rooms have balconies and suites have kitchenettes and sleep sofas. Some rooms have ocean or park views.

🍴 Eating

🍴 Central Encinitas

Swami's Café
CAFE $

(📞760-944-0612; 1163 S Coast Hwy 101; mains $5-10; ⏱7am-5pm; 🚗🪑) This local institution can't be beat for breakfast burritos, multigrain pancakes, stir-fries, salads, smoothies and three-egg *ohm*-lettes (sorry, we couldn't resist). Vegetarians will be satisfied, too. Most of the seating is out on an umbrella-covered patio.

⭐ Trattoria I Trulli
ITALIAN $$

(📞760-943-6800; www.trattoriaitrullisd.com; 830 S Coast Hwy 101; mains lunch $13-21, dinner $14-26; ⏱11:30am-2:30pm daily, 5-10pm Sun-Thu, to 10:30pm Fri & Sat) Country-style seating indoors and great people-watching on the sidewalk. Just one taste of the homemade gnocchi, ravioli or lasagne, salmon in brandy mustard sauce or *pollo uno zero uno* (101; chicken stuffed with cheese, spinach and artichokes in mushroom sauce) and you'll know why this mom-and-pop Italian trattoria is always packed. Reservations are recommended.

El Callejon
MEXICAN $$

(📞760-634-2793; www.el-callejon.com; 345 S Coast Hwy 101; mains $9-22; ⏱11am-9pm Mon-Thu, to 11pm Fri, 10am-11pm Sat, 10am-9pm Sun; 🚗🪑) A raucous, fun, local favorite, this indoor-outdoor candy-colored cantina is at the north end of the town center. The menu is as long as the phone book of a small village, and it would take you over two years of trying a different tequila every day to go through the tequila list.

🍴 North Encinitas/Leucadia

Pannikin Coffee & Tea
CAFE $

(📞760-436-0033; mains $4-8; ⏱6am-6pm) In a sunny, yellow wooden building that used to be the Encinitas train station (transported from its original site), Pannikin is an adorable sprawl of nooks, crannies, balconies and lawns. Muffins and coffees are wonderful, natch, and bagel and lox with steamed scrambled eggs is very attractive indeed.

⭐ Fish 101
SEAFOOD $$

(📞760-634-6221; www.fish101restaurant.com; 1468 N. Coast Hwy 101; mains $10-19) In this roadside shack all growed up, order at the counter, sidle into a butcher block or picnic table, sip craft beer, wine or Mexican Coke from a Mason jar and use paper towels to wipe your face. Simple grilling techniques allow the natural flavors of the fresh catch to show through, and healthy rice bran oil is used for deep frying.

🍷 Drinking

Daley Double
DIVE BAR

(546 S Coast Hwy 101) Once Encinitas' most notorious dive bar, it's now Encinitas' hippest dive bar. Fantastic Old West saloon-style murals make a great backdrop for good old-fashioned sipping and flirting. Expect a line out the door on weekends.

🛈 Getting There & Away

By car, the Encinitas Blvd exit off I-5 is about a quarter mile east of central Encinitas. Encinitas is served by Coaster trains and Breeze buses (www.gonctd.com) connecting San Diego, Oceanside and points between.

Carlsbad

Legoland is by far North County's biggest attraction, but a few miles away sits a quaint downtown enclave and long, sandy beaches great for walking and searching for seashells. Carlsbad has a number of other worthwhile attractions outside the village and Legoland areas – from flowers to musical instruments and go-karts. You pretty much need a car to reach them.

�’ Sights & Activities

Legoland
AMUSEMENT PARK

(📞760-918-5346; http://california.legoland.com; 1 Legoland Dr, Carlsbad; adult/child from $83/73; ⏱daily mid-Mar–Aug, Wed-Sun Sep–mid-Mar;

WORTH A TRIP

SAN DIEGO ZOO SAFARI PARK

Since the early 1960s, the San Diego Zoological Society has been developing this 1800-acre, **open-range zoo** (☑ 760-747-8702; www.sdzsafaripark.org; 15500 San Pasqual Valley Rd, Escondido; admission adult/child $45/36, 2-day pass incl San Diego Zoo $82/64; ☺ mid-Jun–mid-Aug 9am-7pm, other hours vary seasonally; ♿) where herds of giraffes, zebras, rhinos and other animals roam the open valley floor. For an instant safari feel, board the **Africa Tram** ride, which tours you around the second-largest continent in under half an hour.

Elsewhere, animals are in enclosures so naturalistic it's as if the humans are guests, and there's a petting krall and animal shows; pick up a map and schedule. Additional 'safaris,' like zip-lining, a chance to observe a cheetah whizz by while chasing a mechanical rabbit, and even sleepovers (yowza!) are available with reservations and additional payment (from $45).

The park's just north of Hwy 78, 5 miles east of I-15 from the Via Rancho Parkway exit. Parking is $10. Plan on 45 minutes transit by car from San Diego, except in rush hour when that figure can double. For bus information contact **North San Diego County Transit District** (☑ 619-233-3004, from North County 800-266-6883; www.gonctd.com).

ℙ ♿) A fantasy environment built largely of those little colored plastic blocks from Denmark. Many rides and attractions are targeted to elementary schoolers: a junior 'driving school,' a jungle cruise lined with Lego animals, wacky 'sky cruiser' pedal cars on a track, and fairytale, princess, pirate, adventurer and dino-themed escapades. If you have budding scientists (aged 10 and over) with you, sign them up on arrival at the park for an appointment with **Mindstorms**, where they can make computerized Lego robots.

There are also lots of low-thrill activities like face-painting and princess-meeting.

Carlsbad Ranch Flower Fields　　GARDENS
(☑ 760-431-0352; www.theflowerfields.com; 5704 Paseo del Norte; adult/child $12/6; ☺ usually 9am-6pm Mar–mid-May; ℙ) The 50-acre flower fields of Carlsbad Ranch are ablaze in a sea of the carmine, saffron and snow-white blossoms of ranunculuses. Take the Palomar Airport Rd exit off of I-5, head east and turn left on Paseo del Norte.

Batiquitos Lagoon　　PARK
(☑ 760-931-0800; www.batiquitosfoundation. org; 7380 Gabbiano Ln; ☺ nature center 9am-12:30pm Mon-Fri, to 3pm Sat & Sun) One of the last remaining tidal wetlands in California, Batiquitos Lagoon separates Carlsbad from Encinitas. A self-guided tour lets you explore area plants, including the prickly pear cactus, coastal sage scrub and eucalyptus trees, as well as lagoon birds such as the great heron and the snowy egret.

Museum of Making Music　　MUSEUM
(www.museumofmakingmusic.com; 5790 Armada Dr; adult/child & senior $8/5; ☺ 10am-5pm Tue-Sun) Historical exhibits and listening stations of 450 instruments from the 1890s to the present, from manufacturing to the distribution of popular music.

Chopra Center　　MIND-BODY CENTER
(www.chopra.com; 2013 Costa del Mar Rd, Omni La Costa Resort & Spa) Slow down with alternative-health guru Deepak Chopra, who leads seminars on mind-body medicine, complemented by specialized spa treatments.

K1 Speed　　ADVENTURE SPORTS
(www.k1speed.com; Corte Del Abeto; 14-lap race $20; ☺ noon-10pm Mon-Thu, 11am-11pm Fri, 10am-11pm Sat, 10am-8pm Sun) To pick up the pace, this place fills your need for speed with indoor karting (electric drag racing). It supplies all the necessary equipment, including helmet and 'head socks'; first-timers must purchase a special license, $6 extra. Inquire about midweek discounts.

🛏 Sleeping

Below are some of Carlsbad's standout lodgings. Numerous chain motels near the freeway cater to budget travelers.

On Batiquitos Lagoon, two large and luxurious resorts boast golf and extensive fitness and kids' programs: **Omni La Costa Resort & Spa** (☑ 760-438-9111, 800-854-5000; www.lacosta.com; 2100 Costa Del Mar Rd; r from $300; ℙ@🛜🛒🐾) 🏊 has the Chopra Center and a touch of Hollywood history, while the

Park Hyatt Aviara (📞760-603-6800; www.
parkhyattaviara.com; 7100 Aviara Resort Dr; r from
$249; P@🛜🏊🐾) is done up in acres of
marble and has a 15,000-sq-ft spa.

**South Carlsbad State Park
Campground**   CAMPGROUND $
(📞760-438-3143,   reservations   800-444-7275;
www.reserveamerica.com;   7201   Carlsbad   Blvd;
ocean-/street-side campsites $50/35; P) Three
miles south of town and sandwiched between Carlsbad Blvd and the beach, this
campground has over 200 tent and RV sites.

⭐**Legoland Hotel**   HOTEL $$$
(📞877-534-6526,   760-918-5346;   california.lego-
land.com/legoland-hotel; 5885 the Crossings Dr; r
incl breakfast from $369; P✳@🛜🏊) To quote
the *Lego Movie,* 'everything is awesome' at
this new hotel just outside Legoland's main
gate, where Lego designers were let loose.
There are 3500 Lego models (dragons to
surfers) populating the property, and the
elevator turns into a disco between floors.
Each floor has its own theme (pirate, ad-
venture, kingdom) down to the rooms' wall-
paper, props (Lego cannonballs!) even the
shower curtains.

**Hilton Carlsbad Oceanfront
Resort & Spa**   RESORT HOTEL $$$
(📞760-602-0800;   www.carlsbadoceanfrontre-
sortandspa.hilton.com; 1 Ponto Rd; r from $249;
P✳@🛜🏊) Most of Carlsbad's top lodgings are inland, but this swanky new spot
(opened 2012) is an easy walk to the ocean
across Hwy 101. Pools, spa and business and
fitness centers will keep you busy on land.
Chandler's restaurant serves three squares,
including creative dinners like falafel crab-
cakes and diver scallops with artichokes and
smoked almonds. Parking costs $19.

West Inn & Suites   HOTEL $$$
(📞866-431-9378,   760-448-4500;   www.westin-
nandsuites.com; 4970 Avenida Encinas; r incl break-
fast $159-359; P✳@🛜🏊🐾) About halfway
between Legoland and Carlsbad Village, this
hyperfriendly, independently run 86-room
inn caters to both business travelers (note
business and fitness centers) and vacation-
ing families (note the sparkling pool, beach
and Legoland shuttle service and nightly
milk and cookies). Free parking.

✕ Eating & Drinking

All the hotels mentioned have quite decent
restaurants. In town, State St is Carlsbad's
most charming stretch, with a number of

restaurants worth browsing. Nearby are
branches of the brew pub Pizza Port (p445)
and Mexican fave **Las Olas** (📞760-434-5850;
2939 Carlsbad Blvd).

Vigilucci's Cucina Italiana   ITALIAN $$
(📞760-434-2500; 2943 State St; lunch $8-
18, dinner $15-32; ⏱11am-10pm) Enjoy the
white-tablecloth service and the lovely
sidewalk terrace at this State St institution. For lunch try pastas or panini (the
one with parma ham and portobello mushrooms is a fave), while dinner might be
pappardelle with field mushrooms and
seared diver scallops in white truffle and
brandy cream sauce.

Relm   WINE BAR
(📞760-434-9463;   www.thewinerelm.com;   2917
State St; ⏱from 4pm Tue-Sun) This cozy, modernist storefront pours from over 60 bottles
(wine flights $12) and serves cheeseboards
and flatbreads to go with them. When it has
live music, it's irresistible.

ℹ Information

Carlsbad Visitors Center (📞760-434-6093;
www.visitcarlsbad.com; 400 Carlsbad Village
Dr) Housed in the town's original 1887 Santa Fe
train depot.

ℹ Getting There & Away

Carlsbad is a stop on Coaster trains and Breeze
buses (www.gonctd.com). By car, take the
Cannon Dr exit from I-5 for Legoland, the outlet
mall and other sights and lodgings. For Carlsbad
Village, take the Carlsbad Village Dr exit.

Oceanside

The largest North County town, Oceanside
is home to many who work at giant Camp
Pendleton Marine Base just to the north.
The huge military presence mixes with an
attractive natural setting, surf shops and
head shops.

⊙ Sights & Activities

Oceanside Pier   PIER
(per hr/day $5/15) This wooden pier extends
more than 1900ft out to sea. Bait-and-tackle
shops rent poles to the many anglers who
line its wooden fences. Two major surf competitions – the West Coast Pro-Am and the
National Scholastic Surf Association (NSSA) –
take place near the pier each June.

Surfers and would-be surfers can rent equipment from **Asylum Surf** (www.asylumboardshop.com; 310 Mission Ave; surfboards 3hr/full day $20/30, wetsuits $10/15) and take lessons from **Surfcamps USA** (www.surfcampsusa.com; 1202 N Pacific St; lessons per person from $55; ⊕).

★ **California Surf Museum** MUSEUM
(www.surfmuseum.org; 312 Pier View Way; adult/student/child $5/3/free, Tue free; ⊙ 10am-4pm Fri-Wed, to 8pm Thu) It's easy to spend an hour in this heartfelt museum of surf artifacts, ranging from a timeline of surfing history to surf-themed art and a radical collection of boards, including the one chomped by a shark when it ate the arm of surfer Bethany Hamilton. Special exhibits change frequently along different themes (eg women of surfing).

Oceanside Museum of Art MUSEUM
(www.oma-online.org; 704 Pier View Way; adult/senior/student $8/5/3; ⊙ 10am-4pm Tue-Sat, 1-4pm Sun) This museum also underwent a recent revamp and it now stands at an impressive 16,000 sq ft in a modernist, white shell. There are about 10 rotating exhibits a year, with an emphasis on SoCal artists and local cultures.

Mission San Luis Rey de Francia MISSION
(www.sanluisrey.org; 4050 Mission Ave; adult/child & senior $5/4; ⊙ 10am-4pm) About 4.5 miles inland from central Oceanside, this was the largest California mission and the most successful in recruiting Native American converts. At one point some 3000 neophytes lived and worked here. After the Mexican government secularized the missions, San Luis fell into ruin; the adobe walls of the church, from 1811, are the only original parts left. Inside are displays on work and life in the mission, with some original religious art and artifacts.

Helgren's BOAT CHARTERS
(☎ 760-722-2133; www.helgrensportfishing.com; 315 Harbor Dr S) This outfit leads a variety of charter trips for sportfishing (from $55 per half-day) and whale-watching (adult/child $35/20). Phone for details and reservations.

🛏 Sleeping & Eating

★ **Springhill Suites Oceanside Downtown** HOTEL $$
(☎ 760-722-1003; www.shsoceanside.com; 110 N Myers St; r incl breakfast $219-279; P@🛰🏊) Brand new for 2014, this modern, six-story, ocean-view hotel is awash in summery yellows and sea blues in the lobby. Rooms have crisp lines and distressed-wood headboards, and ocean- and pier-view rooms have balconies or patios. Best views are from the pool and hot tub on the top floor, where there's also a fitness center.

Beach Break Café DINER $
(☎ 760-439-6355; 1802 S Coast Hwy; mains $7-12; ⊙ 7am-2pm; P🛶) Fuel up before surfing on omelets, scrambles and pancakes, or afterwards on sandwiches, tacos and salads at this surfers' diner on the east side of the road. A second location by the **harbor** (280 Harbor Dr) serves the same menu in a stellar setting.

101 Café DINER $
(☎ 760-722-5220; 631 S Coast Hwy; mains $6-10; ⊙ 7am-2pm; P🛶) This tiny 1928 streamline moderne diner serves the classics: omelets, burgers etc. If you're lucky, you'll catch the owner and can quiz him about local history.

Hello Betty Fish House SEAFOOD $$
(☎ 760-722-1008; www.hellobettyoceanside.com; 211 Mission Ave; mains $10-24; ⊙ 11am-10pm Sun-Thu, to 11pm Fri & Sat) This new beachfront spot opened in 2014 and locals already love its Baja stone crab and cheese dip, fried and grilled tacos (from $4.50) and salmon burger with Asian slaw and wasabi aioli. Grilled fish platters and other large plates run up to $24. Plus O'side's best views from the bar and deck.

That Boy Good BARBECUE $$
(TBG; ☎ 760-433-4227; www.tbgbbq.com; 207 N Coast Hwy; mains $9-25; ⊙ from 4pm Mon, 11am Tue-Sun) This new shrine to the Mississippi Delta serves belly-busting portions of fried chicken and waffles, pork ribs and the Crossroads Cup (baked beans, mac 'n' cheese, cole slaw topped with your choice of meat). Wash it all down with a craft or canned beer or the BBQ Bloody Mary, topped with a rib.

ℹ Information

California Welcome Center (☎ 760-721-1101, 800-350-7873; www.visitoceanside.org; 928 N Coast Hwy; ⊙ 9am-5pm)

ℹ Getting There & Away

Oceanside Transit Center (235 S Tremont St) Buses and trains all stop here. North County Transit District (NCTD; ☎ 760-966-6500; www.gonctd.com) Breeze Bus 101 departs from UTC in La Jolla (p453) and follows the coastal road to Oceanside. NCTD also operates the Coaster commuter train from San Diego, stopping in Encinitas, Carlsbad and Oceanside. A few Amtrak (p449) Pacific Surfliner trains stop here daily.

Greyhound buses stop at Oceanside and San Diego.

Understand Coastal California

Coastal California Today

Coastal California is today the creative culmination of generations of big dreamers. The fantasies spun by Hollywood and the cutting-edge tech of Silicon Valley have come to dominate the cultural trends of the entire planet. Meanwhile, the state's iconic images of tanned surfers and sunny sands endure, never mind thornier real-life questions about how to manage a burgeoning human population and its accompanying challenges of never-ending traffic gridlock, housing shortages and a sky-high cost of living.

Best on Film

Maltese Falcon (1941) Humphrey Bogart as a San Francisco private eye.
Sunset Boulevard (1950) A classic bonfire of Hollywood vanities.
Vertigo (1958) Alfred Hitchcock's noir thriller, set in SF.
The Graduate (1967) Surviving life in 1960s SoCal suburbia.
Chinatown (1974) LA's brutal 20th-century water wars.
Bladerunner (1982) Ridley Scott's futuristic cyberpunk vision of LA.
Pulp Fiction (1994) Quentin Tarantino's outrageous interlocking LA stories.
LA Confidential (1997) Neo-noir tale of corruption and murder in 1950s LA.
Sideways (2004) Wacky, wine-soaked romantic comedy.

Best in Print

The Tortilla Curtain (TC Boyle; 1995) Mexican-American culture clash and chasing the Californian dream.
My California: Journeys by Great Writers (Angel City Press; 2004) Insightful stories by talented chroniclers.
Where I Was From (Joan Didion; 2003) California-born essayist shatters palm-fringed fantasies.

People & Politics

Even if you've seen it in the movies or on TV, coastal California may still come as a shock to the system. Venice Beach skateboarders, Humboldt hippies, Marin County wild-mushroom hunters, 'Bezerkely' professors and Silicon Valley millionaires aren't on different channels. They all live here, a place where tolerance for other people's beliefs, be they conservative, liberal or wacky, is the necessary social glue.

The most divisive political hot potato of recent years was same-sex marriage, until a voter-approved state constitutional amendment to ban it was struck down for good by the US Supreme Court in 2013. Still controversial elsewhere in the USA, medical marijuana is old news for Californians, who approved a state proposition allowing its use back in 1996 – although the proliferation of raids on MMJ dispensaries and rumors of Mexican cartel intervention have raised eyebrows. Now the burning question is: will California follow Colorado's lead in legalizing marijuana for recreational use? Whoa, dude.

Environmental Roots

There's no denying that California's culture of conspicuous consumption is exported via Hollywood flicks and reality TV (hello, *Real Housewives of Orange County*). But since the 1960s, Californians have trailblazed another, 'greener' way by choosing more sustainable foods and low-impact lifestyles, preserving old-growth forests with tree-sitting activism, declaring urban nuclear-free zones, pushing for environmentally progressive legislation and establishing the biggest US market for hybrid vehicles. Over 60% of Californians admit that yes, they've actually hugged a tree.

That shouldn't really come as a surprise. It was Californians who helped kick-start the world's conservation movement in the midst of the 19th-century industrial revolution, with laws curbing industrial dumping, swaths of prime real estate set aside as urban green space, and pristine wilderness protected by national and state parks. Today, even conservative California politicians may prioritize environmental issues on their agendas – at least as much as the state's ongoing economic recovery and worrying drought allow.

Fast Companies & Economic Recovery
You might not get a word in edgewise when it comes to discussing the environment with a local, but California's technological innovations need no introduction by anyone. Perhaps you've heard of PCs, iPods, Google and the internet? The home of Silicon Valley and a burgeoning biotech industry, Northern California is giving Southern California's gargantuan entertainment industry a serious run for its money as the state's main economic powerhouse.

But even these industries weren't enough to salvage the state's ravaged economy, which spiraled out of control during the US recession beginning in 2007. California's budget crisis brought deep cuts to environmental protections, education, social services and other public programs, including state parks. In the past couple of years, Governor Jerry Brown (Democrat) and state legislators have reversed many of these austerity measures as the economy finally begins to bounce back.

Growing Pains
The biggest problem California faces is growth itself. Because of the Golden State's adaptability and charms, the human wave of domestic migration and international immigration continued to crest until only the last decade. Still, many Americans who heed the mid-19th-century advice to 'Go West, young man!' find themselves winding up on California's shores, as do most of the USA's new foreign-born arrivals.

With this burgeoning humanity come almost unbelievably high costs of living and real estate. Public transportation is often inadequate, so everyone hits the tortured freeways. Meanwhile, the gap between California's richest and poorest citizens dramatically keeps widening. Nowhere in the nation is income inequality greater than in San Francisco, where artists, working-class families and other long-time tenants are being evicted to build luxury condos for wealthy, young tech company employees, whose private commuter buses infuriatingly clog city streets.

Sheer human impaction is a palpable force almost everywhere in coastal California and begs the question that Rodney King asked back in 1992: 'Can we all get along?' Like California's future, the answer to that question remains unknown.

POPULATION: **38.3 MILLION**

AREA: **155,780 SQ MILES**

GDP: **$1.96 TRILLION (12% OF USA)**

AVERAGE PER CAPITA INCOME: **$29,550**

UNEMPLOYMENT: **7.4%**

if California were 100 people

40 would be Caucasian
38 would be Latino
14 would be Asian American
7 would be African American
1 would be other

belief systems
(% of population)

36 Protestant
2 Mormon
3 Jewish
2 Buddhist
1 Muslim
31 Catholic
24 other
1 Hindu

population per sq mile

USA | California | Los Angeles

≈ 80 people

History

When European explorers first arrived in the 16th century, more than 100,000 Native Americans called this land home. Spanish conquistadors and priests marched through in search of a fabled 'city of gold' before establishing Catholic missions and presidios (military forts). After winning independence from Spain, Mexico briefly ruled California, but then got trounced by the fledgling USA just before gold was discovered in 1848, sparking a population boom. Waves of immigrants haven't stopped washing up on these Pacific shores ever since.

Native Californians

The precise etymology of 'California' has never been convincingly established. Many think it derives from a 16th-century Spanish romance novel about a legendary island, fabulously rich in gold and inhabited only by black women warriors ruled by Queen Califía.

Immigration is hardly a new phenomenon here, since human beings have been migrating to California for millennia. Archaeological sites have yielded evidence – from large middens of seashells along the beaches to campfire sites on the Channel Islands – of humans making their homes along this coast as early as 13,000 years ago.

Speaking some 100 distinct languages, California's indigenous people mostly lived in small communities and a few migrated with the seasons. Their diet was largely dependent on acorn meal, supplemented by small game such as rabbits and deer, and fish and shellfish. They were skilled craftspeople, making earthenware pots, animal-skin and plant-fiber clothing, dugout canoes carved from redwood logs, fishing nets, bows, arrows and spears with chipped stone points. The most developed craft was basketry; baskets were often decorated with intricate geometric designs and some were so tightly woven they could hold water.

On the North Coast, fishing communities such as the Ohlone, Miwok and Pomo built subterranean roundhouses and sweat lodges, where they held ceremonies, told stories and gambled. Kumeyaay and Chumash villages dotted the Central Coast, where tribespeople fished and paddled canoes, including out to the Channel Islands. Further south, the nomadic Kumeyaay tribe hunted, foraged and fished near present-day San Diego.

Despite pockets of armed resistance and violent revolts, many indigenous tribespeople were made to construct Spanish missions and presidios in the late 18th and early 19th centuries. Within 100 years after

TIMELINE	20,000 BC	AD 1542	1769
	First people start crossing from Asia into North America via the Bering Strait land bridge. The bones of a human found on California's Santa Rosa Island date back 13,000 years.	Portuguese navigator Juan Rodríguez Cabrillo and his Spanish crew become the first Europeans to sight the mainland of New Spain's west coast, anchoring in today's San Diego Bay.	Spain attempts to colonize California when Padre Junípero Serra and Captain Gaspar de Portolá lead an expedition to establish the first Catholic missions in Alta California, starting in San Diego.

Spanish colonists first arrived in 1769, California's indigenous population had plummeted by 80% to just 20,000 people due to foreign diseases, conscripted labor, violence, hunger and culture shock.

Native Californians were further dispossessed of tribal lands during the Mexican colonial and early American periods. It wasn't until the 20th century – when the US government began recognizing some tribes as sovereign nations, granting Native Americans citizenship and voting rights in 1924 – that California's indigenous population began to rebound.

Political activism, including the 'Red Power' protests of the American Indian Movement (AIM) starting in the late 1960s, led to a cultural renaissance and secured some tribes economic assistance from state and federal agencies. Deprived of their traditional land base and means of livelihood centuries ago, many California tribes have turned to casino gaming to relieve unemployment and poverty on their reservations.

A New World for Europeans

Following the conquest of Mexico in the early 16th century, Spain turned its attention toward exploring the edges of a new empire, fueled by curiosity, lust for power and, above all, greed. In 1542 the Spanish crown engaged Juan Rodríguez Cabrillo, a Portuguese explorer and retired conquistador, to lead an expedition up the West Coast to find the fabled golden land beyond Mexico.

When Cabrillo sailed into what is now San Diego Bay in 1542, he and his crew became the first Europeans to see mainland California. Staring back at them from shore were the Kumeyaay. Cabrillo's ships sat out a storm in the harbor, then sailed northward. They made a stop at the Channel Islands where Cabrillo broke a leg, fell ill, died and was buried on what is now San Miguel Island. The expedition continued as far as Oregon, but returned with no evidence of a city of gold.

Unimpressed Spanish colonial authorities ignored California for the next half century or so, until they decided they needed to secure some ports on the Pacific coast, and sent Sebastián Vizcaíno to find them. Vizcaíno's first expedition was a disaster that didn't get past Baja (Lower) California, but in his second attempt, in 1602, he rediscovered the harbor at San Diego and became the first European to set foot in what Spaniards called Alta (Upper) California.

Meanwhile, the English privateer Sir Francis Drake sailed up the California coast in 1579. He missed the entrance to San Francisco Bay, but pulled in near what is now called Point Reyes to repair his ship. Coastal Miwok tribespeople believed the English mariners to be the spirits of the dead returned from the afterworld. Drake quickly claimed their land for

Find out about the traditions and lifestyles of California's Native American tribes in the readable natural history guide *California Indians and Their Environment* by Kent Lightfoot and Otis Parrish.

1781	1821	1826–32	1848
Spanish governor Felipe de Neve and a tiny band of settlers set out from Mission San Gabriel and trek just 9 miles away to found Los Angeles.	Mexican independence ends Spanish colonial dreams. Mexico inherits 21 Catholic missions in various states of disrepair, but quickly reorganizes Alta California into *ranchos* (land grants).	Teenage Kit Carson helps blaze the Santa Fe Trail, which eventually leads to Los Angeles through 900 miles of rattlesnake-filled high desert and plains guarded by Native American tribes.	After winning the Mexican-American War and signing the Treaty of Guadalupe Hidalgo, the US takes control of Alta California, just as gold is discovered in the Sierra Nevada foothills.

Queen Elizabeth, named it Nova Albion (New England) and sailed on to other adventures, journeying north up the Pacific coast to Alaska.

Spain's Mission Impossible

The distance between each of California's Spanish colonial missions equaled a day's journey by horseback. Learn more about the missions' historical significance and cultural influence at www.missionscalifornia.com.

In the 18th century, as Russian ships came to California's coast in search of sea-otter pelts, and British trappers and explorers spread throughout the West, Spain finally grew worried that its claim to the territory might be challenged. Conveniently, the Catholic Church was anxious to start missionary work among the natives, so the church and Spanish crown combined forces. For the glory of God and the tax coffers of Spain it was decided that Catholic missions would be built across California.

On July 1, 1769, a sorry lot of about 100 missionaries and soldiers, led by the Franciscan priest Junípero Serra and the military commander Gaspar de Portolá, limped ashore at San Diego Bay. They had just spent several weeks at sea sailing from Baja (Lower) California; about half of their cohort had died en route and many of the survivors were sick or near death. It was an inauspicious beginning for Mission San Diego de Alcalá, the first in a chain of 21 Spanish missions in Alta California.

Ostensibly, the presidios' purpose was to protect the missions and deter foreign intruders. The idea was to have Native American converts live inside the missions, learn trade and agricultural skills, and ultimately establish pueblos, which would be like little Spanish towns. Or so the plan went.

But these garrisons created more threats than they deterred, as the soldiers aroused local hostility by raiding and looting tribal camps and kidnapping and raping indigenous women. Not only were the Spanish presidios in Alta California militarily weak, their weaknesses were well known to Russia and Britain, and they didn't much strengthen Spain's claims to California.

Don't-Miss Missions

San Juan Capistrano

Santa Barbara

San Diego

La Purísima

San Carlos Borroméo de Carmelo

Mission Dolores

Ultimately, the mission period was a failure. The Spanish population remained small; the missions achieved little more than mere survival; foreign intruders were not effectively deterred; and more Native Americans died than were converted. Several of California's original Spanish missions still stand today, though a few are in ruins – some toppled by earthquakes, others broken by forced secularization under Mexican rule.

From Mexico to Manifest Destiny

When Mexico gained independence from Spain in 1821, many in that new nation looked to California to satisfy their thirst for private land. By the mid-1830s all but one Spanish mission had been secularized, so that Mexican governors could dole out hundreds of free land grants, or *ranchos*. By law, half of the land grants were supposed to go to Native

1850	1869	1882	1892
After debate about whether it would be a slaveholding or free state (Congress chooses the latter), California enters the Union. Its first constitution is written in both Spanish and English.	A golden spike is nailed in Utah, completing the first transcontinental railroad linking California with the East Coast. Gold is uncovered outside San Diego, unleashing a mini mining frenzy.	The US Chinese Exclusion Act suspends new immigration from China, denies citizenship to those already in the country and sanctions racially targeted laws that stay on the books until 1943.	Oil is discovered by Edward Doheny in downtown LA, near where Dodger Stadium stands today, sparking a major oil boom. Within a decade, LA's population doubles to over 100,000 people.

Californians who worked at the missions, but few actually received their entitlements.

The new landowners, called rancheros or Californios, prospered by raising livestock for the profitable hide and tallow trade. Rancheros became the social, cultural and political elite of Alta California under Mexican rule. Meanwhile, American explorers, trappers, traders, whalers, settlers and other opportunists showed increasing interest in the territory, seizing on economic prospects that the rancheros largely ignored. Some Americans who started businesses here converted to Catholicism, married locals and successfully assimilated into ranchero society.

Impressed by California's untapped riches and hoping to fulfill the promise of Manifest Destiny (the USA's imperialist doctrine of extending its borders from coast to coast), President Andrew Jackson sent an emissary to offer the financially strapped Mexican government $500,000 for California in 1835. Though American settlers were by then showing up in Alta California by the hundreds, Jackson's emissary was tersely rejected. Soon, a political storm was brewing.

In 1836, Texas seceded from Mexico and declared itself an independent republic. When the US annexed Texas in 1845, Mexico broke off diplomatic relations and ordered all foreigners without proper papers to be deported from California. In turn, the US declared war on Mexico and began an invasion. US naval units quickly occupied every port on California's coast, including Monterey, then the capital of Alta California.

Militarily speaking, California remained a sideshow while the war was mostly fought in Mexico. The capture of Mexico City by US troops in September 1847 put an end to hostilities. By signing of the Treaty of Guadalupe Hidalgo on February 2, 1848, the Mexican government ceded much of its northern territory (including Alta California) to the USA, just in time for California's Gold Rush to begin.

Eureka! California's Gold Rush

Gold was discovered at Sutter's Creek, in California's Sierra Nevada foothills, on January 24, 1848. By the next year, surging rivers of wagon trains were creaking into California filled with miners, pioneers, savvy entrepreneurs, outlaws and prostitutes, all seeking their fortunes. In 1850, when California was fast-tracked for admission as the 31st US state, the foreign population had ballooned from 15,000 to 93,000.

With each wave of new arrivals, profits dropped and gold was harder to find. When surface gold became scarce, miners picked, shoveled and dynamited through mountains. Hills were stripped bare, erosion wiped out vegetation, streams silted up and mercury washed down rivers all the way into San Francisco Bay. The city of San Francisco became a hotbed

HISTORY EUREKA! CALIFORNIA'S GOLD RUSH

In 1873 German immigrant and San Francisco store owner Levi Strauss received a patent for his hard-wearing, riveted denim pants, originally designed for California's gold prospectors – and, voilà! – American blue jeans were born.

1906	1913	1934	1942
A massive earthquake levels entire blocks of San Francisco in less than a minute, setting off fires that rage for three days. Survivors start rebuilding immediately.	The Los Angeles Aqueduct, built under the direction of chief engineer William Mulholland, starts supplying a thirsty metropolis with water controversially taken from the eastern Sierra Nevada.	A longshoremen's strike in San Francisco ends with dozens of labor activists shot or beaten by police. After mass funeral processions and a city-wide strike, shipping magnates meet union demands.	During WWII, Executive Order 9066 sends nearly 120,000 Japanese Americans to internment camps. The Japanese American Citizens League files lawsuits, providing legal support for the 1964 Civil Rights Act.

of gambling, prostitution, drink and chicanery, earning it the moniker of 'Barbary Coast,' an allusion to Africa's north coast where pirates preyed.

In the 1860s, California vicariously experienced a second mining boom after the discovery of the Comstock silver lode in present-day Nevada. Exploiting this mother lode required deep-mining techniques, which in turn necessitated California's big-shouldered industrial companies, stocks, trading and speculation. In fact, San Francisco made more money speculating on silver than Nevada did mining it: grandiose mansions sprouted on Nob Hill, and California's new business tycoons became renowned for their unscrupulous audacity.

Riches from Railroads, Real Estate & Oil

The Academy Award–winning 2007 film *There Will Be Blood*, adapted from Upton Sinclair's book *Oil!*, depicts a fictional California oil magnate based on real-life SoCal tycoon Edward Doheny.

Opening the floodgates to massive migration into the West in 1869, the transcontinental railroad shortened the trip from New York to San Francisco from two months to less than four days. Nouveau-riche San Francisco became California's metropolitan center. Meanwhile, Southern California's parched climate, its distance from water resources, and relatively small population made it less attractive to profit-minded railroad moguls, though wheeling and dealing finally resulted in a spur line to LA during the mid-1870s.

By that time, rampant speculation had raised land prices in California to levels no farmer or new immigrant could afford. The railroad brought in products that undersold goods made in California, while some 15,000 Chinese laborers – no longer needed for railroad construction work or mining – flooded the labor market, especially in San Francisco. A period of anti-foreign discrimination and unrest ensued, which culminated in federal legislation banning Chinese immigration outright in 1882.

During the same period, agriculture diversified, with new crops – especially oranges – being grown in Southern California for markets on the East Coast and abroad. As California-grown oranges found their way onto New York grocery shelves, a hard-sell advertising campaign for the Golden State began. Folks back East heeded the self-interested advice of crusading magazine and newspaper editor Horace Greeley to 'Go West, young man.'

Sneakily, much of the land granted to railroads was flipped and sold in big lots to speculators who also acquired, with the help of corrupt politicians and bureaucrats, a majority of the farmland intended for new settlers. A major share of agricultural land was consolidated in the hands of a few city-based landlords, establishing the still-existing pattern of industrial 'agribusiness' (rather than small family farms) dependent on large-scale irrigation projects and cheap migrant farm labor.

LA had other natural resources waiting to be exploited, albeit hidden underground. In 1892 a flat-broke mining prospector and real-estate

1943	1955	1965	1966
Tension between Americans and Mexicans reaches boiling point during the Zoot Suit Riots, which pit US military servicemen against zoot-suit-clad Mexican teens while LA police look on.	In Anaheim, Disneyland opens to bad press, as crowds swarm the theme park, temperatures hit 101°F (38°C), ladies' high-heeled shoes sink into the still-soft asphalt and drinking fountains don't work.	It takes 20,000 National Guards to quell the six-day Watts Riots in LA, which cause death, devastation and over $40 million in property damage.	Ronald Reagan is elected governor of California, setting a career precedent for fading film stars. He served until 1975, then in 1981 became the 40th US President.

speculator named Edward Doheny dug a well near downtown LA that would change Southern California forever. Inside of a year, Doheny's well was producing 40 gallons of 'black gold' (oil) daily, and SoCal's oil industry was born.

Labor & Military Might

The Great Depression saw another wave of immigrants, this time of American farm families who were fleeing the Dust Bowl on the drought-stricken Great Plains. At the end of Route 66 in the promised land of California, they often found social discrimination and only scant pay and deplorable working conditions on company-owned farms, as fictionalized in John Steinbeck's harrowing Pulitzer Prize–winning novel *The Grapes of Wrath*. Outbreaks of social and labor protest led to the rapid growth of the Democratic Party in California, as well as growing trade unions for blue-collar workers.

Many of California's Depression-era public works projects, which were sponsored by the federal government, have had lasting benefits for residents and tourists alike, including the restoration of historic Spanish missions and improvements to highways and public parks. But it was really California's cutting-edge aviation industry – pumped up by billions of dollars from federal military contracts – that helped boost the state out of the Great Depression.

California's workforce permanently changed during WWII, when women and African Americans were recruited for wartime industries and Mexican workers were brought in to fill agricultural labor shortages. After the Japanese bombed Pearl Harbor on December 7, 1941, San Diego became the headquarters of the entire US Pacific Fleet. Throughout WWII, as Southern California's aircraft manufacturing plants turned out planes by the thousands, San Francisco Bay Area workers (including women, nicknamed 'Rosie the Riveters') built hundreds of warships. Military contracts attracted top-notch engineers and scientists, who later launched California's high-tech industry.

After WWII many service people decided to settle permanently on the West Coast. Within a decade after the war, California's population had grown by 40%, reaching 13 million. The state's military-industrial complex continued to prosper during the Cold War era, providing jobs in everything from avionics and missile manufacturing to nuclear submarine maintenance. Military spending peaked in the 1980s under ex-California governor and then US president Ronald Reagan.

Social Movers & Shakers

Unconstrained by the burden of traditions and promoted by film and TV, California has long been a leader in new attitudes and social movements.

> The classic film *Chinatown* (1974) is the fictionalized yet surprisingly realistic account of the brutal early-20th-century water wars that were waged to build Los Angeles.

1968	1969	1977	1989
Presidential candidate Robert Kennedy is assassinated at the Ambassador Hotel in LA by Palestinian immigrant and anti-Zionist Sirhan Sirhan, who remains in jail in San Diego County today.	UCLA professor Len Kleinrock sends data from a computer in Los Angeles to another at Stanford University, typing just two characters before the system crashes. The internet is born.	San Francisco Supervisor Harvey Milk becomes the first openly gay man elected to US public office. Milk sponsors a gay-rights bill before his 1978 murder by political opponent Dan White.	On October 17, the Loma Prieta earthquake hits 6.9 on the Richter scale near Santa Cruz, collapsing a two-level section of Interstate 880 and resulting in 63 deaths and almost 4000 injuries.

During the postwar boom of the 1950s, the Beat movement in San Francisco's North Beach railed against the banality and conformity of suburban life, instead choosing bohemian coffeehouses for jazz, poetry and pot.

When the baby boomers came of age, many hippies took up where the Beat Generation left off, heeding 1960s countercultural icon Timothy Leary's counsel to 'turn on, tune in, and drop out.' Sex, drugs and rock and roll ruled the day. With the foundations for social revolution already laid, protestors up and down California's coast marched against the Vietnam War and for civil rights in the late 1960s, then again for gay liberation starting in the '70s.

Since the 1980s, coastal California has become synonymous with a healthy lifestyle obsession, with more yoga classes and self-actualization workshops than you could shake a shaman's stick at. Remember that in-line skating, snowboarding and mountain biking started here first. Be careful what you scoff at: from pet rocks to soy burgers, California's flavor of the month is often next year's global trend.

To read more about the garage-workshop culture of Silicon Valley go to www.folklore.org, which covers the crashes and personality clashes that made geek history.

High-Tech Booms & Busts

In the 1950s, Stanford University in Palo Alto needed to raise money to finance postwar growth, so it built an industrial park and leased space to high-tech companies like Hewlett-Packard, which formed the nucleus of Silicon Valley. When Hewlett-Packard introduced the first personal computer in 1968, advertisements breathlessly gushed that the 'light' (40lb) machine could 'take on roots of a fifth-degree polynomial, Bessel functions, elliptic integrals and regression analysis' – all for just $4900 (over $33,000 today).

Consumers didn't know quite what to do with computers, but in his 1969 Whole Earth Catalog, author (and former LSD tester for the CIA) Stewart Brand explained that the technology governments used to run countries could empower ordinary people. Hoping to bring computer power to the people, 21-year-old Steve Jobs and Steve Wozniak introduced the Apple II at the 1977 West Coast Computer Faire. Still, the question remained: what would ordinary people do with all that computing power?

By the mid-1990s an entire dot-com industry boomed in Silicon Valley with online start-ups, and suddenly people were getting everything – their mail, news, politics, pet food and, yes, sex – online. But when dot-com profits weren't forthcoming, venture-capital funding dried up and fortunes in stock-options disappeared when the dot-com bubble burst and the NASDAQ plummeted on March 10, 2000. Overnight, 26-year-old vice-presidents and Bay Area service-sector employees alike found themselves jobless. But as online users continued to look for useful informa-

1992	1994	1994	2003
Three of four white police officers charged with beating African American motorist Rodney King are acquitted by a predominantly white jury. Following the trial, Los Angeles endures six days of riots.	Orange County, one of the wealthiest municipalities in the US, declares bankruptcy after the county treasurer loses $1.7 billion investing in risky derivatives and pleads guilty to felony charges.	The 6.7-magnitude Northridge earthquake strikes LA on January 17, killing 72 and causing $20 billion in property damage – one of the costliest natural disasters in US history.	Republican Arnold Schwarzenegger (aka 'The Governator') is elected governor of California. Schwarzenegger breaks party ranks on environmental issues and wins re-election in 2007.

tion – and one another – in those billions of web pages, search engines and social media boomed.

Meanwhile, California's biotech industry also started to take off. In 1976 an upstart company called Genentech was founded in the San Francisco Bay Area, and quickly got to work cloning human insulin and introducing the hepatitis B vaccine. In 2004 California voters approved a $3 billion bond measure for stem-cell research, and by 2008 California had become the USA's biggest funder of stem-cell research, as well as the focus of NASDAQ's new Biotechnology Index.

Recent Recessions & Shaky Recovery

Silicon Valley's internet revolution rewired California's entire economy, so when the dot-com bubble burst in 2000, it plunged the entire state's economy into chaos. That same year also brought widespread power shortages and rolling blackouts to California, which were caused by Enron's illegal manipulation of markets.

In the controversial recall election of 2003, Californians voted to give action-movie star Arnold Schwarzenegger a shot at fixing things. Although a Republican, Schwarzenegger often governed from California's political center. He supported legislation that helped California lead the nation in cutting greenhouse emissions, even as US President and fellow Republican George W Bush rejected the Kyoto Protocol.

Then came the unraveling of the US subprime mortgage-lending crisis, which triggered the stock-market crash of 2008 and mired the nation in a recession with massive unemployment. By 2010 California was so broke that it had issued IOU slips to creditors, and once-again Governor Jerry Brown (a Democrat) was forced to make massive cuts to social services, education and state parks funding. It took several years for the state's economy to start making a real recovery, complicated by the problems of long-term unemployment and a worrying number of years in a row of severe drought. But don't worry: California has always been a comeback kid. Just you wait and see.

Top California History Books

California: A History (Kevin Starr)

Journey to the Sun (Gregory Orfalea)

City of Quartz (Mike Davis)

2004	2005	2008	2013
Google's IPO raises a historic $1.67 billion at $85 per share. Since then share prices have increased over 900% and the company's market value now exceeds $350 billion.	Antonio Villaraigosa is elected mayor of LA, the first Latino to hold that office since 1872. Born poor in East LA, he says in his victory speech, 'I will never forget where I came from.'	A slim majority of California voters pass Proposition 8, defining legal marriage as between a man and a woman. Courts eventually rule the law unconstitutional, and same-sex marriages resume in 2013.	After years of construction delays and engineering controversies, the eastern span of the Bay Bridge opens. At over $6 billion, it is the costliest public works project in California history – so far.

California Flavor

As you graze the Golden State, eating everything from surfer-worthy fish tacos to foraged-ingredient urban tasting menus, you'll often have cause to compliment the chef – and they're quick to turn around and share the praise with local farmers, ranchers, fishers and artisan food producers. Almost anything can and does grow on California's farms: rain-soaked coastal pastures provide grazing territory for livestock; sun-drenched vineyards overflow with prized grapes; and with more than 1000 miles of coastline, seafood just doesn't get any fresher.

California Cuisine: Then & Now

California produces nearly all the nation's almonds, dates, figs, olives and walnuts, 90% of its grapes, 75% of its strawberries and half its tomatoes and lettuce. But dairy products are the real cash cow, bringing in almost $7 billion annually.

To really strike up a conversation with a Californian, skip asking about the weather and instead start right in on the food. Say, 'So where's a good place for a taco around here?' and everyone within earshot will have an opinion. Californians proselytize about their food and idolize homegrown chefs like rock stars. After a few bites, you might begin to understand why.

'Let the ingredients speak for themselves!' is the rallying cry of California cuisine. Heavy French sauces and fussy molecular-gastronomy foams aren't required to make meals memorable, as even haute cuisine is prepared with a light touch. Mulling over menus often means taking a political stand on issues close to many Californians' hearts: organic and non-GMO crops, veganism, grass-fed versus grain-fed meat, biodynamic vineyards and fair-trade coffee. It's no accident that the term 'locavore' – what we call people who buy and eat food grown locally – was invented here.

California's Food Revolutions

Recently seasonal, locavorian eating has become mainstream across the US, but in California the movement started more than 40 years ago. As the turbulent 1960s wound down, many disillusioned idealists concluded that the revolution was not about to be delivered on a platter, but California's pioneering organic farmers weren't about to give up the idea. In 1971, Alice Waters opened Chez Panisse in a converted house in Berkeley, with the then-radical notion of making the most of California's seasonal, all-natural, sustainably produced bounty – and diners quickly tasted the difference.

Cook your own fabulous coastal meals by shopping from produce stalls and artisan food stands at local farmers markets. To find a certified California-grown farmers market near you, search www.cafarmers-markets.com.

Today, Waters' credo of organic, seasonal, sustainably sourced and locally grown ingredients has inspired countless other kitchens to follow suit. Eating 'green' like a slow-food loving 'locavore' isn't a tall order in coastal California, where weekly farmers markets, natural-foods grocery stores and organic farm co-ops abound. Many top chefs make a point of using organic, seasonal produce whenever possible and only order fish, meat or poultry from sustainable regional sources. Bottled water shipped over from Fiji or France? No, thank you – tap water will be just fine.

Food Fight! West Coast vs East Coast

It's true, California's food fixations are easily exaggerated, but not every Californian demands grass-fed burgers with heirloom tomato ketchup.

When New York chefs David Chang and Anthony Bourdain mocked California cuisine as merely putting an organic fig on a plate, Californian chefs turned the tables, saying that New York needs to get out more often and actually try some Mission figs – one of hundreds of heirloom varietals cultivated by Californians since the 18th century.

East–West Coast foodie rivalries are rowdy, with culinary pundits tracking James Beard Awards (the culinary Oscars) like sportscasters ranking pro teams. Competitive California chefs are always breaking new boundaries, expanding beyond historic Cal-Mex and Cal-Italian fusion to more newly minted hyphenated cuisines: Cal-Vietnamese, Cal-Moroccan and even Cal-Ecuadorian. Meanwhile, New York menus have been looking suspiciously Californian, citing local farms and introducing specialty organics from (where else?) California.

Global Fusion Cooking

Beyond its exceptionally rich farmland dirt, California has another culinary advantage: an experimental attitude toward food that dates from its Wild West days. Most mid-19th-century Gold Rush miners were men not accustomed to cooking for themselves, which resulted in such doomed mining-camp experiments as jelly omelets. But the era also introduced California to Cantonese-style dim sum and the US's first Italian restaurant, which opened in San Francisco in 1886.

Some 150 years later, fusion is not a fad but second nature in California, where chefs can hardly resist adding international twists to local flavors, with creative infusions from new immigrant communities. Menus often infuse ingredients and kitchen craft borrowed from neighbors across the Pacific in Asia, from south of the border all across Latin America and from Europe's distant Mediterranean, where the climate and soil are similar to California's.

Keep in mind that California once belonged to Mexico, and Latinos today make up almost 40% of the state's population. Californian takes on Mexican classics remain go-to comfort foods for many people of all ethnicities. Culinary cross-pollination has also yielded wilder fusion experiments: just witness the Californicized burrito (a mega-meal bursting out of a giant flour tortilla) and the Korean taco, with grilled marinated beef and picked vegetables atop Mexican corn tortillas.

Vegetarians, Vegans & Omnivores

To all you beleaguered vegetarians: relax, you are not an afterthought in California cuisine, which revolves around seasonal produce instead of the usual American meat and potatoes. Long before actress Alicia Silverstone (of *Clueless* fame) championed a vegan diet in her cookbook *The Kind Diet,* coastal California restaurants were catering to vegans. Bakeries, bistros, cafes, coffee shops and even mom-and-pop counter joints are

FOOD & WINE FESTIVALS

February

San Francisco Chronicle Wine Competition (www.winejudging.com) The world's stiffest competition of American wines, with tastings and gourmet food.

May

Castroville Artichoke Festival (www.artichoke-festival.org) 3D 'agro-art' sculptures, chefs' demos, a farmers market and field tours near Monterey.

May

Cooking for Solutions (www.montereybayaquarium.org) Celebrity chefs showcase sustainable seafood and farm-fresh produce to benefit the Monterey Bay Aquarium

June

LA Street Food Fest (www.lastreetfoodfest.com) Let the food trucks come to you for a change in Pasadena.

September

Savor the Central Coast (www.savorthecentralcoast.com) Shake hands with artisanal food, winemakers and brewers, then tour farms, ranches and fisheries.

October

Sonoma County Harvest Fair (www.harvestfair.org) Wine competition and tastings, food marketplace, cooking demos and championship grape-stomping in Santa Rosa.

November

San Diego Bay Wine & Food Festival (www.sandiegowine-classic.com) Wine seminars led by master sommeliers, cooking classes and a grand tasting.

CALIFORNIA COOKING CLASSES

Learn how to make California's signature dishes at home, with chefs sharing their culinary secrets in workshops and classes. Some high-end cookware shops such as **Williams-Sonoma** (www.williams-sonoma.com) and **Sur la Table** (www.surlatable.com) also offer casual introductory cooking classes.

Culinary Institute of America at Greystone (http://enthusiasts.ciachef.edu) Weekend baking and cooking classes, chef demonstrations and wine-tasting and pairing seminars in the heart of Napa Valley.

Cheese School of San Francisco (www.cheeseschoolsf.com) This Mission District kitchen lets you experiment with making homemade mozzarella and perfectly pairing artisan cheeses with wine and beer.

Relish Culinary Adventures (www.relishculinary.com) Visit farmers markets with chefs or sign up for hands-on cheese-making and dinner-party workshops around Healdsburg in Sonoma County's wine country.

Cavallo Point Cooking School (www.cavallopoint.com) Seasonal, sustainably themed cooking classes showcase organic, fresh farmers-market fare and an international repertoire of chefs across the Golden Gate Bridge from San Francisco.

Shed (www.healdsburgshed.com) In Sonoma County, Healdsburg's trendy culinary center schedules classes, workshops and guest lectures on anything from bread-making to beekeeping.

Ramekins Sonoma Valley Culinary School (www.ramekins.com) In downtown Sonoma, learn to make your own tamales, take a tour of regional Italian cooking or join a champagne producer or winemaker for dinner.

California Sushi Academy (☑310-231-4499; www.sushi-academy.com; 11310 Nebraska Ave; 3hr class $80-85) Apprentice in the art of finessing raw fish or sake tasting in West LA.

usually prepared for meat-free, dairy-free, gluten-free and/or eggless requests and menu substitutions.

Although California may have more vegetarians and vegans per capita than any other US state, many locals ardently love meat. Trendsetting restaurants' menus proudly herald the names of local farms that supply grass-fed, free-range and hormone-free beef, pork, lamb, chicken, duck and even American heritage-breed turkeys. Not only does being grass-fed improve the meat's texture and flavor, but it's more ecofriendly since livestock aren't forced to consume a crop that requires vast amounts of water, fuel and electricity to grow and process into feed.

To find vegetarian and vegan restaurants and health-food stores throughout coastal California, consult the free online directory at **Happy Cow** (www.happycow.net), now also available as a mobile app.

Regional California Specialties

Calculate the distance between your tomato's origin and your fork: chances are it's shorter than you might think in California. So what are your best bets on local menus? Well, that depends where you are and the time of year. For example, winter can be slim pickings even on fertile Northern California farms, but ideal for Southern California's citrus.

San Francisco Bay Area

Today San Francisco's adventurous eaters support the most award-winning chefs and restaurants per capita of any US city – five times more restaurants than New York, if anyone's keeping score – and 25 farmers markets in San Francisco alone, more than any other US city.

Some San Francisco food novelties have had extraordinary staying power, including ever-popular *cioppino* (seafood stew), chocolate bars invented by the Ghirardelli family, and sourdough bread, with original Gold Rush–era mother dough still yielding local loaves with that distinctive tang.

Nowadays, no Bay Area star chef's extravagant tasting menu is complete without some foraged ingredients – such as wild chanterelle mushrooms found beneath Bay Area oak trees or backyard stinging nettles – and artisan cheeses like Point Reyes blue and freshly harvested oysters from Marin County.

Napa & Sonoma Wine Country

Flush with international acclaim for its vintages since the 1970s, NorCal's wine country also has top-flight restaurateurs and artisan cheese-makers and olive-oil producers to sustain woozy visitors in desperate need of sustenance after a day of tippling. In 1994 Chef Thomas Keller transformed a historic Yountville saloon into the French Laundry, now an international gastronomic landmark, showcasing garden-grown organic produce and casual elegance in multicourse feasts.

Other chefs eager to make their names and fortunes among free-spending wine-country visitors have since flocked to the Napa and Sonoma Valleys, where farm-to-table cuisine is the byword in rustic-chic kitchens. To survey and sample wine country's artisanal food scene, stroll inside Napa's Oxbow Public Market. Sonoma hasn't forgotten its origins as a Mexican *pueblo* (town) either: you can still spot taco trucks rolling by the vineyards.

North Coast

In the 1970s, San Francisco hippies headed back to the land along the North Coast to find a more self-sufficient lifestyle, reviving traditions of making breads and cheeses from scratch and growing their own everything. Early adopters of pesticide-free farming, NorCal's hippie homesteaders innovated hearty, organic cuisine with a health-minded, global-fusion twist that still satisfied the pot-smoking munchies. Today, in pro-medical marijuana Mendocino and Humboldt Counties, local farms are *very* serious about 'No Trespassing' signs – heed them!

You can still taste the influence of traditional Native Californian cuisine on the North Coast. In addition to fishing, hunting game and making bread from acorn flour, tribes such as the Oholone and Miwok also carefully cultivated crops and gathered bonanzas of berries and wildflower honey. Today, fearless foragers have likewise come to appreciate the North Coast's hundreds of edible plants, from wood sorrel to Mendocino sea vegetables, although spots for wild mushrooms remain closely guarded local secrets.

Central California

Most of California's produce is grown in the vast region spreading between the hot, irrigated Central Valley and the more temperate Central Coast. But road-tripping epicureans tend to bolt through the middle of the state to reach SF or LA in time for dinner – if only to make it past the stinky cattle feedlots along Hwy 101 without losing their appetites.

Although much of the inland Central Valley remains dedicated to large-scale agribusiness, both industrial and family-owned farms that have converted to organic production have helped make California the top US producer of organics. Meanwhile along the Central Coast, a cornucopia of weekly farmers markets and local food festivals year-round prove that farm-to-table cooking is not just a passing fancy.

Some of California's more flavorful seafood is caught offshore from Monterey Bay, Morro Bay and San Luis Bay. More rare local seafood delicacies include farm-raised red abalone and oysters. Make pit stops at farm stands all along the Central Coast to bite into prized local produce such as Watsonville strawberries, Cayucos oranges, Carpinteria avocados and Ventura lemons.

CALIFORNIA FLAVOR REGIONAL CALIFORNIA SPECIALTIES

For what's ripe and in season right now at Northern California's farmers markets, along with inspiring recipes by well-known chefs and food writers, check www.cuesa.org/eat-seasonally.

UC Berkeley professor Michael Pollan's ground-breaking book *The Omnivore's Dilemma: A Natural History of Four Meals* (2007) traces exactly where the food a contemporary Bay Area family eats comes from, all the way along the food chain from McDonald's fast food to a DIY foraged, hunted and farmed feast.

FINDING FOOD TRUCKS & POP-UP EATERIES

Taco trucks have been rolling around California for decades. But a new gourmet street-food revolution has taken over the streets, especially in LA and San Francisco. Whatever you're craving, from Korean BBQ tacos to Indian curry naan wraps, haute grilled cheese to good ol' fried chicken, there's probably a restaurant-on-four-wheels serving it. To find trucks coming soon to a curb near you, search for 'food truck' and your location on Twitter. Come prepared with cash and sunblock: most trucks don't accept plastic cards, and lines can be long.

Maverick urban kitchens have also been popping up in such unexpected spaces as art galleries, warehouses and storefronts. Chefs at these 'pop-ups' create experimental meals around a theme, for example, Thai street food or winemakers' dinners. Adventurous eaters seek out these overnight taste sensations on Twitter and websites such as www.eater.com. But there are some downsides: pop-ups often charge restaurant prices, but without menus, quality control, health-inspected facilities or professional service. Bring cash and arrive early, since popular dishes may run out fast.

Los Angeles & Southern California

There's no telling which came first in LA: the chefs or the stars. Perhaps no one has done as much to popularize California's fusion-style cuisine nationwide as peripatetic Austrian-born chef Wolfgang Puck, who began his career as a celebrity restaurateur when he launched Beverly Hill's Spago in 1982. Reservations at chefs' private tables are now as sought-after as entry into velvet-roped nightclub VIP rooms.

As with certain Hollywood blockbusters, trendy LA restaurants don't always live up to the hype – for brutally honest opinions, read reviews by Pulitzer Prize–winning food critic Jonathan Gold in the *Los Angeles Times* or follow him on Twitter (@thejgold). Then join in-the-know locals in Koreatown for flavor-bursting *kalbi* (marinated barbecued beef short ribs), East LA for tacos *al pastor* (marinated, fried pork), the San Gabriel Valley for Chinese dim sum or on West LA's Sawtelle Blvd for ramen noodles made fresh daily, to name just a few foodie detours.

When it comes to seafood, Angelenos were enthusiastically picking up sushi and sashimi with their chopsticks when most of America dismissed raw fish as foreign food not to be trusted. Wanna know the quickest way to start a food fight in LA? Ask Angelenos who they think the city's best sushi chef is. Further south, San Diego may not have an official food, but the entire city obsesses about where to get the best fish tacos. All along SoCal's coast from Malibu to La Jolla, surf-and-sun lovers cruise Hwy 1 in search of the quintessential seafood shack too.

For sustainable choices and items to avoid on local seafood and sushi-bar menus, check the Monterey Bay Aquarium's **Seafood Watch** (www. seafoodwatch. org) website, also available as a free mobile app.

Made in California: Wine, Beer & Beyond

Powerful drink explains a lot about California. Mission vineyards planted in the 18th century gave California a taste for wine, and the mid-19th-century Gold Rush era soon brought a rush on the bar: by 1850, San Francisco had one woman per 100 men, but 500 saloons selling hooch.

Today, California's traditions of wine, beer and cocktails are being reinvented by cult winemakers, craft brewers, micro distillers and saloon revivals. North America's only indigenous beer-brewing style originated right here, and grapes thrive not only in the revered Napa and Sonoma Valleys, but north along the coast to Mendocino and all the way south to Santa Barbara and even San Diego County.

Growing Up on the Grapevine

Mission-grown communion wine was fine for Sundays, but when imported French wine was slow to arrive during California's Gold Rush era, three brothers from Bohemia named Korbel started making their own bubbly in 1882. Today, the Russian River winery they founded has become the biggest US maker of traditional sparkling wines.

Some of California's heritage vines survived federal scrutiny during Prohibition (1920–33), on the specious grounds that grapes were needed for Christian sacramental wines back East – a bootlegging bonanza that kept speakeasies well supplied and saved old vinestock from being torn out by the authorities.

By 1976 California had a lamentable reputation for mass-market plonk and bottled wine spritzers until upstart wineries in Napa Valley and the Santa Cruz Mountains suddenly gained international status. Cabernet Sauvignon from Stag's Leap Wine Cellars and Ridge Monte Bello and Chardonnay from Chateau Montelena beat venerable French wines to take top honors at a landmark blind tasting by international critics now known as the Judgment of Paris.

Nowadays, the Napa and Sonoma Valleys north of San Francisco Bay continue to produce some of California's most prestigious wines, thanks to cool coastal fog, sunny valleys, rocky hillsides and volcanic soils that mimic wine-growing regions across France and Italy.

Sustainable Vines & Wines

During California's dot-com boom of the late 1990s, owning a vineyard became the ultimate Silicon Valley status symbol. Believing the dread phylloxera blight had been conquered with the development of resistant California rootstock AxR1, it seemed like a solid investment – until phylloxera made a catastrophic comeback, and infected vines across the state had to be dug out from the roots. But disaster brought breakthroughs: winemakers rethought their approach from the ground up, replanting organically and trialing biodynamic methods to keep the soil healthy and pests at bay.

Sustainable winemaking processes have now become widespread across California, establishing regional rules for 'green' winemaking and pursuing international Demeter certification for biodynamic wines. Renegade winemakers are experimenting with natural-process winemaking methods such as wild-yeast fermentation, bringing the thrill of the unexpected to their tasting rooms. Owls for pest management, sheep for weed control and solar panels atop LEED-certified buildings are all increasingly common features of California's eco-savvy wineries.

California's Other Wine Countries

Every year California sells more than 500 million gallons of wine – enough to fill over 780 Olympic-sized swimming pools – and California wines now account for nearly 60% of all the wine consumed in the US. What may surprise visitors and wine-tasting neophytes is that most of California's grapes are not grown and most of its wines are not made in the uber-famous Napa and Sonoma Valleys. In fact, California has more than 110 distinct American Viticulture Areas (AVAs), which are known for different varietals and have developed distinct winemaking styles.

Standout lesser-known NorCal wine regions are just a grape's throw (OK, about an hour's drive) from movie-star Napa and Sonoma. In northern Sonoma County, Healdsburg is the gateway to the Alexander Valley, known for its cellar-worthy Cabernet Sauvignon and Chardonnay, while the Dry Creek Valley favors Zinfandel and Sauvignon Blanc. West of Hwy 101 closer to the coast, the Russian River Valley bottles fruit-forward Pinot Noir, accounting for about one in five bottles of that varietal sold statewide. Further north in Mendocino County, follow back roads through the rural Anderson Valley to taste more delicate, soft-spoken Pinot Noir, Riesling and Gewürztraminer.

In SoCal, where ripe avocados, fresh fruits and crunchy nuts grow, there's always something unusual thrown into the salad bowl. Classics invented here include the Cobb salad (first made at Hollywood's Brown Derby Restaurant in the 1930s) and the Chinese chicken salad (popularized in LA during the health-conscious 1970s).

The outlandish film *Sideways* (2004) captures the folly and passion of California's wine-snob scene. It was a critical hit, but California winemakers have a love/hate relationship with it for praising Pinot Noir at Merlot's expense.

CALIFORNIA FLAVOR MADE IN CALIFORNIA: WINE, BEER & BEYOND

WINE-TASTING TIPS

➡ **Swirl** Before tasting a vintage red, swirl your glass to oxygenate the wine and release the flavors.

➡ **Sniff** Dip your nose (without getting it wet) into the glass for a good whiff.

➡ **Swish** Take a swig, and roll it over the front of your teeth and sides of your tongue to get the full effect of complex flavors and textures. After you swallow, breathe out through your nose to appreciate 'the finish.'

➡ **If you're driving or cycling, don't swallow** Sips are hard to keep track of at tastings, so perfect your graceful arc into the spit bucket.

➡ **You don't have to buy anything** No one expects you to buy, especially if you're paying to taste or take a tour; but it is customary to buy a bottle before winery picnics.

➡ **Take it slow & easy** There's no need for speed. Plan to visit three or four wineries a day maximum.

➡ **Don't smoke** Not in the gardens either. Wait until you're off-property.

Down on the Central Coast, the Santa Cruz Mountains produce complex Cabernet Sauvignon and Pinot Noir and shelter some of California's oldest wineries. Around Santa Barbara County, Pinot Noir, Chardonnay and Rhône varietals are blessed with sun, cooling ocean breezes and morning mists. In Paso Robles, one of California's fastest-growing wine regions, risk-taking producers are making the most of their vineyards' sunny dispositions with bold Zinfandel, Syrah and renegade red blends. Around Monterey County and in San Luis Obispo's Edna Valley, smaller family-owned wineries craft crisp Chardonnay and delicate Pinot Noir.

California's southernmost wine region is Temecula, where some vineyards were originally planted by Spanish missionaries in the early 19th century. There, at the edge of the desert outside San Diego, less than 100 miles from Mexico, Rhône and Spanish varietals love the heat.

The movie *Bottle Shock* (2008) takes liberties with the true story of the Judgment of Paris, but it captures the rule-breaking flavor of the early days of winemaking in Sonoma and Napa in the 1970s.

Building Better Brews

Blowing off some steam after work took on new meaning during California's Gold Rush era, when entrepreneurs trying to keep up with the demand for drink started brewing beer at steamy higher temperatures because they lacked ice refrigeration. The result was an amber color, rich, malted flavor and such powerful effervescence that when a keg was tapped, sometimes a mist would rise like steam. San Francisco's Anchor Brewing Company has made its signature Anchor Steam amber ale this way since 1896.

Fast forward to the 21st century: California today boasts nearly 400 craft breweries (more than any other US state), with the most well-established scenes in San Diego and along the North Coast. Snobbery is not just reserved for California's foodies and wine lovers, as many beer drinkers fuss just as much over their monk-brewed triple Belgians and the relative merits of 'hoppiness.' You won't get attitude for ordering beer with a fancy meal – many California sommeliers are happy to suggest beer pairings, and some high-end restaurants offer special tasting menus to accompany signature local beers.

For quality small-batch brews you won't find elsewhere, any self-respecting California city has at least one craft brewery or brewpub of note, while other specialty beer bars proudly offer dozens of California and West Coast microbrews on tap and in bottles. These days, some of California's craft breweries are increasingly experimenting with canning instead of bottling to make their beer cheaper, more ecofriendly and more widely distributed at supermarkets and liquor stores statewide.

The People & Way of Life

In the coastal California dream world, you wake up, have a shot of wheatgrass juice, and roll down to the beach where the surf's up. Lifeguards wave as they go jogging by in bikinis and Speedos. You skateboard down the boardwalk to yoga class, where everyone admires your downward dog. Afterwards, a food truck pulls up with your favorite: *kalbi* (Korean barbecue short-rib) tacos. But wait a sec, can anyone actually make those California dreams come true here?

Living the Dream

Let's keep dreaming. Napping on the beach afterward, you awake to find a casting agent hovering over you, blocking your sunlight, imploring you to star in a movie based on a best-selling comic book. You say you'll have your lawyer look over the papers, and by your lawyer you mean your roommate who plays one on TV. The conversation is cut short when you get a text to meet up with some friends at a bar.

That casting agent was a stress case – she wanted an answer in, like, a month – so you swing by your medical marijuana dispensary and a tattoo parlor to get 'Peace' inscribed on your bicep as a reminder to yourself to stay chill. At the bar, you're called onstage to play a set with the band, and afterward you complain to the drummer about how the casting agent harshed your mellow. She recommends a wine-country getaway, but you're already doing that Big Sur primal-scream chakra-cleansing retreat this weekend.

You head back to your beach house to update your status on your social-networking profile, simultaneously alerting your 10,000 Twitter followers to the major events of the day: 'Killer taco, solid downward dog, peace tattoo, movie offer.' Then you repeat your nightly self-affirmations: 'I am a child of the universe...I am blessed, or at least not a New Yorker... om.'

SoCal inventions include the space shuttle, Mickey Mouse, whitening toothpaste, the hula hoop (or at least its trademark), Barbie, skateboard and surfboard technology, the Cobb salad and the fortune cookie.

Stereotypes vs Reality

Now for the reality check. Any Northern Californian hearing your California dream is bound to get huffy. What, political protests and open-source software inventions don't factor in your dreams? But Southern Californians will also roll their eyes at the silicone-and-spray-tan stereotypes: they didn't create NASA's Jet Propulsion Lab and almost half the world's movies by slacking off.

Still, there is some truth to your California dreamscape. Some 80% of Californians live near the coast rather than inland, even though the beaches aren't always sunny or swimmable (the odds of that increase the further south you go, thus SoCal's inescapable associations with surf, sun and prime-time TV soaps and reality shows). And there's truth in at least one other outdoorsy stereotype: over 60% of Californians admit to having hugged a tree.

Regional Identity

Feel free to believe everything you've ever heard about Californians, just so long as you realize the stereotypes are exaggerated. Sure, tweens snap chewing gum in the shopping malls of the San Fernando Valley north of LA, blond surfers shout 'Dude!' across San Diego beaches, hippies gather for drum circles in San Francisco's Golden Gate Park, and tree huggers toke on joints in the North Coast woods but, all in all, it's hard to peg the coastal population.

San Francisco & North Coast

According to a 2008 Cambridge University study, creativity, imagination, intellectualism and mellowness are all defining personality characteristics of Californians compared with inhabitants of other states. (New Yorkers were found to be 'neurotic' and 'unfriendly.')

In the San Francisco Bay Area, the politics tend to be liberal and the people open-minded, with a strong live-and-let-live ethic and devotion to the Great Outdoors. In overwhelmingly white and wealthy Marin County, civic pride sometimes borders on narcissism. San Francisco is more of a melting pot, but there aren't a lot of lower-income citizens since rents have risen sky-high with the invasion of high-salaried techies. The East Bay, especially Oakland and Berkeley, and San Jose to the south are more ethnically diverse.

Woodsy types live further up the North Coast – think beards and buffalo-plaid flannel. There aren't a lot of people way up there, and there's not a lot of money floating around either (apart from marijuana growers). Conservative radio stations shout on several frequencies, but at the other end of the political spectrum, some of the state's most progressive liberals and borderline eco-fanatics live way up north. If you spot a beat-up old Volvo chugging along the highway, chances are it's running on biodiesel, probably oil recycled from fast-food restaurants.

Central Coast & Santa Barbara

With smaller pockets of population, the hard-to-classify Central Coast starts south of San Francisco near wacky, left-of-center Santa Cruz and stretches all the way down to posh, progressively liberal Santa Barbara. Along the way, coastal Hwy 1 winds past working-class Monterey, made famous by John Steinbeck's novels; the bohemian Big Sur coast, where beatnik artists, hippies and back-to-landers stake their claims; the quaint 'villages' of Carmel-by-the-Sea and Cambria, where the 'newly wed and nearly dead' own multimillion-dollar homes; and the laid-back, liberal college town of San Luis Obispo, over halfway from San Francisco to LA.

THE WAY CALIFORNIANS TALK: IT'S COMPLICATED

Political correctness thrives along the coast. In fact, most people are so determined to get along that it can be hard to find out what somebody really thinks. This increases the further south you go, reaching its Zen-like zenith of 'niceness' in San Diego.

Self-help jargon has thoroughly infiltrated the daily language of coastal Californians. For example, the word 'issue' is constantly bandied about. Generally this is a way to refer to someone else's problems without implying that the person has...well, problems.

The mantra 'Can we all just get along?' flies out the window on busy freeways (almost always called by number, not name, and preceded by 'the' – as in, 'I'm taking the 101 to LA.') Expect to encounter unpredictable drivers with road rage who won't hesitate to cut you off, then flip you the 'bird.'

If someone you just met says, 'Let's get together sometime,' in most parts of the world that means, 'Call me.' Not in California, where it probably means, 'It's been nice talking to you, and now I have to go.' Often the other person never calls and, if you do, you may never hear back. Don't take it too personally.

Wherever you go along the Central Coast, you'll run into people who care passionately about environmental conservation and enthusiastically support local farms, ranchers, winemakers and microbrewers.

Los Angeles & Southern California

Southern California is America at its extremes, with all the good and bad that this entails. Its people are among the nation's richest and poorest, most established and newest arrivals, most refined and roughest, most erudite and most airheaded. What binds them together isn't a shared ethnicity or language, but choosing to be Californian.

Composed of dozens of independent cities, LA is California's most cosmopolitan and racially diverse metro area. Although explosive race-related incidents have received high-profile exposure, as with the riots of 1965 and again in 1992, day-to-day civility between races is the norm. Tensions just as likely reflect the disparity between haves and have-nots, for example, between Beverly Hills mansions and the impoverished inner city of South Central.

Orange County, where beautifully bronzed, buff bodies soak up rays, stretches between LA and San Diego. But make no mistake: it's no beach bums' paradise. Until recent waves of immigration tipped the scales toward liberal voters, the politics 'behind the Orange Curtain' were overwhelmingly conservative. Republicans were welcomed with open arms at $2000-a-plate fundraising dinners, and many people still live in exclusive gated communities that have limited tolerance for outsiders. This conservative sociopolitical trend extends south to San Diego, which also has a sizable US military population.

Lifestyle

Few Californians can afford to spend their entire day tanning, sipping lattes and doing yoga, what with UVA/UVB rays, the rent and gas prices to consider. Most Californians effectively live in their car, commuting an average of 30 minutes each way to work and spending at least $1 out of every $5 earned on car-related expenses. But they have zoomed ahead of the national energy-use curve in their smog-checked cars, buying more hybrid and fuel-efficient cars than any other state.

Few coastal Californians could afford a beach dream-home, and most rent rather than own on a median annual household income of $61,400. Eight of the 10 most expensive US housing markets are in California, and in the two most-expensive areas, Newport Beach and Palo Alto, the average house costs over $1.5 million. Almost half of all Californians reside in cities, but most of the other half live in the suburbs, where the cost of living is just as high, if not higher: San Jose near Silicon Valley has been ranked the most overpriced city in America.

Even so, coastal Californian cities (especially San Francisco and San Diego) consistently top national quality-of-life indexes. Self-help, fitness and body modification are major industries, successfully marketed since the 1970s as 'lite' versions of religious experience – all the agony and ecstasy of the major religious brands, without all those heavy commandments. Exercise and fresh food help keep Californians among the fittest in the nation. Yet almost 250,000 Californians are apparently ill enough to merit prescriptions for medical marijuana. Dispensaries have proliferated up and down the coast, now outnumbering Starbucks coffee shops in some places.

Homelessness is not part of the California dream, but it's a reality for at least 135,000 Californians, representing over 20% of the total US homeless population. The demographic of homeless people is varied, but the largest contingent of homeless Californians are US military veterans, estimated at 31,000 people. What's more, in the 1970s mental health

California Babylon: A Guide to Sites of Scandal, Mayhem and Celluloid in the Golden State (2000) by Kristan Lawson and Anneli Rufus is a guilty-pleasure guide to infamous and bizarre locations throughout the state.

Mike Davis' *City of Quartz* (1990) is an excoriating history of LA and a glimpse into its possible future. Davis and collaborators examine San Diego's underbelly in *Under the Perfect Sun: The San Diego Tourists Never See* (2003).

programs were cut, and state-funded drug treatment programs were dropped in the 1980s, leaving many Californians with mental illnesses and substance-abuse problems no place to go.

Also standing in line at homeless shelters are the working poor, unable to afford to rent even a small apartment on minimum-wage salaries. Rather than addressing the underlying causes of homelessness, some California cities have criminalized loitering, panhandling, even sitting on sidewalks. More than three out of every 1000 Californians already sit in the state's notoriously overcrowded jails, mostly for drug-related crimes.

Population

Immigration

With more than 38 million residents, California is the most populous US state: one in every nine Americans lives here. It's also one of the fastest-growing states, with three of America's 10 biggest cities (Los Angeles, San Diego and San Jose) and over 300,000 newcomers every year. You still don't believe it's crowded here? California's population density is 239 people per sq mile – almost triple the national average.

If you were the average Californian, statistically you'd likely be Latina, aged about 35, living in densely populated LA, Orange or San Diego Counties, and you'd speak more than one language. There's a one in four chance you were born outside the US, and if you were born in the US, the odds are almost 50/50 that you moved here recently from another state.

One of every four immigrants to the US lands in California, with the largest segment coming from Mexico. Most legal immigrants are sponsored by family members who already live here. In addition, an estimated two million undocumented immigrants currently live in California. But this is not a radical new development: before California became a US state in 1850 it was a territory of Mexico and Spain, and historically most of the state's growth has come from immigration.

Multiculturalism

Many coastal Californians idealize their state as an open-minded, easygoing multicultural society that gives everyone a chance to live the American (or Californian) dream. No one should be expected to give up their cultural or personal identity just to become Californian: Chicano pride, Black Power and gay pride all built political bases here.

While equal opportunity may be a shared goal, in practice it's very much a work in progress. Historically, California's Chinatowns, Japantowns and other immigrant enclaves were often created by segregationist sentiment, not by choice. Even racially integrated metro areas of coastal California can be quite segregated in terms of income, language, education and perhaps most surprisingly (given the state's position as a high-tech industry leader in Silicon Valley), internet access.

California's Latino and Asian populations are steadily increasing. More than 30% of the US's Asian American population lives in California, and Latino residents became the state's majority ethnic group in 2014. Latino identity is deeply enmeshed in everyday life in California, from Tejano tunes and taco trucks to J.Lo and Spanish-language TV. Despite being just over 6% of the population and relatively late arrivals with the WWII shipping boom, African Americans have also shaped California's culture, from jazz and hip-hop to fashion, sports and beyond.

New & Old Religions

Religious tolerance is usually the rule. Although Californians are less churchgoing than the American mainstream, and one in five Californians professes no religion at all, it's one of the most religiously diverse states. About a third of residents are Catholic, partly due to a large Latino population, while another third are Protestant. There are also almost two million Muslims and four million Hindus statewide. LA has one of the 10 biggest Jewish communities in the country, and California has the largest number of Buddhists anywhere outside of Asia.

Despite their proportionately small numbers, California's alternative religions and utopian communities dominate the popular imagination, from modern pagans to new-age healers. California made national headlines in the 1960s with gurus from India, in the 1970s with Jim Jones' People's Temple and Erhard Seminars Training (EST), and in the 1990s with Heaven's Gate UFO-millennialist cult in San Diego. The controversial Church of Scientology is still seeking acceptance with celebrity proponents from movie-star Tom Cruise to musician Beck.

California is also a stronghold of fundamentalist and evangelical Christian churches, which have proliferated for the last century, notably in SoCal. In 1924 the world's first broadcast preacher, Aimee Semple McPherson, opened her own radio station to spread the word from LA's Angelus Temple, home of the Foursquare Church, a Pentecostal Christian sect. She pioneered the way for other 20th-century radio and televangelists such as Rick Warren of Orange County's Saddleback Church and the Schuller family of the 'Hour of Power' show, formerly broadcast from the Crystal Cathedral (now called Christ Cathedral) near Anaheim.

> California has thousands of believers in Santeria, a fusion of Catholicism and Yoruba beliefs practiced by West African slaves in the Caribbean and South America. Drop by a *botànica* (herbal folk medicine shop) for charms and candles.

Sports

California has more professional sports teams than any other state. If you doubt that Californians get excited about sports, go ahead and just try to find tickets before they sell out for an Oakland Raiders or San Diego Chargers football, San Francisco Giants or LA Dodgers baseball, or LA Clippers basketball or LA Kings hockey game. You can score less-expensive tickets more easily for pro women's basketball in LA, pro hockey in Anaheim or San Jose, and pro soccer in LA or San Jose.

According to a recent study, Californians are less likely to be couch potatoes than other Americans. Nevertheless, when one of California's professional sports team plays another, the streets are deserted and all eyes glued to the tube. College sports rivalries, such as UC Berkeley's Cal Bears versus Stanford University's Cardinals and the USC Trojans versus the UCLA Bruins, are equally fierce.

> Now an Olympic sport, professional beach volleyball started in Santa Monica in the 1920s. Tournaments are held in SoCal every summer, including at Manhattan Beach in LA's South Bay and at Huntington Beach in Orange County.

The roaring IndyCar race takes over the streets of Long Beach, just south of LA, every April. In San Diego County, Del Mar boasts the state's ritziest horse-racing track, while LA County's historic Santa Anita Racetrack featured in the classic Marx Brothers movie *A Day at the Races* and the short-lived HBO series *Luck*.

Surfing first hit California in 1914, when Irish-Hawaiian surfer George Freeth gave demonstrations at Huntington Beach in Orange County. Today surfing is the coast's coolest spectator sport, with waves sometimes reaching 100ft at the annual Mavericks Invitational competition near Half Moon Bay, south of San Francisco.

Extreme sports date back to the 1970s when skateboarders on LA's Santa Monica–Venice border honed their craft by breaking into dry swimming pools in the backyards of mansions, as chronicled in the 2005 film *Lords of Dogtown*. Extreme sports deities Tony Hawk and Shaun White, both professional skateboarders and X Games champs, hail from San Diego County.

Music & the Arts

Coastal California has long supported thriving music and arts scenes that aren't afraid to be completely independent, even outlandish at times. Californians themselves acknowledge that their music is eclectic, ranging from pitch-perfect opera to off-key punk. Meanwhile, critics have tried and failed to find any consistency in the styles and schools of art and architecture that have flourished here – but taken in the context of the most racially and ethnically diverse US state, that kind of infinite variety makes perfect sense.

Waiting for the Sun: Strange Days, Weird Scenes and the Sound of Los Angeles, by Barney Hoskyns, follows the twists and turns of the SoCal music scene from the Beach Boys to Black Flag.

Music

Much of the American recording industry is based in LA. Today's troubled pop princesses and airbrushed boy bands are only here thanks to all the tuneful revolutions of decades past.

Swing, Jazz, Blues & Soul

In the 1930s and '40s, swingin' big bands sparked a lindy-hopping craze in LA while sailors on shore leave hit San Francisco's underground, integrated jazz clubs. As California's African American community grew with the 'Great Migration' and during the WWII boom, the West Coast blues sound emerged, especially in San Francisco and Oakland.

With Beat poets riffing over improvised bass lines and audiences finger-snapping approval, the cool West Coast jazz of Chet Baker and Dave Brubeck emerged from San Francisco's North Beach neighborhood in the '50s. Meanwhile, in the African American cultural hub of LA's Central Avenue, the hard bop of Charlie Parker and Charles Mingus kept the SoCal scene alive and swinging.

In the 1950s and '60s, doo-wop, rhythm and blues, and soul music were all in steady rotation at nightclubs in South Central LA, considered the 'Harlem of the West.' Soulful singer Sam Cooke started his own hit-making record label, attracting soul and gospel talent to LA.

Early Rock, Folk & Funk

California's first homegrown rock-and-roll talent to make it big in the 1950s was Richie Valens, whose 'La Bamba' was a rockified version of a Mexican folk song. Dick Dale (aka 'The King of the Surf Guitar'), whose recording of 'Miserlou' featured in the movie *Pulp Fiction,* topped the charts with his band the Del-Tones in the early '60s, influencing everyone from the Beach Boys to Jimi Hendrix.

When Joan Baez and Bob Dylan had their Northern California fling in the early '60s, Dylan plugged in his guitar and played folk rock. Janis Joplin and Big Brother & the Holding Company developed their shambling musical stylings in San Francisco, splintering folk rock into psychedelia. Emerging from that same San Francisco mélange, Jefferson Airplane remade Lewis Carroll's children's classic *Alice's Adventures in Wonderland* into the psychedelic hit 'White Rabbit.'

Meanwhile, Jim Morrison and the Doors and the Byrds blew minds on LA's famous Sunset Strip. The epicenter of LA's psychedelic rock scene was the Laurel Canyon neighborhood, just uphill from the Sunset Strip and the legendary Whisky a Go-Go nightclub. The original jam band the Grateful Dead stayed together until guitarist Jerry Garcia's passing in a Marin County rehab clinic in 1995.

The country-influenced pop of The Eagles, Jackson Browne and Linda Ronstadt became America's soundtrack for the early 1970s, joined by the Mexican fusion sounds of Santana from San Francisco and iconic funk bands War from Long Beach and Sly and the Family Stone, who got their groove on in San Francisco before moving to LA.

Punk, Post-Punk & Pop

From the late 1970s to the mid-'80s, LA band X bridged punk and new wave, while local punk radio station KROQ rebelled against the tyranny of pop playlists. San Francisco's punk scene was arty and absurdist, in rare form with Dead Kennedys singer (and future San Francisco mayoral candidate) Jello Biafra howling 'Holiday in Cambodia.'

LA crossover bands such as Bad Religion and Suicidal Tendencies rocked the '80s, as did all-female bands the Bangles and the Go-Gos, new wavers Oingo Boingo and alt-rockers Jane's Addiction. On avant-garde Frank Zappa's 1982 single *Valley Girl*, his 14-year-old daughter Moon Unit taught the rest of America to say 'Omi*g*o-o-od!' like an LA teenager.

By the '90s alternative rock acts such as Beck and Weezer had arrived. Berkeley revived punk in the '90s, including with Grammy Award-winning Green Day. Down south, a key '90s band was ska-punk-alt-rock No Doubt, of Orange County (which later launched the solo career of lead singer Gwen Stefani). SoCal rock stars of the new millennium include San Diego–based pop-punksters Blink 182 and punk-funk sensation Red Hot Chili Peppers, rockin' LA since the '80s.

Rap & Hip-Hop Rhythms

Since the 1980s, LA has been a hotbed for West Coast rap and hip-hop Eazy E, Ice Cube and Dr Dre released the seminal NWA (Niggaz with Attitude) album, *Straight Outta Compton,* in 1989. Death Row Records, cofounded by Dr Dre, has launched megawatt rap talents including Long Beach bad boy Snoop Dog, Warren G, The Game and the late Tupac Shakur, who began his rap career in Marin County of all places.

Throughout the '80s and '90s, California maintained a grassroots hip-hop scene closer to the streets in LA and in Oakland. In the late '90s, the Bay Area birthed the 'hyphy movement,' a reaction against the increasing commercialization of hip-hop, and underground artists like E-40. In LA, no hip-hop band has risen further up the *Billboard* pop charts than the Black Eyed Peas, anchored by Fergie and will.i.am.

On Location: Film & TV

Try to imagine living in a world without Orson Welles whispering 'Rosebud,' Judy Garland clicking her heels three times or the Terminator threatening 'I'll be back.' Shakespeare claimed that 'all the world's a stage,' but in California, it's actually more of a film or TV set. With over 40 TV shows and scores of movies shot here annually, every palm-lined boulevard or beach seems to come with its own IMDb resume.

It's a myth that most movie production ever took place in Hollywood, the social hub of 'the Industry.' Of the major motion-picture studios, only Paramount Pictures is in Hollywood proper, surrounded by block after block of production-related businesses such as lighting and post-production. The high cost of filming has sent location scouts beyond LA's San Fernando Valley (where most movie and TV studios are found) and even north of the border to Canada. A few production companies are based in San Francisco, including Francis Ford Coppola's American Zoetrope, George Lucas' Industrial Light & Magic, and Pixar.

MUSIC & THE ARTS ON LOCATION: FILM & TV

Wanna hear the next breakout indie band before they make it big? Tune into the 'Morning Becomes Eclectic' show on Southern California's KCRW radio station (www.kcrw.com) for live in-studio performances and interviews with the musicians.

Director Alfred Hitchcock set some of his best thrillers in coastal California, including *Vertigo* (1958), with unforgettable shots of San Francisco's Golden Gate Bridge and Muir Woods, and *The Birds* (1963), mostly filmed in Bodega Bay.

HOLLYWOOD'S GOLDEN YEARS

The Industry, as it's called, grew out of the humble orchards of Hollywoodland, a residential neighborhood of Los Angeles, where entrepreneurial moviemakers (including many European immigrants) established studios. In 1913 the first full-length Hollywood feature, a silent Western drama called *The Squaw Man,* was shot by director Cecil B deMille. The silent-movie era gave way to 'talkies' in 1927, the same year that Sid Grauman opened his landmark Chinese Theatre on Hollywood Blvd.

During the 1930s and '40s, American literary lions such as F Scott Fitzgerald, Dorothy Parker, Truman Capote, William Faulkner and Tennessee Williams did stints as Hollywood screenwriters. In the 1950s, during the anti-communist 'Red Scare' of the Cold War era, the federal government's House Un-American Activities Committee investigated and subsequently blacklisted many Hollywood actors, directors and screenwriters, some of whom left for self-imposed exile in Europe, never to return.

With increasing regularity, Hollywood films feature California as both a setting and a topic and, in some cases, almost as a character. LA especially loves to turn the camera on itself, often from a film-noir angle. Meanwhile, SoCal has become a versatile backdrop for both edgy cable TV dramas and vapid reality-TV shows.

Literature

Californians read more than movie scripts: they make up the largest market for books in the US, and read much more than the national average. You've probably already read books by Californians without knowing it: Ray Bradbury's 1950s dystopian classic *Fahrenheit 451,* Alice Walker's Pulitzer Prize–winning *The Color Purple,* Ken Kesey's quintessential '60s novel *One Flew Over the Cuckoo's Nest,* Maxine Hong Kingston's *The Woman Warrior,* Michael Chabon's *The Amazing Adventures of Kavalier and Clay* or something by Bay Area publisher McSweeney's.

A young cartoonist named Walt Disney arrived in LA in 1923, and five years later had his first breakout hit, *Steamboat Willie,* starring a mouse named Mickey, which eventually spawned the entire Disney empire.

Arguably the most influential author to ever emerge from coastal California was social realist John Steinbeck. Published in the 1930s, his first California novel, *Tortilla Flat,* takes place in Monterey's Mexican American community, while his masterpiece, *The Grapes of Wrath,* tells of the struggles of migrant farm workers during the Great Depression.

In the 1930s, San Francisco and LA became capitals of pulp detective novels, which were often turned into Hollywood noir films. Dashiell Hammett *(The Maltese Falcon)* made San Francisco's fog a sinister character. The king of hard-boiled crime writers was Raymond Chandler *(The Big Sleep),* who thinly disguised Santa Monica as shadowy Bay City. In the 1990s, a contemporary renaissance of noir crime fiction was masterminded by James Ellroy *(LA Confidential)* and Walter Mosley *(Devil in a Blue Dress),* whose Easy Rawlins novels are set in South Central LA.

Beginning in the 1950s, the Beat Generation of writers fired up San Francisco's North Beach literary scene, revolving around City Lights Bookstore founded by poet Lawrence Ferlinghetti. Allen Ginsberg's epic poem *Howl* was put on trial for obscenity in 1957, while Jack Kerouac's renegade novel *On the Road* became a cult classic. In the early 1970s, Charles Bukowski's semiautobiographical novel *Post Office* captured down-and-out Downtown LA, while Richard Vasquez's *Chicano* took a dramatic look at LA's Latino barrio. Up north, the serial-style *Tales of the City,* by Armistead Maupin, was a frothy taste of 1970s San Francisco, following the lives of colorful characters, gay and straight.

Few contemporary writers nail California culture as well as Joan Didion. She's best known for her collections of nonfiction essays, *Slouching Towards Bethlehem* and *The White Album,* which take a caustic look at

1960s California flower power with a personal slant. Tom Wolfe also put '60s San Francisco in perspective with *The Electric Kool-Aid Acid Test*, which follows Ken Kesey's band of Merry Pranksters, who began their acid-laced 'magic bus' journey near Santa Cruz.

Architecture

California's architecture was postmodern before the word existed, having long adapted international styles to fit the climate and available materials. Today, unexpected elements are almost everywhere you look: Mayan art-deco facades in LA, chinoiserie streetlamps in San Francisco, English country cottages in Carmel-by-the-Sea, and Japanese hipped roofs on bungalows in Pasadena and Oakland.

Spanish Missions & Victorian Queens

In the late 18th century, the first Spanish missions were built around courtyards, using materials that Native Californians and colonists found on hand: adobe, limestone and grass. Many missions crumbled into disrepair under Mexican rule in the early 19th century, but the style remained practical for the climate and many Californian settlers later adapted it into the rancho adobe style.

Once the Gold Rush got rolling, California's nouveau riche imported materials to construct grand mansions matching European fashions, and raised the stakes with ornamental excess. Many millionaires favored the gilded Queen Anne style. Outrageous examples of Victorian architecture, including 'painted ladies' and 'gingerbread' houses, are seen in San Francisco, Ferndale and Eureka.

Many turn-of-the-20th-century architects rejected frilly Victorian styles in favor of simpler, classical lines. Spanish Colonial Revival architecture, also known as Mission Revival style, hearkened back to early California missions with restrained and functional details: arched doors and windows, long covered porches, fountain courtyards, solid walls and red-tile roofs. Several SoCal train depots showcase this style, as does San Diego's Balboa Park and downtown Santa Barbara.

Arts and Crafts to Art Deco

Simplicity and harmony were hallmarks of California's early-20th-century Arts and Crafts style. Influenced by Japanese design principles and England's Arts and Crafts movement, its woodwork and handmade touches marked a deliberate departure from the Industrial Revolution's mechanization. Pasadena architects Charles and Henry Greene and the Bay Area's Bernard Maybeck and Julia Morgan popularized the versatile one-story bungalow, with overhanging eaves and sleeping porches.

Cosmopolitan California couldn't be limited to any one set of international influences. In the 1920s, the international art-deco style took elements from the ancient world – Mayan glyphs, Egyptian pillars, Babylonian ziggurats – and flattened them into modern motifs to cap stark facades and outline skyscrapers, notably in LA and downtown Oakland. Later, streamline moderne kept decoration to a minimum and mimicked the aerodynamic look of ocean liners and airplanes.

California Modernism

Clothing-optional California has never been shy about showcasing its assets. Starting in the 1960s, California embraced the stripped-down, glass-wall aesthetics of the International Style championed by Bauhaus architects Walter Gropius, Ludwig Mies van der Rohe and Le Corbusier.

In LA, Austrian-born Richard Schindler and Richard Neutra adapted this minimalist modern style to residential houses with open floorplans and floor-to-ceiling windows perfectly suited to SoCal's see-and-be-seen

For a memorable trip through California, join contemporary authors including Pico Iyer and Michael Chabon in *My California: Journeys by Great Writers*. Proceeds from purchases via Angel City Press (www.angelcitypress.com) support the California Arts Council.

Jim Heimann's *California Crazy and Beyond: Roadside Vernacular Architecture* is a romp through the zany, whimsical building-blocks world of California, where lemonade stands look like giant lemons and motels are shaped like tepees.

culture. Neutra and Schindler were also influenced by Frank Lloyd Wright, who designed LA's not quite successful Hollyhock House in a style he dubbed 'California Romanza.'

Together with Charles and Ray Eames, Neutra contributed to the experimental Case Study Houses, several of which still jut out of the LA landscape and are used as filming locations like in *LA Confidential*.

Postmodern Evolutions

True to its anti-establishment nature, California veered away from strict high modernism to add unlikely postmodern shapes to the local landscape. In 1997 Richard Meier made his mark on West LA with the Getty Center, a cresting white wave of a building on a sunburned hilltop. Canadian-born Frank Gehry relocated to Santa Monica, and his billowing, sculptural style for Downtown LA's Walt Disney Concert Hall winks cheekily at shipshape streamline moderne.

Into the 21st century, San Francisco has championed a brand of postmodernism by Pritzker Prize–winning architects that magnifies and mimics California's great outdoors, especially in Golden Gate Park. Swiss architects Herzog & de Meuron clad the MH de Young Memorial Museum in copper, which will slowly oxidize green to match its park setting. Nearby, Renzo Piano literally raised the roof on sustainable design at the LEED platinum-certified California Academy of Sciences, capped by a living-roof garden.

Visual Arts

The earliest European artists to capture California were trained cartographers accompanying Western explorers, although their images of California as an island show more imagination than scientific rigor. This mythologizing tendency continued throughout California's Gold Rush, as artists alternated between caricatures of Wild West debauchery and manifest-destiny propaganda urging pioneers to settle the golden West. The completion of the transcontinental railroad in 1869 brought an influx of romantic painters, who painted epic California wilderness landscapes. In the early 20th century, homegrown colonies of California impressionist plein air painters emerged at Laguna Beach and Carmel-by-the-Sea.

With the invention of photography, the improbable truth of California's landscape and its inhabitants was revealed. Pirkle Jones saw expressive potential in California landscape photography after WWII, while San Francisco–born Ansel Adams' sublime photographs had already started doing justice to Yosemite. Adams founded Group f/64 with Edward Weston from Carmel and Imogen Cunningham in San Francisco. Berkeley-based Dorothea Lange turned her unflinching lens on the plight of Californian migrant workers in the Great Depression, and Japanese Americans forced to enter internment camps in WWII.

As the postwar American West became crisscrossed with freeways and divided into planned communities, Californian painters captured the abstract forms of manufactured landscapes on canvas. In San Francisco, Richard Diebenkorn and David Park became leading proponents of Bay Area Figurative Art, while sculptor Richard Serra captured urban aesthetics in massive, rusting monoliths resembling ship prows and industrial Stonehenges. Pop artists captured SoCal's ethos of conspicuous consumerism through Wayne Thiebaud's still-life gumball machines, British émigré David Hockney's acrylic paintings and Ed Ruscha's canvas and film studies.

To see coastal California's contemporary art at its most experimental, browse the SoCal gallery scenes in Downtown LA and Culver City, then check out San Francisco's Mission District and SOMA neighborhood.

During the Great Depression, murals came to define Californian cityscapes. Mexican muralists Diego Rivera, David Alfaro Siqueiros and José Clemente Orozco sparked an outpouring of murals across LA that today number in the thousands.

Redwoods & Wild Things

From misty redwood forests and rocky headlands to sunny beaches and arid canyons, coastal California is home to a bewildering variety of ecosystems. In fact, 30% of all plant and reptile species and almost half of all bird and mammal species that inhabit the USA are found in California, which boasts the highest biodiversity in North America. This is a land of record-breaking superlatives, starting with the planet's tallest trees.

Native Trees & Wildflowers

Imagine how in centuries past almost all of California's coast, from the Oregon border south to Santa Cruz, was covered with stands of coast redwoods. Today less than 5% of these old-growth forests, whose complexity has been found by scientists to match that of tropical rainforests, remain. Officially the world's tallest trees, coast redwoods are those towering giants with spongy red bark, flat needles and olive-sized cones that rely on fog as their primary water source. On the damp forest floor beneath them, look for western sword ferns, redwood sorrel and velvety green mosses.

Other rare native tree species in coastal California include Monterey and Torrey pines, gnarled trees that have adapted to harsh coastal conditions such as high winds, sparse rainfall and sandy, stony soils. They too derive much of their water from the billowing coastal fog. Today, Torrey pines grow only at Torrey Pines State Reserve near San Diego and in the Channel Islands, home to dozens more endemic plant species. On Catalina Island, you'll also find Catalina ironwood and mahogany trees and the Catalina live-forever (a succulent).

California's myriad flowering plants are both flamboyant and subtle. Many species are so obscure or similar-looking that only a botanist could tell them apart. But in spring you end up with riotous carpets of wildflowers. Those famous 'golden hills' of California are actually the result of many plants drying up in preparation for the long, dry summer. Here plants have adapted to long periods of almost no rain by growing prolifically during California's mild wet winters, springing to life with the first rains in fall and blooming as early as February.

Marine Mammals

Spend even one day along California's coast and you may spot pods of bottle-nosed dolphins and porpoises swimming and doing acrobatics in the ocean. Playful sea otters and harbor seals typically stick closer to shore, especially around public piers and protected bays. Since the 1989 earthquake, loudly barking sea lions have been piling up on San Francisco's Pier 39, much to the delight of ogling tourists. Other excellent places to see wild pinnipeds include Point Lobos State Natural Reserve just south of Monterey, Point Reyes National Seashore in Marin County, and Channel Islands National Park, offshore south of Santa Barbara.

In 2006 the world's tallest tree was discovered in a remote area of Redwood National Park (its location is kept secret to protect it). It's named Hyperion and stands a whopping 379ft tall.

Peak mating season for northern elephant seals along the Pacific coast just happens to coincide with Valentine's Day (February 14).

NATIVE WILDLIFE VS ALIEN INVADERS

Although the staggering numbers of land and sea animals, boundless virgin forests and wildflower fields that greeted California's early settlers are now mostly a thing of the past, it's still possible to see wildlife thriving along the coast in the right places and at the right times of year, from emerald hillsides blanketed by golden poppies to migratory gray whales. However, some of coastal California's endemic species of flora and fauna are but shadow populations today, hovering at the edge of survival, pushed up against the state's ever-burgeoning human population.

Once a biodiverse 'island' protected by the Pacific Ocean and the Sierra Nevada Mountains, California has been overrun by alien species introduced by foreigners ever since the first Spanish colonists arrived in the late 18th century, right up through the Gold Rush era and post-WWII boom. Significantly altered and compromised habitats, both on land and water, have made this coast an easy target for invasive plants and animals, including highly aggressive species that damage both California's ecosystems and the economy.

In San Francisco Bay alone, one of the most important estuaries in the world, there are now over 230 alien species choking the aquatic ecosystem and in some areas they already comprise as much as 95% of the total biomass. Pushing out native flora all along the coast, ice plant – a ropy green ground cover with purple-and-white flowers that creeps over beach dunes and takes over headlands – originally came from South Africa. Volunteers all along the coast are kept busy pulling out invasive plants and restoring native flora.

During construction of California's 19th-century railways, fast-growing eucalyptus trees were imported from Australia to make railroad ties, but the wood proved poor and split when driven through with a stake. The trees now grow like weeds, fueling summertime wildfires with their flammable, explosive seed capsules. Even California's snails come from far away, brought here in the 1850s from France to produce *escargot*. Now they're everywhere, along with Atlantic crabs, which destroy native oyster beds.

Out of necessity but also by choice, California has become a leader in wildlife and ecosystem conservation. The **Monterey Bay National Marine Sanctuary** (http://montereybay.noaa.gov) harbors North America's deepest underwater canyon and protects hundreds of species of fish and over 30 species of marine mammals, including migratory whales. All along the coast, protecting and restoring native habitats, tagging and monitoring endangered wildlife, and innovating captive-breeding-and-release programs are showing hopeful results.

If you can't tell a tufted sea lion from a whiskered harbor seal, pick up one of the excellent *California Natural History Guides* published by the University of California Press (www.california-naturalhistory.com), which are compact enough to carry in a day pack.

Once threatened by extinction, gray whales now migrate in growing numbers along California's coast between December and April. Adult whales live up to 60 years, are longer than a city bus and can weigh up to 40 tons, making quite a splash when they dive below or leap out of the water. Every year they travel from summertime feeding grounds in the arctic Bering Sea, down to southern breeding grounds off Baja California, and then all the way back up again, making a 6000-mile round trip.

Northern elephant seals have made a remarkable comeback along California's coast, after being hunted almost to extinction by the late 19th century for their oil-rich blubber. In winter, the behemoth bulls engage in mock – and sometimes real – combat, all the while making odd guttural grunts, as their harems of female seals and young pups look on. Año Nuevo State Reserve, north of Santa Cruz, is a protected breeding ground, and there's a smaller rookery at Point Reyes, north of San Francisco. California's biggest colony of northern elephant seals hauls out by Point Piedras Blancas near Hearst Castle, south of Big Sur.

Land Mammals

California's most symbolic land animal – it graces the state flag – is the grizzly bear. Grizzlies once roamed California's beaches and grasslands in large numbers, eating everything from whale carcasses to acorns, but were extirpated in the 1920s after relentless persecution. All that remains now are the grizzlies' smaller cousins, black bears. Despite their name, their fur ranges in color from black to dark brown, cinnamon or even blond. These burly omnivores, who feed on berries, nuts, roots, grasses, insects, eggs, small mammals and fish, are rarely seen along the coast, preferring to live in mountainous forests further inland.

As foreign settlers moved into California in the 1800s, many other large mammals fared almost as poorly as grizzly bears. Immense herds of tule elk were hunted to near-extinction by the 1860s. A small remnant herd of tule elk was moved to Point Reyes National Seashore in the 1970s, where the population has since rebounded. Much larger Roosevelt elk once ranged from San Francisco Bay all the way into Canada, but by the 1920s there were only 15 left. Today, species conservation efforts have increased the population to more than 1000 Roosevelt elk, protected by the North Coast's Redwood National and State Parks.

Mountain lions (also called cougars) hunt throughout California, especially in woodsy areas teeming with deer. Solitary lions, which can grow 8ft in length and weigh 175lb, are formidable predators. A few attacks on humans have occurred, usually where human encroachment pushes hungry lions to their limits – for example, at the boundaries between wilderness and rapidly developing suburbs.

The Audubon Society's California chapter website (http://ca.audubon.org) offers helpful birding checklists, descriptions of key species statewide and a newsy Pacific Flyway blog (www.audublog.org).

Birds & Butterflies

California lies on major migratory routes for over 350 species of birds, which either pass through the state or linger during winter. It's an essential stop on the migratory Pacific Flyway between Alaska and Mexico, and almost half of North America's bird species use the state's coastal and inland refuges for rest and refueling. Migration peaks during the wetter winter season, but you can spot an enormous variety of birds year-round at California's coastal beaches, estuaries, wetlands and bays.

Year-round avian residents along California's coast include gulls, grebes, terns, cormorants, sandpipers and little sanderlings that chase receding waves along the shore, looking for critters in the freshly turned sand. A few of California's beaches are closed between March and September to protect endangered western snowy plovers, who lay their eggs in exposed ground scrapes in the sand. Snowy plovers are easily frightened by humans, dogs and noisy off-highway vehicles (OHV), which can cause them to run off and abandon their eggs to burn in the sun.

As you drive along the Big Sur coast, look skyward to spot the largest flying bird in North America, the endangered California condor, which also soars over Pinnacles National Monument and the Los Padres National Forest. Also keep an eye out for regal bald eagles, which have regained a foothold on the Channel Islands, and sometimes spend their winters at Big Bear Lake outside LA. The northern spotted owl, today a threatened species due to destructive logging practices, is protected inside the North Coast's Headwaters Forest Reserve near Eureka.

Another iconic species that takes flight in coastal California, monarch butterflies are gorgeous orange creatures that follow amazing long-distance, multi-generational migration patterns in search of milkweed, their only source of food. Tens of thousands of monarchs hibernate in coastal California during winter, notably along the Central Coast at Santa Cruz, Pacific Grove, Pismo Beach and around Santa Barbara.

Earthquakes & the Land

The third-biggest state after Alaska and Texas, California covers over 155,000 sq miles, making it larger than 85 of the world's smallest nations. It's bordered to the north by woodsy Oregon, to the east by desert-dry Nevada and Arizona, to the south by subtropical Baja California, Mexico, and by 840 miles of Pacific shoreline to the west.

Curious about all the rumbling along the San Andreas Fault? Check out *A Land in Motion* by Michael Collier for a photographic overview of the subject, or get the bejeezus scared out of you by Marc Reisner's part journalistic, part imaginative book, *A Dangerous Place: California's Unsettling Fate.*

Shake, Rattle 'n' Roll

California is a complex geological landscape formed from fragments of rock and earth crust scraped together as the North American continent drifted westward over hundreds of millions of years. The crumpled Coast Ranges, the depressed Central Valley and the still-rising Sierra Nevada mountains all provide evidence of gigantic geological forces exerted as the continental and ocean plates crushed together.

Everything changed about 25 million years ago, when ocean plates stopped colliding and instead started sliding against each other. Today California sits on one of the world's major earthquake fault zones, at the dramatic meeting of two moving plates: the eastern edge of the Pacific Plate, made up of the Pacific Ocean floor and much of California's coastline, and the western edge of the continental North American Plate.

The primary boundary between these two plates is the massive San Andreas Fault, which runs for over 650 miles and has spawned numerous smaller faults that extend their treacherous fingers toward California's shoreline. Because this contact zone doesn't slide smoothly, but catches and slips irregularly, it rattles California with an ongoing succession of tremors and earthquakes.

California's Monster Quakes

In 1906, California's most famous earthquake measured 7.8 on the Richter scale and demolished San Francisco, leaving more than 3000 people dead. The Bay Area made headlines again in 1989 when the Loma Prieta earthquake (magnitude 7.1), which lasted just 15 seconds, caused a section of the Bay Bridge and I-880 in Oakland to collapse. Today, you can walk right up to the epicenter of the Loma Prieta quake in the Forest of Nisene Marks State Park, south of Santa Cruz.

Los Angeles' last 'big one' was in 1994, when the Northridge quake (magnitude 6.7) caused parts of the freeways and the scoreboard at Anaheim Stadium to fall down. With its epicenter in the San Fernando Valley, the Northridge quake's seismic waves were felt as far away as Las Vegas, Nevada. Dozens of deaths, thousands of injuries and estimated damages of $25 billion make it the most costly quake in California history.

Lay of the Land

California's northern boundary lies at the same Mediterranean latitude as Rome, Italy, while its southern edge lies at the same desert latitude

EARTHQUAKE SAFETY TIPS

Earthquakes happen all the time in California, but most are so tiny they are detectable only by sensitive seismological instruments. In the unlikely event that you're caught in a serious shaker:

➡ If indoors, get under a desk or table or stand in a doorway.

➡ Protect your head and stay clear of windows, mirrors or anything that might fall.

➡ Don't head for elevators or go running into the street.

➡ If you're in a shopping mall or large public building, expect the alarm and/or sprinkler systems to come on.

➡ If outdoors, get away from buildings, trees and power lines.

➡ If you're driving, pull over to the side of the road away from bridges, overpasses and power lines. Stay inside the car until the shaking stops.

➡ If you're on a sidewalk near buildings, duck into a doorway to protect yourself from falling bricks, glass and debris.

➡ Prepare for aftershocks.

➡ Turn on the radio and listen for bulletins.

➡ Use the telephone only if absolutely necessary. Keep cell (mobile) phone networks free for emergency services.

as Tel Aviv, Israel. Much of the state remains a biological and geological island cut off from the rest of North America by the Sierra Nevada range.

Much of California's coast is fronted by rugged coastal mountains that capture life-giving moisture from summertime fog and winter's water-laden storms. Called the Coast Ranges, these mountain chains run north and south along most of the shoreline, plunging west into the wild Pacific Ocean and rolling east toward the sea-level Central Valley.

Over 120in of rain a year fall in the northernmost reaches of the Coast Ranges and, in some places, persistent summer fog contributes another 12in of precipitation. Nutrient-rich soils and abundant moisture foster forests of towering trees (where they haven't been logged, that is), including stands of coast redwoods growing as far south as Big Sur and all the way north into Oregon.

San Francisco divides the Coast Ranges roughly in half, with the foggy North Coast remaining sparsely populated. The Central and Southern California coasts have a balmier climate and, as a result, many, many more people, especially in urban areas sprawling from LA to San Diego. South of Santa Barbara, the Coast Ranges are linked to the mightier Sierra Nevada by the Transverse Ranges, one of the USA's only east–west mountain ranges.

Southern California has a hodgepodge of smaller mountain ranges and desert basins. The arid Los Angeles Basin fronts the ocean and is partly surrounded by mountains. San Diego, on the edge of another plateau around 120 miles south of LA, borders Tijuana, Mexico. More mountains just east of San Diego continue south into Mexico and down the spine of northern Baja California.

According to the US Geological Survey, the odds of a magnitude 6.7 or greater earthquake hitting California within the next 30 years is 99.7%. During the same time, sea levels are expected to rise up to 2ft by 2050, due to global warming.

National & State Parks

Most Californians rank outdoor recreation as vital to their quality of life. Statewide, the amount of preserved lands has steadily grown due to important pieces of legislation passed since the 1960s. The landmark 1976 California Coastal Act saved the coastline from further development,

COASTAL CALIFORNIA'S TOP 10 NATIONAL & STATE PARKS

PARK	FEATURES	ACTIVITIES	BEST TIME
Big Sur's State Parks	vertical sea cliffs, pocket beaches, redwood forests, waterfalls, California condors, migrating whales	hiking, horseback riding, beachcombing, bird-watching, swimming	Apr-Oct
Channel Islands National Park	rocky islands with steep cliffs, elephant seals, sea lions, otters, foxes, wildflowers	snorkeling, diving, kayaking, hiking, bird-watching	Apr-Oct
Crystal Cove State Park	sandy beaches, tide pools, woodlands, mule deer, bobcats, great horned lizards, hermit crabs, hummingbirds	swimming, surfing, snorkeling, diving, hiking, mountain biking	Jun-Sep
Golden Gate National Recreation Area	beaches, tide pools, grassy headlands, sand dunes, wetlands, harbor seals, sea lions, migratory whales, brown pelicans, peregrine falcons, Mission Blue butterflies	hiking, cycling, mountain biking, bird-watching, swimming, surfing, kayaking, self-guided historical site tours	May-Sep
Mendocino Headlands State Park	coastal bluffs, rugged beaches, wildflowers, migrating whales	nature walks, beachcombing, hiking, kayaking, fishing	May-Sep
Muir Woods National Monument	towering stands of old-growth redwood trees, black-tailed deer, banana slugs, northern spotted owls	nature walks, hiking	Apr-Oct
Point Lobos State Natural Reserve	rocky headlands, beaches, coves, grassy meadows, woodlands, seals, sea lions, sea otters, migratory whales	hiking, bird-watching, snorkeling, scuba diving, kayaking	Apr-Oct
Point Reyes National Seashore	windswept beaches, lagoons, grassy headlands, tule elk, northern elephant seals, migrating whales	hiking, bird-watching, kayaking, mountain-biking	May-Oct
Redwood National & State Parks	virgin redwood groves, fern forests, pristine beaches, Roosevelt elk, bald eagles, Steller sea lions	hiking, backpacking, kayaking, cycling, scenic drives	May-Sep
Torrey Pines State Natural Reserve	rugged ocean bluffs, saltwater marsh and lagoon, rare Torrey pine tree forest, great blue herons, migrating whales	hiking, bird-watching, swimming, surfing, fishing	Apr-Oct

while the controversial 1994 California Desert Protection Act angered many ranchers, miners and off-roaders.

Today **California State Parks** (www.parks.ca.gov) protects nearly a third of the state's coastline, along with redwood forests, lakes, canyons, waterfalls, wildlife preserves and historical sites. In recent years, federal and state budget shortfalls and chronic underfunding of California's parks have been partly responsible for widespread closures, limited visitor services and increased park-entry and outdoor recreation fees. This continually happens, even though it's in California's economic best interests to keep its parks in business, since revenues from recreational tourism consistently outpace competing 'natural resource extraction' industries such as mining.

Unfortunately, some of California's parks are being loved to death. Too many visitors stresses the environment, and it's increasingly difficult to balance public access with conservation. At popular state beaches in Southern California during summer, it's almost impossible to find a parking space, let alone space on the sand. To avoid the biggest crowds and reduce your impact on parks, try to visit outside of peak season (usually summer) and take public transportation or cycle there.

Other natural areas of coastal California, including those managed by the **National Park Service** (www.nps.gov/state/CA), may go relatively untouched most of the year, which means you won't have to reserve permits, campsites or lodging many months in advance. Just inland from the coast, several national forests in California, managed by the **US Forest Service** (USFS; www.fs.fed.us/r5), are less-trammeled areas worth exploring, including in Big Sur. National wildlife refuges (NWR), especially favored by bird-watchers, are run by the **US Fish & Wildlife Service** (USFWS; www.fws.gov/refuges). More remote wilderness tracts, including the Lost Coast and the Carrizo Plain, are overseen by the **Bureau of Land Management** (BLM; www.blm.gov/ca/st/en.html).

Take a virtual field trip all around the state courtesy of the myriad links compiled online by the California Geological Survey (www.conservation.ca.gov/cgs/geotour).

Taking Steps Toward Sustainability

In California, rapid development and uncontrolled or unplanned growth have often come at great environmental cost. Starting in 1849, Gold Rush miners tore apart the land in their frenzied quest for a lucky strike, ultimately sending more than 1.5 billion tons of debris, and incalculable amounts of poisonous mercury, downstream into the Central Valley, where rivers and streams became clogged and polluted.

Today, tons of particulate matter spew into the air from automobile and diesel emissions, reducing air quality and hiding the sun in urban areas, especially around LA. The ocean is overfished, open-space land is disappearing beneath asphalt and landfills, and tankers occasionally leak oil into the sea. California is now the most-populous US state – with over 70% of residents living in coastal counties – which puts a tremendous strain on its finite natural resources.

So, is this paradise lost? Not yet. California's conservationists and environmental activists, biodynamic farmers and vineyard owners, high-tech innovators in the renewable energy and alternative fuel industries, and progressive-minded legislators, civic leaders and voters are all taking steps together to ensure a greener future for the Golden State.

Water, Water, Where?

Water, or the lack thereof, has long been at the heart of California's epic environmental struggles and catastrophes. Despite campaigning by the state's greatest environmental champion, John Muir, the Tuolumne River was dammed in the 1920s, flooding the Hetch Hetchy Valley inside Yosemite National Park, so that the burgeoning population of San Francisco could have drinking water. Likewise, the diversion of water to Los Angeles from the Eastern Sierra via aqueducts starting in 1913 has contributed to the destruction of Owens Lake and its fertile wetlands, and the degradation of Mono Lake.

Statewide the damming of rivers and capture of water for houses and farms has drained marshlands and destroyed countless salmon runs, including on Native Californian tribal lands along the North Coast. Dams along the Colorado River send millions of acre-feet of water per year to San Diego and much of the rest of Southern California via hundreds of miles of aqueducts, even as they wreak havoc on the local ecosystem and decimate native fish populations.

Regardless of where the water comes from, there never seems to be enough to satisfy the demand of thirsty Californians. Unusually warm temperatures caused by climate change and persistent droughts are critically affecting the state's winter snowpack. If it doesn't snow heavily enough in the Sierra Nevada in winter, there won't be enough snow left in spring to melt and fill the reservoirs that supply coastal cities. Homeowners are slowly learning to conserve water; for example, with outdoor xeriscaping and dry gardens that don't require irrigation. And you can too: look for low-flow showerheads and low-flush toilets in hotel rooms.

Cleaner Air, Land & Energy

Marc Reisner's must-read *Cadillac Desert: the American West and Its Disappearing Water* examines the contentious, sometimes violent, water wars that gave rise to modern California, including coastal cities like Los Angeles.

Although air quality in California has improved markedly in past decades, it still ranks among the worst in the USA. Along much of the coast, air pollution is alleviated by the prevailing westerly winds that blow clean air in off the Pacific. But travel inland, especially across the LA Basin, and the air often takes on a thick haze, obscuring vistas and creating health hazards.

Today, California leads the nation in automobile emissions control and ownership of hybrid and alternative-fuel vehicles, from Priuses and plug-ins to biodiesel cars that chug along on recycled fast-food cooking oil. Toxic clean-up and reclamation of abandoned industrial areas and military sites has also created urban 'green spaces' that help Californians breathe more easily.

Recently, voters have funded construction of solar-power plants, which already produce 500 megawatts of electricity statewide, and there's even talk of harnessing the tremendous tidal flows of the Pacific to generate more 'clean' energy. By law, California's electricity utilities must get 33% of their energy from renewable resources by 2020, the most ambitious target of any US state so far.

Coastal California cities are leading the way when it comes to the eco-conscious mantra 'reduce, reuse, recycle.' Take San Francisco, for example, which plans to recycle *all* of its trash by the year 2020 and has already instituted citywide composting of perishable organic matter under its 'landfill avoidance' policy.

Survival Guide

Directory A–Z

Accommodations

Budget-conscious accommodations include campgrounds, hostels and motels. Midrange motels and hotels generally offer better value for money.

Amenities

➡ In Southern California, nearly all lodgings have air-conditioning, but in Northern California where it rarely gets hot, the opposite is true. In coastal areas as far south as Santa Barbara, only fans may be provided.

➡ Some accommodations offer online computer terminals for guests. A fee may apply (eg at full-service business centers inside hotels).

➡ There may be a fee for wireless internet, especially for in-room access. Look for free wi-fi hot spots in hotel public areas (eg lobby, poolside).

➡ Many lodgings are now exclusively nonsmoking. Where they still exist, smoking rooms are often left unrenovated and in undesirable locations. Expect a hefty 'cleaning fee'

($100 or more) if you light up in designated nonsmoking rooms.

Seasons & Reservations

➡ High season in coastal California is from June to August.

➡ Demand and prices spike even higher around major holidays and for festivals, when some properties may impose multiday minimum stays.

➡ Reservations are recommended for weekend and holiday travel year-round, and every day of the week during high season.

➡ Bargaining may be possible for walk-in guests without reservations, especially at off-peak times.

Rates & Discounts

➡ Quoted rates typically do not include lodging taxes, averaging over 12%.

➡ Generally, midweek rates are lower except at urban hotels geared toward business travelers, which lure leisure travelers with weekend deals.

➡ Discount membership cards (eg AAA, AARP)

may get you about 10% off standard rates at participating hotels and motels.

➡ Look for freebie ad magazines packed with hotel and motel discount coupons at gas stations, highway rest areas and tourist offices.

B&Bs

If you want an atmospheric alternative to impersonal motels and hotels, bed-and-breakfast inns typically inhabit fine old Victorian houses or other heritage buildings, bedecked with floral wallpaper and antique furnishings. People who like privacy may find B&Bs too intimate.

Rates often include a cooked breakfast, but occasionally breakfast is *not* provided (never mind what the name 'B&B' suggests). Amenities vary widely, but rooms with TV and telephone are the exception; the cheapest units share bathrooms.

Standards are high at places certified by the **California Association of Boutique & Breakfast Inns** (www.cabbi.com). Quality varies wildly at hosted and DIY vacation rental properties listed with **Airbnb** (www.airbnb.com) and **Vacation Rentals By Owner** (www.vrbo.com).

Most B&Bs require advance reservations and don't accept drop-in guests; always call ahead. Smoking is generally prohibited and

---

BOOK YOUR STAY ONLINE

For more accommodation reviews by Lonely Planet authors, check out http://lonelyplanet.com/hotels/. You'll find independent reviews, as well as recommendations on the best places to stay. Best of all, you can book online.

children are usually not welcome. Expect minimum-stay requirements, especially on weekends and in high season.

Camping

In coastal California, camping is much more than just a cheap way to spend the night. The best campsites let you wake up on the beach or under a canopy of redwood trees. If you didn't bring your own tent, you can buy (and occasionally rent) camping gear at outdoor outfitters and sporting-goods shops in most cities and some towns.

Most public and private campgrounds in coastal areas are open year-round, including the following types:

Primitive campgrounds Usually campsites have fire pits, picnic tables and access to drinking water and vault toilets; most common in national forests (USFS) and on Bureau of Land Management (BLM) land.

Developed campgrounds Typically found in state and national parks, these offer more amenities, including flush toilets, BBQ grills and occasionally coin-operated hot showers.

Private campgrounds Catering mainly to RVers with full electricity and water hookups and dump stations; tent sites may be sparse and uninviting. Hot showers and coin-op laundry are usually available, and possibly wi-fi, a swimming pool and camping cabins too.

Walk-in (environmental) sites Providing more peace and privacy, and usually cheaper than drive-in campsites. A few state-park campgrounds reserve these sites for long-distance hikers and cyclists only.

CAMPGROUND RATES & RESERVATIONS

Many public and private campgrounds accept reservations for all or some of their sites, while a few are strictly first-come, first-served. Overnight fees range from $10 or less for the most primitive and remote campsites to $60 or more for developed oceanfront sites with RV pull-throughs and full hookups.

Booking services can be used to search for campground locations and amenities, check current availability and make reservations (a fee of up to $10 may apply).

Recreation.gov (☑877-444-6777, 518-885-3639; www.recreation.gov; most tent & RV sites $10-25) Camping and cabin reservations in national parks, national forests (USFS) and other federal recreational lands (eg BLM).

ReserveAmerica (☑916-638-5883, 800-444-7275; www.reserveamerica.com) Reservations for California state-park campgrounds and cabins that accept advance bookings, as well as East Bay and Orange County regional parks and some private campgrounds.

Kampgrounds of America (KOA; ☑888-562-0000; www.koa.com) National chain of reliable but more expensive private campgrounds offering full facilities, including for RVs.

Hostels

Coastal California has 16 hostels affiliated with **Hostelling International USA** (HI-USA; ☑888-464-4872; www.hiusa.org). Dorms in HI hostels are typically gender-segregated and alcohol and smoking are prohibited. HI-USA membership cards ($28 per year) get you $3 off per night.

California also has dozens of independent hostels, particularly in coastal areas. They generally have more relaxed rules and often no curfew. Some hostels include a light breakfast in their rates, arrange local tours or offer pick-ups at transportation hubs. Facilities typically include mixed dorms, semi-private rooms with shared bathrooms, communal kitchens, lockers, internet access and coin-operated laundry.

Some hostels say they accept only international travelers, basically to keep out homeless locals, but Americans who look like travelers (eg you're in possession of an international plane ticket) may be admitted, especially during slow periods.

Dorm-bed rates average $25 to $55 per night, including tax. Reservations are always a good idea, especially in high season. Most hostels take reservations online or by phone. Booking services like www.hostels.com, www.hostelz.com and www.hostelworld.com sometimes offer lower rates than the hostels directly.

Hotels & Motels

➡ At midrange motels and hotels, expect clean, comfortable rooms with a private bathroom and such standard amenities as a cable TV, telephone, coffeemaker and perhaps a microwave and mini fridge.

➡ Top-end hotels and resorts offer more amenities and perhaps a scenic location, high design or historical ambience. Pools, fitness rooms, business centers and full-service restaurants and bars are all standard.

➡ Rooms are often priced by the size and number of beds, rather than the number of occupants. A room with one double or queen-size bed usually costs the same for one or two people, while a room with a king-size bed or two double beds costs more.

➡ There is often a small surcharge for the third and fourth adult, but children under a certain age (this varies) may stay free. Cribs or rollaway cots usually incur an additional fee.

➡ Beware that suites or 'junior suites' may simply be oversized rooms; ask about the layout when booking.

➡ Recently renovated or larger rooms, or those with a view, are likely to cost more. Descriptors like 'oceanfront' and 'oceanview' are liberally used, and may require a periscope to spot the surf.

➡ Rates may include breakfast, which could be just a stale doughnut and wimpy coffee, an all-you-can-eat hot and cold buffet, or anything in between.

➡ Some motels and hotels are now entirely smokefree, meaning you're not allowed to smoke anywhere on the property, or even outdoors within a certain distance of entryways.

Customs Regulations

Currently, non-US citizens and permanent residents may import the following:

➡ 1L of alcohol (if you're over 21 years old)

➡ 200 cigarettes (one carton) or 50 (non-Cuban) cigars (if you're over 18 years old)

➡ $100 worth of gifts Amounts higher than $10,000 cash, traveler's checks, money orders and other cash equivalents must be declared. Don't even think about bringing illegal drugs.

For more complete, up-to-date information, check with **US Customs & Border Protection** (www.cbp.gov).

Discount Cards

'America the Beautiful' Annual Pass (http://store.usgs.gov/pass; 12-month pass $80) Admits four adults and all children under 16 years for free to all national parks and federal recreational lands (eg USFS, BLM) for 12 months from the date of purchase. US citizens and permanent residents aged 62

years and older are eligible for a lifetime Senior Pass ($10), which grants free entry and 50% off some recreational-use fees such as camping.

American Association of Retired Persons (AARP; ☎800-566-0242; www.aarp.org; annual membership $16) Advocacy group for Americans 50 years and older offers member discounts (usually 10%) on hotels, car rentals and more.

American Automobile Association (AAA; ☎877-428-2277; www.aaa.com; annual membership from $57) Members of AAA and its foreign affiliates (eg CAA) qualify for small discounts (usually 10%) on Amtrak trains, car rentals, motels and hotels, chain restaurants and shopping, tours and theme parks.

Go Los Angeles, San Diego & San Francisco Cards (www.smarterdestinations.com; 1-day pass adult/child from $58/50) The Go LA Card and pricier Go San Diego Card include admission to major SoCal theme parks (but not Disneyland). The cheaper Go San Francisco Card covers museums, bicycle rental and a bay cruise. You've got to do a lot of sightseeing over multiple days to make passes even come close to paying off. For discounts, buy online.

International Student Identity & Youth Travel Cards (www.isic.org; 12-month card $25) Offers savings on airline fares, travel insurance and local attractions for full-time students (ISIC) and for nonstudents under 26 years of age (IYTC). Cards are issued by student unions, hosteling organizations and youth-oriented budget travel agencies.

Southern California CityPass (www.citypass.com/southern-california; adult/child from $328/284) If you're visiting SoCal theme parks, CityPass covers three-day admission to Disneyland and Disney California Adventure and one-day admission each to Universal Studios and SeaWorld, with add-ons available for Legoland and the San Diego Zoo or Safari Park.

PRACTICALITIES

➡ **DVDs** Coded region 1 (USA and Canada only)

➡ **Electricity** 110/120V AC, 50/60Hz

➡ **Newspapers** *Los Angeles Times* (www.latimes.com), *San Francisco Chronicle* (www.sfgate.com), *San Jose Mercury News* (www.mercurynews.com)

➡ **Radio** National Public Radio (NPR), lower end of FM dial

➡ **Time** Pacific Standard Time (UTC-8). Clocks are set one hour ahead during daylight saving time (DST), from the second Sunday in March until the first Sunday in November.

➡ **TV** PBS (public broadcasting); cable: CNN (news), ESPN (sports), HBO (movies), Weather Channel

➡ **Weights & measures** Imperial (except 1 US gallon = 0.83 imperial gallons)

Passes are valid for 14 days from the first day of use. It's cheapest to buy them online in advance.

Student Advantage Card (☏800-333-2920; www.studentadvantage.com; 12-month card $22.50) For international and US students, offers 15% savings on Amtrak trains and 20% on Greyhound buses, plus discounts of 10% to 20% on some rental cars and shopping.

Electricity

120V/60Hz

Food

➡ Lunch is generally served between 11:30am and 2:30pm, and dinner between 5pm and 9pm daily, though some restaurants stay open later, especially on Friday and Saturday nights.

➡ If breakfast is served, it's usually between 7:30am and 10:30am. Some diners and cafes keep serving breakfast into the afternoon, or all day. Weekend brunch is a laid-back affair, usually available from 11am until 3pm on Saturday and Sunday.

➡ Like all things Californian, restaurant etiquette tends to be informal. Only a handful of restaurants require more

than a dressy shirt, slacks and a decent pair of shoes; most places require far less.

➡ Tipping 18% to 20% is expected anywhere you receive table service.

➡ Smoking is illegal indoors. Some restaurants have patios or sidewalk tables where smoking is tolerated (ask first, or look around for ashtrays), but don't expect your neighbors to be happy about secondhand smoke.

➡ You can bring your own wine to most restaurants; a 'corkage' fee of $15 to $30 usually applies. Lunches rarely include booze, though a glass of wine or beer, while not common everywhere, is socially acceptable.

➡ If you ask the kitchen to divide a plate between two (or more) people, there may be a small split-plate surcharge.

➡ Vegetarians, vegans and travelers with food allergies or restrictions are in luck – many restaurants are used to catering to specific dietary needs.

Gay & Lesbian Travelers

Coastal California is a magnet for LGBTQ travelers. Hot spots include San Francisco's Castro neighborhood; West Hollywood (WeHo), Silver Lake and Long Beach in LA; the Hillcrest area of San Diego; and Guerneville and Calistoga in Napa Valley.

Same-sex marriage is legal in California. Although homophobic bigotry exists, widespread tolerance is the norm up and down the California coast, except for some small towns, where 'don't ask, don't tell' is still the unspoken social policy.

Resources

Advocate (www.advocate.com/travel) Online news, gay travel features and destination guides.

Damron (www.damron.com) Classic, advertiser-driven gay travel guides and 'Gay Scout' mobile app.

Gay & Lesbian National Hotline (☏888-843-4564; www.glnh.org; ☺1-9pm Mon-Fri, 9am-2pm Sat) For counseling and referrals of any kind.

Gay.net Travel (www.gay.net/travel) City guides, travel news and pride events.

Out Traveler (www.outtraveler.com) Free online magazine with travel tips, destination guides and hotel reviews.

Purple Roofs (www.purpleroofs.com) Online directory of LGBTQ accommodations.

Health

Healthcare & Insurance

➡ Medical treatment in the USA is of the highest caliber, but the expense could kill you. Many healthcare professionals demand payment at the time of service, especially from out-of-towners or international visitors.

→ Except for medical emergencies (in which case call 911 or go to the nearest 24-hour hospital emergency room, or ER), phone around to find a doctor or a walk-in clinic or urgent-care center that will accept your insurance.

→ Some health-insurance policies require you to get pre-authorization over the phone for medical treatment before seeking help. Keep all medical receipts and documentation for billing and insurance claims and reimbursement later.

Insurance
Travel Insurance
Getting travel insurance to cover theft, loss and medical problems is highly recommended. Some policies do not cover 'risky' activities such as scuba diving, motorcycling and skiing so read the fine print. Make sure the policy at least covers hospital stays and an emergency flight home.

Paying for your airline ticket or rental car with a credit card may provide limited travel accident insurance. If you already have private health insurance or a homeowners or renters policy, find out what those policies cover and only get supplemental insurance. If you have pre-paid a large portion of your vacation, trip cancellation insurance may be a worthwhile expense.

Worldwide travel insurance is available at www. lonelyplanet.com/travel-insurance. You can buy, extend and claim online anytime – even if you're already on the road.

Internet Access
→ Cybercafes typically charge $6 to $12 per hour for online access.

→ With branches in coastal cities and most towns,

FedEx Office (☏800-463-3339; www.fedex.com/us/office) offers internet access at self-service computer workstations (30¢ to 40¢ per minute) and sometimes free wi-fi, plus digital-photo printing and CD-burning stations.

→ Free or fee-based wi-fi hot spots can be found at major airports; many hotels, motels and coffee shops (eg Starbucks); and some tourist information centers, campgrounds (eg KOA), stores (eg Apple), bars and restaurants (including fast-food chains such as McDonald's).

→ Free public wi-fi is proliferating (for a list, visit www.ca.gov/wifi) and even some state parks are now wi-fi–enabled (get details at www.parks.ca.gov).

→ Public libraries have internet terminals (online time may be limited, advance sign-up required and a nominal fee charged for out-of-network visitors) and, increasingly, free wi-fi.

Legal Matters
Drugs & Alcohol
→ Possession of less than 1oz of marijuana is a misdemeanor in California. Possession of any other drug or an ounce or more of weed is a felony punishable by lengthy jail time. For foreigners, conviction of any drug offense is grounds for deportation.

→ Police can give roadside sobriety checks to assess if you've been drinking or using drugs. If you fail, they'll require you to take a breath, urine or blood test to determine if your blood alcohol is over the legal limit (0.08%). Refusing to be tested is treated the same as if you had taken and failed the test.

→ Penalties for driving under the influence (DUI) of drugs or alcohol range from license suspension and fines to jail time.

→ It's illegal to carry open containers of alcohol inside a vehicle, even if they're empty. Unless they're full and still sealed, store them in the trunk.

→ Consuming alcohol anywhere other than at a private residence or licensed premises is a no-no, which puts most parks and beaches off-limits (although many campgrounds allow it).

→ Bars, clubs and liquor stores often ask for photo ID to prove you are of legal drinking age (21 years old). Being 'carded' is standard practice, so don't take it personally.

Police & Security
→ For police, fire and ambulance emergencies, dial 911. For nonemergency police assistance, contact the nearest local police station (dial 411 for directory assistance).

→ If you are stopped by the police, be courteous. Don't get out of the car unless asked. Keep your hands where the officer can see them (eg on the steering wheel) at all times.

→ There is no system of paying fines on the spot. Attempting to pay the fine to the officer may lead to a charge of attempted bribery.

→ For traffic violations the ticketing officer will explain the options to you. There is usually a 30-day period to pay a fine; most matters can be handled online or by mail.

→ If you are arrested, you have the right to remain silent and are presumed innocent until proven guilty. Everyone has the right to make one phone call. Foreign travelers who don't have a lawyer, friends or family to help should call their embassy or consulate; the police can provide the number upon request.

➡ Due to security concerns about terrorism, never leave your bags unattended, especially at airports, bus and train stations or on public transportation.

Smoking

➡ Smoking is generally prohibited inside all public buildings, including airports, shopping malls and train and bus stations.

➡ There is no smoking allowed inside restaurants, although it may be tolerated at outdoor patio or sidewalk tables (if you don't see an ashtray, ask first).

➡ At hotels, you must specifically request a smoking room, but note some properties are entirely nonsmoking by law.

➡ In some cities and towns, smoking outdoors within a certain distance of any public business is illegal.

Money

➡ California state sales tax (7.5%) is added to the retail price of most goods and services (gasoline is an exception). Local and city sales taxes may tack on up to an additional 2.5%. Lodging taxes average over 12%.

➡ Most ATMs are connected to international networks and offer decent foreign-exchange rates. Expect a minimum surcharge of around $3 per transaction, plus any fees charged by your home bank.

➡ Exchange cash and traveler's checks (the latter have largely fallen out of use) at major airports, big-city banks and currency-exchange offices such as **American Express** (www. americanexpress.com) or **Travelex** (www.travelex. com).

➡ Outside major cities, exchanging money may be a problem, so make sure you have a credit card

and sufficient cash. Some businesses refuse to accept bills over $20.

➡ Visa, MasterCard and American Express are the most widely accepted credit cards.

Opening Hours

Standard opening hours are as follows:

Banks 9am–5pm Monday–Thursday, to 6pm Friday, sometimes 9am–1pm Saturday

Bars 5pm–2am daily

Business hours (general) 9am–5pm Monday–Friday

Nightclubs 10pm–4am Thursday–Saturday

Post offices 8:30am–4:30pm Monday–Friday, some 9am–noon Saturday

Restaurants 7:30am–10:30am, 11:30am–2:30pm and 5pm–9pm or 10pm daily, some open later Friday and Saturday

Shops 10am–6pm Monday–Saturday, noon–5pm Sunday (malls open later)

Public Holidays

On the following national holidays, banks, schools and government offices (including post offices) are closed, and transportation, museums and other services operate on a Sunday schedule. Holidays falling on a weekend are usually observed the following Monday.

New Year's Day January 1

Martin Luther King Jr Day Third Monday in January

Presidents' Day Third Monday in February

Good Friday Friday before Easter in March/April

Memorial Day Last Monday in May

Independence Day July 4

Labor Day First Monday in September

Columbus Day Second Monday in October

Veterans Day November 11

Thanksgiving Day Fourth Thursday in November

Christmas Day December 25

School Holidays

➡ Schools take a one- or two-week 'spring break' around Easter, sometime in March or April. Some hotels and resorts, especially at beaches and near SoCal's theme parks, raise their rates during this time.

➡ School summer vacations run from mid-June until mid-August, making July and August the busiest travel months.

Safe Travel

Despite its seemingly apocalyptic list of dangers – guns, violent crime, riots – coastal California is a reasonably safe place to visit. The greatest danger is posed by car accidents (buckle up – it's the law). There's also the dramatic, albeit unlikely, possibility of a natural disaster such as a tsunami or a large-magnitude earthquake.

Wildlife

➡ Never feed or approach any wild animals, no matter how harmless they may look. Disturbing or harassing specially protected species (eg many marine mammals) is a crime, subject to enormous fines.

➡ Mountain lion attacks on humans are rare, but can be deadly. If you encounter a mountain lion, stay calm, pick up small children, face the animal and retreat slowly. Make yourself appear larger by raising your arms or grabbing a stick. If the lion behaves menacingly, shout or throw rocks at it. If attacked, fight back aggressively.

➡ Snakes and spiders are common, and not just in wilderness areas. Always look inside your shoes before putting them back on outdoors, especially when camping. Snake bites are rare, but usually occur when a snake is stepped on or provoked (eg picked up or poked with a stick).

Antivenom is available at most hospitals.

Telephone

Dialing Codes

➡ US phone numbers consist of a three-digit area code followed by a seven-digit local number.

➡ When dialing a number within the same area code, only use the seven-digit number (if that doesn't work, try all 10 digits).

➡ For long-distance calls, dial 1 plus the area code plus the local number.

➡ For direct international calls, dial 011 plus the country code plus the area code (usually without the initial '0') plus the local phone number.

➡ If you're calling from abroad, the country code for the US is 1 (the same as Canada, but international rates apply between the two countries).

Cell Phones

➡ You'll need a multiband GSM phone in order to make calls in the USA. Popping in a US prepaid rechargeable SIM card is usually cheaper than using your own network.

➡ SIM cards are sold at telecommunications and electronics stores, which also sell inexpensive prepaid phones, including some airtime.

➡ You can rent a cell phone at Los Angeles (LAX) and San Francisco (SFO) International Airports from **TripTel** (☎877-874-7835; www.triptel. com); pricing plans vary, but typically are expensive.

Payphones & Phonecards

Where payphones still exist, they're usually coin-operated, though some may only accept credit cards (eg in state or national parks). Local calls cost 50¢ minimum. For long-distance and inter-

national calls, prepaid phonecards are sold at convenience stores, supermarkets, newsstands and electronics and convenience stores.

Tourist Information

For pretrip planning, peruse the info-packed website of the **California Travel & Tourism Commission** (☎877-225-4367, 916-444-4429; www.visitcalifornia.com). This state-government agency also runs several **California Welcome Centers** (www. visitcwc.com), where staff dispense maps and brochures and may be able to help find accommodations.

Almost every coastal city and town has a local visitors center or a chamber of commerce where you can pick up free maps, brochures and information.

Travelers with Disabilities

More populated areas of coastal California are reasonably well-equipped for travelers with disabilities, but facilities in smaller towns and rural areas may be limited.

Communications & Accessibility

➡ Telephone companies provide relay operators (dial 711) for those who are hearing impaired.

➡ Most traffic intersections have dropped curbs and sometimes audible crossing signals.

➡ The Americans with Disabilities Act (ADA) requires public buildings built after 1993 to be wheelchair-accessible, including restrooms.

➡ Motels and hotels built after 1993 must have at least one ADA-compliant accessible room; state your specific needs when making reservations.

⇒ For nonpublic buildings built prior to 1993, including hotels, restaurants, museums and theaters, there are no accessibility guarantees; call ahead to find out what to expect.

⇒ Most national and many state parks and some other outdoor recreation areas offer paved or boardwalk nature trails that are wheelchair-accessible.

⇒ Many theme parks go out of their way to be accessible to wheelchairs and guests with mobility limitations and other disabilities.

Transportation

⇒ All major airlines, Greyhound buses and Amtrak trains can accommodate travelers with disabilities, usually with 48 hours advance notice required.

⇒ Major car-rental agencies offer hand-controlled vehicles and vans with wheelchair lifts at no extra charge, but you must reserve these well in advance.

⇒ For wheelchair-accessible van rentals, try **Wheelchair Getaways** (☏800-642-2042; www.wheelchairgetaways.com) or **Mobility Works** (☏877-275-4915; www.mobilityworks.com) in LA and the San Francisco Bay Area.

⇒ Local buses, trains and subway lines usually have wheelchair lifts.

⇒ Seeing-eye dogs can accompany passengers on public transportation.

⇒ Taxi companies have at least one wheelchair-accessible van, but you'll usually need to call for one and then wait a while.

Resources

A Wheelchair Rider's Guide to the California Coast (www.wheelingcalscoast.org) Free accessibility information covering beaches, parks and trails, plus downloadable PDF guides to the San Francisco Bay Area and Los Angeles and Orange County coasts.

Access Northern California (www.accessnca.com) Extensive links to accessible-travel resources, publications, tours and transportation, including outdoor recreation opportunities, plus a searchable lodgings database and an events calendar.

Accessible San Diego (http://access-sandiego.org) Free online city guide (downloadable/print version $4/5) that's updated annually.

California State Parks (http://access.parks.ca.gov) Searchable online map and database of accessible features at state parks.

Los Angeles for Disabled Visitors (www.discoverlosangeles.com/search/site/disabled) Tips for accessible sightseeing, entertainment, museums and transportation.

San Francisco Access Guide (www.sanfrancisco.travel/accessibility/san-francisco-access-guide.html) Free downloadable accessible travel info – dated, but useful.

Theme Park Access Guide (www.mouseplanet.com/tag) An insider's view of Disneyland and other SoCal theme parks 'on wheels.'

Wheelchair Traveling (www.wheelchairtraveling.com) Travel tips, lodging and helpful California destination info.

Visas

⇒ Visa information is highly subject to change. Depending on your country of origin, the rules for entering the USA keep changing. Double-check current visa requirements *before* arriving.

⇒ Currently, under the US Visa Waiver Program (VWP), visas are not required for citizens of 38 countries for stays up to 90 days (no extensions) if you have a machine-readable passport (MRP) that meets current US standards and is valid for six months beyond your intended stay.

⇒ Citizens of VWP countries must still register online with the **Electronic System for Travel Authorization** (ESTA; https://esta.cbp.dhs.gov) at least 72 hours before travel. Once approved, ESTA registration ($14) is valid for up to two years or until your passport expires, whichever comes first.

⇒ For most Canadian citizens traveling with Canadian passports that meet current US standards, a visa for short-term visits (usually up to six months) and ESTA registration aren't required.

⇒ Citizens from all other countries or whose passports don't meet US standards will need to apply for a visa in their home country. The process costs a nonrefundable fee (minimum $160), involves a personal interview and can take several weeks, so apply as early as possible.

⇒ For up-to-date information about entry requirements and eligibility, check the visa section of the **US Department of State website** (http://travel.state.gov) or contact the nearest USA embassy or consulate in your home country.

Transportation

GETTING THERE & AWAY

Getting to California by air or overland by bus, car or train is easy, although it's not always cheap. Flights, cars and tours can be booked online at lonelyplanet.com/bookings.

Entering the Region

Under the US Department of Homeland Security's Orwellian-sounding Office of Biometric Identity Management, almost all visitors to the USA (excluding, for now, many Canadians, some Mexican citizens, children under age 14 and seniors over age 79) will be digitally photographed and have their electronic (inkless) fingerprints scanned upon arrival. Regardless of your visa status, immigration officers have absolute authority to refuse entry to the USA. For more information about entering the USA, visit the **US Customs & Border Protection website** (www.cbp.gov).

California is an important agricultural state. To prevent the spread of pests and diseases, certain food items (including meats, fresh fruit and vegetables) may not be brought into the state. Bakery items, chocolates and hard-cured cheeses are admissible. If you drive into California across the border from Mexico or from the neighboring states of Oregon, Nevada or Arizona, you may have to stop for a quick questioning and inspection by **California Department of Food & Agriculture** (www.cdfa.ca.gov) agents.

Passports

➡ Under the Western Hemisphere Travel Initiative (WHTI), all travelers must have a valid machine-readable (MRP) passport when entering the USA by air, land or sea.

➡ The only exceptions are for most US citizens and some Canadian and Mexican citizens traveling *by land* who can present other WHTI-compliant documents (eg pre-approved 'trusted traveler' cards). For details, visit www.cbp.gov/travel.

➡ All foreign passports must meet current US standards and be valid for at least six months longer than your intended stay in the USA.

➡ MRP passports issued or renewed after October 26, 2006 must be e-passports (ie have a digital photo and integrated chip with biometric data).

Air

➡ To get through airport security checkpoints (30-minute wait times are standard), you'll need a boarding pass and photo ID.

➡ Some travelers may be required to undergo a secondary screening, involving hand pat-downs and carry-on bag searches.

➡ Airport security measures restrict many common items (eg pocketknives, scissors) from being carried on planes. Check current restrictions with the **Transportation Security Administration** (TSA; ☑866-289-9673; www.tsa.gov).

➡ Currently, TSA requires that all carry-on liquids and gels be stored in 3oz or smaller bottles placed inside a quart-sized clear plastic zip-top bag. Exceptions, which must be declared to checkpoint security officers, include medications.

➡ All checked luggage is screened for explosives. TSA may open your suitcase for visual confirmation, breaking the lock if necessary. Leave your bags unlocked or use a TSA-approved lock.

Airports & Airlines

California's major international airports are in Los Angeles and the San Francisco Bay Area. Smaller regional airports are mainly served by domestic US airlines.

Arcata/Eureka Airport (www.co.humboldt.ca.us/aviation; 3561 Boeing Ave, McKinleyville) On the North Coast.

Bob Hope Airport (www.burbankairport.com; 2627 N Hollywood Way, Burbank) About

14 miles northwest of Downtown LA, close to Universal Studios.

John Wayne Airport (www.ocair.com; 18601 Airport Way, Santa Ana) Off the I-405 Fwy in inland Orange County.

Long Beach Airport (www.lgb.org; 4100 Donald Douglas Dr, Long Beach) Easy access to LA and Orange County.

Los Angeles International Airport (LAX; www.lawa.org/lax; 1 World Way) California's largest and busiest airport, 20 miles southwest of Downtown LA, near the beaches.

Mineta San José International Airport (www.flysanjose.com; 1701 Airport Blvd, San Jose) Forty-five miles south of San Francisco, near Silicon Valley.

Monterey Regional Airport (www.montereyairport.com; 200 Fred Kane Dr, Monterey) On the Central Coast, south of Santa Cruz.

Oakland International Airport (OAK; www.oakland-airport.com; 1 Airport Dr) Nationwide domestic service, plus some international flights. The cheapest way to reach downtown San Francisco (15 miles west) from Oakland Airport is via Air-BART trams ($6), which connect to the Coliseum station, where you catch BART to downtown SF ($4.05, 25 minutes).

San Francisco International Airport (www.flysfo.com; S McDonnell Rd) Northern California's major hub, 14 miles south of downtown San Francisco.

San Diego International Airport (www.san.org; 3325 N Harbor Dr) Just 4 miles from downtown San Diego.

San Luis Obispo County Regional Airport (www.sloairport.com; 903 Airport Dr, San Luis Obispo) On the Central Coast, north of Santa Barbara.

Santa Barbara Airport (www.flysba.com; 500 Fowler Rd, Goleta; 🛜) Nine miles west of downtown Santa Barbara, off Hwy 101.

Land

Border Crossings

It's relatively easy crossing from the USA into Mexico; it's crossing back into the USA that can pose problems if you haven't brought all of the required documents. Check the ever-changing passport and visa requirements *before* traveling with the **US Department of State** (http://travel.state.gov).

The **US Customs & Border Protection** (http://bwt.cbp.gov) tracks current wait times at every US border crossing. On the US–Mexico border between San Diego and Tijuana, San Ysidro is the world's busiest border crossing, with average wait times of an hour or more.

US citizens do not require a visa for stays of 72 hours or less within the Mexican border zone (ie as far south as Ensenada). But to re-enter the USA, they need to present a US passport or other WHTI-compliant document (see www.cbp.gov/travel); a regular US driver's license is not enough.

BUS

➡ US-based **Greyhound** (📞800-231-2222; www.greyhound.com) and **Greyhound México** (📞01-800-710-8819; www.greyhound.com.mx) have cooperative service, with direct buses between Mexico and California.

➡ Northbound buses from Mexico can take some time to cross the US border, since US immigration may insist on checking every person on board.

CAR & MOTORCYCLE

➡ Unless you're planning an extended stay in Tijuana, driving across the Mexico border is more trouble than it's worth. Instead take the trolley from San Diego or park your car on the US side and walk across.

➡ If you do decide to drive across, you must purchase Mexican car insurance either beforehand or at the border crossing. Bring your vehicle's registration papers, US liability insurance and driver's license.

➡ If you're renting a car, RV or motorcycle in the USA, ask if the agency allows its vehicles to be taken across the Mexican border – chances are it doesn't.

➡ Occasionally the authorities of either country decide to search a vehicle

---

CLIMATE CHANGE & TRAVEL

Every form of transport that relies on carbon-based fuel generates CO_2, the main cause of human-induced climate change. Modern travel is dependent on airplanes, which might use less fuel per kilometer per person than most cars but travel much greater distances. The altitude at which aircraft emit gases (including CO_2) and particles also contributes to their climate change impact. Many websites offer 'carbon calculators' that allow people to estimate the carbon emissions generated by their journey and, for those who wish to do so, to offset the impact of the greenhouse gases emitted with contributions to portfolios of climate-friendly initiatives throughout the world. Lonely Planet offsets the carbon footprint of all staff and author travel.

WARNING: DRUG CARTELS

As of early 2014, the **US State Department** (http://travel.state.gov) has issued a travel warning about Mexican drug-cartel violence and crime along the US–Mexico border. Travelers should exercise extreme caution in Tijuana, avoid large-scale gatherings and refrain from venturing out after dark. Cars with US license plates can be targets for theft and carjacking.

thoroughly. Remain calm and be polite.

Bus

Greyhound (☑800-231-2222; www.greyhound.com) is the major long-distance bus company, with routes across the USA, including throughout California. It has cut services to many small towns; routes trace major highways and may only stop at larger population centers.

Train

Amtrak (☑800-872-7245; www.amtrak.com) operates a fairly extensive rail system throughout the USA. Trains are comfortable, if a bit slow and occasionally delayed; they're equipped with dining and lounge cars on long-distance routes. Fares vary according to the type of train and seating (eg coach or business class, sleeping compartments).

Amtrak's major long-distance routes to/from California:

California Zephyr Daily service between Chicago and Emeryville (from $163, 52 hours), near San Francisco, via Denver, Salt Lake City, Reno and Sacramento.

Coast Starlight Travels the West Coast daily from Seattle to LA (from $92, 35 hours) via Portland, Sacramento, Oakland, San Luis Obispo and Santa Barbara.

Southwest Chief Daily departures from Chicago and LA (from $135, 43 hours) via Kansas City, Albuquerque and Flagstaff.

Sunset Limited Thrice-weekly service between New Orleans and LA (from $130, 47 hours) via

Houston, San Antonio, El Paso, Tucson and Palm Springs.

GETTING AROUND

Most people drive around California, although you can also fly (if time is limited, but your budget isn't) or save money by taking buses or trains, the latter often following scenic coastal routes.

Air

Several major US carriers fly within California. Flights are often operated by their regional subsidiaries, such as American Eagle, Delta Connection and United Express. Alaska Airlines, Frontier Airlines and Horizon Air serve many regional California airports, as do low-cost airlines Southwest and Spirit. Virgin America currently flies out of Los Angeles, San Francisco and San Diego. JetBlue serves LA County, the San Francisco Bay Area and San Diego.

Bicycle

Although it's a nonpolluting 'green' way to travel, cycling coastal California's roads demands a high level of fitness and the long distances involved make it difficult to cover much ground very fast. Come prepared for weather extremes, from chilly coastal fog and winter rainstorms to intense heat in summer.

Resources

Adventure Cycling Association (www.adventurecycling.org) Online resource for purchasing bicycle-friendly maps and long-distance route guides.

Better World Club (☑866-238-1137; www.betterworldclub.com) Annual membership (from $40) gets you two 24-hour emergency roadside pick-ups and transport within a 30-mile radius.

California Bicycle Coalition (http://calbike.org) Links to cycling route maps, events, safety tips, laws, bike-sharing programs and community nonprofit bicycle shops.

Road Rules

➡ Cycling is allowed on all roads and highways – even along freeways if there's no suitable alternative, such as a smaller parallel frontage road; all mandatory exits are marked.

➡ Some cities have designated bicycle lanes, but make sure you have your wits about you in heavy traffic.

➡ Cyclists must follow the same rules of the road as vehicles. Don't expect drivers to always respect your right of way, however.

➡ Wearing a helmet is mandatory for bicycle riders under 18 years old.

➡ Ensure you have proper lights and reflective gear, especially if you're pedaling at night or in fog.

Transporting Bicycles

➡ Greyhound transports bicycles as luggage (surcharge $30 to $40), provided the bicycle is disassembled and placed in a rigid container ($10 box available at some terminals).

➡ Amtrak's *Pacific Surfliner* trains have onboard racks where you can secure your bike unboxed; try to reserve a spot for your bicycle when buying tickets ($5 surcharge may apply).

➜ On Amtrak trains without racks, bikes must be put in a box ($15 at most staffed terminals) and checked as luggage (fee $10). Not all stations or trains offer checked-baggage service.

➜ Before flying, you'll need to disassemble your bike and box it as checked baggage. Contact airlines directly for details, including surcharges ($75 to $150 or more).

Boat

Boats won't get you around coastal California, although there are a few offshore routes, notably to Catalina Island from LA and Orange County and to Channel Islands National Park from Ventura or Oxnard, north of LA. On San Francisco Bay, regular ferry routes operate between San Francisco and Sausalito, Larkspur, Tiburon, Angel Island, Oakland, Alameda and Vallejo.

Bus

Greyhound (📞800-231-2222; www.greyhound.com) buses are an economical way to travel between major cities and to points along the coast, but won't get you off the beaten path or to national parks or small towns. Frequency of service varies from 'rarely' to 'constantly,' but the main routes have service several times daily.

Greyhound buses are usually clean, comfortable and reliable. The best seats are typically near the front away from the bathroom. Limited amenities include freezing aircon (bring a sweater) and slightly reclining seats; select buses have electrical outlets and wi-fi. Smoking onboard is prohibited. Long-distance buses stop for meal breaks and driver changes.

Bus stations are typically dreary, often in dodgy areas; if you arrive at night, take a taxi into town or to your lodgings. In small towns where

there is no bus station, know exactly where and when the bus arrives, be obvious as you flag it down and pay the driver with exact change.

Costs

You may save money by purchasing tickets at least seven days in advance and by traveling between Monday and Thursday.

Discounts (on unrestricted fares only) are offered to seniors over 62 (5% off), students with a Student Advantage Card (20%) and children aged two to 11 (25%). Tots under two years old ride for free.

Special promotional discounts, such as 50% off companion fares, are often available, though they may come with restrictions or blackout periods. Check the website for current fare specials or ask when buying tickets.

Reservations

It's easy to buy tickets online with a credit card, then pick them up (bring photo ID) at the terminal. You can also buy tickets over the phone or in person from a ticket agent. Greyhound terminal ticket agents accept credit and debit cards, traveler's checks (in US dollars) and cash.

General boarding is first-come, first-served. Buying tickets in advance doesn't guarantee a seat on any particular bus unless you also purchase priority boarding (fee $5), available only at some terminals. Otherwise, arrive at least one hour prior to the scheduled departure to get a seat; allow extra time on weekends and holidays.

Car, Motorcycle & RV

California's love affair with cars runs deep, and it's here to stay: the state is so big, public transportation can't cover it. For flexibility and convenience, you'll want a car, but rental rates and fuel

prices can eat up a good chunk of your trip budget.

Automobile Associations

For 24-hour emergency roadside assistance, free maps and discounts on lodging, attractions, entertainment, car rentals and more, consider joining an auto club.

American Automobile Association (AAA; 📞877-428-2277; www.aaa.com) Walk-in offices throughout California, add-on coverage for RVs and motorcycles, and reciprocal agreements with some international auto clubs (eg CAA in Canada, AA in the UK) – bring your membership card from home.

Better World Club (📞866-238-1137; www.betterworldclub.com) Ecofriendly alternative auto club that supports environmental causes and offers optional emergency roadside assistance for cyclists.

Driver's License

➜ Visitors may legally drive a car in California for up to 12 months with their home driver's license.

➜ If you're from overseas, an International Driving Permit (IDP) will have more credibility with traffic police and simplify the car-rental process, especially if your license doesn't have a photo or isn't written in English.

➜ To drive a motorcycle, you'll need a valid US state motorcycle license or a specially endorsed IDP.

➜ International automobile associations can issue IDPs, valid for one year, for a fee. Always carry your home license together with the IDP.

Fuel

➜ Gas stations in California, nearly all of which are self-service, are ubiquitous, except in national parks and some sparsely populated areas.

➜ Gas is sold in gallons (one US gallon equals 3.78L).

ROAD DISTANCES (miles)

	Anaheim	Los Angeles	Mendocino	Monterey	Napa	Sacramento	San Diego	San Francisco	San Luis Obispo
Los Angeles	25								
Mendocino	555	525							
Monterey	375	320	270						
Napa	425	400	140	150					
Sacramento	410	385	200	185	60				
San Diego	95	120	650	440	520	505			
San Francisco	405	380	155	120	50	85	500		
San Luis Obispo	225	200	380	145	275	290	320	230	
Santa Barbara	120	95	480	250	370	395	215	335	105

At press time, the cost for mid-grade fuel was more than $4.

Insurance

California law requires liability insurance for all vehicles. When renting a car, check your home auto-insurance policy or your international travel-insurance policy to see if you're already covered. If not, expect to pay around $10 to $20 or more per day.

Insurance against damage to the car itself, called Collision Damage Waiver (CDW) or Loss Damage Waiver (LDW), costs another $20 per day; the deductible may require you to pay the first $100 to $500 for any repairs. Some credit cards cover CDW/LDW, provided you charge the entire cost of the car rental to the card. Check with your credit-card issuer first to determine the extent of coverage and policy exclusions.

Rental

CARS

To rent your own wheels, you'll typically need to be at least 25 years old, hold a valid driver's license and have a major credit card, *not* a check or debit card. A few companies may rent to drivers under 25 but over 21 for a hefty surcharge. If you don't have a credit card, large cash deposits are infrequently accepted.

With advance reservations, you can often get an economy-size vehicle with unlimited mileage from around $30 per day, plus insurance, taxes and fees. Weekend and weekly rates are usually the most economical. Airport locations may have cheaper rates but higher add-on fees; if you get a fly-drive package, local taxes may be extra when you pick up the car.

Rates generally include unlimited mileage, but expect surcharges for additional drivers and one-way rentals. Child or infant safety seats are legally required; reserve them when booking for about $10 per day.

If you'd like to minimize your carbon footprint, some major car-rental companies offer 'green' fleets of hybrid or biofueled rental cars, but these fuel-efficient models are in short supply. Reserve those models well in advance

and expect to pay significantly higher rates.

To find and compare independent car-rental companies, try **Car Rental Express** (www.carrentalexpress.com).

Alamo (877-222-9075; www.alamo.com)

Avis (800-633-3469; www.avis.com)

Budget (800-218-7992; www.budget.com)

Dollar (800-800-4000; www.dollar.com)

Enterprise (800-261-7331; www.enterprise.com)

Fox (800-225-4369; www.foxrentacar.com) Locations near LA, Burbank, San Diego, Orange County and San Francisco Bay Area airports.

Hertz (800-654-3131; www.hertz.com)

National (877-222-9058; www.nationalcar.com)

Rent-a-Wreck (877-877-0700; www.rentawreck.com) Minimum rental age and under-25 driver surcharges vary at a dozen locations, mostly around LA and the San Francisco Bay Area.

Simply Hybrid (888-359-0055, 323-653-0011; www.simplyhybrid.com) Rents hybrid, electric and flex-fuel vehicles in LA; ask about free delivery and pick-up.

Super Cheap! Car Rental (www.supercheapcar.com) No surcharge for drivers aged 21 to 24; nominal daily fee applies for drivers aged 18 to 21 (full-coverage insurance required). Locations in the San Francisco Bay Area, LA and Orange County.

Thrifty (800-847-4389; www.thrifty.com)

Zipcar (866-494-7227; www.zipcar.com) Currently available in the San Francisco Bay Area, LA, San Diego, Sacramento, Santa Barbara and Santa Cruz, this car-sharing club charges usage fees (per hour or day), including free gas, insurance (a damage fee of up to $750 may apply) and limited mileage. Apply online (foreign drivers accepted); application fee $25, annual membership from $60.

MOTORCYCLES

Depending on the model, renting a motorcycle costs $100 to $200 per day (plus taxes and fees), including helmets, unlimited miles and liability insurance; one-way rentals and collision insurance (CDW) cost extra. Discounts may be available for multiday and weekly rentals. Security deposits range up to $2000 (credit card required).

California Motorcycle Adventures (☑650-969-6198; www.californiamotorcycleadventures.com; 2554 W Middlefield Rd, Mountain View; ☺9am-6pm Mon-Fri, to 5pm Sat, 10am-5pm Sun) Harley-Davidson rentals in Silicon Valley.

Dubbelju (☑415-495-2774, 866 495 2774; www.dubbelju. com; 689a Bryant St, San Francisco; ☺9am-6pm Mon-Sat) Rents Harley-Davidson, BMW and Japanese and Italian imported motorcycles, as well as scooters.

Eagle Rider (☑310-321-3180, 888-900-9901; www.eaglerider. com) Nationwide rental company with branches in LA, San Diego, Newport Beach, San Francisco and Carmel.

Route 66 Riders (☑888-434-4473, 310-578-0112; www.route66riders.com; 4161 Lincoln Blvd, Marina del Rey; ☺10am-6pm Tue-Sat, 11am-5pm Sun) Harley-Davidson rentals in LA's South Bay.

RECREATIONAL VEHICLES

Gas-guzzling recreational vehicles (RVs) remain popular despite high fuel prices and being cumbersome to drive. That said, they do solve transportation, accommodation and cooking issues in one fell swoop. It's easy to find RV campgrounds with electricity and water hookups, but in cities, RVs are a nuisance, because there are few places to park or plug them in.

Book RVs as far in advance as possible. Rental costs vary by size and model,

but you can expect to pay over $100 per day. Rates often don't include mileage, bedding or kitchen kits, vehicle-prep fees or taxes. If pets are allowed, a surcharge may apply.

Cruise America (☑480-464-7300, 800-671-8042; www.cruiseamerica.com) Nationwide RV rental company with almost two dozen locations statewide.

El Monte (☑562-483-4956, 888-337-2214; www.elmonterv. com) With 15 locations across California, this national RV rental agency offers AAA discounts.

Escape Campervans (☑310-672-9909, 877-270-8267; www.escapecampervans. com) Awesomely painted campervans at economical rates in LA and San Francisco.

Happy Travel Campers (☑855-754-6555, 310-929-5666; www.camperusa.com) Campervan rentals in the San Francisco Bay Area, LA and Las Vegas, NV.

Jucy Rentals (☑800-650-4180; www.jucyrentals.com) Campervan rentals in San Francisco, LA and Las Vegas, NV.

Vintage Surfari Wagons (☑714-585-7565, 949-716-3135; www.vwsurfari.com) VW campervan rentals in Orange County.

Road Conditions & Hazards

For up-to-date highway conditions, including road closures and construction updates, check with the **California Department of Transportation** (CalTrans; ☑800-427-7623; www.dot. ca.gov).

In coastal areas thick fog can often impede driving – slow down and if it's too soupy, get off the road. Along ocean cliffs and on curvy mountain roads, watch out for falling rocks, mudslides and avalanches that could damage or disable your car.

Coastal highways alongside steep, crumbly cliffs may wash out in winter, sometimes for months at

a time. When you see signs that read, 'Expect long delays 40 miles ahead' or 'Hwy 1 closed north of Hearst Castle,' heed the warnings, but don't panic. If you have lodging reservations, call ahead and ask about any available local detours.

Road Rules

➡ Drive on the right-hand side of the road.

➡ Talking or texting on a cell (mobile) phone without a hands-free device while driving is illegal.

➡ The use of seat belts is required for drivers, front-seat passengers and children under age 16.

➡ Infant and child safety seats are required for children under six years old or weighing less than 60lb.

➡ All motorcyclists must wear a helmet. Scooters are not allowed on freeways.

➡ High-occupancy (HOV) lanes marked with a diamond symbol are reserved for cars with multiple occupants, sometimes only during signposted hours.

➡ Unless otherwise posted, the speed limit is 65mph on freeways, 55mph on two-lane undivided highways, 35mph on major city streets and 25mph in business and residential districts and near schools.

➡ Except where indicated, turning right at red lights after coming to a full stop is permitted, although intersecting traffic still has the right of way.

➡ At four-way stop signs, cars proceed in the order in which they arrived; if two cars arrive simultaneously, the one on the right has the right of way. When in doubt, wave the other driver ahead.

➡ When emergency vehicles (eg ambulances, fire trucks) approach from either direction, carefully pull over to the side of the road.

→ Driving under the influence of alcohol or drugs is illegal. It's also illegal to carry open containers of alcohol, even empty ones, inside a vehicle; store them in the trunk.

Local Transportation

California's major coastal cities have relatively cheap local bus, cable-car, trolley, train, light-rail and/or subway systems. Larger coastal towns and counties operate commuter-oriented bus systems, usually with limited evening and weekend services. Public transportation in rural areas and to state and national parks can be sparse.

Bicycle

→ Cycling is a feasible way of getting around smaller cities and beach towns, but it's not much fun in traffic-dense urban areas like LA.

→ San Francisco, Calistoga, Arcata, Santa Cruz, San Luis Obispo, Santa Barbara, Santa Monica and Coronado are among California's most bike-friendly communities, as rated by the **League of American Bicyclists** (www.bikeleague.org).

→ Bicycles may be transported on many local buses and trains, sometimes during off-peak, non-commuter hours only.

→ You can rent bikes by the hour, day or week in most cities and many towns. Rentals start around $10 per day for beach cruisers up to $45 or more for mountain bikes (credit-card security deposit normally required).

Taxi

→ Taxis are metered, with flag-fall fees of $2.50 to $3.50 to start, plus $2 to $3 per mile. Credit cards may be accepted, but bring cash just in case.

→ Taxis may charge extra for baggage and airport pick-ups.

→ Drivers expect a 10% to 15% tip, rounded up to the next dollar.

→ Taxis cruise busy urban areas, but elsewhere you may need to call for one.

Train

Amtrak (☏800-872-7245; www.amtrak.com) runs comfortable, if occasionally tardy, trains to major California cities and some towns. Amtrak's Thruway buses provide onward connections from many train stations. Smoking is prohibited aboard trains and buses.

Amtrak routes serving coastal California:

Coast Starlight Chugs roughly north–south almost the entire length of the state; wi-fi may be available. Daily stops include LA, Burbank, Santa Barbara, San Luis Obispo, Paso Robles, Salinas, San Jose, Oakland and Emeryville.

Pacific Surfliner Eight daily trains ply the San Diego–LA route via Orange County, where stops include San Juan Capistrano and Anaheim, home of Disneyland. Five trains continue north to Santa Barbara via Burbank, Ventura and Carpinteria, with three going all the way to San Luis Obispo. Trains hug the scenic coastline for much of the route. On-board wi-fi may be available.

Costs

Purchase tickets at train stations, by phone or online (in advance for the cheapest fares). Fares depend on the day of travel, the route, the type of seating etc. They may be slightly higher during peak travel periods (eg summer). Round-trip tickets typically cost the same as two one-way tickets.

Usually seniors over 62 and students with an ISIC or Student Advantage Card receive a 15% discount, while up to two children aged two to 15 who are accompanied by an adult get 50% off. AAA members save 10%. Special promotions can become available anytime, so check the website or ask when making reservations.

Reservations

Amtrak reservations can be made up to 11 months prior to departure. In summer and around holidays, trains sell out, so book tickets as early as possible. The cheapest coach fares are usually for unreserved seats, while business-class fares come with guaranteed seats.

Train Passes

Amtrak's California Rail Pass costs $159 ($80 for children aged two to 15) and is valid on all trains (except certain long-distance routes) and most connecting Thruway buses for seven days of travel within a 21-day period. Passholders must reserve each leg of travel in advance and obtain hard-copy tickets prior to boarding.

Behind the Scenes

SEND US YOUR FEEDBACK

We love to hear from travelers – your comments keep us on our toes and help make our books better. Our well-traveled team reads every word on what you loved or loathed about this book. Although we cannot reply individually to your submissions, we always guarantee that your feedback goes straight to the appropriate authors, in time for the next edition. Each person who sends us information is thanked in the next edition – the most useful submissions are rewarded with a selection of digital PDF chapters.

Visit **lonelyplanet.com/contact** to submit your updates and suggestions or to ask for help. Our award-winning website also features inspirational travel stories, news and discussions.

Note: We may edit, reproduce and incorporate your comments in Lonely Planet products such as guidebooks, websites and digital products, so let us know if you don't want your comments reproduced or your name acknowledged. For a copy of our privacy policy visit lonelyplanet.com/privacy.

OUR READERS

Many thanks for the travelers who used the last edition and wrote to us with helpful hints, useful advice and interesting anecdotes:

Rebekah Byrne, Kim Mathes, Leeann Wallett, Mary Winch

AUTHOR THANKS

Sara Benson

Thanks to Suki Gear, Cliff Wilkinson, Alison Lyall and the entire Lonely Planet team, including my co-authors. Family and friends all over California generously gave me insider tips, good company on road trips and most importantly, spare rooms to crash in. Special thanks to my Golden Gate Bridge running partners Beth Kohn (also my Sierra Nevada trail guru) and Derek Wolfgram (home brewer and an expert advisor on Bay Area craft beer).

Andrew Bender

Suki Gear, Cliff Wilkinson, Alison Lyall, Hilary Angel, Juan Flores, Joe Timko, Sarah Weinberg, Suzi Dennett and the good folks at the SPP Help Desk.

Alison Bing

Thanks to Suki Gear, Rana Freedman, Cliff Wilkinson, Katie O'Connell, Melissa Wong, and above all, Marco Flavio Marinucci, for making a Muni bus ride into the adventure of a lifetime.

Celeste Brash

Thanks first to my road trip buddies on this trip, Heather Griggs and Tevai Humbert (who is also my son). On the road I was given all the scoop by local heroes Grant Roden, Audie Theole, Freda Moon, John Vlahides, Kem Pence and Ken Pence. Thanks to Sara Benson for being so passionate about the region and the great Suki Gear for getting me on her last book.

Beth Kohn

Brava to Suki Gear for all her years of work on so many fantastic editions of this guide, and to Sara B, my running, hiking, baking and writing heroine! Thanks to Visit Oakland, Lisa Cesaro of DNC, Kari Cobb in Yosemite National Park and Lara Kaylor at Mammoth Lakes Tourism for their excellent on-the-ground assistance. Jen and Dillon provided worthy campfire s'mores and Claude kept me (reasonably) sane throughout.

Adam Skolnick

Los Angeles is a city I love, full of people I love. LA is home. Still, it's never easy to dissect your own backyard, mostly because you usually know what you're missing. So thanks to Alma Lauer, Trisha Cole, Jessica Ritz, Nina Gregory, Burton Breznick, Tchaiko Omawale, Dan Cohn, Angel Payne, Christine Lazzaro, Liebe Geft, the folks at the Wende Museum, Michael McDowell, Alex Capriotti, and John Moore. Thanks also to all those wild seals, sea lions, dolphins and whales that keep us entertained in the water, and to the LP staff and my cohorts Sara Benson and Andy Bender.

John A Vlahides

I owe great thanks to my commissioning editor, Suki Gear, whom I miss; to my co-author, Sara Benson, for her always-sunny disposition; and to my editor Clifton Wilkinson for giving me free reign – I'm grateful. And to you, dear readers: please accept my most heartfelt gratitude for letting me be your guide to Wine Country. Have fun. I know you will!

ACKNOWLEDGEMENTS

Climate map data adapted from Peel MC, Finlayson BL & McMahon TA (2007) 'Updated World Map of the Köppen-Geiger Climate Classification', Hydrology and Earth System Sciences, 11, 1633¬44.

Illustration pp54–5 by Michael Weldon.

Mural p414–5 *Endangered Species* by Emily Winters 1990, Commissioned by SPARC (Social and Public Art Resource Center) through its Great Walls Unlimited: Neighborhood Pride Program, with support from the Los Angeles Cultural Affairs Department. ©1990 Emily Winters, Artist.

Cover photograph: Surfers at sunset, Malibu; Dean Turner/Getty.

THIS BOOK

This 5th edition of *Coastal California* was researched and written by Sara Benson, Andrew Bender, Alison Bing, Celeste Brash, Beth Kohn, Adam Skolnick and John A Vlahides. Sara, Andrew, Alison, Beth and John also wrote the previous edition, alongside Nate Cavalieri and Bridget Gleeson. This guidebook was commissioned in Lonely Planet's Oakland office, and produced by the following:

Commissioning Editor Suki Gear

Destination Editor Clifton Wilkinson

Product Editor Katie O'Connell

Assisting Editors Gabrielle Innes, Anne Mulvaney

Senior Cartographer Alison Lyall

Book Designer Jennifer Mullins

Cover Image Researcher Naomi Parker

Thanks to Brendan Dempsey, Ryan Evans, Larissa Frost, Tracy Whitney

Index

NOTES

Map Legend

Sights

- Beach
- Bird Sanctuary
- Buddhist
- Castle/Palace
- Christian
- Confucian
- Hindu
- Islamic
- Jain
- Jewish
- Monument
- Museum/Gallery/Historic Building
- Ruin
- Sento Hot Baths/Onsen
- Shinto
- Sikh
- Taoist
- Winery/Vineyard
- Zoo/Wildlife Sanctuary
- Other Sight

Activities, Courses & Tours

- Bodysurfing
- Diving
- Canoeing/Kayaking
- Course/Tour
- Skiing
- Snorkeling
- Surfing
- Swimming/Pool
- Walking
- Windsurfing
- Other Activity

Sleeping

- Sleeping
- Camping

Eating

- Eating

Drinking & Nightlife

- Drinking & Nightlife
- Cafe

Entertainment

- Entertainment

Shopping

- Shopping

Information

- Bank
- Embassy/Consulate
- Hospital/Medical
- Internet
- Police
- Post Office
- Telephone
- Toilet
- Tourist Information
- Other Information

Geographic

- Beach
- Hut/Shelter
- Lighthouse
- Lookout
- Mountain/Volcano
- Oasis
- Park
- Pass
- Picnic Area
- Waterfall

Population

- Capital (National)
- Capital (State/Province)
- City/Large Town
- Town/Village

Transport

- Airport
- BART station
- Border crossing
- Boston T station
- Bus
- Cable car/Funicular
- Cycling
- Ferry
- Metro/Muni station
- Monorail
- Parking
- Petrol station
- Subway/SkyTrain station
- Taxi
- Train station/Railway
- Tram
- Underground station
- Other Transport

Note: Not all symbols displayed above appear on the maps in this book

Routes

- Tollway
- Freeway
- Primary
- Secondary
- Tertiary
- Lane
- Unsealed road
- Road under construction
- Plaza/Mall
- Steps
- Tunnel
- Pedestrian overpass
- Walking Tour
- Walking Tour detour
- Path/Walking Trail

Boundaries

- International
- State/Province
- Disputed
- Regional/Suburb
- Marine Park
- Cliff
- Wall

Hydrography

- River, Creek
- Intermittent River
- Canal
- Water
- Dry/Salt/Intermittent Lake
- Reef

Areas

- Airport/Runway
- Beach/Desert
- Cemetery (Christian)
- Cemetery (Other)
- Glacier
- Mudflat
- Park/Forest
- Sight (Building)
- Sportsground
- Swamp/Mangrove

OUR STORY

A beat-up old car, a few dollars in the pocket and a sense of adventure. In 1972 that's all Tony and Maureen Wheeler needed for the trip of a lifetime – across Europe and Asia overland to Australia. It took several months, and at the end – broke but inspired – they sat at their kitchen table writing and stapling together their first travel guide, *Across Asia on the Cheap*. Within a week they'd sold 1500 copies. Lonely Planet was born.

Today, Lonely Planet has offices in Franklin, London, Melbourne, Oakland, Beijing and Delhi, with more than 600 staff and writers. We share Tony's belief that 'a great guidebook should do three things: inform, educate and amuse'.

OUR WRITERS

Sara Benson

Coordinating Author, Santa Barbara County, Central Coast, Southern California's Best Beaches After graduating from college, Sara jumped on a plane to California with just one suitcase and $100 in her pocket. After driving tens of thousands of miles to every corner of this state, she settled in a little beach town halfway between San Francisco and LA. She's an avid hiker, backpacker, cyclist and all-seasons outdoor enthusiast who has worked for the National Park Service in the Sierra Nevada Mountains. The author of more than 65 travel and nonfiction books, Sara is the lead writer for Lonely Planet's *California*, *California's Best Trips*, *Coastal California* and *Los Angeles, San Diego & Southern California* guides. Follow her latest adventures online at www.indietraveler.blogspot.com, www.indietraveler.net, @indie_traveler on Twitter and indietraveler on Instagram.

Read more about Sara at:
lonelyplanet.com/members/Sara_Benson

Andrew Bender

Disneyland & Orange County, San Diego & Around Andy is a true Angeleno, not because he was born in Los Angeles but because he's made it his own. This native New Englander drove cross-country to work in film production, and eventually realized that the joy was in the journey (and writing about it). He writes the Seat 1A travel site for Forbes, and his writing has also appeared in the *Los Angeles Times*, in-flight magazines and over three dozen LP titles. Current obsessions: discovering SoCal's next great ethnic enclave, and photographing winter sunsets over the Pacific.

Alison Bing

San Francisco Over 10 guidebooks and 20 years in San Francisco, author Alison Bing has spent more time on Alcatraz than some inmates, become an aficionado of drag and burritos, and willfully ignored Muni signs warning that "safety requires avoiding unnecessary conversation."

Celeste Brash

North Coast & Redwoods Celeste's ancestors moved to Northern California in 1906 and this is the region she will always consider home. After 15 years in French Polynesia she now lives in the Pacific Northwest and was thrilled to head south to explore and imbibe the treasures of her old stomping grounds, hike snowy peaks, find petroglyphs in caves, be awed by redwoods and seduced by the wild coast. Find out more about Celeste at www.celestebrash.com.

OVER PAGE | MORE WRITERS

Published by Lonely Planet Publications Pty Ltd
ABN 36 005 607 983
5th edition – March 2015
ISBN 978 1 74220 620 2
© Lonely Planet 2015   Photographs © as indicated 2015
10 9 8 7 6 5 4 3 2 1
Printed in China

Beth Kohn

Marin County & the Bay Area A lucky long-time resident of San Francisco, Beth lives to be playing outside or splashing in big puddles of water. For this and the *California* guide, she hiked and biked Bay Area byways, backpacked Yosemite and Lake Tahoe in winter and soaked in myriad mountain view hot springs. An author of Lonely Planet's *Yosemite, Sequoia & Kings Canyon National Parks* and *Mexico* guides, you can see more of her work at www.bethkohn.com.

Adam Skolnick

Los Angeles Adam Skolnick has written about travel, culture, health, sports, human rights and the environment for Lonely Planet, *New York Times*, *Outside*, *Men's Health*, *Travel & Leisure*, Salon.com, BBC.com and ESPN.com. He has authored or co-authored 25 Lonely Planet guidebooks. Find him on Twitter and Instagram (@adamskolnick).

John A Vlahides

Napa & Sonoma Wine Country John A Vlahides co-hosts the TV series *Lonely Planet: Roads Less Travelled*, screening on National Geographic Channels International. John studied cooking in Paris, with the same chefs who trained Julia Child, and is also a former luxury-hotel concierge and member of Les Clefs d'Or, the international union of the world's elite concierges. He lives in San Francisco, sings tenor with the Grammy-winning San Francisco Symphony, and spends free time biking SF and skiing the Sierra. For more, see JohnVlahides.com, twitter.com/JohnVlahides.